Free Online Access!

The Almanac of American Employers 2017

Your purchase includes access to Book Data and Exports online

As a book purchaser, you can register for free, 1-year, 1-seat online access to the latest data for your book's industry trends, statistics and company profiles. This includes tools to export company data. Simply send us this registration form, and we will send you a user name and password. In this manner, you will have access to our continual updates during the year. Certain restrictions apply.

_____ YES, please register me for free online access. I am the actual, original purchaser. (Proof of purchase may be required.)

Customer Name _____

Title_____

Organization _____

Address _____

City_____State_____Zip_____

Country (if other than USA) _____

Phone_____Fax _____

E-mail _____

Return to: # Plunkett Research®, Ltd.

Attn: Registration
P.O. Drawer 541737, Houston, TX 77254-1737 USA
713.932.0000 · Fax 713.932.7080 · www.plunkettresearch.com
customersupport@plunkettresearch.com

* Purchasers of used books are not eligible to register. Use of online access is subject to the terms of the end user license agreement.

THE ALMANAC OF AMERICAN EMPLOYERS 2017

The Only Guide to America's Hottest, Fastest-Growing Major Corporations

Jack W. Plunkett

Published by:
Plunkett Research®, Ltd., Houston, Texas
www.plunkettresearch.com

THE ALMANAC OF AMERICAN EMPLOYERS
2017

Editor and Publisher:
Jack W. Plunkett

Executive Editor and Database Manager:
Martha Burgher Plunkett

Senior Editors and Researcher:
Isaac Snider

Editors, Researchers and Assistants:
Ashley Bass
John Brucato
Chris Chapin
Gina Sprenkel
Suzanne Zarosky
Shuang Zhou

E-Commerce & Enterprise Accounts Manager:
Jillian Claire Lim

Information Technology Manager:
Seifelnaser Hamed

Video Production:
Uriel Rios

Special Thanks to:
U.S. Department of Labor
Bureau of Labor Statistics
U.S. Department of Commerce
Bureau of Economic Analysis, National Technical Information Service

Plunkett Research®, Ltd.
P. O. Drawer 541737, Houston, Texas 77254 USA
Phone: 713.932.0000   Fax: 713.932.7080
www.plunkettresearch.com

Plunkett Research®, Ltd.
P. O. Drawer 541737
Houston, Texas 77254-1737
Phone: 713.932.0000, Fax: 713.932.7080 www.plunkettresearch.com

ISBN13 # 978-1-62831-419-9 (eBook Edition # 978-1-62831-744-2)

Limited Warranty and Terms of Use:

THE ALMANAC OF AMERICAN EMPLOYERS 2017

CONTENTS

Continued on the next page

Continued from the previous page

INTRODUCTION

THE ALMANAC OF AMERICAN EMPLOYERS is an easy-to-use solution to what would otherwise be a complicated problem: How can you tell, among America's giant companies, which firms are most likely to be hiring? Among those firms, which are the best to work for? No other source provides this book's easy-to-understand comparisons of growth, treatment of employees, salaries, benefits, pension plans, profit sharing and many other items of great importance to job seekers.

Especially helpful is the way in which THE ALMANAC OF AMERICAN EMPLOYERS enables readers with no business background to readily compare the growth potential and benefit plans of large employers. You'll see the mid-term financial record of each firm, along with the impact of earnings, sales and growth plans on each company's potential to provide employment opportunities.

Information is presented in a way that addresses the differing interests of individual employees. You'll find separate listings for dozens of categories of data that you may want to consider. While this book is aimed primarily at job seekers, it will also be of tremendous value to researchers, marketing executives and personnel professionals. THE ALMANAC OF AMERICAN EMPLOYERS is the premier guide to the most successful employers in the nation, their policies and their performance.

THE ALMANAC OF AMERICAN EMPLOYERS is your opportunity to gain valuable knowledge in a matter of minutes. Five hundred of the biggest, most successful corporate employers in America are analyzed in this book. Tens of thousands of pieces of information, gathered from a wide variety of sources, have been researched for these corporations and are presented here in a form that can be easily understood by job seekers of all types.

Thanks to THE ALMANAC OF AMERICAN EMPLOYERS' exclusive data system, potentially confusing considerations have been reduced to simple groups of focused data. By scanning the data groups and the long list of unique indexes, you can find the right employers to fit your personal needs.

The AMERICAN EMPLOYERS 500 are among the best major growth companies to work for in America. Which companies offer the best benefits, are the biggest employers or earn the most profits? Where are these companies operating? All of these things and more are made easy for the reader to determine.

Thousands of observations are made that will be of great interest to prospective employees. For many of the firms, you'll find comments about such items as plans for growth, increases or decreases in the number of employees and charitable programs. You'll also find notes about corporate culture and special programs for the convenience of employees, such as health and recreation facilities, on-site child care, job training or career paths. Finally, you'll find basic information on each company, including the home office address and telephone number; regional, national and international locations; a description of the business; and a list of selected subsidiaries and trade names. In addition, you will find fax numbers and Internet addresses.

Whether you are currently employed by one of these corporate giants or are considering applying for a job with one, you will be able to see how each company compares with the others, even if you don't have the slightest understanding of accounting, finance or employee benefits.

Whatever your purpose for researching corporate employers, you'll find this book to be an indispensable guide. Nonetheless, as is true with all resources, this volume has limitations that the reader should be aware of:

- Financial data and other corporate information can change quickly. A book of this type can be no more current than the data that was available as of the time of editing. Consequently, the financial picture, management and ownership of the firm(s) you are studying may have changed since the date of this book. For example, this almanac includes the most up-to-date sales figures and profits available to the editors as of mid-2016. This means that we have typically used corporate financial data as of the end of 2015.

- Corporate mergers, changes in corporate financial ratings or stability, acquisitions and downsizing are occurring at a very rapid rate. Such events may have created significant change, subsequent to the publishing of this book, within a company you are studying.

- Some of the companies in THE AMERICAN EMPLOYERS 500 are so large in scope and in variety of business endeavors conducted within a parent organization that we have been unable to completely list all subsidiaries, affiliations, divisions and activities within a firm's corporate structure.

- This volume is intended to be a general guide to major employers in numerous industries. That

means that researchers should look to this book for an overview and, when conducting in-depth research, should contact the specific corporations and related industry associations in question for the very latest changes and data. Where possible, we have listed contact information, telephone numbers and Internet addresses for pertinent companies, government agencies and industry associations so that the reader may get further details without unnecessary delay.

- We have used exhaustive efforts to locate and fairly present accurate and complete data. However, when using this book or any other source for business and industry information, the reader should use caution and due diligence by conducting further research where it seems appropriate. We wish you success in your endeavors, and we trust that your experience with this book will be both satisfactory and productive.

- To obtain the best results and to best understand the fields in the company profiles, you should first read the chapter titled "How to Use This Book."

Good luck in your job search. Be patient, do your research and use this book as an important start in the right direction.

Jack W. Plunkett
Houston, Texas
September 2016

HOW TO USE THIS BOOK

Dozens of excellent books already exist to help you choose a career, write a resume, apply for a job and so on. That is not the purpose of THE ALMANAC OF AMERICAN EMPLOYERS. Instead, this book's job is to help you sort through America's giant corporate employers to determine which may be the best for you, or to see how your current employer compares to others. Whether you are entering the job market and looking for your first position, or you are thinking about switching companies in mid-career to find more promising vistas, this book will be a valuable guide.

The two primary sections of the book are devoted first to general information for job seekers (trends analysis and advice on conducting employer research, along with resources, statistics and contacts), followed by the "Individual Data Listings" for THE AMERICAN EMPLOYERS 500. If time permits, you should begin your research in the front chapters of this book. Also, you will find lengthy indexes in Chapter 5 and in the back of the book.

GENERAL INFORMATION FOR JOB SEEKERS

Chapter 1: Major Trends Affecting Job Seekers. This chapter presents an encapsulated view of the major trends in business and the economy that are creating rapid changes in the employment picture at large corporations.

Chapter 2: Statistics. This chapter presents in-depth statistics on employment by education level, sex and race, along with unemployment rates, the fastest-growing occupations and more.

Chapter 3: Research—7 Keys for Job Seekers. This chapter provides a definitive list of items that job seekers should look for when conducting research into major corporate employers.

Chapter 4: Important Contacts for Job Seekers. This chapter covers contacts for important government agencies, professional societies, industry associations, job banks, reference sources and more. Included are Internet sites and contact addresses for a wide variety of job search uses.

THE AMERICAN EMPLOYERS 500

Chapter 5: THE AMERICAN EMPLOYERS 500: Who They Are and How They Were Chosen.

The companies compared in this book were chosen from nearly all industries, on a nationwide basis. They were individually chosen from the largest U.S. employers, based on selected types of business and industry sectors. For a complete description, see Chapter 5.

Individual Data Listings:

Look at one of the companies in THE AMERICAN EMPLOYERS 500's Individual Data Listings. You'll find the following information fields:

Company Name:

The company profiles are in alphabetical order by company name. If you don't find the company you are seeking, it may be a subsidiary or division of one of the firms covered in this book. Try looking it up in the Index by Subsidiaries, Brand Names and Selected Affiliations in the back of the book.

Industry Code:

Industry Group Code: An NAIC code used to group companies within like segments.

Types of Business:

A listing of the primary types of business specialties conducted by the firm.

Brands/Divisions/Affiliations:

Major brand names, operating divisions or subsidiaries of the firm, as well as major corporate affiliations—such as another firm that owns a significant portion of the company's stock. A complete Index by Subsidiaries, Brand Names and Selected Affiliations is in the back of the book.

Contacts:

The names and titles up to 27 top officers of the company are listed, including human resources contacts.

Growth Plans/ Special Features:

Listed here are observations regarding the firm's strategy, hiring plans, plans for growth and product development, along with general information regarding a company's business and prospects.

Financial Data:

Revenue (2016 or the latest fiscal year available to the editors, plus up to five previous years): This figure represents consolidated worldwide sales from all operations. These numbers may be estimates.

R&D Expense (2016 or the latest fiscal year available to the editors, plus up to five previous years): This figure represents expenses associated with the research and development of a company's goods or services. These numbers may be estimates.

Operating Income (2016 or the latest fiscal year available to the editors, plus up to five previous years): This figure represents the amount of profit realized from annual operations after deducting operating expenses including costs of goods sold, wages and depreciation. These numbers may be estimates.

Operating Margin % (2016 or the latest fiscal year available to the editors, plus up to five previous years): This figure is a ratio derived by dividing operating income by net revenues. It is a measurement of a firm's pricing strategy and operating efficiency. These numbers may be estimates.

SGA Expense (2016 or the latest fiscal year available to the editors, plus up to five previous years): This figure represents the sum of selling, general and administrative expenses of a company, including costs such as warranty, advertising, interest, personnel, utilities, office space rent, etc. These numbers may be estimates.

Net Income (2016 or the latest fiscal year available to the editors, plus up to five previous years): This figure represents consolidated, after-tax net profit from all operations. These numbers may be estimates.

Operating Cash Flow (2016 or the latest fiscal year available to the editors, plus up to five previous years): This figure is a measure of the amount of cash generated by a firm's normal business operations. It is calculated as net income before depreciation and after income taxes, adjusted for working capital. It is a prime indicator of a company's ability to generate enough cash to pay its bills. These numbers may be estimates.

Capital Expenditure (2016 or the latest fiscal year available to the editors, plus up to five previous years): This figure represents funds used for investment in or improvement of physical assets such as offices, equipment or factories and the purchase or creation of new facilities and/or equipment. These numbers may be estimates.

EBITDA (2016 or the latest fiscal year available to the editors, plus up to five previous years): This figure is an acronym for earnings before interest, taxes, depreciation and amortization. It represents a company's financial performance calculated as revenue minus expenses (excluding taxes, depreciation and interest), and is a prime indicator of profitability. These numbers may be estimates.

Return on Assets % (2016 or the latest fiscal year available to the editors, plus up to five previous years): This figure is an indicator of the profitability of a company relative to its total assets. It is calculated by dividing annual net earnings by total assets. These numbers may be estimates.

Return on Equity % (2016 or the latest fiscal year available to the editors, plus up to five previous years): This figure is a measurement of net income as a percentage of shareholders' equity. It is also called the rate of return on the ownership interest. It is a vital indicator of the quality of a company's operations. These numbers may be estimates.

Debt to Equity (2016 or the latest fiscal year available to the editors, plus up to five previous years): A ratio of the company's long-term debt to its shareholders' equity. This is an indicator of the overall financial leverage of the firm. These numbers may be estimates.

Address:

The firm's full headquarters address, the headquarters telephone, plus toll-free and fax numbers where available. Also provided is the World Wide Web site address.

Stock Ticker, Exchange: When available, the unique stock market symbol used to identify this firm's common stock for trading and tracking purposes is indicated. Where appropriate, this field may contain "private" or "subsidiary" rather than a ticker symbol. If the firm is a publicly-held company headquartered outside of the U.S., its international ticker and exchange are given.

Total Number of Employees: The approximate total number of employees, worldwide, as of the end of 2016 (or the latest data available to the editors).

Parent Company: If the firm is a subsidiary, its parent company is listed.

Salaries/Bonuses:

(The following descriptions generally apply to U.S. employers only.)

Highest Executive Salary: The highest executive salary paid, typically a 2016 amount (or the latest year available to the editors) and typically paid to the Chief Executive Officer.

Highest Executive Bonus: The apparent bonus, if any, paid to the above person.

Second Highest Executive Salary: The next-highest executive salary paid, typically a 2016 amount (or the latest year available to the editors) and typically paid to the President or Chief Operating Officer.

Second Highest Executive Bonus: The apparent bonus, if any, paid to the above person.

Other Thoughts:

Estimated Female Officers or Directors: It is difficult to obtain this information on an exact basis, and employers generally do not disclose the data in a public way. However, we have indicated what our best efforts reveal to be the apparent number of women who either are in the posts of corporate officers or sit on the board of directors. There is a wide variance from company to company.

Hot Spot for Advancement for Women/Minorities: A "Y" in appropriate fields indicates "Yes." These are firms that appear either to have posted a substantial number of women and/or minorities to high posts or that appear to have a good record of going out of their way to recruit, train, promote and retain women or minorities. (See the Index of Hot Spots For Women and Minorities in the back of the book.) This information may change frequently and can be difficult to obtain and verify. Consequently, the reader should use caution and conduct further investigation where appropriate.

Chapter 1

MAJOR TRENDS AFFECTING JOB SEEKERS

Major trends sweeping through business and the economy that affect job seekers of all types:
1) U.S. Job Market Overview
2) Cost Control Remains a Major Concern at Employers/Consolidation Through Mergers Continues
3) Unemployment in the U.S. Is Down Substantially Compared to the Recent Past
4) Consumers Spend Less, Save More Than During the Last Boom, Affecting a Wide Variety of Companies
5) Technology Continues to Create Sweeping Changes in the Workplace
6) Continued Growth in Outsourcing, Including Supply Chain and Logistics Services
7) Millions Working as Temps
8) Offshoring, Reshoring and the Rebound in American Manufacturing
9) Older Americans Will Delay Retirement and Work Longer/Many Employers Find Older Employees Desirable
10) Employment Sectors that Will Offer an Above-Average Number of Job Opportunities:

Employment Sectors that Will Offer an Above-Average Number of Job Opportunities:
- Automobile Manufacturing and Retailing
- Biotechnology
- Child Care/Children's Products
- Consulting, including Technology Consulting
- Consumer Products
- Cosmetics
- Elder Care, Home Health Care, Nursing Homes and Assisted Living Communities
- Electronic Games, Games for Cell Phones
- Energy Conservation Products and Services
- Health Care Services
- Health Care Products
- Health Care Technology, Including Computerized Patient Records
- Health Foods, Organic Foods, Enhanced Foods
- Home Building
- Hotels
- Insurance
- Internet Services, Server Hosting, Cloud Computing
- Internet of Things: Connected Devices, Remote Wireless Sensors and their Networks, Machine to Machine Communications
- Online Search Services & Social Media, with Advertising Revenues
- Online-based Business and Consumer Sales and Services, including E-Commerce
- Outsourcing, Including Outsourced Business and Computer Services
- Pets: Services and Products
- Pharmaceuticals—Generics
- Restaurants
- Retailing—Basic, Including Drugstores and Supermarkets
- Retailing—Discount and Warehouse Clubs
- Robotics and Factory Automation
- Software—Artificial Intelligence
- Software—Corporate, including Development Tools and Cybersecurity
- Software—Data Analytics and Consumer Scoring
- Software—Mobile Apps
- Software as a Service
- Solar Energy Cells Installation & Maintenance
- Supply Chain Services That Create Cost-Savings
- Water Filtration and Conservation Equipment
- Wireless and Cellular Communications

1) U.S. Job Market Overview

Job seekers in 2017 should see reasonably strong hiring and rising wages, if the low unemployment rates seen in late 2016 continue, and if confidence is reasonably high for both consumers and business leaders. Nonetheless, total growth of the U.S. economy has been disappointing for several years, and this relatively slow growth has a negative effect on hiring and wages.

However, as 2016 was coming to a close, the global economy was dealing with an uncertain financial and business environment in Europe and Japan, and a slowdown in global trade, as well as slowing growth or poor economic results in important developing markets such as Brazil and China. These challenges will have an effect on employment in the U.S., as global trade is of great importance to many of America's largest industrial sectors. (One very bright market in the developing world is India.) On the positive side, during 2016, stock markets had reached impressive highs, house values had bounced back in most American cities and the overall financial conditions of American households was improving.

Meanwhile, job seekers who want good positions with good pay must be extremely well prepared for the process of seeking a job. A large part of the preparation requires that they do meaningful research into prospective employers and the industries in which they operate. The fact remains that several million Americans consider themselves underemployed, and many of them will be looking for better jobs. Competition for highly desirable positions will remain fierce. Many companies receive hundreds or even thousands of resumes for every job opening. Simply sending in a resume and hoping for the best is nowhere near enough for a successful job search.

The good news is that a select set of employers and growth companies will offer superb job opportunities. Sectors such as cloud computing and health care will continue to grow and hire. A few companies with exciting new technologies or cost-saving services will see terrific growth. Salesforce.com, a highly innovative provider of online business services, has been a good example.

Solid companies that do a terrific job of providing the day-to-day needs of consumers and business will continue to hire—Costco, Amazon.com and Southwest Airlines are good examples. Other industry sectors that fall into this category include insurance firms, such as USAA and The Progressive Corporation, along with online services and apps that provide efficient or new ways for consumers and businesses to make purchases, gather data or view entertainment and news.

Growing numbers of consumers prefer to buy from firms that sell goods and services online, offering savings of time, money and car travel. This boosts companies like Amazon.com that offer low prices combined with deep selections and great customer service. Virtually all major retailers, including giants like Wal-Mart and Home Depot, are working hard to provide better online services and choices to their customers. Meanwhile, traditional department stores are in a long, painful period of decline.

The travel industry has been enjoying tremendous growth in revenues over the past few years. Airlines are in much better financial shape than they were in the recent past. Many have shed debt through bankruptcy and successfully reorganized as more financially stable companies. Hotels are enjoying high occupancy rates. Meanwhile, travel has become one of the most successful sectors at selling products and services via the Internet, creating vast numbers of new job opportunities.

The automobile sector is booming as well. New cars have been selling very well, and hiring has been strong at car dealers and manufacturers alike.

Americans who find themselves in the market for a job will need to understand the changes surging through the economy in order to determine which companies to pursue and which to avoid. The U.S. employment market has evolved dramatically, and job seekers must be both knowledgeable and nimble in order to position themselves to find promising careers.

America's job market is looking better than it has in recent years, and job seekers, including new college grads, should see a reasonable level of potential openings. There will be good job opportunities for those who are diligent in seeking top employers in most business sectors.

Economic Factors Affecting the Job Market

Business Productivity: Productivity growth has been positive in recent years, but the increases have been very modest. That is, business can be produced—whether it is goods or services—by utilizing fewer workers than before. This will be extremely beneficial to the U.S. economy in the long run. Productivity is boosted by new technologies, improved management methods and other factors, sometimes as simple as reorganizing the staff and redesigning the workflow to increase output. (It can also receive a quick boost from restrained corporate hiring.) If rising productivity occurs along with rapidly rising sales and profits, then the job market will improve.

Corporate Sales: A trend of rising sales encourages hiring. Reasonable sales growth could lead to an increase. It remains to be seen whether this will occur.

Corporate Profits: When profits increase sharply, companies are inclined to increase both investment and hiring. However, there is still a high level of uncertainty about America's economic future. Much of recent corporate profitability was the result of restrained spending and hiring, and profits were weaker as of late 2016. Hiring is strongest when corporate sales, and accompanying profits, show significant growth, encouraging executives to forecast an extended period of increased demand for their products and services.

In order to compete effectively in today's job market, one of the most important things you can do is arm yourself with knowledge. It is vital for the job seeker to use the best reference tools possible in order to seek out employers that offer a reasonable balance of financial stability, opportunities for advancement and good pay.

Excellent job opportunities always exist if you know where to look. Many of America's most successful firms currently need large numbers of new employees.

Thousands of companies, in technical and non-technical sectors, will need significant numbers of new hires. In particular, companies that offer products or services that save time and/or money will prosper—for example, many types of companies that offer services that help businesses operate more efficiently, will be hiring. Meanwhile, large companies that are not increasing their overall numbers of employees will be hiring on a regular basis due to normal attrition—that is, the loss of employees due to retirement, relocation or other personal circumstances. Massive companies like Walgreen's or Kroger typically need to hire tens of thousands of workers yearly due to normal attrition.

2) Cost Control Remains a Concern at Employers/Consolidation Through Mergers Continues

For most firms, executives have been focusing on cost control as a means to boost profits and financial stability. Employee costs have been targeted as well. Often, companies merge with others in order to seek operating efficiencies or gain access to needed capital. Financing is readily available for large corporate mergers and acquisitions, and the number of mergers has been high. A consolidation of companies via a merger may enable the firms to combine customer bases, administrative staff, sales offices and production facilities, while cutting employees who hold duplicated jobs, in hopes of thereby creating more efficient, more profitable firms. Mergers may be spurred by economic difficulties and falling profits, or they may involve large firms seeking to acquire companies that bring advantages that may boost growth and accelerate profits. For example, online leaders Facebook and Google have acquired numerous firms in order to bring in new technologies.

Because they face tough, global competition, manufacturing firms are frequently involved in such mergers. Good jobs in the U.S. manufacturing sector can be found, despite intense competition from manufacturers in China and other offshore markets. Overall, U.S. factories are running with fewer people per unit of output, thanks to immense investments in factory automation and robotics.

A small, but significant, number of firms are "reshoring" some of their manufacturing, by making products at American plants that were previously manufactured in overseas facilities. Even the American textile industry, which was hit hard by layoffs and bankruptcies during the late 1900s, is enjoying a modest rebound. This is positive, but it is not leading to large numbers of job openings.

Some of the statistical loss in manufacturing employment has been exaggerated by the fact that firms now outsource a good deal of their non-manufacturing operations to services companies. For example, many computer departments, company cafeterias, distribution centers and engineering needs are now outsourced to companies that specialize in such work, thus dramatically reducing the number of in-house jobs at manufacturing firms. This is the long term trend of outsourcing in action.

Also, companies in both manufacturing and service sectors have caught on to management by teams, vastly enhanced supply chain technology (such as the use of the Internet for ordering and tracking components), along with networked management, distribution and manufacturing systems, which all add up to the fact that fewer mid-management, white-collar types are needed to communicate with the people doing the day-to-day work. Production workers have been encouraged to communicate among themselves. In many cases, workers are taking on unprecedented responsibilities, setting their own goals and schedules, tracking costs and output, thereby boosting profits. Historically, these were the tasks of middle managers. Today, vast numbers of those management jobs have been eliminated. Businesses without factories are also undergoing re-engineering and leaps in productivity, often through the streamlining of processes through the use of better computers and software.

3) Unemployment Is Down Substantially Compared to the Recent Past

By the end of September 2016, unemployment in America had dropped to 4.9%, down from 5.1% one year earlier. This improvement in the unemployment rate is encouraging some people to re-enter the workforce.

Today's job market is a vast improvement over that of the dark days of 2008-10, and jobs are now very plentiful in some regions. (The U.S. unemployment rate in August 2007 was down to 4.6%. By the end of 2009, unemployment had soared to 10%, and 8 million jobs were eliminated during the Great Recession.) The job market has been recovering slowly. Nonetheless, many job seekers will be able to find satisfying jobs if they apply themselves to the job hunt, make sure their resumes and self-marketing skills are in superb shape, network effectively and do thorough research. The number of people applying for each job opening is often high. Consequently, it is vital for a job seeker to understand how to best apply for a job online, how to conduct research that will help him or her to shine during an interview and how to create an effective list of prospective employers.

It is also important for job seekers to face the fact that locale has a lot to do with the unemployment rate. There is wide variance in the unemployment rate from state to state and city to city.

4) Consumers Spend Less, Save More Than During the Last Boom, Affecting a Wide Variety of Companies

After piling on debt, running up their credit cards, signing mountains of mortgages and buying new cars at a soaring rate from 2002 through 2007, consumers have completely reversed course. Personal savings rates are much higher than they were during the last boom. Consumer debt has declined dramatically, to much lower, healthier levels. Welcome to a new era of increased frugality and worried consumers.

While increased personal savings and lower debt levels will be very good for America over the long run, it is has been a difficult adjustment for the nation to make, and, for the near term at least, it puts a damper on the job market. Nonetheless, consumer spending has been reasonably strong, with automobile sales and online retailing doing extremely well. Consumers will remain cautious about using debt.

The most successful companies will be those that offer products and services with lasting value, low prices, good customer service, cost-saving strategies or innovative technologies. Excellent examples are Wal-Mart (low prices), Costco (good service and low prices), Amazon (innovative use of online technology to provide convenience and cost-savings), travel firms like Southwest Airlines and Carnival Cruise Lines (good service, low prices, high value) and car makers like Kia and Hyundai (lasting value, low prices).

5) Technology Continues to Create Sweeping Changes in the Workplace

Technology has introduced vast changes throughout industries of all types, greatly boosting productivity and reallocating (or eliminating) workers. A major cause of change for employees, and therefore job seekers, is the tidal wave of new technologies that continues to revolutionize the workplace at all levels. Prospering companies are using new ways to communicate with customers, automate back-office tasks and industrial operations, and push ahead with research and development. There is a never-ending stream of technological innovation. For example, employers have already harnessed the power of networked desktop computers. Today, they are rapidly adopting the use of mobile computing devices such as tablets, Internet-based telephone systems (VOIP and unified communication systems), cloud computing and video conferencing technologies.

The trend of using new practices and technologies while cutting layers of management is largely about communication. This is true whether it is communication between the top offices and the factory floor,

communication with customers, communication between the computers in one corporate office with those in another, or communication from the sales department to the warehouse and the supply chain.

These new technologies mean continuous retraining for much of the workforce. Job seekers who want the best posts must have the training and skills that will let them utilize new technologies effectively. Hundreds of thousands of jobs are remaining unfilled at many companies because of a shortage of technically qualified people. Workforce training is a critical need nationwide.

Jobs in America are shifting to new categories of work based on technologies that didn't exist 20 and 30 years ago. For example, the job title "webmaster" was coined in the 1990s to describe the employee in charge of a firm's Internet sites and intranet operations. Services firms, as well as manufacturers, are placing more and more employees in recently created technical and service positions, while many of the tasks once performed in-house are now provided by outsourced services providers. In the telecommunications industry, digital technology has completely changed the list of job titles while enabling phone service providers to reduce the ratio of employees to customers. In the meantime, hundreds of thousands of jobs have been created at cellular telephone companies. Now, Internet-based telephony, competition from cable providers, fiber to the premises and wireless networks such as Wi-Fi and LTE continue to force telecommunications firms to evolve.

Another excellent example: Retailing, shipping and warehousing are undergoing a technology revolution due to the introduction of Radio Frequency Identification Tags (RFID). This breakthrough in inventory management is based on the placement of digitized product data within product packaging, combined with the use of special sensors in stores and warehouses that can automatically read that data. These sensors can alert a central inventory management system of product movement and the need to restock inventory. From loading docks to shelves to cash registers to parking lots, RFID sensors will eventually track the movement of each pallet or individual item. Many bar codes will eventually be replaced by RFIDs. RFID can even eliminate the need to scan each item at checkout in a retail store. Checkout stations will be equipped with sensors that read RFID-based data such as product code and price, and then automatically calculate purchase totals. Benefits can include less shoplifting and few inventory errors. Another benefit is that firms will be able to reduce overall inventory thanks to better tracking.

As online ordering, tracking and inventory management continue to become more sophisticated and cost-effective, purchasing executives at firms of all types and sizes will accelerate the use of Internet-based systems for management of their supply chains. There are significant opportunities here for e-commerce services and software companies. Likewise, there is great promise for third-party logistics (3PL) companies that combine the power of Internet-based information with strategically located warehouses to fulfill the inventory needs of manufacturers. Robots are being used to a rapidly growing extent in picking inventory within warehouses prior to shipment. Amazon.com is a leader in this regard.

Manufacturing is undergoing its own technology revolution. This is often referred to as factory automation. Advanced technology used with great success on the factory floor includes computer-driven machine tools that require highly skilled operators, along with robotic assemblers that are capable of working nonstop, 24/7 to create and assemble parts into finished goods.

6) Continued Growth in Outsourcing, Including Supply Chain and Logistics Services

Part of the re-engineering process at employers has been a boom in "outsourcing," or the use of outside specialty firms to do chores that firms formerly performed through in-house departments. For example, Pitney Bowes takes over the mailrooms, desktop printers and copiers at major corporations. As part of this turnkey service, Pitney Bowes supplies its own copiers and desktop printers, and then buys toner and paper by the truckload at the best possible price. It trains its employees to keep track of every single copy so its clients can control costs. Copy department employees are transferred from the client firm to Pitney Bowes, the outsourcing firm. There, these employees learn that the head of a Pitney Bowes' copy department can rise to be a regional manager, a vice president or an even higher position within the company. The client firm's costs are lowered and its profits increase. The outsourcing provider makes a tidy profit through its focused expertise. Xerox offers similar services, to the extent that providing services, instead of selling copiers, is now the major part of this firm's business.

One of the largest fields of outsourcing growth has long been in computer departments. IBM and Accenture are among the global leaders in this area. Cloud computing (the use of outsourced, remote servers to run computer functions) is the latest major trend in this regard.

However, many other business functions are commonly outsourced. ServiceMaster takes over janitorial tasks, building management and maintenance functions for giant corporate office campuses and industrial facilities. Another company outsources all of the food warehousing and distribution for nationwide restaurant chains. Why? Because it can run trucks and warehouses more efficiently while its clients concentrate on running restaurants.

While the 1960s, '70s and '80s saw many firms frantically trying to do all tasks in-house, recent trends are quite different. As a period noted for rising productivity and efficiency, the 1990s and 2000s combined were an era of specialization and focus. Companies may do a better job by focusing on their core tasks, while allowing outside firms to provide support and maintenance needs. That trend will continue to be powerful over the long term. Outsourcing, which rapidly gained popularity, will persist in leading the way to higher efficiency and profits. Many

outsourced services companies continue to grow, and they will create (and displace) large numbers of jobs.

Some companies combine outsourcing services with temporary workers. Spherion, a major temporary help firm and one of America's largest employers, is also a leading outsourcing company. Spherion's outsourcing division takes over all human resources administration functions for large clients. This means that Spherion's employees do all of the recruiting, employee records management, benefits management and so on for its client companies. This is a logical extension of Spherion's human resources expertise and good cross-marketing to its roster of corporate clients.

One of the fastest-growing fields in outsourcing has been supply chain and logistics management. Companies offering services in this field include giant transportation companies like UPS. "Supply chain" refers to the entire set of providers of supplies and services that are involved in creating and delivering a component or end product. For example, for an automobile manufacturer like Ford, the supply chain includes companies that make tires, batteries, interior components and engine parts, as well as the trucks and trains that ship these parts and the warehouses that hold them. This supply chain supports Ford's own manufacturing and assembly plants. At the end of Ford's business chain lie the automobile dealers that receive completed cars and deliver them to the end customers. Another example: For a clothing store chain like The Gap, the supply chain includes clothing designers, clothing manufacturers and the warehouses and transportation systems that deliver completed clothes to the stores. The Gap's supply chain is located across dozens of nations.

Logistics is the art of moving goods through the supply chain. Supply chains are so complex and so critical to a company's operations that there are countless ways to automate, improve efficiencies and cut costs. Many manufacturers and retailers are outsourcing all or part of their logistics needs to firms that specialize in creating efficiencies and saving costs. Logistics and supply chain companies have been growing rapidly over the past several years, and creating large numbers of jobs. A concept you should be familiar with is Third Party Logistics ("3PL"), a system whereby a specialist firm in logistics provides a variety of transportation, warehousing and logistics-related services to its clients. These tasks were previously performed in-house by the client. When 3PL services are provided within the client's own facilities, it can also be referred to as "Insourcing." In other words, you might find yourself working for UPS at a site within a distribution company that has no other ties to UPS.

7) Millions Working as Temps

Many major firms, both large and small, are using temporary workers to fill short-term needs, thereby cutting overall employment costs, since temps usually do not receive extensive benefits, bonuses or training. In addition to employees who are placed in temporary jobs by agencies, there are millions of people employed as "independent contractors" and "contract workers." A major development boosting this trend is the "gig economy" or "sharing economy," including companies like the ride service Uber. It now has hundreds of thousands of contract workers. (However, some of these workers are asking the courts to consider whether they are technically employees instead, and a small number of gig economy employers are now treating all of their people as employees, not contractors.)

The largest temporary help agencies tend to have vast global operations. Adecco is a Swiss staffing firm with extensive operations in the U.S., Europe and elsewhere, employing hundreds of thousands of people. Manpower, based in the U.S., does a major part of its business in dozens of nations worldwide. Kelly Services places people in more than 550,000 jobs each year on a worldwide basis.

Demand for temporary workers slows dramatically during economic downturns. The use of temps enables employers to increase the workforce quickly when orders from customers increase, and reduce the workforce rapidly when sales decrease. Temporary workers are also an extremely efficient way to meet needs for one-time projects, fill the slots of permanent employees who are on leave and screen potential candidates for full-time positions by first hiring them on a temporary basis.

In addition, some Americans prefer to work as temporary employees, feeling that this gives them more flexibility in their working lives. Unfortunately, however, many people who end up working in temporary positions would greatly prefer to be employed full-time. Many of these workers have significant experience as well as college degrees. A large percentage of temps work in professional specialties, such as law, finance, engineering or accounting. Also, the number of information technology temps has increased dramatically in the past several years.

Internet Research Tip:
For data on the temporary staffing industry and the temporary workforce in the U.S., see the American Staffing Association (www.americanstaffing.net).

---

8) Offshoring, Reshoring and the Rebound in American Manufacturing

Competition from workers in such nations as Mexico, Indonesia, Thailand and, in particular, China, has been fierce. For several decades, America's manufacturing employment was declining while a vast amount of manufacturing has been sent overseas by U.S. firms.

Today, however, some U.S. industries are experiencing reshoring, or the practice of moving formerly offshored tasks back to America. As wages rise in countries such as China and India, a number of manufacturers are rethinking offshoring, taking into account higher productivity rates among American

workers and higher instances of using cost-effective robotics in manufacturing.

Another factor fueling reshoring is energy costs, which continue to be lower in the U.S. than in many other countries. Savings in energy costs are being augmented by increased manufacturing efficiency. This is due to the growing adoption of robotics. 3-D printing (additive manufacturing) is another technology that is significantly lowering prototyping and product design costs.

While lower employee wages have been a factor in some offshoring, proximity to growing foreign markets is another. Giant multinational companies ranging from Apple to Kraft to General Motors find that a vast portion of their business now lies overseas, often in the rapidly-growing, emerging nations. Many of the world's largest companies find that they need to have local operations throughout the world.

Globalization has a profound effect on Americans—consumer prices become lower, while the U.S. job market changes considerably. Consumer goods are quite inexpensive due to the vast variety of items the U.S. imports from other nations, and prices for many categories of these goods have declined dramatically. Americans can purchase consumer electronics like DVD players and color televisions at extremely low prices, and the price of many types of apparel is much lower thanks to globalization. For example, over 90% of the shoes sold in America are manufactured in low cost nations, especially China.

More than ever before, the world is one vast marketplace. Globalization of business supply chains is a strong trend today and will grow even stronger in the future. Consider the rapid globalization of the automobile industry. The entire global automobile sector is dominated by only a handful of companies, including Toyota, GM, Ford, Daimler, Honda, Volkswagen and Nissan, as well as the increasingly successful Korean automakers Kia and Hyundai. Car manufacturers in China are growing more dominant as well. Car manufacturers commonly have engineering teams collaborating from offices in multiple nations, while parts and components may be imported from a wide variety of suppliers in various countries to undergo final assembly at home.

American companies in many industry sectors have been merging and consolidating on a global basis at a rapid clip. That consolidation will continue. One benefit is that U.S. firms can enter into foreign markets through international acquisitions.

U.S. firms hold leadership positions in several key product and service sectors vital to the rest of the world, including health technology, computers, e-commerce, software and entertainment of all types. The message is clear: global trade and export markets are extremely vital to the health of American business and industry.

A growing middle class in India, China and other emerging nations has been creating demand for goods exported from the U.S., including consumer products bearing desirable brands, as well as luxury automobiles. Also, U.S.-based firms have been enjoying great success in franchising and licensing their methods to startup businesses in China, India and elsewhere, in everything from hotels to fast food to services. American brands such as Nike and Buick are big sellers in China.

Meanwhile, the U.S. is also exporting its expertise in the booming superstore and discount retailing sectors. For instance, hundreds of Wal-Mart's stores are in foreign locations such as Argentina, Brazil, Canada, China, Korea, Mexico, and the U.K. Eventually, Wal-Mart may bring its brand of retailing to virtually all of the world's major markets.

9) Older Americans Will Delay Retirement and Work Longer/Many Employers Find Older Employees Desirable

Certain large employers, particularly national retail chains, have discovered that older workers provide a terrific pool of potential employees. This may be positive for older workers, but to younger job seekers it means more competition for work.

Many members of the immense Baby Boom generation are not planning to retire any time soon. This trend is accelerated by the fact that today's senior citizens will enjoy much longer life spans than earlier generations. Many will continue to work simply because they want to remain active, contributing members of society.

The phrase "Baby Boomer" generally refers to the 78 million Americans born from 1946 to 1964. The term evolved to describe the children of soldiers and war industry workers who were involved in World War II. When those veterans and workers returned to civilian life, they started or added to families in large numbers. As a result, this generation is one of the largest demographic segments in the U.S. Baby Boomers make more than 20% of the U.S. population.

Recently, 2011 marked the year when millions began turning traditional retirement age (65). As Baby Boomers continue to age, America will be experiencing extremely rapid growth in the senior portion of the population. Many Baby Boomers will leave their traditional, long-term jobs and turn to part-time work. Others will continue in their full-time jobs as long as possible.

By the early 2000s, many employers were already developing human resources strategies aimed at hiring or retaining older workers. On the lower end of the pay scale, retailers like Home Depot, a firm that has been known to need tens of thousands of new hires each year, have found older people to be ideal employees. They have knowledge that is extremely useful for providing advice and service to shoppers. They are experienced workers who understand the need to show up on time.

On the higher end of the employment scale, older workers with long-term experience in scientific and engineering tasks will be vital in keeping the gears of business and industry turning. During the 2000s boom, when the airline industry saw good growth, rules were altered in the U.S. to enable commercial airline pilots to keep flying until age 65, instead of facing forced retirement at age 60 as they had in the past.

Industrial firms are dealing with this challenge along two lines: First, how to document and pass along the immense treasure of work-related knowledge that these employees have, and second, how to keep these employees interested in working later into their lives. BASF, a firm with a massive employee base scattered around the world, estimates that by 2020, 50% or more of its employees will be 50 to 65 years old. It has implemented measures ranging from making the workplace more comfortable and safe for older workers, to an intense knowledge transfer program where older workers mentor younger staff members.

10) Employment Sectors that Will Offer an Above-Average Number of Job Opportunities

Job seekers should remain aware of the fact that certain industries will have above-average likelihood to offer job openings. This is due to a number of circumstances, including shifts in consumer tastes and requirements, normal employee turnover and attrition, structural changes within industries, global economic conditions and national policies and priorities.

Below is a list of industries particularly recommended to job seekers.

Employment Sectors that Will Offer an Above-Average Number of Job Opportunities:

- Automobile Manufacturing and Retailing
- Biotechnology
- Child Care/Children's Products
- Consulting, including Technology Consulting
- Consumer Products
- Cosmetics
- Elder Care, Home Health Care, Nursing Homes and Assisted Living Communities
- Electronic Games, Games for Cell Phones
- Energy Conservation Products and Services
- Health Care Services
- Health Care Products
- Health Care Technology, Including Computerized Patient Records
- Health Foods, Organic Foods, Enhanced Foods
- Home Building
- Hotels
- Insurance
- Internet Services, Server Hosting, Cloud Computing
- Internet of Things: Connected Devices, Remote Wireless Sensors and their Networks, Machine to Machine Communications
- Online Search Services & Social Media, with Advertising Revenues
- Online-based Business and Consumer Sales and Services, including E-Commerce

- Outsourcing, Including Outsourced Business and Computer Services
- Pets: Services and Products
- Pharmaceuticals—Generics
- Restaurants
- Retailing—Basic, Including Drugstores and Supermarkets
- Retailing—Discount and Warehouse Clubs
- Robotics and Factory Automation
- Software—Artificial Intelligence
- Software—Corporate, including Development Tools & Cybersecurity
- Software—Data Analytics and Consumer Scoring
- Software—Mobile Apps
- Software as a Service
- Solar Energy Cells Installation & Maintenance
- Supply Chain Services That Create Cost-Savings
- Water Filtration and Conservation Equipment
- Wireless and Cellular Communications

Chapter 2

STATISTICS

Contents:

U.S. Employment Statistics Overview: 2015-2016

(Labor Counts In Thousands; Seasonally Adjusted)

	Jul-15	May-16	Jun-16	Jul-16
Civilian Labor Force, Total	157,115	158,466	158,880	159,287
Employed	148,866	151,030	151,097	151,517
Unemployed	8,249	7,436	7,783	7,770
Persons 16 Years of Age and Over, Not in Labor Force	93,761	94,708	94,517	94,333
Unemployment Rate, All Workers	5.3%	4.7%	4.9%	4.9%
Adult Men (20 years and over)	4.8%	4.3%	4.5%	4.6%
Adult Women (20 years and over)	4.9%	4.2%	4.5%	4.3%
Teenagers (16 to 19 years)	16.3%	16.0%	16.0%	15.6%
White	4.6%	4.1%	4.4%	4.3%
Black or African American	9.1%	8.2%	8.6%	8.4%
Asian	4.0%	4.1%	3.5%	3.8%
Hispanic or Latino	6.8%	5.6%	5.8%	5.4%
Average Hourly Earnings, Private Industry	$25.03	$25.59	$25.61	$25.69
Weekly Earnings, Private Industry	$866.04	$880.30	$880.98	$886.31
Average Work Week, Private Industry (Hours)	34.6	34.4	34.4	34.5
Nonfarm Employment	142,001	143,901	144,193	144,448
Goods-Producing	19,585	19,618	19,623	19,639
Construction	6,437	6,641	6,638	6,652
Manufacturing	12,336	12,281	12,296	12,305
Private Service-Providing	100,394	102,178	102,432	102,633
Retail Trade	15,671	15,920	15,945	15,960
Transportation & Warehousing	4,857	4,890	4,884	4,895
Professional & Business Services	19,707	20,134	20,187	20,257
Education & Health Services	22,075	22,620	22,678	22,714
Leisure & Hospitality	15,125	15,449	15,501	15,546
Government	22,022	22,105	22,138	22,176

Source: U.S. Bureau of Labor Statistics

Plunkett Research,® Ltd.

www.plunkettresearch.com

U.S. Civilian Labor Force:
1997-July 2016

(Persons 16 & Older; In Thousands)

Year	Civilian Workforce Level
1997	136,297
1998	137,673
1999	139,368
2000	142,583
2001	143,734
2002	144,863
2003	146,510
2004	147,401
2005	149,320
2006	151,428
2007	153,124
2008	154,287
2009	154,142
2010	153,889
2011	153,617
2012	154,975
2013	155,389
2014	155,922
2015	157,130
Jul-16	160,705

Note: The civilian labor force consists of employed and unemployed people actively seeking work, but it does not include any Armed Forces personnel.

Source: U.S. Bureau of Labor Statistics

Plunkett Research,® Ltd.

www.plunkettresearch.com

Employment by Major Industry Sector: 2004, 2014 & Projected 2024

Industry Sector	Employment (in Thousands)			Change (in Thousands)		Percent Distribution			Compound Annual Rate of Change	
	2004	2014	2024	2004-14	2014-24	2004	2014	2024	2004-14	2014-24
Total[1]	144,047.0	150,539.9	160,328.8	6,492.9	9,788.9	100.0	100.0	100.0	0.4	0.6
Nonagriculture wage & salary[2]	132,462.2	139,811.5	149,131.6	7,349.3	9,320.1	92.0	92.9	93.0	0.5	0.6
Goods-producing, excluding agriculture	21,815.3	19,170.5	19,227.0	-2,644.8	56.5	15.1	12.7	12.0	-1.3	0.0
Mining	523.2	843.8	924.0	320.6	80.2	0.4	0.6	0.6	4.9	0.9
Construction	6,976.2	6,138.4	6,928.8	-837.8	790.4	4.8	4.1	4.3	-1.3	1.2
Manufacturing	14,315.9	12,188.3	11,374.2	-2,127.6	-814.1	9.9	8.1	7.1	-1.6	-0.7
Services-providing	110,646.9	120,641.0	129,904.6	9,994.1	9,263.6	76.8	80.1	81.0	0.9	0.7
Utilities	563.8	553.0	505.1	-10.8	-47.9	0.4	0.4	0.3	-0.2	-0.9
Wholesale trade	5,663.0	5,826.0	6,151.4	163.0	325.4	3.9	3.9	3.8	0.3	0.5
Retail trade	15,058.2	15,364.5	16,129.1	306.3	764.6	10.5	10.2	10.1	0.2	0.5
Transportation & warehousing	4,248.6	4,640.3	4,776.9	391.7	136.6	2.9	3.1	3.0	0.9	0.3
Information	3,118.3	2,739.7	2,712.6	-378.6	-27.1	2.2	1.8	1.7	-1.3	-0.1
Financial activities	8,105.1	7,979.5	8,486.7	-125.6	507.2	5.6	5.3	5.3	-0.2	0.6
Professional & business services	16,394.9	19,096.2	20,985.5	2,701.3	1,889.3	11.4	12.7	13.1	1.5	0.9
Educational services	2,762.5	3,417.4	3,756.1	654.9	338.7	1.9	2.3	2.3	2.2	0.9
Health care & social assistance	14,429.8	18,057.4	21,852.2	3,627.6	3,794.8	10.0	12.0	13.6	2.3	1.9
Leisure & hospitality	12,493.1	14,710.0	15,651.2	2,216.9	941.2	8.7	9.8	9.8	1.6	0.6
Other services	6,188.3	6,394.0	6,662.0	205.7	268.0	4.3	4.2	4.2	0.3	0.4
Federal government	2,730.0	2,729.0	2,345.6	-1.0	-383.4	1.9	1.8	1.5	0.0	-1.5
State & local government	18,891.3	19,134.0	19,890.1	242.7	756.1	13.1	12.7	12.4	0.1	0.4
Agriculture, forestry, fishing & hunting[3]	2,111.3	2,138.3	2,027.7	26.9	-110.5	1.5	1.4	1.3	0.1	-0.5
Agriculture wage & salary	1,149.0	1,384.0	1,307.3	235.0	-76.7	0.8	0.9	0.8	1.9	-0.6
Agriculture self-employed & unpaid family workers	962.3	754.3	720.4	-208.1	-33.8	0.7	0.5	0.4	-2.4	-0.5
Nonagriculture self-employed & unpaid family workers	9,473.6	8,590.2	9,169.5	-883.4	579.3	6.6	5.7	5.7	-1.0	0.7

[1] Employment data for wage and salary workers are from the BLS Current Employment Statistics survey, which counts jobs, whereas self-employed, unpaid family workers, and agriculture, forestry, fishing, and hunting are from the Current Population Survey (household survey), which counts workers.

[2] Includes wage and salary data from the Current Employment Statistics survey, except private households, which is from the Current Population Survey. Logging workers are excluded.

[3] Includes agriculture, forestry, fishing, and hunting data from the Current Population Survey, except logging, which is from Current Employment Statistics survey. Government wage and salary workers are excluded.

Source: U.S. Bureau of Labor Statistics

Plunkett Research,® Ltd.

www.plunkettresearch.com

Number of People Employed and Unemployed, U.S.:
July 2015 vs. July 2016

(Persons 16 & Older; Numbers In Thousands; Not Seasonally Adjusted)

Occupation	Employed		Unemployed		Unemp. Rates (%)	
	Jul-15	Jul-16	Jul-15	Jul-16	Jul-15	Jul-16
Total*	149,722	152,437	8,805	8,267	5.6	5.1
Management, professional and related	57,392	58,434	1,807	1,782	3.1	3.0
Management, business and financial operations	24,522	24,755	566	609	2.3	2.4
Professional and related	32,870	33,678	1,240	1,174	3.6	3.4
Service	26,843	28,293	1,932	1,626	6.7	5.4
Sales and office	33,366	33,766	1,848	1,691	5.2	4.8
Sales and related	15,677	16,031	966	828	5.8	4.9
Office and administrative support	17,689	17,734	882	863	4.8	4.6
Natural resources, construction and maintenance	14,294	14,467	816	769	5.4	5.0
Farming, fishing and forestry	1,155	1,221	76	99	6.2	7.5
Construction and extraction	7,970	8,354	536	463	6.3	5.3
Installation, maintenance and repair	5,169	4,892	204	207	3.8	4.1
Production, transportation and material moving	17,827	17,477	1,248	1,265	6.5	6.8
Production	8,647	8,235	567	517	6.2	5.9
Transportation and material moving	9,180	9,242	681	749	6.9	7.5

* Persons with no previous work experience and persons whose last job was in the Armed Forces are included in the unemployed total.

Note: Updated population controls are introduced annually with the release of January data.

Source: U.S. Bureau of Labor Statistics

Plunkett Research,® Ltd.

www.plunkettresearch.com

U.S. Labor Force Ages 16 to 24 Years Old by School Enrollment, Educational Attainment, Sex, Race & Ethnicity: October 2015

(Numbers in Thousands, Latest Year Available)	Civilian non-institutional population	Total in Labor Force	Percent of Populace	Employed		Unemployed		Not in Labor Force
				Total	Percent of Populace	Number	Rate (%)	
Total, 16 to 24 years	38,491	21,190	55.1	18,945	49.2	2,245	10.6	17,302
Educational Attainment								
Enrolled in school	21,948	7,943	36.2	7,242	33.0	702	8.8	14,005
Enrolled in high school[1]	9,604	2,050	21.3	1,752	18.2	299	14.6	7,554
Men	4,937	999	20.2	849	17.2	150	15.0	3,939
Women	4,667	1,051	22.5	903	19.3	149	14.1	3,615
White	7,019	1,587	22.6	1,363	19.4	224	14.1	5,431
Black or African American	1,480	251	16.9	213	14.4	37	14.9	1,229
Asian	430	33	7.6	28	6.4	5	-	397
Hispanic or Latino ethnicity	2,190	383	17.5	304	13.9	79	20.7	1,807
Enrolled in college	12,344	5,893	47.7	5,490	44.5	403	6.8	6,451
Enrolled in 2-year college	3,258	1,870	57.4	1,715	52.6	155	8.3	1,387
Enrolled in 4-year college	9,087	4,023	44.3	3,775	41.5	247	6.2	5,064
Full-time students	10,628	4,522	42.5	4,198	39.5	324	7.2	6,106
Part-time students	1,716	1,371	79.9	1,292	75.3	78	5.7	345
Men	5,785	2,627	45.4	2,396	41.4	231	8.8	3,159
Women	6,559	3,266	49.8	3,094	47.2	172	5.3	3,292
White	9,096	4,544	50.0	4,234	46.5	310	6.8	4,552
Black or African American	1,657	773	46.7	713	43.0	60	7.8	884
Asian	1,046	292	27.9	282	27.0	10	3.4	754
Hispanic or Latino ethnicity	2,411	1,207	50.0	1,100	45.6	107	8.8	1,205
Not enrolled in school	16,543	13,246	80.1	11,703	70.7	1,543	11.7	3,297
16 to 19 years	3,098	2,091	67.5	1,705	55.0	386	18.5	1,007
20 to 24 years	13,445	11,155	83.0	9,998	74.4	1,157	10.4	2,290
Sex								
Men	8,670	7,289	84.1	6,436	74.2	853	11.7	1,381
Less than a high school diploma	1,220	799	65.5	584	47.9	216	27.0	420
High school graduates, no college[3]	4,243	3,578	84.3	3,144	74.1	434	12.1	665
Some college or associate degree	2,101	1,855	88.3	1,699	80.9	156	8.4	247
Bachelor's degree and higher[4]	1,106	1,057	95.5	1,009	91.2	48	4.5	49
Women	7,874	5,958	75.7	5,268	66.9	690	11.6	1,916
Less than a high school diploma	1,034	461	44.6	357	34.5	104	22.6	573
High school graduates, no college[3]	3,175	2,302	72.5	1,951	61.4	351	15.2	874
Some college or associate degree	2,147	1,796	83.6	1,669	77.7	127	7.1	351
Bachelor's degree and higher[4]	1,517	1,399	92.3	1,291	85.1	108	7.7	117
Race								
White	12,293	10,001	81.4	9,050	73.6	952	9.5	2,292
Black or African American	2,753	2,117	76.9	1,659	60.3	458	21.6	635
Asian	581	408	70.3	382	65.7	26	6.5	173
Hispanic or Latino ethnicity	3,811	2,947	77.3	2,571	67.5	377	12.8	864

Note: The civilian labor force consists of employed and unemployed people actively seeking work, but it does not include any Armed Forces personnel. Detail for the above race groups do not sum to totals because data are not presented for all races. Persons whose ethnicity is identified as Hispanic or Latino may be of any race. Because of rounding, sums of individual items may not equal totals.

[1] Includes a small number of persons who are in grades below high school. [2] Data not shown where base is less than 75,000. [3] Includes persons with a high school diploma or equivalent. [4] Includes persons with bachelor's, master's, professional, and doctoral degrees.

Source: U.S. Bureau of Labor Statistics

Plunkett Research,® Ltd.

www.plunkettresearch.com

Medical Care Benefits in the U.S.: Access, Participation and Take-Up Rates, March 2016

(All workers = 100 percent)

Characteristics	Private Industry			State/Local Government		
	Access	Particip-ation	Take-up Rate[1]	Access	Particip-ation	Take-up Rate[1]
All workers	67%	49%	73%	88%	73%	83%
Worker Characteristics						
Management, professional and related	86%	66%	77%	89%	73%	82%
Service	39%	23%	58%	82%	69%	84%
Sales and office	66%	47%	71%	89%	75%	83%
Natural resources, construction and maintenance	72%	58%	80%	95%	81%	85%
Production, transportation and material moving	74%	55%	74%	81%	68%	85%
Full time	86%	63%	74%	99%	82%	83%
Part time	19%	11%	59%	24%	17%	71%
Union	93%	78%	85%	95%	79%	84%
Nonunion	65%	46%	71%	81%	67%	82%
Wage percentiles[2]						
Lowest 25 percent	33%	19%	57%	70%	57%	81%
Lowest 10 percent	22%	11%	48%	56%	45%	80%
Second 25 percent	71%	50%	70%	91%	77%	84%
Third 25 percent	85%	65%	77%	94%	78%	83%
Highest 25 percent	92%	72%	78%	97%	80%	82%
Highest 10 percent	93%	72%	78%	96%	80%	83%
Establishment Characteristics						
1 to 99 workers	55%	39%	70%	76%	63%	83%
1 to 49 workers	52%	36%	69%	69%	57%	84%
50 to 99 workers	66%	47%	72%	88%	72%	82%
100 workers or more	82%	62%	75%	89%	74%	83%
100 to 499 workers	79%	58%	74%	85%	70%	82%
500 workers or more	88%	68%	77%	91%	75%	83%

Note: For this table, a worker with access to medical care benefits is defined as having an employer-provided medical plan available for use, regardless of the worker's decision to enroll or participate in the plan. Farm and private household workers, the self-employed and Federal government workers are excluded from the survey.

[1] The take-up rate is a rounded estimate of the percentage of workers with access to a plan who participate in the plan.

[2] Surveyed occupations are classified into wage categories based on the average wage for the occupation, which may include workers with earnings both above and below the threshold. The categories were formed using percentile estimates generated using data from the National Compensation Survey publication, "Employer Costs for Employee Compensation - March 2016."

Source: U.S. Bureau of Labor Statistics

Plunkett Research,® Ltd.

www.plunkettresearch.com

Retirement Benefits in the U.S.: Access, Participation and Take-Up Rates, March 2016

(All workers = 100 percent)

Characteristics	Private Industry			State/Local Government		
	Access	Particip-ation	Take-up Rate[1]	Access	Particip-ation	Take-up Rate[1]
All workers	66%	49%	75%	90%	81%	90%
Worker Characteristics						
Management, professional and related	81%	69%	85%	92%	81%	89%
Service	41%	23%	56%	86%	78%	90%
Sales and office	69%	50%	72%	91%	82%	90%
Natural resources, construction and maintenance	62%	49%	79%	97%	91%	94%
Production, transportation and material moving	70%	53%	75%	85%	78%	91%
Full time	77%	60%	78%	99%	89%	90%
Part time	37%	21%	56%	40%	34%	85%
Union	91%	81%	90%	97%	87%	89%
Nonunion	64%	46%	73%	84%	76%	90%
Wage percentiles[2]						
Lowest 25 percent	42%	22%	52%	76%	68%	89%
Lowest 10 percent	33%	14%	42%	63%	55%	87%
Second 25 percent	65%	45%	69%	93%	84%	90%
Third 25 percent	78%	64%	82%	95%	86%	91%
Highest 25 percent	87%	76%	88%	98%	87%	89%
Highest 10 percent	88%	79%	90%	97%	84%	86%
Establishment Characteristics						
1 to 99 workers	52%	36%	70%	80%	72%	91%
1 to 49 workers	47%	33%	70%	73%	66%	91%
50 to 99 workers	65%	46%	70%	90%	81%	90%
100 workers or more	83%	66%	79%	92%	82%	90%
100 to 499 workers	80%	59%	74%	88%	81%	92%
500 workers or more	90%	76%	85%	93%	83%	89%

Note: Benefits may include defined benefit pension plans as well as defined contribution retirement plans. Workers are considered as having access or as participating if they have access to or participate in at least one of these plan types. Farm and private household workers, the self-employed and Federal government workers are excluded from the survey.

[1] The take-up rate is a rounded estimate of the percentage of workers with access to a plan who participate in the plan.

[2] Surveyed occupations are classified into wage categories based on the average wage for the occupation, which may include workers with earnings both above and below the threshold. The categories were formed using percentile estimates generated using data from the National Compensation Survey publication, "Employer Costs for Employee Compensation - March 2016."

Source: U.S. Bureau of Labor Statistics

Plunkett Research,® Ltd.

www.plunkettresearch.com

Top 15 U.S. Occupations by Numerical Change in Job Growth: 2014-2024

(By Thousands of Employees)

Occupation	Employment		Change		Median annual wage, 2014
	2014	2024	Number	Percent	
Total, all occupations	150,539.9	160,328.8	9,788.9	6.5	$35,540
Personal care aides	1,768.4	2,226.5	458.1	25.9	$20,440
Registered nurses	2,751.0	3,190.3	439.3	16.0	$66,640
Home health aides	913.5	1,261.9	348.4	38.1	$21,380
Combined food preparation and serving workers, including fast food	3,159.7	3,503.2	343.5	10.9	$18,410
Retail salespersons	4,624.9	4,939.1	314.2	6.8	$21,390
Nursing assistants	1,492.1	1,754.1	262.0	17.6	$25,100
Customer service representatives	2,581.8	2,834.8	252.9	9.8	$31,200
Cooks, restaurant	1,109.7	1,268.7	158.9	14.3	$22,490
General and operations managers	2,124.1	2,275.2	151.1	7.1	$97,270
Construction laborers	1,159.1	1,306.5	147.4	12.7	$31,090
Accountants and auditors	1,332.7	1,475.1	142.4	10.7	$65,940
Medical assistants	591.3	730.2	138.9	23.5	$29,960
Janitors and cleaners, except maids and housekeeping cleaners	2,360.6	2,496.9	136.3	5.8	$22,840
Software developers, applications	718.4	853.7	135.3	18.8	$95,510
Laborers and freight, stock, and material movers, hand	2,441.3	2,566.4	125.1	5.1	$24,430

Source: U.S. Bureau of Labor Statistics

Plunkett Research,® Ltd.

www.plunkettresearch.com

Top 15 U.S. Occupations by Percent Change in Job Growth: 2014-2024

(Employment in Thousands)

Occupation	Employment		Change		Median annual wage, 2014
	2014	2024	Number	Percent	
Total, all occupations	150,539.9	160,328.8	9,788.9	6.5	$35,540
Wind turbine service technicians	4.4	9.2	4.8	108.0	$48,800
Occupational therapy assistants	33.0	47.1	14.1	42.7	$56,950
Physical therapist assistants	78.7	110.7	31.9	40.6	$54,410
Physical therapist aides	50.0	69.5	19.5	39.0	$24,650
Home health aides	913.5	1,261.9	348.4	38.1	$21,380
Commercial divers	4.4	6.0	1.6	36.9	$45,890
Nurse practitioners	126.9	171.7	44.7	35.2	$95,350
Physical therapists	210.9	282.7	71.8	34.0	$82,390
Statisticians	30.0	40.1	10.1	33.8	$79,990
Ambulance drivers and attendants, except emergency medical technicians	19.6	26.1	6.5	33.0	$24,080
Occupational therapy aides	8.8	11.6	2.7	30.6	$26,550
Physician assistants	94.4	123.2	28.7	30.4	$95,820
Operations research analysts	91.3	118.9	27.6	30.2	$76,660
Personal financial advisors	249.4	323.2	73.9	29.6	$81,060
Cartographers and photogrammetrists	12.3	15.9	3.6	29.3	$60,930

Source: U.S. Bureau of Labor Statistics

Plunkett Research,® Ltd.

www.plunkettresearch.com

Occupations with the Largest Expected Employment Increases, U.S.: 2014-2024

(By Increase in Number Employed, in Thousands)

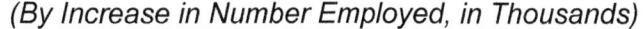

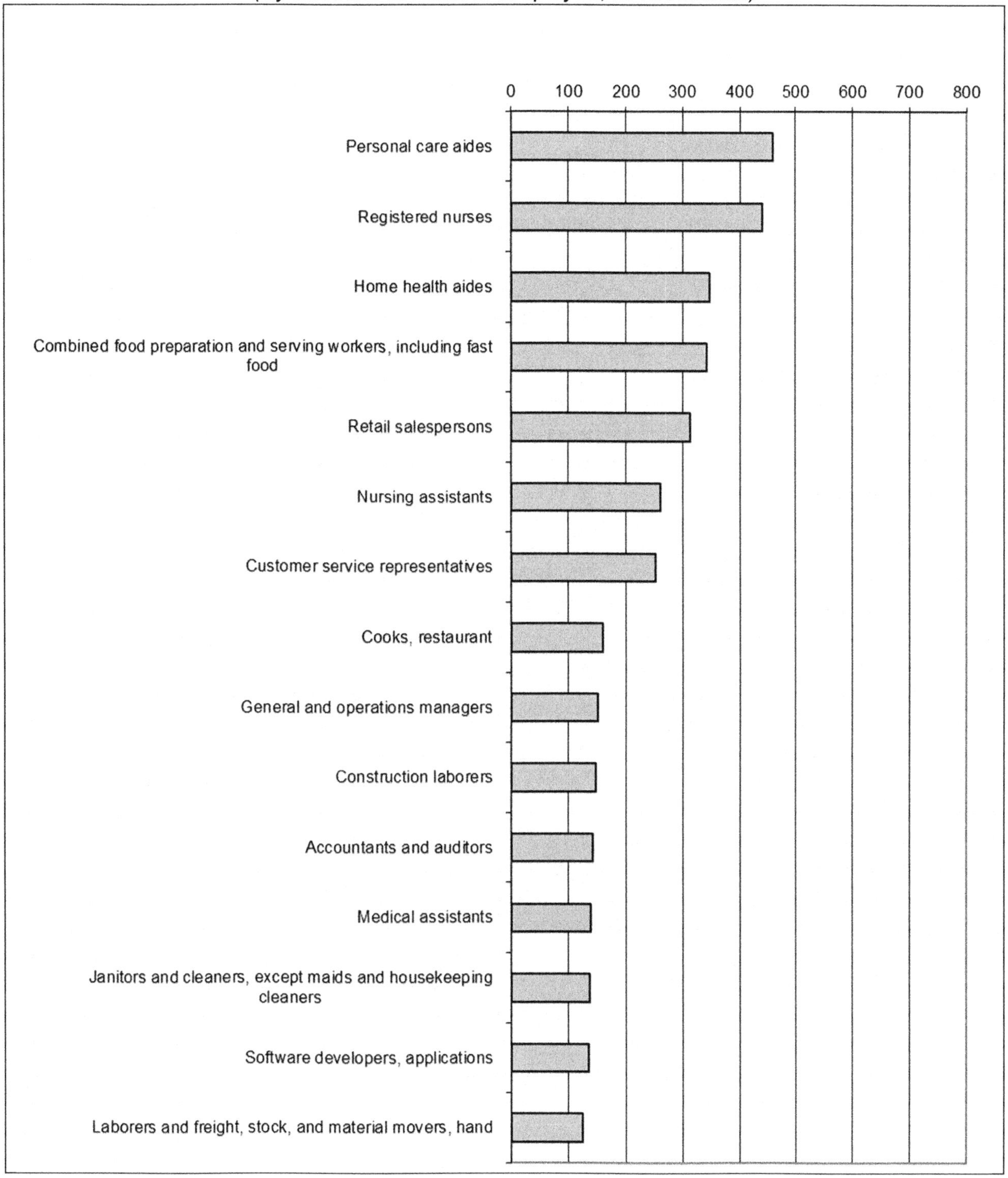

	0	100	200	300	400	500	600	700	800
Personal care aides									
Registered nurses									
Home health aides									
Combined food preparation and serving workers, including fast food									
Retail salespersons									
Nursing assistants									
Customer service representatives									
Cooks, restaurant									
General and operations managers									
Construction laborers									
Accountants and auditors									
Medical assistants									
Janitors and cleaners, except maids and housekeeping cleaners									
Software developers, applications									
Laborers and freight, stock, and material movers, hand									

Source: U.S. Bureau of Labor Statistics

Plunkett Research,® Ltd.

www.plunkettresearch.com

Industries with the Largest Employment Decline, U.S.: 2014-2024

(In Thousands)

Occupation	Major Sector	Employment		Change	
		2014	2024	Number	Compound Annual Rate
Postal Service	Federal government	593.0	427.9	-165.1	-3.2
Federal non-defense government compensation	Federal government	1,514.8	1,404.3	-110.5	-0.8
Newspaper, periodical, book, and directory publishers	Information	412.3	309.0	-103.3	-2.8
Wired telecommunications carriers	Information	607.0	509.2	-97.8	-1.7
Federal defense government compensation	Federal government	522.2	440.0	-82.2	-1.7
Printing and related support activities	Manufacturing	452.7	371.3	-81.4	-2.0
Apparel, leather, and allied manufacturing	Manufacturing	168.5	91.7	-76.8	-5.9
Crop production	Agriculture	765.6	699.9	-65.7	-0.9
Plastics product manufacturing	Manufacturing	541.6	478.5	-63.1	-1.2
Textile mills and textile product mills	Manufacturing	232.1	174.2	-57.9	-2.8
Other miscellaneous manufacturing	Manufacturing	275.2	219.3	-55.9	-2.2
Electric power generation, transmission and distribution	Utilities	392.1	351.3	-40.8	-1.1
Navigational, measuring, electromedical, and control instruments manufacturing	Manufacturing	388.3	353.1	-35.2	-0.9
Semiconductor and other electronic component manufacturing	Manufacturing	367.8	332.7	-35.1	-1.0
Computer and peripheral equipment manufacturing	Manufacturing	162.8	135.5	-27.3	-1.8
Travel arrangement and reservation services	Professional business services	195.7	168.9	-26.8	-1.5
Aerospace product and parts manufacturing	Manufacturing	488.4	464.1	-24.3	-0.5
Communications equipment manufacturing	Manufacturing	93.5	69.5	-24.0	-2.9
Motor vehicle parts manufacturing	Manufacturing	536.6	514.0	-22.6	-0.4
Federal enterprises except the Postal Service and electric utilities	Federal government	81.1	58.9	-22.2	-3.1

Source: U.S. Bureau of Labor Statistics

Plunkett Research,® Ltd.

www.plunkettresearch.com

Chapter 3

RESEARCH: 7 KEYS FOR JOB SEEKERS

How to use your library, college placement office, the Internet and other resources
to become well-informed about a company and its industry
<u>before</u> you ask for an interview

Research is the key to finding appropriate job openings, targeting the best possible employers and performing well when you go to job interviews. Learn what's unique about a company compared to other firms in its industry. Learn why it's prospering–or why it isn't. Where is this company going? Is it favored by stock investors? Is it privately-owned by a family, or has it been acquired by private equity investors who plan to resell it over the mid-term? What are its hottest-selling products and services? Is it investing in research and new facilities so that it may prosper in the future? Also, as many people who have been laid off from failing firms have learned the hard way, determining a company's level of financial stability can be one of the most important factors in making a career decision.

The more you're willing to dig deep at the library or your college's career planning office, and the more adept you are at using the Internet for research, the better your chances of success in a job search. If you are willing to ask questions of knowledgeable businesspeople and of employees who currently work for your target employers, you will enhance your job search even further. The two secrets to successful job research are tenacity and focus. Know what to look for and where to find it.

Once you've landed an interview, you should research both the prospective employer and its industry even further. In this manner, you'll know what questions to ask before you agree to take the job, and you'll present yourself as a knowledgeable potential hire who is truly interested in the company and its business.

Here are the seven keys for research that can lead you to a great employer:

1) Financial Stability
Check bond ratings, credit ratings, debt level, growth in sales and growth in profits, along with the views of stock analysts and business journalists.

2) Growth Plans
Look for new plants, stores or offices to be opened; new technologies, products or divisions to be launched; or plans for strategic acquisitions. (See 3, 4 and 5 below.) Is the employer's growth strategy focused primarily on offshoring work to overseas locations or outsourcing work to outside services providers? Or, does it have a balanced growth strategy that will create good opportunities in its American operations?

3) Research and Development Programs
If the company is a major manufacturer or a technology-based firm, then you should investigate how it invests in R&D (research and development). Is its research and development budget growing? For many types of companies, research is a vital investment in the future.

4) Product Launch and Production
Does the company have the ability to successfully launch new products and services (see 5 below) or to invest in and utilize cutting-edge technologies needed to maintain a competitive edge?

5) Marketing and Distribution Methods
Does the firm utilize an in-house sales force? Does it work through outside dealers and distribution partners? What are its advertising methods? Is it increasing its market share, or are competitors taking customers away? Is the company growing its international sales? Is it adept at using the Internet as a powerful sales tool? Is it successful at selling into vital international markets?

6) Employee Benefits

Are wealth-building benefit plans offered? Will the company match all or part of your deposits to a 401(k) savings plan? Check for tuition reimbursement, pension plans, profit sharing, stock ownership plans, discount stock purchase plans, stock options or performance-based bonuses.

7) Quality-of-Work Factors

Does the company offer continual training, wellness programs, child care, elder care support, promote-from-within policies, flexible work schedules, performance reviews, product discounts or on-site health clubs? Is it a corporate culture that fits your lifestyle?

As a serious job seeker, you should conduct in-depth research and make detailed notes about these key factors for each firm you are considering. Then compare each company's finances, plans and programs to others in the same industry. You'll begin to see what makes some firms outstanding and why those outstanding companies are the best places to make a career investment. For example, if you compare two discount store giants, Wal-Mart and Costco, you will find that Wal-Mart is by far the larger firm, but Costco has an outstanding record of providing superior employee pay and benefits.

Your research goal should be twofold: First, determine whether this is a firm you want to work for. Are the salaries and benefits appealing? Are layoffs likely? Is it planning to expand its workforce in lower-cost nations like India and then lay off U.S. employees? Is the firm growing steadily? A growing company will offer opportunities for you to advance when it launches new locations, services, technologies or product lines. Second, develop a personal understanding of both the company and its industry so you can better sell yourself as a potential employee.

Other Considerations:

Women and Minorities:

Certain industries have a greater tendency to offer advancement opportunities for women or minorities. Historically, the banking and insurance segments have tended to promote both women and minorities, as have retailing, electric utilities, apparel, consumer goods, packaged food and beverages, education, publishing and telephone companies.

Some technology companies have been terrific places for women who want to advance, and many tech companies, such as Hewlett-Packard, IBM, Yahoo, Xerox and eBay, have been known to post women to CEO spots.

Black Enterprise magazine publishes an annual list of the "Most Powerful African Americans in Corporate America," (see www.blackenterprise.com). Meanwhile, the Executive Leadership Council, www.elcinfo.com, a Washington, D.C.-based nonprofit group that conducts programs aimed at filling more executive posts with African Americans, has a unique statistic to report. Its membership is composed of senior-level black executives who have jobs that are no more than three levels below the CEO spot at Fortune 500 companies. When the group was founded in 1986, it had only a handful of members. Today, its membership is about 500 people employed in high-level executive jobs at major corporations (one-third of them are women).

The Hispanic Association on Corporate Responsibility (www.hacr.org) promotes Hispanic advancement in the areas of employment, procurement, philanthropy and governance. Another nonprofit agency, National Hispanic Corporate Achievers (hispanicachievers.org), provides an educational forum for Hispanics working for *Fortune 1000* companies.

Tips on Using Business Magazines, Newspapers and Trade Journals to Find Job Leads and Do Employer Research

Many job seekers overlook the tremendous advantages offered by industry magazines (called "trade journals") and other publications when conducting research.

Industry-specific trade journals frequently have classified ads in the back that list job openings. An example of a great magazine to study is *American Banker,* which can be found at major libraries. Additional information is available at www.americanbanker.com.

Journalists at trade journals and business newspapers continuously interview industry-leading executives regarding their companies' growth plans. New projects and company expansion plans described in these articles provide terrific job leads.

You can also get great contact information from these publications. Read the latest business stories about companies and industries that interest you and you will learn vital information. Best of all, you can glean from stories and interviews the names and titles of executives who lead projects, divisions and subsidiaries.

There are literally hundreds of these trade journals—at least one for each industry sector and sometimes dozens covering the largest industries.

Other great resources include business newspapers such as the *Dallas/Ft. Worth Business Journal, The Wall Street Journal,* the business pages of major newspapers like *The New York Times* and publications written for major investors like *Investor's Business Daily.* At www.bizjournals.com, you can gain access to news stories from business journals from all over the U.S.

Quality-of-Life Benefits:

Many companies offer benefits that help employees balance their personal and professional lives. The concept is that employees who are healthy and comfortable with their personal and family lives make better, more productive employees. To that end, many companies include fitness programs and family services such as extended maternity leaves and child care or elder care, whether on-site or off-site in the form of referral services. Other popular family-friendly benefits include flextime, flexible benefits spending accounts, adoption assistance and telecommuting. In many cases, benefits are listed on employers' web sites.

Work-Life has become a popular phrase for family-friendly benefits and programs among major employers such as Intel, Abbott Laboratories, Baxter International and Aramark. For additional information, you can study such organizations at the Alliance for Work-Life Progress site at www.awlp.org.

Growth Potential and Job Stability:

A firm's growth potential should be among your top priorities. Companies are always trying to maintain or increase productivity, or the ratio of revenues per employee. If a company's sales are sliding, or if it is running out of cash, the job picture starts to collapse. A little extra research into a company's finances and true potential for growth might save you from a future layoff.

Of course, employers sometimes have to resort to layoffs due to conditions outside of their control. The devastating economic recession that officially ran from late 2007 through early 2009 led to millions of layoffs in America.

As a job seeker, you're forced to look out for your own best interests while you sort through thousands of potential employers in dozens of industries. This means that good research is vital. For example, if you put salary at the top of your list, you may have the wrong priorities. From time to time, some of the highest-paying firms have been among those cutting the largest numbers of employees. If you are looking for job stability, your biggest challenge is to pick companies that are more likely to hire now and less likely to have layoffs in the future. That's why a firm's growth outlook should be one of your guiding lights.

However, the goal is *internal* growth caused by expanding sales. Generally less appealing are firms that post a quick spike in growth through big mergers. (In many cases, merged companies lay off people who suddenly find themselves filling jobs duplicated in newly consolidated offices. Also, companies that grow excessively through acquisitions may be taking on loads of debt that can become hard to handle later. However, there are occasional exceptions to this rule, where firms are enjoying soaring demand for products or services and find it difficult to hire quickly enough to keep up.) Companies that are growing rapidly through internal expansion include those opening new stores, distribution centers or offices, developing exciting new products, moving into new markets (including international markets) and creating hot new technologies, retail formats or services. Those types of expansion frequently mean great career

opportunities, including the chance for rapid job promotion.

If you're tenacious, you can find opportunities where others will find only rejection. Identifying real prospects for growth takes more than a quick glance.

Here's an extremely important point for you to remember: You should also look for opportunities in growing divisions that serve special niches, even when the company as a whole is cutting jobs. For example, a firm's online division may be growing, even while its traditional business units are shrinking.

Additional key factors for strong corporate growth, and thereby the best job prospects, include:

1) Companies or divisions with a growing share of a promising market.

Management's ability to anticipate or create change in the marketplace makes for a growing company with great prospects. For example, Sam Walton revolutionized the department store business by realizing that consumers want everyday low prices on name-brand merchandise. He created Wal-Mart, while competitor Sears suffered by maintaining an old-fashioned policy of special sales events on private-label goods. Wal-Mart rapidly became one of the largest creators of new jobs in the private sector. Sears was forced to slash its ranks.

Microsoft made its way to the top with unique products serving a soaring market when it developed highly functional software for personal computers. The software giant created thousands of millionaire employees through the immense increase in the value of its stock plans. HEB, an innovative grocer in Texas, has evolved continually over the decades, constantly introducing improvements to store layouts, and even creating an exciting new HEB Marketplace concept that is a retail industry leader. HEB has large numbers of job openings of many types on a continuous basis.

The point to these stories is that you shouldn't invest your career in a company with mediocre prospects. With perseverance, you can target your own list of employers that are posting growth due to competitive advantages or growing market demand. Your best bets are companies taking reasonable risks in order to move ahead. Those risks may include investments in advertising, research and development, new technology, improved techniques on the manufacturing floor, testing of new products and the opening of new retail store formats. For example, Chico's FAS stores scored a hit by filling a niche in the women's apparel market, and Genentech became a leader in the biotechnology field by risking vast amounts on research. Also, don't overlook the potential of the export market—many American firms find much of their growth by creating products and services that enjoy demand overseas as well as in the U.S.

2) Sales and profits: past and present.

The companies most likely to move along at a good clip are those with an exciting mid-term history. Firms with an average annual growth in sales of 10% to 15% or more over the past several years are generally very promising. Companies that managed to get through the recent recession with only minor drops in revenues may be remarkably stable. Many small and mid-size firms grow at much faster rates and find themselves hiring continuously.

3) Beware of fads.

Unfortunately, a few companies post meteoric growth in businesses that turn out to be mere fads. The restaurant industry suffers from this problem on a regular basis. In recent years, companies selling bagels, frozen yogurt, rotisserie chicken and the like enjoyed impressive, nationwide growth only to collapse like a house of cards a couple of years later.

How to Find and Use Expert Opinions:

Superior sources used by sophisticated job researchers include reports written by: 1) stock analysts; 2) professional market research firms; and 3) journalists at business magazines and industry "trade magazines." Many major libraries have large collections of industry-specific trade magazines that can give you clues that competing job seekers will overlook. Virtually every industry is covered by one or two trade magazines that will give you leads to growing companies. Many articles in these magazines contain the names of executives you may want to contact. Also, most industry trade magazines publish help-wanted ads in the back. It's easy to do an online search for trade magazines, and most of them have terrific web sites that are filled with extremely useful information. For example, a recent search on Google for "pet industry trade magazine" quickly turned up leads to the top magazines for that sector.

Next, move on to reports from experts. Marketing and investment professionals are looking for some of the same clues you should use as a job seeker, and reports written by full-time analysts who cover specific companies or industries can help you find firms that are growing and hiring. You can purchase reports for publicly-traded firms at Yahoo! Finance, http://finance.yahoo.com. First, look up a company by name or ticker symbol. Once you are on the page for that company, look down the left hand column for the link to "Research Reports."

Professionally written market research can be found at Marketresearch.com, www.marketresearch.com. This market research broker charges varying fees for access to the reports. However, many of the reports are reasonably priced, and the insight you gain into industries, markets and leading companies can be extremely helpful. Web sites such as this offer the ability to search for reports by a wide variety of criteria, including company name and industry.

Internet Research Tip:

Be sure to create Google "Alerts" to follow your targeted employers and profession. Google will email results to you daily.

By going to the "more" link at the top of the Google home page, and then selecting "even more" from the drop down list, you can access Google's "Alerts" tool. Here you can arrange to receive email updates on topics of your choice. For example, you can set a general alert about an industry or locale: sales jobs in California, for example. Or something like: opportunities in the American wireless industry. Or even: sales jobs at automobile dealers.

You can use alerts to track specific jobs or employers. For example: openings at Intel. Or: regional sales manager opening Los Angeles. Finally, don't forget that you may want to put a search phrase within quotes to get an exact match to part of your phrase. For example: "loan officer" wanted.

Other Basic Resources:

Annual Reports/10-Ks/S-1s: Companies that sell their stocks to the public, including most of the firms covered in this book, publish annual reports that contain a wealth of information. Annual reports and 10-Ks cover yearly results, financial statements, management practices and other vital information for publicly held firms. S-1s provide the same type of information on companies that are selling stock to the public for the first time. You can find copies of these reports at large libraries. Online, the best place to acquire this information is at typically at the "Investors" tab on the website of the company you are researching. Alternately, try the site of the U.S. Securities and Exchange Commission. They have a user-friendly service that enables you to search for companies and access their financial reports at www.sec.gov. (Look for the "Filings & Forms" section, and then see "Search for Company Filings.") Look especially at the five-year "summary financial statement" in the back of these reports. Also, look for growth in sales and earnings. If these are falling, dig deeper to find out why. Faltering sales or profits can lead to layoffs or to a merger with another firm (which could result in deep job cuts).

Also, you can find a wealth of financial information on publicly-traded firms at Yahoo! Finance, http://finance.yahoo.com.

See Chapter 4, "Important Contacts for Job Seekers," for additional places to get basic corporate data.

Tips on Utilizing Financial Documents Filed by Publicly Held Firms

(Access these documents at the Securities Exchange Commission, www.sec.gov.)

10-K (also called Annual Report on Form 10-K): This is an annual filing required by federal law. It follows a standard format. Information includes a complete description of the business, risk factors, historical financial data and much more. It is vital reading for job seekers. You will find that these documents are written in dry, legal language, but they contain a wealth of information.

DEF 14A Proxy Statement: This is an annual document that gives shareholders certain options to consider at their annual meeting. It names the firm's board of directors and top management. It also gives the dollar value and description of salaries, bonuses, pension plans, stock options and other benefits enjoyed by the company's five highest-paid officers. Job seekers can learn a great deal about a firm's management, pay and benefits from this document. Included is a list of the people or organizations that own more than 5% of the company's stock.

S-1: This is a new registration document for companies that are going public for the first time. In other words, they are creating an IPO (initial public offering). The information includes all of the data found in the 10-K and proxy statement filed annually by companies that have been public for more than one year.

10-Q: This is a quarterly report detailing a company's latest sales, profits and balance sheet.

Press Releases: Most mid-size to large companies issue a continual stream of press releases about new products, technologies and locations; new executive appointments; community activities and a wide variety of other company developments. The best place to find these is online, at the "News" tab on the company's own web site. You can also search popular business press release services such as www.prnewswire.com and www.businesswire.com.

More Ways to Research an Employer's Financial Stability and Growth Plans:

1) Check out its bond rating.

There's no sense in trying to become a financial analyst on your own. Use Internet searches to look for the bond ratings of potential employers. These ratings are based on a company's ability to pay principal and interest when due. If you're considering a major corporation with a bond rating of less than BB (an indicator that a company's debt is riskier than "investment grade"), you should do a lot more investigating before you continue chasing a job at that company.

2) Talk to vendors and current employees.

Talk to employees who work for the employer, or talk to people who do business with it. No one knows what's really going on better than people who are on the scene. If there are problems that are not yet known by the media, or if there are exciting new developments that have not yet been announced, you may find out a lot just by asking around. While you're at it, ask about corporate culture— how well are employees treated?

Popular Job-Search Internet Sites

CareerBuilder	www.careerbuilder.com
Monster	www.monster.com

Tips on Finding Information on Privately Held Employers

Our subscription service, Plunkett Research Online, and our printed Plunkett's industry almanacs, are among the world's most highly regarded sources of profiles of privately-held companies. Check with your library to see if you have access to these tools.

Study back-issue indexes and archives to major newspapers to see what journalists are reporting about a prospective private employer. Many libraries have recent issues of *The Wall Street Journal*, *The New York Times* and other important business newspapers. At major public and university libraries, you may be able to access online databases like ProQuest. These databases have excellent search engines that lead you into online archives of the best publications, including *The Wall Street Journal*, as well as many trade magazines and local business journals.

For smaller firms, go online and try American Journalism Review at www.newslink.org, where you'll be able to search news sites including hometown newspapers across the nation. Likewise, search local business newspapers at www.bizjournals.com, where you'll find links to dozens of major business weeklies like the *Houston Business Journal*.

Finally, consider investing in a credit report. If you really want reassurance, go to Experian SmartBusinessReports, www.smartbusinessreports.com. You can use its links to order a credit report on the employer. These reports are reasonably priced, and they can help you determine whether the company is paying its bills on time or has other problems. This could be vital in helping you determine whether to accept a job at a privately-held firm.

3) Use Internet search engines.

Look up your firm and industry in an Internet search engine such as Google. (You may need to click on "News" instead of relying on a general web search.) There, you may find unusual articles that were recently written about a company's product breakthroughs, treatment of women or minorities, human interest stories, training programs or stories written from other unique slants.

4) Study other business books and guides.

Search at a library or at an online bookseller like Amazon.com for recent books regarding major companies. For example, if you want to apply to biotech leader Genentech for a job, don't fail to read *The Billion Dollar Molecule: One Company's Quest for the Perfect Drug*. With a little research, you can turn up many other excellent books about specific companies, from banks like Bank of America to publishers like Gannett.

Great Places for Industry Research

Plunkett Research, www.plunkettresearch.com. Go to the specific industry of your choice to see an overview of trends and statistics. At our subscription service, www.plunkettresearchonline.com, subscribers have access to thousands of pages of industry analysis, statistics, contacts and company profiles, along with multiple search and export tools.

Quintessentialcareers.com, www.quintessentialcareers.com. Offers a "Career Resources Toolkit."

Wetfeet.com, www.wetfeet.com. Publishes snapshots of hundreds of employers.

Vault.com, www.vault.com. This site publishes insights about careers with hundreds of leading firms.

---

5) Explore industry-specific web sites.

In particular, study the leading industry associations for the sector in which you want to work. You will find listings of hundreds of the most important organizations, professional societies and resources, personally selected by our editors, in the almanacs published by Plunkett Research, Ltd., and in the contacts databases at Plunkett Research Online.

6) Research benefits and pension plans.

For additional information about corporate pension plans, start with the government agency charged with protecting and regulating pensions: the Pension Benefit Guaranty Corporation, 1200 K St. NW, Washington, D.C. 20005-4026, 202-326-4000, www.pbgc.gov. They can answer certain questions over the telephone.

The U.S. Department of Labor publishes a useful book titled "Protect your Pension." They can be contacted at: U.S. Department of Labor, Employee Benefits Security Administration, 200 Constitution Ave. NW, Room N5635, Washington, D.C. 20210, 866-444-3272 or 202-219-8776, www.dol.gov/ebsa/publications/main.html.

The Social Security Administration, 800-772-1213, www.ssa.gov, can provide you with information regarding your potential Social Security benefits.

NOTE: Generally, employees covered by wealth-building benefit plans do not fully own ("vest in") funds contributed on their behalf by the employer until as many

as five years of service with that employer have passed. All pension plans are voluntary—that is, employers are not obligated to offer pensions.

Pension Plans: The type and generosity of these plans vary widely from firm to firm. Caution: Some employers refer to plans as "pension" or "retirement" plans when they are actually 401(k) savings plans that require a contribution by the employee.

Defined Benefit Pension Plans: Pension plans that do not require a contribution from the employee are infrequently offered. However, a few companies, particularly larger employers in high-profit-margin industries, offer defined benefit pension plans where the employee is guaranteed to receive a set pension benefit upon retirement. The amount of the benefit is determined by the years of service with the company and the employee's salary during the later years of employment. The longer a person works for the employer, the higher the retirement benefit. These defined benefit plans are funded entirely by the employer. The benefits, up to a reasonable limit, are guaranteed by the Federal Government's Pension Benefit Guaranty Corporation. These plans are not portable—if you leave the company, you cannot transfer your benefits into a different plan. Instead, upon retirement you will receive the benefits that vested during your service with the company. If your employer offers a pension plan, it must give you a "summary plan description" within 90 days of the date you join the plan. You can also request a "summary annual report" of the plan, and once every 12 months you may request an "individual benefit statement" accounting of your interest in the plan.

Defined Contribution Plans: These are quite different. They do not guarantee a certain amount of pension benefit. Instead, they set out circumstances under which the employer will make a contribution to a plan on your behalf. The most common example is the 401(k) savings plan. Pension benefits are not guaranteed under these plans.

Cash Balance Pension Plans: These plans were recently invented. They are hybrid plans—part defined benefit and part defined contribution. Many employers have converted their older defined benefit plans into cash balance plans. The employer makes deposits (or credits a given amount of money) on the employee's behalf, usually based on a percentage of pay. Employee accounts grow based on a predetermined interest benchmark, such as the interest rate on Treasury Bonds. There are some advantages to these plans, particularly for younger workers: a) The benefits, up to a reasonable limit, are guaranteed by the Pension Benefit Guaranty Corporation. b) Benefits are portable—they can be moved to another plan when the employee changes companies. c) Younger workers and those who spend a shorter number of years with an employer may receive higher benefits than they would under a traditional defined benefit plan.

ESOP Stock Plan (Employees' Stock Ownership Plan): This type of plan is becoming rare, but it can be of great value to employees. Typically, the plan borrows money from a bank and uses those funds to purchase a large block of the corporation's stock. The corporation makes contributions to the plan over a period of time, and the stock purchase loan is eventually paid off. The value of the plan grows significantly as long as the market price of the stock holds up. Qualified employees are allocated a share of the plan based on their length of service and their level of salary. Under federal regulations, participants in ESOPs are allowed to diversify their account holdings in set percentages that rise as the employee ages and gains years of service with the company. In this manner, not all of the employee's assets are tied up in the employer's stock.

Savings Plan, 401(k): Under this type of plan, employees make a tax-deferred deposit into an account. In the best plans, the company makes annual matching donations to the employees' accounts, typically in some proportion to deposits made by the employees themselves. A good plan will match one-half of employee deposits of up to 6% of wages. For example, an employee earning $30,000 yearly might deposit $1,800 (6%) into the plan. The company will match one-half of the employee's deposit, or $900. The plan grows on a tax-deferred basis, similar to an IRA. A very generous plan will match 100% of employee deposits. However, some plans do not call for the employer to make a matching deposit at all. Other plans call for a matching contribution to be made at the discretion of the firm's board of directors. Actual terms of these plans vary widely from firm to firm. Generally, these savings plans allow employees to deposit as much as 15% of salary into the plan on a tax-deferred basis. However, the portion that the company uses to calculate its matching deposit is generally limited to a maximum of 6%. Employees should take care to diversify the holdings in their 401(k) accounts, and most people should seek professional guidance or investment management for their accounts. (Note: when profits are down, many employers exercise their right to suspend their contributions to 401(k)s. Employees may continue to make contributions, but they will not be matched by the employer in these cases.)

Stock Purchase Plan: Qualified employees may purchase the company's common stock at a price below its market value under a specific plan. Typically, the employee is limited to investing a small percentage of wages in this plan. The discount may range from 5% to 15%. Some of these plans allow for deposits to be made through regular monthly payroll deductions. However, new accounting rules for corporations, along with other factors, are leading many companies to curtail these plans—dropping the discount allowed, cutting the maximum yearly stock purchase or otherwise making the plans less generous or appealing.

Profit Sharing: Qualified employees are awarded an annual amount equal to some portion of a company's profits. In a very generous plan, the pool of money awarded to employees would be 15% of profits. Typically,

this money is deposited into a long-term retirement account. Caution: Some employers refer to plans as "profit sharing" when they are actually 401(k) savings plans. True profit sharing plans are rarely offered.

Plunkett Research Online and Plunkett's Industry Reference Books:

1) Internet-Based Services: Plunkett Research Online is a reference service that is subscribed to by the nation's leading university placement offices, libraries and information offices. You can use it to filter prospective employers by location, industry, size and more. You can then export contact information for those companies into spreadsheets or text files. In addition, you can use the site to research the latest editions of our industry analysis. Many additional tools for job seekers are included. For an extensive online tour, see www.plunkettresearch.com.

2) Printed Almanacs: Plunkett Research also publishes industry-specific almanacs for the most important industries. These are top-notch resources for job seekers.

Industry-Specific Books from Plunkett Research:

- Plunkett's Advertising & Branding Industry Almanac
- Plunkett's Airline, Hotel & Travel Industry Almanac
- Plunkett's Almanac of Middle Market Companies
- Plunkett's Apparel & Textiles Industry Almanac
- Plunkett's Automobile Industry Almanac
- Plunkett's Banking, Mortgages & Credit Industry Almanac
- Plunkett's Biotech & Genetics Industry Almanac
- Plunkett's Chemicals, Coatings & Plastics Industry Almanac
- Plunkett's Consulting Industry Almanac
- Plunkett's E-Commerce & Internet Business Almanac
- Plunkett's Education, EdTech and MOOCs Industry Almanac
- Plunkett's Energy Industry Almanac
- Plunkett's Engineering & Research Industry Almanac
- Plunkett's Entertainment & Media Industry Almanac
- Plunkett's Food Industry Almanac
- Plunkett's Games, Apps & Social Media Industry Almanac
- Plunkett's Green Technology Industry Almanac
- Plunkett's Health Care Industry Almanac
- Plunkett's Insurance Industry Almanac
- Plunkett's InfoTech Industry Almanac
- Plunkett's Investment & Securities Industry Almanac

- Plunkett's Manufacturing & Robotics Industry Almanac
- Plunkett's Nanotechnology & MEMS Industry Almanac
- Plunkett's Outsourcing & Offshoring Industry Almanac
- Plunkett's Real Estate & Construction Industry Almanac
- Plunkett's Renewable, Alternative & Hydrogen Energy Industry Almanac
- Plunkett's Restaurant & Hospitality Industry Almanac
- Plunkett's Retail Industry Almanac
- Plunkett's Sports Industry Almanac
- Plunkett's Telecommunications Industry Almanac
- Plunkett's Transportation, Supply Chain & Logistics Industry Almanac
- Plunkett's Wireless & Cellular Telephone Industry Almanac

Publications from Plunkett Research Written Especially for Job Seekers:

- The Almanac of American Employers
- Plunkett's Companion to the Almanac of American Employers

Our books will give you in-depth coverage of specific industries and the leading firms in those industries, along with trends and developments in technology and services. You will find these books in public and academic libraries, college placement offices, human resources offices, corporate libraries and government agency libraries. For sample chapters and additional details, you can preview as well as purchase these books at www.plunkettresearch.com.

The Almanac of American Employers provides profiles and detailed listings of 500 hand-picked, U.S. employers of 2,500 employees or more in size

Plunkett's Companion to The Almanac of American Employers is our book that provides profiles on 500 additional, rapidly growing corporate employers. This companion book covers smaller firms than those in the main volume of *The Almanac of American Employers*.

Chapter 4

IMPORTANT CONTACTS FOR JOB SEEKERS

Contents:

1) Accountants & CPAs Associations
2) Advertising/Marketing Associations
3) Aerospace & Defense Industry Associations
4) Airline & Air Cargo Industry Associations
5) Alternative Energy-Ethanol
6) Alternative Energy-Solar
7) Alternative Energy-Wind
8) Banking Industry Associations
9) Biotechnology & Biological Industry Associations
10) Booksellers Associations
11) Broadcasting, Cable, Radio & TV Associations
12) Careers-Airlines/Flying
13) Careers-Apparel
14) Careers-Banking
15) Careers-Biotech
16) Careers-Coatings
17) Careers-Computers/Technology
18) Careers-Contract & Freelance
19) Careers-First Time Jobs/New Grads
20) Careers-General Job Listings
21) Careers-Health Care
22) Careers-Job Listings for Seniors
23) Careers-Job Listings Hong Kong, China, Singapore, Asia
24) Careers-Job Reference Tools
25) Careers-Restaurants
26) Careers-Science
27) Careers-Sports
28) Careers-Video Games Industry

29) Chemicals Industry Associations
30) Communications Professional Associations
31) Computer & Electronics Industry Associations
32) Consulting Industry Associations
33) Consulting Industry Resources
34) Corporate Information Resources
35) Disabling Conditions
36) Electronic Health Records/Continuity of Care Records
37) Energy Associations-Electric Power
38) Energy Associations-Natural Gas
39) Energy Associations-Other
40) Energy Associations-Petroleum, Exploration, Production, etc.
41) Engineering Industry Associations
42) Engineering, Research & Scientific Associations
43) Entertainment & Amusement Associations-General
44) Film & Theater Associations
45) Fitness Industry Associations
46) Food Industry Associations, General
47) Food Industry Resources, General
48) Food Processor Industry Associations
49) Food Service Industry Associations

50) Games Industry Associations
51) Grocery Industry Associations
52) Health & Nutrition Associations
53) Health Care Business & Professional Associations
54) Health Insurance Industry Associations
55) Hearing & Speech
56) Hotel/Lodging Associations
57) Human Resources Industry Associations
58) Industry Research/Market Research
59) Insurance Industry Associations
60) Insurance Industry Associations-Agents & Brokers
61) Magazines, Business & Financial
62) MBA Resources
63) Online Recruiting & Employment ASPs & Solutions
64) Outsourcing Industry Associations
65) Pensions, Benefits & 401(k) Associations
66) Pensions, Benefits & 401(k) Resources
67) Pharmaceutical Industry Associations (Drug Industry)
68) Pilots Associations
69) Printers & Publishers Associations
70) Real Estate Industry Associations
71) Recording & Music Associations
72) Satellite-Related Professional Organizations
73) Securities Industry Associations

74) Software Industry Associations
75) Stocks & Financial Markets Data
76) Telecommunications Industry Associations
77) Temporary Staffing Firms
78) Testing Resources
79) Textile & Fabric Associations
80) Travel Business & Professional Associations
81) Travel Industry Associations
82) U.S. Government Agencies
83) Water Technologies & Resources
84) Wireless & Cellular Industry Associations
85) Writers, Photographers & Editors Associations

1)   Accountants & CPA Associations

American Institute of CPAs (AICPA)
1211 Ave. of the Americas
New York, NY 10036-8775 US
Phone: 212-596-6200
Fax: 800-362-5066
Toll Free: 888-777-7077
E-mail Address: *service@aicpa.org*
Web Address: www.aicpa.org
American Institute of CPAs (AICPA) represents nearly 370,000 members in 128 countries involved in the accounting profession. Its web site provides information and news for CPAs, news from the organization and a search for accounting firms.

Council of Petroleum Accountants Societies, Inc. (COPAS)
445 Union Blvd., Ste. 207
Lakewood, CO 80228 USA
Phone: 303-300-1131
Toll Free: 877-992-6727
Web Address: www.copas.org
The Council of Petroleum Accountants Societies, Inc. (COPAS) provides a forum for discussing and solving the variety of problems related to accounting for oil and gas. COPAS also provides valuable educational materials related to oil and gas accounting.

International Accounting Standards Board (IASB)
30 Cannon St.
London, EC4M 6XH UK
Phone: 44-20-7246-6410
Fax: 44-20-7246-6411
E-mail Address: info@ifrs.org
Web Address: www.ifrs.org

The International Accounting Standards Board (IASB) website hosts an electronic subscription service to the International Financial Reporting (IFRS) Standards as well access to IFRS summaries.

2)   Advertising/Marketing Associations

4A's (American Association of Advertising Agencies)
1065 Ave. of the Americas, Fl. 16
New York, NY 10018 USA
Phone: 212-682-2500
Web Address: www.aaaa.org
The 4A's (American Association of Advertising Agencies) is the national trade association representing the advertising agency industry in the U.S.

Advertising Women of New York (AWNY)
28 W. 44th St., Ste. 912
New York, NY 10036 USA
Phone: 212-221-7969
E-mail Address: lynn.branigan@awny.org
Web Address: www.awny.org
Advertising Women of New York (AWNY) provides a forum for personal and professional growth, serves as a catalyst for the advancement of women in the communications field and promotes and supports philanthropic endeavors through the AWNY Foundation. The web site also provides content from Women Executives in Public Relations (WERP), such as its a dynamic job board.

American Institute of Graphic Arts (AIGA)
233 Broadway, Fl. 17
New York, NY 10279 USA
Phone: 212-807-1990
Web Address: www.aiga.org
The American Institute of Graphic Arts (AIGA) strives to further excellence in communication design, both as a strategic tool for business and as a cultural force.

American Marketing Association (AMA)
130 E. Randolph St., Fl. 22
Chicago, IL 60601 USA
Phone: 312-542-9000
Fax: 312-542-9001
Toll Free: 800-262-1150
Web Address: www.ama.org
The American Marketing Association (AMA) serves marketing professionals in both business and education and serves all levels of marketing practitioners, educators and students.

Cable & Telecommunications Association for Marketing (CTAM)
120 Waterfront St., Ste. 200
National Harbor, MD 20745 USA
Phone: 301-485-8900
Fax: 301-560-4964
E-mail Address: info@ctam.com
Web Address: www.ctam.com
The Cable & Telecommunications Association for Marketing (CTAM) is dedicated to the discipline and development of consumer marketing excellence in cable television, new media and telecommunications services.

Direct Marketing Association (DMA)
1120 Ave. of the Americas
New York, NY 10036-6700 USA
Phone: 212-768-7277
Web Address: thedma.org
The Direct Marketing Association (DMA) is the oldest and largest trade association for users and suppliers in the direct, database and interactive marketing fields.

3)   Aerospace & Defense Industry Associations

American Institute of Aeronautics and Astronautics (AIAA)
12700 Sunrise Valley Dr., Ste. 200
Reston, VA 20191-5807 USA
Phone: 703-264-7500
Fax: 703-264-7551
Toll Free: 800-639-2422
E-mail Address: custserv@aiaa.org
Web Address: www.aiaa.org
The American Institute of Aeronautics and Astronautics (AIAA) is a nonprofit society aimed at advancing the arts, sciences and technology of aeronautics and astronautics. The institute represents the U.S. in the International Astronautical Federation and the International Council on the Aeronautical Sciences.

4)   Airline & Air Cargo Industry Associations

International Air Transport Association (IATA)
800 Place Victoria
P.O. Box 113
Montreal, QC H4Z 1M1 Canada
Phone: 514-874-0202
Web Address: www.iata.org
The International Air Transport Association (IATA) represents about 260 airlines in order to offer the highest standards of passenger and cargo service.

5) Alternative Energy-Ethanol

Renewable Fuels Association (RFA)
425 3rd St. SW, Ste. 1150
Washington, DC 20024 USA
Phone: 202-289-3835
Fax: 202-289-7519
Web Address: www.ethanolrfa.org
The Renewable Fuels Association (RFA) is a trade organization representing the ethanol industry. It publishes a wealth of useful information, including a listing of biorefineries and monthly U.S. fuel ethanol production and demand.

6) Alternative Energy-Solar

Solar Energy Industries Association (SEIA)
600 14th St. NW, Ste. 400
Washington, DC 20005 USA
Phone: 202-682-0556
E-mail Address: info@seia.org
Web Address: www.seia.org
Established in 1974, the Solar Energy Industries Association is the American trade association of the solar energy industry. Among its operations is a web site that provides news for the solar energy industry, links to related products and companies and solar energy statistics.

7) Alternative Energy-Wind

American Wind Energy Association (AWEA)
1501 M St. NW, Ste. 1000
Washington, DC 20005 USA
Phone: 202-383-2500
Fax: 202-383-2505
Web Address: www.awea.org
The American Wind Energy Association (AWEA) promotes wind energy as a clean source of electricity worldwide. Its website provides excellent resources for research, including an online library, discussions of legislation, and descriptions of wind technologies.

8) Banking Industry Associations

American Bankers Association (ABA)
1120 Connecticut Ave. NW
Washington, DC 20036 USA
Toll Free: 800-226-5377
E-mail Address: custserv@aba.com
Web Address: www.aba.com
The American Bankers Association (ABA) represents banks of all sizes on issues of national importance for financial institutions and their customers. The site offers financial information and solutions, financial news and member access to further advice and content.

9) Biotechnology & Biological Industry Associations

Biotechnology Industry Organization (BIO)
1201 Maryland Ave. SW, Ste. 900
Washington, DC 20024 USA
Phone: 202-962-9200
Fax: 202-488-6301
E-mail Address: info@bio.org
Web Address: www.bio.org
The Biotechnology Industry Organization (BIO) represents members involved in the research and development of health care, agricultural, industrial and environmental biotechnology products. BIO has both small and large member organizations.

10) Booksellers Associations

American Booksellers Association, Inc.
333 Westchester Ave., Ste. S202
White Plains, NY 10604 USA
Phone: 914-406-7500
Fax: 914-417-4013
Toll Free: 800-637-0037
E-mail Address: info@bookweb.org
Web Address: www.bookweb.org
The American Booksellers Association is a nonprofit association representing independent bookstores in the United States.

11) Broadcasting, Cable, Radio & TV Associations

Academy of Television Arts and Sciences
5220 Lankershim Blvd.
North Hollywood, CA 91601-3109 USA
Phone: 818-754-2800
Web Address: www.emmys.tv
The Academy of Television Arts and Sciences is a nonprofit corporation devoted to the advancement of telecommunications arts and sciences and to fostering creative leadership in the telecommunications industry. It is one of three organizations that administer the Emmy Awards. It is responsible for prime time Emmys.

Alliance for Women in Media
1760 Old Meadow Rd., Ste. 500
McLean, VA 22102 USA
Phone: 703-506-3290
Fax: 703-506-3266
E-mail Address:
info@allwomeninmedia.org
Web Address:
www.allwomeninmedia.org/
The Alliance for Women in Media, formerly the American Women in Radio and Television (AWRT), founded in 1951, is a national nonprofit organization dedicated to advancing the role of women in electronic media and related fields.

Association of America's Public Television Stations (APTS)
2100 Crystal Dr., Ste. 700
Arlington, VA 22202 USA
Phone: 202-654-4200
Fax: 202-654-4236
E-mail Address: skarp@apts.org
Web Address: www.apts.org
The Association of America's Public Television Stations (APTS) is a nonprofit membership organization formed to support the continued growth and development of strong and financially sound noncommercial television service for the American public.

Broadcast Education Association (BEA)
1771 N St. NW
Washington, DC 20036-2891 USA
Phone: 202-429-3935
Fax: 202-775-2981
E-mail Address: tbailey@nab.org
Web Address: www.beaweb.org
The Broadcast Education Association (BEA) is the professional association for professors, industry professionals and graduate students interested in teaching and research related to electronic media and multimedia enterprises.

National Academy of Television Arts and Sciences
1697 Broadway, Ste. 404
New York, NY 10019 USA
Phone: 212-586-8424
Fax: 212-246-8129
E-mail Address:
ppillitteri@emmyonline.tv
Web Address: www.emmyonline.org
The National Academy of Television Arts and Sciences is dedicated to the advancement of the arts and sciences of television and the promotion of creative leadership for artistic, educational and technical achievements within the television industry. It is responsible for awarding the Emmy Awards.

National Association of Broadcasters (NAB)
1771 N St. NW
Washington, DC 20036 USA
Phone: 202-429-5300

Toll Free: 800-622-3976
E-mail Address: nab@nab.org
Web Address: www.nab.org
The National Association of Broadcasters
(NAB) represents broadcasters for radio
and television. The organization also
provides benefits to employees of member
companies and to individuals and
companies that provide products and
services to the electronic media industries.

**National Association of Television
Program Executives (NATPE)**
5757 Wilshire Blvd., Penthouse 10
Los Angeles, CA 90036-3681 USA
Phone: 310-857-1601
E-mail Address: jpbommel@natpe.org
Web Address: www.natpe.org
The National Association of Television
Program Executives (NATPE) is the
leading association for content
professionals in the global television
industry. It is dedicated to the growth of
video content development, creations,
production, financing and distribution
across various platforms by providing
education and networking opportunities to
its members.

**National Cable and
Telecommunications Association
(NCTA)**
25 Massachusetts Ave. NW, Ste. 100
Washington, DC 20001-1413 USA
Phone: 202-222-2300
Fax: 202-222-2514
E-mail Address: info@ncta.com
Web Address: www.ncta.com
The National Cable and
Telecommunications Association (NCTA)
is the principal trade association of the
cable television industry in the United
States. It represents cable operators as
well as over 200 cable program networks
that produce TV shows.

**Radio Television Digital News
Association (RTDNA)**
529 14th St. NW, Ste. 1240
Washington, DC 20045 USA
Fax: 202-223-4007
E-mail Address: mikec@rtdna.org
Web Address: www.rtdna.org
The Radio Television Digital News
Association (RTDNA), formerly the
Radio-Television News Directors
Association (RTNDA), is the world's
largest professional organization
exclusively committed to professionals in
electronic journalism.

**Screen Actors Guild, American
Federation of Television and Radio
Artists (SAG-AFTRA)**
5757 Wilshire Blvd., Fl. 7

Los Angeles, CA 90036-3600 USA
Phone: 323-634-8100
Fax: 323-549-6792
Toll Free: 855-724-2387
E-mail Address:
sagaftrainfo@sagaftra.org
Web Address: www.sagaftra.org
The Screen Actors Guild, American
Federation of Television and Radio
Artists (SAG-AFTRA), a product of the
merger of the Screen Actors Guild (SAG)
and the American Federation of
Television and Radio Artists (AFTRA), is
a national labor union representing actors
and other professional performers and
broadcasters in television, radio, sound
recordings, non-broadcast/industrial
programming and new technologies such
as interactive programming and CD-
ROMs.

**Screen Actors Guild-American
Federation of Television and Radio
Artists (SAG-AFTRA)**
5757 Wilshire Blvd., Fl. 7
Los Angeles, CA 90036-3600 USA
Phone: 323-634-8100
Fax: 323-549-6792
Toll Free: 855-724-2387
E-mail Address:
sagaftrainfo@sagaftra.org
Web Address: www.sagaftra.org
The Screen Actors Guild-American
Federation of Television and Radio
Artists (SAG-AFTRA), a product of the
merger of the Screen Actors Guild (SAG)
and the American Federation of
Television and Radio Artists (AFTRA), is
a national labor union representing actors
and other professional performers and
broadcasters in television, radio, sound
recordings, non-broadcast/industrial
programming and new technologies such
as interactive programming and CD-
ROMs.

**Women in Cable &
Telecommunications (WICT)**
14555 Avion Pkwy., Ste. 250
Chantilly, VA 20151 USA
Phone: 703-234-9810
Fax: 703-817-1595
E-mail Address: tgibson@wict.org
Web Address: www.wict.org
Women in Cable & Telecommunications
(WICT) exists to advance the position and
influence of women in media through
leadership programs and services at both
the national and local level.

12) Careers-Airlines/Flying

Aviation/Aerospace Jobs Page
920 Morgan St., Ste. T

Des Moines, IA 50309 USA
Fax: 515-243-5384
Toll Free: 800-292-7731
E-mail Address:
customerservice@nationjob.com
Web Address:
www.nationjob.com/aviation
The Aviation/Aerospace Jobs Page, a
division of NationJob, Inc., features
detailed aviation and aerospace job
listings and company profiles.

AviationJobSearch.com
London Rd.
Sayers Common
West Sussex, BN6 9HS UK
Phone: 44--1273-837538
Fax: 44-1273-837549
E-mail Address:
info@aviationjobsearch.com
Web Address:
www.aviationjobsearch.com
AviationJobSearch.com lists jobs related
to the airline industry.

Avjobs, Inc.
9609 S. University Blvd., Unit 630830
Littleton, CO 80163-3032 USA
Fax: 888-624-8691
E-mail Address: info@avjobs.com
Web Address: www.avjobs.com
Avjobs, Inc. is a group of employers
dedicated to helping individuals obtain
aviation, airline, aerospace and airport
careers.

Flightdeck Recruitment Ltd.
15 High St., W. Mersea
Colchester, Essex CO5 8QA UK
E-mail Address:
contact@flightdeckrecruitment.com
Web Address:
www.flightdeckrecruitment.com
Flightdeck Recruitment Ltd. provides a
link between aviation recruiters who are
looking for flight deck crew and pilots or
flight engineers who are seeking
employment.

13) Careers-Apparel

24 Seven Fashion Recruitment
120 Wooster St., Fl. 4
New York, NY 10012 USA
Phone: 212-966-4426
Fax: 212-966-2313
E-mail Address:
newyork@24seventalent.com
Web Address: www.24seventalent.com
24 Seven Fashion Recruitment is an
employment agency serving the fashion,
beauty, entertainment, advertising,
marketing and retail industries.

Fashion Career Center
950 Tower Ln., Fl. 6
Foster City, CA 94404 USA
Web Address:
www.fashioncareercenter.com
The Fashion Career Center site provides employees and employers with a place to meet and access information about employment in the fashion industry. The FashionCareerCenter.com web site offers links to fashion jobs and fashion schools, as well as offering fashion career advice.

14) Careers-Banking

National Banking & Financial Service Network (NBFSN)
3075 Brickhouse Ct.
Virginia Beach, VA 23452-6860 USA
Phone: 757-463-5766
Fax: 757-340-0826
E-mail Address: smurrell@nbn-jobs.com
Web Address: www.nbn-jobs.com/
The National Banking & Financial Service Network (NBFSN) is made up of recruiting firms in the banking and financial services marketplace. The web site provides job listings.

15) Careers-Biotech

BiotechEmployment.com
E-mail Address:
jobs@Biotechemployment.com
Web Address:
www.biotechemployment.com
BiotechEmployment.com is an online resource for job seekers in biotechnology. The site's features includes resume posting, job search agents and employer profiles. It is part of the eJobstores.com, Inc., which includes the Health Care Job Store sites.

Chase Group (The)
10975 Grandview Dr., Ste. 100
Overland Park, KS 66210 USA
Phone: 913-663-3100
Fax: 913-663-3131
E-mail Address: chase@chasegroup.com
Web Address: www.chasegroup.com
The Chase Group is an executive search firm specializing in biomedical and pharmaceutical placement.

16) Careers-Coatings

CoatingsJobs.com
Web Address: www.coatingsjobs.com
CoatingsJobs.com connects coatings industry job seekers and employers. The web site offers job postings, resume postings, information for job seekers and an employment newsletter.

17) Careers-Computers/ Technology

ComputerJobs.com, Inc.
1995 N. Park Pl., Ste. 375
Atlanta, GA 30339 USA
Toll Free: 800-850-0045
Web Address: www.computerjobs.com
ComputerJobs.com, Inc. is an employment web site that offers users a links to computer-related job opportunities organized by skill and market.

Dice.com
12150 Meredith Dr.
Urbandale, IA 50323 USA
Phone: 515-280-1144
Fax: 515-280-1452
Toll Free: 888-321-3423
E-mail Address: techsupport@dice.com
Web Address: www.dice.com
Dice.com provides free employment services for IT jobs. The site includes advanced job searches by geographic location and category, availability announcements and resume postings, as well as employer profiles, a recruiter's page and career links. It is maintained by Dice Holdings, Inc., a publicly traded company.

Institute for Electrical and Electronics Engineers (IEEE) Job Site
445 Hoes Ln.
Piscataway, NJ 08855-1331 USA
Phone: 732-981-0060
Toll Free: 800-678-4333
E-mail Address:
candidatejobsite@ieee.org
Web Address: careers.ieee.org
The Institute for Electrical and Electronics Engineers (IEEE) Job Site provides a host of employment services for technical professionals, employers and recruiters. The site offers job listings by geographic area, a resume bank and links to employment services.

Pencom Systems, Inc.
152 Remsen St.
Brooklyn, NY 11201 USA
Phone: 718-923-1111
Fax: 718-923-6065
E-mail Address: tom@pencom.com
Web Address: www.pencom.com
Pencom Systems, Inc., an open systems recruiting company, hosts a career web site geared toward high-technology and scientific professionals, featuring an interactive salary survey, career advisor, job listings and technology resources. Its focus is the financial services industry within the New York City area.

18) Careers-Contract & Freelance

Guru.com
5001 Baum Blvd., Ste. 760
Pittsburgh, PA 15213 USA
Toll Free: 888-678-0136
Web Address: www.guru.com
Guru.com provides contract job access for freelancers and contract workers, in fields ranging from interior design to architecture, marketing and web design, among others. Employers can post projects, and freelancers can offer bids on prospective jobs. Many tools are provided to enable freelancers to be completely informed about the scope of the work needed.

19) Careers-First Time Jobs/New Grads

Alumni-Network Recruitment Corporation
Alumni-Network Recruitment Corporation
Oakville, ON Canada
Phone: 905-465-2547
E-mail Address: karen@alumni-network.com
Web Address: www.alumni-network.com
Alumni-Network Recruitment Corporation is a professional search and recruiting firm, specializing in ERP, E-Commerce and Engineering.

CollegeGrad.com, Inc.
950 Tower Ln., Fl. 6
Foster City, CA 94404 USA
E-mail Address: info@quinstreet.com
Web Address: www.collegegrad.com
CollegeGrad.com, Inc. offers in-depth resources for college students and recent grads seeking entry-level jobs.

MonsterCollege
799 Market St., Ste. 500
San Francisco, CA 94103 USA
E-mail Address:
info@college.monster.com
Web Address: www.college.monster.com
MonsterCollege provides information about internships and entry-level jobs, as well as career advice and resume tips, to recent college graduates.

National Association of Colleges and Employers (NACE)
62 Highland Ave.

Bethlehem, PA 18017-9085 USA
Phone: 610-868-1421
E-mail Address:
customer_service@naceweb.org
Web Address: www.naceweb.org
The National Association of Colleges and
Employers (NACE) is a premier U.S.
organization representing college
placement offices and corporate recruiters
who focus on hiring new grads.

20) Careers-General Job Listings

6FigureJobs
25 3rd St., Ste. 230
Stamford, CT 06905 USA
Phone: 203-326-8777
Toll Free: 800-605-5154
E-mail Address: info@6figurejobs.com
Web Address: www.6figurejobs.com
6FigureJobs offers executives a database
of high-level positions. Membership is
free for qualified individuals.

CareerBuilder, Inc.
200 N La Salle St., Ste. 1100
Chicago, IL 60601 USA
Phone: 773-527-3600
Fax: 773-353-2452
Toll Free: 800-891-8880
Web Address: www.careerbuilder.com
CareerBuilder, Inc. focuses on the needs
of companies and also provides a database
of job openings. The site has over 1
million jobs posted by 300,000
employers, and receives an average 23
million unique visitors monthly. The
company also operates online career
centers for 140 newspapers and 9,000
online partners. Resumes are sent directly
to the company, and applicants can set up
a special e-mail account for job-seeking
purposes. CareerBuilder is primarily a
joint venture between three newspaper
giants: The McClatchy Company, Gannett
Co., Inc. and Tribune Company.

CareerOneStop
Toll Free: 877-872-5627
E-mail Address: info@careeronestop.org
Web Address: www.careeronestop.org
CareerOneStop is operated by the
employment commissions of various state
agencies. It contains job listings in both
the private and government sectors, as
well as a wide variety of useful career
resources and workforce information.
CareerOneStop is sponsored by the U.S.
Department of Labor.

Careers Organization (The)
4300 Horton St.
Emeryville, CA 94608 USA

Phone: 510-761-5805
Web Address: www.careers.org
The Career Organization is an online
career resource center with links to jobs
and other career-related web sites, as well
as information regarding colleges and
online degree programs.

CollegeRecruiter.com
3109 W. 50 St., Ste. 121
Minneapolis, MN 55410-2102 USA
Phone: 952-848-2211
Web Address: www.collegerecruiter.com
CollegeRecruiter.com provides college
students with internship, part-time and
summer job listings. Recent graduates can
search for career opportunities by
category and location.

ContractJobHunter
C. E. Publications, Inc.
P.O. Box 3006
Bothell, WA 98041-3006 USA
Phone: 425-806-5200
Fax: 425-806-5585
E-mail Address: staff@cjhunter.com
Web Address: cjhunter.com
ContractJobHunter is a web-based version
of the magazine Contract Employment
Weekly Online. It posts job listings and
links to contract firms in the engineering,
IT and technical fields. Libraries for
reference materials and resume writing
guidelines are also offered. The site is a
service of C. E. Publications, Inc.

eFinancialCareers
1040 Ave. of the Americas, Ste. 16B
New York, NY 10018 USA
Phone: 212-370-8502
Web Address:
www.efinancialcareers.com
eFinancialCareers.com provides
employment listings in the finance
industry, as well as job tools such as
salary surveys, resume writing assistance
and industry news. It is owned DHI
Group, Inc.

EmploymentGuide
4460 Corporation Ln., Ste. 317
Virginia Beach, VA 23462 USA
Toll Free: 877-876-4039
Web Address:
www.employmentguide.com
EmploymentGuide offers general career
resources along with lists of position
openings, company profiles and a resume
database. It also circulates a free print
publication.

EscapeArtist International
300 Caye Financial Center, Coconut Dr.
P.O. Box 11
San Pedro, Belize

Web Address: www.escapeartist.com
EscapeArtist.com provides job searches
for overseas positions, as well as
international working condition resources
and immigration information. It's an
online resource offering information,
analysis and insights for international
expat community in areas of business
opportunities, employment, asset
protection, investments and international
real estate.

ExecuNet, Inc.
295 Westport Ave.
Norwalk, CT 06851 USA
Toll Free: 800-637-3126
E-mail Address:
member.services@execunet.com
Web Address: www.execunet.com
ExecuNet, Inc. is an executive career
management information and contact
service. It's a private career network for
executives at the senior level offering
career advancement, recruitment,
coaching and advisory and peer
networking opportunities.

HigherEdJobs.com
328 Innovation Blvd., Ste. 300
State College, PA 16803 USA
Phone: 814-861-3080
Fax: 814-861-3082
E-mail Address:
sales@HigherEdJobs.com
Web Address: www.higheredjobs.com
HigherEdJobs.com lists job vacancies in
colleges and universities.

IMDiversity, Inc.
201 St. Charles Ave., Ste. 2502
New Orleans, LA 70170 USA
Phone: 281-265-2472
Fax: 281-265-2476
E-mail Address: admin@indiversity.com
Web Address: www.imdiversity.com
IMDiversity, Inc. provides job listings and
career development information for
minorities in the U.S., with a particular
focus on African Americans, Asian
Americans and Pacific Islanders,
Latino/Hispanic Americans, Native
Americans and women.

Indeed.com
6433 Champion Grandview Way
Building 1
Austin, TX 78750 USA
Web Address: www.indeed.com
Indeed.com provides extensive lists of
jobs of all types, with links directly to the
employers. It covers over 60 countries,
including the U.S., Canada, India,
Mexico.

Job Search USA
E-mail Address:
contactjsu@jobsearchusa.org
Web Address: www.jobsearchusa.org
Job Search USA is a major job posting
site that contains job opportunities
classified by a variety of keywords.

Jobs in Logistics
Toll Free: 877-562-7678
Web Address: www.jobsinlogistics.com
Jobs in Logistics is an online job board,
which provides contacts for job seekers in
the transportation, manufacturing, freight
forwarding, warehousing, purchasing,
inventory management and logistics
fields.

JobSearchUSA.org
Web Address: www.jobsearchusa.org
Founded in 2006, Job Search USA is an
all-purpose job search website offering
job listings from various organizations
including not for profits, small businesses,
corporations and educational institutions.
Job Search USA was developed from the
concept of integrating the best features,
design practices and privacy principles of
the leading US job search websites.

LaborMarketInfo (LMI)
Employment Development Dept.
800 Capitol Mall, MIC 83
Sacramento, CA 95814 USA
Phone: 916-262-2162
Fax: 916-262-2352
Web Address:
www.labormarketinfo.edd.ca.gov
LaborMarketInfo (LMI) provides job
seekers and employers a wide range of
resources, namely the ability to find,
access and use labor market information
and services. It provides statistics for
employment demographics on both a local
and regional level, as well as career
searching tools for California residents.
The web site is sponsored by California's
Employment Development Office.

MediaBistro.com
825 Eighth Ave., Fl. 29
New York, NY 10019 USA
E-mail Address:
support@mediabistro.com
Web Address: www.mediabistro.com
MediaBistro.com provides news and
information on current events relating to
the media industry. It also offers an array
of employment resources, including job
listings within the industry.

Monster Worldwide, Inc.
622 Third Ave., Fl. 39
New York, NY 10017 USA
Phone: 212-351-7000

Fax: 646-658-0540
E-mail Address: ir@monster.com
Web Address: www.monster.com
Monster Worldwide, Inc., parent company
of Monster.com, provides online career
and personnel services. The firm operates
in over 40 countries.

MyResumeAgent.com
24 Railroad St.
Kennedy Information, LLC
Keene, NH 03431 USA
Phone: 603-357-8104
Toll Free: 800-531-0007
E-mail Address:
customerservice@kennedyinfo.com
Web Address: www.myresumeagent.com
MyResumeAgent.com allows senior-level
professionals to have their resumes sent to
executive placement firms for a fee. The
site is owned by Kennedy Information,
Inc.

NationJob, Inc.
920 Morgan St., Ste. T
Des Moines, IA 50309 USA
Fax: 515-243-5384
Toll Free: 888-292-7731
E-mail Address:
customerservice@nationjob.com
Web Address: www.nationjob.com
NationJob.com is an online job search
portal. The web site allows users to search
through listings or develop a profile of the
ideal job based on the criterion of
location, industry, salary; and, if they
provide an e-mail address, wait for
appropriate listings to be sent to them
through the firm's PJScout feature.

NETSHARE, Inc.
359 Bel Marin Keys, Ste. 24
Novato, CA 94949 USA
Toll Free: 800-241-5642
E-mail Address: netshare@netshare.com
Web Address: www.netshare.com
Netshare provides access to exclusive
listings of executive jobs that pay
$100,000 and up.

Net-Temps, Inc.
55 Middlesex St., Ste. 220
North Chelmsford, MA 01863 USA
Fax: 978-251-7250
Toll Free: 800-307-0062
E-mail Address: service@net-temps.com
Web Address: www.net-temps.com
Net-Temps, Inc. offers a web site,
operated by professional career
consultants, that features job listings and
job seeking tips.

Recruiters Online Network
E-mail Address: rossi.tony@comcast.net
Web Address: www.recruitersonline.com

The Recruiters Online Network provides
job postings from thousands of recruiters,
Careers Online Magazine, a resume
database, as well as other career
resources.

USAJOBS
1900 E St. NW, Ste. 6500
Washington, DC 20415-0001 USA
Web Address: www.usajobs.gov
USAJOBS, a program of the U.S. Office
of Personnel Management, is the official
job site for the U.S. Federal Government.
It provides a comprehensive list of U.S.
government jobs, allowing users to search
for employment by location; agency; type
of work; or by senior executive positions.
It also has special employment sections
for individuals with disabilities, veterans
and recent college graduates; an
information center, offering resume and
interview tips and other information; and
allows users to create a profile and post a
resume.

21) Careers-Health Care

Health Care Source
100 Sylvan Rd., Ste. 100
Woburn, MA 01801 USA
Phone: 781-368-1033
Fax: 800-829-6600
Toll Free: 800-869-5200
E-mail Address:
solutions@healthcaresource.com
Web Address: www.healthcaresource.com
Health Care Source is a leading provider
of talent management, recruitment and
employment services for healthcare
providers. It offers a comprehensive suite
of solutions, which includes features, such
as applicant tracking and onboarding,
recruitment optimization, reference
checking, behavioral assessments, merit
planning, employee performance and
eLearning courseware among others.

MedicalWorkers.com
Web Address: www.medicalworkers.com
MedicalWorkers.com is an employment
site for medical and health care
professionals.

MedJump.com
E-mail Address: info@medjump.com
Web Address: www.medjump.com
MedJump.com is dedicated to
empowering health care and medical-
related professionals with the necessary
tools to market their abilities and skills.

Medzilla, Inc.
P.O. Box 1710
Marysville, WA 98270 USA

Phone: 360-657-5681
Fax: 425-279-5427
E-mail Address: info@medzilla.com
Web Address: www.medzilla.com
Medzilla, Inc.'s web site offers job
searches, salary surveys, a search agent
and information on employment in the
biotech, pharmaceuticals, healthcare and
science sectors.

Monster Career Advice-Healthcare
133 Boston Post Rd.
Weston, MA 02493 USA
Phone: 978-461-8000
Fax: 978-461-8100
Toll Free: 800-666-7837
Web Address: career-
advice.monster.com/Healthcare/job-
category-3975.aspx
Monster Career Advice-Healthcare, a
service of Monster Worldwide, Inc.,
provides industry-related articles, job
listings, job searches and search agents for
the medical field.

**NationJob Network-Medical and
Health Care Jobs Page**
920 Morgan St., Ste. T
Des Moines, IA 50309 USA
Fax: 515-243-5384
Toll Free: 800-292-7731
E-mail Address:
customerservice@nationjob.com
Web Address:
www.nationjob.com/medical
The NationJob Network-Medical and
Health Care Jobs Page offers information
and listings for health care employment.

Nurse-Recruiter.com
15500 SW Jay St., Ste. 26760
Beaverton, OR 97006-6018 USA
Toll Free: 877-562-7966
Web Address: www.nurse-recruiter.com
Nurse-Recruiter.com is an online job
portal devoted to bringing health care
employers and the nursing community
together.

PracticeLink
415 2nd Ave.
Hinton, WV 25951 USA
Toll Free: 800-776-8383
E-mail Address:
helpdesk@practicelink.com
Web Address: www.practicelink.com
PracticeLink, one of the largest physician
employment web sites, is a free service
with over 1.7 million page views each
month. There are more than 5,000
hospitals, medical groups, private
practices and health systems, posting over
20,000 physician job opportunities on the
web site.

RPh on the Go USA, Inc.
8001 N. Lincoln Ave., Ste. 800
Skokie, IL 60077 USA
Phone: 847-588-7170
Fax: 847-588-7060
Toll Free: 800-553-7359
Web Address: www.rphonthego.com
RPh on the Go USA, Inc. places
temporary and permanent qualified
professionals in the pharmacy community.
This pharmacy staffing firm offers access
to more than 160,000 pharmacy
professionals and matches the right
pharmacy personnel to help meet clients
needs.

22) Careers-Job Listings for Seniors

Dinosaur Exchange
Sutherland House
1759, London Rd.
Leigh-on-Sea, Essex SS9 @RZ UK
Phone: 44-1702--470531
E-mail Address:
CustomerSupport@dinosaur-
exchange.com
Web Address: www.dinosaur-
exchange.com
Dinosaur Exchange, opened in 2003, is a
job forum for the elderly, which allows
seniors to post resumes and be contacted
by employers. Dino-X Ltd. owns and
operates the web site.

**Employment Network for Retired
Government Experts (ENRGE)**
Zavala, Inc.
P.O. Box 1532
N. Falmouth, MA 02556 USA
Phone: 508-564-4140
Web Address: www.enrge.us
The Employment Network for Retired
Government Experts (ENRGE) helps
government employees to remain active in
their professions after retirement.
ENERGE is the business name of Zavala,
Inc.

Senior Job Bank
NHC Group, Inc.
P.O. Box 508
Marlborough, MA 01752 USA
Toll Free: 866-562-2627
E-mail Address:
publisher@seniorjobbank.org
Web Address: www.seniorjobbank.org
The Senior Job Bank web site offers an
easy, effective and free method for senior
citizens to find occasional, part-time,
flexible, temporary or full-time jobs. The
site is owned and managed by NHC
Group, Inc.

Seniors4Hire.org
7071 Warner Ave. F466
Huntington Beach, CA 92647 USA
Phone: 714-848-0996
Fax: 714-848-5445
Toll Free: 800-906-7107
E-mail Address: info@seniors4hire.org
Web Address: www.seniors4hire.org
Seniors4Hire.org is an online career
center with job postings, employment
resources and information on community
service employment programs for older
workers, retirees and senior citizens. The
site is owned and operated by The
Forward Group.

YourEncore
20 N. Meridian St., Ste. 800
Indianapolis, IN 46204 USA
Phone: 317-226-9301
Fax: 317-226-9312
E-mail Address: info@yourencore.com
Web Address: www.yourencore.com
YourEncore is a program that seeks to
employ retirees by matching them with
member companies. The web site utilizes
retirees mainly in the areas of
engineering, science and product
development.

23) Careers-Job Listings Hong Kong, China, Singapore, Asia

CareerJet
Web Address: www.careerjet.hk
CareerJet provides excellent search tools
leading to job listings in Hong Kong,
China and throughout Asia.

Careers@Gov
Web Address: www.careers.gov.sg
Careers@Gov is the government-
sponsored job search site within
Singapore.

CT Good Jobs
Web Address: www.ctgoodjobs.hk
CT Good Jobs provides easy to use job
listings. It also offers online communities
in such areas as retail, human resources
and finance.

HeadHunt
Web Address: www.headhunt.com.sg/
HeadHunt bills itself as an executive job
search site for Singapore.

JobMarket
Web Address: www.jobmarket.com.hk
JobMarket features a very detailed
advanced search option.

JobsCentral Singapore
Web Address: http://jobscentral.com.sg/
JobsCentral Singapore is maintained by
CareerBuilder.

jobsDB
Web Address: http://hk.jobsdb.com/hk
jobsDB provides well organized job
listings in Hong Kong, Indonesia,
Malaysia, Philippines, Singapore,
Thailand and China.

JobStreetWeb Address: www.jobstreet.sg
JobStreet is an extensive job search site
focused in positions within Singapore.

Monster Hong Kong
Web Address: www.monster.com.hk/
Monster Hong Kong provides easy online
access to thousands of jobs in Hong Kong,
Macau, Mainland China and Taiwan.

Monster Singapore
Web Address: www.monster.com.sg/
Monster Singapore is specific to the
Singapore area.

Recruit
Web Address: www.recruit.com.hk
Recruit provides job news, job tips
employer new and job listings in the Hong
Kong area.

Singapore Jobs Online
Web Address:
www.singaporejobsonline.com/
Singapore Jobs Online enables job
searches within Singapore for a wide
variety of job categories.

STJobs
Web Address: www.stjobs.sg/site/index
STJobs is an extensive web site offering
job search within Singapore and the
surrounding area.

24) Careers-Job Reference Tools

CareerXroads (CXR)
7 Clark Ct.
Kendall Park, NJ 08824-1810 USA
Phone: 732-821-6652
E-mail Address: mmc@careerxroads.com
Web Address: www.careerxroads.com
CareerXroads (CXR) publishes an annual
guide on job and resume web sites. It was
cofounded by Gerry Crispin and Mark
Mehler.

Job-Hunt.org
186 Main St.
NETability, Inc.
Marlborough, MA 01752 USA

Phone: 508-624-6261
E-mail Address: info@job-hunt.org
Web Address: www.job-hunt.org
Job-Hunt.org, rather than collecting
resumes or posting job vacancies, offers a
vast list of job listing web sites and links
to helpful job search tools. It is owned by
NETability, Inc.

jobipedia.org
E-mail Address: info@jobipedia.org
Web Address: www.jobipedia.org
jobipedia.org is a public service provided
by the HR Policy Association to help new
entrants into the workforce find jobs.
Every answer you read on jobipedia was
written by someone from a large employer
who actually hires employees for a living.

MBA Career Services Council (CSC)
P.O. Box 47478
Tampa, FL 33646-7478 USA
Phone: 813-220-3191
Fax: 813-319-4952
E-mail Address:
execdirector@mbacsc.org
Web Address: www.mbacsc.org
The MBA Career Services Council (CSC)
is a global professional association for
individuals in the field of MBA career
services and those that recruit directly
from graduate management programs.

Quintessential Careers (QC)
EmpoweringSites.com
DeLand, FL 32720 USA
Phone: 386-740-8872
Fax: 386-740-9764
E-mail Address:
randall@quintcareers.com
Web Address: www.quintcareers.com
Quintessential Careers (QC) provides a
large collection of data and links for job
seekers, including advice, tools and job
postings; it also offers a guide to
researching companies. QC is a subsidiary
of EmpoweringSites.com.

Vault.com, Inc.
132 W. 31st St., Fl. 17
New York, NY 10001 USA
Fax: 212-366-6117
Toll Free: 800-535-2074
E-mail Address:
customerservice@vault.com
Web Address: www.vault.com
Vault.com, Inc. is a comprehensive career
web site for employers and employees,
with job postings and valuable
information on a wide variety of
industries. Its features and content are
largely geared toward MBA degree
holders.

WetFeet.com
254 W 31st St., Fl. 12
New York, NY 10001 USA
Phone: 917-793-0337
Web Address: www.wetfeet.com
WetFeet.com provides an excellent
combination of links and resources for job
seekers. The site is owned by Universum.

What Color is Your Parachute?
E-mail Address:
rnbolles@jobhuntersbible.com
Web Address: www.jobhuntersbible.com
The What Color is Your Parachute?
official web site, JobHuntersBible.com, is
based on the Job-Hunting on the Internet
chapter of Richard (Dick) Bolle's best-
selling book. Designed to aid job hunters
and career changers who want to use the
Internet as part of their job search, the site
provides links to job listing, resume,
career counseling, contacts and research
sites.

25) Careers-Restaurants

FoodService.com
7702 E. Doubletree Ranch Rd., Ste. 300
Scottsdale, AZ 85258 USA
Phone: 602-381-3663
Web Address: www.foodservice.com
FoodService.com, managed and run by
Food Service Interactive, LLC, offers web
site design and job search services for the
food service industry.

Resources in Food, Inc. (RIF)
417 S Lincolnway, Ste. B
North Aurora, IL 60542 USA
Phone: 630-801-0469
Fax: 630-357-7548
Toll Free: 877-743-1100 x1221
E-mail Address: jgrimm@rifood.com
Web Address: www.rifood.com
Resources in Food (RIF) provides
professional management placement for
the hospitality, food manufacturing, food
services, restaurants and wholesale
grocery industry.

26) Careers-Science

Chem Jobs
730 E. Cypress Ave.
Monrovia, CA 91016 USA
Phone: 626-930-0808
Fax: 626-930-0102
E-mail Address: info@chemindustry.com
Web Address: www.chemjobs.net
Chem Jobs is a leading Internet site for
job seekers in chemistry and related
fields, with a particular focus on chemists,
biochemists, pharmaceutical scientists and

chemical engineers. The web site is powered by Chemindustry.com.

New Scientist Jobs
Quadrant House, Sutton
Surrey, SM2 5AS UK
Phone: 781-734-8770
E-mail Address:
nssales@newscientist.com
Web Address: jobs.newscientist.com
New Scientist Jobs is a web site produced by the publishers of New Scientist Magazine that connects jobseekers and employers in the bioscience fields. The site includes a job search engine and a free-of-charge e-mail job alert service.

Science Careers
Phone: 202-312-6375
Web Address: jobs.sciencecareers.org
Science Careers is a web site that contains many useful categories of links, including employment newsgroups, scientific journals, hob postings and placement agencies. It also links to sites containing information regarding internship and fellowship opportunities for high school students, undergrads, graduates, doctoral and post-doctoral students.

27) Careers-Sports

Jobs in Sports
106 Calendar Ave., Ste. 184
LaGrange, IL 60525 USA
Web Address: www.jobsinsports.com
Jobs in Sports is an employment web site that provides job listings in areas including sports marketing, sports media, sales, health and fitness, computers and administration, as well as other job resources.

Sports Careers
Web Address: www.sportscareers.com
Sports Careers offers a range of services to help individuals and employers in the sports industry, including job listings, a resume bank, industry contacts and salary information.

Sports Job Board
Web Address: www.sportsjobboard.com
The Sports Job Board is an employment web site for the sports industry.

WomenSportsJobs.com
Women's Sport Services, LLC
P.O. Box 11
Huntington Beach, CA 92648 USA
Phone: 714-848-1201
Fax: 714-848-5111
E-mail Address:
Feedback@WSServices.com

Web Address:
www.womensportsjobs.com
WomenSportsJobs.com is an employment web site specializing in jobs for women in the sports industry. The site is managed by Women's Sport Services, LLC.

Work in Sports LLC
7335 E. Chauncey Ln., Ste. 115
Phoenix, AZ 85054 USA
Phone: 480-905-7221
Fax: 480-905-7231
Web Address: www.workinsports.com
Work in Sports LLC is an online employment resource for the sports industry that posts hundreds of jobs on its web site.

28) Careers-Video Games Industry

GameJobs
Web Address: www.gamejobs.com
GameJobs.com is independently owned and operated by the Crest Group, LLC, the managers of the Entertainment Consumers Association (ECA), a non-profit membership association. It offers both employers and job seekers in the interactive entertainment industry access to online tools and resources, such as post resume and job openings to accomplish their respective goals.

Video Game Jobs-About.com Career Planning
Web Address:
http://careerplanning.about.com/od/occupations/a/videogamecareer.htm
A useful page on About.com that contains advice and links for people interested in working in the video games industry.

29) Chemicals Industry Associations

American Chemical Society (ACS)
1155 16th St. NW
Washington, DC 20036 USA
Phone: 202-872-4600
Toll Free: 800-227-5558
E-mail Address: help@acs.org
Web Address: www.acs.org
The American Chemical Society (ACS) is a nonprofit organization aimed at promoting the understanding of chemistry and chemical sciences. It represents a wide range of disciplines including chemistry, chemical engineering and other technical fields.

30) Communications Professional Associations

Association for Women In Communications (AWC)
1717 E Republic Rd., Ste. A
Springfield, MO 65804 USA
Phone: 417-886-8606
Fax: 417-886-3685
E-mail Address: members@womcom.org
Web Address: www.womcom.org
The Association for Women In Communications (AWC) is a professional organization that works for the advancement of women across all communications disciplines by recognizing excellence, promoting leadership and positioning its members at the forefront of the communications industry.

Health and Science Communications Association (HeSCA)
P.O. Box 31323
Omaha, NE 68132 USA
Phone: 402-915-5373
E-mail Address: hesca@hesca.org
Web Address: hesca.net
The Health and Science Communications Association (HeSCA) is an organization of communications professionals committed to sharing knowledge and resources in the health sciences arena.

Health Industry Business Communications Council (HIBCC)
2525 E. Arizona Biltmore Cir., Ste. 127
Phoenix, AZ 85016 USA
Phone: 602-381-1091
Fax: 602-381-1093
E-mail Address: info@hibcc.org
Web Address: www.hibcc.org
The Health Industry Business Communications Council (HIBCC) seeks to facilitate electronic communications by developing appropriate standards for information exchange among all health care trading partners.

International Association of Business Communicators (IABC)
155 Montgomery St., Ste. 1210
San Francisco, CA 94111 USA
Phone: 415-544-4700
Fax: 415-544-4747
Toll Free: 800-776-4222
Web Address: www.iabc.com
The International Association of Business Communicators (IABC) is the leading resource for effective business communication practices.

31) Computer & Electronics Industry Associations

Electronics Technicians Association international (ETA International)
5 Depot St.
Greencastle, IN 46135 USA
Phone: 765-653-8262
Fax: 765-653-4287
Toll Free: 800-288-3824
E-mail Address: eta@eta-i.org
Web Address: www.eta-i.org
The Electronics Technicians Association International (ETA International) is a nonprofit professional association for electronics technicians worldwide. The organization provides recognized professional credentials for electronics technicians.

Semiconductor Industry Association (SIA)
1101 K St. NW, Ste. 450
Washington, DC 20005 USA
Phone: 202-446-1700
Fax: 202-216-9745
Toll Free: 866-756-0715
Web Address: www.semiconductors.org
The Semiconductor Industry Association (SIA) is a trade association representing the semiconductor industry in the U.S. Through its coalition of more than 60 companies, SIA members represent roughly 80% of semiconductor production in the U.S. The coalition aims to advance the competitiveness of the chip industry and shape public policy on issues particular to the industry.

32) Consulting Industry Associations

Association of Internal Management Consultants (AIMC)
720 North Collier Blvd., Ste. 201
Marco Island, FL 34145 USA
Phone: 239-642-0580
Web Address: www.aimc.org
The Association of Internal Management Consultants (AIMC) is a professional association representing in-house management consultants. Members work in for-profit corporations, government agencies, educational institutions and nonprofit organizations.

Association of Management Consulting Firms (AMCF)
370 Lexington Ave., Ste. 2209
New York, NY 10017 USA
Phone: 212-262-3055
Fax: 212-262-3054
E-mail Address: info@amcf.org
Web Address: www.amcf.org
The Association of Management Consulting Firms (AMCF) is a recognized leader in promoting the management consulting industry. AMCF represents a diverse list of international members, from large, multinational companies to small, regional firms.

Institute of Management Consultants USA (IMC)
631 U.S. Highway One, Ste. 400
North Palm Beach, FL 33408 USA
Phone: 561-472-0833
Toll Free: 800-837-7321
Web Address: www.imcusa.org
The Institute of Management Consultants USA (IMC) certifies management consultants in accordance with the strict international standards of the International Council of Management Consulting Institutes.

Investment Management Consultant Association (IMCA)
5619 DTC Pkwy., Ste. 500
Greenwood Village, CO 80111 USA
Phone: 303-770-3377
Fax: 303-770-1812
E-mail Address: imca@imca.org
Web Address: www.imca.org
The Investment Management Consultant Association (IMCA) provides information and communication for investment management consultants.

33) Consulting Industry Resources

Consulting Magazine
120 Broadway, Fl.5
New York, NY 10271 USA
Phone: 877-256-2472
Web Address: www.consultingmag.com
Consulting Magazine is a leading online publication for the consulting industry, and features information on consulting careers, thought leadership and corporate strategies. The web site is owned and operated by ALM Media, LLC.

34) Corporate Information Resources

bizjournals.com
120 W. Morehead St., Ste. 400
Charlotte, NC 28202 USA
Web Address: www.bizjournals.com
Bizjournals.com is the online media division of American City Business Journals, the publisher of dozens of leading city business journals nationwide. It provides access to research into the latest news regarding companies both small and large. The organization maintains 42 websites and 64 print publications and sponsors over 700 annual industry events.

Business Wire
101 California St., Fl. 20
San Francisco, CA 94111 USA
Phone: 415-986-4422
Fax: 415-788-5335
Toll Free: 800-227-0845
E-mail Address: info@businesswire.com
Web Address: www.businesswire.com
Business Wire offers news releases, industry- and company-specific news, top headlines, conference calls, IPOs on the Internet, media services and access to tradeshownews.com and BW Connect On-line through its informative and continuously updated web site.

Edgar Online, Inc.
11200 Rockville Pike, Ste. 310
Rockville, MD 20852 USA
Phone: 301-287-0300
Fax: 301-287-0390
Toll Free: 888-870-2316
Web Address: www.edgar-online.com
Edgar Online, Inc. is a gateway and search tool for viewing corporate documents, such as annual reports on Form 10-K, filed with the U.S. Securities and Exchange Commission.

PR Newswire Association LLC
350 Hudson St., Ste. 300
New York, NY 10014-4504 USA
Fax: 800-793-9313
Toll Free: 800-776-8090
E-mail Address: MediaInquiries@prnewswire.com
Web Address: www.prnewswire.com
PR Newswire Association LLC provides comprehensive communications services for public relations and investor relations professionals, ranging from information distribution and market intelligence to the creation of online multimedia content and investor relations web sites. Users can also view recent corporate press releases from companies across the globe. The Association is owned by United Business Media plc.

Silicon Investor
E-mail Address: si.admin@siliconinvestor.com
Web Address: www.siliconinvestor.com
Silicon Investor is focused on providing information about technology companies. Its web site serves as a financial discussion forum and offers quotes, profiles and charts.

35) Disabling Conditions

Job Accommodation Network (JAN)
P.O. Box 6080
Morgantown, WV 26506-6080 USA
Phone: 304-293-7186
Fax: 304-293-5407
Toll Free: 800-526-7234
E-mail Address: jan@askjan.org
Web Address: askjan.org
The Job Accommodation Network (JAN)
is a free consulting service that provides
guidance and information about job
accommodations, the Americans with
Disabilities Act and the employability of
people with disabilities.

36) Electronic Health Records/Continuity of Care Records

**American Health Information
Management Association (AHIMA)**
233 N. Michigan Ave., Fl. 21
Chicago, IL 60601-5809 USA
Phone: 312-233-1100
Fax: 312-233-1090
Toll Free: 800-335-5535
Web Address: www.ahima.org
The American Health Information
Management Association (AHIMA) is a
professional association that consists
health information management
professionals who work throughout the
health care industry.

**American Medical Informatics
Association (AMIA)**
4720 Montgomery Ln., Ste. 500
Bethesda, MD 20814 USA
Phone: 301-657-1291
Fax: 301-657-1296
Web Address: www.amia.org
The American Medical Informatics
Association (AMIA) is a membership
organization of individuals, institutions
and corporations dedicated to developing
and using information technologies to
improve health care.

**College of Healthcare Information
Management Executives (CHIME)**
710 Avis Dr., Ste. 200
Ann Arbor, MI 48108 USA
Phone: 734-665-0000
Fax: 734-665-4922
E-mail Address: staff@cio-chime.org
Web Address: www.cio-chime.org
College of Healthcare Information
Management Executives (CHIME) was
formed with the dual objective of serving
the professional development needs of
health care CIOs and advocating the more

effective use of information management
within health care.

**Healthcare Information and
Management Systems Society (HIMSS)**
33 W Monroe St., Ste. 1700
Chicago, IL 60603-5616 USA
Phone: 312-664-4467
Fax: 312-664-6143
Web Address: www.himss.org
The Healthcare Information and
Management Systems Society (HIMSS)
provides leadership in the optimal use of
technology, information and management
systems for the betterment of health care.

37) Energy Associations-Electric Power

**American Public Power Association
(APPA)**
2451 Crystal Dr., Ste. 1000
Arlington, VA 22202-4804 USA
Phone: 202-467-2900
E-mail Address: info@PublicPower.org
Web Address: www.publicpower.org
The American Public Power Association
(APPA) is a nonprofit service
organization for the country's community-
owned electric utilities, dedicated to
advancing the public policy interests of its
members and their consumers.

Edison Electric Institute (EEI)
701 Pennsylvania Ave. NW
Washington, DC 20004-2696 USA
Phone: 202-508-5000
E-mail Address: feedback@eei.org
Web Address: www.eei.org
The Edison Electric Institute (EEI) is an
association of U.S. shareholder-owned
electric companies as well as worldwide
affiliates and industry associates. Its web
site provides energy news and a link to
Electric Perspectives magazine.

**Women's International Network of
Utility Professionals (WINUP)**
P.O. Box 64
Grove City, OH 43123-0064 USA
Phone: 614-738-0603
E-mail Address: winup@att.net
Web Address: www.winup.org
The Women's International Network of
Utility Professionals (WINUP) provides
networking and support for women in the
utility industry.

38) Energy Associations-Natural Gas

American Gas Association (AGA)
400 N. Capitol St. NW, Ste. 450

Washington, DC 20001 USA
Phone: 202-824-7000
Web Address: www.aga.org
The American Gas Association (AGA)
represents a large number of natural gas
providers, advocating for these companies
and providing a broad range of programs
and services for members.

39) Energy Associations-Other

**American Association of Blacks in
Energy**
1625 K St. NW, Ste. 450
Washington, DC 20006 USA
Phone: 202-371-9530
Fax: 202-371-9218
E-mail Address: info@aabe.org
Web Address: www.aabe.org
The American Association of Blacks in
Energy is dedicated to ensuring the input
of African Americans and other minorities
in discussions and developments of
energy policies, regulations, research and
development technologies and
environmental issues.

40) Energy Associations-Petroleum, Exploration, Production, etc.

**American Association of Professional
Landmen (AAPL)**
800 Fournier St.
Fort Worth, TX 76102 USA
Phone: 817-847-7700
Fax: 817-847-7704
E-mail Address: aapl@landman.org
Web Address: www.landman.org
The American Association of Professional
Landmen (AAPL) promotes the highest
standards of performance for all land
professionals and seeks to advance their
stature and to encourage sound
stewardship of energy and mineral
resources.

American Petroleum Institute (API)
1220 L St. NW
Washington, DC 20005-4070 USA
Phone: 202-682-8000
Web Address: www.api.org
American Petroleum Institute (API)
represents U.S. oil and gas industries and
its web site includes in-depth sections for
energy consumers and energy
professionals.

**Independent Petroleum Association of
America (IPAA)**
1201 15th St. NW, Ste. 300
Washington, DC 20005 USA

Phone: 202-857-4722
Fax: 202-857-4799
E-mail Address: nkirby@ipaa.org
Web Address: www.ipaa.org
The Independent Petroleum Association
of America (IPAA) provides a forum for
the exploration and production segment of
the independent oil and natural gas
business. It also provides information on
the domestic exploration and production
industry.

International Association of Drilling
Contractors (IADC)
10370 Richmond Ave., Ste. 760
Houston, TX 77042 USA
Phone: 713-292-1945
Fax: 713-292-1946
E-mail Address: info@iadc.org
Web Address: www.iadc.org
The International Association of Drilling
Contractors (IADC) represents the
worldwide oil and gas drilling industry
and promotes commitment to safety,
preservation of the environment and
advances in drilling technology.

41) Engineering Industry Associations

National Society of Professional
Engineers (NSPE)
1420 King St.
Alexandria, VA 22314-2794 USA
Fax: 703-836-4875
Toll Free: 888-285-6773
Web Address: www.nspe.org
The National Society of Professional
Engineers (NSPE) represents individual
engineering professionals and licensed
engineers across all disciplines. NSPE
serves approximately 45,000 members
and has more than 500 chapters.

42) Engineering, Research & Scientific Associations

American Association of Petroleum
Geologists (AAPG)
1444 S. Boulder Ave.
Tulsa, OK 74119 USA
Phone: 918-584-2555
Fax: 918-560-2665
Toll Free: 800-364-2274
Web Address: www.aapg.org
The American Association of Petroleum
Geologists (AAPG) is an international
geological organization that supports
educational and scientific programs and
projects related to geosciences.

American Institute of Chemical
Engineers (AIChE)
120 Wall St., Fl. 23
New York, NY 10005-4020 USA
Phone: 203-702-7660
Fax: 203-775-5177
Toll Free: 800-242-4363
Web Address: www.aiche.org
The American Institute of Chemical
Engineers (AIChE) provides leadership in
advancing the chemical engineering
profession. The organization, which is
comprised of more than 50,000 members
from over 100 countries, provides
informational resources to chemical
engineers.

American Society for Healthcare
Engineering (ASHE)
155 N. Wacker Dr., Ste. 400
Chicago, IL 60606 USA
Phone: 312-422-3800
Fax: 312-422-4571
E-mail Address: ashe@aha.org
Web Address: www.ashe.org
The American Society for Healthcare
Engineering (ASHE) is the advocate and
resource for continuous improvement in
the health care engineering and facilities
management professions. It is devoted to
professionals who design, build, maintain
and operate hospitals and other healthcare
facilities.

American Society of Agricultural and
Biological Engineers (ASABE)
2950 Niles Rd.
St. Joseph, MI 49085 USA
Phone: 269-429-0300
Fax: 269-429-3852
Toll Free: 800-371-2723
E-mail Address: hq@asabe.org
Web Address: www.asabe.org
The American Society of Agricultural and
Biological Engineers (ASABE) is a
nonprofit professional and technical
organization interested in engineering
knowledge and technology for food and
agriculture and associated industries.

American Society of Civil Engineers
(ASCE)
1801 Alexander Bell Dr.
Reston, VA 20191-4400 USA
Phone: 703-295-6300
Toll Free: 800-548-2723
Web Address: www.asce.org
The American Society of Civil Engineers
(ASCE) is a leading professional
organization serving civil engineers. It
ensures safer buildings, water systems and
other civil engineering works by
developing technical codes and standards.

American Society of Safety Engineers
(ASSE)
520 N. Northwest Hwy
Park Ridge, IL 60068 USA
Phone: 847-699-2929
E-mail Address:
customerservice@asse.org
Web Address: www.asse.org
The American Society of Safety
Engineers (ASSE) is the world's oldest
and largest professional safety
organization. It manages, supervises and
consults on safety, health and
environmental issues in industry,
insurance, government and education.

Association of Federal Communications
Consulting Engineers (AFCCE)
P.O. Box 19333
Washington, DC 20036 USA
Web Address: www.afcce.org
The Association of Federal
Communications Consulting Engineers
(AFCCE) is a professional organization of
individuals who regularly assist clients on
technical issues before the Federal
Communications Commission (FCC).

Institute of Industrial Engineers (IIE)
3577 Parkway Ln., Ste. 200
Norcross, GA 30092 USA
Phone: 770-449-0460
Fax: 770-441-3295
Toll Free: 800-494-0460
E-mail Address: cs@iienet.org
Web Address: www.iienet2.org
The Institute of Industrial Engineers (IIE)
is an international, non-profit association
dedicated to the education, development,
training and research in the field of
industrial engineering.

Society of Automotive Engineers (SAE)
755 W. Big Beaver, Ste. 1600
Troy, MA 48084 USA
Phone: 248-273-2455
Fax: 248-273-2494
Toll Free: 877-606-7323
E-mail Address: automotive_hq@sae.org
Web Address: www.sae.org
The Society of Automotive Engineers
(SAE) is a resource for technical
information and expertise used in
designing, building, maintaining and
operating self-propelled vehicles for use
on land, sea, air or space.

Society of Broadcast Engineers, Inc.
(SBE)
9102 N. Meridian St., Ste. 150
Indianapolis, IN 46260 USA
Phone: 317-846-9000
E-mail Address: jporay@sbe.org
Web Address: www.sbe.org
The Society of Broadcast Engineers
(SBE) exists to increase knowledge of
broadcast engineering and promote its

interests, as well as to continue the education of professionals in the industry.

Society of Cable Telecommunications Engineers (SCTE)
140 Philips Rd.
Exton, PA 19341-1318 USA
Fax: 610-884-7237
Toll Free: 800-542-5040
E-mail Address: scte@scte.org
Web Address: www.scte.org
The Society of Cable Telecommunications Engineers (SCTE) is a nonprofit professional association dedicated to advancing the careers and serving the industry of telecommunications professionals by providing technical training, certification and information resources.

Society of Hispanic Professional Engineers (SHPE)
13181 Crossroads Pkwy. N., Ste. 450
City of Industry, CA 91746 USA
Phone: 323-725-3970
Fax: 323-725-0316
E-mail Address: shpenational@shpe.org
Web Address: oneshpe.shpe.org
The Society of Hispanic Professional Engineers (SHPE) is a national nonprofit organization that promotes Hispanics in science, engineering and math.

Society of Manufacturing Engineers (SME)
One SME Dr.
Dearborn, MI 48121 USA
Phone: 313-425-3000
Fax: 313-425-3400
Toll Free: 800-733-4763
E-mail Address: communications@sme.org
Web Address: www.sme.org
The Society of Manufacturing Engineers (SME) is a leading professional organization serving engineers in the manufacturing industries.

Society of Motion Picture and Television Engineers (SMPTE)
3 Barker Ave., Fl. 5
White Plains, NY 10601 USA
Phone: 914-761-1100
Fax: 914-761-3115
E-mail Address: marketing@smpte.org
Web Address: www.smpte.org
The Society of Motion Picture and Television Engineers (SMPTE) is the leading technical society for the motion imaging industry. The firm publishes recommended practice and engineering guidelines, as well the SMPTE Journal.

Society of Women Engineers (SWE)
230 N La Salle St., Ste. 1675

Chicago, IL 60601 USA
Toll Free: 877-793-4636
E-mail Address: hq@swe.org
Web Address: societyofwomenengineers.swe.org
The Society of Women Engineers (SWE) is a nonprofit educational and service organization of female engineers.

SPIE
1000 20th St.
Bellingham, WA 98225-6705 USA
Phone: 360-676-3290
Fax: 360-647-1445
Toll Free: 888-504-8171
E-mail Address: customerservice@spie.org
Web Address: www.spie.org
SPIE is a nonprofit technical society aimed at the advancement and dissemination of knowledge in optics, photonics and imaging.

43) Entertainment & Amusement Associations-General

International Association of Amusement Parks and Attractions (IAAPA)
1448 Duke St.
Alexandria, VA 22314 USA
Phone: 703-836-4800
Fax: 703-836-4801
E-mail Address: iaapa@iaapa.org
Web Address: www.iaapa.org
The International Association of Amusement Parks and Attractions (IAAPA) is dedicated to the preservation and prosperity of the amusement industry.

International Special Events Society (ISES)
330 N. Wabash Ave., Ste. 2000
Chicago, IL 60611-4267 USA
Phone: 312-321-6853
Fax: 312-673-6953
Toll Free: 800-688-4737
E-mail Address: info@ises.com
Web Address: www.ises.com
The International Special Events Society (ISES) is comprised of over 7,200 professionals in over 38 countries representing special event planners and producers (from festivals to trade shows), caterers, decorators, florists, destination management companies, rental companies, special effects experts, tent suppliers, audio-visual technicians, event and convention coordinators, balloon artists, educators, journalists, hotel sales managers, specialty entertainers, convention center managers, and many more professional disciplines.

44) Film & Theater Associations

Academy of Motion Picture Arts and Sciences (AMPAS)
8949 Wilshire Blvd.
Beverly Hills, CA 90211-1972 USA
Phone: 310-247-3000
Fax: 310-859-9619
Web Address: www.oscars.org
The Academy of Motion Picture Arts and Sciences (AMPAS) is a professional honorary organization, founded to advance the arts and sciences of motion pictures. Besides hosting the Academy Awards and selecting the winners of the Oscars, AMPAS organizes smaller events highlighting the art of filmmaking, including lectures and seminars, and is currently building the Academy Museum of Motion Pictures.

Alliance of Motion Picture and Television Producers (AMPTP)
15301 Ventura Blvd., Bldg. E
Sherman Oaks, CA 91403 USA
Phone: 818-995-3600
Web Address: www.amptp.org
The Alliance of Motion Picture and Television Producers (AMPTP) is the primary trade association with respect to labor issues in the motion picture and television industry.

American Cinema Editors, Inc. (ACE)
100 Universal City Plz.
Verna Fields Bldg. 2282, Rm. 190
Universal City, CA 91608 USA
Phone: 818-777-2900
E-mail Address: amercinema@earthlink.net
Web Address: www.ace-filmeditors.org
American Cinema Editors (ACE) is an honorary society of motion picture editors that seeks to advance the art and science of the editing profession.

American Society of Cinematographers (ASC)
1782 N. Orange Dr.
Hollywood, CA 90028 USA
Phone: 323-969-4333
Fax: 323-882-6391
Toll Free: 800-448-0145
E-mail Address: office@theasc.com
Web Address: www.theasc.com
The American Society of Cinematographers (ASC) is a trade association for cinematographers in the motion picture industry.

Art Directors Guild (ADG)
11969 Ventura Blvd., Fl. 2
Studio City, CA 91604 USA

Phone: 818-762-9995
Fax: 818-760-4847
E-mail Address: nick@artdirectors.org
Web Address: www.artdirectors.org
The Art Directors Guild (ADG) represents the creative talents that conceive and manage the background and settings for most films and television projects.

Association of Cinema and Video Laboratories (ACVL)
Phone: 805-427-2620
E-mail Address:
peterbulcke@hotmail.com
Web Address: www.acvl.org
The Association of Cinema and Video Laboratories (ACVL) is an international organization whose members are pledged to the highest possible standards of service to the film and video industries.

Independent Film & Television Alliance (IFTA)
10850 Wilshire Blvd., Fl. 9
Los Angeles, CA 90024-4311 USA
Phone: 310-446-1000
Fax: 310-446-1600
E-mail Address: info@ifta-online.org
Web Address: www.ifta-online.org
The Independent Film & Television Alliance (IFTA), formerly the American Film Marketing Association (AFMA), is a trade association whose mission is to provide the independent film and television industry with high-quality, market-oriented services and worldwide representation.

International Alliance of Theatrical Stage Employees (IATSE)
207 W. 25th St., Fl. 4
New York, NY 10001 USA
Phone: 212-730-1770
Fax: 212-730-7809
E-mail Address: webmaster@iatse-intl.org
Web Address: www.iatse-intl.org
The International Alliance of Theatrical Stage Employees (IATSE) is the labor union representing technicians, artisans and crafts workers in the entertainment industry, including live theater, film and television production and trade shows.

International Animated Film Society (ASIFA-Hollywood)
2114 W. Burbank Blvd.
Burbank, CA 91506 USA
Phone: 818-842-8330
E-mail Address: info@asifa-hollywood.org
Web Address: www.asifa-hollywood.org
International Animated Film Society (ASIFA-Hollywood) is a nonprofit

organization dedicated to the advancement of the art of animation.

International Documentary Association (IDA)
3470 Wilshire Blvd., Ste. 980
Los Angeles, CA 90010 USA
Phone: 213-232-1660
Fax: 213-232-1669
E-mail Address:
michael@documentary.org
Web Address: www.documentary.org
The International Documentary Association (IDA) is a nonprofit member service organization, providing publications, benefits and a public forum to its members for issues regarding nonfiction film, video and multimedia.

Motion Picture Association of America (MPAA)
15301 Ventura Blvd., Bldg. E
Sherman Oaks, CA 91403 USA
Phone: 818-995-6600
Fax: 818-285-4403
E-mail Address: ContactUs@mpaa.org
Web Address: www.mpaa.org
The Motion Picture Association of America (MPAA) serves as the voice and advocate of the U.S. motion picture, home video and television industries.

Motion Picture Editors Guild (MPEG)
7715 Sunset Blvd., Ste. 200
Hollywood, CA 90046 USA
Phone: 323-876-4770
Fax: 323-876-0861
Toll Free: 800-705-8700
E-mail Address: social@editorsguild.com
Web Address: www.editorsguild.com
The Motion Picture Editors Guild's (MPEG) web site provides an online directory of editors, a discussion forum and links to related magazines and other organizations that serve the motion picture industry.

Producers Guild of America, Inc. (PGA)
8530 Wilshire Blvd., Ste. 400
Beverly Hills, CA 90211 USA
Phone: 310-358-9020
Fax: 310-358-9520
E-mail Address: info@producersguild.org
Web Address: www.producersguild.org
The Producers Guild of America, Inc. (PGA) is a nonprofit organization for career professionals who initiate, create, coordinate, supervise and control all aspects of the motion picture and television production processes.

SAG-AFTRA
5757 Wilshire Blvd., Fl. 7
Los Angeles, CA 90036-3600 USA

Phone: 323-954-1600
Toll Free: 800-724-2387
Web Address: www.sagaftra.org
The SAG-AFTRA, representing a union of the Screen Actors Guild the American Federation of Television and Radio Artists, represents its members through negotiation and enforcement of collective bargaining agreements that establish equitable levels of compensation, benefits and working conditions for performers. The guild represents 160,000 actors worldwide.

Women In Film (WIF)
6100 Wilshire Blvd., Ste. 710
Los Angeles, CA 90048 USA
Phone: 323-935-2211
Fax: 323-935-2212
E-mail Address: info@wif.org
Web Address: www.wif.org
Women In Film (WIF) strives to empower, promote and mentor women in the entertainment, communication and media industries through a network of contacts, educational programs and events.

45) Fitness Industry Associations

American Fitness Professionals and Associates (AFPA)
1601 Long Beach Blvd.
P.O. Box 214
Ship Bottom, NJ 08008 USA
Phone: 609-978-7583
Fax: 609-978-7582
Toll Free: 800-494-7782
E-mail Address: afpa@afpafitness.com
Web Address: www.afpafitness.com
American Fitness Professionals and Associates (AFPA) offers health and fitness professionals certification programs, continuing education courses, home correspondence courses and regional conventions.

46) Food Industry Associations, General

Institute of Food Technologies (IFT)
525 W. Van Buren, Ste. 1000
Chicago, IL 60607 USA
Phone: 312-782-8424
Fax: 312-782-8348
Toll Free: 800-438-3663
E-mail Address: info@ift.org
Web Address: www.ift.org
The Institute of Food Technologies (IFT) is devoted to the advancement of the science and technology of food through the exchange of knowledge. The site also

provides information and resources for job seekers in the food industry. Members work in food science, food technology and related professions in industry, academia and government.

47) Food Industry Resources, General

Food Manufacturing
199 E. Badger Rd., Ste. 101
Madison, WI 53713 USA
Phone: 973-920-7782
E-mail Address:
tom.lynch@advantagemedia.com
Web Address:
www.foodmanufacturing.com
Food Manufacturing is a trade magazine for companies and employees in the food manufacturing industry. It is published by Advantage Business Media.

48) Food Processor Industry Associations

Grocery Manufacturers Association (GMA)
1350 I St. NW, Ste. 300
Washington, DC 20005 USA
Phone: 202-639-5900
Fax: 202-639-5932
E-mail Address: info@gmaonline.org
Web Address: www.gmaonline.org
The Grocery Manufacturers Association (GMA), formerly the National Food Products Association (NFPA), is the voice of the food, beverage and consumer products industry on scientific and public policy issues involving food safety, food security, nutrition, technical and regulatory matters and consumer affairs.

National Frozen and Refrigerated Foods Association (NFRA)
4755 Linglestown Rd., Ste. 300
Harrisburg, PA 17112 USA
Phone: 717-657-8601
Fax: 717-657-9862
E-mail Address: info@nfraweb.org
Web Address: www.nfraweb.org
The National Frozen and Refrigerated Foods Association (NFRA) promotes the sales and consumption of refrigerated and frozen foods through education, research, training, sales planning and menu development, providing a forum for industry dialogue. It represents manufacturers, sales agents, suppliers, local associations, retailers, wholesalers, distributors and logistic providers involved in the frozen and refrigerated food industry.

49) Food Service Industry Associations

International Flight Services Association (IFSA)
1100 Johnson Ferry Rd., Ste. 300
Atlanta, GA 30342 USA
Phone: 404-303-2969
E-mail Address:
ejohnson@kellencompany.com
Web Address: www.ifsanet.com
The International Flight Services Association (IFSA), formerly the International Inflight Food Service Association, informs the public with respect to educational and career opportunities within the multi-billion-dollar inflight and railway food service industry. IFSA is managed by the Kellen Company.

50) Games Industry Associations

Entertainment Software Association (ESA)
575 7th St. NW, Ste. 300
Washington, DC 20004 USA
Phone: 202-223-2400
E-mail Address: esa@theesa.com
Web Address: www.theesa.com
The Entertainment Software Association (ESA) is a U.S. trade association for companies that publish video and computer games for consoles, personal computers and the Internet. The ESA owns the E3 Media & Business Summit, a major invitation-only annual trade show for the video game industry.

Fantasy Sports Trade Association (FSTA)
600 N. Lake Shore Dr.
Chicago, IL 60611 U.S.A.
Phone: 312-771-7019
E-mail Address: megan@fsta.org
Web Address: www.fsta.org
The Fantasy Sports Trade Association (FSTA) was founded in 1997 to provide a forum for interaction between companies in a unique and growing fantasy sports industry. FSTA represents more than 300 member companies.

Game Manufacturers Association (GAMA)
240 N. Fifth St., Ste. 340
Columbus, OH 43215 USA
Phone: 614-255-4500
Fax: 614-255-4499
E-mail Address: ed@gama.org
Web Address: www.gama.org

The Game Manufacturers Association (GAMA) is an international non-profit trade association serving the hobby games industry. It hosts two annual events, the GAMA Trade Show and Origins Game Fair, and publishes a quarterly information newsletter, GAMATimes.

International Game Developers Association (IGDA)
19 Mantua Rd.
Mt. Royal, NJ 08061 USA
Phone: 856-423-2990
Web Address: www.igda.org
The International Game Developers Association (IGDA) represents members involved in the video game production industry. The firm aims to promote professional development within the gaming industry and advocates for issues that affect the game developer community, including anti-censorship issues.

51) Grocery Industry Associations

National Grocers Association (NGA)
1005 N. Glebe Rd., Ste. 250
Arlington, VA 22201-5758 USA
Phone: 703-516-0700
Fax: 703-516-0115
E-mail Address:
feedback@nationalgrocers.org
Web Address: www.nationalgrocers.org
The National Grocers Association (NGA) is a national trade association representing retail and wholesale grocers that comprise the independent sector of the food distribution industry.

52) Health & Nutrition Associations

Academy of Nutrition and Dietetics
120 S. Riverside Plz., Ste. 2000
Chicago, IL 60606-6995 USA
Phone: 312-899-0040
Toll Free: 800-877-1600
E-mail Address: foundation@eatright.org
Web Address: www.eatright.org
The Academy of Nutrition and Dietetics, formerly known as the American Dietetic Association (ADA) is the world's largest organization of food and nutrition professionals, with nearly 65,000 members. In addition to services for its professional members, this organization's web site offers consumers a respected source for food and nutrition information.

53) Health Care Business & Professional Associations

Advanced Medical Technology Association (AdvaMed)
701 Pennsylvania Ave. NW, Ste. 800
Washington, DC 20004-2654 USA
Phone: 202-783-8700
Fax: 202-783-8750
E-mail Address: info@advamed.org
Web Address: www.advamed.org
The Advanced Medical Technology Association (AdvaMed) strives to be the advocate for a legal, regulatory and economic climate that advances global health care by assuring worldwide access to the benefits of medical technology.

American Academy of Nursing (AAN)
1000 Vermont Ave., Ste. 910
Washington, DC 20005 USA
Phone: 202-777-1170
E-mail Address: info@aannet.org
Web Address: www.aannet.org
The American Academy of Nursing (AAN) works to enhance nursing profession by advancing health policy and practice and generate, synthesize and disseminate nursing knowledge.

American Association of Medical Assistants (AAMA)
20 N. Wacker Dr., Ste. 1575
Chicago, IL 60606 USA
Phone: 312-899-1500
Fax: 312-899-1259
Toll Free: 800-228-2262
Web Address: www.aama-ntl.org
The American Association of Medical Assistants (AAMA) seeks to promote the professional identity and stature of its members and the medical assisting profession through education and credentialing.

American College of Health Care Administrators (ACHCA)
1101 Connecticut Ave. NW, Ste. 450
Washington, DC 20036 USA
Phone: 202-536-5120
Fax: 866-874-1585
E-mail Address: wodonnell@achca.org
Web Address: www.achca.org
The American College of Health Care Administrators (ACHCA) offers educational programming, professional certification and career development opportunities for health care administrators.

American College of Healthcare Executives (ACHE)
1 N. Franklin St., Ste. 1700
Chicago, IL 60606-3529 USA
Phone: 312-424-2800
Fax: 312-424-0023
E-mail Address: contact@ache.org
Web Address: www.ache.org
The American College of Healthcare Executives (ACHE) is an international professional society of health care executives that offers certification and educational programs.

American Dental Association (ADA)
211 E. Chicago Ave.
Chicago, IL 60611-2678 USA
Phone: 312-440-2500
Web Address: www.ada.org
The American Dental Association (ADA) is a nonprofit professional association of dentists committed to enhancing public's oral health with a focus on ethics, science and professional advancement.

American Medical Technologists (AMT)
10700 W. Higgins Rd., Ste. 150
Rosemont, IL 60018 USA
Phone: 847-823-5169
Fax: 847-823-0458
E-mail Address: mail@americanmedtech.org
Web Address: www.americanmedtech.org
American Medical Technologists (AMT) is a nationally and internationally recognized nonprofit certification agency and professional membership association representing allied health professionals. Its members include laboratory health professionals, as well as medical and dental office professionals.

American Medical Women's Association (AMWA)
12100 Sunset Hills Rd., Ste. 130
Reston, VA 20190 USA
Phone: 703-234-4069
Fax: 703-435-4390
Toll Free: 866-564-2483
E-mail Address: associatedirector@amwa-doc.org
Web Address: www.amwa-doc.org
The American Medical Women's Association (AMWA) is an organization of women physicians and medical students dedicated to serving as the unique voice for women's health and the advancement of women in medicine.

American Occupational Therapy Association, Inc. (AOTA)
4720 Montgomery Ln., Ste. 200
Bethesda, MD 20814-3449 USA
Phone: 301-652-6611
Fax: 301-652-7711
Toll Free: 800-377-8555
Web Address: www.aota.org
The American Occupational Therapy Association, Inc. (AOTA) advances the quality, availability, use and support of occupational therapy through standard-setting, advocacy, education and research on behalf of its members and the public.

American Organization of Nurse Executives (AONE)
800 10th St. NW
Two City Center, Suite 400
Washington, DC 20001 USA
Phone: 312-422-2800
E-mail Address: aone@aha.org
Web Address: www.aone.org
The American Organization of Nurse Executives (AONE) is a national organization focused on advancing nursing practice and patient care through leadership, professional development, advocacy and research.

American Public Health Association (APHA)
800 I St. NW
Washington, DC 20001-3710 USA
Phone: 202-777-2742
Fax: 202-777-2534
Web Address: www.apha.org
The American Public Health Association (APHA) is an association of individuals and organizations working to improve the public's health and to achieve equity in health status for all.

American School Health Association (ASHA)
7918 Jones Branch Dr., Ste. 300
McLean, VA 22102 USA
Phone: 703-506-7675
Fax: 703-506-3266
E-mail Address: info@ashaweb.org
Web Address: www.ashaweb.org
The American School Health Association (ASHA) advocates high-quality school health instruction, health services and a healthy school environment.

Dental Trade Alliance (DTA)
4350 N. Fairfax Dr., Ste. 220
Arlington, VA 22203 USA
Phone: 703-379-7755
Fax: 703-931-9429
Web Address: www.dentaltradealliance.org
The Dental Trade Alliance (DTA) represents dental manufacturers, dental dealers and dental laboratories.

Health Industry Distributors Association (HIDA)
310 Montgomery St.
Alexandria, VA 22314-1516 USA
Phone: 703-549-4432
Fax: 703-549-6495

E-mail Address: rowan@hida.org
Web Address: www.hida.org
The Health Industry Distributors
Association (HIDA) is the international
trade association representing medical
products distributors.

**Healthcare Financial Management
Association (HFMA)**
3 Westbrook Corp. Ctr., Ste. 600
Westchester, IL 60154 USA
Phone: 708-531-9600
Fax: 708-531-0032
Toll Free: 800-252-4362
E-mail Address:
memberservices@hfma.org
Web Address: www.hfma.org
The Healthcare Financial Management
Association (HFMA) is one of the nation's
leading personal membership
organizations for health care financial
management executives and leaders.

**Medical Device Manufacturers
Association (MDMA)**
1333 H St., Ste. 400 W.
Washington, DC 20005 USA
Phone: 202-354-7171
Web Address: www.medicaldevices.org
The Medical Device Manufacturers
Association (MDMA) is a national trade
association that represents independent
manufacturers of medical devices,
diagnostic products and health care
information systems.

**Medical Group Management
Association (MGMA)**
104 Inverness Terrace E.
Englewood, CO 80112-5306 USA
Phone: 303-799-1111
Toll Free: 877-275-6462
E-mail Address: support@mgma.com
Web Address: www.mgma.com
Medical Group Management Association
(MGMA) is one of the nation's principal
voices for medical group practice. It
represents over 33,000 administrators and
executives in 18,000 healthcare
organizations in which 385,000
physicians practice.

**National Association of Health Services
Executives (NAHSE)**
1050 Connecticut Ave. NW, Fl. 5
Washington, DC 20036 USA
Phone: 202-772-1030
Fax: 202-772-1072
Web Address: www.nahse.org
The National Association of Health
Services Executives (NAHSE) is a
nonprofit association of black health care
executives who promote the advancement
and development of black health care
leaders and elevate the quality of health

care services rendered to minority and
underserved communities.

**Regulatory Affairs Professionals
Society (RAPS)**
5635 Fishers Ln., Ste. 550
Rockville, MD 20852 USA
Phone: 301-770-2920
Fax: 301-841-7956
E-mail Address: raps@raps.org
Web Address: www.raps.org
The Regulatory Affairs Professionals
Society (RAPS) is an international
professional society representing the
health care regulatory affairs profession
and individual professionals worldwide.

54) Health Insurance Industry Associations

**America's Health Insurance Plans
(AHIP)**
601 Pennsylvania Ave. NW
S. Bldg., Ste. 500
Washington, DC 20004 USA
Phone: 202-778-3200
Fax: 202-331-7487
E-mail Address: ahip@ahip.org
Web Address: www.ahip.org
America's Health Insurance Plans (AHIP)
is a prominent trade association
representing the health care insurance
community. Its members offer health and
supplemental benefits through employer-
sponsored coverage, the individual
insurance market, and public programs
such as Medicare and Medicaid.

55) Hearing & Speech

Hearing Industries Association (HIA)
1444 I St. NW, Ste. 700
Washington, DC 20005 USA
Phone: 202-449-1090
Fax: 202-216-9646
E-mail Address: mjones@bostrom.com
Web Address: www.hearing.org
The Hearing Industries Association (HIA)
represents and unifies the many aspects of
the hearing industry.

56) Hotel/Lodging Associations

**American Hotel and Lodging
Association**
1250 I St., NW, Ste. 1100
Washington, DC 20005-3931 USA
Phone: 202-289-3100
Fax: 202-289-3199
E-mail Address:
informationcenter@ahla.com
Web Address: www.ahla.com

The American Hotel and Lodging
Association is a federation of state
lodging associations throughout the U.S.

57) Human Resources Industry Associations

HR Policy Association
1100 13th St., Ste. 850
Washington, DC 20005 USA
Phone: 202-789-8670
Fax: 202-789-0064
E-mail Address: info@hrpolicy.org
Web Address: www.hrpolicy.org
HR Policy Association is a public policy
organization of chief human resource
officers from major employers. The
association brings together HR
professionals at the highest level of
corporations to discuss changes in public
policy, and to lay out a vision and
advocate for competitive workplace
initiatives that promote job growth and
employment security.

**Society for Human Resource
Management (SHRM)**
1800 Duke St.
Alexandria, VA 22314 USA
Phone: 703-548-3440
Fax: 703-535-6490
Toll Free: 800-283-7476
E-mail Address: shrm@shrm.org
Web Address: www.shrm.org
The Society for Human Resource
Management (SHRM) addresses the
interests and needs of HR professionals
through advocacy, publications, research
and other resource materials. The
organization has 575 affiliate chapters,
both in the U.S. and internationally,
serving over 5,000 members in
approximately 160 countries.

**The Association for Talent
Development (ATD)**
1640 King St.
Alexandria, VA 22313-1443 USA
Phone: 703-683-8100
Fax: 703-299-8723
Toll Free: 800-628-2783
E-mail Address: customercare@td.org
Web Address: www.td.org
The Association for Talent Development
(ATD), formerly American Society for
Training & Development (ASTD) is
dedicated to those professionals in the
fields of training and development. It
provides resources such as research,
analysis, benchmarking, online
information, books and other publications
to training and development professional,
educators and students. Additionally, the
association brings professional together in

conferences, workshops and online, while also offering professional development opportunities, certificate programs and Certified Professional in Learning and Performance (CPLP) credential.

58) Industry Research/ Market Research

Forrester Research
60 Acorn Park Dr.
Cambridge, MA 02140 USA
Phone: 617-613-5730
E-mail Address: press@forrester.com
Web Address: www.forrester.com
Forrester Research is a publicly traded company that identifies and analyzes emerging trends in technology and their impact on business. Among the firm's specialties are the financial services, retail, health care, entertainment, automotive and information technology industries.

MarketResearch.com
11200 Rockville Pike, Ste. 504
Rockville, MD 20852 USA
Phone: 240-747-3093
Fax: 240-747-3004
Toll Free: 800-298-5699
E-mail Address:
customerservice@marketresearch.com
Web Address: www.marketresearch.com
MarketResearch.com is a leading broker for professional market research and industry analysis. Users are able to search the company's database of research publications including data on global industries, companies, products and trends.

Plunkett Research, Ltd.
P.O. Drawer 541737
Houston, TX 77254-1737 USA
Phone: 713-932-0000
Fax: 713-932-7080
E-mail Address:
customersupport@plunkettresearch.com
Web Address: www.plunkettresearch.com
Plunkett Research, Ltd. is a leading provider of market research, industry trends analysis and business statistics. Since 1985, it has served clients worldwide, including corporations, universities, libraries, consultants and government agencies. At the firm's web site, visitors can view product information and pricing and access a large amount of basic market information on industries such as financial services, InfoTech, e-commerce, health care and biotech.

59) Insurance Industry Associations

American Insurance Association (AIA)
2101 L St. NW, Ste.400
Washington, DC 20037 USA
Phone: 202-828-7100
Fax: 202-293-1219
E-mail Address: jbrodt@aiadc.org
Web Address: www.aiadc.org
The American Insurance Association (AIA) is a leading property and casualty insurance trade organization, representing companies that offer all types of property and casualty insurance.

60) Insurance Industry Associations-Agents & Brokers

Council of Insurance Agents & Brokers (CIAB)
701 Pennsylvania Ave. NW, Ste. 750
Washington, DC 20004 USA
Phone: 202-783-4400
Fax: 202-783-4410
E-mail Address: ciab@ciab.com
Web Address: www.ciab.com
The Council of Insurance Agents & Brokers (CIAB) is an association for commercial insurance and employee benefits intermediaries in the U.S. and abroad.

Independent Insurance Agents & Brokers of America, Inc. (IIABA)
127 S. Peyton St.
Alexandria, VA 22314 USA
Fax: 703-683-7556
Toll Free: 800-221-7917
E-mail Address: info@iiaba.org
Web Address:
www.independentagent.com
Independent Insurance Agents & Brokers of America (IIABA) represents its over 300,000 members who are independent insurance agents and brokers.

Professional Insurance Agents (PIA)
25 Chamberlain St.
P.O. Box 997
Glenmont, NY 12077-0997 USA
Fax: 888-225-6935
Toll Free: 800-424-4244
E-mail Address: pia@pia.org
Web Address: www.piaonline.org
Professional Insurance Agents (PIA) is a group of voluntary, membership-based trade associations representing professional, independent property and casualty insurance agents.

61) Magazines, Business & Financial

Bloomberg Businessweek Online
731 Lexington Ave.
New York, NY 10022 USA
Phone: 212-318-2000
Fax: 917-369-5000
Web Address: www.businessweek.com
Business Week Online offers an investor service, global business advice, technology news, small business guides, career information, business school advice, daily news briefs and more.

Forbes Online
60 5th Ave.
New York, NY 10011 USA
Phone: 212-620-2200
E-mail Address:
customerservice@forbes.com
Web Address: www.forbes.com
Forbes Online offers varied stock information, news and commentary on business, technology and personal finance, as well as financial calculators and advice.

Fortune
1271 Ave. of the Americas
Rockefeller Ctr.
New York, NY 10020-1393 USA
Phone: 212-522-8528
Web Address: http://fortune.com/
Fortune, one of the world's premiere business magazines, contains news, business profiles and information on investing, careers, small business, technology and other details of U.S. and international business. Fortune is a publication of Cable News Network (CNN), a Time Warner company.

Investor's Business Daily (IBD)
12655 Beatrice St.
Los Angeles, CA 90066 USA
Phone: 310-448-6000
Toll Free: 800-831-2525
Web Address: www.investors.com
Investor's Business Daily (IBD) offers subscribers information and articles on the stock market, educational resources, advice from analyst William O'Neil, personal portfolios and updates on events and workshops.

Wall Street Journal Online (The)
1211 Ave. of the Americas
New York, NY 10036 USA
Phone: 609-514-0870
Toll Free: 800-568-7625
E-mail Address: support@wsj.com
Web Address: www.wsj.com

The outstanding resources of The Wall Street Journal are available online for a nominal fee.

62) MBA Resources

MBA Depot
Web Address: www.mbadepot.com
MBA Depot is an online community and information portal for MBAs, potential MBA program applicants and business professionals.

63) Online Recruiting & Employment ASPs & Solutions

Hrsoft
2200 Lucien Way, Ste. 201
Maitland, FL 32751 USA
Phone: 407-475-5500
Fax: 407-475-5502
Toll Free: 866-953-8800
E-mail Address:
Michael.Noland@HRsoft.com
Web Address: www.hrsoft.com
HRsoft, formerly Workstream, Inc., creates workforce management solutions through a combination of technology and services designed to integrate an organization.

Insala
2005 NE Green Oaks Blvd., Ste. 110
Arlington, TX 76006 USA
Phone: 817-355-0939
Fax: 817-355-0746
E-mail Address: info@insala.com
Web Address: www.insala.com
Insala provides job search software solutions for the outplacement industry.

Kenexa
650 E. Swedesford Rd., Fl. 2
Wayne, PA 19087 USA
Phone: 877-971-9171
Fax: 610-971-9181
Toll Free: 800-391-9557
E-mail Address: contactus@kenexa.com
Web Address: www.kenexa.com
Kenexa is a back-end recruiting and job-posting service that is used by many companies in building a workforce. Products and services include recruitment software solutions, talent consulting and recruitment process management.

64) Outsourcing Industry Associations

International Association of Outsourcing Professionals (IAOP)
2600 South Rd., Ste. 44-240

Poughkeepsie, NY 12601 USA
Phone: 845-452-0600
Fax: 845-452-6988
E-mail Address:
memberservices@iaop.org
Web Address: www.iaop.org
The International Association of Outsourcing Professionals (IAOP) represents outsourcing leaders and experts from companies of all sizes and industries around the world.

65) Pensions, Benefits & 401(k) Associations

Plan Sponsor Council of America (PSCA)
20 N. Wacker Dr., Ste. 3164
Chicago, IL 60606 USA
Phone: 312-419-1863
Fax: 312-419-1864
E-mail Address: psca@psca.org
Web Address: www.psca.org
The Plan Sponsor Council of America (PSCA), formerly the Profit Sharing/401(k) Council of America (PSCA). is a national nonprofit association of 1,200 companies and their 6 million employees. The group expresses its members' interests to federal policymakers and offers practical, cost-effective assistance with profit sharing and 401(k) plan design, administration, investment, compliance and communication. Its web site offers a thorough glossary, statistics and educational material.

66) Pensions, Benefits & 401(k) Resources

Employee Benefits Security Administration (EBSA)
200 Constitution Ave. NW
Washington, DC 20210 USA
Toll Free: 866-444-3272
Web Address: www.dol.gov/ebsa
The Employee Benefits Security Administration (EBSA) is a division of the U.S. Department of Labor, whose web site features a wealth of benefits information for both employers and employees. Included are the answers to such questions as to how a company's bankruptcy will affect its employees and what one should know about pension rights.

Pension Benefit Guarantee Corporation (PBGC)
1200 K St. NW, Ste. 9429
Washington, DC 20005-4026 USA
Phone: 202-326-4000

Fax: 202-326-4047
Toll Free: 800-400-7242
E-mail Address: webmaster@pbgc.gov
Web Address: www.pbgc.gov
The Pension Benefit Guarantee Corporation (PBGC) is a U.S. Government agency that guarantees a portion of the retirement incomes of about 41 million American workers in about 24,000 private defined benefit pension plans. Its web site contains information regarding this guarantee, along with information on retirement planning and links to several related organizations.

67) Pharmaceutical Industry Associations (Drug Industry)

American Pharmacists Association (AphA)
2215 Constitution Ave. NW
Washington, DC 20037 USA
Phone: 202-628-4410
Fax: 202-783-2351
Toll Free: 800-237-4410
E-mail Address: infocenter@aphanet.org
Web Address: www.pharmacist.com
American Pharmaceutical Association (APhA), formerly American Pharmaceutical Association is a national professional society that provides news and information to pharmacists. Its membership includes over 62,000 practicing pharmacists, pharmaceutical scientists, student pharmacists and pharmacy technicians.

Pharmaceutical Research and Manufacturers of America (PhRMA)
950 F St. NW, Ste. 300
Washington, DC 20004 USA
Phone: 202-835-3400
Web Address: www.phrma.org
Pharmaceutical Research and Manufacturers of America (PhRMA) represents the nation's leading research-based pharmaceutical and biotechnology companies.

68) Pilots Associations

Airline Pilots Association (ALPA)
1625 Massachusetts Ave NW
Washington, DC 20036 USA
Phone: 703-689-2270
E-mail Address: media@alpa.org
Web Address: www.alpa.org
The Airline Pilots Association (ALPA) is an association for professional airline pilots in the United States, in Canada and internationally. ALPA provides airline safety, security, pilot assistance,

representation and advocacy to its members.

69) Printers & Publishers Associations

Epicomm
1800 Diagonal Rd., Ste. 320
Alexandria, VA 22314-2862 USA
Phone: 703-836-9200
Web Address: http://epicomm.org
Epicomm is a non-profit business management association formed in 2014, through the merger of the National Association of Printers & Lithographers (NAPL), National Association of Quick Printers (NAQP) and the Association of Marketing Service Providers (AMSP). It represents the interests of graphic communications industry in the U.S.

In-Plant Printing and Mailing Association (IPMA)
105 S. Jefferson, Ste. B-4
Kearney, MO 64060 USA
Phone: 816-903-4762
Fax: 816-902-4766
E-mail Address: ipmainfo@ipma.org
Web Address: www.ipma.org
The In-Plant Printing and Mailing Association (IPMA), formerly the International Publishing Management Association, is an exclusive not-for-profit organization dedicated to assisting in-house corporate publishing and distribution professionals.

MPA-The Association of Magazine Media
810 7th Ave., Fl. 24
New York, NY 10019 USA
Phone: 212-872-3700
E-mail Address: mpa@magazine.org
Web Address: www.magazine.org
MPA-The Association of Magazine Media (formerly the Magazine Publishers of America, Inc.) is the industry association for consumer magazines in all formats, including printed, mobile and online.

Newspaper Association of America (NAA)
4401 Wilson Blvd., Ste. 900
Arlington, VA 22203-1867 USA
Phone: 571-366-1000
Fax: 571-366-1195
E-mail Address: membsvc@naa.org
Web Address: www.naa.org
The Newspaper Association of America (NAA) is a nonprofit organization representing the newspaper industry.

70) Real Estate Industry Associations

Institute of Real Estate Management (IREM)
430 N. Michigan Ave.
Chicago, IL 60611 USA
Fax: 800-338-4736
Toll Free: 800-837-0706
E-mail Address: getinfo@irem.org
Web Address: www.irem.org
The Institute of Real Estate Management (IREM) seeks to educate real estate managers, certify their competence and professionalism, serve as an advocate on issues affecting the real estate management industry and enhance its members' professional competence so they can better identify and meet the needs of those who use their services.

NAREC
6348 N. Milwaukee Ave., Ste. 103
Chicago, IL 60606 USA
Phone: 773-283-6362
E-mail Address: info@narec.org
Web Address: narec.org
NAREC, formerly PeerSpan and, prior to that, the National Association of Real Estate Companies, is composed of representatives of publicly and privately owned real estate companies, significant subsidiaries of publicly owned companies and public accounting firms.

National Association of Real Estate Brokers (NAREB)
9831 Greenbelt Rd., Ste. 309
Lanham, MD 20706 USA
Phone: 301-552-9340
Fax: 301-552-9216
E-mail Address: info@nareb.com
Web Address: www.nareb.com
The National Association of Real Estate Brokers (NAREB) is a national trade organization dedicated to bringing together the nation's minority professionals in the real estate industry.

National Association of Realtors (NAR)
430 N. Michigan Ave.
Chicago, IL 606-4087 USA
Toll Free: 800-874-6500
Web Address: www.realtor.org
The National Association of Realtors (NAR) is composed of realtors involved in residential and commercial real estate as brokers, salespeople, property managers, appraisers and counselors and in other areas of the industry. NAR also sponsors Realtor.com, operated by Move, Inc.

Women's Council of Realtors (WCR)
430 N. Michigan Ave.
Chicago, IL 60611 USA
Fax: 312-329-3290
Toll Free: 800-245-8512
E-mail Address: wcr@wcr.org
Web Address: www.wcr.org
The Women's Council of Realtors (WCR) is a community of women real estate professionals. It promotes the professional growth of its members through networking, leadership development, resources, infrastructure and accessibility

71) Recording & Music Associations

American Federation of Musicians (AFM)
1501 Broadway, Ste. 600
New York, NY, 10036 USA
Phone: 212-869-1330
Fax: 212-764-6134
Web Address: www.afm.org
The American Federation of Musicians (AFM) is the largest union in the world for music professionals, serving musicians throughout the U.S. and Canada.

American Society of Composers, Authors & Publishers (ASCAP)
1900 Broadway
New York, NY 10023-7142 USA
Phone: 212-621-6000
Fax: 212-621-8453
Web Address: www.ascap.com
American Society of Composers, Authors & Publishers (ASCAP) is a membership association of U.S. composers, songwriters and publishers of every kind of music, with hundreds of thousands of members worldwide.

Content Delivery & Storage Association (CDSA)
39 N. Bayles Ave.
Port Washington, NY 11050 USA
Phone: 516-767-6720
Fax: 516-883-5793
E-mail Address: mporter@CDSAonline.org
Web Address: www.cdsaonline.org
The Content Delivery & Storage Association (CDSA), formerly the International Recording Media Association, is a worldwide trade association encompassing organizations involved in every facet of recording media, including entertainment, information and software content storage. CDSA is under the management of the Media & Entertainment Services Alliance (MESA).

International Association of Audio Information Services (IAAIS)
Toll Free: 800-280-5325
E-mail Address:
Stuart.Holland@state.mn.us
Web Address: www.iaais.org
International Association of Audio Information Services (IAAIS) is an organization that provides audio access to information for people who are print-disabled.

Music Publisher's Association of the United States (MPA)
243 5th Ave., Ste. 236
New York, NY 10016 USA
Phone: 212-327-4044
E-mail Address: admin@mpa.org
Web Address: mpa.org
The Music Publisher's Association of the United States (MPA) serves as a forum for publishers to deal with the music industry's vital issues and is actively involved in supporting and advancing compliance with copyright law, combating copyright infringement and exploring the need for further reform.

Recording Industry Association of America (RIAA)
1025 F St. NW, Fl. 10
Washington, DC 20004 USA
Phone: 202-775-0101
Web Address: www.riaa.com
The Recording Industry Association of America (RIAA) is the trade group that represents the U.S. recording industry.

Society of Professional Audio Recording Services (SPARS)
Fax: 214-722-1442
Toll Free: 800-771-7727
E-mail Address: info@spars.com
Web Address: www.spars.com
The Society of Professional Audio Recording Services (SPARS) is an organization for members of the recording industry to share practical business information about audio and multimedia facility ownership, management and operations.

Songwriters Guild of America
5120 Virginia Way, Ste. C22
Brentwood, TN 37027 USA
Phone: 615-742-9945
Fax: 615-630-7501
Toll Free: 800-524-6742
Web Address: www.songwritersguild.com
The Songwriters Guild of America is the nation's largest and oldest songwriters' organization, providing its members with information and programs to further their careers and understanding of the music industry.

72) Satellite-Related Professional Organizations

Satellite Broadcasting & Communications Association (SBCA)
1100 17th St. NW, Ste. 1150
Washington, DC 20036 USA
Phone: 202-349-3620
Fax: 202-349-3621
Toll Free: 800-541-5981
E-mail Address: info@sbca.org
Web Address: www.sbca.com
The Satellite Broadcasting & Communications Association (SBCA) is the national trade organization representing all segments of the satellite consumer services industry in America.

Society of Satellite Professionals International (SSPI)
250 Park Ave., Fl. 7
The New York Information Technology Ctr.
New York, NY 10177 USA
Phone: 212-809-5199
Fax: 212-825-0075
E-mail Address: rbell@sspi.org
Web Address: www.sspi.org
The Society of Satellite Professionals International (SSPI) is a nonprofit member-benefit society that serves satellite professionals worldwide.

73) Securities Industry Associations

North American Securities Administrators Association, Inc. (NASAA)
750 First St. NE, Ste. 1140
Washington, DC 20002 USA
Phone: 202-737-0900
Fax: 202-783-3571
E-mail Address: ri@nasaa.org
Web Address: www.nasaa.org
The North American Securities Administrators Association (NASAA) is the oldest international organization committed to investor protection. Its web site provides information on franchising and raising capital, as well as state blue sky securities laws and resources for small investment advisors.

Securities Industry and Financial Markets Association (SIFMA)
120 Broadway, Fl. 35
New York, NY 10271-0080 USA
Phone: 212-313-1200
Fax: 212-313-1301
E-mail Address: inquiry@sifma.org
Web Address: www.sifma.org
The Securities Industry and Financial Markets Association (SIFMA), formed by the merger of the Securities Industry Association (SIA) and the Bond Market Association, brings together the shared interests of more than 650 securities and bond industry firms to accomplish common goals.

74) Software Industry Associations

Software & Information Industry Association (SIIA)
1090 Vermont Ave. NW, Fl. 6
Washington, DC 20005-4095 USA
Phone: 202-289-7442
Fax: 202-289-7097
Web Address: www.siia.net
The Software & Information Industry Association (SIIA) is a principal trade association for the software and digital content industry.

75) Stocks & Financial Markets Data

Reuters.com
3 Times Sq.
New York, NY 10036 USA
Phone: 646-223-6890
Web Address: www.reuters.com
Reuters.com, a service of Thomson Reuters, offers information on business and world markets, political and international news and company-specific stock information.

Yahoo! Finance
701 1st Ave.
Yahoo! Inc.
Sunnyvale, CA 94089 USA
Phone: 408-349-3300
Web Address: finance.yahoo.com
Yahoo! Finance provides a wealth of links and a supreme search guide. Users can find just about any financial information concerning both U.S. and world markets. Tax, insurance information, financial news and community research can be conducted through this site, as can searches for other aspects of the financial world.

76) Telecommunications Industry Associations

CompTel
900 17th St. NW, Ste. 400
Washington, DC 20006 USA
Phone: 202-296-6650
E-mail Address: gnorris@comptel.org
Web Address: www.comptel.org

CompTel is a trade organization representing voice, data and video communications service providers and their supplier partners. Members are supported through education, networking, policy advocacy and trade shows.

National Association of Telecommunications Officers and Advisors (NATOA)
3213 Duke St., Ste. 695
Alexandria, VA 22314 USA
Phone: 703-519-8035
Fax: 703-997-7080
E-mail Address: info@natoa.org
Web Address: www.natoa.org
The National Association of Telecommunications Officers and Advisors (NATOA) works to support and serve the telecommunications industry's interests and the needs of local governments.

Telecommunications Industry Association (TIA)
1320 N. Courthouse Rd., Ste. 200
Arlington, VA 22201 USA
Phone: 703-907-7700
Fax: 703-907-7727
E-mail Address:
smontgomery@tiaonline.org
Web Address: www.tiaonline.org
The Telecommunications Industry Association (TIA) is a leading trade association in the information, communications and entertainment technology industry. TIA focuses on market development, trade promotion, trade shows, domestic and international advocacy, standards development and enabling e-business.

United States Telecom Association (USTelecom)
607 14th St. NW, Ste. 400
Washington, DC 20005 USA
Phone: 202-326-7300
Fax: 202-315-3603
E-mail Address:
membership@ustelecom.org
Web Address: www.ustelecom.org
The United States Telecom Association (USTelecom) is a trade association representing service providers and suppliers for the telecom industry.

77) Temporary Staffing Firms

Adecco
Saegereistrasse 10
Glattbrugg, CH-8152 Switzerland
Phone: 41-44-878-88-88
Fax: 41-44-829-88-06

E-mail Address:
press.office@adecco.com
Web Address: www.adecco.com
Adecco maintains human resources and staffing services offices in 70 countries. It provides temporary and permanent personnel.

Advantage Resourcing, Inc.
220 Norwood Park S.
Norwood, MA 02062 USA
Phone: 781-251-8000
Toll Free: 800-343-4314
E-mail Address: M
Web Address: www.hirethinking.com
Advantage Resourcing, Inc., formerly Radia Holdings, Inc., provides integrated human resources services throughout Japan, North America, Europe and Australia. It is one of the largest staffing providers, with over 350 branches and satellite offices.

Allegis Group
7301 Parkway Dr.
Hanover, MD 21076 USA
Toll Free: 800-927-8090
Web Address: www.allegisgroup.com
The Allegis Group provides technical, professional and industrial recruiting and staffing services. Allegis specializes in information technology staffing services. The firm operates in the United Kingdom, Germany and The Netherlands as Aerotek and TEKsystems, and in India as Allegis Group India. Aerotek provides staffing solutions for aviation, engineering, automotive and scientific personnel markets.

CDI Corporation
1717 Arch St., Fl. 35
Philadelphia, PA 19103-2768 USA
Phone: 215-636-1240
E-mail Address:
vince.webb@cdicorp.com
Web Address: www.cdicorp.com
CDI Corporation specializes in engineering and information technology staffing services. Company segments include CDI IT Solutions, specializing in information technology; CDI Engineering Solutions, specializing in engineering outsourcing services; AndersElite Limited, operating in the United Kingdom and Australia; and MRINetwork, specializing in executive recruitment.

Express Employment Professionals
9701 Boardwalk Blvd.
Oklahoma City, OK 73162 USA
Phone: 405-840-5000
Toll Free: 888-923-3797
Web Address: www.expresspros.com

Express Employment Professionals operates through a network of over 550 locations in the United States, Canada, South Africa and Australia. Services include temporary and flexible staffing, evaluation and direct hire, professional and contract staffing, human resource services and online payroll processing (U.S. only).

Glotel Inc.
8700 W. Bryn Mawr Ave., Ste. 400N
Chicago, IL 60631 USA
Phone: 312-612-7480
E-mail Address: info@glotelinc.com
Web Address: www.glotel.com
Glotel is a global technology staffing and managed projects solutions company specializing in the placement of contract and permanent personnel within all areas of technology. Glotel has a network of offices throughout Europe, the U.S. and Asia-Pacific.

Harvey Nash
110 Bishopgate
London, EC2N 4AY UK
Phone: 44-20-7333-0033
Fax: 44-20-7333-0032
E-mail Address:
richard.ashcroft@harveynash.com
Web Address: www.harveynash.com
Harvey Nash provides professional recruitment, interim executive leadership services and outsourcing services. The firm specializes in information technology staffing on a permanent and contract basis in US, UK and Europe. It also offers outsourcing services including offshore software development services, information technology systems management, workforce risk management and managed services for network administration.

Hays plc
250 Euston Rd.
London, NW1 2AF UK
Phone: 44-20-7383-2266
Fax: 44-20-7388-4367
E-mail Address:
customerservice@hays.com
Web Address: www.hays.com
Hays plc is a global leader in specialist recruitment. It places professional candidates in permanent, temporary and interim positions across numerous fields, including accountancy and finance; education; health care; IT and telecom; manufacturing and engineering; pharmaceuticals; professional services; retail, sales and marketing; and support services.

Hudson Highland Group, Inc.
1325 Avenue of the Americas, Fl. 12
New York, NY 10019 USA
Phone: 212-351-7400
Fax: 212-351-7401
Web Address: www.hudson.com
Hudson Highland Group, Inc. provides
permanent recruitment, contract and
human resources consulting and inclusion
solutions. Services range from single
placements to total outsourced solutions.
The company employs professionals
serving clients and candidates in 20
countries.

Kelly Services, Inc.
999 W. Big Beaver Rd.
Troy, MI 48084-4782 USA
Phone: 248-362-4444
E-mail Address: kfirst@kellyservices.com
Web Address: www.kellyservices.com
Kelly Services is a workforce solutions
company offering a wide range of
outsourcing and consulting services, as
well as quality staffing on a temporary,
temporary-to-hire and direct-hire basis
both locally and worldwide.

Kforce, Inc.
1001 E. Palm Ave.
Tampa, FL 33605 USA
Toll Free: 800-395-5575
E-mail Address:
internalstaffing@kforce.com
Web Address: www.kforce.com
Kforce, Inc. is one of America's largest
temporary placement firms, with more
than 70 offices in 44 cities across the U.S.
It specializes in employees for the
following types of jobs: finance and
accounting, scientific, technology, health
care, clinical research, mortgages, title
insurance and real estate.

Labor Ready, Inc.
1015 A St.
Tacoma, WA 98402 USA
Phone: 253-383-9101
Fax: 877-733-0399
Toll Free: 877-733-0430
E-mail Address:
customercare@laborready.com
Web Address: www.laborready.com
Labor Ready, Inc. specializes in
temporary staffing in construction,
manufacturing, hospitality services,
transportation, landscaping, warehousing,
retail and more with almost 700 branches
throughout the U.S., Canada and Puerto
Rico.

Manpower, Inc.
100 Manpower Pl.
Milwaukee, WI 53212 USA
Phone: 414-961-1000

Fax: 414-906-7822
E-mail Address:
Britt.Zarling@manpowergroup.com
Web Address: www.manpower.com
One of the largest temporary staffing
providers in the world, Manpower places
approximately 2 million workers annually
in a variety of positions around the world.

Michael Page International plc
Page House, 1 Dashwood Lang Rd.
Addlestone, Weybridge
Surrey, KT15 2QW UK
Phone: 44-207-831-2000
Web Address: www.michaelpage.co.uk
Michael Page International is one of the
world's leading professional recruitment
consultancies specializing in the
placement of candidates in permanent,
contract, temporary and interim positions.
The Group has operations in the US, UK,
Continental Europe, Asia-Pacific and a
regional presence in France and Australia.
In the US, the firm's focus is on the areas
of financial services, supply chain,
executive searches, marketing, legal and
administrative support.

Pasona Group Inc. (Japan)
Otemachi 2-6-4 Chiyoda-ku
Tokyo, 100-8228 Japan
Web Address: www.pasonagroup.co.jp
Pasona, Inc. provides personnel services,
ranging from temporary
staffing/contracting, placement/recruiting
and outplacement to outsourcing and
training.

Randstad USA
2015 S. Park Pl.
Atlanta, GA 30339 USA
Phone: 770-937-7000
Fax: 770-937-7100
Toll Free: 877-922-2468
E-mail Address: info@us.randstad.com
Web Address: www.us.randstad.com
Randstad provides staffing services in the
office, industrial, technical, creative and
professional markets. It specializes in
temporary and permanent staffing;
recruitment and consultant services; and
human resource services. It operates in 83
countries, primarily in Europe, Asia and
the U.S. Brands include Capac, Yacht,
and Tempo-Team.

Robert Half International Inc. (RHI)
2884 Sand Hill Rd.
Menlo Park, CA 94025 USA
Phone: 650-234-6000
E-mail Address: webmaster@rhi.com
Web Address: www.rhi.com
Robert Half International Inc. (RHI)
specializes in accounting and finance
positions. It also places workers in

administrative, information technology,
legal, advertising and marketing positions
on temporary or permanent bases.

Robert Walters plc
11 Slingsby Pl.
St. Martin's Courtyard
London, WC2E 9AB UK
Phone: 44-20-7379-3333
Fax: 44-20-7509-8714
E-mail Address:
london@robertwalters.com
Web Address: www.robertwalters.com
Robert Walters PLC is a professional
recruitment specialist, outsourcing and
human resource consultant. The firm
provides services for the temporary,
contract and permanent placement of
individuals in the sectors of finance,
operations, legal, information technology,
marketing and administration support. It
has offices in 24 countries including the
US.

Spherion Corporation
33625 Cumberland Blvd., Ste. 600
Atlanta, GA 30339 U.S.A.
Phone: 954-308-6266
E-mail Address: gailferro@spherion.com
Web Address: www.spherion.com
Spherion Corp., a subsidiary of SFN
Group, provides temporary staffing,
recruitment and employee consulting,
primarily in administrative, clerical,
customer service and light industrial
fields.

Synergie SA (France)
11 Ave. du Colonel Bonnet
Paris, 75016 France
Phone: 44-14-90-20
Fax: 45-25-97-10
Web Address: www.synergie.fr
Synergie provides human resource
management services that include
temporary placement, consulting and
training. The firm is most active in
France, but also operates through a
network of 550 agencies in throughout
Europe and Canada.

Tempstaff Co., Ltd. (Japan)
Shinjuku Maynds Twr. 2-1-1
Yoyogi, Shibuya-ku
Tokyo, 151-0053 Japan
Phone: 81-3-5350-1212
Web Address: www.tempstaff.co.jp
Tempstaff Co., Ltd. provides temporary
and permanent placement and recruiting
and outsourcing services. It has 263
offices in Japan and 12 overseas offices
located in Los Angeles, Seattle, Shanghai,
Suzhou, Guangzhou, Hong Kong, Taiwan,
Korea, Singapore and Indonesia.

Volt Information Sciences, Inc.
1133 Ave. of the Americas, Fl. 15
New York, NY 10036 USA
Phone: 212-704-2400
Web Address: www.volt.com
Volt Information Sciences, Inc. provides temporary staffing services, professional search, managed services programs, vendor management systems and recruitment process outsourcing, as well as a wealth of additional support services, in North and South America, Europe and Asia through approximately 400 locations.

78) Testing Resources

CPP, Inc.
1055 Joaquin Rd., Ste. 200
Mountain View, CA 94043 USA
Phone: 650-969-8901
Fax: 650-969-8608
Toll Free: 800-624-1765
E-mail Address: custserv@cpp.com
Web Address: www.cpp.com
CPP, Inc. (formerly known as Consulting Psychologists Press) publishes the Meyers-Briggs Type Indicator, Strong Inventory Test and other psychological assessment-related products. CPP also provides information about the tests and, through division Davies-Black Publishing, offers business-related books and services, including those covering career management and leadership development.

79) Textile & Fabric Associations

International Textile and Apparel Association (ITAA)
P.O. Box 70687
Knoxville, TN 37938-0687 USA
Phone: 865-992-1535
E-mail Address: info@itaaonline.org
Web Address: www.itaaonline.org
The International Textile and Apparel Association (ITAA) is a nonprofit educational and scientific corporation dedicated to providing opportunities to scholars in the retail, textile and apparel industries.

80) Travel Business & Professional Associations

American Society of Travel Agents (ASTA)
1101 King St., Ste. 200
Alexandria, VA 22314 USA
Phone: 703-739-2782
Toll Free: 800-275-2782

E-mail Address: askasta@asta.org
Web Address: www.asta.org
The American Society of Travel Agents (ASTA) is one of the world's largest associations of travel professionals.

Association of Corporate Travel Executives (ACTE)
515 King St., Ste. 440
Alexandria, VA 22314 USA
Phone: 703-683-5322
Fax: 703-683-2720
E-mail Address: info@acte.org
Web Address: www.acte.org
The Association of Corporate Travel Executives (ACTE) serves the specialized travel interests of corporate purchasers and travel service suppliers from nearly 50 countries.

Association of Retail Travel Agents (ARTA)
4320 North Miller Rd.
c/o Travel Destinations, Inc.
Scottsdale, AZ 85251-3606 USA
Fax: 866-743-2087
Toll Free: 866-369-8969
Web Address: www.arta.travel
The Association of Retail Travel Agents (ARTA) is one of the largest nonprofit associations in North America to exclusively represent travel agents.

Association of Travel Marketing Executives (ATME)
P.O. Box 3176
West Tisbury, MA 02575 USA
Phone: 508-693-0550
Fax: 508-693-0115
E-mail Address: kzern@atme.org
Web Address: www.atme.org
The Association of Travel Marketing Executives (ATME) is a global professional association of senior-level travel marketing executives dedicated to providing cutting-edge information, education and opportunities for meaningful networking with peers.

National Society of Minorities in Hospitality
6933 Commons Plz., Ste. 537
Chesterfield, VA 23832 USA
Phone: 703-549-9899
Fax: 703-997-7795
E-mail Address: hq@nsmh.org
Web Address: www.nsmh.org
The National Society of Minorities in Hospitality strives to establish a working relationship between the hospitality industry and minority students.

Network of Executive Women in Hospitality, Inc. (NEWH)
P.O. Box 322

Shawano, WI 54166 USA
Fax: 800-693-6394
Toll Free: 800-593-6394
Web Address: www.newh.org
The Network of Executive Women in Hospitality, Inc. (NEWH) brings together professionals from all facets of the hospitality industry by providing opportunities for education, professional development and networking. Although primarily a U.S.-based organization, NEWH does have international chapters in Toronto and London.

Society of Incentive and Travel Executives
401 N. Michigan Ave.
Chicago, IL 60611-4267 USA
Phone: 312-321-5148
Fax: 312-527-6783
E-mail Address: site@siteglobal.com
Web Address: www.site-intl.org
The Society of Incentive and Travel Executives is a worldwide organization of business professionals dedicated to the recognition and development of motivational and performance improvement strategies in the travel industry.

81) Travel Industry Associations

Destination Marketing Association International
2025 M St. NW, Ste. 500
Washington, DC 20036 USA
Phone: 202-296-7888
Fax: 202-296-7889
E-mail Address:
info@destinationmarketing.org
Web Address:
www.destinationmarketing.org
The Destination Marketing Association International, formerly the International Association of Convention & Visitor Bureaus, strives to enhance the professionalism, effectiveness and image of destination management organizations worldwide. Its members include professionals, industry partners, students and educators from roughly 15 countries.

International Association of Conference Centers (IACC)
243 N. Lindbergh Blvd.
St. Louis, MO 63141 USA
Phone: 314-993-8575
Fax: 314-993-8919
E-mail Address: info@iacconline.org
Web Address: www.iacconline.com
The International Association of Conference Centers (IACC) is a nonprofit, facilities-based organization founded to

promote a greater awareness and understanding of the unique features of conference centers around the world.

National Tour Association (NTA)
101 Prosperous Pl., Ste. 350
Lexington, KY 40509 USA
Phone: 859-264-6540
Fax: 859-266-6570
Toll Free: 800-682-8886
E-mail Address:
NTAwashington@gmail.com
Web Address: www.ntaonline.com
The National Tour Association (NTA) is an association for travel professionals who have an interest in the packaged travel sector of the industry.

U.S. Travel Association
1100 New York Ave. NW, Ste. 450
Washington, DC 20005-3934 USA
Phone: 202-408-8422
Fax: 202-408-1255
E-mail Address: feedback@ustravel.org
Web Address: www.ustravel.org
The U.S. Travel Association is the result of a merger between the Travel Industry Association (TIA) and the Travel Business Roundtable. It is a nonprofit association that represents and speaks for the common interests and concerns of all components of the U.S. travel industry.

82) U.S. Government Agencies

Bureau of Economic Analysis (BEA)
1441 L St. NW
Washington, DC 20230 USA
Phone: 202-606-9900
E-mail Address:
customerservice@bea.gov
Web Address: www.bea.gov
The Bureau of Economic Analysis (BEA), an agency of the U.S. Department of Commerce, is the nation's economic accountant, preparing estimates that illuminate key national, international and regional aspects of the U.S. economy.

Bureau of Labor Statistics (BLS)
2 Massachusetts Ave. NE
Postal Square Building
Washington, DC 20212-0001 USA
Phone: 202-691-5200
Fax: 202-691-7890
Toll Free: 800-877-8339
E-mail Address: blsdata_staff@bls.gov
Web Address: stats.bls.gov
The Bureau of Labor Statistics (BLS) is the principal fact-finding agency for the Federal Government in the field of labor economics and statistics. It is an independent national statistical agency that collects, processes, analyzes and disseminates statistical data to the American public, U.S. Congress, other federal agencies, state and local governments, business and labor. The BLS also serves as a statistical resource to the Department of Labor.

Equal Employment Opportunity Commission (EEOC)
131 M St. NE
Washington, DC 20507-0100 USA
Phone: 202-663-4900
Fax: 202-633-4679
Toll Free: 800-669-4000
E-mail Address: info@eeoc.gov
Web Address: www.eeoc.gov
The Equal Employment Opportunity Commission (EEOC) is a Federal Government agency focused on practices and programs that foster equal opportunity at work and elsewhere. Its web site features details about various protective laws regarding employment. It also provides information on how to file a discrimination claim.

FedStats
Web Address: http://fedstats.sites.usa.gov/
FedStats compiles information for statistics from over 100 U.S. federal agencies. Visitors can sort the information by agency, geography and topic, as well as perform searches.

National Labor Relations Board (NLRB)
1015 Half Street SE
Washington, DC 20570-0001 USA
Phone: 2002-273-1000
Toll Free: 866-667-6572
Web Address: www.nlrb.gov
The National Labor Relations Board (NLRB) provides case reports on labor disputes, searchable by company or union.

U.S. Census Bureau
4600 Silver Hill Rd.
Washington, DC 20233-8800 USA
Phone: 301-763-4636
Toll Free: 800-923-8282
Web Address: www.census.gov
The U.S. Census Bureau is the official collector of data about the people and economy of the U.S. Founded in 1790, it provides official social, demographic and economic information. In addition to the Population & Housing Census, which it conducts every 10 years, the U.S. Census Bureau numerous other surveys annually.

U.S. Department of Commerce (DOC)
1401 Constitution Ave. NW
Washington, DC 20230 USA
Phone: 202-482-2000
E-mail Address: TheSec@doc.gov
Web Address: www.commerce.gov
The U.S. Department of Commerce (DOC) regulates trade and provides valuable economic analysis of the economy.

U.S. Department of Labor (DOL)
200 Constitution Ave. NW
Frances Perkins Bldg.
Washington, DC 20210 USA
Toll Free: 866-487-2365
Web Address: www.dol.gov
The U.S. Department of Labor (DOL) is the government agency responsible for labor regulations.

U.S. Securities and Exchange Commission (SEC)
100 F St. NE
Washington, DC 20549 USA
Phone: 202-942-8088
Web Address: www.sec.gov
The U.S. Securities and Exchange Commission (SEC) is a nonpartisan, quasi-judicial regulatory agency responsible for administering federal securities laws. These laws are designed to protect investors in securities markets and ensure that they have access to disclosure of all material information concerning publicly traded securities. Visitors to the web site can access the EDGAR database of corporate financial and business information.

83) Water Technologies & Resources

American Water Resources Association (AWRA)
P.O. Box 1626
Middleburg, VA 20118 USA
Phone: 540-687-8390
Fax: 540-687-8395
E-mail Address: info@awra.org
Web Address: www.awra.org
The American Water Resources Association (AWRA) represents the interests of professionals involved in water resources and provides a platform for education, research, information exchange on water related issues.

84) Wireless & Cellular Industry Associations

Cellular Telecommunications & Internet Association (CTIA)
1400 16th St. NW, Ste. 600
Washington, DC 20036 USA
Phone: 202-785-0081
Web Address: www.ctia.org

The Cellular Telecommunications & Internet Association (CTIA) is an international nonprofit membership organization that represents a variety of wireless communications sectors including cellular service providers, manufacturers, wireless data and Internet companies. CTIA's industry committees study spectrum allocation, homeland security, taxation, safety and emerging technology.

Wireless Communications Association International (WCAI)
1333 H St. NW, Ste. 700 W
Washington, DC 20005-4754 USA
Phone: 202-452-7823
Web Address: www.wcai.com
The Wireless Communications Association International (WCAI) is the principal nonprofit trade association representing the wireless broadband industry.

85) Writers, Photographers & Editors Associations

American Society of Journalists and Authors, Inc. (ASJA)
355 Lexington Ave., Fl. 15
New York, NY 10017 USA
Phone: 212-997-0947
Web Address: www.asja.org
The American Society of Journalists and Authors (ASJA) is one of the nation's leading organizations of independent nonfiction writers.

American Society of Magazine Editors (ASME)
757 Third Ave., Fl. 11
New York, NY 10017 USA
Phone: 212-872-3700
E-mail Address: mpa@magazine.org
Web Address: www.magazine.org/asme
The American Society of Magazine Editors (ASME) is a professional organization for editors of print and online magazines. ASME is part of the Magazine Publishers of America (MPA).

American Society of News Editors (ASNE)
209 Reynolds Journalism Institute
Missouri School of Journalism
Columbia, MO 65211 USA
Phone: 573-884-2405
Fax: 573-884-3824
Web Address: www.asne.org
The American Society of News Editors (ASNE) is an association that brings together editors of daily newspapers and people directly involved with developing content for daily newspapers.

Association of Opinion Journalists
801 Third St. South
c/o The Poynter Institute
St. Petersburg, FL 33701 USA
Phone: 518-454-5472
E-mail Address: AOJ@poynter.org
Web Address: https://aoj.wildapricot.org/
The Association of Opinion Journalists, formerly known as The National Conference of Editorial Writers (NCEW) strives to stimulate the conscience and improve the quality of opinion writing.

International Women's Writing Guild (IWWG)
274 Madison Ave., Ste. 1202
New York, NY 10016 USA
Phone: 917-720-6959
E-mail Address: iwwgquestions@gmail.com
Web Address: www.iwwg.com
The International Women's Writing Guild (IWWG) is a network for the personal and professional empowerment of women through writing.

Media Communications Association International (MCAI)
c/o MCA-I Chapter
P.O. Box 5135
Madison, WI 53705-0135 USA
Phone: 888-899-6224
E-mail Address: m_k_schaefer@yahoo.com
Web Address: www.mca-i.org
The Media Communications Association International (MCAI) is the leading global community for media communications professionals seeking to drive the convergence of communications and technology for the growth of the profession.

National Association of Hispanic Journalists (NAHJ)
1050 Connecticut Ave. NW, Fl. 10
Washington, DC 20036 USA
Phone: 202-662-7145
E-mail Address: nahj@nahj.org
Web Address: www.nahj.org
The National Association of Hispanic Journalists (NAHJ) is dedicated to the recognition and professional advancement of Hispanics in the news industry.

National Association of Science Writers, Inc. (NASW)
P.O. Box 7905
Berkley, CA 94707 USA
Phone: 510-647-9500
Web Address: www.nasw.org
The National Association of Science Writers (NASW) exists to foster the dissemination of accurate information regarding science through all media devoted to informing the public.

National Federation of Press Women (NFPW)
200 Little Falls St., Ste. 405
Falls Church, VA 22046 USA
Phone: 703-237-9804
Fax: 703-237-9808
E-mail Address: presswomen@aol.com
Web Address: www.nfpw.org
The National Federation of Press Women (NFPW) is an organization of professional journalists and communicators.

National Writers Union (NWU)
256 W. 38th St., Ste. 703
New York, NY 10018 USA
Phone: 212-254-0279
Fax: 212-254-0673
E-mail Address: nwu@nwu.org
Web Address: www.nwu.org
The National Writers Union (NWU) is a labor union that represents freelance writers in all genres, formats and media. It is committed to improving the economic and working conditions of freelance writers.

Society of Children's Book Writers and Illustrators (SCBWI)
4727 Wilshire Blvd., Ste. 301
Los Angeles, CA 90010 USA
Phone: 323-782-1010
Fax: 323-782-1892
E-mail Address: scbwi@scbwi.org
Web Address: www.scbwi.org
The Society of Children's Book Writers and Illustrators (SCBWI) serves people who write, illustrate or share a vital interest in children's literature, including publishers, librarians, booksellers and agents.

Chapter 5

THE AMERICAN EMPLOYERS 500: WHO THEY ARE AND HOW THEY WERE CHOSEN

Note: financial data given for each of the AMERICAN EMPLOYERS 500 firms is for the year ended December 31, 2015, a fiscal year ended in 2015 or the latest figures available to the editors. Telephone numbers, addresses, contact names, Internet addresses and other vital facts were collected in the fall of 2016.

The companies chosen to be listed in THE ALMANAC OF AMERICAN EMPLOYERS are not the same as the "Fortune 500" or any other list of corporations. The AMERICAN EMPLOYERS 500 (the actual number is 503) were chosen specifically for their likelihood to provide new job openings to the greatest number of employees. Complete information about each firm can be found in the "Individual Data Listings," beginning about the middle of this book. They are in alphabetical order.

THE AMERICAN EMPLOYERS 500 includes companies from all parts of the United States and from nearly all industry segments: selected financial services firms, retailers, service companies, wholesalers and distributors, and others, as well as industrial companies, technology firms and manufacturers.

Simply stated, the list contains 500 of the largest, most successful employers in the United States today. In particular, the list contains companies that we have hand-selected to have qualities that we feel will be of greatest interest to job seekers of today who are looking for opportunities to obtain employment with major corporations.

In order to make this reference guide as useful as possible, we are selecting companies for this list by focusing on the type of business, the industry sector served and a company's competitive advantage. To a lesser extent, we are also considering the most recent year's financial performance. We consider industry sector to be a major factor, because some sectors may not offer good career prospects today. Consequently, we have deleted some well-known companies due to the state of their particular markets.

To be included in our list, the firms were selected based on the following criteria:

1) U.S.-based companies. (However, a small number of companies may be subsidiaries of foreign-based firms. Also, a small number of the firms are major U.S. employers that utilize headquarters addresses in other nations.)

2) 2,500 employees or more.

3) These are almost exclusively for-profit companies. However, a small number are major, non-profit health care companies.

4) Selected Type of Business and/or Industry Sector. Companies were chosen based on our analysis of the business potential of their products, services and industrial sectors in light of today's economic conditions and the effects of globalization and technological changes.

The companies were chosen in this manner for the following reasons:

500 COMPANIES so there is a broad base among which to make comparisons and from which you can study potential employers.

LARGER EMPLOYERS (2,500 or more employees) so the information can pertain to as many employees as reasonably possible, and so the companies ranked will tend to create large numbers of job openings. Also, large companies historically have offered significantly higher wages, better benefits and better training than small employers.

FOR-PROFIT so that job seekers using THE ALMANAC OF AMERICAN EMPLOYERS can choose positions in the profit-seeking, private sector, where incentive plans may be available to motivate and reward them, such as profit sharing, stock ownership, bonuses, stock options and the high pay and prestige of top executive posts.

COMPANIES THAT OPERATE IN PROMISING BUSINESS SECTORS because:
1) Companies that are stable or enjoying growing business are much more likely to have job openings. Corporate stability is more important to job seekers today than ever before due to the wave of layoffs and downsizing that continues to sweep through the U.S. (See Chapter 1, "Major Trends Affecting Job Seekers.")
2) These companies are much more likely to offer advancement opportunities. Current employees will benefit from promote-from-within policies when new plants, new stores, new product lines or new offices are opened.

Obviously, some companies are better to work for than others, depending on what you value. Creating this annual list is an arduous task. Generally, our results are very good, but we do occasionally select a company that soon develops problems or announces a layoff. The world of business constantly goes through major changes, and unforeseen events often occur. Nonetheless, it is not easy for a firm to be selected for the AMERICAN EMPLOYERS 500, and the mere presence of a company on the list can be taken as evidence that it has excelled in many ways. To start with, it has to have generated enough business to employ thousands of people–never a simple task. Also, many of these

firms are among the dominant companies in their industries.

INDEX OF COMPANIES WITHIN INDUSTRY GROUPS

The industry codes shown below are based on the 2012 NAIC code system (NAIC is used by many analysts as a replacement for older SIC codes because NAIC is more specific to today's industry sectors, see www.census.gov/NAICS). Companies are given a primary NAIC code, reflecting the main line of business of each firm.

Industry Group	Industry Code	2015 Sales	2015 Profits
Advertising Agencies and Marketing Services			
Interpublic Group of Companies Inc	541810	7,613,799,936	454,600,000
Omnicom Group Inc	541810	15,134,400,512	1,093,900,032
Advertising, Public Relations and Marketing Services			
Acosta Inc	541800	3,300,000,000	
Alliance Data Systems Corporation	541800	6,439,746,048	596,540,992
Valassis Communications Inc (RedPlum)	541800	2,285,000,000	
Air Conditioning and Heating (HVAC) and Commercial Refrigeration Equipment Manufacturing			
Nortek Holdings Inc	333415	2,526,099,968	-26,700,000
Aircraft Components, Parts, Assemblies, Interiors and Systems Manufacturing (Aerospace)			
Spirit Aerosystems Holdings Inc	336413	6,643,899,904	788,700,032
Aircraft Engine and Engine Parts Manufacturing			
United Technologies Corporation	336412	56,098,000,896	7,608,000,000
Aircraft Manufacturing (Aerospace), including Passenger Airliners and Military Aircraft,			
Boeing Company (The)	336411	96,113,999,872	5,176,000,000
General Dynamics Corp	336411	31,469,000,704	2,964,999,936
Lockheed Martin Corp	336411	46,131,998,720	3,604,999,936
Textron Inc	336411	13,422,999,552	697,000,000
Airlines, Scheduled Passenger Air Transportation			
Alaska Air Group Inc	481111	5,598,000,128	848,000,000
American Airlines Group Inc	481111	40,989,999,104	7,609,999,872
Delta Air Lines Inc	481111	40,704,000,000	4,526,000,128
JetBlue Airways Corporation	481111	6,416,000,000	677,000,000
Southwest Airlines Co	481111	19,819,999,232	2,180,999,936
Spirit Airlines Inc	481111	2,141,463,040	317,220,000
United Continental Holdings Inc	481111	37,864,001,536	7,340,000,256
Ambulatory, Outpatient Surgical Clinics, Urgent Care and Emergency Centers			
AMSURG Corporation	621493	2,566,884,096	162,947,008
Apparel and Clothing Brands, Designers, Importers and Distributors			
Hanesbrands Inc	424300	5,731,549,184	428,855,008
Kate Spade & Company Inc	424300	1,242,720,000	17,087,000
Ralph Lauren Corporation	424300	7,619,999,744	702,000,000
Under Armour Inc	424300	3,963,312,896	232,572,992
VF Corp	424300	12,376,743,936	1,231,592,960
Artificial and Synthetic Fibers and Filaments Manufacturing			
Eastman Chemical Company	325220	9,648,000,000	848,000,000

Industry Group	Industry Code	2015 Sales	2015 Profits
Asset Management			
BlackRock Inc	523920	11,400,999,936	3,344,999,936
Fidelity Investments Financial Services	523920	15,900,000,000	3,200,000,000
T Rowe Price Group Inc	523920	4,200,600,064	1,223,000,064
Automobile and Other Motor Vehicle Wholesale Distribution			
JM Family Enterprises Inc	423110	14,500,000,000	
Automobile Dealers (New Cars)			
AutoNation Inc	441110	20,861,999,104	442,600,000
Group 1 Automotive Inc	441110	10,632,505,344	93,999,000
Hendrick Automotive Group	441110	8,400,000,000	
Lithia Motors Inc	441110	7,864,251,904	182,999,008
Penske Automotive Group Inc	441110	19,284,899,840	326,100,000
Automobile Gasoline Engine and Engine Parts Manufacturing			
BorgWarner Inc	336310	8,023,199,744	609,699,968
Automobile Manufacturing			
American Honda Motor Co Inc	336111	60,557,038,000	1,801,247,748
FCA US LLC	336111	11,676,910,000	1,747,498,195
Ford Motor Co	336111	149,558,001,664	7,373,000,192
General Motors Company (GM)	336111	152,355,995,648	9,687,000,064
Mercedes-Benz USA LLC	336111	43,260,000,000	152,378,099
Tesla Motors Inc	336111	4,046,024,960	-888,662,976
Toyota Motor Sales USA Inc (TMS)	336111	93,053,000,000	
Automobile Parts and Accessories Stores			
Advance Auto Parts Inc	441310	9,737,018,368	473,398,016
O'Reilly Automotive Inc	441310	7,966,673,920	931,216,000
Ball Bearing and Roller Bearing Manufacturing			
NN Inc	332991	667,280,000	-7,431,000
Battery Manufacturing, Including Energy Storage Technologies			
APC by Schneider Electric	335911	4,750,000,000	
Integer Holdings Corporation	335911	800,414,016	-7,594,000
Building Material Dealers			
BMC Stock Holdings Inc	444190	1,576,745,984	-4,831,000
Burial Casket Manufacturing			
Matthews International Corporation	339995	1,426,067,968	63,449,000
Cable TV Programming, Cable Networks and Subsciption Video			
Discovery Communications Inc	515210	6,393,999,872	1,034,000,000
Time Warner Inc	515210	28,117,999,616	3,832,999,936
Walt Disney Company (The)	515210	52,465,000,448	8,382,000,128
Candy and Chocolate Manufacturing			
Hershey Co	311351	7,386,626,048	512,951,008
Mars Inc	311351	33,700,000,000	
Car and Truck Parts, Components and Systems Manufacturing, including Engines, Interiors and Electronics,			
Dana Holding Corporation	336300	6,060,000,256	159,000,000
Federal-Mogul Corporation	336300	7,418,999,808	-110,000,000

Industry Group	Industry Code	2015 Sales	2015 Profits
Gentex Corporation	336300	1,543,617,664	318,469,856
Gentherm Inc	336300	856,444,992	95,393,000
Johnson Controls Inc	336300	37,178,998,784	1,563,000,064
Lear Corp	336300	18,211,399,680	745,500,032
LKQ Corporation	336300	7,192,632,832	423,223,008
Modine Manufacturing Company	336300	1,496,400,000	21,800,000
Tenneco Inc	336300	8,208,999,936	247,000,000
TRW Automotive Holdings Corp	336300	16,400,000,000	319,574,976
Car Dealers, Used			
CarMax Inc	441120	14,268,716,032	597,358,016
DriveTime Automotive Group Inc	441120	1,525,000,000	
Car Rental			
Avis Budget Group Inc	532111	8,502,000,128	313,000,000
Dollar Thrifty Automotive Group Inc	532111	1,900,000,000	
Enterprise Holdings Inc	532111	19,400,000,000	
Hertz Global Holdings Inc	532111	10,535,000,064	273,000,000
Car Repair (Repair and Maintenance of Automobiles and Trucks)			
Monro Muffler Brake Inc	811100	894,492,032	61,799,000
Car Reservations (e.g. Uber), Ticket Offices, Time Share and Vacation Club Rentals and Specialty Reservation Services			
Uber Inc	561599	2,000,000,000	
Carpets (Carpeting and Floor Coverings) and Rugs Mills and Manufacturing			
Mohawk Industries Inc	314110	8,071,562,752	615,302,016
Casino Hotels and Casino Resorts			
Las Vegas Sands Corp (The Venetian)	721120	11,688,461,312	1,966,236,032
Pinnacle Entertainment Inc	721120	2,291,847,936	48,887,000
Wynn Resorts Limited	721120	4,075,883,008	195,290,000
Chips (Tortilla, Potato and Corn), Popcorn and Pretzel Manufacturing			
Frito-Lay North America Inc	311919	14,680,000,000	4,304,000,000
Coffee Shops, Doughnut Shops, Ice Cream Parlors, Canteens and Snack Bars			
Starbucks Corporation	722515	19,162,699,776	2,757,400,064
Commercial Banks (Banking)			
Bank of America Corp	522110	82,506,997,760	15,888,000,000
Bank of New York Mellon Corp	522110	15,194,000,384	3,158,000,128
BB&T Corporation	522110	9,610,999,808	2,084,000,000
Capital One Financial Corp	522110	23,413,000,192	4,049,999,872
Citigroup Inc	522110	76,354,002,944	17,241,999,360
Cullen-Frost Bankers Inc	522110	1,065,361,984	279,328,000
FirstMerit Corporation	522110	1,010,292,992	229,484,000
JP Morgan Chase & Co Inc	522110	93,542,998,016	24,441,999,360
US Bancorp	522110	20,092,999,680	5,879,000,064
Wells Fargo & Co	522110	86,057,000,960	22,894,000,128

Industry Group	Industry Code	2015 Sales	2015 Profits
Commercial Real Estate Investment and Operations, Including Office Buildings, Shopping Centers, Industrial Properties and Related REITs			
Jones Lang LaSalle Inc	531120	5,965,670,912	438,672,000
Computer and Data Systems Design, Consulting and Integration Services			
Accenture LLP	541512	14,209,387,000	
CACI International Inc	541512	3,313,452,032	126,195,000
Cognizant Technology Solutions Corp	541512	12,416,000,000	1,623,600,000
MAXIMUS Inc	541512	2,099,821,056	157,772,000
Sapient Corporation	541512	1,562,781,000	
Science Applications International Corp (SAIC)	541512	3,884,999,936	141,000,000
UST Global Inc	541512	455,000,000	
Computer Disks (Discs) and Drives, including Magnetic and Optical Storage Media Manufacturing			
Dell-EMC	334112	24,704,000,000	1,990,000,000
Computer Networking & Related Equipment Manufacturing			
Cisco Systems Inc	334210A	49,160,998,912	8,981,000,192
Computer Peripherals and Accessories, including Printers, Monitors and Terminals Manufacturing			
NCR Corporation	334118	6,373,000,192	-178,000,000
Computer Programming and Custom Software Development and Consulting			
EPAM Systems Inc	541511	914,128,000	84,456,000
Computer Software, Accounting, Banking & Financial			
Concur Technologies Inc	511210Q	724,603,419	-20,571,530
Intuit Inc	511210Q	4,192,000,000	365,000,000
Jack Henry & Associates Inc	511210Q	1,256,189,952	211,220,992
Computer Software, Business Management & ERP			
BMC Software Inc	511210H	2,250,000,000	
Citrix Systems Inc	511210H	3,275,593,984	319,360,992
SAS Institute Inc	511210H	3,160,000,000	
TIBCO Software Inc	511210H	1,000,000,000	
Computer Software, Data Base & File Management			
Oracle Corp	511210J	38,226,001,920	9,937,999,872
Computer Software, Electronic Games, Apps & Entertainment			
Activision Blizzard Inc	511210G	4,664,000,000	892,000,000
Computer Software, Healthcare & Biotechnology			
Allscripts Healthcare Solutions Inc	511210D	1,386,392,960	-2,226,000
Cerner Corporation	511210D	4,425,267,200	539,361,984
eClinicalWorks	511210D	358,000,000	
Epic Systems Corporation	511210D	1,978,000,000	
Medical Information Technology Inc (MEDITECH)	511210D	610,000,000	
Quality Systems Inc	511210D	490,224,992	27,332,000
Computer Software, Multimedia, Graphics & Publishing			
Adobe Systems Inc	511210F	4,795,510,784	629,550,976

Industry Group	Industry Code	2015 Sales	2015 Profits
Computer Software, Network Management, System Testing, & Storage			
F5 Networks Inc	511210B	1,919,822,976	365,014,016
ServiceNow Inc	511210B	1,005,480,000	-198,426,000
VMware Inc	511210B	6,570,999,808	997,000,000
Computer Software, Operating Systems, Languages & Development Tools			
Microsoft Corp	511210I	93,580,001,280	12,193,000,448
Red Hat Inc	511210I	1,789,489,024	180,200,992
Computer Software, Product Lifecycle, Engineering, Design & CAD			
Cadence Design Systems Inc	511210N	1,702,091,008	252,416,992
Mentor Graphics Corp	511210N	1,244,132,992	147,139,008
National Instruments Corp	511210N	1,225,456,000	95,262,000
Synopsys Inc	511210N	2,242,211,072	225,934,000
Computer Software, Sales & Customer Relationship Management			
SalesForce.com Inc	511210K	5,373,585,920	-262,688,000
Computer Software, Security & Anti-Virus			
McAfee Inc	511210E	2,375,000,000	
SunGard Data Systems Inc	511210E	2,950,000,000	
Symantec Corp	511210E	6,508,000,256	878,000,000
Computers, Peripherals, Software and Accessories Distribution			
Arrow Electronics Inc	423430	23,282,020,352	497,726,016
Avnet Inc	423430	27,924,656,128	571,913,024
CDW Corporation	423430	12,988,699,648	403,100,000
Ingram Micro Inc	423430	43,025,850,368	215,104,992
SYNNEX Corp	423430	13,338,396,672	208,524,992
Tech Data Corp	423430	27,670,632,448	175,172,000
Connectors for Electronics Manufacturing			
Belden Inc	334417	2,309,221,888	66,204,000
Molex Inc	334417	3,900,000,000	
Consrtuction of Oil and Gas Pipelines and Structures			
Team Inc	237120	571,718,016	8,878,000
Construction and Mining (except Oil Well) Machinery and Equipment Wholesale Distribution			
Fastenal Co	423810	3,869,187,072	516,360,992
Construction Equipment and Machinery Manufacturing			
Caterpillar Inc	333120	47,011,000,320	2,102,000,000
Hillenbrand Inc	333120	1,596,800,000	111,400,000
Construction of Telecommunications Lines and Systems & Electric Power Lines and Systems			
Quanta Services Inc	237130	7,572,435,968	310,907,008
Construction of Water & Sewer Lines and Systems			
Aegion Corporation	237110	1,333,570,048	-8,067,000
Consulting Services, Human Resources			
Mercer LLC	541612	4,313,000,000	
Resources Connection Inc	541612	590,588,992	27,508,000

Industry Group	Industry Code	2015 Sales	2015 Profits
Verisk Analytics Inc	541612	2,068,009,984	507,576,992
Consulting Services, Marketing			
inVentiv Health Inc	541613	2,350,000,000	
Contract Electronics Manufacturing Services (CEM) and Printed Circuits Assembly			
Jabil Circuit Inc	334418	17,899,196,416	284,019,008
Sanmina Corp	334418	6,374,540,800	377,260,992
Convenience Stores with Gasoline			
Casey's General Stores Inc	447110	7,767,216,128	180,628,000
QuikTrip Corporation	447110	10,960,000,000	
Copper, Lead, Nickel, Bronze, Brass, Beryllium, Magnesium, Titanium and Zinc Foundries (except Die-Casting)			
Precision Castparts Corp	331529	10,005,000,192	1,530,000,000
Cosmetics; Soaps, Detergents & Cleansers; and Personal Care Products, Perfumes & Colognes Manufacturing			
SC Johnson & Son Inc	325600	9,600,000,000	
Couriers, Express and Overnight Delivery			
FedEx Corporation	492110	47,452,999,680	1,050,000,000
United Parcel Service Inc (UPS)	492110	58,362,998,784	4,844,000,256
CPA Firms (Certified Public Accoutants), Accounting			
Deloitte LLP	541211	16,147,000,000	
EY LLP	541211	12,701,000,000	
Grant Thornton LLP	541211	1,450,000,000	
KPMG LLP	541211	9,340,000,000	
PricewaterhouseCoopers (PWC)	541211	35,400,000,000	
Credit Bureaus and Credit Rating Agencies			
Experian North America	561450	2,468,000,000	761,000,000
Moody's Corporation	561450	3,484,499,968	941,299,968
Credit Card Processing, Online Payment Processing, EFT, ACH and Clearinghouses			
American Express Co	522320	32,817,999,872	5,162,999,808
Fidelity National Information Services Inc	522320	6,595,200,000	631,500,032
Fiserv Inc	522320	5,254,000,128	712,000,000
Fleetcor Technologies Inc	522320	1,702,865,024	362,431,008
Heartland Payment Systems Inc	522320	2,682,395,904	84,732,000
MasterCard Inc	522320	9,667,000,320	3,808,000,000
Total System Services Inc (TSYS)	522320	2,779,540,992	364,044,000
Visa Inc	522320	13,880,000,512	6,328,000,000
Cruise Lines			
Carnival Corporation	483112	15,713,999,872	1,756,999,936
Norwegian Cruise Line Holdings Ltd (NCL)	483112	4,345,048,064	427,136,992
Royal Caribbean Cruises Ltd	483112	8,299,074,048	665,782,976
Dairy, Milk and Cheese Product Manufacturing			
Land O'Lakes Inc	311500	13,007,704,000	304,190,000
Data Processing, Business Process Outsourcing (BPO) and Internet Content Hosting Services			
Automatic Data Processing Inc (ADP)	518210	10,938,500,096	1,452,499,968

Industry Group	Industry Code	2015 Sales	2015 Profits
ExlService Holdings Inc	518210	628,492,032	51,565,000
Syntel Inc	518210	968,611,968	252,526,000
Department Stores (except Discount Department Stores)			
Nordstrom Inc	452111	13,505,999,872	720,000,000
Dialysis Centers			
DaVita Healthcare Partners Inc	621492	13,781,836,800	269,732,000
Direct Selling			
Mary Kay Inc	454390	4,000,000,000	
Discount Department Stores			
Kohl's Corporation	452112	19,022,999,552	867,000,000
Distributors of Telecommunications Equipment, Telephones, Cellphones and Electronics Components (Wholesale Distribution)			
Brightstar Corporation	423690	7,600,000,000	
Electric Motor and Power & Motor Generator Manufacturing			
Regal-Beloit Corporation	335312	3,509,700,096	143,300,000
Electric Wiring Device Manufacturing			
Hubbell Inc	335931	3,390,400,000	277,300,000
Electrical Contractors and Other Wiring Installation Contractors			
EMCOR Group Inc	238210	6,718,726,144	172,286,000
Rosendin Electric	238210	1,300,000,000	
Engineering Services, Including Civil, Mechanical, Electronic, Computer and Environmental Engineering			
Black & Veatch Holding Company	541330	3,030,000,000	
Burns & McDonnell	541330	2,700,000,000	
Factory Automation, Industrial Process, Thermostat, Flow Meter and Environmental Quality Monitoring and Control Manufacturing			
Ametek Inc	334513	3,974,295,040	590,859,008
Rockwell Automation Inc	334513	6,307,899,904	827,600,000
Roper Technologies Inc	334513	3,582,394,880	696,067,008
Family Clothing, Apparel and Accessories Stores			
Ross Stores Inc	448140	11,041,677,312	924,723,968
TJX Companies Inc (The)	448140	29,078,407,168	2,215,128,064
Zumiez Inc	448140	811,550,976	43,192,000
Fiber Optic Cable, Connectors and Related Products Manufacturing			
Amphenol Corporation	335921	5,568,699,904	763,500,032
CommScope Inc	335921	3,807,827,968	-70,875,000
Financial Data Publishing - Print & Online			
Bloomberg LP	511120A	9,184,000,000	
Thomson Reuters Corp	511120A	12,209,000,448	1,255,000,064
Fitness Centers, Gyms and Exercise and Fitness Programs			
24 Hour Fitness	713940	1,418,000,000	

Industry Group	Industry Code	2015 Sales	2015 Profits
Food Manufacturing, Processing and Packaging, Diversified			
Ingredion Inc	311000	5,958,000,128	402,000,000
Food Service Contractors			
Aramark	722310	14,329,135,104	235,946,000
HMSHost Corporation	722310	2,800,000,000	
Sodexo Inc	722310	9,200,000,000	
Fossil Fuel Electric Power Generation			
Berkshire Hathaway Energy Company	221112	17,880,000,000	2,400,000,000
DTE Energy Company	221112	10,337,000,448	727,000,000
Duke Energy Corporation	221112	23,459,000,320	2,816,000,000
FirstEnergy Corporation	221112	15,025,999,872	578,000,000
SCANA Corporation	221112	4,380,000,256	746,000,000
Freight Transportation Arrangement			
CH Robinson Worldwide Inc	488510	13,476,083,712	509,699,008
Expeditors International of Washington Inc	488510	6,616,631,808	457,223,008
Park-Ohio Holdings Corp	488510	1,463,800,064	48,100,000
Fruit and Vegetable Canning, Including Juices and Sauces,			
TreeHouse Foods Inc	311421	3,206,405,120	114,910,000
Funeral Homes and Funeral Services			
Service Corporation International Inc	812210	2,986,380,032	233,772,000
General Grocery Products Distributors (Groceries Wholesale Distribution, Excluding Meats, Frozen Foods and Vegetables)			
C&S Wholesale Grocers Inc	424410	30,000,000,000	
SYSCO Corporation	424410	48,680,751,104	686,772,992
United Natural Foods Inc	424410	8,184,977,920	138,734,000
Hazardous Waste Collection			
Stericycle Inc	562112	2,985,907,968	267,046,000
Health Insurance and Medical Insurance Underwriters (Direct Carriers), including Group Health, Supplemental Health and HMOs			
Aetna Inc	524114	60,336,500,736	2,390,200,064
AFLAC Inc	524114	20,871,999,488	2,532,999,936
Amerigroup Corporation	524114	10,000,000,000	
Anthem Inc	524114	79,156,502,528	2,560,000,000
Cigna Corporation	524114	37,875,998,720	2,094,000,000
Health Care Service Corporation (HCSC)	524114	35,000,000,000	
Humana Inc	524114	54,288,998,400	1,276,000,000
UnitedHealth Group Inc	524114	157,106,995,200	5,813,000,192
Heavy Construction, Including Civil Engineering-Construction, Major Construction Projects, Land Subdivision, Infrastructure, Utilities, Highways and Bridges			
Fluor Corp	237000	18,114,048,000	412,512,000
Jacobs Engineering Group Inc	237000	12,114,832,384	302,971,008
Heavy Duty Truck (including Buses) Manufacturing			
Oshkosh Corporation	336120	6,098,100,224	229,500,000
PACCAR Inc	336120	19,115,100,160	1,604,000,000

Industry Group	Industry Code	2015 Sales	2015 Profits
Highway, Street, Tunnel & Bridge Construction			
Tutor Perini Corporation	237310	4,920,472,064	45,292,000
Home Centers, Building Materials			
Home Depot Inc	444110	83,175,997,440	6,344,999,936
Lowe's Companies Inc	444110	56,222,998,528	2,697,999,872
Menard Inc	444110	8,970,000,000	
Home Health Care Services			
Chemed Corporation	621610	1,543,388,032	110,274,000
Lincare Holdings Inc	621610	220,000,000	
Hospitals, General Medical and Surgical			
Adventist Health System	622110	8,400,000,000	
Advocate Health Care	622110	5,329,562,000	78,605,000
Ascension Health	622110	20,538,803,000	562,596,000
Catholic Health Initiatives	622110	15,200,000,000	93,600,000
Cleveland Clinic Foundation (The)	622110	7,156,972,000	480,224,000
Community Health Systems Inc	622110	19,437,000,704	158,000,000
Fairview Health Services	622110	3,867,550,000	64,908,000
HCA Holdings Inc	622110	39,678,001,152	2,128,999,936
Houston Methodist	622110	2,800,000,000	
Kaiser Permanente	622110	61,000,000,000	
LifePoint Health Inc	622110	5,214,300,160	181,900,000
Mayo Foundation for Medical Education and Research	622110	10,315,000,000	526,000,000
MedStar Health	622110	5,030,000,000	160,100,000
Mercy	622110	5,000,000,000	
Providence St. Joseph Health	622110	14,000,000,000	
Spectrum Health	622110	4,625,176,000	367,311,000
Sutter Health Inc	622110	10,998,000,000	81,000,000
Tenet Healthcare Corporation	622110	18,634,000,384	-140,000,000
Trinity Health	622110	15,900,000,000	
Universal Health Services Inc	622110	9,043,450,880	680,528,000
Hospitals, Specialty			
HealthSouth Corporation	622310	3,115,699,968	183,100,000
Select Medical Holdings Corporation	622310	3,742,735,872	130,736,000
Hotels, Motels, Inns and Resorts (Lodging and Hospitality)			
Accor North America	721110	635,410,802	255,037,440
Hilton Worldwide Inc	721110	11,271,999,488	1,404,000,000
Hyatt Hotels Corporation	721110	4,328,000,000	124,000,000
Kimpton Hotel & Restaurant Group LLC	721110	1,200,000,000	
La Quinta Holdings Inc	721110	1,029,974,016	26,365,000
Loews Hotels Holding Corporation	721110	604,000,000	12,000,000
Marriott International Inc	721110	14,485,999,616	859,000,000
Ritz-Carlton Hotel Company LLC (The)	721110	2,400,000,000	
Starwood Hotels & Resorts Worldwide Inc	721110	5,762,999,808	489,000,000
Wyndham Worldwide Corporation	721110	5,536,000,000	612,000,000
Household Dishwasher, Disposal, Trash Compactor and Water Heater Manufacturing			
A.O. Smith Corporation	335228	2,536,499,968	282,900,000

Industry Group	Industry Code	2015 Sales	2015 Profits
Household Laundry Equipment Manufacturing			
Whirlpool Corp	335224	20,891,000,832	783,000,000
Housewares, including Linen, Bath, Kitchen and Cookware			
Bed Bath & Beyond Inc	442299	11,881,176,064	957,473,984
Container Store (The)	442299	781,865,984	22,673,000
Hydroelectric Power Generation			
PG&E Corporation	221111	16,833,000,448	888,000,000
Industrial Equipment and Machinery Distribution			
WW Grainger Inc	423830	9,973,384,192	768,995,968
Industrial Machinery Manufacturing, Other			
Illinois Tool Works Inc	333249	13,404,999,680	1,899,000,064
Insurance Agencies, Risk Management Consultants and Insurance Brokers			
Arthur J Gallagher & Co	524210	5,392,399,872	356,800,000
Brown & Brown Inc	524210	1,660,509,056	243,318,000
Hub International Limited	524210	1,260,000,000	
Marsh & Mclennan Companies Inc	524210	12,892,999,680	1,599,000,064
Insurance Claims Administration and Services			
Athenahealth Inc	524292	924,728,000	14,027,000
Change Healthcare Holdings Inc	524292	1,477,083,000	-96,069,000
Express Scripts Holding Co	524292	101,751,799,808	2,476,400,128
Internet Search Engines, Online Publishing, Sharing and Consumer Services, Online Radio, TV and Entertainment Sites and Social Media			
Airbnb Inc	519130	2,200,000,000	
Expedia Inc	519130	6,672,316,928	764,465,024
Facebook Inc	519130	17,927,999,488	3,688,000,000
Google (Alphabet Inc)	519130	74,989,002,752	16,348,000,256
IAC/InterActiveCorp	519130	3,230,932,992	119,472,000
LinkedIn Corp	519130	2,990,910,976	-166,144,000
Priceline Group Inc (The)	519130	9,223,987,200	2,551,360,000
TripAdvisor Inc	519130	1,492,000,000	198,000,000
Twitter Inc	519130	2,218,032,128	-521,031,008
Investment Banking, and Related Stock Brokerage and Investment Services			
Goldman Sachs Group Inc	523110	33,820,000,256	6,082,999,808
Jefferies LLC	523110	3,274,904,000	121,800,000
Legg Mason Inc	523110	2,819,106,048	237,080,000
Merrill Lynch & Co Inc	523110	14,898,000,000	
Morgan Stanley	523110	35,155,001,344	6,127,000,064
Raymond James Financial Inc	523110	5,200,209,920	502,140,000
Stifel Financial Corp	523110	2,331,593,984	92,336,000
Janitorial Services			
ABM Industries Inc	561720	4,897,800,192	76,300,000
Laboratory Instruments and Lab Equipment Manufacturing			
Waters Corporation	334516	2,042,332,032	469,052,992

Industry Group	Industry Code	2015 Sales	2015 Profits
Life Insurance and Annuity Underwriters (Direct Carriers)			
Hartford Financial Services Group Inc (The)	524113	18,377,000,960	1,682,000,000
Jackson National Life Insurance Company	524113	6,698,142,000	1,400,900,000
Lincoln National Corporation	524113	13,571,999,744	1,154,000,000
MassMutual Financial Group	524113	29,500,000,000	546,000,000
MetLife Inc	524113	69,950,996,480	5,310,000,128
Mutual of Omaha Companies (The)	524113	7,200,000,000	330,000,000
New York Life Insurance Co	524113	26,127,000,000	1,785,000,000
Northwestern Mutual Life Insurance Co	524113	27,880,000,000	
Principal Financial Group (The)	524113	11,964,399,616	1,234,000,000
Prudential Financial Inc	524113	57,118,998,528	5,641,999,872
Trustmark Companies	524113	882,683,041	8,645,781
Linen Supply			
Cintas Corporation	812331	4,476,886,016	430,617,984
Machinery and Engines Manufacturing, Including Construction, Agricultural, Mining, Industrial, Commercial and HVAC			
General Electric Co (GE)	333000	117,386,002,432	-6,126,000,128
Magazine Publishing and Financial Information Publishing			
FactSet Research Systems Inc	511120	1,006,768,000	241,051,008
Management Consulting and General Business Consulting (including Human Resources)			
AT Kearney Inc	541610	1,150,000,000	
Bain & Company Inc	541610	2,300,000,000	
Booz Allen Hamilton Holding Corp	541610	5,274,769,920	232,568,992
Boston Consulting Group Inc (The, BCG)	541610	5,000,000,000	
Deloitte Consulting LLP	541610	7,815,148,000	
FTI Consulting Inc	541610	1,779,149,056	66,053,000
McKinsey & Company Inc	541610	8,300,000,000	
Oliver Wyman Group	541610	1,751,000,000	
Strategy&	541610	1,147,000,000	
Market Research, Business Intelligence and Opinion Polling			
Gartner Inc	541910	2,163,056,128	175,635,008
IMS Health Holdings Inc	541910	2,920,999,936	417,000,000
Nielsen Holdings PLC	541910	6,172,000,256	570,000,000
Mattress Manufacturing			
Select Comfort Corporation	337910	1,213,698,944	50,519,000
Meat Packing and Processing, Including Beef, Pork and Lamb,			
Hillshire Brands Company	311612	4,105,000,000	
Smithfield Foods Inc	311612	14,438,400,000	
Medical Diagnostics, Reagents, Assays and Test Kits Manufacturing			
Bio Rad Laboratories Inc	325413	2,019,441,024	113,093,000
PerkinElmer Inc	325413	2,262,359,040	212,424,992
Medical Equipment and Supplies Manufacturing			
3M Company	339100	30,274,000,896	4,832,999,936

Industry Group	Industry Code	2015 Sales	2015 Profits
Becton Dickinson & Co	339100	10,282,000,384	695,000,000
Boston Scientific Corp	339100	7,477,000,192	-239,000,000
Cooper Companies Inc	339100	1,797,059,968	203,523,008
CR Bard Inc	339100	3,416,000,000	135,400,000
DENTSPLY International Inc	339100	2,674,299,904	251,200,000
Edwards Lifesciences Corporation	339100	2,493,700,096	494,900,000
ResMed Inc	339100	1,678,912,000	352,886,016
St Jude Medical Inc	339100	5,541,000,192	880,000,000
Stryker Corp	339100	9,946,000,384	1,439,000,064
Zimmer Biomet Holdings Inc	339100	5,997,799,936	147,000,000
Medical Imaging and Electromedical (Medical Devices) Equipment, including MRI, Ultrasound, Pacemakers, EKG and CAT			
Danaher Corporation	334510	20,563,099,648	3,357,400,064
IDEXX Laboratories Inc	334510	1,601,891,968	192,078,000
Medtronic Inc	334510	20,260,999,168	2,675,000,064
Varian Medical Systems Inc	334510	3,099,110,912	411,484,992
Medical Laboratories			
Laboratory Corp of America Holdings	621511	8,680,099,840	436,900,000
Quest Diagnostics Inc	621511	7,493,000,192	709,000,000
Medical, Dental and Hospital Equipment and Supplies (Medical Devices) Wholesale Distribution			
Henry Schein Inc	423450	10,629,719,040	479,057,984
Owens & Minor Inc	423450	9,772,946,432	103,409,000
Patterson Companies Inc	423450	4,375,020,032	223,260,992
Thermo Fisher Scientific Inc	423450	16,965,399,552	1,975,399,936
Metal Can Manufacturing			
Crown Holdings Inc	332431	8,762,000,384	393,000,000
Mortgage Loan Servicing, Check Cashing and Money Transmission			
Encore Capital Group Inc	522390	1,161,571,968	45,135,000
Movie (Motion Pictures) Theaters			
Carmike Cinemas Inc	512131	804,368,000	-448,000
New Home Builders (Production Builders)			
DR Horton Inc	236117	10,823,999,488	750,700,032
Lennar Corporation	236117	9,474,008,064	802,894,016
NVR Inc	236117	5,169,562,112	382,927,008
PulteGroup Inc	236117	5,981,963,776	494,089,984
Toll Brothers Inc	236117	4,171,248,128	363,167,008
Nuclear Electric Power Generation			
Exelon Corporation	221113	29,447,000,064	2,268,999,936
Nursing Care Facilities (Skilled Nursing Facilities)			
Kindred Healthcare Inc	623110	7,054,906,880	-93,384,000
Office Administrative Services			
Xerox Corporation	561110	18,044,999,680	474,000,000
Online Shopping, B2B and B2C Sales on the Internet (Ecommerce)			
Amazon.com Inc	454111	107,006,001,152	596,000,000
Liberty Interactive Corp	454111	9,169,000,448	640,000,000

Industry Group	Industry Code	2015 Sales	2015 Profits
Paints and Coatings Manufacturing			
PPG Industries Inc	325510	15,329,999,872	1,406,000,000
Sherwin-Williams Company (The)	325510	11,339,303,936	1,053,849,024
Paper Bag and Coated and Treated Paper Manufacturing			
Sonoco Products Company	322220	4,964,368,896	250,136,000
Personal Care Products; Cosmetics and Makeup; Fragrances and Perfumes; and Hair Care Products Manufacturing			
Estee Lauder Companies Inc (The)	325620	10,780,399,616	1,088,899,968
Pet and Pet Supplies Stores			
Petco Animal Supplies Inc	453910	4,000,000,000	
PetSmart Inc	453910	7,110,000,000	
Petrochemicals Manufacturing			
Chevron Phillips Chemical Company LLC	325110	9,248,000,000	2,651,000,000
ExxonMobil Chemical	325110	24,000,000,000	4,418,000,000
Lubrizol Corporation (The)	325110	7,000,000,000	
Petroleum Refineries			
Koch Industries Inc	324110	115,000,000,000	
Phillips 66	324110	100,949,000,192	4,227,000,064
Pharmaceuticals and Drug Manufacturing			
Abbott Laboratories	325412	20,405,000,192	4,423,000,064
Amgen Inc	325412	21,661,999,104	6,938,999,808
Biogen Inc	325412	10,763,799,552	3,547,000,064
Celgene Corporation	325412	9,255,999,488	1,602,000,000
Gilead Sciences Inc	325412	32,639,000,576	18,108,000,256
Johnson & Johnson	325412	70,073,999,360	15,409,000,448
Lilly (ELI) & Company	325412	19,958,700,032	2,408,399,872
Pfizer Inc	325412	48,851,001,344	6,960,000,000
Pharmaceuticals and Druggists' Merchandise Distributors			
AmerisourceBergen Corp	424210	135,961,804,800	-134,887,008
Cardinal Health Inc	424210	102,530,998,272	1,215,000,064
McKesson Corporation	424210	179,045,007,360	1,476,000,000
Pharmacies and Drug Stores			
CVS Health Corporation	446110	153,289,998,336	5,237,000,192
Rite Aid Corporation	446110	26,528,376,832	2,109,172,992
Walgreens Boots Alliance Inc	446110	103,443,996,672	4,220,000,000
Physicians (except Mental Health Specialists)			
Team Health Holdings Inc	621111	3,597,246,976	82,711,000
Plastics Material and Resin Manufacturing			
Celanese Corporation	325211	5,673,999,872	304,000,000
Huntsman Corporation	325211	10,298,999,808	93,000,000
Pottery, Ceramics and Plumbing Fixture Manufacturing			
Kohler Company	327110	6,000,000,000	
Poultry (Including Chicken, Duck & Turkey) Processing and Packaging			
Tyson Foods Inc	311615	41,372,999,680	1,220,000,000

Industry Group	Industry Code	2015 Sales	2015 Profits
Power, Distribution and Specialty Transformer Manufacturing			
AZZ Inc	335311	816,686,976	64,943,000
Power-Driven Handtool Manufacturing			
Stanley Black & Decker Inc	333991	11,171,800,064	883,699,968
Pressed and Blown Glass and Glassware (except Glass Packaging Containers) Manufacturing			
Corning Inc	327212	9,111,000,064	1,339,000,064
Printing, Commercial			
RR Donnelley & Sons Co	323111	11,256,800,256	151,100,000
Professional Employer Organizations			
Barrett Business Services Inc	561330	740,841,024	25,494,000
Computer Task Group Inc	561330	369,478,016	6,510,000
Property and Casualty (P&C) Insurance Underwriters (Direct Carriers)			
American Financial Group Inc	524126	6,144,999,936	352,000,000
American International Group Inc (AIG)	524126	58,326,999,040	2,196,000,000
Berkshire Hathaway Inc	524126	210,821,005,312	24,082,999,296
Liberty Mutual Group Inc	524126	39,450,000,000	514,000,000
Progressive Corporation (The)	524126	20,853,800,960	1,267,600,000
Safeco Insurance Company of America	524126	1,650,000,000	
State Farm Insurance Companies	524126	80,000,000,000	
Travelers Companies Inc (The)	524126	26,800,001,024	3,439,000,064
USAA	524126	20,971,000,000	2,726,000,000
W R Berkley Corporation	524126	7,206,456,832	503,694,016
Pump and Pumping Equipment Manufacturing			
Graco Inc	333911	1,286,484,992	345,712,992
Radar, Navigation, Sonar, Space Vehicle Guidance, Flight Systems and Marine Instrument Manufacturing			
Trimble Navigation Ltd	334511	2,290,400,000	121,100,000
Radio, Television and Other Electronics Stores			
Best Buy Co Inc	443142	40,339,001,344	1,232,999,936
Railroad Cars, Subways, Trams, Trolleys, Engines and Locomotives Manufacturing			
Greenbrier Companies Inc (The)	336510	2,605,277,952	192,832,000
Trinity Industries Inc	336510	6,392,699,904	796,499,968
Real Estate Agents & Brokers			
CBRE Group Inc	531210	10,855,810,048	547,132,032
Cushman & Wakefield Inc	531210	4,800,000,000	
Reconstituted Wood Product Manufacturing			
Patrick Industries Inc	321219	920,332,992	42,219,000
Recreational Vehicle (RV) Trailer and Camper Manufacturing			
Thor Industries Inc	336214	4,006,819,072	199,384,992
REITs (Real Estate Investment Trusts) - Residential			
Equity Lifestyle Properties Inc	531110A	821,654,016	139,371,008
Restaurants, Fast-Food, Pizza Delivery, Takeout and Family			
Buffalo Wild Wings Inc	722513	1,812,722,048	95,069,000

Industry Group	Industry Code	2015 Sales	2015 Profits
Darden Restaurants Inc	722513	6,764,000,256	709,500,032
McDonald's Corp	722513	25,412,999,168	4,529,299,968
Yum! Brands Inc	722513	13,105,000,448	1,292,999,936
Restaurants, Full-Service, Sit Down			
Brinker International Inc	722511	3,002,277,888	196,694,000
Retirement Communities and Assisted Living Facilities for the Elderly			
Brookdale Senior Living Inc	623310	4,960,608,256	-457,476,992
Scientific Research and Development (R&D) in Life Sciences, Medical Devices, Biotechnology and Pharmaceuticals (Drugs)			
PAREXEL International Corp	541711	2,330,274,048	147,820,992
Pharmaceutical Product Development Inc	541711	1,200,000,000	
Quintiles Transnational Holdings Inc	541711	5,737,618,944	387,204,992
Securities Brokerage, Discount Brokers and Online Stock Brokers			
Charles Schwab Corp (The)	523120	6,368,999,936	1,447,000,064
Edward D Jones & Co LP	523120	6,619,000,000	838,000,000
Seeds, Pesticides, Herbicides and Other Agricultural Chemical Manufacturing			
Scotts Miracle-Gro Co (The)	325320	3,016,499,968	159,800,000
Semiconductor and Solar Cell Manufacturing, Including Chips, Memory, LEDs, Transistors and Integrated Circuits			
Intel Corp	334413	55,354,998,784	11,420,000,256
NVIDIA Corp	334413	4,681,506,816	630,587,008
Qualcomm Inc	334413	25,280,999,424	5,271,000,064
Semiconductor Manufacturing Equipment and Systems (Including Etching, Wafer Processing & Surface Mount) Manufacturing			
Applied Materials Inc	333242	9,658,999,808	1,376,999,936
Lam Research Corp	333242	5,259,312,128	655,577,024
Shoe and Footwear Brands, Designers, Importers and Distributors			
Genesco Inc	424340	2,859,844,096	97,725,000
Nike Inc	424340	30,601,000,960	3,272,999,936
Shoe Stores			
Foot Locker Inc	448210	7,151,000,064	520,000,000
Soap and Other Detergent Manufacturing			
Clorox Company (The)	325611	5,655,000,064	580,000,000
Colgate Palmolive Co	325611	16,033,999,872	1,384,000,000
Soft Drinks (Including Bottled Carbonated and Flavored Water, Bottled Coffee & Tea, Sodas, Pop and Energy Drinks) Manufacturing			
Coca-Cola Bottling Co Consolidated	312111	2,306,458,112	59,002,000
Coca-Cola Company (The)	312111	44,294,000,640	7,351,000,064
PepsiCo Inc	312111	63,055,998,976	5,452,000,256
Specialized Commercial and Service Machinery Manufacturing, Including Cleaning, Laundry and Car Washing Equipment			
Middleby Corporation (The)	333318	1,826,598,016	191,610,000

Industry Group	Industry Code	2015 Sales	2015 Profits
Spices, Seasonings, Salad Dressing, Mayonnaise, Mustard, Catsup and Condiments Manufacturing			
McCormick & Company Inc	311940	4,296,300,032	402,100,000
Sporting Goods Stores			
Academy Sports & Outdoors Ltd	451110	4,600,000,000	
Bass Pro Shops Inc	451110	4,500,000,000	
Cabela's Inc	451110	3,997,701,888	189,330,000
Dick's Sporting Goods Inc	451110	6,814,478,848	344,198,016
Hibbett Sports Inc	451110	913,486,016	73,584,000
Recreational Equipment Inc (REI)	451110	2,423,221,000	35,372,000
Supermarkets and Grocery (except Convenience) Stores			
HEB Grocery Company LP	445110	23,000,000,000	
Kroger Co (The)	445110	108,464,996,352	1,728,000,000
Publix Super Markets Inc	445110	32,618,758,144	1,965,048,064
Safeway Inc	445110	36,980,000,000	
Supervalu Inc	445110	17,820,000,256	192,000,000
Trader Joe's Company Inc	445110	13,000,000,000	
Talent Agencies, Agents and Managers for Athletes and Entertainers			
IMG Worldwide Inc	711410	1,800,000,000	
William Morris Endeavor Entertainment LLC (WME-IMG)	711410	2,200,000,000	
Telecommunications, Telephone and Network Equipment Manufacturing, including PBX, Routers, Switches and Handsets Manufacturing			
NeoPhotonics Corp	334210	339,439,008	3,668,000
Telemarketing Bureaus and Other Contact Centers			
Convergys Corporation	561422	2,950,599,936	169,000,000
Telephone, Internet Access, Broadband, Data Networks, Server Facilities and Telecommunications Services Industry			
AT&T Inc	517110	146,801,000,448	13,345,000,448
CenturyLink Inc	517110	17,899,999,232	878,000,000
Charter Communications Inc	517110	9,754,000,384	-271,000,000
Comcast Corp	517110	74,510,000,128	8,162,999,808
DIRECTV	517110	34,000,000,000	
EchoStar Corp	517110	3,143,714,048	153,356,992
Level 3 Communications Inc	517110	8,229,000,192	3,432,999,936
Liberty Global Inc	517110	17,062,700,032	-1,196,400,000
Mediacom Communications Corp	517110	738,710,000	123,009,000
Rackspace Hosting Inc	517110	2,001,299,968	126,200,000
Verizon Communications Inc	517110	131,620,003,840	17,878,999,040
Television Broadcasting			
CBS Corporation	515120	13,886,000,128	1,412,999,936
Cox Enterprises Inc	515120	18,000,000,000	
Fox Entertainment Group Inc	515120	13,500,000,000	
NBCUniversal LLC	515120	26,000,000,000	5,591,000,000

Industry Group	Industry Code	2015 Sales	2015 Profits
Temporary Staffing, Help and Employment Agencies			
Kelly Services Inc	561320	5,518,199,808	53,800,000
Robert Half International Inc	561320	5,094,932,992	357,796,000
Tire and Tube Wholesale Distribution			
American Tire Distributors	423130	4,800,000,000	-95,800,000
Tire Dealers			
Discount Tire Company	441320	4,200,000,000	
Title Insurance Underwriters (Direct Carriers)			
Fidelity National Financial Inc	524127	9,132,000,256	527,000,000
Truck, Utility Trailer and RV (Recreational Vehicle) Rental and Leasing			
Penske Corporation	532120	23,000,000,000	
Ryder System Inc	532120	6,571,893,248	304,768,000
Trucking and Freight'Long Distance, Full Truckload (FTL)			
JB Hunt Transport Services Inc	484121	6,187,645,952	427,235,008
Trucking and Freight'Long Distance, Less Than Truckload (LTL)			
Old Dominion Freight Line Inc	484122	2,972,442,112	304,689,984
Veterinary Services			
VCA Antech Inc	541940	2,133,675,008	211,048,992
Warehouse Clubs and Super Stores			
Costco Wholesale Corp	452910	116,198,998,016	2,376,999,936
PriceSmart Inc	452910	2,802,603,008	89,124,000
Sam's Club	452910	57,000,000,000	
Wal-Mart Stores Inc (Walmart)	452910	485,650,989,056	16,362,999,808
Waste Collection, Recycling, Treatment and Remediation Services			
Waste Management Inc	562000	12,961,000,448	753,000,000
Watches and Parts (except Crystals) Manufacturing			
Fossil Group Inc	334519A	3,228,836,096	220,636,992
Wireless Communications and Radio and TV Broadcasting Equipment Manufacturing, including Cellphones (Handsets)			
Apple Inc	334220	233,715,007,488	53,394,001,920
Wireless Telecommunications Carriers (except Satellite)			
Agero Inc	517210	625,000,000	
T-Mobile US Inc	517210	32,053,000,192	733,000,000
United States Cellular Corp	517210	3,996,852,992	241,347,008
Women's Clothing, Apparel and Accessories Stores			
Ascena Retail Group Inc	448120	4,802,899,968	-236,800,000
Chico's FAS Inc	448120	2,675,211,008	64,641,000
L Brands Inc	448120	11,454,000,128	1,042,000,000
Victoria's Secret	448120	7,672,000,000	

ALPHABETICAL INDEX

24 Hour Fitness
3M Company
A.O. Smith Corporation
Abbott Laboratories
ABM Industries Inc
Academy Sports & Outdoors Ltd
Accenture LLP
Accor North America
Acosta Inc
Activision Blizzard Inc
Adobe Systems Inc
Advance Auto Parts Inc
Adventist Health System
Advocate Health Care
Aegion Corporation
Aetna Inc
AFLAC Inc
Agero Inc
Airbnb Inc
Alaska Air Group Inc
Alliance Data Systems Corporation
Allscripts Healthcare Solutions Inc
Amazon.com Inc
American Airlines Group Inc
American Express Co
American Financial Group Inc
American Honda Motor Co Inc
American International Group Inc (AIG)
American Tire Distributors
Amerigroup Corporation
AmerisourceBergen Corp
Ametek Inc
Amgen Inc
Amphenol Corporation
AMSURG Corporation
Anthem Inc
APC by Schneider Electric
Apple Inc
Applied Materials Inc
Aramark
Arrow Electronics Inc
Arthur J Gallagher & Co
Ascena Retail Group Inc
Ascension Health
AT Kearney Inc
AT&T Inc
Athenahealth Inc
Automatic Data Processing Inc (ADP)
AutoNation Inc
Avis Budget Group Inc
Avnet Inc
AZZ Inc
Bain & Company Inc
Bank of America Corp
Bank of New York Mellon Corp
Barrett Business Services Inc
Bass Pro Shops Inc
BB&T Corporation
Becton Dickinson & Co
Bed Bath & Beyond Inc
Belden Inc
Berkshire Hathaway Energy Company

Berkshire Hathaway Inc
Best Buy Co Inc
Bio Rad Laboratories Inc
Biogen Inc
Black & Veatch Holding Company
BlackRock Inc
Bloomberg LP
BMC Software Inc
BMC Stock Holdings Inc
Boeing Company (The)
Booz Allen Hamilton Holding Corp
BorgWarner Inc
Boston Consulting Group Inc (The, BCG)
Boston Scientific Corp
Brightstar Corporation
Brinker International Inc
Brookdale Senior Living Inc
Brown & Brown Inc
Buffalo Wild Wings Inc
Burns & McDonnell
C&S Wholesale Grocers Inc
Cabela's Inc
CACI International Inc
Cadence Design Systems Inc
Capital One Financial Corp
Cardinal Health Inc
CarMax Inc
Carmike Cinemas Inc
Carnival Corporation
Casey's General Stores Inc
Caterpillar Inc
Catholic Health Initiatives
CBRE Group Inc
CBS Corporation
CDW Corporation
Celanese Corporation
Celgene Corporation
CenturyLink Inc
Cerner Corporation
CH Robinson Worldwide Inc
Change Healthcare Holdings Inc
Charles Schwab Corp (The)
Charter Communications Inc
Chemed Corporation
Chevron Phillips Chemical Company LLC
Chico's FAS Inc
Cigna Corporation
Cintas Corporation
Cisco Systems Inc
Citigroup Inc
Citrix Systems Inc
Cleveland Clinic Foundation (The)
Clorox Company (The)
Coca-Cola Bottling Co Consolidated
Coca-Cola Company (The)
Cognizant Technology Solutions Corp
Colgate Palmolive Co
Comcast Corp
CommScope Inc
Community Health Systems Inc
Computer Task Group Inc
Concur Technologies Inc
Container Store (The)
Convergys Corporation
Cooper Companies Inc

Corning Inc
Costco Wholesale Corp
Cox Enterprises Inc
CR Bard Inc
Crown Holdings Inc
Cullen-Frost Bankers Inc
Cushman & Wakefield Inc
CVS Health Corporation
Dana Holding Corporation
Danaher Corporation
Darden Restaurants Inc
DaVita Healthcare Partners Inc
Dell-EMC
Deloitte Consulting LLP
Deloitte LLP
Delta Air Lines Inc
DENTSPLY International Inc
Dick's Sporting Goods Inc
DIRECTV
Discount Tire Company
Discovery Communications Inc
Dollar Thrifty Automotive Group Inc
DR Horton Inc
DriveTime Automotive Group Inc
DTE Energy Company
Duke Energy Corporation
Eastman Chemical Company
EchoStar Corp
eClinicalWorks
Edward D Jones & Co LP
Edwards Lifesciences Corporation
EMCOR Group Inc
Encore Capital Group Inc
Enterprise Holdings Inc
EPAM Systems Inc
Epic Systems Corporation
Equity Lifestyle Properties Inc
Estee Lauder Companies Inc (The)
Exelon Corporation
ExlService Holdings Inc
Expedia Inc
Expeditors International of Washington Inc
Experian North America
Express Scripts Holding Co
ExxonMobil Chemical
EY LLP
F5 Networks Inc
Facebook Inc
FactSet Research Systems Inc
Fairview Health Services
Fastenal Co
FCA US LLC
Federal-Mogul Corporation
FedEx Corporation
Fidelity Investments Financial Services
Fidelity National Financial Inc
Fidelity National Information Services Inc
FirstEnergy Corporation
FirstMerit Corporation
Fiserv Inc
Fleetcor Technologies Inc
Fluor Corp
Foot Locker Inc
Ford Motor Co
Fossil Group Inc

Fox Entertainment Group Inc
Frito-Lay North America Inc
FTI Consulting Inc
Gartner Inc
General Dynamics Corp
General Electric Co (GE)
General Motors Company (GM)
Genesco Inc
Gentex Corporation
Gentherm Inc
Gilead Sciences Inc
Goldman Sachs Group Inc
Google (Alphabet Inc)
Graco Inc
Grant Thornton LLP
Greenbrier Companies Inc (The)
Group 1 Automotive Inc
Hanesbrands Inc
Hartford Financial Services Group Inc
(The)
HCA Holdings Inc
Health Care Service Corporation (HCSC)
HealthSouth Corporation
Heartland Payment Systems Inc
HEB Grocery Company LP
Hendrick Automotive Group
Henry Schein Inc
Hershey Co
Hertz Global Holdings Inc
Hibbett Sports Inc
Hillenbrand Inc
Hillshire Brands Company
Hilton Worldwide Inc
HMSHost Corporation
Home Depot Inc
Houston Methodist
Hub International Limited
Hubbell Inc
Humana Inc
Huntsman Corporation
Hyatt Hotels Corporation
IAC/InterActiveCorp
IDEXX Laboratories Inc
Illinois Tool Works Inc
IMG Worldwide Inc
IMS Health Holdings Inc
Ingram Micro Inc
Ingredion Inc
Integer Holdings Corporation
Intel Corp
Interpublic Group of Companies Inc
Intuit Inc
inVentiv Health Inc
Jabil Circuit Inc
Jack Henry & Associates Inc
Jackson National Life Insurance Company
Jacobs Engineering Group Inc
JB Hunt Transport Services Inc
Jefferies LLC
JetBlue Airways Corporation
JM Family Enterprises Inc
Johnson & Johnson
Johnson Controls Inc
Jones Lang LaSalle Inc
JP Morgan Chase & Co Inc

Kaiser Permanente
Kate Spade & Company Inc
Kelly Services Inc
Kimpton Hotel & Restaurant Group LLC
Kindred Healthcare Inc
Koch Industries Inc
Kohler Company
Kohl's Corporation
KPMG LLP
Kroger Co (The)
L Brands Inc
La Quinta Holdings Inc
Laboratory Corp of America Holdings
Lam Research Corp
Land O'Lakes Inc
Las Vegas Sands Corp (The Venetian)
Lear Corp
Legg Mason Inc
Lennar Corporation
Level 3 Communications Inc
Liberty Global Inc
Liberty Interactive Corp
Liberty Mutual Group Inc
LifePoint Health Inc
Lilly (ELI) & Company
Lincare Holdings Inc
Lincoln National Corporation
LinkedIn Corp
Lithia Motors Inc
LKQ Corporation
Lockheed Martin Corp
Loews Hotels Holding Corporation
Lowe's Companies Inc
Lubrizol Corporation (The)
Marriott International Inc
Mars Inc
Marsh & Mclennan Companies Inc
Mary Kay Inc
MassMutual Financial Group
MasterCard Inc
Matthews International Corporation
MAXIMUS Inc
Mayo Foundation for Medical Education
and Research
McAfee Inc
McCormick & Company Inc
McDonald's Corp
McKesson Corporation
McKinsey & Company Inc
Mediacom Communications Corp
Medical Information Technology Inc
(MEDITECH)
MedStar Health
Medtronic Inc
Menard Inc
Mentor Graphics Corp
Mercedes-Benz USA LLC
Mercer LLC
Mercy
Merrill Lynch & Co Inc
MetLife Inc
Microsoft Corp
Middleby Corporation (The)
Modine Manufacturing Company
Mohawk Industries Inc

Molex Inc
Monro Muffler Brake Inc
Moody's Corporation
Morgan Stanley
Mutual of Omaha Companies (The)
National Instruments Corp
NBCUniversal LLC
NCR Corporation
NeoPhotonics Corp
New York Life Insurance Co
Nielsen Holdings PLC
Nike Inc
NN Inc
Nordstrom Inc
Nortek Holdings Inc
Northwestern Mutual Life Insurance Co
Norwegian Cruise Line Holdings Ltd
(NCL)
NVIDIA Corp
NVR Inc
Old Dominion Freight Line Inc
Oliver Wyman Group
Omnicom Group Inc
Oracle Corp
O'Reilly Automotive Inc
Oshkosh Corporation
Owens & Minor Inc
PACCAR Inc
PAREXEL International Corp
Park-Ohio Holdings Corp
Patrick Industries Inc
Patterson Companies Inc
Penske Automotive Group Inc
Penske Corporation
PepsiCo Inc
PerkinElmer Inc
Petco Animal Supplies Inc
PetSmart Inc
Pfizer Inc
PG&E Corporation
Pharmaceutical Product Development Inc
Phillips 66
Pinnacle Entertainment Inc
PPG Industries Inc
Precision Castparts Corp
Priceline Group Inc (The)
PriceSmart Inc
PricewaterhouseCoopers (PWC)
Principal Financial Group (The)
Progressive Corporation (The)
Providence St. Joseph Health
Prudential Financial Inc
Publix Super Markets Inc
PulteGroup Inc
Qualcomm Inc
Quality Systems Inc
Quanta Services Inc
Quest Diagnostics Inc
QuikTrip Corporation
Quintiles Transnational Holdings Inc
Rackspace Hosting Inc
Ralph Lauren Corporation
Raymond James Financial Inc
Recreational Equipment Inc (REI)
Red Hat Inc

Regal-Beloit Corporation
ResMed Inc
Resources Connection Inc
Rite Aid Corporation
Ritz-Carlton Hotel Company LLC (The)
Robert Half International Inc
Rockwell Automation Inc
Roper Technologies Inc
Rosendin Electric
Ross Stores Inc
Royal Caribbean Cruises Ltd
RR Donnelley & Sons Co
Ryder System Inc
Safeco Insurance Company of America
Safeway Inc
SalesForce.com Inc
Sam's Club
Sanmina Corp
Sapient Corporation
SAS Institute Inc
SC Johnson & Son Inc
SCANA Corporation
Science Applications International Corp
(SAIC)
Scotts Miracle-Gro Co (The)
Select Comfort Corporation
Select Medical Holdings Corporation
Service Corporation International Inc
ServiceNow Inc
Sherwin-Williams Company (The)
Smithfield Foods Inc
Sodexo Inc
Sonoco Products Company
Southwest Airlines Co
Spectrum Health
Spirit Aerosystems Holdings Inc
Spirit Airlines Inc
St Jude Medical Inc
Stanley Black & Decker Inc
Starbucks Corporation
Starwood Hotels & Resorts Worldwide Inc
State Farm Insurance Companies
Stericycle Inc
Stifel Financial Corp
Strategy&
Stryker Corp
SunGard Data Systems Inc
Supervalu Inc
Sutter Health Inc
Symantec Corp
SYNNEX Corp
Synopsys Inc
Syntel Inc
SYSCO Corporation
T Rowe Price Group Inc
Team Health Holdings Inc
Team Inc
Tech Data Corp
Tenet Healthcare Corporation
Tenneco Inc
Tesla Motors Inc
Textron Inc
Thermo Fisher Scientific Inc
Thomson Reuters Corp
Thor Industries Inc

TIBCO Software Inc
Time Warner Inc
TJX Companies Inc (The)
T-Mobile US Inc
Toll Brothers Inc
Total System Services Inc (TSYS)
Toyota Motor Sales USA Inc (TMS)
Trader Joe's Company Inc
Travelers Companies Inc (The)
TreeHouse Foods Inc
Trimble Navigation Ltd
Trinity Health
Trinity Industries Inc
TripAdvisor Inc
Trustmark Companies
TRW Automotive Holdings Corp
Tutor Perini Corporation
Twitter Inc
Tyson Foods Inc
Uber Inc
Under Armour Inc
United Continental Holdings Inc
United Natural Foods Inc
United Parcel Service Inc (UPS)
United States Cellular Corp
United Technologies Corporation
UnitedHealth Group Inc
Universal Health Services Inc
US Bancorp
USAA
UST Global Inc
Valassis Communications Inc (RedPlum)
Varian Medical Systems Inc
VCA Antech Inc
Verisk Analytics Inc
Verizon Communications Inc
VF Corp
Victoria's Secret
Visa Inc
VMware Inc
W R Berkley Corporation
Walgreens Boots Alliance Inc
Wal-Mart Stores Inc (Walmart)
Walt Disney Company (The)
Waste Management Inc
Waters Corporation
Wells Fargo & Co
Whirlpool Corp
William Morris Endeavor Entertainment
LLC (WME-IMG)
WW Grainger Inc
Wyndham Worldwide Corporation
Wynn Resorts Limited
Xerox Corporation
Yum! Brands Inc
Zimmer Biomet Holdings Inc
Zumiez Inc

INDEX OF U.S. HEADQUARTERS LOCATION BY STATE

To help you locate members of THE AMERICAN EMPLOYERS 500 geographically, the city and state of the headquarters of each company are in the following index.

ALABAMA
HealthSouth Corporation; Birmingham
Hibbett Sports Inc; Birmingham

ARIZONA
Avnet Inc; Phoenix
Discount Tire Company; Scottsdale
DriveTime Automotive Group Inc; Tempe
PetSmart Inc; Phoenix

ARKANSAS
JB Hunt Transport Services Inc; Lowell
Sam's Club; Bentonville
Tyson Foods Inc; Springdale
Wal-Mart Stores Inc (Walmart); Bentonville

CALIFORNIA
24 Hour Fitness; San Ramon
Activision Blizzard Inc; Santa Monica
Adobe Systems Inc; San Jose
Airbnb Inc; San Francisco
American Honda Motor Co Inc; Torrance
Amgen Inc; Thousand Oaks
Apple Inc; Cupertino
Applied Materials Inc; Santa Clara
Bio Rad Laboratories Inc; Hercules
Cadence Design Systems Inc; San Jose
CBRE Group Inc; Los Angeles
Charles Schwab Corp (The); San Francisco
Cisco Systems Inc; San Jose
Clorox Company (The); Oakland
Cooper Companies Inc; Pleasanton
DIRECTV; El Segundo
Edwards Lifesciences Corporation; Irvine
Encore Capital Group Inc; San Diego
Experian North America; Costa Mesa
Facebook Inc; Menlo Park
Fox Entertainment Group Inc; Los Angeles
Gilead Sciences Inc; Foster City
Google (Alphabet Inc); Mountain View
Ingram Micro Inc; Santa Ana
Intel Corp; Santa Clara
Intuit Inc; Mountain View
Jacobs Engineering Group Inc; Pasadena
Kaiser Permanente; Oakland
Kimpton Hotel & Restaurant Group LLC; San Francisco
Lam Research Corp; Fremont
LinkedIn Corp; Mountain View
McAfee Inc; Santa Clara
McKesson Corporation; San Francisco
NeoPhotonics Corp; San Jose

NVIDIA Corp; Santa Clara
Oracle Corp; Redwood City
Petco Animal Supplies Inc; San Diego
PG&E Corporation; San Francisco
PriceSmart Inc; San Diego
Qualcomm Inc; San Diego
Quality Systems Inc; Irvine
ResMed Inc; San Diego
Resources Connection Inc; Irvine
Robert Half International Inc; Menlo Park
Rosendin Electric; San Jose
Ross Stores Inc; Dublin
Safeway Inc; Pleasanton
SalesForce.com Inc; San Francisco
Sanmina Corp; San Jose
ServiceNow Inc; Santa Clara
Sutter Health Inc; Sacramento
Symantec Corp; Mountain View
SYNNEX Corp; Fremont
Synopsys Inc; Mountain View
Tesla Motors Inc; Palo Alto
TIBCO Software Inc; Palo Alto
Toyota Motor Sales USA Inc (TMS); Torrance
Trader Joe's Company Inc; Monrovia
Trimble Navigation Ltd; Sunnyvale
Tutor Perini Corporation; Sylmar
Twitter Inc; San Francisco
Uber Inc; San Francisco
UST Global Inc; Aliso Viejo
Varian Medical Systems Inc; Palo Alto
VCA Antech Inc; Los Angeles
Visa Inc; San Francisco
VMware Inc; Palo Alto
Walt Disney Company (The); Burbank
Wells Fargo & Co; San Francisco
William Morris Endeavor Entertainment LLC (WME-IMG); Beverly Hills

COLORADO
Arrow Electronics Inc; Centennial
Catholic Health Initiatives; Englewood
DaVita Healthcare Partners Inc; Denver
EchoStar Corp; Englewood
Level 3 Communications Inc; Broomfield
Liberty Global Inc; Englewood
Liberty Interactive Corp; Englewood

CONNECTICUT
Aetna Inc; Hartford
Amphenol Corporation; Wallingford
Charter Communications Inc; Stamford
Cigna Corporation; Bloomfield
EMCOR Group Inc; Norwalk
FactSet Research Systems Inc; Norwalk
Gartner Inc; Stamford
General Electric Co (GE); Fairfield
Hartford Financial Services Group Inc (The); Hartford
Hubbell Inc; Shelton
IMS Health Holdings Inc; Danbury
Priceline Group Inc (The); Norwalk
Stanley Black & Decker Inc; New Britain
United Technologies Corporation; Hartford
W R Berkley Corporation; Greenwich

Xerox Corporation; Norwalk

FLORIDA
Acosta Inc; Jacksonville
Adventist Health System; Altamonte Springs
AutoNation Inc; Fort Lauderdale
Brightstar Corporation; Miami
Brown & Brown Inc; Daytona Beach
Carnival Corporation; Miami
Chico's FAS Inc; Fort Myers
Citrix Systems Inc; Fort Lauderdale
Darden Restaurants Inc; Orlando
Fidelity National Financial Inc; Jacksonville
Fidelity National Information Services Inc; Jacksonville
Hertz Global Holdings Inc; Estero
Jabil Circuit Inc; St. Petersburg
JM Family Enterprises Inc; Deerfield Beach
Lennar Corporation; Miami
Lincare Holdings Inc; Clearwater
Norwegian Cruise Line Holdings Ltd (NCL); Miami
Publix Super Markets Inc; Lakeland
Raymond James Financial Inc; St. Petersburg
Roper Technologies Inc; Sarasota
Royal Caribbean Cruises Ltd; Miami
Ryder System Inc; Miami
Spirit Airlines Inc; Miramar
Tech Data Corp; Clearwater

GEORGIA
AFLAC Inc; Columbus
BMC Stock Holdings Inc; Atlanta
Carmike Cinemas Inc; Columbus
Coca-Cola Company (The); Atlanta
Cox Enterprises Inc; Atlanta
Delta Air Lines Inc; Atlanta
Fleetcor Technologies Inc; Norcross
Home Depot Inc; Atlanta
Mercedes-Benz USA LLC; Atlanta
Mohawk Industries Inc; Calhoun
NCR Corporation; Duluth
PulteGroup Inc; Atlanta
Total System Services Inc (TSYS); Columbus
United Parcel Service Inc (UPS); Atlanta

ILLINOIS
Abbott Laboratories; Abbott Park
Accenture LLP; Chicago
Advocate Health Care; Downers Grove
Allscripts Healthcare Solutions Inc; Chicago
Arthur J Gallagher & Co; Itasca
AT Kearney Inc; Chicago
Boeing Company (The); Chicago
Caterpillar Inc; Peoria
CDW Corporation; Vernon Hills
Equity Lifestyle Properties Inc; Chicago
Exelon Corporation; Chicago
Grant Thornton LLP; Chicago

Health Care Service Corporation (HCSC); Chicago
Hillshire Brands Company; Chicago
Hub International Limited; Chicago
Hyatt Hotels Corporation; Chicago
Illinois Tool Works Inc; Glenview
Ingredion Inc; Westchester
Jones Lang LaSalle Inc; Chicago
LKQ Corporation; Chicago
McDonald's Corp; Oak Brook
Middleby Corporation (The); Elgin
Molex Inc; Lisle
RR Donnelley & Sons Co; Chicago
State Farm Insurance Companies; Bloomington
Stericycle Inc; Lake Forest
Tenneco Inc; Lake Forest
TreeHouse Foods Inc; Oakbrook
Trustmark Companies; Lake Forest
United Continental Holdings Inc; Chicago
United States Cellular Corp; Chicago
Walgreens Boots Alliance Inc; Deerfield
WW Grainger Inc; Lake Forest

INDIANA
Anthem Inc; Indianapolis
Hillenbrand Inc; Batesville
Lilly (ELI) & Company; Indianapolis
Patrick Industries Inc; Elkhart
Thor Industries Inc; Elkhart
Zimmer Biomet Holdings Inc; Warsaw

IOWA
Berkshire Hathaway Energy Company; Des Moines
Casey's General Stores Inc; Ankeny
Principal Financial Group (The); Des Moines

KANSAS
Black & Veatch Holding Company; Overland Park
Koch Industries Inc; Wichita
Spirit Aerosystems Holdings Inc; Wichita

KENTUCKY
Humana Inc; Louisville
Kindred Healthcare Inc; Louisville
Yum! Brands Inc; Louisville

LOUISIANA
CenturyLink Inc; Monroe

MAINE
IDEXX Laboratories Inc; Westbrook

MARYLAND
Discovery Communications Inc; Silver Spring
FTI Consulting Inc; Washington D.C.
HMSHost Corporation; Bethesda
Legg Mason Inc; Baltimore
Lockheed Martin Corp; Bethesda
Marriott International Inc; Bethesda

McCormick & Company Inc; Sparks
MedStar Health; Columbia
Ritz-Carlton Hotel Company LLC (The); Chevy Chase
Sodexo Inc; Gaithersburg
T Rowe Price Group Inc; Baltimore
Under Armour Inc; Baltimore

MASSACHUSETTS
Agero Inc; Medford
Athenahealth Inc; Watertown
Bain & Company Inc; Boston
Biogen Inc; Cambridge
Boston Consulting Group Inc (The, BCG); Boston
Boston Scientific Corp; Marlborough
Dell-EMC; Hopkinton
eClinicalWorks; Westborough
Fidelity Investments Financial Services; Boston
inVentiv Health Inc; Burlington
Liberty Mutual Group Inc; Boston
MassMutual Financial Group; Springfield
Medical Information Technology Inc (MEDITECH); Westwood
PAREXEL International Corp; Waltham
PerkinElmer Inc; Waltham
Sapient Corporation; Boston
Thermo Fisher Scientific Inc; Waltham
TJX Companies Inc (The); Framingham
TripAdvisor Inc; Needham
Waters Corporation; Milford

MICHIGAN
BorgWarner Inc; Auburn Hills
DTE Energy Company; Detroit
FCA US LLC; Auburn Hills
Federal-Mogul Corporation; Southfield
Ford Motor Co; Dearborn
General Motors Company (GM); Detroit
Gentex Corporation; Zeeland
Gentherm Inc; Northville
Jackson National Life Insurance Company; Lansing
Kelly Services Inc; Troy
Lear Corp; Southfield
Penske Automotive Group Inc; Bloomfield Hills
Penske Corporation; Bloomfield Hills
Spectrum Health; Grand Rapids
Stryker Corp; Kalamazoo
Syntel Inc; Troy
Trinity Health; Livonia
TRW Automotive Holdings Corp; Livonia
Valassis Communications Inc (RedPlum); Livonia
Whirlpool Corp; Benton Harbor

MINNESOTA
3M Company; St. Paul
Best Buy Co Inc; Richfield
Buffalo Wild Wings Inc; Minneapolis
CH Robinson Worldwide Inc; Eden Prairie
Fairview Health Services; Minneapolis

Fastenal Co; Winona
Graco Inc; Minneapolis
Land O'Lakes Inc; Arden Hills
Mayo Foundation for Medical Education and Research; Rochester
Medtronic Inc; Minneapolis
Patterson Companies Inc; St. Paul
Select Comfort Corporation; Minneapolis
St Jude Medical Inc; St. Paul
Supervalu Inc; Eden Prairie
UnitedHealth Group Inc; Minnetonka
US Bancorp; Minneapolis

MISSOURI
Aegion Corporation; Chesterfield
Ascension Health; St. Louis
Bass Pro Shops Inc; Springfield
Belden Inc; St. Louis
Burns & McDonnell; Kansas City
Cerner Corporation; North Kansas City
Edward D Jones & Co LP; Des Peres
Enterprise Holdings Inc; St. Louis
Express Scripts Holding Co; St. Louis
Jack Henry & Associates Inc; Monett
O'Reilly Automotive Inc; Springfield
Stifel Financial Corp; St. Louis

NEBRASKA
Berkshire Hathaway Inc; Omaha
Cabela's Inc; Sidney
Mutual of Omaha Companies (The); Omaha

NEVADA
Las Vegas Sands Corp (The Venetian); Las Vegas
Pinnacle Entertainment Inc; Las Vegas
Wynn Resorts Limited; Las Vegas

NEW HAMPSHIRE
C&S Wholesale Grocers Inc; Keene

NEW JERSEY
Ascena Retail Group Inc; Mahwah
Automatic Data Processing Inc (ADP); Roseland
Avis Budget Group Inc; Parsippany
Becton Dickinson & Co; Franklin Lakes
Bed Bath & Beyond Inc; Union
Celgene Corporation; Summit
Cognizant Technology Solutions Corp; Teaneck
CR Bard Inc; Murray Hill
Heartland Payment Systems Inc; Princeton
Johnson & Johnson; New Brunswick
Prudential Financial Inc; Newark
Quest Diagnostics Inc; Madison
Verisk Analytics Inc; Jersey City
Wyndham Worldwide Corporation; Parsippany

NEW YORK
ABM Industries Inc; New York
American Express Co; New York

American International Group Inc (AIG);
New York
Bank of New York Mellon Corp; New
York
BlackRock Inc; New York
Bloomberg LP; New York
CBS Corporation; New York
Citigroup Inc; New York
Colgate Palmolive Co; New York
Computer Task Group Inc; Buffalo
Corning Inc; Corning
Cushman & Wakefield Inc; New York
Deloitte Consulting LLP; New York
Deloitte LLP; New York
Estee Lauder Companies Inc (The); New
York
ExlService Holdings Inc; New York
EY LLP; New York
Foot Locker Inc; New York
Goldman Sachs Group Inc; New York
Henry Schein Inc; Melville
IAC/InterActiveCorp; New York
IMG Worldwide Inc; New York
Interpublic Group of Companies Inc; New
York
Jefferies LLC; New York
JetBlue Airways Corporation; Long Island
City
JP Morgan Chase & Co Inc; New York
Kate Spade & Company Inc; New York
KPMG LLP; New York
Loews Hotels Holding Corporation; New
York
Marsh & Mclennan Companies Inc; New
York
MasterCard Inc; Purchase
McKinsey & Company Inc; New York
Mediacom Communications Corp;
Mediacom Park
Mercer LLC; New York
Merrill Lynch & Co Inc; New York
MetLife Inc; New York
Monro Muffler Brake Inc; Rochester
Moody's Corporation; New York
Morgan Stanley; New York
NBCUniversal LLC; New York
New York Life Insurance Co; New York
Nielsen Holdings PLC; New York
Oliver Wyman Group; New York
Omnicom Group Inc; New York
PepsiCo Inc; Purchase
Pfizer Inc; New York
PricewaterhouseCoopers (PWC); New
York
Ralph Lauren Corporation; New York
Starwood Hotels & Resorts Worldwide Inc;
White Plains
Strategy&; New York
Thomson Reuters Corp; New York
Time Warner Inc; New York
Travelers Companies Inc (The); New York
Verizon Communications Inc; New York

NORTH CAROLINA

American Tire Distributors; Huntersville

Bank of America Corp; Charlotte
BB&T Corporation; Winston-Salem
Coca-Cola Bottling Co Consolidated;
Charlotte
CommScope Inc; Hickory
Duke Energy Corporation; Charlotte
Hanesbrands Inc; Winston-Salem
Hendrick Automotive Group; Charlotte
Laboratory Corp of America Holdings;
Burlington
Lowe's Companies Inc; Mooresville
Old Dominion Freight Line Inc;
Thomasville
Pharmaceutical Product Development Inc;
Wilmington
Quintiles Transnational Holdings Inc;
Durham
Red Hat Inc; Raleigh
SAS Institute Inc; Cary
VF Corp; Greensboro

OHIO

American Financial Group Inc; Cincinnati
Cardinal Health Inc; Dublin
Chemed Corporation; Cincinnati
Cintas Corporation; Cincinnati
Cleveland Clinic Foundation (The);
Cleveland
Convergys Corporation; Cincinnati
Dana Holding Corporation; Maumee
FirstEnergy Corporation; Akron
FirstMerit Corporation; Akron
Kroger Co (The); Cincinnati
L Brands Inc; Columbus
Lubrizol Corporation (The); Wickliffe
Park-Ohio Holdings Corp; Cleveland
Progressive Corporation (The); Mayfield
Village
Scotts Miracle-Gro Co (The); Marysville
Sherwin-Williams Company (The);
Cleveland
Victoria's Secret; Reynoldsburg

OKLAHOMA

Dollar Thrifty Automotive Group Inc;
Tulsa
QuikTrip Corporation; Tulsa

OREGON

Greenbrier Companies Inc (The); Lake
Oswego
Lithia Motors Inc; Medford
Mentor Graphics Corp; Wilsonville
Nike Inc; Beaverton
Precision Castparts Corp; Portland

PENNSYLVANIA

AmerisourceBergen Corp; Chesterbrook
Ametek Inc; Berwyn
Aramark; Philadelphia
Comcast Corp; Philadelphia
Crown Holdings Inc; Philadelphia
DENTSPLY International Inc; York
Dick's Sporting Goods Inc; Coraopolis
EPAM Systems Inc; Newtown

Hershey Co; Hershey
Lincoln National Corporation; Radnor
Matthews International Corporation;
Pittsburgh
PPG Industries Inc; Pittsburgh
Rite Aid Corporation; Camp Hill
Select Medical Holdings Corporation;
Mechanicsburg
SunGard Data Systems Inc; Wayne
Toll Brothers Inc; Horsham
Universal Health Services Inc; King Of
Prussia

RHODE ISLAND

APC by Schneider Electric; West Kingston
CVS Health Corporation; Woonsocket
Nortek Holdings Inc; Providence
Textron Inc; Providence
United Natural Foods Inc; Providence

SOUTH CAROLINA

SCANA Corporation; Cayce
Sonoco Products Company; Hartsville

TENNESSEE

AMSURG Corporation; Nashville
Brookdale Senior Living Inc; Brentwood
Change Healthcare Holdings Inc; Nashville
Community Health Systems Inc; Franklin
Eastman Chemical Company; Kingsport
FedEx Corporation; Memphis
Genesco Inc; Nashville
HCA Holdings Inc; Nashville
LifePoint Health Inc; Brentwood
NN Inc; Johnson City
Team Health Holdings Inc; Knoxville

TEXAS

Academy Sports & Outdoors Ltd; Katy
Accor North America; Carrollton
Alliance Data Systems Corporation; Plano
American Airlines Group Inc; Fort Worth
AT&T Inc; Dallas
AZZ Inc; Fort Worth
BMC Software Inc; Houston
Brinker International Inc; Dallas
Celanese Corporation; Irving
Chevron Phillips Chemical Company LLC;
The Woodlands
Container Store (The); Coppell
Cullen-Frost Bankers Inc; San Antonio
DR Horton Inc; Fort Worth
ExxonMobil Chemical; Spring
Fluor Corp; Irving
Fossil Group Inc; Richardson
Frito-Lay North America Inc; Plano
Group 1 Automotive Inc; Houston
HEB Grocery Company LP; San Antonio
Houston Methodist; Houston
Integer Holdings Corporation; Frisco
La Quinta Holdings Inc; Irving
Mary Kay Inc; Dallas
Mercy; Laredo
National Instruments Corp; Austin
Phillips 66; Houston

Quanta Services Inc; Houston
Rackspace Hosting Inc; San Antonio
Service Corporation International Inc;
Houston
Southwest Airlines Co; Dallas
SYSCO Corporation; Houston
Team Inc; Sugar Land
Tenet Healthcare Corporation; Dallas
Trinity Industries Inc; Dallas
USAA; San Antonio
Waste Management Inc; Houston

UTAH
Huntsman Corporation; Salt Lake City

VIRGINIA
Advance Auto Parts Inc; Roanoke
Amerigroup Corporation; Virginia Beach
Booz Allen Hamilton Holding Corp;
McLean
CACI International Inc; Arlington
Capital One Financial Corp; McLean
CarMax Inc; Richmond
General Dynamics Corp; Falls Church
Hilton Worldwide Inc; McLean
Mars Inc; McLean
MAXIMUS Inc; Reston
NVR Inc; Reston
Owens & Minor Inc; Mechanicsville
Science Applications International Corp
(SAIC); McLean
Smithfield Foods Inc; Smithfield

WASHINGTON
Alaska Air Group Inc; Seattle
Amazon.com Inc; Seattle
Barrett Business Services Inc; Vancouver
Concur Technologies Inc; Bellevue
Costco Wholesale Corp; Issaquah
Danaher Corporation; Washington
Expedia Inc; Bellevue
Expeditors International of Washington
Inc; Seattle
F5 Networks Inc; Seattle
Microsoft Corp; Redmond
Nordstrom Inc; Seattle
PACCAR Inc; Bellevue
Providence St. Joseph Health; Renton
Recreational Equipment Inc (REI); Kent
Safeco Insurance Company of America;
Seattle
Starbucks Corporation; Seattle
T-Mobile US Inc; Bellevue
Zumiez Inc; Lynnwood

WISCONSIN
A.O. Smith Corporation; Milwaukee
Epic Systems Corporation; Verona
Fiserv Inc; Brookfield
Johnson Controls Inc; Milwaukee
Kohler Company; Kohler
Kohl's Corporation; Menomonee Falls
Menard Inc; Eau Claire
Modine Manufacturing Company; Racine

Northwestern Mutual Life Insurance Co;
Milwaukee
Oshkosh Corporation; Oshkosh
Regal-Beloit Corporation; Beloit
Rockwell Automation Inc; Milwaukee
SC Johnson & Son Inc; Racine

Individual Data
Profiles
On Each Of
The AMERICAN EMPLOYERS 500

24 Hour Fitness

NAIC Code: 713940

TYPES OF BUSINESS:

Fitness Centers
Online Nutrition Information
Day Spa

BRANDS/DIVISIONS/AFFILIATES:

AEA Investors LP
Active/Express/Fit Lite
Sport
Super-Sport
Ultra-Sport

CONTACTS: Note: Officers with more than one job title may be intentionally listed here more than once.

Mark Smith, CEO
Jeffrey N. Boyer, COO
Frank Napolitano, Pres.
Patrick Flanagan, CFO
Vicki Davis, Corp. Controller
Danny De La Rosa, Pres., Clubs

GROWTH PLANS/SPECIAL FEATURES:

24 Hour Fitness is one of the world's largest privately owned and operated fitness center chains. The firm, owned by private equity company AEA Investors LP, has nearly 4 million members and over 450 clubs in 17 states. The company operates four types of clubs, including the 24 Hour Fitness Active/Express/Fit Lite club, the Sport club, the Super-Sport club and the Ultra-Sport club. The Fitness/Express/Fit Lite clubs are moderate in size and offer full-body workouts in minutes by using cardio equipment, strength machines and free weights, with most locations offering group exercise classes as well. Sport clubs offer full group exercise schedules, fitness equipment and classes, with most locations providing a sauna, steam room and whirlpool, and some featuring basketball courts and/or swimming pools. Super-Sport clubs offer lots of equipment and functional training areas, with most featuring whirlpools, saunas, towel service, basketball and swimming and some locations offering racquetball. Ultra-Sport clubs are for serious fitness members, offering high-end fitness amenities in prime locations, including group cycling and personal training areas. 24 Hour Fitness offers family memberships, kids' club supervised areas and personal training. 24 Hour Fitness is owned by AEA Investors LP, Ontario Teachers' Pension Plan and Fitness Capital Partners.

FINANCIAL DATA: Note: Data for latest year may not have been available at press time.

In U.S. $	2016	2015	2014	2013	2012	2011
Revenue		1,418,000,000	1,330,000,000	1,300,000,000	1,500,000,000	1,500,000,000
R&D Expense						
Operating Income						
Operating Margin %						
SGA Expense						
Net Income						
Operating Cash Flow						
Capital Expenditure						
EBITDA						
Return on Assets %						
Return on Equity %						
Debt to Equity						

CONTACT INFORMATION:

Phone: 925-543-3100   Fax: 925-543-3200
Toll-Free:
Address: 12647 Alcosta Blvd., Ste. 500, San Ramon, CA 94583 United States

STOCK TICKER/OTHER:

Stock Ticker: Private   Exchange:
Employees: 20,000   Fiscal Year Ends: 12/31
Parent Company: AEA Investors LP

SALARIES/BONUSES:

Top Exec. Salary: $ Bonus: $
Second Exec. Salary: $ Bonus: $

OTHER THOUGHTS:

Estimated Female Officers or Directors: 1
Hot Spot for Advancement for Women/Minorities:

3M Company

www.3m.com

NAIC Code: 339100

TYPES OF BUSINESS:

Health Care Products
Specialty Materials & Textiles
Industrial Products
Safety, Security & Protection Products
Display & Graphics Products
Consumer & Office Products
Electronics & Communications Products
Fuel Cell Technology

BRANDS/DIVISIONS/AFFILIATES:

3M Purification Inc
Thinsulate Acoustic
Scotch
Command
Filtrete
3M

CONTACTS: *Note: Officers with more than one job title may be intentionally listed here more than once.*

Inge Thulin, CEO
Jesse Singh, Senior VP, Divisional
Frank Little, Executive VP, Divisional
James Bauman, Executive VP, Divisional
Michael Roman, Executive VP, Divisional
Michael Vale, Executive VP, Divisional
Joaquin Delgado, Executive VP, Divisional
Hak Shin, Executive VP, Divisional
Ivan Fong, General Counsel
Gregg Larson, Other Corporate Officer
Marlene McGrath, Senior VP, Divisional
Kimberly Price, Senior VP, Divisional
Julie Bushman, Senior VP, Divisional
Jon Lindekugel, Senior VP, Divisional
Paul Keel, Senior VP, Divisional
Khandpur Ashish, Senior VP, Divisional

GROWTH PLANS/SPECIAL FEATURES:

3M Company is involved in the research, manufacturing and marketing of a variety of products. Its operations are organized in five segments: industrial, safety and graphics, electronics and energy, health care and consumer. The industrial business segment serves a range of markets such as automotive, electronics, appliance, paper, printing, food, beverage, and construction. Its major industrial products include Thinsulate Acoustic insulation and 3M paint finishing and detail products. Also, 3M Purification, Inc. provides a line of filtration products. The safety and graphics business segment serves a wide range of markets that increase the safety, security and productivity of people, facilities and systems. Major product offerings include personal protection, traffic safety, border and civil security solutions, commercial graphics sheeting, architectural surface and lighting solutions, cleaning products and roofing granules for asphalt shingles. The electronics and energy business segment serves customers in these markets, including solutions for electronic devices, telecommunications networks, electrical products, power generation and distribution and infrastructure protection. Major products include LCD computer monitors, LCD televisions, hand-held mobile devices, notebook PCs and automotive displays. The health care business segment serves medical clinics, hospitals, pharmaceuticals, dental and orthodontic practitioners, health information systems and food manufacturing and testing. Products include medical and surgical supplies, skin health, infection prevention, inhalation and transdermal drug delivery systems. The consumer segment serves markets that include consumer retail, office retail, home improvement, building maintenance and other markets. Major products include the Scotch tape, Command adhesive and Filtrete filtration family lines of products. In 2015, the firm acquired Polypore's Separations Media business from Polypore International, Inc.; and sold ts Faab Fabricauto business, as well as assets of its North American Library Systems business.

The company offers employees medical and dental insurance, domestic partner benefits, tuition reimbursement, flexible spending accounts, disability coverage, a 401(k) and adoption assistance.

FINANCIAL DATA: *Note: Data for latest year may not have been available at press time.*

In U.S. $	2016	2015	2014	2013	2012	2011
Revenue		30,274,000,000	31,821,000,000	30,871,000,000	29,904,000,000	29,611,000,000
R&D Expense		1,763,000,000	1,770,000,000	1,715,000,000	1,634,000,000	1,570,000,000
Operating Income		6,946,000,000	7,135,000,000	6,666,000,000	6,483,000,000	6,178,000,000
Operating Margin %		22.94%	22.42%	21.59%	21.67%	20.86%
SGA Expense		6,182,000,000	6,469,000,000	6,384,000,000	6,102,000,000	6,170,000,000
Net Income		4,833,000,000	4,956,000,000	4,659,000,000	4,444,000,000	4,283,000,000
Operating Cash Flow		6,420,000,000	6,626,000,000	5,817,000,000	5,300,000,000	5,284,000,000
Capital Expenditure		1,461,000,000	1,493,000,000	1,665,000,000	1,484,000,000	1,379,000,000
EBITDA		8,407,000,000	8,576,000,000	8,078,000,000	7,810,000,000	7,453,000,000
Return on Assets %		15.10%	15.29%	13.81%	13.57%	13.86%
Return on Equity %		38.94%	32.38%	26.56%	26.93%	27.55%
Debt to Equity		0.75	0.51	0.25	0.28	0.29

CONTACT INFORMATION:

Phone: 651 733-1110   Fax: 651 733-9973
Toll-Free: 800-364-3577
Address: 3M Center, St. Paul, MN 55144 United States

STOCK TICKER/OTHER:

Stock Ticker: MMM
Employees: 89,446
Parent Company:

Exchange: NYS
Fiscal Year Ends: 12/31

SALARIES/BONUSES:

Top Exec. Salary:
$1,448,153
Second Exec. Salary:
$653,149

Bonus: $

Bonus: $

OTHER THOUGHTS:

Estimated Female Officers or Directors: 7

Hot Spot for Advancement for Women/Minorities: Y

Sales, profits and employees may be estimates. Financial information, benefits and other data can change quickly and may vary from those stated here.

A.O. Smith Corporation

www.aosmith.com

NAIC Code: 335228

TYPES OF BUSINESS:

Water Heaters
Water Boilers
Solar Water Heating Systems

BRANDS/DIVISIONS/AFFILIATES:

AO Smith
American
GSW
Reliance
State
Takagi
U.S. Craftmaster
Lochinvar

CONTACTS: Note: Officers with more than one job title may be intentionally listed here more than once.

William Vallett, CEO, Subsidiary
Ajita Rajendra, CEO
John Kita, CFO
Daniel Kempken, Chief Accounting Officer
Robert Heideman, Chief Technology Officer
James Stern, Executive VP
Kevin Wheeler, General Manager, Geographical
Wei Ding, General Manager, Subsidiary
Wilfridus Brouwer, President, Subsidiary
Paul Dana, President, Subsidiary
Mark Petrarca, Senior VP, Divisional
Charles Lauber, Senior VP, Divisional
Randall Bednar, Senior VP

GROWTH PLANS/SPECIAL FEATURES:

A. O. Smith Corporation is a manufacturer of water heating equipment serving a diverse mix of residential, commercial and industrial end markets. The firm markets its products under the brand name AO Smith, American, GSW, John Wood, Reliance, State, Takagi, U.S. Craftmaster and Lochinvar. The company operates in two segments: North America and rest of the world. The North America segment markets products mainly in the U.S. In addition, it manufactures and markets specialty commercial condensing and non-condensing boilers and water system tanks. The rest of the world segment caters to China, Europe and India. Moreover, it manufactures and markets water treatment products, primarily for Asia. Both segments manufacture and market comprehensive lines of residential gas, gas tankless and electric water heaters. The firm's residential and commercial water heaters come in sizes ranging from two and a half-gallon (point-of-use) models to 12,500 gallon products with varying efficiency ranges. It offers electric, natural gas and liquid propane models as well as solar tank units. Typical applications include restaurants, hotels and motels, laundries, car washes and small businesses. The company's commercial and residential boilers come in capacities ranging from 40,000 British Thermal Units (BTUs) to 5.0 million BTUs. The boilers are used in hospitals, schools, hotels and other large commercial buildings. Other products include expansion tanks, commercial solar water heating systems, swimming pool and spa heaters and related products and parts.

FINANCIAL DATA: Note: Data for latest year may not have been available at press time.

In U.S. $	2016	2015	2014	2013	2012	2011
Revenue		2,536,500,000	2,356,000,000	2,153,800,000	1,939,300,000	1,710,500,000
R&D Expense						
Operating Income		399,100,000	287,200,000	249,300,000	205,400,000	151,000,000
Operating Margin %		15.73%	12.19%	11.57%	10.59%	8.82%
SGA Expense		610,700,000	572,100,000	524,500,000	450,500,000	372,800,000
Net Income		282,900,000	207,800,000	169,700,000	158,700,000	305,700,000
Operating Cash Flow		344,400,000	263,900,000	279,600,000	143,800,000	58,700,000
Capital Expenditure		72,700,000	86,100,000	97,700,000	69,900,000	53,500,000
EBITDA		472,900,000	352,200,000	301,800,000	297,600,000	217,800,000
Return on Assets %		10.96%	8.46%	7.28%	6.87%	13.70%
Return on Equity %		20.03%	15.33%	13.45%	13.92%	31.07%
Debt to Equity		0.16	0.15	0.13	0.18	0.40

CONTACT INFORMATION:

Phone: 414 359-4000   Fax:
Toll-Free:
Address: 11270 W. Park Place, Milwaukee, WI 53224-9508 United States

STOCK TICKER/OTHER:

Stock Ticker: AOS   Exchange: NYS
Employees: 12,400   Fiscal Year Ends: 12/31
Parent Company:

SALARIES/BONUSES:

Top Exec. Salary: $980,000   Bonus: $
Second Exec. Salary: $522,000   Bonus: $

OTHER THOUGHTS:

Estimated Female Officers or Directors:
Hot Spot for Advancement for Women/Minorities:

Sales, profits and employees may be estimates. Financial information, benefits and other data can change quickly and may vary from those stated here.

Abbott Laboratories

www.abbott.com

NAIC Code: 325412

TYPES OF BUSINESS:

Nutritional Products Manufacturing
Immunoassays
Diagnostics
Consumer Health Products
Medical & Surgical Devices
Generic Pharmaceutical Products
LASIK Devices

BRANDS/DIVISIONS/AFFILIATES:

Multi-Link Vision
ARCHITECT
i-STAT
Similac
Ensure
Pediasure
Zone Perfect

CONTACTS: Note: Officers with more than one job title may be intentionally listed here more than once.

Miles White, CEO
Deepak Nath, Senior VP, Divisional
Robert Funck, Chief Accounting Officer
Richard Ashley, Executive VP
Robert Ford, Executive VP, Divisional
Thomas Freyman, Executive VP, Divisional
Stephen Fussell, Executive VP, Divisional
John Capek, Executive VP, Divisional
Michael Warmuth, Executive VP, Divisional
Heather Mason, Executive VP, Divisional
Brian Blaser, Executive VP, Divisional
Hubert Allen, Executive VP
Jean-Yves Pavee-Callu, Senior VP, Divisional
Roger Bird, Senior VP, Divisional
Andrew Lane, Senior VP, Divisional
Jared Watkin, Senior VP, Divisional
Thomas Frinzi, Senior VP, Divisional

GROWTH PLANS/SPECIAL FEATURES:

Abbott Laboratories develops, manufactures and sells health care products and technologies ranging from pharmaceuticals to medical devices marketed in over 150 countries. It operates in four segments: established pharmaceutical, diagnostics, nutrition and medical devices. Established pharmaceuticals deals with gastroenterology issues, women's health, cardiovascular and metabolic illnesses, pain and the central nervous system, respiratory health and immunization. The Diagnostics segment develops systems and tests to diagnose infectious diseases, cancer, diabetes and genetic conditions, including the ARCHITECT chemistry system and i-STAT hematology systems, which are marketed to hospitals, laboratories, physicians' offices and plasma protein therapeutic companies. The Nutritional segment offers consumer products such as Similac, Ensure, PediaSure and Zone Perfect as well as feeding devices in health care institutions. Medical devices consists of coronary, endovascular and vessel closure devices used in the treatment of vascular disease. Products include the Multi-Link Vision coronary metallic stents, TREK and Voyager balloon dilatation systems and StarClose vessel closure devices. Other products include the FreeStyle line of diabetes products as well as medical devices and products for eye care. In February 2015, Abbott sold its developed markets branded generics pharmaceuticals business to Mylan in exchange for an equity ownership of a newly formed entity that will combine Mylan's existing business and Abbott's developed markets pharmaceuticals business. In February 2016, the firm agreed to acquire Alere, a leading point of care diagnostics company. The following April, Abbott acquired St. Jude Medical Inc. for $25 billion

The firm offers employees medical, dental and vision insurance; flexible spending accounts; adoption assistance; an employee assistance program; legal services; tuition assistance; and life insurance.

FINANCIAL DATA: Note: Data for latest year may not have been available at press time.

In U.S. $	2016	2015	2014	2013	2012	2011
Revenue		20,405,000,000	20,247,000,000	21,848,000,000	39,873,910,000	38,851,260,000
R&D Expense		1,405,000,000	1,345,000,000	1,452,000,000	4,322,182,000	4,129,414,000
Operating Income		2,867,000,000	2,599,000,000	2,629,000,000	8,084,515,000	5,751,948,000
Operating Margin %		14.05%	12.83%	12.03%	20.27%	14.80%
SGA Expense		6,785,000,000	6,530,000,000	6,936,000,000	12,059,500,000	12,756,820,000
Net Income		4,423,000,000	2,284,000,000	2,576,000,000	5,962,920,000	4,728,449,000
Operating Cash Flow		2,966,000,000	3,675,000,000	3,324,000,000	9,314,401,000	8,970,077,000
Capital Expenditure		1,110,000,000	1,077,000,000	1,145,000,000	1,795,289,000	1,491,500,000
EBITDA		4,818,000,000	4,216,000,000	4,397,000,000	9,638,224,000	8,772,677,000
Return on Assets %		10.71%	5.42%	4.67%	9.35%	7.89%
Return on Equity %		20.69%	9.78%	9.92%	23.31%	20.19%
Debt to Equity		0.27	0.15	0.13	0.67	0.49

CONTACT INFORMATION:

Phone: 847 937-6100 Fax: 847 937-1511
Toll-Free:
Address: 100 Abbott Park Rd., Abbott Park, IL 60064-6400 United States

STOCK TICKER/OTHER:

Stock Ticker: ABT Exchange: NYS
Employees: 77,000 Fiscal Year Ends: 12/31
Parent Company:

SALARIES/BONUSES:

Top Exec. Salary: $1,900,000 Bonus: $

Second Exec. Salary: $975,100 Bonus: $

OTHER THOUGHTS:

Estimated Female Officers or Directors: 5

Hot Spot for Advancement for Women/Minorities: Y

ABM Industries Inc

www.abm.com

NAIC Code: 561720

TYPES OF BUSINESS:

Janitorial Services
Parking Facilities
Maintenance Personnel
Security Services
Lighting Services
Billing & Accounting Services
Supplier Management
Energy Efficiency Technology

BRANDS/DIVISIONS/AFFILIATES:

ABM Janitorial Services
Westway Services Holdings Ltd

CONTACTS: Note: Officers with more than one job title may be intentionally listed here more than once.

Diego Scaglione, CFO
Maryellen Herringer, Chairman of the Board
Dean Chin, Chief Accounting Officer
James Mcclure, COO
Scott Salmirs, Director
Sarah McConnell, Executive VP
David Farwell, Senior VP, Divisional
Angelique Carbo, Senior VP, Divisional

GROWTH PLANS/SPECIAL FEATURES:

ABM Industries, Inc. is one of the country's largest facility services providers. ABM provides janitorial, parking, engineering, security and mechanical services to commercial, industrial, institutional and retail facilities throughout the U.S. and 20 additional countries. The company operates through a number of subsidiaries, which are grouped into four segments: janitorial, parking, facility services and building & energy solutions. Janitorial services, operated through ABM Janitorial Services, include floor cleaning and finishing, window washing, furniture polishing and carpet cleaning and dusting. Parking provides parking and transportation services for clients such as commercial office buildings, airports and other transportation centers, education institutions, health facilities, hotels, municipalities, retail centers and stadiums. Facility services provides onsite mechanical engineering and technical services and solutions for facilities and infrastructure systems for a variety of client facilities, including transportation centers, commercial infrastructure, corporate office buildings, data centers, educational institutions, high technology manufacturing facilities, museums, resorts, and shopping centers. Building & energy solutions provides heating, ventilation, air-conditioning, electrical, lighting and other general maintenance and repair services. In 2015, the firm sold its security business to Universal Protection Service, a division of Universal Services of America; and acquired Westway Services Holdings Ltd.

The firm offers employees dental, medical, vision, disability, life, AD&D and business travel accident insurance; flexible spending accounts; workers compensation insurance; 401(k); employee stock plans; employee assistance; tuition reimbursement; and credit union membership.

FINANCIAL DATA: Note: Data for latest year may not have been available at press time.

In U.S. $	2016	2015	2014	2013	2012	2011
Revenue		4,897,800,000	5,032,800,000	4,809,281,000	4,300,265,000	4,246,842,000
R&D Expense						
Operating Income		73,600,000	128,600,000	119,025,000	96,566,000	117,568,000
Operating Margin %		1.50%	2.55%	2.47%	2.24%	2.76%
SGA Expense		390,000,000	363,900,000	348,274,000	327,855,000	324,762,000
Net Income		76,300,000	75,600,000	72,900,000	62,582,000	68,504,000
Operating Cash Flow		145,300,000	120,700,000	135,313,000	150,612,000	159,990,000
Capital Expenditure		26,500,000	37,400,000	32,593,000	28,052,000	22,124,000
EBITDA		139,600,000	192,400,000	185,734,000	153,545,000	174,141,000
Return on Assets %		3.51%	3.50%	3.65%	3.33%	3.99%
Return on Equity %		7.72%	8.01%	8.24%	7.60%	8.92%
Debt to Equity		0.15	0.33	0.34	0.25	0.37

CONTACT INFORMATION:

Phone: 212 297-0200   Fax: 212 297-0375
Toll-Free:
Address: 551 5th Ave., Ste. 300, New York, NY 10176 United States

STOCK TICKER/OTHER:

Stock Ticker: ABM   Exchange: NYS
Employees: 118,000   Fiscal Year Ends: 10/31
Parent Company:

SALARIES/BONUSES:

Top Exec. Salary: $688,931   Bonus: $
Second Exec. Salary: Bonus: $
$688,931

OTHER THOUGHTS:

Estimated Female Officers or Directors: 4
Hot Spot for Advancement for Women/Minorities: Y

Academy Sports & Outdoors Ltd

www.academy.com

NAIC Code: 451110

TYPES OF BUSINESS:

Sporting Goods Stores
Apparel
Footwear
Outdoor Sports Gear
Hunting Licenses

BRANDS/DIVISIONS/AFFILIATES:

KKR & Co LP (Kohlberg Kravis Roberts & Co)

CONTACTS: Note: Officers with more than one job title may be intentionally listed here more than once.

James K. Symancyk, CEO
Rodney Faldyn, Pres.
Beth Menuer, Exec. VP-Footwear
Robert Frennea, Exec. VP-Apparel
Kevin Chapman, Exec. VP-Stores

GROWTH PLANS/SPECIAL FEATURES:

Academy Sports & Outdoors, Ltd., owned by KKR & Co LP, is one of the largest sporting goods retailers in the U.S. The company operates over 209 stores throughout 15 states including Alabama, Florida, Georgia, Arkansas, Louisiana, Indiana, Mississippi, Kansas, Missouri, Kentucky, Oklahoma, North Carolina, South Carolina, Tennessee and Texas. Its retail operations also include a full e-commerce retail store. Academy Sports offers a broad selection of sporting equipment, apparel and footwear. The stores, which range in size from 50,000 to 100,000 square feet, are laid out in a racetrack format with soft goods on the inside, including branded and private label athletic and casual apparel, and hard goods, such as camping, hunting, fishing, marine, footwear and fitness and sporting goods, on the outside. The company distributes merchandise to its stores from its distribution centers located in Katy, Texas and Twiggs County, Georgia. The center utilizes radio frequency identification devices (RFID), automated inventory and replenishment systems and a state-of-the-art warehouse management system to smoothly operate its large processing and inventory space. In 2014, the firm announced that it will begin construction on another distribution center in Cookeville, Tennessee, expected to be operational in early 2016.

The company offers its employees a 401(k) plan; medical, dental and vision insurance; life insurance; short- and long-term disability benefits; tuition reimbursement; merchandise discounts; bereavement leave; continuing education benefits; and business travel accident insurance.

FINANCIAL DATA: Note: Data for latest year may not have been available at press time.

In U.S. $	2016	2015	2014	2013	2012	2011
Revenue		4,600,000,000	4,000,000,000	3,700,000,000	3,254,000,000	2,700,000,000
R&D Expense						
Operating Income						
Operating Margin %						
SGA Expense						
Net Income						
Operating Cash Flow						
Capital Expenditure						
EBITDA						
Return on Assets %						
Return on Equity %						
Debt to Equity						

CONTACT INFORMATION:

Phone: 281-646-5200   Fax: 281-646-5000
Toll-Free: 888-922-2336
Address: 1800 N. Mason Rd., Katy, TX 77449 United States

STOCK TICKER/OTHER:

Stock Ticker: Private   Exchange:
Employees: 23,000   Fiscal Year Ends: 02/28
Parent Company: KKR & Co LP (Kohlberg Kravis Roberts & Co)

SALARIES/BONUSES:

Top Exec. Salary: $ Bonus: $
Second Exec. Salary: $ Bonus: $

OTHER THOUGHTS:

Estimated Female Officers or Directors: 1
Hot Spot for Advancement for Women/Minorities:

Accenture LLP

NAIC Code: 541512

www.accenture.com/us-en

TYPES OF BUSINESS:

IT Consulting
Computer Operations Outsourcing
Supply Chain Technologies
Technology Research
Software Development
Human Resources Consulting
Management Consulting
Research and Development

BRANDS/DIVISIONS/AFFILIATES:

Accenture plc

CONTACTS: Note: Officers with more than one job title may be intentionally listed here more than once.

Pierre Nanterme, CEO
Jo Deblaere, COO
David P. Rowland, CFO
Roxanne Taylor, CMO
Ellyn J. Shook, Human Resources
Paul Daugherty, Chief Technology Officer

GROWTH PLANS/SPECIAL FEATURES:

Accenture LLP, a subsidiary of Accenture plc, is a leading provider of management consulting, technology and outsourcing services, with operations in over 30 U.S. Cities. The firm delivers services through five operating groups: communications, media & technology; financial services; health & public service; products; and resources. Accenture's communications, media & technology group offers technology consulting and systems integration to the electronics, communications and media industries. Its financial services group provides consulting and outsourcing strategies to the insurance, capital markets and banking industries. The firm's health & public service group works with local, state, provincial and national governments to deliver better social, economic and health outcomes to the people they serve. Its products group serves the automotive, life sciences, consumer goods, industrial equipment, retail and transportation and travel services industries. The company's resources group works with the chemicals, energy, natural resources and utilities industries. Additionally, Accenture offers management consulting services in finance & enterprise performance, operations, technology, IT security consulting/outsourcing, cloud computing, business, risk management, sales & growth, customer services, strategy, sustainability and talent & organization.

Accenture offers its employees medical, dental, long-term disability, life and AD&D coverage; nurselines; legal coverage; a profit sharing plan; a 401(k) savings plan; and adoption assistance.

FINANCIAL DATA: Note: Data for latest year may not have been available at press time.

In U.S. $	2016	2015	2014	2013	2012	2011
Revenue		14,209,387,000	12,796,847,000	12,035,847,000	10,200,000,000	9,500,000,000
R&D Expense						
Operating Income						
Operating Margin %						
SGA Expense						
Net Income						
Operating Cash Flow						
Capital Expenditure						
EBITDA						
Return on Assets %						
Return on Equity %						
Debt to Equity						

CONTACT INFORMATION:

Phone: 312-693-0161   Fax: 312-693-0507
Toll-Free: 877-889-9009
Address: 161 North Clark Street, Chicago, IL 60601 United States

STOCK TICKER/OTHER:

Stock Ticker: Subsidiary   Exchange:
Employees: 160,000   Fiscal Year Ends: 08/31
Parent Company: Accenture plc

SALARIES/BONUSES:

Top Exec. Salary: $ Bonus: $
Second Exec. Salary: $ Bonus: $

OTHER THOUGHTS:

Estimated Female Officers or Directors:
Hot Spot for Advancement for Women/Minorities: Y

Accor North America

NAIC Code: 721110

www.accorhotels.com/gb/usa/index.shtml

TYPES OF BUSINESS:

Hotels

BRANDS/DIVISIONS/AFFILIATES:

Accor SA
Sofitel
Novotel
Pullman

CONTACTS: Note: Officers with more than one job title may be intentionally listed here more than once.

Roland de Bonadona, CEO-Americas
Didier Bosc, CFO
Jeff Winslow, CIO
Didier Bosc, Chief Admin. Officer
Alan Rabinowitz, Exec. VP
Jim Amorosia, Pres.
Jeff Winslow, Chief Investment Officer
Robert Moore, Sr. VP-Technical Service

GROWTH PLANS/SPECIAL FEATURES:

Accor North America, a subsidiary of French hotel and human resources conglomerate Accor SA, operates 16 hotels with approximately 4,715 rooms across the U.S. and Canada. The firm's North American hotel chains include seven Sofitel hotels, a French luxury brand that incorporates local culture into its decor. The brand offers visitors first-rate accommodations with upscale restaurants, complete business facilities, fitness centers, fine art and antiques. The Novotel chain is another more upscale offering, which consists of a relaxed modern decor that makes it accessible to both business and leisure travelers. Novotel properties offer rooms with sitting/working areas, mid-scale restaurants and pools and golf course privileges, with eight locations in the U.S. and Canada. In addition, the firm operates one Pullman hotel, which offers upscale, executive lodging for business and leisure stays. Accor incorporates a green policy into all of its chains that consists of water-saving shower heads and faucet aerators, Energy Star program participation, power-reducing heating and cooling systems, recycled paper and soy ink for its directories, energy efficient fluorescent lighting and the use of green Ecolab products for laundry and cleaning.

FINANCIAL DATA: Note: Data for latest year may not have been available at press time.

In U.S. $	2016	2015	2014	2013	2012	2011
Revenue		635,410,802	525,348,522	302,399,520	308,574,820	304,171,460
R&D Expense						
Operating Income						
Operating Margin %						
SGA Expense						
Net Income		255,037,440	269,380,549	153,772,184		
Operating Cash Flow						
Capital Expenditure						
EBITDA						
Return on Assets %						
Return on Equity %						
Debt to Equity						

CONTACT INFORMATION:

Phone: 972-360-9000   Fax: 972-716-6590
Toll-Free: 800-557-3435
Address: 4001 International Pkwy., Carrollton, TX 75007 United States

STOCK TICKER/OTHER:

Stock Ticker: Subsidiary   Exchange:
Employees: 21,563   Fiscal Year Ends: 12/31
Parent Company: Accor SA

SALARIES/BONUSES:

Top Exec. Salary: $ Bonus: $
Second Exec. Salary: $ Bonus: $

OTHER THOUGHTS:

Estimated Female Officers or Directors: 1
Hot Spot for Advancement for Women/Minorities:

Sales, profits and employees may be estimates. Financial information, benefits and other data can change quickly and may vary from those stated here.

Acosta Inc

NAIC Code: 541800

www.acosta.com

TYPES OF BUSINESS:

Marketing Services
Consumer Packaged Goods Sales Research
Retail Sales Support
Integrated Marketing Solutions
Outsourcing
Retail Services

BRANDS/DIVISIONS/AFFILIATES:

Acosta Sales & Marketing
Acosta Marketing Group
LT Acosta Company Inc
Contend
IGNITE Sales Management
Baldwin & Mattson Inc
Neher Sales & Marketing
PacNorth Group (The)

CONTACTS: Note: Officers with more than one job title may be intentionally listed here more than once.

Robert Hill, CEO
Tom Corley, COO
Robert E. Hill, Jr., Pres.
Tim Bensley, CFO
Kevin George, CMO
Margie Arion, Chief Human Resources Officer
Reece Alford, General Counsel
Brian King, Chief Strategy Officer
Vilma Consuegra, VP-Corp. Comm.
Woody Norris, Pres., Client Dev.
Jack Parker, Pres., Grocery Channel Sales
Brian Baldwin, Pres., Strategic Channel Sales
Aidan Tracey, Pres., Acosta Mktg. Group

GROWTH PLANS/SPECIAL FEATURES:

Acosta, Inc., which does business as Acosta Sales & Marketing, is an outsourced sales and marketing agency. Founded in 1927 as single-location food broker L.T. Acosta Company, Inc., the firm serves consumer packaged goods companies and retail groups through offices across the U.S. and Canada. Acosta's client roster includes over 60% of the No. 1 and No. 2 grocery store brands. On behalf of its consumer packaged goods clients, the company offers direct sales of new and existing items to retailers such as Safeway and Kroger. As part of this process, Acosta provides services such as the negotiation of volume and price levels. For retail clients, the firm provides in-store stocking services. It seeks to ensure optimal shelf space location and exposure of its customer's brands in order to maximize the sale of their products. Acosta Marketing Group offers enhanced integrated marketing services including buyer trend reports and customer analytics. In 2015, the firm acquired United Sales Concepts, Escalate, Etherton Sales & Merchandising and LAUNCH! In 2016, it acquired Contend, a data-driven premium content company in Los Angeles; IGNITE Sales Management, which helps manufacturers build and grow profitable brands; Baldwin & Mattson, Inc. and Neher Sales & Marketing, which together will provide personalized service to manufacturers and retailers in the Midwest; and The PacNorth Group, a leading non-food manufacturer agency, which will expand Acosta's non-food coverage in the Northwest region (Washington, Oregon, Idaho and Alaska).

Acosta offers its employees medical, vision and dental insurance; a prescription drug plan; life, disability and AD&D insurance; a 401(k) retirement plan; tuition assistance; gym membership; and cell phone, new car and new computer discounts.

FINANCIAL DATA: Note: Data for latest year may not have been available at press time.

In U.S. $	2016	2015	2014	2013	2012	2011
Revenue		3,300,000,000	3,300,000,000	3,214,322,800	3,032,380,000	2,834,000,000
R&D Expense						
Operating Income						
Operating Margin %						
SGA Expense						
Net Income						
Operating Cash Flow						
Capital Expenditure						
EBITDA						
Return on Assets %						
Return on Equity %						
Debt to Equity						

CONTACT INFORMATION:

Phone: 904-281-9800   Fax: 904-281-9966
Toll-Free:
Address: 6600 Corporate Center Pkwy., Jacksonville, FL 32216 United States

STOCK TICKER/OTHER:

Stock Ticker: Private   Exchange:
Employees: 35,000   Fiscal Year Ends: 07/31
Parent Company: Carlyle Group (The)

SALARIES/BONUSES:

Top Exec. Salary: $ Bonus: $
Second Exec. Salary: $ Bonus: $

OTHER THOUGHTS:

Estimated Female Officers or Directors: 2
Hot Spot for Advancement for Women/Minorities: Y

Activision Blizzard Inc

www.activisionblizzard.com

NAIC Code: 0

TYPES OF BUSINESS:
Computer Software, Electronic Games, Apps & Entertainment
Logistics Services
Apps

BRANDS/DIVISIONS/AFFILIATES:
Activision Publishing Inc
Blizzard Entertainment Inc
Activision Blizzard Distribution
World of Warcraft
Centresoft
Battle.net

CONTACTS: *Note: Officers with more than one job title may be intentionally listed here more than once.*
Eric Hirshberg, CEO, Subsidiary
Riccardo Zacconi, CEO, Subsidiary
Michael Morhaime, CEO, Subsidiary
Robert Kotick, CEO
Dennis Durkin, CFO
Brian Kelly, Chairman of the Board
Wereb Stephen, Chief Accounting Officer
Thomas Tippl, COO
Christopher Walther, Other Executive Officer
Jeffrey Brown, Other Executive Officer

GROWTH PLANS/SPECIAL FEATURES:
Activision Blizzard, Inc. is a leading international publisher and developer of subscription-based massively multiplayer online role-playing games (MMORPGs) and other PC-based, console, handheld and mobile games. The company was formed through the merger of Vivendi Games, owner of Blizzard Entertainment, Inc., and Activision, a leading publisher of interactive entertainment. The company operates in three segments: Activision Publishing, Inc.; Blizzard Entertainment, Inc.; and Activision Blizzard Distribution. Activision Publishing, Inc. publishes interactive entertainment software products and downloadable content. Activision currently offers games that operate on the Sony Computer Entertainment Inc. PlayStation 3, Nintendo Co. Ltd., Wii, Nintendo Wii U and Microsoft Corporation Xbox 360 console systems; the Nintendo Dual Screen and Nintendo 3DS handheld game systems; the PC; and other handheld and mobile devices. Blizzard Entertainment, Inc. publishes real-time strategy, role-playing PC games and online subscription-based games in the massively multiplayer online role-playing game (MMORPG) category. It also internally develops and published PC-based computer games and maintains a proprietary online-game related service, Battle.net. Activision Blizzard Distribution distributes interactive entertainment software and hardware products in Europe through subsidiaries Centresoft and NBG. They provide services to the company's publishing operations and to various third-party publishers, including Sony, Nintendo and Microsoft. Major products of the company include Call of Duty (Activision) and World of Warcraft (Blizzard). In 2015, the firm reached an agreement to acquire King Digital Entertainment for $5.9 billion.

FINANCIAL DATA: *Note: Data for latest year may not have been available at press time.*

In U.S. $	2016	2015	2014	2013	2012	2011
Revenue		4,664,000,000	4,408,000,000	4,583,000,000	4,856,000,000	4,755,000,000
R&D Expense		646,000,000	571,000,000	584,000,000	604,000,000	646,000,000
Operating Income		1,319,000,000	1,183,000,000	1,372,000,000	1,451,000,000	1,328,000,000
Operating Margin %		28.28%	26.83%	29.93%	29.88%	27.92%
SGA Expense		1,114,000,000	1,129,000,000	1,096,000,000	1,139,000,000	1,001,000,000
Net Income		892,000,000	835,000,000	1,010,000,000	1,149,000,000	1,085,000,000
Operating Cash Flow		1,192,000,000	1,292,000,000	1,264,000,000	1,345,000,000	952,000,000
Capital Expenditure		111,000,000	107,000,000	74,000,000	73,000,000	72,000,000
EBITDA		1,813,000,000	1,529,000,000	1,692,000,000	1,579,000,000	1,770,000,000
Return on Assets %		5.87%	5.80%	7.16%	8.36%	8.13%
Return on Equity %		11.51%	12.05%	11.26%	10.53%	10.48%
Debt to Equity		0.50	0.59	0.70		

CONTACT INFORMATION:
Phone: 310 255-2000 Fax: 310 255-2100
Toll-Free:
Address: 3100 Ocean Park Blvd., Santa Monica, CA 90405 United States

STOCK TICKER/OTHER:
Stock Ticker: ATVI
Employees: 6,800
Parent Company:

Exchange: NAS
Fiscal Year Ends: 12/31

SALARIES/BONUSES:
Top Exec. Salary: $2,294,328   Bonus: $
Second Exec. Salary: $1,302,548   Bonus: $

OTHER THOUGHTS:
Estimated Female Officers or Directors:

Hot Spot for Advancement for Women/Minorities:

Sales, profits and employees may be estimates. Financial information, benefits and other data can change quickly and may vary from those stated here.

Adobe Systems Inc

www.adobe.com

NAIC Code: 0

TYPES OF BUSINESS:

Computer Software, Multimedia, Graphics & Publishing
Document Management Software
Photo Editing & Management Software
Graphic Design Software

BRANDS/DIVISIONS/AFFILIATES:

Adobe Acrobat
Adobe Dreamweaver
Adobe Creative Suite
Adobe Creative Cloud
Adobe PostScript
Adobe InDesign
Adobe Stock
Fotolia

CONTACTS: Note: Officers with more than one job title may be intentionally listed here more than once.

Shantanu Narayen, CEO
Ann Lewnes, Chief Marketing Officer
Abhay Parasnis, Chief Technology Officer
Charles Geschke, Co-Chairman
John Warnock, Co-Chairman
Matthew Thompson, Executive VP, Divisional
Mark Garrett, Executive VP
Bradley Rencher, Executive VP
Michael Dillon, General Counsel
Bryan Lamkin, General Manager, Divisional
Donna Morris, Senior VP, Divisional
Richard Rowley, Vice President

GROWTH PLANS/SPECIAL FEATURES:

Adobe Systems, Inc. is one of the largest software companies in the world. It offers a line of creative, business, web and mobile software and services used by creative professionals and developers for creating, managing, delivering, optimizing and engaging with content across multiple operating systems, devices and media. The company operates in three segments: digital media, digital marketing and print & publishing. The digital media division focuses on professional imaging and video products, including the widely used Adobe Creative Suite and Adobe Creative Cloud (CC). Products in this segment also include Adobe Dreamweaver and Adobe InDesign. Digital media's document services business is built around the Adobe Acrobat family of products, the Adobe Reader and a set of integrated cloud-based document services. Adobe PDF documents can be viewed, printed or filled out using the free Adobe Reader. The digital marketing segment consists of the firm's online marketing services including the firm's Adobe Marketing Cloud. The print & publishing segment addresses market opportunities ranging from technical and business publishing to legacy type printing. This segment's Adobe PostScript and Adobe PDF printing technologies provide advanced functionality. Recently-launched Adobe Stock, is the industry's first stock content service to be integrated directly into the content creation process and the tools creatives use every day. It is a curated collection of 40 million quality images deeply integrated into the latest releases of Photoshop CC, InDesign CC, Illustrator CC, Premier Pro CC and After Effects CC. Adobe Stock is available through Adobe Creative Cloud which radically simplifies buying and using stock content including photos, illustrations and graphics. In 2015, the firm acquired privately-held Fotolia, a royalty-free photos, images, graphics and HD video marketplace.

The firm offers employees life, disability, medical, dental, vision and prescription drug insurance; adoption assistance; employee assistance program; product discounts; and a 401(k).

FINANCIAL DATA: Note: Data for latest year may not have been available at press time.

In U.S. $	2016	2015	2014	2013	2012	2011
Revenue		4,795,511,000	4,147,065,000	4,055,240,000	4,403,677,000	4,216,258,000
R&D Expense		862,730,000	844,353,000	826,631,000	742,823,000	738,053,000
Operating Income		903,095,000	412,685,000	422,723,000	1,180,191,000	1,099,299,000
Operating Margin %		18.83%	9.95%	10.42%	26.80%	26.07%
SGA Expense		2,215,161,000	2,195,640,000	2,140,578,000	1,951,141,000	1,800,427,000
Net Income		629,551,000	268,395,000	289,985,000	832,775,000	832,847,000
Operating Cash Flow		1,469,502,000	1,287,482,000	1,151,686,000	1,499,580,000	1,543,314,000
Capital Expenditure		184,936,000	148,332,000	188,358,000	271,076,000	210,294,000
EBITDA		1,277,438,000	734,698,000	744,876,000	1,486,047,000	1,372,387,000
Return on Assets %		5.59%	2.53%	2.84%	8.78%	9.72%
Return on Equity %		9.13%	3.97%	4.33%	13.37%	15.17%
Debt to Equity		0.27	0.13	0.22	0.22	0.26

CONTACT INFORMATION:

Phone: 408 536-6000   Fax: 408 536-6799
Toll-Free: 800-833-6687
Address: 345 Park Ave., San Jose, CA 95110 United States

STOCK TICKER/OTHER:

Stock Ticker: ADBE   Exchange: NAS
Employees: 13,893   Fiscal Year Ends: 11/30
Parent Company:

SALARIES/BONUSES:

Top Exec. Salary: $995,404   Bonus: $
Second Exec. Salary: Bonus: $
$647,013

OTHER THOUGHTS:

Estimated Female Officers or Directors: 5
Hot Spot for Advancement for Women/Minorities: Y

Advance Auto Parts Inc

www.advanceautoparts.com

NAIC Code: 441310

TYPES OF BUSINESS:
Auto Parts & Accessories Stores
Online Sales

BRANDS/DIVISIONS/AFFILIATES:
Advance Auto Parts
Carquest
Worldpac
Autopart International

CONTACTS: *Note: Officers with more than one job title may be intentionally listed here more than once.*
Thomas Greco, CEO
John Brouillard, Chairman of the Board
Jill Livesay, Chief Accounting Officer
Charles Tyson, Executive VP, Divisional
Tammy Finley, Executive VP, Divisional
George Sherman, President
William Carter, Senior VP, Divisional

GROWTH PLANS/SPECIAL FEATURES:

Advance Auto Parts, Inc. is a leading specialty retailer of automotive aftermarket parts, accessories, batteries and maintenance items. The firm primarily operates in the U.S. and serves both do-it-yourself (DIY) and commercial customers. It operates in a single segment comprised of the company's store and branch operations. Advance Auto serves its customers through a variety of channels ranging from brick-and-mortar store locations to self-service eCommerce sites. The company operates under the following store names: Advance Auto Parts, consisting of 4,114 stores that average 7,500 square feet in size; Carquest, consisting of 873 stores that average 7,400 square feet in size; Worldpac, consisting of 122 stores that average 27,000 square feet in size; and Autopart International, consisting of 184 stores that offer approximately 39,000 SKUs. Primary categories of products offered by the company include: parts - alternators, batteries, belts, hoses, brakes, brake pads, chassis parts, climate control parts, clutches, drive shafts, engines, engine parts, ignition parts, lighting, radiators, starters, spark plugs, wires, steering & alignment parts, transmissions, water pumps and windshield wiper blades; accessories â€" air fresheners, auto paint, anti-theft devices, emergency road kits, floor mats, ice scrapers, mirrors, seat & steering wheel covers and vent shades; and chemicals â€" antifreeze, brake & power steering fluids, car wash fluids, car waxes, Freon, fuel additives and windshield washer fluid; and oil â€" transmission fluid and other automotive petroleum products. The company's 5,293 stores are primarily located in the U.S., with 158 located throughout Canada, 28 throughout Puerto Rico and one in the Virgin Islands.

The firm offers employees medical, dental and vision coverage; a 401(k); stock purchase plans; life and AD&D insurance; short- and long-term disability; flexible spending accounts; employee discounts; an employee assistance program; and dependent scholarships.

FINANCIAL DATA: *Note: Data for latest year may not have been available at press time.*

In U.S. $	2016	2015	2014	2013	2012	2011
Revenue		9,737,018,000	9,843,862,000	6,493,814,000	6,205,003,000	6,170,462,000
R&D Expense						
Operating Income		825,780,000	851,710,000	660,318,000	657,315,000	664,642,000
Operating Margin %		8.48%	8.65%	10.16%	10.59%	10.77%
SGA Expense		3,596,992,000	3,601,903,000	2,591,828,000	2,440,721,000	2,404,648,000
Net Income		473,398,000	493,825,000	391,758,000	387,670,000	394,682,000
Operating Cash Flow		689,642,000	708,991,000	545,250,000	685,281,000	828,849,000
Capital Expenditure		234,747,000	228,446,000	195,757,000	271,182,000	268,129,000
EBITDA		1,087,772,000	1,139,495,000	870,811,000	847,459,000	840,134,000
Return on Assets %		5.86%	7.30%	7.69%	9.37%	11.26%
Return on Equity %		21.13%	28.06%	28.73%	37.66%	41.82%
Debt to Equity		0.49	0.81	0.69	0.49	0.48

CONTACT INFORMATION:
Phone: 540-362-4911   Fax:
Toll-Free: 877-238-2623
Address: 5008 Airport Rd., Roanoke, VA 24012 United States

STOCK TICKER/OTHER:
Stock Ticker: AAP
Employees: 73,000
Parent Company:

Exchange: NYS
Fiscal Year Ends: 12/31

SALARIES/BONUSES:
Top Exec. Salary: Bonus: $
$1,034,138
Second Exec. Salary: Bonus: $
$744,715

OTHER THOUGHTS:
Estimated Female Officers or Directors: 3

Hot Spot for Advancement for Women/Minorities: Y

Adventist Health System

www.adventisthealthsystem.com

NAIC Code: 622110

TYPES OF BUSINESS:

General Medical and Surgical Hospitals
Nursing Homes
Home Health Care Services

BRANDS/DIVISIONS/AFFILIATES:

Florida Hospital
Seventh-day Adventist Church

CONTACTS: *Note: Officers with more than one job title may be intentionally listed here more than once.*

Donald L. Jernigan, CEO
Terry D. Shaw, COO
Donald L. Jernigan, Pres.
Terry D. Shaw, CFO
Herb Keller, Sr. VP- CIO
John McLendon, CIO-Information Services
Robert R. Henderschedt, Sr. VP-Admin.
Jeffrey S. Bromme, Chief Legal Officer
Sandra K. Johnson, VP-Bus. Dev., Risk Mgmt. & Compliance
Womack H. Rucker, Jr., VP-Corp. Rel.
Lewis Seifert, Sr. VP-Finance
Amanda Brady, Chief Acct. Officer
Amy L. Zbaraschuk, VP-Finance
T.L. Trimble, VP-Legal Svcs.
Ted Hamilton, VP-Medical Mission
Carlene Jamerson, Sr. VP
John Brownlow, Sr. VP-Managed Care
Celeste M. West, VP-Supply Chain Mgmt.

GROWTH PLANS/SPECIAL FEATURES:

Adventist Health System, sponsored by the Seventh-day Adventist Church, is one of the largest nonprofit Protestant health care organizations in the U.S. The firm operates 46 hospitals in several states, totaling over 8,300 beds, and multiple affiliated extended care centers within the long-term care division. The company serves more than 4.7 million patients annually. Adventist Health's flagship organization, Florida Hospital, is one of the largest health care providers in central Florida and a national leader in cardiac care. The hospital offers more than 2,500 beds across 16 campuses and provides care in the areas of cancer, neurosciences, orthopedics, kidney disease, limb replantation, sports medicine, rehabilitation and women's medicine programs. Adventist Health is a world leader in the use of tissue-sparing radiation based on proton beams, rather than traditional photon-based radiation. The firm is guided by its Christian mission, combining disease treatment, preventative medicine, education and advocacy of a wholesome lifestyle. The hospitals in the Adventist Health group provide a wide range of free or reduced-price services in their communities, including free medical vans and community clinics, free screening and education programs, debt forgiveness, abuse shelters and programs for the homeless and jobless. In August 2016, the firm opened a new NICU (neonatal intensive care unit) at its Florida Hospital Memorial Medical Center in Daytona Beach, which includes private family-centered rooms while sick and premature babies are receiving specialized medical treatment.

FINANCIAL DATA: *Note: Data for latest year may not have been available at press time.*

In U.S. $	2016	2015	2014	2013	2012	2011
Revenue		8,400,000,000	7,955,000,000	7,597,799,000	7,346,597,000	7,054,000,000
R&D Expense						
Operating Income						
Operating Margin %						
SGA Expense						
Net Income			600,000,000	578,818,000	504,958,000	474,200,000
Operating Cash Flow						
Capital Expenditure						
EBITDA						
Return on Assets %						
Return on Equity %						
Debt to Equity						

CONTACT INFORMATION:

Phone: 407-357-1000   Fax:
Toll-Free:
Address: 900 Hope Way, Altamonte Springs, FL 32714 United States

STOCK TICKER/OTHER:

Stock Ticker: Nonprofit   Exchange:
Employees: 80,000   Fiscal Year Ends: 12/31
Parent Company:

SALARIES/BONUSES:

Top Exec. Salary: $ Bonus: $
Second Exec. Salary: $ Bonus: $

OTHER THOUGHTS:

Estimated Female Officers or Directors: 6
Hot Spot for Advancement for Women/Minorities: Y

Advocate Health Care

www.advocatehealth.com

NAIC Code: 622110

TYPES OF BUSINESS:

General Medical and Surgical Hospitals
Clinics & Outpatient Centers
Home Health Care
Physician Groups

BRANDS/DIVISIONS/AFFILIATES:

Advocate BroMenn Medical Center
Advocate Christ Medical Center
Advocate Condell Medical Center
Advocate Good Samaritan Hospital
Advocate Good Shepherd Hospital
Advocate Illinois Masonic Medical Center
Advocate Lutheran General Hospital
Advocate Trinity Hospital

CONTACTS: Note: Officers with more than one job title may be intentionally listed here more than once.

Jim Skogsbergh, CEO
James H. Skogsbergh, Pres.
Kelly Jo Golson, CMO
Lee Sacks, Chief Medical Officer
Gail D. Hasbrouck, General Counsel
Scott Powder, Sr. VP-Strategic Planning & Growth
Dominic Nakis, Treasurer
Lee Sacks, CEO-Advocate Physician Partners
James R. Dan, Pres., Advocate Medical Group
Kathie Bender Schwich, Sr. VP-Mission & Spiritual Care

GROWTH PLANS/SPECIAL FEATURES:

Advocate Health Care is a nonprofit health care network providing acute care and outpatient services in Illinois. The company's operations have over 400 sites of care, with 12 acute care hospitals, including a children's hospital with two campuses. Advocate-branded hospitals include BroMenn Medical Center, Christ Medical Center, Condell Medical Center, Dreyer, Eureka Hospital, Good Samaritan Hospital, Good Shepherd Hospital, Illinois Masonic Medical Center, Lutheran General Hospital, Sherman Hospital, South Suburban Hospital and Trinity Hospital. Its children's hospital is Advocate Children's Hospital, with campuses located at Oak Lawn and Park Ridge. Advocate's outpatient facilities include sites run by its physician groups as well as Advocate Medical Campus Southwest, Advocate Occupational Health, Midwest Center for Day Surgery, Naperville Surgical Center and Tinley Woods Surgery Center. The company utilizes an Electronic Intensive Care Unit program (eICU) that links real-time monitoring from all adult ICU beds in Advocate's hospitals to a central command center staffed by physicians. Advocate sponsors community outreach programs such as school-based health centers; free and reduced cost clinics; nutritional services; and educational programs. The firm is also affiliated with several medical schools and serves as one of the leading trainers of primary care physicians in Illinois. In April 2015, the previously-announced plan for Advocate to merge with NorthShore University Health System was delayed by the Federal Trade Commission in order to take more time before approving what would create the largest not-for-profit health system in the state. In June 2016, the U.S. District Court lifted the FTC's request to block the merger, paving the way for the potential creation of Advocate NorthShore Health Partners.

Advocate's employees receive benefits including medical, dental and vision plans; education assistance; life and disability insurance; and adoption assistance.

FINANCIAL DATA: Note: Data for latest year may not have been available at press time.

In U.S. $	2016	2015	2014	2013	2012	2011
Revenue		5,329,562,000	5,231,393,000	4,940,000,000	4,599,133,000	4,440,464,000
R&D Expense						
Operating Income						
Operating Margin %						
SGA Expense						
Net Income		78,605,000	369,607,000	765,300,000	671,656,000	148,353,000
Operating Cash Flow						
Capital Expenditure						
EBITDA						
Return on Assets %						
Return on Equity %						
Debt to Equity						

CONTACT INFORMATION:

Phone: 630-572-9393   Fax:
Toll-Free:
Address: 3075 Highland Pkwy., Ste. 600, Downers Grove, IL 60515 United States

STOCK TICKER/OTHER:

Stock Ticker: Nonprofit   Exchange:
Employees: 35,000   Fiscal Year Ends: 12/31
Parent Company:

SALARIES/BONUSES:

Top Exec. Salary: $ Bonus: $
Second Exec. Salary: $ Bonus: $

OTHER THOUGHTS:

Estimated Female Officers or Directors: 3
Hot Spot for Advancement for Women/Minorities: Y

Aegion Corporation
NAIC Code: 237110

TYPES OF BUSINESS:
Construction, Heavy & Civil Engineering
Sewer & Pipe Rehabilitation Services

BRANDS/DIVISIONS/AFFILIATES:
Insituform
Brinderson
Underground Solutions Inc

CONTACTS: Note: Officers with more than one job title may be intentionally listed here more than once.
David Martin, CFO
Alfred Woods, Chairman of the Board
Michael White, Controller
Charles Gordon, Director
David Morris, Secretary
John Huhn, Senior VP, Divisional
Stephen Callahan, Senior VP, Divisional

GROWTH PLANS/SPECIAL FEATURES:
Aegion Corporation is a holding company that provides proprietary technologies and pipeline rehabilitation services to the sewer, water, energy and mining infrastructure markets through its various subsidiaries. Most of Aegion's installation operations are project-oriented contracts for municipal entities concerning the maintenance of municipal sewers, commercial pipes and water mains. The company and its subsidiaries operate principally in the U.S., the U.K., Portugal, Chile, Canada, Argentina, Brazil, the UAE, Mexico, Singapore, Saudi Arabia, Oman and Morocco. Aegion has three operating segments: infrastructure solutions, corrosion protection and energy services. Infrastructure solutions consists of the installation and construction of infrastructure, sewer and water rehabilitation activities, as well as the strengthening of pipelines, buildings, bridges, tunnels, industrial developments and waterfront structures. The firm's proprietary Insituform cured-in-place pipe process, a trenchless technology, allows pipelines to be repaired without digging and major service disruptions. The corrosion protection segment undertakes maintenance rehabilitation and corrosion protection services for oil & gas, industrial & mineral piping systems and structures & products for gas release and leak detection systems. Through its subsidiaries, the firm offers fully-integrated corrosion prevention services such as engineering, product & material sales, construction, installation, inspection, monitoring, maintenance and coatings. The energy services segment consists solely of Brinderson and its affiliated entities. Brinderson is based in Costa Mesa, California and provides maintenance, construction, engineering and turnaround activities for the upstream and downstream oil & gas markets. This segment primarily focuses on serving large oil & gas customers in California comprehensive solutions needed for downstream major refinery maintenance, repairs and retrofits. In early 2016, the firm acquired fusible PVC technology provider, Underground Solutions, Inc.; and sold its 51% stake in Bayou Perma-Pipe Canada Ltd.

Employees are offered medical, dental, vision and prescription coverage; retirement plans; 401(k); disability & life insurance; flexible spending; and tuition reimbursement.

FINANCIAL DATA: Note: Data for latest year may not have been available at press time.

In U.S. $	2016	2015	2014	2013	2012	2011
Revenue		1,333,570,000	1,331,421,000	1,091,420,000	1,027,963,000	938,585,000
R&D Expense						
Operating Income		19,946,000	-19,812,000	66,882,000	79,122,000	44,537,000
Operating Margin %		1.49%	-1.48%	6.12%	7.69%	4.74%
SGA Expense		209,477,000	234,105,000	178,483,000	170,882,000	151,764,000
Net Income		-8,067,000	-37,167,000	44,351,000	52,661,000	26,547,000
Operating Cash Flow		132,023,000	80,823,000	84,304,000	110,721,000	22,884,000
Capital Expenditure		30,957,000	34,822,000	28,117,000	46,446,000	22,684,000
EBITDA		61,050,000	21,280,000	112,500,000	116,288,000	82,878,000
Return on Assets %		- .63%	-2.79%	3.43%	4.49%	2.59%
Return on Equity %		-1.33%	-5.56%	6.29%	7.85%	4.25%
Debt to Equity		0.58	0.56	0.51	0.31	0.34

CONTACT INFORMATION:
Phone: 636 530-8000   Fax: 636 519-8010
Toll-Free: 800-234-2992
Address: 17988 Edison Ave., Chesterfield, MO 63005 United States

STOCK TICKER/OTHER:
Stock Ticker: AEGN   Exchange: NAS
Employees: 6,200   Fiscal Year Ends: 12/31
Parent Company:

SALARIES/BONUSES:
Top Exec. Salary: $650,000   Bonus: $
Second Exec. Salary: Bonus: $
$392,000

OTHER THOUGHTS:
Estimated Female Officers or Directors: 2
Hot Spot for Advancement for Women/Minorities: Y

Aetna Inc

NAIC Code: 524114

TYPES OF BUSINESS:

Insurance-Medical & Health
Long-Term Care Insurance
Group Insurance
Pension Products
Dental Insurance
Disability Insurance
Life Insurance

BRANDS/DIVISIONS/AFFILIATES:

CONTACTS: *Note: Officers with more than one job title may be intentionally listed here more than once.*

Mark Bertolini, CEO
Shawn Guertin, CFO
Harold Paz, Chief Medical Officer
Francis Soistman, Executive VP, Divisional
Gary Loveman, Executive VP, Divisional
Margaret McCarthy, Executive VP, Divisional
William Casazza, Executive VP
Karen Lynch, President
Karen Lynch, President
Judith Jones, Secretary
Sharon Virag, Vice President

GROWTH PLANS/SPECIAL FEATURES:

Aetna, Inc. is a health care benefits company, providing a broad range of traditional and consumer-directed health insurance products. These include medical, pharmacy, dental, behavioral health, group life & disability plans and Medicaid health care management capabilities to roughly 46.5 million people. Aetna operates in three segments: health care, group insurance and large case pensions. Health care products include medical insurance plans & products, pharmacy benefits management, dental, behavioral health and vision plans offered on both an insured basis and an employee-funded basis. This division's medical plans include point of service, health maintenance organization, preferred provider organization, health savings accounts and indemnity benefits. Group insurance products primarily comprises life insurance, including group term life insurance coverage and accidental death & dismemberment coverage; disability insurance, including short- and long-term disability; and long-term care insurance products, including the cost of care in private home settings, adult day care, assisted living or nursing facilities. The large case pensions segment primarily manages retirement products for tax-qualified pension plans. Customers include employer groups, individuals, college students, part-time/hourly workers, governmental units, labor groups and expatriates. In 2015, Aetna agreed to buy giant competitor, Humana, for $37 billion. Shareholders of both firms approved the merger that October, but federal regulators had not yet ruled on the deal. In August 2016, Aetna and Humana each agreed to sell certain Medicare Advantage (MA) assets to Molina Healthcare, Inc., which are subject to the completion of Aetna's Humana acquisition. As a result of the transactions, Molina is expected to gain 290,000 MA members in 21 states, preserving robust competition for seniors choosing to receive Medicare through MA plans.

Employee benefits include medical, dental and vision coverage; flexible spending accounts; life and AD&D insurance; short- and long-term disability; employee assistance programs; 401(k) & employee stock purchase plan; and tuition assistance.

FINANCIAL DATA: *Note: Data for latest year may not have been available at press time.*

In U.S. $	2016	2015	2014	2013	2012	2011
Revenue		60,336,500,000	58,003,200,000	47,294,600,000	36,595,900,000	33,779,800,000
R&D Expense						
Operating Income		4,854,600,000	4,253,800,000	3,402,800,000	3,041,100,000	3,445,400,000
Operating Margin %		8.04%	7.33%	7.19%	8.30%	10.19%
SGA Expense		11,649,300,000	10,837,700,000	8,645,400,000	6,876,400,000	6,804,400,000
Net Income		2,390,200,000	2,040,800,000	1,913,600,000	1,657,900,000	1,985,700,000
Operating Cash Flow		3,866,100,000	3,372,800,000	2,278,700,000	1,822,000,000	2,507,800,000
Capital Expenditure		362,900,000	369,600,000	479,100,000	338,200,000	372,000,000
EBITDA		5,270,500,000	4,458,200,000	3,843,300,000	3,264,100,000	3,771,900,000
Return on Assets %		4.47%	3.95%	4.18%	4.14%	5.20%
Return on Equity %		15.62%	14.31%	15.66%	16.15%	19.84%
Debt to Equity		0.48	0.54	0.56	0.62	0.39

CONTACT INFORMATION:

Phone: 860 273-0123   Fax:
Toll-Free: 800-872-3862
Address: 151 Farmington Ave., Hartford, CT 06156 United States

STOCK TICKER/OTHER:

Stock Ticker: AET   Exchange: NYS
Employees: 48,800   Fiscal Year Ends: 12/31
Parent Company:

SALARIES/BONUSES:

Top Exec. Salary: Bonus: $
$1,034,483
Second Exec. Salary: Bonus: $
$919,828

OTHER THOUGHTS:

Estimated Female Officers or Directors: 8

Hot Spot for Advancement for Women/Minorities: Y

AFLAC Inc

NAIC Code: 524114

www.aflac.com

TYPES OF BUSINESS:

Insurance-Supplemental & Specialty Health
Life Insurance
Cancer Insurance
Long-Term Care Insurance
Accident & Disability Insurance
Vision Plans
Dental Plans

BRANDS/DIVISIONS/AFFILIATES:

American Family Life Assurance Company
Continental American Insurance Company
Aflac Group Insurance
AFLAC Japan
EVER

CONTACTS: Note: Officers with more than one job title may be intentionally listed here more than once.

Daniel Amos, CEO
Hiroshi Yamauchi, President, Subsidiary
Charles Lake, Chairman of the Board, Divisional
June Howard, Chief Accounting Officer
Kriss Cloninger, Director
Paul Amos, Director
Kenneth Janke, Executive VP, Divisional
Susan Blanck, Executive VP, Subsidiary
Koji Ariyoshi, Executive VP, Subsidiary
Eric Kirsch, Executive VP, Subsidiary
Frederick Crawford, Executive VP
Audrey Tillman, Executive VP
James Daniels, Other Executive Officer
Teresa White, President, Subsidiary
Joey Loudermilk, Secretary
Robin Wilkey, Senior VP, Divisional
Robin Wilkey, Senior VP, Divisional

GROWTH PLANS/SPECIAL FEATURES:

AFLAC, Inc. is a holding company whose principle subsidiary AFLAC (American Family Life Assurance Company of Columbus), insures more than 50 million people worldwide. The subsidiary is a leading writer of supplemental insurance marketed to employers in the U.S., offering policies for payroll accounts through approximately 13,000 sales agencies, with more than 110,000 sales associates employed by those agencies. AFLAC sells supplemental insurance products, including accident/disability plans, cancer plans, short-term disability plans, sickness & hospital indemnity plans, hospital intensive care plans, fixed-benefit dental plans, vision care plans, long-term care plans and life insurance products. In addition, AFLAC offers specified health event coverage for major medical crises such as heart attack and stroke. U.S. insurance products are designed to provide supplemental coverage to individuals who already have major medical or primary insurance coverage. Through Continental American Insurance Company (branded as Aflac Group Insurance), the company also markets and administers group projects. Subsidiary AFLAC Japan is one of the largest foreign-based insurers in that country. AFLAC Japan's insurance products are designed to help consumers pay for medical and non-medical costs that are not reimbursed under Japan's national health insurance system. EVER, AFLAC Japan's stand-alone medical product, offers a basic level of hospitalization coverage with an affordable premium. AFLAC Japan also sells cancer plans, general medical indemnity plans, medical/sickness riders to its cancer plan, care plans, living benefit life plans, ordinary life insurance plans and annuities. AFLAC Japan accounts for about 70% of AFLAC's annual insurance earnings.

Employee benefits include medical and dental coverage, short- and long-term disability, life insurance, flexible spending accounts, an employee assistance program, employee discount programs and Aflac insurance policies including cancer insurance and hospital confinement indemnity.

FINANCIAL DATA: Note: Data for latest year may not have been available at press time.

In U.S. $	2016	2015	2014	2013	2012	2011
Revenue		20,872,000,000	22,728,000,000	23,939,000,000	25,364,000,000	22,171,000,000
R&D Expense						
Operating Income		3,862,000,000	4,491,000,000	4,816,000,000	4,302,000,000	2,992,000,000
Operating Margin %		18.50%	19.75%	20.11%	16.96%	13.49%
SGA Expense		3,517,000,000	3,697,000,000	3,750,000,000	4,159,000,000	3,950,000,000
Net Income		2,533,000,000	2,951,000,000	3,158,000,000	2,866,000,000	1,964,000,000
Operating Cash Flow		6,776,000,000	6,550,000,000	10,547,000,000	14,952,000,000	10,842,000,000
Capital Expenditure						
EBITDA						
Return on Assets %		2.12%	2.44%	2.50%	2.30%	1.80%
Return on Equity %		14.05%	17.90%	20.64%	19.44%	15.99%
Debt to Equity		0.28	0.28	0.33	0.27	0.24

CONTACT INFORMATION:

Phone: 706 323-3431   Fax:
Toll-Free: 800-235-2667
Address: 1932 Wynnton Rd., Columbus, GA 31999 United States

SALARIES/BONUSES:

Top Exec. Salary: $360,606   Bonus: $1,240,000
Second Exec. Salary: $1,441,100   Bonus: $

STOCK TICKER/OTHER:

Stock Ticker: AFL   Exchange: NYS
Employees: 9,915   Fiscal Year Ends: 12/31
Parent Company:

OTHER THOUGHTS:

Estimated Female Officers or Directors: 8
Hot Spot for Advancement for Women/Minorities: Y

Agero Inc
NAIC Code: 517210

TYPES OF BUSINESS:
Automotive Telematics
Emergency Response Systems
Stolen Vehicle Tracking
Automobile Operational Analysis
Navigation Tools

BRANDS/DIVISIONS/AFFILIATES:
Cross Country Automotive Services
ATX Group
VehicleAssist
ClaimsAssist
Drive360

CONTACTS: *Note: Officers with more than one job title may be intentionally listed here more than once.*
Dave Ferrick, CEO
Jeffrey Blecher, Sr. VP-Strategy
Kate Sweeney, Exec. VP
Cathy Orrico, Sr. VP-Sales
Mark Carbrey, Sr. VP
Peter Necheles, Sr. VP-Corp. Dev.
Jeffrey Blecher, Sr. VP-Strategy
Michael A. Saxton, Sr. Advisor
Tom Metzger, Sr. VP

GROWTH PLANS/SPECIAL FEATURES:
Agero, Inc., a product of the merger of Cross Country Automotive Services and the ATX Group, is a pioneer in the telematics (location-based voice and data communication services) industry as well as a provider of roadside assistance for motorists and claims management services for insurance carriers. With operations throughout North America, the firm's services are used by more than 100 leading corporations, and its technology is incorporated into 75% of new passenger vehicles sold in the U.S. Agero divides its products and services into four segments: mobile offerings, information services, roadside assistance and claims management. The mobile offerings segment offers products that connect customers with their insurance carriers and roadside assistance companies. Products include VehicleAssist, ClaimsAssist and Drive360. The information services segment leverages data and insights to increase process efficiencies. Agero's roadside assistance segment protects over 75 million drivers through its various scalable services and products, such as VehicleAssist. The claims management segment provides accident scene management and vehicle release services.

FINANCIAL DATA: *Note: Data for latest year may not have been available at press time.*

In U.S. $	2016	2015	2014	2013	2012	2011
Revenue		625,000,000	600,000,000	500,000,000	376,000,000	
R&D Expense						
Operating Income						
Operating Margin %						
SGA Expense						
Net Income						
Operating Cash Flow						
Capital Expenditure						
EBITDA						
Return on Assets %						
Return on Equity %						
Debt to Equity						

CONTACT INFORMATION:
Phone: 781-393-9300   Fax: 781-393-6706
Toll-Free:
Address: One Cabot Rd., Medford, MA 02155 United States

STOCK TICKER/OTHER:
Stock Ticker: Private   Exchange:
Employees: 3,000   Fiscal Year Ends: 12/31
Parent Company:

SALARIES/BONUSES:
Top Exec. Salary: $ Bonus: $
Second Exec. Salary: $ Bonus: $

OTHER THOUGHTS:
Estimated Female Officers or Directors: 1
Hot Spot for Advancement for Women/Minorities: Y

Airbnb Inc

NAIC Code: 519130

www.airbnb.com

TYPES OF BUSINESS:

Online Homestay Reservations

BRANDS/DIVISIONS/AFFILIATES:

Airbnb.com

CONTACTS: *Note: Officers with more than one job title may be intentionally listed here more than once.*

Brian Chesky, CEO
Laurence A. Tosi, CFO
Nathan Blecharczyk, CTO

GROWTH PLANS/SPECIAL FEATURES:

Airbnb, Inc., founded in 2008, operates a social networking site for travelers and those who have spare housing space. Through Airbnb.com, members who are willing to let travelers stay in their homes, guest houses, resort properties and other accommodations can post their information, including pricing, photos and amenities. In turn, travelers may search in a given market for members who are willing to accommodate them. Airbnb offers more than 2 million listings in 192 countries. Since its founding, the company has booked over 60 million guest nights. Members are encouraged to write reviews describing the positive and/or negative aspects of their stays. These reviews are partially encouraged so that renters and travelers may view profiles and feedback before staying in homes or letting others stay in their homes, thereby reducing the risk of danger or other negative situations. The Airbnb network is also connected to Facebook, allowing members to search the social networking platform for additional information regarding certain hosts and guests. Airbnb charges room owners a 3% host fee and an additional fee of 6% to 12% per guest. The average commission is about 12% of total revenues. The typical guest stays longer, on average, than a guest in a typical hotel. The firm has a goal of achieving $10 billion in yearly revenues by 2020.

FINANCIAL DATA: *Note: Data for latest year may not have been available at press time.*

In U.S. $	2016	2015	2014	2013	2012	2011
Revenue		2,200,000,000	900,000,000	264,000,000	132,000,000	120,000,000
R&D Expense						
Operating Income						
Operating Margin %						
SGA Expense						
Net Income						
Operating Cash Flow						
Capital Expenditure						
EBITDA						
Return on Assets %						
Return on Equity %						
Debt to Equity						

CONTACT INFORMATION:

Phone: 415-728-0000   Fax:
Toll-Free:
Address: 888 Brannan St., Fl. 4, San Francisco, CA 94107 United States

STOCK TICKER/OTHER:

Stock Ticker: Private   Exchange:
Employees: 4,175   Fiscal Year Ends: 12/31
Parent Company:

SALARIES/BONUSES:

Top Exec. Salary: $ Bonus: $
Second Exec. Salary: $ Bonus: $

OTHER THOUGHTS:

Estimated Female Officers or Directors:
Hot Spot for Advancement for Women/Minorities:

Sales, profits and employees may be estimates. Financial information, benefits and other data can change quickly and may vary from those stated here.

Alaska Air Group Inc

www.alaskaair.com

NAIC Code: 481111

TYPES OF BUSINESS:

Airlines
Air Cargo

BRANDS/DIVISIONS/AFFILIATES:

Alaska Airlines Inc
Horizon Air Industries Inc

CONTACTS: *Note: Officers with more than one job title may be intentionally listed here more than once.*

Bradley Tilden, CEO
Brandon Pedersen, CFO
Christopher Berry, Chief Accounting Officer
Benito Minicucci, COO, Subsidiary
David Campbell, COO, Subsidiary
Kyle Levine, General Counsel
Andrew Harrison, Other Executive Officer
Shannon Alberts, Secretary
Joseph Sprague, Senior VP, Divisional

GROWTH PLANS/SPECIAL FEATURES:

Alaska Air Group, Inc., through its operating subsidiaries Alaska Airlines, Inc. (Alaska) and Horizon Air Industries, Inc. (Horizon), provides passenger air service to more than 32 million passengers per year to over 100 destinations. The firm also provides freight and mail services, primarily to and within Alaska and on the West Coast. Alaska, founded in 1932, operates a fleet of passenger jets and contracts with Horizon, SkyWest Airlines, Inc. and Peninsula Airways, Inc. for regional capacity. Alaska operates an all-Boeing 737 fleet and Horizon operates and all-Bombardier Q400 turboprop fleet. Alaska offers north/south service within the western USA, Canada and Mexico as well as passenger and dedicated cargo services to and within Alaska. It also provides long-haul east/west service to Hawaii and cities in the mid-continental and eastern USA, primarily from Seattle, where it has its largest concentration of departures. Alaska's leading airports are Seattle and Portland. Horizon is the largest regional airline in the Pacific Northwest, representing 90% of Air Group's regional revenue. The subsidiary serves a number of cities in the USA, Canada and Mexico. Horizon's leading airports are within the West Coast and Pacific Northwest regions. New routes in 2015 included Seattle to Milwaukee, Oklahoma City and Washington D.C.; from Las Vegas to Mammoth Lakes; from San Diego to Kona; and from Portland to St. Louis. In April 2016, the firm agreed to acquire Virgin America, Inc. for $2.6 billion.

Both Alaska and Horizon airlines offer employee benefits such as flight privileges, personal time off, health coverage, a 401(k) plan, a profit sharing plan and performance rewards.

FINANCIAL DATA: *Note: Data for latest year may not have been available at press time.*

In U.S. $	2016	2015	2014	2013	2012	2011
Revenue		5,598,000,000	5,368,000,000	5,156,000,000	4,657,000,000	4,317,800,000
R&D Expense						
Operating Income		1,298,000,000	962,000,000	838,000,000	532,000,000	448,900,000
Operating Margin %		23.18%	17.92%	16.25%	11.42%	10.39%
SGA Expense		1,585,000,000	1,705,000,000	1,591,000,000	1,653,000,000	1,237,700,000
Net Income		848,000,000	605,000,000	508,000,000	316,000,000	244,500,000
Operating Cash Flow		1,584,000,000	1,030,000,000	981,000,000	753,000,000	696,000,000
Capital Expenditure		831,000,000	694,000,000	566,000,000	518,000,000	387,400,000
EBITDA		1,640,000,000	1,297,000,000	1,121,000,000	842,000,000	727,900,000
Return on Assets %		13.33%	10.06%	8.95%	5.90%	4.78%
Return on Equity %		37.37%	29.11%	29.44%	24.36%	21.46%
Debt to Equity		0.23	0.32		0.37	0.61	0.93

CONTACT INFORMATION:

Phone: 206 392-5040   Fax:
Toll-Free: 800-252-7522
Address: 19300 Pacific Highway South, Seattle, WA 98188 United States

STOCK TICKER/OTHER:

Stock Ticker: ALK
Employees: 15,143
Parent Company:

Exchange: NYS
Fiscal Year Ends: 12/31

SALARIES/BONUSES:

Top Exec. Salary: $454,254   Bonus: $
Second Exec. Salary: $390,769   Bonus: $

OTHER THOUGHTS:

Estimated Female Officers or Directors: 13
Hot Spot for Advancement for Women/Minorities: Y

Alliance Data Systems Corporation

www.alliancedata.com

NAIC Code: 541800

TYPES OF BUSINESS:

Marketing Services
Credit Services
Transaction Services

BRANDS/DIVISIONS/AFFILIATES:

LoyaltyOne
AIR MILES
Epsilon
World Financial Network National Bank
World Financial Capital Bank
BrandLoyalty Group BV
Conversant Inc

CONTACTS: Note: Officers with more than one job title may be intentionally listed here more than once.

Edward Heffernan, CEO
Charles Horn, CFO
Robert Minicucci, Chairman of the Board
Laura Santillan, Chief Accounting Officer
Melisa Miller, Executive VP
Bryan Kennedy, Executive VP
Bryan Pearson, Executive VP
Joseph Motes, Senior VP

GROWTH PLANS/SPECIAL FEATURES:

Alliance Data Systems Corporation (ADS) is a provider of data-driven and transaction-based marketing and customer loyalty services. The company's products and services are operated through three segments: LoyaltyOne, Epsilon, and card services. The LoyaltyOne segment, which includes the Canadian AIR MILES Reward Program, provides loyalty marketing services, including consumer data, customer-centric retail strategies, direct-to-consumer marketing and loyalty consulting services. More than 170 brand name sponsors participate in the AIR MILES program, including Canada Safeway, Shell Canada, Jean Coutu, RONA, Amex Bank of Canada, Sobey's and Bank of Montreal. Epsilon provides integrated direct marketing solutions that combine database marketing technology and analytics with a broad range of direct marketing services. The firm uses cooperative databases containing consumer transactional data from multi-channel marketers to develop customer acquisition and retention strategies. The card services segment manages over 140 private label credit cards for various retailers. Its operations include account origination, transaction processing, customer care and collections services for the company's private label and other retail credit card programs. Primary subsidiaries in this segment are World Financial Network National Bank and World Financial Capital Bank. ADS' client base includes companies in the retail, financial services, hospitality, telecommunications and health care markets. The firm has 60% ownership in BrandLoyalty Group B.V., a European marketing and advertising company. In 2014, the firm acquired Conversant, Inc., which operates under Epsilon, providing end-to-end marketing services.

The firm offers its employees medical, dental and vision insurance; a 401(k); disability coverage; life, auto and home insurance; flexible spending accounts; an employee stock purchase program; tuition reimbursement; an employee assistance program; prepaid legal services; and adoption assistance.

FINANCIAL DATA: Note: Data for latest year may not have been available at press time.

In U.S. $	2016	2015	2014	2013	2012	2011
Revenue		6,439,746,000	5,302,940,000	4,319,063,000	3,641,390,000	3,173,287,000
R&D Expense						
Operating Income		1,261,860,000	1,098,467,000	1,098,912,000	974,364,000	812,680,000
Operating Margin %		19.59%	20.71%	25.44%	26.75%	25.60%
SGA Expense		203,046,000	141,468,000	109,115,000	108,059,000	95,256,000
Net Income		596,541,000	506,293,000	496,170,000	422,256,000	315,286,000
Operating Cash Flow		1,705,841,000	1,344,159,000	1,003,492,000	1,134,190,000	1,011,347,000
Capital Expenditure		191,683,000	158,694,000	135,376,000	116,455,000	73,502,000
EBITDA		1,754,000,000	1,411,549,000	1,315,031,000	1,141,240,000	965,833,000
Return on Assets %		2.58%	3.02%	3.93%	4.02%	3.65%
Return on Equity %		25.03%	31.13%	71.68%	119.88%	316.77%
Debt to Equity		5.04	3.39	7.01	8.90	21.19

CONTACT INFORMATION:

Phone: 214 494-3000   Fax:
Toll-Free:
Address: 7500 Dallas Pkwy., Ste. 700, Plano, TX 75024 United States

STOCK TICKER/OTHER:

Stock Ticker: ADS   Exchange: NYS
Employees: 15,000   Fiscal Year Ends: 12/31
Parent Company:

SALARIES/BONUSES:

Top Exec. Salary: Bonus: $167,100
$1,114,000
Second Exec. Salary: Bonus: $60,900
$609,000

OTHER THOUGHTS:

Estimated Female Officers or Directors: 5

Hot Spot for Advancement for Women/Minorities: Y

Allscripts Healthcare Solutions Inc

www.allscripts.com

NAIC Code: 0

TYPES OF BUSINESS:

Computer Software, Healthcare & Biotechnology
Interactive Education Services
Clinical Software
Electronic Records Systems
Care Management Software

BRANDS/DIVISIONS/AFFILIATES:

Sunrise Enterprise
Revenue Cycle Management Services

CONTACTS: Note: Officers with more than one job title may be intentionally listed here more than once.

Paul Black, CEO
Melinda Whittington, CFO
Michael Klayko, Director
Dennis Olis, Senior VP, Divisional
James Hewitt, Senior VP, Divisional
Brian Farley, Senior VP

GROWTH PLANS/SPECIAL FEATURES:

Allscripts Healthcare Solutions, Inc. provides clinical software, connectivity and information solutions that physicians and health care providers use to improve service delivery. The firm provides software solutions for hospitals, physician practices and post-acute organizations. For hospitals and health systems, these applications include the Sunrise Enterprise suite of clinical solutions, comprising a full acute care electronic health record (EHR), integrated with financial/administrative solutions including performance management and revenue cycle/access management. Acute care solutions include modules of the Sunrise suite that are available on a stand-alone basis as well as additional stand-alone solutions such as an emergency department information system, care management and discharge management. Allscripts' post-acute tools help smooth the patient transition from hospital to post-acute care facilities, including home health providers, hospices and private duty organizations. For physician practices, the firm's products include integrated EHR and practice management functionality available either via traditional on premise delivery or via Software-as-a-Service; revenue cycle management software and the Revenue Cycle Management Services solution, which enables practices to outsource their full revenue cycle to the firm or address requirements in-house; clearinghouse services; stand-alone electronic prescribing; and document imaging solutions for physician practices. The firm's population health management solution enables hospitals/health systems/ physician practices to connect, transition, analyze, and coordinate care across the entire care community. Additionally, Allscripts offers professional services such as conversion & integration of historical data into its software, training & support services, as well as consulting, remote hosting and IT outsourcing services. In April 2016, the firm established a joint venture, merging its homecare business with Netsmart Technologies, Inc., which together focus on enhancing human services, post-acute care and outcomes.

Allscripts offers its employees medical, dental and vision insurance; flex spending accounts; 401(k); adoption assistance; and education assistance.

FINANCIAL DATA: Note: Data for latest year may not have been available at press time.

In U.S. $	2016	2015	2014	2013	2012	2011
Revenue		1,386,393,000	1,377,873,000	1,373,061,000	1,446,325,000	1,444,077,000
R&D Expense		184,791,000	192,821,000	199,751,000	162,158,000	104,106,000
Operating Income		31,883,000	-39,188,000	-127,601,000	13,271,000	136,544,000
Operating Margin %		2.29%	-2.84%	-9.29%	.91%	9.45%
SGA Expense		339,175,000	358,681,000	419,599,000	384,370,000	387,571,000
Net Income		-2,226,000	-66,453,000	-104,026,000	-1,153,000	73,609,000
Operating Cash Flow		211,579,000	103,496,000	80,987,000	222,670,000	268,754,000
Capital Expenditure		67,586,000	67,099,000	116,156,000	123,131,000	105,054,000
EBITDA		192,977,000	135,443,000	58,524,000	148,961,000	270,629,000
Return on Assets %		-.08%	-2.59%	-4.15%	-.04%	2.92%
Return on Equity %		-.16%	-5.10%	-7.99%	-.08%	4.98%
Debt to Equity		0.43	0.42	0.41	0.28	0.21

CONTACT INFORMATION:

Phone: 866 358-6869   Fax:
Toll-Free: 800-654-0889
Address: 222 Merchandise Mart Plz., Ste. 2024, Chicago, IL 60654 United States

STOCK TICKER/OTHER:

Stock Ticker: MDRX   Exchange: NAS
Employees: 7,200   Fiscal Year Ends: 12/31
Parent Company:

SALARIES/BONUSES:

Top Exec. Salary: Bonus: $
$1,000,000
Second Exec. Salary: Bonus: $
$505,725

OTHER THOUGHTS:

Estimated Female Officers or Directors: 2

Hot Spot for Advancement for Women/Minorities: Y

Sales, profits and employees may be estimates. Financial information, benefits and other data can change quickly and may vary from those stated here.

Amazon.com Inc

NAIC Code: 454111

www.amazon.com

TYPES OF BUSINESS:

Online Retailing and Related Services
Online Books & Music Retail
Online Videos/DVDs Retail
Online Electronics Retail
Online Auctions
Online Household Goods Retail
Online Auto & Industrial Retail
E-Commerce Support & Hosting

BRANDS/DIVISIONS/AFFILIATES:

www.amazon.com
www.amazon.ca
www.amazon.com.mx

CONTACTS: Note: Officers with more than one job title may be intentionally listed here more than once.

Jeffrey Bezos, CEO
Brian Olsavsky, CFO
Shelley Reynolds, Chief Accounting Officer
David Zapolsky, General Counsel
Andrew Jassy, Senior VP, Divisional
Jeffrey Blackburn, Senior VP, Divisional
Diego Piacentini, Senior VP, Divisional
Jeffrey Wilke, Senior VP, Divisional

GROWTH PLANS/SPECIAL FEATURES:

Amazon.com, Inc. is an Internet consumer shopping and cloud computing company headquartered in Seattle, Washington USA. The firm offers millions of new, used, refurbished and collectible items in categories such as books, movies, music games, electronics, computers, home & garden, toys children's goods, grocery, apparel, jewelry, health & beauty sports, outdoors, digital downloads, tools, auto and industrial. Amazon.com is the world's largest provider of cloud infrastructure services. The company, which serves more than 50 million members, operates in three segments: North America, international and Amazon web services (AWS). Each of the company's segments serve primary customer sets consisting of consumers, sellers, developers, enterprises and content creators, as well as advertising services and co-branded credit card agreements. The North American segment derives 60% of annual net sales, and consists primarily of amounts earned from retail sales of consumer products (including from sellers) and subscriptions through North America-focused websites such as www.amazon.com www.amazon.ca and www.amazon.com.mx. The international segment (33%) does the same via Amazon websites serving countries outside the U.S. such as the U.K., Ireland, France Germany, Italy, Spain, Netherlands, Australia, Brazil, Japan China and India. AWS (7%) consists of amounts earned from global sales of compute, storage, database and other AWS service offering for start-ups, enterprises, government agencies and academic institutions. In July 2016, the firm partnered with the U.K. government to explore the steps needed to make the delivery of parcels by small drones a reality, allowing Amazon to trial new methods of testing its delivery systems.

Employee benefits include life, disability, accident, medical dental and vision insurance with domestic partner coverage flexible spending accounts; relocation assistance; paid holiday/vacations; a 401(k); company stock; and several discount programs.

FINANCIAL DATA: Note: Data for latest year may not have been available at press time.

In U.S. $	2016	2015	2014	2013	2012	2011
Revenue		107,006,000,000	88,988,000,000	74,452,000,000	61,093,000,000	48,077,000,000
R&D Expense		12,540,000,000	9,275,000,000	6,565,000,000	4,564,000,000	2,909,000,000
Operating Income		2,233,000,000	178,000,000	745,000,000	676,000,000	862,000,000
Operating Margin %		2.08%	.20%	1.00%	1.10%	1.79%
SGA Expense		20,411,000,000	16,650,000,000	12,847,000,000	9,723,000,000	6,864,000,000
Net Income		596,000,000	-241,000,000	274,000,000	-39,000,000	631,000,000
Operating Cash Flow		11,920,000,000	6,842,000,000	5,475,000,000	4,180,000,000	3,903,000,000
Capital Expenditure		4,589,000,000	4,893,000,000	3,444,000,000	3,785,000,000	1,811,000,000
EBITDA		8,308,000,000	4,845,000,000	3,900,000,000	2,795,000,000	2,082,000,000
Return on Assets %		.99%	-.50%	.75%	-.13%	2.86%
Return on Equity %		4.94%	-2.35%	3.05%	-.48%	8.63%
Debt to Equity		1.05	1.16	0.53	0.46	0.18

CONTACT INFORMATION:

Phone: 206 266-1000   Fax:
Toll-Free:
Address: 410 Terry Ave. N., Seattle, WA 98109 United States

STOCK TICKER/OTHER:

Stock Ticker: AMZN   Exchange: NAS
Employees: 154,100   Fiscal Year Ends: 12/31
Parent Company:

SALARIES/BONUSES:

Top Exec. Salary: $175,000   Bonus: $
Second Exec. Salary: Bonus: $
$172,509

OTHER THOUGHTS:

Estimated Female Officers or Directors: 3
Hot Spot for Advancement for Women/Minorities: Y

American Airlines Group Inc

www.usairways.com

NAIC Code: 481111

TYPES OF BUSINESS:

Airline
Air Freight

BRANDS/DIVISIONS/AFFILIATES:

American Airllines
US Air Group
US Airways Inc
Piedmont Airlines Inc
Envoy Air Inc
PSA Airlines Inc

CONTACTS: Note: Officers with more than one job title may be intentionally listed here more than once.

W. Parker, CEO
Derek Kerr, CFO
Andrew Nocella, Chief Marketing Officer
Robert Isom, COO
Elise Eberwein, Executive VP, Divisional
Stephen Johnson, Executive VP, Divisional
Beverly Goulet, Executive VP
Maya Leibman, Executive VP
J. Kirby, President
Caroline Ray, Secretary

GROWTH PLANS/SPECIAL FEATURES:

American Airlines Group, Inc., a result of the merger of American Airlines and US Air Group, operates one of the largest air carriers in the U.S. Its subsidiaries include US Airways Inc., Piedmont Airlines, Inc., Envoy Air, Inc. and PSA Airlines, Inc. The company operates nearly 6,700 flights per day from its hubs in Charlotte, Chicago, Dallas/Fort Worth, Los Angeles, Miami, New York, Philadelphia, Phoenix and Washington, D.C. The firm offers passenger service to more than 350 destinations in 50 countries. The company's regional airline subsidiaries and affiliates include American Eagle, a network of 10 regional carriers that operate under a codeshare and service agreement with American, and together they operate 3,400 daily flights to 240 destinations in the U.S., Canada, the Caribbean and Mexico; Envoy Air, Inc., which operates 180 aircraft on 900 daily flights to more than 150 destinations in the U.S., Canada and Mexico; Piedmont Airlines, Inc., which operates 300 daily flights to 50 cities in the U.S.; and PSA Airlines, Inc., which operates 500 daily flights to nearly 90 destinations. American and US Airways are members of the oneworld alliance whose members and members-elect serve more than 1,000 destinations with 14,000 daily flights to 150 countries.

US Airways provides employees with auto, home, accident, health, long-term care and critical illness insurance; a 401(k); identity theft protection; travel privileges; employee assistance programs; business resource groups; domestic partner programs; paid vacation; and days off.

FINANCIAL DATA: Note: Data for latest year may not have been available at press time.

In U.S. $	2016	2015	2014	2013	2012	2011
Revenue		40,990,000,000	42,650,000,000	26,743,000,000	24,855,000,000	23,979,000,000
R&D Expense						
Operating Income		6,204,000,000	4,249,000,000	1,399,000,000	107,000,000	-1,054,000,000
Operating Margin %		15.13%	9.96%	5.23%	.43%	-4.39%
SGA Expense		10,918,000,000	10,052,000,000	6,618,000,000	8,483,000,000	8,633,000,000
Net Income		7,610,000,000	2,882,000,000	-1,834,000,000	-1,876,000,000	-1,979,000,000
Operating Cash Flow		6,249,000,000	3,080,000,000	675,000,000	1,279,000,000	680,000,000
Capital Expenditure		6,151,000,000	5,311,000,000	3,114,000,000	1,888,000,000	1,614,000,000
EBITDA		7,105,000,000	5,612,000,000	-304,000,000	-818,000,000	-107,000,000
Return on Assets %		16.51%	6.69%	-5.57%	-7.92%	-8.08%
Return on Equity %		198.79%				
Debt to Equity		3.25	8.01			

CONTACT INFORMATION:

Phone: 817-963-1234   Fax:
Toll-Free:
Address: 4333 Amon Carter Blvd, Fort Worth, TX 76155 United States

STOCK TICKER/OTHER:

Stock Ticker: AAL
Employees: 113,300
Parent Company:

Exchange: NAS
Fiscal Year Ends: 12/31

SALARIES/BONUSES:

Top Exec. Salary: $660,375   Bonus: $
Second Exec. Salary: $609,577   Bonus: $

OTHER THOUGHTS:

Estimated Female Officers or Directors: 7
Hot Spot for Advancement for Women/Minorities: Y

American Express Co

www.americanexpress.com

NAIC Code: 522320

TYPES OF BUSINESS:

Credit Card Processing and Issuing
Travel-Related Services
Lending & Financing
Transaction Services
Bank Holding Company
International Banking Services
Expense Management
Magazine Publishing

BRANDS/DIVISIONS/AFFILIATES:

American Express Travel Related Services Co Inc
American Express Bank FSB
American Express Centurion Bank

CONTACTS: Note: Officers with more than one job title may be intentionally listed here more than once.

Kenneth Chenault, CEO
James Bush, President, Divisional
Jeffrey Campbell, CFO
Marc Gordon, Chief Information Officer
Paul Fabara, Chief Risk Officer
Linda Zukauckas, Controller
Michael ONeill, Executive VP, Divisional
Laureen Seeger, Executive VP
L. Cox, Other Executive Officer
Anre Williams, President, Divisional
Ashwini Gupta, President, Divisional
Douglas Buckminster, President, Divisional
Susan Sobbott, President, Divisional
Carol Schwartz, Secretary
Stephen Squeri, Vice Chairman

GROWTH PLANS/SPECIAL FEATURES:

American Express Co. (AmEx), a bank holding company, is a leading global payments and travel firm. Its principal products are charge and credit payment card products and travel-related services. The firm primarily operates through subsidiary American Express Travel Related Services Company, Inc. AmEx's business is organized into four main segments: U.S. card services, international card services, global commercial services and global network & merchant services. The U.S. card services segment operates through AmEx's USA banking subsidiaries American Express Centurion Bank and American Express Bank, FSB. The division provides a wide array of card products and services to consumers and small businesses in the USA. The firm's international card services division offers these services in countries worldwide. The global commercial services segment offers expense management services to firms and organizations worldwide. Its products and services include corporate purchasing cards, corporate cards, corporate meeting cards, buyer initiated payment programs and business travel accounts. The global network & merchant services division operates a global general-purpose charge and credit card network for both proprietary and issued cards; manages merchant services internationally, which includes signing merchants to accept cards and processing and settling card transactions for those merchants; and offers merchants point-of-sale (POS), servicing/settlement and marketing/information products and services. In June 2016, the 16-year partnership between American Express and Costco dissolved, with Costco no longer accepting American Express credit cards.

FINANCIAL DATA: Note: Data for latest year may not have been available at press time.

In U.S. $	2016	2015	2014	2013	2012	2011
Revenue		32,818,000,000	34,292,000,000	32,974,000,000	31,582,000,000	29,962,000,000
R&D Expense						
Operating Income		7,938,000,000	8,991,000,000	7,888,000,000	6,451,000,000	6,956,000,000
Operating Margin %		24.18%	26.21%	23.92%	20.42%	23.21%
SGA Expense		16,099,000,000	17,168,000,000	16,458,000,000	16,568,000,000	16,182,000,000
Net Income		5,163,000,000	5,885,000,000	5,359,000,000	4,482,000,000	4,935,000,000
Operating Cash Flow		10,972,000,000	10,990,000,000	8,547,000,000	7,082,000,000	10,475,000,000
Capital Expenditure		1,341,000,000	1,195,000,000	1,006,000,000	1,053,000,000	1,189,000,000
EBITDA						
Return on Assets %		3.16%	3.73%	3.49%	2.92%	3.28%
Return on Equity %		24.49%	29.07%	27.92%	23.78%	28.18%
Debt to Equity		2.32	2.80	2.83	3.12	3.16

CONTACT INFORMATION:

Phone: 212 640-2000   Fax: 212 640-2458
Toll-Free: 800-528-4800
Address: 200 Vesey St., World Financial Ctr., New York, NY 10285
United States

STOCK TICKER/OTHER:

Stock Ticker: AXP
Employees: 54,800
Parent Company:

Exchange: NYS
Fiscal Year Ends: 12/31

SALARIES/BONUSES:

Top Exec. Salary:
$1,000,000

Bonus: $4,850,000

Second Exec. Salary:
$800,000

Bonus: $3,858,000

OTHER THOUGHTS:

Estimated Female Officers or Directors: 4

Hot Spot for Advancement for Women/Minorities: Y

American Financial Group Inc

www.afginc.com

NAIC Code: 524126

TYPES OF BUSINESS:

Insurance, Direct Property & Casualty
Long-Term Care Insurance
Annuities
Supplemental Health Insurance
Specialty Insurance
Multi-Peril Crop & Crop Hail Insurance
Car Insurance
Commercial Real Estate

BRANDS/DIVISIONS/AFFILIATES:

Great American Insurance Group
Great American Life Insruance Company
Annuity Investors Life Insurance Company

CONTACTS: *Note: Officers with more than one job title may be intentionally listed here more than once.*

Karl Grafe, Assistant General Counsel
Joseph Consolino, CFO
Michelle Gillis, Chief Administrative Officer
Carl Lindner, Co- President
S. Lindner, Co- President
John Berding, Director
Vito Peraino, General Counsel
Mark Weiss, Vice President

GROWTH PLANS/SPECIAL FEATURES:

American Financial Group, Inc. (AFG) is a holding company that, through subsidiary Great American Insurance Group, is engaged primarily in property and casualty insurance. The company focuses on specialized products for businesses, as well as the sale of fixed and fixed-indexed annuities in the retail, financial institutions and education markets. Property & casualty insurance products include a range of commercial coverages through more than 30 niche insurance businesses that make up Great American Insurance Group. This division's specialized products include, but are not limited to, property & transportation insurance for marine, agriculture and commercial automobile sectors; specialty casualty insurance such as executive/professional liability, umbrella/excess liability, excess & surplus, general liability, targeted programs and workers' compensation; and specialty financial products such as fidelity & surety coverage, as well as lease and loan coverage. AFG sells traditional fixed and fixed-indexed annuities in the retail, financial institutions and education markets through independent producers, as well as through direct relationships with certain financial institutions. This division's operations are conducted primarily through subsidiaries: Great American Life Insurance Company (GALIC) and Annuity Investors Life Insurance Company (AILIC). GALIC comprises 366,000 annuity policies in force with ratings of A and A+ for AM Best and S&P, respectively; and AILIC comprises 122,000 annuity policies inforce with the same ratings as GALIC. Annuities are long-term retirement savings instruments that benefit from income accruing on a tax-deferred basis. Annuity contracts are generally classified as either fixed rate (including fixed-indexed) or variable. Fixed-indexed annuities represent approximately 60% of annuity benefits accumulated each year. In July 2016, the firm agreed to acquire all the outstanding common shares of National Interstate Corporation that it does not currently own.

The firm offers employees medical, dental, vision, disability and life coverage; paid time off; and onsite fitness centers.

FINANCIAL DATA: *Note: Data for latest year may not have been available at press time.*

In U.S. $	2016	2015	2014	2013	2012	2011
Revenue		6,145,000,000	5,713,000,000	5,092,000,000	5,062,000,000	4,750,000,000
R&D Expense						
Operating Income		565,000,000	626,000,000	689,000,000	537,000,000	560,000,000
Operating Margin %		9.19%	10.95%	13.53%	10.60%	11.78%
SGA Expense		1,432,000,000	1,254,000,000	1,108,000,000	1,371,000,000	1,269,000,000
Net Income		352,000,000	452,000,000	471,000,000	488,000,000	343,000,000
Operating Cash Flow		1,357,000,000	1,222,000,000	760,000,000	817,000,000	667,000,000
Capital Expenditure		102,000,000	47,000,000	52,000,000	71,000,000	86,000,000
EBITDA						
Return on Assets %		.72%	1.00%	1.15%	1.29%	1.00%
Return on Equity %		7.43%	9.53%	10.26%	10.69%	7.60%
Debt to Equity		0.22	0.21	0.19	0.20	0.20

CONTACT INFORMATION:

Phone: 513 579-2121   Fax: 513 412-0200
Toll-Free:
Address: 301 E. 4th St., Cincinnati, OH 45202 United States

STOCK TICKER/OTHER:

Stock Ticker: AFG   Exchange: NYS
Employees: 7,000   Fiscal Year Ends: 12/31
Parent Company:

SALARIES/BONUSES:

Top Exec. Salary: Bonus: $
$1,150,000
Second Exec. Salary: Bonus: $
$1,150,000

OTHER THOUGHTS:

Estimated Female Officers or Directors: 3

Hot Spot for Advancement for Women/Minorities: Y

American Honda Motor Co Inc

NAIC Code: 336111

www.hondainamerica.com

TYPES OF BUSINESS:

Automotive Manufacturing
Motorcycles & ATVs
Power Equipment
Marine Engines
Parts Manufacturing & Retail
Research & Development

BRANDS/DIVISIONS/AFFILIATES:

Honda Motor Co Ltd
Honda of America Manufacturing Inc
Honda R&D Americas Inc
Accord
Civic
CR-V
Africa Twin
Gold Wing

CONTACTS: Note: Officers with more than one job title may be intentionally listed here more than once.

Takuji Yamada, CEO
Tom Elliott, Exec. VP-Oper.
Tetsuo Iwamura, Pres.
Hiroyuki Suganuma, CFO
Bruce Smith, Sr. VP-Parts & Svcs. Div.
Michael Accavitti, Sr. VP-Auto Oper.
Steven Center, VP-Environmental Bus. Dev. Office
Sage Marie, Sr. Mgr.-Public Rel.
Michael Ryan, VP-Finance
Robyn Eagles, Mgr.-Honda Public Rel..
Gary Robinson, Mgr.-Acura Advertising
Dave Speck, VP-Tech Coordination Product, Regulatory Office
Tom Peyton, Assistant VP-Auto Advertising

GROWTH PLANS/SPECIAL FEATURES:

American Honda Motor Co., Inc. manufactures and sells automobiles, motorcycles, ATVs, personal watercraft, marine engines, lawn care equipment, snow equipment, generators and water pumps. It is the U.S. subsidiary of Honda Motor Co Ltd. The company's car models include the Accord, Civic, CR-V, CR-Z, FIT, HR-V, Insight, Odyssey, Pilot and Ridgeline. Insight is a gas-electric hybrid car, and Ridgeline is a pickup truck. In addition, Honda owns the Acura brand of vehicles, with 97% of the Honda and Acura vehicles sold in the U.S. being manufactured in North America. American Honda's motorcycle models include Gold Wing, ST1300, Interstate, CTX1300 NM4 and CTX700 touring bikes; VFR1200X, Africa Twin, NC700X, CB500X, CRF250L and XR650L adventure bikes; Gold Wing, Fury, Sabre, Stateline, Interstate, NM4, Shadow, CTX and Rebel cruisers; RC213V, CBR1000RR and CBR600RR supersports; VFR, CB, Interceptor, CBR and GROM sport bikes; and XR650L and CRF250L dual sport bikes. Other Power Sport products include offroad bikes, ATVs, the Side by Side and scooters. Through Honda of America Manufacturing Inc., the firm operates engine, transmission, automobile, motorcycle, ATV and power equipment plants in Ohio, Indiana, Georgia, Alabama, North Carolina and South Carolina. In 2015 the firm produced 1.27 million cars and light trucks, 1.4 million automobile engines, 1.16 million transmissions, 2 million general purpose engines, 505,000 power equipment products and 89,000 ATVs. Through Honda R&D Americas, Inc. American Honda operates office, testing and research/development facilities in North Carolina, Colorado, Ohio, California, Michigan and Toronto. Its 12 manufacturing plants are located in Ohio, Alabama, Georgia, Indiana, South Carolina and North Carolina. Innovation products include ASIMO, the humanoid robot; motorsport vehicles; Walk Assist (a technology for the disabled); and HondaJet, an advanced light business jet.

Employee benefits include tuition reimbursement, comprehensive health care plans, pre-tax spending accounts, retirement plans, same-sex domestic-partner benefits and onsite wellness/fitness facilities.

FINANCIAL DATA: Note: Data for latest year may not have been available at press time.

In U.S. $	2016	2015	2014	2013	2012	2011
Revenue	61,551,806,117	60,557,038,000	52,624,765,000	45,043,300,000	45,029,700,000	50,053,100,000
R&D Expense						
Operating Income						
Operating Margin %						
SGA Expense						
Net Income	1,525,529,259	1,801,247,748	3,330,926,576	2,052,150,000	2,706,720,000	3,631,260,000
Operating Cash Flow						
Capital Expenditure						
EBITDA						
Return on Assets %						
Return on Equity %						
Debt to Equity						

CONTACT INFORMATION:

Phone: 310-783-2000   Fax: 310-783-3023
Toll-Free: 800-999-1009
Address: 1919 Torrance Blvd., Torrance, CA 90501 United States

STOCK TICKER/OTHER:

Stock Ticker: Subsidiary   Exchange:
Employees: 28,000   Fiscal Year Ends: 03/31
Parent Company: Honda Motor Co Ltd

SALARIES/BONUSES:

Top Exec. Salary: $ Bonus: $
Second Exec. Salary: $ Bonus: $

OTHER THOUGHTS:

Estimated Female Officers or Directors: 2
Hot Spot for Advancement for Women/Minorities:

American International Group Inc (AIG)

www.aig.com

NAIC Code: 524126

TYPES OF BUSINESS:

Insurance, Direct Property & Casualty
Life Insurance
Commercial Insurance
Property Insurance

BRANDS/DIVISIONS/AFFILIATES:

CONTACTS: Note: Officers with more than one job title may be intentionally listed here more than once.

Jeffrey Welikson, Assistant General Counsel
Jeffrey Hurd, Executive VP
Seraina Maag, CEO, Divisional
Siddhartha Sankaran, CFO
Robert Miller, Chairman of the Board
Elias Habayeb, Chief Accounting Officer
Philip Fasano, Chief Information Officer
Alessa Quane, Chief Risk Officer
Murli Buluswar, Chief Scientific Officer
Robert Schimek, Executive VP, Divisional
Kevin Hogan, Executive VP, Divisional
Thomas Russo, Executive VP
Martha Gallo, Executive VP
Brian Schreiber, Other Corporate Officer

GROWTH PLANS/SPECIAL FEATURES:

American International Group, Inc. (AIG) is an international insurance organization serving customers in more than 100 countries. The company serves more than 89% of companies included in the Fortune Global 500, and demonstrates strength via its $89 billion in shareholders' equity. AIG distributes insurance products and services across the geographic regions of the Americas (the U.S., Canada, Mexico, South America, the Caribbean and Bermuda), Asia Pacific (Japan, China, Korea, Singapore, Malaysia, Thailand, Australia, Indonesia and others) and EMEA (the U.K., Continental Europe, Russian Federation, India, Middle East and Africa). The firm is the largest commercial insurer in the U.S., the largest U.S.-based property casualty insurer in Europe and the largest foreign property casualty insurer in Asia and the Far East. AIG primarily operates through a single business segment which is composed of two insurance groups: commercial & consumer insurance. The commercial insurance group derives 51% of the company's annual revenue, provides insurance products and services for commercial and institutional property casualty and institutional markets. The consumer insurance group (49%) provides retirement, life and personal insurance products and services. AIG's life insurance premiums and deposits of $32 billion (2015) demonstrate a substantial presence in the U.S. and a healthy share of the Japan market. AIG's corporate & other business segment includes AIG assets and run-off insurance businesses.

FINANCIAL DATA: Note: Data for latest year may not have been available at press time.

In U.S. $	2016	2015	2014	2013	2012	2011
Revenue		58,327,000,000	64,406,000,000	68,678,000,000	65,656,000,000	64,237,000,000
R&D Expense						
Operating Income		3,281,000,000	10,501,000,000	9,368,001,000	9,322,000,000	-1,065,000,000
Operating Margin %		5.62%	16.30%	13.64%	14.19%	-1.65%
SGA Expense		12,686,000,000				
Net Income		2,196,000,000	7,529,000,000	9,085,000,000	3,438,000,000	17,798,000,000
Operating Cash Flow		2,877,000,000	5,007,000,000	5,865,000,000	3,676,000,000	35,000,000
Capital Expenditure						
EBITDA						
Return on Assets %		.43%	1.42%	1.66%	.62%	2.74%
Return on Equity %		2.23%	7.26%	9.15%	3.38%	28.72%
Debt to Equity		0.32	0.29	0.41	0.49	0.71

CONTACT INFORMATION:

Phone: 212 770-7000   Fax: 212 344-6828
Toll-Free: 877-638-4244
Address: 180 Maiden Ln., New York, NY 10038 United States

STOCK TICKER/OTHER:

Stock Ticker: AIG   Exchange: NYS
Employees: 64,000   Fiscal Year Ends: 12/31
Parent Company:

SALARIES/BONUSES:

Top Exec. Salary: Bonus: $4,400,000
$1,038,462
Second Exec. Salary: Bonus: $1,150,000
$1,038,462

OTHER THOUGHTS:

Estimated Female Officers or Directors: 10

Hot Spot for Advancement for Women/Minorities: Y

American Tire Distributors

NAIC Code: 423130

www.atd-us.com

TYPES OF BUSINESS:

Tires & Related Products, Distribution

BRANDS/DIVISIONS/AFFILIATES:

American Tire Distributors Holdings Inc
ATDOnline
TireBuyer.com

CONTACTS: Note: Officers with more than one job title may be intentionally listed here more than once.

Stuart Schuette, CEO
William Berry, Pres.
Jason Yaudes, CFO
Michael Gaither, General Counsel
Phillip Marrett, Exec. VP-Product Planning & Positioning
Daniel Brown, Pres., Tire Pros

GROWTH PLANS/SPECIAL FEATURES:

American Tire Distributors (ATD) is one of the nation's largest suppliers of tires and wheels as well as tools and other automotive service equipment. The company serves the replacement tire market through approximately 140 distribution centers in Canada and the U.S., and more than 1,000 delivery vehicles, delivering products to 70,000 customers. ATD distributes more than 40 million replacement tires each year. ATD offers its tire retailers and service shop clients various tires for passenger vehicles and light trucks, tractor-trailers, buses, farm machinery and specialty and recreational vehicles. The company carries brands including Michelin, Continental, Goodyear and Bridgestone. Its wheel selection ranges from 13- to 30-inch rims for passenger vehicles and light trucks. The firm maintains ATDOnline, which offers dealers access to prices, availability and the ability to place orders 24 hours a day, seven days a week; and TireBuyer.com, where customers can buy tires and wheels as well as choose a dealer location for installation. TireBuyer.com also allows potential purchasers to view tires and wheels on their particular vehicle, using the web site's 3D visualizer. ATD operates as a subsidiary of American Tire Distributors Holdings, Inc.

FINANCIAL DATA: Note: Data for latest year may not have been available at press time.

In U.S. $	2016	2015	2014	2013	2012	2011
Revenue	5,000,000,000	4,800,000,000	5,030,698,000	3,839,269,000	3,455,864,000	1,525,249,000
R&D Expense						
Operating Income						
Operating Margin %						
SGA Expense						
Net Income		-95,800,000	-94,599,999	-6,357,000	-14,346,000	-36,312,000
Operating Cash Flow						
Capital Expenditure						
EBITDA						
Return on Assets %						
Return on Equity %						
Debt to Equity						

CONTACT INFORMATION:

Phone: 704-992-2000   Fax: 704-992-1384
Toll-Free: 800-222-1167
Address: 12200 Herbert Wayne Ct., Ste. 150, Huntersville, NC 28070
United States

STOCK TICKER/OTHER:

Stock Ticker: Subsidiary   Exchange:
Employees: 4,200   Fiscal Year Ends: 01/04
Parent Company: American Tire Distributors Holdings Inc

SALARIES/BONUSES:

Top Exec. Salary: $ Bonus: $
Second Exec. Salary: $ Bonus: $

OTHER THOUGHTS:

Estimated Female Officers or Directors:
Hot Spot for Advancement for Women/Minorities:

Amerigroup Corporation

www.amerigroupcorp.com

NAIC Code: 524114

TYPES OF BUSINESS:

Managed Health Care

BRANDS/DIVISIONS/AFFILIATES:

Anthem Inc

CONTACTS: *Note: Officers with more than one job title may be intentionally listed here more than once.*

Peter D. Haytaian, VP-Anthem
Richard C. Zoretic, Exec. VP
Scott Anglin, CFO-Anthem
Mary T. McCluskey, Exec. VP
Jack Young, VP
Ken Aversa, Sr. VP-Customer Svc. Oper., Medicaid, WellPoint
Georgia Dodds Foley, Chief Compliance Officer, Medicaid, WellPoint
John E. Little, Interim Sr. VP-Gov't Affairs, WellPoint
Aileen McCormick, CEO-Western Region, Medicaid, WellPoint

GROWTH PLANS/SPECIAL FEATURES:

Amerigroup Corporation, the state-sponsored program services division of health benefits company Anthem, Inc., is a managed health care company focused on serving people who receive benefits through publicly-sponsored programs. These programs include Medicaid, Medicare Advantage, Family Care and the Children's Health Insurance Program (CHIP). Since the company does not offer Medicare or commercial products, people served by Amerigroup are generally younger, tend to access health care in an inefficient manner and have a greater percentage of medical expenses related to obstetrics, diabetes, circulatory and respiratory conditions. The firm reduces costs for families and state governments by combining social and behavioral health services to help members obtain health care. Amerigroup's provider networks consist of approximately 136,000 physicians, including primary care physicians, specialists and ancillary providers, and approximately 800 hospitals across all of its markets. The company currently enrolls 3.5 million members in 19 states nationwide.

FINANCIAL DATA: *Note: Data for latest year may not have been available at press time.*

In U.S. $	2016	2015	2014	2013	2012	2011
Revenue		10,000,000,000	9,625,000,000	9,125,000,000	219,000,000	6,318,393,856
R&D Expense						
Operating Income						
Operating Margin %						
SGA Expense						
Net Income						
Operating Cash Flow						
Capital Expenditure						
EBITDA						
Return on Assets %						
Return on Equity %						
Debt to Equity						

CONTACT INFORMATION:

Phone: 757 490-6900   Fax:
Toll-Free: 800-600-4441
Address: 4425 Corporation Lane, Virginia Beach, VA 23462 United States

STOCK TICKER/OTHER:

Stock Ticker: Subsidiary
Employees: 8,000
Parent Company: Anthem Inc

Exchange:
Fiscal Year Ends: 12/31

SALARIES/BONUSES:

Top Exec. Salary: $ Bonus: $
Second Exec. Salary: $ Bonus: $

OTHER THOUGHTS:

Estimated Female Officers or Directors: 3
Hot Spot for Advancement for Women/Minorities: Y

AmerisourceBergen Corp
NAIC Code: 424210

www.amerisourcebergen.com

TYPES OF BUSINESS:
Drug Distribution
Pharmacy Management & Consulting Services
Packaging Solutions
Information Technology
Healthcare Equipment

BRANDS/DIVISIONS/AFFILIATES:
AmerisourceBergen Drug Corporation
AmerisourceBergen Specialty Group
AmerisourceBergen Consulting Services
World Courier
St Francis Group

CONTACTS: Note: Officers with more than one job title may be intentionally listed here more than once.
Steven Collis, CEO
Tim Guttman, CFO
Lazarus Krikorian, Chief Accounting Officer
Dale Danilewitz, Chief Information Officer
Lawrence Marsha, Executive VP, Divisional
Gina Clark, Executive VP
John Chou, Executive VP
June Barry, Executive VP
James Cleary, Executive VP
Kathy Gaddes, General Counsel
Brian Nightengale, President, Divisional
Robert Mauch, President, Divisional
James Frary, President, Divisional
Peyton Howell, President, Divisional

GROWTH PLANS/SPECIAL FEATURES:
AmerisourceBergen Corp. is one of the largest wholesale distributors of pharmaceutical products and services to a wide variety of health care providers and pharmacies. The firm offers brand name and generic pharmaceuticals, supplies and equipment and serves the U.S., Canada and selected global markets. The company's operations are divided into two segments: pharmaceutical distribution and other. Pharmaceutical distribution provides drug distribution and related services designed to reduce health care costs and improve patient outcomes. This segment comprises two operating divisions: the operations of the AmerisourceBergen Drug Corporation (ABDC) and the AmerisourceBergen Specialty Group (ABSG). ABDC provides pharmacy management including distribution of brand-name & generic pharmaceutical products, staffing/consulting services, scalable automated pharmacy dispensing equipment, medication & supply dispensing cabinets and supply management software to a variety of retail & institutional health care providers. ABSG through a number of operating businesses, provides pharmaceutical distribution and other services primarily to physician practices who specialize in a variety of disease states, especially oncology, and to other health care providers such as dialysis clinics. This division also distributes plasma and other blood products, injectable pharmaceuticals and vaccines and provides third-party logistics and outcomes research for biotechnology and pharmaceutical manufacturers. The other segment comprises: AmerisourceBergen Consulting Services (ABCS), which provides commercialization support services such as reimbursement support programs, outcomes research, contract field staffing, patient assistance and copay assistance programs; and World Courier, which is a global specialty transportation and logistics provider for the biopharmaceutical industry. Serving more than 50 countries. In February 2016, the firm acquired St. Francis Group, the U.K.'s largest animal health buying group.

Employee benefits include health care, retirement, life insurance and disability protection.

FINANCIAL DATA: Note: Data for latest year may not have been available at press time.

In U.S. $	2016	2015	2014	2013	2012	2011
Revenue		135,961,800,000	119,569,100,000	87,959,170,000	79,489,600,000	80,217,550,000
R&D Expense						
Operating Income		417,370,000	778,884,000	898,399,000	1,252,728,000	1,202,745,000
Operating Margin %		.30%	.65%	1.02%	1.57%	1.49%
SGA Expense		1,918,045,000	1,587,261,000	1,333,712,000	1,229,495,000	1,197,969,000
Net Income		-134,887,000	276,484,000	433,707,000	718,986,000	706,624,000
Operating Cash Flow		3,920,379,000	1,463,153,000	788,125,000	1,305,449,000	1,167,948,000
Capital Expenditure		231,585,000	264,457,000	202,450,000	164,041,000	167,954,000
EBITDA		625,735,000	943,864,000	1,070,299,000	1,407,550,000	1,335,484,000
Return on Assets %		- .54%	1.36%	2.52%	4.72%	4.80%
Return on Equity %		-10.41%	12.92%	18.16%	27.01%	24.27%
Debt to Equity		5.51	1.01	0.60	0.58	0.33

CONTACT INFORMATION:
Phone: 610 727-7000   Fax: 610 647-0141
Toll-Free: 800-829-3132
Address: 1300 Morris Dr., Chesterbrook, PA 19087 United States

STOCK TICKER/OTHER:
Stock Ticker: ABC   Exchange: NYS
Employees: 17,500   Fiscal Year Ends: 09/30
Parent Company:

SALARIES/BONUSES:
Top Exec. Salary: Bonus: $
$1,190,000
Second Exec. Salary: Bonus: $
$676,539

OTHER THOUGHTS:
Estimated Female Officers or Directors: 7

Hot Spot for Advancement for Women/Minorities: Y

Ametek Inc

NAIC Code: 334513

www.ametek.com

TYPES OF BUSINESS:

Monitoring, Testing, Calibration and Display Electronic Device Manufacturing
ElectromechanicalÂ Device Manufacturing

BRANDS/DIVISIONS/AFFILIATES:

Global Tubes
Brookfield Engineering Laboratories
ESP/SurgeX

CONTACTS: Note: Officers with more than one job title may be intentionally listed here more than once.

David Zapico, CEO
William Burke, CFO
Frank Hermance, Chairman of the Board
Timothy Jones, President, Divisional
John Hardin, President, Divisional
Ronald Oscher, President, Divisional
Thomas Marecic, President, Divisional
Kathryn Sena, Secretary
Thomas Montgomery, Vice President, Divisional

GROWTH PLANS/SPECIAL FEATURES:

Ametek, Inc. is a global manufacturer of electronic instruments and electromechanical devices, with operations in North America, Europe, Asia and South America. The company markets its products worldwide through two operating groups: the electronic instruments group (EIG) and the electromechanical group (EMG). EIG builds monitoring, testing, calibration and display devices for the process, aerospace, industrial and power markets. The group makes significant use of distributors and sales representatives in marketing its products as well as direct sales in some of its more technically sophisticated products. EMG is a supplier of electromechanical devices. EMG produces highly engineered electromechanical connectors for hermetic (moisture-proof) applications, specialty metals for niche markets and brushless air-moving motors, blowers and heat exchangers. Management believes that the firm has several competitive advantages that assist it in sustaining and enhancing its market positions. The company's marketing efforts are generally organized and carried out at the division level. In general, most of the firm's markets are highly competitive. The principal elements of competition for the company's products are price, product technology, distribution, quality and service. AMETEK owns numerous unexpired U.S. patents and foreign patents, including counterparts of its more important U.S. patents, in the major industrial countries of the world. The firm has 85 operating facilities: 52 in the U.S., eight in the U.K., eight in Germany, four in Canada, two in China, two in France, two in Switzerland and one each in Argentina, Austria, Denmark, India, Japan, Mexico and Taiwan. In 2015, the firm acquired Global Tubes, a manufacturer of high-precision, small-diameter metal tubing; and the surface inspection systems division of Cognex Corporation. In 2016, it acquired Brookfield Engineering Laboratories, a manufacturer of viscometers and rheometers; and ESP/SurgeX, a provider of energy intelligence and power protection.

FINANCIAL DATA: Note: Data for latest year may not have been available at press time.

In U.S. $	2016	2015	2014	2013	2012	2011
Revenue		3,974,295,000	4,021,964,000	3,594,136,000	3,334,213,000	2,989,914,000
R&D Expense						
Operating Income		907,716,000	898,586,000	815,079,000	745,872,000	635,941,000
Operating Margin %		22.83%	22.34%	22.67%	22.37%	21.26%
SGA Expense		448,592,000	462,637,000	398,177,000	380,532,000	349,321,000
Net Income		590,859,000	584,460,000	516,999,000	459,132,000	384,464,000
Operating Cash Flow		672,540,000	725,962,000	660,659,000	612,464,000	508,565,000
Capital Expenditure		69,083,000	71,327,000	63,314,000	57,427,000	50,816,000
EBITDA		1,047,635,000	1,023,344,000	917,024,000	843,418,000	712,903,000
Return on Assets %		9.03%	9.50%	9.34%	9.65%	9.44%
Return on Equity %		18.19%	18.33%	18.23%	20.01%	20.08%
Debt to Equity		0.47	0.44	0.36	0.44	0.54

CONTACT INFORMATION:

Phone: 610 647-2121   Fax:
Toll-Free:
Address: 1100 Cassatt Rd., Berwyn, PA 19312-1177 United States

STOCK TICKER/OTHER:

Stock Ticker: AME
Employees: 15,400
Parent Company:

Exchange: NYS
Fiscal Year Ends: 12/31

SALARIES/BONUSES:

Top Exec. Salary: $1,240,575   Bonus: $545,853
Second Exec. Salary: $700,000   Bonus: $216,160

OTHER THOUGHTS:

Estimated Female Officers or Directors:

Hot Spot for Advancement for Women/Minorities:

Sales, profits and employees may be estimates. Financial information, benefits and other data can change quickly and may vary from those stated here.

Amgen Inc

www.amgen.com

NAIC Code: 325412

TYPES OF BUSINESS:
Drugs-Diversified
Oncology Drugs
Nephrology Drugs
Inflammation Drugs
Neurology Drugs

BRANDS/DIVISIONS/AFFILIATES:
Aranesp
EPOGEN
Neulasta
NEUPOGEN
Enbrel
Sensipar
Vectibix
Nplate

CONTACTS: *Note: Officers with more than one job title may be intentionally listed here more than once.*
Robert Bradway, CEO
David Meline, CFO
Annette Such, Chief Accounting Officer
Sean Harper, Executive VP, Divisional
Anthony Hooper, Executive VP, Divisional
Brian Mcnamee, Executive VP, Divisional
Madhu Balachandran, Executive VP, Divisional
Cynthia Patton, Other Executive Officer
Stuart Tross, Senior VP, Divisional
David Piacquad, Senior VP, Divisional
Jonathan Graham, Senior VP

GROWTH PLANS/SPECIAL FEATURES:
Amgen, Inc. is a global biotechnology medicines company that discovers, develops, manufactures and markets human therapeutics based on cellular and molecular biology. Its products are used for treatment in the fields of supportive cancer care, nephrology and inflammation. Amgen's primary products include Aranesp, EPOGEN, Neulasta, NEUPOGEN, Enbrel, XGEVA and Prolia. Aranesp and EPOGEN stimulate the production of red blood cells to treat anemia and belong to a class of drugs referred to as erythropoiesis-stimulating agents. Aranesp is used for the treatment of anemia both in chronic kidney failure and in concomitant chemotherapy. EPOGEN is used to treat anemia associated with end-stage renal disease. Neulasta and NEUPOGEN selectively stimulate the production of neutrophils, one type of white blood cell that helps the body fight infections. Enbrel inhibits tumor necrosis factor (TNF), a substance induced in response to inflammatory and immunological reactions, such as rheumatoid arthritis and psoriasis. XGEVA is approved for the prevention of skeletal-related events for patients with bone metastases from solid tumors, while Prolia is approved for the treatment of men and postmenopausal women with osteoporosis and a high risk of fracture. Other marketed products include Sensipar/Mimpara, which lowers serum calcium levels; Vectibix, used to treat specific progressions of metastatic colorectal cancer; Nplate, used to treat low platelet count; and Kyprolis, used to treat patients with relapsed multiple myeloma. Amgen maintains sales and marketing forces primarily in the U.S., Europe and Canada and markets its products to health care providers such as physicians or their clinics, dialysis centers, hospitals and pharmacies. In September 2015, the firm agreed to acquire Dezima Pharma B.V., a Netherland-based private biotechnology firm.

Amgen offers its employees health, disability and life insurance; paid time off; home and auto insurance; tuition reimbursement; childcare services; telecommuting options; and recreation/fitness classes.

FINANCIAL DATA: *Note: Data for latest year may not have been available at press time.*

In U.S. $	2016	2015	2014	2013	2012	2011
Revenue		21,662,000,000	20,063,000,000	18,676,000,000	17,265,000,000	15,582,000,000
R&D Expense		4,070,000,000	4,297,000,000	4,083,000,000	3,380,000,000	3,167,000,000
Operating Income		8,470,000,000	6,191,000,000	5,867,000,000	5,577,000,000	4,312,000,000
Operating Margin %		39.10%	30.85%	31.41%	32.30%	27.67%
SGA Expense		4,846,000,000	4,699,000,000	5,184,000,000	4,801,000,000	4,486,000,000
Net Income		6,939,000,000	5,158,000,000	5,081,000,000	4,345,000,000	3,683,000,000
Operating Cash Flow		9,077,000,000	8,555,000,000	6,291,000,000	5,882,000,000	5,119,000,000
Capital Expenditure		649,000,000	1,003,000,000	693,000,000	689,000,000	567,000,000
EBITDA		11,181,000,000	8,283,000,000	7,153,000,000	7,150,000,000	5,820,000,000
Return on Assets %		9.87%	7.63%	8.43%	8.42%	7.97%
Return on Equity %		25.76%	21.54%	24.69%	22.81%	17.14%
Debt to Equity		1.04	1.17	1.34	1.26	1.12

CONTACT INFORMATION:
Phone: 805 447-1000   Fax: 805 447-1010
Toll-Free: 800-772-6436
Address: 1 Amgen Center Dr., Thousand Oaks, CA 91320 United States

STOCK TICKER/OTHER:
Stock Ticker: AMGN   Exchange: NAS
Employees: 17,900   Fiscal Year Ends: 12/31
Parent Company:

SALARIES/BONUSES:
Top Exec. Salary: $903,478   Bonus: $1,000,000
Second Exec. Salary: Bonus: $1,427,203
$424,464

OTHER THOUGHTS:
Estimated Female Officers or Directors: 4
Hot Spot for Advancement for Women/Minorities: Y

Amphenol Corporation

www.amphenol.com

NAIC Code: 335921

TYPES OF BUSINESS:

Cables & Connectors
Fiber Optic Cable

BRANDS/DIVISIONS/AFFILIATES:

Times Fiber Communications Inc
Amphenol Fci
FCI Asia Pte Ltd

CONTACTS: *Note: Officers with more than one job title may be intentionally listed here more than once.*

Richard Norwitt, CEO
Craig Lampo, CFO
Martin Loeffler, Director
Edward Wetmore, General Counsel
Luc Walter, General Manager, Divisional
Richard Schneider, General Manager, Divisional
Zachary Raley, General Manager, Divisional
John Treanor, General Manager, Divisional
William Doherty, General Manager, Divisional
Patrick Gillard, Treasurer
David Silverman, Vice President, Divisional
Martin Booker, Vice President, Divisional
Thomas Meotti, Vice President, Divisional
Michael Ivas, Vice President
Jean-Luc Gavelle, Vice President

GROWTH PLANS/SPECIAL FEATURES:

Amphenol Corporation is a leading global designer, manufacturer and marketer of electrical, electronic & fiber optic connectors, interconnect systems and coaxial & flat-ribbon cable. The company has two operating segments: interconnect products & assemblies and cable products & solutions. Interconnect products & assemblies include connectors, which when attached to an electrical, electronic or fiber optic cable; a printed circuit board; or other device, facilitate transmission of power or signal. Value-add systems generally consist of a system of cable, flexible circuits or printed circuit boards and connectors for linking electronic equipment. The cable products & solutions segment primarily designs, manufacturers and markets cable, value-added products and components for use primarily in the broadband communications and information technology markets as well as certain applications in other markets. Amphenol's products are intended for eight primary end markets: automotive, which accounted for 18% of its 2015 sales; broadband communications, 6%; commercial aerospace, 6%; industrial, 17%; information technology and data communications, 16%; military, 10%; mobile devices, 19%; and mobile networks, 8%. Subsidiary Times Fiber Communications, Inc. is one of the world's largest producers of coaxial cable and interconnect products for the cable TV, satellite, data and broadband communications industries. Net sales by geographic region include the U.S., 30%; China, 30%; and other international locations, 40%. Amphenol has international manufacturing and assembly facilities in China, Macedonia, Malaysia, Mexico, India, Indonesia, Eastern Europe and North Africa. In January 2016, the firm acquired FCI Asia Pte. Ltd., an international connector and cable assembly solutions manufacturer, and was renamed Amphenol FCi.

FINANCIAL DATA: *Note: Data for latest year may not have been available at press time.*

In U.S. $	2016	2015	2014	2013	2012	2011
Revenue		5,568,700,000	5,345,500,000	4,614,669,000	4,292,065,000	3,939,786,000
R&D Expense						
Operating Income		1,104,700,000	1,034,600,000	896,813,000	828,345,000	751,678,000
Operating Margin %		19.83%	19.35%	19.43%	19.29%	19.07%
SGA Expense		669,100,000	645,100,000	548,038,000	512,867,000	507,795,000
Net Income		763,500,000	709,100,000	635,672,000	555,317,000	524,191,000
Operating Cash Flow		1,030,500,000	880,900,000	769,050,000	674,679,000	565,207,000
Capital Expenditure		172,100,000	209,100,000	158,448,000	129,099,000	100,222,000
EBITDA		1,292,700,000	1,221,000,000	1,046,680,000	960,233,000	879,220,000
Return on Assets %		10.54%	10.74%	11.16%	11.49%	12.39%
Return on Equity %		24.84%	24.59%	24.03%	24.13%	23.33%
Debt to Equity		0.86	0.91	0.50	0.66	0.63

CONTACT INFORMATION:

Phone: 203 265-8900   Fax: 203 265-8516
Toll-Free: 877-267-4366
Address: 358 Hall Ave., Wallingford, CT 06492 United States

STOCK TICKER/OTHER:

Stock Ticker: APH   Exchange: NYS
Employees: 44,500   Fiscal Year Ends: 12/31
Parent Company:

SALARIES/BONUSES:

Top Exec. Salary: Bonus: $
$1,030,000
Second Exec. Salary: Bonus: $
$530,416

OTHER THOUGHTS:

Estimated Female Officers or Directors: 1

Hot Spot for Advancement for Women/Minorities:

Sales, profits and employees may be estimates. Financial information, benefits and other data can change quickly and may vary from those stated here.

AMSURG Corporation

www.amsurg.com

NAIC Code: 621493

TYPES OF BUSINESS:

Practice-Based Ambulatory Surgery Centers
Physician Services

BRANDS/DIVISIONS/AFFILIATES:

CONTACTS: *Note: Officers with more than one job title may be intentionally listed here more than once.*

Claire Gulmi, CFO
Steven Geringer, Chairman of the Board
Thomas Cigarran, Co-Founder
Phillip Clendenin, Executive VP, Divisional
Robert Coward, Other Executive Officer
Christopher Holden, President
Kevin Eastridge, Senior VP, Divisional

GROWTH PLANS/SPECIAL FEATURES:

AMSURG Corporation is a leading physician-centric surgical center and physician services firm. The company operates in two business segments: ambulatory services and physician services. Ambulatory services, which derives approximately 48% of annual revenues, acquires, develops and operates ambulatory surgery centers (ASCs) in partnerships with physicians. This segment operates more than 250 ASCs in 34 states and the District of Columbia, in partnership with approximately 2,000 physicians. The typical size of a single-specialty ASC is 3,000 to 6,000 square feet; and the size of a multi-specialty ASC is approximately 8,000 to 12,000 square feet. Each center has two or three operating/procedure rooms with areas for reception, preparation, recovery and administration. Each surgery center is specifically tailored to meet the needs of physician partners. Surgery centers perform an average of 7,200 procedures each year. The physician services segment (52%) provides outsourced physician services in multiple specialties to hospitals, ASCs and other healthcare facilities, primarily in the areas of anesthesiology, radiology, children's services and emergency medicine. It provides services to more than 450 healthcare facilities in 29 states. In June 2016, the firm was in talks with Envision Healthcare Holdings, Inc. concerning a merger deal that would bring the two together with a combined value of approximately $10 billion. Envision shareholders would own approximately 53% and AMSURG shareholders would own the remainder. Both boards of directors voted unanimously for the merger.

Employee benefits include medical, vision and dental coverage; a flexible spending account; a health savings account; life and AD&D insurance; short- and long-term disability; long-term care insurance; a 401(k); a wellness program; and employee discounts.

FINANCIAL DATA: *Note: Data for latest year may not have been available at press time.*

In U.S. $	2016	2015	2014	2013	2012	2011
Revenue		2,566,884,000	1,621,949,000	1,079,343,000	928,509,000	786,870,000
R&D Expense						
Operating Income		617,505,000	394,364,000	338,065,000	281,945,000	242,448,000
Operating Margin %		24.05%	24.31%	31.32%	30.36%	30.81%
SGA Expense		1,322,716,000	728,466,000	333,190,000		
Net Income		162,947,000	53,701,000	72,703,000	62,563,000	49,997,000
Operating Cash Flow		537,959,000	412,371,000	332,824,000	295,652,000	243,423,000
Capital Expenditure		60,305,000	40,217,000	28,856,000	28,864,000	22,170,000
EBITDA		714,998,000	454,708,000	371,093,000	312,023,000	268,623,000
Return on Assets %		2.54%	1.27%	3.44%	3.45%	3.65%
Return on Equity %		8.45%	4.32%	10.00%	9.58%	8.47%
Debt to Equity		1.13	1.47	0.76	0.90	0.72

CONTACT INFORMATION:

Phone: 615 665-1283   Fax: 615 665-0755
Toll-Free: 800-945-2301
Address: 1A Burton Hills Blvd., Nashville, TN 37215 United States

STOCK TICKER/OTHER:

Stock Ticker: AMSG   Exchange: NAS
Employees: 10,500   Fiscal Year Ends: 12/31
Parent Company:

SALARIES/BONUSES:

Top Exec. Salary: Bonus: $
$1,000,000
Second Exec. Salary: Bonus: $
$657,280

OTHER THOUGHTS:

Estimated Female Officers or Directors: 2

Hot Spot for Advancement for Women/Minorities: Y

Anthem Inc

www.antheminc.com

NAIC Code: 524114

TYPES OF BUSINESS:

Health Insurance
Health Maintenance Organizations (HMOs)
Point-of-Service Plans
Dental and Vision Plans
Plan Management (ASO) for Self-Insured Organizations
Prescription Plans
Wellness Programs
Medicare Administrative Services

BRANDS/DIVISIONS/AFFILIATES:

Blue Cross and Blue Shield Association
HealthLink
UniCare
CareMore Health Groups Inc
Blue Cross of California
Anthem Blue Cross Blue Shield
Blue Cross Blue Shield of Georgia
Amerigroup

CONTACTS: Note: Officers with more than one job title may be intentionally listed here more than once.

Joseph Swedish, CEO
John Gallina, CFO
Ronald Penczek, Chief Accounting Officer
Gloria McCarthy, Chief Administrative Officer
Thomas Zielinski, Executive VP
Jose Tomas, Executive VP
Craig Samitt, Executive VP
Brian Griffin, Executive VP
Peter Haytaian, President, Divisional
Kathleen Kiefer, Secretary

GROWTH PLANS/SPECIAL FEATURES:

Anthem, Inc. is a health benefits company, serving roughly 38.6 million medical members through its subsidiaries. The firm is an independent licensee of the Blue Cross and Blue Shield Association, an association of independent health benefit plans, and also serves customers throughout the country under the HealthLink and UniCare brands. Anthem serves certain Arizona, California, Nevada, New York and Virginia markets through subsidiary CareMore Health Group, Inc. The firm offers network-based managed care plans to the large and small employer, individual, Medicaid and senior markets. The managed care plans include preferred provider organizations (PPO), health maintenance organizations (HMO), point-of-service (POS) plans, traditional indemnity plans and other hybrid plans including consumer-driven health plans, hospital-only and limited benefit products. In addition, Anthem provides managed care services to self-insured organizations, including claims processing, underwriting, stop loss insurance, actuarial services, provider network access, medical cost management and other administrative services. The company also provides specialty and other products and services, including life and disability insurance benefits; dental, vision and behavioral health benefit services; long-term care insurance; and flexible spending accounts. Subsidiaries include Blue Cross of California, Anthem Blue Cross Blue Shield and Blue Cross Blue Shield of Georgia as well as non-Blue Cross subsidiaries such as HealthLink, Amerigroup and HealthCore. In 2015, competitor CIGNA agreed to acquire Anthem in a deal worth $48 billion. The proposed merger was awaiting federal regulatory approval as of late 2015. In August 2016, the U.S. District judge returned the Anthem-CIGMA case back to the federal court for reassignment in order to help speed the merger process.

The firm offers employees tuition assistance; a 401(k) plan; stock purchase plan; paid time off; long-term care coverage; adoption assistance; an employee assistance program; life insurance; medical, dental and vision coverage; and flexible spending accounts.

FINANCIAL DATA: Note: Data for latest year may not have been available at press time.

In U.S. $	2016	2015	2014	2013	2012	2011
Revenue		79,156,500,000	73,874,100,000	71,023,500,000	61,711,700,000	60,710,700,000
R&D Expense						
Operating Income		4,631,000,000	4,368,100,000	3,840,200,000	3,865,500,000	3,957,900,000
Operating Margin %		5.85%	5.91%	5.40%	6.26%	6.51%
SGA Expense		12,534,800,000	11,748,400,000	9,952,900,000	8,738,300,000	8,435,600,000
Net Income		2,560,000,000	2,569,700,000	2,489,700,000	2,655,500,000	2,646,700,000
Operating Cash Flow		4,116,000,000	3,369,300,000	3,052,300,000	2,744,600,000	3,374,400,000
Capital Expenditure		638,200,000	714,600,000	646,500,000	544,900,000	519,500,000
EBITDA						
Return on Assets %		4.13%	4.22%	4.20%	4.78%	5.18%
Return on Equity %		10.82%	10.48%	10.25%	11.27%	11.23%
Debt to Equity		0.66	0.58	0.54	0.59	0.36

CONTACT INFORMATION:

Phone: 317 488-6000   Fax:
Toll-Free:
Address: 120 Monument Cir., Indianapolis, IN 46204 United States

STOCK TICKER/OTHER:

Stock Ticker: ANTM
Employees: 51,500
Parent Company:

Exchange: NYS
Fiscal Year Ends: 12/31

SALARIES/BONUSES:

Top Exec. Salary: $1,298,077   Bonus: $

Second Exec. Salary: $612,692   Bonus: $300,000

OTHER THOUGHTS:

Estimated Female Officers or Directors: 1

Hot Spot for Advancement for Women/Minorities: Y

APC by Schneider Electric

NAIC Code: 335911

TYPES OF BUSINESS:

Back-Up Power Supplies
Power Protection & Management Products
Consulting Services
PC Accessories
Power Management Software
Fuel Cell-Based Power Backup

BRANDS/DIVISIONS/AFFILIATES:

Schneider Electric SA
Fuel Cell Extended Run
InfraStruXure
American Power Conversion

CONTACTS: Note: Officers with more than one job title may be intentionally listed here more than once.

Jean-Pascal Tricoire, CEO
Julio Rodriguez, COO
Daniel Doimo, Pres.
Karen Miranda, CFO
Olivier Blum, VP-Human Resources
Neil Rasmussen, Sr. VP-Innovation
Hal Grant, VP-IT
Randy Amon, Sr. VP-Customer Care, Quality & Process
Leanne Cunnold, Sr. VP-Bus. Dev. & Strategy
Rob McKernan, Pres., Americas
Mike Maiello, Sr. VP-Home & Bus. Networks
Philippe Arsonneau, Pres., Asia Pacific & Japan
Chenhong Huang, Sr. VP-Greater China
Ed Machala, Sr. VP-Supply Chain, Purchasing & Manufacturing

GROWTH PLANS/SPECIAL FEATURES:

APC by Schneider Electric designs, develops, manufactures and markets power protection and management solutions for computer, communications and electronic applications worldwide. The company's products include uninterruptible power supply (UPS) products, electrical surge protection devices, power distribution products, precision cooling equipment, power management software and accessories, racks and enclosures and various desktop and notebook personal computer accessories. These products are primarily used with sensitive electronic devices, which rely on electric utility power, such as home electronics, PCs, high-performance computer workstations, servers, networking equipment, communications equipment, Internet equipment, data centers, mainframe computers and facilities. APC's UPS products regulate the flow of utility power to the protected equipment and provide seamless back-up power during power interruptions. Back-up power lasts for enough time to continue computer operations, conduct an orderly shutdown, preserve data, work through short power outages or, in some cases, continue operating for several hours or longer. In addition, the firm's Fuel Cell Extended Run (FCXR) product provides hydrogen-based power backup for its proprietary InfraStruXure power, cooling, environmental monitoring and management data center for modular & mobile configurations. The company's security and environmental appliances and accessories protect against environmental or human threats and monitor valuable systems with sensors, cameras and accessories. APC's precision cooling equipment regulates temperature and humidity. Last, the company provides power management software, consulting services and notebook and PC accessories. Its data center software business is responsible for software creation and development, sales, service and marketing programs.

The firm offers employees comprehensive health and dental coverage, short- and long-term disability, flexible spending accounts, life insurance, tuition assistance, a relocation program, leaves of absence, holidays, an employee share plan and a 401(k) plan.

FINANCIAL DATA: Note: Data for latest year may not have been available at press time.

In U.S. $	2016	2015	2014	2013	2012	2011
Revenue		4,750,000,000	4,600,000,000	4,450,000,000	4,300,000,000	4,200,000,000
R&D Expense						
Operating Income						
Operating Margin %						
SGA Expense						
Net Income						
Operating Cash Flow						
Capital Expenditure						
EBITDA						
Return on Assets %						
Return on Equity %						
Debt to Equity						

CONTACT INFORMATION:

Phone: 401-789-2208   Fax: 401-789-3710
Toll-Free: 800-788-2208
Address: 132 Fairgrounds Rd., West Kingston, RI 02892 United States

STOCK TICKER/OTHER:

Stock Ticker: Subsidiary   Exchange:
Employees: 7,580   Fiscal Year Ends: 12/31
Parent Company: Schneider Electric SA

SALARIES/BONUSES:

Top Exec. Salary: $ Bonus: $
Second Exec. Salary: $ Bonus: $

OTHER THOUGHTS:

Estimated Female Officers or Directors: 2
Hot Spot for Advancement for Women/Minorities:

Apple Inc

www.apple.com

NAIC Code: 334220

TYPES OF BUSINESS:

Electronics Design and Manufacturing
Software
Computers and Tablets
Retail Stores
Smartphones
Online Music Store
Apps Store
Home Entertainment Software & Systems

BRANDS/DIVISIONS/AFFILIATES:

iPhone
iPad
Apple Watch
Apple TV
watchOS
tvOS
Mac App Store
iPod

CONTACTS: *Note: Officers with more than one job title may be intentionally listed here more than once.*

Timothy Cook, CEO
Luca Maestri, CFO
Arthur Levinson, Chairman of the Board
Chris Kondo, Chief Accounting Officer
Jeffery Williams, COO
D. Sewell, General Counsel
Craig Federighi, Senior VP, Divisional
Philip Schiller, Senior VP, Divisional
Johny Srouji, Senior VP, Divisional
Eduardo Cue, Senior VP, Divisional
Daniel Riccio, Senior VP, Divisional
Angela Ahrendts, Senior VP, Divisional

GROWTH PLANS/SPECIAL FEATURES:

Apple, Inc. designs, manufactures and markets personal computers, portable digital music players and mobile communication devices and sells a variety of related software, services, peripherals and networking applications. The company's products and services include iPhone, iPad, Mac, iPod, Apple Watch, Apple TV, a portfolio of consumer and professional software applications, the iOS, OS X and watchOS operating systems, iCloud, Apple Pay and a variety of accessory, service and support offerings. The company also sells and delivers digital content and applications through the iTunes Store, App Store, iBookstore, tvOS, Apple TV App Store and Mac App Store. iOS is the company's multi-touch operating system that serves the foundation for iOS devices. OS X is the firm's Mac operating system, built on an open-source UNIX-based foundation and provides an intuitive and integrated computer experience. watchOS is Apple's operating system for Apple Watch, released in September 2015. tvOS is the operating system for the new Apple TV, which became available in October 2015. Peripheral products are sold directly to end-users through its retail and online stores and include printers, storage devices, computer memory, digital video and still camera and other computing products and supplies. Apple's retail stores have been a tremendous success. The iPhone derived 52% of net sales in 2015, with the iPad coming in second deriving 23%, the Mac deriving 6% and other products deriving the rest.

Apple employee benefits include health and life insurance, long-term care insurance, an employee stock purchase plan, a 401(k), short- and long-term disability coverage, paid vacations and holidays, employee discounts, tuition assistance, wellness programs, personal and family counseling, financial education seminars and an onsite fitness center.

FINANCIAL DATA: *Note: Data for latest year may not have been available at press time.*

In U.S. $	2016	2015	2014	2013	2012	2011
Revenue		233,715,000,000	182,795,000,000	170,910,000,000	156,508,000,000	108,249,000,000
R&D Expense		8,067,000,000	6,041,000,000	4,475,000,000	3,381,000,000	2,429,000,000
Operating Income		71,230,000,000	52,503,000,000	48,999,000,000	55,241,000,000	33,790,000,000
Operating Margin %		30.47%	28.72%	28.66%	35.29%	31.21%
SGA Expense		14,329,000,000	11,993,000,000	10,830,000,000	10,040,000,000	7,599,000,000
Net Income		53,394,000,000	39,510,000,000	37,037,000,000	41,733,000,000	25,922,000,000
Operating Cash Flow		81,266,000,000	59,713,000,000	53,666,000,000	50,856,000,000	37,529,000,000
Capital Expenditure		11,488,000,000	9,813,000,000	9,076,000,000	9,402,000,000	7,452,000,000
EBITDA		84,505,000,000	61,813,000,000	57,048,000,000	58,518,000,000	35,604,000,000
Return on Assets %		20.44%	18.00%	19.33%	28.54%	27.06%
Return on Equity %		46.24%	33.61%	30.63%	42.84%	41.67%
Debt to Equity		0.44	0.25	0.13		

CONTACT INFORMATION:

Phone: 408 996-1010   Fax: 408 974-2483
Toll-Free: 800-692-7753
Address: 1 Infinite Loop, Cupertino, CA 95014 United States

STOCK TICKER/OTHER:

Stock Ticker: AAPL   Exchange: NAS
Employees: 92,600   Fiscal Year Ends: 09/30
Parent Company:

SALARIES/BONUSES:

Top Exec. Salary: Bonus: $
$2,000,000
Second Exec. Salary: Bonus: $
$1,000,000

OTHER THOUGHTS:

Estimated Female Officers or Directors:

Hot Spot for Advancement for Women/Minorities:

Applied Materials Inc

www.appliedmaterials.com

NAIC Code: 333242

TYPES OF BUSINESS:

Semiconductor Manufacturing Equipment
LCD Display Technology Equipment
Automation Software
Energy Generation & Conversion Technologies

BRANDS/DIVISIONS/AFFILIATES:

CONTACTS: Note: Officers with more than one job title may be intentionally listed here more than once.

Gary Dickerson, CEO
Robert Halliday, CFO
James Morgan, Chairman Emeritus
Omkaram Nalamasu, Chief Technology Officer
Willem Roelandts, Director
Thomas Larkins, General Counsel
Ali Salehpour, General Manager, Divisional
Ginetto Addiego, Senior VP, Divisional
Charles Read, Vice President

GROWTH PLANS/SPECIAL FEATURES:

Applied Materials, Inc. (AMI), a global leader in the semiconductor industry, provides manufacturing equipment services and software to the global semiconductor, flat panel display, solar photovoltaic (PV) and related industries. AMI operates in four segments: silicon systems, applied global services, display and energy & environmental solutions. The silicon systems group develops, manufactures and sells a range of manufacturing equipment used to fabricate semiconductor chips or integrated circuits. The company offers systems that perform most of the primary processes used in chip fabrication. The applied global services segment provides products and services designed to improve the performance and productivity and reduce environmental impact of the fabrication operations of semiconductor, LCD and solar PV manufacturers. Its services encompass four primary components: fabrication services, automation systems, sub fabrication systems and abatement control systems. The display segment designs, manufactures, sells and services equipment to fabricate thin film transistor LCDs for televisions, computer displays, tablet personal computers, smart phones and other consumer-oriented electronic applications. The energy & environmental solutions segment provides manufacturing solutions for the generation and conservation of energy. The segment is comprised of AMI's products used for fabricating c-Si solar PVs, web products and high throughput roll-to-roll coating systems for flexible electronic products. AMI's products and services utilize nanomanufacturing technology, or the production of ultra-small structures, including the engineering of thin layers of film onto substrates. In October 2015, the firm announced its plan to establish a new R&D lab in Singapore for advanced semiconductor technology in collaboration with the Agency for Science, Technology and Research (A*STAR).

The company offers employees medical, life, AD&D, disability and business travel accident insurance; flexible spending accounts; an employee assistance program; health appraisals; a 401(k) plan; a stock purchase plan; and credit union membership.

FINANCIAL DATA: Note: Data for latest year may not have been available at press time.

In U.S. $	2016	2015	2014	2013	2012	2011
Revenue		9,659,000,000	9,072,000,000	7,509,000,000	8,719,000,000	10,517,000,000
R&D Expense		1,451,000,000	1,428,000,000	1,320,000,000	1,237,000,000	1,118,000,000
Operating Income		1,693,000,000	1,520,000,000	432,000,000	411,000,000	2,398,000,000
Operating Margin %		17.52%	16.75%	5.75%	4.71%	22.80%
SGA Expense		883,000,000	890,000,000	902,000,000	1,076,000,000	901,000,000
Net Income		1,377,000,000	1,072,000,000	256,000,000	109,000,000	1,926,000,000
Operating Cash Flow		1,163,000,000	1,800,000,000	623,000,000	1,851,000,000	2,426,000,000
Capital Expenditure		215,000,000	241,000,000	197,000,000	162,000,000	209,000,000
EBITDA		2,072,000,000	1,918,000,000	855,000,000	833,000,000	2,683,000,000
Return on Assets %		9.66%	8.50%	2.12%	.83%	15.52%
Return on Equity %		17.78%	14.33%	3.57%	1.35%	23.57%
Debt to Equity		0.43	0.24	0.27	0.26	0.22

CONTACT INFORMATION:

Phone: 408 727-5555   Fax: 408 727-9943
Toll-Free:
Address: 3050 Bowers Ave., Santa Clara, CA 95052 United States

SALARIES/BONUSES:

Top Exec. Salary: $995,385   Bonus: $
Second Exec. Salary: Bonus: $
$613,462

STOCK TICKER/OTHER:

Stock Ticker: AMAT   Exchange: NAS
Employees: 15,400   Fiscal Year Ends: 10/31
Parent Company:

OTHER THOUGHTS:

Estimated Female Officers or Directors: 2
Hot Spot for Advancement for Women/Minorities: Y

Aramark

NAIC Code: 722310

www.aramark.com

TYPES OF BUSINESS:

Food Service Contractor
Facilities Management
Uniforms & Career Apparel Rental
Parks & Resorts Concessions & Facilities
Health Care Support Services
Apparel Manufacturing
Clinical Equipment Maintenance

BRANDS/DIVISIONS/AFFILIATES:

Warburg Pincus LLC
GS Capital Partners
CCMP Capital Advisors
J.P. Morgan Partners
Thomas H. Lee Partners LP

CONTACTS: Note: Officers with more than one job title may be intentionally listed here more than once.

Eric Foss, CEO
Stephen Bramlage, CFO
Brian Pressler, Chief Accounting Officer
Lynn McKee, Executive VP, Divisional
Stephen Reynolds, Executive VP
Christina Morrison, Senior VP, Divisional
Christian Dirx, Treasurer

GROWTH PLANS/SPECIAL FEATURES:

Aramark is a leading food, hospitality and facilities management services company. Serving clients in 21 countries, Aramark operates in two main segments: food and support services (FSS) and uniform and career apparel. The FSS segment has two divisions, North America, accounting for 69% of total 2015 sales and international, accounting for 20% of total sales. The FSS segment manages a range of services, including food, hospitality and facility services-for school districts, colleges & universities, healthcare facilities, businesses, sports, entertainment & recreational venues, conference & convention centers, national & state parks and correctional institutions. The facility services consists of plant operations and maintenance, custodial/housekeeping, energy management, clinical equipment maintenance, grounds keeping, and capital project management. The FSS segment offers its services to clients in healthcare, sports, leisure & corrections, business & industry and education sectors. The uniform and career apparel segment provides uniforms and other garments and work clothes and ancillary items such as mats and shop towels in the United States, Puerto Rico, Canada and through a joint venture in Japan. The firm offers full service employee uniform solution, including design, sourcing and manufacturing, delivery, cleaning and maintenance. In addition, this segment offers rental services for uniforms, work clothing, outerwear, particulate-free garments and non-garment items, including industrial towels, floor mats, mops, linen products, and paper products to businesses in a wide range of industries. Aramark is owned by an investor group consisting of GS Capital Partners, CCMP Capital Advisors, J.P. Morgan Partners, Thomas H. Lee Partners and Warburg Pincus LLC.

The company offers its employees medical, dental and vision insurance; a pension plan; life and disability insurance; and an employee assistance plan.

FINANCIAL DATA: Note: Data for latest year may not have been available at press time.

In U.S. $	2016	2015	2014	2013	2012	2011
Revenue		14,329,140,000	14,832,910,000	13,945,660,000	13,505,430,000	13,082,380,000
R&D Expense						
Operating Income		627,938,000	564,563,000	514,474,000	581,775,000	547,089,000
Operating Margin %		4.38%	3.80%	3.68%	4.30%	4.18%
SGA Expense		316,740,000	382,851,000	227,902,000	203,019,000	187,992,000
Net Income		235,946,000	148,956,000	69,356,000	103,551,000	83,846,000
Operating Cash Flow		683,036,000	398,159,000	695,907,000	691,761,000	303,608,000
Capital Expenditure		527,618,000	566,110,000	414,951,000	497,874,000	455,859,000
EBITDA		1,132,290,000	1,085,700,000	1,058,390,000	1,113,264,000	1,078,399,000
Return on Assets %		2.28%	1.43%	.66%	.98%	
Return on Equity %		13.10%	11.36%	7.55%	11.09%	
Debt to Equity		2.76	3.11	6.37	6.39	

CONTACT INFORMATION:

Phone: 215-238-3000   Fax: 215-238-3333
Toll-Free: 800-272-6275
Address: 1101 Market St., ARAMARK Tower, Philadelphia, PA 19107 United States

STOCK TICKER/OTHER:

Stock Ticker: ARMK
Employees: 265,500
Parent Company:

Exchange: NYS
Fiscal Year Ends: 09/30

SALARIES/BONUSES:

Top Exec. Salary: $1,622,625   Bonus: $

Second Exec. Salary: $675,358   Bonus: $

OTHER THOUGHTS:

Estimated Female Officers or Directors: 1

Hot Spot for Advancement for Women/Minorities:

Arrow Electronics Inc

NAIC Code: 423430

www.arrow.com

TYPES OF BUSINESS:

Electronic Components-Distributor
Computer Products-Distributor
Technical Support Services
Supply Chain Services
Design Services
Materials Planning
Assembly Services
Inventory Management

BRANDS/DIVISIONS/AFFILIATES:

CONTACTS: Note: Officers with more than one job title may be intentionally listed here more than once.

Michael Long, CEO
Christopher Stansbury, CFO
Vincent Melvin, Chief Information Officer
Paul Reilly, Executive VP, Divisional
Mary Morris, Other Executive Officer
Sean Kerins, President, Divisional
Andy King, President, Divisional
Gretchen Zech, Senior VP, Divisional
Gregory Tarpinian, Senior VP

GROWTH PLANS/SPECIAL FEATURES:

Arrow Electronics, Inc. is a global provider of products, services and solutions to industrial and commercial users of electronic components and enterprise computing software. The firm offers its clients products and solutions, including materials planning, new product design services, programming and assembly services, inventory management, reverse logistics, electronics asset disposition (EAD) and a variety of online supply chain tools. Arrow serves as a supply channel partner for over 100,000 original equipment manufacturers (OEMs), contract manufacturers and commercial customers through a global network of over 300 locations in 56 countries and territories. Its operations are divided into two segments: global enterprise computing solutions (ECS), representing 37% of sales, and the global components business, 63%. The global ECS segment distributes enterprise IT products, such as servers, software and storage devices, as well as midrange computing products, services and solutions to value added retailers (VARs) in North America and Europe, the Middle East and Africa (EMEA). This segment also provides unified communications products and related services in North America. The global components business segment distributes electronics components and related products to customers in North and South America, EMEA and the Asia-Pacific. Its sales consist of semiconductors; passive, electro-mechanical and interconnect products, such as capacitors, resistors, potentiometers, power supplies, relays, switches and connectors; and computing, memory and other products. The company maintains an aggressive growth strategy based on acquiring competitors and complementary businesses and has completed 13 strategic acquisitions in the last three years.

FINANCIAL DATA: Note: Data for latest year may not have been available at press time.

In U.S. $	2016	2015	2014	2013	2012	2011
Revenue		23,282,020,000	22,768,670,000	21,357,290,000	20,405,130,000	21,390,260,000
R&D Expense						
Operating Income		824,482,000	762,257,000	693,500,000	804,123,000	908,843,000
Operating Margin %		3.54%	3.34%	3.24%	3.94%	4.24%
SGA Expense		1,986,249,000	1,959,749,000	1,873,638,000	1,849,534,000	1,892,592,000
Net Income		497,726,000	498,045,000	399,420,000	506,332,000	598,810,000
Operating Cash Flow		655,079,000	673,301,000	450,691,000	675,033,000	120,883,000
Capital Expenditure		154,800,000	122,505,000	116,162,000	112,224,000	113,941,000
EBITDA		980,236,000	918,305,000	824,641,000	919,473,000	1,019,254,000
Return on Assets %		3.90%	4.06%	3.49%	4.91%	6.16%
Return on Equity %		11.99%	11.95%	9.78%	13.23%	17.30%
Debt to Equity		0.55	0.49	0.53	0.39	0.52

CONTACT INFORMATION:

Phone: 300 824-4000   Fax:
Toll-Free:
Address: 9201 East Dry Creek Road, Centennial, CO 80112 United States

STOCK TICKER/OTHER:

Stock Ticker: ARW
Employees: 18,500
Parent Company:

Exchange: NYS
Fiscal Year Ends: 12/31

SALARIES/BONUSES:

Top Exec. Salary:
$1,150,000
Second Exec. Salary:
$700,000

Bonus: $

Bonus: $

OTHER THOUGHTS:

Estimated Female Officers or Directors: 4

Hot Spot for Advancement for Women/Minorities: Y

Arthur J Gallagher & Co

www.ajg.com

NAIC Code: 524210

TYPES OF BUSINESS:
Insurance Brokerage & Management
Risk Management Services
Employee Benefit Services
Investment Operations
Claims Management
Information Management
Insurance Software
Reinsurance

BRANDS/DIVISIONS/AFFILIATES:

CONTACTS: *Note: Officers with more than one job title may be intentionally listed here more than once.*
J. Gallagher, CEO
Douglas Howell, CFO
Thomas Gallagher, Chairman of the Board, Divisional
Richard Cary, Controller
Walter Bay, General Counsel
Marsha Akin, Other Corporate Officer
Scott Hudson, President, Divisional
Linda Collins, Vice President, Divisional
Susan Pietrucha, Vice President
James Gault, Vice President
James Durkin, Vice President
Joel Cavaness, Vice President

GROWTH PLANS/SPECIAL FEATURES:

Arthur J. Gallagher & Co. and its subsidiaries provide insurance brokerage and third-party claims settlement and administration services to clients in the U.S. and abroad, with Gallagher's brokers, agents and administrators acting as intermediaries between insurers and their customers. The firm operates in three business segments: brokerage, risk management and corporate. The brokerage segment, accounting for 62% of the firm's revenues, is comprised of retail and wholesale brokerage operations. Retail operations focus on property/casualty, employer-provided health and welfare insurance and retirement planning on behalf of middle market commercial, industrial, public, religious and nonprofit clients, while wholesale brokers assist the retail brokers and other non-Gallagher brokers in placing specialized and hard-to-place insurance coverage. The risk management segment (13% of revenues) provides contract claim settlement and administration services for clients that self-insure some or all of their property/casualty coverage and for insurance companies choosing to outsource some or all of their property/casualty claims departments. Gallagher markets its risk management services primarily to Fortune 1000 companies, larger middle market companies, nonprofit organizations and public entities. The corporate segment (25% of revenues) manages the firm's clean energy and tax-advantaged investments and venture capital funds. The majority of the company's revenues are generated in the U.S., with the remaining coming out of the U.K., Australia, Canada and New Zealand. In June 2016, the firm joined the Fortune 500 for the first time.

Employees are offered medical, dental and vision coverage; AD&D; flexible spending account; short- and long-term disability; a 401(k); educational assistance; and an employee stock purchase plan.

FINANCIAL DATA: *Note: Data for latest year may not have been available at press time.*

In U.S. $	2016	2015	2014	2013	2012	2011
Revenue		5,392,400,000	4,626,500,000	3,179,600,000	2,520,300,000	2,134,700,000
R&D Expense						
Operating Income		293,500,000	267,400,000	274,500,000	245,300,000	207,800,000
Operating Margin %		5.44%	5.77%	8.63%	9.73%	9.73%
SGA Expense		840,700,000	767,200,000	552,400,000	483,200,000	419,000,000
Net Income		356,800,000	303,400,000	268,600,000	195,000,000	144,100,000
Operating Cash Flow		652,600,000	402,300,000	349,900,000	343,000,000	283,100,000
Capital Expenditure		99,000,000	81,500,000	93,600,000	51,000,000	40,000,000
EBITDA		730,700,000	615,300,000	503,200,000	428,700,000	363,800,000
Return on Assets %		3.41%	3.59%	4.39%	3.96%	3.56%
Return on Equity %		10.39%	11.41%	14.34%	13.43%	12.26%
Debt to Equity		0.57	0.65	0.39	0.43	

CONTACT INFORMATION:
Phone: 630 773-3800   Fax: 630 285-4000
Toll-Free:
Address: 2 Pierce Pl., Itasca, IL 60143 United States

STOCK TICKER/OTHER:
Stock Ticker: AJG
Employees: 21,500
Parent Company:

Exchange: NYS
Fiscal Year Ends: 12/31

SALARIES/BONUSES:
Top Exec. Salary: $700,000   Bonus: $525,000
Second Exec. Salary: $800,000   Bonus: $200,000

OTHER THOUGHTS:
Estimated Female Officers or Directors: 3
Hot Spot for Advancement for Women/Minorities: Y

Ascena Retail Group Inc

www.ascenaretail.com

NAIC Code: 448120

TYPES OF BUSINESS:

Women's Apparel, Retail
Teen Fashion Stores
Fashion Accessories
Private-Label Credit Cards

BRANDS/DIVISIONS/AFFILIATES:

Justice
Lane Bryant
maurices
dressbarn
Catherines
Ann Inc
Ann Taylor
Loft

CONTACTS: Note: Officers with more than one job title may be intentionally listed here more than once.

Gary Muto, CEO, Subsidiary
David Jaffe, CEO
Robb Giammatteo, CFO
Elliot Jaffe, Co-Founder
Jonathan Pershing, Executive VP
Duane Holloway, General Counsel
Kevin Trolaro, Other Corporate Officer
Ernest Laporte, Senior VP

GROWTH PLANS/SPECIAL FEATURES:

Ascena Retail Group, Inc. operates a national chain of value priced specialty stores offering in-season, moderate to bette quality apparel and accessories. The company ha approximately 3,900 stores throughout the U.S., Puerto Ric and Canada. It now operates in following five segments base on a brand-oriented approach: Justice, Lane Bryant, maurice dressbarn and Catherines. The Justice segment includes 97 specialty retail and outlet stores, e-commerce operations an licensed franchises internationally, offering fashionable appar to girls ages 7-14, designed for an energetic lifestyle. Lan Bryant includes 765 specialty retail and outlet stores and commerce operations, and is a widely recognized brand nam in plus-size fashion. The maurices segment includes 95 specialty retail and outlet stores and e-commerce operation offering up-to-date fashion for women in their 20s and 30s. Th dressbarn segment includes 824 specialty retail and outle stores and e-commerce operations, offering moderate-to better quality career and casual fashion for working wome ranging from their mid-30's to mid-50's. Catherines include 377 specialty retail stores and e-commerce operations, an sells plus-size fashion to women 45 years and older who sho in the moderate price range and are concerned with comfort, and value. Ascena owns distribution centers for its variou brands in Ohio, Iowa, Indiana, Maryland and Wisconsin. 2015, the firm acquired Ann, Inc., the parent of Ann Taylor an Loft.

FINANCIAL DATA: Note: Data for latest year may not have been available at press time.

In U.S. $	2016	2015	2014	2013	2012	2011
Revenue	6,995,400,000	4,802,900,000	4,790,600,000	4,714,900,000	3,353,300,000	2,914,000,000
R&D Expense						
Operating Income	93,800,000	-234,900,000	210,800,000	265,300,000	292,600,000	289,800,000
Operating Margin %		-4.89%	4.40%	5.62%	8.72%	9.94%
SGA Expense	3,398,800,000	2,347,800,000	2,208,600,000	2,172,200,000	1,478,600,000	852,100,000
Net Income	-11,900,000	-236,800,000	133,400,000	151,300,000	162,200,000	170,500,000
Operating Cash Flow	445,400,000	431,300,000	374,700,000	450,000,000	361,500,000	280,800,000
Capital Expenditure	366,500,000	312,500,000	477,500,000	290,900,000	150,400,000	102,100,000
EBITDA	453,700,000	-16,400,000	403,600,000	432,400,000	390,700,000	376,700,000
Return on Assets %		-7.84%	4.45%	5.32%	6.98%	9.76%
Return on Equity %		-14.54%	8.09%	10.44%	12.98%	15.68%
Debt to Equity		0.23	0.09	0.08	0.41	0.14

CONTACT INFORMATION:

Phone: 551-777-6700   Fax:
Toll-Free:
Address: 933 MacArthur Blvd., Mahwah, NJ 07430 United States

STOCK TICKER/OTHER:

Stock Ticker: ASNA
Employees: 48,000
Parent Company:

Exchange: NAS
Fiscal Year Ends: 07/31

SALARIES/BONUSES:

Top Exec. Salary: $1,000,000   Bonus: $

Second Exec. Salary: $500,308   Bonus: $147,766

OTHER THOUGHTS:

Estimated Female Officers or Directors: 2

Hot Spot for Advancement for Women/Minorities: Y

Ascension Health
ascension.org/our-work/subsidiaries/ascension-health
NAIC Code: 622110

TYPES OF BUSINESS:
General Medical and Surgical Hospitals
Acute Care Hospitals
Rehabilitation Hospitals
Psychiatric Hospitals
Pharmacy Management

BRANDS/DIVISIONS/AFFILIATES:
Ascension
Providence Hospital
St. Vincent's Health System
Sacred Heart's Health System
St. Joseph Regional Medical Center
Peyton Manning Children's Hospital
Alexian Brothers
Nazareth Living Care Center

CONTACTS: Note: Officers with more than one job title may be intentionally listed here more than once.
Robert J. Henkel, CEO
Patricia A. Maryland, COO
Robert J. Henkel, Pres.
Ziad Haydar, Chief Medical Officer
Christine Kocot McCoy, General Counsel
Patricia A. Maryland, Pres., Health Care Oper.
Eric S. Engler, Sr. VP-Strategic Planning & Dev.
Jon Glaudemans, Chief Advocacy & Communications Officer
Ann Espoito, Sr. VP
Bonnie Phipps, CEO., St. Agnes HealthCare
Susan L. Davis, New York
Scott Caldwell, Chief Supply Chain Officer

GROWTH PLANS/SPECIAL FEATURES:
Ascension Health, a subsidiary of Ascension, is a leading faith-based, nonprofit health system in the U.S. Its headquarters are in St. Louis, Missouri, and is comprised of 141 hospitals in 24 states as well as in Washington D.C. It has more than 2,500 sites of care and more than 30 senior care facilities. Ascension Health's facilities include Providence Hospital and St. Vincent's Health System of health care facilities in Alabama; Sacred Heart's Health System and St. Vincent's Health facilities in Florida; St. Joseph Regional Medical Center in Idaho; Peyton Manning Children's Hospital at St. Vincent in Indiana; Saint Thomas Health in Kentucky; St. Mary's of Michigan; Alexian Brothers of Missouri; Lourdes Hospital in New York; Seton Manor in Pennsylvania; Nazareth Living Care Center in Texas; and Ministry Health Care facilities in Wisconsin. In addition to Ascension Health, other Ascension subsidiaries provide services and solutions such as physician practice management, venture capital investing, treasury management, biomedical engineering, clinical care management, information services, risk management and contracting. Ascension Health was formed in 1999 when the four provinces of the Daughters of Charity of St. Vincent de Paul that were sponsors of the Daughters of Charity National Health System (now combined into one, the Province of St. Louise) and the Sisters of St. Joseph of Nazareth brought their health systems together.

Ascension Health offers employee benefits such as medical, dental, vision and life insurance; health care and dependent care reimbursement accounts; a retirement savings program and a pension plan; tuition reimbursement; and an employee assistance program.

FINANCIAL DATA: Note: Data for latest year may not have been available at press time.

In U.S. $	2016	2015	2014	2013	2012	2011
Revenue	21,900,000,000	20,538,803,000	19,901,657,000	16,537,000,000	15,293,000,000	14,071,000,000
R&D Expense						
Operating Income						
Operating Margin %						
SGA Expense						
Net Income	219,412,440	562,596,000	1,803,615,000	451,000,000	931,000,000	415,000,000
Operating Cash Flow						
Capital Expenditure						
EBITDA						
Return on Assets %						
Return on Equity %						
Debt to Equity						

CONTACT INFORMATION:
Phone: 314-733-8000   Fax: 314-733-8013
Toll-Free:
Address: 101 South Hanley Rd., Ste 450, St. Louis, MO 63105 United States

STOCK TICKER/OTHER:
Stock Ticker: Subsidiary
Employees: 153,000
Parent Company: Ascension
Exchange:
Fiscal Year Ends: 06/30

SALARIES/BONUSES:
Top Exec. Salary: $ Bonus: $
Second Exec. Salary: $ Bonus: $

OTHER THOUGHTS:
Estimated Female Officers or Directors: 9
Hot Spot for Advancement for Women/Minorities: Y

AT Kearney Inc

www.atkearney.com

NAIC Code: 541610

TYPES OF BUSINESS:

Management Consulting
Technology Consulting
Retail Consulting
Government Consulting
Manufacturing Consulting
Transportation Consulting
Supply Chain Consulting
Industry Research & Publications

BRANDS/DIVISIONS/AFFILIATES:

Global Retail Development Index
Global Business Policy Council
Executive Agenda
AT Kearney Procurement & Analytic Solutions

CONTACTS: *Note: Officers with more than one job title may be intentionally listed here more than once.*

Johan Aurik, Managing Officer
Daniel Mahler, Head-The Americas
Luca Rossi, Head-EMEA
Laura Gurski, Head-Global Practices
Johan Aurik, Chmn.
John Kurtz, Head-Asia Pacific

GROWTH PLANS/SPECIAL FEATURES:

A.T. Kearney, Inc. is a global consulting firm involved in a wide variety of industries. It maintains 62 offices in major business centers across 40 countries. The company specializes in CEO-agenda concerns and provides assistance in analytics marketing & sales, mergers & acquisitions, operations organization & transformation, procurement, strategic IT strategy and sustainability. The industries served by the firm include aerospace & defense, automotive communications/media/technology, consumer products & retail, chemicals, health care, metals & mining, private equity public sector, financial institutions, transportation/travel/infrastructure and utilities. The company produces research in its various areas of interest, with products including business issue papers, the Global Retail Development Index publications and the Executive Agenda biannual publication. A.T. Kearney created and manages the Global Business Policy Council, designed to give a select group of company's prescient information on global market trends. Subsidiary A.T. Kearney Procurement & Analytic Solutions works with clients to assess their current enterprise-wide supply management capabilities, determine the critical gaps in relation to best practices and build a roadmap for improvement.

FINANCIAL DATA: *Note: Data for latest year may not have been available at press time.*

In U.S. $	2016	2015	2014	2013	2012	2011
Revenue		1,150,000,000	1,100,000,000	1,135,000,000	1,050,000,000	969,000,000
R&D Expense						
Operating Income						
Operating Margin %						
SGA Expense						
Net Income						
Operating Cash Flow						
Capital Expenditure						
EBITDA						
Return on Assets %						
Return on Equity %						
Debt to Equity						

CONTACT INFORMATION:

Phone: 312-648-0111　　　Fax: 312-223-6200
Toll-Free:
Address: 222 W. Adams St., Chicago, IL 60606 United States

STOCK TICKER/OTHER:

Stock Ticker: Private　　　　　　　　Exchange:
Employees: 3,600　　　　　　　　　　Fiscal Year Ends: 12/31
Parent Company:

SALARIES/BONUSES:

Top Exec. Salary: $　　　　Bonus: $
Second Exec. Salary: $　　　Bonus: $

OTHER THOUGHTS:

Estimated Female Officers or Directors: 1
Hot Spot for Advancement for Women/Minorities:

AT&T Inc

www.att.com

NAIC Code: 517110

TYPES OF BUSINESS:

Local Telephone Service
Wireless Telecommunications
Long-Distance Telephone Service
Corporate Telecom, Backbone & Wholesale Services
Internet Access
Entertainment & Television via Internet
Satellite TV
VOIP

BRANDS/DIVISIONS/AFFILIATES:

AT&T Mobility LLC
GSF Telecom Holdings SAPI de CV
Iusacell
Nextel Mexico
DIRECTV

CONTACTS: *Note: Officers with more than one job title may be intentionally listed here more than once.*

Stacey Maris, Assistant General Counsel
John Stankey, CEO, Divisional
Ralph De la Vega, CEO, Subsidiary
Randall Stephenson, CEO
John Stephens, CFO
David McAtee, General Counsel
David Huntley, Other Executive Officer
William Blase, Senior Executive VP, Divisional
John Donovan, Senior Executive VP, Divisional
Lori Lee, Senior Executive VP, Divisional
James Cicconi, Senior Executive VP, Subsidiary

GROWTH PLANS/SPECIAL FEATURES:

AT&T, Inc. is one of the world's largest providers of diversified telecommunications services. The company and its subsidiaries offers its communications, digital entertainment services and products to consumers in the U.S., Mexico and Latin America, as well as to businesses and other providers of telecommunications services worldwide. AT&T also owns and operates three regional sports networks. Services & products include wireless communications, data/broadband & Internet services, digital video services, local & long-distance telephone services, telecommunications equipment, managed networking and wholesale services. The company operates through four business segments: business solutions, entertainment, consumer mobility and international. Business solutions provides services to businesses, governmental & wholesale customers and individual subscribers who purchase wireless services through employer-sponsored plans. These solutions include virtual private networks, Ethernet-related products, broadband and data/voice products. The entertainment segment provides video, Internet and voice communication services to residential customers in the U.S. The consumer mobility business provides nationwide wireless service to consumers, as well as to wireless wholesale & resale subscribers located in the U.S. The international business segment provides entertainment services in Latin America and wireless services in Mexico. Via AT&T Mobility LLC, the firm covers all major metropolitan areas and more than 300 million people with its LTE technology. It also provides 4G coverage using HSPA+ technology. In 2015, the firm acquired GSF Telecom Holdings SAPI de CV, Iusacell, Nextel Mexico and DIRECTV.

FINANCIAL DATA: *Note: Data for latest year may not have been available at press time.*

In U.S. $	2016	2015	2014	2013	2012	2011
Revenue		146,801,000,000	132,447,000,000	128,752,000,000	127,434,000,000	126,723,000,000
R&D Expense						
Operating Income		24,785,000,000	11,746,000,000	30,479,000,000	12,997,000,000	9,218,000,000
Operating Margin %		16.88%	8.86%	23.67%	10.19%	7.27%
SGA Expense		32,954,000,000	41,817,000,000	28,414,000,000	41,079,000,000	38,844,000,000
Net Income		13,345,000,000	6,224,000,000	18,249,000,000	7,264,000,000	3,944,000,000
Operating Cash Flow		35,880,000,000	31,338,000,000	34,796,000,000	39,176,000,000	34,648,000,000
Capital Expenditure		20,015,000,000	21,433,000,000	20,944,000,000	19,465,000,000	20,110,000,000
EBITDA		46,828,000,000	31,846,000,000	50,112,000,000	32,026,000,000	28,628,000,000
Return on Assets %		3.83%	2.18%	6.63%	2.67%	1.46%
Return on Equity %		12.76%	7.01%	19.90%	7.34%	3.63%
Debt to Equity		0.96	0.88	0.76	0.71	0.58

CONTACT INFORMATION:

Phone: 210 821-4105   Fax:
Toll-Free:
Address: 208 S. Akard St., Dallas, TX 75202 United States

STOCK TICKER/OTHER:

Stock Ticker: T   Exchange: NYS
Employees: 281,000   Fiscal Year Ends: 12/31
Parent Company:

SALARIES/BONUSES:

Top Exec. Salary: Bonus: $
$1,741,667
Second Exec. Salary: Bonus: $
$941,667

OTHER THOUGHTS:

Estimated Female Officers or Directors: 4

Hot Spot for Advancement for Women/Minorities: Y

Athenahealth Inc

www.athenahealth.com

NAIC Code: 524292

TYPES OF BUSINESS:

Outsourced Health Reimbursement Services
Patient Information Management
Billing & Collection Services for Health Care Providers
Automated Messaging

BRANDS/DIVISIONS/AFFILIATES:

athenaNet
athenaCollector
athenaClinicals
athenaCommunicator
athenaCoordinator
Epocrates
RazorInsights
webOMR

CONTACTS: Note: Officers with more than one job title may be intentionally listed here more than once.

Jonathan Bush, CEO
Karl Stubelis, Chief Accounting Officer
Tim O'Brien, Chief Marketing Officer
Prakash Khot, Chief Technology Officer
Ed Park, COO
Stephen Kahane, Executive VP
Dan Haley, General Counsel
Robert Cosinuke, Other Corporate Officer
Kyle Armbrester, Other Executive Officer

GROWTH PLANS/SPECIAL FEATURES:

Athenahealth, Inc. is a provider of cloud-based business services to physician practices to reduce their administrative work by combining three components: cloud-based software, networked knowledge and back-office work. The firm offers services through its integrated platform, athenaNet. This platform is comprised of four principal tools: athenaCollector, athenaClinicals, athenaCommunicator and athenaCoordinator. athenaCollector, the company's flagship product, is a revenue cycle management service that includes a management platform and automates and manages billing-related functions for physicians' practices. The athenaCollector system tracks, controls and executes claims and billing processes. athenaClinicals, aimed at simplifying electronic medical record (EMR) handling, provides a wholly integrated system for managing the processes of providing and receiving pay for care. athenaCommunicator is an automated message offering that includes automated patient messaging services, live operator services and a patient web portal. athenaCoordinator is designed to streamline the order process between practices and hospitals, optimizing order transmission, pre-certification and pre-registration. The company's Epocrates branded services provide a variety of clinical information & decision support offerings through health care providers' mobile devices, including drug & disease information, medical calculator, tools, clinical guidelines & messaging, market research and formulary hosting. In 2015, athenahealth acquired RazorInsights, a leader in cloud-based electronic health record and financial solutions for rural, critical access and community hospitals; and webOMR, a web-based clinical applications and electronic health record platform.

Employee benefits include medical, vision and dental coverage; flexible spending accounts; an employee assistance program; life and AD&D insurance; short- and long-term disability; 401(k); and an employee stock purchase plan.

FINANCIAL DATA: Note: Data for latest year may not have been available at press time.

In U.S. $	2016	2015	2014	2013	2012	2011
Revenue		924,728,000	752,599,000	595,003,000	422,271,000	324,067,000
R&D Expense		94,254,000	69,461,000	57,639,000	33,792,000	23,343,000
Operating Income		-4,056,000	955,000	5,853,000	34,627,000	32,733,000
Operating Margin %		-.43%	.12%	.98%	8.20%	10.10%
SGA Expense		374,478,000	314,880,000	249,264,000	161,325,000	128,486,000
Net Income		14,027,000	-3,119,000	2,594,000	18,732,000	19,046,000
Operating Cash Flow		163,844,000	149,105,000	93,308,000	70,213,000	60,764,000
Capital Expenditure		184,975,000	129,569,000	67,383,000	39,561,000	24,475,000
EBITDA		142,704,000	94,637,000	67,989,000	63,771,000	53,803,000
Return on Assets %		1.36%	-.36%	.42%	4.82%	6.24%
Return on Equity %		2.75%	-.71%	.73%	6.83%	9.35%
Debt to Equity		0.52	0.33	0.44		

CONTACT INFORMATION:

Phone: 617 402-1000   Fax: 617 402-1099
Toll-Free: 800-981-5084
Address: 311 Arsenal St., Watertown, MA 02472 United States

STOCK TICKER/OTHER:

Stock Ticker: ATHN
Employees: 4,668
Parent Company:

Exchange: NAS
Fiscal Year Ends: 12/31

SALARIES/BONUSES:

Top Exec. Salary: $612,692   Bonus: $
Second Exec. Salary: Bonus: $
$509,980

OTHER THOUGHTS:

Estimated Female Officers or Directors: 1
Hot Spot for Advancement for Women/Minorities:

Automatic Data Processing Inc (ADP)

www.adp.com

NAIC Code: 518210

TYPES OF BUSINESS:

Data Processing Services
Business Outsourcing Solutions
Information Services
Payroll Processing

BRANDS/DIVISIONS/AFFILIATES:

ADP TotalSource

CONTACTS: Note: Officers with more than one job title may be intentionally listed here more than once.

Carlos Rodriguez, CEO
Deborah Dyson, Vice President, Divisional
Jan Siegmund, CFO
Brock Albinson, Chief Accounting Officer
John Jones, Director
Edward Flynn, Executive VP, Divisional
Michael Bonarti, General Counsel
Dermot OBrien, Other Executive Officer
Donald Weinstein, Other Executive Officer
John Ayala, President, Divisional
Douglas Politi, President, Divisional
Maria Black, President, Divisional
Mark Benjamin, President, Divisional
Thomas Perrotti, President, Geographical
Michael Eberhard, Treasurer
Stuart Sackman, Vice President, Divisional

GROWTH PLANS/SPECIAL FEATURES:

Automatic Data Processing, Inc. (ADP) is one of the world's largest providers of cloud-based human capital management (HCM) solutions to employers, as well as business outsourcing services, analytics and compliance expertise. The company serves approximately 650,000 clients in more than 110 countries. ADP operates in two segments: employer services and professional employer organization (PEO) services. The employer services segment offers a comprehensive range of business outsourcing and HCM solutions including payroll services, benefits administration, recruiting and talent management, human resource management, time and attendance management, insurance services, retirement services and compliance and payment solutions. The PEO services segment, which operates as ADP TotalSource, provides small and medium sized businesses with comprehensive employment administration outsourcing solutions (through a co-employment relationship), including payroll, payroll tax filing, human resources guidance, 401(k) plan administration, benefits administration, compliance services, health and workers' compensation coverage and other supplemental benefits for employees. ADP TotalSource has approximately 9,700 clients in all 50 states; the businesses it serves have a combined total of 439,000 worksite employees.

Employee benefits in the U.S. include medical, dental and vision insurance; health care and dependent care flexible spending accounts; life, AD&D and disability coverage; a pension and 401(k) plan; a stock purchase and stock option plan; auto & home insurance programs; tuition reimbursement; and a scholarship program.

FINANCIAL DATA: Note: Data for latest year may not have been available at press time.

In U.S. $	2016	2015	2014	2013	2012	2011
Revenue	11,667,800,000	10,938,500,000	12,206,500,000	11,310,100,000	10,665,200,000	9,879,500,000
R&D Expense						
Operating Income	2,190,500,000	2,014,000,000	2,222,700,000	1,997,200,000	1,959,000,000	1,824,700,000
Operating Margin %	18.77%	18.41%	18.20%	17.65%	18.36%	18.46%
SGA Expense	2,637,000,000	2,496,900,000	2,762,400,000	2,620,600,000	2,466,200,000	2,323,300,000
Net Income	1,492,500,000	1,452,500,000	1,515,900,000	1,405,800,000	1,388,500,000	1,254,200,000
Operating Cash Flow	1,859,900,000	1,905,600,000	1,821,400,000	1,577,200,000	1,910,200,000	1,705,800,000
Capital Expenditure	386,000,000	335,500,000	367,700,000	282,900,000	249,600,000	277,700,000
EBITDA	2,579,500,000	2,355,100,000	2,616,900,000	2,410,400,000	2,453,100,000	2,259,500,000
Return on Assets %	3.88%	4.45%	4.71%	4.45%	4.26%	4.10%
Return on Equity %	32.13%	25.30%	23.57%	22.85%	22.90%	21.83%
Debt to Equity	0.44					

CONTACT INFORMATION:

Phone: 973 974-5000   Fax: 973 974-5390
Toll-Free: 800-225-5237
Address: 1 ADP Blvd., Roseland, NJ 07068 United States

STOCK TICKER/OTHER:

Stock Ticker: ADP
Employees: 55,000
Parent Company:

Exchange: NAS
Fiscal Year Ends: 06/30

SALARIES/BONUSES:

Top Exec. Salary: $1,000,000   Bonus: $

Second Exec. Salary: $590,000   Bonus: $

OTHER THOUGHTS:

Estimated Female Officers or Directors: 1

Hot Spot for Advancement for Women/Minorities: Y

Sales, profits and employees may be estimates. Financial information, benefits and other data can change quickly and may vary from those stated here.

AutoNation Inc

NAIC Code: 441110

www.autonation.com

TYPES OF BUSINESS:

Auto Dealer
Online Auto Sales
Vehicle Maintenance & Repair Services
Vehicle Parts
Extended Service Contracts
Vehicle Protection Products

BRANDS/DIVISIONS/AFFILIATES:

CONTACTS: Note: Officers with more than one job title may be intentionally listed here more than once.

Cheryl Miller, CFO
William Berman, COO
Jonathan Ferrando, Executive VP, Divisional
Michael Jackson, President
Donna Parlapiano, Senior VP, Divisional
Christopher Cade, Vice President

GROWTH PLANS/SPECIAL FEATURES:

AutoNation, Inc. is one of the largest automobile retailers in the U.S. It owns and operates 342 new vehicle franchises from 254 stores located in major metropolitan markets, predominantly in the Sunbelt region of the U.S. The company offers a diversified range of automotive products and services, including new vehicles, which generated 57.5% of the firm's 2015 revenue; used vehicles, 22.9%; parts and automotive services, 15%; and automotive finance, insurance products and other 4.8%. The firm also arranges financing for vehicle purchases through third-party finance sources. The core brands of vehicles, representing approximately 95% of the new vehicles the firm sold in 2015, are manufactured by Toyota, Ford, Honda, Nissan, General Motors, Mercedes, BMW, Volkswagen and Chrysler. AutoNation operates in three segments: domestic, import and premium luxury. Domestic is comprised of franchises that sell new General Motors, Jeep, Lincoln, Cadillac, Chevrolet, Ford and Chrysler among other brands. Import includes franchises that sell Toyota, Honda, Infiniti, Hyundai, Subaru, Volvo, Scion, Fiat, Acura, Mitsubishi, Mazda, Volkswagen and Nissan vehicles. Premium Luxury includes retailers that sell Land Rover, Mini, smart, Audi, Bentley, Porsche, Maserati, Mercedes, BMW, Alfa Romeo and Lexus franchises. In 2015, The domestic segment accounted for 34% of the company's total new vehicle unit sales; import, 34%; and premium luxury, 32%. The company's website offers prospective buyers the ability to evaluate current trade-in values of vehicles, explore nearby car lots, read automotive reviews and even arrange for the purchase of an automobile online.

The firm offers employees health, dental, life and disability insurance; longevity bonuses; a 401(k) plan; and an employee vehicle purchase program.

FINANCIAL DATA: Note: Data for latest year may not have been available at press time.

In U.S. $	2016	2015	2014	2013	2012	2011
Revenue		20,862,000,000	19,108,800,000	17,517,600,000	15,668,800,000	13,832,300,000
R&D Expense						
Operating Income		873,100,000	820,800,000	740,300,000	645,300,000	572,000,000
Operating Margin %		4.18%	4.29%	4.22%	4.11%	4.13%
SGA Expense		2,263,500,000	2,079,600,000	1,935,000,000	1,749,500,000	1,649,400,000
Net Income		442,600,000	418,700,000	374,900,000	316,400,000	281,400,000
Operating Cash Flow		507,200,000	485,100,000	484,100,000	316,600,000	376,400,000
Capital Expenditure		247,600,000	209,200,000	160,800,000	160,600,000	149,100,000
EBITDA		999,300,000	929,200,000	841,400,000	736,500,000	653,700,000
Return on Assets %		4.92%	5.13%	4.95%	4.72%	4.62%
Return on Equity %		20.02%	20.25%	19.99%	17.66%	14.16%
Debt to Equity		0.74	1.01	0.87	1.22	0.86

CONTACT INFORMATION:

Phone: 954 769-6000   Fax:
Toll-Free:
Address: 200 SW 1st Ave., Ste.1600, Fort Lauderdale, FL 33301 United States

STOCK TICKER/OTHER:

Stock Ticker: AN   Exchange: NYS
Employees: 24,000   Fiscal Year Ends: 12/31
Parent Company:

SALARIES/BONUSES:

Top Exec. Salary: $1,250,000   Bonus: $
Second Exec. Salary: $700,000   Bonus: $

OTHER THOUGHTS:

Estimated Female Officers or Directors: 2

Hot Spot for Advancement for Women/Minorities:

Avis Budget Group Inc

www.avisbudgetgroup.com

NAIC Code: 532111

TYPES OF BUSINESS:

Automobile Rental
Franchising
Truck Rental

BRANDS/DIVISIONS/AFFILIATES:

Avis
Budget
ZipCar
Payless
Apex
Maggiore Group

CONTACTS: *Note: Officers with more than one job title may be intentionally listed here more than once.*

Larry De Shon, CEO
David Wyshner, CFO
Ronald Nelson, Chairman of the Board
David Calabria, Chief Accounting Officer
W. Deaver, Executive VP
Michael Tucker, Executive VP
Edward Linnen, Executive VP
Joseph Ferraro, President, Divisional
Mark Servodidio, President, Divisional
Jean Sera, Secretary
Bryon Koepke, Senior VP

GROWTH PLANS/SPECIAL FEATURES:

Avis Budget Group, Inc. (ABG) operates in the global vehicle rental industry through Avis, Budget, Zipcar, Payless and Apex. Avis is a rental car supplier to the premium commercial and leisure segments of the travel industry. Budget is a rental car supplier to the price-conscious segments of the travel industry. Its fleet of approximately 21,000 Budget trucks are rented through a network of approximately 1,000 dealer-operated and 450 company-operated locations throughout the continental USA. Zipcar is the world's leading car sharing company, with nearly 1 million members in the USA, Canada and Europe. Payless is a rental car supplier comprised of 200 vehicle rental locations worldwide. These include 80 company-operated locations and 100 locations operated by licensees. Apex operates in New Zealand and Australia via 20 locations. ABG's operations include approximately 11,000 car and truck rental locations in the USA, Canada, Australia, New Zealand, Latin America, the Caribbean and parts of Asia, with a fleet of more than 580,000 vehicles. It completed more than 38 million vehicle rental transactions worldwide in 2015. The company operates in three segments: North America, which provides car rentals in the USA, vehicle rentals in Canada, and operates ABG's car sharing business in North America; international, which provides and licenses ABG's brands to third parties for vehicle rentals and ancillary products and services primarily in Europe, the Middle East, Asia, South America, Central America, the Caribbean, Australia and New Zealand, and also operates ABG's car sharing business in select markets; and truck rental, which provides truck rentals and ancillary products and services to consumers and commercial users in the USA. In 2015, the firm acquired Maggiore Group, Italy's fourth-largest vehicle rental business.

The company offers its employees medical, dental and vision coverage; life insurance; flexible spending accounts; short-and long-term disability, AD&D; and 401(k).

FINANCIAL DATA: *Note: Data for latest year may not have been available at press time.*

In U.S. $	2016	2015	2014	2013	2012	2011
Revenue		8,502,000,000	8,485,000,000	7,937,000,000	7,357,000,000	5,900,000,000
R&D Expense						
Operating Income		974,000,000	978,000,000	589,000,000	300,000,000	36,000,000
Operating Margin %		11.45%	11.52%	7.42%	4.07%	.61%
SGA Expense		1,093,000,000	1,080,000,000	1,070,000,000	959,000,000	1,011,000,000
Net Income		313,000,000	245,000,000	16,000,000	290,000,000	-29,000,000
Operating Cash Flow		2,584,000,000	2,579,000,000	2,253,000,000	1,889,000,000	1,578,000,000
Capital Expenditure		12,127,000,000	12,057,000,000	11,051,000,000	11,199,000,000	8,724,000,000
EBITDA		2,750,000,000	3,059,000,000	2,552,000,000	2,461,000,000	2,031,000,000
Return on Assets %		1.80%	1.47%	.10%	2.06%	-.24%
Return on Equity %		56.70%	34.12%	2.09%	49.61%	-7.05%
Debt to Equity		28.00	17.30	13.80	12.75	21.19

CONTACT INFORMATION:

Phone: 973 496-4700   Fax: 212 413-1924
Toll-Free:
Address: 6 Sylvan Way, Parsippany, NJ 07054 United States

STOCK TICKER/OTHER:

Stock Ticker: CAR   Exchange: NAS
Employees: 30,000   Fiscal Year Ends: 12/31
Parent Company:

SALARIES/BONUSES:

Top Exec. Salary: Bonus: $
$1,244,521
Second Exec. Salary: Bonus: $
$748,836

OTHER THOUGHTS:

Estimated Female Officers or Directors: 2

Hot Spot for Advancement for Women/Minorities:

Sales, profits and employees may be estimates. Financial information, benefits and other data can change quickly and may vary from those stated here.

Avnet Inc

NAIC Code: 423430

TYPES OF BUSINESS:

Components-Distributor
Marketing Services
Supply Chain Advisory Services

BRANDS/DIVISIONS/AFFILIATES:

MSC Investoren GmbH
Nisko Semiconductors Ltd
Seamless Technologies Inc

CONTACTS: *Note: Officers with more than one job title may be intentionally listed here more than once.*

William Amelio, CEO
Kevin Moriarty, CFO
William Schumann, Chairman of the Board
Steven Phillips, Chief Information Officer
Michael Buseman, Other Executive Officer
MaryAnn Miller, Other Executive Officer
Patrick Zammit, President, Divisional
Gerald Fay, President, Divisional
Michael McCoy, Secretary
Erin Lewin, Senior VP

GROWTH PLANS/SPECIAL FEATURES:

Avnet, Inc. is one of the world's largest value-added distributors of electronic components, enterprise computer and storage products, software and embedded subsystems. The firm connects more than 800 suppliers to over 100,000 original equipment manufacturers (OEMs), electronic manufacturing services (EMS) providers, original design manufacturers (ODMs) and value-added resellers (VARs). Additionally, the firm provides engineering design, materials management and logistics services, system integration and configuration and supply chain services. The company divides its business into two divisions, technology solutions and electronics marketing, which operate throughout the Americas, Europe, the Middle East, Africa and Asia/Pacific. The technology solutions division markets and sells servers, data storage, software and related services to resellers and mid to high-end users as well as focusing on the worldwide OEM market. The electronics marketing division markets and sells semiconductors and interconnect, passive and electromechanical devices (IP&E) to a customer base whose end-markets include automotive, communications, computer hardware and peripheral, industrial and manufacturing, medical equipment, military and aerospace. Avnet pursues growth through strategic acquisitions to expand its geographic and market coverage. During 2014, the firm acquired MSC Investoren GmbH, Nisko Semiconductors Ltd. and Seamless Technologies, Inc. In September 2016, Avnet agreed to sale its technology solutions unit to Tech Data Corp. for approximately $2.6 billion.

Avnet employees receive life, AD&D, disability, travel accident, medical, dental and vision insurance; flexible spending accounts; a pension plan; a 401(k); an employee stock purchase plan; and tuition reimbursement.

FINANCIAL DATA: *Note: Data for latest year may not have been available at press time.*

In U.S. $	2016	2015	2014	2013	2012	2011
Revenue	26,219,280,000	27,924,660,000	27,499,650,000	25,458,920,000	25,707,520,000	26,534,410,000
R&D Expense						
Operating Income	787,669,000	827,673,000	789,940,000	625,981,000	884,165,000	929,979,000
Operating Margin %	3.00%	2.96%	2.87%	2.45%	3.43%	3.50%
SGA Expense	2,170,524,000	2,274,642,000	2,341,168,000	2,204,319,000	2,092,807,000	2,100,650,000
Net Income	506,531,000	571,913,000	545,604,000	450,073,000	567,019,000	669,069,000
Operating Cash Flow	224,315,000	583,883,000	237,418,000	696,197,000	528,718,000	278,079,000
Capital Expenditure	147,548,000	174,374,000	123,242,000	97,379,000	128,652,000	148,707,000
EBITDA	896,043,000	955,949,000	943,138,000	777,594,000	982,977,000	1,044,807,000
Return on Assets %	4.59%	5.18%	5.02%	4.36%	5.64%	7.56%
Return on Equity %	10.80%	11.94%	11.88%	10.98%	14.24%	18.93%
Debt to Equity	0.28	0.35	0.24	0.28	0.32	0.31

CONTACT INFORMATION:

Phone: 480 643-2000　　　Fax: 480 643-7370
Toll-Free: 800-409-1483
Address: 2211 S. 47th St., Phoenix, AZ 85034 United States

STOCK TICKER/OTHER:

Stock Ticker: AVT　　　　　　　Exchange: NYS
Employees: 19,000　　　　　　　Fiscal Year Ends: 06/30
Parent Company:

SALARIES/BONUSES:

Top Exec. Salary: $950,000　　Bonus: $
Second Exec. Salary:　　　　　Bonus: $
$600,000

OTHER THOUGHTS:

Estimated Female Officers or Directors: 2
Hot Spot for Advancement for Women/Minorities: Y

AZZ Inc

NAIC Code: 335311

www.azz.com

TYPES OF BUSINESS:

Electrical Equipment Manufacturing
Galvanizing Services

BRANDS/DIVISIONS/AFFILIATES:

US Galvanizing LLC
Alpha Galvanizing Inc

CONTACTS: Note: Officers with more than one job title may be intentionally listed here more than once.

Tom Ferguson, CEO
Paul Fehlman, CFO
Kevern Joyce, Chairman of the Board
Robert Steines, Chief Accounting Officer
Matthew Emery, Chief Information Officer
Tara Mackey, Other Executive Officer
Tim Pendley, Senior VP, Divisional
Chris Bacius, Vice President, Divisional

GROWTH PLANS/SPECIAL FEATURES:

AZZ, Inc. is a global provider of galvanizing services, welding solutions, specialty electrical equipment and highly engineered services to the power generation, transmission, distribution, refining and industrial markets. The firm operates through two business segments: galvanizing and energy. The galvanizing segment provides hot dip galvanizing to the steel fabrication industry. Hot dip galvanizing is a metallurgical process in which molten zinc is applied to steel. The zinc alloying renders corrosion protection to fabricated steel for extended periods of up to 50 years. AZZ operates 43 galvanizing plants located across 19 states in U.S. and three Canadian provinces. The products are used in agriculture, construction, recreation, electrical utility, petrochemical and bridge and highway application. The energy segment offers specialized products and services designed to support industrial, nuclear and electrical applications. Products under this segment include electrical enclosures, medium and high voltage bus ducts, custom switchgear, explosion proof and hazardous duty lighting, nuclear safety-related equipment and tubular products. The products are also used in oil, gas, petrochemical, power generation, power transmission and utility power distribution. In 2015, the firm acquired U.S. Galvanizing, LLC, including its six galvanizing facilities. In 2016, it acquired Alpha Galvanizing, Inc., which serves steel fabrication companies; and agreed to acquire Power Electronics, Inc., a manufacturer and integrator of electrical enclosure systems.

AZZ offers its employees medical, dental and vision coverage, along with a 401(k) plan and other benefits.

FINANCIAL DATA: Note: Data for latest year may not have been available at press time.

In U.S. $	2016	2015	2014	2013	2012	2011
Revenue	903,192,000	816,687,000	751,723,400	570,594,200	469,112,400	380,649,400
R&D Expense						
Operating Income	122,288,000	106,825,000	100,113,800	94,368,830	75,722,010	54,958,020
Operating Margin %	13.53%	13.08%	13.31%	16.53%	16.14%	14.43%
SGA Expense	107,823,000	98,871,000	105,591,200	66,188,580	48,864,890	46,645,120
Net Income	76,790,000	64,943,000	59,597,050	60,456,210	40,735,800	34,962,640
Operating Cash Flow	143,589,000	118,157,000	107,275,300	92,737,620	64,064,830	42,085,360
Capital Expenditure	39,861,000	29,377,000	43,471,530	24,922,990	19,783,760	16,410,870
EBITDA	166,940,000	152,780,000	155,622,800	136,804,600	100,174,700	84,854,660
Return on Assets %	7.99%	6.87%	7.23%	9.29%	6.94%	7.37%
Return on Equity %	17.04%	16.31%	16.79%	19.45%	14.98%	14.45%
Debt to Equity	0.63	0.75	1.02	0.58	0.73	0.87

CONTACT INFORMATION:

Phone: 817 810-0095   Fax: 817 336-5354
Toll-Free:
Address: One Museum Place, 3100 W. 7th St., Ste. 500, Fort Worth, TX 76107 United States

STOCK TICKER/OTHER:

Stock Ticker: AZZ   Exchange: NYS
Employees: 3,244   Fiscal Year Ends: 02/28
Parent Company:

SALARIES/BONUSES:

Top Exec. Salary: $690,000   Bonus: $
Second Exec. Salary: $360,591   Bonus: $

OTHER THOUGHTS:

Estimated Female Officers or Directors: 1
Hot Spot for Advancement for Women/Minorities:

Bain & Company Inc

NAIC Code: 541610

www.bain.com

TYPES OF BUSINESS:

Management Consulting
Technology Consulting
Merger & Acquisition Consulting

BRANDS/DIVISIONS/AFFILIATES:

CONTACTS: *Note: Officers with more than one job title may be intentionally listed here more than once.*

Bob Bechek, Worldwide Managing Dir.
Dave Johnson, Managing Dir.-The Americas
Dale Cottrell, Managing Dir.-Asia Pacific
Orit Gadiesh, Chmn.
Paul Meehan, Managing Dir.-EMEA

GROWTH PLANS/SPECIAL FEATURES:

Bain & Company, Inc. provides business consulting services on a global level. From approximately 53 offices in 34 countries, the firm's consultants work with top management executives from thousands of companies to help them outperform market competitors and create sustained financial growth and stability. Most of the company's offices are located in the heavily industrialized economies of the U.S. and Europe, but offices in locations such as Brazil, Argentina, South Africa, India, China, Japan, Singapore and Australia are also key parts of the firm's business. Consultants typically help executives make important decisions in areas such as corporate strategy, change management, company organization, operations, performance improvement, marketing and sale of a company's unprofitable businesses; develop strategies to create profitable ones; penetrate new product segments; seize new business opportunities; and identify flawed business strategies. Services are provided to clients in industries such as technology, telecom, financial services, retail, media, consumer products, transportation, nonprofit and public sector, energy and utilities, private equity and health care. In appropriate situations, Bain consultants assist clients in implementing the changes they decide to make to their business structures or processes.

The firm tends to hire college graduates with either liberal arts degrees, MBA degrees or both. Positions often involve extensive travel and sometimes major relocation, the costs of which are reimbursed by Bain.

FINANCIAL DATA: *Note: Data for latest year may not have been available at press time.*

In U.S. $	2016	2015	2014	2013	2012	2011
Revenue		2,300,000,000	2,100,000,000	2,086,000,000	2,010,000,000	1,863,000,000
R&D Expense						
Operating Income						
Operating Margin %						
SGA Expense						
Net Income						
Operating Cash Flow						
Capital Expenditure						
EBITDA						
Return on Assets %						
Return on Equity %						
Debt to Equity						

CONTACT INFORMATION:

Phone: 617-572-2000   Fax: 617-572-2427
Toll-Free:
Address: 131 Dartmouth St., Boston, MA 02116 United States

STOCK TICKER/OTHER:

Stock Ticker: Private   Exchange:
Employees: 5,700   Fiscal Year Ends: 12/31
Parent Company:

SALARIES/BONUSES:

Top Exec. Salary: $ Bonus: $
Second Exec. Salary: $ Bonus: $

OTHER THOUGHTS:

Estimated Female Officers or Directors: 1
Hot Spot for Advancement for Women/Minorities:

Bank of America Corp

www.bankofamerica.com

NAIC Code: 522110

TYPES OF BUSINESS:

Banking
Asset Management
Investment & Brokerage Services
Mortgages
Credit Cards
Insurance Agency

BRANDS/DIVISIONS/AFFILIATES:

CONTACTS: *Note: Officers with more than one job title may be intentionally listed here more than once.*

Brian Moynihan, CEO
Thong Nguyen, President, Divisional
Paul Donofrio, CFO
Rudolf Bless, Chief Accounting Officer
Andrea Smith, Chief Administrative Officer
Geoffrey Greener, Chief Risk Officer
Thomas Montag, COO
Catherine Bessant, COO
David Leitch, General Counsel
Ross Jeffries, General Counsel
Dean Athanasia, President, Divisional
Gary Lynch, Vice Chairman
Terrence Laughlin, Vice Chairman, Divisional

GROWTH PLANS/SPECIAL FEATURES:

Bank of America Corp. is a global provider of a diversified range of banking and financial services. The company operates through five business segments: consumer banking, global wealth & investment management (GWIM), global banking, global markets, legacy assets & servicing (LAS) and other. Consumer banking provides deposit and lending services, as well as small business client management services, consumer & small business credit card services, debit card services, consumer vehicle lending and home loan options. GWIM offers Merrill Lynch global wealth management, as well as U.S. trust services and private wealth management services. Global banking offers investment banking, global corporate banking, global commercial banking and business banking services. The global markets segment offers fixed income and equity market products. LAS provides mortgage servicing, owned legacy home equity loan portfolios and legacy mortgage exposures. Other activities by Bank of America include equity investments, international consumer cards, merchant services, liquidating services, residual expense allocation services and more.

The company offers its employees benefits including tuition and adoption reimbursement; medical, dental and vision insurance plans; employee assistance programs; and health care and dependent care flexible spending accounts.

FINANCIAL DATA: *Note: Data for latest year may not have been available at press time.*

In U.S. $	2016	2015	2014	2013	2012	2011
Revenue		82,507,000,000	84,247,000,000	88,942,000,000	83,334,000,000	93,454,000,000
R&D Expense						
Operating Income		22,154,000,000	6,855,000,000	16,172,000,000	3,072,000,000	-230,000,000
Operating Margin %		26.85%	8.13%	18.18%	3.68%	-.24%
SGA Expense		47,962,000,000	65,324,000,000	58,623,000,000	60,416,000,000	64,474,000,000
Net Income		15,888,000,000	4,833,000,000	11,431,000,000	4,188,000,000	1,446,000,000
Operating Cash Flow		27,730,000,000	26,739,000,000	92,817,000,000	-13,858,000,000	64,490,000,000
Capital Expenditure			1,160,000,000	521,000,000		1,307,000,000
EBITDA						
Return on Assets %		.67%	.18%	.46%	.12%	
Return on Equity %		6.28%	1.70%	4.60%	1.28%	.04%
Debt to Equity		1.01	1.08	1.13	1.26	1.75

CONTACT INFORMATION:

Phone: 704 386-5681   Fax:
Toll-Free: 800-432-1000
Address: 100 N. Tryon St., 18th Fl., Charlotte, NC 28255 United States

STOCK TICKER/OTHER:

Stock Ticker: BAC
Employees: 242,000
Parent Company:

Exchange: NYS
Fiscal Year Ends: 12/31

SALARIES/BONUSES:

Top Exec. Salary: $1,000,000   Bonus: $5,800,000
Second Exec. Salary: $850,000   Bonus: $3,960,000

OTHER THOUGHTS:

Estimated Female Officers or Directors: 8

Hot Spot for Advancement for Women/Minorities: Y

Bank of New York Mellon Corp

www.bnymellon.com

NAIC Code: 522110

TYPES OF BUSINESS:

Asset Management & Securities Services
Investment & Wealth Management
Private Banking
Shareowner Services
Broker-Dealer Services
Issuer Services
Treasury Services

BRANDS/DIVISIONS/AFFILIATES:

Bank of New York Mellon (The)
BNY Mellon NA
Bank of New York Mellon Trust Company
BNY Mellon Trust of Delaware
BNY Mellon Investment Servicing Trust Co
BNY Mellon Trust Company of Illinois
Pershing LLC

CONTACTS: Note: Officers with more than one job title may be intentionally listed here more than once.

Mitchell Harris, CEO, Divisional
Gerald Hassell, CEO
Thomas Gibbons, CFO
Kurtis Kurimsky, Chief Accounting Officer
J. Mccarthy, General Counsel, Subsidiary
Michelle Neal, Managing Director
James Wiener, Other Executive Officer
Monique Herena, Other Executive Officer
Karen Peetz, President
Craig Beazer, Secretary
Brian Shea, Vice Chairman

GROWTH PLANS/SPECIAL FEATURES:

Bank of New York Mellon Corp. (BNYM) is a global investment company providing asset management and securities services for individual investors, institutions and corporations in 35 countries and more than 100 markets. In addition, BNYM offers financial solutions for individuals, including investment and wealth management, private banking and shareowner services. The company works with consultants and advisors to help them select the services that best meet their customers needs. The firm has two principal banking subsidiaries: The Bank of New York Mellon and BNY Mellon NA, which provide trust & custody activities, investment management services, banking services and various securities-related activities. Additionally, the firm has four other U.S. bank and/or trust company subsidiaries concentrating on trust products and services across the nation: The Bank of New York Mellon Trust Company, National Association, BNY Mellon Trust of Delaware, BNY Mellon Investment Servicing Trust Company and BNY Mellon Trust Company of Illinois. Most of the asset management businesses are direct or indirect non-bank subsidiaries of BNY Mellon. Through Pershing LLC, the firm offers broker-dealer and advisor services. Pershing is a provider of clearing, execution and financial business solutions to institutional and retail financial organizations and independent registered investment advisors. BNYM's issuer service offerings include global corporate trust services, depositary receipt services and shareowner services. The company also offers treasury services. BNYM has approximately $1.7 trillion in assets under management and $28.5 trillion in assets under administration or custody. Customers include corporations, foundations, governments, unions, endowments, mutual funds and high-net-worth individuals.

Employees are offered medical, vision and dental health plans; life insurance; and an array of retirement plans varying by location.

FINANCIAL DATA: Note: Data for latest year may not have been available at press time.

In U.S. $	2016	2015	2014	2013	2012	2011
Revenue		15,194,000,000	15,692,000,000	14,983,000,000	14,555,000,000	14,730,000,000
R&D Expense						
Operating Income		4,235,000,000	3,563,000,000	3,712,000,000	3,302,000,000	3,617,000,000
Operating Margin %		27.87%	22.70%	24.77%	22.68%	24.55%
SGA Expense		7,115,000,000	7,447,000,000	7,330,000,000	6,706,000,000	6,627,000,000
Net Income		3,158,000,000	2,567,000,000	2,111,000,000	2,445,000,000	2,516,000,000
Operating Cash Flow		4,127,000,000	4,484,000,000	-642,000,000	1,629,000,000	2,211,000,000
Capital Expenditure		601,000,000	791,000,000	609,000,000	652,000,000	642,000,000
EBITDA						
Return on Assets %		.77%	.64%	.55%	.70%	.87%
Return on Equity %		8.43%	6.82%	5.74%	7.05%	7.65%
Debt to Equity		0.62	0.58	0.57	0.56	0.66

CONTACT INFORMATION:

Phone: 212 495-1784 Fax:
Toll-Free:
Address: 1 Wall St., New York, NY 10286 United States

STOCK TICKER/OTHER:

Stock Ticker: BK
Employees: 51,100
Parent Company:

Exchange: NYS
Fiscal Year Ends: 12/31

SALARIES/BONUSES:

Top Exec. Salary:
$1,000,000

Bonus: $

Second Exec. Salary:
$650,000

Bonus: $

OTHER THOUGHTS:

Estimated Female Officers or Directors: 6

Hot Spot for Advancement for Women/Minorities: Y

Barrett Business Services Inc

www.barrettbusiness.com

NAIC Code: 561330

TYPES OF BUSINESS:

Human Resources Management
Staffing Services
Professional Employer Services (PEO)

BRANDS/DIVISIONS/AFFILIATES:

CONTACTS: *Note: Officers with more than one job title may be intentionally listed here more than once.*

Michael Elich, CEO
Gary Kramer, CFO
Gerald Blotz, COO, Divisional
Gregory Vaughn, COO, Divisional
Anthony Meeker, Director

GROWTH PLANS/SPECIAL FEATURES:

Barrett Business Services, Inc. is a human resources management company that provides staffing services and professional employer services. Originally founded in 1951, Barrett is headquartered in Vancouver, Washington and has more than 50 offices in Washington, California, Oregon, Idaho, Arizona, Nevada, Utah, Colorado, Maryland, Delaware and North Carolina. The firm's outsourced services help clients deal with issues concerning employment laws and regulations, payroll processing, employee benefits and administration, workers' compensation coverage, effective risk management, workplace safety programs and human resource administration. Barrett's staffing services include short-term, temporary-to-permanent and permanent placements in areas including clerical/administrative work, light industrial assignments, technical work, onsite management assignments and other specialties. The firm has been offering professional employer services since 1990, focusing on human resource management services for small and mid-sized companies. The company's professional employer services arrangement allows Barrett to enter a contractual agreement with the client's customer(s), thereby becoming a co-employer with the client company. This enables Barrett to assume responsibility for many or all of the human resource management duties, such as payroll/taxes, employee benefits, health insurance, workers' compensation, workplace safety, federal/state employment laws, labor regulatory requirements and other administrative tasks. The firm serves customers in a variety of markets, including electronics manufacturers, various light-manufacturing industries, forest products and agriculture-based companies, transportation and shipping enterprises, food processing, telecommunications, public utilities, general contractors in numerous construction-related fields and various professional services firms.

The company provides its employees medical and dental insurance as well as a 401(k) plan.

FINANCIAL DATA: *Note: Data for latest year may not have been available at press time.*

In U.S. $	2016	2015	2014	2013	2012	2011
Revenue		740,841,000	636,184,000	532,844,000	402,652,000	314,874,000
R&D Expense						
Operating Income		36,428,000	-45,910,000	24,426,000	18,787,000	3,934,000
Operating Margin %		4.91%	-7.21%	4.58%	4.66%	1.24%
SGA Expense		90,177,000	73,821,000	60,061,000	46,450,000	38,174,000
Net Income		25,494,000	-27,084,000	17,892,000	13,131,000	14,318,000
Operating Cash Flow		100,631,000	69,596,000	70,196,000	45,657,000	31,355,000
Capital Expenditure		2,996,000	4,632,000	4,097,000	3,712,000	1,247,000
EBITDA		39,962,000	-42,658,000	27,177,000	20,264,000	5,278,000
Return on Assets %		5.39%	-7.11%	6.59%	5.81%	6.96%
Return on Equity %		54.70%	-48.70%	28.29%	16.88%	14.53%
Debt to Equity			0.51	0.06	0.09	

CONTACT INFORMATION:

Phone: 360 828-0700   Fax: 360-828-0701
Toll-Free: 800-494-5669
Address: 8100 NE Parkway Dr., Ste. 200, Vancouver, WA 98662 United States

STOCK TICKER/OTHER:

Stock Ticker: BBSI   Exchange: NAS
Employees: 93,040   Fiscal Year Ends: 12/31
Parent Company:

SALARIES/BONUSES:

Top Exec. Salary: $650,000   Bonus: $
Second Exec. Salary: $400,000   Bonus: $70,000

OTHER THOUGHTS:

Estimated Female Officers or Directors:
Hot Spot for Advancement for Women/Minorities:

Bass Pro Shops Inc

www.basspro.com

NAIC Code: 451110

TYPES OF BUSINESS:

Sporting Goods, Retail
Sport Boats
Hunting & Fishing Equipment
Catalog & Online Sales
Outdoor Apparel
Resort Operations
Television Production

BRANDS/DIVISIONS/AFFILIATES:

Outdoor World
RedHead
American Rod & Gun
Big Cedar Lodge
Bass Pro Shop
Dogwood Canyon
Offshore Angler
White River Fly Shops

CONTACTS: Note: Officers with more than one job title may be intentionally listed here more than once.

James Hagale, CEO
James Hagale, COO
James Hagale, Pres.
Martin G. MacDonald, Dir.-Conservation
John L. Morris, Chmn.

GROWTH PLANS/SPECIAL FEATURES:

Bass Pro Shops, Inc. is a leader in sporting goods retail. The company markets its products through 89 retail stores in the U.S. and five in Canada, a mail-order catalog and its Internet sites. The firm is dedicated to providing outdoor recreational products, including specialty apparel, and also aims to inspire environmental conservation among its customers. The sporting goods superstores operate under the Bass Pro Shop and Outdoor World brand names. Products include boats and campers as well as fishing, hunting, camping, automobile and marine supplies. Many of these stores have a variety of unique features and attractions to draw more customers, including restaurants, snack bars, archery ranges, indoor fish tanks, waterfalls and video arcades. Aside from its stores, the company sells goods over the Internet and through catalogs/sales flyers under the Bass Pro Shops, RedHead, Offshore Angler and White River Fly Shops brand names. Its wholesale operations consist of Tracker Marine Group, a leader in sport boat manufacturing, and American Rod & Gun, one of the largest wholesale hunting and fishing distributors in the country. In addition to offering a variety of hunting and fishing trips and contests, Bass Pro runs the Wonders of Wildlife facility, a museum and conservation education center near its corporate headquarters, and Big Cedar Lodge, an outdoors-themed vacation spot in Missouri located near the company's own nature park, Dogwood Canyon. The company also produces a weekly television program on The Outdoor Channel and an international radio show.

FINANCIAL DATA: Note: Data for latest year may not have been available at press time.

In U.S. $	2016	2015	2014	2013	2012	2011
Revenue		4,500,000,000	4,250,000,000	4,200,000,000	4,150,000,000	4,000,000,000
R&D Expense						
Operating Income						
Operating Margin %						
SGA Expense						
Net Income						
Operating Cash Flow						
Capital Expenditure						
EBITDA						
Return on Assets %						
Return on Equity %						
Debt to Equity						

CONTACT INFORMATION:

Phone: 417-873-5000   Fax: 417-873-5060
Toll-Free: 800-227-7776
Address: 2500 E. Kearney St., Springfield, MO 65898 United States

STOCK TICKER/OTHER:

Stock Ticker: Private   Exchange:
Employees: 20,000   Fiscal Year Ends: 12/31
Parent Company:

SALARIES/BONUSES:

Top Exec. Salary: $ Bonus: $
Second Exec. Salary: $ Bonus: $

OTHER THOUGHTS:

Estimated Female Officers or Directors:
Hot Spot for Advancement for Women/Minorities:

BB&T Corporation

www.bbt.com

NAIC Code: 522110

TYPES OF BUSINESS:

Banking
Mortgages
Consumer Loans
Commercial Loans
Investment Services
Securities Lending
Insurance
Leasing

BRANDS/DIVISIONS/AFFILIATES:

Branch Bank
BB&T Equipment Finance Corporation
BB&T Investment Services Inc
BB&T Insurance Services Inc
CRC Insurance Services Inc
Grandbridge Real Estate Capital LLC
McGriff, Seibels & Williams Inc
BB&T Securities

CONTACTS: Note: Officers with more than one job title may be intentionally listed here more than once.

Kelly King, CEO
Robert Johnson, General Counsel
Daryl Bible, CFO
Cynthia Powell, Chief Accounting Officer
Steven Wiggs, Chief Marketing Officer
Clarke Starnes, Chief Risk Officer
Christopher Henson, COO
William Yates, Other Corporate Officer
David Weaver, Other Corporate Officer
Donna Goodrich, Other Corporate Officer

GROWTH PLANS/SPECIAL FEATURES:

BB&T Corp. is a financial holding company that conducts the majority of its operations primarily through its commercial bank subsidiary, Branch Bank, and other nonbank subsidiaries. Services and products include those for community banking, residential mortgage banking, dealer financial services, specialized lending, insurance services and financial services. BB&T's largest subsidiary, Branch Bank, provides a wide range of banking and trust services for retail and commercial clients including small and mid-size businesses, public agencies, local governments and individuals, through 2,139 offices. Branch Bank's principal operating subsidiaries include: BB&T Equipment Finance Corporation, providing loan and lease financing to commercial and small businesses; BB&T Investment Services, Inc., offering non-deposit investment alternatives; BB&T Insurance Services, Inc., offering property and casualty, life, health, employee benefits, commercial general liability, surety, title and other insurance products; CRC Insurance Services, Inc., a nationwide wholesale insurance broker; Grandbridge Real Estate Capital LLC which arranges & services commercial mortgage loans; and McGriff, Seibels & Williams, Inc., providing insurance products on an agency basis to large commercial clients. BB&T's non-bank subsidiaries include: BB&T Securities, a registered investment banking and full-service brokerage firm; Regional Acceptance Corporation, specializing in indirect financing for consumer purchases of primarily mid-model and late-model used automobiles; American Coastal Insurance Company, a Florida specialty insurance company that underwrites property insurance risks for commercial condominium or cooperative associations; and Sterling Capital Management LLC, providing a full range of investment strategies, including domestic and international equity, alternative investment products and strategies and fixed income investing. In April 2016, the firm acquired National Penn Bancshares, Inc.; and CGSC North America Holdings Corporation.

Employee benefits include 401(k) & pension plans; medical, vision and dental coverage; disability, life and AD&D insurance; health savings account; and wellness program.

FINANCIAL DATA: Note: Data for latest year may not have been available at press time.

In U.S. $	2016	2015	2014	2013	2012	2011
Revenue		9,611,000,000	9,158,000,000	9,553,000,000	9,677,000,000	8,620,000,000
R&D Expense						
Operating Income		2,917,000,000	2,986,000,000	3,124,000,000	2,792,000,000	1,628,000,000
Operating Margin %		30.35%	32.60%	32.70%	28.85%	18.88%
SGA Expense		4,047,000,000	3,802,000,000	3,594,000,000	3,705,000,000	3,284,000,000
Net Income		2,084,000,000	2,151,000,000	1,679,000,000	1,979,000,000	1,289,000,000
Operating Cash Flow		2,915,000,000	3,258,000,000	5,339,000,000	3,698,000,000	4,565,000,000
Capital Expenditure					145,000,000	224,000,000
EBITDA						
Return on Assets %		.97%	1.08%	.85%	1.06%	.77%
Return on Equity %		8.33%	9.56%	7.96%	10.51%	7.61%
Debt to Equity		0.96	1.07	1.06	1.00	1.25

CONTACT INFORMATION:

Phone: 336 733-2000   Fax:
Toll-Free: 800-226-5228
Address: 200 W. 2nd St., Winston-Salem, NC 27101 United States

STOCK TICKER/OTHER:

Stock Ticker: BBT   Exchange: NYS
Employees: 33,400   Fiscal Year Ends: 12/31
Parent Company:

SALARIES/BONUSES:

Top Exec. Salary: Bonus: $
$1,056,250
Second Exec. Salary: Bonus: $
$691,250

OTHER THOUGHTS:

Estimated Female Officers or Directors: 3

Hot Spot for Advancement for Women/Minorities: Y

Sales, profits and employees may be estimates. Financial information, benefits and other data can change quickly and may vary from those stated here.

Becton Dickinson & Co

www.bd.com

NAIC Code: 339100

TYPES OF BUSINESS:

Medical Equipment-Injection/Infusion
Drug Delivery Systems
Infusion Therapy Products
Diabetes Care Products
Surgical Products
Microbiology Products
Diagnostic Products
Consulting Services

BRANDS/DIVISIONS/AFFILIATES:

BD Medical
BD Life Sciences
CareFusion Corporation
BD Vacutainer
BD Hypak
Cellular Research Inc
CRISI Medical Systems

CONTACTS: Note: Officers with more than one job title may be intentionally listed here more than once.

Vincent Forlenza, CEO
Linda Tharby, Executive VP
Christopher Reidy, CFO
John Gallagher, Chief Accounting Officer
Nabil Shabshab, Chief Marketing Officer
Ellen Strahlman, Chief Medical Officer
Joseph Mercurio, Controller
William Kozy, COO
Stephen Sichak, Executive VP, Divisional
Gary Cohen, Executive VP
Thomas Polen, Executive VP
James Lim, Executive VP
Jeffrey Sherman, General Counsel
Alexandre Conroy, President, Geographical

GROWTH PLANS/SPECIAL FEATURES:

Becton, Dickinson & Co. (BD) manufactures and sells a broad line of medical supplies, devices and diagnostic systems used by health care professionals, medical research institutions and the general public. The company operates in two worldwide business segments: BD Medical and BD Life Sciences. BD Medical offers products, including specially designed devices for diabetes care; pre-fillable drug delivery systems; and infusion therapy products. It also offers anesthesia and surgical products, ophthalmic surgery devices, critical care systems, elastic support products, respiratory ventilation and diagnostic equipment and thermometers. BD Life Sciences offers products for safe collection and transport of diagnostics specimens; instruments and reagent systems to detect a broad range of infectious diseases; and research and clinical tools that facilitate the study of cells in order to get a comprehensive understanding of normal and disease processes. Some of the products are integrated systems for specimen collection, molecular testing systems for infectious diseases and fluorescence-activated cell sorters and analyzers. Two of BD's most popular products are BD Hypak pre-fillable syringes and BD Vacutainer blood-collection products. Outside of the U.S., the company's products are manufactured and sold in Europe, the Middle East, Africa, Japan, Mexico, Brazil, Asia Pacific and Canada. In 2015, it acquired medical technology company CRISI Medical Systems; medical technology firm, CareFusion Corporation; and acquired Cellular Research, Inc., a biotechnology research and development company. In January 2016, the company sold its BD Rx business to Fresenius Kabi.

The firm offers employees medical, dental, vision and prescription drug coverage; a flexible spending account; an employee assistance program; and at select locations, onsite services such as fitness centers, walking trails, banks and cafeterias.

FINANCIAL DATA: Note: Data for latest year may not have been available at press time.

In U.S. $	2016	2015	2014	2013	2012	2011
Revenue		10,282,000,000	8,446,000,000	8,054,000,000	7,708,382,000	7,828,904,000
R&D Expense		632,000,000	550,000,000	494,000,000	471,755,000	476,496,000
Operating Income		1,074,000,000	1,606,000,000	1,255,000,000	1,557,885,000	1,763,282,000
Operating Margin %		10.44%	19.01%	15.58%	20.21%	22.52%
SGA Expense		2,563,000,000	2,145,000,000	2,422,000,000	1,923,354,000	1,851,774,000
Net Income		695,000,000	1,185,000,000	1,293,000,000	1,169,927,000	1,270,994,000
Operating Cash Flow		1,730,000,000	1,746,000,000	1,717,000,000	1,760,228,000	1,716,000,000
Capital Expenditure		633,000,000	653,000,000	588,000,000	553,644,000	605,257,000
EBITDA		2,001,000,000	2,219,000,000	1,849,000,000	2,118,004,000	2,304,371,000
Return on Assets %		3.53%	9.63%	10.99%	10.73%	12.65%
Return on Equity %		11.37%	23.47%	28.17%	26.10%	24.76%
Debt to Equity		1.58	0.74	0.74	0.90	0.51

CONTACT INFORMATION:

Phone: 201 847-6800   Fax:
Toll-Free: 800-284-6845
Address: 1 Becton Dr., Franklin Lakes, NJ 07417 United States

STOCK TICKER/OTHER:

Stock Ticker: BDX
Employees: 49,517
Parent Company:

Exchange: NYS
Fiscal Year Ends: 09/30

SALARIES/BONUSES:

Top Exec. Salary: $1,045,000   Bonus: $

Second Exec. Salary: $749,840   Bonus: $

OTHER THOUGHTS:

Estimated Female Officers or Directors: 6

Hot Spot for Advancement for Women/Minorities: Y

Sales, profits and employees may be estimates. Financial information, benefits and other data can change quickly and may vary from those stated here.

Bed Bath & Beyond Inc

www.bedbathandbeyond.com

NAIC Code: 442299

TYPES OF BUSINESS:

Linens & Housewares, Retail
Small Appliances
Home Accessories
Health & Beauty Care
Baby & Toddler Merchandise

BRANDS/DIVISIONS/AFFILIATES:

Bed Bath & Beyond
Harmon
buybuy BABY
Christmas Tree Shops and That!
World Market
Cost Plus World Market
Linen Holdings
One Kings Lane Inc

CONTACTS: Note: Officers with more than one job title may be intentionally listed here more than once.

Steven Temares, CEO
Susan Lattmann, CFO
Warren Eisenberg, Co-Chairman
Leonard Feinstein, Co-Chairman
Eugene Castagna, COO
Arthur Stark, Other Executive Officer
Matthew Fiorilli, Senior VP, Divisional

GROWTH PLANS/SPECIAL FEATURES:

Bed Bath & Beyond, Inc. (BBB) is one of the nation's largest operators of domestic superstores, with approximately 1,530 stores in 50 states as well as Washington D.C., Canada and Puerto Rico. BBB operates six retail entities: Bed Bath & Beyond; Harmon and Harmon Face Values; buybuy BABY; Christmas Tree Shops and That!; World Market or Cost Plus World Market and One Kings Lane. Bed Bath & Beyond stores offer a full line of domestic merchandise and home furnishings, including bed linens, bath accessories and kitchen tiles, as well as furniture, dinnerware and glassware. Harmon or Harmon Face Values sells beauty care products in 51 stores. Buybuy BABY is a retailer of infant and toddler merchandise with 105 stores in 32 states. Christmas Tree Shops and That! stores offer gifts, household items and furnishings through 78 locations in 21 states. World Market or Cost Plus World Market retails home decorating items, furniture, holiday and other seasonal items as well as specialty food and beverages with 258 stores in 30 states. One Kings Lane is a home decor and design business. The company also operates Linen Holdings, a provider of a variety of textile products, amenities and other goods to institutional customers in the hospitality, cruise line, food service, healthcare and other industries. Through a joint venture, BBB operates seven stores in Mexico under the Bed Bath & Beyond name. BBB relies on paid advertising and uses circulars and mailing pieces as its primary marketing vehicles. In addition, the company has distribution facilities, which ship merchandise to stores or customers, totaling approximately 6.1 million square feet. Moreover, the firm offers a wide variety of products through its network of web sites including www.buybuybaby.com, www.harmondiscount.com, www.worldmarket.com, www.bedbathandbeyond.com and www.onekingslane.com. In June 2016, the firm acquired One Kings Lane, Inc.

FINANCIAL DATA: Note: Data for latest year may not have been available at press time.

In U.S. $	2016	2015	2014	2013	2012	2011
Revenue	12,103,890,000	11,881,180,000	11,503,960,000	10,914,580,000	9,499,890,000	8,758,503,000
R&D Expense						
Operating Income	1,414,903,000	1,554,293,000	1,614,587,000	1,638,218,000	1,568,369,000	1,288,458,000
Operating Margin %	11.68%	13.08%	14.03%	15.00%	16.50%	14.71%
SGA Expense	3,205,407,000	3,065,486,000	2,950,995,000	2,750,537,000	2,362,564,000	2,334,471,000
Net Income	841,489,000	957,474,000	1,022,290,000	1,037,788,000	989,537,000	791,333,000
Operating Cash Flow	1,012,184,000	1,185,848,000	1,383,186,000	1,192,990,000	1,225,284,000	987,407,000
Capital Expenditure	328,395,000	330,637,000	317,180,000	354,682,000	243,374,000	183,474,000
EBITDA	1,688,850,000	1,793,486,000	1,833,396,000	1,832,946,000	1,752,242,000	1,472,278,000
Return on Assets %	12.69%	14.60%	16.18%	17.29%	17.40%	14.65%
Return on Equity %	31.73%	28.64%	25.49%	25.93%	25.19%	20.86%
Debt to Equity	0.58	0.54				

CONTACT INFORMATION:

Phone: 908 688-0888   Fax: 908 810-8813
Toll-Free: 800-462-3966
Address: 650 Liberty Ave., Union, NJ 07083 United States

STOCK TICKER/OTHER:

Stock Ticker: BBBY   Exchange: NAS
Employees: 60,000   Fiscal Year Ends: 02/28
Parent Company:

SALARIES/BONUSES:

Top Exec. Salary: $3,967,500   Bonus: $
Second Exec. Salary: $1,811,154   Bonus: $

OTHER THOUGHTS:

Estimated Female Officers or Directors: 1

Hot Spot for Advancement for Women/Minorities:

Belden Inc

NAIC Code: 334417

www.belden.com

TYPES OF BUSINESS:

Cable & Wire Connectors Manufacturing
Electronic Products
Broadcasting Equipment
Aerospace & Automotive Electronics
Enclosures

BRANDS/DIVISIONS/AFFILIATES:

Tripwire

CONTACTS: *Note: Officers with more than one job title may be intentionally listed here more than once.*

John Stroup, CEO
Henk Derksen, CFO
Bryan Cressey, Chairman of the Board
Douglas Zink, Chief Accounting Officer
Christopher Gusenleitner, Executive VP, Divisional
Dhrupad Trivedi, Executive VP, Divisional
Glenn Pennycook, Executive VP, Divisional
Roel Vestjens, Executive VP, Divisional
Brian Anderson, General Counsel
Dean McKenna, Senior VP, Divisional
Ross Rosenberg, Senior VP, Divisional
Steven Biegacki, Senior VP, Divisional

GROWTH PLANS/SPECIAL FEATURES:

Belden, Inc. designs, manufactures and markets signal transmission products, including cable, connectivity and networking components. The company is divided into four segments: broadcast solutions, enterprise connectivity solutions, industrial connectivity solutions and industrial IT solutions. Broadcast solutions provides production, distribution and connectivity systems for the television broadcast, cable, satellite and IPTV industries. Products are used in a variety of applications, including live production signal management, program playout for broadcasters, monitoring for pay-TV operators and broadband connectivity. Broadcast products include camera mounted fiber solutions, interfaces and routers, broadcast and audio-visual cable solutions, monitoring systems, playout systems, outside plant connectivity products and other cable and connectivity products. The enterprise connectivity solutions segment provides infrastructure and connectivity solutions for enterprise customers. Products include fiber and copper connectivity products; fiber optic and copper cable products; and wiring racks, panels and enclosures as well as interconnecting hardware, intelligent patching devices and cable management solutions for complete end-to-end network structured wiring systems. The industrial connectivity solutions segment provides infrastructure components and connectivity systems for industrial automation applications. Products include industrial and input/output (I/O) connectors, industrial cables, IP and networking cables, I/O modules, distribution boxes, customer specific wiring solutions and load-moment indicators for the mobile crane market. The industrial IT segment provides mission-critical networking systems. Products include security devices, Ethernet switches and related equipment, routers and gateways, network management software and wireless systems. In early 2015, Belden acquired Tripwire for $710 million, a leader in security and vulnerability management.

FINANCIAL DATA: *Note: Data for latest year may not have been available at press time.*

In U.S. $	2016	2015	2014	2013	2012	2011
Revenue		2,309,222,000	2,308,265,000	2,069,193,000	1,840,739,000	1,981,953,000
R&D Expense		148,311,000	113,914,000	83,277,000	65,410,000	55,711,000
Operating Income		140,553,000	163,119,000	201,262,000	108,497,000	187,006,000
Operating Margin %		6.08%	7.06%	9.72%	5.89%	9.43%
SGA Expense		527,288,000	487,945,000	378,009,000	345,926,000	325,950,000
Net Income		66,204,000	74,449,000	103,313,000	194,490,000	114,345,000
Operating Cash Flow		236,410,000	194,028,000	164,601,000	139,388,000	184,563,000
Capital Expenditure		54,969,000	45,459,000	40,209,000	41,010,000	40,053,000
EBITDA		290,895,000	265,864,000	294,595,000	116,435,000	238,191,000
Return on Assets %		2.01%	2.47%	3.87%	8.89%	6.56%
Return on Equity %		8.11%	9.05%	12.53%	25.82%	17.15%
Debt to Equity		2.12	2.18	1.63	1.39	0.79

CONTACT INFORMATION:

Phone: 314 854-8000   Fax: 314 854-8001
Toll-Free: 800-235-3361
Address: 1 N. Brentwood Blvd., 15/Fl, St. Louis, MO 63105 United States

STOCK TICKER/OTHER:

Stock Ticker: BDC   Exchange: NYS
Employees: 8,100   Fiscal Year Ends: 12/31
Parent Company:

SALARIES/BONUSES:

Top Exec. Salary: $850,000   Bonus: $
Second Exec. Salary: Bonus: $
$486,023

OTHER THOUGHTS:

Estimated Female Officers or Directors: 2
Hot Spot for Advancement for Women/Minorities: Y

Berkshire Hathaway Energy Company

www.berkshirehathawayenergyco.com/

NAIC Code: 221112

TYPES OF BUSINESS:

Utilities-Electricity & Natural Gas
Pipelines
Wind Generation
Hydroelectric Generation
Thermal Solar Generation
Real Estate Brokerage
Solar Power

BRANDS/DIVISIONS/AFFILIATES:

PacifiCorp
Rocky Mountain Power
Pacific Power
PacifiCorp Transmission
MidAmerican Energy Company
Northern Natural Gas Company
Kern River Gas Transmission Company
BHE U.S. Transmission

CONTACTS: *Note: Officers with more than one job title may be intentionally listed here more than once.*

Gregory E. Abel, CEO
Gregory E. Abel, Pres.
Patrick J. Goodman, CFO
Maureen E. Sammon, Chief Admin. Officer
Douglas L. Anderson, General Counsel
Gregory E. Abel, Chmn.

GROWTH PLANS/SPECIAL FEATURES:

Berkshire Hathaway Energy Company generates, transmits, stores, distributes and supplies energy through its subsidiaries to roughly 11.6 million customers. The company has 14 primary subsidiaries. PacifiCorp serves roughly 1.8 million customers, operating in three business units: Rocky Mountain Power, which delivers electricity in Wyoming, Utah and Idaho; Pacific Power, delivering electricity in Oregon, Washington and California; and PacifiCorp Transmission, which constitutes the company's electric generation, energy trading and coal mining operations. MidAmerican Energy Company generates, transmits and sells electricity to over 752,000 customers and supplies natural gas to over 733,000 customers in Illinois, Nebraska, Iowa and South Dakota. Northern Natural Gas Company owns a 14,700-mile interstate natural gas pipeline system extending from Texas to the upper Midwest, serving 81 utility companies. Kern River Gas Transmission Company owns 1,700 miles of interstate pipeline and delivers natural gas to Nevada, Utah and California. Homeservices of America, Inc. is a leading U.S. residential real estate brokerage firm. NV Energy Inc. serves 1.2 million customers in Nevada, serving approximately 90% of the state as well as 25-,000 natural gas service customers in select areas. Northern Powergrid offers 3.9 million users electricity in the Northeastern part of England. Berkshire Hathaway Energy supplies electricity to over 10.7 million customers and natural gas to nearly 1 million. BHE Renewables' 3,877 megawatts total capacity of owned and under construction clean energy includes 1,278 MW solar, 1,153 MW wind, 338 MW geothermal, 138 MW hydro and 970 MW natural gas. AltaLink is the largest regulated transmission company in Alberta, owning 13,000 kilometers of transmission lines and more than 300 substations. Finally, BHE U.S. Transmission provides transmission solutions for wholesale customers.

The company offers employees medical, dental, vision, disability and life insurance; a 401(k) plan; a profit sharing plan; an employee assistance program; flexible spending accounts; tuition reimbursement; and adoption assistance.

FINANCIAL DATA: *Note: Data for latest year may not have been available at press time.*

In U.S. $	2016	2015	2014	2013	2012	2011
Revenue		17,880,000,000	17,326,000,000	12,635,000,000	11,548,000,000	11,173,000,000
R&D Expense						
Operating Income						
Operating Margin %						
SGA Expense						
Net Income		2,400,000,000	2,095,000,000	1,636,000,000	1,472,000,000	1,331,000,000
Operating Cash Flow						
Capital Expenditure						
EBITDA						
Return on Assets %						
Return on Equity %						
Debt to Equity						

CONTACT INFORMATION:

Phone: 515-242-3022   Fax:
Toll-Free:
Address: 666 Grand Ave., Des Moines, IA 50306-0657 United States

STOCK TICKER/OTHER:

Stock Ticker: Subsidiary   Exchange:
Employees: 21,000   Fiscal Year Ends: 12/31
Parent Company: Berkshire Hathaway Inc

SALARIES/BONUSES:

Top Exec. Salary: $ Bonus: $
Second Exec. Salary: $ Bonus: $

OTHER THOUGHTS:

Estimated Female Officers or Directors: 1
Hot Spot for Advancement for Women/Minorities:

Sales, profits and employees may be estimates. Financial information, benefits and other data can change quickly and may vary from those stated here.

Berkshire Hathaway Inc

www.berkshirehathaway.com

NAIC Code: 524126

TYPES OF BUSINESS:

Insurance--Property & Casualty, Specialty, Surety
Retail Operations
Foodservice Operations
Building Products & Services
Apparel & Footwear
Technology Training
Manufactured Housing & RVs
Business Jet Flexible Ownership Services

BRANDS/DIVISIONS/AFFILIATES:

General Re Corporation
GEICO Corporation
Berkshire Hathaway Reinsurance Group
Berkshire Hathaway Primary Group
Clayton Homes Inc
Acme Building Brands
FlightSafety International Inc
Precision Castparts Corp

CONTACTS: Note: Officers with more than one job title may be intentionally listed here more than once.

Warren Buffett, CEO
Marc Hamburg, CFO
Daniel Jaksich, Chief Accounting Officer
Charles Munger, Director
Sharon Heck, Secretary

GROWTH PLANS/SPECIAL FEATURES:

Berkshire Hathaway, Inc. is a holding company that owns subsidiaries engaged in diverse business activities, most importantly insurance and reinsurance. Berkshire provides property & casualty insurance and reinsurance, as well as life, accident and health reinsurance, through U.S. and foreign businesses. The company conducts its insurance underwriting business through four divisions. General Re Corporation, through its subsidiaries, conducts global reinsurance business in 51 cities and provides reinsurance worldwide. GEICO Corporation mainly provides private passenger auto insurance to individuals in all 50 U.S. states and Washington, D.C. The Berkshire Hathaway Reinsurance Group underwrites excess-of-loss and quota-share reinsurance for insurers and reinsurers; and Berkshire Hathaway Primary Group offers insurance for property and casualty. The company's financial subsidiaries include Clayton Homes, Inc., a manufactured housing company; XTRA Corporation, a provider of transportation equipment leases; and furniture rental company CORT Business Services Corporation. Berkshire's apparel and footwear businesses include Fruit of the Loom, Russell, Vanity Fair, Garan, Fechheimer Brothers, H.H. Brown Shoe Company, Brooks Sports and Justin Brands. The firm manufactures and distributes building products through Acme Building Brands, Benjamin Moore & Co., Johns Manville, Shaw and MiTek. Subsidiary FlightSafety International, Inc. provides training to aircraft and ship pilots, while NetJets, Inc. offers fractional ownership programs for aircraft. In addition, subsidiary International Dairy Queen services approximately 6,700 DQ Grill and Chill, Dairy Queen and Orange Julius stores. Borsheim Jewelry Company, Inc. is a retailer of fine jewelry, watches, crystal, china, stemware, flatware, gifts and collectibles. Other non-insurance operations include grocery and foodservice distribution, furniture retailing, carpet manufacturing, utilities and energy, newspapers, cleaning products, confectioneries, agricultural equipment, kitchen tools and recreational vehicles. In 2016, the firm acquired complex metal components manufacturer, Precision Castparts Corp.

FINANCIAL DATA: Note: Data for latest year may not have been available at press time.

In U.S. $	2016	2015	2014	2013	2012	2011
Revenue		210,821,000,000	194,673,000,000	182,150,000,000	162,463,000,000	143,688,000,000
R&D Expense						
Operating Income		34,946,000,000	28,105,000,000	28,796,000,000	22,236,000,000	15,314,000,000
Operating Margin %		16.57%	14.43%	15.80%	13.68%	10.65%
SGA Expense		45,874,000,000	43,099,000,000	11,917,000,000	10,503,000,000	8,670,000,000
Net Income		24,083,000,000	19,872,000,000	19,476,000,000	14,824,000,000	10,254,000,000
Operating Cash Flow		31,491,000,000	32,010,000,000	27,704,000,000	20,950,000,000	20,476,000,000
Capital Expenditure		16,082,000,000	15,185,000,000	11,087,000,000	9,775,000,000	8,191,000,000
EBITDA						
Return on Assets %		4.46%	3.93%	4.26%	3.61%	2.68%
Return on Equity %		9.71%	8.60%	9.51%	8.41%	6.36%
Debt to Equity		0.32	0.33	0.32	0.33	0.36

CONTACT INFORMATION:

Phone: 402 346-1400   Fax: 402 346-3375
Toll-Free:
Address: 3555 Farnam St., Omaha, NE 68131 United States

STOCK TICKER/OTHER:

Stock Ticker: BRK.A   Exchange: NYS
Employees: 316,000   Fiscal Year Ends: 12/31
Parent Company:

SALARIES/BONUSES:

Top Exec. Salary: Bonus: $
$1,350,000
Second Exec. Salary: Bonus: $
$100,000

OTHER THOUGHTS:

Estimated Female Officers or Directors:

Hot Spot for Advancement for Women/Minorities:

Best Buy Co Inc

NAIC Code: 443142

TYPES OF BUSINESS:

Consumer Electronics Stores
Retail Music & Video Sales
Personal Computers
Office Supplies
Cell Phones and Accessories
Appliances
Cameras
Consumer Electronics Installation & Service

BRANDS/DIVISIONS/AFFILIATES:

Geek Squad
Best Buy Mobile
Best Buy Express
Magnolia Home Theater
Pacific Kitchen and Home
Best Buy
Best Buy Canada
Best Buy Direct

CONTACTS: Note: Officers with more than one job title may be intentionally listed here more than once.

Hubert Joly, CEO
Corie Barry, CFO
Greg Revelle, Chief Marketing Officer
Mathew Watson, Controller
Keith Nelsen, General Counsel
Paula Baker, Other Executive Officer
R. Mohan, Other Executive Officer
Shari Ballard, President, Divisional
Mary Kelley, President, Divisional

GROWTH PLANS/SPECIAL FEATURES:

Best Buy Co., Inc. is a leading retailer of name-brand consumer electronics, appliances and home office and entertainment products and services. The company conducts business in both the domestic and international markets. The domestic market includes all of the firm's U.S. businesses, operating under such brands as Best Buy; Best Buy Direct; Best Buy Express; Best Buy Mobile; Geek Squad, which provides computer repair and installation services; Magnolia Home Theater; and Pacific Kitchen and Home. The international segment, which is comprised of the firm's businesses in Canada and Mexico, operates under brand names such as Best Buy, Best Buy Express, Best Buy Mobile and Geek Squad. The company's products include home office equipment, cameras, computer and audio/video equipment, computer upgrades and car audio and security system installation. The firm operates 1,200 large-format and 400 small-format Best Buy stores in the U.S. and internationally. In 2015 Best Buy Direct, subsidiary Best Buy Canada announced it was consolidating its Future Shop chain by closing 66 Future Shop locations and transitioning an additional 65 Future Shop stores to the Best Buy Brand.

Employee benefits include medical, dental, vision, life, disability, health care and dependent care spending accounts. Wealth benefits include 401(k) accounts, an employee stock purchase plan and bonus/incentive programs.

FINANCIAL DATA: Note: Data for latest year may not have been available at press time.

In U.S. $	2016	2015	2014	2013	2012	2011
Revenue	39,528,000,000	40,339,000,000	42,410,000,000	45,085,000,000	50,705,000,000	50,272,000,000
R&D Expense						
Operating Income	1,375,000,000	1,450,000,000	1,140,000,000	-125,000,000	1,085,000,000	2,114,000,000
Operating Margin %	3.47%	3.59%	2.68%		2.13%	4.20%
SGA Expense	7,618,000,000	7,592,000,000	8,391,000,000	9,502,000,000	10,242,000,000	10,325,000,000
Net Income	897,000,000	1,233,000,000	532,000,000	-441,000,000	-1,231,000,000	1,277,000,000
Operating Cash Flow	1,322,000,000	1,935,000,000	1,094,000,000	1,454,000,000	3,293,000,000	1,190,000,000
Capital Expenditure	649,000,000	561,000,000	547,000,000	705,000,000	766,000,000	744,000,000
EBITDA	2,047,000,000	2,133,000,000	1,903,000,000	758,000,000	2,122,000,000	3,143,000,000
Return on Assets %	6.23%	8.42%	3.79%		-7.27%	7.06%
Return on Equity %	19.14%	27.45%	13.34%		-23.79%	19.76%
Debt to Equity	0.30	0.31	0.40		0.44	0.10

CONTACT INFORMATION:

Phone: 612 291-1000   Fax: 612 292-4001
Toll-Free:
Address: 7601 Penn Ave. S., Richfield, MN 55423 United States

STOCK TICKER/OTHER:

Stock Ticker: BBY   Exchange: NYS
Employees: 125,000   Fiscal Year Ends: 02/28
Parent Company:

SALARIES/BONUSES:

Top Exec. Salary: Bonus: $
$1,175,000
Second Exec. Salary: Bonus: $
$925,000

OTHER THOUGHTS:

Estimated Female Officers or Directors: 5

Hot Spot for Advancement for Women/Minorities: Y

Bio Rad Laboratories Inc

www.bio-rad.com

NAIC Code: 325413

TYPES OF BUSINESS:

Clinical Diagnostics Products
Medical Equipment
Analytical Instruments
Laboratory Devices
Biomaterials
Imaging Products
Assays
Software

BRANDS/DIVISIONS/AFFILIATES:

CONTACTS: *Note: Officers with more than one job title may be intentionally listed here more than once.*

John Cassingham, Assistant Secretary
Norman Schwartz, CEO
Christine Tsingos, CFO
James Stark, Chief Accounting Officer
John Goetz, COO
Michael Crowley, Executive VP, Divisional
Giovanni Magni, Executive VP
John Hertia, Executive VP
Shannon Hall, Executive VP
Ronald Hutton, Executive VP

GROWTH PLANS/SPECIAL FEATURES:

Bio-Rad Laboratories, Inc. supplies the research, health care and analytical chemistry markets with a broad range of life science research and clinical diagnostic products and systems. These are used to separate complex chemical and biological materials and to identify, analyze and purify components. The company operates in two industry segments: clinical diagnostics and life science. The clinical diagnostics division encompasses an array of technologies incorporated into a variety of tests used to detect, identify and quantify substances in blood or other body fluids and tissues. The test results are used as aids for medical diagnosis, detection, evaluation, monitoring and treatment of diseases and other conditions. This division is known for diabetes monitoring products, quality control systems, blood virus testing, blood typing, toxicology, genetic disorders products, molecular pathology and Internet-based software. The firm's life science division develops, manufactures and markets more than 5,000 products for applications including electrophoresis, image analysis, molecular detection, chromatography, gene transfer, sample preparation and amplification. Products include a range of laboratory instruments, apparatuses and consumables used for research in genomics, proteomics and food safety. The life science division provides its services to universities, medical schools, pharmaceutical manufacturers, industrial research organizations, food testing laboratories, government agencies and biotechnology researchers.

FINANCIAL DATA: *Note: Data for latest year may not have been available at press time.*

In U.S. $	2016	2015	2014	2013	2012	2011
Revenue		2,019,441,000	2,175,044,000	2,132,694,000	2,069,235,000	2,073,529,000
R&D Expense		192,972,000	220,333,000	210,952,000	214,040,000	186,439,000
Operating Income		166,708,000	149,984,000	169,456,000	257,200,000	295,156,000
Operating Margin %		8.25%	6.89%	7.94%	12.42%	14.23%
SGA Expense		761,990,000	808,200,000	798,070,000	682,898,000	696,294,000
Net Income		113,093,000	88,845,000	77,790,000	163,778,000	178,223,000
Operating Cash Flow		186,210,000	273,312,000	175,476,000	278,898,000	259,816,000
Capital Expenditure		113,372,000	136,478,000	113,698,000	154,197,000	103,324,000
EBITDA		299,339,000	303,588,000	320,856,000	404,443,000	409,897,000
Return on Assets %		3.20%	2.64%	2.27%	5.01%	5.78%
Return on Equity %		4.83%	4.06%	3.70%	8.72%	10.86%
Debt to Equity		0.17	0.19	0.19	0.36	0.41

CONTACT INFORMATION:

Phone: 510 724-7000   Fax: 510 741-5817
Toll-Free: 800-424-6723
Address: 1000 Alfred Nobel Dr., Hercules, CA 94547 United States

STOCK TICKER/OTHER:

Stock Ticker: BIO   Exchange: NYS
Employees: 7,600   Fiscal Year Ends: 12/31
Parent Company:

SALARIES/BONUSES:

Top Exec. Salary: $885,558   Bonus: $
Second Exec. Salary: $666,125   Bonus: $

OTHER THOUGHTS:

Estimated Female Officers or Directors: 3
Hot Spot for Advancement for Women/Minorities: Y

Biogen Inc

www.biogenidec.com

NAIC Code: 325412

TYPES OF BUSINESS:

Drugs-Immunology, Neurology & Oncology
Autoimmune & Inflammatory Disease Treatments
Drugs-Multiple Sclerosis
Drugs-Cancer

BRANDS/DIVISIONS/AFFILIATES:

AVONEX
PLEGRIDY
RITUXAN
TECFIDERA
FAMPYRA
ELOCTATE
GAZYVA
Biogen Idec Inc

CONTACTS: *Note: Officers with more than one job title may be intentionally listed here more than once.*

Paul Clancy, CFO
Gregory Covino, Chief Accounting Officer
Alfred Sandrock, Chief Medical Officer
Spyridon Artavanis-Tsakonas, Chief Scientific Officer
Stelios Papadopoulos, Director
Steven Holtzman, Executive VP, Divisional
Kenneth Dipietro, Executive VP, Divisional
Adam Koppel, Executive VP, Divisional
Adriana Karaboutis, Executive VP, Divisional
Susan Alexander, Executive VP

GROWTH PLANS/SPECIAL FEATURES:

Biogen, Inc. (formerly Biogen Idec, Inc.) is a biotechnology company focused on discovering, developing, manufacturing and marketing therapies for the treatment of multiple sclerosis (MS) and other autoimmune disorders, neurodegenerative diseases and hemophilia. Biogen's marketed products for MS include: AVONEX, an intramuscular injectable therapy designed to treat relapsing forms of the disease and is one of the most prescribed forms of treatment worldwide; PLEGRIDY, a subcutaneous injectable therapy in the U.S. for the treatment of relapsing forms of MS and in the European Union (EU) for relapsing remitting MS (RRMS); TECFIDERA, an oral therapy in the U.S. for the treatment of relapsing forms of MS and in the EU for people with RRMS; TYSABRI, a monoclonal antibody for the treatment of RRMS and also U.S. approved to treat Crohn's disease; and FAMPYRA, which aids in improving adult patients with MS-related walking disabilities. Principal marketed products for hemophilia A and B include: ELOCTATE, a recombinant DNA-derived, antihemophilic factor in the U.S. for the treatment of adults and children with hemophilia A for control and prevention of bleeding episodes; and ALPROLIX, a recombinant DNA-derived, coagulation Factor IX concentrate in the U.S. for the treatment of adults and children with hemophilia B for control and prevention of bleeding episodes. Biogen collaborates with Genentech, Inc. on the development and commercialization of RITUXAN, a widely prescribed monoclonal antibody used to treat non-Hodgkin's lymphoma, rheumatoid arthritis, chronic lymphocytic leukemia (CLL) and two forms of ANCA-associated vasculitis; and shares operating profits and losses relating to GAZYVA with Genentech. GAZYVA, in combination with chlorambucil, is for the treatment of patients with previously untreated CLL, and is FDA approved. In 2015, the firm changed its name to just Biogen, Inc.

Biogen offers employees medical, dental and vision insurance; tuition reimbursement; flexible spending accounts; and an employee assistance program.

FINANCIAL DATA: *Note: Data for latest year may not have been available at press time.*

In U.S. $	2016	2015	2014	2013	2012	2011
Revenue		10,763,800,000	9,703,324,000	6,932,199,000	5,516,461,000	5,048,634,000
R&D Expense		2,012,800,000	1,893,422,000	1,444,053,000	1,334,919,000	1,219,602,000
Operating Income		4,891,000,000	3,955,656,000	2,515,509,000	1,855,849,000	1,724,691,000
Operating Margin %		45.43%	40.76%	36.28%	33.64%	34.16%
SGA Expense		2,113,100,000	2,232,342,000	1,797,408,000	1,595,360,000	1,373,904,000
Net Income		3,547,000,000	2,934,784,000	1,862,341,000	1,380,033,000	1,234,428,000
Operating Cash Flow		3,716,100,000	2,942,115,000	2,345,078,000	1,879,897,000	1,727,741,000
Capital Expenditure		643,000,000	287,751,000	3,509,000,000	261,182,000	252,175,000
EBITDA		5,463,200,000	4,664,283,000	3,044,219,000	2,257,253,000	2,103,147,000
Return on Assets %		20.97%	22.42%	16.93%	14.39%	14.40%
Return on Equity %		35.15%	30.21%	23.90%	20.61%	20.88%
Debt to Equity		0.69	0.05	0.06	0.09	0.16

CONTACT INFORMATION:

Phone: 617-679-2000   Fax: 619 679-2617
Toll-Free:
Address: 225 Binney Street, Cambridge, MA 02142 United States

STOCK TICKER/OTHER:

Stock Ticker: BIIB
Employees: 7,350
Parent Company:

Exchange: NAS
Fiscal Year Ends: 12/31

SALARIES/BONUSES:

Top Exec. Salary:
$1,538,462
Second Exec. Salary:
$747,498

Bonus: $

Bonus: $

OTHER THOUGHTS:

Estimated Female Officers or Directors: 4

Hot Spot for Advancement for Women/Minorities: Y

Sales, profits and employees may be estimates. Financial information, benefits and other data can change quickly and may vary from those stated here.

Black & Veatch Holding Company

www.bv.com

NAIC Code: 541330

TYPES OF BUSINESS:

Heavy & Civil Engineering, Construction
Infrastructure & Energy Services
Environmental & Hydrologic Engineering
Consulting Services
IT Services
Power Plant Engineering and Construction
LNG and Gas Processing Plant Engineering
Climate Change Services

BRANDS/DIVISIONS/AFFILIATES:

RCC Consultants

CONTACTS: *Note: Officers with more than one job title may be intentionally listed here more than once.*

Steven L. Edwards, CEO
Steven L. Edwards, Pres.
Karen L. Daniel, CFO
Lori Kelleher, Chief Human Resources Officer
James R. Lewis, Chief Admin. Officer
Timothy W. Triplett, General Counsel
Cindy Wallis-Lage, Pres., Water
O.H. Oskvig, CEO-Energy Business
William R. Van Dyke, Pres., Federal Svcs.
Steven L. Edwards, Chmn.
Hoe Wai Cheong, Sr. VP-Water-Asia Pacific
John E. Murphy, Pres., Construction & Procurement

GROWTH PLANS/SPECIAL FEATURES:

Black & Veatch Holding Company (B&V) is an engineering consulting and construction company specializing in infrastructure development for the energy, water telecommunications, federal, management consulting and environmental markets. The company is employee-owned and operates over 100 offices worldwide. B&V divides its service offerings into 13 categories. The firm's asset management services include power and water asset optimization solutions. Its environmental services encompass energy optimization water planning, greenhouse gas services, climate economic and government services. The company provides construction services for energy facilities, water and wastewater treatment facilities, water distribution systems, desalination facilities wireless sites and aerospace and defense sites. The construction management service segment offers tailored services aimed at reducing costs while improving quality. Design-build services cover engineering, procurement and construction. Engineering and design services include power delivery, siting, new generation engineering, power plant upgrade and bulk materials handling services. The nexus of water and energy segment addresses the interdependency of water and energy, reducing costs for both. Management consulting services comprise enterprise management and utility efficiency solutions. Procurement services include project procurement strategy, transportation logistics and inspection services. The program management segment manages energy, water, telecom and federal programs. Smart grid/smart utility services include utilities planning, system modeling distribution automation and field construction. The security services segment offers cyber, electronic and physical security to the communications and utility industries. B&V also offers consulting and planning services. In August 2015, the firm acquired RCC Consultants, a global engineering and consulting firm.

The company offers employees medical, dental, vision and prescription drug coverage; flexible spending accounts employee assistance programs; tuition reimbursement adoption assistance; and credit union membership.

FINANCIAL DATA: *Note: Data for latest year may not have been available at press time.*

In U.S. $	2016	2015	2014	2013	2012	2011
Revenue		3,030,000,000	3,600,000,000	3,560,000,000	3,279,000,000	2,600,000,000
R&D Expense						
Operating Income						
Operating Margin %						
SGA Expense						
Net Income						
Operating Cash Flow						
Capital Expenditure						
EBITDA						
Return on Assets %						
Return on Equity %						
Debt to Equity						

CONTACT INFORMATION:

Phone: 913-458-2000   Fax: 913-458-2934
Toll-Free:
Address: 11401 Lamar Ave., Overland Park, KS 66211 United States

STOCK TICKER/OTHER:

Stock Ticker: Private
Employees: 10,285
Parent Company:

Exchange:
Fiscal Year Ends: 12/31

SALARIES/BONUSES:

Top Exec. Salary: $ Bonus: $
Second Exec. Salary: $ Bonus: $

OTHER THOUGHTS:

Estimated Female Officers or Directors: 4
Hot Spot for Advancement for Women/Minorities: Y

BlackRock Inc

www.blackrock.com

NAIC Code: 523920

TYPES OF BUSINESS:

Investment Management
Risk Management Services
Investment System Services

BRANDS/DIVISIONS/AFFILIATES:

Aladdin
iShares
BlackRock Solutions
BlackRock Investment Institute
Infraestructura Institucional S de RL de CV
Grandview

CONTACTS: Note: Officers with more than one job title may be intentionally listed here more than once.

Laurence Fink, CEO
Robert Kapito, Director
Ryan Stork, Chairman of the Board, Geographical
Mark McCombe, Chairman of the Board, Subsidiary
Marc Comerchero, Chief Accounting Officer
Joseph Feliciani, COO, Divisional
Robert Goldstein, COO
J. Kushel, Other Corporate Officer
Jeffrey Smith, Other Corporate Officer
David Blumer, Other Corporate Officer

GROWTH PLANS/SPECIAL FEATURES:

BlackRock, Inc. and its subsidiaries form one of the largest investment management firms in the U.S., with $4.6 trillion worth of assets under management. The company manages more than 70 offices in 30 countries. The firm acts as a fiduciary on behalf of institutional and individual investors worldwide through a variety of fixed income, cash management, equity and balanced and alternative investment accounts and funds. The company also provides risk management, investment system outsourcing and financial advisory services. BlackRock's Aladdin platform is an operating system for investment managers that combines risk analytics with portfolio management, trading and operations tools. Its clients include a diverse group of taxable, tax-exempt and official institutions, retail investors and high-net-worth individuals globally. Institutional clients include pension funds, official institutions, foundations, endowments and charities, insurance companies, banks, sub-advisory relationships and private banks. Products are offered directly through intermediaries that include open-end and closed-end mutual funds, iShares exchange-traded funds (ETFs), collective investment funds and separate accounts. The firm also offers risk management, investment systems and advisory services to institutional investors through its BlackRock Solutions (BRS) product line. The firm's global platform, BlackRock Investment Institute, leverages its expertise in markets, asset classes and client segments in order to produce information that makes the company's portfolio managers better investors. In late 2015, the firm acquired Infraestructura Institucional S de RL de CV. In 2016, it sold Asia Square Tower 1 in Singapore for approximately $2.45 billion; and acquired GE Energy Financial Services' 50% interest in Grandview wind project in Texas. Grandview is now jointly-owned by BlackRock and E.ON Climate and Renewables North America.

The company offers employees health care, disability and life coverage; retirement benefits; and tuition assistance.

FINANCIAL DATA: Note: Data for latest year may not have been available at press time.

In U.S. $	2016	2015	2014	2013	2012	2011
Revenue		11,401,000,000	11,081,000,000	10,180,000,000	9,337,000,000	9,081,000,000
R&D Expense						
Operating Income		4,664,000,000	4,474,000,000	3,857,000,000	3,524,000,000	3,249,000,000
Operating Margin %		40.90%	40.37%	37.88%	37.74%	35.77%
SGA Expense		6,152,000,000	6,030,000,000	5,757,000,000	5,237,000,000	5,177,000,000
Net Income		3,345,000,000	3,294,000,000	2,932,000,000	2,458,000,000	2,337,000,000
Operating Cash Flow		3,004,000,000	3,081,000,000	3,642,000,000	2,240,000,000	2,826,000,000
Capital Expenditure		221,000,000	66,000,000	94,000,000	150,000,000	247,000,000
EBITDA		5,053,000,000	4,905,000,000	4,475,000,000	3,980,000,000	3,610,000,000
Return on Assets %		1.43%	1.43%	1.39%	1.29%	1.30%
Return on Equity %		11.97%	12.23%	11.30%	9.74%	9.13%
Debt to Equity		0.17	0.30	0.27	0.31	0.25

CONTACT INFORMATION:

Phone: 212 810-5300   Fax: 212 754-3123
Toll-Free:
Address: 40 E. 52nd St., New York, NY 10022 United States

STOCK TICKER/OTHER:

Stock Ticker: BLK   Exchange: NYS
Employees: 12,200   Fiscal Year Ends: 12/31
Parent Company:

SALARIES/BONUSES:

Top Exec. Salary: $900,000   Bonus: $8,720,000
Second Exec. Salary: $750,000   Bonus: $7,085,000

OTHER THOUGHTS:

Estimated Female Officers or Directors: 5
Hot Spot for Advancement for Women/Minorities: Y

Bloomberg LP

NAIC Code: 0

www.bloomberg.com

TYPES OF BUSINESS:

Financial Data Publishing-Print & Online
Magazine Publishing
Management Software
Multimedia Presentation Services
Broadcast Television
Radio Broadcasting
Electronic Exchange Systems
Software

BRANDS/DIVISIONS/AFFILIATES:

QuickTake
Bloomberg Terminal
Bloomberg Tradebook
Bloomberg Vault
Bloomberg Government
Bloomberg New Energy Finance
Bloomberg Television
Bloomberg Content Services

CONTACTS: Note: Officers with more than one job title may be intentionally listed here more than once.

Michael R. Bloomberg, CEO
Elizabeth Mazzeo, COO
Daniel L. Doctoroff, Pres.
Jason Schechter, Chief Communications Officer
Matthew Winkler, Editor-in-Chief, Bloomberg News
Thomas Secunda, Vice Chmn.
Matthew Winkler, Vice Chmn.

GROWTH PLANS/SPECIAL FEATURES:

Bloomberg LP is an information services, news and media company, serving the financial services industry, government offices and agencies, corporations and news organizations. The company operates in six segments: communications, financial products, enterprise products, industry products, media and media services. Communications provides press announcements involving Bloomberg through its worldwide press contact centers, including the Americas, Europe/Middle East/Africa and Asia Pacific. Bloomberg's QuickTake franchise offers Q&A-style explainers to help readers quickly navigate breaking news and understand a story's fundamentals as news develops. Financial products comprises the Bloomberg Terminal, a platform for financial professionals who need real-time data, news and analytics to make fast and informed decisions; and the Bloomberg Tradebook, a global agency broker that provides anonymous direct market access and algorithmic trading to more than 125 global liquidity venues across 43 countries. This division also includes Bloomberg Briefs, Bloomberg Indexes, Bloomberg SEF and Bloomberg Institute. Enterprise provides enterprise solutions such as enterprise data, distribution and information; and trading solutions that address workflow with front-end portfolio, inventory, sales and trading, as well as middle and back office operations solutions for buy-side and sell-side firms. This division's Bloomberg Vault is a secure, managed service for information governance, data analytics and trade reconstruction across the enterprise. Industry products include Bloomberg Government, a web-based information service for professionals who interact with the federal government; Bloomberg Law/BNA and Bloomberg Big Law for legal, tax and regulatory professionals; and Bloomberg New Energy Finance for decision-makers in the energy system. Media delivers business and political news through Bloomberg Business, Bloomberg Politics, Bloomberg View, Bloomberg Television, Bloomberg Radio, Bloomberg Mobile Apps and news bureaus. Media Services includes advertising, Bloomberg Content Service and Bloomberg Live Conferences.

FINANCIAL DATA: Note: Data for latest year may not have been available at press time.

In U.S. $	2016	2015	2014	2013	2012	2011
Revenue		9,184,000,000	9,000,000,000	8,275,000,000	8,300,000,000	7,700,000,000
R&D Expense						
Operating Income						
Operating Margin %						
SGA Expense						
Net Income			2,650,000,000	2,500,000,000	2,300,000,000	2,150,000,000
Operating Cash Flow						
Capital Expenditure						
EBITDA						
Return on Assets %						
Return on Equity %						
Debt to Equity						

CONTACT INFORMATION:

Phone: 212-318-2000   Fax: 917-369-5000
Toll-Free:
Address: 731 Lexington Ave., New York, NY 10022 United States

STOCK TICKER/OTHER:

Stock Ticker: Private   Exchange:
Employees: 19,000   Fiscal Year Ends: 12/31
Parent Company:

SALARIES/BONUSES:

Top Exec. Salary: $ Bonus: $
Second Exec. Salary: $ Bonus: $

OTHER THOUGHTS:

Estimated Female Officers or Directors: 1
Hot Spot for Advancement for Women/Minorities:

BMC Software Inc

www.bmc.com

NAIC Code: 0

TYPES OF BUSINESS:

Computer Software-Mainframe Related
Systems Management Software
e-Business Software
Consulting & Training Services

BRANDS/DIVISIONS/AFFILIATES:

Cloud IT Ops
BMC Remedyforce
BMC HR Case Management
BMC MyIT

CONTACTS: Note: Officers with more than one job title may be intentionally listed here more than once.

Robert E. Beauchamp, CEO
Robert E. Beauchamp, Pres.
Stephen B. Solcher, CFO
Nick Utton, Sr. VP
Monika Fahlbusch, Chief People Officer
Kia Behnia, CTO
Hollie Castro, Sr. VP-Admin.
Patrick K. Tagtow, General Counsel
Steve Goddard, Sr. VP-Bus. Oper.
Ken Berryman, Sr. VP-Strategy & Corp. Dev.
Ann Duhon, Mgr.-Comm.
Derrick Vializ, VP-Investor Rel.
T. Cory Bleuer, Chief Acct. Officer
Patrick K. Tagtow, Chief Compliance Officer
Paul Avenant, Sr. VP-Solutions
Robert E. Beauchamp, Chmn.

GROWTH PLANS/SPECIAL FEATURES:

BMC Software, Inc. is a software vendor company that provides system management, service management and automation solutions primarily for large companies. Its software products span mainframe systems, IT service management, cloud management, IT operations, workload automation and IT automation. The firm offers digital enterprise management, which includes digital service management, digital infrastructure optimization, digital enterprise automations and digital service assurance. The digital service management enhances employee productivity through automation and compliance tracking. Products in this unit include BMC Remedyforce, BMC HR Case Management and BMC MyIT. The digital infrastructure optimization solutions focus on offering services to match digital infrastructure, such as servers, private and hybrid clouds and virtual infrastructures. The digital enterprise automations allows users to centrally orchestrate the automation of services and significantly reduce delivery time across a range of technologies, including networks, mobile devices, middleware, cloud, big data, apps and applications. The digital service assurance combines sophisticated data collection and analytic capabilities allowing businesses to take action based on customer online posts and complaints. BMC's customers include manufacturers, telecommunication companies, financial service providers, educational institutions, retailers, distributors, hospitals, government agencies and channel partners, including resellers, distributors and system integrators. Over 10,000 customers worldwide use BMC products, including 100% of the Forbes Global 100 companies. In 2015, the firm acquired Cloud IT Ops technology from Boundary.

FINANCIAL DATA: Note: Data for latest year may not have been available at press time.

In U.S. $	2016	2015	2014	2013	2012	2011
Revenue		2,250,000,000	2,205,000,000	2,201,000,000	2,172,000,000	2,065,299,968
R&D Expense						
Operating Income						
Operating Margin %						
SGA Expense						
Net Income			234,000,000	331,000,000	401,000,000	456,200,000
Operating Cash Flow						
Capital Expenditure						
EBITDA						
Return on Assets %						
Return on Equity %						
Debt to Equity						

CONTACT INFORMATION:

Phone: 713 918-8800   Fax: 713 918-8000
Toll-Free: 800-841-2031
Address: 2101 Citywest Blvd., Houston, TX 77042 United States

SALARIES/BONUSES:

Top Exec. Salary: $ Bonus: $
Second Exec. Salary: $ Bonus: $

STOCK TICKER/OTHER:

Stock Ticker: Private   Exchange:
Employees: 6,700   Fiscal Year Ends: 03/31
Parent Company: Bain Capital

OTHER THOUGHTS:

Estimated Female Officers or Directors: 2
Hot Spot for Advancement for Women/Minorities: Y

BMC Stock Holdings Inc

www.buildwithbmc.com

NAIC Code: 444190

TYPES OF BUSINESS:

Building Materials & Hardware Stores, Retail
Building & Construction Services

BRANDS/DIVISIONS/AFFILIATES:

BMC
Ready-Frame
BMC Design
BMC Timber Truss
Building Materials Holding Corp
Stock Building Supply Holdings Inc

CONTACTS: Note: Officers with more than one job title may be intentionally listed here more than once.

Peter Alexander, CEO
James Major, CFO
William Gay, Chief Accounting Officer
Paul Street, Chief Administrative Officer
David Bullock, Director
Lisa Hamblet, Executive VP, Divisional
Thomas Barnes, Senior VP, Divisional
C. Ball, Senior VP
Walter Randolph, Vice President, Divisional
Duff Wakefield, Vice President, Divisional

GROWTH PLANS/SPECIAL FEATURES:

BMC Stock Holdings, Inc. (formerly Building Materials Holding Corp.) is a diversified lumber and building materials distributor and solutions provider that sells to new construction, repair and remodeling contractors. The company carries a wide range of products via operations in 17 U.S. states. Its primary products include lumber, lumber sheet goods, millwork, doors, flooring, windows, structural components (engineered wood products, trusses and wall panels) and other exterior products. BMC's solution-based services include design, product specification, installation and installation management services. The firm also offers a broad range of products sourced through a network of suppliers, which together with various solution-based services, represent approximately 50% of the construction cost of a typical new home. BMC serves its customers from 147 locations, which include 91 distribution and retail operations, 47 millwork fabrication operations, 35 structural components fabrication operations and 13 flooring operations. Brands of the company include BMC, Ready Frame, BMC Design and BMC Timber Truss. In December 2015, Building Materials Holding Corp. merged with and into Stock Building Supply Holdings, Inc., forming the newly combined BMC Stock Holdings, Inc. The company trades on NASDAQ under the BMCH ticker symbol.

FINANCIAL DATA: Note: Data for latest year may not have been available at press time.

In U.S. $	2016	2015	2014	2013	2012	2011
Revenue		1,576,746,000	1,295,716,000	1,197,037,000	942,398,000	759,982,000
R&D Expense						
Operating Income		12,248,000	18,324,000	761,000	-18,907,000	-59,301,000
Operating Margin %		.77%	1.41%	.06%	-2.00%	-7.80%
SGA Expense		306,843,000	279,717,000	254,935,000	221,192,000	213,036,000
Net Income		-4,831,000	10,419,000	-4,635,000	-14,533,000	-42,133,000
Operating Cash Flow		743,000	16,941,000	-40,264,000	-12,243,000	-7,001,000
Capital Expenditure		31,319,000	43,306,000	7,448,000	2,741,000	1,339,000
EBITDA		37,621,000	32,454,000	13,694,000	-6,860,000	-44,707,000
Return on Assets %		- .55%	3.02%	-2.14%	-8.88%	-18.19%
Return on Equity %		-1.25%	7.75%	-7.99%	-56.11%	-90.07%
Debt to Equity		0.67	0.68	0.50	0.16	0.01

CONTACT INFORMATION:

Phone: 678-222-1219   Fax: 678-222-1316
Toll-Free:
Address: Two Lakeside Commons, 980 Hammond Drive NE, Ste 500, Atlanta, GA 30328 United States

STOCK TICKER/OTHER:

Stock Ticker: BMCH
Employees: 9,600
Parent Company:

Exchange: NAS
Fiscal Year Ends: 12/31

SALARIES/BONUSES:

Top Exec. Salary: $700,000   Bonus: $1,000,000
Second Exec. Salary: $425,000   Bonus: $

OTHER THOUGHTS:

Estimated Female Officers or Directors: 2
Hot Spot for Advancement for Women/Minorities:

Boeing Company (The)

www.boeing.com

NAIC Code: 336411

TYPES OF BUSINESS:

Aircraft Manufacturing
Aerospace Technology & Manufacturing
Military Aircraft
Satellite Manufacturing
Communications Products & Services
Air Traffic Management Technology
Financing Services
Research & Development

BRANDS/DIVISIONS/AFFILIATES:

Boeing 777
Boeing 737
Boeing 787 Dreamliner
Boeing Capital Corporation
Boeing 747-8

CONTACTS: Note: Officers with more than one job title may be intentionally listed here more than once.

Michael Lohr, Assistant General Counsel
Thomas Downey, Senior VP, Divisional
Christopher Chadwick, CEO, Divisional
Raymond Conner, CEO, Divisional
Gregory Smith, CFO
Robert Verbeck, Chief Accounting Officer
John Tracy, Chief Technology Officer
Dennis Muilenburg, Director
J. Luttig, Executive VP
Bertrand-Marc Allen, President, Subsidiary
Anthony Parasida, Senior VP, Divisional
Timothy Keating, Senior VP, Divisional
Diana Sands, Senior VP, Divisional
Heidi Capozzi, Vice President, Divisional

GROWTH PLANS/SPECIAL FEATURES:

The Boeing Company is one of the world's major aerospace firms. The company operates in the following segments: commercial airplanes; defense, space & security (BDS), which is further subdivided into Boeing military aircraft (BMA), network & space systems (N&SS) and global services & support (GS&S); and Boeing Capital Corporation (BCC). The commercial airplanes segment develops, produces and markets commercial jet aircraft and related support services. Its family of jet aircraft includes the 737 narrow-body model, the 767 and 777 wide-body models, the 787 Dreamliner and the 747-8 intercontinental and freighter models. The BDS BMA subdivision is focused on the development of military aircraft and precision engagement as well as mobility products and services. The N&SS subdivision provides products and services to assist customers in transforming operations through network integration, intelligence and surveillance systems, communications and space exploration. The GS&S subdivision is engaged in operations, maintenance and logistics support functions for military platforms. BCC provides financing to commercial aircraft customers. In 2015, the company signed the second phase of a performance-based contract with the U.S. Defense Logistics Agency that reduces combat logistics support costs while enhancing warfighter readiness. As a result, Boeing will provide support for 11 different aircraft including the F/A-18 Super Hornet, AH-64 Apache, AV-8B Harrier, B-52 Stratofortress and C-17 Globemaster III. Also in 2015, the firm won the contract to sustain the Minuteman III intercontinental ballistic missile (ICBM) guidance system for the U.S. Air Force.

The company offers its employees benefits including medical, dental, life, AD&D and disability insurance; flexible spending accounts; pension and retirement savings plans; tuition assistance; and onsite and on-the-job training.

FINANCIAL DATA: Note: Data for latest year may not have been available at press time.

In U.S. $	2016	2015	2014	2013	2012	2011
Revenue		96,114,000,000	90,762,000,000	86,623,000,000	81,698,000,000	68,735,000,000
R&D Expense		3,331,000,000	3,047,000,000	3,071,000,000	3,298,000,000	3,918,000,000
Operating Income		7,443,000,000	7,473,000,000	6,562,000,000	6,311,000,000	5,844,000,000
Operating Margin %		7.74%	8.23%	7.57%	7.72%	8.50%
SGA Expense		3,525,000,000	3,767,000,000	3,956,000,000	3,717,000,000	3,408,000,000
Net Income		5,176,000,000	5,446,000,000	4,585,000,000	3,900,000,000	4,018,000,000
Operating Cash Flow		9,363,000,000	8,858,000,000	8,179,000,000	7,508,000,000	4,023,000,000
Capital Expenditure		2,450,000,000	2,236,000,000	2,238,000,000	1,710,000,000	1,713,000,000
EBITDA		9,263,000,000	9,376,000,000	8,462,000,000	8,184,000,000	7,551,000,000
Return on Assets %		5.34%	5.67%	5.05%	4.61%	5.40%
Return on Equity %		68.95%	46.21%	44.20%	83.13%	127.94%
Debt to Equity		1.37	0.93	0.54	1.52	2.85

CONTACT INFORMATION:

Phone: 312 544-2000   Fax:
Toll-Free:
Address: 100 N. Riverside Plz., Chicago, IL 60606 United States

STOCK TICKER/OTHER:

Stock Ticker: BA
Employees: 165,500
Parent Company:

Exchange: NYS
Fiscal Year Ends: 12/31

SALARIES/BONUSES:

Top Exec. Salary:
$1,719,962
Second Exec. Salary:
$1,354,269

Bonus: $

Bonus: $

OTHER THOUGHTS:

Estimated Female Officers or Directors: 7

Hot Spot for Advancement for Women/Minorities: Y

Booz Allen Hamilton Holding Corp

www.boozallen.com

NAIC Code: 541610

TYPES OF BUSINESS:

Strategy Consulting
Engineering & IT Consulting
Supply Chain Management
Industry Research & Publications
War Gaming & Strategic Simulation

BRANDS/DIVISIONS/AFFILIATES:

Carlyle Group (The)

CONTACTS: Note: Officers with more than one job title may be intentionally listed here more than once.

Horacio Rozanski, CEO
Lloyd Howell, CFO
Ralph Shrader, Chairman of the Board
Karen Dahut, Executive VP
Susan Penfield, Executive VP
Joseph Logue, Executive VP
John Mayer, Executive VP
Elizabeth Thompson, Executive VP
Joseph Mahaffee, Executive VP
Nancy Laben, Secretary

GROWTH PLANS/SPECIAL FEATURES:

Booz Allen Hamilton Holding Corp. (BAH), founded in 1914, is a strategy and technology consulting firm, providing services to the U.S. government in the defense, intelligence and civil sectors. BAH's major areas of expertise include business analytics, information technology, cyber security, operations and logistics, organization and change, service innovation, public sector mission effectiveness, strategy and leadership and systems engineering and integration. It derives substantially all of its revenue from services provided under contracts and task orders with the U.S. government. The company's work with national governments around the world has included projects to enhance national security, economic well-being and the health and safety of citizens. Some of BAH's largest clients have included the U.S. Department of Defense; the U.S. Air Force, Army, Navy and Marine Corps; the U.S. Intelligence Community & civil agencies such as the Department of Homeland Security, the Department of Health and Human Services and the Department of the Treasury. The company's international clients are primarily in the Middle East as well as in south-east Asia. The company also publishes books, reports and studies on industry subjects ranging from information technology to leadership. The firm maintains offices across the U.S. as well as strategic locations overseas. Investment firm, The Carlyle Group, maintains a majority interest in the company.

The company offers employees dental, medical and vision insurance; life insurance; medical flexible spending accounts; tuition assistance; an employee assistance program; and health and wellness programs.

FINANCIAL DATA: Note: Data for latest year may not have been available at press time.

In U.S. $	2016	2015	2014	2013	2012	2011
Revenue	5,405,738,000	5,274,770,000	5,478,693,000	5,758,059,000	5,859,218,000	5,591,296,000
R&D Expense						
Operating Income	444,584,000	458,822,000	460,611,000	446,234,000	387,432,000	319,444,000
Operating Margin %	8.22%	8.69%	8.40%	7.74%	6.61%	5.71%
SGA Expense	2,319,592,000	2,159,439,000	2,229,642,000	2,366,576,000	2,446,543,000	2,354,294,000
Net Income	294,094,000	232,569,000	232,188,000	219,058,000	239,955,000	84,694,000
Operating Cash Flow	249,234,000	309,958,000	332,718,000	464,654,000	360,046,000	296,339,000
Capital Expenditure	66,635,000	36,041,000	20,905,000	33,113,000	76,925,000	88,784,000
EBITDA	511,813,000	520,410,000	531,144,000	512,604,000	467,157,000	340,559,000
Return on Assets %	9.99%	7.87%	7.58%	6.74%	7.57%	2.78%
Return on Equity %	98.85%	127.93%	116.55%	31.02%	22.93%	11.95%
Debt to Equity	3.63	8.41	9.23	7.31	0.77	1.06

CONTACT INFORMATION:

Phone: 703 902-5000   Fax: 703 902-3333
Toll-Free:
Address: 8283 Greensboro Dr., McLean, VA 22102 United States

STOCK TICKER/OTHER:

Stock Ticker: BAH
Employees: 22,500
Parent Company:

Exchange: NYS
Fiscal Year Ends:

SALARIES/BONUSES:

Top Exec. Salary:
$1,437,500
Second Exec. Salary:
$1,250,000

Bonus: $

Bonus: $

OTHER THOUGHTS:

Estimated Female Officers or Directors: 4

Hot Spot for Advancement for Women/Minorities: Y

BorgWarner Inc

www.bwauto.com

NAIC Code: 336310

TYPES OF BUSINESS:
Gasoline Engine and Engine Parts Manufacturing
Motor Vehicle Transmissions
Power Train Parts
Turbochargers
Cooling Systems
Chain Systems
Industrial Equipment

BRANDS/DIVISIONS/AFFILIATES:
BorgWarner Emissions Systems Inc
NSK-Warner Kabushiki Kaisha
HY-VO
MORSE TEC
DualTronic
Remy International Inc

CONTACTS: Note: Officers with more than one job title may be intentionally listed here more than once.
James Verrier, CEO
Ronald Hundzinski, CFO
Alexis Michas, Chairman of the Board
Steve Carlson, Chief Accounting Officer
John Gasparovic, General Counsel
Stefan Demmerle, General Manager, Subsidiary
Daniel Paterra, General Manager, Subsidiary
Frederic Lissalde, General Manager, Subsidiary
Joseph Fadool, General Manager, Subsidiary
Brady Ericson, General Manager, Subsidiary
Robin Kendrick, General Manager, Subsidiary
Thomas McGill, Treasurer
Kim Jenett, Vice President, Divisional

GROWTH PLANS/SPECIAL FEATURES:
BorgWarner, Inc. manufactures and sells engineered systems and components, designed to improve fuel efficiency, air quality and vehicle stability, to original equipment manufacturers (OEMs) of passenger cars, SUVs, trucks, commercial transportation products and industrial equipment worldwide. BorgWarner operates manufacturing and technical facilities at 74 locations in 19 countries, serving customers in North America, South America, Europe and Asia. Products fall into two operating segments: engine and drivetrain. The engine group produces turbochargers, timing systems, emissions systems, thermal systems, diesel cold start and gasoline ignition technology. Brand names developed by the engine group include the HY-VO front-wheel drive transmission and four-wheel drive (4WD) chain and the MORSE TEC chain system for light vehicles. This division is operated through subsidiary BorgWarner Emissions Systems, Inc., which manufactures the engine group's products. The drivetrain group produces transmission components and systems as well as all-wheel drive (AWD) torque management systems. Products include friction plates, one-way clutches, transmission bands and torque converter lock-up clutches. The company's Japanese joint-venture, NSK-Warner Kabushiki Kaisha, is one of the leading producers of friction pads and one way clutches in Japan. The drivetrain group's DualTronic transmission technology, used by the entire VW Group vehicle family, provides smooth-shifting convenience through a two-clutch wet-friction system. In November 2015, the firm acquired Remy International, Inc., which manufactures rotating electrical components such as alternators, starter motors and electric traction motors for the automotive and commercial vehicle industry. Remy operates in 10 countries on five continents.

FINANCIAL DATA: Note: Data for latest year may not have been available at press time.

In U.S. $	2016	2015	2014	2013	2012	2011
Revenue		8,023,200,000	8,305,100,000	7,436,600,000	7,183,200,000	7,114,700,000
R&D Expense						
Operating Income		939,700,000	963,700,000	855,200,000	752,900,000	797,500,000
Operating Margin %		11.71%	11.60%	11.49%	10.48%	11.20%
SGA Expense		687,700,000	698,900,000	645,600,000	629,300,000	621,000,000
Net Income		609,700,000	655,800,000	624,300,000	500,900,000	550,100,000
Operating Cash Flow		867,900,000	801,800,000	718,800,000	878,700,000	708,200,000
Capital Expenditure		577,300,000	563,000,000	417,800,000	407,400,000	393,700,000
EBITDA		1,307,400,000	1,346,900,000	1,202,900,000	1,089,000,000	1,123,500,000
Return on Assets %		7.58%	9.27%	9.37%	8.10%	9.55%
Return on Equity %		17.00%	18.27%	18.79%	18.31%	23.67%
Debt to Equity		0.59	0.19	0.28	0.26	0.31

CONTACT INFORMATION:
Phone: 248 754-9200   Fax:
Toll-Free:
Address: 3850 Hamlin Rd., Auburn Hills, MI 48326 United States

STOCK TICKER/OTHER:
Stock Ticker: BWA   Exchange: NYS
Employees: 30,000   Fiscal Year Ends: 12/31
Parent Company:

SALARIES/BONUSES:
Top Exec. Salary: Bonus: $
$1,150,000
Second Exec. Salary: Bonus: $
$612,250

OTHER THOUGHTS:
Estimated Female Officers or Directors: 4

Hot Spot for Advancement for Women/Minorities: Y

Sales, profits and employees may be estimates. Financial information, benefits and other data can change quickly and may vary from those stated here.

Boston Consulting Group Inc (The, BCG)

www.bcg.com

NAIC Code: 541610

TYPES OF BUSINESS:

Management Consulting
Marketing Consulting
Corporate Strategy Research

BRANDS/DIVISIONS/AFFILIATES:

Strategy Institute (The)
Center for Health Care Value
Talent Revolution

CONTACTS: Note: Officers with more than one job title may be intentionally listed here more than once.

Rich Lesser, CEO
Rich Lesser, Pres.
Debbie Simpson, CFO
Jeremy Barton, General Counsel
Miki Tsusaka, Sr. Partner
Sharon Marcil, Sr. Partner
Matthew Krentz, Sr. Partner
Hans-Paul Burkner, Chmn.
Vaishali Rastogi, Partner

GROWTH PLANS/SPECIAL FEATURES:

The Boston Consulting Group, Inc. (BCG) provides international strategy and general management consulting services with the aim of helping businesses create and sustain competitive advantages. With more than 85 offices in 48 countries, BCG is one of the world's largest consulting organizations. Most of its offices are located in Europe and Asia, though the firm does have a significant North American presence. Areas of consulting expertise include automotive, consumer markets, corporate development, the energy industry, e-commerce, financial services, globalization, health care, industrial goods, information technology, operations, organization, pricing, retail, strategy, technology, communications, travel and tourism. BCG also publishes extensive reports on many aspects of multiple industries and is constantly developing new ideas on business structure and efficiency. This written material is stored on the company's web site and can be searched from multiple angles. BCG has established The Strategy Institute, a collaboration between certain current BCG consultants and professors and PhDs at higher-education institutions such as Harvard Business School, the National War College, the Said Business School of Oxford University and the University of California, Berkley. The institute does research on various subjects such as the relationship between poetry and strategic thinking, creating projects concerning learning, as well as the relationship between religion and culture in shaping identity. The company also operates the Center for Health Care Value, which collects data in order to establish fair health care prices in response to the trend of rising costs. In 2015, the firm partnered with Google Digital Academy to drive an industry-wide initiative, the Talent Revolution, to significantly enhance digital marketing skills for leading companies. The data from its annual company surveys will identify key gaps in digital marketing skills, and will then be used to inform and help companies build their skills in order to keep pace with rapid changes.

FINANCIAL DATA: Note: Data for latest year may not have been available at press time.

In U.S. $	2016	2015	2014	2013	2012	2011
Revenue		5,000,000,000	4,200,000,000	3,710,000,000	3,625,000,000	3,550,000,000
R&D Expense						
Operating Income						
Operating Margin %						
SGA Expense						
Net Income						
Operating Cash Flow						
Capital Expenditure						
EBITDA						
Return on Assets %						
Return on Equity %						
Debt to Equity						

CONTACT INFORMATION:

Phone: 617-973-1200   Fax: 617-973-1399
Toll-Free:
Address: 1 Exchange Place, 30th & 31st Fl., Boston, MA 02109 United States

STOCK TICKER/OTHER:

Stock Ticker: Private   Exchange:
Employees: 12,000   Fiscal Year Ends: 12/31
Parent Company:

SALARIES/BONUSES:

Top Exec. Salary: $ Bonus: $
Second Exec. Salary: $ Bonus: $

OTHER THOUGHTS:

Estimated Female Officers or Directors: 4
Hot Spot for Advancement for Women/Minorities: Y

Boston Scientific Corp

NAIC Code: 339100

www.bostonscientific.com

TYPES OF BUSINESS:

Supplies-Surgery
Interventional Medical Products
Catheters
Guide wires
Stents
Oncology Research

BRANDS/DIVISIONS/AFFILIATES:

Promus
SYNERGY
Charger PTA
WallFlex
ADVANTIO
Resolution
Precision Spinal Cord Stimulation
OptiCross

CONTACTS: *Note: Officers with more than one job title may be intentionally listed here more than once.*

Michael Mahoney, CEO
Karen Prange, President, Divisional
Daniel Brennan, CFO
Timothy Pratt, Chief Administrative Officer
Keith Dawkins, Chief Medical Officer
John Abele, Director Emeritus
Edward Mackey, Executive VP, Divisional
Joseph Fitzgerald, Executive VP
Michael Phalen, Executive VP
Supratim Bose, Executive VP
David Pierce, President, Divisional
Maulik Nanavaty, President, Divisional
Kevin Ballinger, President, Divisional
Jeffrey Mirviss, President, Divisional
Eric Thepaut, President, Geographical
John Sorenson, Senior VP, Divisional
Wendy Carruthers, Senior VP, Divisional

GROWTH PLANS/SPECIAL FEATURES:

Boston Scientific Corp. is a worldwide developer, manufacturer and marketer of medical devices that are used in a broad range of interventional medical specialties. Cardiovascular products include Promus, EPIC, WALLSTENT, Innova and SYNERGY brands of stent systems; OptiCross and iLab ultrasound imaging systems; Mustang percutaneous transluminal angioplasty (PTA) balloon; Coyote and Charger PTA balloon catheter; Rubicon support catheter; Direxion torqueable microcatheter; and Renegade HI-FLO Fathom microcatheter system. Cardia rhythm pacemaker brands include INGENIO and ADVANTIO. Endoscopy surgical brands include SpyGlass, WallFlex, Resolution, Expect and RX Biliary System. Boston Scientific operates in seven segments: cardiac rhythm management, which offers implantable devices that monitor the heart and deliver electricity to treat cardiac abnormalities; interventional cardiology, which sells coronary stent systems and products for the treatment of peripheral diseases; electrophysiology, which develops less-invasive medical technologies used in the diagnosis and treatment of rate and rhythm disorders of the heart; endoscopy, which sells products for the treatment of a variety of digestive diseases; urology/women's health, which offers products for the treatment of urinary stone disease, benign prostatic hyperplasia (BPH), stress urinary incontinence and other conditions; peripheral interventions, which include balloon catheters, stents, wires vena cava filters and peripheral embolization devices used to treat patients with peripheral diseases; and neuromodulation, which sells the Precision Spinal Cord Stimulation system for the treatment of chronic intractable pain management of the trunk and/or limbs. In 2015, the firm acquired the American Medical Systems urology portfolio, which includes the Men's Health and Prostate Health businesses, from Endo International plc. That same year it agreed to acquire interventional radiology portfolio of CeloNova Biosciences, a developer of endovascular and interventional cardiology technologies.

The firm offers employees medical, dental, vision and life insurance; educational assistance; and flexible spending accounts.

FINANCIAL DATA: *Note: Data for latest year may not have been available at press time.*

In U.S. $	2016	2015	2014	2013	2012	2011
Revenue		7,477,000,000	7,380,000,000	7,143,000,000	7,249,000,000	7,622,000,000
R&D Expense		876,000,000	817,000,000	861,000,000	886,000,000	895,000,000
Operating Income		-327,000,000	-301,000,000	120,000,000	-3,868,000,000	904,000,000
Operating Margin %		-4.37%	-4.07%	1.67%	-53.35%	11.86%
SGA Expense		2,987,000,000	3,013,000,000	2,814,000,000	2,688,000,000	2,659,000,000
Net Income		-239,000,000	-119,000,000	-121,000,000	-4,068,000,000	441,000,000
Operating Cash Flow		600,000,000	1,269,000,000	1,082,000,000	1,260,000,000	1,008,000,000
Capital Expenditure		247,000,000	259,000,000	245,000,000	226,000,000	304,000,000
EBITDA		439,000,000	432,000,000	790,000,000	-3,163,000,000	1,640,000,000
Return on Assets %		-1.35%	-.70%	-.71%	-21.16%	2.03%
Return on Equity %		-3.74%	-1.83%	-1.80%	-44.64%	3.89%
Debt to Equity		0.89	0.59	0.64	0.61	0.37

CONTACT INFORMATION:

Phone: 508 683-4000   Fax: 508 647-2200
Toll-Free: 888-272-1001
Address: 300 Boston Scientific Way, Marlborough, MA 01752-1234
United States

STOCK TICKER/OTHER:

Stock Ticker: BSX
Employees: 24,000
Parent Company:

Exchange: NYS
Fiscal Year Ends: 12/31

SALARIES/BONUSES:

Top Exec. Salary: $967,740   Bonus: $
Second Exec. Salary: $638,563   Bonus: $

OTHER THOUGHTS:

Estimated Female Officers or Directors: 5
Hot Spot for Advancement for Women/Minorities: Y

Sales, profits and employees may be estimates. Financial information, benefits and other data can change quickly and may vary from those stated here.

Brightstar Corporation

NAIC Code: 423690

www.brightstar.com

TYPES OF BUSINESS:

Telecommunication Supply Chain & Distribution Services
Wireless Device & Accessories Distribution
Wireless Device Manufacturing
Supply Chain, Marketing and Retail Consultation

BRANDS/DIVISIONS/AFFILIATES:

eSecuritel
Virtual Care
Mobile Phone Xchange
Consensus
WirelessWorks
SoftBank Group Corp

CONTACTS: Note: Officers with more than one job title may be intentionally listed here more than once.

Jaymin Patel, CEO
Dennis J. Strand, Pres., Brightstar Financial Svcs.
Catherine Smith, Sr. VP
Bela Lainck, Pres., Buy-Back & Trade-In Solutions
Rafael M. de Guzman, III, VP-Strategy
Oscar J. Fumagali, Chief Treas. Officer
Oscar J. Rojas, Pres., Brightstar Latin America
Arturo A. Osorio, Pres., Asia Pacific, Middle East & Africa
Jeff Gower, Pres., Brightstar U.S. & Canada
David Leach, CEO-eSecuritel
Ronald D. Fisher, Chmn.
Michael Singer, Sr. VP-Global Strategy & New Bus. Dev.
Ramon Colomina, Pres., Supply Chain Solutions

GROWTH PLANS/SPECIAL FEATURES:

Brightstar Corporation is a global distributor and provider of value-added supply chain services to the wireless and telecommunications industry. It also designs and manufactures products under licensing agreements with leading manufacturers. The company's supply chain services include customer return management and device return, recycling and resale. The firm works with its allied companies Genco and Teleplan to provide these solutions. It also distributes handsets, accessories, wireless data, fixed wireless, wireless broadband and prepaid wireless products, working with allied companies Boinc, Starscriber and Trikomsel. The firm operates its handset protection and service for devices through its subsidiaries eSecuritel and Virtual care. For buy back and trade in, it depends on subsidiary Mobile Phone Xchange and through subsidiary Consensus to provide multi-channel retail solutions. Brightstar's wireless data and telecom solutions division addresses vertical market needs through products and services within cellular infrastructure, broadband infrastructure, 2.5G and 3G modems, modules and PCMCIA (personal computer memory card international association) cards, content applications and wireless PDAs. The firm operates facilities in 50 countries worldwide, with the majority located in Central and South America. Brightstar's customer base includes more than 200 wireless operators, 100 electronic manufactures and over 50,000 retailers worldwide. In October 2015, the firm acquired Ontario-based WirelessWorks, a specialized consulting and solutions provider for mobile network operators and device manufacturers.

FINANCIAL DATA: Note: Data for latest year may not have been available at press time.

In U.S. $	2016	2015	2014	2013	2012	2011
Revenue		7,600,000,000	7,200,000,000	7,228,000,000	6,300,000,000	5,700,000,000
R&D Expense						
Operating Income						
Operating Margin %						
SGA Expense						
Net Income						
Operating Cash Flow						
Capital Expenditure						
EBITDA						
Return on Assets %						
Return on Equity %						
Debt to Equity						

CONTACT INFORMATION:

Phone: 305-421-6000   Fax:
Toll-Free:
Address: 9725 NW 117th Ave., #300, Miami, FL 33178 United States

STOCK TICKER/OTHER:

Stock Ticker: Subsidiary
Employees: 9,000
Parent Company: SoftBank Group Corp

Exchange:
Fiscal Year Ends: 12/31

SALARIES/BONUSES:

Top Exec. Salary: $ Bonus: $
Second Exec. Salary: $ Bonus: $

OTHER THOUGHTS:

Estimated Female Officers or Directors: 1
Hot Spot for Advancement for Women/Minorities:

Brinker International Inc

www.brinker.com

NAIC Code: 722511

TYPES OF BUSINESS:

Casual Dining Restaurants

BRANDS/DIVISIONS/AFFILIATES:

Chili's Grill and Bar
Maggiano's Little Italy

CONTACTS: Note: Officers with more than one job title may be intentionally listed here more than once.

Thomas Edwards, CFO
David Doyle, Chief Information Officer
Doug Comings, COO, Subsidiary
Wyman Roberts, Director
Joseph Depinto, Director
John Cywinski, Executive VP, Divisional
Scarlett May, General Counsel
Tony Bridwell, Other Executive Officer
Kelli Valade, President, Subsidiary
Steve Provost, President, Subsidiary
Homero Ortegon, Senior VP, Divisional
Krista Gibson, Senior VP

GROWTH PLANS/SPECIAL FEATURES:

Brinker International, Inc. owns, operates, develops and franchises over 1,632 casual dining restaurant chains in 30 countries under two brands, Chili's Grill & Bar and Maggiano's Little Italy. Chili's Grill & Bar serves lunch and dinner, while also offering a To-Go menu. Entree selections for Chili's range in price from approximately $6 to $17.69. The company owns 15,550 Chili's restaurants in 50 states and 30 countries internationally. All company-owned Chili's restaurants are outfitted with Ziosk multi-functional table top tablets that provide entertainment, ordering, guest surveys and pay-at-the-table capabilities. Maggiano's Little Italy is a classic Italian-American restaurant, featuring individual and family style menus and extensive banquet facilities. Entree selections for Maggiano's range in price from approximately $12.95 to $42.50. Brinker International currently owns 49 domestic Maggiano's locations. Brinker International's growth plans include expansion through franchises and joint ventures, most revolving around Chili's Grill & Bar. In particular, it plans to focus its international growth in emerging markets, such as India, China, Brazil and Russia.

The firm offers employees medical, dental, vision, life and short-term disability insurance; disability coverage; prescription discounts; health and dependent care flexible spending accounts; an employee assistance program; a long-term care plan; a 401(k); discounts at company restaurants; and reimbursement programs.

FINANCIAL DATA: Note: Data for latest year may not have been available at press time.

In U.S. $	2016	2015	2014	2013	2012	2011
Revenue	3,257,489,000	3,002,278,000	2,905,452,000	2,846,098,000	2,820,722,000	2,761,386,000
R&D Expense						
Operating Income	317,476,000	311,202,000	242,165,000	256,775,000	231,837,000	205,420,000
Operating Margin %	9.74%	10.36%	8.33%	9.02%	8.21%	7.43%
SGA Expense	130,897,000	134,649,000	137,647,000	136,773,000	143,388,000	132,834,000
Net Income	200,745,000	196,694,000	154,039,000	163,359,000	151,232,000	141,060,000
Operating Cash Flow	394,700,000	368,611,000	359,842,000	290,688,000	303,438,000	259,988,000
Capital Expenditure	112,788,000	140,262,000	161,066,000	131,531,000	125,226,000	70,361,000
EBITDA	475,329,000	458,525,000	380,460,000	390,914,000	360,663,000	340,087,000
Return on Assets %	13.80%	13.44%	10.46%	11.31%	10.35%	8.45%
Return on Equity %		145.01%	71.14%	40.39%	24.16%	
Debt to Equity		13.19	5.22	1.89	1.14	

CONTACT INFORMATION:

Phone: 972 980-9917   Fax: 972 770-9593
Toll-Free:
Address: 6820 LBJ Freeway, Dallas, TX 75240 United States

STOCK TICKER/OTHER:

Stock Ticker: EAT   Exchange: NYS
Employees: 53,000   Fiscal Year Ends: 06/30
Parent Company:

SALARIES/BONUSES:

Top Exec. Salary: $947,307   Bonus: $
Second Exec. Salary: $570,801   Bonus: $

OTHER THOUGHTS:

Estimated Female Officers or Directors: 3
Hot Spot for Advancement for Women/Minorities: Y

Brookdale Senior Living Inc

www.brookdaleliving.com

NAIC Code: 623310

TYPES OF BUSINESS:

Assisted Living Facilities
Retirement Communities
Assisted Living Communities
Continued Care Retirement Communities (CCRCs)
Managed Facilities

BRANDS/DIVISIONS/AFFILIATES:

CONTACTS: Note: Officers with more than one job title may be intentionally listed here more than once.

T. Smith, CEO
Lucinda Baier, CFO
Dawn Kussow, Chief Accounting Officer
Bryan Richardson, Chief Administrative Officer
Labeed Diab, COO
Daniel Decker, Director
Kristin Ferge, Executive VP
Mary Patchett, Executive VP, Divisional
H. Kaestner, Executive VP, Divisional
George Hicks, Executive VP, Divisional
Glenn Maul, Executive VP
Chad White, General Counsel
Mark Ohlendorf, President
Ross Roadman, Senior VP, Divisional
Julie Davis, Vice President, Divisional

GROWTH PLANS/SPECIAL FEATURES:

Brookdale Senior Living, Inc. (BSL) is one of the largest senior living facility operators in the U.S. It operates 1,123 owned, leased or managed senior living facilities in 47 states that can serve approximately 108,000 residents. BSL operates five business segments: retirement centers, assisted living, continuing care retirement communities (CCRCs) rentals, Brookdale ancillary services and management services. It has 130 retirement center communities with 24,486 units, 915 assisted living communities with 62,567 units and 78 rental CCRC communities with 21,367 units. The facilities strive to offer residents a home-like setting and typically feature assistance with daily living, multiple forms of therapy and various home health services. BSL offers a full spectrum of care options, including independent living, personalized assisted living, rehabilitation and skilled nursing. It operates memory care communities, which are freestanding assisted living communities designed for residents with Alzheimer's disease and other dementias. The company maintains its own culinary arts institute, which offers a training ground for chefs and dining staff. Leased communities generated the largest share (48.7%) of 2015 revenues, followed by owned communities (38.8%). BSL generated 81.9% of its 2015 revenue from private pay customers, with the remainder generated by Medicare, Medicaid and other various third-party payer programs. In June 2015, Brookdale acquired a portfolio of 35 private pay senior housing communities from Chartwell Retirement Residences, in which Brookdale owns 90% and HCP, Inc. 10%, respectively.

FINANCIAL DATA: Note: Data for latest year may not have been available at press time.

In U.S. $	2016	2015	2014	2013	2012	2011
Revenue		4,960,608,000	3,831,706,000	2,891,966,000	2,770,085,000	2,457,918,000
R&D Expense						
Operating Income		-165,206,000	-84,905,000	131,288,000	82,286,000	90,180,000
Operating Margin %		-3.33%	-2.21%	4.53%	2.97%	3.66%
SGA Expense		822,548,000	671,046,000	461,277,000	451,270,000	423,185,000
Net Income		-457,477,000	-148,990,000	-3,584,000	-65,645,000	-68,175,000
Operating Cash Flow		292,366,000	242,652,000	366,121,000	290,969,000	268,427,000
Capital Expenditure		411,051,000	304,245,000	257,527,000	208,412,000	160,131,000
EBITDA		570,768,000	461,969,000	421,382,000	353,544,000	340,971,000
Return on Assets %		-4.44%	-1.95%	-.07%	-1.43%	-1.51%
Return on Equity %		-17.13%	-7.63%	-.35%	-6.42%	-6.49%
Debt to Equity		2.52	2.07	2.38	2.16	2.26

CONTACT INFORMATION:

Phone: 615 221-2250   Fax: 615 221-2289
Toll-Free: 866-785-9025
Address: 111 Westwood Place, Ste. 400, Brentwood, TN 37027 United States

STOCK TICKER/OTHER:

Stock Ticker: BKD
Employees: 82,000
Parent Company:

Exchange: NYS
Fiscal Year Ends: 12/31

SALARIES/BONUSES:

Top Exec. Salary: $76,500   Bonus: $1,000,000
Second Exec. Salary: $48,654   Bonus: $1,000,000

OTHER THOUGHTS:

Estimated Female Officers or Directors: 1
Hot Spot for Advancement for Women/Minorities:

Brown & Brown Inc

www.bbinsurance.com

NAIC Code: 524210

TYPES OF BUSINESS:

Insurance-Property & Casualty
Risk Management Services
Professional Liability Insurance
Third-Party Administration & Consulting
Managed Care & Utilization Management Services
Reinsurance
Life Insurance
Health Insurance

BRANDS/DIVISIONS/AFFILIATES:

CONTACTS: Note: Officers with more than one job title may be intentionally listed here more than once.

R. Watts, CFO
J. Brown, Chairman of the Board
Richard Freebourn, Executive VP, Divisional
Robert Lloyd, Executive VP
J. Penny, Other Executive Officer
Anthony Strianese, President, Divisional
Chris Walker, President, Divisional
J. Brown, President

GROWTH PLANS/SPECIAL FEATURES:

Brown & Brown, Inc. is a diversified insurance agency, wholesale brokerage, insurance programs and service organization. The firm markets and sells insurance products and services, primarily in the property, casualty and employee benefit areas. The company operates through 236 locations in 41 states, as well as international offices in London, England; Hamilton, Bermuda; and George Town, Cayman Islands. It operates through four segments: retail, wholesale brokerage, national programs and services. The retail segment provides a range of insurance products and services to commercial, public entity, professional and individual customers. The wholesale brokerage division markets and sells excess and surplus commercial and personal insurance and reinsurance, primarily through independent agents and brokers. The national programs division consists of two units: professional programs, which provides professional liability and related package products for certain medical, financial, real estate and law professionals; and special programs, which markets targeted products and services designated for specific industries, trade groups, public entities and market niches. The services division provides clients with third-party claims administration, consulting for the workers' compensation insurance markets, comprehensive medical utilization management services and Medicare Secondary Payer statute compliance-related services. The retail division generates the majority (52%) of the company's revenue, followed by the national programs division (26%), the wholesale brokerage division (13%), and the services division (9%).

FINANCIAL DATA: Note: Data for latest year may not have been available at press time.

In U.S. $	2016	2015	2014	2013	2012	2011
Revenue		1,660,509,000	1,575,796,000	1,363,279,000	1,200,032,000	1,013,542,000
R&D Expense						
Operating Income		444,810,000	378,095,000	357,609,000	304,811,000	270,521,000
Operating Margin %		26.78%	23.99%	26.23%	25.40%	26.69%
SGA Expense		856,952,000	811,112,000	705,603,000	624,371,000	519,869,000
Net Income		243,318,000	206,896,000	217,112,000	184,045,000	163,995,000
Operating Cash Flow		411,848,000	385,019,000	389,374,000	220,315,000	237,531,000
Capital Expenditure		18,375,000	24,923,000	16,366,000	24,028,000	13,608,000
EBITDA		550,118,000	471,993,000	459,466,000	399,854,000	351,800,000
Return on Assets %		4.76%	4.80%	6.40%	6.41%	6.54%
Return on Equity %		11.14%	10.04%	11.38%	10.66%	10.41%
Debt to Equity		0.50	0.54	0.18	0.24	0.15

CONTACT INFORMATION:

Phone: 386 252-9601   Fax: 386 239-7252
Toll-Free:
Address: 220 S. Ridgewood Ave., Daytona Beach, FL 32114 United States

STOCK TICKER/OTHER:

Stock Ticker: BRO   Exchange: NYS
Employees: 7,591   Fiscal Year Ends: 12/31
Parent Company:

SALARIES/BONUSES:

Top Exec. Salary: Bonus: $
$1,029,422
Second Exec. Salary: Bonus: $
$600,000

OTHER THOUGHTS:

Estimated Female Officers or Directors: 3

Hot Spot for Advancement for Women/Minorities: Y

Sales, profits and employees may be estimates. Financial information, benefits and other data can change quickly and may vary from those stated here.

Buffalo Wild Wings Inc

www.buffalowildwings.com

NAIC Code: 722513

TYPES OF BUSINESS:

Limited-Service Restaurants

BRANDS/DIVISIONS/AFFILIATES:

Buffalito
B-Dubs
Buffalo Wild Wings Grill & Bar
Jammin' Jalapeno
Thai Curry
PizzaRev
B-Dubs Radio
Rusty Taco Inc

CONTACTS: *Note: Officers with more than one job title may be intentionally listed here more than once.*

Sally Smith, CEO
Jeffrey Sorum, CFO
James Schmidt, COO
James Damian, Director
Judith Shoulak, Executive VP, Divisional
Kathleen Benning, Executive VP, Divisional
Emily Decker, General Counsel
Lee Patterson, Senior VP, Divisional
Andrew Block, Senior VP, Divisional

GROWTH PLANS/SPECIAL FEATURES:

Buffalo Wild Wings, Inc. is the owner, operator and franchisor of Buffalo Wild Wings Grill & Bar restaurants, also known as B-Dubs. The company operates more than 1,080 restaurants in the U.S., Mexico and Canada. The restaurants' proprietary item is its Buffalo, New York-style chicken wings spun in any of its 16 signature sauces, including Jammin' Jalapeno and Thai Curry; and five signature seasonings, such as Sweet BBQ, Desert Heat, Buffalo and Blazin. Orders can range from 6 wings to 100, with larger orders available for parties. Additionally, the company's menu also features items such as chicken tenders, salads, Wild Flatbreads, sandwiches, popcorn shrimp, specialty hamburgers, wraps, Buffalito soft tacos and appetizers, which are made to order and are available for dine-in and take-out. The restaurants are geared toward both sports fans and families and feature a full bar, up to 10 projection screens where sporting events are shown as well as 50 additional television sets where customers can play Buzztime trivia and video games. Buffalo Wild Wings restaurants feature anywhere from 20-30 domestic, imported and craft beers on tap, and additionally sell bottled beers, wines and liquor. Restaurant operations generally are open on a daily basis from 11 am-2 pm, with franchising agreements requiring franchisees to operate the establishments for at least twelve hours a day. In 2014, the firm launched a B-Dubs Radio station on iHeartRadio, featuring music with sports programming; acquired a majority interest in Rusty Taco, Inc.; and opened its first PizzaRev franchise in Minneapolis, with a build-your-own pizza concept. In 2015, the company opened its first restaurant in Philippines, as well as in Dubai.

FINANCIAL DATA: *Note: Data for latest year may not have been available at press time.*

In U.S. $	2016	2015	2014	2013	2012	2011
Revenue		1,812,722,000	1,516,223,000	1,266,719,000	1,040,530,000	784,478,000
R&D Expense						
Operating Income		138,487,000	135,724,000	100,861,000	82,614,000	72,784,000
Operating Margin %		7.63%	8.95%	7.96%	7.93%	9.27%
SGA Expense		143,287,000	131,582,000	110,829,000	98,779,000	87,253,000
Net Income		95,069,000	94,094,000	71,554,000	57,275,000	50,426,000
Operating Cash Flow		237,260,000	217,866,000	179,360,000	145,188,000	148,260,000
Capital Expenditure		172,548,000	137,466,000	138,735,000	130,542,000	130,127,000
EBITDA		265,990,000	234,178,000	185,839,000	150,076,000	122,697,000
Return on Assets %		9.87%	12.06%	11.03%	10.54%	11.51%
Return on Equity %		15.47%	18.10%	16.85%	16.33%	17.54%
Debt to Equity		0.10				

CONTACT INFORMATION:

Phone: 952 593-9943   Fax: 952 593-9787
Toll-Free: 800-499-9586
Address: 5500 Wayzata Blvd., Ste. 1600, Minneapolis, MN 55416 United States

STOCK TICKER/OTHER:

Stock Ticker: BWLD   Exchange: NAS
Employees: 37,200   Fiscal Year Ends: 12/31
Parent Company:

SALARIES/BONUSES:

Top Exec. Salary: $841,346   Bonus: $
Second Exec. Salary: $511,837   Bonus: $

OTHER THOUGHTS:

Estimated Female Officers or Directors: 5
Hot Spot for Advancement for Women/Minorities: Y

Burns & McDonnell

www.burnsmcd.com

NAIC Code: 541330

TYPES OF BUSINESS:

Engineering Services
Construction
Consulting
Environmental Consulting
Architecture & Design
Energy Transmission

BRANDS/DIVISIONS/AFFILIATES:

CONTACTS: *Note: Officers with more than one job title may be intentionally listed here more than once.*

Greg Graves, CEO
Greg Graves, Pres.
Dennis W. (Denny) Scott, CFO
Rich Miller, Dir-IT
Mark Taylor, Treas.
Don Greenwood, Pres., Construction
Ray Kowalik, VP
John Nobles, Pres., Process & Industrial
Greg Graves, Chmn.

GROWTH PLANS/SPECIAL FEATURES:

Burns & McDonnell provides engineering, architectural, construction, environmental and consulting services across the U.S. and worldwide. The company divides its businesses into several global practice units. The architecture unit designs & builds plants, facilities and buildings such as federal/military facilities, food/consumer factories, health care facilities, information technology facilities and laboratories. The commissioning unit provides verification of new construction, its subsystems for mechanical, plumbing, electrical, fire/life safety, building envelopes, interior systems such as laboratory units, co-generation utility plants, sustainable systems and more. The construction unit, through a general contractor, designs & builds infrastructure for air quality control, aviation, chemicals, oil & gas, electric power generation, electrical transmission/distribution, manufacturing/industrial, environmental, federal/military, food & consumer products and water sectors. The consulting unit provides insight and understanding concerning the engineering, architecture, construction and environmental features of facilities and buildings. The engineering unit provides integrated engineering services across a variety of disciplines and industries. The operations & maintenance unit helps to streamline and optimize the process of operating and maintaining facilities. The planning unit takes the vision and helps put the facilities, operations and systems in place to make it happen. The studies unit provides critical support for business decision, including financial, environmental and functionality. Burns & McDonnell is a 100% employee-owned company, with more than 35 offices worldwide.

The firm offers employees health and life insurance, short- and long-term disability, flexible spending accounts, personal time off, eight paid holidays, educational seminars and tuition assistance. The company is 100% employee-owned through its employee stock ownership plan.

FINANCIAL DATA: *Note: Data for latest year may not have been available at press time.*

In U.S. $	2016	2015	2014	2013	2012	2011
Revenue		2,700,000,000	2,645,000,000	2,300,000,000	1,500,000,000	1,174,000,000
R&D Expense						
Operating Income						
Operating Margin %						
SGA Expense						
Net Income						
Operating Cash Flow						
Capital Expenditure						
EBITDA						
Return on Assets %						
Return on Equity %						
Debt to Equity						

CONTACT INFORMATION:

Phone: 816-333-9400   Fax: 816-822-3028
Toll-Free:
Address: 9400 Ward Pkwy., Kansas City, MO 64114 United States

STOCK TICKER/OTHER:

Stock Ticker: Private   Exchange:
Employees: 4,900   Fiscal Year Ends: 12/31
Parent Company:

SALARIES/BONUSES:

Top Exec. Salary: $ Bonus: $
Second Exec. Salary: $ Bonus: $

OTHER THOUGHTS:

Estimated Female Officers or Directors:
Hot Spot for Advancement for Women/Minorities:

C&S Wholesale Grocers Inc

www.cswg.com

NAIC Code: 424410

TYPES OF BUSINESS:

Wholesale Food Distribution
Warehousing
Wholesale Food Distribution
Produce
Meat
Health & Beauty Aids
Dairy Products
Fresh/Frozen Bakery Items

BRANDS/DIVISIONS/AFFILIATES:

Par Logistics Management System
FreshKO Produce Services Inc

CONTACTS: Note: Officers with more than one job title may be intentionally listed here more than once.

Rick Cohen, CEO
Kevin McNamara, CFO
Bob Palmer, Exec. VP-Procurement & Sales
Asad Husain, Chief Human Resources Officer
George Dramalis, CIO
Mike Newbold, Chief Admin. Officer
Bruce Johnson, Chief Organization Effectiveness Officer
Peter Fiore, Exec. VP-Distribution Services
Rick Cohen, Chmn.
Bob Palmer, Exec. VP-Procurement & Sales

GROWTH PLANS/SPECIAL FEATURES:

C&S Wholesale Grocers, Inc. provides grocery retailers with warehousing, distribution and logistics service solutions. C&S delivers food and non-food items to approximately 6,500 locations in 15 states, including supermarket chains, independent supermarkets, mass marketers and wholesale clubs. It also distributes to military bases and retail stores. The company supplies over 170,000 items including private label products, such as produce, meat, dairy products, delicatessen products, frozen products, tobacco, beauty items and candy. The company's warehouse locations include facilities in Maryland, Alabama, Vermont, New York, Pennsylvania, California, Florida, Indiana, Louisiana, Hawaii, Massachusetts, New Hampshire, South Carolina, New Jersey and Connecticut. C&S has customers that include Giant of Carlisle, Giant of Landover, Safeway, Stop & Shop and Target. Through its subsidiaries and affiliates, C&S provides licensing trademark services and automated warehouse technologies to retail grocery stores and assists large food manufacturers in developing logistical solutions. The company's Par Logistics Management System allows the firm real time visibility and remote control over all of the refrigerated trucks in its fleet. In November 2015, the firm acquired FreshKO Produce Services Inc., a provider of high-quality produce.

FINANCIAL DATA: Note: Data for latest year may not have been available at press time.

In U.S. $	2016	2015	2014	2013	2012	2011
Revenue		30,000,000,000	25,900,000,000	24,200,000,000	23,000,000,000	21,400,000,000
R&D Expense						
Operating Income						
Operating Margin %						
SGA Expense						
Net Income						
Operating Cash Flow						
Capital Expenditure						
EBITDA						
Return on Assets %						
Return on Equity %						
Debt to Equity						

CONTACT INFORMATION:

Phone: 603-354-7000   Fax:
Toll-Free:
Address: 7 Corporate Dr., Keene, NH 03431 United States

STOCK TICKER/OTHER:

Stock Ticker: Private   Exchange:
Employees: 25,000   Fiscal Year Ends: 09/30
Parent Company:

SALARIES/BONUSES:

Top Exec. Salary: $ Bonus: $
Second Exec. Salary: $ Bonus: $

OTHER THOUGHTS:

Estimated Female Officers or Directors:
Hot Spot for Advancement for Women/Minorities:

Cabela's Inc

NAIC Code: 451110

www.cabelas.com

TYPES OF BUSINESS:

Sporting Goods Stores
Hunting & Fishing Supplies
Camping Equipment
Outdoor Apparel
Catalog & Online Sales
Credit Card Programs

BRANDS/DIVISIONS/AFFILIATES:

World's Foremost Bank
Cabela's CLUB Visa

CONTACTS: *Note: Officers with more than one job title may be intentionally listed here more than once.*

Sean Baker, CEO, Subsidiary
Thomas Millner, CEO
Ralph Castner, CFO
James Cabela, Chairman of the Board
Charles Baldwin, Chief Administrative Officer
Douglas Means, Executive VP
Scott Williams, President
Brent LaSure, Secretary

GROWTH PLANS/SPECIAL FEATURES:

Cabela's, Inc. is a leading retailer of outdoor and hunting supply merchandise. Through its web site, mail-order catalogs and retail stores, the company supplies hunting, marine, automobile & ATV, fishing and camping equipment as well as brand-name casual clothing and home fashion accessories. It operates in three divisions: retail, direct and financial services. The retail division manages 57 retail stores in 31 states and seven stores in Canada. The stores, which are considered tourist attractions, receive millions of visitors per year. They are designed to communicate an outdoor lifestyle environment characterized by the outdoor feel of the lighting, wood or tile flooring, cedar wood beams, open ceilings and lodge-style atmosphere. The retail-format stores range between 40,000 to 246,000 square feet, contain a mountain and pond with museum-quality taxidermy and native game fish, gun libraries featuring high-quality firearms, archery training systems, virtual shooting arcades, museums or educational centers and restaurants and banquet and meeting facilities. The direct segment of Cabela's is responsible for the company's catalog and Internet sales channel operations. Its Cabelas.com website is a cost-effective medium to offer a convenient, user-friendly and secure online shopping option for new and existing customers. Through its wholly-owned subsidiary World's Foremost Bank, the financial services division offers the Cabela's CLUB Visa credit card, a rewards-based program that allows customers to earn and redeem points by using their credit card. The firm currently has over 1.8 million active credit accounts.

FINANCIAL DATA: *Note: Data for latest year may not have been available at press time.*

In U.S. $	2016	2015	2014	2013	2012	2011
Revenue		3,997,702,000	3,647,650,000	3,599,577,000	3,112,682,000	2,811,166,000
R&D Expense						
Operating Income		307,792,000	335,395,000	361,361,000	275,699,000	231,548,000
Operating Margin %		7.69%	9.19%	10.03%	8.85%	8.23%
SGA Expense		1,387,647,000	1,251,325,000	1,201,519,000	1,046,861,000	954,125,000
Net Income		189,330,000	201,715,000	224,390,000	173,513,000	142,620,000
Operating Cash Flow		326,991,000	257,979,000	345,004,000	234,629,000	366,468,000
Capital Expenditure		412,716,000	440,891,000	333,009,000	214,267,000	126,740,000
EBITDA		450,214,000	453,434,000	458,824,000	361,106,000	310,237,000
Return on Assets %		2.34%	2.86%	3.69%	3.18%	2.95%
Return on Equity %		10.38%	11.78%	15.04%	13.57%	12.93%
Debt to Equity		1.84	1.68	1.72	1.56	1.11

CONTACT INFORMATION:

Phone: 308 254-5505   Fax: 308 254-4800
Toll-Free: 800-237-4444
Address: 1 Cabela Dr., Sidney, NE 69160 United States

STOCK TICKER/OTHER:

Stock Ticker: CAB
Employees: 19,300
Parent Company:

Exchange: NYS
Fiscal Year Ends: 12/31

SALARIES/BONUSES:

Top Exec. Salary: $989,000   Bonus: $
Second Exec. Salary: $503,846   Bonus: $

OTHER THOUGHTS:

Estimated Female Officers or Directors: 2
Hot Spot for Advancement for Women/Minorities:

CACI International Inc

www.caci.com

NAIC Code: 541512

TYPES OF BUSINESS:

Consulting-InfoTech Related
Engineering Simulation Software
Custom Software Engineering
Managed Network Services
Information Management Tools
Knowledge Management
Systems Integration
Radio Frequency Identification (RFID)

BRANDS/DIVISIONS/AFFILIATES:

CACI Limited
CACI BV
LTC Engineering Associates Inc
L-3 National Security Solutions Inc

CONTACTS: Note: Officers with more than one job title may be intentionally listed here more than once.

Kenneth Asbury, CEO
Thomas Mutryn, CFO
J. London, Chairman of the Board
Gregory Buckis, Chief Accounting Officer

GROWTH PLANS/SPECIAL FEATURES:

CACI International, Inc. is a technology development company that provides IT and network services to defense, intelligence and other government departments. Contracts with the U.S. government make up approximately 94% of the company's annual revenue. CACI's domestic operations provide business solutions that combine federal domain expertise with technology solutions; command & control (C2) solutions, consisting of hardware, software and interfaces for seamless C2 capabilities; communications solutions for soldier systems, mobile platforms, fixed facilities and the enterprise; cyber security solutions; enterprise IT solutions; health delivery systems, integrating electronic health records, sharpening emergency responsiveness and improving costs; intelligence services that converts data collected into knowledge for decision-making; investigation & litigation support; logistics & material readiness solutions for the secure global flow & storage of goods, services and information in support of U.S. government agencies; and the integration of surveillance & reconnaissance technologies into platforms that enhance soldier & unit situational awareness, mobility, lethality, interoperability and survivability. International operations are conducted primarily through the firm's European subsidiaries, CACI Limited and CACI BV, which provide a diverse mix of IT services and proprietary data & software products. This division serves commercial and government customers throughout the U.K., continental Europe and around the world. In 2015, the firm acquired LTC Engineering Associates, Inc., a specialized provider of technical engineering solutions and services to the Intelligence and Department of Defense communities in the areas of software engineering, cybersecurity, signals intelligence, communications intelligence, as well as digital signals processing. In February 2016, the firm acquired L-3 National Security Solutions, Inc., expanding its business in enterprise IT, intelligence services and other key market areas.

The company offers employees medical, dental and vision insurance; life and AD&D insurance; short- and long-term disability coverage; flexible spending accounts; health club discounts; a 401(k); a discount stock purchase plan; credit union membership; tuition reimbursement; a group legal plan; an employee assistance program; a commuter benefit program; pet care discounts; and merchandise discounts.

FINANCIAL DATA: Note: Data for latest year may not have been available at press time.

In U.S. $	2016	2015	2014	2013	2012	2011
Revenue	3,744,053,000	3,313,452,000	3,564,562,000	3,681,990,000	3,774,473,000	3,577,780,000
R&D Expense						
Operating Income	264,750,000	236,381,000	257,403,000	270,841,000	299,849,000	251,401,000
Operating Margin %	7.07%	7.13%	7.22%	7.35%	7.94%	7.02%
SGA Expense						
Net Income	142,799,000	126,195,000	135,316,000	151,689,000	167,454,000	144,218,000
Operating Cash Flow	242,577,000	223,215,000	198,643,000	249,331,000	266,688,000	225,964,000
Capital Expenditure	20,835,000	17,444,000	15,279,000	15,439,000	18,284,000	14,388,000
EBITDA	329,502,000	302,464,000	322,584,000	324,919,000	355,811,000	307,468,000
Return on Assets %	3.94%	3.81%	4.61%	6.19%	7.10%	6.31%
Return on Equity %	9.25%	8.89%	10.56%	12.81%	13.56%	11.64%
Debt to Equity	0.87	0.69	0.91	0.24	0.45	0.30

CONTACT INFORMATION:

Phone: 703 841-7800   Fax: 703 841-7882
Toll-Free:
Address: 1100 N. Glebe Rd., Arlington, VA 22201 United States

STOCK TICKER/OTHER:

Stock Ticker: CACI   Exchange: NYS
Employees: 16,600   Fiscal Year Ends: 06/30
Parent Company:

SALARIES/BONUSES:

Top Exec. Salary: $835,417   Bonus: $
Second Exec. Salary: Bonus: $
$598,041

OTHER THOUGHTS:

Estimated Female Officers or Directors: 5
Hot Spot for Advancement for Women/Minorities: Y

Sales, profits and employees may be estimates. Financial information, benefits and other data can change quickly and may vary from those stated here.

Cadence Design Systems Inc

www.cadence.com

NAIC Code: 0

TYPES OF BUSINESS:

Software-Electronic Design Automation
Training & Support Services
Design & Methodology Services

BRANDS/DIVISIONS/AFFILIATES:

Forte Design Systems
Jasper Design Automation Inc

CONTACTS: *Note: Officers with more than one job title may be intentionally listed here more than once.*

Lip-Bu Tan, CEO
Geoffrey Ribar, CFO
John Shoven, Chairman of the Board
James Cowie, General Counsel
Chi-Ping Hsu, Other Executive Officer
Thomas Beckley, Senior VP, Divisional
Anirudh Devgan, Senior VP, Divisional
Neil Zaman, Senior VP, Divisional

GROWTH PLANS/SPECIAL FEATURES:

Cadence Design Systems, Inc. is a leading provider of system design enablement solutions and electronic design automation software/hardware used by semiconductor & electronic system customers to develop and design integrated circuits (ICs) and electronic devices. It licenses, sells and leases its hardware technology and provides design and methodology services throughout the world to help manage and accelerate electronic product development processes. Cadence combines its design technologies into platforms for five major design activities: functional verification, digital IC, custom IC, system interconnect & analysis and IP (intellectual property). Functional verification products are used to verify that the circuitry designed by customers will perform as intended. Digital IC design offerings are used by customers to create logical representations of a digital circuit or an IC that can be verified for correctness prior to implementation. Once the logic is verified, the design is converted to a format ready for silicon manufacturing. This division's signoff offering is comprised of tools used to signoff the design as ready for manufacture by a silicon foundry, which provides certification for this step. Custom IC design and verification offerings are used to create schematic & physical representations of circuits down to the transistor level for analog, mixed-signal, custom digital, memory and RF designs. System interconnect & analysis offerings are used to develop PCBs and IC packages. IP offerings consist of pre-verified, customizable functional blocks which customers integrate into their system-on-a-chips to accelerate the development process and to reduce the risk of errors in the design process. In 2014, the company acquired high-speed interface IP assets of TranSwitch Corporation; Forte Design Systems; and Jasper Design Automation, Inc.

Cadence employees receive medical, dental and vision coverage; retiree health access; short- and long-term disability; life insurance; domestic partner coverage; a 401(k); an employee stock purchase plan; and tuition reimbursement.

FINANCIAL DATA: *Note: Data for latest year may not have been available at press time.*

In U.S. $	2016	2015	2014	2013	2012	2011
Revenue		1,702,091,000	1,580,932,000	1,460,116,000	1,326,424,000	1,149,835,000
R&D Expense		637,567,000	603,006,000	534,022,000	454,085,000	400,745,000
Operating Income		285,430,000	206,644,000	189,007,000	211,672,000	120,377,000
Operating Margin %		16.76%	13.07%	12.94%	15.95%	10.46%
SGA Expense		512,414,000	513,307,000	499,471,000	454,354,000	416,661,000
Net Income		252,417,000	158,898,000	164,243,000	439,948,000	72,229,000
Operating Cash Flow		378,200,000	316,722,000	367,605,000	315,994,000	240,342,000
Capital Expenditure		44,808,000	39,810,000	44,929,000	35,966,000	31,421,000
EBITDA		414,072,000	330,757,000	294,885,000	312,230,000	230,099,000
Return on Assets %		9.07%	5.63%	6.96%	21.73%	4.13%
Return on Equity %		18.63%	12.76%	15.85%	66.34%	21.00%
Debt to Equity		0.25	0.26			0.32

CONTACT INFORMATION:

Phone: 408 943-1234   Fax: 408 428-5001
Toll-Free: 800-746-6223
Address: 2655 Seely Ave., Bldg. 5, San Jose, CA 95134 United States

STOCK TICKER/OTHER:

Stock Ticker: CDNS
Employees: 6,100
Parent Company:

Exchange: NAS
Fiscal Year Ends: 12/31

SALARIES/BONUSES:

Top Exec. Salary: $650,000   Bonus: $
Second Exec. Salary: $400,000   Bonus: $

OTHER THOUGHTS:

Estimated Female Officers or Directors: 2
Hot Spot for Advancement for Women/Minorities:

Sales, profits and employees may be estimates. Financial information, benefits and other data can change quickly and may vary from those stated here.

Capital One Financial Corp

NAIC Code: 522110

www.capitalone.com

TYPES OF BUSINESS:

Credit Card Issuing
Credit Card Products & Services
Mortgage Services
Consumer Lending
Health Care Financing
Small Business Loans
Mortgages
Commercial Banking

BRANDS/DIVISIONS/AFFILIATES:

Capital One Bank National Association
Capital One National Association

CONTACTS: Note: Officers with more than one job title may be intentionally listed here more than once.

Richard Fairbank, CEO
R. Blackley, CFO
Robert Alexander, Chief Information Officer
Kevin Borgmann, Chief Risk Officer
John Finneran, General Counsel
Stephen Crawford, Other Corporate Officer
Jory Berson, Other Executive Officer
Frank LaPrade, Other Executive Officer
Jonathan Witter, President, Divisional
Sanjiv Yajnik, President, Divisional
Michael Slocum, President, Divisional
Ryan Schneider, President, Divisional

GROWTH PLANS/SPECIAL FEATURES:

Capital One Financial Corp. is a financial holding company whose banking and non-banking subsidiaries market a variety of financial products and services. The business operates in three segments: credit cards, commercial banking and consumer banking. The credit cards segment includes domestic consumer and small business card lending, domestic small business lending, closed end installment lending and the international card lending businesses in Canada and the U.K. Commercial banking is comprised of lending, deposit gathering and treasury management services provided to commercial real estate and middle market customers. This segment also includes a portfolio of small commercial real estate loans that are in run-off mode. Consumer banking includes branch-based lending and deposit gathering activities for small business customers as well as consumer deposit gathering and lending activities, auto financing and mortgage lending. The company's principle subsidiaries are Capital One Bank National Association (COBNA) and Capital One National Association (CONA). COBNA offers consumers credit and debit card services, as well as lending and deposit products. CONA offers banking products and financial services to consumers, small businesses and commercial clients. In December 2015, the firm acquired GE Capital's U.S. healthcare financial services unit.

Employees of Capital One receive flex spending accounts; medical, dental, vision, prescription drug and employee assistance programs; a 401(k); life, long-term care and disability insurance; military and parental leave; adoption assistance; and an employee discount stock purchase program.

FINANCIAL DATA: Note: Data for latest year may not have been available at press time.

In U.S. $	2016	2015	2014	2013	2012	2011
Revenue		23,413,000,000	22,290,000,000	22,384,000,000	21,396,000,000	16,279,000,000
R&D Expense						
Operating Income		5,881,000,000	6,569,000,000	6,417,000,000	5,035,000,000	4,587,000,000
Operating Margin %		25.11%	29.47%	28.66%	23.53%	28.17%
SGA Expense		8,368,000,000	6,952,000,000	7,993,000,000	7,288,000,000	5,041,000,000
Net Income		4,050,000,000	4,428,000,000	4,159,000,000	3,517,000,000	3,147,000,000
Operating Cash Flow		10,127,000,000	9,304,001,000	9,984,000,000	9,060,000,000	7,455,000,000
Capital Expenditure		532,000,000	502,000,000	818,000,000	560,000,000	315,000,000
EBITDA						
Return on Assets %		1.20%	1.43%	1.34%	1.34%	1.54%
Return on Equity %		8.38%	10.00%	9.94%	9.93%	11.10%
Debt to Equity		1.22	1.05	0.95	1.20	0.91

CONTACT INFORMATION:

Phone: 703 720-1000   Fax:
Toll-Free: 800-801-1164
Address: 1680 Capital One Dr., McLean, VA 22102 United States

STOCK TICKER/OTHER:

Stock Ticker: COF
Employees: 46,000
Parent Company:

Exchange: NYS
Fiscal Year Ends: 12/31

SALARIES/BONUSES:

Top Exec. Salary: $ Bonus: $2,677,500
Second Exec. Salary: Bonus: $
$1,549,462

OTHER THOUGHTS:

Estimated Female Officers or Directors: 3
Hot Spot for Advancement for Women/Minorities: Y

Cardinal Health Inc

www.cardinal.com

NAIC Code: 424210

TYPES OF BUSINESS:

Healthcare Products & Services
Supply Chain Services
Medical Products

BRANDS/DIVISIONS/AFFILIATES:

Cardinal.com
Cardinal Health at Home
Access Closure Inc
Harvard Drugs Group (The)
Cordis
naviHealth Holdings LLC

CONTACTS: *Note: Officers with more than one job title may be intentionally listed here more than once.*

Donald Casey, CEO, Divisional
Jon Giacomin, CEO, Divisional
George Barrett, CEO
Michael Kaufmann, CFO
Stuart Laws, Chief Accounting Officer
Patricia Morrison, Chief Information Officer
Pamela Kimmet, Other Executive Officer
Craig Morford, Other Executive Officer

GROWTH PLANS/SPECIAL FEATURES:

Cardinal Health, Inc. is a provider of products and services that improve the safety and productivity of health care. The company operates in two segments: pharmaceuticals and medical products. The pharmaceutical segment distributes a broad line of branded and generic pharmaceutical products, specialty pharmaceutical, over-the-counter health care products and consumer products. It is also a full-service wholesale distributor to retail customers, hospitals and alternate care providers located throughout the U.S. In addition, this segment operates nuclear pharmacies and cyclotron facilities, provides pharmacy operations, medication therapy management and patient outcomes services to hospitals and other healthcare providers. The segment offers a broad range of support services including computerized order entry provided through Cardinal.com; generic sourcing programs; product movement, inventory and management reports; and consultation on store operations and merchandising. Through its medical products segment, the company distributes a broad range of medical, surgical and laboratory products to hospitals, ambulatory surgery centers, clinical laboratories, physician offices and other healthcare providers in the U.S., Canada and China and to patients in the home in the U.S. through its Cardinal Health at Home division. This segment also manufactures, sources and develops its own line of private brand medical and surgical products which include: single-use surgical drapes, gowns and apparel, exam and surgical gloves and fluid suction and collection systems; and manufactures extravascular closure devices. In 2015, the firm acquired The Harvard Drug Group; acquired the Cordis business from Ethicon, Inc.; and acquired a 71% stake in naviHealth Holdings LLC.

Employee benefits include medical, dental and vision coverage; a 401(k); flexible spending accounts; short- and long-term disability; life insurance; travel insurance; an employee assistance program; adoption assistance; and tuition reimbursement.

FINANCIAL DATA: *Note: Data for latest year may not have been available at press time.*

In U.S. $	2016	2015	2014	2013	2012	2011
Revenue	121,546,000,000	102,531,000,000	91,084,000,000	101,093,000,000	107,552,000,000	102,644,200,000
R&D Expense						
Operating Income	2,459,000,000	2,161,000,000	1,885,000,000	996,000,000	1,792,000,000	1,514,000,000
Operating Margin %	2.02%	2.10%	2.06%	.98%	1.66%	1.47%
SGA Expense	3,648,000,000	3,240,000,000	3,028,000,000	2,875,000,000	2,677,000,000	2,594,800,000
Net Income	1,427,000,000	1,215,000,000	1,166,000,000	334,000,000	1,069,000,000	959,000,000
Operating Cash Flow	2,971,000,000	2,540,000,000	2,524,000,000	1,727,000,000	1,176,000,000	1,394,600,000
Capital Expenditure	465,000,000	300,000,000	249,000,000	195,000,000	263,000,000	291,300,000
EBITDA	3,100,000,000	2,612,000,000	2,344,000,000	1,393,000,000	2,118,000,000	1,924,400,000
Return on Assets %	4.44%	4.32%	4.49%	1.33%	4.53%	4.47%
Return on Equity %	22.27%	19.19%	18.84%	5.46%	17.68%	17.24%
Debt to Equity	0.75	0.83	0.49	0.61	0.38	0.37

CONTACT INFORMATION:

Phone: 614 757-5000   Fax:
Toll-Free: 800-234-8701
Address: 7000 Cardinal Pl., Dublin, OH 43017 United States

STOCK TICKER/OTHER:

Stock Ticker: CAH   Exchange: NYS
Employees: 34,500   Fiscal Year Ends: 06/30
Parent Company:

SALARIES/BONUSES:

Top Exec. Salary: Bonus: $
$1,320,000
Second Exec. Salary: Bonus: $
$793,973

OTHER THOUGHTS:

Estimated Female Officers or Directors: 8

Hot Spot for Advancement for Women/Minorities: Y

Sales, profits and employees may be estimates. Financial information, benefits and other data can change quickly and may vary from those stated here.

CarMax Inc

NAIC Code: 441120

www.carmax.com

TYPES OF BUSINESS:

Used Auto Dealers, Retail
New Auto Dealers
Online Sales
Vehicle Repair Services
Financial Services

BRANDS/DIVISIONS/AFFILIATES:

CarMax Auto Finance

CONTACTS: *Note: Officers with more than one job title may be intentionally listed here more than once.*

Thomas Reedy, CFO
Thomas Folliard, Chairman of the Board
Natalie Wyatt, Chief Accounting Officer
Shamim Mohammad, Chief Information Officer
Edwin Hill, Executive VP, Divisional
William Wood, Executive VP
Eric Margolin, General Counsel
Celeste Gunter, Other Corporate Officer
William Nash, President
Jon Daniels, Senior VP, Divisional
James Lyski, Senior VP

GROWTH PLANS/SPECIAL FEATURES:

CarMax, Inc. is a leading retailer of used cars in the U.S. The firm purchases, reconditions and sells used vehicles through 158 used car superstores located in 78 metropolitan markets across the U.S. CarMax vehicles are typically 0 to 10 years old, have more than 100,000 miles and range in price from $12,000 to $35,000. The firm also sells new vehicles at four of its locations under franchise agreements with three car manufacturers. The company offers a wide selection of makes and models of both domestic and imported vehicles to appeal to diverse consumer preferences and budgets, including popular brands from manufacturers such as Chrysler, Ford, General Motors, Honda, Hyundai, Kia, Mazda, Nissan, Toyota and Volkswagen, and luxury brands such as Acura, BMW, Infiniti, Lexus and Mercedes-Benz. The company will also transfer any used vehicle in its nationwide inventory to a local superstore. In 2014, approximately 30% of vehicles sold were transferred at customer request. Vehicles purchased through the company's in-store appraisal process that fall short of retail standards are sold at onsite wholesale auctions restricted to licensed automobile dealers. All store locations provide vehicle repair service and used-car warranty service. In addition, through the company's web site, customers can search new and used cars as well as find information on Kelley Blue Book figures, car buying tips, rebates and incentives. CarMax offers financing options through CarMax Auto Finance, including revolving credit and automobile installment loans. The firm retailed approximately 619,900 used vehicles in fiscal 2016 as well as 394,437 wholesale vehicles it sold through onsite auctions.

CarMax offers its employees a benefits package including educational assistance, a daycare savings account, life insurance, adoption assistance, an associate discount program and an employee assistance program.

FINANCIAL DATA: *Note: Data for latest year may not have been available at press time.*

In U.S. $	2016	2015	2014	2013	2012	2011
Revenue	15,149,670,000	14,268,720,000	12,574,300,000	10,962,820,000	10,003,600,000	8,975,554,000
R&D Expense						
Operating Income	1,058,861,000	997,096,000	493,486,000	732,595,000	700,160,000	616,120,000
Operating Margin %	6.98%	6.98%	3.92%	6.68%	6.99%	6.86%
SGA Expense	1,351,935,000	1,257,725,000	1,155,215,000	1,031,034,000	940,786,000	905,091,000
Net Income	623,428,000	597,358,000	492,586,000	434,284,000	413,795,000	380,878,000
Operating Cash Flow	-148,893,000	-968,130,000	-613,163,000	-778,441,000	-62,164,000	-17,198,000
Capital Expenditure	315,584,000	309,817,000	310,317,000	235,707,000	172,616,000	76,580,000
EBITDA	1,183,662,000	1,108,977,000	930,067,000	828,991,000	783,436,000	676,021,000
Return on Assets %	4.50%	4.79%	4.56%	4.76%	5.45%	8.10%
Return on Equity %	20.56%	18.45%	15.54%	15.25%	16.66%	18.02%
Debt to Equity	3.56	2.79	2.21	1.99	1.81	1.70

CONTACT INFORMATION:

Phone: 804 747-0422   Fax: 804 747-5848
Toll-Free: 800-519-1511
Address: 12800 Tuckahoe Creek Pkwy., Richmond, VA 23238 United States

STOCK TICKER/OTHER:

Stock Ticker: KMX
Employees: 22,064
Parent Company:

Exchange: NYS
Fiscal Year Ends: 02/28

SALARIES/BONUSES:

Top Exec. Salary: $1,257,747
Bonus: $

Second Exec. Salary: $660,769
Bonus: $

OTHER THOUGHTS:

Estimated Female Officers or Directors: 9

Hot Spot for Advancement for Women/Minorities: Y

Carmike Cinemas Inc

www.carmike.com

NAIC Code: 512131

TYPES OF BUSINESS:
Movie Theaters

BRANDS/DIVISIONS/AFFILIATES:
Hollywood Connection
Eastwynn Theatres Inc
George G Kerasotes Corporation
GKC Theatres Inc
GKC Indiana Theatres Inc
GKC Michigan Theatres Inc
Military Services Inc

CONTACTS: Note: Officers with more than one job title may be intentionally listed here more than once.
Richard Hare, CFO
Roland Smith, Chairman of the Board
Gregory Wiggins, Chief Accounting Officer
Jeffrey Cole, Controller
Fred Van Noy, COO
S. Passman, Director
Daniel Ellis, General Counsel
A. Mayo, President, Divisional
Robert Collins, President, Divisional
John Lundin, Vice President, Divisional

GROWTH PLANS/SPECIAL FEATURES:
Carmike Cinemas, Inc. is a major chain of movie theaters in the U.S. The company operates 275 theaters with 2,942 screens located in 41 states. In addition, the company operates two family entertainment centers under the name Hollywood Connection, which feature multiplex theaters and other forms of entertainment. All of Carmike's screens operate on a digital-based platform, and many theatres are equipped for 3-D. Occasionally, the firm converts under-performing theaters to discount theaters. It currently operates 14 theaters with 100 screens as discount theaters. Carmike also offers Big D, IMAX and MuviXL format auditoriums, featuring wall to wall screens, 7.1 surround sound and digital projection for 2D and 3D features. Carmike targets small to mid-sized non-urban communities. It chooses these areas due to lower operating costs and the communities' decreased access to alternative forms of entertainment. The sale of movie tickets account for 62% of the company's revenues, while concessions and other revenues account for 38%. Carmike owns several subsidiaries, including Eastwynn Theatres, Inc.; George G Kerasotes Corporation; GKC Theatres, Inc.; GKC Indiana Theatres, Inc.; GKC Michigan Theatres, Inc.; and Military Services, Inc. In 2015, Carmike entered into a partnership with Fathom Events to bring enhanced alternative programming offerings to 150 Carmike locations in 31 states. The alternative programming includes sporting events, great performances and other unique entertainment from around the world. In February 2016, the firm acquired two movie theaters from AMC Entertainment Holdings, Inc. for $5.4 million. That March, Carmike agreed to be acquired by AMC Entertainment Holdings, Inc. for $1.1 billion. The deal is awaiting regulatory approval.

FINANCIAL DATA: Note: Data for latest year may not have been available at press time.

In U.S. $	2016	2015	2014	2013	2012	2011
Revenue		804,368,000	689,929,000	634,835,000	539,324,000	482,209,000
R&D Expense						
Operating Income		65,388,000	41,044,000	59,554,000	54,712,000	35,158,000
Operating Margin %		8.12%	5.94%	9.38%	10.14%	7.29%
SGA Expense		135,231,000	124,222,000	25,838,000	25,020,000	19,929,000
Net Income		-448,000	-8,942,000	5,753,000	96,308,000	-7,710,000
Operating Cash Flow		101,007,000	39,003,000	70,789,000	52,385,000	69,887,000
Capital Expenditure		54,211,000	59,679,000	37,812,000	35,059,000	19,282,000
EBITDA		104,218,000	90,279,000	102,090,000	83,233,000	67,523,000
Return on Assets %		-.04%	-1.02%	.73%	16.96%	-1.75%
Return on Equity %		-.15%	-3.34%	2.91%	133.93%	
Debt to Equity		1.53	1.52	1.82	2.87	

CONTACT INFORMATION:
Phone: 706 576-3400   Fax: 706 576-3441
Toll-Free:
Address: 1301 First Ave., Columbus, GA 31901 United States

STOCK TICKER/OTHER:
Stock Ticker: CKEC
Employees: 7,800
Parent Company:

Exchange: NAS
Fiscal Year Ends: 12/31

SALARIES/BONUSES:
Top Exec. Salary: $770,000   Bonus: $120,120
Second Exec. Salary: $440,000   Bonus: $34,320

OTHER THOUGHTS:
Estimated Female Officers or Directors: 1
Hot Spot for Advancement for Women/Minorities:

Carnival Corporation

NAIC Code: 483112

TYPES OF BUSINESS:

Cruise Line
On-Board Casinos
Tours
Resort Hotels

BRANDS/DIVISIONS/AFFILIATES:

Carnival Cruise Lines
Princess Cruises
Holland America Line
Seabourn Cruise Line
Costa Cruises
P&O Cruises
Cunard
AIDA Cruises

CONTACTS: Note: Officers with more than one job title may be intentionally listed here more than once.

David Noyes, CEO, Geographical
Michael Thamm, CEO, Subsidiary
Stein Kruse, CEO, Subsidiary
Arnold Donald, CEO
David Bernstein, CFO
Micky Arison, Chairman of the Board
Larry Freedman, Chief Accounting Officer
Josh Leibowitz, Chief Strategy Officer
Alan Buckelew, COO
Arnaldo Perez, Secretary

GROWTH PLANS/SPECIAL FEATURES:

Carnival Corporation is a leading provider of cruises and vacation packages to destinations worldwide. The firm is linked with its sister company Carnival plc. The firm divides its cruise brands into two segments: North America, which includes Carnival Cruise Lines, Princess Cruises, Holland America Line and Seabourn Cruise Line; and Europe, Australia & Asia (EAA), comprised of Costa Cruises, P&O Cruises, Cunard and AIDA Cruises. In total, the company operated 99 ships and 10.8 million guests in 2015. Carnival Cruise Lines operates 24 ships and is based in North America. Princess is a global cruise and tour company operating 18 ships. Holland America Line serves the industry's premium segment, with 13 ships sailing to all seven continents. Seabourn offers luxury cruises on its three luxury yachts. Costa Cruises is a leading cruise company in Europe, Spain and South America, operating a modern fleet of 15 ships. P&O Cruises, which operates from the U.K. and Australia, sails to destinations in the Caribbean, South America, Scandinavia, the Mediterranean and Atlantic Islands as well as Round the World cruises. Cunard operates the Queen Mary 2, Queen Elizabeth and Queen Victoria ships. AIDA operates in the German-speaking cruise market via a fleet of 10 ships. The company also owns Holland America Princess Alaska Tours, a leading tour operator in Alaska and the Canadian Yukon, offering lodging (at 11 owned hotels and lodges), chartered motorcoaches, rail cars, luxury day boats and sightseeing packages. In 2016, the firm commenced operations of its new brand called fathom Cruise Line, a social travel category that offers consumers meaningful impact travel experiences to work alongside locals as they tackle community needs.

FINANCIAL DATA: Note: Data for latest year may not have been available at press time.

In U.S. $	2016	2015	2014	2013	2012	2011
Revenue		15,714,000,000	15,884,000,000	15,456,000,000	15,382,000,000	15,793,000,000
R&D Expense						
Operating Income		2,574,000,000	1,792,000,000	1,352,000,000	1,642,000,000	2,255,000,000
Operating Margin %		16.38%	11.28%	8.74%	10.67%	14.27%
SGA Expense		2,067,000,000	2,054,000,000	1,879,000,000	1,720,000,000	1,717,000,000
Net Income		1,757,000,000	1,236,000,000	1,078,000,000	1,298,000,000	1,912,000,000
Operating Cash Flow		4,545,000,000	3,430,000,000	2,834,000,000	2,999,000,000	3,766,000,000
Capital Expenditure		2,294,000,000	2,583,000,000	2,149,000,000	2,332,000,000	2,696,000,000
EBITDA		3,642,000,000	3,168,000,000	2,979,000,000	3,165,000,000	3,799,000,000
Return on Assets %		4.46%	3.10%	2.72%	3.33%	5.02%
Return on Equity %		7.31%	5.06%	4.44%	5.43%	8.16%
Debt to Equity		0.31	0.30	0.32	0.29	0.33

CONTACT INFORMATION:

Phone: 305 599-2600   Fax: 305 471-4700
Toll-Free:
Address: 3655 NW 87th Ave., Miami, FL 33178 United States

STOCK TICKER/OTHER:

Stock Ticker: CCL   Exchange: NYS
Employees: 12,900   Fiscal Year Ends: 11/30
Parent Company:

SALARIES/BONUSES:

Top Exec. Salary: Bonus: $
$1,000,000
Second Exec. Salary: Bonus: $
$825,000

OTHER THOUGHTS:

Estimated Female Officers or Directors: 1

Hot Spot for Advancement for Women/Minorities: Y

Casey's General Stores Inc

www.caseys.com

NAIC Code: 447110

TYPES OF BUSINESS:

Convenience Stores
Franchising
Gas Stations

BRANDS/DIVISIONS/AFFILIATES:

Casey's General Store
Casey's Distribution Center
Casey's Marketing Company
Casey's Services Company
Casey's Retail Company
CGS Sales Corporation
Tobacco City Inc

CONTACTS: Note: Officers with more than one job title may be intentionally listed here more than once.

Terry Handley, CEO
William Walljasper, CFO
Robert Myers, Chairman of the Board
Julia Jackowski, General Counsel
Brian Johnson, Secretary
John Soupene, Senior VP, Divisional
Jay Soupene, Senior VP, Divisional
Cindi Summers, Senior VP, Divisional

GROWTH PLANS/SPECIAL FEATURES:

Casey's General Stores, Inc. has 1,931 stores in 14 Midwestern states, primarily Iowa, Missouri and Illinois, operating under the Casey's General Store banner. The company's general stores carry more than 3,000 items, including a broad selection of food, beverages, tobacco products, health and beauty aids, automotive products and other non-food items. In addition, all but one location offers gasoline for sale on a self-service basis. During the firm's fiscal 2016 year, 51 stores were newly constructed and three were closed down. Additionally, five stores were acquired, of which four were opened and the fifth is scheduled to open in 2017. About 57% of Casey's stores are located in markets with a population of less than 5,000, and approximately 18% of its stores are in communities with more than 20,000 persons. Casey's Distribution Center is adjacent to its corporate headquarters in Ankeny, Iowa. Casey's General Stores seek to meet the needs of residents of small towns by combining the features of a general store with a convenience store. Wholly-owned subsidiaries include Casey's Marketing Company, which oversees wholesale operations including the distribution center; Casey's Services Company, which provides store construction and transportation services; Casey's Retail Company, which holds the rights to the Casey's trademark; CGS Sales Corporation, which operates one store in Iowa and one in Nebraska; and Tobacco City, Inc., which operates one store in North Dakota. In July 2016, the firm announced a commitment to work closely with its suppliers to source 100% of its eggs from cage-free hens by 2025, based upon available supply and affordability to its customers.

Employees are offered medical, vision and dental; life insurance; short- and long-term disability; flexible spending accounts; a 401(k); a stock purchase plan; advancement opportunities; wellness programs; a scholarship program; accident insurance; critical illness insurance; and half-priced meals on the job.

FINANCIAL DATA: Note: Data for latest year may not have been available at press time.

In U.S. $	2016	2015	2014	2013	2012	2011
Revenue	7,122,086,000	7,767,216,000	7,840,255,000	7,250,840,000	6,987,804,000	5,635,240,000
R&D Expense						
Operating Income	388,879,000	323,250,000	245,802,000	210,177,000	218,707,000	191,084,000
Operating Margin %	5.46%	4.16%	3.13%	2.89%	3.12%	3.39%
SGA Expense	1,053,805,000	960,424,000	857,297,000	760,365,000	688,431,000	607,628,000
Net Income	225,982,000	180,628,000	134,514,000	110,625,000	116,791,000	94,623,000
Operating Cash Flow	464,709,000	341,682,000	314,160,000	286,328,000	294,879,000	261,443,000
Capital Expenditure	392,839,000	360,734,000	308,633,000	305,301,000	240,874,000	214,573,000
EBITDA	559,816,000	479,680,000	377,259,000	322,195,000	315,606,000	263,077,000
Return on Assets %	8.69%	7.58%	6.28%	5.88%	6.89%	6.30%
Return on Equity %	23.07%	22.64%	20.34%	19.96%	25.67%	15.40%
Debt to Equity	0.75	0.95	1.18	1.08	1.31	1.68

CONTACT INFORMATION:

Phone: 515 965-6100   Fax: 515 965-6205
Toll-Free:
Address: 1 Convenience Blvd., Ankeny, IA 50021 United States

STOCK TICKER/OTHER:

Stock Ticker: CASY   Exchange: NAS
Employees: 29,749   Fiscal Year Ends: 04/30
Parent Company:

SALARIES/BONUSES:

Top Exec. Salary: Bonus: $
$1,125,000
Second Exec. Salary: Bonus: $
$770,000

OTHER THOUGHTS:

Estimated Female Officers or Directors: 3

Hot Spot for Advancement for Women/Minorities: Y

Caterpillar Inc

NAIC Code: 333120

TYPES OF BUSINESS:

Machinery-Earth Moving & Agricultural
Diesel and Turbine Engines
Financing
Fuel Cell Manufacturing
Rail Car Maintenance
Engine & Equipment Remanufacturing
Locomotive Manufacturing and Maintenance

BRANDS/DIVISIONS/AFFILIATES:

Progress Rail Services
Solar Turbines

CONTACTS: Note: Officers with more than one job title may be intentionally listed here more than once.

Douglas Oberhelman, CEO
Bradley Halverson, CFO
Jananne Copeland, Chief Accounting Officer
James Buda, Executive VP, Divisional
Robert Charter, President, Divisional
D. Umpleby, President, Divisional
Thomas Pellette, President, Divisional
Edward Rapp, President, Divisional
Christopher Reitz, Secretary
David Bozeman, Senior VP
Denise Johnson, Vice President

GROWTH PLANS/SPECIAL FEATURES:

Caterpillar, Inc. is a leading manufacturer of construction and mining equipment. The company's principal lines of business are machinery, energy & transportation and financial products. The machinery, energy & transportation segments consist of the firm's construction industries, resource industries, energy & transportation and all other operations. Construction industry products include pipe layers, motor graders, wheel tractor-scrapers, excavators, backhoe loaders, mining shovels, log skidders and loaders and skid steer loaders, among others. Resource industry products consist of electric rope shovels, draglines, hydraulic shovels, drills, highwall miners, underground mining equipment, off-highway trucks, articulated trucks, paving products, wheel dozers and forestry products. The energy & transportation business primarily provides support services for customers using reciprocating engines, turbines, diesel-electric locomotives, integrated systems and solutions, and related parts across industries serving oil and gas, power generation, industrial and marine applications as well as rail-related businesses. This business line, through subsidiary Progress Rail Services, is also responsible for the design, manufacture, remanufacture and maintenance of rail-related products. The financial products business provides customers retail and wholesale financing alternatives for Caterpillar products. The firm's Solar Turbines subsidiary is a leader in industrial gas turbine power system engines. Its dealer network consists of 175 dealer locations worldwide, serving 182 countries.

Employees of the company receive benefits including a 401(k), health coverage, an employee assistance program and flexible spending accounts.

FINANCIAL DATA: Note: Data for latest year may not have been available at press time.

In U.S. $	2016	2015	2014	2013	2012	2011
Revenue		47,011,000,000	55,184,000,000	55,656,000,000	65,875,000,000	60,138,000,000
R&D Expense		2,165,000,000	2,135,000,000	2,046,000,000	2,466,000,000	2,297,000,000
Operating Income		3,256,000,000	5,328,000,000	5,628,000,000	8,573,000,000	7,153,000,000
Operating Margin %		6.92%	9.65%	10.11%	13.01%	11.89%
SGA Expense		5,199,000,000	5,697,000,000	5,547,000,000	5,919,000,000	5,203,000,000
Net Income		2,102,000,000	3,695,000,000	3,789,000,000	5,681,000,000	4,928,000,000
Operating Cash Flow		6,675,000,000	8,057,000,000	10,191,000,000	5,241,000,000	7,010,000,000
Capital Expenditure		3,261,000,000	3,379,000,000	4,446,000,000	5,076,000,000	3,924,000,000
EBITDA		6,995,000,000	9,354,000,000	9,407,000,000	12,313,000,000	10,474,000,000
Return on Assets %		2.57%	4.35%	4.34%	6.65%	6.77%
Return on Equity %		13.32%	19.67%	19.76%	37.35%	41.57%
Debt to Equity		1.70	1.65	1.28	1.58	1.93

CONTACT INFORMATION:

Phone: 309 675-1000   Fax: 309 675-4332
Toll-Free:
Address: 100 NE Adams St., Peoria, IL 61629 United States

STOCK TICKER/OTHER:

Stock Ticker: CAT   Exchange: NYS
Employees: 105,700   Fiscal Year Ends: 12/31
Parent Company:

SALARIES/BONUSES:

Top Exec. Salary: Bonus: $
$1,600,008
Second Exec. Salary: Bonus: $300,000
$729,768

OTHER THOUGHTS:

Estimated Female Officers or Directors: 11

Hot Spot for Advancement for Women/Minorities: Y

Catholic Health Initiatives

www.catholichealthinitiatives.org

NAIC Code: 622110

TYPES OF BUSINESS:

General Medical and Surgical Hospitals
Long-Term Care
Assisted & Independent Living Facilities
Community Health Organizations
Home Care Services
Occupational Health Clinic
Cancer Prevention Institute

BRANDS/DIVISIONS/AFFILIATES:

CHI
Centura Health
Mercy Health Network
KentuckyOne Health Inc
Sylvania Franciscan Health
TriHealth Inc
Premier Health Partners

CONTACTS: *Note: Officers with more than one job title may be intentionally listed here more than once.*

Kevin E. Lofton, CEO
Michael T. Rowan, COO
Kevin E. Lofton, Pres.
J. Dean Swindle, CFO
Patricia G. Webb, Chief Human Resource Officer
Stephen L. Moore, Chief Medical Officer
Michael O'Rourke, CIO
Mitch H. Melfi, General Counsel
John F. DiCola, Sr. VP-Strategy & Bus. Dev.
Joyce M. Ross, Sr. VP-Comm.
Philip L. Foster, Sr. VP
A. Michelle Cooper, Corp. Responsibility Officer
Kathleen Sanford, Chief Nursing Officer
Joseph W. Wilczek, Sr. VP-Div. Oper.
Christopher Lowney, Chmn.
Steven C. Kehrberg, Sr. VP-Supply Chain

GROWTH PLANS/SPECIAL FEATURES:

Catholic Health Initiatives (CHI) is a national faith-based, nonprofit health care organization focused on strengthening and advancing the Catholic health ministry. The organization operates 103 hospitals in 18 states, including academic medical centers & teaching hospitals, critical-access facilities, community health services organizations, accredited nursing colleges, home-health agencies, and other facilities that span the inpatient/outpatient continuum of care. CHI's family of hospitals and facilities comprise the following names: CHI, Centura Health, Mercy Health Network, KentuckyOne Health, Inc., Sylvania Franciscan Health, TriHealth, Inc. and Premier Health Partners.

Employee benefits include medical, dental and vision coverage; flexible spending accounts; life and AD&D insurance; short- and long-term disability; a retirement plan; 403(b) and 457(b) plans; and tuition and adoption assistance.

FINANCIAL DATA: *Note: Data for latest year may not have been available at press time.*

In U.S. $	2016	2015	2014	2013	2012	2011
Revenue		15,713,280,000	13,888,673,000	10,708,225,000	9,844,271,000	9,004,978,000
R&D Expense						
Operating Income						
Operating Margin %						
SGA Expense						
Net Income		137,793,000	633,967,000	-54,943,000	311,818,000	335,326,000
Operating Cash Flow						
Capital Expenditure						
EBITDA						
Return on Assets %						
Return on Equity %						
Debt to Equity						

CONTACT INFORMATION:

Phone: 303-298-9100   Fax:
Toll-Free:
Address: 198 Inverness Drive West, Englewood, CO 80112 United States

STOCK TICKER/OTHER:

Stock Ticker: Nonprofit   Exchange:
Employees: 86,000   Fiscal Year Ends: 06/30
Parent Company:

SALARIES/BONUSES:

Top Exec. Salary: $ Bonus: $
Second Exec. Salary: $ Bonus: $

OTHER THOUGHTS:

Estimated Female Officers or Directors: 6
Hot Spot for Advancement for Women/Minorities: Y

CBRE Group Inc

NAIC Code: 531210

www.cbre.com

TYPES OF BUSINESS:

Real Estate Brokerage
Real Estate Management Services
Mortgage Banking
Investment Management
Consulting Services

BRANDS/DIVISIONS/AFFILIATES:

CBRE Inc
CBRE Capital Markets
CBRE Ltd
CBRE Global Investors LLC
Trammell Crow Company LLC
Sitehawk Retail Real Estate
Forum Analytics LLC
Tax Credit Group

CONTACTS: *Note: Officers with more than one job title may be intentionally listed here more than once.*

William Concannon, CEO, Divisional
T. Ferguson, CEO, Divisional
Calvin Frese, CEO, Geographical
Robert Sulentic, CEO
James Groch, CFO
Ray Wirta, Chairman of the Board
Gil Borok, Chief Accounting Officer
J. Kirk, Chief Administrative Officer
Michael Lafitte, COO
Laurence Midler, Executive VP
Steve Iaco, Other Corporate Officer

GROWTH PLANS/SPECIAL FEATURES:

CBRE Group, Inc. is one of the world's largest commercial real estate services companies, with over 400 offices in more than 50 countries. It offers services to occupiers, owners lenders/investors in office, retail, industrial, multi-family and other commercial real estate assets. The firm's core services include commercial property and corporate facilities management, tenant representation, property/agency leasing property sales, valuation, real estate investment management commercial mortgage origination and servicing, capital markets (equity and debt), development services and proprietary research. CBRE operates in five segments. Americas, which accounted for 57% of its 2015 revenue. Europe, Middle East and Africa (EMEA), 27.7%; Asia Pacific 10.5%; global investment management, 4.2%; and development services, 0.6%. Americas operates primarily through CBRE, Inc.; CBRE Capital Markets, Inc.; and CBRE Ltd. EMEA has offices in 43 countries, with its largest located in the France, Germany, Italy, the Netherlands, Russia, Spain and the U.K. Asia Pacific operates in 14 countries, including Australia and New Zealand, China, Hong Kong, India, Japan, Korea and Singapore. In addition, the company has agreements with affiliated offices in Cambodia, Malaysia, the Philippines and Thailand that generate royalty fees and support cross-referral arrangements. Global investment management is handled by subsidiary CBRE Global Investors, LLC. Through the Trammell Crow Company LLC, the firm provides development services primarily in the U.S. to users of and investors in commercial real estate. During 2015, the firm acquired Global Workplace Solutions business from Johnson Controls, Inc.; Sitehawk Retail Real Estate, a retail real estate services firm; Forum Analytics, LLC, provider of sophisticated modeling and mapping solutions; and Tax Credit Group, provider of advisory, investment sales, debt and structured finance services.

The company offers its employees medical, dental and vision insurance; a 401(k); flexible spending accounts; an employee assistance program; and paid vacation and holidays.

FINANCIAL DATA: *Note: Data for latest year may not have been available at press time.*

In U.S. $	2016	2015	2014	2013	2012	2011
Revenue		10,855,810,000	9,049,918,000	7,184,794,000	6,514,099,000	5,905,411,000
R&D Expense						
Operating Income		835,944,000	792,254,000	616,128,000	585,081,000	462,862,000
Operating Margin %		7.70%	8.75%	8.57%	8.98%	7.83%
SGA Expense		2,633,609,000	2,438,960,000	2,104,310,000	2,002,914,000	1,882,666,000
Net Income		547,132,000	484,503,000	316,538,000	315,555,000	239,162,000
Operating Cash Flow		651,897,000	661,780,000	745,108,000	291,081,000	361,219,000
Capital Expenditure		139,464,000	171,242,000	156,358,000	150,232,000	147,980,000
EBITDA		1,312,706,000	1,154,398,000	835,337,000	835,451,000	696,717,000
Return on Assets %		5.86%	6.61%	4.27%	4.19%	3.87%
Return on Equity %		22.00%	23.31%	18.43%	23.45%	23.22%
Debt to Equity		0.97	0.81	0.98	1.65	2.26

CONTACT INFORMATION:

Phone: 213-613-3333   Fax: 213 438-4820
Toll-Free:
Address: 400 South Hope Street, 25th Fl, Los Angeles, CA 90071 United States

STOCK TICKER/OTHER:

Stock Ticker: CBG
Employees: 52,000
Parent Company:

Exchange: NYS
Fiscal Year Ends: 12/31

SALARIES/BONUSES:

Top Exec. Salary: $967,500   Bonus: $607,130
Second Exec. Salary: $752,500   Bonus: $500,000

OTHER THOUGHTS:

Estimated Female Officers or Directors: 2
Hot Spot for Advancement for Women/Minorities:

Sales, profits and employees may be estimates. Financial information, benefits and other data can change quickly and may vary from those stated here.

CBS Corporation

www.cbscorporation.com

NAIC Code: 515120

TYPES OF BUSINESS:

Television Broadcasting
News Organization
Outdoor Advertising
Radio Networks & Programming
Television Production
Cable TV Networks
Book Publishing

BRANDS/DIVISIONS/AFFILIATES:

CBS Television Network
CBS Television Studios
CBS Television Stations
CBS Radio
Movie Channel (The)
CBS Sports Network
Smithsonian Institution
Simon & Schuster

CONTACTS: Note: Officers with more than one job title may be intentionally listed here more than once.

Leslie Moonves, CEO
Sumner Redstone, Chairman Emeritus
Lawrence Liding, Chief Accounting Officer
Anthony Ambrosio, Chief Administrative Officer
Joseph Ianniello, COO
Shari Redstone, Director
Richard Jones, Executive VP
Jonathan Anschell, Executive VP
Gil Schwartz, Other Executive Officer
Lawrence Tu, Other Executive Officer

GROWTH PLANS/SPECIAL FEATURES:

CBS Corporation is a leading mass media company in the U.S. The firm operates through four segments: entertainment, accounting for 61% of 2015 revenues; local broadcasting, 19%; cable networks, 16%; and publishing, 4%. The entertainment division is composed of the following: CBS Television Network, CBS Television Studios, CBS Global Distribution Group (which itself is composed of CBS Studios International and CBS Television Distribution), CBS Interactive and CBS Films. The local broadcasting segment is composed of CBS Television Stations, the company's 30 owned broadcast television stations; and CBS Radio, through which CBS owns and operates 117 radio stations in 26 U.S. markets. The cable networks segment is composed of a digital streaming subscription offerings; Showtime Networks, which operates the firm's premium subscription program services: Showtime, The Movie Channel and Flix; CBS Sports Network, the company's cable network which focuses on college athletics and other sports; and Smithsonian Networks, a venture between Showtime Networks and Smithsonian Institution, which operates Smithsonian Channel, a basic cable program service. The publishing segment is composed of Simon & Schuster, which publishes and distributes consumer books under imprints such as Simon & Schuster, Pocket Books, Scribner, Gallery Books, Touchstone and Atria Books.

CBS offers its employees health, vision, dental & life insurance; a 401(k) plan; short & long term disability; flexible spending accounts; adoption assitance; eldercare programs; and paid leave to care for a terminally ill family member.

FINANCIAL DATA: Note: Data for latest year may not have been available at press time.

In U.S. $	2016	2015	2014	2013	2012	2011
Revenue		13,886,000,000	13,806,000,000	15,284,000,000	14,089,000,000	14,245,000,000
R&D Expense						
Operating Income		2,417,000,000	2,896,000,000	3,259,000,000	2,983,000,000	2,529,000,000
Operating Margin %		17.40%	20.97%	21.32%	21.17%	17.75%
SGA Expense		2,455,000,000	2,462,000,000	2,735,000,000	2,634,000,000	2,755,000,000
Net Income		1,413,000,000	2,959,000,000	1,879,000,000	1,574,000,000	1,305,000,000
Operating Cash Flow		1,394,000,000	1,275,000,000	1,873,000,000	1,815,000,000	1,749,000,000
Capital Expenditure		193,000,000	206,000,000	270,000,000	254,000,000	265,000,000
EBITDA		2,679,000,000	2,808,000,000	3,730,000,000	3,438,000,000	3,067,000,000
Return on Assets %		5.90%	11.72%	7.11%	5.97%	4.98%
Return on Equity %		22.54%	34.94%	18.62%	15.64%	13.22%
Debt to Equity		1.47	0.93	0.59	0.57	0.60

CONTACT INFORMATION:

Phone: 212 975-4321   Fax: 212 975-4516
Toll-Free:
Address: 51 W. 52nd St., New York, NY 10019 United States

STOCK TICKER/OTHER:

Stock Ticker: CBS   Exchange: NYS
Employees: 17,310   Fiscal Year Ends: 12/31
Parent Company:

SALARIES/BONUSES:

Top Exec. Salary: $3,500,000   Bonus: $19,000,000
Second Exec. Salary: $2,500,000   Bonus: $8,073,000

OTHER THOUGHTS:

Estimated Female Officers or Directors: 3

Hot Spot for Advancement for Women/Minorities: Y

CDW Corporation

www.cdw.com

NAIC Code: 423430

TYPES OF BUSINESS:

Computer Products, Direct Selling
Online Sales
Custom Installation & Repair-Computers

BRANDS/DIVISIONS/AFFILIATES:

CDW Government LLC
CDW Canada Inc

CONTACTS: *Note: Officers with more than one job title may be intentionally listed here more than once.*

Thomas Richards, CEO
Ann Ziegler, CFO
Neil Fairfield, Chief Accounting Officer
Jonathan Stevens, Chief Information Officer
Neal Campbell, Chief Marketing Officer
Christine Leahy, Other Executive Officer
Dennis Berger, Other Executive Officer
Christina Rother, Senior VP, Divisional
Matthew Troka, Senior VP, Divisional
Christina Corley, Senior VP, Divisional
Douglas Eckrote, Senior VP, Divisional

GROWTH PLANS/SPECIAL FEATURES:

CDW Corporation is one of the leading providers of multi-branded information technology products and services to business, government, education and health care customers in the U.S. and Canada. The firm offers over 100,000 products from over 1,000 leading technology brands, in addition to customized solution design and management with focus areas including notebooks, desktops, printers, servers and storage, unified communications, security, wireless, power and cooling, networking, software licensing, cloud computing, data center optimization and mobility solutions. The company manages its inventory through a 450,000-square-foot distribution center in Vernon Hills, Illinois, and a 513,000-square-foot distribution center in Las Vegas, Nevada. CDW offers customers free access to certified technicians for telephone support and complete custom installation and repair services via the company's configuration center, in addition to access to a database of frequently asked technical questions and direct links to manufacturers' tech support web sites. Its CDW Government LLC subsidiary provides specialized product offerings and services to federal, state and local governments as well as the educational sector. CDW Canada, Inc. serves commercial and public sector customers in Canada.

The company offers its employees medical, dental and vision insurance; a 401(k) plan; a profit sharing plan; life and AD&D insurance; flexible spending accounts; tuition reimbursement; short- and long-term disability insurance; and an employee assistance program.

FINANCIAL DATA: *Note: Data for latest year may not have been available at press time.*

In U.S. $	2016	2015	2014	2013	2012	2011
Revenue		12,988,700,000	12,074,500,000	10,768,600,000	10,128,200,000	9,602,400,000
R&D Expense						
Operating Income		742,000,000	673,000,000	508,600,000	510,600,000	470,700,000
Operating Margin %		5.71%	5.57%	4.72%	5.04%	4.90%
SGA Expense		1,373,800,000	1,248,300,000	1,251,700,000	1,159,000,000	1,116,700,000
Net Income		403,100,000	244,900,000	132,800,000	119,000,000	17,100,000
Operating Cash Flow		277,500,000	435,000,000	366,300,000	317,400,000	214,700,000
Capital Expenditure		90,100,000	55,000,000	47,100,000	41,400,000	45,700,000
EBITDA		969,400,000	880,900,000	716,800,000	720,800,000	675,600,000
Return on Assets %		6.27%	4.07%	2.28%	2.03%	.28%
Return on Equity %		39.66%	29.71%	31.31%	184.21%	
Debt to Equity		2.94	3.38	4.50	27.33	

CONTACT INFORMATION:

Phone: 847-465-6000   Fax: 847-465-6800
Toll-Free: 800-750-4239
Address: 200 N. Milwaukee Ave., Vernon Hills, IL 60061 United States

STOCK TICKER/OTHER:

Stock Ticker: CDW   Exchange: NAS
Employees: 7,000   Fiscal Year Ends: 12/31
Parent Company:

SALARIES/BONUSES:

Top Exec. Salary: $851,587   Bonus: $
Second Exec. Salary: $516,806   Bonus: $

OTHER THOUGHTS:

Estimated Female Officers or Directors: 10
Hot Spot for Advancement for Women/Minorities: Y

Celanese Corporation

www.celanese.com

NAIC Code: 325211

TYPES OF BUSINESS:

Manufacturing-Acetyl Intermediate Chemicals
Industrial Products
Technical & High-Performance Polymers
Sweeteners & Sorbates
Ethanol Production
Food Ingredients
Cellulose Derivative Fibers

BRANDS/DIVISIONS/AFFILIATES:

GUR

CONTACTS: Note: Officers with more than one job title may be intentionally listed here more than once.

Mark Rohr, CEO
Kevin Oliver, Chief Accounting Officer
James Peacock, Deputy General Counsel
Scott Sutton, Executive VP
Patrick Quarles, Executive VP
Gjon Nivica, General Counsel
Lori Johnston, Senior VP, Divisional
Christopher Jensen, Senior VP, Divisional

GROWTH PLANS/SPECIAL FEATURES:

Celanese Corporation produces a line of industrial chemicals and advanced materials. It manufactures acetyl products, which are intermediate chemicals for nearly all major industries, and also produces high-performance engineered polymers. The company operates through two segments: materials solutions and the acetyl chain. Together, these segments utilize raw materials, technology, integrated systems and research resources in order to increase efficiency and respond to market needs. Materials solutions is further divided into two units: advanced engineered materials, which includes polyoxymethylene, ultra-high molecular weight polyethylene, polybutylene terephthalate, long-fiber thermoplastics and liquid crystal polymers; and consumer specialties, which includes acetate tow, acetate flake, acetate film, acesulfame potassium, potassium sorbate, sorbic acid and sweetener systems. These materials are used for fuel system components, automotive safety systems, medical applications, industrial applications, battery separators, consumer electronics, filtration, films, packaging, confections, telecommunications and more. The acetyl chain segment is further divided into two units: industrial specialties, which includes conventional emulsions, vinyl acetate ethylene emulsions, ethylene vinyl acetate resins/compounds and low-density polyethylene resins; and acetyl intermediates, which includes acetic acid, vinyl acetate monomer, acetaldehyde, ethyl acetate, fomaldehyde, butyl acetate and ethanol. These materials are used for paints, coatings, adhesives, textiles, paper finishing, packaging, lamination, medical applications, automotive parts, pharmaceuticals, inks and more. Headquartered in Irving, Texas, the company's operations are primarily located in North America, Europe and Asia, consisting of 23 global production facilities and eight affiliate production facilities. In 2015, Celanese sold its atmosphere emulsions unit based in Tarragona, Spain; and commenced methanol production at its Clear Lake, Texas facility, with an annual capacity of 1.4 million tons. In January 2016, the firm announced plans to expand manufacturing production capacity for its GUR brand of ultra-high molecular weight polyethylene product at the company's Bishop, Texas facility. Expansion was expected to be completed May 2016.

FINANCIAL DATA: Note: Data for latest year may not have been available at press time.

In U.S. $	2016	2015	2014	2013	2012	2011
Revenue		5,674,000,000	6,802,000,000	6,510,000,000	6,418,000,000	6,763,000,000
R&D Expense		119,000,000	86,000,000	85,000,000	102,000,000	96,000,000
Operating Income		326,000,000	758,000,000	1,508,000,000	511,000,000	690,000,000
Operating Margin %		5.74%	11.14%	23.16%	7.96%	10.20%
SGA Expense		506,000,000	758,000,000	311,000,000	507,000,000	536,000,000
Net Income		304,000,000	624,000,000	1,101,000,000	605,000,000	607,000,000
Operating Cash Flow		862,000,000	962,000,000	762,000,000	722,000,000	638,000,000
Capital Expenditure		520,000,000	678,000,000	377,000,000	410,000,000	204,000,000
EBITDA		970,000,000	1,386,000,000	2,100,000,000	1,162,000,000	1,287,000,000
Return on Assets %		3.49%	6.99%	12.22%	6.90%	7.22%
Return on Equity %		11.70%	22.62%	49.71%	39.40%	53.55%
Debt to Equity		1.03	0.92	1.06	1.69	2.14

CONTACT INFORMATION:

Phone: 972 443-4000   Fax: 972 332-9373
Toll-Free:
Address: 222 West Las Colinas Blvd, Ste 900N, Irving, TX 75039-5421 United States

STOCK TICKER/OTHER:

Stock Ticker: CE   Exchange: NYS
Employees: 7,081   Fiscal Year Ends: 12/31
Parent Company:

SALARIES/BONUSES:

Top Exec. Salary: $1,100,000   Bonus: $

Second Exec. Salary: $525,000   Bonus: $

OTHER THOUGHTS:

Estimated Female Officers or Directors: 1

Hot Spot for Advancement for Women/Minorities: Y

Sales, profits and employees may be estimates. Financial information, benefits and other data can change quickly and may vary from those stated here.

Celgene Corporation

NAIC Code: 325412

TYPES OF BUSINESS:

Cancer & Immune-Inflammatory Related Diseases Drugs

BRANDS/DIVISIONS/AFFILIATES:

Revlimid
Abraxane
Pomalyst/Imnovid
Vidaza
Thalomid
Otezla
Quanticel Pharmaceuticals Inc
Receptos Inc

CONTACTS: Note: Officers with more than one job title may be intentionally listed here more than once.

Mark Alles, CEO
Peter Kellogg, CFO
Thomas Daniel, Chairman of the Board, Subsidiary
Robert Hugin, Chairman of the Board
Robert Hershberg, Chief Scientific Officer
Julia Haller, DirectorKaplan
Scott Smith, President, Divisional
Rupert Vessey, President, Divisional
Jacqualyn Fouse, President

GROWTH PLANS/SPECIAL FEATURES:

Celgene Corporation is a global biopharmaceutical company involved in discovering, developing and commercializing cancer and immune-inflammatory related disease treatment therapies. Celgene's commercial stage products include Revlimid, Abraxane, Pomalyst/Imnovid, Vidaza, Thalomid, Otezla and Istodax. Revlimid is in several Phase 3 trials across a range of hematological malignances. Abraxane is in various stages of investigation for breast, pancreatic and non-small cell lung cancers. Pomalyst/Imnovid was approved in the U.S. and the European Union for indications in multiple myeloma based on Phase 2 and 3 trial results, with an additional Phase 3 trial currently underway in relapsed and refractory multiple myeloma. Vidaza is a pyrimidine nucleoside analog that has been shown to reverse the effects of DNA hypermethylation and promote subsequent gene re-expression. It is marketed in the U.S. as well as many international markets for the treatment of myelodysplastic syndromes (MDS), chronic myelomonocytic leukemia and acute myeloid leukemia. Thalomid is sold as Thalomid or Thalidomide Celgene outside the U.S., and as Thalomid REMS in the U.S. It is administered orally for the treatment of multiple myeloma and erythema nodosum leprosum. Otezla is being evaluated in Phase 3 trials for Behcet's disease and expanded indications in psoriatic arthritis and psoriasis. Istodax is administered by intravenous infusion for the treatment of cutaneous T-cell lymphoma (CTCL) and peripheral T-cell lymphoma (PTCL). Additionally, it has received orphan drug designation for the treatment of non-Hodgkin's T-cell lymphomas, including CTCL and PTCL. Celgene's current preclinical and clinical-stage pipeline of new drug candidates and cell therapies include both small molecule and biologic therapeutic agents designed to selectively regulate disease-associated genes and proteins. In 2015, the firm acquired Quanticel Pharmaceuticals, Inc., a biotechnology company focused on cancer drug discovery; and acquired Receptos, Inc., whose lead drug candidate, ozanimod, is a small molecule that modulates sphingosine 1-phosphate 1 and 5 receptors.

FINANCIAL DATA: Note: Data for latest year may not have been available at press time.

In U.S. $	2016	2015	2014	2013	2012	2011
Revenue		9,255,999,000	7,670,400,000	6,493,900,000	5,506,713,000	4,842,070,000
R&D Expense		3,697,300,000	2,430,600,000	2,226,200,000	1,724,156,000	1,600,264,000
Operating Income		2,254,600,000	2,519,000,000	1,808,900,000	1,746,442,000	1,442,753,000
Operating Margin %		24.35%	32.84%	27.85%	31.71%	29.79%
SGA Expense		2,305,400,000	2,027,900,000	1,684,500,000	1,373,541,000	1,226,314,000
Net Income		1,602,000,000	1,999,900,000	1,449,900,000	1,456,180,000	1,318,150,000
Operating Cash Flow		2,483,900,000	2,806,300,000	2,225,900,000	2,018,553,000	1,808,685,000
Capital Expenditure		286,300,000	175,100,000	139,100,000	160,389,000	132,119,000
EBITDA		2,743,000,000	2,877,100,000	2,131,100,000	2,028,143,000	1,825,110,000
Return on Assets %		7.21%	13.02%	11.54%	13.39%	13.06%
Return on Equity %		25.74%	33.01%	25.69%	25.98%	22.93%
Debt to Equity		2.40	0.96	0.75	0.48	0.23

CONTACT INFORMATION:

Phone: 908 673-9000   Fax: 908 673-9001
Toll-Free:
Address: 86 Morris Ave., Summit, NJ 07901 United States

STOCK TICKER/OTHER:

Stock Ticker: CELG   Exchange: NAS
Employees: 6,971   Fiscal Year Ends: 12/31
Parent Company:

SALARIES/BONUSES:

Top Exec. Salary: Bonus: $
$1,483,333
Second Exec. Salary: Bonus: $
$871,250

OTHER THOUGHTS:

Estimated Female Officers or Directors: 3

Hot Spot for Advancement for Women/Minorities: Y

CenturyLink Inc

NAIC Code: 517110

www.centurylink.com

TYPES OF BUSINESS:

Local Telephone Service
Long-Distance Services
Internet Service Provider
Business Information Services
Fiber Network Services
Satellite TV
IPTV

BRANDS/DIVISIONS/AFFILIATES:

CenturyLink
Cognilytics

CONTACTS: Note: Officers with more than one job title may be intentionally listed here more than once.

Glen Post, CEO
R. Ewing, CFO
William Owens, Chairman of the Board
David Cole, Chief Accounting Officer
Stacey Goff, Chief Administrative Officer
Harvey Perry, Director
Maxine Moreau, Executive VP, Divisional
Scott Trezise, Executive VP, Divisional
Aamir Hussain, Executive VP
Girish Varma, President, Divisional
Dean Douglas, President, Divisional

GROWTH PLANS/SPECIAL FEATURES:

CenturyLink, Inc. is an integrated communications company engaged primarily in providing an array of communications services, including local and long distance voice, wholesale local network access, high-speed Internet access, other data services and video services. The company divides its operations in two segments: consumer and business. The consumer segment offers strategic and legacy products and services to residential customers that include broadband, wireless, video and Prism TV services. The business segment consists of products and services for commercial, global and governmental customers, and include its private line, broadband, Ethernet, MPLS (multiprotocol label switching), Voice over Internet Protocol (VoIP), network management services, colocation, managed hosting and cloud hosting services. The company provides products and services to customers through its telecommunication network, which consists of voice and data switches, copper cables, fiber-optic cables and other equipment, serving approximately 12.4 million access lines. The company operates over 55 data centers in the U.S., Europe and Asia. Most of CenturyLink's services are sold under the CenturyLink brand, with satellite TV service offered under a co-branded agreement under the DIRECTV brand name and wireless services offered under the firm's agency agreement with Verizon Wireless under the Verizon Wireless name. In December 2014, it acquired Cognilytics, a provider of advanced predictive analytics and big data solutions.

Employee benefits include medical, dental, prescription and vision coverage; an employee assistance program; retirement plans and a 401(k); flexible spending accounts; life and AD&D insurance; short-and long-term disability; and career development programs.

FINANCIAL DATA: Note: Data for latest year may not have been available at press time.

In U.S. $	2016	2015	2014	2013	2012	2011
Revenue		17,900,000,000	18,031,000,000	18,095,000,000	18,376,000,000	15,351,000,000
R&D Expense						
Operating Income		2,605,000,000	2,410,000,000	1,453,000,000	2,713,000,000	2,025,000,000
Operating Margin %		14.55%	13.36%	8.02%	14.76%	13.19%
SGA Expense		3,328,000,000	3,347,000,000	3,502,000,000	3,244,000,000	2,975,000,000
Net Income		878,000,000	772,000,000	-239,000,000	777,000,000	573,000,000
Operating Cash Flow		5,152,000,000	5,188,000,000	5,559,000,000	6,065,000,000	4,201,000,000
Capital Expenditure		2,872,000,000	3,047,000,000	3,048,000,000	2,919,000,000	2,411,000,000
EBITDA		6,817,000,000	6,849,000,000	6,063,000,000	7,349,000,000	6,046,000,000
Return on Assets %		1.79%	1.51%	-.45%	1.41%	1.46%
Return on Equity %		6.03%	4.79%	-1.31%	3.87%	3.76%
Debt to Equity		1.33	1.33	1.17	1.00	1.02

CONTACT INFORMATION:

Phone: 318 388-9000   Fax: 318 789-8656
Toll-Free:
Address: 100 CenturyLink Dr., Monroe, LA 71203 United States

STOCK TICKER/OTHER:

Stock Ticker: CTL   Exchange: NYS
Employees: 45,000   Fiscal Year Ends: 12/31
Parent Company:

SALARIES/BONUSES:

Top Exec. Salary: Bonus: $
$1,250,000
Second Exec. Salary: Bonus: $
$663,138

OTHER THOUGHTS:

Estimated Female Officers or Directors: 5

Hot Spot for Advancement for Women/Minorities: Y

Sales, profits and employees may be estimates. Financial information, benefits and other data can change quickly and may vary from those stated here.

Cerner Corporation

www.cerner.com

NAIC Code: 0

TYPES OF BUSINESS:

Computer Software, Healthcare & Biotechnology
Medical Information Systems
Application Hosting
Integrated Delivery Networks
Access Management
Consulting Services
Safety & Risk Management

BRANDS/DIVISIONS/AFFILIATES:

Cerner Millennium
HealtheIntent
Cerner Health Services
CernerWorks

CONTACTS: *Note: Officers with more than one job title may be intentionally listed here more than once.*

Neal Patterson, CEO
Marc Naughton, CFO
Michael Battaglioli, Chief Accounting Officer
Clifford Illig, Co-Founder
Michael Nill, COO
Jeffrey Townsend, Executive VP
Julia Wilson, Other Executive Officer
Randy Sims, Other Executive Officer
Zane Burke, President

GROWTH PLANS/SPECIAL FEATURES:

Cerner Corporation designs, develops, installs and supports information technology and content applications for health care organizations, consumers and physicians. Cerner's applications are designed to help eliminate error, variance and waste in the care process as well as provide appropriate health information and knowledge to care givers, clinicians and consumers, and appropriate management information to health care administrations. Cerner solutions are offered on the unified Cerner Millennium architecture and on the HealtheIntent cloud-based platform. The Millennium framework combines clinical, financial and management information systems and provides secure access to an individual's electronic medical record at the point of care, and organizes and proactively delivers information to meet the specific needs of the physician, nurse, laboratory technician, pharmacist or other care provider, front- and back-office professionals as well as consumers. The HealtheIntent platform offers EHR-agnostic solutions based on sophisticated, statistical algorithms to help providers predict and improve outcomes, control costs, improve quality and manage the health of their patients. Cerner also offers a broad range of services including implementation and training, remote hosting, operational management services, revenue cycle services, support and maintenance, health care data analysis, clinical process optimization, transaction processing, employer health centers, employee wellness programs and third-party administrator (TPA) services for employer-based health plans. Cerner Health Services offers a portfolio of enterprise-level clinical & financial health care information technology solutions, as well as departmental, connectivity, population health and care coordination solutions globally. CernerWorks is the company's remote-hosting business. Roughly more than 18,000 facilities around the world license Cerner's products. These facilities include hospitals; physician practices; ambulatory facilities such as laboratories, ambulatory centers, cardiac facilities, radiology clinics and surgery centers; home health facilities; and retail pharmacies. In 2015, Cerner acquired Siemens AG's health services business, now referred to as Cerner Health Services.

FINANCIAL DATA: *Note: Data for latest year may not have been available at press time.*

In U.S. $	2016	2015	2014	2013	2012	2011
Revenue		4,425,267,000	3,402,703,000	2,910,748,000	2,665,436,000	2,203,153,000
R&D Expense		539,799,000	289,358,000	338,786,000	219,639,000	286,801,000
Operating Income		781,136,000	763,084,000	576,012,000	571,662,000	459,798,000
Operating Margin %		17.65%	22.42%	19.78%	21.44%	20.87%
SGA Expense		2,262,024,000	1,642,437,000	1,481,228,000	1,184,207,000	1,014,882,000
Net Income		539,362,000	525,433,000	398,354,000	397,232,000	306,627,000
Operating Cash Flow		947,526,000	847,027,000	695,865,000	708,314,000	546,294,000
Capital Expenditure		648,220,000	467,901,000	584,331,000	306,488,000	208,357,000
EBITDA		1,233,361,000	1,080,520,000	855,818,000	815,356,000	687,591,000
Return on Assets %		10.68%	12.17%	10.21%	11.84%	11.30%
Return on Equity %		14.50%	15.60%	13.27%	15.44%	14.54%
Debt to Equity		0.14	0.01	0.03	0.04	0.03

CONTACT INFORMATION:

Phone: 816 221-1024   Fax:
Toll-Free:
Address: 2800 Rockcreek Pkwy., North Kansas City, MO 64117 United States

STOCK TICKER/OTHER:

Stock Ticker: CERN
Employees: 15,800
Parent Company:

Exchange: NAS
Fiscal Year Ends: 12/31

SALARIES/BONUSES:

Top Exec. Salary: Bonus: $
$1,025,000
Second Exec. Salary: Bonus: $
$623,654

OTHER THOUGHTS:

Estimated Female Officers or Directors: 13

Hot Spot for Advancement for Women/Minorities: Y

CH Robinson Worldwide Inc

www.chrobinson.com

NAIC Code: 488510

TYPES OF BUSINESS:

3PL Third Party Logistics
Produce Sourcing
Expedited Services
Fuel Purchasing Management Services
Warehousing
Customs Brokerage
Freight Transportation Arrangements

BRANDS/DIVISIONS/AFFILIATES:

Robinson Fresh
Pink Ribbon Watermelon
ChemSolutions
Freightquote.com

CONTACTS: Note: Officers with more than one job title may be intentionally listed here more than once.

John Wiehoff, CEO
Andrew Clarke, CFO
Chad Lindbloom, Chief Information Officer
Angela Freeman, Other Executive Officer
Christopher OBrien, Other Executive Officer
Ben Campbell, Other Executive Officer
James Lemke, President, Divisional
Jordan Kass, President, Divisional
Jereon Eijsink, President, Divisional
Mike Short, President, Divisional
Robert Biesterfeld, President, Divisional
Thomas Mahlke, Vice President

GROWTH PLANS/SPECIAL FEATURES:

C.H. Robinson Worldwide, Inc. (CHRW) is one of the world's largest third-party logistics (3PL) providers and a global provider of multimodal transportation services. It maintains over 280 offices around the world. CHRW operates in two main sectors: transportation and logistics services and sourcing. In the transportation and logistics services sector, the company (which does not own any of its own equipment) maintains one of the largest global networks of motor carrier capacity through contracts with approximately 66,000 carriers. Annually, CHRW serves more than 46,000 customers and handles over 12.7 million shipments. The group also contracts air carriers, oceans carriers and specialty motor carriers. In addition, it provides value-added logistics services, supply chain analysis, freight consolidation, core carrier program management and information reporting. The sourcing sector focuses on procuring fresh produce for retailers, wholesalers and foodservice operators nationwide. CHRW markets its own brands of produce under Robinson Fresh and Pink Ribbon Watermelon brands, which are sourced through various growers and packed through contract agreements with other packaging firms. Additionally, the company maintains exclusive licensing agreements to distribute fresh produce under various third-party brand names, such as Tropicana, Welch's and Mott's. The company's ChemSolutions division provides logistics services to chemical manufacturing and distribution customers globally. CHRW's division, TMC, offers managed global transportation management system (TMS) software and consulting services, including cloud-based TMS technology. In 2015, the firm acquired Freightquote.com, Inc., a privately-held freight broker.

The firm offers employees medical, dental and vision insurance; a 401(k); an employee stock purchase plan; flexible spending accounts; an employee assistance plan; and employee discounts.

FINANCIAL DATA: Note: Data for latest year may not have been available at press time.

In U.S. $	2016	2015	2014	2013	2012	2011
Revenue		13,476,080,000	13,470,070,000	12,752,080,000	11,359,110,000	10,336,350,000
R&D Expense						
Operating Income		858,310,000	748,418,000	682,650,000	675,320,000	692,730,000
Operating Margin %		6.36%	5.55%	5.35%	5.94%	6.70%
SGA Expense		1,410,170,000	1,259,234,000	1,153,445,000	1,042,251,000	939,928,000
Net Income		509,699,000	449,711,000	415,904,000	593,804,000	431,612,000
Operating Cash Flow		718,336,000	513,426,000	347,777,000	460,342,000	429,712,000
Capital Expenditure		44,642,000	29,502,000	48,206,000	50,656,000	52,806,000
EBITDA		924,719,000	805,427,000	739,532,000	713,410,000	725,228,000
Return on Assets %		15.93%	14.94%	14.83%	24.02%	20.88%
Return on Equity %		46.38%	45.27%	34.03%	43.14%	35.19%
Debt to Equity		0.43	0.47	0.53		

CONTACT INFORMATION:

Phone: 952 937-8500   Fax: 952 937-6714
Toll-Free:
Address: 14701 Charlson Rd., Eden Prairie, MN 55347 United States

STOCK TICKER/OTHER:

Stock Ticker: CHRW   Exchange: NAS
Employees: 13,159   Fiscal Year Ends: 12/31
Parent Company:

SALARIES/BONUSES:

Top Exec. Salary: $291,667   Bonus: $196,063
Second Exec. Salary: $458,750   Bonus: $

OTHER THOUGHTS:

Estimated Female Officers or Directors: 4
Hot Spot for Advancement for Women/Minorities: Y

Change Healthcare Holdings Inc

www.emdeon.com

NAIC Code: 524292

TYPES OF BUSINESS:

Healthcare Business & Administration Management
Claims Processing & Billing

BRANDS/DIVISIONS/AFFILIATES:

Blackstone Group (The)
Intelligent Healthcare Network

CONTACTS: *Note: Officers with more than one job title may be intentionally listed here more than once.*

Neil de Crescenzo, CEO
Randy Giles, CFO
Alex Choy, CIO
Miriam Paramore, Exec. VP-Prod. Mgmt. & Strategy
Gregory T. Stevens, General Counsel
Frank Manzella, Sr. VP-Corp. Dev.
Kevin Mahoney, Exec. VP-Pharmacy Svcs.
Gary D. Stuart, Exec. VP-Payer Svcs.
Sajid Khan, Exec. VP-Ambulatory Svcs.
T. Ulrich Brechbuhl, Exec. VP-Revenue Cycle Solutions

GROWTH PLANS/SPECIAL FEATURES:

Change Healthcare Holdings, Inc. provides technology-enables services for the health care industry. Through its Intelligent Healthcare Network, the firm helps connect payers, providers and patients and then leverages the data needed to deliver predictive insights to clients. Clients then utilize the knowledge to solve problems and to capitalize on business opportunities. The company's solutions include tools and resources that provide actionable insights, exchange mission-critical information, revenue opportunities, cost-effective strategies, increase of cash flow and management of complex healthcare workflows. Specific solutions for providers include patient access, coding, claims/denials, remittance, receivables, revenue discovery, medical networking, clinical networking, ePrescribing networking, self-pay coverage, as well as consulting services. Solutions for payers include coding, integrated pricing, payment accuracy insight, investigations, audit & recovery, third-party liability, changing providers, Medicare/Medicaid, social security, payment, settlement, risk and consultation. Solutions for pharmacies include Medicaid benefit advisory, processing, MedRX advisory, pharmacy networking, pharmacy payer networking and RX claim advisory. In June 2016, the firm, along with McKesson Corporation, announced the creation of a new healthcare information technology company which will be jointly-owned by Change Healthcare (30%) and McKesson (70%). The entity will combine substantially all of Change Healthcare's business and the majority of McKesson Technology Solutions, and is expected to generate in excess of $150 million in annual synergies by the second year following the close of the transaction. Change Healthcare is currently majority-owned by The Blackstone Group.

FINANCIAL DATA: *Note: Data for latest year may not have been available at press time.*

In U.S. $	2016	2015	2014	2013	2012	2011
Revenue		1,477,083,000	1,350,413,000	1,242,567,000	1,152,313,000	1,119,648,000
R&D Expense						
Operating Income						
Operating Margin %						
SGA Expense						
Net Income		-96,069,000	-75,854,000	-74,458,000	-78,335,000	-42,144,000
Operating Cash Flow						
Capital Expenditure						
EBITDA						
Return on Assets %						
Return on Equity %						
Debt to Equity						

CONTACT INFORMATION:

Phone: 615-932-3000   Fax:
Toll-Free:
Address: 3055 Lebanon Pike, Nashville, TN 37214 United States

STOCK TICKER/OTHER:

Stock Ticker: Private   Exchange:
Employees: 4,100   Fiscal Year Ends: 12/31
Parent Company:

SALARIES/BONUSES:

Top Exec. Salary: $ Bonus: $
Second Exec. Salary: $ Bonus: $

OTHER THOUGHTS:

Estimated Female Officers or Directors: 1
Hot Spot for Advancement for Women/Minorities:

Charles Schwab Corp (The)

www.schwab.com

NAIC Code: 523120

TYPES OF BUSINESS:

Stock Brokerage-Retail, Online & Discount
Investment Services
Financial Services
Mutual Funds
Wealth Management
Financial Information
Banking
Online Trading Platform

BRANDS/DIVISIONS/AFFILIATES:

Charles Schwab & Co Inc
Charles Schwab Bank
Charles Schwab Investment Management Inc

CONTACTS: Note: Officers with more than one job title may be intentionally listed here more than once.

Joseph Martinetto, CEO, Subsidiary
Marie Chandoha, CEO, Subsidiary
Walter Bettinger, CEO
Charles Schwab, Chairman of the Board
Nigel Murtagh, Executive VP, Divisional
Terri Kallsen, Executive VP, Divisional
Bernard Clark, Executive VP, Divisional
David Garfield, Executive VP

GROWTH PLANS/SPECIAL FEATURES:

The Charles Schwab Corp. (CSC) engages in securities brokerage, banking, money management and related financial advisory services. The company has managed $2.51 trillion in client brokerage accounts, 9.8 million active brokerage accounts, 1.5 million corporate retirement plan participants and 1 million banking accounts through its primary subsidiary, Charles Schwab & Co., Inc. (Schwab). Schwab is a securities broker-dealer with more than 325 domestic branch offices in 45 states, as well as a branch in each of the Commonwealth of Puerto Rico and London, England. It serves clients in Hong Kong through CSC subsidiaries Charles Schwab Bank, a federal savings bank located in Reno, Nevada; and Charles Schwab Investment Management, Inc., an investment advisor for the company's proprietary mutual and exchange-traded funds. CSC provides its financial services and products such as brokerage, banking, trust, advice and mutual/exchange trade funds to individuals and institutional clients through two segments: investor services and advisor services. Investor services provides retail brokerage and banking services to individual investors, retirement plan services and corporate brokerage services. Advisor services provides custodial, trading and support services to independent investment advisors (IAs), and retirement business services to independent retirement plan advisors and record keepers whose plan assets are held at Schwab Bank.

The firm offers employees medical, dental, life, AD&D and vision insurance; health and dependent care flexible spending accounts; disability coverage; a 401(k) plan; a legal services plan; an employee discount program; an employee stock purchase plan; discounts on company products; and an employee assistance program.

FINANCIAL DATA: Note: Data for latest year may not have been available at press time.

In U.S. $	2016	2015	2014	2013	2012	2011
Revenue		6,369,000,000	6,054,000,000	5,434,000,000	4,899,000,000	4,709,000,000
R&D Expense						
Operating Income		2,279,000,000	2,115,000,000	1,705,000,000	1,450,000,000	1,392,000,000
Operating Margin %		35.78%	34.93%	31.37%	29.59%	29.56%
SGA Expense		2,723,000,000	2,652,000,000	2,504,000,000	2,264,000,000	2,180,000,000
Net Income		1,447,000,000	1,321,000,000	1,071,000,000	928,000,000	864,000,000
Operating Cash Flow		1,246,000,000	2,348,000,000	1,656,000,000	1,266,000,000	2,464,000,000
Capital Expenditure		266,000,000	400,000,000	249,000,000	148,000,000	180,000,000
EBITDA						
Return on Assets %		.80%	.84%	.72%	.72%	.85%
Return on Equity %		11.92%	12.33%	11.07%	10.74%	12.39%
Debt to Equity		0.24	0.17	0.20	0.18	0.25

CONTACT INFORMATION:

Phone: 415 667-7000   Fax: 415 627-8894
Toll-Free: 800-648-5300
Address: 211 Main Street, San Francisco, CA 94105 United States

STOCK TICKER/OTHER:

Stock Ticker: SCHW   Exchange: NYS
Employees: 15,300   Fiscal Year Ends: 12/31
Parent Company:

SALARIES/BONUSES:

Top Exec. Salary: Bonus: $
$1,000,000
Second Exec. Salary: Bonus: $
$610,417

OTHER THOUGHTS:

Estimated Female Officers or Directors: 6

Hot Spot for Advancement for Women/Minorities: Y

Charter Communications Inc

www.charter.com

NAIC Code: 517110

TYPES OF BUSINESS:

Cable TV Service
Internet Access
Advanced Broadband Cable Services
Telephony Services
Voice Over Internet Protocol

BRANDS/DIVISIONS/AFFILIATES:

Charter Security Suite
Charter.net

CONTACTS: *Note: Officers with more than one job title may be intentionally listed here more than once.*

Daniel Bollinger, Assistant General Counsel
Catherine Bohigian, Executive VP, Divisional
Thomas Rutledge, CEO
Christopher Winfrey, CFO
Kevin Howard, Chief Accounting Officer
Jonathan Hargis, Chief Marketing Officer
John Bickham, COO
David Kline, Executive VP, Divisional
Paul Marchand, Executive VP, Divisional
Kathleen Mayo, Executive VP, Divisional
Thomas Adams, Executive VP, Divisional
James Blackley, Executive VP, Divisional
Scott Weber, Executive VP, Divisional
James Nuzzo, Executive VP, Divisional
Richard DiGeronimo, Executive VP, Divisional
Richard Dykhouse, Executive VP

GROWTH PLANS/SPECIAL FEATURES:

Charter Communications, Inc. operates broadband communications businesses in the U.S., offering traditional cable video programming, high-speed Internet access and voice service as well as advanced broadband services. The company serves approximately 4.3 million video customers, 5.2 million high-speed Internet customers and 2.6 million telephone customers. Roughly 61% of these customers are bundle service subscribers. The firm's video services include offerings such as basic video, online video, digital video, premium channels, pay-per-view, On Demand and Subscription On Demand, high definition television (HDTV) and digital video recorder (DVR). The firm offers several tiers of high-speed Internet services with speeds ranging from 30 megabytes per second (Mbps) to 120 Mbps. The company offers the Charter Security Suite, an Internet portal, and Charter.net services. The firm provides voice communications services, primarily using VoIP (voice over Internet protocol) technology, as well as telephone services. Residential video, Internet and voice services generate approximately 83% of Charter's revenue. Commercial services generate approximately 11% of the company's total revenues and include scalable and tailored broadband communications solutions for business organizations, ranging from small businesses to carrier wholesales. Sale of advertising generates the remainder of Charter's total revenues. In May 2016, the company, Time Warner Cable Inc. and Bright House Networks LLC together received final approval from the California Public Utilities Commission for Charter to merge with Time Warner Cable, as well as to acquire Bright House from parent Advance/Newhouse Partnership. The combined company will take on the Charter Communications, Inc. name, and the transaction was expected to close by the end of the month (May 2016).

Employee benefits include medical, dental and vision coverage; a 401(k); flexible spending accounts; health savings accounts; life and AD&D insurance; short- and long-term disability; adoption reimbursement; tuition reimbursement; and employee discounts.

FINANCIAL DATA: *Note: Data for latest year may not have been available at press time.*

In U.S. $	2016	2015	2014	2013	2012	2011
Revenue		9,754,000,000	9,108,000,000	8,155,000,000	7,504,000,000	7,204,000,000
R&D Expense						
Operating Income		1,114,000,000	971,000,000	925,000,000	916,000,000	1,041,000,000
Operating Margin %		11.42%	10.66%	11.34%	12.20%	14.45%
SGA Expense		691,000,000	529,000,000		422,000,000	1,426,000,000
Net Income		-271,000,000	-183,000,000	-169,000,000	-304,000,000	-369,000,000
Operating Cash Flow		2,359,000,000	2,359,000,000	2,158,000,000	1,876,000,000	1,737,000,000
Capital Expenditure		1,812,000,000	2,188,000,000	1,749,000,000	1,732,000,000	1,343,000,000
EBITDA		3,239,000,000	3,073,000,000	2,779,000,000	2,573,000,000	2,485,000,000
Return on Assets %		- .84%	- .87%	-1.02%	-1.94%	-2.35%
Return on Equity %		-542.00%	-123.23%	-112.66%	-108.96%	-39.10%
Debt to Equity			143.99	93.91	85.95	31.43

CONTACT INFORMATION:

Phone: 203-905-7801   Fax:
Toll-Free:
Address: 400 Atlantic Street, Stamford, CT 06901 United States

STOCK TICKER/OTHER:

Stock Ticker: CHTR   Exchange: NAS
Employees: 23,200   Fiscal Year Ends: 12/31
Parent Company:

SALARIES/BONUSES:

Top Exec. Salary: Bonus: $
$2,000,000
Second Exec. Salary: Bonus: $
$1,375,000

OTHER THOUGHTS:

Estimated Female Officers or Directors: 1

Hot Spot for Advancement for Women/Minorities:

Chemed Corporation

www.chemed.com

NAIC Code: 621610

TYPES OF BUSINESS:

Home Health Care Services
Plumbing Services

BRANDS/DIVISIONS/AFFILIATES:

VITAS Healthcare Corporation
Roto-Rooter Corporation

CONTACTS: *Note: Officers with more than one job title may be intentionally listed here more than once.*

Nicholas Westfall, CEO, Subsidiary

GROWTH PLANS/SPECIAL FEATURES:

Chemed Corporation, through its wholly-owned subsidiaries VITAS Healthcare Corporation and Roto-Rooter Corporation, offers hospice care and plumbing services, respectively. VITAS is one of the largest national providers of hospice care and end-of-life services. Its team members include registered nurses, licensed practical nurses, home health aides, physicians, social workers, chaplains and other caregiving professionals. VITAS provides hospice care services in the patient's home, including music therapy and pet visits. Additionally, the firm manages inpatient hospice units, providing service in hospitals, nursing homes and assisted living communities/residential care facilities. More than 90% of VITAS' service revenues consist of payments from Medicare and Medicaid. Roto-Rooter supports the maintenance needs of residential and commercial markets by providing services such as plumbing, drain cleaning, high-pressure water jetting, underground leak and line detection, video camera pipe inspections, grease trap and liquid waste pumping, backflow protection, emergency services, automated drain care programs and pipe repair and replacement. One of the largest businesses of its type in North America, Roto-Rooter operates hundreds of company-owned and franchises throughout the U.S. and in parts of Canada. Moreover, the subsidiary has licensed master franchisees in Japan, Mexico, Hong Kong/China, the U.K., Philippines, Indonesia and Singapore. Concerning revenues, Roto-Rooter's largest share is generated by plumbing repair and maintenance, followed by sewer & drain cleaning, HVAC (heating, ventilation and air conditioning) repair and other products and services.

Employee benefits include medical, prescription and dental coverage; life insurance; short- and long-term disability; a 401(k); profit sharing; flexible spending accounts; and tuition reimbursement.

FINANCIAL DATA: *Note: Data for latest year may not have been available at press time.*

In U.S. $	2016	2015	2014	2013	2012	2011
Revenue		1,543,388,000	1,456,282,000	1,413,329,000	1,430,043,000	1,355,970,000
R&D Expense						
Operating Income		184,458,000	168,419,000	133,394,000	156,419,000	153,727,000
Operating Margin %		11.95%	11.56%	9.43%	10.93%	11.33%
SGA Expense		237,821,000	220,118,000	212,518,000	208,656,000	202,260,000
Net Income		110,274,000	99,317,000	77,227,000	89,304,000	85,979,000
Operating Cash Flow		171,500,000	110,279,000	150,847,000	131,768,000	174,343,000
Capital Expenditure		44,135,000	43,571,000	29,324,000	35,252,000	29,592,000
EBITDA		217,270,000	204,041,000	171,252,000	191,063,000	183,943,000
Return on Assets %		12.88%	11.32%	8.80%	10.78%	10.57%
Return on Equity %		22.86%	22.06%	17.12%	20.60%	19.63%
Debt to Equity		0.16	0.31		0.38	0.40

CONTACT INFORMATION:

Phone: 513 762-6900   Fax: 513 762-6919
Toll-Free:
Address: 255 E. 5th St., 2600 Chemed Ctr., Cincinnati, OH 45202 United States

STOCK TICKER/OTHER:

Stock Ticker: CHE   Exchange: NYS
Employees: 14,406   Fiscal Year Ends: 12/31
Parent Company:

SALARIES/BONUSES:

Top Exec. Salary: $968,167   Bonus: $
Second Exec. Salary: $661,833   Bonus: $

OTHER THOUGHTS:

Estimated Female Officers or Directors: 3
Hot Spot for Advancement for Women/Minorities: Y

Sales, profits and employees may be estimates. Financial information, benefits and other data can change quickly and may vary from those stated here.

Chevron Phillips Chemical Company LLC

www.cpchem.com

NAIC Code: 325110

TYPES OF BUSINESS:

Petrochemical & Plastics Manufacturing
Olefins & Polyolefins
Aromatics & Styrenics
Specialty Chemicals

BRANDS/DIVISIONS/AFFILIATES:

K-Resin SBC
Aromax
Track Tek
Soltex
Chevron Corporation
Phillips 66

CONTACTS: Note: Officers with more than one job title may be intentionally listed here more than once.

Peter Cella, CEO
Peter Cella, Pres.
Tim D. Leveille, CFO
Greg Wagner, VP-Human Resources
Dennis Holtermann, VP-Research & Tech.
Peggy Colsman, CIO
Rick Roberts, Sr. VP-Mfg.
Tim Hill, General Counsel
Ron Corn, VP-Corp. Planning & Dev.
Brian Cain, Head-Corp. Comm.
Tim D. Leveille, Controller
Dan Coombs, Sr. VP-Specialties, Aromatics & Styrenics
Mark Lashier, Exec. VP-Olefins & Polyolefins
Trevor Roberts, Treas.
David Morgan, VP-Polyethylene

GROWTH PLANS/SPECIAL FEATURES:

Chevron Phillips Chemical Company LLC (CPChem) is the combined petrochemical businesses of Chevron Corporation and Phillips 66, both 50% owners. With 34 production and two research centers worldwide, CPChem is an international producer of olefins and polyalphaolefins. It is also a supplier of aromatics, alpha olefins, styrenics, specialty chemicals, polyethylene pipe and proprietary plastics. The company manufactures chemical products that are vital in the various production processes of over 70,000 consumer and industrial products. Its business is separated into two divisions: olefins & polyalphaolefins; and aromatics, styrenics &specialty products. Products in the olefins & polyalphaolefins family consist of ethylene, propylene and their polymer derivatives; olefins & polyalphaolefins; and high-density polyethylene pipe, conduit and pipe fitting. These products are sold as building blocks for other chemicals and as ingredients for use in a variety of end-products, including motor oils, lubricants, plastics, coatings, textiles and packaging. CPChem's aromatics and styrenics include cyclohexane, paraxylene, benzene, styrene, polystyrene and K-Resin SBC, a unique type of copolymer. Aromax is the company's proprietary benzene production process. Aromatics & styrenics are used in the manufacturing of insulation products, housewares, food packaging, electronic parts and media enclosures. Specialty chemicals are used in various applications, including electronics, automobiles, oil and gas well drilling, appliances, agriculture and pharmaceuticals. This division sells TrackTek brand racing fuels and Soltex drill mud additive.

The firm offers employees medical, dental and vision benefits; educational assistance; an employee assistance program; discounts on personal items; and relocation assistance.

FINANCIAL DATA: Note: Data for latest year may not have been available at press time.

In U.S. $	2016	2015	2014	2013	2012	2011
Revenue		9,248,000,000	13,416,000,000	13,147,000,000	13,243,000,000	13,935,000,000
R&D Expense						
Operating Income						
Operating Margin %						
SGA Expense						
Net Income		2,651,000,000	3,288,000,000	2,743,000,000	2,403,000,000	1,970,000,000
Operating Cash Flow						
Capital Expenditure						
EBITDA						
Return on Assets %						
Return on Equity %						
Debt to Equity						

CONTACT INFORMATION:

Phone: 832-813-4100   Fax:
Toll-Free: 800-231-1212
Address: 10001 Six Pines Dr., The Woodlands, TX 77380 United States

STOCK TICKER/OTHER:

Stock Ticker: Joint Venture   Exchange:
Employees: 5,000   Fiscal Year Ends: 12/31
Parent Company: Chevron Corporation

SALARIES/BONUSES:

Top Exec. Salary: $ Bonus: $
Second Exec. Salary: $ Bonus: $

OTHER THOUGHTS:

Estimated Female Officers or Directors: 1
Hot Spot for Advancement for Women/Minorities: Y

Sales, profits and employees may be estimates. Financial information, benefits and other data can change quickly and may vary from those stated here.

Chico's FAS Inc

NAIC Code: 448120

www.chicosfas.com

TYPES OF BUSINESS:

Women's Apparel, Retail
Online & Catalog Sales
Franchising

BRANDS/DIVISIONS/AFFILIATES:

Chico's
White House/Black Market
Soma Intimates
Passport

CONTACTS: *Note: Officers with more than one job title may be intentionally listed here more than once.*

Todd Vogensen, Assistant Secretary
Shelley Broader, CEO
David Oliver, Chief Accounting Officer
Eric Singleton, Chief Information Officer
Ross Roeder, Director
Susan Lanigan, Executive VP
Sara Stensrud, Executive VP
Donna Colaco, President, Divisional
Laurie Van Brunt, President, Divisional
Cynthia Murray, President, Divisional
Sheryl Clark, President, Subsidiary
Sean McCartney, Senior VP, Divisional
Jennifer Adkins, Vice President, Divisional

GROWTH PLANS/SPECIAL FEATURES:

Chico's FAS, Inc. retails exclusively-designed, private label, casual-to-formal clothing, complementary accessories, intimate apparel and gift items for women under the Chico's, White House/Black Market and Soma Intimates brands. Chico's FAS currently operates a total of 1,518 retail stores in 48 states, the U.S. Virgin Islands and Puerto Rico, as well as eCommerce sites for all its brands. The firm also sells merchandise through franchise 37 locations in Mexico. Chico's primarily targets women aged 30 and over with moderate to high income levels. Currently, there are more than 600 Chico's boutique stores and 115 Chico's outlet stores. The majority of the firm's products are designed and developed by its Product Development Team, headquartered in Fort Myers, Florida. The company offers a Passport club membership free of charge, in which customers can receive additional benefits after spending a fixed amount. Chico's FAS also operates the White House/Black Market chain of more than 430 boutiques and over 70 outlet locations that focus on women aged 35 and older who lead active work and social lives with moderate to high income levels. White House/Black Market offers clothes predominately in shades of white and black, although the stores do offer clothing in other colors and a line of denim jeans as well. The Soma Intimates line currently consists of nearly 270 boutique-style stores and over 15 outlet locations. Soma Intimates offers foundation products in intimate apparel, sleepwear, body wear and active wear. In January 2016, the firm sold its Boston Proper direct-to-consumer business to Brentwood Associates, and closed its stores.

FINANCIAL DATA: *Note: Data for latest year may not have been available at press time.*

In U.S. $	2016	2015	2014	2013	2012	2011
Revenue	2,642,309,000	2,675,211,000	2,586,037,000	2,581,057,000	2,196,360,000	1,904,954,000
R&D Expense						
Operating Income	-13,084,000	116,343,000	141,183,000	287,538,000	222,377,000	177,082,000
Operating Margin %	-.49%	4.34%	5.45%	11.14%	10.12%	9.29%
SGA Expense	1,282,585,000	1,263,134,000	1,202,068,000	1,161,105,000	998,861,000	889,625,000
Net Income	1,946,000	64,641,000	65,883,000	180,219,000	140,874,000	115,394,000
Operating Cash Flow	196,991,000	282,483,000	236,682,000	368,273,000	255,181,000	239,626,000
Capital Expenditure	84,841,000	119,817,000	138,510,000	164,690,000	131,757,000	73,045,000
EBITDA	105,716,000	238,612,000	259,486,000	396,009,000	321,807,000	271,195,000
Return on Assets %	.14%	4.60%	4.46%	11.99%	9.91%	8.43%
Return on Equity %	.24%	6.97%	6.58%	17.14%	13.58%	11.27%
Debt to Equity	0.12					

CONTACT INFORMATION:

Phone: 239 277-6200   Fax: 239 277-5237
Toll-Free: 888-550-5559
Address: 11215 Metro Pkwy., Fort Myers, FL 33966 United States

STOCK TICKER/OTHER:

Stock Ticker: CHS   Exchange: NYS
Employees: 23,800   Fiscal Year Ends: 01/31
Parent Company:

SALARIES/BONUSES:

Top Exec. Salary: $950,000   Bonus: $
Second Exec. Salary: Bonus: $400,000
$338,462

OTHER THOUGHTS:

Estimated Female Officers or Directors: 11
Hot Spot for Advancement for Women/Minorities: Y

Cigna Corporation

NAIC Code: 524114

TYPES OF BUSINESS:

Insurance-Medical & Health, HMOs & PPOs
Indemnity Insurance
Investment Management Services
Group Life, Accident & Disability

BRANDS/DIVISIONS/AFFILIATES:

CONTACTS: Note: Officers with more than one job title may be intentionally listed here more than once.

David Cordani, CEO
Thomas McCarthy, CFO
Isaiah Harris, Chairman of the Board
Mary Hoeltzel, Chief Accounting Officer
Mark Boxer, Chief Information Officer
Lisa Bacus, Chief Marketing Officer
John Murabito, Executive VP, Divisional
Nicole Jones, Executive VP
Matthew Manders, President, Divisional
Jason Sadler, President, Divisional
Herbert Fritch, President, Subsidiary
Neil Tanner, Secretary

GROWTH PLANS/SPECIAL FEATURES:

Cigna Corporation is a global health services organization. Along with its insurance subsidiaries, the company is a major provider of medical, dental, disability, life and accident insurance and related products and services, the majority of which are offered through employers and other groups. Cigna operates in three segments: global health care, global supplemental benefits and group disability & life. The global health care segment accounts for 80% of annual revenue, and is comprised of two divisions: commercial and government. The commercial division consists of global health benefits, products and services designed to meet the needs of local and multinational companies and organizations, along with their domestic and globally mobile employees and dependents. The government division offers Medicare Advantage and Medicare Part D plans to seniors, as well as Medicaid plans. The global supplemental benefits segment accounts for 9% of annual revenue, and offers supplemental health, life and accident insurance products mainly in Asia, Europe and the United States. In addition, it offers services to globally mobile individuals and local citizens through partnerships and local licensing. In China, India and Turkey, products are offered through joint ventures. The group disability & life segment accounts for 11% of annual revenue, and provides group long-term and short-term disability insurance, group life insurance and accident and specialty insurance. These products and services are provided by the firm's subsidiaries. Cigna's other operations include corporate-owned life insurance, deferred gains, run-off reinsurance and its run-off settlement annuity business. In 2015, Cigna agreed to acquire giant competitor Anthem, Inc. in a deal worth $48 billion. In July 2016, the U.S. Department of Justice challenged the merger, causing Cigna to announce the merger would close in 2017 at the earliest, if at all.

Employee benefits include child/dependent care, adoption assistance, onsite health centers and an employee assistance program.

FINANCIAL DATA: Note: Data for latest year may not have been available at press time.

In U.S. $	2016	2015	2014	2013	2012	2011
Revenue		37,876,000,000	34,914,000,000	32,380,000,000	29,119,000,000	21,998,000,000
R&D Expense						
Operating Income		3,327,000,000	3,304,000,000	2,176,000,000	2,477,000,000	1,968,000,000
Operating Margin %		8.78%	9.46%	6.72%	8.50%	8.94%
SGA Expense		2,134,000,000	10,011,000,000	7,566,000,000	7,187,000,000	5,901,000,000
Net Income		2,094,000,000	2,102,000,000	1,476,000,000	1,623,000,000	1,327,000,000
Operating Cash Flow		2,717,000,000	1,994,000,000	719,000,000	2,350,000,000	1,491,000,000
Capital Expenditure		510,000,000	473,000,000	527,000,000	408,000,000	422,000,000
EBITDA						
Return on Assets %		3.70%	3.81%	2.73%	3.09%	2.74%
Return on Equity %		18.36%	19.69%	14.51%	17.92%	17.70%
Debt to Equity		0.41	0.46	0.47	0.51	0.59

CONTACT INFORMATION:

Phone: 860 226-6000   Fax: 215 761-3596
Toll-Free: 800-997-1654
Address: 900 Cottage Grove Rd., Bloomfield, CT 06002 United States

STOCK TICKER/OTHER:

Stock Ticker: CI   Exchange: NYS
Employees: 37,200   Fiscal Year Ends: 12/31
Parent Company:

SALARIES/BONUSES:

Top Exec. Salary: Bonus: $
$1,189,615
Second Exec. Salary: Bonus: $
$1,000,000

OTHER THOUGHTS:

Estimated Female Officers or Directors: 4

Hot Spot for Advancement for Women/Minorities: Y

Cintas Corporation

www.cintas.com

NAIC Code: 812331

TYPES OF BUSINESS:

Linen & Uniform Supply
Uniform Rental, Sales & Cleaning
Uniform Design & Manufacturing
Outsourcing Services
Dust Control Services
Restroom Cleaning Services
First Aid & Safety Products

BRANDS/DIVISIONS/AFFILIATES:

CONTACTS: *Note: Officers with more than one job title may be intentionally listed here more than once.*

Scott Farmer, CEO
J. Hansen, CFO
Richard Farmer, Chairman Emeritus
Robert Kohlhepp, Chairman of the Board
J. Holloman, COO
Thomas Frooman, General Counsel
Paul Adler, Vice President

GROWTH PLANS/SPECIAL FEATURES:

Cintas Corporation provides highly specialized products and services to corporate customers in North America. The company is a leading corporate identity uniform supplier, as well as a supplier of entrance and logo mats, restroom supplies, promotional products, first aid, safety, fire protection products and industrial carpet/tile cleaning services. Cintas operates through two business primary segments: uniform rental & facilities services and first aid & safety services. The uniform rental & facility services segment consists of the rental and servicing of uniforms and other garments, including flame-resistant clothing, mats, mops, shop towels and other ancillary items. This segment also provides restroom cleaning supplies and services; carpet and tile cleaning services; and the sale of items from Cintas' catalogs. The first aid & safety services segment consists of first aid and safety products and services, as well as fire protection products and services. The company provides these products and services to over 900,000 businesses of all types, from small service and manufacturing companies to major corporations that employ thousands of people. In October 2015, the firm sold its investment in Shred-it International, Inc. to Stericycle, Inc.

Employee benefits include flexible spending accounts; medical, prescription drug, dental and vision coverage; disability; and wellness programs.

FINANCIAL DATA: *Note: Data for latest year may not have been available at press time.*

In U.S. $	2016	2015	2014	2013	2012	2011
Revenue	4,905,458,000	4,476,886,000	4,551,812,000	4,316,471,000	4,102,000,000	3,810,384,000
R&D Expense						
Operating Income	781,748,000	696,407,000	567,010,000	565,211,000	539,627,000	440,343,000
Operating Margin %	15.93%	15.55%	12.45%	13.09%	13.15%	11.55%
SGA Expense	1,348,122,000	1,224,930,000	1,302,752,000	1,221,856,000	1,198,981,000	1,168,944,000
Net Income	693,520,000	430,618,000	374,442,000	315,442,000	297,637,000	246,989,000
Operating Cash Flow	465,845,000	580,276,000	607,969,000	552,748,000	469,862,000	340,886,000
Capital Expenditure	275,385,000	217,720,000	145,580,000	196,486,000	160,802,000	182,592,000
EBITDA	947,923,000	864,061,000	841,900,000	731,284,000	697,400,000	593,259,000
Return on Assets %	16.71%	9.95%	8.50%	7.41%	6.99%	5.93%
Return on Equity %	36.74%	20.87%	17.04%	14.53%	13.40%	10.21%
Debt to Equity	0.56	0.67	0.59	0.59	0.49	0.55

CONTACT INFORMATION:

Phone: 513 459-1200   Fax: 513 573-4030
Toll-Free:
Address: 6800 Cintas Blvd., Cincinnati, OH 45262 United States

STOCK TICKER/OTHER:

Stock Ticker: CTAS   Exchange: NAS
Employees: 32,000   Fiscal Year Ends: 05/31
Parent Company:

SALARIES/BONUSES:

Top Exec. Salary: $1,000,000   Bonus: $

Second Exec. Salary: $643,966   Bonus: $

OTHER THOUGHTS:

Estimated Female Officers or Directors: 1

Hot Spot for Advancement for Women/Minorities:

Sales, profits and employees may be estimates. Financial information, benefits and other data can change quickly and may vary from those stated here.

Cisco Systems Inc

www.cisco.com

NAIC Code: 0

TYPES OF BUSINESS:
Computer Networking Equipment
Routers & Switches
Real-Time Conferencing Technology
Server Virtualization Software
Data Storage Products
Security Products
Teleconference Systems and Technology
Unified Communications Systems

BRANDS/DIVISIONS/AFFILIATES:
Cisco Unified Computing System
Embrane
MaintenanceNet
Portcullis Computer Security
ParStream
OpenDNS

CONTACTS: Note: Officers with more than one job title may be intentionally listed here more than once.
Charles Robbins, CEO
John Chambers, Chairman of the Board
Prat Bhatt, Chief Accounting Officer
Karen Walker, Chief Marketing Officer
Chris Dedicoat, Executive VP, Divisional
Kelly Kramer, Executive VP
Mark Chandler, General Counsel
Rebecca Jacoby, Other Executive Officer

GROWTH PLANS/SPECIAL FEATURES:
Cisco Systems, Inc. designs and sells broad lines of products provides services and delivers integrated solutions to develop and connect networks around the world, building the Internet The company is organized into three geographic segments: the Americas; Europe, Middle East & Africa (EMEA); and Asia Pacific, Japan & China (APJC). Its products and technologies are grouped into: switching, next-generation network routing, collaboration, service provider video, data center, wireless and security. Switching is an integral networking technology used in campuses, branch offices and data centers. It is used within buildings in local-area networks (LANs) and across great distances in wide-area networks (WANs). Switching products offer forms of connectivity to end users, workstations, IP phones, wireless access points and servers. NGN routing technology interconnects public and private wireline and mobile networks for mobile, data, voice and video applications This segment's portfolio of hardware & software solutions consists of physical & virtual routers, as well as routing and optical systems. Collaboration integrates voice, video, data and mobile applications on fixed & mobile networks across a wide range of devices and related IT equipment. Service provider video systems and digital interactive devices enable service providers and content originators to deliver entertainment information & communication services to consumers and businesses worldwide. Data center's Cisco Unified Computing System enables fast IT and scalability for workloads, data analytics and cloud-native applications and infrastructures Wireless access via wireless fidelity (Wi-Fi) is a technology that provides indoor & outdoor coverage with seamless roaming for voice, video and data applications. Security aims to protect the digital economy of Cisco customers. During 2015, the firm announced its intent to acquire Acano Limited and Lancope Inc. It acquired Embrane, MaintenanceNet, Portcullis Computer Security, ParStream and OpenDNS; and divested its television set-top-box and cable modem business to Technicolor SA.

FINANCIAL DATA: Note: Data for latest year may not have been available at press time.

In U.S. $	2016	2015	2014	2013	2012	2011
Revenue	49,247,000,000	49,161,000,000	47,142,000,000	48,607,000,000	46,061,000,000	43,218,000,000
R&D Expense	6,296,000,000	6,207,000,000	6,294,000,000	5,942,000,000	5,488,000,000	5,823,000,000
Operating Income	12,660,000,000	10,770,000,000	9,345,000,000	11,196,000,000	10,065,000,000	7,674,000,000
Operating Margin %	25.70%	21.90%	19.82%	23.03%	21.85%	17.75%
SGA Expense	11,433,000,000	11,861,000,000	11,437,000,000	11,802,000,000	11,969,000,000	11,720,000,000
Net Income	10,739,000,000	8,981,000,000	7,853,000,000	9,983,000,000	8,041,000,000	6,490,000,000
Operating Cash Flow	13,570,000,000	12,552,000,000	12,332,000,000	12,894,000,000	11,491,000,000	10,079,000,000
Capital Expenditure	1,146,000,000	1,227,000,000	1,275,000,000	1,160,000,000	1,126,000,000	1,174,000,000
EBITDA	15,746,000,000	14,209,000,000	12,711,000,000	14,161,000,000	13,357,000,000	10,939,000,000
Return on Assets %	9.13%	8.21%	7.61%	10.34%	8.99%	7.71%
Return on Equity %	17.42%	15.43%	13.56%	18.08%	16.32%	14.18%
Debt to Equity	0.38	0.35	0.36	0.21	0.31	0.34

CONTACT INFORMATION:
Phone: 408 526-4000   Fax: 408 526-4100
Toll-Free: 800-553-6387
Address: 170 W. Tasman Dr., San Jose, CA 95134 United States

STOCK TICKER/OTHER:
Stock Ticker: CSCO   Exchange: NAS
Employees: 71,833   Fiscal Year Ends: 07/31
Parent Company:

SALARIES/BONUSES:
Top Exec. Salary: $632,866   Bonus: $500,000
Second Exec. Salary: Bonus: $
$1,100,000

OTHER THOUGHTS:
Estimated Female Officers or Directors: 10
Hot Spot for Advancement for Women/Minorities: Y

Citigroup Inc

www.citigroup.com

NAIC Code: 522110

TYPES OF BUSINESS:

Banking
Commercial, Residential & Consumer Lending
Credit Cards
Investment Banking
Insurance
Brokerage Services
Equity
Cash Management

BRANDS/DIVISIONS/AFFILIATES:

Citicorp
Citi Holdings
Citi
Citibank
CitiMortgage
Banamex

CONTACTS: Note: Officers with more than one job title may be intentionally listed here more than once.

Stephen Bird, CEO, Divisional
James Forese, CEO, Divisional
William Mills, CEO, Geographical
Jim Cowles, CEO, Geographical
Francisco Aristeguieta, CEO, Geographical
Jane Fraser, CEO, Geographical
Barbara Desoer, CEO, Subsidiary
Michael Corbat, CEO
John Gerspach, CFO
Michael ONeill, Chairman of the Board
Jeffrey Walsh, Chief Accounting Officer
Bradford Hu, Chief Risk Officer
Rohan Weerasinghe, General Counsel

GROWTH PLANS/SPECIAL FEATURES:

Citigroup, Inc. is a diversified financial services holding company and one of the largest banking organizations in the world. The firm is organized into two segments: Citicorp and Citi Holdings. Citicorp consists of the company's global consumer banking business, which provides retail banking, local commercial banking, investment services and Citi-branded credit cards; and the institutional clients group, which provides investment banking, debt & equity, lending, real estate, cash management, clearing and trade services. This segment also includes corporate/other, which comprises the firm's treasury operations, its technology & global staff functions, as well as other corporate expenses. Citicorp has operations in North America, Europe, Latin America, Middle East, Africa and Asia. Half of its loans, deposits, revenues and net income are generated from outside the U.S. Citi Holdings operates the company's brokerage and asset management and local consumer lending businesses as well as managing a special asset pool. Citigroup has a number of brands including Citibank, which offers banking services from more than 2,994 branches in 24 countries worldwide; CitiMortgage, which offers a variety of mortgage products; and Banamex, a major commercial bank in Mexico. In 2015, Citigroup sold its retail banking and credit cards businesses in Japan; and sold personal loan provider, OneMain Financial. In 2016, the firm was in talks with Itau Unibanco Holding SA to sell its Brazilian consumer banking operations, and announced plans to also sell its consumer operations in Argentina and Colombia. That same year, it sold its 20% stake in China Guangfa Bank to China Life Insurance Company Ltd.; and announced plans to delist from Tokyo Stock Exchange.

FINANCIAL DATA: Note: Data for latest year may not have been available at press time.

In U.S. $	2016	2015	2014	2013	2012	2011
Revenue		76,354,000,000	76,882,000,000	76,366,000,000	70,173,000,000	78,353,000,000
R&D Expense						
Operating Income		24,826,000,000	14,364,000,000	19,497,000,000	7,936,000,000	14,624,000,000
Operating Margin %		32.51%	18.68%	25.53%	11.30%	18.66%
SGA Expense		29,897,000,000	32,239,000,000	31,991,000,000	33,342,000,000	33,167,000,000
Net Income		17,242,000,000	7,313,000,000	13,673,000,000	7,541,000,000	11,067,000,000
Operating Cash Flow		39,737,000,000	45,434,000,000	57,410,000,000	14,271,000,000	44,741,000,000
Capital Expenditure		3,198,000,000	3,386,000,000	3,490,000,000	3,604,000,000	3,448,000,000
EBITDA						
Return on Assets %		.90%	.35%	.71%	.40%	.58%
Return on Equity %		8.02%	3.36%	7.01%	4.12%	6.48%
Debt to Equity		0.98	1.11	1.11	1.28	1.82

CONTACT INFORMATION:

Phone: 212 559-1000   Fax: 212 816-8913
Toll-Free: 800-285-3000
Address: 388 Greenwich Street, New York, NY 10013 United States

STOCK TICKER/OTHER:

Stock Ticker: C   Exchange: NYS
Employees: 231,000   Fiscal Year Ends: 12/31
Parent Company:

SALARIES/BONUSES:

Top Exec. Salary: Bonus: $6,000,000
$1,500,000
Second Exec. Salary: Bonus: $6,201,315
$496,712

OTHER THOUGHTS:

Estimated Female Officers or Directors: 5

Hot Spot for Advancement for Women/Minorities: Y

Sales, profits and employees may be estimates. Financial information, benefits and other data can change quickly and may vary from those stated here.

Citrix Systems Inc

www.citrix.com

NAIC Code: 0

TYPES OF BUSINESS:

Computer Software-Application Server
Consulting Services
Training & Technical Support
Online Services

BRANDS/DIVISIONS/AFFILIATES:

XenApp
XenDesktop
XenServer
Citrix NetScaler
GoToMeeting
Subscription Advantage
ByteMobile Smart Capacity
Citrix CloudPlatform

CONTACTS: Note: Officers with more than one job title may be intentionally listed here more than once.

Robert Calderoni, Chairman of the Board
Jessica Soisson, Chief Accounting Officer
Timothy Minahan, Chief Marketing Officer
David Henshall, COO
Kirill Tatarinov, Director
William Burley, Former General Manager, Divisional
Antonio Gomes, General Counsel
Christopher Hylen, General Manager, Divisional
Klaus Oestermann, General Manager, Divisional
Jesse Lipson, General Manager, Divisional
Carlos Sartorius, Senior VP, Geographical

GROWTH PLANS/SPECIAL FEATURES:

Citrix Systems, Inc. designs, develops and markets products that allow applications to be delivered, supported and shared on demand. The firm's desktop virtualization solutions, XenApp and XenDesktop, reduce the complexity and cost of desktop management by virtualizing the desktop and applications in the datacenter. XenApp runs the business logic of applications on a central server, transmitting only screen pixels, keystrokes and mouse movements through an encrypted channel to users' computers. XenDesktop streams desktop images through multiple virtual machines. The firm's Software as a Service (SaaS) division includes products such as GoToMyPC, GoToMeeting, GoToTraining, GoToMyAssist, Podio and GoToWebinar, which are designed to provide web-based access to office resources for offsite locations. The datacenter and cloud solutions product groups include virtual infrastructure and application networking products. Virtual infrastructure includes the XenServer, a server virtualization solution that aggregates a pool of computing and storage resources. Networking and cloud applications, through products including Citrix NetScalar, ByteMobile Smart Capacity, Citrix CloudPlatform, Citrix XenServer and Citrix CloudBridge, are designed to improve application performance, access datacenter resources in offsite locations and deliver local area network-like performance over a wide area network. The technical services division provides consulting services, technical support and product training to support Citrix products. In addition, Subscription Advantage allows customers to budget for product updates and update software versions as they become available. One year of Subscription Advantage is bundled in with the purchase of any product. In November 2015, the firm announced plans to spin off its GoTo family of products into a separate, publicly-traded company by mid-2016.

Citrix offers employees medical, dental, prescription and vision benefits; onsite fitness centers; flex-hours; a company matched 401(k); and paid time off.

FINANCIAL DATA: Note: Data for latest year may not have been available at press time.

In U.S. $	2016	2015	2014	2013	2012	2011
Revenue		3,275,594,000	3,142,856,000	2,918,434,000	2,586,123,000	2,206,392,000
R&D Expense		563,975,000	553,817,000	516,338,000	450,571,000	343,727,000
Operating Income		350,085,000	302,311,000	380,717,000	390,778,000	416,966,000
Operating Margin %		10.68%	9.61%	13.04%	15.11%	18.89%
SGA Expense		1,538,027,000	1,600,187,000	1,476,916,000	1,306,088,000	1,147,088,000
Net Income		319,361,000	251,723,000	339,523,000	352,547,000	356,322,000
Operating Cash Flow		1,034,548,000	845,981,000	928,343,000	818,527,000	679,122,000
Capital Expenditure		172,228,000	179,093,000	175,042,000	150,718,000	127,369,000
EBITDA		748,909,000	634,308,000	648,217,000	605,651,000	576,221,000
Return on Assets %		5.81%	4.69%	6.78%	7.92%	9.13%
Return on Equity %		15.40%	9.16%	10.54%	12.04%	13.48%
Debt to Equity		0.67	0.59			

CONTACT INFORMATION:

Phone: 954 267-3000   Fax: 954 267-9319
Toll-Free: 800-424-8749
Address: 851 W. Cypress Creek Rd., Fort Lauderdale, FL 33309 United States

STOCK TICKER/OTHER:

Stock Ticker: CTXS   Exchange: NAS
Employees: 10,081   Fiscal Year Ends: 12/31
Parent Company:

SALARIES/BONUSES:

Top Exec. Salary: $740,057   Bonus: $
Second Exec. Salary: $690,000   Bonus: $

OTHER THOUGHTS:

Estimated Female Officers or Directors: 2
Hot Spot for Advancement for Women/Minorities:

Sales, profits and employees may be estimates. Financial information, benefits and other data can change quickly and may vary from those stated here.

Cleveland Clinic Foundation (The)

www.clevelandclinic.org

NAIC Code: 622110

TYPES OF BUSINESS:

General Medical and Surgical Hospitals

BRANDS/DIVISIONS/AFFILIATES:

Glickman Urological & Kidney Institute
Lerner Research Institute
Lerner College of Medicine

CONTACTS:

Note: Officers with more than one job title may be intentionally listed here more than once.

Delos M. Cosgrove, CEO
Delos M. Cosgrove, Pres.
Steven C. Glass, CFO
Paul Matsen, CMO
Robert Wyllie, Chief Medical Oper. Officer
C. Martin Harris, CIO
Cindy Hundorfean, Chief Admin. Officer-Clinical Svcs.
David W. Rowan, Chief Legal Officer
William M. Peacock, III, Chief-Oper.
Michael Harrington, Chief Acct. Officer
Kristen D.W. Morris, Chief Gov't. & Community Rel. Officer
Linda McHugh, Exec. Admin.-CEO & Board of Governors
K. Kelly Hancock, Interim Exec. Chief Nursing Officer
Ann Huston, Chief Strategy Officer
Robert E. Rich, Jr., Chmn.

GROWTH PLANS/SPECIAL FEATURES:

The Cleveland Clinic Foundation is a nonprofit clinic in Ohio that combines medical care with education and research. It is noted for very advanced surgical techniques and advanced care. Founded in 1921, it serves 5.1 million patients per year across the nation and internationally. The Cleveland Clinic has over 4,500 beds across its system, and over 3,400 scientists and physicians work within the system. Facilities include the main hospital; more than 150 outpatient regional care centers, including 18 full-service family health centers and three health & wellness centers in Ohio. Additionally, there are Cleveland Clinics in Florida, comprising hospital, emergency and outpatient services, as well as cancer, neurological care, family health and wellness centers; in Nevada, which has a center for brain health, as well as the Glickman Urological & Kidney Institute; in Canada, with 28,000 square feet of offices in Toronto offering health, sports health and lifestyle management programs; and Abu Dhabi, which has 4.4 million square feet, up to 490 beds, a heart and vascular center, a digestive disease center, an eye center, a neurological center and a respiratory and critical care center. Cleveland's Lerner Research Institute is home of all laboratory-based research by the firm, as well as many translational and clinical studies. The institute comprises 1,500 scientists and support personnel, and is actively involved in programs such as cardiovascular, oncologic, neurologic, allergic, immunologic, musculoskeletal, metabolic, infectious diseases and eye diseases. The Lerner College of Medicine has an enrollment of 160 students obtaining MD degrees with an emphasis on clinical research skills.

Employee benefits include pension and savings plans; health, dental and vision insurance; life insurance; short- and long-term disability; adoption assistance; and an employee wellness program.

FINANCIAL DATA:

Note: Data for latest year may not have been available at press time.

In U.S. $	2016	2015	2014	2013	2012	2011
Revenue		7,156,972,000	6,687,379,000	6,450,159,000	6,187,137,000	6,000,000,000
R&D Expense						
Operating Income						
Operating Margin %						
SGA Expense						
Net Income		480,224,000	467,543,000	293,995,000	157,069,000	200,000,000
Operating Cash Flow						
Capital Expenditure						
EBITDA						
Return on Assets %						
Return on Equity %						
Debt to Equity						

CONTACT INFORMATION:

Phone: 216-444-2200   Fax:
Toll-Free:
Address: 2049 E. 100th St., Cleveland, OH 44195 United States

STOCK TICKER/OTHER:

Stock Ticker: Nonprofit   Exchange:
Employees: 41,000   Fiscal Year Ends: 12/31
Parent Company:

SALARIES/BONUSES:

Top Exec. Salary: $ Bonus: $
Second Exec. Salary: $ Bonus: $

OTHER THOUGHTS:

Estimated Female Officers or Directors: 22
Hot Spot for Advancement for Women/Minorities: Y

Clorox Company (The)

NAIC Code: 325611

www.thecloroxcompany.com

TYPES OF BUSINESS:

Cleaning/Laundry Products-Manufacturing
Automotive Care Products
Pesticides
Cat Litter
Water Filtration Products
Charcoal
Domestic Plastics
Dressings & Sauces

BRANDS/DIVISIONS/AFFILIATES:

Clorox
Clorox 2
Tilex
Liquid-Plumr
Formula 409
Hidden Valley
Ayudin
Renew Life

CONTACTS: Note: Officers with more than one job title may be intentionally listed here more than once.

Stephen Robb, CFO
Kirsten Marriner, Other Executive Officer
Thomas Johnson, Chief Accounting Officer
Manjit Singh, Chief Information Officer
Eric Reynolds, Chief Marketing Officer
Dawn Willoughby, COO, Divisional
Nikolaos Vlahos, COO, Divisional
Benno Dorer, Director
George Harad, Director
James Foster, Executive VP, Divisional
Laura Stein, Executive VP, Divisional
Jon Balousek, General Manager, Divisional
Matthew Laszlo, Other Executive Officer
Denise Garner, Other Executive Officer
William Bailey, Senior VP, Divisional
Linda Rendle, Senior VP, Divisional
Michael Costello, Senior VP, Divisional

GROWTH PLANS/SPECIAL FEATURES:

The Clorox Company is a leading producer of consumer and institutional products. Its operations consist of four business segments: cleaning, lifestyle, household and international. Cleaning consists of laundry, home-care and professional products that are sold in the U.S. These products include Clorox branded bleaches; Clorox 2 branded color boosters and stain fighters; home-care products sold under the Pine-Sol S.O.S., Tilex, Liquid-Plumr and Formula 409 brands; and natural cleaning products sold under the Green Works brand name. The lifestyle segment consists of food products, water-filtration systems, filters and all-natural personal care products. These products include sauces and dressing marketed under the KC Masterpiece and Hidden Valley brands, Brita water-filtration systems and filters and Burt's Bees natural personal care products. The household segment consists of charcoal, cat litter, plastic bags, wraps and container products. Brands in this division include Glad, Kingsford, Match Light, Ever Clean Scoop Away and Fresh Step. The international segment includes brands and products marketed outside the U.S. Clorox sells its products internationally under such brand names as Ayudin, PinoLuz, Bon Bril and Lestoil. Clorox's products are manufactured in over 12 countries and are sold through grocery stores, retail outlets and mass merchandisers to consumers in more than 100 countries. Within the U.S., the company also sells institutional, janitorial, health care and food-service versions of many of its products through distributors as well as natural personal care products through the Internet. In March 2016, the firm acquired Renew Life, a leading brand in dietary health, with an emphasis on the digestive system.

FINANCIAL DATA: Note: Data for latest year may not have been available at press time.

In U.S. $	2016	2015	2014	2013	2012	2011
Revenue	5,761,000,000	5,655,000,000	5,591,000,000	5,623,000,000	5,468,000,000	5,231,000,000
R&D Expense	141,000,000	136,000,000	125,000,000	130,000,000	121,000,000	115,000,000
Operating Income	1,064,000,000	1,000,000,000	958,000,000	966,000,000	903,000,000	659,000,000
Operating Margin %	18.46%	17.68%	17.13%	17.17%	16.51%	12.59%
SGA Expense	1,393,000,000	1,321,000,000	1,269,000,000	1,307,000,000	1,280,000,000	1,237,000,000
Net Income	648,000,000	580,000,000	558,000,000	572,000,000	541,000,000	557,000,000
Operating Cash Flow	778,000,000	874,000,000	767,000,000	775,000,000	612,000,000	698,000,000
Capital Expenditure	172,000,000	125,000,000	138,000,000	194,000,000	192,000,000	228,000,000
EBITDA	1,236,000,000	1,190,000,000	1,144,000,000	1,157,000,000	1,094,000,000	859,000,000
Return on Assets %	14.92%	13.77%	13.02%	13.20%	12.70%	12.77%
Return on Equity %	312.28%	426.47%	372.00%	10400.00%		
Debt to Equity	6.05	15.22	10.35	14.86		

CONTACT INFORMATION:

Phone: 510 271-7000   Fax: 510 832-1463
Toll-Free:
Address: 1221 Broadway, Oakland, CA 94612-1888 United States

STOCK TICKER/OTHER:

Stock Ticker: CLX
Employees: 8,000
Parent Company:

Exchange: NYS
Fiscal Year Ends: 06/30

SALARIES/BONUSES:

Top Exec. Salary: $1,154,423   Bonus: $

Second Exec. Salary: $789,762   Bonus: $

OTHER THOUGHTS:

Estimated Female Officers or Directors: 3

Hot Spot for Advancement for Women/Minorities: Y

Coca-Cola Bottling Co Consolidated

www.cokeconsolidated.com

NAIC Code: 312111

TYPES OF BUSINESS:

Beverages-Soft Drink Manufacturing
Bottling Services

BRANDS/DIVISIONS/AFFILIATES:

Coca Cola Company (The)
Dr. Pepper
Country Breeze
Tum-E Yummies
POWERade
Monster Energy
Dasani
Bean and Body

CONTACTS: Note: Officers with more than one job title may be intentionally listed here more than once.

J. Harrison, CEO
Clifford Deal, CFO
William Billiard, Chief Accounting Officer
Umesh Kasbekar, Director
Morgan Everett, Director
James Harris, Executive VP, Divisional
Robert Chambless, Executive VP, Divisional
David Katz, Executive VP, Divisional
Henry Flint, President
Lauren Steele, Senior VP, Divisional
Kimberly Kuo, Senior VP, Divisional
Michael Strong, Senior VP, Divisional

GROWTH PLANS/SPECIAL FEATURES:

Coca-Cola Bottling Co. Consolidated (CCB), founded in 1902, is a nonalcoholic beverage manufacturer and distributor. The firm primarily produces, markets and distributes products of The Coca-Cola Company, which owns approximately 34.8% of CCB. The company manufactures products in two categories: sparkling beverages, which consist of beverages with carbonation, including energy drinks; and still beverages, including bottled water, tea, ready-to-drink coffee, enhanced water, juices and sports drinks. CCB distributes and markets still beverages of The Coca-Cola Company such as POWERade, Dasani water, vitaminwater and Minute Maid Juices To Go in certain regions. It also produces and markets Dr. Pepper, Monster Energy and Sundrop in some of its regions. In addition, the company markets and distributes certain products which it owns, including Country Breeze tea and diet Country Breeze tea; Bean and Body coffee beverages; Fuel in a Bottle power shots; and Tum-E Yummies, a vitamin C enhanced flavored drink. The company's principal soft drink is Coca-Cola classic, and products of The Coca-Cola Company generate more than half of CCB's bottle/can volume to retail customers. CCB holds bottling rights from The Coca-Cola Company covering the majority of North Carolina, South Carolina and West Virginia as well as portions of Alabama, Mississippi, Tennessee, Kentucky, Virginia, Pennsylvania, Georgia and Florida. The main packaging materials for the firm's beverages are plastic bottles and aluminum cans. In addition, the company provides restaurants and other immediate consumption outlets with fountain products. The company operates 46 sales locations and five manufacturing facilities across eleven states.

The firm offers employees medical, dental and vision insurance as well as a 401(k) plan.

FINANCIAL DATA: Note: Data for latest year may not have been available at press time.

In U.S. $	2016	2015	2014	2013	2012	2011
Revenue		2,306,458,000	1,746,369,000	1,641,331,000	1,614,433,000	1,561,239,000
R&D Expense						
Operating Income		98,144,000	85,967,000	73,647,000	88,686,000	87,530,000
Operating Margin %		4.25%	4.92%	4.48%	5.49%	5.60%
SGA Expense		802,888,000	619,272,000	584,993,000	565,623,000	541,713,000
Net Income		59,002,000	31,354,000	27,675,000	27,217,000	28,608,000
Operating Cash Flow		108,290,000	91,903,000	96,374,000	83,172,000	109,650,000
Capital Expenditure		163,887,000	84,364,000	61,432,000	53,271,000	53,156,000
EBITDA		179,040,000	147,097,000	132,318,000	150,545,000	149,648,000
Return on Assets %		3.59%	2.31%	2.16%	2.05%	2.14%
Return on Equity %		27.65%	16.72%	16.94%	20.42%	22.07%
Debt to Equity		2.76	2.70	2.28	3.45	3.60

CONTACT INFORMATION:

Phone: 704 557-4400   Fax: 704 551-4451
Toll-Free: 800-777-2653
Address: 4100 Coca-Cola Plz., Charlotte, NC 28211 United States

STOCK TICKER/OTHER:

Stock Ticker: COKE   Exchange: NAS
Employees: 7,300   Fiscal Year Ends: 12/31
Parent Company:

SALARIES/BONUSES:

Top Exec. Salary: $239,608   Bonus: $1,126,449
Second Exec. Salary: $943,700   Bonus: $

OTHER THOUGHTS:

Estimated Female Officers or Directors: 3
Hot Spot for Advancement for Women/Minorities: Y

Sales, profits and employees may be estimates. Financial information, benefits and other data can change quickly and may vary from those stated here.

Coca-Cola Company (The)

www.coca-cola.com

NAIC Code: 312111

TYPES OF BUSINESS:

Soft Drink Manufacturing
Concentrates & Syrups
Sports Drinks
Bottled Water
Fruit Juices

BRANDS/DIVISIONS/AFFILIATES:

Coca-Cola
Odwalla
Hellenic Partners GmbH
Sprite
Gold Peak
Multon
Beverage Partners Worldwide
Ilko Coffee International Srl

CONTACTS: Note: Officers with more than one job title may be intentionally listed here more than once.

Gloria Bowden, Assistant General Counsel
Irial Finan, Executive VP
Muhtar Kent, CEO
Kathy Waller, CFO
Alexander Cummings, Chief Administrative Officer
Ed Steinike, Chief Information Officer
Marcos De Quinto, Chief Marketing Officer
Ed Hays, CTO
James Quincey, COO
Ahmet Bozer, Executive VP
J. Douglas, Executive VP
Bernhard Goepelt, General Counsel
Mark Randazza, Other Corporate Officer

GROWTH PLANS/SPECIAL FEATURES:

The Coca-Cola Company manufactures, distributes and markets nonalcoholic beverages, beverage concentrates and markets nonalcoholic beverages, beverage concentrates and beverage syrups in over 200 countries. The company sells beverage concentrates and syrups to bottling and canning operations, fountain wholesalers and some fountain retailers. Additionally, it sells finished and sparkling beverages. Coca-Cola owns or licenses over 3,600 products, including diet and light beverages, waters, enhanced waters, juices and juice drinks, teas, coffees and energy and sports drinks. Coca-Cola's carbonated products include Coca-Cola Classic, Diet Coke, Coca-Cola Zero, Fanta, Sprite, Diet Sprite, Sprite Zero, Sprite Light, Fresca and Barq's. The firm also produces, distributes and markets juice and juice-drink products including Minute Maid, Simply, Odwalla, Five Alive, Bacardi mixers and Hi-C. Coca-Cola has a license to manufacture and sell concentrates for Seagram's mixers, a line of sparkling drinks. The firm has ownership interests in numerous joint ventures, bottling operations and canning operations, although most of these operations are independently owned and managed. Multon, a Russian juice business operated as a joint venture with Coca-Cola Hellenic Bottling Company SA, markets juice products in Russia, Ukraine and Belarus. Beverage Partners Worldwide, a joint venture with Nestle SA, markets tea products under trademarks including Yuan Ye, Gold Peak, Nestea and Frestea; and coffee products under Nescafe, Taster's Choice and Georgia. Other joint ventures include Ilko Coffee International Srl, formed in cooperation with illycafe SpA; and Hellenic Partners GmbH, a joint venture between Coca-Cola Hellenic and Ilko Coffee. In 2014, the company acquired a 16.7% stake in Monster Beverage Corp. In September 2015, the firm announced that it will sell 9 U.S. bottling facilities to three of its largest independent bottlers. The company plans to focus on its higher profit margin businesses and reduce its costs.

FINANCIAL DATA: Note: Data for latest year may not have been available at press time.

In U.S. $	2016	2015	2014	2013	2012	2011
Revenue		44,294,000,000	45,998,000,000	46,854,000,000	48,017,000,000	46,542,000,000
R&D Expense						
Operating Income		8,728,001,000	9,708,000,000	10,228,000,000	10,779,000,000	10,154,000,000
Operating Margin %		19.70%	21.10%	21.82%	22.44%	21.81%
SGA Expense		10,237,000,000	17,218,000,000	17,310,000,000	17,738,000,000	17,440,000,000
Net Income		7,351,000,000	7,098,000,000	8,584,000,000	9,019,000,000	8,572,000,000
Operating Cash Flow		10,528,000,000	10,615,000,000	10,542,000,000	10,645,000,000	9,474,000,000
Capital Expenditure		2,553,000,000	2,406,000,000	2,550,000,000	2,780,000,000	2,920,000,000
EBITDA		12,431,000,000	11,784,000,000	13,917,000,000	14,188,000,000	13,810,000,000
Return on Assets %		8.07%	7.79%	9.74%	10.85%	11.21%
Return on Equity %		26.31%	22.35%	26.02%	27.99%	27.36%
Debt to Equity		1.11	0.62	0.57	0.44	0.43

CONTACT INFORMATION:

Phone: 404 676-2121   Fax:
Toll-Free: 800-438-2653
Address: 1 Coca-Cola Plz., Atlanta, GA 30313 United States

STOCK TICKER/OTHER:

Stock Ticker: KO
Employees: 129,200
Parent Company:

Exchange: NYS
Fiscal Year Ends: 12/31

SALARIES/BONUSES:

Top Exec. Salary: Bonus: $
$1,600,000
Second Exec. Salary: Bonus: $
$884,844

OTHER THOUGHTS:

Estimated Female Officers or Directors: 6

Hot Spot for Advancement for Women/Minorities: Y

Cognizant Technology Solutions Corp

www.cognizant.com

NAIC Code: 541512

TYPES OF BUSINESS:

Computer Systems Design Services
Outsourced Services
Software Engineering

BRANDS/DIVISIONS/AFFILIATES:

Process Space
TZ US Parent Inc
Cadient Group Inc

CONTACTS: Note: Officers with more than one job title may be intentionally listed here more than once.

Rajeev Mehta, CEO, Divisional
Francisco DSouza, CEO
Karen McLoughlin, CFO
John Klein, Chairman of the Board
Sridhar Thiruvengadam, COO
Lakshmi Narayanan, Director
Malcolm Frank, Executive VP, Divisional
Steven Schwartz, Executive VP
Sumithra Gomatam, Executive VP
Venkat Krishnaswamy, Executive VP
Debashis Chatterjee, Executive VP
Ramakrishna Chintamaneni, Executive VP
Dharmendra Sinha, Executive VP
Gordon Coburn, President
Ramakrishnan Chandrasekaran, Vice Chairman, Subsidiary

GROWTH PLANS/SPECIAL FEATURES:

Cognizant Technology Solutions Corp. specializes in custom IT design, development, integration and maintenance services. The firm provides these services primarily to Global 2000 companies located in the U.S., Europe and Asia. The company's core competencies include complex systems development and integration, application maintenance, infrastructure management, enterprise software package implementation and maintenance, technology consulting, data warehousing, business intelligence and analytics, application testing and knowledge process outsourcing. Cognizant operates in four business segments: financial services, which provides services to customers in the banking and insurance industries; health care, which provides services to health care and life science industries; manufacturing, retail & logistics, which provides services to those industries; and other, which covers communications, information services, media, entertainment and high technology. Cognizant provides its IT services using an integrated onsite/offshore business model. This business model combines technical and account management teams located onsite at the customer location and offshore at dedicated development centers located primarily in India, Argentina, the U.S., the Philippines, China, France, Canada and Hungary. The firm has developed proprietary methodologies for integrating onsite and offshore teams, including its Process Space software engineering process, which is available to all onsite and offshore programmers. Process Space is used as part of an initial assessment that allows the firm to define the scope and risks of the project and subdivide the project into smaller phases with frequent deliverables and feedback from customers. In 2014, the company completed several acquisitions it believes will accelerate its ability to provide multi-service integrated solutions to the health care industry, as well as to enhance its overall digital delivery capabilities. Acquisitions include TZ US Parent Inc. and Cadient Group Inc.

FINANCIAL DATA: Note: Data for latest year may not have been available at press time.

In U.S. $	2016	2015	2014	2013	2012	2011
Revenue		12,416,000,000	10,262,680,000	8,843,189,000	7,346,472,000	6,121,156,000
R&D Expense						
Operating Income		2,142,000,000	1,884,878,000	1,677,910,000	1,361,496,000	1,136,468,000
Operating Margin %		17.25%	18.36%	18.97%	18.53%	18.56%
SGA Expense		2,508,600,000	2,037,021,000	1,727,609,000	1,557,646,000	1,328,665,000
Net Income		1,623,600,000	1,439,267,000	1,228,578,000	1,051,263,000	883,618,000
Operating Cash Flow		2,153,300,000	1,473,010,000	1,423,776,000	1,172,583,000	875,152,000
Capital Expenditure		272,800,000	212,203,000	261,626,000	334,465,000	288,221,000
EBITDA		2,511,300,000	2,134,566,000	1,857,840,000	1,518,084,000	1,260,643,000
Return on Assets %		13.10%	14.44%	16.68%	17.47%	17.51%
Return on Equity %		19.08%	20.74%	22.35%	23.87%	23.44%
Debt to Equity		0.09	0.12			

CONTACT INFORMATION:

Phone: 201 801-0233   Fax: 201 801-0243
Toll-Free: 888-937-3277
Address: 500 Frank W. Burr Blvd., Teaneck, NJ 07666 United States

STOCK TICKER/OTHER:

Stock Ticker: CTSH   Exchange: NAS
Employees: 211,500   Fiscal Year Ends: 12/31
Parent Company:

SALARIES/BONUSES:

Top Exec. Salary: $645,000   Bonus: $
Second Exec. Salary: $613,500   Bonus: $

OTHER THOUGHTS:

Estimated Female Officers or Directors: 1
Hot Spot for Advancement for Women/Minorities:

Colgate Palmolive Co

NAIC Code: 325611

www.colgatepalmolive.com

TYPES OF BUSINESS:

Toothpaste & Oral Care Products Manufacturer
Household Cleaning Products
Soap Products
Baby Care Products
Pet Food
Hair Products
Shaving Products

BRANDS/DIVISIONS/AFFILIATES:

Softsoap
Palmolive
Ajax
Hill's Prescription Diet
Tom's of Maine
Lady Speed Stick
Hill's Pet Nutrition
Irish Spring

CONTACTS: *Note: Officers with more than one job title may be intentionally listed here more than once.*

Ian Cook, CEO
Dennis Hickey, CFO
Mukul Deoras, Chief Marketing Officer
Patricia Verduin, Chief Technology Officer
Victoria Dolan, Controller
Jennifer Daniels, Other Executive Officer
John Huston, Other Executive Officer
P. Skala, President, Geographical
Noel Wallace, President, Geographical
Daniel Marsili, Senior VP, Divisional
Delia Thompson, Senior VP, Divisional
Franck Moison, Vice Chairman, Divisional

GROWTH PLANS/SPECIAL FEATURES:

Colgate-Palmolive Co. (Colgate), founded in 1806, is a consumer products company whose merchandise is marketed in over 200 countries and territories throughout the world. The company manages its business in two product segments: oral personal & home care and pet nutrition. Colgate oral care products include toothbrushes, toothpaste, tooth whitener mouth rinses, dental floss and pharmaceutical products for dentists and other oral health professionals. The segment also markets bar & liquid hand soaps, shower gels, shampoos conditioners, deodorants, antiperspirants and shave products. The firm's Softsoap and Palmolive brands are two U.S. market leaders in liquid soaps. Other major products include household care products such as Ajax and Palmolive dishwashing liquids and Murphy's Oil Soap. Additional oral personal and home care brands include Irish Spring, Tom's of Maine and Lady Speed Stick. Colgate also supplies specialty pet nutrition products for dogs and cats through subsidiary Hill's Pet Nutrition, with products marketed in over 95 countries. Pet foods are marketed primarily under the Hill's Science Diet and Hill's Prescription Diet trademarks. Hill's Science Diet is sold by authorized pet supply retailers, breeders and veterinarians for everyday nutritional needs, while Hill's Prescription Diet includes a range of therapeutic products sold by veterinarians to help nutritionally manage disease conditions in dogs and cats.

Employee benefits include medical, dental and vision coverage; flexible spending accounts; short- and long-term disability; life insurance; 401(k) with company match; profit sharing; a company funded retirement plan; and tuition assistance.

FINANCIAL DATA: *Note: Data for latest year may not have been available at press time.*

In U.S. $	2016	2015	2014	2013	2012	2011
Revenue		16,034,000,000	17,277,000,000	17,420,000,000	17,085,000,000	16,734,000,000
R&D Expense						
Operating Income		2,789,000,000	3,557,000,000	3,556,000,000	3,889,000,000	3,841,000,000
Operating Margin %		17.39%	20.58%	20.41%	22.76%	22.95%
SGA Expense		5,464,000,000	5,982,000,000	6,223,000,000	5,930,000,000	5,758,000,000
Net Income		1,384,000,000	2,180,000,000	2,241,000,000	2,472,000,000	2,431,000,000
Operating Cash Flow		2,949,000,000	3,298,000,000	3,204,000,000	3,196,000,000	2,896,000,000
Capital Expenditure		691,000,000	757,000,000	670,000,000	565,000,000	537,000,000
EBITDA		3,345,000,000	4,105,000,000	4,132,000,000	4,379,000,000	4,269,000,000
Return on Assets %		10.89%	15.95%	16.43%	18.92%	20.34%
Return on Equity %		327.18%	126.37%	99.73%	108.32%	96.27%
Debt to Equity			4.92	2.06	2.25	1.86

CONTACT INFORMATION:

Phone: 212 310-2000   Fax: 212 310-3284
Toll-Free: 800-468-6502
Address: 300 Park Ave., New York, NY 10022 United States

STOCK TICKER/OTHER:

Stock Ticker: CL
Employees: 37,700
Parent Company:

Exchange: NYS
Fiscal Year Ends: 12/31

SALARIES/BONUSES:

Top Exec. Salary: Bonus: $
$1,309,000
Second Exec. Salary: Bonus: $
$938,333

OTHER THOUGHTS:

Estimated Female Officers or Directors: 29

Hot Spot for Advancement for Women/Minorities: Y

Comcast Corp

NAIC Code: 517110

www.corporate.comcast.com

TYPES OF BUSINESS:

Cable Television
VoIP Service
Cable Network Programming
High-Speed Internet Service
Video-on-Demand
Advertising Services
Interactive Program Schedules
Wireless Services

BRANDS/DIVISIONS/AFFILIATES:

XFINITY
NBC
Telemundo
Universal
Comcast Spectator
Philadelphia Flyers
Wells Fargo Center

CONTACTS: Note: Officers with more than one job title may be intentionally listed here more than once.

Neil Smit, CEO, Subsidiary
Stephen Burke, CEO, Subsidiary
Brian Roberts, CEO
Michael Cavanagh, CFO
Lawrence Salva, Chief Accounting Officer
Arthur Block, Executive VP
David Cohen, Senior Executive VP

GROWTH PLANS/SPECIAL FEATURES:

Comcast Corp. provides information, entertainment and communications products and services. Comcast operates through five segments: cable communications, cable networks, broadcast television, filmed entertainment and theme parks. The cable communications segment maintains the firm's video, high-speed internet and voice servicing operations, serving residential customers under the XFINITY brand. This division also sells advertising, as well as video, high-speed internet, voice and other services to small- and medium-sized businesses. The cable networks segment includes the firm's national cable networks, its regional sports & news networks, its international cable networks and its cable television production operations. The broadcast television segment consists primarily of the company's NBC and Telemundo broadcast networks, its 10 NBC- and 17 Telemundo-owned local broadcast television stations and its broadcast television production operations. Filmed entertainment comprises the studio operations of Universal Pictures, which produces, acquires, markets and distributes filmed entertainment worldwide. Theme parks comprises the Universal theme parks in Orlando, Florida and Hollywood, California. Additionally, the firm's subsidiary Comcast Spectator owns the Philadelphia Flyers and the Wells Fargo Center in Philadelphia, Pennsylvania. In February 2014 the company agreed to acquire Time Warner Cable. However, the deal was called off in 2015.

FINANCIAL DATA: Note: Data for latest year may not have been available at press time.

In U.S. $	2016	2015	2014	2013	2012	2011
Revenue		74,510,000,000	68,775,000,000	64,657,000,000	62,570,000,000	55,842,000,000
R&D Expense						
Operating Income		15,998,000,000	14,904,000,000	13,563,000,000	12,179,000,000	10,721,000,000
Operating Margin %		21.47%	21.67%	20.97%	19.46%	19.19%
SGA Expense		27,282,000,000	24,940,000,000	23,553,000,000	22,664,000,000	16,727,000,000
Net Income		8,163,000,000	8,380,000,000	6,816,000,000	6,203,000,000	4,160,000,000
Operating Cash Flow		18,778,000,000	16,945,000,000	14,160,000,000	14,854,000,000	14,345,000,000
Capital Expenditure		9,869,000,000	8,542,000,000	7,605,000,000	6,637,000,000	6,261,000,000
EBITDA		24,754,000,000	23,101,000,000	21,560,000,000	21,928,000,000	18,348,000,000
Return on Assets %		5.00%	5.26%	4.21%	3.84%	3.01%
Return on Equity %		15.55%	16.20%	13.62%	12.83%	9.08%
Debt to Equity		0.93	0.83	0.87	0.77	0.80

CONTACT INFORMATION:

Phone: 215 286-1700   Fax:
Toll-Free: 800-266-2278
Address: 1 Comcast Ctr., Philadelphia, PA 19103 United States

STOCK TICKER/OTHER:

Stock Ticker: CMCSA
Employees: 153,000
Parent Company:

Exchange: NAS
Fiscal Year Ends: 12/31

SALARIES/BONUSES:

Top Exec. Salary: $2,928,748   Bonus: $
Second Exec. Salary: $2,718,813   Bonus: $

OTHER THOUGHTS:

Estimated Female Officers or Directors: 16

Hot Spot for Advancement for Women/Minorities: Y

Sales, profits and employees may be estimates. Financial information, benefits and other data can change quickly and may vary from those stated here.

CommScope Inc
NAIC Code: 335921

TYPES OF BUSINESS:
Cable-Coaxial & Fiber Optic
Local Area Network Products
Wireless Products

BRANDS/DIVISIONS/AFFILIATES:
Systimax
Uniprise
Airvana LP

CONTACTS: *Note: Officers with more than one job title may be intentionally listed here more than once.*
Mark Olson, CFO
Frank Drendel, Chairman of the Board
Robert Granow, Chief Accounting Officer
Randall Crenshaw, COO
Frank Wyatt, General Counsel
Marvin Edwards, President
Joanne Townsend, Senior VP, Divisional
Peter Karlsson, Senior VP, Divisional
Philip Armstrong, Senior VP, Divisional

GROWTH PLANS/SPECIAL FEATURES:
CommScope, Inc. is a global leader in connectivity solutions for communications networks. It provides infrastructure solutions for wireless, residential broadband, business enterprise and carrier wireline networks. CommScope's operations are divided into four major product segments: broadband, enterprise, wireless and broadband network solutions (BNS). CommScope's broadband division produces coaxial cable, fiber optic cable and conduit for cable television system operators. These products support multi-channel video, voice and high-speed data services for residential and commercial customers using hybrid fiber coaxial (HFC) architecture. The firm is one of the world's largest manufacturers of coaxial cable and a leading North American supplier of fiber optic cable. The enterprise segment markets systems under the Systimax and Uniprise brand names. It consists of structured cabling systems for business enterprise applications, connectivity solutions for wired and wireless networks within organizations and coaxial cable for various video and data applications that are not related to cable television. Wireless provides merchant radio frequency (RF) wireless network connectivity solutions and small cell distributed antenna system (DAS) solutions to enable carriers' 2G, 3G and 4G networks. The BNS segment provides fiber optic & copper connectivity for wireline and wireless networks, as well as small-cell distributed antenna system solutions for the wireless market. CommScope's focus on research and innovation has led to over 10,000 patents and patent applications, and over 3,000 registered trademarks. In 2015, the firm acquired TE Connectivity's BNS business for $3 billion. That October, CommScope acquired Airvana LP for about $45 million, a provider of 4G LTE and 3G small cell solutions that enable communication and access information and entertainment in challenging & high-value environments (offices, public venues and homes).

The firm offers employees a 401(k) plan; educational assistance; medical, dental and vision insurance; life and AD&D insurance; short- and long-term disability; and an employee assistance program.

FINANCIAL DATA: *Note: Data for latest year may not have been available at press time.*

In U.S. $	2016	2015	2014	2013	2012	2011
Revenue		3,807,828,000	3,829,614,000	3,480,117,000	3,321,885,000	3,186,446,000
R&D Expense		135,964,000	125,301,000	126,431,000	121,718,000	112,904,000
Operating Income		181,593,000	577,449,000	329,714,000	238,238,000	-134,719,000
Operating Margin %		4.76%	15.07%	9.47%	7.17%	-4.22%
SGA Expense		687,389,000	484,891,000	502,275,000	461,149,000	517,903,000
Net Income		-70,875,000	236,772,000	19,396,000	5,353,000	-252,308,000
Operating Cash Flow		302,060,000	289,418,000	237,701,000	286,135,000	135,749,000
Capital Expenditure		56,501,000	36,935,000	36,780,000	27,957,000	38,792,000
EBITDA		476,160,000	755,502,000	541,400,000	488,555,000	120,242,000
Return on Assets %		-1.13%	4.88%	.40%	.11%	
Return on Equity %		-5.60%	19.76%	1.70%	.45%	
Debt to Equity		4.27	2.06	2.30	2.08	

CONTACT INFORMATION:
Phone: 828-324-2200   Fax:
Toll-Free: 800-982-1708
Address: 1100 CommScope Place SE, Hickory, NC 28602 United States

STOCK TICKER/OTHER:
Stock Ticker: COMM
Employees: 13,000
Parent Company:

Exchange: NAS
Fiscal Year Ends: 12/31

SALARIES/BONUSES:
Top Exec. Salary: $983,750   Bonus: $ 200
Second Exec. Salary: $690,000   Bonus: $ 800

OTHER THOUGHTS:
Estimated Female Officers or Directors: 2
Hot Spot for Advancement for Women/Minorities:

Community Health Systems Inc

www.chs.net

NAIC Code: 622110

TYPES OF BUSINESS:

General Medical and Surgical Hospitals
Surgical & Emergency Services
Acute Care Services
Internal Medicine
Obstetrics
Emergency Room Services
Diagnostic Services
Ambulatory Surgery Centers

BRANDS/DIVISIONS/AFFILIATES:

Quorum Health Corporation
Quorum Health Resources LLC

CONTACTS: *Note: Officers with more than one job title may be intentionally listed here more than once.*

Wayne Smith, CEO
W. Cash, CFO
Kevin Hammons, Chief Accounting Officer
Tim Hingtgen, Executive VP, Divisional
Rachel Seifert, Executive VP
Lynn Simon, Other Executive Officer
Martin Bonick, President, Divisional
Thomas Miller, President, Divisional
Michael Portacci, President, Divisional
John McClellan, President, Divisional
David Miller, President
Tomi Galin, Senior VP, Divisional
Robert Horrar, Vice President, Divisional
P. Smith, Vice President, Divisional

GROWTH PLANS/SPECIAL FEATURES:

Community Health Systems, Inc. is one of the largest operators of hospitals in the U.S. The company owns, leases and operates 159 hospitals in 22 states, with approximately 27,000 licensed beds. Community Health Systems provides health care for local residents, offering a wide range of diagnostic, medical and surgical services in in-patient and out-patient settings. In April 2016, the firm spun off Quorum Health Corporation, which became an independent public company listed on the NYSE under ticker symbol QHC. The transaction created two health care companies, with QHC owning or leasing a portfolio of 38 hospitals with an aggregate of 3,582 licensed beds. QHC also operates Quorum Health Resources LLC, a leading hospital management advisory and consulting services business.

The company offers employees medical, dental and vision insurance; flexible spending accounts; life and disability insurance; and a 401(k) savings plan.

FINANCIAL DATA: *Note: Data for latest year may not have been available at press time.*

In U.S. $	2016	2015	2014	2013	2012	2011
Revenue		19,437,000,000	18,639,000,000	12,997,690,000	13,028,980,000	13,626,170,000
R&D Expense		68,000,000				
Operating Income		1,337,000,000	1,380,000,000	899,763,000	1,210,124,000	1,134,485,000
Operating Margin %		6.87%	7.40%	6.92%	9.28%	8.32%
SGA Expense		9,447,999,000	9,052,000,000	6,505,159,000	6,376,760,000	5,832,706,000
Net Income		158,000,000	92,000,000	141,203,000	265,640,000	201,948,000
Operating Cash Flow		921,000,000	1,615,000,000	1,088,719,000	1,280,120,000	1,261,908,000
Capital Expenditure		1,010,000,000	3,944,000,000	613,992,000	768,790,000	1,192,073,000
EBITDA		2,511,000,000	2,501,000,000	1,703,684,000	1,852,262,000	1,780,272,000
Return on Assets %		.58%	.41%	.83%	1.66%	1.35%
Return on Equity %		3.93%	2.60%	4.86%	10.35%	8.80%
Debt to Equity		4.18	4.16	3.02	3.46	3.66

CONTACT INFORMATION:

Phone: 615 465-7000   Fax: 615 645-7001
Toll-Free:
Address: 4000 Meridian Blvd., Franklin, TN 37067 United States

STOCK TICKER/OTHER:

Stock Ticker: CYH   Exchange: NYS
Employees: 135,000   Fiscal Year Ends: 12/31
Parent Company:

SALARIES/BONUSES:

Top Exec. Salary: Bonus: $
$1,600,000
Second Exec. Salary: Bonus: $
$850,000

OTHER THOUGHTS:

Estimated Female Officers or Directors: 18

Hot Spot for Advancement for Women/Minorities: Y

Computer Task Group Inc

www.ctg.com

NAIC Code: 561330

TYPES OF BUSINESS:

IT Staffing & Outsourcing
Integration Services
Application Management
Information Security
Help Desk Services
Facilities Management

BRANDS/DIVISIONS/AFFILIATES:

Computer Task Group of Canada Inc
Computer Task Group Belgium NV
CTG ITS SA
Computer Task Group IT Solutions SA
Computer Task Group Luxembourg PSF
Computer Task Group (UK) Ltd
etrinity NV

CONTACTS: *Note: Officers with more than one job title may be intentionally listed here more than once.*

Brendan Harrington, CFO
Daniel Sullivan, Director
Arthur Crumlish, Director
Alfred Hamilton, General Manager, Divisional
Filip Gyde, General Manager, Geographical
Peter Radetich, Senior VP
John Laubacker, Treasurer

GROWTH PLANS/SPECIAL FEATURES:

Computer Task Group, Inc. (CTG) provides consulting and staffing services to information technology (IT) companies. The company has seven operating subsidiaries: Computer Task Group of Canada, Inc., providing services in Canada; and Computer Task Group Belgium NV, CTG ITS SA, Computer Task Group IT Solutions SA, Computer Task Group Luxembourg PSF, Computer Task Group (UK) Ltd. and etrinity NV, each primarily providing services in Europe. Services provided in North America are primarily performed by the parent corporation, CTG. The firm's IT solutions include engagements with a fixed duration and deliverables that achieve value-based outcomes by applying the right IT solutions to address clients' business needs. These include the implementation of packaged software applications; the development & deployment of customized software and solutions designed to fit the needs of a specific client or market and the design & distribution of complex technology components. IT and other staffing services address a range of IT and business resource needs, such as filling specific talent gaps to managing high-volume staffing programs. CTG recruits, retains and manages IT for its clients, which are primarily large technology service providers and companies with multiple locations. Its strategic consulting delivers customized recommendations and plans that address business & IT challenges and maximize the realization of benefits.

The firm offers employees medical, dental and vision insurance; tuition reimbursement; short- and long-term disability coverage; and flexible spending accounts.

FINANCIAL DATA: *Note: Data for latest year may not have been available at press time.*

In U.S. $	2016	2015	2014	2013	2012	2011
Revenue		369,478,000	393,268,000	419,036,000	424,415,000	396,275,000
R&D Expense						
Operating Income		10,637,000	17,152,000	24,727,000	24,462,000	19,310,000
Operating Margin %		2.87%	4.36%	5.90%	5.76%	4.87%
SGA Expense		56,523,000	62,186,000	63,982,000	66,867,000	64,981,000
Net Income		6,510,000	10,350,000	15,679,000	16,165,000	11,938,000
Operating Cash Flow		-4,685,000	6,708,000	18,991,000	21,156,000	8,605,000
Capital Expenditure		1,901,000	3,093,000	3,952,000	1,872,000	1,948,000
EBITDA		12,924,000	20,237,000	27,581,000	28,805,000	21,812,000
Return on Assets %		3.89%	5.99%	9.20%	10.30%	8.59%
Return on Equity %		5.69%	9.20%	14.47%	16.87%	14.32%
Debt to Equity		0.01				

CONTACT INFORMATION:

Phone: 716 882-8000   Fax:
Toll-Free: 800-992-5350
Address: 800 Delaware Ave., Buffalo, NY 14209 United States

STOCK TICKER/OTHER:

Stock Ticker: CTG   Exchange: NAS
Employees: 3,800   Fiscal Year Ends: 12/31
Parent Company:

SALARIES/BONUSES:

Top Exec. Salary: $369,863   Bonus: $
Second Exec. Salary: Bonus: $
$336,384

OTHER THOUGHTS:

Estimated Female Officers or Directors:
Hot Spot for Advancement for Women/Minorities:

Concur Technologies Inc

NAIC Code: 0

TYPES OF BUSINESS:

Software Manufacturer-Expense Reporting
Corporate Expense Management Solutions
Professional Services
Travel and Entertainment Expense Reporting Software
Meeting Expense Reporting Software

BRANDS/DIVISIONS/AFFILIATES:

Concur Travel & Expense
SAP SE

CONTACTS: Note: Officers with more than one job title may be intentionally listed here more than once.

Steve Singh, CEO
Elena Donio, Pres.
Frank Pelzer, CFO
Jessica Shapiro, VP-CMO
Mark Nelson, Chief Technology Officer
John Torrey, Executive VP, Divisional
Robert Cavanaugh, Executive VP
Elena Donio, Executive VP

GROWTH PLANS/SPECIAL FEATURES:

Concur Technologies, Inc. provides business automation process services and software products for the management of travel- and meeting-related corporate expenses. The firm's product solutions cover three primary aspects of corporate travel management: travel procurement, expense management and itinerary management. Travel procurement software automates corporate travel booking and processing functions and can be tailored to a company's specific travel policies and preferred vendors. Employees using Concur's travel procurement solutions are able to set their own travel preferences while organizations set policy through technology filters to retain control. Expense management solutions simplify the expense reporting process, while reducing costs and improving internal controls. Its software automatically imports corporate or personal credit card charges to create expense reports and reconciles transaction data from itinerary data captured at the time of booking, corporate card charges incurred during travel and electronic receipts captured directly from the supplier. Concur's itinerary management solutions enable individual business travelers and their organizations to manage and share travel itinerary information and can be imported into other Concur solutions to provide greater insight and control over travel and expense spend for organizations. Its flagship product, Concur Travel & Expense, integrates online travel booking with automated expense reporting to provide unified end-to-end corporate travel procurement and expense reporting. The firm also offers value-added services and software that integrate with the company's primary products. Additionally, Concur offers professional services including consulting, customer support and training. The company has more than 20,000 customers worldwide. Concur is owned by German software giant SAP SE, and operates as a business unit within SAP.

The firm offers employees life, disability, medical, dental and vision insurance; flexible spending accounts; and a 401(k).

FINANCIAL DATA: Note: Data for latest year may not have been available at press time.

In U.S. $	2016	2015	2014	2013	2012	2011
Revenue		724,603,419	702,588,032	545,800,000	439,825,984	349,488,000
R&D Expense						
Operating Income						
Operating Margin %						
SGA Expense						
Net Income		-20,571,530	-118,295,000	-24,394,000	-7,006,000	-10,743,000
Operating Cash Flow						
Capital Expenditure						
EBITDA						
Return on Assets %						
Return on Equity %						
Debt to Equity						

CONTACT INFORMATION:

Phone: 425 590-5000   Fax: 425 702-8828
Toll-Free: 800-401-8412
Address: 601 108th Avenue NE, Suite 1000, Bellevue, WA 98004 United States

STOCK TICKER/OTHER:

Stock Ticker: Subsidiary
Employees: 2,741
Parent Company: SAP SE

Exchange:
Fiscal Year Ends: 12/31

SALARIES/BONUSES:

Top Exec. Salary: $ Bonus: $
Second Exec. Salary: $ Bonus: $

OTHER THOUGHTS:

Estimated Female Officers or Directors: 2
Hot Spot for Advancement for Women/Minorities:

Container Store (The)

www.containerstore.com

NAIC Code: 442299

TYPES OF BUSINESS:

Home Organization Products, Retail
Luggage
Packing Materials
Specialty Boxes
Online Sales

BRANDS/DIVISIONS/AFFILIATES:

Leonard Green & Partners LP
Container Store (The)
Elfa International AB
Elfa
Contained Home

CONTACTS: Note: Officers with more than one job title may be intentionally listed here more than once.

Per von Mentzer, CEO, Subsidiary
William Tindell, CEO
Jodi Taylor, CFO
Melissa Reiff, COO
Sharon Tindell, Director
Peter Lodwick, General Counsel
Jeffrey Miller, Vice President

GROWTH PLANS/SPECIAL FEATURES:

The Container Store, owned by private equity firm Leonard Green & Partners LP, is a national retailer selling organizational and storage products. Products include drawer & cabinet organizers, luggage, tool racks, packing materials, specialty & shipping boxes and locker organizers, among many other household objects designed to manage space efficiently. Store interiors have an open layout which is divided into sections with brightly colored banners such as Closet, Kitchen and Laundry. The company's operations are divided into two segments: The Container Store, made up of retail stores, website and call center; and Elfa, a design and manufacturing business. The firm's stores average 25,000 square feet and carry more than 11,000 items. The majority of the company's approximately 79 stores are located in 28 states and Washington, D.C. The Container Store processes and ships its entire product line from its 725,000-square-foot distribution center in Coppell, Texas. The company's web site allows customers to view and order store products, plan organizational and storage projects and receive free customized assistance from in-store space planning experts. In 2015, this segment made up approximately 91% of the firm's total net sales. The firm is the exclusive distributor of Elfa International AB, a wholly owned Swedish subsidiary, which designs and manufactures component-based shelving and drawer systems, as well as made-to-measure sliding doors. Elfa represented 9% of total net sales, and has four manufacturing facilities located in Sweden (2), Finland, and Poland. Contained Home, the firm's in-home, customized design and organization service, where expert organizers go directly to customer homes, launched in 2015.

The company offers its employees a 40% discount on merchandise; 401(k); paid vacation; employee assistance program; domestic partner benefits; corporate wellness program; transportation benefits; pet insurance; paid pregnancy disability leave; and medical, life, dental and vision insurance.

FINANCIAL DATA: Note: Data for latest year may not have been available at press time.

In U.S. $	2016	2015	2014	2013	2012	2011
Revenue	794,630,000	781,866,000	748,538,000	706,757,000	633,619,000	568,820,000
R&D Expense						
Operating Income	24,861,000	46,971,000	31,027,000	24,142,000	-6,628,000	-14,918,000
Operating Margin %	3.12%	6.00%	4.14%	3.41%	-1.04%	-2.62%
SGA Expense	404,399,000	382,439,000	376,080,000	338,942,000	298,868,000	271,221,000
Net Income	5,142,000	22,673,000	8,166,000	-130,000	-30,671,000	-45,053,000
Operating Cash Flow	42,307,000	64,625,000	50,762,000	45,186,000	42,203,000	48,764,000
Capital Expenditure	46,431,000	48,740,000	48,565,000	48,559,000	40,953,000	18,175,000
EBITDA	59,091,000	77,982,000	60,151,000	46,359,000	20,823,000	9,436,000
Return on Assets %	.67%	2.92%	-6.71%	-12.06%	-14.63%	
Return on Equity %	2.51%	11.36%	-23.96%	-38.80%	-46.88%	
Debt to Equity	1.55	1.61	1.66	1.18	1.25	

CONTACT INFORMATION:

Phone: 972-538-6900   Fax: 972-538-7623
Toll-Free: 800-733-3532
Address: 500 Freeport Pkwy., Coppell, TX 75019 United States

STOCK TICKER/OTHER:

Stock Ticker: TCS
Employees: 4,900
Parent Company: Leonard Green & Partners LP

Exchange: NYS
Fiscal Year Ends: 03/31

SALARIES/BONUSES:

Top Exec. Salary: $675,000   Bonus: $
Second Exec. Salary: $625,000   Bonus: $

OTHER THOUGHTS:

Estimated Female Officers or Directors: 5
Hot Spot for Advancement for Women/Minorities: Y

Convergys Corporation

www.convergys.com

NAIC Code: 561422

TYPES OF BUSINESS:

Call Centers
Outsourced Customer Care

BRANDS/DIVISIONS/AFFILIATES:

Stream Global Services Inc

CONTACTS: *Note: Officers with more than one job title may be intentionally listed here more than once.*

Andrea Ayers, CEO
Andre Valentine, CFO
Jeffrey Fox, Chairman of the Board
Taylor Greenwald, Chief Accounting Officer
Jarrod Pontius, Chief Administrative Officer
Marjorie Connelly, COO

GROWTH PLANS/SPECIAL FEATURES:

Convergys Corporation is a global provider of customer care and outsourced contact center services. The firm's customer management business provides outsourced agent-assisted and self-service customer care services as well as consulting and technology services to the in-house customer care market. Phone- and web-based agent-assisted service channels provide customers with assistance across the entire customer lifecycle. The company delivers these services using a variety of tools, including computer telephony integration, interactive voice response, advanced speech recognition, knowledge-based management and the Internet through agent-assisted and self-service channels. The firm has around 150 contact centers located in 31 countries, assisting customers in approximately 58 languages. These contact centers average approximately 65,000 square feet each, and have approximately 89,900 production workstations that provide service 24 hours a day, 365 days a year. Annually, it handles more than 4 billion customer contacts. Convergys primarily services companies in the automotive, communications, financial services, government, health care, manufacturing, retail, technology and transportation sectors. Its largest client, AT&T, accounts for approximately 15.3% of its annual revenue. Other significant clients include Comcast Corp. and DIRECTV Group, Inc. In 2014, the company acquired Stream Global Services, Inc., a business process outsourcing (BPO) company. In 2015, the firm announced a strategic partnership with Nexidia, a leading provider of customer interaction analytics technology solutions.

The firm offers its employees life, AD&D, medical, dental and vision insurance; a 401(k) plan; an employee stock purchase plan; tuition reimbursement; an employee assistance program; and an employee discount program.

FINANCIAL DATA: *Note: Data for latest year may not have been available at press time.*

In U.S. $	2016	2015	2014	2013	2012	2011
Revenue		2,950,600,000	2,855,500,000	2,046,100,000	2,005,000,000	2,262,000,000
R&D Expense		7,100,000	7,700,000	8,200,000	10,800,000	49,300,000
Operating Income		194,400,000	150,800,000	137,400,000	38,600,000	168,300,000
Operating Margin %		6.58%	5.28%	6.71%	1.92%	7.44%
SGA Expense		695,900,000	714,800,000	467,700,000	477,200,000	527,400,000
Net Income		169,000,000	120,000,000	60,900,000	100,600,000	334,800,000
Operating Cash Flow		249,300,000	261,000,000	210,000,000	113,000,000	196,600,000
Capital Expenditure		109,200,000	116,700,000	63,800,000	98,400,000	88,300,000
EBITDA		363,700,000	316,200,000	233,300,000	131,600,000	559,800,000
Return on Assets %		6.93%	5.36%	3.04%	4.61%	15.04%
Return on Equity %		13.50%	9.53%	4.57%	7.22%	25.79%
Debt to Equity		0.26	0.35	0.04	0.04	0.08

CONTACT INFORMATION:

Phone: 513 723-7000   Fax: 513 723-2048
Toll-Free:
Address: 201 E. Foruth St., Cincinnati, OH 45202 United States

STOCK TICKER/OTHER:

Stock Ticker: CVG   Exchange: NYS
Employees: 125,000   Fiscal Year Ends: 12/31
Parent Company:

SALARIES/BONUSES:

Top Exec. Salary: $900,000   Bonus: $
Second Exec. Salary: Bonus: $
$545,616

OTHER THOUGHTS:

Estimated Female Officers or Directors: 3
Hot Spot for Advancement for Women/Minorities: Y

Sales, profits and employees may be estimates. Financial information, benefits and other data can change quickly and may vary from those stated here.

Cooper Companies Inc

www.coopercos.com

NAIC Code: 339100

TYPES OF BUSINESS:

Medical Devices
Contact Lenses
Gynecological Instruments
Diagnostic Products

BRANDS/DIVISIONS/AFFILIATES:

CooperVision Inc
CooperSurgical Inc
Proclear
Phosphorylcholine (PC) Technology
Genesis Genetics

CONTACTS: Note: Officers with more than one job title may be intentionally listed here more than once.

Robert Weiss, CEO
Gregory Matz, CFO
A. Bender, Chairman of the Board
Tina Maloney, Chief Accounting Officer
Carol Kaufman, Chief Administrative Officer
Daniel McBride, COO
Allan Rubenstein, Director
Albert White, Executive VP
Randal Golden, General Counsel
Paul Remmell, President, Subsidiary
Kim Duncan, Vice President, Divisional

GROWTH PLANS/SPECIAL FEATURES:

Cooper Companies, Inc. develops, manufactures and markets health care products, primarily medical devices. The company operates through two business units: CooperVision, Inc. (CVI) and CooperSurgical, Inc. (CSI). CVI develops, manufactures and markets a broad range of contact lenses, including disposable spherical and specialty contact lenses. It is a leading manufacturer of toric lenses, which correct astigmatism; multifocal lenses for presbyopia, the blurring of vision due to advancing age; and spherical lenses, including hydrogel lenses, which correct the most common near- and far-sighted visual defects. CVI offers single-use, two-week, monthly and quarterly disposable sphere and toric lenses as well as custom toric lenses to correct a high degree of astigmatism. CVI's Proclear line of spherical, toric and multifocal lenses are manufactured with omafilcon, a material that incorporates its proprietary Phosphorylcholine (PC) Technology to enhance tissue-device compatibility. CVI's products are primarily manufactured at its facilities in the U.S., the U.K., Hungary and Puerto Rico. It distributes its products out of West Henrietta, New York; Fareham, U.K.; Liege, Belgium; and various smaller international distribution facilities. CSI develops, manufactures and markets medical devices, diagnostic products and surgical instruments and accessories used primarily by gynecologists and obstetricians. The subsidiary manufactures and distributes its products at its facilities in Trumbull, Connecticut; Malov, Denmark; Pasadena, California; Stafford, Texas; and Berlin, Germany. In 2016, the firm acquired Genesis Genetics, a genetics laboratory specializing in preimplantation genetic screening and diagnosis; and the commercial assets of Recombine, Inc., a clinical genetic testing company specializing in carrier screening.

FINANCIAL DATA: Note: Data for latest year may not have been available at press time.

In U.S. $	2016	2015	2014	2013	2012	2011
Revenue		1,797,060,000	1,717,776,000	1,587,725,000	1,445,136,000	1,330,835,000
R&D Expense		69,589,000	66,259,000	58,827,000	51,730,000	43,581,000
Operating Income		236,671,000	306,486,000	305,945,000	283,398,000	227,556,000
Operating Margin %		13.16%	17.84%	19.26%	19.61%	17.09%
SGA Expense		712,543,000	683,115,000	610,735,000	564,903,000	513,138,000
Net Income		203,523,000	269,856,000	296,151,000	248,339,000	175,430,000
Operating Cash Flow		390,970,000	454,823,000	415,925,000	315,121,000	336,281,000
Capital Expenditure		243,023,000	238,065,000	178,127,000	99,779,000	103,665,000
EBITDA		424,991,000	442,700,000	446,788,000	398,437,000	308,255,000
Return on Assets %		4.56%	7.10%	9.74%	8.92%	6.81%
Return on Equity %		7.77%	10.84%	12.88%	12.02%	9.73%
Debt to Equity		0.41	0.49	0.12	0.15	0.16

CONTACT INFORMATION:

Phone: 925 460-3600   Fax: 949 597-0662
Toll-Free:
Address: 6140 Stoneridge Mall Rd., Ste. 590, Pleasanton, CA 94588
United States

STOCK TICKER/OTHER:

Stock Ticker: COO
Employees: 9,460
Parent Company:

Exchange: NYS
Fiscal Year Ends: 10/31

SALARIES/BONUSES:

Top Exec. Salary: $875,000   Bonus: $218,750
Second Exec. Salary: Bonus: $86,625
$495,000

OTHER THOUGHTS:

Estimated Female Officers or Directors: 2
Hot Spot for Advancement for Women/Minorities: Y

Corning Inc

www.corning.com

NAIC Code: 327212

TYPES OF BUSINESS:

Glass & Optical Fiber Manufacturing
Glass Substrates for LCDs
Optical Switching Products
Photonic Modules & Components
Networking Devices
Semiconductor Materials
Laboratory Supplies
Emissions Control Products

BRANDS/DIVISIONS/AFFILIATES:

Samsung Corning Precision Materials Co Ltd
Vascade
LEAF
SMF-28e
ClearCurve
InfiniCor
ClearCurve VSDN
Gorilla

CONTACTS: *Note: Officers with more than one job title may be intentionally listed here more than once.*

Wendell Weeks, CEO
James Clappin, President, Divisional
R. Tripeny, CFO
Edward Schlesinger, Chief Accounting Officer
Lisa Ferrero, Chief Administrative Officer
David Morse, Chief Technology Officer
Clark Kinlin, Executive VP
Eric Musser, Executive VP, Divisional
Martin Curran, Executive VP
Lewis Steverson, General Counsel
Lawrence McRae, Other Corporate Officer
Jeffrey Evenson, Other Executive Officer
Linda Jolly, Secretary
Christine Pambianchi, Senior VP, Divisional
Mark Rogus, Senior VP

GROWTH PLANS/SPECIAL FEATURES:

Corning, Inc. is an international technology-based corporation. The firm operates in five business segments: display technologies, optical communications, specialty materials, environmental technologies and life sciences. The display technologies segment manufactures glass substrates for active matrix liquid crystal displays (LCDs), used in notebook computers, flat panel desktop monitor and LCD televisions. Corning owns 57.5% of Samsung Corning Precision Materials Co. Ltd., which produces glass substrates using a proprietary fusion process. The optical communications segment is divided into carrier network and enterprise network. The carrier network products include Vascade submarine optical fibers for use in submarine networks; LEAF optical fiber for long-haul, regional and metropolitan networks; SMF-28e single mode optical fiber for additional transmission wavelengths in metropolitan and access networks, and ClearCurve fiber for use in multiple dwelling units. The enterprise network product portfolio includes ClearCurve ultra-bendable multimode fiber for data centers and other enterprise network applications; InfiniCor fibers for local area networks; and ClearCurve VSDN ultra-bendable optical fiber designed to support emerging high-speed interconnects between computers and other consumer electronics devices. The specialty materials segment offers products such as glass windows for space shuttles and optical components for high-tech industries and includes the firm's Gorilla glass product line of protective cover glass for portable display devices. In its environmental technologies segment, Corning produces ceramic products for emissions and pollution control, such as gasoline/diesel substrate and filter products. The company's life sciences segment manufactures laboratory products such as consumables (plastic vessels, specialty surfaces and media), as well as general labware and equipment used for cell culture research, bioprocessing, genomics, drug discovery, microbiology and chemistry.

FINANCIAL DATA: *Note: Data for latest year may not have been available at press time.*

In U.S. $	2016	2015	2014	2013	2012	2011
Revenue		9,111,000,000	9,715,000,000	7,819,000,000	8,012,000,000	7,890,000,000
R&D Expense		769,000,000	815,000,000	710,000,000	745,000,000	671,000,000
Operating Income		1,322,000,000	1,931,000,000	1,371,000,000	1,321,000,000	1,694,000,000
Operating Margin %		14.50%	19.87%	17.53%	16.48%	21.47%
SGA Expense		1,523,000,000	1,211,000,000	1,126,000,000	1,165,000,000	1,033,000,000
Net Income		1,339,000,000	2,472,000,000	1,961,000,000	1,728,000,000	2,805,000,000
Operating Cash Flow		2,809,000,000	4,709,000,000	2,787,000,000	3,206,000,000	3,189,000,000
Capital Expenditure		1,250,000,000	1,076,000,000	1,019,000,000	1,801,000,000	2,432,000,000
EBITDA		2,810,000,000	4,891,000,000	3,595,000,000	3,225,000,000	4,259,000,000
Return on Assets %		4.23%	8.44%	6.77%	6.03%	10.45%
Return on Equity %		6.93%	12.22%	9.19%	8.11%	13.86%
Debt to Equity		0.23	0.16	0.15	0.15	0.11

CONTACT INFORMATION:

Phone: 607 974-9000   Fax: 607 974-8688
Toll-Free:
Address: 1 Riverfront Plz., Corning, NY 14831 United States

STOCK TICKER/OTHER:

Stock Ticker: GLW   Exchange: NYS
Employees: 35,700   Fiscal Year Ends: 12/31
Parent Company:

SALARIES/BONUSES:

Top Exec. Salary: $1,353,096   Bonus: $
Second Exec. Salary: $942,454   Bonus: $

OTHER THOUGHTS:

Estimated Female Officers or Directors: 1

Hot Spot for Advancement for Women/Minorities: Y

Costco Wholesale Corp

www.costco.com

NAIC Code: 452910

TYPES OF BUSINESS:

Warehouse Clubs, Retail
Food
Health & Beauty Products
Electronics
Furniture
Apparel
Automotive Supplies
Gasoline Sales

BRANDS/DIVISIONS/AFFILIATES:

Costco Wholesale Industries
Kirkland Signature

CONTACTS: *Note: Officers with more than one job title may be intentionally listed here more than once.*

Jeffrey Brotman, Chairman of the Board
James Sinegal, Co-Founder
Douglas Schutt, COO, Divisional
Dennis Zook, COO, Divisional
Joseph Portera, COO, Divisional
John McKay, COO, Divisional
James Murphy, COO, Divisional
W. Jelinek, Director
Franz Lazarus, Executive VP, Divisional
Timothy Rose, Executive VP, Divisional
Richard Galanti, Executive VP
Paul Moulton, Executive VP
John Sullivan, Secretary
David Petterson, Senior VP

GROWTH PLANS/SPECIAL FEATURES:

Costco Wholesale Corp. operates membership warehouses based on the concept that offering members very low prices on a limited selection of branded and private-label products will produce high sales volumes and rapid inventory turnover. This rapid turnover, combined with volume purchasing, efficient distribution and reduced handling of merchandise in self-service warehouse facilities, allows the firm to operate at significantly lower margins than traditional discount retailers. Costco buys the majority of its merchandise directly from manufacturers for shipment to warehouses or to consolidation points, minimizing freight and handling costs. Products include health & beauty aids, cleaning supplies, foods, alcohol, appliances, electronics, tools, office supplies, furniture, automotive supplies, apparel, cameras, house wares and books. Stores contain other features, including pharmacies, print shops, photo labs and gas stations. Costco's private products are marketed under the Kirkland Signature label brand. It has three types of memberships: executive, business and gold star. Memberships are designed to build customer loyalty and start at $55 per year (for U.S. and Canadian operations). The firm operates 686 warehouses, including 480 in the U.S. and Puerto Rico, 27 in the U.K., 89 in Canada, seven in Australia, 12 in Korea, 36 in Mexico, 11 in Taiwan, 23 in Japan and one in Spain. The stores average approximately 144,000 square feet and stock distinct products including upscale items such as jewelry and wines. Costco Wholesale Industries, a division of the company, operates manufacturing businesses, including special food packaging, optical laboratories, meat processing and jewelry distribution. The company also operates eCommerce web sites in the U.S., Canada, the U.K. and Mexico.

Costco offers employees health care, dental, vision and prescription coverage; 401(k); employee assistance, employee stock purchase and dependent care assistance plan; short- and long-term disability; life insurance; health care reimbursement; and long-term care insurance.

FINANCIAL DATA: *Note: Data for latest year may not have been available at press time.*

In U.S. $	2016	2015	2014	2013	2012	2011
Revenue		116,199,000,000	112,640,000,000	105,156,000,000	99,137,000,000	88,915,000,000
R&D Expense						
Operating Income		3,624,000,000	3,220,000,000	3,053,000,000	2,759,000,000	2,439,000,000
Operating Margin %		3.11%	2.85%	2.90%	2.78%	2.74%
SGA Expense		11,510,000,000	10,962,000,000	10,155,000,000	9,555,000,000	8,728,001,000
Net Income		2,377,000,000	2,058,000,000	2,039,000,000	1,709,000,000	1,462,000,000
Operating Cash Flow		4,285,000,000	3,984,000,000	3,437,000,000	3,057,000,000	3,198,000,000
Capital Expenditure		2,393,000,000	1,993,000,000	2,083,000,000	1,480,000,000	1,290,000,000
EBITDA		4,855,000,000	4,339,000,000	4,096,000,000	3,770,000,000	3,354,000,000
Return on Assets %		7.15%	6.50%	7.10%	6.34%	5.78%
Return on Equity %		20.74%	17.79%	17.58%	14.02%	12.80%
Debt to Equity		0.45	0.41	0.46	0.11	0.10

CONTACT INFORMATION:

Phone: 425 313-8100   Fax: 425 313-8103
Toll-Free: 800-774-2678
Address: 999 Lake Dr., Issaquah, WA 98027 United States

STOCK TICKER/OTHER:

Stock Ticker: COST   Exchange: NAS
Employees: 205,000   Fiscal Year Ends: 08/31
Parent Company:

SALARIES/BONUSES:

Top Exec. Salary: $699,810   Bonus: $188,800
Second Exec. Salary: Bonus: $188,800
$650,000

OTHER THOUGHTS:

Estimated Female Officers or Directors: 4
Hot Spot for Advancement for Women/Minorities: Y

Cox Enterprises Inc

www.coxenterprises.com

NAIC Code: 515120

TYPES OF BUSINESS:
Cable Television and Internet Services
Television Broadcasting
Newspaper Publishing
Radio Stations
Online News, Information and Services Sites
Auctions
Automotive E-Commerce
Technology Products

BRANDS/DIVISIONS/AFFILIATES:
Cox Communications Inc
Cox Business Services
Managed IP PBX
Cox Media
Valpak
Kudzu.com
G1GABLASTSM

CONTACTS:
Note: Officers with more than one job title may be intentionally listed here more than once.

John M. Dyer, CEO
Alexander C. Taylor, Exec. VP
Jimmy W. Hayes, Pres.
Marybeth N. Leamer, Exec. VP-Human Resources
Gregory B. Morrison, CIO
Marybeth N. Leamer, Exec. VP-Admin.
Shauna Sullivan Muhl, VP-Legal
Roberto I. Jimenez, VP-Corp. Comm. & Public Affairs
J. Lacey Lewis, Sr. VP-Finance
Patrick J. Esser, Pres., Cox Comm.
Sanford Schwartz, Pres., Manheim
Bill Hoffman, Pres., Cox Media Group
Kathy Decker, Treas.
James Cox Kennedy, Chmn.

GROWTH PLANS/SPECIAL FEATURES:
Cox Enterprises, Inc., through subsidiary Cox Communications, Inc., is a broadband communications and entertainment company, serving millions of customers throughout the U.S. Cox offers advanced digital video, high speed Internet and local & long distance telephone services over its own nationwide IP network. Cox Business Services provides data, video and voice solutions to small and regional businesses such as schools & universities, government organizations and financial institutions. The firm's Managed IP PBX service provides small business customers that have limited internal information technology departments with telecommunication systems that are monitored and managed around the clock by Cox Business. Cox Media offers national and local cable advertising in traditional spot and new media formats, along with promotional opportunities and production services, and owns Valpak, a leading direct marketing company in the U.S. The company also maintains Kudzu.com, an online directory that aggregates user reviews and ratings on local businesses, merchants and service providers. The company's recent G1GABLASTSM offering is a residential gigabit Internet service that features speeds 100 times faster than the average speed. G1GABLASTSM is available in select U.S. states, with plans to be available in all of its markets by the end of 2016.

FINANCIAL DATA:
Note: Data for latest year may not have been available at press time.

In U.S. $	2016	2015	2014	2013	2012	2011
Revenue		18,000,000,000	17,000,000,000	15,920,000,000	15,300,000,000	14,700,000,000
R&D Expense						
Operating Income						
Operating Margin %						
SGA Expense						
Net Income						
Operating Cash Flow						
Capital Expenditure						
EBITDA						
Return on Assets %						
Return on Equity %						
Debt to Equity						

CONTACT INFORMATION:
Phone: 678-645-0000 Fax:
Toll-Free:
Address: 6205 Peachtree Dunwoody Rd. 1400 Lake Hearn Dr., Atlanta, GA 30328 United States

STOCK TICKER/OTHER:
Stock Ticker: Private
Employees: 55,000
Parent Company:
Exchange:
Fiscal Year Ends: 12/31

SALARIES/BONUSES:
Top Exec. Salary: $ Bonus: $
Second Exec. Salary: $ Bonus: $

OTHER THOUGHTS:
Estimated Female Officers or Directors: 7
Hot Spot for Advancement for Women/Minorities: Y

CR Bard Inc

NAIC Code: 339100

www.crbard.com

TYPES OF BUSINESS:

Equipment-Urological Catheters
Diagnostic and Interventional Products
Minimally Invasive Vascular Products
Surgical Specialty Products
Supply Chain and Business Services
Oncology Products
Urology Products

BRANDS/DIVISIONS/AFFILIATES:

Unltraverse
LifeStent
PowerPICC
PowerPort
Statlock
PerFix
Ventralex
OptiFix

CONTACTS: *Note: Officers with more than one job title may be intentionally listed here more than once.*

Timothy Ring, CEO
Christopher Holland, CFO
Frank Lupisella, Chief Accounting Officer
Timothy Collins, President, Divisional
Jim Beasley, President, Divisional
John Groetelaars, President, Divisional
John Weiland, President
John DeFord, Senior VP, Divisional
Samrat Khichi, Senior VP
Betty Larson, Vice President, Divisional
Sharon Luboff, Vice President, Divisional
Patricia Christian, Vice President, Divisional

GROWTH PLANS/SPECIAL FEATURES:

C.R. Bard, Inc. designs, manufactures, packages, distributes and sells medical, surgical, diagnostic and patient care devices. The company markets its products in five categories, four primary ones: vascular, accounting for 28% of 2015 net sales; oncology, 27%, urology, 25%; surgical specialties, 17%; and other, 3%. C.R. Bard's line of minimally-invasive vascular products include percutaneous transluminal angioplasty (PTA) catheters, guidewires, introducers and accessories, peripheral vascular stents, vena cava filters and biopsy devices. Some of the brands in the vascular division are Ultraverse, Crosser, CTO, VascuTrakPTA, Flair AV, LifeStar and LifeStent. Additional products include cardiac mapping and electrophysiology laboratory systems as well as diagnostic and temporary pacing electrode catheters, fabrics and meshes and implantable blood vessel replacements. C.R. Bard's oncology products include the PowerPICC and PowerPort devices which eliminate the need for unnecessary catheters. The urology segment markets products that include the Foley catheter and the Statlock catheter stabilization line. The firm's surgical specialties products include meshes for vessel and hernia repair; irrigation devices for orthopedic, laparoscopic and gynecological procedures; and products for topical hemostasis. These products include the PerFix plug, Ventralex, Ventrio, and Allomax hernia patches; and the OptiFix and Capsure fixation devices. C.R. Bard's products are distributed in the U.S. directly to hospitals and other health care institutions as well as through numerous hospital/surgical supply and other medical specialty distributors.

U.S. employee benefits include medical, prescription, dental and vision coverage; a wellness program; life and AD&D insurance; short-and long-term disability; flexible spending accounts; a 401(k); and an employee stock purchase plan.

FINANCIAL DATA: *Note: Data for latest year may not have been available at press time.*

In U.S. $	2016	2015	2014	2013	2012	2011
Revenue		3,416,000,000	3,323,600,000	3,049,500,000	2,958,100,000	2,896,400,000
R&D Expense		259,200,000	302,000,000	295,700,000	203,200,000	185,400,000
Operating Income		349,400,000	781,500,000	1,265,900,000	812,300,000	560,400,000
Operating Margin %		10.22%	23.51%	41.51%	27.46%	19.34%
SGA Expense		1,012,100,000	981,500,000	920,300,000	817,300,000	1,041,100,000
Net Income		135,400,000	294,500,000	689,800,000	530,100,000	328,000,000
Operating Cash Flow		798,100,000	660,000,000	1,123,300,000	661,200,000	721,500,000
Capital Expenditure		103,800,000	139,900,000	103,000,000	92,000,000	89,300,000
EBITDA		587,400,000	664,700,000	1,404,800,000	908,300,000	662,300,000
Return on Assets %		2.66%	5.81%	15.00%	13.11%	9.23%
Return on Equity %		8.18%	15.12%	34.37%	28.59%	19.21%
Debt to Equity		0.78	0.77	0.67	0.73	0.50

CONTACT INFORMATION:

Phone: 908 277-8000   Fax: 908 277-8278
Toll-Free: 800-367-2273
Address: 730 Central Ave., Murray Hill, NJ 07974 United States

STOCK TICKER/OTHER:

Stock Ticker: BCR
Employees: 14,900
Parent Company:

Exchange: NYS
Fiscal Year Ends: 12/31

SALARIES/BONUSES:

Top Exec. Salary: $1,092,000
Bonus: $

Second Exec. Salary: $909,175
Bonus: $

OTHER THOUGHTS:

Estimated Female Officers or Directors: 6

Hot Spot for Advancement for Women/Minorities: Y

Crown Holdings Inc

www.crowncork.com

NAIC Code: 332431

TYPES OF BUSINESS:

Metal Can Manufacturing
Food and Beverage Cans
Plastic Containers

BRANDS/DIVISIONS/AFFILIATES:

CONTACTS: *Note: Officers with more than one job title may be intentionally listed here more than once.*

Timothy Donahue, CEO
Thomas Kelly, CFO
John Conway, Chairman of the Board
David Beaver, Controller
William Gallagher, General Counsel
Caesar Sweitzer, Independent Director
Djalma Novaes, President, Divisional
Gerard Gifford, President, Divisional
Robert Bourque, President, Divisional
Adam Dickstein, Secretary

GROWTH PLANS/SPECIAL FEATURES:

Crown Holdings, Inc. is a worldwide leader in the design, manufacture and sale of packaging products for consumer goods. Its primary products include steel and aluminum cans for food, beverage, household and other consumer products and metal vacuum closures and caps. The company operates 147 plants, along with sales and service facilities in 37 countries. Crown is organized geographically within three divisions: Americas, Europe and Asia Pacific. The Americas division includes operations in the U.S., Brazil, Canada, the Caribbean, Colombia and Mexico. Within this region, the company produces aluminum beverage cans and ends and steel crowns, commonly referred to as bottle caps, as well as steel and aluminum food cans and ends and metal vacuum closures. The European division includes operations in Eastern and Western Europe, the Middle East and North Africa, and produces beverage, food and aerosol cans and ends, specialty packaging and metal vacuum closures and caps. This division includes 68 plants in 24 countries. The Asia Pacific division consists of beverage can operations in Cambodia, China, Malaysia, Singapore, Thailand and Vietnam and non-beverage can operations, primarily including food cans and specialty packaging in China, Singapore, Thailand and Vietnam. In this region, Crown operates 30 plants in six countries. The firm supplies beverage cans and ends and other packaging products to a variety of beverage and beer companies, including Anheuser-Busch InBev, Carlsberg, Coca-Cola, Cott Beverages, Dr Pepper Snapple Group, Heineken, Molson Coors, Pepsi-Cola and SAB Miller, among others. Customers for its food packaging products include Abbot Laboratories, Bonduelle, Cecab, Faribault Foods, Mars, Simmons Foods, Nestle and Princes Group, among others. The firm primarily supplies aerosol cans to Colgate Palmolive, Procter & Gamble, Friesland Campina, SC Johnson and Unilever.

FINANCIAL DATA: *Note: Data for latest year may not have been available at press time.*

In U.S. $	2016	2015	2014	2013	2012	2011
Revenue		8,762,000,000	9,097,000,000	8,656,000,000	8,470,000,000	8,644,000,000
R&D Expense						
Operating Income		927,000,000	810,000,000	917,000,000	812,000,000	842,000,000
Operating Margin %		10.57%	8.90%	10.59%	9.58%	9.74%
SGA Expense		416,000,000	398,000,000	425,000,000	417,000,000	395,000,000
Net Income		393,000,000	387,000,000	324,000,000	557,000,000	282,000,000
Operating Cash Flow		956,000,000	912,000,000	885,000,000	621,000,000	379,000,000
Capital Expenditure		354,000,000	328,000,000	275,000,000	324,000,000	401,000,000
EBITDA		1,146,000,000	959,000,000	946,000,000	1,042,000,000	995,000,000
Return on Assets %		3.98%	4.36%	4.17%	7.75%	4.09%
Return on Equity %		298.85%	629.26%			
Debt to Equity		36.49	42.07	867.25		

CONTACT INFORMATION:

Phone: 215 698-5100   Fax:
Toll-Free:
Address: One Crown Way, Philadelphia, PA 19154-4599 United States

STOCK TICKER/OTHER:

Stock Ticker: CCK
Employees: 23,000
Parent Company:

Exchange: NYS
Fiscal Year Ends: 12/31

SALARIES/BONUSES:

Top Exec. Salary: $1,075,000   Bonus: $
Second Exec. Salary: $645,000   Bonus: $

OTHER THOUGHTS:

Estimated Female Officers or Directors: 3

Hot Spot for Advancement for Women/Minorities: Y

Cullen-Frost Bankers Inc

www.frostbank.com

NAIC Code: 522110

TYPES OF BUSINESS:

Banking
Insurance
Loans
Discount Brokerage
Trust Services
Cash Management
Investment Services

BRANDS/DIVISIONS/AFFILIATES:

Frost Bank
Frost Insurance Agency Inc
Frost Brokerage Services Inc
Frost Investment Advisors LLC
Tri-Frost Corporation
Main Plaza Corporation
Cullen/Frost Capital Trust
WNB Capital Trust

CONTACTS: Note: Officers with more than one job title may be intentionally listed here more than once.

Richard Evans, CEO
Paul Bracher, Executive VP, Subsidiary
Jerry Salinas, CFO
Phillip Green, Director
Patrick Frost, Director
Robert Berman, Executive VP, Subsidiary
Gary McKnight, Executive VP, Subsidiary
Candace Wolfshohl, Executive VP, Subsidiary
Annette Alonzo, Executive VP, Subsidiary
Paul Olivier, Executive VP, Subsidiary
William Perotti, Executive VP, Subsidiary
Stanley McCormick, Executive VP
Michael Milich, Other Corporate Officer
Vernon Torgerson, Senior Executive Vice President

GROWTH PLANS/SPECIAL FEATURES:

Cullen/Frost Bankers, Inc., with $28.6 billion in assets in 2015, is a financial holding company and a bank holding company headquartered in San Antonio, Texas. Through its subsidiaries, Cullen/Frost provides an array of products and services throughout numerous Texas markets, offering commercial & consumer banking services, as well as trust & investment management, insurance, brokerage, mutual funds, leasing, treasury management, capital markets advisory and item processing services. Cullen/Frost serves a variety of industries, including energy, manufacturing, services, construction, retail, telecommunications, healthcare, military and transportation. The company's loan portfolio has a significant concentration of energy-related loans totaling approximately 15.3% of total loans, but is not dependent upon any single industry or customer. Subsidiaries of the firm include Frost Bank, the principal operating subsidiary and sole banking subsidiary of Cullen/Frost; Frost Insurance Agency, Inc.; Frost Brokerage Services, Inc.; Frost Investment Advisors, LLC; Tri-Frost Corporation, which holds securities for investment purposes; Main Plaza Corporation, a loan provider; Cullen/Frost Capital Trust I, II; and WNB Capital Trust I.

Cullen/Frost offers its employees life, medical, dental and vision insurance; long-term disability insurance; a 401(k) plan; a flexible spending account; banking benefits; an employee assistance program; tuition reimbursement; the Tom Frost Scholarship ($5,000 to qualifying child of employee); and a profit sharing plan.

FINANCIAL DATA: Note: Data for latest year may not have been available at press time.

In U.S. $	2016	2015	2014	2013	2012	2011
Revenue		1,065,362,000	1,007,078,000	923,373,000	893,648,000	871,778,000
R&D Expense						
Operating Income		319,799,000	336,024,000	290,881,000	308,475,000	286,235,000
Operating Margin %		30.01%	33.36%	31.50%	34.51%	32.83%
SGA Expense		451,981,000	365,732,000	347,781,000	327,474,000	317,681,000
Net Income		279,328,000	277,977,000	237,866,000	237,952,000	217,535,000
Operating Cash Flow		393,471,000	286,670,000	173,606,000	299,999,000	274,369,000
Capital Expenditure		147,129,000	131,970,000	39,599,000	24,891,000	26,719,000
EBITDA						
Return on Assets %		.95%	1.02%	.97%	1.09%	1.14%
Return on Equity %		9.91%	10.63%	9.65%	10.09%	10.01%
Debt to Equity		0.08	0.08	0.09	0.09	0.09

CONTACT INFORMATION:

Phone: 210 220-4011   Fax: 210 220-5578
Toll-Free: 877-513-7678
Address: 100 W. Houston St., San Antonio, TX 78205 United States

STOCK TICKER/OTHER:

Stock Ticker: CFR   Exchange: NYS
Employees: 4,211   Fiscal Year Ends: 12/31
Parent Company:

SALARIES/BONUSES:

Top Exec. Salary: $975,000   Bonus: $
Second Exec. Salary: Bonus: $
$565,000

OTHER THOUGHTS:

Estimated Female Officers or Directors: 3
Hot Spot for Advancement for Women/Minorities: Y

Cushman & Wakefield Inc

www.cushmanwakefield.com

NAIC Code: 531210

TYPES OF BUSINESS:

Real Estate Brokerage
Property Management
Real Estate Documentation Web Site
Advisory Services
Research Services
Property Valuation

BRANDS/DIVISIONS/AFFILIATES:

DTZ
Cushman & Wakefield Sonnenblick Goldman

CONTACTS: Note: Officers with more than one job title may be intentionally listed here more than once.

Brett White, CEO
John Santora, COO
Edward C. Forst, Pres.
Duncan Palmer, CFO
Gene Boxer, Global General Counsel
James M. Underhill, CEO-Americas
Sanjay Verma, CEO-Asia Pacific
John Busi, Exec. VP-Valuation & Advisory
Brett White, Chmn.
Carlo Sant'Albano, CEO-Int'l

GROWTH PLANS/SPECIAL FEATURES:

Cushman & Wakefield, Inc. (C&W) is a global commercial real estate brokerage and services company. C&W provides advisory services related to asset buying, selling, financing and leasing, and also provides strategic planning, portfolio analysis and space location services. Agency and brokerage services assist clients with marketing and positioning properties through landlord representation, lease advisory, offices, retail services, supply chain, tenant representation and industrial solutions. Its capital markets group offers real estate buying, financing and investment clients various advisory services, including agency execution, investment management and corporate disposition practice. Global consulting services comprise market access, office platform, retail consulting and supply chain solutions for business customers and transaction and portfolio consulting for real estate customers. The practice groups division serves clients in select industries, including energy and resources, health care, hospitality, law firms, life sciences, mission critical facilities and Japanese multinational corporations. The research division offers property research, market analysis and forecasting solutions. The firm's valuation and advisory services include appraisal, portfolio valuation, development strategy, occupancy strategy and property tax services for real estate. Subsidiary Cushman & Wakefield Sonnenblick Goldman provides real estate financial services, specializing in debt structuring and debt and equity placement. C&W's corporate occupier and investor services manage real estate portfolios through account, transaction and project management, lease administration and facilities management. In 2015, the company was acquired by DTZ (formerly Cassidy Turley), and is now a global firm with 43,000 employees and revenues of $5 billion. The combined firms use the Cushman & Wakefield name.

C&W provides its employees with benefits such as medical, dental, vision, legal, disability and life insurance; domestic partner benefits; educational assistance; 401(k) plans; commuter program; and discounted gym memberships.

FINANCIAL DATA: Note: Data for latest year may not have been available at press time.

In U.S. $	2016	2015	2014	2013	2012	2011
Revenue		4,800,000,000	2,849,000,000	2,498,600,000	2,050,000,000	2,000,000,000
R&D Expense						
Operating Income						
Operating Margin %						
SGA Expense						
Net Income			61,600,000	46,200,000	18,202,800	14,900,000
Operating Cash Flow						
Capital Expenditure						
EBITDA						
Return on Assets %						
Return on Equity %						
Debt to Equity						

CONTACT INFORMATION:

Phone: 212-841-7500   Fax: 212-841-5002
Toll-Free:
Address: 1290 Avenue of the Americas, New York, NY 10104 United States

STOCK TICKER/OTHER:

Stock Ticker: Subsidiary   Exchange:
Employees: 43,000   Fiscal Year Ends: 12/31
Parent Company: DTZ

SALARIES/BONUSES:

Top Exec. Salary: $ Bonus: $
Second Exec. Salary: $ Bonus: $

OTHER THOUGHTS:

Estimated Female Officers or Directors: 2
Hot Spot for Advancement for Women/Minorities:

Sales, profits and employees may be estimates. Financial information, benefits and other data can change quickly and may vary from those stated here.

CVS Health Corporation

cvshealth.com

NAIC Code: 446110

TYPES OF BUSINESS:

Drug Stores
Pharmacy Benefits Management
Online Pharmacy Services

BRANDS/DIVISIONS/AFFILIATES:

CVS.com
Navarro.com
Onofre.com.br
CVS Pharmacy
CVS
Longs Drugs
Navarro Discount
Drogaria Onofre

CONTACTS: Note: Officers with more than one job title may be intentionally listed here more than once.

Larry Merlo, CEO
Colleen McIntosh, Senior VP
David Denton, CFO
David Dorman, Chairman of the Board
Eva Boratto, Chief Accounting Officer
Troyen Brennan, Chief Medical Officer
Per Lofberg, Executive VP
J. Joyner, Executive VP
Thomas Moriarty, Executive VP
Robert Kraft, Executive VP
Jonathan Roberts, Executive VP
Helena Foulkes, Executive VP
Lisa Bisaccia, Other Executive Officer
Steven Gold, Other Executive Officer
Andrew Sussman, Other Executive Officer

GROWTH PLANS/SPECIAL FEATURES:

CVS Health Corporation is a leading provider of prescription and related health care services in the U.S. It operates in three segments: corporate, retail/LTC and pharmacy services. The corporate segment provides management and administrative services to support the company's overall operations. The retail/LTC (long-term care) segment includes over 9,655 retail stores, of which 7,897 are stores that operated a pharmacy and 1,672 are CVS pharmacies located within Target Corporation stores. This division also includes CVS online retail pharmacy web sites (CVS.com, Navarro.com and Onofre.com.br), 32 on-site pharmacy stores, LTC pharmacy operations and retail health care clinics. The retail stores are located in 49 states, the District of Columbia, Puerto Rico and Brazil operating under the CVS Pharmacy, CVS, Longs Drugs, Navarro Discount Pharmacy and Drogaria Onofre names. The pharmacy services segment provides a full range of pharmacy benefit management services, including mail order pharmacy services plan design and administration, formulary management, claims processing and health management programs. Through subsidiary SilverScript Insurance Company, the division is a national provider of drug benefits to eligible beneficiaries under Medicare Part D. The segment operates a national retail pharmacy network with 24 retail specialty pharmacy stores; 11 specialty mail order pharmacies; five mail order dispensing services; and 83 branches with 73 ambulatory infusion suites. In December 2015, the firm acquired Target's pharmacies and clinics for $1.9 billion. Target's 1,672 drugstores were rebranded as CVS/pharmacy, while its 79 medical clinics were rebranded as MinuteClinics.

Employee benefits include medical, dental, vision and prescription coverage; free health screenings at MinuteClinic; a 401(k); employee stock purchase plan; short- and long-term disability; employee discounts; education reimbursement; an employee assistance program; and flexible spending accounts.

FINANCIAL DATA: Note: Data for latest year may not have been available at press time.

In U.S. $	2016	2015	2014	2013	2012	2011
Revenue		153,290,000,000	139,367,000,000	126,761,000,000	123,133,000,000	107,100,000,000
R&D Expense						
Operating Income		9,454,000,000	8,799,000,000	8,037,000,000	7,228,000,000	6,330,000,000
Operating Margin %		6.16%	6.31%	6.34%	5.87%	5.91%
SGA Expense		17,074,000,000	16,568,000,000	15,746,000,000	15,278,000,000	14,231,000,000
Net Income		5,237,000,000	4,644,000,000	4,592,000,000	3,877,000,000	3,461,000,000
Operating Cash Flow		8,412,000,000	8,137,000,000	5,783,000,000	6,671,000,000	5,856,000,000
Capital Expenditure		2,367,000,000	2,136,000,000	1,984,000,000	2,030,000,000	1,872,000,000
EBITDA		11,567,000,000	10,224,000,000	9,915,000,000	8,633,000,000	7,902,000,000
Return on Assets %		6.23%	6.37%	6.68%	5.94%	5.46%
Return on Equity %		13.93%	12.23%	12.14%	10.23%	9.13%
Debt to Equity		0.70	0.30	0.33	0.24	0.24

CONTACT INFORMATION:

Phone: 401 765-1500   Fax: 401 762-2137
Toll-Free: 888-746-7287
Address: 1 CVS Dr., Woonsocket, RI 02895 United States

STOCK TICKER/OTHER:

Stock Ticker: CVS   Exchange: NYS
Employees: 202,000   Fiscal Year Ends: 12/31
Parent Company:

SALARIES/BONUSES:

Top Exec. Salary: Bonus: $
$1,560,000
Second Exec. Salary: Bonus: $
$937,500

OTHER THOUGHTS:

Estimated Female Officers or Directors: 4

Hot Spot for Advancement for Women/Minorities: Y

Dana Holding Corporation

www.dana.com

NAIC Code: 336300

TYPES OF BUSINESS:

Automotive Products, Motors & Parts Manufacturing
Engine Systems
Fluid Systems
Heavy Vehicle Technologies
Brake Components
Chassis & Drive Train Components
Filtration Products
Financial Services

BRANDS/DIVISIONS/AFFILIATES:

Dana Spicer Thailand
Magnum Gaskets

CONTACTS: Note: Officers with more than one job title may be intentionally listed here more than once.

Jonathan Collins, CFO
Rodney Filcek, Chief Accounting Officer
George Constand, Chief Technology Officer
Joseph Muscari, Director
James Kamsickas, Director
Mark Wallace, Executive VP
Marc Levin, General Counsel
Aziz Aghili, President, Divisional
Dwayne Matthews, President, Divisional
Robert Pyle, President, Divisional

GROWTH PLANS/SPECIAL FEATURES:

Dana Holding Corporation supplies high technology driveline, sealing and thermal management products for global vehicle manufacturers. The company operates 100 facilities in 25 countries. Dana divides its operations into four segments: light vehicle, commercial vehicle, off-highway and power technologies. In the light vehicles segment, Dana engages in the manufacturing of component parts for light trucks, crossover utility vehicles, sport utility vehicles, vans and passenger cars. Products include front axles, rear axles, driveshafts, differentials, torque couplings and modular assemblies. Largest customers in this segment are Ford, Hyundai, Tata, Nissan, Toyota and Chrysler. The commercial vehicle segment manufactures parts for the medium/heavy duty vehicle market, including medium duty trucks, heavy duty trucks, buses and specialty vehicles. Products include axles, driveshafts, steering shafts, suspensions and tire management systems. Major customers include PACCAR, Volvo, Volkswagen, Ford and Daimler. The off-highway segment manufactures axels, driveshafts, end-fittings, transmissions, torque converters and electronic controls for off-highway use such as construction, earth moving, agriculture, mining, forestry, rail and material handling. Major customers include Deere & Company, AGCO, Manitou, Fiat and Oshkosh. Finally, the power technologies segment manufactures parts for the light vehicle, medium/heavy vehicle and off-highway markets. Products include gaskets, cover module, heat shields, engine sealing systems, cooling and heat transfer products. Major customers include Ford, General Motors, Volkswagen, Caterpillar and Cummins. In 2015, the firm opened its 16th technology center, located in Cedar Park, Texas; and opened the Dana Spicer Thailand gear manufacturing facility. In February 2016, Dana acquired Magnum Gaskets, a U.S.-based supplier of aftermarket gaskets and sealing products for automotive and commercial-vehicle applications.

FINANCIAL DATA: Note: Data for latest year may not have been available at press time.

In U.S. $	2016	2015	2014	2013	2012	2011
Revenue		6,060,000,000	6,617,000,000	6,769,000,000	7,224,000,000	7,592,000,000
R&D Expense						
Operating Income		444,000,000	471,000,000	412,000,000	448,000,000	375,000,000
Operating Margin %		7.32%	7.11%	6.08%	6.20%	4.93%
SGA Expense		391,000,000	411,000,000	410,000,000	434,000,000	409,000,000
Net Income		159,000,000	319,000,000	244,000,000	300,000,000	219,000,000
Operating Cash Flow		406,000,000	510,000,000	577,000,000	339,000,000	370,000,000
Capital Expenditure		260,000,000	234,000,000	209,000,000	164,000,000	196,000,000
EBITDA		579,000,000	591,000,000	729,000,000	725,000,000	682,000,000
Return on Assets %		3.43%	6.20%	-.25%	5.14%	3.61%
Return on Equity %		17.58%	30.93%	-1.28%	25.94%	19.71%
Debt to Equity		2.13	1.49	1.67	0.73	0.84

CONTACT INFORMATION:

Phone: 419 887-3000   Fax: 419 535-4643
Toll-Free: 800-537-8823
Address: 3939 Technology Dr., Maumee, OH 43537 United States

STOCK TICKER/OTHER:

Stock Ticker: DAN   Exchange: NYS
Employees: 22,600   Fiscal Year Ends: 12/31
Parent Company:

SALARIES/BONUSES:

Top Exec. Salary: Bonus: $
$1,025,000
Second Exec. Salary: Bonus: $500,000
$430,833

OTHER THOUGHTS:

Estimated Female Officers or Directors:

Hot Spot for Advancement for Women/Minorities: Y

Danaher Corporation

www.danaher.com

NAIC Code: 334510

TYPES OF BUSINESS:
Medical Diagnostic Equipment
Environmental Management Products
Test & Calibration Equipment
Automotive Components & Repair Equipment
Motors & Drives
Bar Code Equipment
Security & Defense Products

BRANDS/DIVISIONS/AFFILIATES:
TrojanUV
Hach
ChemTreat
Dexis
Gendex
Sciex
Beckman Coulter
Fortive Corporation

CONTACTS: Note: Officers with more than one job title may be intentionally listed here more than once.
Thomas P. Joyce, CEO

GROWTH PLANS/SPECIAL FEATURES:

Danaher Corporation designs, manufactures and markets professional, medical, industrial and commercial products. The company is a global science and technology innovator committed to helping customers solve complex challenges and improve quality of life. Danaher operates through four business divisions: environmental, dental, life sciences & diagnostics and industrial technologies. The environmental division provides products that help protect the global water supply. Its TrojanUV offering treats 2.24 billion gallons a day of drinking water for New York City. This division's platform provides instrumentation and disinfection systems that help analyze, treat and manage the quality of ultra-pure, potable, waste, ground and ocean water in residential, commercial, industrial and natural resource applications. Other brands within this segment include Hach, ChemTreat and McCrometer. The dental division develops products used to diagnose, treat and prevent disease and ailments of the teeth, gums and supporting bone, as well as improve the aesthetics of the human smile. Brands within this division include Dexis, Gendex, i-CAT, Instrmentarium, KaVo, Kerr, Ormco, Pelton & Crane, Soredex, KerrTotalCare and Nobel Biocare. Life sciences & diagnostics offers a range of research and clinical tools that scientists use to study cells and cell components in order to understand the cause of disease, identify new therapies and test new drugs and vaccines. Brands within this segment include Sciex, Beckman Coulter, Leica Biosystems, Leica Microsystems, Molecular Devices, Radiometer, HemoCue and Pall. Industrial technologies develops and manufactures equipment, consumables and software for various printing, marking, coding, design and color management applications on consumer and industrial products. Brands include Esko, Linx, Pantone, VideoJet, X-Rite and Foba. In July 2016, the firm separated its test & measurement segment, Industrial Technologies segment and retail/commercial petroleum platform through the spin-off of Fortive Corporation. Fortive is now a standalone company trading on the NASDAQ under the symbol FTV.

FINANCIAL DATA: Note: Data for latest year may not have been available at press time.

In U.S. $	2016	2015	2014	2013	2012	2011
Revenue		20,563,100,000	19,913,800,000	19,118,000,000	18,260,400,000	16,090,540,000
R&D Expense		1,239,100,000	1,314,200,000	1,249,900,000	1,137,900,000	1,018,526,000
Operating Income		3,469,100,000	3,431,300,000	3,274,900,000	3,165,100,000	2,617,226,000
Operating Margin %		16.87%	17.23%	17.12%	17.33%	16.26%
SGA Expense		6,054,300,000	5,697,000,000	5,432,800,000	5,181,200,000	4,607,692,000
Net Income		3,357,400,000	2,598,400,000	2,695,000,000	2,392,200,000	2,172,264,000
Operating Cash Flow		3,801,800,000	3,758,400,000	3,585,300,000	3,415,000,000	2,626,267,000
Capital Expenditure		633,000,000	597,500,000	551,500,000	458,300,000	334,471,000
EBITDA		4,538,100,000	4,543,000,000	4,606,900,000	4,008,100,000	3,224,420,000
Return on Assets %		7.87%	7.25%	7.97%	7.60%	8.32%
Return on Equity %		14.26%	11.35%	13.01%	13.31%	14.19%
Debt to Equity		0.50	0.14	0.15	0.27	0.30

CONTACT INFORMATION:
Phone: 202 828-0850   Fax: 202 828-0860
Toll-Free:
Address: 2200 Pennsylvania Ave. NW, Ste. 800W, Washington, WA 20006 United States

STOCK TICKER/OTHER:
Stock Ticker: DHR
Employees: 81,000
Parent Company:

Exchange: NYS
Fiscal Year Ends: 12/31

SALARIES/BONUSES:
Top Exec. Salary: $1,000,000   Bonus: $
Second Exec. Salary: $575,300   Bonus: $300,000

OTHER THOUGHTS:
Estimated Female Officers or Directors: 2

Hot Spot for Advancement for Women/Minorities: Y

Darden Restaurants Inc

www.darden.com

NAIC Code: 722513

TYPES OF BUSINESS:
Limited-Service Restaurants

BRANDS/DIVISIONS/AFFILIATES:
Red Lobster
Olive Garden
Capital Grille (The)
Bahama Breeze
LongHorn Steakhouse
Seasons 52
Eddie V's Prime Seafood
Yard House

CONTACTS: *Note: Officers with more than one job title may be intentionally listed here more than once.*
Eugene Lee, CEO
Ricardo Cardenas, CFO
Charles Sonsteby, Chairman of the Board
John Madonna, Chief Accounting Officer
Matthew Broad, General Counsel
Danielle Kirgan, Other Executive Officer
Todd Burrowes, President, Divisional
David George, President, Divisional
Harald Herrmann, Senior VP, Divisional

GROWTH PLANS/SPECIAL FEATURES:
Darden Restaurants, Inc. is a leading publicly held casual dining company in the U.S. It owns and operates nearly 1,500 restaurants throughout the U.S. and Canada. Darden operates seven restaurant chains: Olive Garden, LongHorn Steakhouse, The Capital Grille, Bahama Breeze, Eddie V's, Yard House and Seasons 52. Olive Garden, with over 800 restaurants, is a casual dining Italian restaurant in the U.S. and Canada. Its menu includes a variety of Italian foods, including antipasti; soups, salad and garlic breadsticks; baked pastas; sauteed chicken, seafood and vegetables; grilled meats; and a variety of desserts. It also offers imported Italian wines, coffee and espresso. LongHorn Steakhouse restaurants, with over 450 locations, are full-service establishments serving both lunch and dinner with American West-themed decor. The Capital Grille chain of upscale full-service restaurants dry-ages its steaks on the premises and flies in fresh seafood daily to its 54 locations as well as featuring a 350-selection wine list. The company's 38 Bahama Breeze locations offer guests an island dining experience with a menu featuring Caribbean-style beef, chicken and seafood. Eddie V's is a steak and seafood restaurant with 13 locations in Texas, Florida, California, Illinois, Virginia and Arizona. Yard House is a casual American-style restaurant with over 54 locations. Seasons 52, with 42 restaurants, is a fresh grill and wine bar with seasonally inspired menus, offering nutritionally balanced meals lower in calories than comparable restaurant meals. Additionally, the firm has 52 restaurants operated by independent third parties. In November 2015, the firm completed its previously announced spin-off of select real estate and restaurant assets into Four Corners Property Trust, Inc.

FINANCIAL DATA: *Note: Data for latest year may not have been available at press time.*

In U.S. $	2016	2015	2014	2013	2012	2011
Revenue	6,933,500,000	6,764,000,000	6,285,600,000	8,551,900,000	7,998,700,000	7,500,200,000
R&D Expense						
Operating Income	622,200,000	367,600,000	327,200,000	648,300,000	739,600,000	745,900,000
Operating Margin %	8.97%	5.43%	5.20%	7.58%	9.24%	9.94%
SGA Expense	622,900,000	673,500,000	663,500,000	847,800,000	746,800,000	738,000,000
Net Income	375,000,000	709,500,000	286,200,000	411,900,000	475,500,000	476,300,000
Operating Cash Flow	820,400,000	471,000,000	770,100,000	949,300,000	762,200,000	892,600,000
Capital Expenditure	228,300,000	296,500,000	414,800,000	685,600,000	639,700,000	547,700,000
EBITDA	913,500,000	687,500,000	631,600,000	1,044,000,000	1,093,500,000	1,058,900,000
Return on Assets %	7.09%	10.83%	4.07%	6.39%	8.33%	8.89%
Return on Equity %	17.50%	31.60%	13.57%	21.11%	25.17%	24.87%
Debt to Equity	0.22	0.62	1.17	1.23	0.81	0.75

CONTACT INFORMATION:
Phone: 407 245-4000   Fax: 407 245-4989
Toll-Free:
Address: 1000 Darden Ctr. Dr., Orlando, FL 32837 United States

STOCK TICKER/OTHER:
Stock Ticker: DRI
Employees: 150,000
Parent Company:

Exchange: NYS
Fiscal Year Ends: 05/31

SALARIES/BONUSES:
Top Exec. Salary: $953,750   Bonus: $
Second Exec. Salary: $576,539   Bonus: $

OTHER THOUGHTS:
Estimated Female Officers or Directors: 7
Hot Spot for Advancement for Women/Minorities: Y

DaVita Healthcare Partners Inc

www.davita.com

NAIC Code: 621492

TYPES OF BUSINESS:

Renal Care Services
Clinical Research

BRANDS/DIVISIONS/AFFILIATES:

HealthCare Partners
DaVita Kidney Care
DaVita (Shandong) Kidney Disease Hospital Co Ltd

CONTACTS: Note: Officers with more than one job title may be intentionally listed here more than once.

Javier Rodriguez, CEO, Divisional
Joseph Mello, CEO, Divisional
Dennis Kogod, CEO, Divisional
Kent Thiry, CEO
James Hilger, Chief Accounting Officer
Michael Staffieri, COO, Divisional
Jeanine Jiganti, Other Executive Officer
Kathleen Waters, Other Executive Officer
Martha Ha, Secretary
Leanne Zumwalt, Vice President, Divisional

GROWTH PLANS/SPECIAL FEATURES:

DaVita HealthCare Partners, Inc. is a leading provider of dialysis services in the U.S. for patients suffering from chronic kidney failure, also known as end stage renal disease (ESRD). The company operates through a network of 2,251 outpatient dialysis centers located in 46 states and Washington, D.C., serving approximately 180,000 patients. The firm also provides acute inpatient dialysis services in approximately 900 hospitals and related laboratory services. DaVita's dialysis and related lab services business accounted for approximately 62% of the firm's 2015 revenue. DaVita HealthCare Partners' secondary business is its HealthCare Partners (HCP) services, which provides integrated health care delivery and management. HCP operates through contracts, with 807,400 members under its care in 2015. In addition, HCP also provides a stand-alone dialysis center in Malaysia. DaVita's ancillary services and strategic initiatives include pharmacy services, vascular access services and clinical research, which conduct research trials with dialysis patients. Subsidiary DaVita Kidney Care has a joint venture kidney care specialty hospital chain in Shandong, China, called DaVita (Shandong) Kidney Disease Hospital Co Ltd. In 2015, DaVita agreed to acquire Renal Ventures Limited LLC, including a 100% interest in all its dialysis centers. The transaction is subject to Federal Trade Commission approval and expected to close by the end of 2016. In May 2016, DaVita agreed to acquire Family Health Care of Central Florida, a primary care group serving the Orlando metro area for more than 30 years.

The firm offers employees medical, dental and vision insurance; short- and long-term disability insurance; life insurance; a 401(k) plan; tuition reimbursement; flexible spending accounts; and an employee assistance program.

FINANCIAL DATA: Note: Data for latest year may not have been available at press time.

In U.S. $	2016	2015	2014	2013	2012	2011
Revenue		13,781,840,000	12,795,110,000	11,764,050,000	8,186,280,000	6,982,214,000
R&D Expense						
Operating Income		1,170,695,000	1,815,141,000	1,550,134,000	1,297,084,000	1,130,782,000
Operating Margin %		8.49%	14.18%	13.17%	15.84%	16.19%
SGA Expense		1,452,135,000	1,261,506,000	1,176,485,000	980,412,000	691,243,000
Net Income		269,732,000	723,114,000	633,446,000	536,017,000	478,001,000
Operating Cash Flow		1,557,200,000	1,459,407,000	1,773,341,000	1,100,848,000	1,180,046,000
Capital Expenditure		707,998,000	642,348,000	617,597,000	550,146,000	400,156,000
EBITDA		1,769,540,000	2,310,902,000	2,083,658,000	1,633,766,000	1,401,079,000
Return on Assets %		1.47%	4.12%	3.82%	4.30%	5.62%
Return on Equity %		5.37%	15.06%	15.45%	18.15%	23.20%
Debt to Equity		1.84	1.62	1.83	2.21	2.06

CONTACT INFORMATION:

Phone: 303 405-2100   Fax: 310 792-8928
Toll-Free:
Address: 2000 16th St., Denver, CO 80202 United States

STOCK TICKER/OTHER:

Stock Ticker: DVA   Exchange: NYS
Employees: 41,000   Fiscal Year Ends: 12/31
Parent Company:

SALARIES/BONUSES:

Top Exec. Salary: Bonus: $
$1,200,000
Second Exec. Salary: Bonus: $
$800,000

OTHER THOUGHTS:

Estimated Female Officers or Directors: 3

Hot Spot for Advancement for Women/Minorities: Y

Dell-EMC
NAIC Code: 334112

www.emc.com

TYPES OF BUSINESS:
Networked Computer Storage Systems
Virtual Server Software
Management Protection Software
Consulting Services
Storage Management Services

BRANDS/DIVISIONS/AFFILIATES:
VMware Inc
Pivotal Software Inc
Pivotal Big Data Suite
EMC Global Services
VMware Virtual Infrastructure
Cloudscaling Group Inc (The)
Spanning Cloud Apps Inc
Maginatics Inc

CONTACTS: Note: Officers with more than one job title may be intentionally listed here more than once.
David Goulden, CEO, Divisional
Robert Mee, CEO, Divisional
Joseph Tucci, CEO
Denis Cashman, CFO
Paul Maritz, Chairman of the Board, Divisional
Howard Elias, COO, Divisional
Erin McSweeney, Executive VP, Divisional
Paul Dacier, Executive VP
Harry You, Executive VP
Jeremy Burton, President, Divisional
Amit Yoran, President, Divisional
William Scannell, President, Divisional
William Teuber, Vice Chairman

GROWTH PLANS/SPECIAL FEATURES:
Dell-EMC, formerly EMC Corp., develops, delivers and supports systems, software and services for the storage, management and protection of electronic information. Dell-EMC operates in three business divisions: EMC Information Infrastructure, Pivotal and VMware Virtual Infrastructure. The Information Infrastructure business is divided into three segments: information storage, information intelligence and RSA information security. The information storage segment provides a range of networked information storage systems, software and services to support customers' information storage and management strategies. The information intelligence segment helps customers optimize business processes and create, manage and archive information such as documents, e-mail, web pages, records and application data. The RSA information security segment, delivers intelligence-driven security solutions designed to help organizations reduce the risk of operating in a digital world. RSA solutions provide the ability to detect, investigate & respond to advanced threats; confirm & manage identities; and ultimately prevent intellectual property theft, fraud and cybercrime. Majority-owned Pivotal Software, Inc. is a provider of annual subscription-based software & maintenance package Pivotal Big Data Suite, which bundles Pivotal Greenplum Database, Pivotal GemFire, Pivotal HAWQ and Pivotal HD next-generation products that can run across a variety of infrastructures, clouds and devices. The VMware Virtual Infrastructure division, represented by a majority stake in VMware, Inc., provides virtual infrastructure software from the desktop to the data center, supporting a range of operating systems. Additionally, EMC Global Services offers consulting services, technology deployment managed services, customer support services, training and certification through more than 16,000 support-service professionals as well as a global network of alliances and partners. In 2014, the firm acquired three cloud technology companies: The Cloudscaling Group, Inc.; Maginatics, Inc.; and Spanning Cloud Apps, Inc. In September 2016, Dell acquired EMC in a deal valued at $67 billion. VMware, Inc. will remain an independent, publicly-traded company.

FINANCIAL DATA: Note: Data for latest year may not have been available at press time.

In U.S. $	2016	2015	2014	2013	2012	2011
Revenue		24,704,000,000	24,440,000,512	23,221,999,616	21,713,901,568	20,007,587,840
R&D Expense						
Operating Income						
Operating Margin %						
SGA Expense						
Net Income		1,990,000,000	2,713,999,872	2,888,999,936	2,732,613,120	2,461,337,088
Operating Cash Flow						
Capital Expenditure						
EBITDA						
Return on Assets %						
Return on Equity %						
Debt to Equity						

CONTACT INFORMATION:
Phone: 508 435-1000   Fax: 508 435-5222
Toll-Free:
Address: 176 South St., Hopkinton, MA 01748 United States

STOCK TICKER/OTHER:
Stock Ticker: Subsidiary   Exchange:
Employees: 70,000   Fiscal Year Ends: 12/31
Parent Company: Dell Technologies Inc

SALARIES/BONUSES:
Top Exec. Salary: $ Bonus: $
Second Exec. Salary: $ Bonus: $

OTHER THOUGHTS:
Estimated Female Officers or Directors: 2
Hot Spot for Advancement for Women/Minorities: Y

Deloitte Consulting LLP www2.deloitte.com/us/en/services/consulting.html

NAIC Code: 541610

TYPES OF BUSINESS:

Management Consulting
Technology Integration Consulting
Human Resources Consulting
Business Strategy Consulting
Outsourcing Services
Strategic Consulting
Software

BRANDS/DIVISIONS/AFFILIATES:

Deloitte Touche Tohmatsu
Deloitte LLP

CONTACTS: *Note: Officers with more than one job title may be intentionally listed here more than once.*

Janet Foutty, CEO
Janet Foutty, Chmn.

GROWTH PLANS/SPECIAL FEATURES:

Deloitte Consulting LLP offers a range of expert consulting services from offices worldwide. The company is a subsidiary of Deloitte LLP, which is itself a subsidiary of Deloitte Touche Tohmatsu. Deloitte Consulting operates through three service categories: human capital, strategy & operations and technology. The human capital division's services leverage research, analytics and industry insights to help design and execute critical programs from business-driven human resources to innovative talent, leadership and change programs. Its services include actuarial, rewards, analytics, research-based membership programs, advisory services, HR transformation organization transformation & talent, employee experience enhancement and management consulting. Strategy & operations works with senior executives to help solve complex problems by bringing an approach to executable strategy that combines deep industry knowledge, rigorous analysis and insight to enable confident action. This division offers business model transformation, finance, mergers & acquisitions, service operations, social impact, supply chain operations and manufacturing operations consulting. The technology category transforms business via technology from strategy to implementation, this division delivers technology solutions that help drive transformation, improve productivity and streamline business operations. Solutions include application management services, digital engagement solutions, digital marketing, analytics, information management, application upgrades, financial transformation, product lifecycle management, supply chain management, cloud services, systems integration, systems development, IT mergers & acquisitions, IT strategy and technology infrastructure transformation.

Deloitte LLP offers employees medical, dental and prescription coverage; short- and long-term disability; tuition and employee assistance; emergency backup daycare; and flexible spending accounts.

FINANCIAL DATA: *Note: Data for latest year may not have been available at press time.*

In U.S. $	2016	2015	2014	2013	2012	2011
Revenue		7,815,148,000	7,111,116,000	6,200,000,000	5,888,000,000	5,400,000,000
R&D Expense						
Operating Income						
Operating Margin %						
SGA Expense						
Net Income						
Operating Cash Flow						
Capital Expenditure						
EBITDA						
Return on Assets %						
Return on Equity %						
Debt to Equity						

CONTACT INFORMATION:

Phone: 212-492-4000   Fax: 212-489-1687
Toll-Free:
Address: 30 Rockefeller Plaza, New York, NY 10112 United States

STOCK TICKER/OTHER:

Stock Ticker: Subsidiary   Exchange:
Employees: 64,884   Fiscal Year Ends: 05/31
Parent Company: Deloitte Touche Tohmatsu

SALARIES/BONUSES:

Top Exec. Salary: $ Bonus: $
Second Exec. Salary: $ Bonus: $

OTHER THOUGHTS:

Estimated Female Officers or Directors:
Hot Spot for Advancement for Women/Minorities: Y

Deloitte LLP

www.deloitte.com

NAIC Code: 541211

TYPES OF BUSINESS:

Accounting Services
Management Consulting
Risk Management Services
Financial Advisory Services
Outsourcing Services
Legal & Compliance Advisory Services

BRANDS/DIVISIONS/AFFILIATES:

Deloitte Touche Tohmatsu
Deloitte & Touche LLP
Deloitte Consulting LLP
Deloitte Financial Advisory Services LLP
Deloitte Tax LLP
Deloitte Foundation
Deloitte Doctoral Fellowship Program
Trueblood Seminars for Professors

CONTACTS: *Note: Officers with more than one job title may be intentionally listed here more than once.*

Cathy Engelbert, CEO
Michael Fucci, Chmn.

GROWTH PLANS/SPECIAL FEATURES:

Deloitte LLP, the U.S. division of global accounting firm Deloitte Touche Tohmatsu, offers a variety of financial and consulting services. The firm operates through several subsidiaries, including Deloitte & Touche LLP, Deloitte Consulting LLP, Deloitte Financial Advisory Services LLP and Deloitte Tax LLP. The company divides its services into 11 categories: audit, consulting, financial advisory, human capital, mergers & acquisitions, operations, regulatory, risk, strategy, tax and technology. Additionally, the firm has expertise in offering complementary services, such as legal and compliance advising involving litigation, ethics, management and disclosure issues. Industries served by the company include consumer business, energy & resources, financial services, life sciences & health care, manufacturing, public sector, real estate and technology/media & telecommunications. The firm also funds the Deloitte Foundation, dedicated to supporting accounting, business and related fields of study in the U.S. The foundation funds the Deloitte Doctoral Fellowship Program and Trueblood Seminars for Professors, among other higher education initiatives. In addition, the company conducts and publishes research concerning consumer spending patterns and economic growth.

Deloitte LLP offers employees medical, dental and prescription drug coverage; short- and long-term disability; life and travel accident insurance; a group legal plan; tuition assistance; flexible work arrangements; an employee assistance program; adoption assistance and reimbursement; emergency backup daycare; sabbaticals; flexible spending accounts; and a professional development program.

FINANCIAL DATA: *Note: Data for latest year may not have been available at press time.*

In U.S. $	2016	2015	2014	2013	2012	2011
Revenue		16,147,000,000	14,910,000,000	13,894,000,000	13,067,000,000	11,939,000,000
R&D Expense						
Operating Income						
Operating Margin %						
SGA Expense						
Net Income						
Operating Cash Flow						
Capital Expenditure						
EBITDA						
Return on Assets %						
Return on Equity %						
Debt to Equity						

CONTACT INFORMATION:

Phone: 212-489-1600   Fax: 212-489-1687
Toll-Free:
Address: 1633 Broadway, Paramount Bldg., New York, NY 10019-6754
United States

STOCK TICKER/OTHER:

Stock Ticker: Subsidiary   Exchange:
Employees: 70,603   Fiscal Year Ends: 05/31
Parent Company: Deloitte Touche Tohmatsu

SALARIES/BONUSES:

Top Exec. Salary: $ Bonus: $
Second Exec. Salary: $ Bonus: $

OTHER THOUGHTS:

Estimated Female Officers or Directors: 18
Hot Spot for Advancement for Women/Minorities: Y

Delta Air Lines Inc

NAIC Code: 481111

TYPES OF BUSINESS:

Airline
Air Freight

BRANDS/DIVISIONS/AFFILIATES:

Virgin Atlantic Airways Ltd

CONTACTS: Note: Officers with more than one job title may be intentionally listed here more than once.

Paul Jacobson, CFO
Craig Meynard, Chief Accounting Officer
Edward Bastian, Director
Steven Sear, Executive VP, Divisional
Joanne Smith, Executive VP
Peter Carter, Executive VP
Glen Hauenstein, President
Wayne West, Senior Executive VP

GROWTH PLANS/SPECIAL FEATURES:

Delta Air Lines, Inc. is a major air carrier that provides scheduled air transportation domestically and internationally for freight and more than 180 million passengers annually From its multiple hubs (Atlanta, Cincinnati, Detroit, Los Angeles, Boston, Minneapolis/St. Paul, New York-JFK, New York-LaGuardia, Salt Lake City, Seattle, Amsterdam, Paris-Charles de Gaulle and Tokyo-Narita), the company serves 337 destinations in 62 countries. The firm has a total 809 aircraft in fleet, with 618 being company owned and 191 being leased Delta is a founding member of the SkyTeam international alliance, a global airline alliance that provides customers with 1,000 worldwide destinations, flights and services. Delta also has trans-Atlantic joint ventures with both Air France KLM Group and Alitalia in addition to a trans-Pacific joint venture with Virgin Australia. The company also holds a 49% interest in Virgin Atlantic Airways Ltd., giving Delta a more competitive stance in the vital New York City to London Heathrow route.

Delta offers its employees medical, dental, vision and life insurance; flexible spending accounts; a 401(k) plan; profit sharing; credit union membership; employee assistance programs; adoption assistance, paid holiday and vacation; and free and reduced rate travel benefits for employees and their close family members.

FINANCIAL DATA: Note: Data for latest year may not have been available at press time.

In U.S. $	2016	2015	2014	2013	2012	2011
Revenue		40,704,000,000	40,362,000,000	37,773,000,000	36,670,000,000	35,115,000,000
R&D Expense						
Operating Income		7,802,000,000	2,206,000,000	3,400,000,000	2,175,000,000	1,975,000,000
Operating Margin %		19.16%	5.46%	9.00%	5.93%	5.62%
SGA Expense		11,938,000,000	10,905,000,000	9,829,000,000	9,228,000,000	8,839,999,000
Net Income		4,526,000,000	659,000,000	10,540,000,000	1,009,000,000	854,000,000
Operating Cash Flow		7,927,000,000	4,947,000,000	4,504,000,000	2,476,000,000	2,834,000,000
Capital Expenditure		2,945,000,000	2,249,000,000	2,568,000,000	1,968,000,000	1,254,000,000
EBITDA		9,637,000,000	3,977,000,000	5,058,000,000	3,402,000,000	3,193,000,000
Return on Assets %		8.43%	1.23%	21.77%	2.29%	1.97%
Return on Equity %		46.03%	6.44%	221.61%		
Debt to Equity		0.62	0.97	0.84		

CONTACT INFORMATION:

Phone: 404 715-2600   Fax: 404 715-1400
Toll-Free: 866-715-2170
Address: 1030 Delta Blvd., Atlanta, GA 30320 United States

STOCK TICKER/OTHER:

Stock Ticker: DAL
Employees: 83,000
Parent Company:

Exchange: NYS
Fiscal Year Ends: 12/31

SALARIES/BONUSES:

Top Exec. Salary: $800,000   Bonus: $
Second Exec. Salary: Bonus: $
$625,000

OTHER THOUGHTS:

Estimated Female Officers or Directors: 2
Hot Spot for Advancement for Women/Minorities: Y

DENTSPLY International Inc

www.dentsply.com

NAIC Code: 339100

TYPES OF BUSINESS:

Dental Consumable Products
Dental Specialty Products
Dental Laboratory products

BRANDS/DIVISIONS/AFFILIATES:

Ankylos
Delton
Esthet.X
In-Ovation
Maillefer
Palodent
Sani-Tip
Xylocaine

CONTACTS: Note: Officers with more than one job title may be intentionally listed here more than once.

Ulrich Michel, CFO
Bret Wise, Chairman of the Board
Christopher Clark, COO, Divisional
James Mosch, COO, Divisional
Jeffrey Slovin, Director
Rainer Berthan, Executive VP, Divisional
Jonathan Friedman, General Counsel
Maureen MacInnis, Other Executive Officer
Albert Sterkenburg, Senior VP
Robert Size, Senior VP

GROWTH PLANS/SPECIAL FEATURES:

DENTSPLY International, Inc. designs, manufactures and markets a broad range of products for the professional dental market. It offers products in four principal categories: dental consumables, dental laboratory products, dental specialty products and consumable medical device products. The dental consumables category consists of dental sundries and small equipment used in dental offices. Dental sundries in this category include dental anesthetics, prophylaxis or prophylaxis paste, tooth sealants, impression materials, restorative materials, tooth whiteners and topical fluoride. Small equipment products include dental diagnostic systems, high- and low-speed dental handpieces, intraoral curing light systems and ultrasonic scalers and polishers. The dental laboratory category includes products and equipment used in preparation of dental appliances by dental laboratories such as dental prosthetics, precious metal dental alloys, dental ceramics and crown and bridge materials. Equipment includes computer-aided machining ceramic systems and porcelain furnaces. Dental specialty products, used within dental offices and laboratory settings, include endodontic instruments and materials, dental implants and related products, bone grafting materials and orthodontic appliances and accessories. Consumable medical device products consist mainly of urological products including catheters, certain surgical products, medical drills and other nonmedical products. Some of DENTSPLY's brand names include Ankylos, Aquasil, Caulk, Delton, Esthet.X, In-Ovation, Maillefer, Origo, Palodent, Rinn, Sani-Tip, Sultan and Xylocaine. The firm maintains manufacturing and distribution facilities in the U.S. located in Delaware, Florida, Illinois, Massachusetts, Ohio, Pennsylvania and Tennessee. It also has international facilities in Belgium, Brazil, China, France, Germany, Italy, Japan, Mexico, the Netherlands, Poland, Puerto Rico, Sweden and Switzerland.

Employee benefits include medical, dental, vision, disability and life insurance; flexible spending accounts; an employee stock ownership plan; a 401(k); and an employee assistance program.

FINANCIAL DATA: Note: Data for latest year may not have been available at press time.

In U.S. $	2016	2015	2014	2013	2012	2011
Revenue		2,674,300,000	2,922,620,000	2,950,770,000	2,928,429,000	2,537,718,000
R&D Expense						
Operating Income		375,200,000	445,600,000	419,166,000	381,939,000	300,728,000
Operating Margin %		14.02%	15.24%	14.20%	13.04%	11.85%
SGA Expense		1,077,300,000	1,143,106,000	1,144,890,000	1,148,731,000	936,847,000
Net Income		251,200,000	322,854,000	313,192,000	314,213,000	244,520,000
Operating Cash Flow		497,400,000	560,401,000	417,846,000	369,685,000	393,469,000
Capital Expenditure		72,000,000	105,767,000	101,421,000	95,401,000	74,254,000
EBITDA		508,500,000	580,360,000	546,863,000	516,729,000	384,960,000
Return on Assets %		5.54%	6.63%	6.23%	6.46%	6.10%
Return on Equity %		10.78%	13.29%	13.20%	15.49%	13.26%
Debt to Equity		0.48	0.49	0.46	0.55	0.80

CONTACT INFORMATION:

Phone: 717 845-7511   Fax: 717 854-2343
Toll-Free: 800-877-0020
Address: 221 W. Philadelphia St., York, PA 17405 United States

STOCK TICKER/OTHER:

Stock Ticker: XRAY
Employees: 11,400
Parent Company:

Exchange: NAS
Fiscal Year Ends: 12/31

SALARIES/BONUSES:

Top Exec. Salary: $975,000   Bonus: $
Second Exec. Salary: $636,500   Bonus: $

OTHER THOUGHTS:

Estimated Female Officers or Directors: 5
Hot Spot for Advancement for Women/Minorities: Y

Sales, profits and employees may be estimates. Financial information, benefits and other data can change quickly and may vary from those stated here.

Dick's Sporting Goods Inc

www.dickssportinggoods.com

NAIC Code: 451110

TYPES OF BUSINESS:

Sporting Goods Stores
Outdoor Apparel
Footwear
Hunting & Fishing Supplies
Golf Supplies
Bicycles
Online Sales

BRANDS/DIVISIONS/AFFILIATES:

Dick's Sporting Goods
Golf Galaxy
Field & Stream
Maxfli
Reebok
Golf Galaxy LLC
True Runner
Chelsea Collective

CONTACTS: Note: Officers with more than one job title may be intentionally listed here more than once.

Edward Stack, CEO
Joseph Oliver, Chief Accounting Officer
Lauren Hobart, Chief Marketing Officer
William Colombo, Director
Michele Willoughby, Executive VP, Divisional
Lee Belitsky, Executive VP, Divisional
Andre Hawaux, Executive VP
Deborah Victorelli, Senior VP, Divisional
John Hayes, Senior VP

GROWTH PLANS/SPECIAL FEATURES:

Dick's Sporting Goods, Inc. (DSG) is a retail sporting goods chain that operates 645 Dick's Sporting Goods stores in 46 states as well as 79 Golf Galaxy stores in 29 states. The company offers a broad assortment of sporting goods equipment, footwear and apparel under national and private-label brands Aciscs, Callaway Golf, Columbia, Nike, Remington, TaylorMade-adidas Golf, The North Face and Under Armour. DSG also offers private brands and products through exclusive licenses such as adidas, DBX, Field & Stream, Fitness Gear, Maxfli, Nickent, Primed, Quest, Reebok, Slazenger, Top-Flite, Umbro and Walter Hagen. Each of the Dick's Sporting Goods locations typically contains six store-within-a-store specialty units: footwear, team sports, outdoor lodge, golf, fitness and athletic apparel. In addition to apparel and equipment sales, its stores offer a variety of services such as golf club fitting, repair and grip replacement; tennis and lacrosse racket stringing; ice skate sharpening; bicycle repair and servicing; scope mounting and bore sighting; and CO_2 tank filling for paintball. The company owns Golf Galaxy LLC, which operates the Golf Galaxy stores designed for serious golf enthusiasts and include artificial bent grass putting greens, golf simulators and private lessons. In addition to its retail locations, the firm maintains separate catalog and e-commerce sites for its chains. DGS also owns and operates 10 Field & Stream stores, a specialized outdoor concept; three True Runner store, a specialized footwear concept; and Chelsea Collective, a women's specialty retail fitness boutique.

FINANCIAL DATA: Note: Data for latest year may not have been available at press time.

In U.S. $	2016	2015	2014	2013	2012	2011
Revenue	7,270,965,000	6,814,479,000	6,213,173,000	5,836,119,000	5,211,802,000	4,871,492,000
R&D Expense						
Operating Income	535,192,000	554,059,000	536,812,000	523,674,000	432,020,000	309,249,000
Operating Margin %	7.36%	8.13%	8.63%	8.97%	8.28%	6.34%
SGA Expense	1,647,695,000	1,532,607,000	1,407,138,000	1,313,489,000	1,162,861,000	1,139,781,000
Net Income	330,391,000	344,198,000	337,598,000	290,709,000	263,906,000	182,077,000
Operating Cash Flow	643,514,000	605,978,000	403,870,000	438,284,000	410,421,000	389,967,000
Capital Expenditure	370,028,000	349,007,000	285,668,000	219,026,000	201,807,000	159,067,000
EBITDA	728,481,000	738,660,000	703,964,000	620,955,000	562,475,000	421,921,000
Return on Assets %	9.44%	10.57%	11.33%	9.88%	9.43%	7.51%
Return on Equity %	18.24%	19.53%	20.58%	18.05%	17.61%	14.88%
Debt to Equity					0.09	0.10

CONTACT INFORMATION:

Phone: 724 273-3400   Fax:
Toll-Free: 877-846-9997
Address: 345 Court St., Coraopolis, PA 15108 United States

STOCK TICKER/OTHER:

Stock Ticker: DKS   Exchange: NYS
Employees: 37,200   Fiscal Year Ends: 01/31
Parent Company:

SALARIES/BONUSES:

Top Exec. Salary: $1,000,000   Bonus: $

Second Exec. Salary: $768,606   Bonus: $

OTHER THOUGHTS:

Estimated Female Officers or Directors: 4

Hot Spot for Advancement for Women/Minorities: Y

Sales, profits and employees may be estimates. Financial information, benefits and other data can change quickly and may vary from those stated here.

DIRECTV

www.directv.com

NAIC Code: 517110

TYPES OF BUSINESS:

Satellite Broadcasting
Commercial Satellite Fleet
Satellite-Based Internet Services
Digital Television

BRANDS/DIVISIONS/AFFILIATES:

AT&T Inc
DIRECTV Holdings LLC
DIRECTV Latin American Holdings Inc
PanAmericana
Sky Brasil Servicos Ltda
Innova S de RL de CV
Sky Mexico
Game Show Network LLC

CONTACTS: *Note: Officers with more than one job title may be intentionally listed here more than once.*

Michael White, CEO
Patrick Doyle, CFO
Romulo Pontual, Chief Technology Officer
Larry Hunter, Executive VP
Joseph Bosch, Executive VP
Bruce Churchill, Executive VP
Steven Adams, Senior VP
Fazal Merchant, Senior VP

GROWTH PLANS/SPECIAL FEATURES:

DIRECTV is a leading provider of digital television entertainment throughout the U.S. and Latin America. The company's three business segments, DIRECTV U.S., DIRECTV Latin America and DIRECTV Sports Networks, and their subsequent subsidiaries are engaged in digital entertainment programming via satellite for residential and commercial subscribers. DIRECTV U.S., operating through DIRECTV Holdings LLC, provides direct-to-home digital television services, with 37 million subscribers. It offers one of the nation's most comprehensive selections of HD channels, 3D programming and Video on Demand services. It has a fleet of owned and leased satellites. The company operates more than 50 customer service centers. DIRECTV Latin America, operated by DIRECTV Latin American Holdings, Inc., is comprised of PanAmericana; its 93%-owned subsidiary Sky Brasil Servicos Ltda.; and its 41% investment in Innova, S de RL de CV (known as Sky Mexico). DIRECTV Sports Networks, operating through DIRECTV Sports Networks LLC, is comprised primarily of three regional sports television networks based in Seattle, Denver and Pittsburgh, each of which operates under the Root Sports brand name. Additionally, DIRECTV owns a 42% interest in Game Show Network LLC, a basic television network dedicated to game-related programming and Internet interactive game playing. In July 2015, the firm was acquired by AT&T, Inc.

Employees receive medical, dental and vision coverage; flexible spending accounts; wellness plans; employee assistance programs; free DIRECTV service; discounted DIRECTV services for friends and family; and a 401(k) savings plan with a matching contribution opportunity.

FINANCIAL DATA: *Note: Data for latest year may not have been available at press time.*

In U.S. $	2016	2015	2014	2013	2012	2011
Revenue		34,000,000,000	33,260,000,000	31,754,000,000		
R&D Expense						
Operating Income						
Operating Margin %						
SGA Expense						
Net Income			3,102,000,000	2,995,000,000		
Operating Cash Flow						
Capital Expenditure						
EBITDA						
Return on Assets %						
Return on Equity %						
Debt to Equity						

CONTACT INFORMATION:

Phone: 310-964-5000   Fax:
Toll-Free:
Address: 2260 E. Imperial Hwy., El Segundo, CA 90245 United States

STOCK TICKER/OTHER:

Stock Ticker: Subsidiary   Exchange:
Employees: 31,000   Fiscal Year Ends: 12/31
Parent Company: AT&T Inc

SALARIES/BONUSES:

Top Exec. Salary: $ Bonus: $
Second Exec. Salary: $ Bonus: $

OTHER THOUGHTS:

Estimated Female Officers or Directors: 3
Hot Spot for Advancement for Women/Minorities: Y

Discount Tire Company

www.discounttire.com

NAIC Code: 441320

TYPES OF BUSINESS:

Tire Stores
Mail-Order & Online Tire Sales
Roadside Assistance

BRANDS/DIVISIONS/AFFILIATES:

Discount Tire
America's Tire Co
CarCareONE

CONTACTS: *Note: Officers with more than one job title may be intentionally listed here more than once.*

Michael Zuieback, CEO
Michael Zuieback, Pres.
Christian Roe, CFO
Don G. Majors, Jr., VP-Mktg.
Charlie Baugh, CIO
Bruce T. Halle, Chmn.

GROWTH PLANS/SPECIAL FEATURES:

Discount Tire Company, based in Arizona, is one of the largest independent tire dealers in the U.S. The firm operates over 920 stores in 31 U.S. states. These stores operate under the Discount Tire name as well as under the America's Tire Co name in certain parts of California. Discount Tire carries leading tire brands such as BF Goodrich, Michelin, Goodyear, Pirelli and GT Radial as well in-house exclusive brands Road Hugger, Arizonian, MB Wheels and Pathfinder tires and wheels. The company also repairs tires, offers tire rotations and balancing and provides free air pressure checking to its customers. In addition, the firm sells and delivers tires through its mail-order/online division (Discount Tire direct), which provides fast free shipping to a customer's door as well as through its web site. This web site also provides extensive information for its customers on all aspects of wheel and tire care. The company offers a Discount Tire/America's Tire CarCareONE card, a credit card that also provides emergency roadside assistance. The CarCareONE card is underwritten by Synchrony Financial.

Discount Tires offers its employees benefits including flexible spending accounts; an employee assistance program; medical, vision, life and dental insurance; paid vacation; a 401(k) plan and profit sharing plans. Part-time employees are eligible for medical insurance and a 401(k).

FINANCIAL DATA: *Note: Data for latest year may not have been available at press time.*

In U.S. $	2016	2015	2014	2013	2012	2011
Revenue		4,200,000,000	3,900,000,000	3,500,000,000	3,300,000,000	3,100,000,000
R&D Expense						
Operating Income						
Operating Margin %						
SGA Expense						
Net Income						
Operating Cash Flow						
Capital Expenditure						
EBITDA						
Return on Assets %						
Return on Equity %						
Debt to Equity						

CONTACT INFORMATION:

Phone: 480-606-6000   Fax: 480-951-8619
Toll-Free:
Address: 20225 N. Scottsdale Rd., Scottsdale, AZ 85254 United States

STOCK TICKER/OTHER:

Stock Ticker: Private   Exchange:
Employees: 17,955   Fiscal Year Ends: 12/31
Parent Company:

SALARIES/BONUSES:

Top Exec. Salary: $ Bonus: $
Second Exec. Salary: $ Bonus: $

OTHER THOUGHTS:

Estimated Female Officers or Directors:
Hot Spot for Advancement for Women/Minorities:

Discovery Communications Inc

corporate.discovery.com

NAIC Code: 515210

TYPES OF BUSINESS:

Cable TV Networks
Digital Media
Catalog & Online Sales
Educational Products
E-commerce
Merchandising

BRANDS/DIVISIONS/AFFILIATES:

Discovery Channel
TLC
Hub (The)
Oprah Winfrey Network (OWN, The)
3net
Investigation Discovery
Military Channel
Velocity

CONTACTS: *Note: Officers with more than one job title may be intentionally listed here more than once.*

David Zaslav, CEO
Andrew Warren, CFO
Robert Miron, Chairman of the Board
Kurt Wehner, Chief Accounting Officer
Adria Romm, Other Corporate Officer
Paul Guyardo, Other Executive Officer
Bruce Campbell, Other Executive Officer
David Leavy, Other Executive Officer
Jean-Briac Perrette, President, Divisional
Stephanie Marks, Secretary

GROWTH PLANS/SPECIAL FEATURES:

Discovery Communications, Inc. is a global media and entertainment company that produces and distributes original and purchased programming across multiple platforms to 2.6 billion cumulative subscribers across the globe. Discovery spans a variety of diverse genres, including exploration, survival, natural history, environment, technology, docu-series, health and wellness and space. The firm operates in four segments: U.S. networks, international networks, education and other. The U.S. networks segment operates and owns ten national TV networks: Discovery Channel, TLC, Animal Planet, Investigation Discovery, Science, Military Channel, Discovery Fit & Health and Velocity. The division also includes the firm's interests in The Oprah Winfrey Network (OWN), The Hub and 3net, a 24/7 3D TV network. The firm's international networks reach more than 220 countries and territories around the world and are distributed in over 40 languages. Networks include Discovery Channel, Animal Planet, Discovery Home & Health, Turbo, Quest, Discovery en Espanol and Discovery Famillia. Education offers a suite of curriculum-based tools and educator enhancement resources that promote the integration of media and technology in the classroom. Other is largely comprised of production studios that develop television content for our networks and television service providers throughout the world. The company's portfolio also includes web sites, retail, merchandising and various digital media products and services. In July 2015, Discovery announced an agreement to acquire full ownership of Eurosport, leading sports channels across Europe and Asia, from TF1 Group.

FINANCIAL DATA: *Note: Data for latest year may not have been available at press time.*

In U.S. $	2016	2015	2014	2013	2012	2011
Revenue		6,394,000,000	6,265,000,000	5,535,000,000	4,487,000,000	4,235,000,000
R&D Expense						
Operating Income		1,985,000,000	2,061,000,000	1,998,000,000	1,855,000,000	1,799,000,000
Operating Margin %		31.04%	32.89%	36.09%	41.34%	42.47%
SGA Expense		1,669,000,000	1,692,000,000	1,575,000,000	1,291,000,000	1,183,000,000
Net Income		1,034,000,000	1,139,000,000	1,075,000,000	943,000,000	1,132,000,000
Operating Cash Flow		1,277,000,000	1,318,000,000	1,285,000,000	1,099,000,000	1,100,000,000
Capital Expenditure		103,000,000	120,000,000	115,000,000	77,000,000	58,000,000
EBITDA		2,219,000,000	2,404,000,000	2,318,000,000	1,883,000,000	2,732,000,000
Return on Assets %		5.08%	5.82%	7.70%	7.59%	9.87%
Return on Equity %		14.66%	15.29%	17.22%	14.72%	17.77%
Debt to Equity		1.39	1.07	1.04	0.82	0.64

CONTACT INFORMATION:

Phone: 240 662-2000   Fax: 240 662-1868
Toll-Free:
Address: 1 Discovery Pl., Silver Spring, MD 20910 United States

STOCK TICKER/OTHER:

Stock Ticker: DISCA   Exchange: NAS
Employees: 5,700   Fiscal Year Ends: 12/31
Parent Company:

SALARIES/BONUSES:

Top Exec. Salary: Bonus: $
$3,115,385
Second Exec. Salary: Bonus: $
$1,557,692

OTHER THOUGHTS:

Estimated Female Officers or Directors: 1

Hot Spot for Advancement for Women/Minorities: Y

Dollar Thrifty Automotive Group Inc

www.thrifty.com/AboutUs/content.aspx

NAIC Code: 532111

TYPES OF BUSINESS:

Automobile Rental
Used Car Sales
Financial Services

BRANDS/DIVISIONS/AFFILIATES:

Hertz Global Holdings Inc
Thrifty Rental
Dollar Rent A Car

CONTACTS: Note: Officers with more than one job title may be intentionally listed here more than once.

Scott L. Thompson, Pres.
H. Clofford Buster, CFO
Rick L. Morris, CIO
Scott L. Thompson, Chmn.

GROWTH PLANS/SPECIAL FEATURES:

Dollar Thrifty Automotive Group, Inc. (DTG) is a holding company for rental car agencies Thrifty Car Rental and Dollar Rent A Car. These wholly-owned subsidiaries comprise one of the largest car rental companies in the world. DTG itself is a wholly-owned subsidiary of Hertz Global Holdings, Inc. Through corporately-owned and franchised stores, the Thrifty and Dollar operate more than 1,000 locations in 77 countries throughout North, Central and South America, Africa, the Middle East, the Caribbean, Asia and the Pacific. DTG also sells vehicle rental franchises worldwide, and provides sales & marketing, reservations, data processing systems, insurance and other services to franchisees. DTG provides customers supplemental equipment and optional products, including global positioning system equipment, ski racks, infant & child seats, as well as rent-a-toll products for electronic toll payments.

The company offers employees medical, dental and vision coverage; domestic partner benefits; flexible spending accounts; a wellness program; short- and long-term disability; life and AD&D insurance; an employee assistance program; a 401(k); tuition reimbursement; and employee discounts.

FINANCIAL DATA: Note: Data for latest year may not have been available at press time.

In U.S. $	2016	2015	2014	2013	2012	2011
Revenue		1,900,000,000	1,910,000,000	1,875,000,000	1,700,000,000	1,548,928,000
R&D Expense						
Operating Income						
Operating Margin %						
SGA Expense						
Net Income						
Operating Cash Flow						
Capital Expenditure						
EBITDA						
Return on Assets %						
Return on Equity %						
Debt to Equity						

CONTACT INFORMATION:

Phone: 918-660-7700   Fax: 918-669-2934
Toll-Free: 888-700-9803
Address: 5330 E. 31st St., Tulsa, OK 74135 United States

SALARIES/BONUSES:

Top Exec. Salary: $ Bonus: $
Second Exec. Salary: $ Bonus: $

STOCK TICKER/OTHER:

Stock Ticker: Subsidiary   Exchange:
Employees: 5,900   Fiscal Year Ends: 12/31
Parent Company: Hertz Global Holdings Inc

OTHER THOUGHTS:

Estimated Female Officers or Directors: 2
Hot Spot for Advancement for Women/Minorities:

DR Horton Inc

www.drhorton.com

NAIC Code: 236117

TYPES OF BUSINESS:

Construction, Home Building and Residential
Mortgages
Title Insurance

BRANDS/DIVISIONS/AFFILIATES:

DHI Mortgage

CONTACTS: Note: Officers with more than one job title may be intentionally listed here more than once.

Thomas Montano, Assistant Secretary
Bill Wheat, CFO
Donald Horton, Chairman of the Board
Michael Murray, COO
David Auld, President

GROWTH PLANS/SPECIAL FEATURES:

D.R. Horton, Inc. is a leading national builder of single-family homes with a diversified set of holdings and operating divisions in 27 states and 79 metropolitan markets. The firm generally builds homes between 1,000 to 4,000 square feet, ranging in price from $100,000 to over 1 million. In 2015, the company closed approximately 36,736 homes, with an average closing sales price approximating $285,700. The company is divided into six regional homebuilding segments and one financial services segment. The homebuilding segments are East, operating in eight states; Midwest, four states; Southeast, five states; South Central, three states; Southwest, two states; and West, six states. The building services section constructs residences, tailored to the particular community where they are being built, including single-family residential homes, townhouses, condominiums, duplexes and triplexes. Detached homes sales accounted for 90% of the firm's 2015 revenues. Subcontractors under the supervision of D. R. Horton do substantially all of the actual building. The financial services segment of the company provides mortgage financing and title insurance through its wholly-owned subsidiary, DHI Mortgage. The home builder's current business strategy is to enter into new lot option contracts to purchase finished lots in selected communities to potentially increase sales volumes and profitability. The firm plans to renegotiate existing lot option contracts as necessary to reduce lot costs and better match the scheduled lot purchases with new home demand in each community. The company also manages inventory of homes under construction by selectively starting construction on unsold homes to capture new home demand while monitoring the number and aging of unsold homes and aggressively marketing its unsold, completed homes in inventory. In 2015, the company acquired the homebuilding operations of Pacific Ridge Homes in Seattle, Washington.

FINANCIAL DATA: Note: Data for latest year may not have been available at press time.

In U.S. $	2016	2015	2014	2013	2012	2011
Revenue		10,824,000,000	8,024,900,000	6,259,300,000	4,354,000,000	3,636,800,000
R&D Expense						
Operating Income		1,092,500,000	790,900,000	654,400,000	242,900,000	12,100,000
Operating Margin %		10.09%	9.85%	10.45%	5.57%	.33%
SGA Expense		1,186,000,000	965,400,000	766,300,000	614,100,000	556,300,000
Net Income		750,700,000	533,500,000	462,700,000	956,300,000	71,800,000
Operating Cash Flow		700,400,000	-661,400,000	-1,231,100,000	-298,100,000	14,900,000
Capital Expenditure		56,100,000	100,200,000	58,000,000	33,600,000	16,300,000
EBITDA		1,177,500,000	852,600,000	685,600,000	288,600,000	83,900,000
Return on Assets %		7.03%	5.59%	5.74%	15.17%	1.27%
Return on Equity %		13.63%	11.63%	12.09%	30.78%	2.74%
Debt to Equity		0.64	0.71	0.86	0.69	0.65

CONTACT INFORMATION:

Phone: 817-390-8200   Fax: 817 856-8429
Toll-Free:
Address: 301 Commerce St., Ste. 500, Fort Worth, TX 76102 United States

STOCK TICKER/OTHER:

Stock Ticker: DHI   Exchange: NYS
Employees: 6,230   Fiscal Year Ends: 09/30
Parent Company:

SALARIES/BONUSES:

Top Exec. Salary: $500,000   Bonus: $950,000
Second Exec. Salary: Bonus: $
$1,000,000

OTHER THOUGHTS:

Estimated Female Officers or Directors: 1
Hot Spot for Advancement for Women/Minorities:

DriveTime Automotive Group Inc

www.drivetime.com

NAIC Code: 441120

TYPES OF BUSINESS:

Used Auto Dealers
Auto Financing
Auto Leasing

BRANDS/DIVISIONS/AFFILIATES:

DriveCare Powertrain Protection Plan
Bridgecrest Acceptance Company

CONTACTS: Note: Officers with more than one job title may be intentionally listed here more than once.

Ray Fidel, CEO
Ray Fidel, Pres.
Mark G. Sauder, CFO
Paul I. Kaplan, CIO
Jon Ehlinger, General Counsel
Jon Ehlinger, VP-Public Rel.
Al Appelman, VP-Risk & Customer Analytics
Ernest C. Garcia II, Chmn.

GROWTH PLANS/SPECIAL FEATURES:

DriveTime Automotive Group, Inc. is a leading chain of buy-here-pay-here used car dealerships. The company targets its products and services to the sub-prime segment of the automobile financing industry. This segment serves customers with limited credit histories, low income or past credit problems who cannot access traditional financing. Advantages of buy-here-pay-here dealerships include the ability to offer customers expanded credit opportunities and flexible payment terms as well as the ability to make payments at the dealership. For each used vehicle sold, the company offers a 30-day limited warranty, 5-day return guarantee, autocheck history report and a certified multi-point inspection. The firm finances all of the used cars through retail installment contracts. DriveTime currently operates 139 dealerships nationwide. The dealerships are located in high-visibility, high-traffic commercial areas and maintain an average inventory of 60-70 used cars, featuring a wide selection of makes and models. The ages of the cars typically range from three to seven years. DriveTime acquires its inventory primarily from used vehicle auctions. After purchase, the cars are delivered to one of the company's centers, where they are inspected thoroughly and reconditioned for sale. The company offers its DriveCare Powertrain Protection Plan to customers interested in extended protection coverage. Besides flexible auto loan financing, no-commitment lease options are also offered. In 2016, the firm launched Bridgecrest Acceptance Company, a licensed third-party servicer that will service loans for DriveTime and other affiliated finance companies. All credit scoring, risk decision analytics and verifications remain the responsibility of DriveTime.

DriveTime offers its employees benefits including medical, dental, vision, disability and life insurance; paid time off; a 401(k); flexible spending accounts; and tuition reimbursement.

FINANCIAL DATA: Note: Data for latest year may not have been available at press time.

In U.S. $	2016	2015	2014	2013	2012	2011
Revenue		1,525,000,000	1,475,000,000	1,400,896,000	1,221,064,000	1,121,967,000
R&D Expense						
Operating Income						
Operating Margin %						
SGA Expense						
Net Income						
Operating Cash Flow						
Capital Expenditure						
EBITDA						
Return on Assets %						
Return on Equity %						
Debt to Equity						

CONTACT INFORMATION:

Phone: Fax:
Toll-Free: 888-418-1212
Address: 1720 W. Rio Salado Pkwy, Tempe, AZ 85281 United States

STOCK TICKER/OTHER:

Stock Ticker: Private   Exchange:
Employees: 4,200   Fiscal Year Ends: 12/31
Parent Company:

SALARIES/BONUSES:

Top Exec. Salary: $ Bonus: $
Second Exec. Salary: $ Bonus: $

OTHER THOUGHTS:

Estimated Female Officers or Directors:
Hot Spot for Advancement for Women/Minorities:

Sales, profits and employees may be estimates. Financial information, benefits and other data can change quickly and may vary from those stated here.

DTE Energy Company

www.dteenergy.com

NAIC Code: 221112

TYPES OF BUSINESS:

Utilities-Electricity & Natural Gas
Energy Management
Wholesale Energy Trading
Fuel Supply Services
Hydroelectric Power
Nuclear Power
Coal Shipping-Rail & Boat
Consulting Services

BRANDS/DIVISIONS/AFFILIATES:

DTE Electric
DTE Gas

CONTACTS: Note: Officers with more than one job title may be intentionally listed here more than once.

Gerard Anderson, CEO
Peter Oleksiak, CFO
Donna England, Chief Accounting Officer
David Meador, Chief Administrative Officer
Mark Stiers, COO, Subsidiary
Trevor Lauer, COO, Subsidiary
Gerardo Norcia, COO
Lisa Muschong, Director
Bruce Peterson, General Counsel
David Ruud, President, Divisional
Larry Steward, Senior VP
Steve Kurmas, Vice Chairman

GROWTH PLANS/SPECIAL FEATURES:

DTE Energy Company is a diversified energy and energy technology company that develops merchant power and industrial energy projects and works in energy trading, selling electricity, natural gas, coal, chilled water, landfill gas and steam. DTE is also one of the nation's largest purchasers, transporters and marketers of coal. The company's operations are divided into four segments: electric, gas, non-utility operations and corporate & other. The electric segment consists of DTE Electric, which is engaged in the generation, purchase, distribution and sale of electricity to approximately 2.2 million residential, commercial and industrial customers in southeastern Michigan. The gas segment is represented by DTE Gas, which buys, stores, transports and distributes natural gas to 1.2 million residential, commercial and industrial customers. The firm's non-utility operations segment include gas storage & pipelines, encompassing DTE's interstate gas transmission pipelines and storage facilities; power & industrial projects, primarily consisting of energy product delivery, coal transportation, as well as marketing and electricity provided by biomass-fueled energy projects; and energy trading, which buys, sells and trades electricity, coal and natural gas, and provides risk management services such as energy marketing and trading operations. The corporate & other segment consists of various holding company activities, certain non-utility debt and energy-related investments. In 2016, the firm retired three coal-fired generating units among its plants, and announced plans to close eight additional coal-fired generators at three plants in Michigan by 2023, replacing them with renewable energy.

DTE offers its employees medical, dental and vision coverage; comprehensive wellness programs; a 401(k) plan; flexible spending accounts; an employee assistance program; long-term care insurance; life, disability and AD&D insurance; and flex time.

FINANCIAL DATA: Note: Data for latest year may not have been available at press time.

In U.S. $	2016	2015	2014	2013	2012	2011
Revenue		10,337,000,000	12,301,000,000	9,661,000,000	8,791,000,000	8,897,000,000
R&D Expense						
Operating Income		1,239,000,000	1,590,000,000	1,203,000,000	1,279,000,000	1,423,000,000
Operating Margin %		11.98%	12.92%	12.45%	14.54%	15.99%
SGA Expense						
Net Income		727,000,000	905,000,000	661,000,000	610,000,000	711,000,000
Operating Cash Flow		1,911,000,000	1,839,000,000	2,154,000,000	2,209,000,000	2,008,000,000
Capital Expenditure		2,020,000,000	2,049,000,000	1,876,000,000	1,820,000,000	1,484,000,000
EBITDA		2,252,000,000	2,849,000,000	2,452,000,000	2,418,000,000	2,476,000,000
Return on Assets %		2.56%	3.35%	2.52%	2.33%	2.79%
Return on Equity %		8.50%	11.13%	8.64%	8.48%	10.35%
Debt to Equity		1.00	1.00	0.91	0.95	1.02

CONTACT INFORMATION:

Phone: 313 235-4000 Fax: 313 235-6743
Toll-Free: 866-966-5555
Address: 1 Energy Plaza, Detroit, MI 48226 United States

STOCK TICKER/OTHER:

Stock Ticker: DTE Exchange: NYS
Employees: 10,000 Fiscal Year Ends: 12/31
Parent Company:

SALARIES/BONUSES:

Top Exec. Salary:
$1,268,269
Bonus: $

Second Exec. Salary:
$674,615
Bonus: $

OTHER THOUGHTS:

Estimated Female Officers or Directors: 8

Hot Spot for Advancement for Women/Minorities: Y

Sales, profits and employees may be estimates. Financial information, benefits and other data can change quickly and may vary from those stated here.

Duke Energy Corporation

www.duke-energy.com

NAIC Code: 221112

TYPES OF BUSINESS:

Utilities-Electricity & Natural Gas
Merchant Power Generation
Natural Gas Transportation & Storage
Electricity Transmission
Energy Marketing
Real Estate
Telecommunications
Facility & Plant Services

BRANDS/DIVISIONS/AFFILIATES:

Duke Energy International LLC
National Methanol Company
Duke Energy Renewables
Mesquite Creek Wind

CONTACTS: *Note: Officers with more than one job title may be intentionally listed here more than once.*

Lynn Good, CEO
Steven Young, CFO
William Currens, Chief Accounting Officer
A.R. Mullinax, Executive VP, Divisional
Lloyd Yates, Executive VP, Divisional
Julie Janson, Executive VP
Douglas Esamann, Executive VP
Dhiaa Jamil, Executive VP
Melissa Anderson, Other Executive Officer
Brian Savoy, Senior VP, Divisional

GROWTH PLANS/SPECIAL FEATURES:

Duke Energy Corporation is an energy services provider that offers delivery and management of electricity and natural gas throughout the U.S. The company operates in three segments: regulated utilities, international energy and commercial power. The regulated utilities segment provides regulated electric and gas services to 7.4 million customers in Ohio, Indiana, Kentucky, Florida and the Carolinas. This segment relies on a fuel mix of 29% coal, 27% nuclear, 23.1% oil & gas and 0.8% hydroelectric & solar. The international energy segment owns, operates and manages power generation facilities and sells and markets electric power and natural gas outside the U.S. Subsidiary Duke Energy International LLC operates power generation plants primarily in Latin America. Additionally, the segment includes a 25% interest in National Methanol Company, a large regional producer of methanol and methyl tertiary butyl ether located in Saudi Arabia. The commercial power segment owns, operates and manages wind & solar renewable generation and energy transmission projects throughout U.S. Additionally, it builds and operates high voltage power and natural gas transmission projects. This segment relies on wind and solar resources for its generation of electric energy; and includes Duke Energy Renewables, which develops wind and solar energy projects in the U.S. In September 2015, the firm acquired a 50% stake in Mesquite Creek Wind, a 211-megawatt (MW) wind power project near Lamesa, Texas, through its joint venture partnership with Sumitomo Corp. of America. That October, Duke Energy announced plans to acquire Piedmont Natural Gas Company, Inc. for $4.9 billion. The transaction is contingent upon approval by the North Carolina Utilities Commission.

The firm offers employees life, disability, medical, dental and vision insurance; retirement benefits; and wellness programs.

FINANCIAL DATA: *Note: Data for latest year may not have been available at press time.*

In U.S. $	2016	2015	2014	2013	2012	2011
Revenue		23,459,000,000	23,925,000,000	24,598,000,000	19,624,000,000	14,529,000,000
R&D Expense						
Operating Income		5,367,000,000	5,258,000,000	4,982,000,000	3,110,000,000	2,777,000,000
Operating Margin %		22.87%	21.97%	20.25%	15.84%	19.11%
SGA Expense						
Net Income		2,816,000,000	1,883,000,000	2,665,000,000	1,768,000,000	1,706,000,000
Operating Cash Flow		6,676,000,000	6,586,000,000	6,382,000,000	5,244,000,000	3,672,000,000
Capital Expenditure		6,766,000,000	5,384,000,000	5,526,000,000	5,501,000,000	4,372,000,000
EBITDA		9,363,000,000	9,263,000,000	8,695,000,000	6,345,000,000	5,350,000,000
Return on Assets %		2.32%	1.59%	2.33%	2.00%	2.80%
Return on Equity %		6.98%	4.58%	6.49%	5.56%	7.53%
Debt to Equity		0.94	0.91	0.92	0.89	0.82

CONTACT INFORMATION:

Phone: 704-382-3853 Fax: 704-382-3814
Toll-Free: 800-873-3853
Address: 550 S. Tryon St., Charlotte, NC 28202 United States

STOCK TICKER/OTHER:

Stock Ticker: DUK Exchange: NYS
Employees: 28,344 Fiscal Year Ends: 12/31
Parent Company:

SALARIES/BONUSES:

Top Exec. Salary:
$1,225,758

Bonus: $

Second Exec. Salary:
$670,833

Bonus: $

OTHER THOUGHTS:

Estimated Female Officers or Directors: 8

Hot Spot for Advancement for Women/Minorities: Y

Eastman Chemical Company

www.eastman.com

NAIC Code: 325220

TYPES OF BUSINESS:

Chemicals, Fibers & Plastics
Coatings, Adhesives & Additives
Performance & Intermediate Chemicals
Acetate Fibers & Textiles
Gasification Services
Food Safety Diagnostics
Logistics Services
PET, Polyethylene & Polymers

BRANDS/DIVISIONS/AFFILIATES:

Estrobond
Estron
Chromspun

CONTACTS: Note: Officers with more than one job title may be intentionally listed here more than once.

Brian Henry, Assistant Secretary
Curtis Espeland, CFO
Scott King, Chief Accounting Officer
Stephen Crawford, Chief Technology Officer
Mark Costa, Director
Brad Lich, Executive VP
David Golden, Other Executive Officer
Mark Cox, Other Executive Officer
Perry Stuckey, Other Executive Officer
Michael Chung, Other Executive Officer
Damon Warmack, Senior VP, Divisional
Lucian Boldea, Senior VP, Divisional

GROWTH PLANS/SPECIAL FEATURES:

Eastman Chemical Company manufactures and sells a broad portfolio of chemicals, plastics and fibers through 51 manufacturing sites in 15 countries. The firm has five operating segments: additives & functional products (AFP); fibers; adhesives & plasticizers (A&P); advanced materials; and specialty fluids & intermediates. The AFP segment manufactures specialty polymers and solvents as well as rubber additivers. The fibers segment manufactures Estron acetate and Estrobond triacetin plasticizers for use in cigarette filters; Estron natural and Chromspun solution-dyed acetate yarns for the apparel, home furnishing and industrial fabrics industries; and cellulose acetate and acetyl raw materials for other acetate fiber producers. The A&P segment manufactures resins and plasticizers used in consumables, building and construction, durable goods, health and wellness as well as industrial chemicals and processing. The advanced materials segment produces specialized co-polyesters, cellulosic plastics, aftermarket window films, polyvinyl butyral sheets and resins used in industries including transportation, consumables, building and construction. The specialty fluids & intermediates segment produces chemicals and fluids for industrial, health and wellness, energy, consumables and agricultural applications.

The company offers employees health, life, dependent life and disability insurance; a 401(k); and an employee stock purchase plan.

FINANCIAL DATA: Note: Data for latest year may not have been available at press time.

In U.S. $	2016	2015	2014	2013	2012	2011
Revenue		9,648,000,000	9,527,000,000	9,350,000,000	8,102,000,000	7,178,000,000
R&D Expense		251,000,000	227,000,000	193,000,000	198,000,000	158,000,000
Operating Income		1,384,000,000	1,162,000,000	1,862,000,000	800,000,000	1,021,000,000
Operating Margin %		14.34%	12.19%	19.91%	9.87%	14.22%
SGA Expense		762,000,000	755,000,000	645,000,000	644,000,000	469,000,000
Net Income		848,000,000	751,000,000	1,165,000,000	437,000,000	696,000,000
Operating Cash Flow		1,612,000,000	1,408,000,000	1,297,000,000	1,128,000,000	625,000,000
Capital Expenditure		652,000,000	596,000,000	488,000,000	470,000,000	466,000,000
EBITDA		1,963,000,000	1,627,000,000	2,292,000,000	1,152,000,000	1,313,000,000
Return on Assets %		5.35%	5.38%	9.93%	4.90%	11.43%
Return on Equity %		22.76%	20.55%	34.57%	18.15%	39.80%
Debt to Equity		1.67	2.06	1.12	1.62	0.77

CONTACT INFORMATION:

Phone: 423 229-2000   Fax: 423 229-2145
Toll-Free:
Address: 200 S. Wilcox Dr., Kingsport, TN 37662 United States

STOCK TICKER/OTHER:

Stock Ticker: EMN   Exchange: NYS
Employees: 15,000   Fiscal Year Ends: 12/31
Parent Company:

SALARIES/BONUSES:

Top Exec. Salary: Bonus: $
$1,117,070
Second Exec. Salary: Bonus: $
$799,754

OTHER THOUGHTS:

Estimated Female Officers or Directors: 2

Hot Spot for Advancement for Women/Minorities: Y

EchoStar Corp

NAIC Code: 517110

www.echostar.com

TYPES OF BUSINESS:

Digital Set-Top Boxes & Related Products
Fixed Satellite Services

BRANDS/DIVISIONS/AFFILIATES:

EchoStar Technologies LLC
Echostar Satellite Services LLC
Hughes Communications Inc
EchoStar Mobile Limited
EchoStar XXI
Solaris Mobile

CONTACTS: Note: Officers with more than one job title may be intentionally listed here more than once.

Michael Dugan, CEO
David Rayner, CFO
Charles Ergen, Chairman of the Board
Pradman Kaul, Director
Kenneth Carroll, Executive VP, Divisional
Sandra Kerentoff, Executive VP, Divisional
Kranti Kilaru, Executive VP, Divisional
Dean Manson, Executive VP
Mark Jackson, President, Subsidiary
Anders Johnson, President, Subsidiary

GROWTH PLANS/SPECIAL FEATURES:

EchoStar Corp. is a global provider of satellite operations, video delivery solutions and broadband satellite technologies and services for home and office, delivering innovative network technologies, managed services and solutions for enterprises and governments. The company operates in three business segments: Hughes Communications, Inc., EchoStar Technologies and EchoStar Satellite Services. Hughes provides satellite broadband Internet to North American consumers and broadband network services and equipment to domestic and international enterprise markets. The Hughes segment also offers managed services to large enterprises, as well as solutions to customers for mobile satellite systems. EchoStar Technologies designs, develops, and distributes set top boxes and related products and technology primarily for satellite TV service providers, telecommunication and international cable companies and directly to consumers. This segment additionally provides digital broadcast operations such as satellite uplinking/downlinking, transmission services, signal processing and conditional access management primarily to DISH Network Corporation and its subsidiaries. EchoStar Technologies offer its TV Anywhere technology through Slingbox units directly to consumers via retail outlets and online, as well as to the pay-TV operator market. EchoStar Satellite Services provides satellite services on a full-time and occasional-use basis primarily to DISH Network, Dish Mexico, U.S. government service providers, Internet service providers, broadcast news organizations, programmers and private enterprise customers. Subsidiary EchoStar Mobile Limited (formerly Solaris Mobile) is based in Ireland and licensed by the European Union (EU) to provide mobile satellite service/complementary ground component (MSS/CGC) services covering the entire EU using S-band spectrum. This division is scheduled to launch EchoStar XXI in mid-2016, in order to provide space segment capacity to EchoStar Mobile.

The firm offers employees medical, dental and vision plans; tuition reimbursement; discounted employee products and services; disability and life insurance; a 401(k) plan; and an employee stock purchase program.

FINANCIAL DATA: Note: Data for latest year may not have been available at press time.

In U.S. $	2016	2015	2014	2013	2012	2011
Revenue		3,143,714,000	3,445,578,000	3,282,452,000	3,121,704,000	2,761,431,000
R&D Expense		73,717,000	60,886,000	67,942,000	69,649,000	50,966,000
Operating Income		356,033,000	328,090,000	103,587,000	99,886,000	80,838,000
Operating Margin %		11.32%	9.52%	3.15%	3.19%	2.92%
SGA Expense		378,686,000	372,010,000	358,499,000	372,644,000	303,276,000
Net Income		153,357,000	152,874,000	2,525,000	211,048,000	3,639,000
Operating Cash Flow		776,451,000	840,131,000	450,507,000	505,149,000	447,018,000
Capital Expenditure		729,275,000	680,026,000	433,621,000	611,482,000	377,172,000
EBITDA		871,796,000	906,358,000	665,629,000	805,039,000	494,262,000
Return on Assets %		2.25%	2.36%	.03%	3.21%	.07%
Return on Equity %		4.52%	4.89%	.07%	6.82%	.12%
Debt to Equity		0.59	0.65	0.73	0.77	0.81

CONTACT INFORMATION:

Phone: 303 706-4000   Fax:
Toll-Free:
Address: 100 Inverness Terrace E., Englewood, CO 80112 United States

STOCK TICKER/OTHER:

Stock Ticker: SATS   Exchange: NAS
Employees: 4,400   Fiscal Year Ends: 12/31
Parent Company:

SALARIES/BONUSES:

Top Exec. Salary: $850,013   Bonus: $
Second Exec. Salary: Bonus: $
$761,646

OTHER THOUGHTS:

Estimated Female Officers or Directors: 1
Hot Spot for Advancement for Women/Minorities:

eClinicalWorks

www.eclinicalworks.com

NAIC Code: 0

TYPES OF BUSINESS:

Computer Software, Healthcare & Biotechnology
Electronic Prescription Filing
Patient Flow Management
Claims Submission & Management Software
Business Optimization Software

BRANDS/DIVISIONS/AFFILIATES:

Enterprise Business Optimizer
eClinicalWorks HMS
eClinicalWorks CCMR
eClinicalWorks Patient Portal

CONTACTS: Note: Officers with more than one job title may be intentionally listed here more than once.

Girish Kumar Navani, CEO

GROWTH PLANS/SPECIAL FEATURES:

eClinicalWorks is a private company operating in the ambulatory clinical systems market. The company primarily provides electronic medical record (EMR) and practice management (PM) tools for its clients, including physicians; large and small health systems; large and medium medical group practices, including federally qualified health centers (FQHCs) and community health centers (CHCs); and small, solo provider practices. The firm's customer base consists of more than 115,000 physicians and over 850,000 medical professionals in all 50 states and 24 countries. eClinicalWorks' EMR cloud solution provides patient flow management, patient record access, registry reporting, electronic prescription request, referring physician communication and clinical data transfers, all while keeping the data private. When used with the firm's PM system, this system enables clients to review patient history, current medications, allergies and diagnostic tests; streamline medical billing management; check patient insurance eligibility; electronically submit and manage claims; and perform clinical and financial analyses through its Enterprise Business Optimizer (eBO) tool. eClinicalWorks HMS is a web-based product that covers the clinical, administrative and financial areas of an integrated healthcare delivery system. Other suites include eClinicalWorks CCMR, a population health program across all functional ACO categories; healow (health and online wellness) suite, which offer tools that facilitates secure communication between providers and patients; and the RCM (revenue cycle management) console assists in processing claims, financial analytics, reimbursement evaluation and six levels of clearinghouse integrations. The company also maintains a web-based patient portal, eClinicalWorks Patient Portal, allowing patients to access their physician's systems to view their own lab results and appointment information as well as request prescription refills and communicate with doctors and nurses.

eClinicalWorks offers its employees health, dental, vision, life and disability insurance; flexible spending accounts; and a 401(k) plan.

FINANCIAL DATA: Note: Data for latest year may not have been available at press time.

In U.S. $	2016	2015	2014	2013	2012	2011
Revenue		358,000,000	333,000,000	300,000,000	255,000,000	204,700,000
R&D Expense						
Operating Income						
Operating Margin %						
SGA Expense						
Net Income						
Operating Cash Flow						
Capital Expenditure						
EBITDA						
Return on Assets %						
Return on Equity %						
Debt to Equity						

CONTACT INFORMATION:

Phone: 508-836-2700   Fax: 508-836-4466
Toll-Free: 866-888-6929
Address: 2 Technology Dr., Westborough, MA 01581 United States

STOCK TICKER/OTHER:

Stock Ticker: Private   Exchange:
Employees: 4,500   Fiscal Year Ends: 12/31
Parent Company:

SALARIES/BONUSES:

Top Exec. Salary: $ Bonus: $
Second Exec. Salary: $ Bonus: $

OTHER THOUGHTS:

Estimated Female Officers or Directors:
Hot Spot for Advancement for Women/Minorities:

Edward D Jones & Co LP

www.edwardjones.com

NAIC Code: 523120

TYPES OF BUSINESS:

Stock Brokerage
Financial Planning
Retirement & Estate Planning
Life Insurance
Banking Services
Annuities

BRANDS/DIVISIONS/AFFILIATES:

Jones Financial Companies LLLP (The)
Edward Jones

CONTACTS: *Note: Officers with more than one job title may be intentionally listed here more than once.*

James D. Weddle, Managing Partner
Kavin D. Bastien, CFO
Norman Eaker, Principal-Firm Admin.
James A. Tricarico, General Counsel

GROWTH PLANS/SPECIAL FEATURES:

Edward D. Jones & Co. L.P., which trades under the name Edward Jones, is an investment brokerage network specifically focused on individual investors, most of whom are retired, as well as small-business owners in rural communities and suburbs. The firm serves nearly 7 million clients and has a network of approximately 11,500 offices in the U.S. and Canada. Edward Jones keeps its offices continuously connected through satellite uplinks. Edward Jones brokers focus on conservative long-term investors with the intention of buying and holding stocks in relatively low-risk investment portfolios in government bonds, blue-chip stocks and high-quality mutual funds. Other products from the company include annuities, college saving programs, estate planning, life insurance, retirement plans and traditional banking services, such as savings and checking accounts. The firm also maintains a research department to provide specific investment recommendations and market information for retail customers. Edward Jones' web site offers financial planning for life events, including buying a home, expecting a child, changing jobs and the loss of a loved one.

The company offers employees medical and dental benefits, 401(k) plans, life and disability insurance, a profit sharing plan and tuition reimbursement.

FINANCIAL DATA: *Note: Data for latest year may not have been available at press time.*

In U.S. $	2016	2015	2014	2013	2012	2011
Revenue		6,619,000,000	6,278,000,000	5,657,000,000	4,965,200,000	4,509,861,000
R&D Expense						
Operating Income						
Operating Margin %						
SGA Expense						
Net Income		838,000,000	770,000,000	674,338,000	555,000,000	481,783,000
Operating Cash Flow						
Capital Expenditure						
EBITDA						
Return on Assets %						
Return on Equity %						
Debt to Equity						

CONTACT INFORMATION:

Phone: 314-515-2000   Fax: 314-515-2622
Toll-Free:
Address: 12555 Manchester Rd., Des Peres, MO 63131 United States

STOCK TICKER/OTHER:

Stock Ticker: Subsidiary   Exchange:
Employees: 40,000   Fiscal Year Ends: 12/31
Parent Company: Jones Financial Companies LLP (The)

SALARIES/BONUSES:

Top Exec. Salary: $ Bonus: $
Second Exec. Salary: $ Bonus: $

OTHER THOUGHTS:

Estimated Female Officers or Directors: 3
Hot Spot for Advancement for Women/Minorities: Y

Edwards Lifesciences Corporation

www.edwards.com

NAIC Code: 339100

TYPES OF BUSINESS:

Supplies-Cardiovascular Disease Related
Cardiac Surgery Products
Critical Care Products
Vascular Products
Heart Valve Implants

BRANDS/DIVISIONS/AFFILIATES:

PERIMOUNT
Edwards Intuity Valve System
Edwards SAPIEN
Swan-Ganz
FloTrac
ClearSight
PreSep
EV1000

CONTACTS: Note: Officers with more than one job title may be intentionally listed here more than once.

Denise Botticelli, Assistant General Counsel
Michael Mussallem, CEO
Scott Ullem, CFO
Robert Sellers, Chief Accounting Officer
Larry Wood, Vice President, Divisional
Donald Bobo, Vice President, Divisional
Catherine Szyman, Vice President, Divisional
Bernard Zovighian, Vice President, Divisional
Huimin Wang, Vice President, Geographical
Patrick Verguet, Vice President, Geographical

GROWTH PLANS/SPECIAL FEATURES:

Edwards Lifesciences Corporation designs products for cardiovascular diseases, such as heart valve disease, coronary artery disease, peripheral vascular disease (PVD) and congestive heart failure. The firm operates in three main areas: surgical heart valve therapy (28% of 2015 net sales), transcatheter heart valves (47%) and critical care (13%). Surgical heart valve products include the PERIMOUNT line of pericardial heart valves made from biologically inert porcine tissue, often on a wire-form stent; and valve repair therapies, such as the Edwards Intuity Valve System, a minimally-invasive aortic system designed to enable a faster procedure and a smaller incision. Transcatheter heart valves are designed to treat heart valves disease using catheter-based approaches. Its main products are the Edwards SAPIEN, Sapien XT and Sapien 3 transcatheter aortic heart valves and delivery systems used to treat heart valve disease using catheter-based approaches for patients deemed at high risk for traditional open-heart surgery. The aortic heart valves are available for sale in more than 65 countries. The company's critical care products include the Swan-Ganz brand hemodynamic monitoring devices used during surgery; FloTrac, a minimally invasive continuous cardiac output monitoring system; ClearSight hemodynamic monitor that provides real-time, beat-to-beat information; PreSep, a venous oximetry catheter for measuring central venous oxygen saturation; and EV1000 clinical monitoring platform which displays a patient's physiological status and integrates many of the firm's sensors and catheters into one platform. The firm sells its products in approximately 100 countries, including Australia, Brazil, Canada, France, Germany, Italy, Japan, the Netherlands, Spain and the U.K.

Employee benefits include medical, dental and vision coverage; 401(k); an employee stock purchase plan; short- and long-term disability; and adoption assistance.

FINANCIAL DATA: Note: Data for latest year may not have been available at press time.

In U.S. $	2016	2015	2014	2013	2012	2011
Revenue		2,493,700,000	2,322,900,000	2,045,500,000	1,899,600,000	1,678,600,000
R&D Expense		383,100,000	346,500,000	323,000,000	291,300,000	246,300,000
Operating Income		635,700,000	1,233,200,000	454,500,000	408,400,000	278,500,000
Operating Margin %		25.49%	53.08%	22.21%	21.49%	16.59%
SGA Expense		850,700,000	858,000,000	745,600,000	705,300,000	642,400,000
Net Income		494,900,000	811,100,000	391,700,000	293,200,000	236,700,000
Operating Cash Flow		549,700,000	1,022,300,000	472,700,000	373,800,000	314,500,000
Capital Expenditure		106,500,000	93,700,000	110,100,000	127,700,000	90,600,000
EBITDA		705,400,000	1,229,800,000	593,800,000	452,800,000	344,700,000
Return on Assets %		13.05%	25.95%	15.83%	13.95%	12.63%
Return on Equity %		21.08%	43.25%	25.78%	20.81%	17.89%
Debt to Equity		0.23	0.27	0.38	0.12	0.11

CONTACT INFORMATION:

Phone: 949 250-2500   Fax: 949 250-2525
Toll-Free: 800-424-3278
Address: 1 Edwards Way, Irvine, CA 92614 United States

SALARIES/BONUSES:

Top Exec. Salary: $973,077   Bonus: $
Second Exec. Salary: $503,846   Bonus: $300,000

STOCK TICKER/OTHER:

Stock Ticker: EW   Exchange: NYS
Employees: 8,600   Fiscal Year Ends: 12/31
Parent Company:

OTHER THOUGHTS:

Estimated Female Officers or Directors: 3
Hot Spot for Advancement for Women/Minorities: Y

Sales, profits and employees may be estimates. Financial information, benefits and other data can change quickly and may vary from those stated here.

EMCOR Group Inc

NAIC Code: 238210

www.emcorgroup.com

TYPES OF BUSINESS:

Electric, Heating and AC Contractors
Mechanical Contracting
Technical Consulting Services
Facilities Management

BRANDS/DIVISIONS/AFFILIATES:

CONTACTS: Note: Officers with more than one job title may be intentionally listed here more than once.

Anthony Guzzi, CEO
Mark Pompa, CFO
Stephen Bershad, Chairman of the Board
R. Matz, Executive VP, Divisional
Maxine Mauricio, Executive VP
Sheldon Cammaker, Vice Chairman

GROWTH PLANS/SPECIAL FEATURES:

EMCOR Group, Inc. is a global leader in mechanical and electrical contracting and facilities services. The company offers its services through more than 70 subsidiaries and join ventures and more than 170 offices located throughout the U.S as well as in Canada, the U.K. and the Middle East. Services provided to its customers include the design, integration installation, start up, operation and maintenance of systems fo generation and distribution of electrical power; lighting systems; low-voltage systems, such as fire alarm, security communications and process control systems; voice and data communication systems; heating, ventilation, air conditioning refrigeration and clean-room process ventilation systems plumbing, process and high-purity piping systems; water and wastewater treatment systems; and central plant heating and cooling systems. In addition to its construction services EMCOR offers facilities services, such as site-based operations and maintenance, mobile maintenance and service facilities management, installation and support for building systems, technical consulting and diagnostic services, small modification and retrofit projects and program developmen and management for energy systems. Most of the firm's business is done with corporations, municipalities and other government agencies, owner/developers and building tenants Additional services are provided to a range of general and specialty contractors, with EMCOR operating as a subcontractor.

EMCOR offers its employees benefits including medical, vision and dental coverage; life insurance; flexible spending accounts; disability income; employee wellness and assistance programs; and a 401(k) and stock purchase options.

FINANCIAL DATA: Note: Data for latest year may not have been available at press time.

In U.S. $	2016	2015	2014	2013	2012	2011
Revenue		6,718,726,000	6,424,965,000	6,417,158,000	6,346,679,000	5,613,459,000
R&D Expense						
Operating Income		287,082,000	289,878,000	210,292,000	249,967,000	210,793,000
Operating Margin %		4.27%	4.51%	3.27%	3.93%	3.75%
SGA Expense		656,573,000	626,478,000	591,063,000	556,242,000	518,121,000
Net Income		172,286,000	168,664,000	123,792,000	146,584,000	130,826,000
Operating Cash Flow		266,666,000	246,657,000	150,069,000	184,408,000	149,425,000
Capital Expenditure		35,460,000	38,035,000	35,497,000	37,875,000	29,581,000
EBITDA		361,944,000	365,210,000	278,758,000	312,489,000	266,389,000
Return on Assets %		4.96%	4.92%	3.76%	4.78%	4.53%
Return on Equity %		11.91%	11.70%	8.80%	11.35%	10.95%
Debt to Equity		0.20	0.22	0.22	0.11	0.12

CONTACT INFORMATION:

Phone: 203 849-7800   Fax: 203 849-7900
Toll-Free: 866-890-7794
Address: 301 Merritt Seven, Norwalk, CT 06851 United States

STOCK TICKER/OTHER:

Stock Ticker: EME   Exchange: NYS
Employees: 27,000   Fiscal Year Ends: 12/31
Parent Company:

SALARIES/BONUSES:

Top Exec. Salary: Bonus: $
$1,050,000
Second Exec. Salary: Bonus: $
$650,000

OTHER THOUGHTS:

Estimated Female Officers or Directors: 3

Hot Spot for Advancement for Women/Minorities: Y

Encore Capital Group Inc

www.encorecapital.com

NAIC Code: 522390

TYPES OF BUSINESS:

Credit Card Receivables
Debt Collections

BRANDS/DIVISIONS/AFFILIATES:

Atlantic Credit & Finance Inc
Cabot Credit Management Limited
Refinancia SA
Propel Acquisition LLC
Hillesden Securities Ltd
Baycorp Holdings Pty Ltd

CONTACTS: Note: Officers with more than one job title may be intentionally listed here more than once.

Kenneth Vecchione, CEO
Jonathan Clark, CFO
Willem Mesdag, Chairman of the Board
Ashish Masih, Executive VP, Divisional
Gregory Call, General Counsel
Paul Grinberg, Other Corporate Officer

GROWTH PLANS/SPECIAL FEATURES:

Encore Capital Group, Inc. is an international specialty finance company providing debt recovery solutions for consumers and property owners across a broad range of financial assets. Encore operates through two business segments: portfolio purchasing & recovery (PP&R) and tax liens. PP&R acquires portfolios of defaulted consumer receivables at deep discounts to face value and manage them by working with individuals as they repay their obligations and work toward financial recovery. Defaulted receivables are consumers' unpaid financial commitments to credit originators, including banks, credit unions, consumer finance companies, commercial retailers and telecommunication companies. Subsidiaries within this division include wholly-owned Atlantic Credit & Finance Inc., a U.S.-based firm that specializes in collecting high-balance receivables by forging collaborative relationships with consumers majority-owned; majority-owned Cabot Credit Management Limited, a market leader in debt management in the U.K. and Ireland; majority-owned Grove Holdings, a U.K.-based specialty investment firm focused on consumer non-performing loans in the U.K. and bank and non-bank receivables in Spain; and majority-owned Refinancia SA, a market leader in the management of non-performing loans in Colombia and Peru. The tax lien segment is operated through subsidiary Propel Acquisition LLC, and its subsidiaries, which acquire and service residential and commercial tax liens on real property. Propel works directly with property owns to structure affordable payment plans by paying delinquent property taxes on behalf of the property owners in exchange for payment agreements collateralized by a tax lien on the property. Propel also purchases tax liens directly from taxing authorities in various other states. This segment's portfolio of tax liens and other assets extends through 22 U.S. states. In 2015, the firm acquired Hillesden Securities Ltd.; and a majority stake in Baycorp Holdings Pty. Ltd. In February 2016, the firm agreed to sell Propel.

FINANCIAL DATA: Note: Data for latest year may not have been available at press time.

In U.S. $	2016	2015	2014	2013	2012	2011
Revenue		1,161,572,000	1,072,789,000	773,364,000	555,872,000	467,371,000
R&D Expense						
Operating Income		245,302,000	319,444,000	198,359,000	154,176,000	120,774,000
Operating Margin %		21.11%	29.77%	25.64%	27.73%	25.84%
SGA Expense		734,866,000	631,537,000	494,809,000	346,917,000	302,160,000
Net Income		45,135,000	103,726,000	75,299,000	69,477,000	60,958,000
Operating Cash Flow		114,425,000	111,544,000	74,775,000	98,520,000	84,579,000
Capital Expenditure		28,647,000	23,238,000	13,423,000	6,265,000	5,564,000
EBITDA		281,482,000	347,506,000	207,684,000	164,997,000	126,874,000
Return on Assets %		1.13%	3.22%	3.90%	7.00%	7.87%
Return on Equity %		7.40%	17.36%	15.40%	17.87%	18.08%
Debt to Equity		5.39	4.45	3.23	1.73	1.04

CONTACT INFORMATION:

Phone: 877 445-4581   Fax:
Toll-Free: 877-445-4581
Address: 3111 Camino Del Rio N., Ste. 103, San Diego, CA 92108 United States

STOCK TICKER/OTHER:

Stock Ticker: ECPG   Exchange: NAS
Employees: 5,400   Fiscal Year Ends: 12/31
Parent Company:

SALARIES/BONUSES:

Top Exec. Salary: $860,000   Bonus: $
Second Exec. Salary: $550,000   Bonus: $

OTHER THOUGHTS:

Estimated Female Officers or Directors: 2
Hot Spot for Advancement for Women/Minorities:

Enterprise Holdings Inc

NAIC Code: 532111

www.enterpriseholdings.com

TYPES OF BUSINESS:

Car & Truck Rental
Vanpool Services

BRANDS/DIVISIONS/AFFILIATES:

Alamo Rent A Car
National Car Rental
Enterprise Rent-A-Car
Enterprise Car Sales
Enterprise Truck Rental
Enterprise CarShare
Enterprise Rideshare
Zimride

CONTACTS: *Note: Officers with more than one job title may be intentionally listed here more than once.*

Pamela Nicholson, CEO
Christine Taylor, COO
Pamela Nicholson, Pres.
Rick Short, CFO
Patrick T. Farrell, Chief Mktg. Officer
Edward Adams, Sr. VP-Human Resources
Craig Kennedy, CIO
Lee Kaplan, Chief Admin. Officer
Matthew G. Darrah, Exec. VP-North American Oper.
Greg Stubblefield, Chief Strategy Officer
Patrick T. Farrell, Chief Comm. Officer
Rose Langhorst, Treas.
Steve Bloom, Pres., Enterprise Fleet Mgmt.
Jo Ann Taylor Kindle, Pres., Enterprise Holdings Foundation
Andrew C. Taylor, Chmn.
Greg Stubblefield, Exec. VP-Global Sales & Mktg.

GROWTH PLANS/SPECIAL FEATURES:

Enterprise Holdings, Inc. is the parent company of Alamo Rent A Car, National Car Rental and Enterprise Rent-A-Car car rental agencies. The company also owns Enterprise Car Sales, Enterprise Truck Rental, as well as car/ride sharing programs Enterprise CarShare, Enterprise Rideshare and Zimride by Enterprise. The company's combined rental fleet is the largest in the world, at 1.5 million vehicles. It serves more than 6,000 retail and airport locations in the U.S., and approximately 8,6000 worldwide, including Mexico, the Caribbean, Latin America, Canada, Ireland, the U.K., Germany and Asia. Alamo Rent A Car is a budget rental car company catering to leisure and vacation customers, particularly international travelers visiting North America. It operates self-service kiosks at 63 U.S. locations. National Car Rental is a premium rental brand that serves frequent business travelers and offers the Emerald Club frequent-renter benefits program. Enterprise Rent-A-Car boasts over 5,500 retail and airport offices in the U.S. Enterprise Car Sales is a used-car reseller that provides non-negotiable pricing and after-market warranties on used cars acquired through trade-in or extracted from the rental fleet. Enterprise Truck Rental provides commercial-grade trucks such as $\frac{3}{4}$- to 1-ton pickups, cargo vans, straight trucks, as well as stakebed trucks (from 16 to 26 feet long), all equipped for commercial use. Enterprise CarShare is a car sharing program that allows customers to rent a car for flexible periods of time through an online membership portal. Enterprise Rideshare specializes in customized vanpool programs and commuter services for individuals and/or companies. Zimride is a ride-sharing platform for companies and universities. In June 2016, the firm acquired vRide, a vanpooling company that has been serving U.S. commuters for nearly 40 years.

Enterprise Holdings offers its employees medical, dental and vision insurance; prescription drug coverage; flexible spending accounts; life insurance; and long-term disability plans.

FINANCIAL DATA: *Note: Data for latest year may not have been available at press time.*

In U.S. $	2016	2015	2014	2013	2012	2011
Revenue		19,400,000,000	17,800,000,000	16,400,000,000	15,400,000,000	14,100,000,000
R&D Expense						
Operating Income						
Operating Margin %						
SGA Expense						
Net Income						
Operating Cash Flow						
Capital Expenditure						
EBITDA						
Return on Assets %						
Return on Equity %						
Debt to Equity						

CONTACT INFORMATION:

Phone: 314-512-2880   Fax: 314-512-4706
Toll-Free:
Address: 600 Corporate Park Dr., St. Louis, MO 63105 United States

STOCK TICKER/OTHER:

Stock Ticker: Private   Exchange:
Employees: 93,000   Fiscal Year Ends: 03/31
Parent Company:

SALARIES/BONUSES:

Top Exec. Salary: $ Bonus: $
Second Exec. Salary: $ Bonus: $

OTHER THOUGHTS:

Estimated Female Officers or Directors: 5
Hot Spot for Advancement for Women/Minorities: Y

EPAM Systems Inc

www.epam.com

NAIC Code: 541511

TYPES OF BUSINESS:

Software Engineering
Customer Relationship Management
Consulting
Technical Writing

BRANDS/DIVISIONS/AFFILIATES:

Alliance Global Services

CONTACTS: *Note: Officers with more than one job title may be intentionally listed here more than once.*

Arkadiy Dobkin, CEO
Anthony Conte, CFO
Elaina Shekhter, Chief Marketing Officer
Ginger Mosier, General Counsel
Balazs Fejes, Senior VP, Divisional

GROWTH PLANS/SPECIAL FEATURES:

EPAM Systems is an IT outsourcing company that provides software services through offices located across Europe, Asia and North America with a business focus on Central and Eastern Europe. It offers software development and related services, including technology consulting, custom software development, software product development, embedded software development and low-level programming, technical writing and documentation, application testing, application maintenance, application reengineering and offshore development center setup services. The firm's technology consulting expertise includes IT strategy development, enterprise application integration strategy, business and technical analysis and technology-specific support. EPAM's software development services include product research, prototyping, development, quality assurance and testing, deployment, performance tuning, maintenance and support, customization, porting and cross-platform migration and component design and integration. The company's mobile application development services include development for iPhone, Android, Blackberry, Windows Mobile and other mobile platforms. The firm's technical writing and documentation services cover software documentation, online help, product specifications, proofreading, software localization and translation. The company's application testing services include functional testing, automated testing and continuous integration for distributed software project implementation. The company serves clients in various industries, including software and technology; health care and insurance; travel and hospitality; financial services; media, entertainment, research, publishing and online learning; energy, oil, metal, manufacturing and construction; retail and consumer goods; telecommunications; and high tech. In November 2015, the firm acquired Alliance Global Services, a software product development services and test automation solutions firm.

FINANCIAL DATA: *Note: Data for latest year may not have been available at press time.*

In U.S. $	2016	2015	2014	2013	2012	2011
Revenue		914,128,000	730,027,000	555,117,000	433,799,000	334,528,000
R&D Expense						
Operating Income		105,967,000	86,183,000	76,493,000	66,006,000	55,008,000
Operating Margin %		11.59%	11.80%	13.77%	15.21%	16.44%
SGA Expense		222,759,000	163,666,000	116,497,000	85,868,000	64,930,000
Net Income		84,456,000	69,641,000	61,994,000	54,484,000	44,353,000
Operating Cash Flow		76,393,000	104,874,000	58,225,000	48,499,000	54,520,000
Capital Expenditure		17,964,000	15,840,000	15,920,000	27,077,000	17,093,000
EBITDA		123,362,000	103,666,000	91,613,000	76,888,000	60,367,000
Return on Assets %		12.30%	13.56%	15.82%	17.44%	5.78%
Return on Equity %		15.67%	16.57%	18.71%	26.82%	14.58%
Debt to Equity		0.05				

CONTACT INFORMATION:

Phone: 267 759-9000   Fax: 267 759-8989
Toll-Free:
Address: 41 University Dr., Ste. 202, Newtown, PA 18940 United States

STOCK TICKER/OTHER:

Stock Ticker: EPAM   Exchange: NYS
Employees: 14,109   Fiscal Year Ends: 12/31
Parent Company:

SALARIES/BONUSES:

Top Exec. Salary: $400,000   Bonus: $500,000
Second Exec. Salary: $280,000   Bonus: $250,000

OTHER THOUGHTS:

Estimated Female Officers or Directors: 2
Hot Spot for Advancement for Women/Minorities:

Epic Systems Corporation

NAIC Code: 0

TYPES OF BUSINESS:

Computer Software, Healthcare & Biotechnology
Information Networks
Support Services

BRANDS/DIVISIONS/AFFILIATES:

Epicenter
EpicCare
Epic Europe BV
Community Library Exchange
Lucy PHR

CONTACTS: Note: Officers with more than one job title may be intentionally listed here more than once.

Judy Faulkner, CEO
Carl D. Dvorak, COO
Robert M. Fahrenbach, CFO
Carl Dvorak, Exec. VP

GROWTH PLANS/SPECIAL FEATURES:

Epic Systems Corporation is a developer of health industry clinical, access and revenue software for mid-size and large medical groups, hospitals, academic facilities, children's organizations, multi-hospital systems and integrated health care organizations. All Epic software applications are designed to share a single database, called Epicenter, so that each viewer can access all available patient data through a single interface from anywhere in the organization. The firm's clinical software products include integrated inpatient and ambulatory systems under the EpicCare brand as well as health information management tools and specialty information systems. The firm's interoperability service, Lucy PHR, allows patients to organize and access their medical history independently of any one facility. Other products offer access services, including scheduling, inpatient and ambulatory registration, call management and nurse triage; revenue cycle services, such as hospital and professional billing; health plan and managed care administration systems; clinical and financial data repositories; enterprise reporting; patient medical record access systems; and connectivity tools, including voice recognition, interfacing and patient monitoring devices. In conjunction with its software applications, the company provides extensive client services, including training, process engineering, tailoring of applications to the client's situation and access to network specialists who plan and implement client systems. In addition, Epic hosts Community Library Exchange, an online collection of application tools and pre-made content that allows clients to share report and registration templates, custom forms, enterprise report formats and documentation shortcuts. Epic also operates in the Netherlands under Epic Europe BV.

Employees of the firm are offered medical, dental, vision, life and disability insurance; a 401(k) plan; and flexible spending accounts.

FINANCIAL DATA: Note: Data for latest year may not have been available at press time.

In U.S. $	2016	2015	2014	2013	2012	2011
Revenue		1,978,000,000	1,856,000,000	1,750,000,000	1,526,000,000	1,190,000,000
R&D Expense						
Operating Income						
Operating Margin %						
SGA Expense						
Net Income						
Operating Cash Flow						
Capital Expenditure						
EBITDA						
Return on Assets %						
Return on Equity %						
Debt to Equity						

CONTACT INFORMATION:

Phone: 608-271-9000   Fax: 608-271-7237
Toll-Free:
Address: 1979 Milky Way, Verona, WI 53593 United States

STOCK TICKER/OTHER:

Stock Ticker: Private   Exchange:
Employees: 9,000   Fiscal Year Ends: 12/31
Parent Company:

SALARIES/BONUSES:

Top Exec. Salary: $ Bonus: $
Second Exec. Salary: $ Bonus: $

OTHER THOUGHTS:

Estimated Female Officers or Directors: 1
Hot Spot for Advancement for Women/Minorities:

Equity Lifestyle Properties Inc

www.equitylifestyle.com

NAIC Code: 0

TYPES OF BUSINESS:
Real Estate Investment Trust
Manufactured Home & RV Communities

BRANDS/DIVISIONS/AFFILIATES:
MHC Operating Limited Partnership

CONTACTS: Note: Officers with more than one job title may be intentionally listed here more than once.
Thomas Heneghan, CEO, Subsidiary
Paul Seavey, CFO
Samuel Zell, Chairman of the Board
Patrick Waite, COO
Howard Walker, Director
Roger Maynard, Executive VP, Divisional
David Eldersveld, Executive VP
Marguerite Nader, President
Ann Wallin, Vice President

GROWTH PLANS/SPECIAL FEATURES:
Equity Lifestyle Properties, Inc. (ELS) is an integrated real estate investment trust (REIT) that owns and operates communities of developed residential sites as well as recreational vehicle (RV) resorts. The company primarily operates through MHC Operating Limited Partnership. The firm owns or has an interest in 387 properties throughout the U.S. and Canada, consisting of about 143,887 residential sites. The heaviest concentrations of these properties are located in Florida, California and Arizona, with 122, 49 and 42 properties respectively. Additional U.S. sites are located in Texas, Pennsylvania, Washington, Colorado, Wisconsin, Oregon, North Carolina, Delaware, Indiana, Nevada, New York, Virginia, New Jersey, Illinois, Maine, Massachusetts, Idaho, Michigan, Minnesota, New Hampshire, South Carolina, Utah, Maryland, North Dakota, Ohio, Tennessee, Alabama, Connecticut and Kentucky. These communities are designed and improved for the placement of detached, single-family manufactured homes that are produced offsite, then installed and set on residential sites within the communities. The owner of each home leases the site on which it is located, while the firm handles property infrastructure issues, such as water, sewage and power. Sites typically contain centralized entrances, paved streets, curbs, gutters, parkways, clubhouses for social activities and recreation, swimming pools, shuffleboard courts, tennis courts, laundry facilities and cable television service, among other amenities. Each community is designed to attract, and is marketed to, retirees, empty-nesters, families or first-time homeowners. The company focuses on owning properties in or near large metropolitan markets as well as popular retirement and vacation destinations.

FINANCIAL DATA: Note: Data for latest year may not have been available at press time.

In U.S. $	2016	2015	2014	2013	2012	2011
Revenue		821,654,000	776,809,000	728,375,000	709,877,000	580,073,000
R&D Expense						
Operating Income		146,423,000	137,520,000	75,208,000	67,963,000	40,556,000
Operating Margin %		17.82%	17.70%	10.32%	9.57%	6.99%
SGA Expense		47,016,000	42,476,000	43,493,000	37,302,000	51,354,000
Net Income		139,371,000	128,005,000	116,199,000	69,391,000	36,598,000
Operating Cash Flow		352,882,000	285,745,000	255,349,000	236,459,000	175,641,000
Capital Expenditure		117,486,000	145,112,000	182,421,000	99,473,000	713,121,000
EBITDA		370,941,000	367,418,000	308,214,000	310,314,000	226,818,000
Return on Assets %		3.79%	3.47%	3.14%	1.58%	.82%
Return on Equity %		16.63%	15.48%	14.44%	7.55%	4.77%
Debt to Equity		2.71	2.85	2.89	3.13	3.14

CONTACT INFORMATION:
Phone: 312 279-1400   Fax: 312 279-1710
Toll-Free:
Address: 2 N. Riverside Plz., Ste. 800, Chicago, IL 60606 United States

STOCK TICKER/OTHER:
Stock Ticker: ELS
Employees: 3,900
Parent Company:

Exchange: NYS
Fiscal Year Ends: 12/31

SALARIES/BONUSES:
Top Exec. Salary: $385,000   Bonus: $
Second Exec. Salary: Bonus: $
$350,000

OTHER THOUGHTS:
Estimated Female Officers or Directors: 3
Hot Spot for Advancement for Women/Minorities: Y

Sales, profits and employees may be estimates. Financial information, benefits and other data can change quickly and may vary from those stated here.

Estee Lauder Companies Inc (The)

www.elcompanies.com

NAIC Code: 325620

TYPES OF BUSINESS:

Cosmetics
Cosmetic & Fragrance Sales
Retail Cosmetics Stores
Hair Care Products

BRANDS/DIVISIONS/AFFILIATES:

Aveda
La Mer
Clinique
Estee Lauder
Bobbie Brown
Aramis
Editions de Parfums Frederic Malle
GLAMGLOW

CONTACTS: Note: Officers with more than one job title may be intentionally listed here more than once.

Fabrizio Freda, CEO
John Demsey, President, Divisional
Tracey Travis, CFO
Leonard Lauder, Chairman Emeritus
William Lauder, Chairman of the Board
Ronald Lauder, Chairman, Divisional
Michael OHare, Executive VP, Divisional
Carl Haney, Executive VP, Divisional
Gregory Polcer, Executive VP, Divisional
Alexandra Trower, Executive VP, Divisional
Sara Moss, Executive VP
Cedric Prouve, President, Divisional

GROWTH PLANS/SPECIAL FEATURES:

The Estee Lauder Companies, Inc. is a global manufacturer and marketer of skin care, cosmetic, fragrance and hair care products. The company's products are sold in over 150 countries and territories under brand names such as Estee Lauder, Aramis, Clinique, Origins, M.A.C., Bobbi Brown, La Mer and Aveda. The firm is also the global licensee for fragrances and cosmetics sold under the Tommy Hilfiger, Donna Karan, Michael Kors, Tom Ford, Tory Burch and Coach brand names. Estee Lauder sells its products principally through 30,000 points of sale, including upscale department stores, specialty retailers, upscale perfumeries and pharmacies and prestige salons and spas as well as freestanding company-owned stores and spas, authorized retailer web sites, stores on cruise ships, television direct marketing, in-flight and duty-free shops and self-select outlets. The founding Lauder family still controls 86.7% of the company's voting shares. The firm operates on a global basis, with over half of its sales generated outside the U.S. Skin care products currently account for roughly 42% of the company's sales; makeup products, 40%; fragrance products, 13%; and hair care items, 5%. In 2015, the firm acquired Editions de Parfums Frederic Malle, a fragrance brand; and GLAMGLOW, a skin care brand.

FINANCIAL DATA: Note: Data for latest year may not have been available at press time.

In U.S. $	2016	2015	2014	2013	2012	2011
Revenue	11,262,300,000	10,780,400,000	10,968,800,000	10,181,700,000	9,713,601,000	8,810,000,000
R&D Expense						
Operating Income	1,610,300,000	1,606,300,000	1,827,600,000	1,526,000,000	1,311,700,000	1,089,400,000
Operating Margin %	14.29%	14.90%	16.66%	14.98%	13.50%	12.36%
SGA Expense	7,337,800,000	7,073,500,000	6,985,900,000	6,597,000,000	6,324,800,000	5,696,700,000
Net Income	1,114,600,000	1,088,900,000	1,204,100,000	1,019,800,000	856,900,000	700,800,000
Operating Cash Flow	1,788,700,000	1,943,300,000	1,535,200,000	1,226,300,000	1,126,700,000	1,027,000,000
Capital Expenditure	525,300,000	473,000,000	510,200,000	461,000,000	420,700,000	351,000,000
EBITDA	2,040,600,000	2,029,900,000	2,212,200,000	1,886,000,000	1,618,000,000	1,383,800,000
Return on Assets %	12.76%	13.51%	16.03%	14.84%	13.31%	12.07%
Return on Equity %	30.89%	29.04%	33.71%	33.87%	31.95%	30.61%
Debt to Equity	0.53	0.44	0.34	0.40	0.39	0.41

CONTACT INFORMATION:

Phone: 212 572-4200   Fax: 212 572-3941
Toll-Free:
Address: 767 5th Ave., New York, NY 10153 United States

STOCK TICKER/OTHER:

Stock Ticker: EL   Exchange: NYS
Employees: 44,000   Fiscal Year Ends: 06/30
Parent Company:

SALARIES/BONUSES:

Top Exec. Salary: Bonus: $
$1,800,000
Second Exec. Salary: Bonus: $
$1,500,000

OTHER THOUGHTS:

Estimated Female Officers or Directors: 10

Hot Spot for Advancement for Women/Minorities: Y

Exelon Corporation

www.exeloncorp.com

NAIC Code: 221113

TYPES OF BUSINESS:

Electric Power Generation-Nuclear
Energy Marketing

BRANDS/DIVISIONS/AFFILIATES:

Exelon Generation Company LLC
Constellation Energy Group Inc
Atlantic City Electric
Baltimore Gas and Electric Company
Commonwealth Edison Company
Delmarva Power & Light Company
PECO Energy Company
Pepco Holdings Inc

CONTACTS: *Note: Officers with more than one job title may be intentionally listed here more than once.*

Denis OBrien, CEO, Divisional
Calvin Butler, CEO, Subsidiary
Joseph Nigro, CEO, Subsidiary
Kenneth Cornew, CEO, Subsidiary
Anne Pramaggiore, CEO, Subsidiary
Craig Adams, CEO, Subsidiary
Christopher Crane, CEO
Bryan Wright, CFO, Subsidiary
Phillip Barnett, CFO, Subsidiary
Joseph Trpik, CFO, Subsidiary
David Vahos, CFO, Subsidiary
Scott Bailey, Chief Accounting Officer, Subsidiary
Gerald Kozel, Chief Accounting Officer
Duane DesParte, Chief Accounting Officer
Paymon Aliabadi, Chief Risk Officer
Matthew Bauer, Controller, Subsidiary
Robert Aiken, Controller, Subsidiary
Terence Donnelly, COO, Subsidiary
Michael Pacilio, COO, Subsidiary
Stephen Woerner, COO, Subsidiary
Michael Innocenzo, COO, Subsidiary

GROWTH PLANS/SPECIAL FEATURES:

Exelon Corporation is a Fortune 100 utility services holding company, delivering electricity and natural gas to 10 million customers. The firm's primary subsidiaries include Exelon Generation Company LLC, Constellation Energy Group, Inc., Atlantic City Electric (ACE), Baltimore Gas & Electric Company (BGE), Commonwealth Edison Company (ComEd), Delmarva Power & Light Company, PECO Energy Company and Pepco Holdings, Inc. Together, these companies serve U.S. customers located in Delaware, the District of Columbia, Illinois, Maryland, New Jersey and Pennsylvania. Exelon Generation is a power generator with approximately 35,000 megawatts (MW) of owned capacity comprising one of the nations' cleanest and lowest-cost power generation fleets. It is also a major owner and operator of nuclear plants in the U.S., operating 23 reactors at 14 facilities. Constellation is a retail and wholesale supplier of power, natural gas and energy products and services for homes and businesses. ACE provides energy to nearly 550,000 customers in southern New Jersey. BGE is Maryland's largest electricity provider, with more than 1.2 million residential electric customers; and also provides gas to more than 650,000 customers. ComEd has more than 3.8 million customers across the northern Illinois region, and has launched one of the nation's largest grid modernization and SmartGrid program. Delmarva serves more than 520,000 electric customers in Delaware and eastern Maryland, as well as nearly 130,000 natural gas customers in northern Delaware. PECO serves more than 1.6 million electric and 506,000 natural gas customers in southeastern Pennsylvania. Pepco provides electric service to approximately 842,000 customers in Maryland and Washington, D.C. In March 2016, the firm acquired Pepco Holdings, making Exelon the largest regulated utility in the U.S. by customer count and total revenue.

Exelon offers employees health and life insurance, disability coverage, a 401(k) and an employee stock purchase plan.

FINANCIAL DATA: *Note: Data for latest year may not have been available at press time.*

In U.S. $	2016	2015	2014	2013	2012	2011
Revenue		29,447,000,000	27,429,000,000	24,888,000,000	23,489,000,000	18,924,000,000
R&D Expense						
Operating Income		4,409,000,000	3,096,000,000	3,656,000,000	2,380,000,000	4,480,000,000
Operating Margin %		14.97%	11.28%	14.68%	10.13%	23.67%
SGA Expense						
Net Income		2,269,000,000	1,623,000,000	1,719,000,000	1,160,000,000	2,495,000,000
Operating Cash Flow		7,616,000,000	4,457,000,000	6,343,000,000	6,131,000,000	4,853,000,000
Capital Expenditure		7,624,000,000	6,077,000,000	5,395,000,000	5,810,000,000	4,042,000,000
EBITDA		8,396,000,000	7,419,000,000	6,593,000,000	6,805,000,000	6,982,000,000
Return on Assets %		2.49%	1.94%	2.16%	1.73%	4.64%
Return on Equity %		9.37%	7.15%	7.78%	6.47%	17.85%
Debt to Equity		0.94	0.88	0.80	0.85	0.84

CONTACT INFORMATION:

Phone: 312 394-7398   Fax: 312 394-7945
Toll-Free: 800-483-3220
Address: 10 S. Dearborn St., 48th Fl., Chicago, IL 60680-5379 United States

STOCK TICKER/OTHER:

Stock Ticker: EXC
Employees: 29,762
Parent Company:

Exchange: NYS
Fiscal Year Ends: 12/31

SALARIES/BONUSES:

Top Exec. Salary: $1,224,808
Second Exec. Salary: $836,558

Bonus: $

Bonus: $

OTHER THOUGHTS:

Estimated Female Officers or Directors: 6

Hot Spot for Advancement for Women/Minorities: Y

ExlService Holdings Inc

NAIC Code: 518210

www.exlservice.com

TYPES OF BUSINESS:

Business Process Outsourcing
Contact Center Operations
Collections, Cash Management & Loan Servicing
Customer Support Services
Claims Processing & Servicing

BRANDS/DIVISIONS/AFFILIATES:

RPM Data Solutions LLC
RPM Direct LLC
Business EXLerator Framework

CONTACTS: Note: Officers with more than one job title may be intentionally listed here more than once.

Rohit Kapoor, CEO
Vishal Chhibbar, CFO
Pavan Bagai, COO
Garen Staglin, Director
Nancy Saltzman, Executive VP
Vikas Bhalla, Executive VP
Rembert de Villa, Executive VP
Nalin Miglani, Executive VP

GROWTH PLANS/SPECIAL FEATURES:

ExlService Holdings, Inc. (EXL) provides outsourcing and transformation services primarily to companies in the insurance, health care, banking & financial services, transportation & logistics, travel and utilities industries. The firm operates in two business segments: operations management and analytics. The operations management segment consists of select business operations of a client such as claims processing, clinical operations, or financial transaction processing. Solutions in this segment includes operating and delivery model based on Business EXLerator Framework, which allows the firm to offer advanced automation, such as robotics, workflow management, data visualization and embedded analytics for better business outcomes. The Business EXLerator Framework correlates data from multiple sources to create actionable insights for front-line operations and makes use of embedded technology tools, applications and platforms. The analytics segment focuses on generating data-driven insights across all parts of customers' business. It offers predictive and prescriptive analytics in the areas of customer acquisition and lifecycle management, risk underwriting and pricing, operational effectiveness, credit and operational risk monitoring and governance, regulatory reporting and data management. Services offered by this segment include design and implementation of solutions enabling data visualization and management; integrations of data insights; deployment of analytics professionals and data scientists; and identification, cleansing, matching and use of structured, semi-structured and unstructured data. In 2015, it acquired analytics firms RPM Direct LLC and RPM Data Solutions LLC.

FINANCIAL DATA: Note: Data for latest year may not have been available at press time.

In U.S. $	2016	2015	2014	2013	2012	2011
Revenue		628,492,000	499,278,000	478,452,000	442,930,000	360,541,000
R&D Expense						
Operating Income		67,343,000	34,040,000	67,420,000	57,232,000	41,318,000
Operating Margin %		10.71%	6.81%	14.09%	12.92%	11.46%
SGA Expense		126,767,000	104,675,000	95,173,000	88,199,000	76,242,000
Net Income		51,565,000	32,445,000	48,097,000	41,836,000	34,780,000
Operating Cash Flow		96,691,000	66,659,000	82,792,000	65,782,000	56,235,000
Capital Expenditure		25,585,000	27,678,000	15,916,000	18,804,000	19,468,000
EBITDA		108,579,000	62,068,000	92,337,000	82,855,000	64,312,000
Return on Assets %		8.42%	6.25%	10.69%	10.28%	10.18%
Return on Equity %		11.65%	8.26%	13.53%	13.43%	13.19%
Debt to Equity		0.12	0.12			0.01

CONTACT INFORMATION:

Phone: 212 277-7100   Fax: 212 277-7111
Toll-Free:
Address: 280 Park Ave., 38th Fl., New York, NY 10017 United States

STOCK TICKER/OTHER:

Stock Ticker: EXLS   Exchange: NAS
Employees: 22,800   Fiscal Year Ends: 12/31
Parent Company:

SALARIES/BONUSES:

Top Exec. Salary: $600,000   Bonus: $
Second Exec. Salary: Bonus: $
$450,000

OTHER THOUGHTS:

Estimated Female Officers or Directors: 2
Hot Spot for Advancement for Women/Minorities:

Expedia Inc

NAIC Code: 519130

www.expedia.com

TYPES OF BUSINESS:

Online Travel Services
Online Reservations
Corporate Travel Services
Vacation Packages
Retail Travel Services Kiosks
Destination Activities & Tours
Online Travel Information

BRANDS/DIVISIONS/AFFILIATES:

Expedia.com
Hotwire.com
Venere
Expedia CruiseShipCenters
trivago GmbH
Travelocity
HomeAway Inc
Orbtiz Worldwide Inc

CONTACTS: Note: Officers with more than one job title may be intentionally listed here more than once.

Dara Khosrowshahi, CEO
Mark Okerstrom, CFO
Barry Diller, Chairman of the Board
Lance Soliday, Chief Accounting Officer
Victor Kaufman, Director
Robert Dzielak, Executive VP

GROWTH PLANS/SPECIAL FEATURES:

Expedia, Inc. is an online travel service offering travel shopping and reservation services, publishing schedules, pricing and availability information for numerous airlines, lodging properties, car rental companies, cruise lines and multiple-destination service providers, including restaurants, attractions and tours. The company's travel portfolio includes more than 269,000 properties, 1.2 million live vacation rental listings in 200 countries, as well as 400 airlines. The Expedia brand web sites, for both USA (Expedia.com) and international travelers, offer a large variety of travel products and services available directly to travelers. It also operates as a merchant by directly contracting from suppliers and selling discounted products directly to the consumer. The firm owns Hotels.com, which provides a full portfolio of hotel contacts around the world, and Hotwire.com, a web site that offers travelers discount airfare. Other subsidiaries include Venere, a resource for European hotels; Classic Vacations, a premium vacation packaging agency; eLong, an online travel service based in Beijing, China; Egencia, a travel management service for corporate customers; Expedia CruiseShipCenters, a network of cruise vacation retail locations; Expedia Local Expert, which specializes in local tours and attractions; Expedia Affiliate Network, which powers bookings for leading airlines and hotels; trivago GmbH, an online hotel metasearch company; wotif.com Holdings Limited, an operator of travel brands in the Asia Pacific; and CarRentals.com, an online car rental booking company. In 2015, Expedia acquired Travelocity, HomeAway, Inc. and Orbitz Worldwide, Inc.

The company offers employees medical, life, AD&D, disability, dental and vision insurance; flexible spending accounts; onsite flu shots; a 401(k); adoption assistance; an employee assistance program; a group legal program; tuition reimbursement; travel assistance; business travel accident insurance; pet insurance; and discounts for auto and home insurance.

FINANCIAL DATA: Note: Data for latest year may not have been available at press time.

In U.S. $	2016	2015	2014	2013	2012	2011
Revenue		6,672,317,000	5,763,485,000	4,771,259,000	4,030,347,000	3,449,009,000
R&D Expense		830,244,000	686,154,000		484,898,000	380,999,000
Operating Income		413,566,000	517,764,000	366,060,000	431,724,000	479,609,000
Operating Margin %		6.19%	8.98%	7.67%	10.71%	13.90%
SGA Expense		3,850,412,000	3,275,241,000	3,151,043,000	2,183,416,000	1,805,204,000
Net Income		764,465,000	398,097,000	232,850,000	280,171,000	472,294,000
Operating Cash Flow		1,368,045,000	1,366,959,000	763,200,000	1,229,575,000	1,030,072,000
Capital Expenditure		787,041,000	328,387,000	308,581,000	235,697,000	207,837,000
EBITDA		1,552,502,000	908,162,000	671,526,000	633,797,000	647,724,000
Return on Assets %		6.23%	4.75%	3.14%	4.12%	7.17%
Return on Equity %		22.99%	20.26%	10.52%	12.50%	19.38%
Debt to Equity		0.65	0.97	0.58	0.54	0.56

CONTACT INFORMATION:

Phone: 425 679-7200   Fax: 425 564-7240
Toll-Free: 800-397-3342
Address: 333 108th Ave. NE, Bellevue, WA 98004 United States

STOCK TICKER/OTHER:

Stock Ticker: EXPE
Employees: 18,210
Parent Company:

Exchange: NAS
Fiscal Year Ends: 12/31

SALARIES/BONUSES:

Top Exec. Salary: $1,000,000   Bonus: $2,750,000

Second Exec. Salary: $750,000   Bonus: $1,750,000

OTHER THOUGHTS:

Estimated Female Officers or Directors: 1

Hot Spot for Advancement for Women/Minorities:

Expeditors International of Washington Inc www.expeditors.com

NAIC Code: 488510

TYPES OF BUSINESS:

Freight Transportation Arrangement
Online Services
Logistics Software
Freight Consolidation
Customs Brokerage

BRANDS/DIVISIONS/AFFILIATES:

exp.o
exp.o Booking
exp.o ISF
CDM (Container Delivery Management)
TradeFlow
Expeditors Tradewin LLC
Certuspact LLC

CONTACTS: Note: Officers with more than one job title may be intentionally listed here more than once.

Jeffrey Musser, CEO
Bradley Powell, CFO
Christopher McClincy, Chief Information Officer
James Wang, Co-Founder
Robert Wright, Director
Benjamin Clark, General Counsel
Philip Coughlin, President, Divisional
Daniel Wall, President, Divisional
Eugene Alger, President, Divisional

GROWTH PLANS/SPECIAL FEATURES:

Expeditors International of Washington, Inc. provides global logistics services through an international network spanning 253 locations in 110 countries, which includes four regional headquarters in London, Sao Paulo, Beirut and Shanghai. The company's services include consolidation or forwarding of air and ocean freight, customs brokerage, distribution management, vendor consolidation, cargo insurance, purchase order management and customized logistics information. Ocean freight services account for 33% of the firm's revenue, airfreight accounts for 42%, and customs brokerage and other services account for 25%. Expeditors International does not compete for domestic freight, overnight courier or small parcel business and does not own aircraft or steamships. The company provides many services over the Internet. Expeditors International's web-based tracking system, exp.o, possesses query capabilities to find the status of inbound shipments or orders and to view customs details. Linked to exp.o, exp.o Booking is the company's web-based electronic booking tool that provides notifications, pick-up arrangements, shipment tracking and document generation. exp.o ISF (importer security filing) assists importers in fulfilling U.S. Customs Importer Security Filing requirements. CDM (Container Delivery Management) enables carriers to enter container delivery status and location information that customers can view on exp.o. Through web access to international tariff data and rules, TradeFlow helps international companies reduce the risks and manage the costs associated with importing and exporting. The firm's subsidiaries include Expeditors Tradewin LLC, providingcustoms consulting services; and Certuspact LLC, a billing verification company.

Expeditors International offers its employees a comprehensive benefits package, a 401(k) plan and a stock purchase plan.

FINANCIAL DATA: Note: Data for latest year may not have been available at press time.

In U.S. $	2016	2015	2014	2013	2012	2011
Revenue		6,616,632,000	6,564,721,000	6,080,257,000	5,980,943,000	6,150,498,000
R&D Expense						
Operating Income		721,484,000	594,648,000	552,073,000	530,798,000	618,327,000
Operating Margin %		10.90%	9.05%	9.07%	8.87%	10.05%
SGA Expense		1,287,971,000	1,206,264,000	1,164,281,000	1,117,280,000	1,116,997,000
Net Income		457,223,000	376,888,000	348,526,000	333,360,000	385,679,000
Operating Cash Flow		564,712,000	394,966,000	407,536,000	370,126,000	457,131,000
Capital Expenditure		44,383,000	37,472,000	53,411,000	47,626,000	78,115,000
EBITDA		767,496,000	643,940,000	600,144,000	591,584,000	676,930,000
Return on Assets %		16.70%	12.76%	11.67%	11.45%	13.90%
Return on Equity %		25.68%	19.06%	16.94%	16.53%	20.59%
Debt to Equity						

CONTACT INFORMATION:

Phone: 206 674-3400   Fax: 206 674-3459
Toll-Free:
Address: 1015 3rd Ave., 12th Fl., Seattle, WA 98104 United States

STOCK TICKER/OTHER:

Stock Ticker: EXPD   Exchange: NAS
Employees: 15,397   Fiscal Year Ends: 12/31
Parent Company:

SALARIES/BONUSES:

Top Exec. Salary: $100,000   Bonus: $
Second Exec. Salary: Bonus: $
$100,000

OTHER THOUGHTS:

Estimated Female Officers or Directors: 2
Hot Spot for Advancement for Women/Minorities:

Experian North America

www.experian.com

NAIC Code: 561450

TYPES OF BUSINESS:

Credit Bureau
Customer Relationship Software & Solutions
Marketing Software & Solutions
Business & Consumer Internet Sites
Online Services
Risk Management Services, Automotive

BRANDS/DIVISIONS/AFFILIATES:

Experian plc
Experian.com
CreditReport.com
freecreditscore.com

CONTACTS: *Note: Officers with more than one job title may be intentionally listed here more than once.*

Brian Cassin, CEO-Experian plc
Don Robert, CEO-Experian plc
Kerry Williams, Pres., Credit Svcs. & Experian Latin America
Brian Cassin, CFO-Experian plc
John Peace, Chmn.-Experian plc
Don Robert, Chmn.

GROWTH PLANS/SPECIAL FEATURES:

Experian North America, a subsidiary of Experian plc, is a leading credit-reporting agency in the U.S., Canada and Mexico. It also helps organizations find, develop and manage customer relationships by providing information, decision-making solutions and processing services. Experian operates through four segments: credit services, decision analytics, marketing services and consumer services. The credit services unit provides clients with solutions that optimize processes in acquiring new customers, prospecting for customers, customer portfolio management tools and collections services. Decision analytics provides analytical software and services to help clients optimize their lending strategies, allowing companies to manage credit risk, maintain regulatory compliance, predict behavior, prevent and detect fraud and allow for more efficient decision making. The marketing services unit provides customer acquisition, retention and growth and marketing strategy services to the advertising and media, automotive, banking, catalog, retail, financial services, consumer products and travel and hospitality markets. Finally, the consumer services segment offers consumers access to their credit histories and financial management tools through various web sites, including Experian.com, CreditReport.com and freecreditscore.com.

Parent company Experian offers its employees health, dental and vision care plans; flexible spending accounts; education assistance; credit union membership; an employee assistance program; referral bonuses; employee discounts; adoption assistance; and fitness reimbursement.

FINANCIAL DATA: *Note: Data for latest year may not have been available at press time.*

In U.S. $	2016	2015	2014	2013	2012	2011
Revenue		2,468,000,000	2,404,000,000	2,258,000,000		
R&D Expense						
Operating Income						
Operating Margin %						
SGA Expense						
Net Income		761,000,000	757,000,000	662,000,000		
Operating Cash Flow						
Capital Expenditure						
EBITDA						
Return on Assets %						
Return on Equity %						
Debt to Equity						

CONTACT INFORMATION:

Phone: 714-830-7000 Fax: 714-830-2449
Toll-Free: 888-397-3742
Address: 475 Anton Blvd., Costa Mesa, CA 92626 United States

STOCK TICKER/OTHER:

Stock Ticker: Subsidiary Exchange:
Employees: 6,700 Fiscal Year Ends: 03/31
Parent Company: Experian plc

SALARIES/BONUSES:

Top Exec. Salary: $ Bonus: $
Second Exec. Salary: $ Bonus: $

OTHER THOUGHTS:

Estimated Female Officers or Directors:
Hot Spot for Advancement for Women/Minorities:

Express Scripts Holding Co

www.express-scripts.com

NAIC Code: 524292

TYPES OF BUSINESS:

Pharmacy Benefits Management
Mail & Internet Pharmacies
Formulary Management
Integrated Drug & Medical Data Analysis
Market Research Programs
Medical Information Management
Workers' Compensation Programs
Informed-Decision Counseling

BRANDS/DIVISIONS/AFFILIATES:

CuraScript Specialty Distribution
Freedom Fertility
Accredo Health Group
United BioSource

CONTACTS: Note: Officers with more than one job title may be intentionally listed here more than once.

George Paz, Chairman of the Board
Donald Fotsch, Senior VP, Divisional
Chris McGinnis, Chief Accounting Officer
Gary Wimberly, Chief Information Officer
Steven Miller, Chief Medical Officer
Eric Slusser, Executive VP
Martin Akins, General Counsel
Sara Wade, Other Executive Officer
Glen Stettin, Other Executive Officer
Timothy Wentworth, President
David Norton, Senior VP, Divisional
David Queller, Senior VP, Divisional
Christine Houston, Senior VP, Divisional
Everett Neville, Senior VP, Divisional
Phyllis Anderson, Senior VP

GROWTH PLANS/SPECIAL FEATURES:

Express Scripts Holding Co. is one of the largest independent pharmacy benefit managers in the U.S. The firm provides pharmacy service and pharmacy benefit plan design consultation for clients including HMOs, health insurers, third party administrators, employers, unions and government health care plans. The company operates in two segments: pharmacy benefit management (PBM) and other business operations. The PBM division offers retail network pharmacy management and retail drug card programs; home delivery and specialty pharmacy services; patient care contact centers; rebate programs; electronic claims processing and drug utilization review; information reporting and analysis programs; consumer health and drug information; assistance programs for low-income patients; benefit plan design and consultation; and drug formulary management, compliance and therapy management programs. It dispenses drugs to patients from several home delivery fulfillment pharmacies and maintains partnerships with over 70,000 retail pharmacies. This segment also provides fertility services to both providers and patients through its subsidiary, Freedom Fertility. Subsidiary, Accredo Health Group focuses on dispensing injectable, infused, oral or inhaled drugs that require a higher level of clinical service and support. Express Scripts' other business operations includes the following brands that service patients through multiple paths: subsidiary CuraScript Specialty Distribution offers specialty medical supplies and pharmaceuticals to treat rare and orphan diseases directly to providers, hospitals and clinics in the U.S.; and subsidiary United BioSource provides consulting services for pharmaceutical manufacturers to collect scientific evidence to guide the safe, effective and affordable use of medicines. The segment also assists with eligibility review, prior authorization coordination, re-pricing, utilization management, monitoring and reporting.

The firm offers employees a comprehensive health package, a 401(k), a stock purchase plan, financial counseling and paid time off.

FINANCIAL DATA: Note: Data for latest year may not have been available at press time.

In U.S. $	2016	2015	2014	2013	2012	2011
Revenue		101,751,800,000	100,887,100,000	104,098,800,000	93,858,100,000	46,128,300,000
R&D Expense						
Operating Income		4,339,300,000	3,602,400,000	3,551,700,000	2,784,500,000	2,311,700,000
Operating Margin %		4.26%	3.57%	3.41%	2.96%	5.01%
SGA Expense		4,062,600,000	4,322,700,000	4,580,700,000	4,545,700,000	898,200,000
Net Income		2,476,400,000	2,007,600,000	1,844,600,000	1,312,900,000	1,275,800,000
Operating Cash Flow		4,848,300,000	4,549,000,000	4,757,500,000	4,781,600,000	2,192,000,000
Capital Expenditure		295,900,000	436,600,000	423,000,000	160,200,000	144,400,000
EBITDA		6,723,200,000	5,892,000,000	6,073,400,000	4,682,600,000	2,577,500,000
Return on Assets %		4.62%	3.74%	3.30%	3.56%	9.75%
Return on Equity %		13.23%	9.58%	8.15%	10.15%	41.96%
Debt to Equity		0.80	0.54	0.56	0.64	2.86

CONTACT INFORMATION:

Phone: 314-996-0900   Fax: 314-770-0303
Toll-Free:
Address: 1 Express Way, St. Louis, MO 63121 United States

STOCK TICKER/OTHER:

Stock Ticker: ESRX   Exchange: NAS
Employees: 29,500   Fiscal Year Ends: 12/31
Parent Company:

SALARIES/BONUSES:

Top Exec. Salary: Bonus: $
$1,324,058
Second Exec. Salary: Bonus: $
$901,250

OTHER THOUGHTS:

Estimated Female Officers or Directors: 3

Hot Spot for Advancement for Women/Minorities: Y

ExxonMobil Chemical

NAIC Code: 325110

www.exxonmobilchemical.com

TYPES OF BUSINESS:

Plastics & Rubber Manufacturing
Petrochemicals
Catalyst Technology
Polypropylene

BRANDS/DIVISIONS/AFFILIATES:

Univation Technologies LLC
Badger Licensing LLC
XyMax
PxMax
Exxon Mobil Corporation (ExxonMobil)
UNIPOL PE Process
New Exceed

CONTACTS: Note: Officers with more than one job title may be intentionally listed here more than once.

Rex W. Tillerson, CEO
Neil A. Chapman, Pres.
Sherman J. Glass Jr., Pres., ExxonMobil Refining & Amp
Donald D. Humphreys, Sr. VP
Rex W. Tillerson, Chmn.

GROWTH PLANS/SPECIAL FEATURES:

ExxonMobil Chemical, a division of Exxon Mobil Corporation, is one of the world's largest petrochemical companies, manufacturing and marketing olefins, aromatics, fluids, synthetic rubber, polyethylene, polypropylene, oriented polypropylene packaging films, plasticizers, synthetic lubricant base-stocks, additives for fuels and lubricants, zeolite catalysts and other petrochemical products. The firm is one of the only major olefins producers with proprietary pyrolysis-reactor technology, which delivers the highest olefin yields in the industry. The unit's XyMax and PxMax aromatics utilize proprietary zeolite shape-selective catalyst technology. This technology increases conversion and reduces losses versus other technologies in the production of higher olefins. Univation Technologies, LLC, a joint venture company owned by ExxonMobil Chemical and Dow Chemical Co., has developed the UNIPOL PE Process for manufacturing linear low-density polyethylene and high-density polyethelene. The joint venture also furnishes catalysts for metallocene and bimodal resins. Badger Licensing, LLC, a joint venture with The Shaw Group, licenses alkylation technologies. ExxonMobil Chemical's recent New Exceed metallocene polyethylene resins were introduced as a new, globally available grade for extrusion coating and lamination applications. This grade has a range of applications, including drink cartons, lamitubes and flexible packaging.

FINANCIAL DATA: Note: Data for latest year may not have been available at press time.

In U.S. $	2016	2015	2014	2013	2012	2011
Revenue		24,000,000,000	24,235,000,000	24,063,000,000	24,159,000,000	25,006,000,000
R&D Expense						
Operating Income						
Operating Margin %						
SGA Expense						
Net Income		4,418,000,000	4,315,000,000	3,828,000,000	3,900,000,000	4,383,000,000
Operating Cash Flow						
Capital Expenditure						
EBITDA						
Return on Assets %						
Return on Equity %						
Debt to Equity						

CONTACT INFORMATION:

Phone: 281-870-6000 Fax: 281-870-6661
Toll-Free:
Address: 22777 Springwoods Village Pkwy., Spring, TX 77389-1425
United States

STOCK TICKER/OTHER:

Stock Ticker: Subsidiary
Employees: 25,000
Parent Company: Exxon Mobil Corporation (EXXONMOBIL)

Exchange:
Fiscal Year Ends: 12/31

SALARIES/BONUSES:

Top Exec. Salary: $ Bonus: $
Second Exec. Salary: $ Bonus: $

OTHER THOUGHTS:

Estimated Female Officers or Directors:
Hot Spot for Advancement for Women/Minorities:

EY LLP

NAIC Code: 541211

TYPES OF BUSINESS:

Accounting
Risk Management
Tax Preparation Services
Human Resources Management
IT Services
Transaction Support Services
Industry Publications

BRANDS/DIVISIONS/AFFILIATES:

EY

CONTACTS: Note: Officers with more than one job title may be intentionally listed here more than once.

Chris Hamilton, Managing Partner
Michael Inserra, Regional Managing Partner-Financial Svcs.
Tom Hough, Vice Chair-Assurance Svcs.
Richard Jeanneret, Vice Chair-Transaction Advisory Svcs.
Jean-Yves, Vice Chair-Quality & Risk Mgmt.
Tom McGrath, Sr. Vice Chair-Accounts
Ronen Barel, Chmn.

GROWTH PLANS/SPECIAL FEATURES:

EY LLP, the U.S. branch of the global accounting firm EY (Ernst & Young), is a professional services company. The firm provides advisory, tax, assurance, transaction and specialty services. Advisory services include actuarial, customer, cyber security, finance, risk management, internal audit, people advisory, program management, risk assurance, risk transformation, strategy, supply chain & operations and technology. Tax services include global tax, country tax, cross border tax, global trade, global compliance & reporting, human capital, private client, law, tax accounting, tax performance, tax policy & controversy, transaction tax, sales tax, transfer pricing and operating model effectiveness. Assurance services include accounting compliance, reporting, climate change, sustainability, financial accounting, financial statement audit, fraud investigation and dispute services. Transaction services include corporate development, divesture, lead advisory, operational transaction, restructuring, strategy, transaction support, transaction tax, valuation and business modeling. Specialty services include climate change & sustainability, CertifyPoint, China overseas investment, family business, French business, global business and Japan business. Industries served by EY LLP include automotive & transportation, health, oil & gas, technology, consumer products & retail, life sciences, power & utilities, telecommunications, financial services, media & entertainment, private equity, government & public sector, mining & metals, real estate, hospitality and construction. Clients of the firm have included Best Buy, British Petroleum, Coca-Cola, FedEx, Google, Lockheed Martin, McDonald's, Target Corporation and Whole Foods Markets, among others.

FINANCIAL DATA: Note: Data for latest year may not have been available at press time.

In U.S. $	2016	2015	2014	2013	2012	2011
Revenue		12,701,000,000	11,542,000,000	10,750,000,000	9,820,000,000	8,981,000,000
R&D Expense						
Operating Income						
Operating Margin %						
SGA Expense						
Net Income						
Operating Cash Flow						
Capital Expenditure						
EBITDA						
Return on Assets %						
Return on Equity %						
Debt to Equity						

CONTACT INFORMATION:

Phone: 212-773-3000   Fax: 212-773-6350
Toll-Free:
Address: 5 Times Sq., 14th Fl., New York, NY 10036 United States

STOCK TICKER/OTHER:

Stock Ticker: Subsidiary   Exchange:
Employees: 65,457   Fiscal Year Ends: 06/30
Parent Company: EY

SALARIES/BONUSES:

Top Exec. Salary: $ Bonus: $
Second Exec. Salary: $ Bonus: $

OTHER THOUGHTS:

Estimated Female Officers or Directors: 5
Hot Spot for Advancement for Women/Minorities: Y

F5 Networks Inc

www.f5.com

NAIC Code: 0

TYPES OF BUSINESS:
Computer Software, Network Management, System Testing & Storage
Internet Traffic Management Solutions
Firewall Software
File Virtualization

BRANDS/DIVISIONS/AFFILIATES:
BIG-IP
VIPRION
FirePass
Application Security Manager
iControl
ARX

CONTACTS: Note: Officers with more than one job title may be intentionally listed here more than once.
Andrew Reinland, CFO
Alan Higginson, Director
John McAdam, Director
John Dilullo, Executive VP, Divisional
Ryan Kearny, Executive VP, Divisional
Edward Eames, Executive VP
Scot Rogers, Executive VP

GROWTH PLANS/SPECIAL FEATURES:

F5 Networks, Inc. provides application delivery networking products that improve the security, availability and performance of network applications. Its core products, the BIG-IP controller, VIPRION, FirePass controller data manager, Application Security Manager (ASM) firewall and iControl, help manage traffic to servers and network devices in a way that maximizes availability and throughput. BIG-IP products share a common full-proxy operating system that enables them to inspect and modify traffic flow to and from servers and has built-in functionality to secure, optimize and ensure the availability of application traffic. VIPRION is the firm's chassis-based application delivery controller that uses modular blades that can be added or removed without disturbing current application settings. The company's FirePass product offers a secure socket layer-virtual private network that allows enterprises to provide authorized users with secure remote access to corporate networks and applications. The ASM firewall provides content-based, application-level security against attacks. The iControl software interface products enable communication with one another and allow integration with third-party products, including custom and commercial enterprise applications. Intelligent file virtualization manages file storage infrastructure through non-disruptive data migration, automated storage tiering, dynamic load balancing and efficient data replication though the ARX product family. The company sells its products and services to large enterprise customers and service providers through a variety of channels, including distributors, value-added resellers and systems integrators. In 2014, the firm acquired cloud-based security services provider, Defense.Net, Inc.

Employee benefits include medical, dental and vision coverage; flexible spending accounts; life and disability insurance; an employee stock purchase plan; a 401(k) with company match; tuition assistance; and an employee assistance program.

FINANCIAL DATA: Note: Data for latest year may not have been available at press time.

In U.S. $	2016	2015	2014	2013	2012	2011
Revenue		1,919,823,000	1,732,046,000	1,481,314,000	1,377,247,000	1,151,834,000
R&D Expense		296,583,000	263,792,000	209,614,000	177,406,000	138,910,000
Operating Income		552,899,000	493,557,000	430,818,000	426,303,000	350,662,000
Operating Margin %		28.79%	28.49%	29.08%	30.95%	30.44%
SGA Expense		738,080,000	664,738,000	585,442,000	537,370,000	454,258,000
Net Income		365,014,000	311,183,000	277,314,000	275,186,000	241,397,000
Operating Cash Flow		684,541,000	548,992,000	499,693,000	495,437,000	416,938,000
Capital Expenditure		67,086,000	22,718,000	26,583,000	30,117,000	36,160,000
EBITDA		605,482,000	539,678,000	470,823,000	461,442,000	371,549,000
Return on Assets %		16.23%	14.09%	13.39%	15.81%	16.47%
Return on Equity %		27.17%	21.40%	19.33%	22.60%	22.89%
Debt to Equity						

CONTACT INFORMATION:
Phone: 206 272-5555   Fax: 206 272-5556
Toll-Free: 888-882-4447
Address: 401 Elliott Ave. W., Seattle, WA 98119 United States

STOCK TICKER/OTHER:
Stock Ticker: FFIV   Exchange: NAS
Employees: 4,178   Fiscal Year Ends: 09/30
Parent Company:

SALARIES/BONUSES:
Top Exec. Salary: $718,386   Bonus: $
Second Exec. Salary: $534,759   Bonus: $1,500

OTHER THOUGHTS:
Estimated Female Officers or Directors: 3
Hot Spot for Advancement for Women/Minorities: Y

Facebook Inc

NAIC Code: 519130

TYPES OF BUSINESS:

Social Networking
Advertising Services
Developer Tools
Online Video
3-D Headset Manufacturing
Apps

BRANDS/DIVISIONS/AFFILIATES:

Facebook Platform
WhatsApp Inc
Instagram
Oculus VR
LiveRail
Messenger

CONTACTS: Note: Officers with more than one job title may be intentionally listed here more than once.

Jan Koum, CEO, Subsidiary
Mark Zuckerberg, CEO
David Wehner, CFO
Jas Athwal, Chief Accounting Officer
Michael Schroepfer, Chief Technology Officer
Sheryl Sandberg, COO
Christopher Cox, Other Executive Officer
David Fischer, Vice President, Divisional
Colin Stretch, Vice President

GROWTH PLANS/SPECIAL FEATURES:

Facebook, Inc. owns and operates a free social networking utility for communicating online with family, friends and acquaintances. As of August 2015, the company had 1.18 billion monthly active users in general, and 745 million daily active users who specifically used the company's mobile products. Some of the site's core functions and applications include individual profiles and home pages; friend lists; group pages; and photos, videos, events and other shared items. Communication is enabled through means such as in-site instant messaging, personal messages, public posts and status updates. Third-party applications (such as games, quizzes and personality tests) can also be added to users' pages to further personalize the site. For privacy, the firm gives users the ability to limit, to some extent, who can view their profile, postings and other personal information. The company's Facebook Platform is a set of development tools and application programming interfaces that enable developers to integrate with Facebook to create social apps and websites. More than 10 million apps and websites have been integrated as part of the platform. Facebook generates the majority of its revenues from advertising, which can be customized to reach specifically targeted audiences by accessing information users provide the company on their individual profiles. Subsidiary Instagram is a mobile phone-based photo-sharing service that makes it simple for users to upload photos to their profiles. Messenger is a mobile-to-mobile messaging application available on Android, iOS and Windows Phone devices; and WhatsApp Messenger is a cross-platform mobile messaging app that allows people to exchange messages on iOS, Android, BlackBerry, Windows Phone and Nokia devices. In 2014, Facebook acquired 3-D headset maker Oculus VR; LiveRail, an advertising technology company; and WhatApp, Inc.

Facebook provides its employees with health coverage; life and disability insurance; 401(k); parental leave and daycare reimbursements; vacation pay; and an employee assistance program. The firm's Palo Alto headquarters features an onsite cafeteria serving free breakfast, lunch and dinner daily.

FINANCIAL DATA: Note: Data for latest year may not have been available at press time.

In U.S. $	2016	2015	2014	2013	2012	2011
Revenue		17,928,000,000	12,466,000,000	7,872,000,000	5,089,000,000	3,711,000,000
R&D Expense		4,816,000,000	2,666,000,000	1,415,000,000	1,399,000,000	388,000,000
Operating Income		6,225,000,000	4,994,000,000	2,804,000,000	538,000,000	1,756,000,000
Operating Margin %		34.72%	40.06%	35.61%	10.57%	47.31%
SGA Expense		4,020,000,000	2,653,000,000	1,778,000,000	1,788,000,000	707,000,000
Net Income		3,688,000,000	2,940,000,000	1,500,000,000	53,000,000	1,000,000,000
Operating Cash Flow		8,599,000,000	5,457,000,000	4,222,000,000	1,612,000,000	1,549,000,000
Capital Expenditure		2,523,000,000	1,831,000,000	1,362,000,000	1,235,000,000	606,000,000
EBITDA		8,162,000,000	6,176,000,000	3,821,000,000	1,194,000,000	2,060,000,000
Return on Assets %		8.19%	10.07%	9.03%	.29%	14.33%
Return on Equity %		9.13%	11.34%	10.95%	.39%	22.91%
Debt to Equity				0.01	0.16	0.09

CONTACT INFORMATION:

Phone: 650 543-4800　　　Fax:
Toll-Free:
Address: 1601 Willo Road, Menlo Park, CA 94025 United States

STOCK TICKER/OTHER:

Stock Ticker: FB　　　　　　　　　　Exchange: NAS
Employees: 12,691　　　　　　　　　Fiscal Year Ends: 12/31
Parent Company:

SALARIES/BONUSES:

Top Exec. Salary: $715,385　　Bonus: $1,265,193
Second Exec. Salary:　　　　　Bonus: $943,360
$639,423

OTHER THOUGHTS:

Estimated Female Officers or Directors: 2
Hot Spot for Advancement for Women/Minorities: Y

FactSet Research Systems Inc

www.factset.com

NAIC Code: 511120

TYPES OF BUSINESS:
Online Financial & Economic Data
Financial Software
Consulting Services

BRANDS/DIVISIONS/AFFILIATES:

CONTACTS: *Note: Officers with more than one job title may be intentionally listed here more than once.*
Maurizio Nicolelli, CFO
Philip Hadley, Chairman of the Board
Mark Hale, Executive VP
Scott Miller, Executive VP
Rachel Stern, General Counsel
Edward Baker-Greene, Other Executive Officer
Philip Snow, President

GROWTH PLANS/SPECIAL FEATURES:

FactSet Research Systems, Inc. supplies financial information and analytical applications to global investors, including portfolio managers, performance analysts, risk managers, sell-side equity researchers, investment bankers and fixed income professionals. Headquartered in Norwalk, Connecticut, the company operates 38 locations in 21 countries. FactSet currently has 62,205 users and 2,976 clients in over 50 countries worldwide, with access to data from more than 220 data suppliers, 100 news sources and 80 exchanges. It combines the content of tens of thousands of companies from multiple sources (stock markets, research firms, governments and others) into a single online platform of information and analytics. The firm integrates content from premier providers such as Thomson Reuters, Standard & Poor's, Axioma, Inc., Interactive Data Corporation LLC, Dow Jones & Company, Inc., Northfield Information Services, Inc., Barclays Capital, Intex Solutions, Inc. and many more. FactSet's operations are organized into three reportable segments based on geographic operations: the U.S., Europe and Asia Pacific. The majority of fiscal revenue is derived from its U.S. clients, with Europe being next and Asia Pacific the remainder. The U.S. segment services finance professionals including financial institutions throughout the Americas, while the European and Asia Pacific segments service investment professionals located throughout Europe and Asia, respectively. The European segment is headquartered in London, England and maintains offices in France, Germany, the Netherlands, Latvia, Dubai and Italy. The Asia Pacific segment is headquartered in Tokyo, Japan with offices in Hong Kong, Australia and India. FactSet's client retention rate is over 95%. In July 2016, the firm sold its market research business (Market Metrics and Matrix Solutions) to Asset International for $165 million.

FactSet offers U.S. employees tuition assistance; medical, dental, life, disability, vision, AD&D and business travel insurance; wellness programs; disability and maternity leave; counseling services; flexible spending accounts; 401(k); and employee stock purchase plan.

FINANCIAL DATA: *Note: Data for latest year may not have been available at press time.*

In U.S. $	2016	2015	2014	2013	2012	2011
Revenue		1,006,768,000	920,335,000	858,112,000	805,793,000	726,510,000
R&D Expense						
Operating Income		331,918,000	302,219,000	269,419,000	272,990,000	238,335,000
Operating Margin %		32.96%	32.83%	31.39%	33.87%	32.80%
SGA Expense		269,511,000	264,430,000	282,314,000	257,266,000	243,552,000
Net Income		241,051,000	211,543,000	198,637,000	188,809,000	171,046,000
Operating Cash Flow		306,442,000	265,023,000	269,809,000	231,965,000	207,136,000
Capital Expenditure		25,682,000	17,743,000	18,517,000	22,520,000	29,343,000
EBITDA		363,267,000	336,654,000	305,198,000	306,769,000	275,182,000
Return on Assets %		34.43%	31.26%	28.69%	27.93%	26.27%
Return on Equity %		46.23%	40.18%	36.31%	35.37%	33.61%
Debt to Equity		0.06				

CONTACT INFORMATION:
Phone: 203 810-1000   Fax: 203 810-1001
Toll-Free:
Address: 601 Merritt 7, 3rd Fl., Norwalk, CT 06851 United States

STOCK TICKER/OTHER:
Stock Ticker: FDS   Exchange: NYS
Employees: 7,360   Fiscal Year Ends: 08/31
Parent Company:

SALARIES/BONUSES:
Top Exec. Salary: $338,000   Bonus: $1,200,000
Second Exec. Salary: Bonus: $1,250,000
$169,000

OTHER THOUGHTS:
Estimated Female Officers or Directors: 3
Hot Spot for Advancement for Women/Minorities: Y

Fairview Health Services

www.fairview.org

NAIC Code: 622110

TYPES OF BUSINESS:

General Medical and Surgical Hospitals
Specialty Clinics
Home Care
Hospice Services
Children's Services
Cancer Care
Senior Care
Academic Teaching Hospital

BRANDS/DIVISIONS/AFFILIATES:

Fairview Lakes Medical Center
Maple Grove Medical Center
Fairview Northland Medical Center
Fairview Ridges Hospital
Fairview Southdale Hospital
Ebenezer
Fairview Foundation (The)

CONTACTS: Note: Officers with more than one job title may be intentionally listed here more than once.

David Murphy, Interim CEO
Bob Beacher, Pres.
Daniel Fromm, CFO
Carolyn Jacobson, Chief Human Resources Officer
Brent Asplin, Chief Clinical Officer
Alistair Jacques, CIO
Mark Hansberry, VP-Strategic Planning
Mark Hansberry, VP-Comm.
Brent Asplin, Pres., Fairview Medical Group
Daniel K. Anderson, Pres., Fairview Community Hospitals
Bob Beacher, Pres., Fairview Pharmacy Services
Richard Howard, Pres., Fairview Foundation
David Murphy, Chmn.
Mark Thomas, Pres., Senior Services

GROWTH PLANS/SPECIAL FEATURES:

Fairview Health Services is an integrated health network. It serves the Minneapolis-St. Paul area of Minnesota and suburbs; the Red Wing, Northland, Lakes and Range areas of Minnesota; the Minnesota Valley; and Wyoming. The system contains acute care hospitals; primary care, specialty care and occupational health clinics; senior care and housing facilities; freestanding surgery centers; ambulatory care facilities; retail and specialty pharmacies; counseling centers, home health care programs; and various foundations supporting health-related services. The company's hospitals include Fairview Lakes Medical Center, Maple Grove Medical Center, Fairview Northland Medical Center, Fairview Ridges Hospital and Fairview Southdale Hospital. Fairview also has an academic partnership with the University of Minnesota and University of Minnesota Physicians. Through these partnerships, Fairview Health operates from the University of Minnesota Academic Health Center, which consists of six schools and colleges that educate and train researchers, physicians and other health care professionals; the University of Minnesota Physicians, a group practice with more than 800 physicians and 1,600 health care professionals who apply clinical breakthroughs for patients at University of Minnesota Medical Center and University of Minnesota Masonic Children's Hospital, as well as hospitals and clinics throughout the community. Through its subsidiary Ebenezer, Fairview provides senior housing facilities such as apartments, assisted living complexes, cooperatives, condominiums, a memory care facility for patients living with Alzheimer's or other early-stage dementias and adult and intergenerational daycare programs. The Fairview Foundation is the group's funding entity for operations, special projects, programs, allocations and endowments.

Fairview offers its employees life, disability, health and dental insurance; assistance program; wellness, disease management, spiritual health, smoking cessation and weight management services; health club discounts; 529 college savings; adoption and day care assistance; 403(b) and 401(k); continuing education programs; tuition reimbursement; a Sallie Mae partnership; and medical mission grants.

FINANCIAL DATA: Note: Data for latest year may not have been available at press time.

In U.S. $	2016	2015	2014	2013	2012	2011
Revenue		3,867,550,000	3,560,832,000	3,318,513,000	3,218,081,000	3,011,509,000
R&D Expense						
Operating Income						
Operating Margin %						
SGA Expense						
Net Income		64,908,000	166,695,000	244,300,000	108,039,000	16,667,000
Operating Cash Flow						
Capital Expenditure						
EBITDA						
Return on Assets %						
Return on Equity %						
Debt to Equity						

CONTACT INFORMATION:

Phone: 612-672-7272   Fax: 612-672-7186
Toll-Free: 800-824-1953
Address: 2450 Riverside Ave., Minneapolis, MN 55454 United States

STOCK TICKER/OTHER:

Stock Ticker: Nonprofit   Exchange:
Employees: 21,500   Fiscal Year Ends: 12/31
Parent Company:

SALARIES/BONUSES:

Top Exec. Salary: $ Bonus: $
Second Exec. Salary: $ Bonus: $

OTHER THOUGHTS:

Estimated Female Officers or Directors: 9
Hot Spot for Advancement for Women/Minorities: Y

Fastenal Co

www.fastenal.com

NAIC Code: 423810

TYPES OF BUSINESS:
Construction and Mining (except Oil Well) Machinery and Equipment Merchant Wholesalers
Office Equipment Merchant Wholesalers

BRANDS/DIVISIONS/AFFILIATES:
FNL
FNL G9
Aspect
Rock River
Blackstone
Tritan
FMT
PowerPhase

CONTACTS: Note: Officers with more than one job title may be intentionally listed here more than once.
Daniel Florness, CEO
Sheryl Lisowski, Controller
Willard Oberton, Director
Reyne Wisecup, Director
James Jansen, Executive VP, Divisional
Nicholas Lundquist, Executive VP, Divisional
Gary Polipnick, Executive VP, Divisional
Ashok Singh, Executive VP, Divisional
John Soderberg, Executive VP, Divisional
Charles Miller, Executive VP, Divisional
Holden Lewis, Executive VP
Terry Owen, Senior Executive VP, Divisional
Leland Hein, Senior Executive VP, Divisional

GROWTH PLANS/SPECIAL FEATURES:
Fastenal Co. is a retailer and wholesaler of industrial and construction supplies. The firm operates roughly 2,622 store locations, the majority of which are located in all 50 U.S. states. The remaining stores are located in Canada, Mexico, Puerto Rico, Dominican Republic, Panama, Brazil, Colombia, Chile, Singapore, Malaysia, Thailand, China, India, The Netherlands, Hungary, the U.K., Germany, Czech Republic, Italy, Poland, Romania, Sweden and South Africa. The company also operates 14 North American distribution centers (11 in the U.S., two in Canada and one in Mexico) from which it distributes products to its store and in-plant locations. The firm sells 11 types of products: fasteners, sold under brands such as FNL, FNL G9, Holo-Krome and Rock River; tools through the FMT and Rock River brands; cutting tools, marketed under the FMT and Tritan labels; office supplies through its Aspect brand; welding supplies through its Blackstone brand; hydraulics and pneumatics through StrongHold and Dynaflo; janitorial supplies under the Clean Choice brand; material handling items, sold under the EquipRite label; electrical supplies through PowerPhase; metals under the Fastenal label; and safety supplies through the Bodyguard brand. Threaded fasteners account for approximately 90% of Fastenal's total sales. Of the firm's over 1 million standard stock items, roughly 95% are manufactured by other companies; Fastenal manufactures the other 5% of its products.

Fastenal offers its employees medical, dental, life, disability and AD&D insurance; a retirement savings plan; company profit sharing; and employee discount programs.

FINANCIAL DATA: Note: Data for latest year may not have been available at press time.

In U.S. $	2016	2015	2014	2013	2012	2011
Revenue		3,869,187,000	3,733,507,000	3,326,106,000	3,133,577,000	2,766,859,000
R&D Expense						
Operating Income		828,755,000	787,590,000	712,657,000	673,691,000	574,609,000
Operating Margin %		21.41%	21.09%	21.42%	21.49%	20.76%
SGA Expense		1,121,590,000	1,110,776,000	1,007,431,000	941,236,000	859,369,000
Net Income		516,361,000	494,150,000	448,636,000	420,536,000	357,929,000
Operating Cash Flow		546,940,000	499,392,000	416,120,000	396,292,000	268,489,000
Capital Expenditure		155,168,000	189,474,000	206,540,000	138,406,000	120,043,000
EBITDA		915,726,000	861,021,000	777,772,000	727,743,000	619,315,000
Return on Assets %		21.11%	22.28%	23.05%	24.02%	22.70%
Return on Equity %		27.78%	26.79%	26.92%	27.85%	26.11%
Debt to Equity		0.16				

CONTACT INFORMATION:
Phone: 507 454-5374   Fax: 507 453-8049
Toll-Free:
Address: 2001 Theurer Blvd., Winona, MN 55987-0978 United States

STOCK TICKER/OTHER:
Stock Ticker: FAST   Exchange: NAS
Employees: 20,746   Fiscal Year Ends: 12/31
Parent Company:

SALARIES/BONUSES:
Top Exec. Salary: $572,292   Bonus: $
Second Exec. Salary: Bonus: $
$523,333

OTHER THOUGHTS:
Estimated Female Officers or Directors: 2
Hot Spot for Advancement for Women/Minorities:

FCA US LLC

www.fcanorthamerica.com/company/AboutUs/Pages/AboutUs.aspx

NAIC Code: 336111

TYPES OF BUSINESS:

Automobile Manufacturing
Research & Development
Nanotechnology-Coatings
Light Truck Manufacturing
Financial Services

BRANDS/DIVISIONS/AFFILIATES:

Fiat Chrysler Automobiles NV
Chrysler
Jeep
Android Auto
Uconnect
AppleCarPlay
Pacifica Hybrid
Dodge

CONTACTS: Note: Officers with more than one job title may be intentionally listed here more than once.

Sergio Marchionne, CEO
Robert E. Lee, VP-Engine, Powertrain & Electrified Propulsion
Ralph V. Gilles, Sr. VP-Prod. Design
Mark M. Chernoby, Sr. VP-Eng.
Mauro Pino, Sr. VP-Mfg. & World Class Mfg.
Peter Grady, VP-Network Dev. & Fleet
Marjorie Loeb, General Counsel
Barbara J. Pilarski, VP-Bus. Dev.
Gualberto Ranieri, Sr. VP-Comm.
Laurie A. Macaddino, VP-Audit
Doug D. Betts, Sr. VP-Quality
Alistair Gardner, Pres.
Reid Bigland, Head-U.S. Sales
Steven G. Beahm, Sr. VP-Supply Chain Mgmt.

GROWTH PLANS/SPECIAL FEATURES:

FCA US LLC, also known as Chrysler, is a North American automaker headquartered in Michigan. It is a member of the Fiat Chrysler Automobiles NV family of companies. FCA US designs, engineers, manufactures and sells vehicles under the Chrysler, Jeep, Dodge, Ram and Fiat brands as well as the street and racing technology (SRT) performance vehicle designation. The company also distributes the Alfa Romeo 4C model and Mopar products. FCA is one of the largest automakers in the world based on total annual vehicle sales. FCA's fourth-generation Uconnect system brings interactive ability to the in-car radio and telemetric-like controls to car settings. The 2016 models feature AppleCarPlay and Android Auto, providing a safer way to use a smartphone inside a car. Other concepts the firm is exploring for future Uconnect models include predictive technology that monitors the driver's daily habits; Vehicle-to-X communication, enabling vehicles to communicate with each other and the roadside; and privacy mode, which detects when a passenger is present in the vehicle. FCA's 2017 Chrysler Pacifica and Pacifica Hybrid have been re-engineered from the ground up on an all-new platform for class-leading ride, handling and noise, vibration & harshness, and will boast 115 minivan innovations. The hybrid will offer up to 80 miles per gallon equivalent (MPGe) in city driving. The firm sold 2.24 million vehicles in 2015 and has 37 manufacturing facilities, 12 regional business centers, 22 parts distribution centers and eight training & test facilities. In 2014 Fiat Group acquired 100% of Chrysler, merged Fiat SpA into Chrysler and renamed it FCA US LLC.

The firm offers employees medical, prescription, vision & dental coverage; life insurance; discounted auto and home insurance; discount new vehicle purchase programs; and educational & personal development programs.

FINANCIAL DATA: Note: Data for latest year may not have been available at press time.

In U.S. $	2016	2015	2014	2013	2012	2011
Revenue		11,676,910,000	10,913,000,000	72,140,000,000	65,800,000,000	55,000,000,000
R&D Expense						
Operating Income						
Operating Margin %						
SGA Expense						
Net Income		1,747,498,195	1,587,005,793	2,760,000,000	1,700,000,000	183,000,000
Operating Cash Flow						
Capital Expenditure						
EBITDA						
Return on Assets %						
Return on Equity %						
Debt to Equity						

CONTACT INFORMATION:

Phone: 248-576-5741   Fax:
Toll-Free: 800-992-1997
Address: 1000 Chrysler Dr., Auburn Hills, MI 48326-2766 United States

STOCK TICKER/OTHER:

Stock Ticker: Private   Exchange:
Employees: 65,535   Fiscal Year Ends: 12/31
Parent Company: Fiat Chrysler Automobiles NV

SALARIES/BONUSES:

Top Exec. Salary: $ Bonus: $
Second Exec. Salary: $ Bonus: $

OTHER THOUGHTS:

Estimated Female Officers or Directors: 3
Hot Spot for Advancement for Women/Minorities: Y

Federal-Mogul Corporation

www.federalmogul.com

NAIC Code: 336300

TYPES OF BUSINESS:

Aftermarket Products & Services
Powertrain Products
Sealing Systems
Vehicle Safety & Performance Products

BRANDS/DIVISIONS/AFFILIATES:

CONTACTS: *Note: Officers with more than one job title may be intentionally listed here more than once.*

Michelle Taigman, Assistant Secretary
Rainer Jueckstock, CEO, Divisional
Daniel Ninivaggi, CEO, Subsidiary
Martin Hendricks, President, Divisional
Scott Pepin, Senior VP, Divisional
Jerome Rouquet, Senior VP
John Patouhas, Vice President

GROWTH PLANS/SPECIAL FEATURES:

Federal-Mogul Corporation is a supplier of vehicle and industrial products for fuel economy, alternative energies, environment and safety systems. The company operates two divisions: powertrain, which accounted for 57% of annual sales; and motorparts, 43%. Powertrain focuses on original equipment (OE) products for automotive, heavy duty and industrial applications. This segment offers its customers a diverse array of market-leading products for OE applications, including pistons, piston rings, piston pins, cylinder liners, valve seats & guides, ignition products, dynamic seals, bonded piston seals, combustion & exhaust gaskets, static gaskets & seals, rigid heat shields, engine bearings, industrial bearings, brushings & washers, plus element resistant systems protection sleeving products, acoustic shielding and flexible heat shields. The motorparts segment sells and distributes a broad portfolio of products manufactured by Powertrain. Motorparts' products include brake disc pads, brake linings, brake linings, brake blocks, brake system components, chassis products, wipers and other product lines to OE and aftermarket customers. Federal-Mogul maintains manufacturing facilities and distribution centers in 26 countries. In January 2016, the firm terminated its previously announced spin-off of its motorparts division.

The firm offers employees medical, dental, prescription drug, vision and hearing insurance; flexible spending accounts; life and AD&D insurance; disability coverage; a 401(k) plan; tuition assistance; and a pension plan.

FINANCIAL DATA: *Note: Data for latest year may not have been available at press time.*

In U.S. $	2016	2015	2014	2013	2012	2011
Revenue		7,419,000,000	7,317,000,000	6,786,000,000	6,664,000,000	6,910,000,000
R&D Expense						
Operating Income		1,000,000	232,000,000	254,000,000	-121,000,000	-50,000,000
Operating Margin %		.01%	3.17%	3.74%	-1.81%	-.72%
SGA Expense		794,000,000	776,000,000	719,000,000	712,000,000	689,000,000
Net Income		-110,000,000	-168,000,000	41,000,000	-117,000,000	-90,000,000
Operating Cash Flow		38,000,000	278,000,000	418,000,000	-53,000,000	241,000,000
Capital Expenditure		440,000,000	418,000,000	380,000,000	387,000,000	348,000,000
EBITDA		342,000,000	566,000,000	552,000,000	278,000,000	345,000,000
Return on Assets %		-1.53%	-2.35%	.58%	-1.67%	-1.25%
Return on Equity %		-13.95%	-14.63%	3.70%	-13.94%	-8.07%
Debt to Equity		3.79	3.17	0.60	3.76	2.87

CONTACT INFORMATION:

Phone: 248 354-7700   Fax: 248 354-8950
Toll-Free:
Address: 27300 West 11 Mile road, Southfield, MI 48034 United States

STOCK TICKER/OTHER:

Stock Ticker: FDML   Exchange: NAS
Employees: 53,700   Fiscal Year Ends: 12/31
Parent Company:

SALARIES/BONUSES:

Top Exec. Salary: $2,332,400   Bonus: $
Second Exec. Salary: $823,077   Bonus: $

OTHER THOUGHTS:

Estimated Female Officers or Directors: 1

Hot Spot for Advancement for Women/Minorities:

Sales, profits and employees may be estimates. Financial information, benefits and other data can change quickly and may vary from those stated here.

FedEx Corporation

www.fedex.com

NAIC Code: 492110

TYPES OF BUSINESS:

Couriers and Express Delivery Services
Ground Delivery Services
Freight Services
Document Solutions & Business Services
International Trade Services

BRANDS/DIVISIONS/AFFILIATES:

Federal Express Corp
FedEx Ground Package System Inc
FedEx Freight Inc
TNT
FedEx SupplyChain System
FedEx Trade Networks Inc
FedEx SmartPost Inc
FedEx Custom Critical Inc

CONTACTS: Note: Officers with more than one job title may be intentionally listed here more than once.

David Bronczek, CEO, Subsidiary
Michael Ducker, CEO, Subsidiary
Henry Maier, CEO, Subsidiary
Frederick Smith, CEO
Robert Carter, Chief Information Officer
T. Glenn, Executive VP, Divisional
Alan Graf, Executive VP
Christine Richards, Executive VP
John Merino, Vice President

GROWTH PLANS/SPECIAL FEATURES:

FedEx Corporation is a global provider of shipping, transportation, e-commerce and business services. It operates through a number of subsidiaries, including Federal Express Corp. (FedEx Express); FedEx Ground Package System, Inc. (FedEx Ground); FedEx Freight, Inc. (FedEx Freight); and FedEx Corporate Services, Inc. (FedEx Services). FedEx Express is an express transportation company offering time-certain delivery within one to three business days. The division also includes FedEx SupplyChain System; FedEx Trade Networks, Inc., which provides international trade services, specializing in custom brokerage and Bongo International, LLC, which is provides cross-border enablement technology and solutions. FedEx Ground offers small-package ground delivery service. It provides service to almost every business address in the U.S. and Canada as well as residential delivery to nearly 100% of U.S. residents through FedEx Home Delivery. Other subsidiaries are FedEx SmartPost, Inc., which specializes in the consolidation and delivery of high volumes of low-weight, less time-sensitive business-to-consumer packages using the U.S. Postal Service or Canada Post for final delivery to residences; and GENCO Distribution System, Inc., a third-party logistics provider. FedEx Freight provides less-than-truckload (LTL) freight services through its FedEx Freight Priority and its FedEx Freight Economy. The division also includes FedEx Custom Critical, Inc., a time-specific, critical shipment carrier. FedEx Services serves other FedEx companies with sales, marketing and IT support in addition to customer service through FedEx TechConnect as well as document and business services through FedEx Office and Print Services. In May 2016, FedEx acquired European package delivery firm TNT. This gives FedEx very broad capabilities in ground delivery within the European market.

FedEx Corporation offers its employees medical, dental and vision care insurance; short- and long-term disability; worker's compensation; life insurance; a pension plan; and a retirement savings plan.

FINANCIAL DATA: Note: Data for latest year may not have been available at press time.

In U.S. $	2016	2015	2014	2013	2012	2011
Revenue	50,365,000,000	47,453,000,000	45,567,000,000	44,287,000,000	42,680,000,000	39,304,000,000
R&D Expense						
Operating Income	3,077,000,000	1,867,000,000	3,446,000,000	2,551,000,000	3,186,000,000	2,378,000,000
Operating Margin %	6.10%	3.93%	7.56%	5.76%	7.46%	6.05%
SGA Expense	20,079,000,000	19,576,000,000	16,555,000,000	17,230,000,000	16,099,000,000	15,276,000,000
Net Income	1,820,000,000	1,050,000,000	2,097,000,000	1,561,000,000	2,032,000,000	1,452,000,000
Operating Cash Flow	5,708,000,000	5,366,000,000	4,264,000,000	4,688,000,000	4,835,000,000	4,041,000,000
Capital Expenditure	4,818,000,000	4,347,000,000	3,533,000,000	3,375,000,000	4,007,000,000	3,434,000,000
EBITDA	5,707,000,000	4,473,000,000	6,036,000,000	4,923,000,000	5,306,000,000	4,324,000,000
Return on Assets %	4.37%	2.99%	6.29%	4.91%	7.09%	5.55%
Return on Equity %	12.64%	6.93%	12.83%	9.71%	13.57%	10.00%
Debt to Equity	1.00	0.48	0.31	0.15	0.08	0.10

CONTACT INFORMATION:

Phone: 901 818-7500   Fax: 901 346-1013
Toll-Free:
Address: 942 S. Shady Grove Rd., Memphis, TN 38120 United States

STOCK TICKER/OTHER:

Stock Ticker: FDX   Exchange: NYS
Employees: 166,000   Fiscal Year Ends: 05/31
Parent Company:

SALARIES/BONUSES:

Top Exec. Salary: Bonus: $
$1,279,632
Second Exec. Salary: Bonus: $
$960,936

OTHER THOUGHTS:

Estimated Female Officers or Directors: 3

Hot Spot for Advancement for Women/Minorities: Y

Fidelity Investments Financial Services

www.fidelity.com

NAIC Code: 523920

TYPES OF BUSINESS:

Mutual Funds
Human Resources Administration Services
Employee Benefits Services
Online Brokerage
Outsourced Staffing and Recruiting Services
Clearing and Execution Products and Services
Real Estate Investments
Institutional Account Management and Services

BRANDS/DIVISIONS/AFFILIATES:

Fidelity Advisor
Fidelity Management & Research Company
Pyramis Global Advisors
Fidelity Brokerage Services

CONTACTS: *Note: Officers with more than one job title may be intentionally listed here more than once.*

Kathleen Murphy, Pres.
Jim Speros, Chief Creative Officer
Steve A. Scullen, III, Pres., Corp. Oper.
Lori Kalahar Johnson, VP-Online Strategy
Michael A. Jones, CEO
Jacques Perold, Pres., Fidelity Management & Research Company
Charles Morrison, Pres., Asset Mgmt.
Nancy D. Prior, Pres., Fixed Income Div.

GROWTH PLANS/SPECIAL FEATURES:

Fidelity Investments Financial Services (FIFS) is one of the nation's largest mutual fund companies and one of the world's largest providers of financial services. With over $5.2 trillion in assets under administration, the company offers more than 560 mutual funds and numerous other investment vehicles for individual, corporate and other institutional investors. FIFS is one of the largest providers of 401(k) retirement savings plans in the U.S. and a leading provider of 403(b), 457 and 401(a) retirement plans for nonprofits, colleges, universities, health care institutions, state agencies and local governments. In addition, the firm provides IRAs, CDs, money market accounts, insurance, bill pay services, checking accounts and annuities as well as market news and analysis. Fidelity Management & Research Company, with more than 500 analysts and traders, is the investment advisor to FIFS' funds. Through its employer solutions division, FIFS administers benefit plans for over 21,000 employers and offers human resources administration and employee benefits services. The company also provides investment management products and services such as the Fidelity Advisor family of mutual funds. Through Fidelity Brokerage Services, individual investors can buy and sell stocks, bonds, options and more than 4,000 mutual funds. FIFS's Pyramis Global Advisors unit is a spin-off designed to enhance services and investment products for institutional investors such as corporate and public retirement funds, endowments and foundations. The company serves retail customers by phone and through over 180 investor centers located throughout the U.S. The firm has additional operations in South America, Europe, Asia, the Middle East, Africa and Australia.

FINANCIAL DATA: *Note: Data for latest year may not have been available at press time.*

In U.S. $	2016	2015	2014	2013	2012	2011
Revenue		15,900,000,000	14,900,000,000	13,600,000,000	13,000,000,000	12,800,000,000
R&D Expense						
Operating Income						
Operating Margin %						
SGA Expense						
Net Income		3,200,000,000	3,400,000,000	2,600,000,000	3,400,000,000	3,300,000,000
Operating Cash Flow						
Capital Expenditure						
EBITDA						
Return on Assets %						
Return on Equity %						
Debt to Equity						

CONTACT INFORMATION:

Phone: 617-563-7000   Fax:
Toll-Free: 800-343-3548
Address: 82 Devonshire St., Boston, MA 02109 United States

STOCK TICKER/OTHER:

Stock Ticker: Private   Exchange:
Employees: 38,000   Fiscal Year Ends: 12/31
Parent Company:

SALARIES/BONUSES:

Top Exec. Salary: $ Bonus: $
Second Exec. Salary: $ Bonus: $

OTHER THOUGHTS:

Estimated Female Officers or Directors: 2
Hot Spot for Advancement for Women/Minorities:

Fidelity National Financial Inc

NAIC Code: 524127

www.fnf.com

TYPES OF BUSINESS:

Title Insurance
Escrow Services
Collection & Trust Activities
Electronic Data Interchange Software
Payment Processing
Equipment Lease Services
Insurance Claims Management

BRANDS/DIVISIONS/AFFILIATES:

Fidelity National Title Insurance Company
Chicago Title Insurance Company
Commonwealth Land Title Insurance Company
Alamo Title Insurance
National Title Insurance of New York Inc
Black Knight Financial Services Inc
ServiceLink Holdings LLC
American Blue Ribbon Holdings LLC

CONTACTS: *Note: Officers with more than one job title may be intentionally listed here more than once.*

Raymond Quirk, CEO
Anthony Park, CFO
William Foley, Chairman of the Board
Roger Jewkes, Co-COO
Frank Willey, Director
Brent Bickett, Executive VP, Divisional
Michael Gravelle, Executive VP
Peter Sadowski, Executive VP
Michael Nolan, President

GROWTH PLANS/SPECIAL FEATURES:

Fidelity National Financial, Inc. (FNF) is a holding company that provides title insurance, technology and transaction services to the real estate and mortgage industries. The firm claims to be the nation's largest title insurance company through the following title insurance underwriters: Fidelity National Title Insurance Company, Chicago Title Insurance Company, Commonwealth Land Title Insurance Company, Alamo Title Insurance and National Title Insurance of New York, Inc. FNF also provides mortgage technology solutions and transaction services through its majority-owned subsidiaries: Black Knight Financial Services, Inc. and ServiceLink Holdings LLC. FNF owns majority and minority equity investment stakes in a number of entities, including American Blue Ribbon Holdings LLC, Ceridian HCM, Inc., Fleetcor Technologies, Inc. and Digital Insurance, Inc. Black Knight provides integrated technology, services, data and analytics that lenders and servicers use to manage the life cycle of their loans. American Blue Ribbon Holdings operates company and franchise family and casual dining restaurants in more than 40 states. Ceridian offers business service and software solutions that help organizations control costs, save time, optimize their workforce and grow revenue. Digital Insurance is the nation's leading employee benefits agency specializing in insurance for small businesses and mid-sized companies. In 2016, the firm sold its Max & Erma's restaurant concept; and agreed to acquire Commissions, Inc., an end-to-end SaaS lead management software platform focused on high-performing residential real estate agents and agent teams.

FINANCIAL DATA: *Note: Data for latest year may not have been available at press time.*

In U.S. $	2016	2015	2014	2013	2012	2011
Revenue		9,132,000,000	8,024,000,000	8,565,000,000	7,201,700,000	4,839,600,000
R&D Expense						
Operating Income		867,000,000	392,000,000	651,000,000	843,400,000	414,800,000
Operating Margin %		9.49%	4.88%	7.60%	11.71%	8.57%
SGA Expense		5,597,000,000	5,231,000,000	6,074,000,000	4,596,000,000	2,988,800,000
Net Income		527,000,000	583,000,000	402,000,000	606,500,000	369,500,000
Operating Cash Flow		917,000,000	567,000,000	484,000,000	620,000,000	124,900,000
Capital Expenditure		241,000,000	210,000,000	145,000,000	79,200,000	35,900,000
EBITDA						
Return on Assets %		3.88%	1.75%	3.93%	6.82%	4.69%
Return on Equity %		9.19%	3.86%	8.61%	15.35%	10.46%
Debt to Equity		0.48	0.47	0.26	0.31	0.25

CONTACT INFORMATION:

Phone: 904 854-8100   Fax: 904 357-1007
Toll-Free: 888-934-3354
Address: 601 Riverside Ave., Jacksonville, FL 32204 United States

STOCK TICKER/OTHER:

Stock Ticker: FNF
Employees: 54,091
Parent Company:

Exchange: NYS
Fiscal Year Ends: 12/31

SALARIES/BONUSES:

Top Exec. Salary: $471,538   Bonus: $750,000
Second Exec. Salary: $850,000   Bonus: $

OTHER THOUGHTS:

Estimated Female Officers or Directors: 1
Hot Spot for Advancement for Women/Minorities:

Fidelity National Information Services Inc   www.fisglobal.com

NAIC Code: 522320

TYPES OF BUSINESS:

Payment & Transaction Processing Services
IT Consulting
Outsourcing Services
Due Diligence Services
Mortgage Loan Processing

BRANDS/DIVISIONS/AFFILIATES:

Capco
SunGard Data Systems Inc

CONTACTS: *Note: Officers with more than one job title may be intentionally listed here more than once.*

Gary Norcross, CEO
James Woodall, CFO
Frank Martire, Chairman of the Board
Michael Nussbaum, Chief Accounting Officer
Michael Oates, Chief Administrative Officer
Gregory Montana, Chief Risk Officer
Marianne Brown, Co-COO
Anthony Jabbour, COO
William Foley, Director

GROWTH PLANS/SPECIAL FEATURES:

Fidelity National Information Services, Inc. (FIS) offers banking/payments technology solutions, processing services and information-based services. Headquartered in Jacksonville, Florida, FIS maintains a global presence, serving more than 20,000 financial institutions through offices in over 130 countries worldwide. Through its Capco brand, the firm provides core financial institution processing, card issuer and transaction processing services as well as outsourcing services to financial institutions and retailers worldwide. The company operates in three segments: integrated financial solutions (IFS), global financial solutions (GFS) and corporate and other. IFS serves the North America regional and community bank market for transaction and account processing, payment solutions, channel solutions, digital channels, risk and compliance solutions and services. This segment's solutions include core processing and ancillary applications, digital solutions (internet, mobile and eBanking), fraud and risk management, compliance, electronic funds transfer, credit cards, item processing, output services, government payment, ePayment and retail check authorization. GFS serves the largest financial institutions worldwide with banking and payments solutions, as well as consulting and transformation services. This segment also delivers an array of capital markets and asset management solutions and services, as well as insurance and public sector and education solutions and services. GFS solutions include retail banking, payment services, securities processing, finance, asset management, global trading, corporate liquidity, insurance, wealth management, global commercial services, strategic consulting, as well as domain-specific, mission critical enterprise resource planning and administrative software to state and local governments and K-12 educational institutions. The corporate and other segment consists of overhead expense, leveraged functions and miscellaneous expenses not included in the operating segments. In November 2015, the firm acquired financial software creator SunGard Data Systems, Inc. for $9.1 billion.

FINANCIAL DATA: *Note: Data for latest year may not have been available at press time.*

In U.S. $	2016	2015	2014	2013	2012	2011
Revenue		6,595,200,000	6,413,800,000	6,070,700,000	5,807,600,000	5,745,700,000
R&D Expense						
Operating Income		1,099,200,000	1,270,600,000	1,064,400,000	1,079,200,000	1,066,800,000
Operating Margin %		16.66%	19.81%	17.53%	18.58%	18.56%
SGA Expense		1,102,800,000	810,500,000	920,700,000	781,500,000	671,800,000
Net Income		631,500,000	679,100,000	493,100,000	461,200,000	469,600,000
Operating Cash Flow		1,136,900,000	1,164,900,000	1,060,300,000	1,046,700,000	1,171,500,000
Capital Expenditure		415,300,000	371,200,000	336,200,000	296,100,000	300,300,000
EBITDA		1,905,500,000	1,852,500,000	1,638,200,000	1,695,300,000	1,646,300,000
Return on Assets %		3.09%	4.76%	3.58%	3.36%	3.35%
Return on Equity %		7.95%	10.33%	7.45%	7.01%	7.27%
Debt to Equity		1.23	0.77	0.65	0.63	0.69

CONTACT INFORMATION:

Phone: 904 438-6000   Fax: 904 357-1105
Toll-Free: 888-323-0310
Address: 601 Riverside Ave., Jacksonville, FL 32204 United States

STOCK TICKER/OTHER:

Stock Ticker: FIS   Exchange: NYS
Employees: 40,000   Fiscal Year Ends: 12/31
Parent Company:

SALARIES/BONUSES:

Top Exec. Salary: Bonus: $
$1,000,000
Second Exec. Salary: Bonus: $
$800,000

OTHER THOUGHTS:

Estimated Female Officers or Directors: 3

Hot Spot for Advancement for Women/Minorities: Y

Sales, profits and employees may be estimates. Financial information, benefits and other data can change quickly and may vary from those stated here.

FirstEnergy Corporation

www.firstenergycorp.com

NAIC Code: 221112

TYPES OF BUSINESS:

Electric Utility
Power Generation
Energy Management
Telecommunications

BRANDS/DIVISIONS/AFFILIATES:

Ohio Edison Company
Cleveland Electric Illuminating Co (The)
Toledo Edison Co (The)
Pennsylvania Electric Company
Jersey Central Power & Light Co
Metropolitan Edison Company
Allegheny Energy Supply Co
FirstEnergy Transmission LLC

CONTACTS: *Note: Officers with more than one job title may be intentionally listed here more than once.*

Charles Jones, CEO
Gary Benz, Senior VP, Subsidiary
James Pearson, CFO
K. Taylor, Chief Accounting Officer
George Smart, Director
Leila Vespoli, Executive VP, Divisional
Lynn Cavalier, Other Executive Officer
Bennett Gaines, Other Executive Officer
Donald Schneider, President, Subsidiary
Steven Strah, President, Subsidiary
Rhonda Ferguson, Secretary
M. Dowling, Senior VP, Divisional
Charles Lasky, Senior VP, Subsidiary
Dennis Chack, Senior VP, Subsidiary
Charles Lasky, Senior VP, Subsidiary

GROWTH PLANS/SPECIAL FEATURES:

FirstEnergy Corporation is a diversified energy services holding company involved in the generation, transmission and distribution of electricity, energy management and other energy-related services. The firm operates 15 principal electric utility subsidiaries: Ohio Edison Company, The Cleveland Electric Illuminating Co., The Toledo Edison Co., Pennsylvania Electric Company, Jersey Central Power & Light Co., Metropolitan Edison Company, Pennsylvania Power Company, First Energy Service Company, First Energy Solutions Corp., Allegheny Energy Supply Co., Monongahela Power Company, The Potomac Edison Company, West Penn Power Company, FirstEnergy Transmission LLC and Allegheny Energy Service Corp. FirstEnergy is one of the largest investor-owned electric systems, serving 6 million customers in a service area that ranges over 65,000 square miles of Ohio, Pennsylvania, West Virginia, Maryland, New Jersey and New York. Generation is conducted through a variety of methods, including coal, nuclear power, wind, solar, gas, oil and hydroelectric generation. Other FirstEnergy subsidiaries include FELHC, Inc.; FirstEnergy Nuclear Generation LLC; FirstEnergy Properties, Inc.; FirstEnergy Ventures Corp.; and GPU, Inc.

Employee benefits include medical, prescription, dental and vision coverage; flexible spending accounts; life insurance; long-term care insurance; long-term disability; a 401(k) savings plan; pension plan; education assistance; adoption assistance; an employee assistance program; and employee discounts.

FINANCIAL DATA: *Note: Data for latest year may not have been available at press time.*

In U.S. $	2016	2015	2014	2013	2012	2011
Revenue		15,026,000,000	15,049,000,000	14,917,000,000	15,303,000,000	16,258,000,000
R&D Expense						
Operating Income		2,292,000,000	1,062,000,000	1,607,000,000	2,176,000,000	1,698,000,000
Operating Margin %		15.25%	7.05%	10.77%	14.21%	10.44%
SGA Expense		3,991,000,000	4,797,000,000	3,337,000,000	4,378,000,000	3,909,000,000
Net Income		578,000,000	299,000,000	392,000,000	770,000,000	885,000,000
Operating Cash Flow		3,447,000,000	2,713,000,000	2,662,000,000	2,320,000,000	3,063,000,000
Capital Expenditure		2,894,000,000	3,312,000,000	2,638,000,000	2,678,000,000	2,278,000,000
EBITDA		3,744,000,000	2,626,000,000	2,713,000,000	3,377,000,000	3,572,000,000
Return on Assets %		1.10%	.58%	.77%	1.57%	2.15%
Return on Equity %		4.65%	2.38%	3.04%	5.84%	8.11%
Debt to Equity		1.54	1.54	1.24	1.16	1.18

CONTACT INFORMATION:

Phone: 800 736-3402   Fax:
Toll-Free: 800-633-4766
Address: 76 S. Main St., Akron, OH 44308 United States

STOCK TICKER/OTHER:

Stock Ticker: FE
Employees: 15,781
Parent Company:

Exchange: NYS
Fiscal Year Ends: 12/31

SALARIES/BONUSES:

Top Exec. Salary:
$1,118,558
Second Exec. Salary:
$752,789

Bonus: $

Bonus: $

OTHER THOUGHTS:

Estimated Female Officers or Directors: 6

Hot Spot for Advancement for Women/Minorities: Y

FirstMerit Corporation

www.firstmerit.com

NAIC Code: 522110

TYPES OF BUSINESS:

Banking
Mortgage Loans & Loan Services
Credit Life, Credit Accident & Health Insurance
Consumer & Business Loans
Equipment Leasing & Financing
Securities Brokerage Services
Life Insurance
Financial Consulting

BRANDS/DIVISIONS/AFFILIATES:

FirstMerit Bank NA
FirstMerit Mortgage Corporation
CPHCSUB LLC
CREPD LLC
FirstMerit Equipment Finance Company Inc
FirstMerit Insurance Group Inc
FirstMerit Insurance Agency Inc
FirstMerit Title Agency Ltd

CONTACTS: *Note: Officers with more than one job title may be intentionally listed here more than once.*

Paul Greig, CEO
Chistopher Maurer, Executive VP
Terrence Bichsel, CFO
Sandra Pierce, Chairman, Divisional
Nancy Worman, Chief Accounting Officer
William Richgels, Chief Credit Officer
Mark Quinlan, Chief Information Officer
Brian Williams, Chief Risk Officer
N Brocklehurst, Executive VP, Divisional
Michael Robinson, Executive VP, Divisional
Carlton Langer, Executive VP
Mark DuHamel, Executive VP
David Goodall, Other Executive Officer

GROWTH PLANS/SPECIAL FEATURES:

FirstMerit Corporation is a holding company that operates as a regional banking organization through its principal subsidiary FirstMerit Bank NA (FMB). FMB provides commercial and consumer banking services through 366 banking offices and 400 automated teller locations in Ohio, Michigan, Pennsylvania, Illinois and Wisconsin. The bank offers checking, savings and money market accounts as well as commercial and consumer loans for the financing of both real estate and personal property. In addition, it provides personal and corporate trust services, personal financial services, cash management services and international banking services. FMB is the parent company of 22 wholly-owned subsidiaries, including FirstMerit Mortgage Corporation, a mortgage loan provider; FirstMerit Equipment Finance Company Inc., a commercial lease finance company; CPHCSUB LLC and CREPD LLC, each of which hold foreclosed commercial and construction properties; FirstMerit Insurance Group Inc., a life insurance and financial consulting firm; FirstMerit Insurance Agency Inc., which is licensed to sell life insurance products and annuities; and FirstMerit Title Agency Ltd., a title insurance provider. In January 2016, the firm agreed to be acquired by Huntington Bancshares, Inc., and will subsequently merge with and into Huntington. FMB will merge into The Huntington National Bank, a wholly-owned subsidiary of Huntington. That July, FirstMerit announced that, in connection with the proposed merger, FMB would sell 13 branches within Stark and Ashtabula counties (Ohio) to First Commonwealth Bank.

The company offers its employees benefits including medical, dental, vision, long- and short-term disability and life insurance; flexible spending accounts; a 401(k) plan; a retirement investment plan; a profit sharing account; tuition reimbursement; and an employee assistance program.

FINANCIAL DATA: *Note: Data for latest year may not have been available at press time.*

In U.S. $	2016	2015	2014	2013	2012	2011
Revenue		1,010,292,992	1,057,091,968	981,128,000	695,433,984	704,384,000
R&D Expense						
Operating Income						
Operating Margin %						
SGA Expense						
Net Income		229,484,000	237,951,008	183,684,000	134,106,000	119,558,000
Operating Cash Flow						
Capital Expenditure						
EBITDA						
Return on Assets %						
Return on Equity %						
Debt to Equity						

CONTACT INFORMATION:

Phone: 330 996-6300   Fax: 330 253-1849
Toll-Free: 888-554-4362
Address: 3 Cascade Plaza, 7/Fl, Akron, OH 44308 United States

STOCK TICKER/OTHER:

Stock Ticker: FMER   Exchange: NAS
Employees: 4,112   Fiscal Year Ends: 12/31
Parent Company:

SALARIES/BONUSES:

Top Exec. Salary: $ Bonus: $
Second Exec. Salary: $ Bonus: $

OTHER THOUGHTS:

Estimated Female Officers or Directors: 4
Hot Spot for Advancement for Women/Minorities: Y

Fiserv Inc
NAIC Code: 522320

TYPES OF BUSINESS:
Financial Services
Investment Services
Online Banking
Electronic Billing & Payment
Software Applications & Investment Management Solutions

BRANDS/DIVISIONS/AFFILIATES:
ACI Worldwide

CONTACTS: Note: Officers with more than one job title may be intentionally listed here more than once.
Jeffery Yabuki, CEO
Kenneth Best, Chief Accounting Officer
Robert Hau, Chief Financial Officer
Mark Ernst, COO
Daniel Kearney, Director
Rahul Gupta, President, Divisional
Kevin Schultz, President, Divisional
Steven Tait, President, Divisional
Byron Vielehr, President, Divisional
Kevin Gregoire, President, Divisional
Lynn McCreary, Secretary

GROWTH PLANS/SPECIAL FEATURES:
Fiserv, Inc. provides integrated data processing and information management systems to more than 13,000 financial services providers, including banks, thrifts, credit unions, investment management firms, leasing and finance companies, retailers, merchants and government agencies. It operates in two primary segments: financial institution services (financial) and payments & industry products (payments). The financial segment provides banks, thrifts and credit unions with account processing services, item processing services, loan origination and servicing products, cash management and consulting services as well as other products and services that support a variety of financial transactions. The payments segment provides products and services that address a range of technology needs for the financial services industry, including Internet banking, electronic bill payment, electronic funds transfer and debit processing, fraud and risk management capabilities, card and print personalization services, check imaging and investment account processing services for separately managed accounts. The company operates centers nationwide for full-service data processing, software development, item processing and check imaging, technology support and related product businesses. It operates support centers located in approximately 120 cities located in South America, Europe and the Asia Pacific. In March 2016, the firm acquired ACI Worldwide's community financial services business.

FINANCIAL DATA: Note: Data for latest year may not have been available at press time.

In U.S. $	2016	2015	2014	2013	2012	2011
Revenue		5,254,000,000	5,066,000,000	4,814,000,000	4,482,000,000	4,337,000,000
R&D Expense						
Operating Income		1,311,000,000	1,210,000,000	1,061,000,000	1,056,000,000	996,000,000
Operating Margin %		24.95%	23.88%	22.03%	23.56%	22.96%
SGA Expense		1,034,000,000	975,000,000	977,000,000	829,000,000	799,000,000
Net Income		712,000,000	754,000,000	648,000,000	611,000,000	472,000,000
Operating Cash Flow		1,346,000,000	1,307,000,000	1,039,000,000	835,000,000	953,000,000
Capital Expenditure		359,000,000	292,000,000	236,000,000	195,000,000	192,000,000
EBITDA		1,643,000,000	1,615,000,000	1,465,000,000	1,417,000,000	1,266,000,000
Return on Assets %		7.62%	7.99%	7.19%	7.16%	5.60%
Return on Equity %		23.91%	21.91%	18.50%	18.30%	14.55%
Debt to Equity		1.61	1.12	1.04	0.94	0.98

CONTACT INFORMATION:
Phone: 262 879-5000   Fax: 262 879-5275
Toll-Free: 800-872-7882
Address: 255 Fiserv Dr., Brookfield, WI 53045 United States

STOCK TICKER/OTHER:
Stock Ticker: FISV   Exchange: NAS
Employees: 21,000   Fiscal Year Ends: 12/31
Parent Company:

SALARIES/BONUSES:
Top Exec. Salary: $840,000   Bonus: $
Second Exec. Salary: Bonus: $
$600,000

OTHER THOUGHTS:
Estimated Female Officers or Directors: 1
Hot Spot for Advancement for Women/Minorities:

Fleetcor Technologies Inc

NAIC Code: 522320

www.fleetcor.com

TYPES OF BUSINESS:
Payment & Transaction Processing Services

BRANDS/DIVISIONS/AFFILIATES:
Travelcard Nederland BV
Servicos e Tecnologia de Pagamentos SA

CONTACTS: Note: Officers with more than one job title may be intentionally listed here more than once.
Ronald Clarke, CEO
Eric Dey, CFO
John Reed, Chief Information Officer
Charles Freund, Executive VP, Divisional
John Coughlin, Executive VP, Divisional
Andrew Blazye, President, Divisional
David Maxsimic, President, Divisional
Todd House, President, Divisional
Timothy Downs, President, Divisional
Armando Netto, President, Divisional
Gregory Secord, President, Divisional
Kurt Adams, President, Divisional
Alexey Gavrilenya, President, Geographical

GROWTH PLANS/SPECIAL FEATURES:
FleetCor Technologies, Inc. is a leading independent global provider of fuel cards, workforce payment products and services to businesses, commercial fleets, major oil companies, petroleum marketers and government entities in countries throughout North America, Latin America and Europe. The company's payment programs enable customers to better manage and control employee spending and provide card-accepting merchants with a high volume customer base that can increase their sales. In 2015, FleetCor processed approximately 1.9 billion transactions on its proprietary networks and third-party networks. The company sells a range of customized fleet and lodging payment programs directly and indirectly through partners such as major oil companies and petroleum marketers. It provides customers with various card products that typically function like a charge card to purchase fuel, lodging and related products and services at participating locations. Depending on the customer's and partner's needs, the firm provides these services in a variety of outsourced solutions ranging from end-to-end solutions (encompassing issuing, processing and network services) to limited back office processing services. Other services include the company's proprietary equipment which, when installed at the fueling site and on the vehicle, reduces the chances of unauthorized or fraudulent transactions; a telematics solution in Europe that combines GPS, satellite tracking and other wireless technology to allow fleet operators to monitor their vehicles; and prepaid fuel and food vouchers in Mexico. In order to deliver its payment programs and services, FleetCor owns and operates proprietary closed-loop networks in North America and internationally. In March 2016, the firm agreed to acquire Servicos e Tecnologia de Pagamentos SA. That August, it acquired Travelcard Nederland BV.

FINANCIAL DATA: Note: Data for latest year may not have been available at press time.

In U.S. $	2016	2015	2014	2013	2012	2011
Revenue		1,702,865,000	1,199,390,000	895,171,000	707,534,000	519,591,000
R&D Expense						
Operating Income		667,534,000	565,449,000	420,632,000	324,928,000	226,334,000
Operating Margin %		39.20%	47.14%	46.98%	45.92%	43.56%
SGA Expense		406,790,000	281,490,000	199,629,000	156,551,000	121,371,000
Net Income		362,431,000	368,707,000	284,501,000	216,199,000	147,335,000
Operating Cash Flow		754,584,000	608,334,000	375,685,000	135,460,000	279,625,000
Capital Expenditure		41,875,000	27,070,000	20,785,000	19,111,000	13,454,000
EBITDA		860,987,000	677,810,000	493,369,000	375,843,000	260,425,000
Return on Assets %		4.37%	5.84%	8.55%	8.56%	7.73%
Return on Equity %		12.98%	18.44%	26.37%	25.06%	20.50%
Debt to Equity		0.72	0.78	0.38	0.53	0.34

CONTACT INFORMATION:
Phone: 770 449-0479 Fax: 770 449-3471
Toll-Free: 800-877-9019
Address: 5445 Triangle Pkwy, Ste. 400, Norcross, GA 30092 United States

STOCK TICKER/OTHER:
Stock Ticker: FLT
Employees: 4,780
Parent Company:

Exchange: NYS
Fiscal Year Ends: 12/31

SALARIES/BONUSES:
Top Exec. Salary: $1,000,000
Bonus: $
Second Exec. Salary: $280,048
Bonus: $210,561

OTHER THOUGHTS:
Estimated Female Officers or Directors:

Hot Spot for Advancement for Women/Minorities:

Sales, profits and employees may be estimates. Financial information, benefits and other data can change quickly and may vary from those stated here.

Fluor Corp
NAIC Code: 237000

TYPES OF BUSINESS:
Heavy Construction and Engineering
Power Plant Construction and Management
Facilities Management
Procurement Services
Consulting Services
Project Management
Asset Management
Staffing Services

BRANDS/DIVISIONS/AFFILIATES:
ServiTrade
Ameco
Fluor Constructors International Inc

CONTACTS: *Note: Officers with more than one job title may be intentionally listed here more than once.*
David Seaton, CEO
Biggs Porter, CFO
Robin Chopra, Chief Accounting Officer
Peter Oosterveer, COO
Glenn Gilkey, Executive VP, Divisional
Garry Flowers, Executive VP, Divisional
Ray Barnard, Executive VP, Divisional
Jose Luis Bustamante, Executive VP, Divisional
Carlos Hernandez, Executive VP
Bruce Stanski, President, Divisional

GROWTH PLANS/SPECIAL FEATURES:
Fluor Corp., through its subsidiaries, is a global provider of engineering, procurement, construction and maintenance services, with offices in over 25 countries. The company provides logistics services in both Afghanistan and Iraq. Besides being a primary service provider to the U.S. federal government, Fluor serves a diverse set of industries including oil and gas, chemical and petrochemicals, transportation, mining and metals, power, life sciences and manufacturing. It operates in five business segments: oil and gas, industrial and infrastructure, government, global services and power. The oil and gas segment offers design, engineering, procurement, construction and project management services to energy-related industries. Industrial and infrastructure provides design, engineering and construction services to the transportation, mining, life sciences, telecommunications, manufacturing, microelectronics and health care sectors. The government segment provides project management services, including environmental restoration, engineering, construction, site operations and maintenance, to the U.S. government, particularly to the Department of Energy, the Department of Homeland Security and the Department of Defense. Global services provides operations, maintenance and construction services as well as industrial fleet outsourcing, plant turnaround services, temporary staffing, procurement services and construction-related support. The power segment provides such services as engineering, procurement, construction, program management, start-up, commissioning and maintenance to the gas fueled, solid fueled, renewable and nuclear marketplaces. Separate from the rest of the businesses, Fluor Constructors International, Inc. provides unionized management and construction services in the U.S. and Canada. Subsidiary Ameco provides integrated mobile equipment and tool solutions and includes Mozambique construction equipment company, Servitrade. In December 2015, the firm agreed to acquire Stork Holding B.V., a Netherland-based provider of maintenance, modification and asset integrity services.

Fluor offers its employees health, dental, vision, life and accident insurance; disability coverage; savings and retirement plans; a tax savings account; and educational assistance.

FINANCIAL DATA: *Note: Data for latest year may not have been available at press time.*

In U.S. $	2016	2015	2014	2013	2012	2011
Revenue		18,114,050,000	21,531,580,000	27,351,570,000	27,577,140,000	23,381,400,000
R&D Expense						
Operating Income		926,367,000	1,216,322,000	1,190,043,000	733,987,000	985,456,000
Operating Margin %		5.11%	5.64%	4.35%	2.66%	4.21%
SGA Expense		168,329,000	182,711,000	175,148,000	151,010,000	163,460,000
Net Income		412,512,000	510,909,000	667,711,000	456,330,000	593,728,000
Operating Cash Flow		849,132,000	642,574,000	788,906,000	628,378,000	889,769,000
Capital Expenditure		240,220,000	324,704,000	288,487,000	254,747,000	338,167,000
EBITDA		961,060,000	1,427,184,000	1,411,584,000	974,124,000	1,219,356,000
Return on Assets %		5.21%	6.18%	8.04%	5.51%	7.47%
Return on Equity %		13.50%	14.87%	18.81%	13.54%	17.22%
Debt to Equity		0.33	0.31	0.13	0.15	0.15

CONTACT INFORMATION:
Phone: 469 398-7000   Fax: 469 398-7255
Toll-Free:
Address: 6700 Las Colinas Blvd., Irving, TX 75039 United States

STOCK TICKER/OTHER:
Stock Ticker: FLR   Exchange: NYS
Employees: 38,758   Fiscal Year Ends: 12/31
Parent Company:

SALARIES/BONUSES:
Top Exec. Salary: Bonus: $
$1,333,302
Second Exec. Salary: Bonus: $350,000
$721,180

OTHER THOUGHTS:
Estimated Female Officers or Directors: 3

Hot Spot for Advancement for Women/Minorities: Y

Foot Locker Inc

www.footlocker-inc.com

NAIC Code: 448210

TYPES OF BUSINESS:

Athletic Shoes, Retail
Athletic Apparel
Catalogs
Online Sales
Athletic Equipment

BRANDS/DIVISIONS/AFFILIATES:

Foot Locker
Lady Foot Locker
Kids Foot Locker
Champs Sports
Eastbay Inc
Footaction
SIX:02
final-score.com

CONTACTS: Note: Officers with more than one job title may be intentionally listed here more than once.

Stephen Jacobs, CEO, Divisional
Lewis Kimble, CEO, Divisional
Lauren Peters, CFO
Giovanna Cipriano, Chief Accounting Officer
Peter Brown, Chief Information Officer
Pawan Verma, Chief Information Officer
Richard Johnson, Director
Robert Mchugh, Executive VP, Divisional
Paulette Alviti, Other Executive Officer
Jeffrey Berk, Senior VP, Divisional
Sheilagh Clarke, Senior VP
John Maurer, Treasurer

GROWTH PLANS/SPECIAL FEATURES:

Foot Locker, Inc. is one of the largest athletic footwear and apparel retailers in the world, operating approximately 3,423 stores in the U.S., Canada, Europe, Australia and New Zealand. The company operates several store formats, including Foot Locker, Lady Foot Locker, Kids Foot Locker, Champs Sports, Footaction and SIX:02. Foot Locker stores offer athletic-inspired performance products, manufactured primarily by the leading athletic brands. These stores offer products for activities such as running, basketball and cross-training. Lady Foot Locker is a U.S. retailer of athletic footwear, apparel and accessories for active women. Kids Foot Locker offers brand name athletic footwear, apparel and accessories for infants, boys and girls. Champs Sports is a mall-based retailer of specialty athletic footwear and apparel as well as an assortment of sporting equipment. Footaction stores offer athletic footwear and clothing with a street-inspired fashion style. The primary customers of Footaction are young males. SIX:02 is a fitness apparel brand and retailer marketed to women for any activity, style or body type. Retail locations also feature fitness zones, fitting lounge areas and a trained Fit Crew. In addition to its retail stores, the direct-to-customers segment, through affiliates such as Eastbay, Inc., sells merchandise through catalogs and web sites, including eastbay.com, final-score.com, eastbayteamsales.com, runnerspoint.com and sp24.com, as well as all Foot Locker web sites. In 2014, the CCS brand was transferred under the Eastbay banner.

FINANCIAL DATA: Note: Data for latest year may not have been available at press time.

In U.S. $	2016	2015	2014	2013	2012	2011
Revenue	7,412,000,000	7,151,000,000	6,505,000,000	6,182,000,000	5,623,000,000	5,049,000,000
R&D Expense						
Operating Income	942,000,000	809,000,000	666,000,000	610,000,000	437,000,000	262,000,000
Operating Margin %	12.70%	11.31%	10.23%	9.86%	7.77%	5.18%
SGA Expense	1,415,000,000	1,426,000,000	1,334,000,000	1,294,000,000	1,244,000,000	1,138,000,000
Net Income	541,000,000	520,000,000	429,000,000	397,000,000	278,000,000	169,000,000
Operating Cash Flow	745,000,000	712,000,000	530,000,000	416,000,000	497,000,000	326,000,000
Capital Expenditure	228,000,000	190,000,000	206,000,000	163,000,000	152,000,000	97,000,000
EBITDA	996,000,000	948,000,000	799,000,000	736,000,000	552,000,000	368,000,000
Return on Assets %	14.71%	14.72%	12.51%	12.37%	9.35%	5.91%
Return on Equity %	21.43%	20.83%	17.60%	17.69%	13.44%	8.50%
Debt to Equity	0.05	0.05	0.05	0.05	0.06	0.06

CONTACT INFORMATION:

Phone: 212 720-3700   Fax: 212 553-7026
Toll-Free: 800-991-6815
Address: 112 W. 34th St., New York, NY 10120 United States

STOCK TICKER/OTHER:

Stock Ticker: FL   Exchange: NYS
Employees: 47,025   Fiscal Year Ends: 01/31
Parent Company:

SALARIES/BONUSES:

Top Exec. Salary: Bonus: $
$1,037,500
Second Exec. Salary: Bonus: $
$673,000

OTHER THOUGHTS:

Estimated Female Officers or Directors: 3

Hot Spot for Advancement for Women/Minorities: Y

Ford Motor Co

NAIC Code: 336111

www.ford.com

TYPES OF BUSINESS:

Automobile Manufacturing
Automobile Financing
Fuel-Cell & Hybrid Research

BRANDS/DIVISIONS/AFFILIATES:

Ford
Lincoln
Ford Motor Credit Co
Ford Mustang
Ford F150
Ford Focus
Lincoln Navigator SUV
Ford Escape Hybrid SUV

CONTACTS: Note: Officers with more than one job title may be intentionally listed here more than once.

Corey MacGillivray, Assistant Secretary
Joseph Hinrichs, Executive VP
John Lawler, CEO, Divisional
Bernard Silverstone, CEO, Subsidiary
Mark Fields, CEO
Robert Shanks, CFO
James Hackett, Chairman of the Board, Subsidiary
William Ford, Chairman of the Board
Raj Nair, CTO
Stephen Odell, Executive VP, Divisional
James Farley, Executive VP
Nigel Harris, President, Divisional
Dave Schoch, President, Geographical
Jonathan Osgood, Secretary

GROWTH PLANS/SPECIAL FEATURES:

Ford Motor Co. is a designer and manufacturer of automobiles and automotive systems. The firm operates in two segments: automotive and financial services. The automotive segment designs, manufactures, sells and services cars and trucks under the brands Ford and Lincoln. The company sells its vehicles to the public via independently owned dealerships, including roughly 10,727 Ford; 360 Lincoln; and 884 Ford/Lincoln dealerships. These dealerships are located in North America, South America, Europe, Asia Pacific and Africa. In addition to new car sales, the firm also sells vehicles to its dealerships for sale to fleet customers, including commercial fleet customers, daily rental car companies and governments, and sells parts and accessories to authorized parts distributors. The firm's financial services segment, operating through Ford Motor Credit Co., offers vehicle-related financing, leasing and insurance. Some of Ford's most popular vehicles include the Ford Mustang sports car, the Ford F150 truck, the compact Ford Focus, the Lincoln Navigator SUV and the Ford Escape Hybrid SUV. The company hopes to quickly introduce fully electric vehicles to the U.S. market. In 2015, Ford secured more than 1,000 U.S. jobs by starting production of its all-new F-650 and F-750 medium-duty trucks at its Ohio, U.S. assembly plant, a $168 million investment. The company's trucks are previously built in Mexico. In 2016, the firm announced it would be closing its Australian manufacturing base and its entire operation in Indonesia (including their dealer network) that same year.

FINANCIAL DATA: Note: Data for latest year may not have been available at press time.

In U.S. $	2016	2015	2014	2013	2012	2011
Revenue		149,558,000,000	144,077,000,000	146,917,000,000	134,252,000,000	136,264,000,000
R&D Expense						
Operating Income		8,064,000,000	3,745,000,000	5,439,000,000	6,291,000,000	11,374,000,000
Operating Margin %		5.39%	2.59%	3.70%	4.68%	8.34%
SGA Expense		14,999,000,000	14,117,000,000	13,176,000,000	12,182,000,000	11,578,000,000
Net Income		7,373,000,000	3,187,000,000	7,155,000,000	5,665,000,000	20,213,000,000
Operating Cash Flow		16,170,000,000	14,507,000,000	10,444,000,000	9,045,000,000	9,784,001,000
Capital Expenditure		7,196,000,000	7,463,000,000	6,597,000,000	5,488,000,000	4,293,000,000
EBITDA		18,991,000,000	12,575,000,000	14,286,000,000	13,637,000,000	17,368,000,000
Return on Assets %		3.40%	1.55%	3.64%	3.07%	11.78%
Return on Equity %		27.58%	12.45%	33.80%	36.57%	281.61%
Debt to Equity		3.13	3.22	2.90	4.15	3.93

CONTACT INFORMATION:

Phone: 313 322-3000	Fax: 313 222-4177
Toll-Free: 800-392-3673
Address: 1 American Rd., Dearborn, MI 48126 United States

STOCK TICKER/OTHER:

Stock Ticker: F
Employees: 187,000
Parent Company:

Exchange: NYS
Fiscal Year Ends: 12/31

SALARIES/BONUSES:

Top Exec. Salary: $2,000,000
Second Exec. Salary: $1,750,000

Bonus: $

Bonus: $

OTHER THOUGHTS:

Estimated Female Officers or Directors: 4

Hot Spot for Advancement for Women/Minorities: Y

Fossil Group Inc

www.fossil.com

NAIC Code: 0

TYPES OF BUSINESS:

Watches and Parts (except crystals) Manufacturing
Accessories
Online Sales
Leather Goods
Belts
Handbags
Jewelry
Retail Stores

BRANDS/DIVISIONS/AFFILIATES:

Fossil
Relic
Skagen
Zodiac
Misfit Inc

CONTACTS: Note: *Officers with more than one job title may be intentionally listed here more than once.*

Kosta Kartsotis, CEO
Dennis Secor, CFO
Darren Hart, Executive VP, Divisional
Randy Belcher, Executive VP, Geographical
Hans-Peter Gehmacher, Executive VP, Geographical
John White, Executive VP
Gregory McKelvey, Executive VP

GROWTH PLANS/SPECIAL FEATURES:

Fossil Group, Inc. designs, develops, markets and distributes fashion accessories. The company's principal offerings include a line of men's and women's watches and jewelry sold under proprietary and licensed brands, handbags, leather goods, sunglasses and apparel. In the watch and jewelry product category, Fossil has a diverse portfolio of globally recognized brands such as Fossil, Relic, Skagen and Zodiac. Also, through license agreements, the company utilizes prestigious brand names such as Burberry, DKNY, Michael Kors, Marc Jacobs, Adidas and Emporio Armani. The company distributes products through various channels including wholesale and export as well as directly to the consumer. Domestically, the company sells its products through a distribution network that includes Neiman Marcus, Nordstrom, Macy's, Dillard's, JCPenney, Kohl's, Saks Fifth Avenue, Wal-Mart and Target. The firm also sells its products through a network of domestic company-owned stores, which includes 99 retail and 139 outlet stores. Additionally, the company offers an extensive collection of Fossil brand products through its catalog and web site as well as proprietary and licensed watch and jewelry brands through other managed and affiliate web sites. Internationally, products are sold to department stores and specialty stores in over 150 countries through 23 company-owned foreign sales subsidiaries and through approximately 80 independent distributors. The firm's network of international company-owned stores include 250 retail stores and 131 outlet stores. In December 2015, the firm acquired Misfit, Inc., an innovator in wearable technology and stylish connected devices.

FINANCIAL DATA: Note: *Data for latest year may not have been available at press time.*

In U.S. $	2016	2015	2014	2013	2012	2011
Revenue		3,228,836,000	3,509,691,000	3,259,971,000	2,857,508,000	2,567,302,000
R&D Expense						
Operating Income		291,234,000	566,536,000	561,596,000	488,840,000	471,991,000
Operating Margin %		9.01%	16.14%	17.22%	17.10%	18.38%
SGA Expense		1,437,833,000	1,434,636,000	1,300,090,000	1,117,703,000	967,195,000
Net Income		220,637,000	376,707,000	378,152,000	343,401,000	294,702,000
Operating Cash Flow		360,771,000	387,883,000	411,682,000	451,600,000	251,267,000
Capital Expenditure		83,497,000	104,182,000	110,052,000	122,804,000	131,496,000
EBITDA		419,339,000	669,907,000	652,951,000	562,918,000	505,875,000
Return on Assets %		9.67%	16.97%	18.57%	19.70%	18.94%
Return on Equity %		23.23%	36.81%	32.85%	29.35%	27.41%
Debt to Equity		0.85	0.62	0.46	0.06	

CONTACT INFORMATION:

Phone: 972 234-2525   Fax: 972 234-4669
Toll-Free: 800-449-3056
Address: 901 S. Central Expy., Richardson, TX 75080 United States

STOCK TICKER/OTHER:

Stock Ticker: FOSL   Exchange: NAS
Employees: 15,200   Fiscal Year Ends: 12/31
Parent Company:

SALARIES/BONUSES:

Top Exec. Salary: $676,346   Bonus: $
Second Exec. Salary: Bonus: $
$623,654

OTHER THOUGHTS:

Estimated Female Officers or Directors: 4
Hot Spot for Advancement for Women/Minorities: Y

Sales, profits and employees may be estimates. Financial information, benefits and other data can change quickly and may vary from those stated here.

Fox Entertainment Group Inc

NAIC Code: 515120

TYPES OF BUSINESS:

Broadcast Television
Film Distribution and Production
Television Programming
Online Communities and Game Sites
Professional Sports
Electronic Games
Cable TV Programming
Online Entertainment

BRANDS/DIVISIONS/AFFILIATES:

Twenty-First Century Fox Inc
Fox Sports Enterprises
STATS LLC
FX
National Geographic Channel
SPEED
Fox College Sports
Big Ten Network

CONTACTS: *Note: Officers with more than one job title may be intentionally listed here more than once.*

Mohinder Walia, Managing Dir.

GROWTH PLANS/SPECIAL FEATURES:

Fox Entertainment Group, Inc., a wholly-owned subsidiary of Twenty-First Century Fox, Inc., is a conglomerate focused on film and television entertainment. The company engages in feature film and television production and distribution principally through the following businesses: filmed entertainment, television stations, a television broadcast network and cable networks. The filmed entertainment business finances, develops, produces, distributes and markets motion pictures, as well as television and home entertainment programming. The television stations business owns and operates network broadcast groups, comprised of 28 stations in 17 markets and covering more than 37% of U.S. television homes. These markets include: New York, Los Angeles, Chicago, Dallas, San Francisco, Washington, D.C. and Houston. The television broadcast network operates entertainment channels in the U.S. and internationally. The network provides nearly 20 hours of regularly-scheduled network programming on a weekly basis; 15 hours of prime time programming; an hour of late-night programming; and weekend programming timeslots. Programming includes, but is not limited to, adult animation, children's programming, news and sports. The cable networks business includes 36 domestic programming services that together reach more than 550 million subscribing television homes. Cable networks include FX, National Geographic Channel, Fox Reality Channel, Fox Movie Channel, Fuel TV, FSN, SPEED, Fox Soccer Channel, Fox College Sports, Fox Sports en Espanol and the Big Ten Network. This division also includes Fox Sports Enterprises, which manages interests in sports franchises and leading statistical information provider STATS LLC.

FINANCIAL DATA: *Note: Data for latest year may not have been available at press time.*

In U.S. $	2016	2015	2014	2013	2012	2011
Revenue		13,500,000,000	13,300,000,000			
R&D Expense						
Operating Income						
Operating Margin %						
SGA Expense						
Net Income						
Operating Cash Flow						
Capital Expenditure						
EBITDA						
Return on Assets %						
Return on Equity %						
Debt to Equity						

CONTACT INFORMATION:

Phone: 310-369-1000   Fax: 310-969-3300
Toll-Free:
Address: 10201 W. Pico Blvd., Bldg. 100, Ste. 3220, Los Angeles, CA 90035 United States

STOCK TICKER/OTHER:

Stock Ticker: Subsidiary   Exchange:
Employees: 12,500   Fiscal Year Ends: 06/30
Parent Company: Twenty-First Century Fox Inc

SALARIES/BONUSES:

Top Exec. Salary: $ Bonus: $
Second Exec. Salary: $ Bonus: $

OTHER THOUGHTS:

Estimated Female Officers or Directors:
Hot Spot for Advancement for Women/Minorities:

Frito-Lay North America Inc

www.fritolay.com

NAIC Code: 311919

TYPES OF BUSINESS:

Snack Products
Salsas/Dips
Chips
Cookies

BRANDS/DIVISIONS/AFFILIATES:

PepsiCo Inc
Doritos
Cheetos
Lay's
Rold Gold
SunChips
Grandma's
Ruffles

CONTACTS: Note: Officers with more than one job title may be intentionally listed here more than once.

Tomas Greco, CEO
Tom Greco, Pres.
Hari Avula, CFO
Ram Krishnan, CMO
Patrick McLaughlin, Sr. VP-Human Resources
Mike Zbuchalski, Sr. VP-R&D
Kristen Blum, CIO
Marc Kesselman, General Counsel
Christopher Wyse, VP-Public Affairs
Randy Melville, Gen. Mgr.-Central Bus. Unit
Vivek Sankaran, Chief Customer Officer
Dave Scalera, Sr. VP-Go-to-Market Capability & Productivity
Ted Herrod, Gen. Mgr.-West Bus. Unit
Marc Guay, Pres., PepsiCo Foods Canada
Leslie Starr Keating, Sr. VP-Supply Chain

GROWTH PLANS/SPECIAL FEATURES:

Frito-Lay North America, Inc., a subsidiary of PepsiCo, Inc., manufactures, markets, sells and distributes branded snacks. The firm's proprietary products include: Lay's potato chips, Doritos tortilla chips, Tostitos tortilla chips, Cheetos cheese-flavored snacks, Fritos corn chips, Ruffles potato chips, SunChips and multigrain snacks. Additionally, the company's brand portfolio includes: Rold Gold pretzels; Baked! Cheetos, Lay's, Ruffles and Tostitos; Grandma's cookies; Cracker Jack candy-coated popcorn; Matador beef jerky; Funyuns onion rings; Sabritones puffed wheat snacks; El Isleno plantain chips; Stacy's pita chips and 100 calorie mini bite portion control snack packs. The firm's joint venture with Strauss Group markets refrigerated spreads and dips under the Sabra brand name, including hummus, salsas and guacamole. The firm recently updated the Lay's Classic Potato Chips recipe to feature only potatoes, healthier oils such as corn and sunflower oil and a dash of salt; and updated the Tostitos and SunChips brands to feature healthier recipes with no MSG, artificial preservatives or artificial flavorings. The company offers a gluten-free recipe section on its web site for customers with Celiac Disease or gluten sensitivities.

Employee benefits include medical, dental and vision coverage; life insurance; disability coverage; a flexible spending account; wellness programs; an employee assistance program; tuition reimbursement; a pension plan; a retirement plan; a discount stock purchase plan; discounts on electronics, entertainment and automobiles; childcare and elderly care; and commuter reimbursement.

FINANCIAL DATA: Note: Data for latest year may not have been available at press time.

In U.S. $	2016	2015	2014	2013	2012	2011
Revenue		14,680,000,000	14,502,000,000	14,126,000,000	13,574,000,000	13,322,000,000
R&D Expense						
Operating Income						
Operating Margin %						
SGA Expense						
Net Income		4,304,000,000	4,054,000,000	3,877,000,000	3,646,000,000	3,621,000,000
Operating Cash Flow						
Capital Expenditure						
EBITDA						
Return on Assets %						
Return on Equity %						
Debt to Equity						

CONTACT INFORMATION:

Phone: 972-334-7000   Fax: 972-334-2019
Toll-Free: 800-352-4477
Address: 7701 Legacy Dr., Plano, TX 75024 United States

STOCK TICKER/OTHER:

Stock Ticker: Subsidiary
Employees: 48,000
Parent Company: Pepsico Inc

Exchange:
Fiscal Year Ends: 12/31

SALARIES/BONUSES:

Top Exec. Salary: $ Bonus: $
Second Exec. Salary: $ Bonus: $

OTHER THOUGHTS:

Estimated Female Officers or Directors: 3
Hot Spot for Advancement for Women/Minorities: Y

FTI Consulting Inc

NAIC Code: 541610

www.fticonsulting.com

TYPES OF BUSINESS:

Bankruptcy & Restructuring Consulting
Interim Management Staffing
Corporate Recovery Services
Litigation Assistance
Forensic Accounting
Data Mining
Technology Consulting
Software Development

BRANDS/DIVISIONS/AFFILIATES:

Ringtail

CONTACTS: Note: Officers with more than one job title may be intentionally listed here more than once.

Steven Gunby, CEO
Gerard Holthaus, Chairman of the Board
Catherine Freeman, Chief Accounting Officer
Matthew Pachman, Chief Risk Officer
Curtis Lu, General Counsel
Heather Klink, General Counsel
Joanne Catanese, Other Corporate Officer
Paul Linton, Other Executive Officer
Holly Paul, Other Executive Officer

GROWTH PLANS/SPECIAL FEATURES:

FTI Consulting, Inc. is a global consulting firm that provides turnaround, restructuring, bankruptcy and other related consulting services. The firm works in industries including retail, insurance, media and entertainment and energy and utilities. It operates 48 U.S. offices in 19 states and 28 foreign countries, including the U.K., Russia, France, Japan and China. FTI divides its operations into five segments: corporate finance & restructuring, forensic & litigation consulting, economic consulting, technology and strategic communications. The corporate finance & restructuring segment's services include turnaround and restructuring services, which consist of providing advisory services to debtors, creditors and stakeholders confronted with liquidity problems, underperformance and over-expansion; interim key executive staffing; and mergers and acquisitions services, which include financial accounting, investment banking and tax advice. Forensic & litigation consulting includes forensic accounting and financial investigations; trial services, which include providing advice and support for clients in complex civil trials; and pre-, in- and post-trial dispute advisory services. Economic consulting includes analyses of complex economic issues in legal and regulatory proceedings. The technology segment includes FTI's proprietary Ringtail software for document review, litigation support and information management. Strategic communications includes financial & brand communications, media relations, public affairs and business consulting.

The firm offers employees life, disability, AD&D, medical, dental and vision insurance; health and dependent care flexible spending accounts; a 401(k); and an employee assistance program.

FINANCIAL DATA: Note: Data for latest year may not have been available at press time.

In U.S. $	2016	2015	2014	2013	2012	2011
Revenue		1,779,149,000	1,756,212,000	1,652,432,000	1,576,871,000	1,566,768,000
R&D Expense						
Operating Income		164,511,000	147,426,000	81,439,000	59,036,000	205,447,000
Operating Margin %		9.24%	8.39%	4.92%	3.74%	13.11%
SGA Expense		432,668,000	433,845,000	394,681,000	378,016,000	373,295,000
Net Income		66,053,000	58,807,000	-10,594,000	-36,986,000	103,903,000
Operating Cash Flow		139,920,000	135,401,000	193,271,000	120,188,000	173,828,000
Capital Expenditure		31,399,000	39,256,000	42,544,000	27,759,000	31,091,000
EBITDA		191,272,000	202,743,000	138,779,000	116,350,000	262,704,000
Return on Assets %		2.83%	2.45%	-.45%	-1.57%	4.30%
Return on Equity %		5.87%	5.48%	-1.00%	-3.40%	9.14%
Debt to Equity		0.43	0.63	0.68	0.67	0.58

CONTACT INFORMATION:

Phone: 202-312-9100   Fax: 202-312-9101
Toll-Free: 800-334-5701
Address: 1101 K Street NW, Washington D.C., MD 20005 United States

STOCK TICKER/OTHER:

Stock Ticker: FCN
Employees: 4,634
Parent Company:

Exchange: NYS
Fiscal Year Ends: 12/31

SALARIES/BONUSES:

Top Exec. Salary: $212,500   Bonus: $1,000,000
Second Exec. Salary: $1,038,462   Bonus: $

OTHER THOUGHTS:

Estimated Female Officers or Directors: 3
Hot Spot for Advancement for Women/Minorities: Y

Gartner Inc

NAIC Code: 541910

www.gartner.com

TYPES OF BUSINESS:

Research-Computer Hardware & Software
Industry Research
IT Symposia & Conferences
Measurement & Advisory Services

BRANDS/DIVISIONS/AFFILIATES:

Gartner Symposium
SircleIT Inc
Market-Visio Oy
Software Advice Inc
Capterra

CONTACTS: Note: Officers with more than one job title may be intentionally listed here more than once.

Eugene Hall, CEO
Craig Safian, CFO
James Smith, Chairman of the Board
Alwyn Dawkins, Senior VP, Divisional
Per Waern, Senior VP, Divisional
Robin Kranich, Senior VP, Divisional
Peter Sondergaard, Senior VP, Divisional
David McVeigh, Senior VP, Divisional
David Godfrey, Senior VP, Divisional
Thomas Christopher, Senior VP, Divisional
Kendall Davis, Senior VP, Divisional
Daniel Peale, Senior VP

GROWTH PLANS/SPECIAL FEATURES:

Gartner, Inc. is a research and advisory firm that offers independent research and analysis on IT, computer hardware, software, communications and related technology industries. With consultants in 85 countries, it provides coverage of the IT industry to roughly 10,000 organizations. The company operates in three segments: research, consulting and events. The research segment, the main service of the company, provides research content and advice for IT professionals, technology companies and the investment community in the form of reports and briefings as well as peer networking services and membership programs designed specifically for CIOs and other senior executives. The consulting division consists primarily of consulting, measurement engagements and strategic advisory services (paid one-day analyst engagements known as SAS), which provide assessments of cost, performance, efficiency and quality focused on the IT industry. This division seeks to accomplish three major outcomes for its clients: applying IT to drive improvements in business performance; creating sustainable IT efficiency that ensures a constant return on IT investments; and strengthening the IT organization and operations to ensure high-value services to the client's lines of business and to enable the client to adapt to business changes. The events group delivers various symposia, conferences and exhibitions focused on the IT industry. The group offers a range of membership-only peer networking programs designed to bring together business executives and IT professionals in order to outline the key business drivers and best practices for the new economy. The segment hosts events such as Gartner Symposium and other conferences on specialized topics such as outsourcing, mobile wireless, customer relationship management, application integration and business intelligence. In 2014, the firm acquired SircleIT, Inc.; Market-Visio Oy; and Software Advice, Inc. In September 2015, it acquired Capterra.

FINANCIAL DATA: Note: Data for latest year may not have been available at press time.

In U.S. $	2016	2015	2014	2013	2012	2011
Revenue		2,163,056,000	2,021,441,000	1,784,213,000	1,615,808,000	1,468,588,000
R&D Expense						
Operating Income		287,997,000	286,162,000	275,492,000	245,707,000	214,062,000
Operating Margin %		13.31%	14.15%	15.44%	15.20%	14.57%
SGA Expense		962,677,000	876,067,000	760,458,000	678,843,000	613,707,000
Net Income		175,635,000	183,766,000	182,801,000	165,903,000	136,902,000
Operating Cash Flow		345,561,000	346,779,000	315,654,000	279,813,000	255,566,000
Capital Expenditure		46,128,000	38,486,000	36,498,000	44,337,000	41,954,000
EBITDA		341,890,000	326,395,000	311,269,000	275,272,000	245,464,000
Return on Assets %		8.61%	9.96%	10.73%	11.05%	10.27%
Return on Equity %		1220.91%	70.34%	54.73%	67.92%	74.23%
Debt to Equity			2.38	0.37	0.37	0.82

CONTACT INFORMATION:

Phone: 203 316-1111   Fax:
Toll-Free:
Address: 56 Top Gallant Rd., Stamford, CT 06902-7700 United States

STOCK TICKER/OTHER:

Stock Ticker: IT   Exchange: NYS
Employees: 7,834   Fiscal Year Ends: 12/31
Parent Company:

SALARIES/BONUSES:

Top Exec. Salary: $875,324   Bonus: $
Second Exec. Salary: $491,520   Bonus: $

OTHER THOUGHTS:

Estimated Female Officers or Directors: 3
Hot Spot for Advancement for Women/Minorities: Y

General Dynamics Corp

www.generaldynamics.com

NAIC Code: 336411

TYPES OF BUSINESS:

Aircraft Manufacturing
Combat Vehicles & Systems
Telecommunications Systems
Naval Vessels & Submarines
Ship Management Services
Information Systems & Technology
Defense Systems & Services
Business Jets

BRANDS/DIVISIONS/AFFILIATES:

Gulfstream Aerospace Corp
M1A1 Abrams Tank
Gulfstream
G500
G600

CONTACTS: *Note: Officers with more than one job title may be intentionally listed here more than once.*

Phebe Novakovic, CEO
Phebe Novakovic, Chmn.

GROWTH PLANS/SPECIAL FEATURES:

General Dynamics Corp. (GDC) is one of the world's largest aerospace and defense contractors, with a portfolio of over 60 businesses. Its customers include the U.S. military, other government organizations, armed forces of allied nations and a diverse base of corporate and industrial buyers. The firm's operations are divided into four segments: information systems and technology (IST), marine systems, combat systems and aerospace. The IST group designs, manufactures and delivers tactical and strategic mission systems, information technology and mission services as well as intelligence mission systems to the U.S. Department of Defense and other customers. The marine systems division provides the U.S. Navy with combat vessels, including nuclear submarines, surface combatants and auxiliary ships. The segment also provides ship management services, such as overhaul, repair and lifecycle support services, and builds commercial ships. The combat systems group provides design, development, production, support and enhancement for tracked and wheeled military vehicles, weapons systems and munitions, with product lines including medium armored vehicles, main battle tanks, munitions, rockets and missile components and armament and detection systems. It is the leading builder of armored vehicles and makes products such as the M1A1 Abrams Tank. The aerospace group designs, manufactures and provides services for technologically advanced business jet aircraft under the Gulfstream name. In February 2016, wholly-owned Gulfstream Aerospace Corp. announced its Gulfstream G500 completed flutter testing. The G500 is a new family of clean-sheet aircraft which can fly 5,000 nautical miles at Mach 0.85, and carry up to 19 passengers. The G500 is expected to receive type certification from the U.S. Federal Aviation Administration and Aviation Safety Agency in 2017. It is scheduled to enter service in 2018, with the G600 following in 2019.

FINANCIAL DATA: *Note: Data for latest year may not have been available at press time.*

In U.S. $	2016	2015	2014	2013	2012	2011
Revenue		31,469,000,000	30,852,000,000	31,218,000,000	31,513,000,000	32,677,000,000
R&D Expense						
Operating Income		4,178,000,000	3,889,000,000	3,685,000,000	833,000,000	3,826,000,000
Operating Margin %		13.27%	12.60%	11.80%	2.64%	11.70%
SGA Expense		1,952,000,000	1,984,000,000	2,079,000,000	2,276,000,000	2,030,000,000
Net Income		2,965,000,000	2,533,000,000	2,357,000,000	-332,000,000	2,526,000,000
Operating Cash Flow		2,499,000,000	3,728,000,000	3,106,000,000	2,685,000,000	3,238,000,000
Capital Expenditure		569,000,000	521,000,000	440,000,000	450,000,000	458,000,000
EBITDA		4,682,000,000	4,401,000,000	4,266,000,000	1,317,000,000	4,465,000,000
Return on Assets %		8.80%	7.15%	6.75%	-.95%	7.49%
Return on Equity %		26.27%	19.24%	18.20%	-2.69%	19.02%
Debt to Equity		0.26	0.28	0.26	0.34	0.29

CONTACT INFORMATION:

Phone: 703 876-3000   Fax: 703 876-3125
Toll-Free:
Address: 2941 Fairview Park Dr., Ste. 100, Falls Church, VA 22042 United States

STOCK TICKER/OTHER:

Stock Ticker: GD   Exchange: NYS
Employees: 99,900   Fiscal Year Ends: 12/31
Parent Company:

SALARIES/BONUSES:

Top Exec. Salary: $1,583,750   Bonus: $4,850,000
Second Exec. Salary: $716,250   Bonus: $1,020,000

OTHER THOUGHTS:

Estimated Female Officers or Directors: 3

Hot Spot for Advancement for Women/Minorities: Y

Sales, profits and employees may be estimates. Financial information, benefits and other data can change quickly and may vary from those stated here.

General Electric Co (GE)

NAIC Code: 333000

TYPES OF BUSINESS:

Machinery and Equipment Manufacturing
Energy Systems & Consulting
Business Leasing & Finance
Industrial & Electrical Equipment
Transportation, Aircraft Engines, Rail Systems & Truck Fleet Management
Real Estate Investments & Finance
Medical Equipment

BRANDS/DIVISIONS/AFFILIATES:

GE Capital
GE Capital Aviation Services

CONTACTS: *Note: Officers with more than one job title may be intentionally listed here more than once.*

John Rice, CEO, Divisional
Keith Sherin, CEO, Subsidiary
Jeffrey Immelt, CEO
Jeffrey Bornstein, CFO
Jan Hauser, Chief Accounting Officer
Alexander Dimitrief, General Counsel
Susan Peters, Senior VP, Divisional
Elizabeth Comstock, Vice Chairman, Divisional

GROWTH PLANS/SPECIAL FEATURES:

General Electric Co. (GE) is one of the larger technology, media and financial services corporations. The firm operates through several divisions: power & water, oil & gas, energy management, aviation, health care, transportation, appliances & lighting and GE Capital. Power & water is a leader in the field of development, implementation and improvement of products and technologies that harness resources such as wind, oil, gas and water to produce electric power. Oil & gas helps oil and gas companies make more efficient and sustainable use of the world's energy resources. Energy management (5%) designs, manufactures and services leading technology solutions for the delivery, management, conversion and optimization of electrical power for customers across multiple energy-intensive industries. Aviation is one of the world's leading providers of jet engines and related services with operations in North America, Europe, Asia and South America. Health care provides essential health care technologies to developed, developing and emerging countries. Transportation is a global technology leader and supplier to the railroad, marine, drilling and mining industries. Appliances & lighting manufactures, sells and services major home appliances, including refrigerators, freezers and residential water systems; and lighting products such as automotive, decorative and specialty bulbs. GE Capital manages all of the lending and financial services units of GE, including commercial lending and leasing, consumer lending, real estate activities, energy financial services and commercial aircraft leasing and finance (through GE Capital Aviation Services). In 2015, GE announced plans to sell off nearly all of GE Capital's assets and business interests, but not its aircraft leasing business or energy finance business, and that it would create a company, Current, to house its developing energy business. In January 2016, the firm agreed to sell its appliance business to Qingdao Haier Co., Ltd.

FINANCIAL DATA: *Note: Data for latest year may not have been available at press time.*

In U.S. $	2016	2015	2014	2013	2012	2011
Revenue		117,386,000,000	148,589,000,000	146,045,000,000	147,359,000,000	147,300,000,000
R&D Expense						
Operating Income		16,862,000,000	26,711,000,000	26,267,000,000	29,914,000,000	34,643,000,000
Operating Margin %		14.36%	17.97%	17.98%	20.30%	23.51%
SGA Expense		17,831,000,000	30,572,000,000	37,819,000,000	39,244,000,000	40,296,000,000
Net Income		-6,126,000,000	15,233,000,000	13,057,000,000	13,641,000,000	14,151,000,000
Operating Cash Flow		19,891,000,000	27,710,000,000	28,579,000,000	31,331,000,000	33,359,000,000
Capital Expenditure		7,309,000,000	13,727,000,000	13,458,000,000	15,126,000,000	12,650,000,000
EBITDA		16,496,000,000	35,994,000,000	36,029,000,000	39,260,000,000	43,828,000,000
Return on Assets %		-1.07%	2.33%	1.94%	1.94%	1.78%
Return on Equity %		-5.41%	11.77%	10.29%	11.39%	11.14%
Debt to Equity		1.50	1.73	1.85	2.08	2.25

CONTACT INFORMATION:

Phone: 203 373-2211   Fax: 203 373-3131
Toll-Free:
Address: 3135 Easton Turnpike, Fairfield, CT 06828 United States

STOCK TICKER/OTHER:

Stock Ticker: GE   Exchange: NYS
Employees: 333,000   Fiscal Year Ends: 12/31
Parent Company:

SALARIES/BONUSES:

Top Exec. Salary: $3,800,000   Bonus: $5,400,000
Second Exec. Salary: $2,500,000   Bonus: $5,232,500

OTHER THOUGHTS:

Estimated Female Officers or Directors: 10

Hot Spot for Advancement for Women/Minorities: Y

General Motors Company (GM)   www.gm.com

NAIC Code: 336111

TYPES OF BUSINESS:

Automobile Manufacturing
Security & Information Services
Automotive Electronics
Financing & Insurance
Parts & Service
Transmissions
Engines
Locomotives

BRANDS/DIVISIONS/AFFILIATES:

Chevrolet
Buick
Cadillac
GMC
Opel
Vauxhall
Holden
SAIC-GMAC Automotive Finance Co Ltd

CONTACTS: *Note: Officers with more than one job title may be intentionally listed here more than once.*

Mary Barra, CEO
Jaime Ardila, Executive VP
Charles Stevens, CFO
Karl-Thomas Neumann, Chairman of the Board, Subsidiary
Thomas Timko, Chief Accounting Officer
James DeLuca, Executive VP, Divisional
Mark Reuss, Executive VP, Divisional
Stefan Jacoby, Executive VP, Divisional
Craig Glidden, Executive VP
Matthew Tsien, Executive VP
Carel De Nysschen, Executive VP
Alan Batey, Executive VP
Barry Engle, Executive VP
Jill Sutton, Other Corporate Officer
Daniel Ammann, President

GROWTH PLANS/SPECIAL FEATURES:

General Motors Company (GM) is engaged in the worldwide development, production and marketing of cars, trucks, automotive systems and locomotives. The firm's major North American brands include Chevrolet, Buick, Cadillac and GMC. Besides its North American brands, GM markets vehicles internationally under the following brands: Opel, via Adam Opel AG; Vauxhall, via Vauxhall Motors Ltd.; and Holden, via GM. The company is organized into four geographically-based segments: General Motors North America (GMNA), focused on U.S., Canada, and Mexico; General Motors international operations (GMIO), focused primarily on Egypt, Australia, the Middle East and Asia; General Motors Europe (GME), centered on European operations; and General Motors South America (GMSA), with operations primarily in Brazil, Argentina, Colombia and Venezuela. GM's equity ownership stakes through various regional subsidiaries in Asia design, manufacture and market vehicles under the Alpheon, Baojun, Buick, Cadillac, Chevrolet, Jiefang and Wuling brands. The firm has 20,252 dealerships worldwide, with 4,886 locations in North America. In 2015, GM acquired an equity interest in SAIC-GMAC Automotive Finance Co. Ltd., based in China. In March 2016, the firm agreed to acquire Cruise Automation to add Cruise's deep software talent and rapid development capability to further accelerate GM's development of autonomous vehicle technology.

FINANCIAL DATA: *Note: Data for latest year may not have been available at press time.*

In U.S. $	2016	2015	2014	2013	2012	2011
Revenue		152,356,000,000	155,929,000,000	155,427,000,000	152,256,000,000	150,276,000,000
R&D Expense						
Operating Income		4,897,000,000	1,530,000,000	5,131,000,000	-30,363,000,000	5,656,000,000
Operating Margin %		3.21%	.98%	3.30%	-19.94%	3.76%
SGA Expense		13,405,000,000	12,158,000,000	12,382,000,000	13,593,000,000	12,163,000,000
Net Income		9,687,000,000	3,949,000,000	5,346,000,000	6,188,000,000	9,190,000,000
Operating Cash Flow		11,978,000,000	10,058,000,000	12,630,000,000	10,605,000,000	8,166,000,000
Capital Expenditure		7,874,000,000	7,091,000,000	7,565,000,000	9,118,000,000	7,078,000,000
EBITDA		16,178,000,000	11,887,000,000	15,833,000,000	8,994,000,000	13,869,000,000
Return on Assets %		5.20%	1.63%	2.38%	3.30%	5.35%
Return on Equity %		25.71%	7.48%	11.53%	18.13%	28.34%
Debt to Equity		1.09	0.89	0.55	0.40	0.42

CONTACT INFORMATION:

Phone: 313 556-5000   Fax:
Toll-Free:
Address: 300 Renaissance Ctr., Detroit, MI 48265-3000 United States

STOCK TICKER/OTHER:

Stock Ticker: GM   Exchange: NYS
Employees: 219,000   Fiscal Year Ends: 12/31
Parent Company:

SALARIES/BONUSES:

Top Exec. Salary: Bonus: $
$1,750,000
Second Exec. Salary: Bonus: $
$1,200,000

OTHER THOUGHTS:

Estimated Female Officers or Directors: 8

Hot Spot for Advancement for Women/Minorities: Y

Genesco Inc

www.genesco.com

NAIC Code: 424340

TYPES OF BUSINESS:

Shoes, Retail
Retail Stores
Men's Accessories
Wholesale Operations
Hats, Retail
Catalog & Online Operations
Athletic Team Products

BRANDS/DIVISIONS/AFFILIATES:

Journeys
Lids Sports
Schuh
Johnston & Murphy
Little Burgundy

CONTACTS: Note: Officers with more than one job title may be intentionally listed here more than once.

Robert Dennis, CEO
Mimi Vaughn, CFO
Paul Williams, Chief Accounting Officer
Roger Sisson, Secretary
James Estepa, Senior VP
Jonathan Caplan, Senior VP
Parag Desai, Senior VP, Divisional
Matthew Johnson, Treasurer

GROWTH PLANS/SPECIAL FEATURES:

Genesco, Inc. is a leading specialty retailer of footwear, apparel and accessories through 2,852 retail stores worldwide. These include 2,824 footwear, headwear and sports apparel and accessory stores in the U.S. and Puerto Rico; 151 headwear and sports apparel and accessory stores and 82 footwear stores in Canada; and 125 footwear stores in the U.K., Ireland and Germany. The company operates five business segments: Journeys, Lids Sports, Schuh, Johnston & Murphy and licensed brands. The Journey's segment operates 1,222 stores, including Journeys, Journeys Kidz, Shi by Journeys, Little Burgundy and Underground by Journeys retail stores, catalog and e-commerce operations. This segment accounts for 41% of Genesco's net sales. The stores average 1,920 square feet, and sell footwear and accessories for young men, women and children. The Lids Sports segment accounts for 32% of net sales, and operates 1,332 stores, including 919 Lids stores, 228 Lids Locker room and Clubhouse stores and 185 Locker Room by Lids leased departments. The stores average 1,175 square feet, and sell core headwear, apparel, accessories and novelties. The Schuh segment accounts for 14% of net sales, and operates 115 stores which average 5,000 square feet in both street-level and mall locations within the U.K., Ireland and Germany. Schuh stores sell men's and women's casual and athletic footwear. This division plans to open Schuh Kids stores in 2017. The Johnston & Murphy segment accounts for 9% of net sales, and operate 173 retail shops and factory stores in the U.S. and Canada. The stores average 1,875 square feet, and sell footwear, apparel and accessories primarily for men and women aged between 35 and 55. The licensed brands segment generates 4% of net sales from licensed brands such as Dockers, SureGrip Footwear and G.H. Bass. In 2016, the firm acquired Little Burgundy, a retail footwear chain based in Canada, from Aldo Group, Inc.

Employee benefits include medical, prescription, vision and dental coverage; 401(k) plan; stock purchase plan; life insurance; short- and long-term disability; employee discounts; flexible spending accounts; and adoption assistance.

FINANCIAL DATA: Note: Data for latest year may not have been available at press time.

In U.S. $	2016	2015	2014	2013	2012	2011
Revenue	3,022,234,000	2,859,844,000	2,624,972,000	2,604,817,000	2,291,987,000	1,789,839,000
R&D Expense						
Operating Income	151,251,000	167,266,000	163,435,000	167,970,000	143,870,000	86,083,000
Operating Margin %	5.00%	5.84%	6.22%	6.44%	6.27%	4.80%
SGA Expense	1,284,322,000	1,230,864,000	1,134,274,000	1,113,340,000	1,007,502,000	807,197,000
Net Income	94,569,000	97,725,000	92,653,000	110,536,000	81,959,000	53,211,000
Operating Cash Flow	145,118,000	189,764,000	139,999,000	123,210,000	144,960,000	102,608,000
Capital Expenditure	100,652,000	103,111,000	98,456,000	71,737,000	49,456,000	29,299,000
EBITDA	234,958,000	234,652,000	230,636,000	231,762,000	197,672,000	133,829,000
Return on Assets %	6.05%	6.46%	6.68%	8.59%	7.45%	5.83%
Return on Equity %	9.70%	10.23%	10.77%	14.59%	12.32%	8.89%
Debt to Equity	0.10	0.01	0.02	0.05	0.04	

CONTACT INFORMATION:

Phone: 615 367-7000   Fax: 615 367-8278
Toll-Free:
Address: 1415 Murfreesboro Rd., Nashville, TN 37217 United States

STOCK TICKER/OTHER:

Stock Ticker: GCO   Exchange: NYS
Employees: 27,325   Fiscal Year Ends: 01/31
Parent Company:

SALARIES/BONUSES:

Top Exec. Salary: $877,000   Bonus: $
Second Exec. Salary: $625,000   Bonus: $

OTHER THOUGHTS:

Estimated Female Officers or Directors: 2
Hot Spot for Advancement for Women/Minorities:

Sales, profits and employees may be estimates. Financial information, benefits and other data can change quickly and may vary from those stated here.

Gentex Corporation

www.gentex.com

NAIC Code: 336300

TYPES OF BUSINESS:

Specialty Automobile Parts Manufacturer
Electro-Optic Technology
Rearview Mirrors & Mirror Sub-Assemblies
Headlight Systems
Smoke Alarms & Smoke Detectors
Electrochromic Window Shades

BRANDS/DIVISIONS/AFFILIATES:

SmartBeam
HomeLink
Alteos

CONTACTS: *Note: Officers with more than one job title may be intentionally listed here more than once.*

Scott Ryan, Assistant General Counsel
Fred Bauer, CEO
Kevin Nash, Chief Accounting Officer
James Hollars, Independent Director
Steve Downing, Senior VP
Joseph Matthews, Vice President, Divisional
Neil Boehm, Vice President, Divisional

GROWTH PLANS/SPECIAL FEATURES:

Gentex Corporation designs, develops, manufactures and markets proprietary products for the automotive, aviation and fire protection industry. The firm is organized into three operating segments: automotive, fire protection and aerospace. The automotive division is the firm's largest business segment and builds products such as interior and exterior electrochromic automatic-dimming rearview mirrors and automotive electronics. The company also has an exterior auto-dimming mirror sub-assembly, which works as a complete glare-control system with the interior mirror. Automatic-dimming mirrors include the SmartBeam driver-assist feature for headlamp lighting control; HomeLink mirror electronics; LED map lamps; compass and temperature displays; telematics; hands-free communication; rear camera display and full display interior mirrors; CMOS imager-based video cameras for rear vision with high dynamic range; proprietary exterior turn signals; and side blind zone indicators. Gentex supplies automatic-dimming rearview mirrors for Rolls Royce, Cadillac, Buick, Chevrolet, Renault, Ford, Kia, Audi, BMW, Toyota and other manufacturers. The fire protection segment produces photoelectric smoke detectors and alarms; visual signaling alarms; electrochemical carbon monoxide alarms and detectors; audible and visual signaling alarms; and bells and speakers for use in fire detection systems in commercial and residential buildings. The firm's aerospace segment manufactures interactive windows which are sold under the Alteos brand of interactive window systems. The windows feature electrochromic window shades that are used in both commercial and business aircraft passenger cabins. Gentex also makes dimmable aircraft windows for the passenger compartment of the Boeing 787 Dreamliner series and the Hawker Beechcraft King Air 350i.

Gentex offers its employees health, dental, life and disability insurance; a 401(k) plan; tuition reimbursement; profit sharing bonus; adoption assistance; access to a wellness center; and an employee stock purchase plan.

FINANCIAL DATA: *Note: Data for latest year may not have been available at press time.*

In U.S. $	2016	2015	2014	2013	2012	2011
Revenue		1,543,618,000	1,375,501,000	1,171,864,000	1,099,560,000	1,023,762,000
R&D Expense		88,392,920	84,175,740	76,495,050	85,003,600	81,634,160
Operating Income		458,766,400	398,834,200	304,741,800	234,455,200	231,367,900
Operating Margin %		29.72%	28.99%	26.00%	21.32%	22.59%
SGA Expense		56,616,700	55,879,780	49,496,040	48,359,720	48,578,250
Net Income		318,469,900	288,604,600	222,930,000	168,586,800	164,668,200
Operating Cash Flow		351,578,400	327,223,100	317,338,800	257,846,000	141,668,700
Capital Expenditure		97,941,760	72,518,980	55,380,460	117,474,400	120,177,700
EBITDA		539,365,600	476,210,500	367,596,000	284,635,000	274,002,600
Return on Assets %		15.26%	15.24%	14.71%	13.80%	15.11%
Return on Equity %		19.33%	19.91%	18.20%	15.69%	17.14%
Debt to Equity		0.13	0.16	0.20		

CONTACT INFORMATION:

Phone: 616 772-1800   Fax: 616 772-7348
Toll-Free:
Address: 600 N. Centennial St., Zeeland, MI 49464 United States

STOCK TICKER/OTHER:

Stock Ticker: GNTX   Exchange: NAS
Employees: 4,757   Fiscal Year Ends: 12/31
Parent Company:

SALARIES/BONUSES:

Top Exec. Salary: $523,102   Bonus: $118,033
Second Exec. Salary: Bonus: $42,699
$299,261

OTHER THOUGHTS:

Estimated Female Officers or Directors: 1
Hot Spot for Advancement for Women/Minorities:

Gentherm Inc

www.gentherm.com

NAIC Code: 336300

TYPES OF BUSINESS:

Automobile Parts Manufacturing
Thermoelectric Devices
Climate Control Seats
Temperature Controlled Mattresses

BRANDS/DIVISIONS/AFFILIATES:

Gentherm GmbH
Gentherm Global Power Technologies
Gentherm North America
Gentherm Asia Electronics
Global Thermoelectric Inc

CONTACTS: Note: Officers with more than one job title may be intentionally listed here more than once.

Barry Steele, CFO
Oscar Marx, Chairman of the Board
Frithjof Oldorff, COO, Subsidiary
Kenneth Phillips, General Counsel
Erin Ascher, Other Executive Officer
Daniel Coker, President
Ryan Gaul, Vice President, Divisional
Greg Steinl, Vice President, Divisional
John Marx, Vice President, Divisional
Darren Schumacher, Vice President, Divisional

GROWTH PLANS/SPECIAL FEATURES:

Gentherm, Inc. designs, develops and markets products based on its advanced, proprietary thermoelectric device (TED) technologies for a wide range of global markets and heating and cooling applications. The firm's current principal product is its climate control seat (CCS), which it sells to automobile and light truck original equipment manufacturers (OEMs) or Tier 1 suppliers. The CCS actively heats and cools the passenger by using TED technologies. The CCS product is currently offered as a standard or optional feature on automobiles produced by Ford, General Motors, Toyota, Nissan, Hyundai, Volkswagen, Fiat Chrysler, BMW, Daimler, Honda and Jaguar/Land Rover. The firm also offers a heated-only variant of the CCS, which has a lower price and is targeted to certain lower cost vehicle models and certain geographical markets. Other products the firm has developed include a line of actively heated and cooled luxury mattresses and an automotive heated and cooled cup holder for the 2011 Dodge Charger. Additionally, through its majority-owned subsidiary Gentherm GmbH, the firm produces automotive cable systems used to connect automotive components to sources of power. Subsidiary Gentherm Global Power Technologies is a global market leader and developer of thermoelectric generators, and is also the company's advanced research and product development division. Other subsidiaries include Gentherm North America and Gentherm Asia Electronics. Gentherm holds 403 issued patents, of which 186 are U.S. and 217 are non-U.S. patents. In April 2014, Gentherm acquired Global Thermoelectric, Inc., a firm involved in industrial thermoelectric generator systems and remote power generation.

FINANCIAL DATA: Note: Data for latest year may not have been available at press time.

In U.S. $	2016	2015	2014	2013	2012	2011
Revenue		856,445,000	811,300,000	662,082,000	554,979,000	369,588,000
R&D Expense		59,604,000	57,526,000	49,873,000	40,950,000	28,440,000
Operating Income		121,319,000	98,434,000	49,580,000	36,058,000	18,881,000
Operating Margin %		14.16%	12.13%	7.48%	6.49%	5.10%
SGA Expense		95,456,000	84,647,000	72,895,000	64,919,000	42,110,000
Net Income		95,393,000	70,119,000	33,820,000	17,872,000	10,344,000
Operating Cash Flow		104,712,000	80,335,000	59,794,000	36,865,000	35,370,000
Capital Expenditure		55,490,000	38,887,000	35,861,000	26,793,000	11,816,000
EBITDA		162,577,000	132,512,000	80,829,000	67,435,000	42,233,000
Return on Assets %		15.83%	13.48%	6.99%	2.73%	.92%
Return on Equity %		28.11%	26.64%	16.34%	9.90%	3.49%
Debt to Equity		0.24	0.29	0.26	0.24	0.97

CONTACT INFORMATION:

Phone: 248-504-0500   Fax: 248-348-9735
Toll-Free:
Address: 21680 Haggerty Rd., Ste. 101, Northville, MI 48167 United States

STOCK TICKER/OTHER:

Stock Ticker: THRM   Exchange: NAS
Employees: 8,607   Fiscal Year Ends: 12/31
Parent Company:

SALARIES/BONUSES:

Top Exec. Salary: $700,000   Bonus: $682,500
Second Exec. Salary: $404,575 Bonus: $299,838

OTHER THOUGHTS:

Estimated Female Officers or Directors: 1
Hot Spot for Advancement for Women/Minorities:

Gilead Sciences Inc

www.gilead.com

NAIC Code: 325412

TYPES OF BUSINESS:

Viral & Bacterial Infections Drugs
Respiratory & Cardiopulmonary Diseases Drugs

BRANDS/DIVISIONS/AFFILIATES:

Atripla
Complera
Harvoni
Zydelig
Letairis
Ranexa
Cayston
AmBisome

CONTACTS: *Note: Officers with more than one job title may be intentionally listed here more than once.*

John Milligan, CEO
Robin Washington, CFO
John Martin, Chairman of the Board
Kevin Young, COO
Paul Carter, Executive VP, Divisional
Gregg Alton, Executive VP, Divisional
Norbert Bischofberger, Executive VP, Divisional
Brett Pletcher, General Counsel

GROWTH PLANS/SPECIAL FEATURES:

Gilead Sciences, Inc. is a biopharmaceutical company that discovers, develops and commercializes therapeutics for the treatment of life-threatening diseases such as viral and bacterial infections as well as respiratory and cardiopulmonary diseases. The firm maintains research, development, manufacturing, sales and marketing facilities in the U.S., Europe and Australia and operates through its subsidiaries in over 30 countries. Gilead's current products on the market consist of: Atripla, Complera, Emtriva, Stribild, Truvada, Tybost, Viread and Vitekta, which are oral medicines used as part of a combination therapy to treat HIV/AIDS; Harvoni, Hepsera, Sovaldi and Viread, which are oral medicines to treat liver diseases; Zydelig, an oral medicine for oncology purposes; Letairis, Ranexa (oral medicines) and Lexiscan (injection medicine), for cardiovascular purposes; Cayston inhalation solution and oral medicine Tamiflu, for respiratory purposes; AmBisome, an injection medicine to treat meningitis in HIV infected patients; and Macugen, an injection medicine to treat neovascular age-related macular degeneration. In January 2015, the firm acquired Phenex Pharmaceuticals' Farnesoid X Receptor (FXR) program, comprising small molecular FXR agonists for treatment of liver diseases including nonalcoholic steatohepatitis (NASH). In May of same year, Gilead Aciences acquired EpiTherapeutics ApS, a privately-held Danish company, which develops novel innovative cancer drugs based on epigenetics.

The company offers its employees medical, vision, dental, disability, life and AD&D insurance; a 401(k); a stock purchase plan; an entertainment discount program; an employee assistance plan; and tuition reimbursement.

FINANCIAL DATA: *Note: Data for latest year may not have been available at press time.*

In U.S. $	2016	2015	2014	2013	2012	2011
Revenue		32,639,000,000	24,890,000,000	11,201,690,000	9,702,517,000	8,385,385,000
R&D Expense		3,014,000,000	2,854,000,000	2,119,756,000	1,759,945,000	1,229,151,000
Operating Income		22,193,000,000	15,265,000,000	4,523,999,000	4,010,175,000	3,789,841,000
Operating Margin %		67.99%	61.32%	40.38%	41.33%	45.19%
SGA Expense		3,426,000,000	2,983,000,000	1,699,431,000	1,461,034,000	1,241,983,000
Net Income		18,108,000,000	12,101,000,000	3,074,808,000	2,591,566,000	2,803,637,000
Operating Cash Flow		20,329,000,000	12,818,000,000	3,104,988,000	3,194,716,000	3,639,010,000
Capital Expenditure		747,000,000	557,000,000	190,782,000	397,046,000	131,904,000
EBITDA		23,445,000,000	16,318,000,000	4,859,817,000	4,251,102,000	4,158,654,000
Return on Assets %		41.86%	42.34%	14.06%	13.44%	19.40%
Return on Equity %		106.64%	90.32%	29.73%	32.29%	44.49%
Debt to Equity		1.14	0.77	0.34	0.75	1.12

CONTACT INFORMATION:

Phone: 650 574-3000   Fax: 650 578-9264
Toll-Free: 800-445-3235
Address: 333 Lakeside Dr., Foster City, CA 94404 United States

STOCK TICKER/OTHER:

Stock Ticker: GILD
Employees: 7,000
Parent Company:

Exchange: NAS
Fiscal Year Ends: 12/31

SALARIES/BONUSES:

Top Exec. Salary:
$1,727,423
Second Exec. Salary:
$1,186,154

Bonus: $

Bonus: $

OTHER THOUGHTS:

Estimated Female Officers or Directors: 4

Hot Spot for Advancement for Women/Minorities: Y

Goldman Sachs Group Inc

www.goldmansachs.com

NAIC Code: 523110

TYPES OF BUSINESS:

Investment Banking
Securities & Investment Management
Financial Services
Asset Management
Bank Holding Company

BRANDS/DIVISIONS/AFFILIATES:

CONTACTS: Note: Officers with more than one job title may be intentionally listed here more than once.

Beverly OToole, Assistant Secretary
Michael Sherwood, CEO, Subsidiary
Lloyd Blankfein, CEO
Harvey Schwartz, CFO
Mark Schwartz, Chairman, Divisional
Sarah Smith, Chief Accounting Officer
Gregory Palm, Executive VP
Alan Cohen, Executive VP
Edith Cooper, Executive VP
John Rogers, Executive VP
Gary Cohn, President
John Weinberg, Vice Chairman

GROWTH PLANS/SPECIAL FEATURES:

Goldman Sachs Group, Inc. is a financial holding company regulated by the Board of Governors of the Federal Reserve System, operating in over 30 countries. The firm has four main business divisions: institutional client services, investment management, investment banking and investing & lending. The institutional client services division, totaling 44% in revenues, accounted for the majority of the company's 2014 profits. It provides clients with services regarding fixed income currency and commodities execution on a variety of products such as interest rate and credit products, mortgages, currencies and commodities. The investment management segment, 17% of revenues, provides investment and wealth advisory services on a range of asset classes and investment plans, including equity, fixed income, hedge funds, private equity, real estate, currencies, commodities and asset allocation of strategies to institutions and high-net-worth individuals who access the companies' products through third-party distributors. The investment banking division, 19%, provides financial advisory services including strategic advisory assignments with respect to mergers and acquisitions, divestitures, corporate defense activities, risk management, debt and equity underwriting, restructurings and spin-offs to corporate and government clients around the world. The investing & lending sector, 20%, manages a portfolio of investments consisting of equity and debt securities in addition to other investments in privately negotiated transactions, leveraged buyouts, acquisitions and investment funds managed by external parties. In addition, the Goldman Sachs Prime Brokerage program in Europe and the U.S. delivers investment research, products and execution services to brokerage firms.

The firm offers employees medical, prescription, life, disability, accident, travel, dental and vision insurance; a 401(k); adoption assistance; and employee investing services.

FINANCIAL DATA: Note: Data for latest year may not have been available at press time.

In U.S. $	2016	2015	2014	2013	2012	2011
Revenue		33,820,000,000	34,528,000,000	34,206,000,000	34,163,000,000	28,811,000,000
R&D Expense						
Operating Income		8,778,000,000	12,357,000,000	11,737,000,000	11,207,000,000	6,169,000,000
Operating Margin %		25.95%	35.78%	34.31%	32.80%	21.41%
SGA Expense		14,041,000,000	14,019,000,000	14,106,000,000	14,833,000,000	14,220,000,000
Net Income		6,083,000,000	8,477,000,000	8,040,000,000	7,475,000,000	4,442,000,000
Operating Cash Flow		6,961,000,000	-7,623,000,000	4,543,000,000	12,879,000,000	21,645,000,000
Capital Expenditure		1,833,000,000	678,000,000	706,000,000	961,000,000	1,184,000,000
EBITDA						
Return on Assets %		.64%	.91%	.83%	.78%	.27%
Return on Equity %		7.46%	11.15%	10.97%	10.66%	3.64%
Debt to Equity		2.65	2.58	2.60	2.86	3.13

CONTACT INFORMATION:

Phone: 212 902-1000   Fax: 212 902-3000
Toll-Free:
Address: 200 West St., New York, NY 10282 United States

STOCK TICKER/OTHER:

Stock Ticker: GS
Employees: 36,800
Parent Company:

Exchange: NYS
Fiscal Year Ends: 12/31

SALARIES/BONUSES:

Top Exec. Salary: $2,000,000
Bonus: $6,300,000

Second Exec. Salary: $1,850,000
Bonus: $5,745,000

OTHER THOUGHTS:

Estimated Female Officers or Directors: 5

Hot Spot for Advancement for Women/Minorities: Y

Sales, profits and employees may be estimates. Financial information, benefits and other data can change quickly and may vary from those stated here.

Google (Alphabet Inc)

www.google.com

NAIC Code: 519130

TYPES OF BUSINESS:

Search Engine-Internet
Paid Search Listing Advertising Services
Online Software and Productivity Tools
Online Video and Photo Services
Travel Booking
Analytical Tools
Venture Capital
Online Maps

BRANDS/DIVISIONS/AFFILIATES:

Google.com
AdWords
AdSense
Google Ventures
YouTube
Double Click
Alphabet Inc
Alphabet

CONTACTS: Note: Officers with more than one job title may be intentionally listed here more than once.

Kent Walker, Assistant Secretary
Sundar Pichai, CEO, Subsidiary
Larry Page, CEO
Ruth Porat, CFO
Eric Schmidt, Chairman of the Board
Sergey Brin, Director
Diane Greene, Director
David Drummond, Other Executive Officer

GROWTH PLANS/SPECIAL FEATURES:

Google (Alphabet, Inc.) operates Google.com, a global leader in technology and a provider of the most used search engine, which connects people to information by indexing the content of billions of Internet pages. The company's business operates in four different areas: search, advertising, operating systems and platforms and enterprise. While end-users can use Google's search engine for free, the company profits from charging fees to other sites that use its search technology through an auction-based program that enables business clients to bid for ad space. Businesses use the AdWords program to promote their products and services. In addition, third-party web sites that comprise the Google Network use the AdSense program to deliver ads that generate revenue and are relevant to search results. Advertising revenue is also generated from other web-based applications that include Google Display, a program that provides clients with delivery of display services; Double Click, an advertising technology that creates a real-time auction marketplace where advertisers can trade display ad space; Google Mobile, a free and open source smartphone operating system; and Google Local, a tool that allows consumers to locate local information via the web. The company's operating systems and platforms division develops proprietary products such as the Android market, Google Chrome, Google TV and Google Books. The enterprise division creates productivity and content sharing tools, such as Google Docs, Gmail, Blogger, Google Play, Google+ and YouTube. In August 2015, the firm announced that it has created a new holding company named Alphabet. Google's search business, YouTube and the Android and Chrome software units will operate as one unit under the holding company. Sundar Pichai will run that unit. Other businesses, mainly in development stage will operate as separate units under Alphabet. These businesses include Nest, Google Ventures, Google Fiber and Calico.

FINANCIAL DATA: Note: Data for latest year may not have been available at press time.

In U.S. $	2016	2015	2014	2013	2012	2011
Revenue		74,989,000,000	66,001,000,000	59,825,000,000	50,175,000,000	37,905,000,000
R&D Expense		12,282,000,000	9,831,999,000	7,952,000,000	6,793,000,000	5,162,000,000
Operating Income		19,360,000,000	16,496,000,000	13,966,000,000	12,760,000,000	11,742,000,000
Operating Margin %		25.81%	24.99%	23.34%	25.43%	30.97%
SGA Expense		15,183,000,000	13,982,000,000	12,049,000,000	9,988,000,000	7,813,000,000
Net Income		16,348,000,000	14,444,000,000	12,920,000,000	10,737,000,000	9,737,000,000
Operating Cash Flow		26,024,000,000	22,376,000,000	18,659,000,000	16,619,000,000	14,565,000,000
Capital Expenditure		9,915,000,000	10,959,000,000	7,358,000,000	3,273,000,000	3,438,000,000
EBITDA		24,818,000,000	22,339,000,000	18,518,000,000	16,432,000,000	14,235,000,000
Return on Assets %		11.36%	11.93%	12.62%	12.90%	14.93%
Return on Equity %		14.07%	15.06%	16.24%	16.53%	18.65%
Debt to Equity		0.01	0.03	0.02	0.04	0.05

CONTACT INFORMATION:

Phone: 650 253-0000   Fax: 650 253-0001
Toll-Free:
Address: 1600 Amphitheatre Pkwy., Mountain View, CA 94043 United States

STOCK TICKER/OTHER:

Stock Ticker: GOOG   Exchange: NAS
Employees: 61,814   Fiscal Year Ends: 12/31
Parent Company:

SALARIES/BONUSES:

Top Exec. Salary: $1,254,808   Bonus: $6,000,000
Second Exec. Salary: $395,000   Bonus: $5,000,000

OTHER THOUGHTS:

Estimated Female Officers or Directors: 3

Hot Spot for Advancement for Women/Minorities: Y

Sales, profits and employees may be estimates. Financial information, benefits and other data can change quickly and may vary from those stated here.

Graco Inc

www.graco.com

NAIC Code: 333911

TYPES OF BUSINESS:
Pump and Pumping Equipment Manufacturing

BRANDS/DIVISIONS/AFFILIATES:
High Pressure Equipment
White Knight Fluid Handling

CONTACTS: *Note: Officers with more than one job title may be intentionally listed here more than once.*
Patrick McHale, CEO
Lee Mitau, Chairman of the Board
Caroline Chambers, Chief Accounting Officer
David Lowe, Executive VP, Divisional
Mark Sheahan, General Manager, Divisional
Mark Eberlein, General Manager, Divisional
Peter OShea, General Manager, Divisional
Brian Zumbolo, General Manager, Geographical
Bernard Moreau, General Manager, Geographical
Jeffrey Johnson, General Manager, Geographical
Christian Rothe, Treasurer
David Ahlers, Vice President, Divisional
Charles Rescorla, Vice President, Divisional
Dale Johnson, Vice President
Karen Gallivan, Vice President

GROWTH PLANS/SPECIAL FEATURES:
Graco, Inc. provides fluid handling solutions to customers in the manufacturing, processing, construction and maintenance industries throughout the world. The company operates in three segments: industrial, contractor and process. The industrial segment includes the industrial products and the applied fluid technologies divisions. The industrial products division markets equipment and services to customers who manufacture, assemble, maintain, repair and refinish products such as appliances, vehicles, airplanes, electronics, cabinets and furniture. The applied fluid technologies division designs and sells equipment for use by industrial customers, including systems used to spray polyurethane foam and polyuria coatings. The contractor segment markets a complete line of airless paint and texture sprayers; accessories such as spray guns, hoses and filters; and spare parts such as tips and seals. The process segment includes process, oil & natural gas and lubrication divisions. Process markets pumps, valves, meters and accessories to move and dispense chemicals, oil & natural gas, water, wastewater, petroleum, food lubricants and other fluids. Markets served include food, beverage, dairy, oil & natural gas, pharmaceutical, cosmetics, semi-conductor, electronics, wastewater, mining, fast oil change facilities, service garages, fleet service centers, automobile dealerships and industrial lubrication applications. Oil & natural gas markets chemical injection pumping solutions, high pressure and ultra-high pressure valves. The lubrication division designs and sells equipment for use in vehicle servicing, supplying pumps, hose reels, meters, valves and accessories. It also offers systems, components and accessories for the automatic lubrication of bearings, gears and generators in industrial and commercial equipment, compressors, turbines and on- and off-road vehicles. In 2015, the firm acquired High Pressure Equipment (HiP), a manufacturer of valves, fittings and other flow control equipment; acquired White Knight Fluid Handling, a pump manufacturer; and sold its liquid finishing business to Carlisle for $590 million.

FINANCIAL DATA: *Note: Data for latest year may not have been available at press time.*

In U.S. $	2016	2015	2014	2013	2012	2011
Revenue		1,286,485,000	1,221,130,000	1,104,024,000	1,012,456,000	895,283,000
R&D Expense		58,559,000	54,246,000	51,428,000	48,921,000	41,554,000
Operating Income		302,125,000	308,925,000	279,769,000	224,677,000	219,514,000
Operating Margin %		23.48%	25.29%	25.34%	22.19%	24.51%
SGA Expense		324,016,000	303,565,000	276,258,000	276,932,000	239,137,000
Net Income		345,713,000	225,573,000	210,822,000	149,126,000	142,328,000
Operating Cash Flow		189,639,000	241,255,000	243,055,000	189,682,000	162,044,000
Capital Expenditure		41,749,000	30,636,000	23,319,000	18,234,000	24,785,000
EBITDA		536,963,000	369,321,000	344,285,000	275,361,000	251,342,000
Return on Assets %		23.54%	15.70%	15.91%	13.58%	20.26%
Return on Equity %		56.14%	36.66%	38.73%	38.39%	48.50%
Debt to Equity		0.61	1.03	0.64	1.22	0.92

CONTACT INFORMATION:
Phone: 612 623-6000   Fax: 612 623-6777
Toll-Free:
Address: 88 11th Ave. NE, Minneapolis, MN 55413 United States

STOCK TICKER/OTHER:
Stock Ticker: GGG   Exchange: NYS
Employees: 3,100   Fiscal Year Ends: 12/31
Parent Company:

SALARIES/BONUSES:
Top Exec. Salary: $750,400   Bonus: $
Second Exec. Salary: $366,100   Bonus: $150,000

OTHER THOUGHTS:
Estimated Female Officers or Directors:
Hot Spot for Advancement for Women/Minorities:

Sales, profits and employees may be estimates. Financial information, benefits and other data can change quickly and may vary from those stated here.

Grant Thornton LLP

www.grantthornton.com

NAIC Code: 541211

TYPES OF BUSINESS:

Accounting & Auditing Services
Financial Services
Administration Consulting

BRANDS/DIVISIONS/AFFILIATES:

Grant Thornton International Ltd

CONTACTS: Note: Officers with more than one job title may be intentionally listed here more than once.

Mike McGuire, CEO
Russell Wieman, CFO
Manish Tomar, CIO
J. Michael McGuire, Nat'l Managing Partner-Oper.
Trent Gazzaway, Managing Partner-Audit Svcs.
Doreen Griffith, Managing Partner-Tax Svcs.
Steve Lukens, Managing Partner-Advisory Svcs.

GROWTH PLANS/SPECIAL FEATURES:

Grant Thornton LLP is the U.S. arm of Grant Thornton International Ltd., and provides advisory, audit and tax services to both public and private corporations. The company's advisory services include business consulting; forensic investigative and dispute services; governance, risk and compliance; restructuring and turnaround; technology solutions; transaction advisory; and valuation. Its audit solutions include employee benefit plan audit, financial statement audit, fresh start accounting, international financial reporting standards reporting and resources and public finance. Tax services include the Affordable Care Act, compensation & benefits consulting, international tax, private wealth services, SALT alerts, state and local tax, strategic federal tax, tax accounting/risk advisory, tax compliance and tax hot topics. Industries served by the firm include construction, distribution, energy, financial services, food and beverage, health care, hospitality and restaurants, life sciences, manufacturing, not-for-profit organizations, private equity, public sector, real estate, retail, technology and transportation. Grant Thornton LLP has 58 offices across 29 states and the District of Columbia.

Grant Thornton's employee benefits include medical and dental plans, reimbursement accounts and a 401(k) plan.

FINANCIAL DATA: Note: Data for latest year may not have been available at press time.

In U.S. $	2016	2015	2014	2013	2012	2011
Revenue		1,450,000,000	1,354,000,000	1,300,000,000	1,260,000,000	1,175,000,000
R&D Expense						
Operating Income						
Operating Margin %						
SGA Expense						
Net Income						
Operating Cash Flow						
Capital Expenditure						
EBITDA						
Return on Assets %						
Return on Equity %						
Debt to Equity						

CONTACT INFORMATION:

Phone: 312-856-0200   Fax: 312-602-8099
Toll-Free:
Address: 171 N. Clark St., Ste. 200, Chicago, IL 60601 United States

SALARIES/BONUSES:

Top Exec. Salary: $ Bonus: $
Second Exec. Salary: $ Bonus: $

STOCK TICKER/OTHER:

Stock Ticker: Private   Exchange:
Employees: 6,400   Fiscal Year Ends: 07/31
Parent Company: Grant Thornton International Ltd

OTHER THOUGHTS:

Estimated Female Officers or Directors: 2
Hot Spot for Advancement for Women/Minorities:

Greenbrier Companies Inc (The)

www.gbrx.com

NAIC Code: 336510

TYPES OF BUSINESS:

Railcar Manufacturing
Railcar Maintenance
Marine Barge Manufacturing
Railcar Leasing
Railcar Management

BRANDS/DIVISIONS/AFFILIATES:

Greenbrier Europe BV
Greenbrier Management Services LLC
Greenbrier Railcar LLC
Gunderson LLC
Gunderson Marine LLC
Autostack Company LLC
GBW Railcar Services LLC

CONTACTS: Note: Officers with more than one job title may be intentionally listed here more than once.

William Furman, CEO
Lorie Tekorius, CFO
Adrian Downes, Chief Accounting Officer
Anne Manning, Controller
Mark Rittenbaum, Executive VP, Divisional
Victoria McManus, Executive VP
Martin Baker, General Counsel
Walter Hannan, Other Executive Officer
Alejandro Centurion, President, Divisional
James Sharp, President, Subsidiary
Sherrill Corbett, Secretary

GROWTH PLANS/SPECIAL FEATURES:

The Greenbrier Companies, Inc. (TGC) designs, manufactures and markets railroad freight car equipment in North America and Europe. TGC operates in four segments: manufacturing; wheels & parts; GBW joint venture; and leasing & services. The manufacturing operations are focused on intermodal double-stack railcars, which can be transported by multiple types of carriers; conventional railcars, including a variety of boxcars, flat cars and hopper cars; and tank cars, including cars designed for the transportation of ethanol, methanol and other commodities. This segment also includes European railcar manufacturing, including pressurized and non-pressurized tank cars, flat cars, coil cars, coal cars, gondolas, sliding wall cars and automobile transporter cars. In addition, operations includes the fabrication of ocean-going vessels, including conventional deck barges, double-hull tank barges, railcar/deck barges, barges for heavy industrial products and ocean-going dump barges. The wheels & parts segment operates from nine locations and is engaged in complete wheel services including reconditioning of wheels and axles in addition to new axle machining and finishing and axle downsizing. The component parts facilities offers services including, reconditioning and manufacturing railcar cushioning units, couplers, yokes, side frames, bolsters and various other parts. It also makes roofs, doors and associated parts for boxcars. The GBW joint venture, through GBW Railcar Services LLC, oversees the railcar repair, refurbishment, maintenance and retrofitting operations. The leasing and services segment is facilitated by the company's ownership of a lease fleet of roughly 9,300 railcars. Management services offered by the firm include railcar maintenance management; railcar accounting services; car hire receivable and payable administration; fleet management, including railcar tracking using proprietary software; and railcar remarketing. TGC provides management services for approximately 269,000 railcars. Subsidiaries of the company include Greenbrier Europe BV, Greenbrier Management Services LLC, Greenbrier Railcar LLC, Gunderson LLC, Gunderson Marine LLC and Autostack Company LLC.

FINANCIAL DATA: Note: Data for latest year may not have been available at press time.

In U.S. $	2016	2015	2014	2013	2012	2011
Revenue		2,605,278,000	2,203,962,000	1,756,418,000	1,807,716,000	1,243,290,000
R&D Expense						
Operating Income		386,892,000	239,520,000	41,651,000	118,788,000	67,574,000
Operating Margin %		14.85%	10.86%	2.37%	6.57%	5.43%
SGA Expense		151,791,000	125,270,000	103,175,000	104,596,000	80,326,000
Net Income		192,832,000	111,919,000	-11,048,000	58,708,000	6,466,000
Operating Cash Flow		192,333,000	135,907,000	104,592,000	116,056,000	-34,252,000
Capital Expenditure		105,989,000	70,227,000	60,827,000	117,885,000	84,302,000
EBITDA		439,844,000	279,553,000	80,143,000	158,824,000	83,373,000
Return on Assets %		11.65%	7.97%	-.82%	4.37%	.54%
Return on Equity %		30.99%	23.82%	-2.56%	14.80%	1.99%
Debt to Equity		0.44	0.87	0.87	0.99	1.18

CONTACT INFORMATION:

Phone: 503 684-7000   Fax: 503 684-7553
Toll-Free:
Address: 1 Centerpointe Dr., Ste. 200, Lake Oswego, OR 97035 United States

STOCK TICKER/OTHER:

Stock Ticker: GBX   Exchange: NYS
Employees: 10,689   Fiscal Year Ends: 08/31
Parent Company:

SALARIES/BONUSES:

Top Exec. Salary: $916,667   Bonus: $
Second Exec. Salary: $501,667   Bonus: $

OTHER THOUGHTS:

Estimated Female Officers or Directors: 5
Hot Spot for Advancement for Women/Minorities: Y

Sales, profits and employees may be estimates. Financial information, benefits and other data can change quickly and may vary from those stated here.

Group 1 Automotive Inc

NAIC Code: 441110

www.group1auto.com

TYPES OF BUSINESS:

Auto Dealers
Auto Repair Services
Insurance Services
Automotive Replacement Parts
Financing Services
Collision Service Centers

BRANDS/DIVISIONS/AFFILIATES:

Spire Automotive Group

CONTACTS: *Note: Officers with more than one job title may be intentionally listed here more than once.*

Earl Hesterberg, CEO
John Rickel, CFO
John Adams, Chairman of the Board
Darryl Burman, General Counsel
Beth Sibley, Secretary
Frank Grese, Senior VP, Divisional
Peter DeLongchamps, Vice President, Divisional

GROWTH PLANS/SPECIAL FEATURES:

Group 1 Automotive, Inc. is a leading operator in the U.S., U.K. and Brazil automotive retailing industries. The company, through its subsidiaries, sells new and used cars and light trucks, provides maintenance and repair services, sells replacement parts and arranges vehicle financing and insurance through its 199 franchises. The franchises include 152 dealership locations and 35 collision centers. The dealerships offer 32 different brands, which include Toyota, BMW, Ford, Mercedes-Benz, Honda, Nissan, Lexus, Chevrolet, Audi, Hyundai, Acura, Jeep, MINI, GMC, Volkswagen, RAM, Kia, Cadillac, Dodge, Subaru, Land Rover, Buick, Sprinter, Chrysler, Scion, Peugeot, Mazda, Lincoln, Porsche, smart, Volvo, Jaguar and Renault. Group 1's dealerships have taken several steps toward building customer confidence in their used vehicle inventory, including participation in manufacturer certification processes. These processes make used vehicles eligible for new vehicle benefits such as new vehicle finance rates and extended manufacturer warranties. In addition to its dealerships, the company owns 28 collision service centers. In 2016, the firm acquired Spire Automotive Group, based in London, England; and sold three U.S. dealerships, which included Mercedes-Benz and Volkswagen of Freehold, New Jersey and Ira Toyota of Milford, Massachusetts.

FINANCIAL DATA: *Note: Data for latest year may not have been available at press time.*

In U.S. $	2016	2015	2014	2013	2012	2011
Revenue		10,632,510,000	9,937,889,000	8,918,581,000	7,476,100,000	6,079,765,000
R&D Expense						
Operating Income		278,338,000	302,110,000	273,322,000	229,996,000	193,503,000
Operating Margin %		2.61%	3.04%	3.06%	3.07%	3.18%
SGA Expense		1,120,833,000	1,061,964,000	976,856,000	848,446,000	735,229,000
Net Income		93,999,000	93,004,000	113,992,000	100,209,000	82,394,000
Operating Cash Flow		141,047,000	198,288,000	52,372,000	-75,322,000	199,316,000
Capital Expenditure		120,252,000	150,392,000	102,858,000	88,491,000	60,558,000
EBITDA		325,577,000	298,051,000	308,359,000	261,530,000	220,566,000
Return on Assets %		2.11%	2.33%	3.33%	3.64%	3.52%
Return on Equity %		9.53%	9.23%	12.02%	12.01%	10.35%
Debt to Equity		1.31	1.03	0.64	0.64	0.59

CONTACT INFORMATION:

Phone: 713 647-5700   Fax: 713 647-5858
Toll-Free:
Address: 800 Gessner, Ste. 500, Houston, TX 77024 United States

STOCK TICKER/OTHER:

Stock Ticker: GPI
Employees: 12,886
Parent Company:

Exchange: NYS
Fiscal Year Ends: 12/31

SALARIES/BONUSES:

Top Exec. Salary: $1,100,000   Bonus: $

Second Exec. Salary: $583,500   Bonus: $

OTHER THOUGHTS:

Estimated Female Officers or Directors:

Hot Spot for Advancement for Women/Minorities: Y

Sales, profits and employees may be estimates. Financial information, benefits and other data can change quickly and may vary from those stated here.

Hanesbrands Inc

www.hanesbrands.com

NAIC Code: 424300

TYPES OF BUSINESS:

Apparel and Clothing Brands, Designers, Importers and Distributors
Outerwear
Hosiery
Internet Sales
Catalogs

BRANDS/DIVISIONS/AFFILIATES:

Champion
Hanes
Playtex
Lilyette
Just My Size
Wonderbra
Maidenform
Knights Apparel

CONTACTS: Note: Officers with more than one job title may be intentionally listed here more than once.

Richard Noll, CEO
Richard Moss, CFO
M. Scott Lewis, Chief Accounting Officer
Gerald Evans, COO
Joia Johnson, General Counsel
Elizabeth Burger, Other Executive Officer
Michael Faircloth, Other Executive Officer
John Marsh, President, Divisional
W. Upchurch, President, Divisional

GROWTH PLANS/SPECIAL FEATURES:

Hanesbrands, Inc. designs, manufactures, sources and sells apparel including t-shirts, bras, panties, men's underwear, kids' underwear, socks, hosiery, casual wear and active wear. The company is organized into four operating segments: innerwear, which accounted for 46% of its 2015 revenue; activewear, 27%; direct-to-consumer, 7%; and international, 20%. Hanesbrands' innerwear segment produces bras, panties, men's underwear, kids' underwear and socks marketed under the Hanes, Playtex, Bali, Just My Size, Maidenform, L'eggs, Lilyette, Donna Karan and Wonderbra brands. Hanesbrands also maintains a licensing agreement with Polo Ralph Lauren to produce underwear. The activewearwear segment produces t-shirts, fleece, athletic uniforms, thermals sleepwear and casual wear marketed under the Hanes, Champion, Hanes Beefy-T, Duofold and Just My Size brands. The direct-to-consumer segment operates 252 outlet stores as well as catalogs and e-commerce channels. The international segment includes sales in Europe, Asia, Latin America, Canada, Australia, the Middle East, Africa and the Caribbean, with the company's largest international markets comprising Europe, Canada, Japan, Mexico, Brazil and Australia. During 2015, sales in the U.S. accounted for 80% of its revenue, while international sales accounted for the remainder. Its largest customers are Wal-Mart, Target and Kohl's, which accounted for 23%, 15% and 5%, respectively, of total revenue. Hanesbrands engages in manufacturing through both company-owned and operated facilities and third-party contractors. The firm's design, research and product development activities are primarily located in a North Carolina facility, with some activities in New York City and Lenexa, Kansas. In April 2015, the company acquired Knights Apparel, a seller of licensed collegiate logo apparel.

FINANCIAL DATA: Note: Data for latest year may not have been available at press time.

In U.S. $	2016	2015	2014	2013	2012	2011
Revenue		5,731,549,000	5,324,746,000	4,627,802,000	4,525,721,000	4,637,143,000
R&D Expense						
Operating Income		595,118,000	563,954,000	515,186,000	440,115,000	478,281,000
Operating Margin %		10.38%	10.59%	11.13%	9.72%	10.31%
SGA Expense		1,541,214,000	1,340,453,000	1,096,507,000	979,932,000	1,062,090,000
Net Income		428,855,000	404,519,000	330,494,000	164,681,000	266,688,000
Operating Cash Flow		227,007,000	508,090,000	591,281,000	548,902,000	167,957,000
Capital Expenditure		99,375,000	64,311,000	43,627,000	40,994,000	90,099,000
EBITDA		699,021,000	662,156,000	606,076,000	533,151,000	569,006,000
Return on Assets %		7.91%	8.68%	8.56%	4.29%	6.81%
Return on Equity %		32.21%	30.91%	31.21%	21.00%	42.88%
Debt to Equity		1.76	1.16	1.19	1.48	2.65

CONTACT INFORMATION:

Phone: 336 519-8080   Fax: 312 726-3712
Toll-Free:
Address: 1000 E. Hanes Mill Rd., Winston-Salem, NC 27105 United States

STOCK TICKER/OTHER:

Stock Ticker: HBI   Exchange: NYS
Employees: 65,300   Fiscal Year Ends: 12/31
Parent Company:

SALARIES/BONUSES:

Top Exec. Salary: Bonus: $
$1,200,000
Second Exec. Salary: Bonus: $
$750,000

OTHER THOUGHTS:

Estimated Female Officers or Directors: 4

Hot Spot for Advancement for Women/Minorities: Y

Hartford Financial Services Group Inc (The) www.thehartford.com

NAIC Code: 524113

TYPES OF BUSINESS:

Life Insurance
Mutual Funds
Property & Casualty Insurance
Group Life & Accident Insurance
Reinsurance
Employee Benefits Administration
Asset Management
Bank Holding Company

BRANDS/DIVISIONS/AFFILIATES:

Hartford Life Insurance Company
Talcott Resolution

CONTACTS: Note: Officers with more than one job title may be intentionally listed here more than once.

Christopher Swift, CEO
Beth Bombara, CFO
Scott Lewis, Chief Accounting Officer
Kathleen Bromage, Chief Marketing Officer
Robert Rupp, Chief Risk Officer
William Bloom, Executive VP, Divisional
Martha Gervasi, Executive VP, Divisional
Raymond Sprague, Executive VP, Divisional
David Robinson, Executive VP
Brion Johnson, Executive VP
James Davey, Executive VP
Douglas Elliot, President
Donald Hunt, Vice President

GROWTH PLANS/SPECIAL FEATURES:

The Hartford Financial Services Group, Inc. is a diversified insurance and financial services company that offers insurance and investment products. Through Hartford Life Insurance Company and its many subsidiaries, it is a leading provider of investment products, individual life, group life and group disability insurance products and property and casualty insurance products in the U.S., Canada and select overseas markets. The Hartford is organized into six major divisions: commercial lines, personal lines, property & casualty and other operations (P&C/other), group benefits, mutual funds and Talcott Resolution. Commercial lines provides standard workers' compensation, property, automobile, liability, marine, livestock and umbrella coverages as well as a variety of customized insurance products and risk management services. Personal lines provides standard automobile, homeowners and home-based business coverages, including a special program designed for members of AARP. P&C/other includes certain property and casualty operations, currently managed by the company, that have discontinued writing new business and substantially all of the company's asbestos and environmental exposure coverage. Group benefits offers group life, accident and disability coverage as well as group retiree health and voluntary benefits to individual members of employer groups. Mutual funds offers investment management, administration, distribution and related services to investors through investment products in both domestic and international markets. Talcott Resolution is comprised of run-off business from the company's U.S. annuity, international annuity and institutional and private-placement life insurance businesses. In 2016, the firm agreed to acquire Northern Homelands Company, the holding company of Maxum Specialty Insurance Group, for $170 million; and agreed to sell its U.K. property & casualty run-off subsidiaries, Downlands Liability Management Limited and Hartford Financial Products International Limited, to Catalina Holdings UK Limited.

The firm offers employees medical, dental and vision insurance; a wellness program; investment, savings, stock & bond purchase plans; and short- and long-term disability.

FINANCIAL DATA: Note: Data for latest year may not have been available at press time.

In U.S. $	2016	2015	2014	2013	2012	2011
Revenue		18,377,000,000	18,614,000,000	26,236,000,000	26,412,000,000	21,859,000,000
R&D Expense						
Operating Income		1,978,000,000	1,699,000,000	63,000,000	-527,000,000	230,000,000
Operating Margin %		10.76%	9.12%	.24%	-1.99%	1.05%
SGA Expense		3,772,000,000	4,028,000,000	4,280,000,000	5,237,000,000	4,398,000,000
Net Income		1,682,000,000	798,000,000	176,000,000	-38,000,000	662,000,000
Operating Cash Flow		2,756,000,000	1,886,000,000	1,237,000,000	2,681,000,000	2,274,000,000
Capital Expenditure		307,000,000	121,000,000			
EBITDA						
Return on Assets %		.71%	.30%	.05%	-.02%	.19%
Return on Equity %		9.25%	4.24%	.81%	-.36%	2.94%
Debt to Equity		0.28	0.30	0.32	0.31	0.29

CONTACT INFORMATION:

Phone: 860 547-5000   Fax: 860 720-6097
Toll-Free:
Address: 690 Asylum Ave., 1 Hartford Plaza, Hartford, CT 06115 United States

STOCK TICKER/OTHER:

Stock Ticker: HIG   Exchange: NYS
Employees: 17,500   Fiscal Year Ends: 12/31
Parent Company:

SALARIES/BONUSES:

Top Exec. Salary: Bonus: $
$1,000,000
Second Exec. Salary: Bonus: $
$900,000

OTHER THOUGHTS:

Estimated Female Officers or Directors: 1

Hot Spot for Advancement for Women/Minorities: Y

HCA Holdings Inc

NAIC Code: 622110

www.hcahealthcare.com

TYPES OF BUSINESS:
General Medical and Surgical Hospitals
Outpatient Surgery Centers
Sub-Acute Care
Psychiatric Hospitals
Rehabilitation Services
Hospital Management Services

BRANDS/DIVISIONS/AFFILIATES:

CONTACTS: Note: Officers with more than one job title may be intentionally listed here more than once.
R. Johnson, CEO
Charles Hall, President, Divisional
William Rutherford, CFO
Martin Paslick, Chief Information Officer
Jonathan Perlin, Chief Medical Officer
Donald Stinnett, Controller
Samuel Hazen, COO
Robert Waterman, General Counsel
Joseph Sowell, Other Executive Officer
Alan Yuspeh, Other Executive Officer
Jane Englebright, Other Executive Officer
Michael Cuffe, President, Divisional
Jon Foster, President, Divisional
A. Moore, President, Divisional
John Franck, Secretary
Victor Campbell, Senior VP
Jana Davis, Senior VP, Divisional

GROWTH PLANS/SPECIAL FEATURES:

HCA Holdings, Inc. owns and operates approximately 168 hospitals and 116 freestanding surgery centers in 20 states and the U.K. The company's acute care hospitals provide a full range of services, including internal medicine, general surgery, neurosurgery, orthopedics, obstetrics, cardiac care, diagnostic services, emergency services, radiology, respiratory therapy, cardiology and physical therapy. The psychiatric hospitals provide therapeutic programs including child, adolescent and adult psychiatric care and adult and adolescent alcohol and drug abuse treatment and counseling. The outpatient health care facilities operated by HCA include surgery centers, diagnostic and imaging centers, comprehensive outpatient rehabilitation and physical therapy centers. The company's hospitals do not engage in extensive medical research and education programs; however, some facilities are affiliated with medical schools and may participate in the clinical rotation of medical interns and residents. In addition, HCA provides a variety of management services to health care facilities such as patient safety programs; ethics and compliance programs; national supply contracts; equipment purchasing and leasing contracts; and accounting, financial and clinical systems. Other services include governmental reimbursement assistance, construction planning and coordination, information technology systems, legal counsel, human resource services and internal audit.

Employee benefits include medical, vision and dental coverage; a 401(k); life insurance; disability; and financial education resources.

FINANCIAL DATA: Note: Data for latest year may not have been available at press time.

In U.S. $	2016	2015	2014	2013	2012	2011
Revenue		39,678,000,000	36,918,000,000	34,182,000,000	33,013,000,000	32,506,000,000
R&D Expense						
Operating Income		5,918,000,000	5,565,000,000	2,946,000,000	4,852,000,000	4,338,000,000
Operating Margin %		14.91%	15.07%	8.61%	14.69%	13.34%
SGA Expense		18,115,000,000	16,641,000,000	15,646,000,000	15,089,000,000	13,440,000,000
Net Income		2,129,000,000	1,875,000,000	1,556,000,000	1,605,000,000	2,465,000,000
Operating Cash Flow		4,734,000,000	4,448,000,000	3,680,000,000	4,175,000,000	3,933,000,000
Capital Expenditure		2,375,000,000	2,176,000,000	1,943,000,000	1,862,000,000	1,679,000,000
EBITDA		7,526,000,000	7,044,000,000	6,547,000,000	6,371,000,000	7,063,000,000
Return on Assets %		6.65%	6.24%	5.46%	5.83%	9.71%
Return on Equity %						
Debt to Equity						

CONTACT INFORMATION:
Phone: 615 344-9551   Fax: 615 320-2266
Toll-Free:
Address: 1 Park Plaza, Nashville, TN 37203 United States

STOCK TICKER/OTHER:
Stock Ticker: HCA
Employees: 225,000
Parent Company:

Exchange: NYS
Fiscal Year Ends: 12/31

SALARIES/BONUSES:
Top Exec. Salary: $1,283,309   Bonus: $
Second Exec. Salary: $945,815   Bonus: $

OTHER THOUGHTS:
Estimated Female Officers or Directors: 2

Hot Spot for Advancement for Women/Minorities:

Health Care Service Corporation (HCSC)

www.hcsc.com

NAIC Code: 524114

TYPES OF BUSINESS:

Insurance-Medical & Health, HMOs & PPOs
Traditional Indemnity Plans
Medicare Supplemental Health
Life Insurance
Dental & Vision Insurance
Electronic Claims & Information Network
Workers' Compensation
Retirement Services

BRANDS/DIVISIONS/AFFILIATES:

Blue Cross and Blue Shield of Illinois
Blue Cross and Blue Shield of Texas
Blue Cross and Blue Shield of New Mexico
Blue Cross and Blue Shield of Oklahoma
Blue Cross and Blue Shield of Montana
Prime Therapeutics LLC
Dental Network of America Inc
TMG Health

CONTACTS: Note: Officers with more than one job title may be intentionally listed here more than once.

Paula Steiner, CEO
Colleen Reitan, Exec.VP-Plan Oper.
Eric Feldstein, Sr.VP
Nazneen Razi, Chief Human Resources Officer
Stephen Ondra, Chief Medical Officer
Karen Atwood, Exec. VP-IT
John Cannon, Chief Admin. Officer
Deborah Dorman-Rodriguez, Corp. Sec.
Martin G. Foster, Pres., Plan Oper.
Paula A. Steiner, Chief Strategy Officer
Ross Blackstone, Contact-Media
Ted Haynes, Pres., Oklahoma Div.
Kurt Shipley, Pres., New Mexico Div.
Karen M. Atwood, Pres., Illinois Div.
Bert E. Marshall, Pres., Texas Div.

GROWTH PLANS/SPECIAL FEATURES:

Health Care Service Corporation (HCSC) is a customer-owned health insurer which operates through its Blue Cross and Blue Shield divisions in Illinois, Montana, Texas, New Mexico and Oklahoma. It also has several subsidiaries that offer a variety of health and life insurance products and related services to employers and individuals. It provides PPOs, HMOs, POS plans, traditional indemnity and Medicare supplemental health plans to over 15 million members through Blue Cross and Blue Shield of Illinois, Blue Cross and Blue Shield of Oklahoma, Blue Cross and Blue Shield of Texas, Blue Cross and Blue Shield of Montana and Blue Cross and Blue Shield of New Mexico. Through its non-Blue Cross and Blue Shield subsidiaries, the company offers prescription drug plans, Medicare supplemental insurance, dental and vision coverage, life and disability insurance, workers' compensation, retirement services and medical financial services. One such subsidiary, Dental Network of America, Inc., functions as a third-party administrator for all company dental programs and is registered in every state except Florida. It also offers a dental discount card program. Availity, LLC, a partially-owned subsidiary, operates a health care clearinghouse and provides Internet-based health information services. TMG Health offers business process outsourcing (BPO) for Medicare and Medicaid. Dearborn National operates as the brand name for HCSC's ancillary benefits subsidiaries, offering group life, disability, dental, worksite and voluntary products. Other subsidiaries include Medecisions, Inc.; HCSC Insurance Service Company; Prime Therapeutics, LLC; and TriWest Healthcare Alliance.

Employee benefits include medical coverage, 401(k), a pension plan, life & AD&D insurance, dependent life coverage, short- and long-term disability, educational assistance, flexible spending accounts, transportation reimbursement, group legal service, an employee assistance program, adoption assistance and a wellness program.

FINANCIAL DATA: Note: Data for latest year may not have been available at press time.

In U.S. $	2016	2015	2014	2013	2012	2011
Revenue		35,000,000,000	31,200,000,000	22,690,000,000	20,714,282,000	19,958,096,000
R&D Expense						
Operating Income						
Operating Margin %						
SGA Expense						
Net Income		-65,800,000	-281,000,000	684,300,000	1,007,066,000	1,203,879,000
Operating Cash Flow						
Capital Expenditure						
EBITDA						
Return on Assets %						
Return on Equity %						
Debt to Equity						

CONTACT INFORMATION:

Phone: 312-653-6000   Fax: 312-819-1220
Toll-Free: 800-654-7385
Address: 300 E. Randolph St., Chicago, IL 60601 United States

STOCK TICKER/OTHER:

Stock Ticker: Mutual Company   Exchange:
Employees: 23,000   Fiscal Year Ends: 12/31
Parent Company:

SALARIES/BONUSES:

Top Exec. Salary: $ Bonus: $
Second Exec. Salary: $ Bonus: $

OTHER THOUGHTS:

Estimated Female Officers or Directors: 6
Hot Spot for Advancement for Women/Minorities: Y

HealthSouth Corporation

www.healthsouth.com

NAIC Code: 622310

TYPES OF BUSINESS:

Rehabilitation Facilities
Long-term Care Hospitals
Home Health Programs

BRANDS/DIVISIONS/AFFILIATES:

Cardinal Hill Rehabilitation Hospital
Reliant Hospital Partners LLC
CareSouth Health System Inc

CONTACTS: *Note: Officers with more than one job title may be intentionally listed here more than once.*

April Anthony, CEO, Subsidiary
Jay Grinney, CEO
Douglas Coltharp, CFO
Andrew Price, Chief Accounting Officer
Elissa Charbonneau, Chief Medical Officer
Mark Tarr, COO
Leo Higdon, Director
Cheryl Levy, Other Executive Officer
John Darby, Secretary
Edmund Fay, Senior VP

GROWTH PLANS/SPECIAL FEATURES:

HealthSouth Corporation is a major provider of post-acute healthcare services. The company offers both facility-based and home-based post-acute services in 34 states and Puerto Rico through its network of inpatient rehabilitation hospitals, home health agencies and hospice agencies. HealthSouth manages its operations via two segments: inpatient rehabilitation and home health & hospice. Inpatient rehabilitation comprises 121 hospitals with more than 8,000 licensed beds. This segment provides specialized rehabilitation treatment on both an inpatient and outpatient basis. Inpatient rehabilitation hospitals offer specialized rehabilitative care across an array of diagnosis and deliver comprehensive, high-quality, cost-effective patient care services. During 2015, this segment discharged more than 149,000 patients and had over 577,000 outpatient visits. Home health & hospice comprises 186 home health locations and 27 hospice locations. It is the nation's fourth largest provider of Medicare-certified home nursing services to adult patients in need of care. These services include, among others, skilled nursing, physical/occupational/speech therapy, medical social work and home health aide services. Home health admitted more than 74,000 patients and home hospice admitted 2,452 patients in 2015. In 2015, the firm acquired Cardinal Hill Rehabilitation Hospital in Lexington, Kentucky; and acquired both Reliant Hospital Partners LLC and the home health agency operations of CareSouth Health System, Inc.

The firm offers employees medical, dental and vision insurance; flexible spending accounts; life and disability insurance; a 401(k) plan; a 529 college savings plan; pre-paid legal services; and an employee assistance plan.

FINANCIAL DATA: *Note: Data for latest year may not have been available at press time.*

In U.S. $	2016	2015	2014	2013	2012	2011
Revenue		3,115,700,000	2,374,300,000	2,247,200,000	2,134,900,000	2,026,900,000
R&D Expense						
Operating Income		546,700,000	467,400,000	482,300,000	416,900,000	386,400,000
Operating Margin %		17.54%	19.68%	21.46%	19.52%	19.06%
SGA Expense		1,997,200,000	1,449,300,000	1,347,200,000	1,331,700,000	1,252,400,000
Net Income		183,100,000	222,000,000	323,600,000	185,000,000	208,700,000
Operating Cash Flow		484,800,000	444,900,000	470,300,000	411,500,000	342,700,000
Capital Expenditure		156,500,000	187,900,000	216,500,000	159,700,000	109,100,000
EBITDA		678,200,000	603,800,000	590,300,000	516,600,000	441,100,000
Return on Assets %		4.52%	7.25%	9.31%	6.82%	7.86%
Return on Equity %		33.46%	59.53%	230.07%		
Debt to Equity		5.12	4.46	5.98		

CONTACT INFORMATION:

Phone: 205 967-7116   Fax: 205 969-4740
Toll-Free: 800-765-4772
Address: 3660 Grandview Pkwy., Ste. 200, Birmingham, AL 35243
United States

STOCK TICKER/OTHER:

Stock Ticker: HLS   Exchange: NYS
Employees: 24,100   Fiscal Year Ends: 12/31
Parent Company:

SALARIES/BONUSES:

Top Exec. Salary: $1,000,000   Bonus: $
Second Exec. Salary: $625,000   Bonus: $

OTHER THOUGHTS:

Estimated Female Officers or Directors: 8

Hot Spot for Advancement for Women/Minorities: Y

Heartland Payment Systems Inc   www.heartlandpaymentsystems.com

NAIC Code: 522320

TYPES OF BUSINESS:

Financial Processing Services
Credit/Debit Processing
Payroll Processing Services
Processing Equipment Provider
Micropayments

BRANDS/DIVISIONS/AFFILIATES:

HPS Exchange
Heartland Payroll Company
Heartland Marketing Solutions
Dinerware
pcAmerica
Payroll 1
Digital Dining
Beanstalk Data

CONTACTS: Note: Officers with more than one job title may be intentionally listed here more than once.

Robert Carr, CEO
Samir Zabaneh, CFO
Charles Kallenbach, General Counsel
David Gilbert, President, Divisional
Michael Lawler, President, Divisional
Robert Baldwin, Vice Chairman

GROWTH PLANS/SPECIAL FEATURES:

Heartland Payment Systems, Inc. (HPS) is a provider of credit/debit card, payroll and other associated processing services to approximately 182,526 U.S. bankcard merchants. HPS primarily serves restaurant, hospitality, hotel and retail merchants throughout the U.S. The firm's services include credit/debit card processing, payroll services and the HPS Exchange, while products include gift cards (with company logos), terminals, printers and other processing equipment. Its credit/debit card processing services allow clients to extend a variety of payment options to customers; the firm processes all major credit cards, including Visa, MasterCard, American Express, Diners Club, JCB and Discover, 24 hours per day 365 days a year. The company's payroll services, which it provides through Heartland Payroll Company, entail calculation of payroll checks (which includes taxes, voluntary reductions, retirement plans and direct deposit), tax returns/filing concerns and additional services, such as reimbursement checks and automated check signing. The HPS Exchange is a company-developed transaction processing platform with added features unique to HPS. The platform features fast transaction processing, customized reports/receipts and online merchant management, which allows retailers to immediately view transaction processing details in real time. Additional products and services offered by the firm include K-12 school solutions, primarily school nutrition programs and point of sale (POS) systems at over 34,000 schools; micropayment services; campus solutions, which include networked payment solutions for college campuses; and loyalty and Heartland Marketing Solutions, which comprise loyalty and gift card programs. During 2015, the firm acquired POS companies Dinerware and pcAmerica; Payroll 1; and Digital Dining. In early 2016, the company acquired Beanstalk Data, a provider of customer engagement platform.

HPS offers its employees health, dental and life insurance; short- and long-term disability; flexible spending and dependent care accounts; and the option to add additional life insurance for spouses and dependents.

FINANCIAL DATA: Note: Data for latest year may not have been available at press time.

In U.S. $	2016	2015	2014	2013	2012	2011
Revenue		2,682,395,904	2,311,380,992	2,135,372,032	2,013,436,032	1,996,950,016
R&D Expense						
Operating Income						
Operating Margin %						
SGA Expense						
Net Income		84,732,000	33,879,000	78,626,000	65,889,000	43,939,000
Operating Cash Flow						
Capital Expenditure						
EBITDA						
Return on Assets %						
Return on Equity %						
Debt to Equity						

CONTACT INFORMATION:

Phone: 609 683-3831   Fax: 609 683-3815
Toll-Free: 888-963-3600
Address: 90 Nassau St., Princeton, NJ 08542 United States

STOCK TICKER/OTHER:

Stock Ticker: Subsidiary   Exchange:
Employees: 3,734   Fiscal Year Ends: 12/31
Parent Company: Global Payments Inc

SALARIES/BONUSES:

Top Exec. Salary: $ Bonus: $
Second Exec. Salary: $ Bonus: $

OTHER THOUGHTS:

Estimated Female Officers or Directors: 2
Hot Spot for Advancement for Women/Minorities:

HEB Grocery Company LP

www.heb.com

NAIC Code: 445110

TYPES OF BUSINESS:

Supermarkets
Grocery Stores
Gourmet Food Stores
Dairy Processing
Bakery
Pharmacy Services

BRANDS/DIVISIONS/AFFILIATES:

H-E-B
Central Market
H-E-B plus!
Joe V's Smart Shop
Temple Retail Support Center

CONTACTS: Note: Officers with more than one job title may be intentionally listed here more than once.

Charles C. Butt, CEO
Craig Boyan, COO
Craig Boyan, Pres.
Martin Otto, CFO
Martin Otto, Chief Merchant
Judy Lindquist, General Counsel
Lynette Padalecki, VP-Corp. Planning & Analysis
Winell Herron, VP-Public Affairs & Diversity
Scott McClelland, Pres., Houston Food & Drug Stores Div.
Suzanne Wade, Pres., San Antonio Food & Drug Stores Div.
William Fry, VP-Quality Assurance & Environmental Affairs
Roxanne Orsak, Exec. VP-Drug
Charles C. Butt, Chmn.
Mike Graham, Sr. VP-Logistics & Supply Chain

GROWTH PLANS/SPECIAL FEATURES:

HEB Grocery Company LP is one of the largest regional food retailers in the southwestern U.S. and Mexico. It operates over 370 grocery stores in 150 communities in Texas and Mexico under the H-E-B brand name. The firm owns one of the largest milk plants in Texas as well as a large bread bakery, a meat plant, a pastry bakery, an ice cream plant, a chip plant and a photo processing lab. The stores carry a wide variety of merchandise, including a line of products under the H-E-B brand. H-E-B also operates nine Central Market stores, with locations in Houston, Dallas, Fort Worth, Plano, San Antonio, Southlake and Austin. Central Markets are gourmet specialty stores featuring large prepared foods-to-go areas, eat-in areas, comprehensive wine departments, specialty butcher and fish counters, a European bakery, a deli with meats, a large selection of cheeses from around the globe and a juice and ice cream bar. H-E-B plus! stores offer additional departments including Cook & Grill, Card & Party and a Tortilleria. The firm also owns a series of seven discount stores in the Houston and Baytown, Texas area known as Joe V's Smart Shop. HEB Grocery owns and operates a retail support center in Monterrey, Mexico, as well as the Temple Retail Support Center, a 450,000 square foot warehouse and transportation facility in central Texas.

Employees of the firm are offered a variety of benefits, including discounts on groceries and a prescription plan. In 2015, the company launched a benefit whereby qualified employees receive an annual grant of shares of nonvoting stock equal to 3% of wages.

FINANCIAL DATA: Note: Data for latest year may not have been available at press time.

In U.S. $	2016	2015	2014	2013	2012	2011
Revenue		23,000,000,000	22,000,000,000	20,400,000,000	19,750,000,000	19,125,000,000
R&D Expense						
Operating Income						
Operating Margin %						
SGA Expense						
Net Income						
Operating Cash Flow						
Capital Expenditure						
EBITDA						
Return on Assets %						
Return on Equity %						
Debt to Equity						

CONTACT INFORMATION:

Phone: 210-938-8000   Fax: 210-938-8169
Toll-Free: 800-432-3113
Address: 646 S. Main Ave, San Antonio, TX 78204 United States

STOCK TICKER/OTHER:

Stock Ticker: Private   Exchange:
Employees: 96,000   Fiscal Year Ends: 10/31
Parent Company:

SALARIES/BONUSES:

Top Exec. Salary: $ Bonus: $
Second Exec. Salary: $ Bonus: $

OTHER THOUGHTS:

Estimated Female Officers or Directors: 5
Hot Spot for Advancement for Women/Minorities: Y

Hendrick Automotive Group

www.hendrickauto.com

NAIC Code: 441110

TYPES OF BUSINESS:

Auto Dealers, Retail
Parts & Service
Accessories
Racing & Motorsports

BRANDS/DIVISIONS/AFFILIATES:

Hendrick Motorsports
Hendrick Marrow Program
Hendrick Autoguard
Hendrick KIA Charlotte

CONTACTS: Note: Officers with more than one job title may be intentionally listed here more than once.

Edward J. Brown, III, CEO
Edward J. Brown, III, Pres.
Brian Williams, VP-Mktg. & Advertising
Veronica Zayatz, VP-Acct., Audits & Taxes
Rick Hendrick, Chmn.

GROWTH PLANS/SPECIAL FEATURES:

Hendrick Automotive Group sells new and used automobiles from 29 automakers, including Acura, Lincoln, Subaru, Toyota, Ford, Audi, KIA, Fiat, Scion, Hyundai, Honda, GMC, Porsche, BMW, Cadillac and Volvo. It boasts a network of 102 dealerships in 14 states across the U.S. as well as 143 franchise locations. The firm's automobile offerings include cars as well as light trucks. Hendrick Automotive offers other services, including financing, maintenance, body repair and parts and accessories. The group has 29 collision centers and four accessories distributor installers located across the U.S. Customers can access a database of pre-owned and new cars on the company web site. Through the Hendrick Autoguard partner, the company offers warranty and vehicle protection plans for new and used cars and trucks. Hendrick Automotive also supports charitable operations including the Hendrick Marrow Program, which recruits potential matching marrow donors, raises funds for tissue typing and offers support for those suffering from leukemia and other blood-related diseases. In addition, Hendrick Automotive operates Hendrick Motorsports, which sponsors a number of NASCAR teams. In February 2016, the firm acquired North Carolina-based Folger KIA East from Folger Automotive, relocated it to East Independence Blvd. and subsequently renamed it Hendrick KIA Charlotte.

FINANCIAL DATA: Note: Data for latest year may not have been available at press time.

In U.S. $	2016	2015	2014	2013	2012	2011
Revenue		8,400,000,000	7,500,000,000	7,000,000,000	5,900,000,000	4,900,000,000
R&D Expense						
Operating Income						
Operating Margin %						
SGA Expense						
Net Income						
Operating Cash Flow						
Capital Expenditure						
EBITDA						
Return on Assets %						
Return on Equity %						
Debt to Equity						

CONTACT INFORMATION:

Phone: 704-568-5550   Fax: 704-566-3295
Toll-Free:
Address: 6000 Monroe Rd., Ste. 100, Charlotte, NC 28212 United States

STOCK TICKER/OTHER:

Stock Ticker: Private   Exchange:
Employees: 10,000   Fiscal Year Ends: 12/31
Parent Company:

SALARIES/BONUSES:

Top Exec. Salary: $ Bonus: $
Second Exec. Salary: $ Bonus: $

OTHER THOUGHTS:

Estimated Female Officers or Directors: 1
Hot Spot for Advancement for Women/Minorities:

Henry Schein Inc

www.henryschein.com

NAIC Code: 423450

TYPES OF BUSINESS:

Health Care Products Distribution
Dental Supplies Distribution
Veterinary Products Distribution
Electronic Catalogs

BRANDS/DIVISIONS/AFFILIATES:

Henry Schein Animal Health
Oasis
Dentrix
EXACT
MicroMD
RxWorks Inc
Dental Cremer SA
Custom Automated Prosthetics

CONTACTS: *Note: Officers with more than one job title may be intentionally listed here more than once.*

Lonnie Shoff, CEO, Divisional
Michael Ettinger, Secretary
James Breslawski, CEO, Divisional
Stanley Bergman, CEO
Steven Paladino, CFO
Gerald Benjamin, Chief Administrative Officer
James Harding, Chief Technology Officer
Mark Mlotek, Director
Walter Siegel, General Counsel
Stanley Komaroff, Other Corporate Officer
Michael Racioppi, Other Executive Officer
Peter McCarthy, President, Divisional
Robert Minowitz, President, Divisional
David McKinley, President, Divisional
Paul Rose, Senior VP, Divisional
Lorelei McGlynn, Senior VP, Divisional
Paul Rose, Senior VP, Divisional

GROWTH PLANS/SPECIAL FEATURES:

Henry Schein, Inc. distributes products and services to office-based health care practitioners in North America and Europe. The firm has more than 1 million customers worldwide and distributes more than 110,000 national and Henry Schein private-brand products and 150,000 special-order items. The company operates in two segments: health care distribution and technology. The health care distribution segment, which accounts for roughly 96.6% of annual revenue, aggregates the dental, medical and animal health divisions. This segment distributes branded and generic pharmaceuticals, small equipment, laboratory products, large dental equipment, consumable products, infection-control products, vaccines, diagnostic tests, surgical products and vitamins. Through Henry Schein Animal Health, a majority-owned subsidiary, the firm distributes animal health products in Europe as well as the U.S., Australia and New Zealand. The technology segment provides software, technology and other value-added services to health care practitioners, primarily in the U.S. and Canada. Value-added solutions include practice-management software systems for dental and medical practitioners and animal health clinics. Practice-management software solutions include Oasis, Dentrix, EXACT and Easy Dental for dental practices; DVM Manager and AVImark for veterinary clinics; and MicroMD for physician usage. The technology group also provides financial services and continuing education for practitioners. In 2016, the firm acquired the following: RxWorks, Inc., provider of veterinary practice management software; a majority stake in Dental Cremer SA, a distributor of dental supplies and equipment; and Custom Automated Prosthetics, a digital laboratory supply company.

The company offers employees medical, dental, vision, life, AD&D and disability insurance; flexible spending accounts; 401(k); college savings plan; tuition assistance; and paid time off.

FINANCIAL DATA: *Note: Data for latest year may not have been available at press time.*

In U.S. $	2016	2015	2014	2013	2012	2011
Revenue		10,629,720,000	10,371,390,000	9,560,647,000	8,939,967,000	8,530,242,000
R&D Expense						
Operating Income		733,972,000	715,142,000	677,054,000	618,961,000	582,149,000
Operating Margin %		6.90%	6.89%	7.08%	6.92%	6.82%
SGA Expense		2,243,356,000	2,196,173,000	1,978,960,000	1,873,360,000	1,835,906,000
Net Income		479,058,000	466,077,000	431,554,000	388,076,000	367,661,000
Operating Cash Flow		586,841,000	592,504,000	664,175,000	408,099,000	554,625,000
Capital Expenditure		71,684,000	82,116,000	60,215,000	51,237,000	45,176,000
EBITDA		905,893,000	885,607,000	820,267,000	760,412,000	715,580,000
Return on Assets %		7.57%	7.92%	7.87%	7.70%	7.91%
Return on Equity %		16.81%	16.64%	15.98%	15.38%	15.18%
Debt to Equity		0.16	0.19	0.16	0.18	0.14

CONTACT INFORMATION:

Phone: 631 843-5500   Fax: 631 843-5665
Toll-Free:
Address: 135 Duryea Rd., Melville, NY 11747 United States

STOCK TICKER/OTHER:

Stock Ticker: HSIC
Employees: 19,000
Parent Company:

Exchange: NAS
Fiscal Year Ends: 12/31

SALARIES/BONUSES:

Top Exec. Salary: $1,353,308   Bonus: $

Second Exec. Salary: $704,692   Bonus: $

OTHER THOUGHTS:

Estimated Female Officers or Directors: 6

Hot Spot for Advancement for Women/Minorities: Y

Sales, profits and employees may be estimates. Financial information, benefits and other data can change quickly and may vary from those stated here.

Hershey Co

NAIC Code: 311351

www.hersheys.com

TYPES OF BUSINESS:

Candy Manufacturing
Baking Supplies
Chocolate Products
Confectionaries & Snacks
Amusement Parks
Resorts/Hotels

BRANDS/DIVISIONS/AFFILIATES:

Kit Kat
Reese's
Hershey Kisses
Hershey's Chocolate World
Scharffen Berger
Artisan Confections Company
Hershey India Confectionery Private Limited
Allan Candy Company

CONTACTS: Note: Officers with more than one job title may be intentionally listed here more than once.

Michele Buck, COO

GROWTH PLANS/SPECIAL FEATURES:

Hershey Co. is one of the largest candy makers in the U.S. manufacturing more than 80 brand names in the chocolate sweets and refreshment business. The company's products are marketed in approximately 70 countries worldwide. Its operations are aggregated into two segments: North America and International & Other. Hershey's principal product groups include chocolate and non-chocolate confectionery products such as Reese's, Kit Kat, Hershey Bars and Hershey Kisses packaged items; and grocery products, such as baking ingredients, chocolate drink mixes, peanut butter, dessert toppings and beverages. Its products are sold primarily to wholesale distributors, chain grocery stores, mass merchandisers, chain drug stores, vending companies, wholesale clubs, convenience stores, dollar stores, concessionaires, department stores and natural food stores. Its direct retail operations, including Hershey's Chocolate World in Hershey, Pennsylvania, and Hershey's retail stores in New York City, Chicago, Niagara Falls (Ontario), Shanghai, Dubai and Singapore, are managed by The Hershey Experience. Wholly-owned subsidiary Artisan Confections Company produces Scharffen Berger high-cacao dark chocolate products and Dagoba natural and organic chocolate products. Hershey also produces products in China through Lotte Shanghai Foods Company; markets its Van Houten brand products in the Middle East and Asia; and also markets through Godrej Hershey Ltd., a wholly-owned subsidiary known as Hershey India Confectionery Private Limited. In December 2014, the firm acquired the Canadian confectionery manufacturer Allan Candy Company. In January 2015 Hershey announced it will acquire KRAVE Pure Foods, Inc. manufacturer of KRAVE jerky.

The firm offers employees health, dental and vision insurance; an employee assistance program; life insurance; disability coverage; onsite fitness centers; gym membership reimbursement; a 401(k) plan; retirement contributions; an employee stock purchase plan; health care and dependent care spending accounts; store discounts; adoption assistance and tuition reimbursement.

FINANCIAL DATA: Note: Data for latest year may not have been available at press time.

In U.S. $	2016	2015	2014	2013	2012	2011
Revenue		7,386,626,000	7,421,768,000	7,146,079,000	6,644,252,000	6,080,788,000
R&D Expense						
Operating Income		1,037,759,000	1,389,575,000	1,339,675,000	1,111,148,000	1,055,028,000
Operating Margin %		14.04%	18.72%	18.74%	16.72%	17.35%
SGA Expense		2,064,114,000	1,900,970,000	1,922,508,000	1,703,796,000	1,477,750,000
Net Income		512,951,000	846,912,000	820,470,000	660,931,000	628,962,000
Operating Cash Flow		1,214,456,000	838,221,000	1,188,405,000	1,094,827,000	580,867,000
Capital Expenditure		356,810,000	370,789,000	350,911,000	277,966,000	347,567,000
EBITDA		1,227,758,000	1,605,173,000	1,543,866,000	1,324,125,000	1,273,388,000
Return on Assets %		9.34%	15.41%	16.22%	14.41%	14.48%
Return on Equity %		41.82%	55.35%	62.11%	70.09%	71.82%
Debt to Equity		1.56	1.06	1.11	1.47	2.05

CONTACT INFORMATION:

Phone: 717 534-4200   Fax: 717 531-6161
Toll-Free: 800-468-1714
Address: 100 Crystal A Dr., Hershey, PA 17033 United States

STOCK TICKER/OTHER:

Stock Ticker: HSY   Exchange: NYS
Employees: 14,800   Fiscal Year Ends: 12/31
Parent Company:

SALARIES/BONUSES:

Top Exec. Salary: Bonus: $
$1,204,616
Second Exec. Salary: Bonus: $
$655,310

OTHER THOUGHTS:

Estimated Female Officers or Directors: 4

Hot Spot for Advancement for Women/Minorities: Y

Sales, profits and employees may be estimates. Financial information, benefits and other data can change quickly and may vary from those stated here.

Hertz Global Holdings Inc

www.hertz.com

NAIC Code: 532111

TYPES OF BUSINESS:

Automobile Rental
Truck Rental
Claims Management
Heavy Equipment Rental
Used Automobile Sales
Leasing
Actuarial Services
Franchising

BRANDS/DIVISIONS/AFFILIATES:

Hertz Claims Management
Hertz
Dollar
Thrifty
Firefly
Donlen
Donlen Corporation

CONTACTS: *Note: Officers with more than one job title may be intentionally listed here more than once.*

Lawrence Silber, CEO, Subsidiary
John Tague, CEO
Thomas Kennedy, CFO
Robin Kramer, Chief Accounting Officer
Tyler Best, Chief Information Officer
Linda Levinson, Director
Robert Stuart, Executive VP, Divisional
Richard Frecker, Other Corporate Officer
Jeffrey Foland, Other Executive Officer
Michel Taride, President, Divisional

GROWTH PLANS/SPECIAL FEATURES:

Hertz Global Holdings, Inc. owns one of the largest worldwide airport general-use car rental brands and one of the largest equipment rental businesses in the U.S. and Canada. Hertz is the number one airport car rental brand in the U.S. and at 125 major airports in Europe. The company operates in four segments: U.S. car rental, international car rental, worldwide equipment rental and other operations. U.S. car rental rents cars, crossovers and light trucks, and also provides ancillary products and services. This segment has franchises and associates that operate rental locations under the Hertz, Dollar, Thrifty, Firefly and Donlen brands throughout the USA. International car rental rents the same vehicles and provides the same products and services as the U.S. division, only internationally. This segment maintains a network of company-operated car rental locations, a majority of which are in Europe. Its franchisees and associates also operate rental locations in approximately 150 countries and jurisdictions. Worldwide equipment rental rents industrial, construction, material handling and other equipment. It rents a broad range of earthmoving, material handling, aerial and electrical equipment, air compressors, power generators, pumps, small tools, compaction equipment, construction-related trucks and other types of commercial vehicles. This division's Hertz Entertainment Services unit rents studio and production equipment products used primarily in the U.S. entertainment industry. Other operations comprise the firm's Donlen Corporation, which provides fleet leasing and management services; and subsidiary Hertz Claims Management, which provides claim management services. U.S. car rental derives 60% of company revenues, international car rental derives 20%, worldwide equipment derives 14% and other operations derives 6%. In June 2016, the firm reached an agreement with Lyft to supply rental car rates for drivers who can either use the cars for Lyft business or for personal driving. Lyft provides ridesharing in more than 200 U.S. cities.

FINANCIAL DATA: *Note: Data for latest year may not have been available at press time.*

In U.S. $	2016	2015	2014	2013	2012	2011
Revenue		10,535,000,000	11,046,000,000	10,771,900,000	9,020,807,000	8,298,380,000
R&D Expense						
Operating Income		832,000,000	610,000,000	1,472,200,000	450,545,000	1,080,985,000
Operating Margin %		7.89%	5.52%	13.66%	4.99%	13.02%
SGA Expense		1,045,000,000	1,088,000,000	1,022,200,000	945,784,000	745,278,000
Net Income		273,000,000	-82,000,000	346,200,000	243,079,000	176,170,000
Operating Cash Flow		3,332,000,000	3,452,000,000	3,589,600,000	2,717,983,000	2,233,339,000
Capital Expenditure		12,985,000,000	11,663,000,000	10,612,200,000	312,786,000	9,736,006,000
EBITDA		3,874,000,000	3,930,000,000	4,150,900,000	3,425,493,000	3,061,645,000
Return on Assets %		1.15%	- .33%	1.44%	1.18%	1.00%
Return on Equity %		12.17%	-3.13%	13.11%	10.25%	8.10%
Debt to Equity		7.87	6.49	5.88	6.16	5.06

CONTACT INFORMATION:

Phone: 239-301-7000   Fax:
Toll-Free: 800-654-3131
Address: 8501 Williams Road, Estero, FL 33928 United States

STOCK TICKER/OTHER:

Stock Ticker: HTZ   Exchange: NYS
Employees: 30,400   Fiscal Year Ends: 12/31
Parent Company:

SALARIES/BONUSES:

Top Exec. Salary: $800,962   Bonus: $2,647,500
Second Exec. Salary: Bonus: $2,780,000
$553,846

OTHER THOUGHTS:

Estimated Female Officers or Directors: 6
Hot Spot for Advancement for Women/Minorities: Y

Hibbett Sports Inc

NAIC Code: 451110

www.hibbett.com

TYPES OF BUSINESS:

Sporting Goods Stores
Sports Apparel
Athletic Shoes
Training Equipment

BRANDS/DIVISIONS/AFFILIATES:

Hibbett Sports
Hibbett Team Sales Inc
Sports Additions

CONTACTS: Note: Officers with more than one job title may be intentionally listed here more than once.

Jeffry Rosenthal, CEO
Scott Bowman, CFO
Michael Newsome, Chairman of the Board
Jared Briskin, Other Executive Officer
Elaine Rodgers, Secretary
Cathy Pryor, Senior VP, Divisional

GROWTH PLANS/SPECIAL FEATURES:

Hibbett Sports, Inc. is an operator of sporting goods stores in small to mid-sized markets predominantly in the Southeast, Southwest, Midwest and Mid-Atlantic U.S. Its stores offer a broad assortment of athletic equipment, footwear and apparel. The company's merchandise assortment features a broad selection of brand name merchandise emphasizing team sports complemented by localized apparel and accessories designed to appeal to a wide range of customers. Hibbett operates a total of 1000 stores in 32 states. The firm's primary retail format is Hibbett Sports, a 5,000-square-foot store model located in strip centers frequently within in close proximity to Wal-Mart stores. Sports Additions stores are mall-based stores averaging 2,500 square feet with roughly 90% of merchandise consisting of athletic footwear and the remainder consisting of caps and a limited assortment of apparel. Sports Additions stores offer a broader assortment of athletic footwear, with a greater emphasis on fashion than the athletic footwear choices offered by traditional Hibbett Sports stores. Subsidiary Hibbett Team Sales, Inc. supplies customized athletic apparel, equipment and footwear to school, athletic and youth programs in Alabama, Georgia, Mississippi and Florida. It sells its merchandise directly to educational institutions and youth associations.

The firm offers employees life, disability, medical and dental insurance; a vision care plan; a stock purchase plan; a 401(k) plan; employee discounts; and a 529 college savings plan.

FINANCIAL DATA: Note: Data for latest year may not have been available at press time.

In U.S. $	2016	2015	2014	2013	2012	2011
Revenue	943,104,000	913,486,000	851,965,000	818,700,000	732,645,000	664,954,000
R&D Expense						
Operating Income	112,004,000	118,146,000	113,891,000	115,981,000	93,531,000	73,547,000
Operating Margin %	11.87%	12.93%	13.36%	14.16%	12.76%	11.06%
SGA Expense	203,673,000	192,648,000	181,527,000	169,872,000	155,672,000	143,232,000
Net Income	70,528,000	73,584,000	70,877,000	72,582,000	59,060,000	46,400,000
Operating Cash Flow	58,479,000	102,392,000	53,301,000	87,124,000	54,921,000	61,918,000
Capital Expenditure	25,147,000	22,873,000	50,507,000	21,970,000	12,997,000	10,476,000
EBITDA	129,073,000	134,158,000	127,749,000	129,024,000	106,761,000	87,212,000
Return on Assets %	15.76%	16.94%	17.86%	21.00%	18.81%	15.70%
Return on Equity %	22.19%	23.40%	26.09%	32.77%	29.24%	24.73%
Debt to Equity	0.01				0.01	0.01

CONTACT INFORMATION:

Phone: 205 942-4292   Fax: 205 912-7290
Toll-Free:
Address: 2700 Milan Court, Birmingham, AL 35211 United States

STOCK TICKER/OTHER:

Stock Ticker: HIBB   Exchange: NAS
Employees: 8,900   Fiscal Year Ends: 01/31
Parent Company:

SALARIES/BONUSES:

Top Exec. Salary: $510,000   Bonus: $
Second Exec. Salary: Bonus: $
$395,000

OTHER THOUGHTS:

Estimated Female Officers or Directors: 3
Hot Spot for Advancement for Women/Minorities: Y

Hillenbrand Inc

NAIC Code: 333120

www.hillenbrandinc.com

TYPES OF BUSINESS:
Materials Handling Equipment
Burial Caskets and Cases Manufacturing
Conveying Equipment
Size Reduction Equipment

BRANDS/DIVISIONS/AFFILIATES:
Batesville Casket Company
Coperion K-Tron
Coperion GmbH
Rotex Global LLC
TerraSource Global
ABEL Pumps LP
Abel GmbH & Co KG
Red Valve Company

CONTACTS: Note: Officers with more than one job title may be intentionally listed here more than once.
Joe Raver, CEO
F. Loughrey, Chairman of the Board
Eric Teegarden, Chief Accounting Officer
Diane Bohman, Chief Administrative Officer
Nicholas Farrell, General Counsel
Tory Flynn, Other Corporate Officer
John Zerkle, Other Corporate Officer
Kimberly Ryan, President, Divisional
Christopher Trainor, President, Subsidiary
Scott George, Senior VP, Divisional
William Canady, Senior VP, Divisional
Kristina Cerniglia, Senior VP
Theodore Haddad, Treasurer

GROWTH PLANS/SPECIAL FEATURES:
Hillenbrand, Inc. is a holding company involved in funeral products and bulk solid material handling equipment. The firm operates through two primary business platforms: Batesville and process equipment group. Batesville, which includes subsidiary Batesville Casket Company, manufactures and sells non-gasketed steel, hardwood and veneer hardwood caskets as well as cloth-covered and all-wood caskets. Additional products include urns, containers and other similar products. The company's hardwood caskets are made from mahogany, cherry, walnut, maple, pile, oak, pecan, poplar and sycamore woods, and are manufactured to resist the entrance of outside elements as well as rust and corrosion. Urns and containers are primarily made of hardwoods, fiberboard, bronze, acrylic and marble. Brands within this segment include Batesville, Marsellus, Dimensions and Cremation Options. The process equipment group segment designs, produces, markets, sells and services feeders and pneumatic conveying equipment as well as equipment that is used to reduce materials in size, such as coal-crushing tools. The segment consists of four companies: Coperion GmbH, which is involved in compounding and extruding equipment, bulk materials handling systems and related engineering services; Coperion K-Tron, a subsidiary of Coperion that focuses on feeding and pneumatic conveying equipment; Rotex Global LLC, which manufactures separation equipment, such as gyratory and vibratory screeners and sifters; and TerraSource Global, a creator of size reduction equipment, conveying systems and screening equipment, operating under the Pennsylvania Crusher, Gundlach and Jeffrey Rader brands. In October 2015, the firm acquired both ABEL Pumps LP and Abel GmbH & Co. KG from Roper Technologies for about $107 million. In February 2016, it acquired Red Valve Company, Inc. for $131.9 million.

FINANCIAL DATA: Note: Data for latest year may not have been available at press time.

In U.S. $	2016	2015	2014	2013	2012	2011
Revenue		1,596,800,000	1,667,200,000	1,553,400,000	983,200,000	883,400,000
R&D Expense						
Operating Income		194,000,000	174,500,000	118,100,000	148,800,000	158,600,000
Operating Margin %		12.14%	10.46%	7.60%	15.13%	17.95%
SGA Expense		348,300,000	414,700,000	409,100,000	240,100,000	211,300,000
Net Income		111,400,000	109,700,000	63,400,000	104,800,000	106,100,000
Operating Cash Flow		105,000,000	179,600,000	127,200,000	138,200,000	189,500,000
Capital Expenditure		31,000,000	23,600,000	29,900,000	20,900,000	21,900,000
EBITDA		240,400,000	241,600,000	207,100,000	187,700,000	204,900,000
Return on Assets %		5.97%	5.59%	4.10%	9.24%	9.50%
Return on Equity %		18.92%	19.05%	11.79%	22.07%	26.03%
Debt to Equity		0.87	0.93	1.15	0.53	0.97

CONTACT INFORMATION:
Phone: 812 934-7500   Fax: 812 934-7613
Toll-Free:
Address: 1 Batesville Blvd., Batesville, IN 47006 United States

STOCK TICKER/OTHER:
Stock Ticker: HI
Employees: 5,900
Parent Company:

Exchange: NYS
Fiscal Year Ends: 09/30

SALARIES/BONUSES:
Top Exec. Salary: $482,158   Bonus: $180,000
Second Exec. Salary: $645,205   Bonus: $

OTHER THOUGHTS:
Estimated Female Officers or Directors: 3
Hot Spot for Advancement for Women/Minorities: Y

Hillshire Brands Company

www.hillshirefarm.com/

NAIC Code: 311612

TYPES OF BUSINESS:

Processed Meats

GROWTH PLANS/SPECIAL FEATURES:

Hillshire Brands Company manufactures and markets brand-name meat products for retail and food service markets worldwide. The company produces a variety of smoked sausages, lunch meats, cocktail links, link sausages, summer sausages and hams, all under the Hillshire Farm brand. Hillshire's more nutritious product line includes thin-sliced lower sodium meats, smoked chicken sausages and turkey sausages. The company's www.hillshirefarm.com website provides a recipe link that features 15-minute sensations, healthy recipes, as well as appetizer, breakfast, lunch, dinner, soup and salad suggestions using Hillshire Farm meat products. In 2014, the firm was acquired by Tyson Foods, Inc. and operates as its wholly-owned subsidiary.

BRANDS/DIVISIONS/AFFILIATES:

Tyson Foods Inc
Hillshire Farm

CONTACTS: *Note: Officers with more than one job title may be intentionally listed here more than once.*

Donnie Smith, CEO - Tyson
Sean Connolly, Pres.
Jeff George, Sr. VP-R&D
Kent Magill, General Counsel
Brian Davidson, Sr. VP-Corp. Strategy & Dev.
Jon Harris, Chief Communications Officer
Andy Callahan, Pres., Retail
Donald C. Davis, Pres., Sara Lee Foodservice
Sally Grimes, Chief Innovation Officer
Thomas P. Hayes, Chief Supply Chain Officer

FINANCIAL DATA: *Note: Data for latest year may not have been available at press time.*

In U.S. $	2016	2015	2014	2013	2012	2011
Revenue		4,105,000,000	4,000,000,000	3,920,000,000	4,094,000,128	4,019,000,000
R&D Expense						
Operating Income						
Operating Margin %						
SGA Expense						
Net Income			258,000,000	252,000,000	84,500,000	56,000,000
Operating Cash Flow						
Capital Expenditure						
EBITDA						
Return on Assets %						
Return on Equity %						
Debt to Equity						

CONTACT INFORMATION:

Phone: 312-614-6000   Fax:
Toll-Free:
Address: 400 S. Jefferson St., Chicago, IL 60607 United States

STOCK TICKER/OTHER:

Stock Ticker: Subsidiary   Exchange:
Employees: 9,100   Fiscal Year Ends: 06/30
Parent Company: Tyson Foods Inc

SALARIES/BONUSES:

Top Exec. Salary: $ Bonus: $
Second Exec. Salary: $ Bonus: $

OTHER THOUGHTS:

Estimated Female Officers or Directors: 4
Hot Spot for Advancement for Women/Minorities: Y

Hilton Worldwide Inc

www.hiltonworldwide.com

NAIC Code: 721110

TYPES OF BUSINESS:

Hotels & Resorts
Timeshare Properties
Conference Centers
Franchising
Management Services
Online Reservations

BRANDS/DIVISIONS/AFFILIATES:

Blackstone Group LP (The)
Hilton Grand Vacations Co LLC
Hilton
Hhonors
DoubleTree
Embassy Suites
Homewood Suites
Hampton Inn

CONTACTS: Note: Officers with more than one job title may be intentionally listed here more than once.

Christopher Nassetta, CEO
Kevin Jacobs, CFO
Jonathan Gray, Chairman of the Board
Michael Duffy, Chief Accounting Officer
James Holthouser, Executive VP, Divisional
Mark Wang, Executive VP, Divisional
Kristin Campbell, Executive VP
Matthew Schuyler, Executive VP
Christopher Silcock, Executive VP
Ian Carter, Executive VP

GROWTH PLANS/SPECIAL FEATURES:

Hilton Worldwide, Inc. owns, manages and develops hotels, resorts and timeshare properties and franchises lodging properties worldwide. Hilton Worldwide consists of 12 hotel brands and more than 4,610 hotels in 100 countries, ranging from affordable focus-service hotels to luxury extended stay suites. Hotel brands include Hilton, Hilton Garden Inn, DoubleTree, Embassy Suites, Homewood Suites, Home2 Suites, Hampton Inn, Conrad Hotels, Curio A Collection by Hilton, tru by Hilton, Canopy by Hilton and The Waldorf Astoria Collection. Additionally, Hilton Grand Vacations Co., LLC is the firm's timeshare brand in which ownership of a deeded real estate interest with club membership points provides members with a lifetime of vacation advantages. Hhonors, the firm's loyalty enrollment program for returning customers, has over 44 million members and includes partner benefits with several airlines. In addition, Hilton Worldwide offers architecture and construction and management services to individuals interested in developing their own properties. The Blackstone Group LP owns 45.9% of the firm's stock. In 2015, Hilton sold Waldorf Astoria New York, and signed agreements to redeploy the proceeds to add five landmark properties: Hilton Orlando Bonnet Creek, Waldorf Astoria Orlando, The Reach in Key West, Casa Marina in Key West (all in Florida) and Parc 55 in San Francisco, California. In February 2016, the firm announced plans to split into three companies by years' end, spinning off its real estate and vacation/timeshare businesses, while retaining its present hotel business.

FINANCIAL DATA: Note: Data for latest year may not have been available at press time.

In U.S. $	2016	2015	2014	2013	2012	2011
Revenue		11,272,000,000	10,502,000,000	9,735,000,000	9,276,000,000	8,783,000,000
R&D Expense						
Operating Income		2,071,000,000	1,673,000,000	1,102,000,000	1,100,000,000	975,000,000
Operating Margin %		18.37%	15.93%	11.32%	11.85%	11.10%
SGA Expense		547,000,000	491,000,000	748,000,000	460,000,000	416,000,000
Net Income		1,404,000,000	673,000,000	415,000,000	352,000,000	253,000,000
Operating Cash Flow		1,394,000,000	1,366,000,000	2,101,000,000	1,110,000,000	1,167,000,000
Capital Expenditure		372,000,000	337,000,000	332,000,000	536,000,000	482,000,000
EBITDA		2,763,000,000	2,393,000,000	1,921,000,000	1,692,000,000	1,403,000,000
Return on Assets %		5.41%	2.55%	1.54%	1.29%	.92%
Return on Equity %		26.15%	14.76%	12.45%	16.88%	13.54%
Debt to Equity		1.72	2.43	2.90	6.77	8.78

CONTACT INFORMATION:

Phone: 703-883-1000   Fax:
Toll-Free: 800-445-8667
Address: 7930 Jones Branch Dr., Ste. 1100, McLean, VA 22102 United States

STOCK TICKER/OTHER:

Stock Ticker: HLT
Employees: 157,000
Parent Company:

Exchange: NYS
Fiscal Year Ends: 12/31

SALARIES/BONUSES:

Top Exec. Salary: $1,246,154   Bonus: $
Second Exec. Salary: $748,077   Bonus: $

OTHER THOUGHTS:

Estimated Female Officers or Directors: 2

Hot Spot for Advancement for Women/Minorities:

Sales, profits and employees may be estimates. Financial information, benefits and other data can change quickly and may vary from those stated here.

HMSHost Corporation

www.hmshost.com

NAIC Code: 722310

TYPES OF BUSINESS:

Food Service Contractors
Food, Beverage & Retail Concessions
Travel Plazas
Food Courts

BRANDS/DIVISIONS/AFFILIATES:

Autogrill SpA
Ciao Gourmet Market
La Tapenade Mediterranean
Z Market
Wicker Park Seafood & Sushi Bar
Beaudevin
Jose Cuervo Tequileria

CONTACTS: Note: Officers with more than one job title may be intentionally listed here more than once.

Steve Johnson, CEO
Silvano Delnegro, COO
Tom Fricke, Pres.
Mark Ratych, CFO
Laura E. FitzRandolph, Exec. VP-Human Resources
Sarah Naqvi, Exec. VP-CIO

GROWTH PLANS/SPECIAL FEATURES:

HMSHost Corporation, a wholly-owned subsidiary of Italy-based Autogrill SpA, is a leading provider of food and beverage concessions for travelers. The firm operates facilities in over 120 airports worldwide as well as 99 roadside travel plazas along major U.S. and Canada toll roads and turnpikes in the Northeast and Midwest. HMSHost also serves tourist destinations such as Space Center Houston and the Empire State Building. The company's international airport operations include food service outlets at major and regional airports in Canada, Australia, Singapore, Ireland, India, Denmark, Sweden, the Netherlands, the U.K., Malaysia, France, Finland, Russia, the Middle East, Vietnam, Indonesia and New Zealand. HMSHost is engaged in a range of national and local brand licensing and franchising relationships, providing its food service with well-known brands ranging from Wolfgang Puck, Quiznos Sub to Starbucks, Pizza Hut and the Chili's Too. The company also develops proprietary branded concepts including Ciao Gourmet Market, La Tapenade Mediterranean, Z Market, Wicker Park Seafood & Sushi Bar, Beaudevin and Jose Cuervo Tequileria. In June 2016, the firm agreed to acquire Concession Management Services, Inc.'s airport restaurants, which would transform the operations of 16 dining locations at Los Angeles International Airport and McCarran International Airport (Las Vegas).

FINANCIAL DATA: Note: Data for latest year may not have been available at press time.

In U.S. $	2016	2015	2014	2013	2012	2011
Revenue		2,800,000,000	2,704,700,000	2,759,400,000	2,700,000,000	2,679,000,000
R&D Expense						
Operating Income						
Operating Margin %						
SGA Expense						
Net Income			86,500,000	76,900,000		
Operating Cash Flow						
Capital Expenditure						
EBITDA						
Return on Assets %						
Return on Equity %						
Debt to Equity						

CONTACT INFORMATION:

Phone: 240-694-4100   Fax: 240-694-4790
Toll-Free:
Address: 6905 Rockledge Dr., Bethesda, MD 20817 United States

SALARIES/BONUSES:

Top Exec. Salary: $ Bonus: $
Second Exec. Salary: $ Bonus: $

STOCK TICKER/OTHER:

Stock Ticker: Subsidiary   Exchange:
Employees: 37,000   Fiscal Year Ends: 12/31
Parent Company: Autogrill SpA

OTHER THOUGHTS:

Estimated Female Officers or Directors: 1
Hot Spot for Advancement for Women/Minorities:

Home Depot Inc

www.homedepot.com

NAIC Code: 444110

TYPES OF BUSINESS:

Home Centers, Retail
Home Improvement Products
Building Materials
Lawn & Garden Products
Online & Catalog Sales
Tool & Truck Rental
Installation & Design Services

BRANDS/DIVISIONS/AFFILIATES:

Hampton Bay Lighting
Husky
Behr Premium Plus
Vigoro
RIDGID
Ryobi
Glacier Bay
Interline Brands Inc

CONTACTS: Note: Officers with more than one job title may be intentionally listed here more than once.

Carol Tome, CFO
Matthew Carey, Chief Information Officer
Mark Holifield, Executive VP, Divisional
Edward Decker, Executive VP, Divisional
Marc Powers, Executive VP, Divisional
Timothy Crow, Executive VP, Divisional
Teresa Roseborough, Executive VP
Craig Menear, President

GROWTH PLANS/SPECIAL FEATURES:

Home Depot, Inc. is one of the world's largest home improvement retailers. The company operates approximately 2,274 Home Depot stores throughout the U.S., Canada, Guam, Puerto Rico, the Virgin Islands and Mexico. A typical store encompasses 104,000 square feet of enclosed space with a 24,000 square foot outdoor garden center; these locations usually stock between 30,000 and 40,000 items. These stores sell an assortment of building materials, plumbing materials, electrical materials, kitchen products, hardware, seasonal items, paint, flooring and wall coverings. The firm's proprietary brands include Hampton Bay lighting, Husky hand tools, Behr Premium Plus paint, Vigoro lawn care products, RIDGID and Ryobi power tools and Glacier Bay bath fixtures. Home Depot markets its products primarily to three types of customers: professional customers, such as remodelers, contractors, repairmen and small business owners; do-it-for-me shoppers, who are homeowners that personally purchase Home Depot products but hire third-party individuals for installation and/or project completion; and do-it-yourself (DIY) customers, who are homeowners that both shop for and personally install and/or utilize the firm's materials. In 2015, the firm acquired Interline Brands, Inc. from P2 Capital Partners for $1.6 billion.

The company offers its employees medical, dental, vision, life, AD&D and disability insurance; a 401(k) plan; a stock purchase plan; adoption, education and relocation assistance; flexible spending accounts; a legal services plan; auto and homeowners insurance; and veterinary coverage.

FINANCIAL DATA: Note: Data for latest year may not have been available at press time.

In U.S. $	2016	2015	2014	2013	2012	2011
Revenue	88,519,000,000	83,176,000,000	78,812,000,000	74,754,000,000	70,395,000,000	67,997,000,000
R&D Expense						
Operating Income	11,774,000,000	10,469,000,000	9,166,000,000	7,766,000,000	6,661,000,000	5,839,000,000
Operating Margin %	13.30%	12.58%	11.63%	10.38%	9.46%	8.58%
SGA Expense	16,801,000,000	16,834,000,000	16,597,000,000	16,508,000,000	16,028,000,000	15,849,000,000
Net Income	7,009,000,000	6,345,000,000	5,385,000,000	4,535,000,000	3,883,000,000	3,338,000,000
Operating Cash Flow	9,373,000,000	8,242,000,000	7,628,000,000	6,975,000,000	6,651,000,000	4,585,000,000
Capital Expenditure	1,503,000,000	1,442,000,000	1,389,000,000	1,312,000,000	1,221,000,000	1,096,000,000
EBITDA	13,803,000,000	12,592,000,000	10,935,000,000	9,537,000,000	8,356,000,000	7,521,000,000
Return on Assets %	16.99%	15.77%	13.19%	11.11%	9.63%	8.24%
Return on Equity %	89.64%	58.09%	35.54%	25.42%	21.11%	17.43%
Debt to Equity	3.30	1.80	1.17	0.53	0.60	0.46

CONTACT INFORMATION:

Phone: 770 433-8211   Fax: 770 431-2707
Toll-Free: 800-553-3199
Address: 2455 Paces Ferry Rd. N.W., Atlanta, GA 30339 United States

STOCK TICKER/OTHER:

Stock Ticker: HD   Exchange: NYS
Employees: 385,000   Fiscal Year Ends: 01/31
Parent Company:

SALARIES/BONUSES:

Top Exec. Salary: $1,300,000   Bonus: $
Second Exec. Salary: $1,051,923   Bonus: $

OTHER THOUGHTS:

Estimated Female Officers or Directors: 7

Hot Spot for Advancement for Women/Minorities: Y

Houston Methodist

NAIC Code: 622110

www.methodisthealth.com

TYPES OF BUSINESS:

General Medical and Surgical Hospitals

GROWTH PLANS/SPECIAL FEATURES:

Houston Methodist is a nonprofit health care organization that owns and operates several hospitals and facilities located in Houston. Its hospitals include Houston Methodist Hospital, Houston Methodist Sugar Land Hospital, Houston Methodist West Hospital, Houston Methodist Willowbrook Hospital, Houston San Jacinto Methodist Hospital, Houston Methodist St. John Hospital, Houston Methodist St. Catherine Hospital and Houston Methodist The Woodlands Hospital (scheduled to open in 2017). Each campus is staffed by highly-trained specialists who provide advanced treatment as well as follow-up care. Some of the Methodist hospital's areas of focus include breast care, heart care, neuroscience, orthopedics and oncology. Houston Methodist Hospital, the system's flagship, is among U.S. News & World Report's best hospitals. Other centers include Houston Methodist Emergency Care Centers, the Houston Methodist Imaging Center, the Houston Methodist Breast Care Center and the Houston Methodist Outpatient Center. Houston Methodist Research Institute is home to physicians that collaborate on more than 800 clinical trials. The Houston Methodist Institute for Technology, Innovation and Education is a 35,000-square-foot surgical training center and virtual hospital which provides ongoing education. Houston Methodist Hospital Foundation accepts all gifts on Houston Methodist's behalf and views donor contribution as essential to its growth and success. Houston Methodist Community Benefits support individuals and organizations that provide financial and medical assistance to more than 150,000 patients on an annual basis. Houston Methodist Specialty Physician Group are physicians employed by Houston Methodist that are rooted in an academic and research environment where teaching and continued education are encouraged. Last, Houston Methodist Primary Care Group is dedicated to providing patient care for the entire family.

BRANDS/DIVISIONS/AFFILIATES:

Houston Methodist Hospital,
Houston Methodist Sugar Land Hospital
Houston Methodist West Hospital
Houston Methodist Willowbrook Hospital
Houston San Jacinto Methodist Hospital
Houston Methodist St. John Hospital
Houston Methodist Emergency Care Centers
Houston Methodist Breast Care Center

CONTACTS: Note: Officers with more than one job title may be intentionally listed here more than once.

Marc L. Boom, CEO
Marc L. Boom, Pres.
Gregory Nelson, Sec.
Carlton Caucum, Treas.
Joseph Walter III, Assistant Treas.
Robert K. Moses, Jr., Assistant Sec.
Ewing Werlein, Jr., Chmn.

FINANCIAL DATA: Note: Data for latest year may not have been available at press time.

In U.S. $	2016	2015	2014	2013	2012	2011
Revenue		2,800,000,000	2,616,170,000	2,616,169,000	2,331,041,000	2,285,000,000
R&D Expense						
Operating Income						
Operating Margin %						
SGA Expense						
Net Income				683,525,000		
Operating Cash Flow						
Capital Expenditure						
EBITDA						
Return on Assets %						
Return on Equity %						
Debt to Equity						

CONTACT INFORMATION:

Phone: 713-790-3311   Fax:
Toll-Free:
Address: 6565 Fannin St., Houston, TX 77030 United States

STOCK TICKER/OTHER:

Stock Ticker: Nonprofit   Exchange:
Employees: 20,000   Fiscal Year Ends: 12/31
Parent Company:

SALARIES/BONUSES:

Top Exec. Salary: $ Bonus: $
Second Exec. Salary: $ Bonus: $

OTHER THOUGHTS:

Estimated Female Officers or Directors: 5
Hot Spot for Advancement for Women/Minorities: Y

Hub International Limited
www.hubinternational.com

NAIC Code: 524210

TYPES OF BUSINESS:
Insurance Brokerage & Management
Risk Management
Property & Casualty Insurance
Employee Benefit Services
Investments & Financial Planning
Life Insurance
Health & Disability Insurance

BRANDS/DIVISIONS/AFFILIATES:

CONTACTS:
Note: Officers with more than one job title may be intentionally listed here more than once.

Martin P. Hughes, CEO
Richard A. Gulliver, Pres.
Joseph C. Hyde, CFO
Trey Biggs, Chief Sales Officer
Deborah Deters, Sr. VP-Human Resources
Scott Goodreau, Chief Legal Officer
Roy H. Taylor, Pres., West Region
Lawrence J. Lineker, Pres., Canadian Region
Scott Goodreau, Pres., Central Region
Deborah Deters, Sr. VP
Martin P. Hughes, Chmn.
James Barton, Pres., Canada & Midwest Regions

GROWTH PLANS/SPECIAL FEATURES:

Hub International Limited is an insurance brokerage providing an array of property, casualty, life and health insurance as well as employee benefits, investment and risk management products and services. The company focuses primarily on middle-market commercial accounts in the U.S. and Canada, and operates through more than 330 offices using a variety of retail and wholesale distribution channels. Hub operates through four divisions: personal insurance, business insurance, employee benefits and risk services. Personal insurance includes homeowner's, condominiums, co-op housing, health and renter's insurance; auto, boat, collector car, recreational vehicle and travel insurance; and specialty insurance such as personal excess liability and aviation. Business insurance includes aviation, business owners, commercial auto, employment practices, marine, professional liability, boiler & machinery, business property, cyber liability, director/officer liability, executive liability, environmental protection, financial services, workers' compensation, business travel, trade credit & political risk, surety bonds, mergers & acquisitions, general liability and contest and prize insurance. Employee benefits comprises group medical plans, disability, group life insurance, voluntary benefits, dental plans, individual health, employee benefits consulting, absence management, wellness programs, health advocacy and benefits administration. Risk services include regulatory compliance assistance, safety management, emergency response planning, business continuity, fleet safety management, property protection, claim data analysis, disability management, claim reporting guidance, return-to-work planning, crisis management and webinars. During 2015, the firm acquired and integrated more than 25 brokerages. By mid-2016, it acquired and integrated 15 brokerages.

FINANCIAL DATA:
Note: Data for latest year may not have been available at press time.

In U.S. $	2016	2015	2014	2013	2012	2011
Revenue		1,260,000,000	1,230,000,000	1,147,560,000	988,700,000	878,321,552
R&D Expense						
Operating Income						
Operating Margin %						
SGA Expense						
Net Income						
Operating Cash Flow						
Capital Expenditure						
EBITDA						
Return on Assets %						
Return on Equity %						
Debt to Equity						

CONTACT INFORMATION:
Phone: 312-922-5000   Fax: 877-402-6606
Toll-Free: 877-402-4187
Address: 300 N. LaSalle St., 17/F, Chicago, IL 60654 United States

STOCK TICKER/OTHER:
Stock Ticker: Private   Exchange:
Employees: 7,000   Fiscal Year Ends: 12/31
Parent Company: Hellman & Friedman LLC

SALARIES/BONUSES:
Top Exec. Salary: $ Bonus: $
Second Exec. Salary: $ Bonus: $

OTHER THOUGHTS:
Estimated Female Officers or Directors: 1
Hot Spot for Advancement for Women/Minorities: Y

Hubbell Inc

NAIC Code: 335931

www.hubbell.com

TYPES OF BUSINESS:

Current-Carrying Wiring Device Manufacturing

BRANDS/DIVISIONS/AFFILIATES:

Hubbell
Hubbell Building Automation
Hubbell Outdoor Lighting
Raco
Victor
Alera Lighting
Ohio Brass
Quazite

CONTACTS: *Note: Officers with more than one job title may be intentionally listed here more than once.*

Megan Preneta, Assistant General Counsel
David Nord, CEO
William Sperry, CFO
Joseph Capozzoli, Chief Accounting Officer
An-Ping Hsieh, General Counsel
Darrin Wegman, President, Divisional
Kevin Poyck, President, Divisional
Rodd Ruland, President, Divisional
William Tolley, Senior VP, Divisional
Maria Lee, Treasurer
Stephen Mais, Vice President, Divisional
Gerben Bakker, Vice President, Divisional

GROWTH PLANS/SPECIAL FEATURES:

Hubbell, Inc. designs, manufactures and distributes electrical and electronic products for a range of non-residential and residential construction, industrial and utility applications. The company operates in two segments: electrical and power. The electrical segment is comprised of businesses that sell stock and custom products including standard and special application wiring device products, rough-in electrical products, connector and grounding products, lighting fixtures and controls, as well as other electrical equipment. The products are typically used in and around industrial, commercial and institutional facilities by electrical contractors, maintenance personnel, electricians and telecommunications companies. Hubbell's products are supplied principally to industrial, non-residential and residential customers. These products are sold under brand and trademarks including, such as Hubbell, Raco, Victor, Kellems, Bell, Wiegmann, Gleason Reel, Hawke, Hipotronics, Chalmit and Austdac. Hubbell manufactures and sells lighting fixtures and controls for indoor and outdoor applications within residential, commercial, institutional and industrial markets. These products are sold under a number of brand and trademarks, such as Kim Lighting, Sportsliter Solutions, Kurt Versen, Beacon Products, Hubbell Building Automation, Spaulding Lighting, Alera Lighting, Dual-Lite and Hubbell Outdoor Lighting. The power segment consists of operations that design and manufacture various transmission, distribution, substation and telecommunications products mainly used by the electrical utility industry. Hubbell manufactures and sells a number of electrical distribution, transmission, and substation products. These products are sold under a number of brand and trademarks, such as Ohio Brass, Chance, Anderson, Fargo, Hubbell, Quazite, Electro Composites, Hot Box, PCORE and Delmar.

FINANCIAL DATA: *Note: Data for latest year may not have been available at press time.*

In U.S. $	2016	2015	2014	2013	2012	2011
Revenue		3,390,400,000	3,359,400,000	3,183,900,000	3,044,400,000	2,871,600,000
R&D Expense						
Operating Income		474,600,000	517,400,000	507,600,000	471,800,000	423,800,000
Operating Margin %		13.99%	15.40%	15.94%	15.49%	14.75%
SGA Expense		617,200,000	591,600,000	562,900,000	540,400,000	499,900,000
Net Income		277,300,000	325,300,000	326,500,000	299,700,000	267,900,000
Operating Cash Flow		331,100,000	391,500,000	381,800,000	349,100,000	335,000,000
Capital Expenditure		77,100,000	60,300,000	58,800,000	49,100,000	55,400,000
EBITDA		534,800,000	595,900,000	575,200,000	539,400,000	488,900,000
Return on Assets %		8.46%	9.99%	10.64%	10.34%	9.61%
Return on Equity %		15.08%	16.97%	18.30%	19.15%	18.23%
Debt to Equity		0.34	0.31	0.31	0.35	0.40

CONTACT INFORMATION:

Phone: 475 882-4000   Fax: 203 799-4333
Toll-Free:
Address: 40 Waterview Drive, Shelton, CT 06484 United States

STOCK TICKER/OTHER:

Stock Ticker: HUBB
Employees: 15,400
Parent Company:

Exchange: NYS
Fiscal Year Ends: 12/31

SALARIES/BONUSES:

Top Exec. Salary: $968,700   Bonus: $
Second Exec. Salary: $505,000   Bonus: $

OTHER THOUGHTS:

Estimated Female Officers or Directors:
Hot Spot for Advancement for Women/Minorities:

Humana Inc

www.humana.com

NAIC Code: 524114

TYPES OF BUSINESS:

Insurance-Medical & Health, HMOs & PPOs
Insurance-Dental
Employee Benefit Plans
Insurance-Group Life
Wellness Programs

BRANDS/DIVISIONS/AFFILIATES:

CONTACTS: *Note: Officers with more than one job title may be intentionally listed here more than once.*

Bruce Broussard, CEO
Brian Kane, CFO
Kurt Hilzinger, Chairman of the Board
Cynthia Zipperle, Chief Accounting Officer
Brian LeClaire, Chief Information Officer
Roy Beveridge, Chief Medical Officer
James Murray, COO
Timothy Huval, Other Executive Officer
Christopher Hunter, Other Executive Officer
Jody Bilney, Other Executive Officer
Joan Lenahan, Secretary
Heidi Margulis, Senior VP, Divisional
Christopher Todoroff, Senior VP
Christopher Kay, Senior VP

GROWTH PLANS/SPECIAL FEATURES:

Humana, Inc. is a leading health benefits company in the U.S., serving approximately 14.2 million medical benefit plan members and 7.2 million specialty products members in the U.S. and Puerto Rico. It operates in three segments: retail, employer group and health care services. The retail segment consists of Medicare and commercial fully-insured medical and specialty health insurance benefits, including dental, vision and other supplemental health and financial protection products, marketed directly to individuals. The employer group segment consists of Medicare and commercial fully-insured medical and specialty health insurance benefits, including dental, vision and other supplemental health and financial protection products as well as administrative services-only products marketed to employer groups. Humana provides health benefits and related services to companies ranging from fewer than 10 to over 10,000 employees. The health care services segment includes services offered to health plan members as well as to third parties that promote health and wellness, including provider services, pharmacies, integrated wellness and home care services. Other businesses consists of military services, primarily the TRICARE South Region, Medicaid and closed-block long-term care businesses as well as the firm's contract with the Centers for Medicare and Medicaid Services to administer the Limited Income Newly Eligible Transition program, known as LI-NET. Many of its products are offered through HMOs (health maintenance organizations), Private Fee-For-Service (PFFS) and preferred provider organizations (PPOs). In 2015, Humana sold Concentra Inc. for $1 billion. Also, Humana agreed to be acquired by competitor Aetna in a deal worth $37 billion, with the shareholders of both firms approving the deal. In August 2016, Aetna and Humana agreed to individually sell certain of their respective Medicare Advantage assets to Molina Healthcare, Inc. These transactions are subject to the successful completion of the Aetna-Humana acquisition.

The firm offers employees an array of comprehensive benefits.

FINANCIAL DATA: *Note: Data for latest year may not have been available at press time.*

In U.S. $	2016	2015	2014	2013	2012	2011
Revenue		54,289,000,000	48,500,000,000	41,313,000,000	39,126,000,000	36,832,000,000
R&D Expense						
Operating Income		2,431,000,000	2,170,000,000	1,921,000,000	1,911,000,000	2,235,000,000
Operating Margin %		4.47%	4.47%	4.64%	4.88%	6.06%
SGA Expense		7,318,000,000	7,639,000,000	6,355,000,000	5,830,000,000	5,395,000,000
Net Income		1,276,000,000	1,147,000,000	1,231,000,000	1,222,000,000	1,419,000,000
Operating Cash Flow		868,000,000	1,618,000,000	1,716,000,000	1,923,000,000	2,079,000,000
Capital Expenditure		523,000,000	528,000,000	441,000,000	410,000,000	346,000,000
EBITDA						
Return on Assets %		5.29%	5.18%	6.04%	6.48%	8.39%
Return on Equity %		12.76%	12.09%	13.55%	14.45%	18.93%
Debt to Equity		0.36	0.39	0.27	0.29	0.20

CONTACT INFORMATION:

Phone: 502 580-1000   Fax: 502 580-1441
Toll-Free:
Address: 500 W. Main St., Louisville, KY 40202 United States

STOCK TICKER/OTHER:

Stock Ticker: HUM   Exchange: NYS
Employees: 57,000   Fiscal Year Ends: 12/31
Parent Company:

SALARIES/BONUSES:

Top Exec. Salary: Bonus: $
$1,243,087
Second Exec. Salary: Bonus: $
$842,105

OTHER THOUGHTS:

Estimated Female Officers or Directors: 3

Hot Spot for Advancement for Women/Minorities: Y

Huntsman Corporation

NAIC Code: 325211

www.huntsman.com

TYPES OF BUSINESS:

Chemicals Manufacturing
Polyurethane Manufacturing
Advanced Materials & Surface Technologies
Performance Chemicals
Pigments

BRANDS/DIVISIONS/AFFILIATES:

Huntsman International LLC
Tecnoelastomeri

CONTACTS: *Note: Officers with more than one job title may be intentionally listed here more than once.*

Troy Keller, Assistant General Counsel
John Heskett, Treasurer
Anthony Hankins, CEO, Geographical
Peter Huntsman, CEO
J. Esplin, CFO
Jon Huntsman, Chairman of the Board
Randy Wright, Chief Accounting Officer
Maria Csiba-Womersley, Chief Information Officer
Nolan Archibald, Director
David Stryker, Executive VP
Russ Stolle, Other Corporate Officer
Simon Turner, President, Divisional
Paul Hulme, President, Divisional
Monte Edlund, President, Divisional
James Huntsman, President, Divisional
Stewart Monteith, President, Divisional
Brian Ridd, Senior VP, Divisional
R. Rogers, Senior VP, Divisional
Ronald Gerrard, Senior VP, Divisional
Kurt Ogden, Vice President, Divisional
Kevin Hardman, Vice President, Divisional
Steven Jorgensen, Vice President, Divisional

GROWTH PLANS/SPECIAL FEATURES:

Huntsman Corporation is a global manufacturer o differentiated organic chemical products and inorganic chemical products. The company operates all of its businesses through wholly-owned subsidiary Huntsman International LLC The firm operates in five business segments: polyurethanes advanced materials, textile effects, performance products and pigments and additives. The polyurethanes segment (accounting for 37% of 2015 revenues) produces MD (Methylene diphenyl diisocyanate) products, propylene oxide polyols, propylene glycol, thermoplastic urethane, aniline and methyl tert-butyl ether products. The advanced materials segment (10% of revenues) manufactures epoxy resin compounds and formulations; cross-linking, matting and curing agents; and epoxy, acrylic and polyurethane-based adhesives The textile effects division (8% of revenues) produces textile chemicals and dyes. The firm's performance products segment (24% of revenues) is organized around three market groups performance specialties, performance intermediates and maleic anhydride and licensing. It produces amines carbonates and certain specialty surfactants; consumes internally produced and third-party-sourced base petrochemicals in the manufacture of its surfactants and ethanolamines products; licenses maleic anhydride manufacturing technology (mainly used in the production o fiberglass reinforced resins); and supplies butane fixed bec catalyst used in the manufacture of maleic anhydrides Huntsman's pigments and additives segment (21% o revenues) manufactures titanium dioxide, used in paints and coatings, plastics, paper, printing inks, fibers and ceramics. Ir June 2015, the firm acquired Tecnoelastomeri, an Italiar manufacturer of MDI systems, finished elastomer parts and machines for processing elastomers.

FINANCIAL DATA: *Note: Data for latest year may not have been available at press time.*

In U.S. $	2016	2015	2014	2013	2012	2011
Revenue		10,299,000,000	11,578,000,000	11,079,000,000	11,187,000,000	11,221,000,000
R&D Expense		160,000,000	158,000,000	140,000,000	152,000,000	166,000,000
Operating Income		405,000,000	633,000,000	510,000,000	845,000,000	606,000,000
Operating Margin %		3.93%	5.46%	4.60%	7.55%	5.40%
SGA Expense		982,000,000	974,000,000	942,000,000	951,000,000	921,000,000
Net Income		93,000,000	323,000,000	128,000,000	363,000,000	247,000,000
Operating Cash Flow		575,000,000	760,000,000	708,000,000	774,000,000	365,000,000
Capital Expenditure		663,000,000	601,000,000	471,000,000	412,000,000	330,000,000
EBITDA		780,000,000	1,054,000,000	958,000,000	1,205,000,000	1,048,000,000
Return on Assets %		.89%	3.19%	1.41%	4.13%	2.84%
Return on Equity %		5.77%	17.19%	6.82%	21.13%	14.31%
Debt to Equity		3.20	2.77	1.83	1.92	2.24

CONTACT INFORMATION:

Phone: 801 584-5700   Fax: 801 584-5781
Toll-Free:
Address: 500 Huntsman Way, Salt Lake City, UT 84108 United States

STOCK TICKER/OTHER:

Stock Ticker: HUN   Exchange: NYS
Employees: 16,000   Fiscal Year Ends: 12/31
Parent Company:

SALARIES/BONUSES:

Top Exec. Salary: Bonus: $
$1,675,000
Second Exec. Salary: Bonus: $
$1,325,000

OTHER THOUGHTS:

Estimated Female Officers or Directors: 2

Hot Spot for Advancement for Women/Minorities:

Hyatt Hotels Corporation

NAIC Code: 721110

www.hyatt.com

TYPES OF BUSINESS:

Hotel Ownership & Management
Timeshares
Golf Courses
Gaming
Retirement Communities
Motels & Inns
Hotel Franchising

BRANDS/DIVISIONS/AFFILIATES:

Hyatt Regency
Grand Hyatt
Hyatt Place
Hyatt Gold Passport
Andaz
Hyatt House
Hyatt Residence Club
Park Hyatt

CONTACTS: Note: Officers with more than one job title may be intentionally listed here more than once.

Mark Hoplamazian, CEO
Thomas Pritzker, Chairman of the Board
Bradley OBryan, Chief Accounting Officer
Patrick Grismer, Executive VP
Maryam Banikarim, Executive VP
Rena Reiss, Executive VP
H. Floyd, Executive VP
Peter Sears, Executive VP
David Udell, Executive VP
Peter Fulton, Executive VP
Stephen Haggerty, Other Corporate Officer
Robert Webb, Other Executive Officer

GROWTH PLANS/SPECIAL FEATURES:

Hyatt Hotels Corporation (Hyatt) owns, operates, manages and franchises full-service luxury hotels in 52 countries across the globe. The company owns, manages or franchises approximately 599 hotels with approximately 156,336 rooms. Hyatt's operations consist of several brands. Hyatt and Hyatt Regency host business and leisure travelers, although Hyatt Regency caters mainly to larger groups. Grand Hyatt hotels cater to leisure and business travelers and include accommodations for banquets and conferences. Park Hyatt hotels are smaller, full-service luxury hotels featuring world class art and restaurants in a few of the world's most visited cities. The Andaz branded hotels are boutique-style hotels that feature restaurants and bars aimed at local clientele as well as single travelers. The two select service brands, Hyatt House and Hyatt Place, are extended-stay brands designed to feel more like home. Hyatt Residence Club provides vacation ownership and vacation rental opportunities, offering members timeshare or points-based resort vacation opportunities. Hyatt Ziva and Hyatt Zilara are the company's all-inclusive resort brands which are developed, sold and managed as part of the Hyatt Residence club. Hyatt's guest loyalty program, Hyatt Gold Passport, has over 20 million members.

The firm offers employees complementary hotel rooms; medical, dental, vision and prescription drug coverage; and tuition assistance.

FINANCIAL DATA: Note: Data for latest year may not have been available at press time.

In U.S. $	2016	2015	2014	2013	2012	2011
Revenue		4,328,000,000	4,415,000,000	4,184,000,000	3,949,000,000	3,698,000,000
R&D Expense						
Operating Income		323,000,000	279,000,000	233,000,000	159,000,000	153,000,000
Operating Margin %		7.46%	6.31%	5.56%	4.02%	4.13%
SGA Expense		308,000,000	349,000,000	323,000,000	316,000,000	283,000,000
Net Income		124,000,000	344,000,000	207,000,000	88,000,000	113,000,000
Operating Cash Flow		538,000,000	473,000,000	456,000,000	499,000,000	393,000,000
Capital Expenditure		269,000,000	253,000,000	232,000,000	301,000,000	331,000,000
EBITDA		582,000,000	950,000,000	731,000,000	518,000,000	445,000,000
Return on Assets %		1.57%	4.21%	2.61%	1.16%	1.53%
Return on Equity %		2.87%	7.32%	4.31%	1.82%	2.27%
Debt to Equity		0.26	0.29	0.27	0.25	0.25

CONTACT INFORMATION:

Phone: 312 750-1234   Fax:
Toll-Free: 800-323-7249
Address: 71 S. Wacker Dr., 12th Fl., Chicago, IL 60606 United States

STOCK TICKER/OTHER:

Stock Ticker: H   Exchange: NYS
Employees: 45,000   Fiscal Year Ends: 12/31
Parent Company:

SALARIES/BONUSES:

Top Exec. Salary: Bonus: $
$1,060,833
Second Exec. Salary: Bonus: $
$727,083

OTHER THOUGHTS:

Estimated Female Officers or Directors: 3

Hot Spot for Advancement for Women/Minorities: Y

IAC/InterActiveCorp

www.iac.com

NAIC Code: 519130

TYPES OF BUSINESS:

E-Commerce, Online Advertising & Search Engines
Online Personals & Dating Services
Online Entertainment & Shopping Directories
Service Provider Listings Online

BRANDS/DIVISIONS/AFFILIATES:

Match Group
OKCupid
Tinder
Princeton Review (The)
CollegeHumor
About.com
Dictionary.com
ShoeBuy

CONTACTS: *Note: Officers with more than one job title may be intentionally listed here more than once.*

Barry Diller, Chairman of the Board
Joseph Levin, Director
Glenn Schiffman, Executive VP
Gregg Winiarski, General Counsel
Michael Schwerdtman, Senior VP
Victor Kaufman, Vice Chairman

GROWTH PLANS/SPECIAL FEATURES:

IAC/InterActiveCorp. (IAC) is a leading media and Internet company. It is organized into four segments: Match Group, which includes business brands Match, OKCupid, Tinder and The Princeton Review; search & applications includes About.com, Ask.com, Dictionary.com and Investopedia; media includes Vimeo, Electus, The Daily Beast and CollegeHumor; and eCommerce includes HomeAdvisor and ShoeBuy. Match Group's dating businesses operate in North America via Match, Chemistry, People Media, OK Cupid, Tinder and more in the U.S. and Canada; and internationally via Meetic and Tender. Its non-dating businesses include online test preparation and tutoring sites, The Princeton Review and Tutor.com, as well as streaming fitness and workout videos via DailyBurn. Search & application's About.com provides detailed information and content written by independent, freelance subject matter experts across hundreds of vertical categories; Ask.com is a question and answer social network; Dictionary.com provides online and mobile dictionary and reference services; and Investopedia is a resource for investment and personal finance education and information. The media division's Vimeo business operates a global video sharing platform for creators and their audiences; Electus provides production and producer services for both unscripted and scripted television, feature film and digital content; The Daily Beast is a website dedicated to news, commentary, culture and entertainment that curates and publishes existing and original online content from its own roster of contributors in the U.S.; and CollegeHumor features daily original comedy videos and articles created by its in-house writing and production team, in addition to user-submitted videos, pictures, articles and links. eCommerce's HomeAdvisor is an online marketplace for matching consumers with home services professionals in the U.S.; and Shoebuy is an Internet retailer of footwear and related accessories. The company is headquartered in New York City and has offices worldwide. In late-2015, the firm went public with its Match Group matchmaking division, including the business' web sites and apps.

FINANCIAL DATA: *Note: Data for latest year may not have been available at press time.*

In U.S. $	2016	2015	2014	2013	2012	2011
Revenue		3,230,933,000	3,109,547,000	3,022,987,000	2,800,933,000	2,059,444,000
R&D Expense		185,766,000	160,515,000	141,330,000	101,869,000	78,760,000
Operating Income		179,588,000	378,727,000	426,203,000	323,568,000	197,762,000
Operating Margin %		5.55%	12.17%	14.09%	11.55%	9.60%
SGA Expense		1,871,205,000	1,568,047,000	1,336,601,000	1,294,774,000	942,902,000
Net Income		119,472,000	414,873,000	285,784,000	159,266,000	174,233,000
Operating Cash Flow		349,405,000	424,048,000	410,961,000	351,055,000	372,386,000
Capital Expenditure		62,049,000	57,233,000	80,311,000	51,201,000	39,954,000
EBITDA		418,666,000	445,325,000	568,649,000	383,463,000	255,728,000
Return on Assets %		2.51%	9.75%	7.10%	4.41%	5.08%
Return on Equity %		6.29%	22.55%	17.10%	8.94%	8.03%
Debt to Equity		0.96	0.54	0.64	0.35	0.05

CONTACT INFORMATION:

Phone: 212 314-7300   Fax: 212 314-7399
Toll-Free:
Address: 555 W. 18th St., New York, NY 10011 United States

STOCK TICKER/OTHER:

Stock Ticker: IAC   Exchange: NAS
Employees: 5,000   Fiscal Year Ends: 12/31
Parent Company:

SALARIES/BONUSES:

Top Exec. Salary: $500,000   Bonus: $2,200,000
Second Exec. Salary: Bonus: $1,000,000
$575,000

OTHER THOUGHTS:

Estimated Female Officers or Directors: 6
Hot Spot for Advancement for Women/Minorities: Y

IDEXX Laboratories Inc

www.idexx.com

NAIC Code: 334510

TYPES OF BUSINESS:

Veterinary Laboratory Testing Equipment
Point-of-Care Diagnostic Products
Veterinary Pharmaceuticals
Information Management Software
Food & Water Testing Products
Laboratory Testing Services
Consulting

BRANDS/DIVISIONS/AFFILIATES:

VetTest
VetLyte
VetStat
LaserCyte Dx
SNAPshot DX
Coag Dx
Colisure
ProCyte Dx Hematology Analyzer

CONTACTS: Note: Officers with more than one job title may be intentionally listed here more than once.

Jonathan Ayers, CEO
Brian Mckeon, CFO
Jay Mazelsky, Executive VP
Michael Williams, Executive VP
Jacqueline Studer, Vice President

GROWTH PLANS/SPECIAL FEATURES:

IDEXX Laboratories, Inc. develops, manufactures and distributes products and provides services for the veterinary and the food and water testing markets. The company operates in three business segments: companion animal group (CAG), which provides diagnostic and information technology-based products and services for the veterinary markets; water quality products; and livestock, poultry and diary (LPD), which provides diagnostic products and services for livestock and poultry health, and to ensure the quality and safety of milk and food. IDEXX markets an integrated and flexible suite of in-house laboratory analyzers for use in veterinary practices, which is referred to as the VetLab suite of analyzers. The suite includes several instrument systems as well as associated proprietary consumable products such as VetTest, VetLyte, VetStat and LaserCyte Dx analyzers; the IDEXX SNAPshot Dx; the ProCyte Dx Hematology Analyzer; and the Coag Dx Analyzer, among other offerings. In addition, the company provides assay kits, software and instrumentation for accurate assessment of infectious disease in production animals, such as cattle, swine and poultry. Water quality products include Colilert, Colilert-18 and Colisure tests, which simultaneously detect total coliforms and E. coli in water. IDEXX's principal product for use in testing for antibiotic residue in milk is the SNAP Beta-Lactam test, which detects penicillin, amoxicillin, ampicillin, ceftiofur and cephapirin residues. SNAPduo Beta-Tetra ST detects certain tetracycline antibiotic residues in addition to those detected by the Beta-Lactam test kits. Moreover, IDEXX's other operating segment combines and presents products for the human point-of-care medical diagnostics market with its pharmaceutical product line and out-licensing arrangements. Sales of products and services to customers outside the U.S. account for 39% of the company's overall revenue.

IDEXX offers its employees health, dental and life insurance; a401(k) and employee stock purchase plans; short- and long-term disability; flexible spending accounts; and sick days, vacation and paid holidays.

FINANCIAL DATA: Note: Data for latest year may not have been available at press time.

In U.S. $	2016	2015	2014	2013	2012	2011
Revenue		1,601,892,000	1,485,807,000	1,377,058,000	1,293,338,000	1,218,689,000
R&D Expense		99,681,000	98,263,000	88,003,000	82,014,000	76,042,000
Operating Income		299,912,000	260,255,000	266,762,000	262,563,000	236,225,000
Operating Margin %		18.72%	17.51%	19.37%	20.30%	19.38%
SGA Expense		482,465,000	457,598,000	401,353,000	354,571,000	334,239,000
Net Income		192,078,000	181,906,000	187,800,000	178,267,000	161,786,000
Operating Cash Flow		216,364,000	235,846,000	245,996,000	230,282,000	220,700,000
Capital Expenditure		82,921,000	60,698,000	78,636,000	66,392,000	53,464,000
EBITDA		371,336,000	320,872,000	323,243,000	316,873,000	286,171,000
Return on Assets %		13.43%	13.91%	16.09%	16.70%	16.78%
Return on Equity %		1150.47%	57.23%	32.53%	30.32%	29.05%
Debt to Equity			2.97	0.29		

CONTACT INFORMATION:

Phone: 207 556-0300   Fax: 207 856-0346
Toll-Free: 800-548-6733
Address: 1 Idexx Dr., Westbrook, ME 04092 United States

STOCK TICKER/OTHER:

Stock Ticker: IDXX   Exchange: NAS
Employees: 6,400   Fiscal Year Ends: 12/31
Parent Company:

SALARIES/BONUSES:

Top Exec. Salary: $800,000   Bonus: $
Second Exec. Salary: $516,923   Bonus: $

OTHER THOUGHTS:

Estimated Female Officers or Directors: 2
Hot Spot for Advancement for Women/Minorities: Y

Sales, profits and employees may be estimates. Financial information, benefits and other data can change quickly and may vary from those stated here.

Illinois Tool Works Inc

NAIC Code: 333249

TYPES OF BUSINESS:

Industrial Products & Equipment
Steel, Plastic & Paper Products
Power Systems & Electronics
Transportation-Related Components, Fasteners, Fluids & Polymers
Construction-Related Fasteners & Tools
Food Equipment & Adhesives
Decorative Surfacing Materials
Adhesives, Sealants & Lubrication

BRANDS/DIVISIONS/AFFILIATES:

CONTACTS: Note: Officers with more than one job title may be intentionally listed here more than once.

David Parry, Vice Chairman

GROWTH PLANS/SPECIAL FEATURES:

Illinois Tool Works, Inc. (ITW) is a multinational manufacturer of a diversified range of industrial products and equipment, with operations in 57 countries. It operates in seven primary segments: automotive OEM, test & measurement and electronics, food equipment, polymers & fluids, welding construction products and specialty products. The automotive OEM segment produces components and fasteners for automotive-related applications. Products include plastic and metal components, fasteners and assemblies for automobiles light trucks and other industrial uses. The test & measurement segment produces equipment, consumables and related software for testing and measuring of materials and structures as well as equipment and consumables used in the production of electronic subassemblies and microelectronics. The food equipment division provides commercial food equipment and related services. Products include warewashing equipment cooking and refrigeration equipment; food processing equipment; and kitchen exhaust, ventilation and pollution control systems. The polymer & fluids segment offers adhesives, sealants, lubrication and cutting fluids, janitorial and hygiene products and fluids and polymers for auto aftermarket maintenance and appearance. The welding segment produces arc welding equipment, consumables and accessories for a wide array of industrial and commercial applications. The construction products segment produces tools, fasteners and other products for construction applications. Products include packaged hardware, fasteners, anchors and other products for retail. Finally, the specialty products segment produces beverage packaging equipment and consumables; product coding and marking equipment and consumables; and appliance components and fasteners. In January 2016, the company agreed to acquire the Engineered Fasteners and Components business from ZF TRW.

FINANCIAL DATA: Note: Data for latest year may not have been available at press time.

In U.S. $	2016	2015	2014	2013	2012	2011
Revenue		13,405,000,000	14,484,000,000	14,135,000,000	17,924,000,000	17,786,580,000
R&D Expense						
Operating Income		2,867,000,000	2,888,000,000	2,514,000,000	2,847,000,000	2,731,008,000
Operating Margin %		21.38%	19.93%	17.78%	15.88%	15.35%
SGA Expense		2,417,000,000	2,678,000,000	2,815,000,000	3,332,000,000	3,282,352,000
Net Income		1,899,000,000	2,946,000,000	1,679,000,000	2,870,000,000	2,071,384,000
Operating Cash Flow		2,299,000,000	1,616,000,000	2,528,000,000	2,072,000,000	1,956,008,000
Capital Expenditure		284,000,000	361,000,000	368,000,000	382,000,000	353,408,000
EBITDA		3,422,000,000	3,456,000,000	3,199,000,000	4,430,000,000	3,378,856,000
Return on Assets %		11.36%	15.65%	8.55%	15.39%	12.10%
Return on Equity %		31.53%	35.66%	16.57%	27.89%	21.36%
Debt to Equity		1.32	0.87	0.28	0.43	0.34

CONTACT INFORMATION:

Phone: 847 724-7500   Fax: 847 657-4261
Toll-Free:
Address: 155 Harlem Avenue, Glenview, IL 60025 United States

STOCK TICKER/OTHER:

Stock Ticker: ITW   Exchange: NYS
Employees: 48,000   Fiscal Year Ends: 12/31
Parent Company:

SALARIES/BONUSES:

Top Exec. Salary: Bonus: $
$1,155,379
Second Exec. Salary: Bonus: $
$739,850

OTHER THOUGHTS:

Estimated Female Officers or Directors: 4

Hot Spot for Advancement for Women/Minorities: Y

IMG Worldwide Inc

img.com

NAIC Code: 711410

TYPES OF BUSINESS:

Agents-Athletes
Agents-Models
Agents-Writers, Artists & Musicians
Event Marketing
Corporate Marketing Consulting Services
Sports Television Programming
Sports Schools & Training

BRANDS/DIVISIONS/AFFILIATES:

William Morris Endeavor Entertainment LLC
Trans World International
CSI Sports
Tigress Productions Limited
Nunet AG
WME/IMG
Kovert Creative

CONTACTS: Note: Officers with more than one job title may be intentionally listed here more than once.

Ari Emanuel, Co-CEO
Patrick Whitesell, Co-CEO
Michel Masquelier, Pres., IMG Media
George Pyne, Pres., IMG Sports & Entertainment

GROWTH PLANS/SPECIAL FEATURES:

IMG Worldwide, Inc. is one of largest sports and lifestyle marketing and management agencies in the world. The company represents some of the world's top athletes, broadcasters, models, classical musicians, authors and newsmakers from offices in over 25 countries. The agency operates in a number of industries, including professional sports, college sports, fashion, entertainment, media and other various entertainment categories. Its sports operations handle everything from events and sponsorships to client representation and training. The company owns, produces and manages several prestigious sporting events, including events at Wimbledon and Nobel Prize functions. Sports clients have included tennis player Venus Williams, baseball player Derek Jeter, basketball player Charles Barkley and hockey player Jaromir Jagr. IMG's fashion and entertainment operations handle a multitude of events and personalities, including models Gisele Bundchen and Cindy Crawford. Its media operations create, distribute, sell and represent content across every medium. IMG's media division, along with the firm's subsidiaries TWI (Trans World International), CSI Sports, Tigress Productions Limited and Nunet AG, is one of the world's largest independent producers and distributors of televised sports programming. Annually, the company produces and distributes original programming to over 130 countries. IMG is a subsidiary of William Morris Endeavor Entertainment LLC (WME), with some of its work and solutions branded as WME/IMG. In January 2016, WME/IMG partnered with Joseph Assad and Lewis Kay to form Kovert Creative, a creative agency that brings together brands and talent in the core areas of digital services, personal & brand marketing and communications. Kovert Creative has offices in New York and Los Angeles.

FINANCIAL DATA: Note: Data for latest year may not have been available at press time.

In U.S. $	2016	2015	2014	2013	2012	2011
Revenue		1,800,000,000	1,705,000,000	1,650,000,000	1,500,000,000	1,400,000,000
R&D Expense						
Operating Income						
Operating Margin %						
SGA Expense						
Net Income						
Operating Cash Flow						
Capital Expenditure						
EBITDA						
Return on Assets %						
Return on Equity %						
Debt to Equity						

CONTACT INFORMATION:

Phone: 212-489-8300   Fax: 646-558-8399
Toll-Free:
Address: 200 5th Ave., Fl. 7, New York, NY 10010 United States

STOCK TICKER/OTHER:

Stock Ticker: Subsidiary   Exchange:
Employees: 3,500   Fiscal Year Ends: 12/31
Parent Company: William Morris Endeavor Entertainment LLC

SALARIES/BONUSES:

Top Exec. Salary: $ Bonus: $
Second Exec. Salary: $ Bonus: $

OTHER THOUGHTS:

Estimated Female Officers or Directors:
Hot Spot for Advancement for Women/Minorities:

IMS Health Holdings Inc

www.imshealth.com

NAIC Code: 541910

TYPES OF BUSINESS:

Market Research - Pharmaceuticals
Pharmaceutical Sales Tracking
Health Care Databases
Software-Sales Management & Market Research
Physician Profiling
Industry Audits
Prescription Tracking Reporting Services

BRANDS/DIVISIONS/AFFILIATES:

IMS One
IMS Health AETracker
Quintiles Transnational Holdings Inc
Quintiles IMS Holdings

CONTACTS: *Note: Officers with more than one job title may be intentionally listed here more than once.*

Ari Bousbib, CEO
Ronald Bruehlman, CFO
Harshan Bhangdia, Chief Accounting Officer
Harvey Ashman, General Counsel
Kevin Knightly, Senior VP, Divisional
Robert Chu, Senior VP, Divisional
Jose Fernandez, Senior VP, Divisional
Clinton Wolfe, Vice President, Divisional

GROWTH PLANS/SPECIAL FEATURES:

IMS Health Holdings, Inc. is a global information and technology services company for the health care industry. IMS Health is active in more than 100 countries, its scaled data set contains over 15 petabytes of unique data and over 500 million patient records. In 2015, 61% of generated revenue was derived from outside the U.S. IMS serves key health care organizations and decision makers around the world that span the breadth of life science companies, including pharmaceutical, biotechnology, consumer health and medical device manufacturers, as well as distributors, providers, payers, government agencies, policymakers, researchers and the financial community. The company leverages its proprietary information assets to develop technology and services with a health care-focused workforce. These capabilities include a health care-specific global IT infrastructure; a staff of more than 15,000 professionals; its cloud IMS One, which opens the IT infrastructure to clients; and a set of proprietary applications that include commercial applications, real-world evidence solutions, payer-provider solutions and clinical solutions. In 2015, the firm acquired certain relationship management and strategic data businesses of Cegedim. In March 2016, it launched IMS Health AETracker, an application for Hootsuite that enables life sciences companies to drive compliance and engagement with patients and healthcare providers on social media channels. The app is available on the Hootsuite App Directory and integrates with IMS Health's technology solution, AETracker. In May 2016, the firm agreed to merge with Quintiles Transnational Holdings, Inc. in an all-stock deal worth about $8.75 billion. The merged firm will be called Quintiles IMS Holdings.

FINANCIAL DATA: *Note: Data for latest year may not have been available at press time.*

In U.S. $	2016	2015	2014	2013	2012	2011
Revenue		2,921,000,000	2,641,000,000	2,544,000,000	2,443,000,000	2,364,000,000
R&D Expense						
Operating Income		364,000,000	208,000,000	354,000,000	239,000,000	219,000,000
Operating Margin %		12.46%	7.87%	13.91%	9.78%	9.26%
SGA Expense		712,000,000	721,000,000	596,000,000	579,000,000	604,000,000
Net Income		417,000,000	-189,000,000	82,000,000	-42,000,000	111,000,000
Operating Cash Flow		490,000,000	110,000,000	400,000,000	399,000,000	334,000,000
Capital Expenditure		183,000,000	167,000,000	122,000,000	108,000,000	104,000,000
EBITDA		727,000,000	377,000,000	694,000,000	638,000,000	608,000,000
Return on Assets %		5.70%	-2.49%	1.01%	-.50%	1.32%
Return on Equity %		26.78%	-15.58%	6.39%	-1.80%	3.73%
Debt to Equity		2.63	2.42	5.54	2.46	0.98

CONTACT INFORMATION:

Phone: 203-448-4600   Fax:
Toll-Free:
Address: 83 Wooster Heights Rd., Danbury, CT 06810 United States

STOCK TICKER/OTHER:

Stock Ticker: IMS   Exchange: NYS
Employees: 10,200   Fiscal Year Ends: 12/31
Parent Company:

SALARIES/BONUSES:

Top Exec. Salary: $1,600,000   Bonus: $
Second Exec. Salary: $487,562   Bonus: $

OTHER THOUGHTS:

Estimated Female Officers or Directors: 1

Hot Spot for Advancement for Women/Minorities: Y

Ingram Micro Inc

www.ingrammicro.com

NAIC Code: 423430

TYPES OF BUSINESS:

Microcomputers, Distribution
Networking Equipment
Software & Accessories Distribution
Supply Chain Management Services
Online Marketing Services

BRANDS/DIVISIONS/AFFILIATES:

ANOVO
CANAI Group
Clarity Technology
Odin Service Automation

CONTACTS: *Note: Officers with more than one job title may be intentionally listed here more than once.*

Alain Monie, CEO
William Humes, CFO
Dale Laurance, Chairman of the Board
Paul Read, COO
Larry Boyd, Executive VP
Shailendra Gupta, President, Divisional
Scott Sherman, Vice President, Divisional

GROWTH PLANS/SPECIAL FEATURES:

Ingram Micro, Inc. is a global distributor of IT products. The company markets microcomputer hardware, networking equipment and software products to over 200,000 resellers in approximately 160 countries. Ingram provides a comprehensive inventory of hundreds of thousands of distinct items from approximately 1,400 vendors. Its products are sold in five primary segments: IT peripherals, systems, software, networking and mobility. IT peripherals include printers, scanners, displays, projectors, monitors, panels, mass storage, tape, digital signage products, digital cameras, digital video disc players, game consoles, TVs, audio products, small appliances, media management, home control systems, barcode/card printers, AIDC scanners & software, wireless infrastructure products, physical security products, processors, motherboards, hard drives, memory, as well as ink & toner supplies, paper, carrying cases and anti-glare screens. Systems products include rack, tower & blade servers; desktops; and portable personal computers and tablets. Software products include business application software, operating system software, entertainment software, middleware, developer software tools, security software, storage software and virtualization software. Networking products include networking hardware, communication products and network security hardware such as switches, hubs, routers, wireless local area networks, wireless wide area networks, network interface cards, cellular data cards, network-attached storage and storage area networks. Mobility products include mobile handsets, tablets, navigation devices, aircards, SIM cards, flash memory and other mobile companion products, including health & fitness bands, wearables, app-cessories and services. Ingram also offers supply chain management services such as sales and marketing, customer care, financial services and logistics to suppliers and resellers. In February 2016, the firm agreed to be acquired by Tianjin Tianhai, a China-based shipping and distribution group.

Ingram offers its employees medical, dental and vision coverage; a 401(k) plan; adoption assistance; tuition reimbursement; and an employee assistance program.

FINANCIAL DATA: *Note: Data for latest year may not have been available at press time.*

In U.S. $	2016	2015	2014	2013	2012	2011
Revenue		43,025,850,000	46,487,430,000	42,553,920,000	37,827,300,000	36,328,700,000
R&D Expense						
Operating Income		415,316,000	487,262,000	514,875,000	462,352,000	458,646,000
Operating Margin %		.96%	1.04%	1.20%	1.22%	1.26%
SGA Expense		2,076,528,000	2,025,948,000	1,891,573,000	1,542,650,000	1,444,505,000
Net Income		215,105,000	266,691,000	310,583,000	305,909,000	244,240,000
Operating Cash Flow		1,455,953,000	-490,102,000	466,040,000	45,721,000	295,859,000
Capital Expenditure		122,918,000	88,651,000	95,639,000	92,300,000	122,188,000
EBITDA		531,436,000	618,507,000	624,179,000	522,290,000	497,662,000
Return on Assets %		1.71%	2.16%	2.66%	2.96%	2.67%
Return on Equity %		5.28%	6.57%	8.21%	8.88%	7.49%
Debt to Equity		0.27	0.26	0.20	0.26	0.09

CONTACT INFORMATION:

Phone: 714 566-1000   Fax: 714 566-7604
Toll-Free:
Address: 1600 E. St. Andrew Pl., Santa Ana, CA 92705-4926 United States

STOCK TICKER/OTHER:

Stock Ticker: IM
Employees: 21,700
Parent Company:

Exchange: NYS
Fiscal Year Ends: 12/31

SALARIES/BONUSES:

Top Exec. Salary: $1,000,000   Bonus: $
Second Exec. Salary: $734,999   Bonus: $

OTHER THOUGHTS:

Estimated Female Officers or Directors: 2

Hot Spot for Advancement for Women/Minorities: Y

Ingredion Inc

NAIC Code: 311000

www.ingredion.us/Pages/default.aspx

TYPES OF BUSINESS:

Food Products, Manufacturing
Wet Milling
Food Ingredients
Starch-Based Products
Cornstarch
Liquid Sweeteners

BRANDS/DIVISIONS/AFFILIATES:

Penford Corporation

CONTACTS: *Note: Officers with more than one job title may be intentionally listed here more than once.*

Ilene Gordon, CEO
James Zallie, Executive VP, Divisional
Jack Fortnum, Executive VP
Christine Castellano, General Counsel
Anthony Delio, Other Executive Officer
Robert Stefansic, Other Executive Officer
Jorgen Kokke, President, Geographical
Martin Sonntag, Senior VP, Divisional
Diane Frisch, Senior VP, Divisional
Matthew Galvanoni, Vice President, Divisional
Stephen Latreille, Vice President

GROWTH PLANS/SPECIAL FEATURES:

Ingredion Inc. is one of the world's largest corn refiners and a major supplier of food ingredients and industrial products derived from wet milling and processing of corn and other starch-based materials such as tapioca, potatoes and rice. Corn processing is a two-step process. During the front-end process, corn is steeped in a water-based solution and separated into starch and other co-products such as animal feed and germ. The starch is then dried for sale or further processed to make sweeteners and other ingredients that serve the particular needs of various industries. The company's sweetener products, which account for 39% of sales, include high fructose corn syrup, glucose corn syrups, high maltose corn syrups, caramel color, dextrose, polyols, maltodextrins and glucose and corn syrup solids. Starch-based products (43% of sales) include both industrial and food-grade starches. Ingredion's specialty ingredients (24% of sales) comprise select starch and sweetener ingredients that provide clean-label solutions that enable front-of-pack claims for customers. The firm serves customers in many diverse industries including the food and beverage, pharmaceutical, paper products, laminated paper, textile and brewing industries as well as the global animal feed and corn oil markets. Ingredion supplies a broad range of customers, including food, beverage, brewing, pharmaceutical, paper/corrugated products, textile, personal care, animal feed and corn oil markets. Ingredion owns and operates 36 manufacturing facilities within North America, South America, Asia Pacific and the EMEA. In 2015, the firm acquired Penford Corporation, a U.S-based specialty ingredients for food and non-food applications.

FINANCIAL DATA: *Note: Data for latest year may not have been available at press time.*

In U.S. $	2016	2015	2014	2013	2012	2011
Revenue		5,958,000,000	5,668,000,000	6,653,000,000	6,868,000,000	6,219,000,000
R&D Expense						
Operating Income		660,000,000	581,000,000	613,000,000	668,000,000	671,000,000
Operating Margin %		11.07%	10.25%	9.21%	9.72%	10.78%
SGA Expense		562,000,000	525,000,000	534,000,000	556,000,000	543,000,000
Net Income		402,000,000	355,000,000	396,000,000	428,000,000	416,000,000
Operating Cash Flow		686,000,000	731,000,000	619,000,000	732,000,000	300,000,000
Capital Expenditure		280,000,000	276,000,000	298,000,000	313,000,000	263,000,000
EBITDA		862,000,000	788,000,000	815,000,000	889,000,000	885,000,000
Return on Assets %		7.90%	6.79%	7.23%	7.84%	8.00%
Return on Equity %		18.60%	15.49%	16.36%	18.85%	20.39%
Debt to Equity		0.84	0.82	0.71	0.70	0.85

CONTACT INFORMATION:

Phone: 708-551-2600   Fax: 708-551-2700
Toll-Free: 800-443-2746
Address: 5 Westbrook Corporate Ctr., Westchester, IL 60154 United States

STOCK TICKER/OTHER:

Stock Ticker: INGR
Employees: 11,000
Parent Company:

Exchange: NYS
Fiscal Year Ends: 12/31

SALARIES/BONUSES:

Top Exec. Salary:
$1,145,460
Second Exec. Salary:
$590,812

Bonus: $

Bonus: $

OTHER THOUGHTS:

Estimated Female Officers or Directors: 7

Hot Spot for Advancement for Women/Minorities: Y

Integer Holdings Corporation

NAIC Code: 335911

TYPES OF BUSINESS:

Battery Manufacturing
Implantable Medical Device Components

BRANDS/DIVISIONS/AFFILIATES:

Greatbatch
Lake Region
Electrochem
Greatbatch Inc
QiG Group LLC
Nuvectra Corporation

CONTACTS: Note: Officers with more than one job title may be intentionally listed here more than once.

Thomas Hook, CEO
Thomas Mazza, Chief Accounting Officer
Bill Sanford, Director
Mauricio Arellano, Executive VP, Divisional
Kristin Trecker, Executive VP
Timothy McEvoy, General Counsel
Antonio Gonzalez, President, Divisional
Declan Smyth, President, Divisional
Jeremy Friedman, President, Divisional
Jennifer Bolt, President, Subsidiary
Michael Dinkins, Senior VP

GROWTH PLANS/SPECIAL FEATURES:

Integer Holdings Corporation (formerly Greatbatch, Inc.) is one of the largest medical device outsource manufacturers in the world. Integer comprises the following brands: Greatbatch, Lake Region and Electrochem. Greatbach develops and manufactures medical devices and components for cardiac rhythm management, neuromodulation, vascular and orthopedics. Lake Region develops and manufactures medical devices and components for the cardio & vascular and advanced surgical markets, including solutions for electrophysiology, vascular access, cardiovascular, urology, oncology, orthopedics, laparoscopy, biopsy/drug delivery and arthroscopy. Electrochem provides customized battery power and management solutions, charging/docking stations and power supplies for energy, military and environmental applications. In October 2015, Greatbatch acquired Lake Region Medical for $1.73 billion, and subsequently merged with Lake Region to form a new company called Integer Holdings Corporation, which became effective July 1, 2016. Additionally, in February 2016, former Greatbatch spun off subsidiary QiG Group LLC and changed its name to Nuvectra Corporation. Nuvectra focuses on the design and development of medical device systems and components.

FINANCIAL DATA: Note: Data for latest year may not have been available at press time.

In U.S. $	2016	2015	2014	2013	2012	2011
Revenue		800,414,016	687,787,008	663,945,024	646,177,024	568,822,016
R&D Expense						
Operating Income						
Operating Margin %						
SGA Expense						
Net Income		-7,594,000	55,458,000	36,267,000	-4,799,000	33,122,000
Operating Cash Flow						
Capital Expenditure						
EBITDA						
Return on Assets %						
Return on Equity %						
Debt to Equity						

CONTACT INFORMATION:

Phone: 716 759-5600   Fax: 716 759-5654
Toll-Free:
Address: 2595 Dallas Parkway, Ste. 310, Frisco, TX 75034 United States

STOCK TICKER/OTHER:

Stock Ticker: GB   Exchange: NYS
Employees: 9,559   Fiscal Year Ends: 12/31
Parent Company:

SALARIES/BONUSES:

Top Exec. Salary: $ Bonus: $
Second Exec. Salary: $ Bonus: $

OTHER THOUGHTS:

Estimated Female Officers or Directors:
Hot Spot for Advancement for Women/Minorities:

Intel Corp

NAIC Code: 334413

TYPES OF BUSINESS:

Microprocessors
Semiconductors
Circuit Boards
Flash Memory Products
Software Development
Home Network Equipment
Digital Imaging Products
Healthcare Products

BRANDS/DIVISIONS/AFFILIATES:

Ultrabook
McAfee LiveSafe
Intel Edison
McAfee Inc

CONTACTS: *Note: Officers with more than one job title may be intentionally listed here more than once.*

Brian Krzanich, CEO
Kirk Skaugen, General Manager, Divisional
Stacy Smith, CFO
Andy Bryant, Chairman of the Board
Thomas Kilroy, Executive VP, Divisional
William Holt, Executive VP
Venkata Renduchintala, Executive VP
Gregory Pearson, General Manager, Divisional
Sohail Ahmed, General Manager, Divisional
Josh Walden, General Manager, Divisional
Christopher Young, General Manager, Divisional
Amir Faintuch, General Manager, Divisional
Hermann Eul, General Manager, Divisional
Aicha Evans, General Manager, Divisional
Mike Bell, General Manager, Divisional
Ann Kelleher, General Manager, Subsidiary
Suzan Miller, Other Corporate Officer
Richard Taylor, Other Corporate Officer

GROWTH PLANS/SPECIAL FEATURES:

Intel Corp. is a global semiconductor chip maker that develops advanced integrated digital technology platforms for the computing and communications industries. It operates in five divisions: client computing group, data center group, Internet of Things group, software and services operating segments and other. The client computing group provides Intel architecture-based products and platforms for notebooks, including the Ultrabook system, home gateway products, set-top box components and desktops for businesses and consumers. The data center group provides technology for virtualization, energy efficiency and performance of servers, storage and workstation platforms. The Internet of Things group offers platforms for customers to design products for the retail, transportation, industrial and buildings and home market segments. It also focuses on establishing an end-to-end architecture that captures information for consumers. It launched the Intel Edison development platform designed to empower wearables, robotics and other small devices by connecting, creating and consuming data. The software and services operating segments, including its McAfee LiveSafe service, develops platforms that can be used across many operating systems, applications and all Intel products, delivering a comprehensive security suite that offers consumer protection. The all other segment primarily consists of revenue from its non-volatile memory solutions group, its netbook group and its new devices group segments. Subsidiary McAfee, Inc. offers software and hardware and hardware products that provide security solutions to protect systems in consumer, mobile and corporate environments from malicious virus attacks and loss of data. In March 2016, the firm acquired Altera Corp.

FINANCIAL DATA: *Note: Data for latest year may not have been available at press time.*

In U.S. $	2016	2015	2014	2013	2012	2011
Revenue		55,355,000,000	55,870,000,000	52,708,000,000	53,341,000,000	53,999,000,000
R&D Expense		12,128,000,000	11,537,000,000	10,611,000,000	10,148,000,000	8,350,000,000
Operating Income		14,002,000,000	15,347,000,000	12,291,000,000	14,638,000,000	17,477,000,000
Operating Margin %		25.29%	27.46%	23.31%	27.44%	32.36%
SGA Expense		7,930,000,000	8,136,000,000	8,088,000,000	8,057,000,000	7,670,000,000
Net Income		11,420,000,000	11,704,000,000	9,620,000,000	11,005,000,000	12,942,000,000
Operating Cash Flow		19,017,000,000	20,418,000,000	20,776,000,000	18,884,000,000	20,963,000,000
Capital Expenditure		7,446,000,000	10,197,000,000	10,747,000,000	11,842,000,000	10,764,000,000
EBITDA		23,260,000,000	23,896,000,000	20,887,000,000	22,485,000,000	23,886,000,000
Return on Assets %		11.71%	12.70%	10.88%	14.15%	19.27%
Return on Equity %		19.52%	20.51%	17.57%	22.66%	27.14%
Debt to Equity		0.32	0.21	0.22	0.25	0.15

CONTACT INFORMATION:

Phone: 408 765-8080   Fax: 408 765-2633
Toll-Free: 800-628-8686
Address: 2200 Mission College Blvd., Santa Clara, CA 95054 United States

STOCK TICKER/OTHER:

Stock Ticker: INTC
Employees: 107,300
Parent Company:

Exchange: NAS
Fiscal Year Ends: 12/31

SALARIES/BONUSES:

Top Exec. Salary:
$1,100,000
Second Exec. Salary:
$850,000

Bonus: $

Bonus: $

OTHER THOUGHTS:

Estimated Female Officers or Directors: 10

Hot Spot for Advancement for Women/Minorities: Y

Interpublic Group of Companies Inc

www.interpublic.com

NAIC Code: 541810

TYPES OF BUSINESS:

Advertising Services
Marketing & Branding
Market Research
Public Relations
Online Marketing
Direct Marketing
Promotions & Events
Sports & Entertainment Marketing

BRANDS/DIVISIONS/AFFILIATES:

Foote, Cone & Belding
IPG Mediabrands
MullenLowe Group
McCann Worldgroup
Weber Shandwick
Cassidy
DeVries

CONTACTS: *Note: Officers with more than one job title may be intentionally listed here more than once.*

Michael Roth, CEO
Frank Mergenthaler, CFO
Christopher Carroll, Chief Accounting Officer
Julie Connors, Chief Risk Officer
Philippe Krakowsky, Executive VP
Andrew Bonzani, General Counsel
Ellen Johnson, Senior VP, Divisional

GROWTH PLANS/SPECIAL FEATURES:

Interpublic Group of Companies, Inc. (IPG) is a group comprising of hundreds of advertising and specialized marketing and communications services companies that combined represent one of the largest resources of advertising and marketing expertise in the world, with offices and affiliations in over 100 countries. The firm operates through two divisions: integrated agency networks (IAN) and constituency management group (CMG). IAN is comprised of Foote, Cone & Belding (FCB), IPG Mediabrands, MullenLowe Group and McCann Worldgroup, its digital specialist and domestic integrated agencies. IAN agencies provide an array of global communications and marketing services, each offering a distinctive range of solutions for clients. Its digital specialist agencies provide digital capabilities, and its domestic integrated agencies provide advertising, marketing, communications services and/or marketing services and partner with the firm's global operating divisions as needed. CMG is comprised of a number of specialist marketing service offerings which includes Weber Shandwick, Cassidy, DeVries, Golin, FutureBrand, Jack Morton and Octagon Worldwide. These marketing service subsidiaries provide clients with public relations, meeting and event production, sports and entertainment marketing, corporate and brand identity and marketing consulting. IPG's five largest clients are General Motors, Johnson & Johnson, L'Oreal, Samsung and Unilever. In 2015, IPG acquired majority stake in the Russian affiliates of the company's three global creative networks, McCann, Mullen Lowe and FCB, from ADV, its long-term partner in the country.

FINANCIAL DATA: *Note: Data for latest year may not have been available at press time.*

In U.S. $	2016	2015	2014	2013	2012	2011
Revenue		7,613,800,000	7,537,100,000	7,122,300,000	6,956,200,000	7,014,600,000
R&D Expense						
Operating Income		871,900,000	788,400,000	598,300,000	678,300,000	687,200,000
Operating Margin %		11.45%	10.46%	8.40%	9.75%	9.79%
SGA Expense		6,742,700,000	6,748,500,000	6,463,400,000	6,277,900,000	6,326,400,000
Net Income		454,600,000	477,100,000	267,900,000	446,700,000	532,300,000
Operating Cash Flow		674,000,000	669,500,000	592,900,000	357,200,000	273,500,000
Capital Expenditure		161,100,000	148,700,000	173,000,000	169,200,000	140,300,000
EBITDA		1,005,000,000	968,600,000	748,100,000	956,000,000	1,026,100,000
Return on Assets %		3.58%	3.71%	1.96%	3.29%	4.01%
Return on Equity %		22.27%	22.02%	11.74%	19.60%	22.89%
Debt to Equity		0.81	0.76	0.51	0.93	0.54

CONTACT INFORMATION:

Phone: 212 704-1200   Fax: 212 399-8130
Toll-Free:
Address: 909 Third Ave., New York, NY 10022 United States

STOCK TICKER/OTHER:

Stock Ticker: IPG   Exchange: NYS
Employees: 45,400   Fiscal Year Ends: 12/31
Parent Company:

SALARIES/BONUSES:

Top Exec. Salary: Bonus: $
$1,500,000
Second Exec. Salary: Bonus: $
$1,000,000

OTHER THOUGHTS:

Estimated Female Officers or Directors: 9

Hot Spot for Advancement for Women/Minorities: Y

Intuit Inc
NAIC Code: 0

www.intuit.com

TYPES OF BUSINESS:
Computer Software-Financial Management
Business Accounting Software
Consumer Finance Software
Tax Preparation Software
Online Financial Services

BRANDS/DIVISIONS/AFFILIATES:
QuickBooks
TurboTax
Lacerte
ProSeries
ProFile
Intuit Tax Online
QuickBooks Pro
QuickBooks Desktop for Mac

CONTACTS: Note: Officers with more than one job title may be intentionally listed here more than once.
R. Williams, CFO
William Campbell, Chairman Emeritus
Brad Smith, Chairman of the Board
Mark Flournoy, Chief Accounting Officer
H. Stansbury, Chief Technology Officer
Daniel Wernikoff, Executive VP
Laura Fennell, Executive VP
Scott Cook, Founder
Sasan Goodarzi, General Manager, Divisional

GROWTH PLANS/SPECIAL FEATURES:
Intuit, Inc. is a provider of software and web-based services specializing in financial management and tax solutions. The company has three business segments: small business consumer tax and professional tax. The small business segment targets small businesses and the accounting professionals who serve them. This division includes QuickBooks financial and business management online services and desktop software, payroll solutions and payment processing solutions. QuickBooks is a desktop software portfolio which includes QuickBooks Pro and QuickBooks Desktop for Mac, providing accounting functionality for small businesses; and QuickBooks Premier, providing small businesses with advanced accounting functionality and business planning tools. The consumer tax segment targets consumers, and includes TurboTax income tax preparation products and services. TurboTax products and services are designed to enable individuals to prepare and file their own federal and state personal income tax returns quickly and accurately. The professional tax segment targets professional accountants in the U.S. and Canada, and includes Lacerte ProSeries, ProFile and Intuit Tax Online professional tax products and services. Lacerte is designed for full service accounting firms who handle more complex returns. ProSeries offers two software versions: ProSeries Professional Edition designed for year-round tax practices handling moderately complex tax returns; and ProSeries Basic Edition, for the needs of smaller and seasonal tax practices. ProFile is a Canadian tax offering which werves year-round full service accounting firms for both consumer and business tax returns. Intuit Tax Online is the firm's cloud-based solution designed for year-round practices who prepared moderately complex consumer and small business returns and integrates with the QuickBooks Online offerings. The firm sold its Intuit Health business in early 2014. During 2015, it divested its Demandforce and QuickBase businesses.

Intuit employees receive health, dental and life insurance; a 401(k) savings plan; an employee stock purchase plan; and an employee assistance program.

FINANCIAL DATA: Note: Data for latest year may not have been available at press time.

In U.S. $	2016	2015	2014	2013	2012	2011
Revenue	4,694,000,000	4,192,000,000	4,506,000,000	4,171,000,000	4,151,000,000	3,851,000,000
R&D Expense	881,000,000	798,000,000	758,000,000	685,000,000	669,000,000	634,000,000
Operating Income	1,242,000,000	738,000,000	1,314,000,000	1,233,000,000	1,177,000,000	1,007,000,000
Operating Margin %	26.45%	17.60%	29.16%	29.56%	28.35%	26.14%
SGA Expense	1,807,000,000	1,771,000,000	1,746,000,000	1,641,000,000	1,506,000,000	1,465,000,000
Net Income	979,000,000	365,000,000	907,000,000	858,000,000	792,000,000	634,000,000
Operating Cash Flow	1,401,000,000	1,504,000,000	1,446,000,000	1,366,000,000	1,246,000,000	1,013,000,000
Capital Expenditure	522,000,000	261,000,000	201,000,000	209,000,000	196,000,000	228,000,000
EBITDA	1,476,000,000	970,000,000	1,542,000,000	1,472,000,000	1,443,000,000	1,267,000,000
Return on Assets %	21.24%	7.17%	16.97%	16.87%	16.17%	12.30%
Return on Equity %	56.05%	13.49%	27.44%	27.34%	29.55%	23.32%
Debt to Equity	0.42	0.21	0.16	0.14	0.18	0.19

CONTACT INFORMATION:
Phone: 650 944-6000   Fax: 650 944-3060
Toll-Free: 800-446-8848
Address: 2700 Coast Ave, Mountain View, CA 94043 United States

STOCK TICKER/OTHER:
Stock Ticker: INTU
Employees: 7,900
Parent Company:

Exchange: NAS
Fiscal Year Ends: 07/31

SALARIES/BONUSES:
Top Exec. Salary:
$1,000,000
Second Exec. Salary:
$700,000

Bonus: $

Bonus: $

OTHER THOUGHTS:
Estimated Female Officers or Directors: 5

Hot Spot for Advancement for Women/Minorities: Y

inVentiv Health Inc

www.inventivhealth.com

NAIC Code: 541613

TYPES OF BUSINESS:

Marketing-Life Sciences & Pharmaceuticals
Sales & Marketing Outsourcing
Clinical Staffing
Health Care Communications
Advertising Services
Data Services
Sales Force Deployment
Clinical Research Services

BRANDS/DIVISIONS/AFFILIATES:

inVentiv Health Clinical Division
Addison Whitney
inVentiv Health Public Relations Group
Navicor
Adheris Health
inVentiv Group Holdings Inc
inVentiv Therapeutics Institute
inVentiv Recruitment Solutions

CONTACTS: Note: Officers with more than one job title may be intentionally listed here more than once.

Michael Bell, CEO
Jonathan E. Bicknell, CFO
Rachel Stahler, CIO
Eric M. Sherbet, General Counsel
Sydney Rubin, Chief Comm. Officer
Paul Mignon, Pres., inVentiv Health Selling Solutions
Ray Hill, Exec. VP
Mark Dmytruk, Pres., inVentiv Health Patient Outcomes
Kelly Gratz, Pres., inVentiv Health Commercial Solutions
Michael Bell, Chmn.

GROWTH PLANS/SPECIAL FEATURES:

inVentiv Health, Inc. is a clinical services and marketing services provider for the pharmaceutical and life sciences industries. Services include sales and marketing, clinical staffing, planning and analytics, marketing support, professional development and training and data collection and management. The company operates in six core business units: commercial, clinical, communication, consulting, patient outcomes and selling solutions. Commercial specializes in providing sales teams and sales support services, including clinical educators, medical science liaisons and sales staffing and training; marketing and communications, such as advertising, branding, PR, patient education and digital and social media strategies; and patient outcomes, which include services related to patient adherence, assistance and reimbursement as well as disease management and cost containment. Clinical is comprised of inVentiv Health Clinical Division, which is a clinical research organization (CRO) that provides global drug development services to pharmaceutical, biotechnology, generic drug and medical device companies, with capabilities in Phase I-IV clinical development, bioanalytical services and strategic resourcing. The communications unit consists of Addison Whitney, a full-service brand identity consultancy; GSW Worldwide, a full-service healthcare communications agency; inVentiv Health Public Relations Group, which is comprised five of global health communications agencies: Ilidura Consumer, Biosector 2, Chamberlain Healthcare PR, Chandler Chicco Agency and Haas & Health Partner ; Navicor, a healthcare advertising agency; and PALIO advertising agency. The consulting unit, through Campbell Alliance, offers specialized consulting services to clients in the pharmaceutical and biotech industries. The patient outcomes unit consists of Adheris Health, a provider of tailored, direct-to-patient medication adherence programs. The selling solutions unit is comprised of inVentiv Health Selling Solutions; inVentiv Recruitment Solutions; and inVentiv Therapeutics Institute. The firm s privately owned by inVentiv Group Holdings, Inc., an organization sponsored by affiliates of Thomas H. Lee Partners, L.P., Liberty Lane Partners and members of the inVentiv Health management team.

FINANCIAL DATA: Note: Data for latest year may not have been available at press time.

In U.S. $	2016	2015	2014	2013	2012	2011
Revenue		2,350,000,000	2,200,000,000	2,180,000,000	2,070,000,000	1,930,000,000
R&D Expense						
Operating Income						
Operating Margin %						
SGA Expense						
Net Income						
Operating Cash Flow						
Capital Expenditure						
EBITDA						
Return on Assets %						
Return on Equity %						
Debt to Equity						

CONTACT INFORMATION:

Phone: 800-416-0555   Fax:
Toll-Free:
Address: 1 Van de Graaff Dr., Burlington, MA 01803 United States

STOCK TICKER/OTHER:

Stock Ticker: Private   Exchange:
Employees: 14,000   Fiscal Year Ends: 12/31
Parent Company: inVentiv Group Holdings Inc

SALARIES/BONUSES:

Top Exec. Salary: $ Bonus: $
Second Exec. Salary: $ Bonus: $

OTHER THOUGHTS:

Estimated Female Officers or Directors: 1
Hot Spot for Advancement for Women/Minorities: Y

Jabil Circuit Inc

NAIC Code: 334418

www.jabil.com

TYPES OF BUSINESS:

Contract Electronics Manufacturing
Maintenance & Support Services
Custom Design Services

BRANDS/DIVISIONS/AFFILIATES:

Plasticos Castella

CONTACTS: Note: Officers with more than one job title may be intentionally listed here more than once.

Michael Loparco, CEO, Divisional
Alessandro Parimbelli, CEO, Divisional
Courtney Ryan, CEO, Subsidiary
Mark Mondello, CEO
Forbes Alexander, CFO
Timothy Main, Chairman of the Board
Meheryar Dastoor, Controller
William Muir, COO
Thomas Sansone, Director
Joseph Mcgee, Executive VP, Divisional
Scott Slipy, Executive VP, Divisional
Robert Paver, General Counsel
William Peters, President
Sergio Cadavid, Senior VP

GROWTH PLANS/SPECIAL FEATURES:

Jabil Circuit, Inc. (JBL) is a provider of worldwide electronic manufacturing services. It provides electronics design, production and product management services to a broad range of companies. JBL divides its operations into two segments: diversified manufacturing services (DMS) and electronics manufacturing services (EMS). DMS is focused on providing engineering solutions and on material sciences & technologies. This segment includes customers primarily in the consumer lifestyles & wearable technologies, defense & aerospace, emerging growth, health care, mobility and packaging industries. EMS is focused around leveraging information technology, supply chain design & engineering, technologies largely centered on core electronics, sharing of JBL's large-scale manufacturing infrastructure and the ability to serve a broad range of end markets. This segment includes customers primarily in the automotive, digital home, industrial & energy, networking & telecommunications, point of sale, printing and storage industries. The firm maintains facilities located worldwide, including Austria, Belgium, Brazil, Canada, China, Finland, France, Germany, Hungary, India, Ireland, Israel, Italy, Japan, Malaysia, Mexico, The Netherlands, Poland, Russia, Scotland, Singapore, South Korea, Spain, Taiwan, Ukraine, the U.S. and Vietnam. Its largest customers include Apple, Inc.; Cisco Systems, Inc.; LM Ericsson Telephone Company; General Electric Company; Hewlett-Packard Company; Ingenico SA; NetApp, Inc.; Sony Mobile Communications, Inc.; Valeo SA; and Zebra Technologies Corporation. In 2015, the firm acquired Plasticos Castella, a European manufacturer of plastic products for the food, beverage and consumer product goods industries.

FINANCIAL DATA: Note: Data for latest year may not have been available at press time.

In U.S. $	2016	2015	2014	2013	2012	2011
Revenue		17,899,200,000	15,762,150,000	18,336,890,000	17,151,940,000	16,518,830,000
R&D Expense		27,645,000	28,611,000	28,468,000	25,837,000	25,034,000
Operating Income		555,411,000	204,074,000	511,438,000	621,931,000	578,734,000
Operating Margin %		3.10%	1.29%	2.78%	3.62%	3.50%
SGA Expense		862,647,000	675,730,000	688,752,000	644,452,000	604,179,000
Net Income		284,019,000	241,313,000	371,482,000	394,687,000	381,063,000
Operating Cash Flow		1,240,282,000	498,857,000	1,213,889,000	634,226,000	828,009,000
Capital Expenditure		963,145,000	624,060,000	736,858,000	497,697,000	458,989,000
EBITDA		1,088,913,000	687,456,000	925,243,000	968,521,000	898,059,000
Return on Assets %		3.14%	2.73%	4.38%	5.31%	5.67%
Return on Equity %		12.46%	10.54%	16.73%	19.87%	22.12%
Debt to Equity		0.58	0.74	0.72	0.78	0.59

CONTACT INFORMATION:

Phone: 727 577-9749 Fax: 727 579-8529
Toll-Free:
Address: 10560 Dr. Martin Luther King Jr. St. N., St. Petersburg, FL 33716 United States

STOCK TICKER/OTHER:

Stock Ticker: JBL
Employees: 161,000
Parent Company:

Exchange: NYS
Fiscal Year Ends: 08/31

SALARIES/BONUSES:

Top Exec. Salary: $1,050,000 Bonus: $
Second Exec. Salary: $670,000 Bonus: $

OTHER THOUGHTS:

Estimated Female Officers or Directors:

Hot Spot for Advancement for Women/Minorities: Y

Jack Henry & Associates Inc

www.jackhenry.com

NAIC Code: 0

TYPES OF BUSINESS:

Software-Data Processing
Financial Services Software
Consulting Services
Hardware Sales

BRANDS/DIVISIONS/AFFILIATES:

Silverlake
CIF 20/20
Core Director
Episys
Symitar
ProfitStars
Banno
Bayside Business Solutions

CONTACTS: *Note: Officers with more than one job title may be intentionally listed here more than once.*

Kevin Williams, CFO
John Prim, Chairman of the Board
Mark Forbis, Chief Technology Officer
Matthew Flanigan, Director
David Foss, President
Robert Schendel, Secretary

GROWTH PLANS/SPECIAL FEATURES:

Jack Henry & Associates, Inc. (JHA) is a provider of integrated computer systems relating to data processing and management information for banks, credit unions and other financial institutions in the U.S. The company serves nearly 10,900 financial institutions and corporate entities. It provides products and services through three marketed brands: Jack Henry Banking, Symitar and ProfitStars. Jack Henry Banking currently supports more than 1,200 commercial banks with information and transaction processing platforms that provide enterprise-wide automation. Its core banking software platforms include SilverLake, an IBM System i-based product designed for commercial-focused banks with assets ranging from $500 million to $30 billion; CIF 20/20, an IBM-System i-based system that supports nearly 570 banks ranging from new institutions to those with assets exceeding $2 billion; and Core Director, a Windows-based client/server system that serves more than 200 banks ranging from new institutions to banks with assets over $1 billion. The Symitar brand supports credit unions through its two core platforms: Episys, an IBM System p-based program designed for credit unions with more than $50 million in assets; and Cruise, designed for credit unions with less than $50 million in assets. Profit Stars provides specialized products and services to nearly 10,500 financial services organizations. Products include business intelligence and management applications, retail delivery products, business banking systems, electronic funds transfer products, Internet banking products, risk management and protection programs, document imaging products and professional services and education products. In 2014, the firm acquired Banno, a provider of data-enriched web and transaction marketing services. In July 2015, it acquired Bayside Business Solutions, a portfolio management systems provider.

The firm offers employees medical, dental and vision insurance; flexible spending accounts; and education assistance.

FINANCIAL DATA: *Note: Data for latest year may not have been available at press time.*

In U.S. $	2016	2015	2014	2013	2012	2011
Revenue	1,354,646,000	1,256,190,000	1,210,053,000	1,129,386,000	1,027,109,000	966,897,000
R&D Expense	81,234,000	71,495,000	66,748,000	63,202,000	60,876,000	63,395,000
Operating Income	361,659,000	317,865,000	311,999,000	265,547,000	236,235,000	216,317,000
Operating Margin %	26.69%	25.30%	25.78%	23.51%	23.00%	22.37%
SGA Expense	157,593,000	146,494,000	139,882,000	148,243,000	126,619,000	119,622,000
Net Income	248,867,000	211,221,000	201,136,000	176,645,000	154,984,000	137,471,000
Operating Cash Flow	365,116,000	373,790,000	341,659,000	309,174,000	264,550,000	240,132,000
Capital Expenditure	164,562,000	145,301,000	111,667,000	97,774,000	80,034,000	59,039,000
EBITDA	491,614,000	437,030,000	420,147,000	366,528,000	332,030,000	306,956,000
Return on Assets %	13.62%	12.20%	12.36%	10.87%	9.91%	8.95%
Return on Equity %	25.04%	20.81%	19.06%	17.18%	16.63%	16.86%
Debt to Equity		0.05			0.10	0.14

CONTACT INFORMATION:

Phone: 417 235-6652   Fax:
Toll-Free: 800-299-4222
Address: 663 W. Hwy. 60, Monett, MO 65708 United States

STOCK TICKER/OTHER:

Stock Ticker: JKHY   Exchange: NAS
Employees: 5,822   Fiscal Year Ends: 06/30
Parent Company:

SALARIES/BONUSES:

Top Exec. Salary: $606,934   Bonus: $
Second Exec. Salary: $461,891   Bonus: $

OTHER THOUGHTS:

Estimated Female Officers or Directors: 3
Hot Spot for Advancement for Women/Minorities: Y

Jackson National Life Insurance Company   www.jnl.com

NAIC Code: 524113

TYPES OF BUSINESS:

Life Insurance
Financial Services
Annuities
Asset Management
Retail Brokerage Services

BRANDS/DIVISIONS/AFFILIATES:

Prudential plc
Jackson National Asset Management
SII Investments Inc
National Planning Holdings Inc
PPM America Inc
Jackson National Life Insurance Company

CONTACTS: Note: Officers with more than one job title may be intentionally listed here more than once.

James R. Sopha, Pres.
P. Chad Myers, CFO
Machelle A. McAdory, Chief Human Resources Officer
Keith R. Moore, Group Chief Tech. Officer
Laura L. Prieskorn, Chief Admin. Officer
Thomas J. Meyer, General Counsel
Kenneth H. Stewart, Sr. VP-Corp. Dev.
Richard A. Ash, Chief Actuary
Leandra R. Knes, CEO
Michael A. Bell, CEO
Greg P. Cicotte, Pres., Jackson National Life Distributors LLC
Barry L. Stowe, Chmn.

GROWTH PLANS/SPECIAL FEATURES:

Jackson National Life Insurance Company, an indirect wholly owned subsidiary of U.K. firm Prudential plc, offers life insurance and financial services such as fixed, indexed and variable annuities. In addition, through subsidiaries and affiliated firms, the company offers asset management and retail brokerage services. The firm is comprised of more than 5,000 associates, over 138,000 advisors and more than 4 million policies and contracts as of December 2015. Jackson National markets its products throughout the U.S. through wholesalers and broker/dealers. Subsidiary Jackson National Asset Management provides investment advisory, transfer agency, fund accounting and administration services for funds and separate accounts that support Jackson's variable products and employee 401(k) retirement plan. SII Investments, Inc. is a broker/dealer to financial advisors. National Planning Holdings, Inc. is Jackson National's affiliated network of independent broker-dealers. Subsidiary PPM America, Inc. is an asset manager that provides investment services for a variety of institutional mandates and retail products sourced primarily from affiliates, including Jackson as well as affiliates in the U.K. and Asia. Jackson National Life Insurance Company of New York offers an array of products, primarily variable and fixed annuities, designed to help customers plan for retirement.

Employee benefits include health, dental and vision coverage; flexible spending accounts; an employee assistance program; 401(k) with company match; a profit sharing program; life insurance; short- and long-term disability; employee discounts; tuition reimbursement; and subsidized onsite day care.

FINANCIAL DATA: Note: Data for latest year may not have been available at press time.

In U.S. $	2016	2015	2014	2013	2012	2011
Revenue		6,698,142,000	4,472,890,000	5,396,953,000	5,106,904,000	4,184,800,000
R&D Expense						
Operating Income						
Operating Margin %						
SGA Expense						
Net Income		1,400,900,000	350,769	755,162,000	937,755,000	697,153,000
Operating Cash Flow						
Capital Expenditure						
EBITDA						
Return on Assets %						
Return on Equity %						
Debt to Equity						

CONTACT INFORMATION:

Phone: 517-381-5500   Fax: 800-701-0125
Toll-Free:
Address: 1 Corporate Way, Lansing, MI 48951 United States

STOCK TICKER/OTHER:

Stock Ticker: Subsidiary   Exchange:
Employees: 5,000   Fiscal Year Ends: 12/31
Parent Company: Prudential plc

SALARIES/BONUSES:

Top Exec. Salary: $ Bonus: $
Second Exec. Salary: $ Bonus: $

OTHER THOUGHTS:

Estimated Female Officers or Directors: 3
Hot Spot for Advancement for Women/Minorities: Y

Jacobs Engineering Group Inc

www.jacobs.com

NAIC Code: 237000

TYPES OF BUSINESS:

Engineering & Design Services
Facility Management
Construction & Field Services
Technical Consulting Services
Environmental Services

BRANDS/DIVISIONS/AFFILIATES:

J L Patterson & Associates

CONTACTS: Note: Officers with more than one job title may be intentionally listed here more than once.

Kevin Berryman, CFO
Noel Watson, Chairman of the Board
Santo Rizzuto, Executive VP, Divisional
Michael Tyler, General Counsel
Andrew Kremer, President, Divisional
Terence Hagen, President, Divisional
Joseph Mandel, President, Divisional
Steven Demetriou, President
Cora Carmody, Senior VP, Divisional
Lori Sundberg, Senior VP, Divisional

GROWTH PLANS/SPECIAL FEATURES:

Jacobs Engineering Group, Inc. offers technical, professional and construction services to industrial, commercial and governmental clients throughout North America, Europe, Asia, South America, India, the U.K. and Australia. Jacobs provides project services, which include engineering, design and architecture; process, scientific and systems consulting services; operations and maintenance services; and construction services, which include direct-hire construction and management services. Services are offered to industry groups such as oil & gas exploration, production and refining; pharmaceuticals & biotechnology; chemicals & polymers; buildings, which includes projects in the fields of health care and education as well as civic, governmental and other buildings; infrastructure; technology; energy; consumer & forest products; automotive & industrial; and environmental programs. Jacobs also provides pricing studies, project feasibility reports and automation & control system analysis for U.S. government agencies involved in defense and aerospace programs. In addition, the company is one of the leading providers of environmental engineering and consulting services in the U.S. and abroad, providing support in such areas as underground storage tank removal, contaminated soil and water remediation and long-term groundwater monitoring. Jacobs also designs, builds, installs, operates and maintains various types of soil and groundwater cleanup systems. In December 2015, the firm acquired J. L. Patterson & Associates, a consulting and professional services engineering firm specializing in rail planning, environmental permitting, design and construction management.

Jacobs offers its employees medical, disability, life and AD&D insurance; an employee stock purchase plan; and tuition reimbursement.

FINANCIAL DATA: Note: Data for latest year may not have been available at press time.

In U.S. $	2016	2015	2014	2013	2012	2011
Revenue		12,114,830,000	12,695,160,000	11,818,380,000	10,893,780,000	10,381,660,000
R&D Expense						
Operating Income		445,527,000	528,068,000	668,979,000	596,073,000	518,918,000
Operating Margin %		3.67%	4.15%	5.66%	5.47%	4.99%
SGA Expense		1,522,811,000	1,545,716,000	1,173,340,000	1,130,916,000	1,040,575,000
Net Income		302,971,000	328,108,000	423,093,000	378,954,000	331,029,000
Operating Cash Flow		484,572,000	721,716,000	448,516,000	299,805,000	236,490,000
Capital Expenditure		88,404,000	132,146,000	127,270,000	102,574,000	98,749,000
EBITDA		598,932,000	699,015,000	773,328,000	705,846,000	620,830,000
Return on Assets %		3.73%	4.17%	5.99%	5.88%	6.16%
Return on Equity %		6.91%	7.55%	10.66%	10.77%	10.72%
Debt to Equity		0.13	0.17	0.09	0.14	

CONTACT INFORMATION:

Phone: 626 578-3500   Fax: 626 578-6988
Toll-Free:
Address: 155 N. Lake Ave., Pasadena, CA 91101 United States

STOCK TICKER/OTHER:

Stock Ticker: JEC   Exchange: NYS
Employees: 49,900   Fiscal Year Ends: 09/30
Parent Company:

SALARIES/BONUSES:

Top Exec. Salary: $125,000   Bonus: $5,650,000
Second Exec. Salary: $544,832   Bonus: $1,500,000

OTHER THOUGHTS:

Estimated Female Officers or Directors: 1
Hot Spot for Advancement for Women/Minorities: Y

Sales, profits and employees may be estimates. Financial information, benefits and other data can change quickly and may vary from those stated here.

JB Hunt Transport Services Inc

www.jbhunt.com

NAIC Code: 484121

TYPES OF BUSINESS:

General Trucking
Logistics Services
Intermodal Services
Dedicated Fleet Services

BRANDS/DIVISIONS/AFFILIATES:

CONTACTS: Note: Officers with more than one job title may be intentionally listed here more than once.

Kevin Bracy, Assistant Secretary
John Roberts, CEO
David Mee, CFO
Kirk Thompson, Chairman of the Board
John Kuhlow, Chief Accounting Officer
Stuart Scott, Chief Information Officer
Shelley Simpson, Chief Marketing Officer
Craig Harper, Executive VP
Nicholas Hobbs, Executive VP
Terrence Matthews, Executive VP

GROWTH PLANS/SPECIAL FEATURES:

J.B. Hunt Transport Services, Inc. is a North American truckload transportation and logistics company servicing the U.S., Canada and Mexico. The firm's operations are organized into four business segments: intermodal (JBI), dedicated contract services (DCS), full truckload dry-van freight (JBT) and integrated capacity solutions (ICS). The JBI segment utilizes agreements with rail carriers under which those carriers provide for railway movement of goods, while J.B. Hunt provides for the drayage (i.e. transport of goods by truck to and from rail terminals). The segment operates 73,298 company-controlled containers system wide. It also manages a fleet of 3,916 company-owned tractors. The DCS segment involves the provision of customized services governed by long-term contracts and currently includes dry-van, flatbed, temperature-controlled, dump trailers and local inner-city operations. This segment specializes in the design, development and execution of customer-specific fleet services, including private fleet conversion, dedicated fleet creation and transportation system augmentation. It operates 6,425 company-owned trucks, 448 customer-owned trucks and 7 independent contractor trucks. The JBT segment consists of conventional truck transport services in which company-controlled tractors pick up, transport and deliver cargo. J.B. Hunt dedicates 1,296 company-owned tractors to this segment. The segment also has 590 independent contractors, some of whom lease company-owned tractors. The ICS division provides non-asset and asset-light transportation solutions to customers through relationships with third-party carriers and integration with company-owned equipment.

The firm offers employees life, disability, auto, home, medical, dental and vision insurance; a 401(k) plan; and health care and dependent care reimbursement accounts.

FINANCIAL DATA: Note: Data for latest year may not have been available at press time.

In U.S. $	2016	2015	2014	2013	2012	2011
Revenue		6,187,646,000	6,165,441,000	5,584,571,000	5,054,980,000	4,526,842,000
R&D Expense						
Operating Income		715,694,000	631,542,000	576,708,000	530,200,000	444,233,000
Operating Margin %		11.56%	10.24%	10.32%	10.48%	9.81%
SGA Expense		1,466,761,000	1,341,000,000	1,183,682,000	1,064,757,000	1,030,853,000
Net Income		427,235,000	374,792,000	342,382,000	310,354,000	257,006,000
Operating Cash Flow		873,308,000	646,779,000	574,351,000	548,044,000	635,692,000
Capital Expenditure		725,122,000	808,569,000	493,431,000	439,494,000	502,282,000
EBITDA		1,055,393,000	926,125,000	830,157,000	759,367,000	658,184,000
Return on Assets %		12.14%	12.05%	12.95%	13.11%	12.15%
Return on Equity %		34.11%	33.81%	37.95%	45.66%	45.06%
Debt to Equity		0.77	0.56	0.45	0.73	1.23

CONTACT INFORMATION:

Phone: 479 820-0000   Fax:
Toll-Free: 800-643-3622
Address: 615 J.B. Hunt Corporate Dr., Lowell, AR 72745-0130 United States

STOCK TICKER/OTHER:

Stock Ticker: JBHT
Employees: 21,562
Parent Company:

Exchange: NAS
Fiscal Year Ends: 12/31

SALARIES/BONUSES:

Top Exec. Salary: $796,132   Bonus: $
Second Exec. Salary: $478,946   Bonus: $

OTHER THOUGHTS:

Estimated Female Officers or Directors: 4
Hot Spot for Advancement for Women/Minorities: Y

Jefferies LLC

www.jefferies.com

NAIC Code: 523110

TYPES OF BUSINESS:

Stock Brokerage/Investment Banking
Corporate Finance
Asset Management
Mergers & Acquisitions Advising
Execution Services

BRANDS/DIVISIONS/AFFILIATES:

Leucadia National Corporation
Jefferies International Limited
Jefferies Investment Advisers LLC

CONTACTS: *Note: Officers with more than one job title may be intentionally listed here more than once.*

Richard B. Handler, CEO
Peregrine Broadbent, CFO
Michael J. Sharp, General Counsel
Steven R. Black, Global Head-Equities Research
Patrice Blanc, CEO-Jefferies Bache
Tim Cronin, Head-Int'l Fixed Income
Benjamin D. Lorello, Global Head-Investment Banking & Capital Markets
Richard B. Handler, Chmn.
David Weaver, Head-European Capital Markets

GROWTH PLANS/SPECIAL FEATURES:

Jefferies LLC, a wholly owned subsidiary of Leucadia National Corporation, is an international full-service investment bank and institutional securities firm. The company provides insight, expertise and execution to investors, companies and government entities. Jefferies offer deep sector expertise across a full range of products and services in investment banking, equities, fixed income, commodities and wealth management in the Americas, Europe, the Middle East and Asia. For corporate clients, the firm is a merger and acquisition (M&A) and restructuring advisor and underwriter of debt and equity issues. For institutional investors and high-end individuals, the firm is a leading provider of trade execution and liquidity in equity, convertible and high yield securities and a market maker of fixed income and commodity-linked products. Jefferies also offers top-tier wealth management, prime services and securities finance. The company's investment banking division offers debt capital markets, equity capital markets, mergers and acquisitions, restructuring and recapitalization and U.K. corporate brokering. This segment's deep sector products include consumer and retail, energy, financial institutions, financial sponsors, health care, industrials, media and telecom, public finance, real estate, gaming, lodging and technology. Its equities division provide cash equities, electronic trading solutions, equity derivatives, convertibles, prime services and corporate access. Fixed income products consist of government securities, mortgage- and asset-backed securities, corporate credit, emerging markets, municipal securities and capital markets. Jefferies' research and strategy division offers insight to clients on market strategy, economics, equity, fixed income, foreign exchange and commodities in the Americas, Europe and Asia. Asset management is provided through various investment advisory entities including Jefferies Investment Advisers, LLC and Jefferies International Limited. Wealth management services include portfolio management services, executive services and family office services.

FINANCIAL DATA: *Note: Data for latest year may not have been available at press time.*

In U.S. $	2016	2015	2014	2013	2012	2011
Revenue		3,274,904,000	3,846,265,000	2,930,000,000	2,998,784,000	2,545,190,912
R&D Expense						
Operating Income						
Operating Margin %						
SGA Expense						
Net Income		121,800,000	303,021,000	341,000,000	323,149,000	284,617,984
Operating Cash Flow						
Capital Expenditure						
EBITDA						
Return on Assets %						
Return on Equity %						
Debt to Equity						

CONTACT INFORMATION:

Phone: 212 284-2300   Fax: 212 284-2111
Toll-Free:
Address: 520 Madison Ave., New York, NY 10022 United States

STOCK TICKER/OTHER:

Stock Ticker: Subsidiary   Exchange:
Employees: 3,797   Fiscal Year Ends: 11/30
Parent Company: Leucadia National Corporation

SALARIES/BONUSES:

Top Exec. Salary: $ Bonus: $
Second Exec. Salary: $ Bonus: $

OTHER THOUGHTS:

Estimated Female Officers or Directors:
Hot Spot for Advancement for Women/Minorities:

JetBlue Airways Corporation

NAIC Code: 481111

www.jetblue.com

TYPES OF BUSINESS:

Airline
In-Flight Entertainment

BRANDS/DIVISIONS/AFFILIATES:

JetBlue Getaways
TrueBlue
Mint
Blue
Blue Plus
Blue Flex

CONTACTS: *Note: Officers with more than one job title may be intentionally listed here more than once.*

Mark Powers, CFO
Joel Peterson, Chairman of the Board
Alexander Chatkewitz, Chief Accounting Officer
Frank Sica, Director
Martin St George, Executive VP, Divisional
James Hnat, Executive VP, Divisional
Robin Hayes, President

GROWTH PLANS/SPECIAL FEATURES:

JetBlue Airways Corporation is a low-fare, low-cost passenge
airline. It primarily operates on point-to-point routes with its flee
of Airbus A321, Airbus A320 and EMBRAER 190 aircraft types
It serves 87 cities in the U.S., Caribbean and Latin America
The majority of its average 900 daily flights have as an origir
or destination one of the company's six focus cities: Boston
Fort Lauderdale, Los Angeles/Long Beach, New York, Orlando
and San Juan, Puerto Rico. The company's flights are single
class, but feature leather seats and seat-back televisions with
36 channels of free DirecTV programming, 100 stations of free
SiriusXM satellite radio and movie channel offerings from
JetBlue Features. JetBlue sells vacation packages through
JetBlue Getaways, a one-stop website designed to mee
customers' demand for packaged travel planning. The firm also
participates in three major global distribution systems: Sabre
Galileo and Amadeus; and four major online travel agents
(OTAs): Expedia, Travelocity, Orbitz and Priceline. JetBlue
also offers customers a choice to purchase tickets from three
branded fares: Blue, Blue Plus and Blue Flex. Each fare
includes different offerings such as free checked bags, reduced
change fees and additional TrueBlue rewards points. The
company's premium transcontinental product, Mint, includes 16
fully lie-flat seats in select Airbus aircraft, four of which are ir
suites with a privacy door.

JetBlue offers employees medical, dental, vision and life
insurance; short- and long-term disability insurance; a group
legal plan; flexible spending accounts; pilot loss of license
health risk assessments; disease management programs; ar
airline credit union; a 401(k) plan; a Roth 401(k) plan; self
directed accounts; a profit sharing plan; a stock purchase plan
and free and reduced rate standby travel on JetBlue flights.

FINANCIAL DATA: *Note: Data for latest year may not have been available at press time.*

In U.S. $	2016	2015	2014	2013	2012	2011
Revenue		6,416,000,000	5,817,000,000	5,441,000,000	4,982,000,000	4,504,000,000
R&D Expense						
Operating Income		1,216,000,000	515,000,000	428,000,000	376,000,000	322,000,000
Operating Margin %		18.95%	8.85%	7.86%	7.54%	7.14%
SGA Expense		1,804,000,000	1,525,000,000	1,358,000,000	1,248,000,000	1,146,000,000
Net Income		677,000,000	401,000,000	168,000,000	128,000,000	86,000,000
Operating Cash Flow		1,598,000,000	912,000,000	758,000,000	698,000,000	614,000,000
Capital Expenditure		941,000,000	857,000,000	637,000,000	828,000,000	528,000,000
EBITDA		1,562,000,000	1,082,000,000	733,000,000	646,000,000	566,000,000
Return on Assets %		8.20%	5.28%	2.33%	1.81%	1.25%
Return on Equity %		23.59%	17.19%	8.35%	7.02%	5.04%
Debt to Equity		0.43	0.77	0.99	1.30	1.62

CONTACT INFORMATION:

Phone: 718 286-7900   Fax: 718 709-3621
Toll-Free: 800-538-2583
Address: 27-01 Queens Plaza North, Long Island City, NY 11101 United
States

STOCK TICKER/OTHER:

Stock Ticker: JBLU
Employees: 16,862
Parent Company:

Exchange: NAS
Fiscal Year Ends: 12/31

SALARIES/BONUSES:

Top Exec. Salary: $542,500   Bonus: $
Second Exec. Salary: Bonus: $
$424,917

OTHER THOUGHTS:

Estimated Female Officers or Directors: 5
Hot Spot for Advancement for Women/Minorities: Y

JM Family Enterprises Inc

www.jmfamily.com

NAIC Code: 423110

TYPES OF BUSINESS:

Automobile Distribution-Wholesale
Automobile Dealer
Parts Distribution
Financing & Insurance
Dealership Financing
Consulting Services

BRANDS/DIVISIONS/AFFILIATES:

JM Lexus
JM&A Group
JM Service Center
Southeast Toyota Distributors LLC
World Omni Financial Corp

CONTACTS: Note: Officers with more than one job title may be intentionally listed here more than once.

Colin Brown, CEO
Brent Burns, COO
Colin Brown, Pres.
Ron Coombs, CFO
Carmen Johnson, General Counsel
Frank Armstrong, Exec. VP
Ron Coombs, Sr. VP
Forrest Heathcott, Exec. VP
Ed Sheehy, Exec. VP

GROWTH PLANS/SPECIAL FEATURES:

JM Family Enterprises, Inc. is a leading family-owned diversified automotive company. Through its subsidiaries, JM is a distributor of Toyotas and Scions, a diversified financial services company, a provider of finance and insurance products, a provider of integrated software systems for automotive dealers and a Lexus dealership. Subsidiary JM Lexus is one of the highest volume Lexus dealerships in the world, selling roughly 10,043 new and 2,508 pre-owned vehicles in 2015. The firm's JM&A Group subsidiary is a leading independent provider of finance and insurance products in the automotive industry, currently servicing over 7,800 dealer customers nationwide. This division sold 3,403,814 contracts in 2015, with a total 11.5 million active contracts and nearly $2 billion in invested reserves. JM Service Center (JMSC) is JM's internal shared services center. Its Southeast Toyota Distributors LLC subsidiary is an independent distributor of Toyotas and Scions, distributing cars, trucks, vans, parts and accessories to 176 independent Toyota dealers. Southeast Toyota sold 480,351 vehicles in 2015, including fleet and retail sales. Subsidiary World Omni Financial Corp. (WOFC) is a diversified financial services company and a leading provider in the areas of indirect consumer retail and lease financing; commercial dealership financing; third-party portfolio management and servicing; remarketing services; wholesale floorplan accounting and risk management systems; and field services, such as floorplan audit services and vehicle inspection services. This division set an all-time volume record in 2015, with 220,092 retail and lease contracts funded.

JM offers its employees educational assistance and development programs; flextime; adoption assistance; an onsite fitness center and access to a cafeteria and credit union; massage therapy; health and dependent care spending accounts; and medical, dental, vision, prescription, life and disability insurance.

FINANCIAL DATA: Note: Data for latest year may not have been available at press time.

In U.S. $	2016	2015	2014	2013	2012	2011
Revenue		14,500,000,000	13,750,000,000	12,500,000,000	11,500,000,000	9,300,000,000
R&D Expense						
Operating Income						
Operating Margin %						
SGA Expense						
Net Income						
Operating Cash Flow						
Capital Expenditure						
EBITDA						
Return on Assets %						
Return on Equity %						
Debt to Equity						

CONTACT INFORMATION:

Phone: 954-429-2000   Fax: 954-429-2300
Toll-Free:
Address: 100 Jim Moran Blvd., Deerfield Beach, FL 33442 United States

STOCK TICKER/OTHER:

Stock Ticker: Private   Exchange:
Employees: 4,100   Fiscal Year Ends: 12/31
Parent Company:

SALARIES/BONUSES:

Top Exec. Salary: $ Bonus: $
Second Exec. Salary: $ Bonus: $

OTHER THOUGHTS:

Estimated Female Officers or Directors: 1
Hot Spot for Advancement for Women/Minorities:

Johnson & Johnson

NAIC Code: 325412

www.jnj.com

TYPES OF BUSINESS:

Personal Health Care & Hygiene Products
Sterilization Products
Surgical Products
Pharmaceuticals
Skin Care Products
Baby Care Products
Contact Lenses
Medical Equipment

BRANDS/DIVISIONS/AFFILIATES:

Motrin
Band-Aid
Listerine
Tylenol
Neosporin
Pepcid AC
XO1 Limited
Novira Therapeutics Inc

CONTACTS: *Note: Officers with more than one job title may be intentionally listed here more than once.*

Lacey Elberg, Assistant Secretary
Alex Gorsky, CEO
Dominic Caruso, CFO
Sandra Peterson, Chairman of the Board, Divisional
Paulus Stoffels, Chairman of the Board, Divisional
Ronald Kapusta, Chief Accounting Officer
Michael Ullmann, General Counsel
Douglas Chia, Secretary
Peter Fasolo, Vice President, Divisional

GROWTH PLANS/SPECIAL FEATURES:

Johnson & Johnson, founded in 1886, is one of the world's most comprehensive and well-known researchers, developers and manufacturers of health care products. Johnson & Johnson's worldwide operations are divided into three segments: consumer, pharmaceuticals and medical devices & diagnostics. The company's principal consumer goods are personal care and hygiene products, including baby care, skin care, oral care, wound care and women's health care products as well as nutritional and over-the-counter pharmaceutical products. Major consumer brands include Motrin, Band-Aid, Listerine, Tylenol, Neosporin, Aveeno and Pepcid AC. The pharmaceutical segment covers a wide spectrum of health fields, including anti-infective, antipsychotic, contraceptive, dermatology, gastrointestinal, hematology, immunology, neurology, oncology, pain management and virology. Among its pharmaceutical products are Risperdal, an antipsychotic used to treat schizophrenia, and Remicade for the treatment of immune mediated inflammatory diseases. In the medical devices & diagnostics segment, Johnson & Johnson makes a number of products including orthopedic joint reconstruction devices, surgical care, advanced sterilization products, blood glucose monitoring devices, diagnostic products and disposable contact lenses. The firm owns more than 265 companies across 60 countries and is headquartered in New Brunswick, New Jersey. During 2015, the firm acquired XO1 Limited, as well as Novira Therapeutics, Inc.

FINANCIAL DATA: *Note: Data for latest year may not have been available at press time.*

In U.S. $	2016	2015	2014	2013	2012	2011
Revenue		70,074,000,000	74,331,000,000	71,312,000,000	67,224,000,000	65,030,000,000
R&D Expense		9,046,000,000	8,672,000,000	8,183,000,000	7,665,000,000	7,548,000,000
Operating Income		18,065,000,000	20,959,000,000	18,377,000,000	15,869,000,000	16,153,000,000
Operating Margin %		25.77%	28.19%	25.76%	23.60%	24.83%
SGA Expense		21,203,000,000	21,954,000,000	21,830,000,000	20,869,000,000	20,969,000,000
Net Income		15,409,000,000	16,323,000,000	13,831,000,000	10,853,000,000	9,671,999,000
Operating Cash Flow		19,279,000,000	18,471,000,000	17,414,000,000	15,396,000,000	14,298,000,000
Capital Expenditure		3,463,000,000	3,714,000,000	3,595,000,000	2,934,000,000	2,893,000,000
EBITDA		23,494,000,000	24,991,000,000	20,057,000,000	17,973,000,000	16,090,000,000
Return on Assets %		11.65%	12.37%	10.88%	9.23%	8.93%
Return on Equity %		21.87%	22.70%	19.91%	17.80%	17.01%
Debt to Equity		0.18	0.21	0.17	0.17	0.22

CONTACT INFORMATION:

Phone: 732 524-0400   Fax: 732 214-0332
Toll-Free:
Address: 1 Johnson & Johnson Plz., New Brunswick, NJ 08933 United States

STOCK TICKER/OTHER:

Stock Ticker: JNJ
Employees: 126,500
Parent Company:

Exchange: NYS
Fiscal Year Ends: 12/31

SALARIES/BONUSES:

Top Exec. Salary:
$1,613,462
Second Exec. Salary:
$1,158,385

Bonus: $

Bonus: $

OTHER THOUGHTS:

Estimated Female Officers or Directors: 4

Hot Spot for Advancement for Women/Minorities: Y

Johnson Controls Inc

www.johnsoncontrols.com

NAIC Code: 336300

TYPES OF BUSINESS:
Automobile Parts & Controls
Automotive Batteries
Facilities Management
Automotive Interior Components
Energy Management Services
Building Security, Lighting & HVAC Systems

BRANDS/DIVISIONS/AFFILIATES:
Metasys Building Management System
Optima
Varta
Helia
LTH
Global WorkPlace Solutions

CONTACTS: *Note: Officers with more than one job title may be intentionally listed here more than once.*
Alex Molinaroli, CEO
Suzanne Vincent, Chief Accounting Officer
Kimberley Metcalf-Kupres, Chief Marketing Officer
Susan Davis, Executive VP, Geographical
Brian Stief, Executive VP
R. McDonald, Executive VP
Simon Davis, Other Executive Officer
Michael Bartschat, Other Executive Officer
Grady Crosby, Other Executive Officer
Joseph Walicki, President, Divisional
William Jackson, President, Divisional
George Oliver, President
Frank Voltolina, Treasurer
Jeffrey Williams, Vice President, Divisional
Brian Cadwallader, Vice President

GROWTH PLANS/SPECIAL FEATURES:
Johnson Controls, Inc. (JCI) is a leader in automotive interiors/batteries, building efficiency and facility management. Its operations are divided into three segments: automotive experience, building efficiency and power solutions. The firm's automotive experience segment designs and manufactures concept cars; complete seat systems; seating components; electronics; instrument panels; overhead, door and cargo management systems; cockpits; and interior trim for manufacturers of cars and light trucks. The division operates approximately 230 wholly- and majority-owned manufacturing/assembly plants in 32 countries. The building efficiency division operates in 52 countries, supplying systems designed for HVAC (heating, ventilation and air conditioning), lighting, security and fire management. The U.S. Department of Defense utilizes JCI for the Pentagon's energy management and environmental control systems. Global WorkPlace Solutions provides companies with a real-estate based approach to shareholder value. The building efficiency division also offers facility management services using its patented Metasys Building Management System. It handles school districts, hospitals, factories, airports and government facilities. JCI's power solutions division manufactures and replaces automotive batteries, focusing on innovations for hybrid electric vehicles. Its battery brands include Optima, Varta, Heliar (in South America) and LTH (in Mexico). The segment produces roughly 146 million lead-acid batteries annually in approximately 61 wholly- and majority-owned manufacturing/assembly facilities in 22 countries. In January 2016, the firm announced plans to merge with Tyco International PLC. The resulting company would be named Johnson Controls PLC and the firm's shareholders would control 56%.

JCI offers employees benefits including health care coverage, tuition reimbursement and a 401(k).

FINANCIAL DATA: *Note: Data for latest year may not have been available at press time.*

In U.S. $	2016	2015	2014	2013	2012	2011
Revenue		37,179,000,000	42,828,000,000	42,730,000,000	41,955,000,000	40,833,000,000
R&D Expense						
Operating Income		2,064,000,000	2,319,000,000	2,813,000,000	1,483,000,000	1,987,000,000
Operating Margin %		5.55%	5.41%	6.58%	3.53%	4.86%
SGA Expense		3,986,000,000	4,308,000,000	3,965,000,000	4,438,000,000	4,183,000,000
Net Income		1,563,000,000	1,215,000,000	1,178,000,000	1,226,000,000	1,624,000,000
Operating Cash Flow		1,600,000,000	2,395,000,000	2,686,000,000	1,559,000,000	1,076,000,000
Capital Expenditure		1,135,000,000	1,199,000,000	1,377,000,000	1,831,000,000	1,325,000,000
EBITDA		3,299,000,000	3,244,000,000	3,673,000,000	2,647,000,000	3,016,000,000
Return on Assets %		5.00%	3.77%	3.77%	4.04%	5.86%
Return on Equity %		14.41%	10.28%	9.87%	10.85%	15.38%
Debt to Equity		0.55	0.56	0.37	0.46	0.41

CONTACT INFORMATION:
Phone: 414 524-1200   Fax:
Toll-Free: 800-524-6220
Address: 5757 N. Green Bay Ave., Milwaukee, WI 53209 United States

STOCK TICKER/OTHER:
Stock Ticker: JCI
Employees: 48,000
Parent Company:

Exchange: NYS
Fiscal Year Ends: 09/30

SALARIES/BONUSES:
Top Exec. Salary: $1,575,000   Bonus: $

Second Exec. Salary: $1,000,000   Bonus: $

OTHER THOUGHTS:
Estimated Female Officers or Directors: 4

Hot Spot for Advancement for Women/Minorities: Y

Jones Lang LaSalle Inc

NAIC Code: 531120

www.us.jll.com

TYPES OF BUSINESS:

Real Estate Rental, Leasing & Management
Investment Management
Project Management
Consulting Services
Real Estate Investment Banking
Properties Brokerage

BRANDS/DIVISIONS/AFFILIATES:

LaSalle Investment Management
Oak Grove Capital
Corrigo
Tansei Mall Management
Propell National Valuers
Lodgetax
Bill Goold Realty
Washington Partners Inc

CONTACTS: Note: Officers with more than one job title may be intentionally listed here more than once.

Alastair Hughes, CEO, Divisional
James Jasionowski, Executive VP
Jeff Jacobson, CEO, Divisional
Gregory OBrien, CEO, Divisional
John Forrest, CEO, Divisional
Guy Grainger, CEO, Geographical
Chris Ireland, CEO, Geographical
Colin Dyer, CEO
Christie Kelly, CFO
David Johnson, Chief Information Officer
Charles Doyle, Chief Marketing Officer
Louis Bowers, Controller
Sheila Penrose, Director
Parikshat Suri, Executive VP
Allan Frazier, Executive VP
Patricia Maxson, Executive VP
Mark Ohringer, Executive VP
Joseph Romenesko, Executive VP
Grace Chang, Managing Director, Divisional

GROWTH PLANS/SPECIAL FEATURES:

Jones Lang LaSalle, Inc. (JLL) is a real estate money management firm that provides integrated real estate and investment management expertise on a local, regional and global level to owner, occupier and investor clients. The firm is active in the area of property and corporate facility management services, with a portfolio encompassing roughly 4 billion square feet worldwide. JLL offers its real estate services across three geographically-aligned business segments: the Americas; Europe, the Middle East and Africa (EMEA); and Asia Pacific. The company's range of real estate service areas includes agency leasing, property management, project and development management, valuations, brokerage of properties, capital markets, real estate investment banking and merchant banking, corporate finance, hotel advisory, space acquisition and disposition, facilities management, strategic consulting, energy management and sustainability, value recovery and receivership services as well as money management. These services are offered to for-profit and not-for-profit firms as well as to governmental entities and public private partnerships across a wide variety of property categories, including offices, hotels, industrial, retail, multi-family residential, hospitals, data centers, sporting facilities, cultural institutions and transportation centers. A fourth business segment encompasses the operations of subsidiary LaSalle Investment Management, a diversified real estate investment management firm with $56.4 billion in assets under management. JLL has operations in over 1,000 locations in 80 countries worldwide, including 230 corporate offices. In 2015 the firm completed 20 acquisitions including Oak Grove Capital; Corrigo; Tansei Mall Management; Lodgetax and Propell National Valuers among others. In early 2016, the firm acquired Bill Goold Realty and Washington Partners, Inc.

FINANCIAL DATA: Note: Data for latest year may not have been available at press time.

In U.S. $	2016	2015	2014	2013	2012	2011
Revenue		5,965,671,000	5,429,603,000	4,461,591,000	3,932,830,000	3,584,544,000
R&D Expense						
Operating Income		529,798,000	465,664,000	368,819,000	289,403,000	251,205,000
Operating Margin %		8.88%	8.57%	8.26%	7.35%	7.00%
SGA Expense		5,293,615,000	4,827,097,000	3,994,604,000	3,519,196,000	3,194,380,000
Net Income		438,672,000	386,063,000	269,865,000	208,050,000	164,384,000
Operating Cash Flow		375,769,000	498,861,000	293,167,000	327,698,000	211,338,000
Capital Expenditure		196,703,000	156,927,000	110,684,000	94,758,000	91,538,000
EBITDA		715,415,000	608,266,000	448,672,000	424,346,000	374,424,000
Return on Assets %		7.77%	7.97%	6.02%	5.01%	4.50%
Return on Equity %		17.27%	16.89%	13.04%	11.39%	10.06%
Debt to Equity		0.19	0.11	0.19	0.22	0.27

CONTACT INFORMATION:

Phone: 312 782-5800   Fax: 312 782-4339
Toll-Free:
Address: 200 E. Randolph Dr., Chicago, IL 60601 United States

STOCK TICKER/OTHER:

Stock Ticker: JLL   Exchange: NYS
Employees: 58,100   Fiscal Year Ends: 12/31
Parent Company:

SALARIES/BONUSES:

Top Exec. Salary: $750,000   Bonus: $
Second Exec. Salary: Bonus: $
$400,000

OTHER THOUGHTS:

Estimated Female Officers or Directors: 2
Hot Spot for Advancement for Women/Minorities: Y

JP Morgan Chase & Co Inc

www.jpmorganchase.com

NAIC Code: 522110

TYPES OF BUSINESS:

Banking
Mortgages
Investment Banking
Stock Brokerage
Credit Cards
Business Finance
Mutual Funds
Annuities

BRANDS/DIVISIONS/AFFILIATES:

JPMorgan Chase Bank NA
Chase Bank USA NA
JP Morgan Securities LLC
One Equity Partners

CONTACTS: Note: Officers with more than one job title may be intentionally listed here more than once.

Gordon Smith, CEO, Divisional
Mary Erdoes, CEO, Divisional
Daniel Pinto, CEO, Divisional
Douglas Petno, CEO, Divisional
James Dimon, CEO
Marianne Lake, CFO
Mark ODonovan, Chief Accounting Officer
Ashley Bacon, Chief Risk Officer
Matthew Zames, COO
Stacey Friedman, General Counsel
John Donnelly, Other Corporate Officer
Anthony Horan, Secretary
Stephen Cutler, Vice Chairman

GROWTH PLANS/SPECIAL FEATURES:

J.P. Morgan Chase & Co., Inc. (JPM) is one of the largest banking institutions in the world, with operations in over 60 countries and over $2.4 trillion in assets. JPM's principal subsidiaries include JPMorgan Chase Bank, NA, a national banking association with operations in 23 states; Chase Bank USA, NA, a leading provider of retail banking services and credit cards; and J.P. Morgan Securities LLC, an investment banking firm. JPM operates its business through five segments: consumer and community banking (CCB), corporate and investment banking (CIB), commercial banking, asset management and corporate/private equity. The CCB segment serves consumers and businesses through personal service at bank branches and through ATMs, online, mobile and telephone banking. The CIB segment, comprised of banking and markets and investor services, offers a broad range of investment banking, market-making, prime brokerage, and treasury and securities products and services to a global client base. The commercial banking segment provides local expertise and service to U.S. and U.S. multinational clients, including corporations, municipalities, financial institutions and nonprofit entities with annual revenue generally ranging from $20 million to $2 billion. The asset management segment is a global leader in investment and wealth management. The corporate/private equity segment measures, monitors, reports and manages the firm's liquidity, funding and structural interest rate and foreign exchange risks. In 2015, the firm spun out its One Equity Partners (OEP) equity business.

The company offers employees benefits including medical, dental, vision, life, disability and accident insurance; adoption assistance; an employee assistance program; tuition assistance; 401(k) and retirement plans; an employee stock purchase plan; and discounts on banking services.

FINANCIAL DATA: Note: Data for latest year may not have been available at press time.

In U.S. $	2016	2015	2014	2013	2012	2011
Revenue		93,543,000,000	94,205,000,000	96,606,000,000	97,031,000,000	97,234,000,000
R&D Expense						
Operating Income		30,702,000,000	29,792,000,000	25,914,000,000	28,917,000,000	26,749,000,000
Operating Margin %		32.82%	31.62%	26.82%	29.80%	27.50%
SGA Expense		38,651,000,000	38,514,000,000	38,735,000,000	38,386,000,000	37,127,000,000
Net Income		24,442,000,000	21,762,000,000	17,923,000,000	21,284,000,000	18,976,000,000
Operating Cash Flow		73,466,000,000	36,593,000,000	107,953,000,000	25,079,000,000	95,932,000,000
Capital Expenditure						
EBITDA						
Return on Assets %		.90%	.80%	.69%	.85%	.80%
Return on Equity %		10.33%	9.75%	8.40%	10.72%	10.21%
Debt to Equity		1.39	1.44	1.47	1.41	1.46

CONTACT INFORMATION:

Phone: 212 270-6000   Fax: 212 270-1648
Toll-Free: 877-242-7372
Address: 270 Park Ave., New York, NY 10017 United States

SALARIES/BONUSES:

Top Exec. Salary: $750,000   Bonus: $7,100,000
Second Exec. Salary: $750,000   Bonus: $6,900,000

STOCK TICKER/OTHER:

Stock Ticker: JPM
Employees: 251,196
Parent Company:

Exchange: NYS
Fiscal Year Ends: 12/31

OTHER THOUGHTS:

Estimated Female Officers or Directors: 3
Hot Spot for Advancement for Women/Minorities: Y

Sales, profits and employees may be estimates. Financial information, benefits and other data can change quickly and may vary from those stated here.

Kaiser Permanente

NAIC Code: 622110

www.kaiserpermanente.org

TYPES OF BUSINESS:

General Medical and Surgical Hospitals
General & Specialty Hospitals
Outpatient Facilities
HMO
Health Insurance
Integrated Health Care System
Physician Networks
Clinical Record Management

BRANDS/DIVISIONS/AFFILIATES:

Kaiser Foundation Health Plan Inc
Kaiser Foundation Hospitals
Permanente Medical Groups
Kaiser Permanente Health Research
KP HealthConnect

CONTACTS: Note: Officers with more than one job title may be intentionally listed here more than once.

Bernard Tyson, CEO
Kathy Lancaster, CFO
Chuck Columbus, Chief Human Resources Officer
Raymond J. Baxter, Sr. VP-Community Benefit, Research & Health Policy
Richard D. Daniels, CIO
Mark S. Zemelman, General Counsel
Arthur M. Southam, Exec. VP-Health Plan Oper.
Chris Grant, Sr. VP-Corp. Dev. & Care Delivery Strategy
Diane Gage Lofgren, Sr. VP
Cynthia Powers Overmyer, Sr. VP-Internal Audit Svcs.
Daniel P. Garcia, Chief Compliance Officer
Anthony Barrueta, Sr. VP-Gov't Rel.
Amy Compton-Phillips, Associate Exec. Dir.-Quality, Permanente
Bernard Tyson, Chmn.

GROWTH PLANS/SPECIAL FEATURES:

Kaiser Permanente is a nonprofit company dedicated to providing integrated health care coverage. The firm operates in California, Colorado, Georgia, Hawaii, Maryland, Washington D.C., Oregon, Virginia and Washington. It serves more than 10.6 million members of which most are in California. Kaiser has three main operating divisions: Kaiser Foundation Health Plan, Inc., which contracts with individuals and groups to provide medical coverage; Kaiser Foundation Hospitals and their subsidiaries, operating community hospitals and outpatient facilities in several states; and Permanente Medical Groups, the company's network of physicians providing health care to its members. The company's resources include approximately 38 medical centers, including hospitals and outpatient facilities; 619 medical offices; and 18,600 physicians. Kaiser Foundation Hospitals also fund medical and health-related research. In addition, Kaiser Permanente Health Research has eight research centers across the country, which conduct clinical trials of new drugs and medical devices and specialize in epidemiological studies. The firm, as a participant in the Medicare program, cares for over 1.3 million Medicare members, making it one of the largest health plans serving the Medicare program. The KP HealthConnect program integrates clinical records with appointments, registration and billing, thereby significantly improving care delivery and patient satisfaction.

Employees of the firm are offered medical, vision, dental and life insurance; a prescription plan; paid time off for vacations; designated holidays; sick leave; disability benefits; retirement plans; tuition reimbursement; employee assistance programs; and transit spending account options. Kaiser Permanente's employee health care coverage extends to spouses, domestic partners and unmarried children.

FINANCIAL DATA: Note: Data for latest year may not have been available at press time.

In U.S. $	2016	2015	2014	2013	2012	2011
Revenue		61,000,000,000	56,400,000,000	53,100,000,000	50,600,000,000	47,900,000,000
R&D Expense						
Operating Income						
Operating Margin %						
SGA Expense						
Net Income		1,900,000,000	3,100,000,000	2,700,000,000	2,600,000,000	1,600,000,000
Operating Cash Flow						
Capital Expenditure						
EBITDA						
Return on Assets %						
Return on Equity %						
Debt to Equity						

CONTACT INFORMATION:

Phone: 510-271-5910   Fax: 510-267-7524
Toll-Free:
Address: 1 Kaiser Plaza, Fl. 19, Oakland, CA 94612 United States

STOCK TICKER/OTHER:

Stock Ticker: Nonprofit   Exchange:
Employees: 174,415   Fiscal Year Ends: 12/31
Parent Company:

SALARIES/BONUSES:

Top Exec. Salary: $ Bonus: $
Second Exec. Salary: $ Bonus: $

OTHER THOUGHTS:

Estimated Female Officers or Directors: 9
Hot Spot for Advancement for Women/Minorities: Y

Kate Spade & Company Inc

www.katespadeandcompany.com

NAIC Code: 424300

TYPES OF BUSINESS:

Apparel and Clothing Brands, Designers, Importers and Distributors
Apparel Marketing
Jewelry Design & Marketing

BRANDS/DIVISIONS/AFFILIATES:

kate spade new york
Jack Spade
Adelington Design Group
Globalluxe Kate Spade HK Limited
Fifth & Pacific Companies Inc
Kate Spade & Company

CONTACTS: *Note: Officers with more than one job title may be intentionally listed here more than once.*

Craig Leavitt, CEO
Thomas Linko, CFO
Linda Yanussi, Chief Information Officer
Nancy Karch, Director
Deborah Lloyd, Other Executive Officer
George Carrara, President
William Higley, Senior VP, Divisional
Timothy Michno, Senior VP

GROWTH PLANS/SPECIAL FEATURES:

Kate Spade & Company, Inc. designs and markets a portfolio of retail-based, premium accessories and apparel brands including kate spade new york and Jack Spade. Kate spade new york offers fashion products for women and children, as well as home products. These include handbags, small leather goods, fashion accessories, jewelry and fragrances, as well as footwear, swimwear, watches, optics, tabletop products, legwear, electronics cases, bedding and stationery. Jack Spade offers fashion products for men, including briefcases, travel bags, small leather goods, fashion accessories and apparel. The firm also owns the Adelington Design Group, a private jewelry design and development group, which markets brands through department stores and serves JCPenney via exclusive supplier agreements for the Liz Claiborne and Monet jewelry lines and Kohl's via an exclusive supplier agreement for Dana Buchman jewelry. In addition, the company has licenses for the Liz Claiborne New York brand, available at QVC and Lizwear, which is distributed through the club store channel. Kate Spade operates in North America, as well as internationally, including Japan, Southeast Asia, Europe and Latin America. In 2014, it sold its Lucky Brand Jeans business to an affiliate of Leonard Green & Partners, L.P. (LGP) for $225 million; and acquired the Kate Spade businesses in Hong Kong, Macau, Taiwan, Malaysia, Singapore, Indonesia and Thailand from Globalluxe Kate Spade HK Limited. That same year, parent Fifth & Pacific Companies, Inc. changed its name to Kate Spade & Company to reflect the company's brand portfolio. In 2015, Kate Spade discontinued its Kate Spade Saturday business and began to absorb its key offerings into the kate spade new york label; and closed its company-owned Jack Spade retail stores in order to reimagine the brand as an e-commerce label. That October, the firm introduced its comprehensive home furnishings collection of furniture, lighting, rugs and fabric.

FINANCIAL DATA: *Note: Data for latest year may not have been available at press time.*

In U.S. $	2016	2015	2014	2013	2012	2011
Revenue		1,242,720,000	1,138,603,000	1,264,935,000	1,505,094,000	1,518,721,000
R&D Expense						
Operating Income		66,398,000	33,472,000	-45,513,000	-34,451,000	-96,252,000
Operating Margin %		5.34%	2.93%	-3.59%	-2.28%	-6.33%
SGA Expense		687,709,000	645,266,000	766,103,000	877,426,000	904,619,000
Net Income		17,087,000	159,160,000	72,995,000	-74,505,000	-171,687,000
Operating Cash Flow		105,576,000	14,364,000	-24,031,000	11,358,000	-17,028,000
Capital Expenditure		60,207,000	99,953,000	78,114,000	82,792,000	73,653,000
EBITDA		116,335,000	87,910,000	14,419,000	70,103,000	-10,283,000
Return on Assets %		1.79%	16.71%	7.76%	-8.04%	-15.55%
Return on Equity %		7.68%	190.46%			
Debt to Equity		1.61	2.00			

CONTACT INFORMATION:

Phone: 212-354-4900   Fax:
Toll-Free:
Address: 2 Park Ave., New York, NY 10016 United States

STOCK TICKER/OTHER:

Stock Ticker: KATE   Exchange: NYS
Employees: 3,500   Fiscal Year Ends: 12/31
Parent Company: Kate Spade & Company

SALARIES/BONUSES:

Top Exec. Salary: Bonus: $
$1,900,000
Second Exec. Salary: Bonus: $
$1,500,000

OTHER THOUGHTS:

Estimated Female Officers or Directors: 6

Hot Spot for Advancement for Women/Minorities: Y

Kelly Services Inc

NAIC Code: 561320

www.kellyservices.com

TYPES OF BUSINESS:

Staffing & Temporary Help
Human Resources Consulting
Outsourcing Solutions
Permanent Hiring Programs
Call Center Services
Benefits & Payroll Outsourcing

BRANDS/DIVISIONS/AFFILIATES:

CONTACTS: Note: Officers with more than one job title may be intentionally listed here more than once.

Carl Camden, CEO
Terence Adderley, Chairman of the Board
Laura Lockhart, Chief Accounting Officer
Peter Quigley, Chief Administrative Officer
George Corona, COO
Teresa Carroll, General Manager, Divisional
Natalia Shuman-Fabbri, General Manager, Geographical
James Polehna, Secretary
Antonina Ramsey, Senior VP
Olivier Thirot, Senior VP

GROWTH PLANS/SPECIAL FEATURES:

Kelly Services, Inc. is a staffing and services company that offers temporary staffing services, staff leasing, outsourcing and full-time placement. Kelly's workforce solutions are provided to customers through offices in three regions: the Americas; Europe, the Middle East and Africa (EMEA); and Asia Pacific. It operates in seven segments: Americas commercial, Americas professional and technical (Americas PT), EMEA commercial, EMEA PT, Asia Pacific commercial, Asia Pacific PT and the outsourcing and consulting group (OCG). Americas commercial specialties include providing trained staff, employees and support roles for offices, including data entry, clerical & administrative; contact centers, including technical support hotlines & telemarketing units; education, supplying schools; marketing, including seminars, as well as sales & trade shows; electronic assembly, including assemblers, quality control inspectors and technicians; and light industrial, including maintenance workers, material handlers and assemblers. Americas PT provides staffing services for the following sectors: science, engineering, IT, creative services, finance/accounting, health care and law. EMEA commercial provides staffing services similar to Americas commercial, including the following sectors: office, contact center, temporary-to-hire, catering, hospitality and industrial. EMEA PT provides staffing services similar to Americas PT, including engineering, finance/accounting, health care, IT and science. Asia Pacific commercial provides staffing similar to the Americas and EMEA commercial, including permanent placement, temporary staffing and temporary-to-full-time staffing. Asia Pacific PT provides similar staffing as Americas and EMEA PT, including engineering, IT and science. OCG delivers integrated talent management solutions to meet customer needs across multiple regions, skill sets and the entire spectrum of talent categories. Services in this segment include contingent workforce outsourcing, business process outsourcing, recruitment process outsourcing, independent contractor solutions, payroll process outsourcing, career transition and executive coaching/development and executive search.

FINANCIAL DATA: Note: Data for latest year may not have been available at press time.

In U.S. $	2016	2015	2014	2013	2012	2011
Revenue		5,518,200,000	5,562,700,000	5,413,100,000	5,450,500,000	5,551,000,000
R&D Expense						
Operating Income		66,700,000	21,900,000	53,300,000	72,300,000	57,700,000
Operating Margin %		1.20%	.39%	.98%	1.32%	1.03%
SGA Expense		853,600,000	886,500,000	834,500,000	821,200,000	836,400,000
Net Income		53,800,000	23,700,000	58,900,000	50,100,000	63,700,000
Operating Cash Flow		23,500,000	-70,000,000	115,300,000	61,100,000	19,100,000
Capital Expenditure		16,900,000	21,700,000	20,000,000	21,500,000	15,400,000
EBITDA		88,600,000	41,300,000	72,000,000	94,500,000	92,400,000
Return on Assets %		2.78%	1.27%	3.43%	3.15%	4.37%
Return on Equity %		6.22%	2.86%	7.53%	7.07%	9.80%
Debt to Equity						

CONTACT INFORMATION:

Phone: 248 362-4444   Fax: 248 362-2258
Toll-Free:
Address: 999 W. Big Beaver Rd., Troy, MI 48084 United States

STOCK TICKER/OTHER:

Stock Ticker: KELYA   Exchange: NAS
Employees: 7,000   Fiscal Year Ends: 12/31
Parent Company:

SALARIES/BONUSES:

Top Exec. Salary: Bonus: $
$1,000,000
Second Exec. Salary: Bonus: $
$655,000

OTHER THOUGHTS:

Estimated Female Officers or Directors: 11

Hot Spot for Advancement for Women/Minorities: Y

Kimpton Hotel & Restaurant Group LLC   www.kimptonhotels.com

NAIC Code: 721110

TYPES OF BUSINESS:

Hotels
Restaurants
Hotel Management Services

BRANDS/DIVISIONS/AFFILIATES:

InterContinental Hotels Group PLC
Area 31
Hotel Vintage Plaza
Hotel Burnham
Cafe Pescatore
Sazerac
Silverleaf Tavern
Scala's Bistro

CONTACTS: Note: Officers with more than one job title may be intentionally listed here more than once.

Mike DeFrino, CEO
Judy Miles, General Counsel
Joe Long, Exec. VP-Dev.
Lisa Demoney, Sr. Dir.-Digital Mktg. & Media
Stephanie Moustirats, Dir.-Hotel Public Rel.
James Alderman, Sr. VP-Acquisitions & Dev.
James Lin, Sr. VP-Restaurant Oper.
Barry Pollard, Sr. VP-Hotel Oper.
Christine Lawson, Sr. VP-Hotel Sales & Catering

GROWTH PLANS/SPECIAL FEATURES:

Kimpton Hotel & Restaurant Group LLC, based in San Francisco, owns 59 lifestyle boutique hotels in 30 U.S. cities. Its holdings also consist of more than 60 restaurants and bars next to or within its hotels. The firm specializes in renovating old, disused buildings to transform them into unique hotels as well as small, European-style restaurants. Its themed hotels include Hotel Vintage Plaza in Portland, Oregon, which has an Italian romance theme; Hotel Vintage in Seattle, highlighting local Washington wines; and Hotel Burnham in Chicago, which focuses on its significance in Chicago's history. Some notable restaurants run by Kimpton include San Francisco bistros Cafe Pescatore, Scala's Bistro and Puccini & Pinetti; Sazerac in Seattle; Atwood Cafe in Chicago; Area 31 in Miami; Firefly in Washington, D.C.; Ruby Room in Boston; and Silverleaf Tavern in New York City. The company also offers full service spas at some of its locations. Special services offered by its hotels include the Mind, Body, Spa Program, which offers in-room massage, yoga, Pilates and meditation; pet packages, which include pet-friendly amenities and services; and Hosted Evening Wine Hour. The company is also engaged in comprehensive management services for other companies, offering everything from financial management to facilities renovation. The company is owned by hotel giant InterContinental Hotels Group PLC. Kimpton plans to open eight additional hotels, located in California, Colorado, Illinois, North Carolina, Ohio, Wisconsin, as well as in the Cayman Islands. It plans to open another in Nashville, Tennessee in 2017. In January 2016, Kimpton announced the signing of its first Kimpton Hotels & Restaurants hotel outside the Americas, debuting in Amsterdam. After a complete renovation, the 270-room hotel will open in 2017.

The firm offers employees medical, dental, vision and life insurance; long- and short-term disability; paid vacation time; tuition reimbursement; and employee discounts.

FINANCIAL DATA: Note: Data for latest year may not have been available at press time.

In U.S. $	2016	2015	2014	2013	2012	2011
Revenue		1,200,000,000	1,049,880,000	1,000,000,000	945,000,000	905,000,000
R&D Expense						
Operating Income						
Operating Margin %						
SGA Expense						
Net Income						
Operating Cash Flow						
Capital Expenditure						
EBITDA						
Return on Assets %						
Return on Equity %						
Debt to Equity						

CONTACT INFORMATION:

Phone: 415-397-5572   Fax: 415-296-8031
Toll-Free: 800-546-7866
Address: 222 Kearny St., Ste. 200, San Francisco, CA 94108 United States

STOCK TICKER/OTHER:

Stock Ticker: Subsidiary   Exchange:
Employees: 7,754   Fiscal Year Ends: 12/31
Parent Company: InterContinental Hotels Group PLC

SALARIES/BONUSES:

Top Exec. Salary: $ Bonus: $
Second Exec. Salary: $ Bonus: $

OTHER THOUGHTS:

Estimated Female Officers or Directors: 9
Hot Spot for Advancement for Women/Minorities: Y

Sales, profits and employees may be estimates. Financial information, benefits and other data can change quickly and may vary from those stated here.

Kindred Healthcare Inc

www.kindredhealthcare.com

NAIC Code: 623110

TYPES OF BUSINESS:

Nursing Care Facilities
Nursing Centers
Contract Rehabilitation Services

BRANDS/DIVISIONS/AFFILIATES:

Gentiva Health Services Inc

CONTACTS: Note: Officers with more than one job title may be intentionally listed here more than once.

Stephen Farber, CFO
Stephen Cunanan, Chief Administrative Officer
Kent Wallace, COO
Phyllis Yale, Director
William Altman, Executive VP, Divisional
David Causby, Executive VP
Jon Rousseau, Executive VP
Joseph Landenwich, General Counsel
Steven Monaghan, President, Divisional
Michael Beal, President, Divisional
Pete Kalmey, President, Divisional
Benjamin Breier, President
John Lucchese, Senior VP
Paul Diaz, Vice Chairman of the Board

GROWTH PLANS/SPECIAL FEATURES:

Kindred Healthcare, Inc. is a health care services company. The firm is organized into four operating divisions: hospital, Kindred at Home, Kindred Rehabilitation Services and nursing center. The hospital division operates 95 transitional care hospitals (certified as long-term acute care (LTAC) under the Medicare program) in 22 U.S. states. Kindred at Home provides home health, hospice and community care services from 604 locations in 40 states. Kindred Rehabilitation Services operates 18 inpatient rehabilitation hospitals (IRFs) and 100 hospital-based acute rehabilitation units, providing rehabilitation services primarily in hospitals and long-term care settings in 46 states. The nursing center division operates 90 nursing centers and seven assisted-living facilities in 18 states. In 2015, the firm acquired Gentiva Health Services, Inc. In 2016, Kindred sold two of its transitional care hospitals to Select Medical Holdings Corp., and acquired four LTAC hospitals from Select in an exchange transaction. That same year, Kindred and Palomar Health created a joint venture to construct and operate a 52-bed inpatient rehabilitation hospital in Escondido, California.

The firm offers employees medical, dental and vision coverage; flexible spending accounts; and a 401(k) plan.

FINANCIAL DATA: Note: Data for latest year may not have been available at press time.

In U.S. $	2016	2015	2014	2013	2012	2011
Revenue		7,054,907,000	5,027,599,000	4,900,510,000	6,181,291,000	5,521,763,000
R&D Expense						
Operating Income		134,929,000	170,125,000	-58,016,000	113,583,000	5,322,000
Operating Margin %		1.91%	3.38%	-1.18%	1.83%	.09%
SGA Expense		1,777,897,000	1,290,862,000	318,077,000	428,979,000	399,257,000
Net Income		-93,384,000	-79,837,000	-168,492,000	-40,367,000	-53,481,000
Operating Cash Flow		163,262,000	105,471,000	199,412,000	262,562,000	153,706,000
Capital Expenditure		141,862,000	96,338,000	112,732,000	165,497,000	220,558,000
EBITDA		296,109,000	335,071,000	232,422,000	316,121,000	183,138,000
Return on Assets %		-1.53%	-1.66%	-4.11%	-.96%	-1.65%
Return on Equity %		-6.34%	-6.32%	-14.40%	-3.17%	-4.60%
Debt to Equity		2.09	1.97	1.45	1.31	1.18

CONTACT INFORMATION:

Phone: 502 596-7300   Fax: 502 596-4170
Toll-Free: 800-545-0749
Address: 680 S. 4th St., Louisville, KY 40202 United States

STOCK TICKER/OTHER:

Stock Ticker: KND   Exchange: NYS
Employees: 61,500   Fiscal Year Ends: 12/31
Parent Company:

SALARIES/BONUSES:

Top Exec. Salary: $486,551   Bonus: $1,000,000
Second Exec. Salary: Bonus: $350,000
$596,171

OTHER THOUGHTS:

Estimated Female Officers or Directors: 4
Hot Spot for Advancement for Women/Minorities: Y

Koch Industries Inc

www.kochind.com

NAIC Code: 324110

TYPES OF BUSINESS:

Petroleum Refining
Chemicals
Textiles
Pipelines
Fertilizer Production
Chemical Equipment
Asphalt & Paving Supplies
Beef Production

BRANDS/DIVISIONS/AFFILIATES:

Flint Hills Resources
Koch Minerals LLC
Koch Ag & Energy Solutions LLC
Matador Cattle Company (The)
Koch Chemical Technology Group LLC
INVISTA BV
Koch Agriculture Company
Georgia-Pacific LLC

CONTACTS: Note: Officers with more than one job title may be intentionally listed here more than once.

Charles G. Koch, CEO
David L. Robertson, COO
David H. Koch, VP
Don Clay, Managing Dir.-Environmental & Regulatory Affairs
Michael William Hofmann, Chief Risk Officer
Charles G. Koch, Chmn.

GROWTH PLANS/SPECIAL FEATURES:

Koch Industries, Inc. is a diversified group of companies with operations in markets such as refining and chemicals; process and pollution control equipment and technologies; minerals and fertilizers; polymers and fibers; commodity and financial trading and services; and forest and consumer products. It also conducts operations in venture capital investments, municipal finance, capital market investments and business development. Subsidiary Flint Hills Resources operates petroleum refineries in Alaska, Minnesota and Texas, with a combined crude oil processing capacity of more than 600,000 barrels per day. These plants produce petrochemicals, fuels, asphalt and base oils. Koch Minerals, LLC supplies coal and petroleum coke as well as cement, pulp and paper, sulfur and related products internationally. Koch Ag & Energy Solutions, LLC owns or has interests in nitrogen fertilizer plants capable of marketing and distributing more than 13 million metric tons of nitrogen products annually. The Matador Cattle Company, a division of the Koch Agriculture Company, operates three ranches in Kansas, Montana and Texas totaling 460,000 acres. Koch Pipeline Company, LP operates a 4,000-mile network of pipelines. Koch Chemical Technology Group, LLC designs, manufactures, sells, installs and services process and pollution control equipment. INVISTA BV is a global producer and marketer of polymers and fibers, primarily for nylon, spandex and polyester applications. Georgia-Pacific LLC manufactures and markets tissue, packaging, paper, building products, related chemicals and fluff, filter and market pulp under such brand names as Quilted Northern, Angel Soft, Brawny, Sparkle and Dixie.

Employee benefits include a 401(k), pension, medical and dental coverage, flexible spending accounts, life and AD&D insurance, business travel accident insurance, short- and long-term disability and educational assistance.

FINANCIAL DATA: Note: Data for latest year may not have been available at press time.

In U.S. $	2016	2015	2014	2013	2012	2011
Revenue		115,000,000,000	115,500,000,000	114,000,000,000	112,500,000,000	110,000,000,000
R&D Expense						
Operating Income						
Operating Margin %						
SGA Expense						
Net Income			10,600,000,000	10,500,000,000	10,000,000,000	8,500,000,000
Operating Cash Flow						
Capital Expenditure						
EBITDA						
Return on Assets %						
Return on Equity %						
Debt to Equity						

CONTACT INFORMATION:

Phone: 316-828-5500   Fax: 316-828-5739
Toll-Free:
Address: 4111 E. 37th St. N., Wichita, KS 67220 United States

STOCK TICKER/OTHER:

Stock Ticker: Private   Exchange:
Employees: 100,000   Fiscal Year Ends: 12/31
Parent Company:

SALARIES/BONUSES:

Top Exec. Salary: $ Bonus: $
Second Exec. Salary: $ Bonus: $

OTHER THOUGHTS:

Estimated Female Officers or Directors:
Hot Spot for Advancement for Women/Minorities:

Kohler Company

NAIC Code: 327110

TYPES OF BUSINESS:

Plumbing Fixtures
Resorts
Kitchen & Bath Products
Building Materials

BRANDS/DIVISIONS/AFFILIATES:

Kohler
Sterling
Kallista
Ann Sacks
Robern
Kohler Engines
Lombardini
Somo

CONTACTS: Note: Officers with more than one job title may be intentionally listed here more than once.

David Kohler, CEO
Herbert V. Kohler, Jr., Chmn.

GROWTH PLANS/SPECIAL FEATURES:

Kohler Company founded in 1873, is an American manufacturer that operates on six continents worldwide. The firm has four divisions: kitchen & bath, power systems, interiors and hospitality. Kitchen & bath offers products under the Kohler, Sterling, Kallista, Ann Sacks and Robern brands. Products include fashionable sinks, faucets, toilets, bidets, vanities, medicine cabinets, accessories and commercial products. The products can include a number of features including luxury design, automated systems, stainless steel and touchless products. Power systems include: Kohler Engines, Lombardini, Kohler Power, Somo and Kohler Power Uninterruptible. Products include private and commercial agricultural equipment, including lawn mowers; maritime equipment, such as marine generators; home generators; and uninterruptible power solutions. Interiors include the Baker, McGuire, Ann Sacks, Kallista and Mark David brands. Products include furniture, lighting, home accessories, textiles, artesian stone design, plumbing products and high-end hospitality furnishings. Hospitality includes golf destinations and hospitality products. Hospitality includes the American Club Resort (Kohler, Wisconsin) and Old Course Hotel (St. Andrews, Scotland) offer spa services, golf, lodgings and high-end cuisine to their guests. Additional hospitality services include Kohler Original Chocolates and Kohler At Home, offering high end bedding & spa-like products for home use.

Kohler offers its employees medical, dental, life and prescription insurance; dependent and health care spending accounts; a wellness program; a pension plan; a 401(k) plan with company matching; annual bonuses; paid time off; and employee discounts.

FINANCIAL DATA: Note: Data for latest year may not have been available at press time.

In U.S. $	2016	2015	2014	2013	2012	2011
Revenue		6,000,000,000	5,210,000,000	5,000,000,000	4,800,000,000	4,500,000,000
R&D Expense						
Operating Income						
Operating Margin %						
SGA Expense						
Net Income						
Operating Cash Flow						
Capital Expenditure						
EBITDA						
Return on Assets %						
Return on Equity %						
Debt to Equity						

CONTACT INFORMATION:

Phone: 920-457-4441   Fax:
Toll-Free: 800-456-4537
Address: 444 Highland Dr., Kohler, WI 53044 United States

STOCK TICKER/OTHER:

Stock Ticker: Private   Exchange:
Employees: 30,000   Fiscal Year Ends:
Parent Company:

SALARIES/BONUSES:

Top Exec. Salary: $ Bonus: $
Second Exec. Salary: $ Bonus: $

OTHER THOUGHTS:

Estimated Female Officers or Directors:
Hot Spot for Advancement for Women/Minorities:

Kohl's Corporation

www.kohls.com

NAIC Code: 452112

TYPES OF BUSINESS:

Discount Department Stores
Online Sales

BRANDS/DIVISIONS/AFFILIATES:

Kohls.com
Off-Aisle by Kohl

CONTACTS: Note: Officers with more than one job title may be intentionally listed here more than once.

Kevin Mansell, CEO
Kevin Mansell, Pres.

GROWTH PLANS/SPECIAL FEATURES:

Kohl's Corporation operates family-oriented specialty department stores. The company currently operates 1,164 stores in 49 states, with three store formats: prototype (approximately 88,000 square feet of retail space), small (approximately 68,000 square feet of retail space) and urban (approximately 125,000 square feet of retail space). Kohl's stores offer apparel, shoes and accessories for women, children and men; soft home products, such as sheets and pillows; and other home products, such as small electronics and luggage. Brands sold include Dockers, Lee, Levi's, Jockey, Candie's, Nike, Dana Buchman, LC Lauren Conrad, Simply Vera Vera Wang, Dana Buchman Food Network and FILA Sport. Approximately 30% of Kohl's' merchandise is marketed towards women, 20% is marketed towards men, 18% is comprised of home furnishing products, 13% is designed for children, 10% is comprised of accessories and 9% is comprised of footwear. In addition to its physical retail locations, the company also markets its products through its e-commerce site, Kohls.com. The firm maintains nine distribution centers located in Ohio, Texas, Virginia, Missouri, New York, California, Georgia and Illinois, and e-commerce fulfillment centers in Monroe, Ohio; Edgewood, Maryland; DeSoto, Texas; and San Bernardino, California. Kohl's has started an off-price format called Off-Aisle by Kohl, in which all sales are final. In July 2016, the firm partnered with Under Armour to propel its active wear business. Under Armour is a provider of performance footwear, apparel and equipment.

The company offers its employees medical, dental and vision insurance; long-term disability and life insurance; a 401(k) plan; tuition reimbursement; onsite fitness classes, farmers market, child care, dry cleaning and food service; adoption assistance; parental leave; vacation; and merchandise discounts.

FINANCIAL DATA: Note: Data for latest year may not have been available at press time.

In U.S. $	2016	2015	2014	2013	2012	2011
Revenue	19,204,000,000	19,023,000,000	19,031,000,000	19,279,000,000	18,804,000,000	18,391,000,000
R&D Expense						
Operating Income	1,553,000,000	1,689,000,000	1,742,000,000	1,890,000,000	2,158,000,000	1,914,000,000
Operating Margin %	8.08%	8.87%	9.15%	9.80%	11.47%	10.40%
SGA Expense	4,452,000,000	4,350,000,000	4,313,000,000	4,267,000,000	4,243,000,000	4,462,000,000
Net Income	673,000,000	867,000,000	889,000,000	986,000,000	1,167,000,000	1,114,000,000
Operating Cash Flow	1,474,000,000	2,024,000,000	1,884,000,000	1,265,000,000	2,143,000,000	1,676,000,000
Capital Expenditure	690,000,000	682,000,000	643,000,000	785,000,000	927,000,000	761,000,000
EBITDA	2,487,000,000	2,575,000,000	2,631,000,000	2,723,000,000	2,940,000,000	2,579,000,000
Return on Assets %	4.80%	6.01%	6.28%	7.04%	8.43%	8.33%
Return on Equity %	11.72%	14.48%	14.78%	15.70%	15.97%	13.96%
Debt to Equity	0.83	0.77	0.78	0.73	0.63	0.20

CONTACT INFORMATION:

Phone: 262 703-7000   Fax: 262 703-6373
Toll-Free:
Address: N56 W17000 Ridgewood Dr., Menomonee Falls, WI 53051 United States

STOCK TICKER/OTHER:

Stock Ticker: KSS
Employees: 137,000
Parent Company:

Exchange: NYS
Fiscal Year Ends: 01/31

SALARIES/BONUSES:

Top Exec. Salary: $1,378,075
Second Exec. Salary: $187,500

Bonus: $
Bonus: $1,000,000

OTHER THOUGHTS:

Estimated Female Officers or Directors:

Hot Spot for Advancement for Women/Minorities: Y

Sales, profits and employees may be estimates. Financial information, benefits and other data can change quickly and may vary from those stated here.

KPMG LLP

NAIC Code: 541211

www.kpmg.com/US/en/Pages/default.aspx

TYPES OF BUSINESS:

Accounting Services
Human Resource Advisory Services
Accounting Technology
Publications
Risk Management

BRANDS/DIVISIONS/AFFILIATES:

KPMG International
Audit Committee Institute
KPMG TaxWatch

CONTACTS: Note: Officers with more than one job title may be intentionally listed here more than once.

John Veihmeyer, CEO
George Ledwith, Dir.-Global Comm.
John Veihmeyer, Chmn.

GROWTH PLANS/SPECIAL FEATURES:

KPMG LLP, the U.S. subsidiary of global accounting cooperative KPMG International, is a leading provider of audit, advisory and tax services within the U.S. The firm's audit operations are based on a multidisciplinary approach focused on compliance tools, technological assistance and cultural values. KPMG founded and maintains the Audit Committee Institute, designed to educate audit committee members about governance, accounting, financial reporting and other audit issues. KPMG's tax services segment provides tax assistance in the following areas: economic and valuation services, exempt organizations tax, federal tax, inbound tax services, international corporate tax, international executive services, legislative and regulatory services, mergers and acquisitions, state and local tax and trade and customs. The company also provides tax-related news through its KPMG TaxWatch podcast series and tax-related newsletters and publications. The firm's advisory services division assists its clients in achieving strengthened governance, reporting and internal controls; early identification and assessment of risk and control issues; improved efficiency and effectiveness of key business processes; and informed responses to existing and proposed regulatory requirements. With offices in more than 80 locations across the U.S., KPMG serves companies and organizations in such major industry sectors as financial services; industrial markets; consumer markets; information, communications and entertainment; government; and health care. The firm also maintains a special focus group that has industry experience with the issues Japanese companies face in the U.S. as well as both Japanese and U.S. business cultures, practices and standards.

KPMG offers employees medical, dental and vision coverage; short- and long-term disability; life and long-term care insurance; a 401(k) plan; a pension plan; flexible spending accounts; and discounts on cars, insurance, jewelry, retailers, transit passes and other programs.

FINANCIAL DATA: Note: Data for latest year may not have been available at press time.

In U.S. $	2016	2015	2014	2013	2012	2011
Revenue		9,340,000,000	8,376,440,000	7,880,000,000	7,450,000,000	7,050,000,000
R&D Expense						
Operating Income						
Operating Margin %						
SGA Expense						
Net Income						
Operating Cash Flow						
Capital Expenditure						
EBITDA						
Return on Assets %						
Return on Equity %						
Debt to Equity						

CONTACT INFORMATION:

Phone: 212-758-9700   Fax: 212-751-2109
Toll-Free:
Address: 345 Par Ave., New York, NY 10154-0102 United States

STOCK TICKER/OTHER:

Stock Ticker: Subsidiary   Exchange:
Employees: 23,000   Fiscal Year Ends: 09/30
Parent Company: KPMG International

SALARIES/BONUSES:

Top Exec. Salary: $ Bonus: $
Second Exec. Salary: $ Bonus: $

OTHER THOUGHTS:

Estimated Female Officers or Directors:
Hot Spot for Advancement for Women/Minorities:

Kroger Co (The)

NAIC Code: 445110

TYPES OF BUSINESS:

Grocery Stores
Convenience Stores
Jewelry Stores
Pharmacies
Food Processing
Gas Stations
Department Stores

BRANDS/DIVISIONS/AFFILIATES:

Kroger
City Market
Dillons
Food 4 Less
Fred Meyer
Fry's
Smith's
Axium Pharmacy Holdings Inc

CONTACTS: Note: Officers with more than one job title may be intentionally listed here more than once.

W. Mcmullen, CEO
Stuart Aitken, Vice President
J. Schlotman, CFO
M. Van Oflen, Chief Accounting Officer
Christopher Hjelm, Chief Information Officer
Frederick Morganthall, Executive VP, Divisional
Michael Donnelly, Executive VP, Divisional
Sukanya Madlinger, Senior VP
Mark Tuffin, Senior VP
Alessandro Tosolini, Senior VP, Divisional
Robert Clark, Senior VP, Divisional
Kathleen Barclay, Senior VP, Divisional
M. Perry, Senior VP, Divisional
Todd Foley, Treasurer
Jessica Adelman, Vice President, Divisional
Timothy Massa, Vice President, Divisional
Erin Sharp, Vice President, Divisional

GROWTH PLANS/SPECIAL FEATURES:

The Kroger Co. is one of the largest supermarket operators in the U.S. The company operates 2,778 supermarkets under a variety of names such as Kroger, City Market, Dillons, Jay C, Food 4 Less, Fred Meyer, Fry's and Smith's. More than 1,300 of these stores have fuel centers. Kroger's supermarkets operate under one of four store formats: combination food and drug stores, multi-department stores, marketplace stores and price impact warehouses. The combo stores are the primary food store format and typically draw customers from a 2 to 2.5 mile radius; multi-department stores are larger in size than combos and sell merchandise such as apparel, home furnishings, dÃ©cor, outdoor living, electronics, automotive products, toys and fine jewelry; marketplace stores offer full-service grocery, pharmacy and beauty care departments, as well as general merchandise; and price impact warehouses offer low cost promotions for grocery, health and beauty items. The firm also operates 784 convenience stores under the Quik Stop, Loaf N' Jug, Tom Thumb, Turkey Hill, Kwik Shop and Smith's Express names. Kroger's 323 fine jewelry stores operate under the Fred Meyer brand. Kroger manages a number of walk-in medical clinics located in its stores. The company operates 38 manufacturing plants, which supply approximately 40% of the corporate brand units sold in its retail outlets. These plants consist of 17 dairies, 10 deli or bakery plants, five grocery product plants, two beverage plants, two meat plants and two cheese plants. In July 2016, the firm agreed to acquire Modern HC Holdings, Inc., and will merge it with wholly-owned Axium Pharmacy Holdings, Inc. to create a combined specialty pharmacy operating as a wholly-owned subsidiary of The Kroger Co.

FINANCIAL DATA: Note: Data for latest year may not have been available at press time.

In U.S. $	2016	2015	2014	2013	2012	2011
Revenue	109,830,000,000	108,465,000,000	98,375,000,000	96,751,000,000	90,374,000,000	82,189,000,000
R&D Expense						
Operating Income	3,576,000,000	3,137,000,000	2,725,000,000	2,764,000,000	1,278,000,000	2,182,000,000
Operating Margin %	3.25%	2.89%	2.76%	2.85%	1.41%	2.65%
SGA Expense	18,669,000,000	17,868,000,000	15,809,000,000	15,477,000,000	15,964,000,000	14,462,000,000
Net Income	2,039,000,000	1,728,000,000	1,519,000,000	1,497,000,000	602,000,000	1,116,000,000
Operating Cash Flow	4,833,000,000	4,163,000,000	3,380,000,000	2,833,000,000	2,658,000,000	3,366,000,000
Capital Expenditure	3,349,000,000	2,831,000,000	2,330,000,000	2,062,000,000	1,898,000,000	1,919,000,000
EBITDA	5,665,000,000	5,085,000,000	4,428,000,000	4,416,000,000	2,916,000,000	3,782,000,000
Return on Assets %	6.32%	5.77%	5.63%	6.22%	2.56%	4.78%
Return on Equity %	33.33%	32.01%	31.67%	36.56%	12.97%	22.03%
Debt to Equity	1.42	1.80	1.79	1.46	1.72	1.37

CONTACT INFORMATION:

Phone: 513 762-4000   Fax: 513 762-1575
Toll-Free: 866-221-4141
Address: 1014 Vine St., Cincinnati, OH 45202 United States

STOCK TICKER/OTHER:

Stock Ticker: KR   Exchange: NYS
Employees: 400,000   Fiscal Year Ends: 01/31
Parent Company:

SALARIES/BONUSES:

Top Exec. Salary: Bonus: $
$1,216,665
Second Exec. Salary: Bonus: $
$793,825

OTHER THOUGHTS:

Estimated Female Officers or Directors: 5

Hot Spot for Advancement for Women/Minorities: Y

L Brands Inc

NAIC Code: 448120

TYPES OF BUSINESS:

Apparel, Retail
Contract Manufacturing
Apparel Importing
Catalog & Online Sales
Lingerie
Cosmetics
Fragrances
Candles

BRANDS/DIVISIONS/AFFILIATES:

Victoria's Secret
Bath & Body Works
Victoria's Secret U.K.
White Barn Candle Company
C.O. Bigelow
La Senza
Henri Bendel
VictoriasSecret.com

CONTACTS: Note: Officers with more than one job title may be intentionally listed here more than once.

Charles McGuigan, CEO, Divisional
Nicholas Coe, CEO, Divisional
Stuart Burgdoerfer, CFO
Leslie Wexner, Founder

GROWTH PLANS/SPECIAL FEATURES:

L Brands, Inc. is an apparel, lingerie, personal care products, accessories and fragrances retailer operating under various brand names, including Victoria's Secret and Bath & Body Works. The company operates approximately 3,005 retail stores. Victoria's Secret and Victoria's Secret U.K., with more than 1,100 stores in the U.S., Canada and the U.K., are specialty retailers of women's intimate apparel, beauty products and related accessories. Victoria's Secret's direct marketing segment is in charge of the firm's catalog. Bath & Body Works, with 1,600 stores in the U.S. and Canada, features personal care products and also operates White Barn Candle Company to supply its candle needs and C.O. Bigelow in Chicago for body products. L Brands also retains full ownership of the approximately 29 Henri Bendel women's personal care, apparel and accessory stores. In addition, the company operates La Senza, a Canadian lingerie company with more than 120 stores in Canada. L Brands runs four e-commerce sites: VictoriasSecret.com, HenriBendel.com, LaSenza.com and BathandBodyWorks.com. In 2015, the firm sold its remaining ownership interest in its third-party apparel sourcing business to Sycamore Partners.

L Brands offers its employees medical, dental, prescription, life and vision insurance; short- and long-term disability coverage; an employee assistance program; flexible spending; a retirement plan; a 401(k); a stock purchase plan; product discounts; tuition assistance; paid time off; and adoption assistance.

FINANCIAL DATA: Note: Data for latest year may not have been available at press time.

In U.S. $	2016	2015	2014	2013	2012	2011
Revenue	12,154,000,000	11,454,000,000	10,773,000,000	10,459,000,000	10,364,000,000	9,613,000,000
R&D Expense						
Operating Income	2,192,000,000	1,953,000,000	1,743,000,000	1,573,000,000	1,238,000,000	1,284,000,000
Operating Margin %	18.03%	17.05%	16.17%	15.03%	11.94%	13.35%
SGA Expense	3,012,000,000	2,855,000,000	2,686,000,000	2,720,000,000	2,698,000,000	2,341,000,000
Net Income	1,253,000,000	1,042,000,000	903,000,000	753,000,000	850,000,000	805,000,000
Operating Cash Flow	1,869,000,000	1,786,000,000	1,248,000,000	1,351,000,000	1,266,000,000	1,284,000,000
Capital Expenditure	727,000,000	715,000,000	691,000,000	588,000,000	426,000,000	274,000,000
EBITDA	2,725,000,000	2,398,000,000	2,167,000,000	1,986,000,000	1,864,000,000	1,853,000,000
Return on Assets %	15.62%	14.13%	13.66%	12.41%	13.53%	11.81%
Return on Equity %					105.39%	44.00%
Debt to Equity		264.72			25.40	1.69

CONTACT INFORMATION:

Phone: 614 415-7000   Fax: 614 479-7440
Toll-Free:
Address: 3 Limited Pkwy., Columbus, OH 43230 United States

STOCK TICKER/OTHER:

Stock Ticker: LB   Exchange: NYS
Employees: 80,100   Fiscal Year Ends: 01/31
Parent Company:

SALARIES/BONUSES:

Top Exec. Salary: Bonus: $
$1,985,385
Second Exec. Salary: Bonus: $
$1,488,846

OTHER THOUGHTS:

Estimated Female Officers or Directors: 1

Hot Spot for Advancement for Women/Minorities: Y

La Quinta Holdings Inc

www.lq.com

NAIC Code: 721110

TYPES OF BUSINESS:

Hotels, Motels & Suites
Hotel Management
Franchising

BRANDS/DIVISIONS/AFFILIATES:

La Quinta Properties
La Quinta Inns
La Quinta Inns and Suites
Blackstone Group LP

CONTACTS: Note: Officers with more than one job title may be intentionally listed here more than once.

James Forson, CFO
Mitesh Shah, Chairman of the Board
Julie Cary, Chief Marketing Officer
John Cantele, COO
Mark Chloupek, Executive VP
Rajiv Trivedi, Executive VP
Keith Cline, President

GROWTH PLANS/SPECIAL FEATURES:

La Quinta Holdings, Inc., owned by the Blackstone Group LP, is the operator of the La Quinta motels and suites properties. La Quinta is a leading limited-service lodging brand that provides comfortable guest rooms in convenient locations at affordable prices. The firm is one of the largest owners and operators of limited-service hotels in the U.S. It maintains 886 hotels and 87,500 rooms in 48 states, as well as Canada, Mexico and Honduras, under the brands La Quinta Inns and La Quinta Inns and Suites. The firm also licenses its brand name to franchisees for royalties and other fees. The company markets its services to both leisure guests and business travelers. All of the firm's hotels are owned through La Quinta Properties, a real estate investment trust (REIT). A typical La Quinta Inn features approximately 130 guest rooms with amenities including movies-on-demand, interactive video games, free high-speed Internet, complimentary continental breakfast, a swimming pool, fax services and 24-hour front desk message services. La Quinta Inn and Suites properties also feature deluxe two-room suites with microwaves and refrigerators as well as fitness centers, courtyards and expanded food offerings. The Blackstone Group LP holds a 28.3% interest in the company and can currently appoint 20% of the company's directors. Currently, La Quinta has a pipeline of 228 franchised hotels to be located in the U.S., Mexico, Columbia, Nicaragua, Guatemala and Chile. In May 2015, the firm expanded into the Latin American market with a franchise agreement for an LQ Hotel by La Quinta in Chile. In September of the same year, the firm sold 24 geographically dispersed hotels

The firm offers employees medical, dental and vision coverage; life insurance; long-term disability; an employee assistance program; flexible spending accounts; a 401(k) plan; tuition reimbursement; an internal referral bonus program; and room rate discounts.

FINANCIAL DATA: Note: Data for latest year may not have been available at press time.

In U.S. $	2016	2015	2014	2013	2012	2011
Revenue		1,029,974,000	976,938,000	873,893,000	818,012,000	751,541,000
R&D Expense						
Operating Income		128,071,000	136,669,000	156,181,000	129,595,000	101,849,000
Operating Margin %		12.43%	13.98%	17.87%	15.84%	13.55%
SGA Expense		250,677,000	261,781,000	190,055,000	180,987,000	154,949,000
Net Income		26,365,000	-337,297,000	3,976,000	-30,954,000	63,513,000
Operating Cash Flow		290,495,000	286,082,000	232,858,000	248,187,000	220,429,000
Capital Expenditure		100,776,000	78,630,000	115,632,000	102,899,000	96,152,000
EBITDA		311,489,000	311,690,000	321,570,000	292,328,000	267,571,000
Return on Assets %		.84%	-10.48%	.12%	-.90%	1.82%
Return on Equity %		3.40%	-59.99%	1.25%	-12.26%	33.50%
Debt to Equity		2.27	2.31		9.00	15.17

CONTACT INFORMATION:

Phone: 214-492-6600   Fax: 214-492-6616
Toll-Free:
Address: 909 Hidden Ridge, Ste. 600, Irving, TX 75038 United States

STOCK TICKER/OTHER:

Stock Ticker: LQ
Employees: 7,719
Parent Company: Blackstone Group LP

Exchange: NYS
Fiscal Year Ends: 12/31

SALARIES/BONUSES:

Top Exec. Salary: $832,403   Bonus: $
Second Exec. Salary: $479,912   Bonus: $

OTHER THOUGHTS:

Estimated Female Officers or Directors: 2
Hot Spot for Advancement for Women/Minorities:

Laboratory Corp of America Holdings

www.labcorp.com

NAIC Code: 621511

TYPES OF BUSINESS:

Clinical Laboratory Testing
Diagnostics
Urinalyses
Blood Cell Counts
Blood Chemistry Analysis
HIV Tests
Genetic Testing
Specialty & Niche Tests

BRANDS/DIVISIONS/AFFILIATES:

Center for Molecular Biology and Pathology
National Genetics Institute Inc
Viromed Laboratories Inc
DIANON Systems Inc
Correlagen Diagnostics
DNA Identity Lab
LabCorp

CONTACTS: Note: Officers with more than one job title may be intentionally listed here more than once.

Deborah Keller, CEO, Divisional
David King, CEO
Lance Berberian, Chief Information Officer
Glenn Eisenberg, Executive VP
Lisa Uthgenannt, Other Executive Officer
F. Eberts, Other Executive Officer
Edward Dodson, Senior VP

GROWTH PLANS/SPECIAL FEATURES:

Laboratory Corp. of America Holdings (LabCorp) is a leading independent clinical laboratory company in the U.S. Its tests are used primarily for routine screening, patient diagnosis and the monitoring and treatment of disease. The company operates a nationwide network of 39 primary testing laboratories and approximately 1,700 service centers, consisting of branches, patient service centers and STAT labs, which can perform routine tests quickly and report results to the physician immediately. LabCorp's testing services include routine testing, specialty testing and new test development. The most frequently requested routine tests offered by the firm include blood chemistry analyses, thyroid tests, urinalyses, blood cell counts, pap tests, HIV tests, microbiology cultures and substance-abuse tests. Specialty testing businesses in which LabCorp offers its services include infectious diseases, diagnostic genetics, oncology testing, clinical trials testing, identity testing, allergy testing and occupational testing. Its Center for Molecular Biology and Pathology is a leading molecular diagnostics and polymerase chain reaction (PCR) technology firm. The company's National Genetics Institute, Inc. subsidiary is a leading developer of PCR assays for Hepatitis C. Viromed Laboratories, Inc. provides molecular microbial testing using real time PCR platforms. Additional specialty testing subsidiaries include anatomic pathology/oncology testing firm DIANON Systems, Inc.; forensics through Cellmark Forensics; paternity testing firm DNA Identity Lab; and molecular diagnosis of cardiac disease company Correlagen Diagnostics. LabCorp processes an average of over 500,000 specimens per day and provides clinical laboratory services in all 50 states, as well as in Belgium, Canada, China, Japan, Singapore, the U.K. and the United Arab Emirates. In August 2016, the firm agreed to acquire Sequenom, Inc., a provider of non-invasive prenatal testing, for approximately $371 million.

Employee benefits include medical, dental and vision coverage; flexible spending accounts; 401(k) and stock purchase plan; life and AD&D insurance; and short- and long-term disability.

FINANCIAL DATA: Note: Data for latest year may not have been available at press time.

In U.S. $	2016	2015	2014	2013	2012	2011
Revenue		8,680,100,000	6,011,600,000	5,808,300,000	5,671,400,000	5,542,300,000
R&D Expense						
Operating Income		1,002,900,000	910,400,000	990,900,000	1,023,500,000	948,400,000
Operating Margin %		11.55%	15.14%	17.06%	18.04%	17.11%
SGA Expense		1,622,000,000	1,198,200,000	1,128,800,000	1,114,600,000	1,159,600,000
Net Income		436,900,000	511,200,000	573,800,000	583,100,000	519,700,000
Operating Cash Flow		982,400,000	739,000,000	818,700,000	841,400,000	855,600,000
Capital Expenditure		255,800,000	203,500,000	202,200,000	176,300,000	145,700,000
EBITDA		1,464,800,000	1,181,700,000	1,242,200,000	1,268,500,000	1,185,000,000
Return on Assets %		4.05%	7.16%	8.33%	9.01%	8.43%
Return on Equity %		11.25%	19.24%	22.03%	22.33%	20.91%
Debt to Equity		1.21	0.95	1.15	0.80	0.83

CONTACT INFORMATION:

Phone: 336 229-1127   Fax: 336 229-7717
Toll-Free:
Address: 358 S. Main St., Burlington, NC 27215 United States

STOCK TICKER/OTHER:

Stock Ticker: LH   Exchange: NYS
Employees: 36,000   Fiscal Year Ends: 12/31
Parent Company:

SALARIES/BONUSES:

Top Exec. Salary: Bonus: $
$1,044,481
Second Exec. Salary: Bonus: $
$645,263

OTHER THOUGHTS:

Estimated Female Officers or Directors: 3

Hot Spot for Advancement for Women/Minorities: Y

Sales, profits and employees may be estimates. Financial information, benefits and other data can change quickly and may vary from those stated here.

Lam Research Corp

www.lamrc.com

NAIC Code: 333242

TYPES OF BUSINESS:

Semiconductor Manufacturing Equipment
Etch Processing Systems
Chemical Mechanical Planarization Systems
Wafer Cleaning Equipment & Services
Support Services

BRANDS/DIVISIONS/AFFILIATES:

Flex
Versys
Kiyo
Syndion
Silfex Inc
Multi-Station Sequential Deposition
VECTOR
ALTUS

CONTACTS: Note: Officers with more than one job title may be intentionally listed here more than once.

Martin Anstice, CEO
Douglas Bettinger, CFO
Timothy Archer, COO
Stephen Newberry, Director
Richard Gottscho, Executive VP, Divisional
Sarah ODowd, Other Executive Officer

GROWTH PLANS/SPECIAL FEATURES:

Lam Research Corp. supplies wafer fabrication equipment and services to semiconductor companies worldwide. The firm designs, manufactures, markets and services semiconductor processing equipment used in semiconductor device fabrication. The company's etch products are used to deposit special films on silicon wafers and to selectively etch away portions of these films utilizing plasma-based technologies, creating an integrated circuit (IC). Its products include the Flex product family for dielectric etch, the Versys metal and Kiyo product families for conductor etch and the Syndion product family for three-dimensional ICs. Lam's VECTOR family of plasma-enhanced chemical vapor deposition and atomic layer deposition systems delivers superior thin film quality, wafer-to-water uniformity, productivity and low cost of ownership. The firm also offers wafer cleaning services and equipment that employs proprietary technology and can be used throughout the semiconductor manufacturing process. Lam's ALTUS product family deposits a highly conformal atomic layer for advanced tungsten metallization applications. The patented Multi-Station Sequential Deposition architecture enables a nucleation layer to be formed using pulsed nucleation layer technology. Additionally, through Silfex, Inc., the firm supplies high-purity custom silicon components and assemblies to various high-technology markets. Lam developed several industry firsts, including the patented TCP (Transformer Coupled Plasma) source technology, the first inductive plasma source technology with a planar coil; dual frequency confined technology for dielectric etch; the 200/300mm capable etch product line with a 200mm comparable footprint; decoupling plasma density and bias power for conductor etch; and providing technologies to control parameters that impact critical dimension uniformity.

The firm offers employees life, disability, AD&D, medical, dental and vision insurance; flexible spending accounts; group legal service plans; educational assistance; gym membership reimbursements; an employee assistance program; adoption aid; and access to a credit union.

FINANCIAL DATA: Note: Data for latest year may not have been available at press time.

In U.S. $	2016	2015	2014	2013	2012	2011
Revenue	5,885,893,000	5,259,312,000	4,607,309,000	3,598,916,000	2,665,192,000	3,237,693,000
R&D Expense	913,712,000	825,242,000	716,471,000	683,688,000	444,559,000	373,293,000
Operating Income	1,074,256,000	788,039,000	677,669,000	118,071,000	237,733,000	804,285,000
Operating Margin %	18.25%	14.98%	14.70%	3.28%	8.91%	24.84%
SGA Expense	630,954,000	591,611,000	613,341,000	599,487,000	400,052,000	308,075,000
Net Income	914,049,000	655,577,000	632,289,000	113,879,000	168,723,000	723,748,000
Operating Cash Flow	1,350,277,000	785,503,000	717,049,000	719,933,000	499,089,000	881,028,000
Capital Expenditure	175,330,000	198,265,000	145,503,000	160,795,000	107,272,000	127,495,000
EBITDA	1,385,918,000	1,092,452,000	1,077,309,000	431,182,000	344,205,000	881,015,000
Return on Assets %	8.44%	7.55%	8.29%	1.49%	2.79%	22.11%
Return on Equity %	16.62%	12.93%	13.28%	2.36%	4.43%	34.15%
Debt to Equity	0.57	0.19	0.16	0.17	0.14	0.29

CONTACT INFORMATION:

Phone: 510 572-0200   Fax: 510 572-6454
Toll-Free: 800-526-7678
Address: 4650 Cushing Pkwy., Fremont, CA 94538 United States

STOCK TICKER/OTHER:

Stock Ticker: LRCX
Employees: 7,500
Parent Company:

Exchange: NAS
Fiscal Year Ends: 06/30

SALARIES/BONUSES:

Top Exec. Salary: $906,646   Bonus: $
Second Exec. Salary: $604,431   Bonus: $

OTHER THOUGHTS:

Estimated Female Officers or Directors: 3
Hot Spot for Advancement for Women/Minorities: Y

Land O'Lakes Inc

www.landolakesinc.com

NAIC Code: 311500

TYPES OF BUSINESS:

Dairy Products, Manufacturing
Animal Feed & Pet Food
Plant Food
Crop Protection Products
Food Ingredients
Agronomy Products
Crop Seed
Eggs

BRANDS/DIVISIONS/AFFILIATES:

Kozy Shack
Alpine Lace
Land O'Lakes Purina Feed LLC
Purina Mills LLC
MoArk LLC
Land O'Lakes Finance Company
Northwest Food Products Transportation
CROPLAN GENETICS

CONTACTS: Note: Officers with more than one job title may be intentionally listed here more than once.

Chris Policinski, CEO
Beth Ford, COO
Dan Knutson, CFO
Tim Scott, CMO
Loren Heeringa, Chief Human Resources Officer
Peter Janzen, Chief Admin. Officer
Peter Janzen, General Counsel
Barry Wolfish, Chief Corp. Strategy
Karen Grabow, Sr. VP-Bus. Dev. Svcs.
Carol Kitchen, Sr. VP-Global Ingredients
Beth Ford, Chief Supply Chain Officer

GROWTH PLANS/SPECIAL FEATURES:

Land O'Lakes, Inc. (LOL) is a dairy cooperative and a leading producer of dairy and agricultural products in the U.S. and more than 50 countries. The dairy foods segment produces butter spreads, cheese and related products, marketed under national and regional brands including Land O'Lakes and Alpine Lace cheese. Through its subsidiary Kozy Shack, the firm produces milk-based desserts such as rice pudding, tapioca pudding, bread pudding and flan. LOL's customer base includes major national supermarket and supercenter chains, industrial customers and food service customers. The Land O'Lakes name is licensed to many other businesses that distribute sour cream, yogurt, cocoa mix, milks, creams, juices, eggs, cottage cheese and other milk-based products under the brand. Land O'Lakes Purina Feed LLC produces animal feed for both the commercial and non-commercial sectors of the feed market in North America through its wholly owned subsidiary Purina Mills LLC. Products include complete feeds, supplements, premixes, milk replacers and ingredients. LOL also sells crop seed for a variety of crops, including alfalfa, soybeans, corn and forage and turf grasses. Crop seed products and crop protection are sold under the brands CROPLAN GENETICS, Agrisolutions and Origin. WinField Solutions supports the firm's Expert Seller web site, which offers customers marketing and sales tools, educational information and promotional items. This division markets and distributes seeds produced by Syngenta and Monsanto companies with which LOL has strategic alliances. In addition, the firm has a business development and marketing segment available to its cooperative members. Additional subsidiaries include MoArk LLC, Land O'Lakes Finance Company and Northwest Food Products Transportation. In 2015, the firm acquired assets of FLM+, an agriculture marketing communications company.

Employees of the firm receive benefits including medical, dental, vision, disability, life and AD&D coverage; an employee assistance program; and 401(k).

FINANCIAL DATA: Note: Data for latest year may not have been available at press time.

In U.S. $	2016	2015	2014	2013	2012	2011
Revenue		13,007,704,000	14,965,516,000	14,236,449,000	13,642,019,000	12,426,283,000
R&D Expense						
Operating Income						
Operating Margin %						
SGA Expense						
Net Income		304,190,000	266,495,000	305,953,000	240,365,000	182,156,000
Operating Cash Flow						
Capital Expenditure						
EBITDA						
Return on Assets %						
Return on Equity %						
Debt to Equity						

CONTACT INFORMATION:

Phone: 651-481-2222   Fax: 651-481-2000
Toll-Free: 800-328-9680
Address: 4001 N. Lexington Ave., Arden Hills, MN 55126 United States

STOCK TICKER/OTHER:

Stock Ticker: Cooperative
Employees: 10,000
Parent Company:

Exchange:
Fiscal Year Ends: 12/31

SALARIES/BONUSES:

Top Exec. Salary: $ Bonus: $
Second Exec. Salary: $ Bonus: $

OTHER THOUGHTS:

Estimated Female Officers or Directors: 3
Hot Spot for Advancement for Women/Minorities: Y

Sales, profits and employees may be estimates. Financial information, benefits and other data can change quickly and may vary from those stated here.

Las Vegas Sands Corp (The Venetian)   www.lasvegassands.com

NAIC Code: 721120

TYPES OF BUSINESS:

Hotel Casinos
Convention & Conference Centers
Shopping Center Development
Casino Property Development

BRANDS/DIVISIONS/AFFILIATES:

Venetian Resort Hotel Casino (The)
Sands Expo and Convention Center (The)
Sands China Ltd
Sands Macao Casino (The)
Palazzo Resort Hotel Casino (The)
Venetian Macao Resort Hotel (The)
Marina Bay Sands Pte Ltd
Cotai Strip

CONTACTS: Note: Officers with more than one job title may be intentionally listed here more than once.

George Tanasijevich, CEO, Subsidiary
Sheldon Adelson, CEO
Patrick Dumont, CFO
Randy Hyzak, Chief Accounting Officer
George Markantonis, COO, Subsidiary
Robert Goldstein, COO
Ira Raphaelson, Executive VP
Stephanie Marz, Vice President, Divisional

GROWTH PLANS/SPECIAL FEATURES:

Las Vegas Sands Corp. (LVSC) is an international hotel, resort and casino firm. Its flagship property is The Venetian Resort Hotel Casino, which is connected to The Palazzo Resort Hotel Casino. Together, The Venetian and The Palazzo offer 225,000 square feet of gaming space, with 240 table games and 2,350 slot machines, as well as 7,092 hotel suites. LVSC also runs the 1.2 million square foot convention and trade show facility, The Sands Expo and Convention Center, and a supplemental event and conference center. Additionally, the firm operates the Sands Casino Resort Bethlehem in eastern Pennsylvania, which features 145,000 square feet of gaming space, a 300-room hotel, 150,000 square feet of retail space and other amenities. Outside the U.S., LVSC has operations in Macao, through majority-owned subsidiary Sands China Ltd., and Singapore, through Marina Bay Sands Pte. Ltd. The company's largest development project, the multi-billion dollar Cotai Strip, is a collection of hotel properties, casinos and entertainment venues in Macao. Sands China runs The Sands Macao and The Venetian Macao Resort Hotel, the anchor property on the Cotai Strip. Other properties on the Cotai Strip include the Four Seasons Macao and the Plaza Casino. Its Singapore property, Marina Bay Sands features three 55-story hotel towers, gaming space, convention space, two state-of-the-art theaters and The Shoppes at Marina Bay Sands.

FINANCIAL DATA: Note: Data for latest year may not have been available at press time.

In U.S. $	2016	2015	2014	2013	2012	2011
Revenue		11,688,460,000	14,583,850,000	13,769,880,000	11,131,130,000	9,410,745,000
R&D Expense		10,372,000	14,325,000	15,809,000	19,958,000	11,309,000
Operating Income		2,841,475,000	4,099,226,000	3,408,243,000	2,311,382,000	2,389,887,000
Operating Margin %		24.31%	28.10%	24.75%	20.76%	25.39%
SGA Expense		1,491,093,000	1,459,113,000	1,532,614,000	1,412,760,000	1,131,809,000
Net Income		1,966,236,000	2,840,629,000	2,305,997,000	1,524,093,000	1,560,123,000
Operating Cash Flow		3,449,971,000	4,832,844,000	4,439,412,000	3,057,757,000	2,662,496,000
Capital Expenditure		1,528,642,000	1,178,656,000	943,982,000	1,449,234,000	1,508,593,000
EBITDA		3,924,666,000	5,138,481,000	4,422,191,000	3,213,186,000	3,172,176,000
Return on Assets %		9.07%	12.60%	10.27%	6.86%	5.86%
Return on Equity %		28.02%	38.18%	31.31%	20.44%	18.39%
Debt to Equity		1.37	1.37	1.22	1.43	1.21

CONTACT INFORMATION:

Phone: 702 414-1000   Fax: 702 414-4884
Toll-Free:
Address: 3355 Las Vegas Blvd. S., Las Vegas, NV 89109 United States

STOCK TICKER/OTHER:

Stock Ticker: LVS   Exchange: NYS
Employees: 48,500   Fiscal Year Ends: 12/31
Parent Company:

SALARIES/BONUSES:

Top Exec. Salary: Bonus: $
$3,250,000
Second Exec. Salary: Bonus: $
$1,538,462

OTHER THOUGHTS:

Estimated Female Officers or Directors:

Hot Spot for Advancement for Women/Minorities:

Lear Corp

NAIC Code: 336300

www.lear.com

TYPES OF BUSINESS:

Automobile Components
Automotive Interiors
Electrical Systems
Instrument Panels
Seat Systems
Flooring Systems
Entertainment & Wireless Systems
Keyless Entry Systems

BRANDS/DIVISIONS/AFFILIATES:

Solid State Smart Junction Box
Eagle Ottawa

CONTACTS: Note: Officers with more than one job title may be intentionally listed here more than once.

Matthew Simoncini, CEO
Jeffrey Vanneste, CFO
Henry Wallace, Chairman of the Board
James Murawski, Chief Accounting Officer
Terrence Larkin, Executive VP, Divisional
Raymond Scott, Executive VP
Shari Burgess, Other Executive Officer
Frank Orsini, President, Divisional
Jay Kunkel, President, Divisional
Thomas DiDonato, Senior VP, Divisional
Melvin Stephens, Senior VP, Divisional

GROWTH PLANS/SPECIAL FEATURES:

Lear Corp. is one of the world's largest automotive interior systems suppliers. The firm serves every major automotive manufacturer, including General Motors, Ford, BMW, Fiat Chrysler and Volkswagen. The company currently operates 145 facilities in 22 countries. Its business is conducted through two segments: seating and electrical power management systems (EPMS). The seating segment consists of the design, engineering, just-in-time assembly and delivery of complete seat systems as well as the manufacture of all major seat components, including seat structures and mechanisms, seat covers, seat forms and headrests. The segment produces seat systems that are fully assembled and ready for installation in automobiles and light trucks. These include luxury and performance automotive seating required by premium automakers, including Alfa Romeo, Audi, Lamborghini, BMW, Cadillac, Ferrari, Jaguar Land Rover, Lincoln, Maserati, Mercedes-Benz and Porsche. The EPMS segment consists of the design, manufacture, assembly and supply of electrical distribution systems and components for traditional powertrain vehicles as well as for hybrid and electric vehicles. This segment is able to provide customers with design and engineering solutions involving manufactured systems, modules and components that optimally integrate a vehicle's entire electrical distribution system, consisting of wiring, terminals and connectors, junction boxes and electronic modules. This includes the Solid State Smart Junction Box, which integrates advancement in terminal and connector technology, junction box and electronic control module capability and complete electrical distribution system expertise. As of December 2016, the company had 24 operating joint ventures located in seven countries, including 16 in Asia, seven in North America (including one that is dedicated to serving Asian automotive manufacturers) and one in Europe. During 2015, Lear acquired Eagle Ottawa, a supplier of automotive leather; acquired intellectual property and technology from Autonet Mobile; and opened its first automotive plant in Macedonia, in Gostivar.

FINANCIAL DATA: Note: Data for latest year may not have been available at press time.

In U.S. $	2016	2015	2014	2013	2012	2011
Revenue		18,211,400,000	17,727,300,000	16,234,000,000	14,567,000,000	14,156,500,000
R&D Expense						
Operating Income		1,186,800,000	929,200,000	736,600,000	705,200,000	679,600,000
Operating Margin %		6.51%	5.24%	4.53%	4.84%	4.80%
SGA Expense		580,500,000	529,900,000	528,700,000	479,300,000	485,600,000
Net Income		745,500,000	672,400,000	431,400,000	1,282,800,000	540,700,000
Operating Cash Flow		1,271,100,000	927,800,000	820,100,000	729,800,000	790,300,000
Capital Expenditure		485,800,000	424,700,000	460,600,000	458,300,000	329,500,000
EBITDA		1,466,000,000	1,165,800,000	964,000,000	938,300,000	901,700,000
Return on Assets %		8.03%	7.69%	5.22%	16.87%	7.93%
Return on Equity %		25.33%	22.39%	13.20%	43.31%	22.08%
Debt to Equity		0.65	0.49	0.34	0.17	0.28

CONTACT INFORMATION:

Phone: 248 447-1500　　Fax:
Toll-Free: 800-413-5327
Address: 21557 Telegraph Rd., Southfield, MI 48033 United States

STOCK TICKER/OTHER:

Stock Ticker: LEA　　　　　　　　Exchange: NYS
Employees: 136,200　　　　　　　Fiscal Year Ends: 12/31
Parent Company:

SALARIES/BONUSES:

Top Exec. Salary:　　　　Bonus: $
$1,306,125
Second Exec. Salary:　　Bonus: $
$834,942

OTHER THOUGHTS:

Estimated Female Officers or Directors: 1

Hot Spot for Advancement for Women/Minorities:

Sales, profits and employees may be estimates. Financial information, benefits and other data can change quickly and may vary from those stated here.

Legg Mason Inc

www.leggmason.com

NAIC Code: 523110

TYPES OF BUSINESS:

Stock Brokerage/Investment Banking
Mutual Funds

BRANDS/DIVISIONS/AFFILIATES:

Legg Mason Funds
Royce Funds (The)
QS Investors Holdings LLC
RARE Infrastructure Limited
Western Asset Funds

CONTACTS: *Note: Officers with more than one job title may be intentionally listed here more than once.*

Joseph Sullivan, CEO
Peter Nachtwey, CFO
Ursula Schliessler, Chief Administrative Officer
Thomas Merchant, Executive VP
Terence Johnson, Executive VP
Thomas Hoops, Other Corporate Officer

GROWTH PLANS/SPECIAL FEATURES:

Legg Mason, Inc. is a global asset management company with consolidated assets under management totaling $696 billion. Operating through its subsidiaries, the firm provides investment management and related services to institutional and individual clients, company-sponsored mutual funds and other pooled investment vehicles. The company offers these products and services directly and through various financial intermediaries. The firm conducts its business primarily through several asset managers, housed in independent subsidiaries owned by Legg Mason. Asset managers provide a range of separate account investment management services to institutional clients, including pension and other retirement plans, corporations, insurance companies, endowments, foundations and governments as well as to high-net-worth individuals and families. Asset managers also sponsor and manage various groups of U.S. mutual funds, including the Legg Mason Funds and The Royce Funds. The Legg Mason Funds consist of 121 mutual funds and 31 closed-end funds in the U.S., all of which are sub-advised by subsidiary asset managers. The Royce Funds consist of 29 mutual funds and three closed-end funds, most of which invest primarily in smaller-cap company stocks using a value approach. Funds which previously comprised the company's Western Asset Funds are now included in the Legg Mason Funds. Outside the U.S., the firm manages, supports and distributes funds across a wide array of global fixed income, liquidity and equity investment strategies. International funds include a broad range of cross border funds that are domiciled in Ireland and Luxembourg and are sold in a number of countries across Asia, Europe and Latin America. In 2014, the firm acquired QS Investors Holdings, LLC, based in Delaware. In October 2015, it acquired a majority stake in RARE Infrastructure Limited, based in Sydney, Australia.

The company offers employees paid time off, health care coverage, commuter discounts, a 401(k) plan, a profit sharing plan, a stock purchase plan, adoption assistance and tuition reimbursement.

FINANCIAL DATA: *Note: Data for latest year may not have been available at press time.*

In U.S. $	2016	2015	2014	2013	2012	2011
Revenue	2,660,844,000	2,819,106,000	2,741,757,000	2,612,650,000	2,662,574,000	2,784,317,000
R&D Expense						
Operating Income	50,831,000	498,219,000	430,893,000	-434,499,000	338,753,000	386,808,000
Operating Margin %	1.91%	17.67%	15.71%	-16.63%	12.72%	13.89%
SGA Expense	2,070,994,000	2,119,704,000	2,102,563,000	2,110,700,000	2,113,576,000	2,198,022,000
Net Income	-25,032,000	237,080,000	284,784,000	-353,327,000	220,817,000	253,923,000
Operating Cash Flow	454,451,000	568,118,000	437,324,000	303,332,000	496,769,000	412,140,000
Capital Expenditure	40,330,000	45,773,000	40,452,000	38,351,000	31,822,000	32,904,000
EBITDA	83,542,000	481,353,000	535,397,000	-359,840,000	484,462,000	560,102,000
Return on Assets %	- .37%	3.25%	3.96%	-4.46%	2.55%	2.93%
Return on Equity %	- .62%	5.01%	5.96%	-6.73%	3.85%	4.37%
Debt to Equity	0.41	0.23	0.21	0.27	0.24	0.25

CONTACT INFORMATION:

Phone: 410 539-0000   Fax: 410 454-4174
Toll-Free: 800-822-5544
Address: 100 International Dr., Baltimore, MD 21202 United States

STOCK TICKER/OTHER:

Stock Ticker: LM
Employees: 3,066
Parent Company:

Exchange: NYS
Fiscal Year Ends: 02/28

SALARIES/BONUSES:

Top Exec. Salary: $500,000   Bonus: $3,320,000
Second Exec. Salary: $339,300   Bonus: $1,855,167

OTHER THOUGHTS:

Estimated Female Officers or Directors: 2
Hot Spot for Advancement for Women/Minorities:

Lennar Corporation

NAIC Code: 236117

TYPES OF BUSINESS:

Construction, Home Building and Residential
Mortgages
Title Insurance & Services

BRANDS/DIVISIONS/AFFILIATES:

Universal American Mortgage Company LLC
Eagle Home Mortgage LLC
Railto Investments
Lennar

CONTACTS: Note: Officers with more than one job title may be intentionally listed here more than once.

Stuart Miller, CEO
Bruce Gross, CFO
David Collins, Chief Accounting Officer
Jonathan Jaffe, COO
Richard Beckwitt, President
Mark Sustana, Secretary
Diane Bessette, Vice President

GROWTH PLANS/SPECIAL FEATURES:

Lennar Corporation is a U.S. homebuilder and provider of financial services operating in 20 states. The firm sells single family attached and detached homes and, to a lesser extent multi-level residential buildings primarily under the Lennar brand name in communities targeted to first-time, move-up and active adult homebuyers. The company also purchases develops and sells residential land. Lennar divides its homebuilding operations into six segments: East (which includes Florida, Georgia, Maryland, New Jersey, North Carolina, South Carolina and Virginia); Central (including Arizona, Colorado and Texas, excluding Houston); West (California and Nevada); Houston, Texas; Southeast Florida and other (including Illinois, Minnesota, Tennessee, Oregon and Washington). Lennar's homes have an average sale price of about $344,000. In 2015, it delivered 24,292 homes to buyers. Lennar generally supervises and controls the development of land and the design and building of its residential communities with a relatively small labor force hiring subcontractors for site improvements and virtually all of the work involved in the construction of homes. Through its financial services subsidiaries, Universal American Mortgage Company, LLC and Eagle Home Mortgage, LLC, the firm provides mortgage financing, title insurance and closing services for both buyers of its homes and third parties. Lennar's subsidiaries provide loans to 82% of its homebuyers who obtain mortgage financing in areas where it offers services. The Rialto Investments division provides advisory services ongoing asset management services and acquisition and monetization services related to distressed loans and securities portfolios. The Lennar multifamily segment, currently under development, will focus on developing a portfolio of multifamily rental properties in select U.S. markets.

The company offers employees medical, dental and vision insurance; home and auto insurance; mortgage and title benefits; short-and long-term disability; and life insurance.

FINANCIAL DATA: Note: Data for latest year may not have been available at press time.

In U.S. $	2016	2015	2014	2013	2012	2011
Revenue		9,474,008,000	7,779,812,000	5,935,095,000	4,104,706,000	3,095,385,000
R&D Expense						
Operating Income		1,086,016,000	922,038,000	685,836,000	322,176,000	103,934,000
Operating Margin %		11.46%	11.85%	11.55%	7.84%	3.35%
SGA Expense		216,244,000	177,161,000	146,060,000	127,338,000	95,256,000
Net Income		802,894,000	638,916,000	479,674,000	679,124,000	92,199,000
Operating Cash Flow		-419,646,000	-788,488,000	-807,714,000	-424,648,000	-259,135,000
Capital Expenditure		17,623,000	14,278,000	8,126,000	2,822,000	9,936,000
EBITDA		1,265,736,000	1,044,877,000	806,203,000	344,548,000	210,124,000
Return on Assets %		5.80%	5.20%	4.43%	6.95%	1.02%
Return on Equity %		15.16%	14.03%	12.65%	22.22%	3.47%
Debt to Equity		0.98	0.93	0.99	1.18	1.40

CONTACT INFORMATION:

Phone: 305 559-4000   Fax: 305 227-7115
Toll-Free: 800-741-4663
Address: 700 NW 107th Ave., Ste. 400, Miami, FL 33172 United States

STOCK TICKER/OTHER:

Stock Ticker: LEN
Employees: 7,749
Parent Company:

Exchange: NYS
Fiscal Year Ends: 11/30

SALARIES/BONUSES:

Top Exec. Salary:
$1,000,000

Bonus: $

Second Exec. Salary:
$800,000

Bonus: $

OTHER THOUGHTS:

Estimated Female Officers or Directors: 3

Hot Spot for Advancement for Women/Minorities: Y

Level 3 Communications Inc

www.level3.com

NAIC Code: 517110

TYPES OF BUSINESS:

Private Data Networks-Fiber Optic
Broadband Network Services
Managed Modem Access Services
Digital Media Capture and Distribution
High-Speed Content Upload
Server Facilities

BRANDS/DIVISIONS/AFFILIATES:

Softswitch

CONTACTS: Note: Officers with more than one job title may be intentionally listed here more than once.

Jeffrey Storey, CEO
Sunit Patel, CFO
Eric Mortensen, Chief Accounting Officer
James Ellis, Director
Hector Alonso, President, Divisional
Andrew Crouch, President, Divisional
John Ryan, Secretary

GROWTH PLANS/SPECIAL FEATURES:

Level 3 Communications, Inc. is a leading provider of integrated communications services. Its primary business is the provision of communications services over its extensive broadband networks in North America, Europe and Latin America, consisting of approximately 106,000 intercity route miles. The networks supply a portfolio of services including Internet protocol (IP) services (Internet access, Ethernet and virtual private network services), broadband transport and colocation services to enterprises and other organization in more than 60 countries. Its patented Softswitch-based managed modem and voice services, which use a distributed computer system to emulate traditional circuit switches, provide customers with voice over IP (VoIP) technology. Level 3 divides its core network services into four segments according to customer base: wholesale markets, enterprises, government customers and content customers. Wholesale customers include domestic and international carriers; voice service providers, which include calling card companies, conferencing providers and contact centers that use VoIP technology to better manage costs and enable advanced applications; wireless providers; and broadband cable television operators. Enterprise customers include large multinational customers; enterprises that purchase communications services; portals and large search enterprises, regional service providers; systems integrators; and software service providers. Government customers comprise government departments and agencies, including states and municipalities, for the U.S. and other countries, as well as research and educational consortia. Content customers comprise subgroups of customers such as digital entertainment (online gaming/social networking/technology/Internet video providers), media and entertainment (conglomerates/programmers/studios/production companies/broadcast stations) and sports teams (professional/college and stadiums/venues).

The firm offers employees a 401(k) plan; educational assistance; flexible spending accounts; and medical, dental and vision coverage.

FINANCIAL DATA: Note: Data for latest year may not have been available at press time.

In U.S. $	2016	2015	2014	2013	2012	2011
Revenue		8,229,000,000	6,777,000,000	6,313,000,000	6,376,000,000	4,333,000,000
R&D Expense						
Operating Income		1,331,000,000	1,013,000,000	666,000,000	575,000,000	52,000,000
Operating Margin %		16.17%	14.94%	10.54%	9.01%	1.20%
SGA Expense		1,467,000,000	1,181,000,000	2,376,000,000	2,416,000,000	1,759,000,000
Net Income		3,433,000,000	314,000,000	-109,000,000	-422,000,000	-756,000,000
Operating Cash Flow		1,855,000,000	1,161,000,000	713,000,000	578,000,000	384,000,000
Capital Expenditure		1,229,000,000	910,000,000	760,000,000	743,000,000	494,000,000
EBITDA		2,091,000,000	1,700,000,000	1,378,000,000	1,108,000,000	735,000,000
Return on Assets %		15.22%	1.85%	-.83%	-3.18%	-7.01%
Return on Equity %		41.63%	8.07%	-8.44%	-35.70%	-145.94%
Debt to Equity		1.08	1.72	5.90	7.27	7.02

CONTACT INFORMATION:

Phone: 720 888-1000   Fax: 720 888-5088
Toll-Free: 877-253-8353
Address: 1025 Eldorado Blvd., Broomfield, CO 80021 United States

STOCK TICKER/OTHER:

Stock Ticker: LVLT   Exchange: NYS
Employees: 13,500   Fiscal Year Ends: 12/31
Parent Company:

SALARIES/BONUSES:

Top Exec. Salary: Bonus: $2,379,300
$1,246,154
Second Exec. Salary: Bonus: $2,446,154
$569,039

OTHER THOUGHTS:

Estimated Female Officers or Directors: 2

Hot Spot for Advancement for Women/Minorities: Y

Sales, profits and employees may be estimates. Financial information, benefits and other data can change quickly and may vary from those stated here.

Liberty Global Inc

NAIC Code: 517110

www.lgi.com

TYPES OF BUSINESS:

Video, Voice & Broadband Internet Access Services
Telephony Services
VoIP Services
Mobile Telephony Services
Video on Demand Services

BRANDS/DIVISIONS/AFFILIATES:

Unitymedia KabelBW GmbH
UPC Holding BV
VTR Global Com SA
Telenet Group Holding NV
Liberty Puerto Rico
Choice Cable TV
Ziggo NV
VTR GlobalCom SpA

CONTACTS: Note: Officers with more than one job title may be intentionally listed here more than once.

Michael Fries, CEO
John Malone, Chairman of the Board
Balan Nair, Chief Technology Officer
Bernard Dvorak, Co-CFO
Charles Bracken, Co-CFO
Bryan Hall, Executive VP
Diederik Karsten, Executive VP
Leonard Stegman, Managing Director

GROWTH PLANS/SPECIAL FEATURES:

Liberty Global, Inc. (LGI) is an international provider of video, voice and broadband Internet services, with consolidated broadband communications and/or direct-to-home (DTH) satellite operations in 14 countries around the world, primarily in Europe and Chile. LGI has 27 million customers and 56 million video, voice and/or Internet subscribers. Its products include Video on Demand, high definition TV, Digital Video Recorders (DVRs), VoIP telephony services and broadband Internet service featuring downstream speeds of up to 500 megabytes per second (Mbps). The firm conducts its business operations through various subsidiaries. Through indirect wholly-owned subsidiary UPC Holding BV, the firm provides video, voice and broadband Internet services in nine European countries and in Chile. The European broadband communications operations and DTH operations of UPC Holding, along with the German broadband communications operations of subsidiary Unitymedia KabelBW GmbH, are collectively referred to as the UPC/Unity division. UPC's broadband communication operations in Chile are provided through VTR Global Com SA, an 80%-owned subsidiary. Through its 57.4% indirect majority interest in Telenet Group Holding NV, LGI provides broadband communications services in Belgium. LGI also has consolidated broadband communications operations in Puerto Rico and consolidated programming business interests in Europe and Argentina. Liberty Puerto Rico is the company's brand in Puerto Rico. In 2014, the company acquired Ziggo NV, a Dutch cable operator; acquired the remaining shares in both VTR GlobalCom SpA and VTR Wireless SpA, Chile's largest cable operator; and sold its Chellomedia division. In 2015, the firm acquired Choice Cable TV, a cable and broadband services provider in Puerto Rico; and agreed to acquire Cable & Wireless Communications Plc.

FINANCIAL DATA: Note: Data for latest year may not have been available at press time.

In U.S. $	2016	2015	2014	2013	2012	2011
Revenue		17,062,700,000	18,248,300,000	14,474,200,000	10,310,800,000	9,510,800,000
R&D Expense						
Operating Income		2,101,100,000	2,228,200,000	2,012,100,000	1,983,100,000	1,818,400,000
Operating Margin %		12.31%	12.21%	13.90%	19.23%	19.11%
SGA Expense		2,973,500,000	3,172,800,000	2,616,500,000	1,936,100,000	1,780,400,000
Net Income		-1,196,400,000	-695,000,000	-963,900,000	322,800,000	-772,700,000
Operating Cash Flow		5,399,300,000	5,603,200,000	3,931,300,000	2,919,700,000	2,736,300,000
Capital Expenditure		2,272,300,000	2,684,400,000	2,481,500,000	1,883,600,000	1,927,000,000
EBITDA		7,116,600,000	6,988,900,000	6,036,800,000	3,885,200,000	3,336,400,000
Return on Assets %		-1.74%	-.98%	-1.81%	.86%	-2.21%
Return on Equity %		-9.51%	-5.19%	-13.54%	12.87%	-26.41%
Debt to Equity		4.03	3.03	3.63	12.29	8.75

CONTACT INFORMATION:

Phone: 303 220-6600   Fax: 720 875-5401
Toll-Free:
Address: 12300 Liberty Blvd., Englewood, CO 80112 United States

STOCK TICKER/OTHER:

Stock Ticker: LBTYA   Exchange: NAS
Employees: 38,000   Fiscal Year Ends: 12/31
Parent Company:

SALARIES/BONUSES:

Top Exec. Salary: Bonus: $
$2,115,000
Second Exec. Salary: Bonus: $
$1,057,500

OTHER THOUGHTS:

Estimated Female Officers or Directors: 3

Hot Spot for Advancement for Women/Minorities: Y

Liberty Interactive Corp

www.libertyinteractive.com

NAIC Code: 454111

TYPES OF BUSINESS:

Online and Internet Businesses
e-Commerce

BRANDS/DIVISIONS/AFFILIATES:

QVC Inc
Backcountry.com Inc
Bodybuilding.com LLC
CommerceHub
Evite Inc
LMC Right Start Inc
Liberty Expedia Holdings Inc
zulily inc

CONTACTS: *Note: Officers with more than one job title may be intentionally listed here more than once.*

Michael George, CEO, Subsidiary
Gregory Maffei, CEO
Christopher Shean, CFO
John Malone, Chairman of the Board
Pamela Coe, Other Corporate Officer
Richard Baer, Other Executive Officer
Albert Rosenthaler, Other Executive Officer

GROWTH PLANS/SPECIAL FEATURES:

Liberty Interactive Corp. is a holding company with interests primarily in e-commerce businesses. The firm's largest business is QVC, Inc., which markets and sells a wide variety of consumer products in the U.S. and several foreign countries primarily through live televised shopping programs and via the Internet through its U.S. and international web sites. Additionally, Liberty Interactive owns entire or majority interests in online commerce retailers Backcountry.com Inc., Bodybuilding.com LLC, CommerceHub, Evite Inc. and LMC Right Start Inc. Backcountry operates websites that offer sports gear and outdoor clothing; Bodybuilding manages website related to sports nutrition, body building and fitness; CommerceHub provides software-as-a-service platform for online retailers and their suppliers to sell products to consumers without physically owning inventory nor managing the fulfillment of those products; Evite is an online invitation and social event planning service on the web; and Right Start is a retailer of products for infants through toddlers such as strollers, car seats, nursery and feeding accessories. Affiliates include Expedia, Inc., an online travel company; HSN, Inc., an interactive multi-channel retailer; FTD Companies, Inc., a floral and gifting company; Interval Leisure Group, Inc., a global provider of membership and leisure services to the vacation industry; and LendingTree, Inc., an owner of several brands and businesses that provide information, tools, advice, products and services for critical transactions in customers' lives. LendingTree brands include LendingTree, GetSmart, DegreeTree, LendingTreeAutos, DoneRight, ServiceTree and InsuranceTree. In 2014, the firm spun off wholly-owned Liberty TripAdvisor Holdings, Inc.; and sold Provide Commerce, Inc. In November 2015, it obtained board authorization to spin off both wholly-owned CommerceHub and Liberty Expedia Holdings, Inc., which are expected to occur by mid-2016. Also in 2015, the firm acquired zulily, inc.

FINANCIAL DATA: *Note: Data for latest year may not have been available at press time.*

In U.S. $	2016	2015	2014	2013	2012	2011
Revenue		9,169,000,000	10,028,000,000	10,307,000,000	10,018,000,000	9,616,000,000
R&D Expense						
Operating Income		1,170,000,000	1,206,000,000	1,131,000,000	1,124,000,000	1,133,000,000
Operating Margin %		12.76%	12.02%	10.97%	11.21%	11.78%
SGA Expense		1,495,000,000	1,794,000,000	1,909,000,000	1,810,000,000	1,728,000,000
Net Income		640,000,000	520,000,000	438,000,000	466,000,000	912,000,000
Operating Cash Flow		981,000,000	1,204,000,000	972,000,000	1,470,000,000	914,000,000
Capital Expenditure		218,000,000	226,000,000	295,000,000	338,000,000	312,000,000
EBITDA		1,918,000,000	1,835,000,000	1,745,000,000	1,799,000,000	2,007,000,000
Return on Assets %		4.54%	3.73%	2.92%	2.87%	5.42%
Return on Equity %		13.50%	9.75%	6.54%	6.90%	14.27%
Debt to Equity		1.18	1.36	0.79	0.61	0.74

CONTACT INFORMATION:

Phone: 720 875-5400   Fax: 720 875-7469
Toll-Free: 866-876-0461
Address: 12300 Liberty Blvd., Englewood, CO 80112 United States

STOCK TICKER/OTHER:

Stock Ticker: QVCA
Employees: 20,000
Parent Company:

Exchange: NAS
Fiscal Year Ends: 12/31

SALARIES/BONUSES:

Top Exec. Salary:
$1,125,509
Second Exec. Salary:
$960,750

Bonus: $

Bonus: $

OTHER THOUGHTS:

Estimated Female Officers or Directors: 1

Hot Spot for Advancement for Women/Minorities:

Liberty Mutual Group Inc

NAIC Code: 524126

TYPES OF BUSINESS:

Insurance, Direct Property & Casualty
Rehabilitation Services
Disability Care Management
Homeowners' Insurance
Auto Insurance
Group Life Insurance
Asset Management & Investment Products
Workers' Compensation

BRANDS/DIVISIONS/AFFILIATES:

Liberty Life Assurance Company of Boston
Liberty Mutual Benefits
Liberty International Underwriters
Liberty Mutual Surety
Liberty Specialty Markets
Research Institute for Safety

CONTACTS: Note: Officers with more than one job title may be intentionally listed here more than once.

David H. Long, CEO
David H. Long, Pres.
Dennis J. Langwell, CFO
Melanie M. Foley, Sr. VP-Human Resources
James M. McGlennon, CIO
Melanie M. Foley, Sr. VP-Admin.
James F. Kelleher, Sr. VP
Paul G. Alexander, Mgr.-Comm.
Laurance H.S. Yahia, Treas.
J. Paul Condrin III, Exec. VP
A. Alexander Fontanes, Exec. VP
Christopher L. Peirce, Exec. VP
Timothy M. Sweeney, Exec. VP
David H. Long, Chmn.
Luis Bonell, Exec. VP

GROWTH PLANS/SPECIAL FEATURES:

Liberty Mutual Group, Inc. is a group of insurance companie:
with offices in 21 countries and $19.2 billion in assets. Libert
Mutual has four strategic business units: personal insurance
commercial insurance, Liberty international and globa
specialty. The company's personal insurance business uni
provides private passenger automobile, homeowners, valuable
possessions, identity theft and personal liability coverage
through its U.S. offices. This unit also offers traditional and
variable life insurance and annuity products through subsidiary
Liberty Life Assurance Company of Boston. The company':
commercial insurance business unit offers property, casualty
employee benefits and specialty lines for businesses of al
types and sizes through subsidiary Liberty Mutual Benefits. The
firm's Liberty international business unit provides property
casualty, health and life insurance products to individuals and
businesses in countries throughout Europe, Asia, India and
Latin America. The global specialty unit is comprised of Liberty
International Underwriters, Liberty Mutual Surety and Liberty
Specialty Markets which provide a wide array of specialty
insurance and reinsurance products. This division focuses on
increasing return on equity, expanding analytics capabilities
risk engineering, as well as broker relationship managemen
and training. Liberty Mutual also operates the Research
Institute for Safety, which conducts original investigations o
job-related accidents and publishes its findings in a range o
peer-reviewed journals.

Employees are offered medical, dental and vision insurance; a
401(k) plan; a pension plan; tuition reimbursement; flexible
spending accounts; disability insurance; and life insurance.

FINANCIAL DATA: Note: Data for latest year may not have been available at press time.

In U.S. $	2016	2015	2014	2013	2012	2011
Revenue		37,617,000,000	37,721,000,000	36,556,000,000	36,325,000,000	34,671,000,000
R&D Expense						
Operating Income						
Operating Margin %						
SGA Expense						
Net Income		514,000,000	1,833,000,000	1,743,000,000	829,000,000	365,000,000
Operating Cash Flow						
Capital Expenditure						
EBITDA						
Return on Assets %						
Return on Equity %						
Debt to Equity						

CONTACT INFORMATION:

Phone: 617-357-9500   Fax: 617-350-7648
Toll-Free: 800-837-5254
Address: 175 Berkeley St., Boston, MA 02116 United States

SALARIES/BONUSES:

Top Exec. Salary: $ Bonus: $
Second Exec. Salary: $ Bonus: $

STOCK TICKER/OTHER:

Stock Ticker: Mutual Company   Exchange:
Employees: 51,000   Fiscal Year Ends: 12/31
Parent Company:

OTHER THOUGHTS:

Estimated Female Officers or Directors: 4
Hot Spot for Advancement for Women/Minorities: Y

LifePoint Health Inc

www.lifepointhospitals.com

NAIC Code: 622110

TYPES OF BUSINESS:

General Medical and Surgical Hospitals

BRANDS/DIVISIONS/AFFILIATES:

Providence Hospitals
Frye Regional Medical Center
St. Francis Hospital
LifePoint Hospitals Inc

CONTACTS: Note: Officers with more than one job title may be intentionally listed here more than once.

William Carpenter, CEO
Leif Murphy, CFO
John Bumpus, Chief Administrative Officer
Russell Holman, Chief Medical Officer
David Dill, COO
Paul Gilbert, Executive VP
Christy Green, Other Corporate Officer
Victor Giovanetti, President, Divisional
Jeffrey Seraphine, President, Divisional
R. Raplee, President, Divisional
Michael Coggin, Senior VP

GROWTH PLANS/SPECIAL FEATURES:

LifePoint Health, Inc., formerly LifePoint Hospitals, Inc., is a holding company that owns and operates general acute care hospitals in non-urban communities in the U.S. The firm operates 72 hospitals, with over 8,500 beds, as well as 1,700 physician practices, 40 post-acute facilities and 30 outpatient centers located in 22 states across the country. The company's hospitals typically provide the range of medical and surgical services commonly available in hospitals in non-urban markets. These services generally include internal medicine; obstetrics; general surgery; emergency room, psychiatric, diagnostic and coronary care; radiology; oncology; rehabilitation and pediatric services; and, in some hospitals, specialized services such as open-heart surgery, skilled nursing and neuro-surgery. In many markets, LifePoint also provides outpatient services such as one-day surgery, laboratory, x-ray, respiratory therapy, imaging, sports medicine and lithotripsy. Post-acute services and facilities include home health and hospice services, long-term care services, nursing homes and assisted living establishments. Outpatient centers and services include urgent care centers, diagnostic imaging centers, ambulatory surgery centers and radiation oncology programs. In 2015, the firm changed its name to LifePoint Health in order to reflect its evolution from a hospital operator to a health care company. In 2016, it acquired Providence Hospitals for about $132 million; Frye Regional Medical Center for $190.9 million; and St. Francis Hospital for $257.1 million.

The company offers its employees medical, dental, vision, life and disability insurance; adoption assistance; flexible spending accounts; a wellness program; a Wells Fargo Employee Home Mortgage Program; and a 401(k) plan.

FINANCIAL DATA: Note: Data for latest year may not have been available at press time.

In U.S. $	2016	2015	2014	2013	2012	2011
Revenue		5,214,300,000	4,483,100,000	3,678,300,000	3,391,800,000	3,026,100,000
R&D Expense						
Operating Income		426,700,000	383,700,000	308,500,000	352,500,000	370,400,000
Operating Margin %		8.18%	8.55%	8.38%	10.39%	12.24%
SGA Expense		3,439,500,000	2,134,500,000	2,628,300,000	586,000,000	514,800,000
Net Income		181,900,000	126,100,000	128,200,000	151,900,000	162,900,000
Operating Cash Flow		627,100,000	412,300,000	354,000,000	382,200,000	401,500,000
Capital Expenditure		274,700,000	207,100,000	185,200,000	221,400,000	219,900,000
EBITDA		705,700,000	634,200,000	553,900,000	565,200,000	556,000,000
Return on Assets %		3.17%	2.28%	2.48%	3.34%	3.82%
Return on Equity %		8.23%	5.77%	6.01%	7.60%	8.50%
Debt to Equity		1.16	1.02	0.81	0.82	0.82

CONTACT INFORMATION:

Phone: 615 920-7000   Fax:
Toll-Free:
Address: 330 Seven Springs Way, Brentwood, TN 37027 United States

STOCK TICKER/OTHER:

Stock Ticker: LPNT   Exchange: NAS
Employees: 38,000   Fiscal Year Ends: 12/31
Parent Company:

SALARIES/BONUSES:

Top Exec. Salary: Bonus: $
$1,150,000
Second Exec. Salary: Bonus: $
$670,000

OTHER THOUGHTS:

Estimated Female Officers or Directors: 1

Hot Spot for Advancement for Women/Minorities: Y

Lilly (ELI) & Company

NAIC Code: 325412

TYPES OF BUSINESS:

Pharmaceuticals Discovery & Development
Veterinary Products

BRANDS/DIVISIONS/AFFILIATES:

Novartis Animal Health
Humulin
Gemzar
Comfortis
Cialis
ReoPro
Tylan
Denagard

CONTACTS: Note: Officers with more than one job title may be intentionally listed here more than once.

John Lechleiter, CEO

GROWTH PLANS/SPECIAL FEATURES:

Lilly (Eli) & Company researches, develops, manufactures and sells pharmaceuticals designed to treat a variety of conditions. The firm operates through two segments: human pharmaceutical products and animal health products. Human pharmaceutical products are grouped into four divisions: endocrinology, neuroscience, oncology and cardiovascular. Endocrinology products include Humalog, Humulin, Trajenta, Jentadueto, Jardiance, Trulicity and Glyxambi, for the treatment of diabetes; Forteo and Evista, for osteoporosis in women; Humatrope, for human growth hormone deficiency; and Axiron, a topical solution of testosterone. Neuroscience products include Cymbalta and Prozac, for major depressive disorder; Zyprexa, for schizophrenia; Strattera, for attention-deficit hyperactivity disorder; and Amyvid, a radioactive diagnostic agent for brain imaging of people with cognitive decline. Oncology products include Alimta, for non-small cell lung cancer; Erbitux, for colorectal cancers; Gemzar, for pancreatic cancer/metastatic breast cancer/ovarian cancer/bladder cancer; and Cyramza, for advanced or metastatic gastric cancer. Cardiovascular products include Cialis, for erectile dysfunction; Effient, for reduction of thrombotic cardiovascular events; and ReoPro, for the prevention of cardiac ischemic complications. Animal health products are grouped into two divisions: food animals and companion animals. Food animal products include Rumensin, a cattle feed additive; Psoliac, a protein supplement; Paylean, Optaflexx and Surmax, leanness and/or performance enhancers; Tylan, Micotil and Pulmotil, antibiotics; and Coban, Monteban and Maxiban, anticoccidial agents. Companion animal products include Trifexis and Comfortis chewable tablets are manufactured for flea prevention. Wholly-owned Novartis Animal Health's products include Denagard, Milbemax, Sentinel, Atopica and Fortekor. In January 2016, the FDA approved Humulin R U-500 KwikPen, a highly concentrated formulation of insulin used to treat high blood sugar in people with type 1 & 2 diabetes.

Eli Lilly offers employees life, health, prescription drug and dental insurance; domestic partner benefits; an employee assistance program; paid maternity leave; a 401(k); flexible spending accounts; adoption assistance; and tuition reimbursement.

FINANCIAL DATA: Note: Data for latest year may not have been available at press time.

In U.S. $	2016	2015	2014	2013	2012	2011
Revenue		19,958,700,000	19,615,600,000	23,113,100,000	22,603,400,000	24,286,500,000
R&D Expense		5,331,400,000	4,733,600,000	5,531,300,000	5,278,100,000	5,020,800,000
Operating Income		3,057,100,000	3,328,700,000	5,370,400,000	5,408,200,000	5,528,500,000
Operating Margin %		15.31%	16.96%	23.23%	23.92%	22.76%
SGA Expense		6,533,000,000	6,620,800,000	7,125,600,000	7,513,500,000	7,879,900,000
Net Income		2,408,400,000	2,390,500,000	4,684,800,000	4,088,600,000	4,347,700,000
Operating Cash Flow		2,772,800,000	4,367,100,000	5,735,000,000	5,304,800,000	7,234,500,000
Capital Expenditure		1,066,200,000	1,470,900,000	1,093,300,000	1,044,200,000	1,692,900,000
EBITDA		4,484,800,000	4,528,100,000	7,495,000,000	7,048,200,000	6,909,100,000
Return on Assets %		6.62%	6.60%	13.45%	12.01%	13.44%
Return on Equity %		16.08%	14.48%	28.92%	28.88%	33.49%
Debt to Equity		0.54	0.34	0.23	0.37	0.40

CONTACT INFORMATION:

Phone: 317 276-2000   Fax:
Toll-Free:
Address: Lilly Corp. Ctr., Indianapolis, IN 46285 United States

STOCK TICKER/OTHER:

Stock Ticker: LLY   Exchange: NYS
Employees: 39,135   Fiscal Year Ends: 12/31
Parent Company:

SALARIES/BONUSES:

Top Exec. Salary: Bonus: $
$1,500,000
Second Exec. Salary: Bonus: $
$1,045,200

OTHER THOUGHTS:

Estimated Female Officers or Directors: 8

Hot Spot for Advancement for Women/Minorities: Y

Sales, profits and employees may be estimates. Financial information, benefits and other data can change quickly and may vary from those stated here.

Lincare Holdings Inc

NAIC Code: 621610

TYPES OF BUSINESS:

Home Health Care-Oxygen & Other Respiratory Therapy Services
Durable Medical Equipment
Home Infusion Therapies

BRANDS/DIVISIONS/AFFILIATES:

Linde AG
American HomePatient Inc

CONTACTS: *Note: Officers with more than one job title may be intentionally listed here more than once.*

Kristen Hoefer, CEO
Greg McCarthy, COO
Shawn S. Schabel, Pres.
Crispin Teufel, CFO

GROWTH PLANS/SPECIAL FEATURES:

Lincare Holdings, Inc. provides oxygen and other respiratory therapy services to in-home patients. The firm serves over 800,000 customers in 48 states and Canada through 1,000 operating centers. The company also provides durable medical equipment and home infusion therapies in certain geographic markets. The firm's customers typically suffer from chronic obstructive pulmonary diseases (COPD), such as emphysema, chronic bronchitis or asthma, and require supplemental oxygen or other respiratory therapy services in order to alleviate the symptoms and discomfort of respiratory dysfunction. Lincare's home oxygen equipment comes in two variations: oxygen concentrators and liquid oxygen systems. Oxygen concentrators are stationary units that provide a continuous flow of oxygen by filtering ordinary room air and are often supplemented with portable gaseous oxygen cylinders or liquid oxygen systems to meet the ambulatory or emergency needs of the customer. Liquid oxygen systems are thermally insulated containers of liquid oxygen; they generally consist of a stationary unit and a portable unit. Other respiratory therapy services offered by the company include nebulizers and associated respiratory medications; non-invasive ventilation; ventilators and continuous positive airway pressure devices, which maintain open airways in customers suffering from obstructive sleep apnea by providing airflow at prescribed pressures during sleep. Lincare's home infusion therapy products and services include chemotherapy, continuous pain management, intravenous antibiotic therapy, parenteral nutrition, dobutamine infusions, enteral nutrition, immunoglobulin therapy and central catheter management. Therapies for enteral therapy are available at certain Lincare locations with a licensed dietitian on staff. The firm also offers pediatric respiratory services, where medical professionals work hand in hand with a child and its caregivers to instruct the child on how to treat their illness. Lincare is a subsidiary of German technology firm, Linde AG. In February 2016, the firm acquired American HomePatient, Inc.

FINANCIAL DATA: *Note: Data for latest year may not have been available at press time.*

In U.S. $	2016	2015	2014	2013	2012	2011
Revenue		220,000,000	2,100,000,000	2,000,000,000	1,900,000,000	1,847,520,000
R&D Expense						
Operating Income						
Operating Margin %						
SGA Expense						
Net Income						
Operating Cash Flow						
Capital Expenditure						
EBITDA						
Return on Assets %						
Return on Equity %						
Debt to Equity						

CONTACT INFORMATION:

Phone: 727-530-7700   Fax: 727-532-9692
Toll-Free:
Address: 19387 US 19 N., Clearwater, FL 33764 United States

SALARIES/BONUSES:

Top Exec. Salary: $ Bonus: $
Second Exec. Salary: $ Bonus: $

STOCK TICKER/OTHER:

Stock Ticker: Subsidiary   Exchange:
Employees: 11,000   Fiscal Year Ends: 12/31
Parent Company: Linde AG

OTHER THOUGHTS:

Estimated Female Officers or Directors:
Hot Spot for Advancement for Women/Minorities:

Lincoln National Corporation

NAIC Code: 524113

www.lfg.com

TYPES OF BUSINESS:

Life Insurance
Investment Management
Retirement Plans
Mutual Funds
Financial Planning
Annuities

BRANDS/DIVISIONS/AFFILIATES:

Lincoln Financial Group

CONTACTS: *Note: Officers with more than one job title may be intentionally listed here more than once.*

Dennis Glass, CEO
Randal Freitag, CFO
Kenneth Solon, Chief Information Officer
William Cunningham, Director
Kirkland Hicks, Executive VP
Ellen Cooper, Executive VP
Lisa Buckingham, Executive VP
Mark Konen, President, Divisional
Wilford Fuller, President, Subsidiary
Christine Janofsky, Senior Vice President and Chief Accounting Officer

GROWTH PLANS/SPECIAL FEATURES:

Lincoln National Corporation is a holding company operating multiple insurance and retirement businesses. The operations of the firm's subsidiaries, collectively known as Lincoln Financial Group, are divided into four operating businesses: retirement plan services, life insurance, annuities and group protection. Retirement plan services provides employers with retirement plan products and services, with a focus on defined contribution retirement plans. The life insurance segment offers life insurance products including term insurances, a linked benefit product, indexed Universal Life insurance (UL) and both single and survivorship versions of UL and variable UL products (VUL). In a UL contract, contract holders typically have flexibility in the timing and amount of premium payments and the amount of death benefit, provided there is sufficient account value to cover all policy charges. VUL products are UL products that provide a return on account values linked to an underlying investment portfolio of variable funds offered through the products. The annuities segment offers fixed and variable annuities to its clients. Group protection offers employers non-medical insurance products, principally term life, disability and dental. The company's other operations include financial data for operations that are not directly related to the business segments, investment income and its run-off institutional pension business.

Lincoln National offers its employees benefits including disability, life, medical, dental and vision insurance; domestic partner benefits; tuition reimbursement; a 401(k) with matching contributions; an employee assistance program; and flexible work arrangements.

FINANCIAL DATA: *Note: Data for latest year may not have been available at press time.*

In U.S. $	2016	2015	2014	2013	2012	2011
Revenue		13,572,000,000	13,554,000,000	11,969,000,000	11,532,000,000	10,636,000,000
R&D Expense						
Operating Income		1,430,000,000	1,997,000,000	1,631,000,000	1,568,000,000	599,000,000
Operating Margin %		10.53%	14.73%	13.62%	13.59%	5.63%
SGA Expense		4,318,000,000	4,079,000,000	3,701,000,000		
Net Income		1,154,000,000	1,515,000,000	1,244,000,000	1,313,000,000	294,000,000
Operating Cash Flow		2,243,000,000	2,526,000,000	799,000,000	1,269,000,000	1,277,000,000
Capital Expenditure						
EBITDA						
Return on Assets %		.45%	.61%	.54%	.62%	.14%
Return on Equity %		7.86%	10.37%	8.75%	9.01%	2.18%
Debt to Equity		0.40	0.33	0.39	0.36	0.38

CONTACT INFORMATION:

Phone: 484 583-1400   Fax: 215 448-3962
Toll-Free: 877-275-5462
Address: 150 N. Radnor Chester Rd., Ste. A305, Radnor, PA 19087 United States

STOCK TICKER/OTHER:

Stock Ticker: LNC
Employees: 9,312
Parent Company:

Exchange: NYS
Fiscal Year Ends: 12/31

SALARIES/BONUSES:

Top Exec. Salary: $1,169,050
Bonus: $

Second Exec. Salary: $663,320
Bonus: $

OTHER THOUGHTS:

Estimated Female Officers or Directors: 2

Hot Spot for Advancement for Women/Minorities: Y

LinkedIn Corp

www.linkedin.com

NAIC Code: 519130

TYPES OF BUSINESS:

Business-Oriented Social Networking
Advertising Services
Recruiting Tools

BRANDS/DIVISIONS/AFFILIATES:

LinkedIn.com
lynda.com

CONTACTS: Note: Officers with more than one job title may be intentionally listed here more than once.

Jeffrey Weiner, CEO
Reid Hoffman, Chairman of the Board
Susan Taylor, Chief Accounting Officer
Michael Gamson, Senior VP, Divisional
Patricia Wadors, Senior VP, Divisional
James Scott, Senior VP, Divisional
Shannon Stubo, Senior VP, Divisional
Steven Sordello, Senior VP
Michael Callahan, Senior VP

GROWTH PLANS/SPECIAL FEATURES:

LinkedIn Corp. is an online social networking site targeting the business and professional community. Through its web site, LinkedIn.com, users can post profiles, connect with co-workers, post resumes and search for job openings. Other features on the site include Company Pages, which allows companies to showcase brands and products; and a suite of products for corporate recruitment initiatives, including sourcing and pipelining, a referral engine, career pages and recruitment ads. The site generates revenue through ad sales, user subscription fees on premium accounts and enterprise hiring software licensing fees. The company offers a range of solutions to its members, including free solutions, such as stay connected & informed, advance my career and ubiquitous access; and monetized solutions, such as talent, marketing and premium subscription. Its membership base exceeds more than 400 million users in over 200 countries and territories and is available in multiple languages including English, French, German, Italian, Portuguese, Spanish, Japanese, Korean, Russian, Arabic and Turkish. It is currently expanding its international scope, opening offices in London, Amsterdam, Singapore, Tokyo and Mumbai. In 2015, the firm acquired lynda.com, an online learning company that teaches business, technology and creative skills to help people achieve their professional goals. In June 2016, LInkedIn agreed to be acquired by Microsoft.

FINANCIAL DATA: Note: Data for latest year may not have been available at press time.

In U.S. $	2016	2015	2014	2013	2012	2011
Revenue		2,990,911,000	2,218,767,000	1,528,545,000	972,309,000	522,189,000
R&D Expense		775,660,000	536,184,000	395,643,000	257,179,000	132,222,000
Operating Income		-150,942,000	36,135,000	47,812,000	56,862,000	25,845,000
Operating Margin %		-5.04%	1.62%	3.12%	5.84%	4.94%
SGA Expense		1,526,863,000	1,115,705,000	747,666,000	452,898,000	239,574,000
Net Income		-166,144,000	-15,747,000	26,769,000	21,610,000	11,912,000
Operating Cash Flow		806,975,000	568,951,000	436,473,000	267,070,000	133,424,000
Capital Expenditure		507,246,000	547,633,000	278,019,000	125,420,000	96,382,000
EBITDA		256,624,000	274,948,000	182,328,000	136,711,000	68,945,000
Return on Assets %		-2.67%	-.35%	1.13%	1.91%	2.14%
Return on Equity %		-4.26%	-.52%	1.51%	2.81%	3.69%
Debt to Equity		0.25	0.32			

CONTACT INFORMATION:

Phone: 650 687-3600 Fax:
Toll-Free:
Address: 2029 Stierlin Ct., Mountain View, CA 94043 United States

STOCK TICKER/OTHER:

Stock Ticker: LNKD   Exchange: NYS
Employees: 9,372   Fiscal Year Ends: 12/31
Parent Company:

SALARIES/BONUSES:

Top Exec. Salary: $966,538   Bonus: $
Second Exec. Salary: Bonus: $
$582,115

OTHER THOUGHTS:

Estimated Female Officers or Directors: 4
Hot Spot for Advancement for Women/Minorities: Y

Lithia Motors Inc

www.lithia.com

NAIC Code: 441110

TYPES OF BUSINESS:

Auto Dealers, Retail
Automotive Repair & Maintenance
Insurance & Financing

BRANDS/DIVISIONS/AFFILIATES:

DCH Toyota/Scion of Milford

CONTACTS: Note: Officers with more than one job title may be intentionally listed here more than once.

Bryan Deboer, CEO
Christopher Holzshu, CFO
Sidney Deboer, Chairman of the Board
John North, Chief Accounting Officer
M.L. Heimann, Director Emeritus
Scott Hillier, Senior VP, Divisional
Chun-Wai Liang, Senior VP, Subsidiary

GROWTH PLANS/SPECIAL FEATURES:

Lithia Motors, Inc. is a leading operator of automotive dealerships, retailing both new and used vehicles through 139 stores in the U.S. and over the Internet. The company operates stores in Oregon, California, Texas, Washington, Hawaii, Iowa, Idaho, Alaska, Montana, North Dakota, Nevada and New Mexico. California and Oregon represent the firm's two largest markets, with 31 and 24 locations respectively. The firm sells new and used cars and light trucks; sells replacement parts; provides vehicle maintenance, warranty, paint and repair services; and arranges related financing, service contracts, protection products and credit insurance for its automotive customers. Lithia's dealerships offer customers vehicles in 30 domestic and imported brands, including Ford, Toyota, BMW, Suzuki and Hyundai. Chrysler, which includes Chrysler, Dodge, Ram and Jeep, accounts for the largest single revenue share of the company, at approximately 20.6%. Lithia also operates 17 collision repair centers. The company markets its parts and service products by notifying the owners of vehicles purchased at its franchises when their vehicles are due for periodic service. The firm's other marketing efforts include direct-mail ads to previous customers as well as newspaper, television and radio ads. The Lithia web site offers users several services, such as viewing new and used vehicle inventories and scheduling service appointments. The company also offers financing and insurance to customers that purchase new or used vehicles. In February 2016, the firm acquired Ira Toyota/Scion of Milford, Massachusetts, and renamed it DCH Toyota/Scion of Milford.

Lithia offers employees medical, dental and vision insurance; short- and long-term disability coverage; life insurance; an employee stock purchase plan; a 401(k) plan; and employee discounts.

FINANCIAL DATA: Note: Data for latest year may not have been available at press time.

In U.S. $	2016	2015	2014	2013	2012	2011
Revenue		7,864,252,000	5,390,326,000	4,005,749,000	3,316,487,000	2,699,360,000
R&D Expense						
Operating Income		302,735,000	231,899,000	183,518,000	148,369,000	111,991,000
Operating Margin %		3.84%	4.30%	4.58%	4.47%	4.14%
SGA Expense		811,175,000	563,207,000	427,400,000	373,688,000	327,545,000
Net Income		182,999,000	138,720,000	106,000,000	80,362,000	58,860,000
Operating Cash Flow		74,209,000	30,319,000	32,059,000	-212,476,000	-766,000
Capital Expenditure		83,244,000	85,983,000	50,025,000	64,584,000	31,673,000
EBITDA		343,329,000	261,461,000	206,546,000	168,208,000	129,635,000
Return on Assets %		5.99%	6.02%	6.58%	6.09%	5.55%
Return on Equity %		24.37%	22.97%	22.01%	20.21%	17.12%
Debt to Equity		0.73	0.90	0.45	0.67	0.75

CONTACT INFORMATION:

Phone: 541 776-6401   Fax: 541 776-6362
Toll-Free: 877-331-3084
Address: 150 N. Bartlett St., Medford, OR 97501 United States

STOCK TICKER/OTHER:

Stock Ticker: LAD
Employees: 8,827
Parent Company:

Exchange: NYS
Fiscal Year Ends: 12/31

SALARIES/BONUSES:

Top Exec. Salary: $882,000   Bonus: $
Second Exec. Salary: $840,000   Bonus: $

OTHER THOUGHTS:

Estimated Female Officers or Directors:
Hot Spot for Advancement for Women/Minorities:

LKQ Corporation

www.lkqcorp.com

NAIC Code: 336300

TYPES OF BUSINESS:
Remanufactured OEM Parts
Aftermarket Replacement Parts
Vehicle Salvage
Scrap/Bulk Automotive Parts
Refurbished Aluminum Wheels

BRANDS/DIVISIONS/AFFILIATES:
Pittsburgh Glass Works LLC

CONTACTS: Note: Officers with more than one job title may be intentionally listed here more than once.
John Quinn, CEO, Divisional
Robert Wagman, CEO
Sukhpal Ahluwalia, Chairman of the Board, Subsidiary
Michael Clark, Controller
Joseph Holsten, Director
Dominick Zarcone, Executive VP
Victor Casini, General Counsel
Walter Hanley, Senior VP, Divisional
Robert Alberico, Senior VP, Divisional
Justin Jude, Senior VP, Divisional
Steven Greenspan, Senior VP, Divisional

GROWTH PLANS/SPECIAL FEATURES:

LKQ Corporation is a global distributor of vehicle products, including replacement parts, components and systems used in the repair and maintenance of vehicles. The company also distributes specialty vehicle products and accessories. LKQ operates through three segments: wholesale North America, Europe and specialty. Within the wholesale North America segment, LKQ distributes its wholesale automotive products from 348 facilities. Its engine remanufacturing operations are conducted primarily at its facilities located in Mexico. Products within this segment include aftermarket, recycled, remanufactured, refurbished and original manufacture equipment (OEM) parts, which are distributed to professional collision and mechanical automobile repair businesses. This division's sales include more than 110, SKUs of aftermarket automotive products, for the most common models of domestic and foreign automobiles and light trucks, between three to 12 years old. The Europe segment distributes automotive aftermarket parts in the U.K. This division operates 218 selling locations, supported by three national distribution centers and 17 regional hubs. Sales include more than 300,000 SKUs annually, with inventory mainly composed of mechanical aftermarket parts for the repair of vehicles three to 15 years old. Top-selling products include brake pads, discs, sensors, clutches, spark plugs, batteries, steering & suspension products, filters, oil and automotive fluids. The specialty segment distributes and markets vehicle aftermarket equipment and accessories in North America, serving the truck, off-road, speed & performance, recreational vehicle (RV), towing, wheels/tires, performance handling and accessories markets. Annual sales include more than 250,000 SKUs, with top-selling products including trailer hitches, satellite antennas, generators, sealants, RV systems and water pumps. In April 2016, the acquired Pittsburgh Glass Works LLC, a global distributor and manufacturer of automotive glass products.

FINANCIAL DATA: Note: Data for latest year may not have been available at press time.

In U.S. $	2016	2015	2014	2013	2012	2011
Revenue		7,192,633,000	6,740,064,000	5,062,528,000	4,122,930,000	3,269,862,000
R&D Expense						
Operating Income		704,627,000	649,868,000	530,180,000	437,953,000	361,483,000
Operating Margin %		9.79%	9.64%	10.47%	10.62%	11.05%
SGA Expense		1,987,271,000	1,866,520,000	1,454,080,000	1,219,343,000	972,991,000
Net Income		423,223,000	381,519,000	311,623,000	261,225,000	210,264,000
Operating Cash Flow		529,837,000	370,897,000	428,056,000	206,190,000	211,772,000
Capital Expenditure		170,490,000	140,950,000	90,186,000	88,255,000	86,416,000
EBITDA		835,082,000	777,867,000	613,474,000	510,761,000	414,583,000
Return on Assets %		7.54%	7.56%	7.56%	7.54%	7.64%
Return on Equity %		14.50%	15.04%	14.44%	14.47%	13.75%
Debt to Equity		0.49	0.66	0.53	0.53	0.56

CONTACT INFORMATION:
Phone: 312 621-1950   Fax: 312 621-1969
Toll-Free: 877-557-2677
Address: 500 W. Madison St., Ste. 2800, Chicago, IL 60661 United States

STOCK TICKER/OTHER:
Stock Ticker: LKQ   Exchange: NAS
Employees: 29,500   Fiscal Year Ends: 12/31
Parent Company:

SALARIES/BONUSES:
Top Exec. Salary: $904,932   Bonus: $
Second Exec. Salary: $548,972   Bonus: $

OTHER THOUGHTS:
Estimated Female Officers or Directors:
Hot Spot for Advancement for Women/Minorities:

Lockheed Martin Corp

NAIC Code: 336411

www.lockheedmartin.com

TYPES OF BUSINESS:

Aircraft Manufacturing
Military Aircraft
Defense Electronics
Systems Integration & Technology Services
Communications Satellites & Launch Services
Undersea, Shipboard, Land & Airborne Systems & Subsystems

BRANDS/DIVISIONS/AFFILIATES:

Aegis Combat System
MK-41 Vertical Launching System
Sikorsky Aircraft

CONTACTS: Note: Officers with more than one job title may be intentionally listed here more than once.

Stephen Piper, Assistant General Counsel
Marillyn Hewson, CEO
Brian Colan, Chief Accounting Officer
Orlando Carvalho, Executive VP, Divisional
Richard Edwards, Executive VP, Divisional
Dale Bennett, Executive VP, Divisional
Richard Ambrose, Executive VP, Divisional
Sondra Barbour, Executive VP, Divisional
Patrick Dewar, Executive VP, Divisional
Bruce Tanner, Executive VP
Maryanne Lavan, General Counsel
Kenneth Possenriede, Vice President

GROWTH PLANS/SPECIAL FEATURES:

Lockheed Martin Corp. specializes in developing and servicing advanced technological systems. It serves domestic and international customers with products and services that have defense, civil and commercial applications, with principal customers including agencies of the U.S. government (72% of its annual sales). The company operates in five segments: aeronautics, information systems & global services (IS&GS), missiles & fire control (MFC), mission systems & training (MST) and space systems. The aeronautics segment is engaged in the design, research and development, systems integration, production, sustainment, support and upgrade of advanced military aircraft, air vehicles and related technologies. Major products include the F-35 stealth fighter, the F-22 fighter and the C-130 tactical airlifter. The IS&GS segment provides federal services, IT solutions and technology expertise across a broad spectrum of applications and customers. The MFC segment provides air & missile defense systems, tactical missiles & air-to-ground precision strike weapon systems, fire control systems and manned & unmanned ground vehicles, amongst other things. Major programs in this segment include air and missile defense programs, such as The Patriot Advanced Capability-3 and Terminal High Altitude Area Defense air and missile defense programs; and the Multiple Launch Rocket System, Hellfire, Joint Air-to-Surface Standoff Missile and Javelin tactical missile programs. MST offers services such as surface ship & submarine combat systems, sea & land-based missile defense systems, radar systems and military & commercial training systems. Products in this segment include Aegis Combat System and MK-41 Vertical Launching System. The space systems segment designs, researches, develops, engineers and produces satellites, strategic and defensive missile systems and space transportation systems. In 2015, Lockheed acquired Sikorsky Aircraft for $9 billion. In January 2016, it sold its government information technology unit to Leidos Holdings, Inc. for $5 billion, so that it could better focus on building military jets, helicopters and missiles.

FINANCIAL DATA: Note: Data for latest year may not have been available at press time.

In U.S. $	2016	2015	2014	2013	2012	2011
Revenue		46,132,000,000	45,600,000,000	45,358,000,000	47,182,000,000	46,499,000,000
R&D Expense						
Operating Income		5,436,000,000	5,592,000,000	4,505,000,000	4,196,000,000	3,980,000,000
Operating Margin %		11.78%	12.26%	9.93%	8.89%	8.55%
SGA Expense						
Net Income		3,605,000,000	3,614,000,000	2,981,000,000	2,745,000,000	2,655,000,000
Operating Cash Flow		5,101,000,000	3,866,000,000	4,546,000,000	1,561,000,000	4,253,000,000
Capital Expenditure		939,000,000	845,000,000	836,000,000	942,000,000	987,000,000
EBITDA		6,492,000,000	6,592,000,000	5,495,000,000	5,443,000,000	4,993,000,000
Return on Assets %		8.36%	9.86%	7.96%	7.17%	7.27%
Return on Equity %		110.97%	86.89%	120.27%	527.88%	112.76%
Debt to Equity		4.61	1.81	1.25	157.89	6.45

CONTACT INFORMATION:

Phone: 301 897-6000   Fax: 301 897-6083
Toll-Free:
Address: 6801 Rockledge Dr., Bethesda, MD 20817 United States

STOCK TICKER/OTHER:

Stock Ticker: LMT   Exchange: NYS
Employees: 123,000   Fiscal Year Ends: 12/31
Parent Company:

SALARIES/BONUSES:

Top Exec. Salary: Bonus: $
$1,603,221
Second Exec. Salary: Bonus: $
$937,436

OTHER THOUGHTS:

Estimated Female Officers or Directors: 5

Hot Spot for Advancement for Women/Minorities: Y

Loews Hotels Holding Corporation

www.loewshotels.com

NAIC Code: 721110

TYPES OF BUSINESS:

Hotels, Luxury
Hotel Management Services

BRANDS/DIVISIONS/AFFILIATES:

Loews Corporation
Loews Miami Beach Hotel
Loews Santa Monica Beach Hotel
Loews Royal Pacific Resort at Universal Orlando
Loews Portofino Bay Hotel at Universal Orlando
Loews Don CeSar Beach Resort & Spa
Loews Boston Hotel
Loews Chicago Hotel

CONTACTS: Note: Officers with more than one job title may be intentionally listed here more than once.

Kirk Kinsell, CEO
Jack Adler, Pres.
Shawn Hauver, VP-Oper.
Lark-Marie Anton, Sr. VP-Public Rel. & Mktg. Comm.

GROWTH PLANS/SPECIAL FEATURES:

Loews Hotels Holding Corporation, a subsidiary of the Loews Corporation, currently has a portfolio of 26 owned and/or operated luxury hotels and resorts. Located in 21 cities throughout the U.S. and Canada, the firm's properties include the 790-room Loews Miami Beach Hotel in Florida, the 581-room Loews Philadelphia Hotel, the 347-room Loews Santa Monica Beach Hotel in Southern California and the 142-room Loews Hotel Vogue in Montreal. Loews Hotels operates three joint venture hotels with Universal Studios in Orlando, Florida: Loews Royal Pacific Resort at Universal Orlando, its largest hotel with 1,000 rooms; the 750-room Loews Portofino Bay Hotel at Universal Orlando; the 650-room Hard Rock Hotel at Universal Orlando; and the 277-room Loews Don CeSar Beach Resort in St. Pete Beach, Florida. Loews Hotels' business amenities include high-speed Internet access, a power breakfast with notable business leaders, notarization services, private dining rooms, boardrooms and concierge services. The YouFirst Loyalty Program rewards guests based on number of stays and offers free Internet access, late checkout, guaranteed rooms and upgrades for guests who visit at least twice a year. Loews Hotels offers facilities for weddings, meetings and special events; and special programs and services designed for people traveling with pets, children and teenagers. Recently, the company completed renovations on its Boston-based hotel, located in the city's Back Bay area. Following its reopening, the hotel was renamed the Loews Boston Hotel. In early 2015, the firm agreed to purchase the 158-room Mandarin Oriental San Francisco Hotel, and the new Loews Chicago Hotel opened for business.

FINANCIAL DATA: Note: Data for latest year may not have been available at press time.

In U.S. $	2016	2015	2014	2013	2012	2011
Revenue		604,000,000	472,659,000	380,000,000	397,938,000	337,000,000
R&D Expense						
Operating Income						
Operating Margin %						
SGA Expense						
Net Income		12,000,000	11,000,000	141,000,000	61,000,000	13,000,000
Operating Cash Flow						
Capital Expenditure						
EBITDA						
Return on Assets %						
Return on Equity %						
Debt to Equity						

CONTACT INFORMATION:

Phone: 212-521-2000   Fax: 212-521-2525
Toll-Free: 800-235-6397
Address: 667 Madison Ave., New York, NY 10021 United States

STOCK TICKER/OTHER:

Stock Ticker: Subsidiary   Exchange:
Employees: 7,500   Fiscal Year Ends: 12/31
Parent Company: Loews Corporation

SALARIES/BONUSES:

Top Exec. Salary: $ Bonus: $
Second Exec. Salary: $ Bonus: $

OTHER THOUGHTS:

Estimated Female Officers or Directors: 2
Hot Spot for Advancement for Women/Minorities: Y

Lowe's Companies Inc

NAIC Code: 444110

TYPES OF BUSINESS:

Home Centers, Retail
Home Improvement Products
Home Installation Services
Special Order Sales

BRANDS/DIVISIONS/AFFILIATES:

Orchard Supply Hardware
Iris
Kobalt
Blue Hawk
Utilitech
Aquasource
Lowes.com
Rona Inc

CONTACTS: Note: Officers with more than one job title may be intentionally listed here more than once.

Robert Hull, CFO
Paul Ramsay, Chief Information Officer
Marshall Croom, Chief Risk Officer
Rick Damron, COO
Ross Mccanless, General Counsel
N. Peace, Other Corporate Officer
Richard Maltsbarger, Other Corporate Officer
Michael Jones, Other Executive Officer
Jennifer Weber, Other Executive Officer
Robert Niblock, President
Matthew Hollifield, Senior VP

GROWTH PLANS/SPECIAL FEATURES:

Lowe's Companies, Inc. is one of the largest home improvement retailers in the world. The company owns roughly 1,857 stores in 50 U.S. states, Mexico and Canada, each carrying approximately 36,000 products and 202 million square feet of retail space. The company also operates 80 stores under the recently acquired Orchard Supply Hardware name in California and Oregon. Hundreds of thousands of items are also available through the firm's special order system. Lowe's stores chiefly serve do-it-yourself (DIY) homeowners and commercial business customers, including contractors, landscapers, electricians, painters and plumbers. Its home improvement product categories include building materials, lighting, cabinets and countertops, seasonal living, millwork, lumber, flooring, lawn and landscaping items, hardware, fashion and rough plumbing, appliances, paint, tools, plants and plant pots, outdoor power equipment, rough electrical, home environment and organization and windows and walls. Each Lowe's store carries a wide selection of national brand name merchandise such as Samsung, Whirlpool, Stainmaster, GE, Valspar, Sylvania, Dewalt, Owens Corning and Johns Manville; and exclusive brand names such as Kobalt, allen+roth, Blue Hawk, Utilitech and Aquasource. The company's Lowes.com web site facilitates customers researching, comparing and buying Lowe's products, and also allows customers to special order products not carried in its physical store locations. Lowe's entered the smarthome market with Iris, an affordable, cloud-based home management system, which allows users to interact and control their home's security cameras, thermostat, locks, lighting and appliances remotely from a smart phone or computer. In May 2016, the firm acquired Rona, Inc. for $2.4 billion, creating one of the largest home improvement retailers in Canada.

Lowe's offers its employees life, short- and long-term disability, accident, auto, home, medical, dental and vision insurance; family assistance programs; stock purchase plan; tuition reimbursement; paid time off; 401(k); and flexible spending accounts.

FINANCIAL DATA: Note: Data for latest year may not have been available at press time.

In U.S. $	2016	2015	2014	2013	2012	2011
Revenue	59,074,000,000	56,223,000,000	53,417,000,000	50,521,000,000	50,208,000,000	48,815,000,000
R&D Expense						
Operating Income	4,971,000,000	4,792,000,000	4,149,000,000	3,560,000,000	3,277,000,000	3,560,000,000
Operating Margin %	8.41%	8.52%	7.76%	7.04%	6.52%	7.29%
SGA Expense	14,115,000,000	13,281,000,000	12,865,000,000	12,244,000,000	12,593,000,000	12,006,000,000
Net Income	2,546,000,000	2,698,000,000	2,286,000,000	1,959,000,000	1,839,000,000	2,010,000,000
Operating Cash Flow	4,784,000,000	4,929,000,000	4,111,000,000	3,762,000,000	4,349,000,000	3,852,000,000
Capital Expenditure	1,197,000,000	880,000,000	940,000,000	1,211,000,000	1,829,000,000	1,329,000,000
EBITDA	6,563,000,000	6,385,000,000	5,719,000,000	5,211,000,000	4,862,000,000	5,256,000,000
Return on Assets %	8.03%	8.30%	6.99%	5.91%	5.46%	6.02%
Return on Equity %	28.75%	24.58%	17.78%	12.89%	10.61%	10.81%
Debt to Equity	1.50	1.08	0.85	0.65	0.42	0.36

CONTACT INFORMATION:

Phone: 704 758-1000   Fax: 336 658-4766
Toll-Free: 800-445-6937
Address: 1000 Lowe's Blvd., Mooresville, NC 28117 United States

STOCK TICKER/OTHER:

Stock Ticker: LOW   Exchange: NYS
Employees: 270,000   Fiscal Year Ends: 01/31
Parent Company:

SALARIES/BONUSES:

Top Exec. Salary: $1,300,000   Bonus: $

Second Exec. Salary: $790,000   Bonus: $

OTHER THOUGHTS:

Estimated Female Officers or Directors: 3

Hot Spot for Advancement for Women/Minorities: Y

Lubrizol Corporation (The)

www.lubrizol.com

NAIC Code: 325110

TYPES OF BUSINESS:
Manufacturing-Specialty Chemicals
Fuel & Lubricant Additives
Polymers
Performance Coatings, Resins & Additives
Plastic Plumbing, Automobile Molded Parts & Film
Rubber, Plastic & Lubricants Additives

BRANDS/DIVISIONS/AFFILIATES:
Lubrizol Advanced Materials Inc
TempRite
Estane
Lubrizol Specialty Products Inc
Weatherford International

CONTACTS: *Note: Officers with more than one job title may be intentionally listed here more than once.*
James L. Hambrick, CEO
Brian A. Valentine, CFO
Andrew B. Panega, Corp. VP-Human Resources
John J. King, Corp. VP-Info. Solutions & Bus. Processes
James L. Hambrick, Chmn.

GROWTH PLANS/SPECIAL FEATURES:
The Lubrizol Corporation, a subsidiary of Berkshire Hathaway, Inc., is a manufacturer and marketer of specialty chemicals and additives for the transportation, consumer and industrial markets. The company maintains production facilities throughout the Americas, Europe, the Middle East & Africa and Asia Pacific. It operates through three segments: Lubrizol Additives (LA), Lubrizol Advanced Materials (LAM) and Lubrizol Oilfield Solutions (LOS). LA produces engine additives such as passenger car, construction equipment, motorcycle and marine vessel motor oils; diesel engine oils; fuel additives; driveline additives; and industrial additives. This segment also offers toll manufacturing, custom testing and consulting services. LA products are aimed at enhancing engine performance, increasing fuel economy and extending engine life. The LAM segment contains three primary product lines: engineered polymers, synthetic rheology modifiers and performance coatings. Engineered polymers include TempRite chlorinated polyvinyl chloride (CPVC) resins and compounds for use in exterior building materials, fire sprinkler systems and industrial piping; and Estane thermoplastic elastomers, used in medical tubing and other applications. The synthetic rheology coatings segment produces specialty chemicals focusing on the personal care, home care, food and pharmaceutical industries. Performance coatings supplies specialty resins, additives and polymers. LOS combines the capabilities of Lubrizol Specialty Products Inc. with the firm's solutions for its oilfield customers, as well as with the oilfield chemistry and technology businesses of subsidiary Weatherford International. Products in this segment include oilfield chemicals, refinery chemicals, water treatment chemicals, as well as pipeline flow improvers.

Lubrizol employee benefits vary by country but include health care and disability coverage, retirement planning and time off.

FINANCIAL DATA: *Note: Data for latest year may not have been available at press time.*

In U.S. $	2016	2015	2014	2013	2012	2011
Revenue		7,000,000,000	7,000,000,000	6,400,000,000	6,100,000,000	5,800,000,000
R&D Expense						
Operating Income						
Operating Margin %						
SGA Expense						
Net Income						
Operating Cash Flow						
Capital Expenditure						
EBITDA						
Return on Assets %						
Return on Equity %						
Debt to Equity						

CONTACT INFORMATION:
Phone: 440-943-4200   Fax: 440-943-5337
Toll-Free:
Address: 29400 Lakeland Blvd., Wickliffe, OH 44092 United States

STOCK TICKER/OTHER:
Stock Ticker: Subsidiary
Employees: 8,924
Parent Company: Berkshire Hathaway Inc

Exchange:
Fiscal Year Ends: 12/31

SALARIES/BONUSES:
Top Exec. Salary: $ Bonus: $
Second Exec. Salary: $ Bonus: $

OTHER THOUGHTS:
Estimated Female Officers or Directors: 1
Hot Spot for Advancement for Women/Minorities:

Marriott International Inc
NAIC Code: 721110

www.marriott.com

TYPES OF BUSINESS:
Hotels & Resorts
Suites Hotels
Corporate Apartments
Extended Stay Lodging
Luxury Hotels
Business Hotels

BRANDS/DIVISIONS/AFFILIATES:
Marriott Hotels
Ritz-Carlton Hotel Company LLC (The)
Starwood Hotels & Resorts Worldwide Inc
Renaissance Hotels
Courtyard by Marriott
Fairfield Inn & Suites by Marriott
TownePlace Suites by Marriott
JW Marriott

CONTACTS: Note: Officers with more than one job title may be intentionally listed here more than once.
Bancroft Gordon, Assistant General Counsel
David Grissen, President, Divisional
Arne Sorenson, CEO
Kathleen Oberg, CFO
J. Marriott, Chairman of the Board
Stephanie Linnartz, Chief Marketing Officer
Bao Giang Val Bauduin, Controller
Sterling Colton, Director Emeritus
William Shaw, Director Emeritus
Edward Ryan, Executive VP
Anthony Capuano, Executive VP
David Rodriguez, Executive VP
Amy McPherson, Managing Director, Geographical
Argiris Kyriakidis, Managing Director, Geographical
Craig Smith, Managing Director, Geographical

GROWTH PLANS/SPECIAL FEATURES:
Marriott International, Inc. operates 4,424 hotels and related lodging facilities in 79 countries and territories, totaling nearly 760,000 rooms. The company operates through three segments: North American full-service lodging, North American limited-service lodging and international. Marriott develops operates and franchises hotels under various brand names including Marriott Hotels, JW Marriott, The Ritz-Carlton BuVLGARI Hotels and Resorts, Renaissance Hotels Courtyard by Marriott, Residence Inn by Marriott, Fairfield Inn & Suites, SpringHill Suites by Marriott, EDITION, Autograph Collection Hotels, Marriott Executive Apartments, Marriott Vacation Club, Gaylor Hotels, AC Hotels by Marriott, Protea Hotels, Moxy Hotels and TownePlace Suites by Marriott. The firm also operates 41 home and condominium projects and 28 Marriott Executive Apartments located in 15 countries. Additionally, Marriott Golf manages 35 golf resorts worldwide. The company operates 15 system-wide hotel reservation centers: six in the U.S. and Canada and nine in other countries and territories. In 2015, Marriott debuted its first property in Italy, on a private island called JW Marriott Venice Resort & Spa. In February 2016, it expanded its footprint in Chhattisgarh, India with Courtyard by Marriott Raipur; signed for five hotels to open in Japan by 2018 with Mori Trust Group, which will be under the Marriott Hotels brand; and announced plans to open two new hotels in Cartagena, Colombia by 2018. In September 2016, Marriott completed the acquisition of Starwood Hotels & Resorts Worldwide, Inc.

FINANCIAL DATA: Note: Data for latest year may not have been available at press time.

In U.S. $	2016	2015	2014	2013	2012	2011
Revenue		14,486,000,000	13,796,000,000	12,784,000,000	11,814,000,000	12,317,000,000
R&D Expense						
Operating Income		1,350,000,000	1,159,000,000	988,000,000	940,000,000	526,000,000
Operating Margin %		9.31%	8.40%	7.72%	7.95%	4.27%
SGA Expense		634,000,000	659,000,000	726,000,000	645,000,000	752,000,000
Net Income		859,000,000	753,000,000	626,000,000	571,000,000	198,000,000
Operating Cash Flow		1,430,000,000	1,224,000,000	1,140,000,000	989,000,000	1,089,000,000
Capital Expenditure		426,000,000	476,000,000	465,000,000	690,000,000	257,000,000
EBITDA		1,561,000,000	1,351,000,000	1,144,000,000	1,131,000,000	688,000,000
Return on Assets %		13.26%	11.02%	9.53%	9.32%	2.65%
Return on Equity %						49.25%
Debt to Equity						

CONTACT INFORMATION:
Phone: 301 380-3000   Fax: 301 380-3967
Toll-Free: 800-721-7033
Address: 10400 Fernwood Rd., Bethesda, MD 20817 United States

STOCK TICKER/OTHER:
Stock Ticker: MAR   Exchange: NAS
Employees: 123,500   Fiscal Year Ends: 12/31
Parent Company:

SALARIES/BONUSES:
Top Exec. Salary: Bonus: $
$3,000,000
Second Exec. Salary: Bonus: $
$1,236,000

OTHER THOUGHTS:
Estimated Female Officers or Directors: 7

Hot Spot for Advancement for Women/Minorities: Y

Mars Inc

www.mars.com

NAIC Code: 311351

TYPES OF BUSINESS:

Chocolate & Confectionery Manufacturing
Snack Foods & Candy Bars
Pet Nutrition
Drink Vending Systems
Prepared Foods
Information Technology Services

BRANDS/DIVISIONS/AFFILIATES:

M&Ms
M&M World
Milky Way
Twix
Seeds of Change
Cesar
Uncle Ben's
Wm Wrigley Jr Company

CONTACTS: *Note: Officers with more than one job title may be intentionally listed here more than once.*

Grant F. Reid, Pres.
Reuben Gamoran, CFO
Bruce McColl, CMO
Richard Ware, VP-R&D
John Donofrio, General Counsel
David Kamenetzky, VP-Corp. Affairs
Frank Mars, Pres., Symbioscience
Martin Radvan, Pres., Wrigley
Grant Reid, Pres., Chocolate
Poul Weihrauch, Pres., Food
Steven Badger, Chmn.
Richard Ware, VP-Supply & Procurement

GROWTH PLANS/SPECIAL FEATURES:

Mars, Inc., founded in 1911, is a family-owned company that operates through six business divisions: chocolate, pet care, food, drinks, Symbioscience and Wm. Wrigley Jr. Company, which produces Wrigley gum and sugar. The company's chocolate segment makes some of the world's most popular and widely available snacks and confectionery products, including M&Ms, Mars, Snickers, Milky Way, Twix, Dove, 3 Musketeers, Kudos bars and combo snacks. The company has a branded retail store called M&M World, with four locations in the U.S and one in London. The pet care unit offers products for cats and dogs, including such brands as Cesar, Whiskas, Pedigree, Royal Canine, Banfield Pet Hospital, Greenies, The Good Life Recipes, Temptations and Crave. In the food division, Mars produces rice, entrees, sauces and condiments under the Uncle Ben's, Dolmio, Suzi-Wan, Royco, Raris, Seeds of Change and Ebly brands. The firm's drinks segment distributes Mars' KLIX, Bright Tea Co., Dove/Galaxy hot chocolate, Alterra coffee and FLAVIA drink vending machine systems, which are industry leading products that provide in-cup drinks such as fresh ground coffee, leaf tea and hot chocolate. The Symbioscience unit offers products such as Mars Botanical Cocoapro, Cocoa-Via, and Mars Veterinary-Wisdom Panel MX. The Wrigley Gum and Sugar division offers snacks such as Starburst, Skittles, Juicy Fruit gum, Life Savers and Altoids. Mars operates approximately manufacturing facilities throughout the U.S., as well as facilities in Bolton and Newmarket, Ontario. In 2015, the firm agreed to distribute Peet's Coffee and Tea products across North America; and agreed to acquire Mexican chocolate manufacturer, Grupo Turin.

FINANCIAL DATA: *Note: Data for latest year may not have been available at press time.*

In U.S. $	2016	2015	2014	2013	2012	2011
Revenue		33,700,000,000	33,500,000,000	33,200,000,000	31,500,000,000	31,000,000,000
R&D Expense						
Operating Income						
Operating Margin %						
SGA Expense						
Net Income						
Operating Cash Flow						
Capital Expenditure						
EBITDA						
Return on Assets %						
Return on Equity %						
Debt to Equity						

CONTACT INFORMATION:

Phone: 703-821-4900   Fax: 703-448-9678
Toll-Free: 800-627-7852
Address: 6885 Elm St., McLean, VA 22101 United States

STOCK TICKER/OTHER:

Stock Ticker: Private   Exchange:
Employees: 75,000   Fiscal Year Ends: 12/31
Parent Company:

SALARIES/BONUSES:

Top Exec. Salary: $ Bonus: $
Second Exec. Salary: $ Bonus: $

OTHER THOUGHTS:

Estimated Female Officers or Directors: 1
Hot Spot for Advancement for Women/Minorities:

Marsh & Mclennan Companies Inc

www.marshmac.com

NAIC Code: 524210

TYPES OF BUSINESS:

Insurance Brokerage
Consulting Services
Risk Management
Benefits Administration
Human Resources Services

BRANDS/DIVISIONS/AFFILIATES:

Marsh Inc
Guy Carpenter & Company LLC
Mercer Inc
Oliver Wyman Group
Lippincott
NERA Economic Consulting
CPSG Partners

CONTACTS: Note: Officers with more than one job title may be intentionally listed here more than once.

Carey Roberts, Assistant General Counsel
Peter Zaffino, CEO, Subsidiary
Alexander Moczarski, CEO, Subsidiary
Julio Portalatin, CEO, Subsidiary
Scott McDonald, CEO, Subsidiary
Mark McGivney, CFO
E. Gilbert, Chief Information Officer
Robert Rapport, Controller
H. Hanway, Director
Daniel Glaser, Director
Peter Beshar, Executive VP
Laurie Ledford, Other Executive Officer

GROWTH PLANS/SPECIAL FEATURES:

Marsh & McLennan Companies, Inc. (MMC) is a global professional services firm. The company provides insurance and management and consulting services in the areas of risk, strategy and human capital to clients in over 130 countries. It is the parent company of a number of leading risk experts and specialty consultants, including Marsh, Inc., an insurance broker, intermediary and risk advisor; Guy Carpenter & Company LLC, a risk and reinsurance specialist; Mercer, Inc., a provider of HR and related financial advice and services; and Oliver Wyman Group, a management consultancy. MMC operates in two divisions: risk & insurance services and consulting. The risk & insurance services segment generated 53% of the firm's total revenue and is primarily composed of Marsh and Guy Carpenter. The consulting segment was responsible for 47% of the firm's total revenue and operates through Mercer and Oliver Wyman. The Mercer division offers investment consulting services and specialized management and economic consulting services as well as human resources consulting and related outsourcing. Oliver Wyman includes Lippincott, a consulting firm that helps clients with branding and corporate image; and NERA Economic Consulting, one of the world's largest consulting groups that focuses on economics and deploys professional economists. In 2016, the firm acquired CPSG Partners, a leading Workday services partner.

MMC offers employees medical, dental and vision insurance; spending accounts; life insurance; business travel accident insurance; disability coverage; an employee stock purchase plan; a 401(k) plan; a retirement plan; tuition assistance; auto and home insurance; pet insurance; a legal assistance plan; and an employee assistance program.

FINANCIAL DATA: Note: Data for latest year may not have been available at press time.

In U.S. $	2016	2015	2014	2013	2012	2011
Revenue		12,893,000,000	12,951,000,000	12,261,000,000	11,924,000,000	11,526,000,000
R&D Expense						
Operating Income		2,419,000,000	2,301,000,000	2,077,000,000	1,829,000,000	1,638,000,000
Operating Margin %		18.76%	17.76%	16.93%	15.33%	14.21%
SGA Expense		7,334,000,000	7,515,000,000	7,226,000,000	7,134,000,000	6,969,000,000
Net Income		1,599,000,000	1,465,000,000	1,357,000,000	1,176,000,000	993,000,000
Operating Cash Flow		1,888,000,000	2,112,000,000	1,341,000,000	1,322,000,000	1,705,000,000
Capital Expenditure		325,000,000	368,000,000	401,000,000	320,000,000	280,000,000
EBITDA		2,893,000,000	2,610,000,000	2,498,000,000	2,226,000,000	1,935,000,000
Return on Assets %		8.86%	8.41%	8.15%	7.40%	6.45%
Return on Equity %		23.57%	19.58%	18.78%	18.92%	16.21%
Debt to Equity		0.67	0.47	0.33	0.40	0.45

CONTACT INFORMATION:

Phone: 212 345-5000   Fax: 212 345-4809
Toll-Free:
Address: 1166 Ave. of the Americas, New York, NY 10036 United States

STOCK TICKER/OTHER:

Stock Ticker: MMC
Employees: 57,000
Parent Company:

Exchange: NYS
Fiscal Year Ends: 12/31

SALARIES/BONUSES:

Top Exec. Salary:
$1,400,000

Bonus: $

Second Exec. Salary:
$1,000,000

Bonus: $

OTHER THOUGHTS:

Estimated Female Officers or Directors: 3

Hot Spot for Advancement for Women/Minorities: Y

Mary Kay Inc

NAIC Code: 454390

www.marykay.com

TYPES OF BUSINESS:

Cosmetics & Beauty Supplies, Direct Selling
Online Retail
Fragrances
Over-the-Counter Drugs
Cosmetics & Beauty Supplies, Manufacturing

BRANDS/DIVISIONS/AFFILIATES:

Thinking of You
MK High Intensity
Belara
Domain
Velocity
Journey
Mary Kay Museum

CONTACTS: Note: Officers with more than one job title may be intentionally listed here more than once.

David Holl, CEO
David B. Holl, Pres.
Deborah Gibbins, CFO
Sheryl Adkins-Green, CMO
Melinda Foster Sellers, Chief People Officer
Kregg Jodie, CIO
Nathan Moore, Chief Legal Officer
Darrell Overcash, Pres., North America Region
Tara Eustace, Pres., European Region
Jose Smeke, Pres., Latin American Region
Richard R. Rogers, Exec. Chmn.
K.K. Chua, Pres., Asia Pacific Region
Dennis Greaney, Chief Supply Chain Officer

GROWTH PLANS/SPECIAL FEATURES:

Mary Kay, Inc. is one of the largest direct sellers of skin care products in the U.S. The company's merchandise includes more than 200 products across several categories, including skin care, color cosmetics, spa and body care and fragrances. Skin care includes anti-aging creams; cleansers; moisturizers; basic skin care for different skin types; products for specific needs, such as acne treatment and oil control; and lip and eye care. Color cosmetics products include lip, eyes, cheeks, nails, foundations and powder color enhancers as well as travel sets and applicators. The Mary Kay fragrance line has specialty scents for both men and women, including Journey, Belara and Thinking of You for women, and Domain, MK High Intensity and Velocity for men. Mary Kay develops, tests, manufactures and packages the majority of its products at its own plants. Most inventory is manufactured at the Dallas site, where the company headquarters and the Mary Kay Museum are located. An additional manufacturing facility is located in China. With FDA approval, the company also manufactures and distributes certain products classified as over-the-counter drugs, such as sunscreens and acne treatment products. There are about 3.5 million Mary Kay independent beauty consultants serving customers in more than 35 countries worldwide. About 40% of new sales recruits are relatively young, aged 18 to 30. A new recruit pays $100 for a basic starter kit in order to begin selling Mary Kay products. Independent beauty consultants may eventually become independent sales directors and/or independent national sales directors. Mary Kay has more than 1,200 patents for products, technologies and packaging designs in its global portfolio.

FINANCIAL DATA: Note: Data for latest year may not have been available at press time.

In U.S. $	2016	2015	2014	2013	2012	2011
Revenue		4,000,000,000	3,200,000,000	3,100,000,000	3,000,000,000	2,900,000,000
R&D Expense						
Operating Income						
Operating Margin %						
SGA Expense						
Net Income						
Operating Cash Flow						
Capital Expenditure						
EBITDA						
Return on Assets %						
Return on Equity %						
Debt to Equity						

CONTACT INFORMATION:

Phone: 972-687-6300   Fax: 972-687-1611
Toll-Free: 800-627-9529
Address: 16251 Dallas Pkwy., Dallas, TX 75001 United States

STOCK TICKER/OTHER:

Stock Ticker: Private
Employees: 5,000
Parent Company:

Exchange:
Fiscal Year Ends: 12/31

SALARIES/BONUSES:

Top Exec. Salary: $ Bonus: $
Second Exec. Salary: $ Bonus: $

OTHER THOUGHTS:

Estimated Female Officers or Directors: 3
Hot Spot for Advancement for Women/Minorities: Y

MassMutual Financial Group

www.massmutual.com

NAIC Code: 524113

TYPES OF BUSINESS:

Life Insurance
Pension Products
Real Estate Equity Management
Disability Insurance
Investment Management Products
Mutual Fund Management
Investor Services

BRANDS/DIVISIONS/AFFILIATES:

Massachusetts Mutual Life Insurance Co
Oppenheimer Funds Inc
Cornerstone Real Estate Advisers
Babson Capital Management LLC
Baring Asset Management Limited
MassMutual International LLC
MetLife Premier Client Group

CONTACTS: *Note: Officers with more than one job title may be intentionally listed here more than once.*

Roger W. Crandall, CEO
Roger W. Crandall, Pres.
Elizabeth A. Ward, CFO
Eddie Ahmed, Exec. VP-Human Resources
Robert J. Casale, CIO
Mark D. Roellig, General Counsel
Sharmaine Miller, VP-New Bus. Oper.
Douglas G. Russell, Sr. VP-Strategy & Corp. Dev.
Elizabeth A. Ward, Chief Enterprise Risk Officer
William F. Glavin, Jr., CEO
Elaine A. Sarsynski, Chmn.
Susan M. Cicco, VP
Roger W. Crandall, Chmn.
Elaine A. Sarsynski, CEO

GROWTH PLANS/SPECIAL FEATURES:

MassMutual Financial Group, a marketing name for Massachusetts Mutual Life Insurance Co. and its affiliated companies, is a global, growth oriented, diversified financial services organization. With its affiliates, it boasts more than 3 million customers and over $650 billion in managed assets. The mutually owned company offers financial protection, accumulation and income management by providing life insurance, annuities, disability income insurance, long-term care insurance, retirement planning products, income management and other products and services for individuals, business owners, corporations and institutions. It operates through several subsidiaries. MassMutual's investment group provides investment management products, such as securities and real estate as well as mutual fund management and real estate equities management services primarily through Oppenheimer Funds, Inc. and Cornerstone Real Estate Advisers. Subsidiary Babson Capital Management LLC offers individual and institutional investor services. Baring Asset Management Limited is an international investment management firm with offices, clients and business lines throughout the world's major markets. MassMutual International LLC offers insurance, savings and retirement products, as well as other financial services. MassMutual Ventures LLC is a venture capital firm with the mandate to back startups and entrepreneurial businesses. In July 2016, the firm acquired MetLife's U.S. retail advisor division, the MetLife Premier Client Group.

The firm offers employees life, health, dental, disability and vision insurance; flexible spending accounts; and a 401(k).

FINANCIAL DATA: *Note: Data for latest year may not have been available at press time.*

In U.S. $	2016	2015	2014	2013	2012	2011
Revenue		29,500,000,000	26,400,000,000	27,560,000,000	26,710,000,000	19,687,000,000
R&D Expense						
Operating Income						
Operating Margin %						
SGA Expense						
Net Income		546,000,000	799,000,000	-113,000,000	872,000,000	459,000,000
Operating Cash Flow						
Capital Expenditure						
EBITDA						
Return on Assets %						
Return on Equity %						
Debt to Equity						

CONTACT INFORMATION:

Phone: 413-744-1000   Fax: 413-744-6005
Toll-Free: 800-767-1000
Address: 1295 State St., Springfield, MA 01111 United States

STOCK TICKER/OTHER:

Stock Ticker: Mutual Company   Exchange:
Employees: 10,000   Fiscal Year Ends: 12/31
Parent Company:

SALARIES/BONUSES:

Top Exec. Salary: $ Bonus: $
Second Exec. Salary: $ Bonus: $

OTHER THOUGHTS:

Estimated Female Officers or Directors: 8
Hot Spot for Advancement for Women/Minorities: Y

MasterCard Inc

www.mastercard.com

NAIC Code: 522320

TYPES OF BUSINESS:
Credit Card Issuer
Transaction Processing Services

BRANDS/DIVISIONS/AFFILIATES:
MasterCard
Maestro
Cirrus
Mastercard Network
VocaLink Holdings Limited

CONTACTS: *Note: Officers with more than one job title may be intentionally listed here more than once.*
Ajaypal Banga, CEO
Walt Macnee, Vice Chairman
Martina Hund-Mejean, CFO
Richard Haythornthwaite, Chairman of the Board
Andrea Forster, Chief Accounting Officer
Timothy Murphy, General Counsel
Ronald Garrow, Other Executive Officer
Michael Miebach, Other Executive Officer
Ann Cairns, President, Divisional
Robert Reeg, President, Divisional
Gary Flood, President, Divisional
Craig Vosburg, President, Geographical
Raghu Malhotra, President, Geographical
Janet McGinness, Secretary

GROWTH PLANS/SPECIAL FEATURES:
MasterCard, Inc. is a global payment solutions company that provides services to support the credit, debit and related payment programs of thousands of financial institutions. The company develops and markets payment solutions and processes payment transactions; it also provides consulting services to customers and merchants. MasterCard manages payment card brands including MasterCard, Maestro and Cirrus. A typical transaction processed over the MasterCard Network involves four parties in addition to the firm: the cardholder, the merchant, the issuer (the cardholder's financial institution) and the acquirer (the merchant's financial institution). The company's customers are the financial institutions that act as issuers and acquirers. MasterCard generates revenues from the fees that it charges customers for providing these transaction processing and other payment-related services by assessing their customers based on their volume of dollar activity. The company's credit and debit cards are accepted at more than 150 currencies in 210 countries worldwide. In July 2016, the firm announced that Citicard MasterCards stopped supporting Paypass completely, and that existing plastic and keyfobs would continue to work until their expiration date. No new Paypass-enabled hardware would be issued to U.S. customers from July 2016 forward. Also in 2016, MasterCard acquired a majority stake (92.4%) of VocaLink Holdings Limited, a payment systems company headquartered in the U.K., for approximately $290 million.

The firm offers employees medical, dental and vision coverage; life, disability and AD&D insurance; child care options; flexible work hours; adoption assistance; financial wellness programs; and personal services and discounts.

FINANCIAL DATA: *Note: Data for latest year may not have been available at press time.*

In U.S. $	2016	2015	2014	2013	2012	2011
Revenue		9,667,000,000	9,473,000,000	8,346,000,000	7,391,000,000	6,714,000,000
R&D Expense						
Operating Income		5,078,000,000	5,106,000,000	4,503,000,000	3,937,000,000	2,713,000,000
Operating Margin %		52.52%	53.90%	53.95%	53.26%	40.40%
SGA Expense		4,244,000,000	4,046,000,000	3,490,000,000	3,204,000,000	3,037,000,000
Net Income		3,808,000,000	3,617,000,000	3,116,000,000	2,759,000,000	1,906,000,000
Operating Cash Flow		4,043,000,000	3,407,000,000	4,135,000,000	2,948,000,000	2,684,000,000
Capital Expenditure		342,000,000	334,000,000	299,000,000	218,000,000	177,000,000
EBITDA		5,385,000,000	5,448,000,000	4,772,000,000	4,182,000,000	2,965,000,000
Return on Assets %		24.10%	24.46%	23.33%	23.83%	19.51%
Return on Equity %		59.41%	50.67%	43.27%	43.16%	34.42%
Debt to Equity		0.54	0.22			

CONTACT INFORMATION:
Phone: 914 249-2000   Fax: 914 249-4206
Toll-Free: 800-627-8372
Address: 2000 Purchase St., Purchase, NY 10577 United States

STOCK TICKER/OTHER:
Stock Ticker: MA
Employees: 10,300
Parent Company:

Exchange: NYS
Fiscal Year Ends: 12/31

SALARIES/BONUSES:
Top Exec. Salary: $1,200,000   Bonus: $
Second Exec. Salary: $665,633   Bonus: $

OTHER THOUGHTS:
Estimated Female Officers or Directors: 2

Hot Spot for Advancement for Women/Minorities: Y

Matthews International Corporation

www.matw.com

NAIC Code: 339995

TYPES OF BUSINESS:

Burial Caskets and Cases Manufacturing

BRANDS/DIVISIONS/AFFILIATES:

SGK Brand Solutions
Schawk Inc
Aurora Products Group LLC

CONTACTS: Note: Officers with more than one job title may be intentionally listed here more than once.

Joseph Bartolacci, CEO
Steven Nicola, CFO
John Turner, Chairman of the Board
David Beck, Controller
David Schawk, Director
Brian Dunn, Executive VP, Divisional
Brian Walters, General Counsel
Paul Rahill, President, Divisional
Steven Gackenbach, President, Divisional
Robert Marsh, Treasurer
Marcy Campbell, Vice President, Divisional

GROWTH PLANS/SPECIAL FEATURES:

Matthews International Corporation is a designer, manufacturer and marketer of memorialization products and brand solutions. Memorialization products consist primarily of bronze memorials and other memorialization products, caskets and cremation equipment for the cemetery and funeral home industries. The company's products and operations are comprised of three business segments: SGK Brand Solutions, memorialization and industrial. SGK Brand Solutions is comprised of the graphics imaging business, including wholly-owned Schawk, Inc., and Matthews' merchandising solutions operations. This segment provides brand development, brand management, pre-media services, printing plates & cylinders, embossing tools and creative design services to consumer packaged goods, retail and packaging industries. The memorialization segment manufactures and markets a full line of memorialization products used primarily in cemeteries, funeral homes and crematories. These products are sold primarily in the U.S., Europe, Canada and Australia, and include cast bronze memorials, granite memorials, caskets, cremation equipment and other memorialization products. This division also manufactures and markets architectural products used to identify or commemorate people, places, events and accomplishments. The industrial segment designs, manufactures and distributes an array of marking, coding and industrial automation solutions, order fulfillment systems and related consumables. Manufacturers, suppliers and distributors worldwide rely on Matthews' integrated systems to identify, track, control and pick their products. In 2015, the firm acquired Aurora Products Group LLC from Kohlberg & Company for $214 million, subject to a working capital adjustment.

FINANCIAL DATA: Note: Data for latest year may not have been available at press time.

In U.S. $	2016	2015	2014	2013	2012	2011
Revenue		1,426,068,000	1,106,597,000	985,357,000	900,317,000	898,821,000
R&D Expense						
Operating Income		105,023,000	82,891,000	95,792,000	93,577,000	118,516,000
Operating Margin %		7.36%	7.49%	9.72%	10.39%	13.18%
SGA Expense		424,352,000	309,605,000	260,726,000	242,993,000	233,144,000
Net Income		63,449,000	43,674,000	54,888,000	55,843,000	72,372,000
Operating Cash Flow		141,064,000	92,399,000	109,326,000	82,123,000	95,564,000
Capital Expenditure		48,251,000	29,237,000	24,924,000	33,236,000	22,440,000
EBITDA		172,882,000	123,288,000	132,226,000	124,218,000	147,918,000
Return on Assets %		3.02%	2.69%	4.68%	5.01%	6.92%
Return on Equity %		8.40%	6.57%	10.68%	11.85%	15.62%
Debt to Equity		1.21	0.91	0.63	0.62	0.64

CONTACT INFORMATION:

Phone: 412-442-8200   Fax: 412-442-8290
Toll-Free:
Address: Two Northshore Center, Pittsburgh, PA 15212-5851 United States

STOCK TICKER/OTHER:

Stock Ticker: MATW   Exchange: NAS
Employees: 9,400   Fiscal Year Ends: 09/30
Parent Company:

SALARIES/BONUSES:

Top Exec. Salary: $765,346   Bonus: $
Second Exec. Salary: $595,000   Bonus: $

OTHER THOUGHTS:

Estimated Female Officers or Directors:
Hot Spot for Advancement for Women/Minorities:

MAXIMUS Inc

www.maximus.com

NAIC Code: 541512

TYPES OF BUSINESS:

Consulting-Government Agencies
Outsourced Program Management
IT Systems Management
Consulting

BRANDS/DIVISIONS/AFFILIATES:

Acentia
Ascend

CONTACTS: *Note: Officers with more than one job title may be intentionally listed here more than once.*

Richard Montoni, CEO
Richard Nadeau, CFO
Peter Pond, Chairman of the Board
Raymond Ruddy, Director
David Francis, General Counsel
Akbar Piloti, General Manager, Divisional
Mark Andrekovich, Other Executive Officer
Bruce Caswell, President

GROWTH PLANS/SPECIAL FEATURES:

MAXIMUS, Inc. provides business process services (BPS) to government health and human services agencies. MAXIMUS is one of the largest pure-play health and human services BPS providers to governments in the U.S., the U.K., Australia, Canada, Saudi Arabia and New Zealand. The company is divided into three segments: health services, accounting for 53% of 2015 revenue; human services, 23%; and U.S. federal services, 24%. Health services provides BPS and consulting services for state, provincial and federal government programs, such as Medicaid, CHIP (children's health insurance programs) and the Affordable Care Act, in the U.S.; Health Insurance BC (British Columbia), in Canada; and Health Assessment Advisory Service and Fit for Work Services, in the U.K. Human services provides national, state and local human services agencies with a variety of BPS and related consulting services for government programs such as welfare-to-work, child support higher education and K-12 special education. The U.S. federal services segment provides BPS and program management for large government programs, independent health review and appeals services for both the U.S. federal government and similar state-based programs. This division also offers technology solutions for civilian federal programs. In 2015, the firm acquired Acentia, a provider of technology and management solutions. In March 2016, it acquired independent and specialized health assessment provider Ascend.

The company offers its employees medical, dental, vision, life and AD&D insurance; flexible spending accounts; long-term care policies; legal services; employee assistance; 401(k); paid time off; discounts on childcare; and credit union accounts.

FINANCIAL DATA: *Note: Data for latest year may not have been available at press time.*

In U.S. $	2016	2015	2014	2013	2012	2011
Revenue		2,099,821,000	1,700,912,000	1,331,279,000	1,050,145,000	929,633,000
R&D Expense						
Operating Income		259,832,000	225,308,000	186,208,000	127,575,000	122,401,000
Operating Margin %		12.37%	13.24%	13.98%	12.14%	13.16%
SGA Expense		238,792,000	226,815,000	197,859,000	157,402,000	132,866,000
Net Income		157,772,000	145,440,000	116,731,000	76,133,000	81,168,000
Operating Cash Flow		206,217,000	213,600,000	120,938,000	115,160,000	96,860,000
Capital Expenditure		105,149,000	47,148,000	62,176,000	23,148,000	26,114,000
EBITDA		317,414,000	273,976,000	222,024,000	154,035,000	145,246,000
Return on Assets %		14.46%	16.53%	15.03%	12.07%	14.85%
Return on Equity %		27.00%	26.79%	23.80%	18.44%	22.76%
Debt to Equity		0.34				

CONTACT INFORMATION:

Phone: 703 251-8500   Fax:
Toll-Free: 800-629-4687
Address: 1891 Metro Center Dr., Reston, VA 20190 United States

STOCK TICKER/OTHER:

Stock Ticker: MMS
Employees: 17,000
Parent Company:

Exchange: NYS
Fiscal Year Ends: 09/30

SALARIES/BONUSES:

Top Exec. Salary: $725,000   Bonus: $
Second Exec. Salary: $425,000   Bonus: $225,000

OTHER THOUGHTS:

Estimated Female Officers or Directors: 3
Hot Spot for Advancement for Women/Minorities: Y

Mayo Foundation for Medical Education and Research

www.mayo.edu
NAIC Code: 622110

TYPES OF BUSINESS:
General Medical and Surgical Hospitals
Physician Practice Management
Medical Research
Health Care Education

BRANDS/DIVISIONS/AFFILIATES:
Mayo Clinic
St. Marys Hospital
Dan Abraham Healthy Living Center
Birdsall Medical Research Building
Mayo Clinic Hospital
Mayo Clinic Specialty Building

CONTACTS: Note: Officers with more than one job title may be intentionally listed here more than once.
John H. Noseworthy, CEO
John H. Noseworthy, Pres.
Kedrick D. Adkins Jr, CFO
Shirley A. Weis, Chief Admin. Officer
Jonathan J. Oviatt, Chief Legal Officer
Harry N. Hoffman, Treas.
William C. Rupp, VP
Wyatt W. Decker, VP
Robert F. Brigham, Assistant Sec.
Sherry L. Hubert, Assistant Sec.
Samuel A. Di Piazza Jr., Chmn.

GROWTH PLANS/SPECIAL FEATURES:

Mayo Foundation for Medical Education and Research is a nonprofit health care organization providing medical treatment physician management, health care education, research and other specialized medical services through a network of clinics and hospitals in Minnesota, Arizona and Florida. The three primary clinics, which house physician group practices, are located in Rochester, Minnesota; Jacksonville, Florida; and Scottsdale and Phoenix, Arizona. The Rochester campus is comprised of the Mayo, The Hilton and Stabile buildings as well as St. Mary's Hospital. This facility is a fully integrated medical research and education center. The Dan Abraham Healthy Living Center, located on the Rochester campus, is a state-of-the-art wellness and fitness facility. The Jacksonville campus is centered around the Davis and Mayo buildings, in conjunction with the Birdsall Medical Research Building. The Mayo Clinic Hospital, located on the Jacksonville campus offers 304 beds and 22 operating rooms. In addition, it offers care in more than 35 medical and surgical specialties. The Scottsdale campus is centered around a five-story outpatient clinic. The Mayo Clinic Hospital, located in Phoenix, contains 268 beds, 21 operating rooms, an outpatient surgery center, a patient education library, a pharmacy, a full service laboratory and an endoscopy suite. The Mayo Clinic Specialty Building is an outpatient clinic building connected to the Mayo Clinic Hospital on the Phoenix campus. In 2015, the firm entered into a license agreement with TapImmune Inc., to commercialize a proprietary folate receptor alpha vaccine technology for all cancer indications.

Employees of the firm are offered medical, dental, vision, AD&D, life, disability and prescription drug plans; an employee assistance program; flexible spending accounts; tuition assistance; a scholarship plan; elder, adult and child care; a pension plan; relocation reimbursement; and a variety of other benefits. Benefits may vary by location.

FINANCIAL DATA: Note: Data for latest year may not have been available at press time.

In U.S. $	2016	2015	2014	2013	2012	2011
Revenue		10,315,000,000	9,760,600,000	9,420,800,000	8,843,900,000	8,475,700,000
R&D Expense						
Operating Income						
Operating Margin %						
SGA Expense						
Net Income		526,000,000	834,800,000	612,100,000	395,400,000	610,200,000
Operating Cash Flow						
Capital Expenditure						
EBITDA						
Return on Assets %						
Return on Equity %						
Debt to Equity						

CONTACT INFORMATION:
Phone: 507-284-2511   Fax: 507-284-0161
Toll-Free: 800-660-4582
Address: 200 First St. SW, Rochester, MN 55905 United States

STOCK TICKER/OTHER:
Stock Ticker: Nonprofit   Exchange:
Employees: 64,000   Fiscal Year Ends: 12/31
Parent Company:

SALARIES/BONUSES:
Top Exec. Salary: $ Bonus: $
Second Exec. Salary: $ Bonus: $

OTHER THOUGHTS:
Estimated Female Officers or Directors: 5
Hot Spot for Advancement for Women/Minorities: Y

McAfee Inc

www.mcafee.com

NAIC Code: 0

TYPES OF BUSINESS:

Computer Software, Security & Anti-Virus
Virus Protection Software
Network Management Software

BRANDS/DIVISIONS/AFFILIATES:

Intel Security
Intel Corp
McAfee Total Protection
McAfee LiveSafe
McAfee AntiVirus Plus
Intel Security Partner Program
Security for Business
SaaS Email Security

CONTACTS: Note: Officers with more than one job title may be intentionally listed here more than once.

Michael DeCesare, Pres.
Penny Baldwin, Exec. VP
Patty Hatter, CIO
Michael Fey, CTO
Bryan Reed Barney, Exec. VP-Prod. Dev.
Ari Jaaksi, Sr. VP
Louis Riley, General Counsel
Tom Fountain, Sr. VP
Edward Hayden, Sr. VP-Finance & Acct.
Steve Redman, Exec. VP-Global Sales
Ken Levine, Sr. VP
Gert-Jan Schenk, Pres., EMEA
Barry McPherson, Exec. VP-Worldwide Delivery & Support Svcs.
Todd Gebhart, Vice Chmn.
Jean-Claude Broido, Pres., McAfee Japan
Barry McPherson, Exec. VP-Supply Chain & Facilities

GROWTH PLANS/SPECIAL FEATURES:

McAfee, Inc., operating under the brand Intel Security, is a subsidiary of Intel Corp. The firm is a global developer and supplier of software-based computer security systems that prevent intrusions on networks and protect computer systems from attacks. It allows home users, businesses, government agencies, service providers and partners to block attacks, prevent disruptions and continuously track and improve their security. The company's products are categorized for consumers, small business, partners and enterprise. Consumer products are geared toward users who work from home on one or multiple devices such as computers, tablets, laptops and smartphones. Products consist of PC protection software such as McAfee Total Protection, which works as an anti-virus and maintains an enhanced firewall, McAfee LiveSafe and McAfee AntiVirus Plus. Small business products are designed for businesses with 250 or less devices ranging from PCs, tablets, servers and smartphones. Products categories in this segment includes desktops, email and web and popular products are Security for Business, SaaS Email Security and SaaS Web & Email Protection among others. Partners consists of Intel Security Partner Program, which offers special security solutions through resale or technology partnerships. The resale partnerships include resellers and managed service providers and the technology partnerships include global, OEM and security innovation alliances. Enterprise security products are geared toward companies with hundreds to tens of thousands computers. Products cover email and web security, mobile and network security, endpoint protection, database security and data protection and encryption. In 2014, Intel CEO Brian Krzanich announced that it will be rebranding McAfee as Intel Security, but will keep McAfee's red shield logo.

FINANCIAL DATA: Note: Data for latest year may not have been available at press time.

In U.S. $	2016	2015	2014	2013	2012	2011
Revenue		2,375,000,000	2,216,000,000	2,190,000,000	2,072,000,000	2,200,000,000
R&D Expense						
Operating Income						
Operating Margin %						
SGA Expense						
Net Income			55,000,000	24,000,000	12,000,000	
Operating Cash Flow						
Capital Expenditure						
EBITDA						
Return on Assets %						
Return on Equity %						
Debt to Equity						

CONTACT INFORMATION:

Phone: 972-963-8000   Fax:
Toll-Free: 855-380-6445
Address: 2821 Mission College Blvd., Santa Clara, CA 95054 United States

STOCK TICKER/OTHER:

Stock Ticker: Subsidiary
Employees: 7,923
Parent Company: INTEL CORP

Exchange:
Fiscal Year Ends: 12/31

SALARIES/BONUSES:

Top Exec. Salary: $ Bonus: $
Second Exec. Salary: $ Bonus: $

OTHER THOUGHTS:

Estimated Female Officers or Directors: 3
Hot Spot for Advancement for Women/Minorities: Y

Sales, profits and employees may be estimates. Financial information, benefits and other data can change quickly and may vary from those stated here.

McCormick & Company Inc

www.mccormick.com

NAIC Code: 311940

TYPES OF BUSINESS:

Herbs, Spices & Seasonings

BRANDS/DIVISIONS/AFFILIATES:

Wuhan
McCormick
Simply Asia
Zatarain's
Thai Kitchen
Lawry's
Club House
Ducros

CONTACTS: *Note: Officers with more than one job title may be intentionally listed here more than once.*

Gordon Stetz, CFO
Christina Mcmullen, Chief Accounting Officer
Lawrence Kurzius, Director
Alan Wilson, Director
Brendan Foley, President, Divisional
Malcolm Swift, President, Divisional
Nneka Rimmer, Senior VP, Divisional
Lisa Manzone, Senior VP, Divisional
Michael Smith, Senior VP, Divisional
Jeffery Schwartz, Vice President

GROWTH PLANS/SPECIAL FEATURES:

McCormick & Company, Inc., founded in 1889, is a global manufacturer, marketer and distributor of spices, seasonings and flavorings to the entire food industry, including retail outlets, food manufacturers and food service businesses. The firm operates in two segments: consumer and industrial. The consumer segment sells spices, herbs, seasoning blends and other flavors to retail outlets, including grocery, mass merchandise, warehouse clubs, discount and drug stores. Its leading brands are McCormick, Lawry's and Club House, with ethnic brands consisting of Zatarain's, Simply Asia, Thai Kitchen and Wuhan, as well as global brands such as Ducros, Vahine, Silvo and Schwartz. The industrial segment sells seasoning blends, natural spices and herbs, wet flavors, coating systems and compound flavors to other food manufacturers and the food service industry, both directly and indirectly through distributors. The company's major sales, distribution and production facilities are located in the North America, Europe and China as well as additional facilities in Australia, Mexico, India, Singapore, Central America, Thailand and South Africa.

McCormick offers its employees medical and dental insurance, life and disability insurance, adoption assistance, a profit sharing plan, an employee stock purchase plan, an employee assistance program and tuition assistance.

FINANCIAL DATA: *Note: Data for latest year may not have been available at press time.*

In U.S. $	2016	2015	2014	2013	2012	2011
Revenue		4,296,300,000	4,243,200,000	4,123,400,000	4,014,200,000	3,697,600,000
R&D Expense						
Operating Income		548,400,000	603,000,000	550,500,000	578,300,000	540,300,000
Operating Margin %		12.76%	14.21%	13.35%	14.40%	14.61%
SGA Expense		1,127,400,000	1,122,000,000	1,075,000,000	1,039,500,000	982,200,000
Net Income		402,100,000	437,900,000	387,700,000	407,800,000	374,200,000
Operating Cash Flow		590,000,000	503,600,000	465,200,000	455,000,000	340,000,000
Capital Expenditure		128,400,000	132,700,000	99,900,000	110,300,000	96,700,000
EBITDA		655,400,000	706,800,000	658,700,000	683,500,000	640,900,000
Return on Assets %		9.01%	9.88%	9.00%	9.88%	9.96%
Return on Equity %		23.22%	23.51%	21.44%	24.83%	24.49%
Debt to Equity		0.63	0.56	0.52	0.46	0.64

CONTACT INFORMATION:

Phone: 410-771-7301   Fax:
Toll-Free:
Address: 18 Loveton Cir., Sparks, MD 21152 United States

STOCK TICKER/OTHER:

Stock Ticker: MKC   Exchange: NYS
Employees: 10,000   Fiscal Year Ends: 11/30
Parent Company:

SALARIES/BONUSES:

Top Exec. Salary: Bonus: $
$1,033,716
Second Exec. Salary: Bonus: $
$660,421

OTHER THOUGHTS:

Estimated Female Officers or Directors: 1

Hot Spot for Advancement for Women/Minorities: Y

McDonald's Corp

www.mcdonalds.com

NAIC Code: 722513

TYPES OF BUSINESS:

Fast Food Restaurants
Home-Meal Replacement Restaurants
Franchising

BRANDS/DIVISIONS/AFFILIATES:

Big Mac
Quarter Pounder
Filet O'Fish
Happy Meal
Egg McMuffin
McDonald's Next
Create Your Taste

CONTACTS: *Note: Officers with more than one job title may be intentionally listed here more than once.*

Peter Bensen, Chief Administrative Officer
Douglas Goare, President, Geographical
Enrique Hernandez, Director
Stephen Easterbrook, Director
Christopher Kempczinski, Executive VP, Divisional
Jim Sappington, Executive VP, Divisional
Robert Gibbs, Executive VP, Divisional
Kevin Ozan, Executive VP
Silvia Lagnado, Executive VP
David Fairhurst, Executive VP
Gloria Santona, Executive VP
Ian Borden, President, Divisional
Michael Andres, President, Geographical
David Hoffmann, President, Geographical
Brian Mullens, Senior VP

GROWTH PLANS/SPECIAL FEATURES:

McDonald's Corp. operates more than 36,000 fast-food restaurants in over 100 countries, serving approximately 68 million customers per day. McDonald's has expanded by its franchising model, whereby independent businessmen and women provide capital by initially investing in equipment, signs, seating and decor of restaurants and personally operating them. The company shares the investment by owning or leasing the land and buildings. Approximately 80% of McDonald's worldwide restaurants are franchises, the rest being operated directly by the company or under joint-venture agreements. The McDonald's menu includes items such as hamburgers, cheeseburgers, fish and chicken sandwiches, chicken nuggets, French fries, salads, milkshakes, desserts and soft drinks. McDonald's restaurants are also open during breakfast hours and offer egg sandwiches, hotcakes, biscuit and bagel sandwiches and muffins. Brand names include the Big Mac, Quarter Pounder, Filet O'Fish, Happy Meal and Egg McMuffin. As part of a multi-year beverage business strategy designed to take advantage of the significant and growing beverage category, the company is introducing hot specialty coffee offerings on a market-by-market basis, all of which serve as a platform for the recent introduction of smoothies, frappes and other beverage options in a number of markets. The company is continually working to provide nutritious additions to its menu, including salads, apple slices, oatmeal and low fat yogurt. In 2015, the firm announced plans to fully transition to cage-free eggs for its nearly 16,000 restaurants in the U.S. and Canada over the next 10 years; and opened its first McDonald's Next open-concept store in Hong Kong, offering Create Your Taste digital ordering, as well as free mobile device charging & table service after 6:00 pm.

The firm offers qualified employees medical, dental and vision insurance; short- and long-term disability; profit sharing and savings plans; adoption assistance; vacation and holiday pay; and a child care discount.

FINANCIAL DATA: *Note: Data for latest year may not have been available at press time.*

In U.S. $	2016	2015	2014	2013	2012	2011
Revenue		25,413,000,000	27,441,300,000	28,105,700,000	27,567,000,000	27,006,000,000
R&D Expense						
Operating Income		7,145,500,000	7,949,200,000	8,764,300,000	8,604,600,000	8,529,700,000
Operating Margin %		28.11%	28.96%	31.18%	31.21%	31.58%
SGA Expense		2,434,300,000	2,487,900,000	2,385,600,000	2,455,200,000	2,393,700,000
Net Income		4,529,300,000	4,757,800,000	5,585,900,000	5,464,800,000	5,503,100,000
Operating Cash Flow		6,539,100,000	6,730,300,000	7,120,700,000	6,966,100,000	7,150,100,000
Capital Expenditure		1,813,900,000	2,583,400,000	2,824,700,000	3,049,200,000	2,729,800,000
EBITDA		8,749,700,000	9,587,000,000	10,311,500,000	10,084,100,000	9,920,000,000
Return on Assets %		12.54%	13.41%	15.51%	15.98%	16.94%
Return on Equity %		45.42%	32.96%	35.68%	36.82%	37.92%
Debt to Equity		3.40	1.16	0.88	0.89	0.84

CONTACT INFORMATION:

Phone: 630 623-3000   Fax: 630 623-5700
Toll-Free: 800-244-6227
Address: 1 McDonald's Plz., Oak Brook, IL 60523 United States

SALARIES/BONUSES:

Top Exec. Salary: $1,025,000   Bonus: $
Second Exec. Salary: $941,667   Bonus: $

STOCK TICKER/OTHER:

Stock Ticker: MCD   Exchange: NYS
Employees: 420,000   Fiscal Year Ends: 12/31
Parent Company:

OTHER THOUGHTS:

Estimated Female Officers or Directors: 4

Hot Spot for Advancement for Women/Minorities: Y

Sales, profits and employees may be estimates. Financial information, benefits and other data can change quickly and may vary from those stated here.

McKesson Corporation

www.mckesson.com

NAIC Code: 424210

TYPES OF BUSINESS:

Pharmaceutical Distribution
Medical-Surgical Products Distribution
Health Care Management Software
Consulting
Outsourcing

BRANDS/DIVISIONS/AFFILIATES:

InterQual
US Pharmaceutical Distribution
McKesson Canada Corp
McKesson Specialty Health
McKesson Pharmacy Technology & Services
RelayHealth
Rexall

CONTACTS: *Note: Officers with more than one job title may be intentionally listed here more than once.*

John Hammergren, CEO
James Beer, CFO
Kathleen McElligott, Chief Information Officer
Jorge Figueredo, Executive VP, Divisional
Bansi Nagji, Executive VP, Divisional
Lori Schechter, Executive VP
Paul Julian, Executive VP
Patrick Blake, Executive VP
Erin Lampert, Senior VP
Brian Moore, Senior VP

GROWTH PLANS/SPECIAL FEATURES:

McKesson Corporation provides medicines, pharmaceutical supplies, information and care management products and services to the health care industry. The company operates in two segments: distribution solutions and technology solutions. The distribution solutions segment distributes ethical and proprietary drugs, medical-surgical supplies and equipment and health and beauty care products throughout North America and internationally. This segment also provides specialty pharmaceutical solutions to biotech and pharmaceutical manufacturers, sells pharmacy software and provides consulting and outsourcing services. The technology solutions segment delivers clinical, patient care, financial, supply chain and strategic management software solutions as well as pharmacy automation for hospitals and connectivity and outsourcing services. This segment, which includes InterQual, also provides clinical auditing and compliance systems, as well as claims payment solutions. The company's subsidiaries include U.S. Pharmaceutical Distribution, McKesson Canada Corp., McKesson Specialty Health, McKesson Pharmacy Technology & Services and RelayHealth. In late-2015, the firm agreed to sell its Brazilian pharmaceutical distribution business, as well as small businesses from its distribution and technology segments. The sale is expected to close mid-2017. In 2016, McKesson acquired Canadian pharmacy chain, Rexall, for $3 billion; and acquired the pharmaceutical distribution business of UDG Healthcare Plc, based in Ireland, for $412 million. Also, in June 2016, McKesson and Change Healthcare Holdings, Inc. announced plans to create a new healthcare information technology company, combining all of Change Healthcare's business and the majority of McKesson Technology Solutions. McKesson will own about 70% and Change 30% of the standalone company when the transaction closes.

Employee benefits include medical, dental, vision, AD&D and dependent life insurance; an employee assistance program and flexible spending accounts.

FINANCIAL DATA: *Note: Data for latest year may not have been available at press time.*

In U.S. $	2016	2015	2014	2013	2012	2011
Revenue	190,884,000,000	179,045,000,000	137,609,000,000	122,455,000,000	122,734,000,000	112,084,000,000
R&D Expense	392,000,000	392,000,000	456,000,000	480,000,000	440,000,000	407,000,000
Operating Income	3,545,000,000	2,968,000,000	2,367,000,000	2,315,000,000	2,149,000,000	1,821,000,000
Operating Margin %	1.85%	1.65%	1.72%	1.89%	1.75%	1.62%
SGA Expense	7,276,000,000	7,901,000,000	5,418,000,000	4,198,000,000	3,829,000,000	3,529,000,000
Net Income	2,258,000,000	1,476,000,000	1,263,000,000	1,338,000,000	1,403,000,000	1,202,000,000
Operating Cash Flow	3,672,000,000	3,112,000,000	3,136,000,000	2,483,000,000	2,950,000,000	2,338,000,000
Capital Expenditure	677,000,000	545,000,000	415,000,000	406,000,000	403,000,000	388,000,000
EBITDA	4,488,000,000	4,048,000,000	3,103,000,000	2,750,000,000	2,721,000,000	1,996,000,000
Return on Assets %	4.08%	2.79%	2.91%	3.94%	4.38%	4.06%
Return on Equity %	26.68%	17.86%	16.20%	19.25%	19.97%	16.29%
Debt to Equity	0.73	1.02	1.05	0.63	0.44	0.49

CONTACT INFORMATION:

Phone: 415 983-8300   Fax: 415 983-8453
Toll-Free: 800-826-9360
Address: 1 Post St., San Francisco, CA 94104 United States

STOCK TICKER/OTHER:

Stock Ticker: MCK   Exchange: NYS
Employees: 70,400   Fiscal Year Ends: 03/31
Parent Company:

SALARIES/BONUSES:

Top Exec. Salary: Bonus: $
$1,680,000
Second Exec. Salary: Bonus: $
$1,065,000

OTHER THOUGHTS:

Estimated Female Officers or Directors: 4

Hot Spot for Advancement for Women/Minorities: Y

McKinsey & Company Inc

www.mckinsey.com

NAIC Code: 541610

TYPES OF BUSINESS:

Management Consulting
Strategic & Logistics Consulting
Industry-Specific Consulting
Business Research
Business Publications

BRANDS/DIVISIONS/AFFILIATES:

McKinsey Global Institute
McKinsey Quarterly

CONTACTS: Note: Officers with more than one job title may be intentionally listed here more than once.

Dominic Barton, Managing Dir.

GROWTH PLANS/SPECIAL FEATURES:

McKinsey & Company, Inc. is a privately-held international management consulting firm established in 1926. Headquartered in New York, the firm maintains more than 100 offices in over 50 countries. McKinsey provides consulting services for leading businesses, governments, non-governmental organizations and non-profits. The company helps clients make improvements to their performance at every level of their organization. Business functions include analytics, business technology, digital technology, implementation, learning programs for clients, marketing & sales, operations, organization, recover & transformation services, risk, strategy & corporate finance, as well as sustainability & resource productivity. Industries served by McKinsey include advanced electronics, aerospace & defense, automotive & assembly, chemicals, consumer packaged goods, electric power & natural gas, financial services, healthcare systems & services, high tech, infrastructure, media & entertainment, metals & mining, oil & gas, paper & forest products, pharmaceuticals & medical products, private equity & principal investors, public sector, retail, semiconductors, social sector, telecommunications and travel/transport/logistics. The McKinsey Global Institute helps leaders in multiple sectors develop deeper understanding of the global economy. The firm's flagship business publication, McKinsey Quarterly, has been defining and informing the senior-management agenda since 1964.

FINANCIAL DATA: Note: Data for latest year may not have been available at press time.

In U.S. $	2016	2015	2014	2013	2012	2011
Revenue		8,300,000,000	8,000,000,000	7,150,000,000	6,375,000,000	5,450,000,000
R&D Expense						
Operating Income						
Operating Margin %						
SGA Expense						
Net Income						
Operating Cash Flow						
Capital Expenditure						
EBITDA						
Return on Assets %						
Return on Equity %						
Debt to Equity						

CONTACT INFORMATION:

Phone: 212-446-7000   Fax: 212-446-8575
Toll-Free:
Address: 55 E. 52nd St., 21st Fl., New York, NY 10022 United States

STOCK TICKER/OTHER:

Stock Ticker: Private   Exchange:
Employees: 17,000   Fiscal Year Ends: 12/31
Parent Company:

SALARIES/BONUSES:

Top Exec. Salary: $ Bonus: $
Second Exec. Salary: $ Bonus: $

OTHER THOUGHTS:

Estimated Female Officers or Directors: 2
Hot Spot for Advancement for Women/Minorities: Y

Sales, profits and employees may be estimates. Financial information, benefits and other data can change quickly and may vary from those stated here.

Mediacom Communications Corp

www.mediacomcc.com

NAIC Code: 517110

TYPES OF BUSINESS:

Cable TV Service
Internet Service
Digital Cable
Telephone Service

BRANDS/DIVISIONS/AFFILIATES:

Mediacom Online
Mediacom Online Ultra
Mediacom Phone
Home Controller

CONTACTS: *Note: Officers with more than one job title may be intentionally listed here more than once.*

Rocco B. Commisso, CEO
John G. Pascarelli, VP-Operations
Mark E. Stephan, CFO
David M. McNaughton, Sr. VP-Mktg.
Italia Commisso Weinand, Sr. VP-Human Resources & Programming
J.R. Walden, Sr. VP-Tech.
Joseph E. Young, General Counsel
John G. Pascarelli, Exec. VP-Oper.
Jack Griffin, Dir.-Corp. Finance
Edward S. Pardini, Sr. VP-Divisional Oper.-North Central Division
Brian M. Walsh, Sr. VP
Tapan Dandnaik, Sr. VP-Customer Service & Financial Oper.
Steve Litwer, Sr. VP-Advertising Sales, OnMedia Div.
Rocco B. Commisso, Chmn.

GROWTH PLANS/SPECIAL FEATURES:

Mediacom Communications Corp., a leading local cable company, supplies an array of broadband products and services to more than 1,500 communities throughout the U.S. The firm offers its customers a full array of traditional video services, which includes basic service, digital video service, pay-per-view service, high definition television, digital video recorders and video-on-demand. In addition, the company offers Mediacom Online, which offers three levels of high-speed Internet access, ranging from 3 Mbps to 20 Mbps. Mediacom's premium Internet service, Mediacom Online Ultra, allows maximum downstream and upstream speeds of 150 Mbps and 20 Mbps respectively. The firm's Mediacom Phone offers customers unlimited local, regional and long-distance calling within the U.S., Puerto Rico, U.S. Virgin Islands and Canada. It is delivered over voice over Internet protocol (VoIP) that digitizes voice signals and routes them as data packets through Mediacom's controlled broadband cable systems. It includes features such as Caller ID with name and number, call waiting, three-way calling and enhanced Emergency 911 dialing. Mediacom also offers video, HSD (high speed data), phone, network and transport services to commercial and large enterprise customers. It offers large enterprise customers who require high-bandwidth connections solutions such as the point-to-point circuits required by wireless communications providers. Additionally, Mediacom offers a home security product, Home Controller, which provides 24-hour-a-day monitoring from a UL-approved facility. In May 2016, the firm announced it would be adding a wide variety of foreign language programming, including Filipino, French, German, Italian, Korean, Russian, South-Asian and Vietnamese. Each of the channels can be purchased a la carte by any Mediacom customer subscribing to the LocalPlus TV or higher tier of video service.

FINANCIAL DATA: *Note: Data for latest year may not have been available at press time.*

In U.S. $	2016	2015	2014	2013	2012	2011
Revenue		738,710,000	711,634,000	698,861,000	681,683,000	1,550,400,000
R&D Expense						
Operating Income						
Operating Margin %						
SGA Expense						
Net Income		123,009,000	75,219,000	90,446,000	68,491,000	
Operating Cash Flow						
Capital Expenditure						
EBITDA						
Return on Assets %						
Return on Equity %						
Debt to Equity						

CONTACT INFORMATION:

Phone: 855-633-4226   Fax: 845-698-4069
Toll-Free: 800-479-2082
Address: 1 Mediacom Way, Mediacom Park, NY 10918 United States

STOCK TICKER/OTHER:

Stock Ticker: Private   Exchange:
Employees: 4,410   Fiscal Year Ends: 12/31
Parent Company:

SALARIES/BONUSES:

Top Exec. Salary: $ Bonus: $
Second Exec. Salary: $ Bonus: $

OTHER THOUGHTS:

Estimated Female Officers or Directors: 1
Hot Spot for Advancement for Women/Minorities:

Medical Information Technology Inc (MEDITECH)

www.meditech.com

NAIC Code: 0

TYPES OF BUSINESS:

Computer Software, Healthcare & Biotechnology

BRANDS/DIVISIONS/AFFILIATES:

MEDITECH 6.1 Release
Health Care Information System
MEDITECH Medication Management
Medical and Practice Management Solution
CAUTI Prevention Toolkit

CONTACTS: Note: Officers with more than one job title may be intentionally listed here more than once.

Howard Messing, CEO
Michelle O'Connor, COO
Howard Messing, Pres.
Barbara A. Manzolillo, CFO
Helen Waters, VP-Mktg. & Sales
Scott Radner, VP-Advanced Technology
Chris Anschuetz, VP-Tech.
Michelle O'Connor, Exec. VP-Prod. Dev.
Hoda Sayed-Friel, Exec. VP-Strategy & Mktg.
Barbara A. Manzolillo, Treas.
Robert Gale, Sr. VP-Prod. Dev.
Leah Farina, VP-Client Svcs. & Int'l
Scott Radner, VP-Advanced Tech.
A. Neil Pappalardo, Chmn.
Steven Koretz, Sr. VP- Int'l & Client Svcs.

GROWTH PLANS/SPECIAL FEATURES:

Medical Information Technology, Inc. (MEDITECH) develops and markets information system software for the health care industry. MEDITECH's software products automate a variety of hospital functions as well as provide products for long-term care facilities, ambulatory care centers, acute-care hospitals, emergency rooms and pharmacies, as well as imaging, therapeutic service and behavioral health facilities. The company specifies aggregate components for each hospital and suggests typical configurations from selected hardware vendors pertaining to its software needs. The firm's software products include MEDITECH 6.1 Release, an organizational interface tool; Health Care Information System, which provides health care groups with reporting tools for managing organizational performance quality; MEDITECH Medication Management, a closed loop system designed to aid in all aspects of medication delivery; Medical and Practice Management Solution software, which manages order entry, provides bedside medication verification, handles operating room management, provides nursing interface systems, creates enterprise medical records and provides patient education and discharge instructions; and software designed for long-term and home care needs. In addition, MEDITECH's corporate software can consolidate a hospital's human resources and general accounting needs, among others. In 2015, the firm launched its CAUTI Prevention Toolkit, a catheter-associated urinary tract infection (CAUTI) product that supports prevention and early detection of CAUTI events via catheter data, guidance and clinical decision support notifications.

The firm offers employees benefits such as medical, dental, AD&D, life and long-term disability insurance; educational assistance; paid time off; a profit sharing plan; and an annual bonus.

FINANCIAL DATA: Note: Data for latest year may not have been available at press time.

In U.S. $	2016	2015	2014	2013	2012	2011
Revenue		610,000,000	590,000,000	582,000,000	597,800,000	545,224,384
R&D Expense						
Operating Income						
Operating Margin %						
SGA Expense						
Net Income						
Operating Cash Flow						
Capital Expenditure						
EBITDA						
Return on Assets %						
Return on Equity %						
Debt to Equity						

CONTACT INFORMATION:

Phone: 781-821-3000   Fax: 781-821-2199
Toll-Free:
Address: Meditech Circle, Westwood, MA 02090 United States

STOCK TICKER/OTHER:

Stock Ticker: Private   Exchange:
Employees: 4,068   Fiscal Year Ends: 12/31
Parent Company:

SALARIES/BONUSES:

Top Exec. Salary: $ Bonus: $
Second Exec. Salary: $ Bonus: $

OTHER THOUGHTS:

Estimated Female Officers or Directors: 10
Hot Spot for Advancement for Women/Minorities: Y

MedStar Health

NAIC Code: 622110

www.medstarhealth.org

TYPES OF BUSINESS:

General Medical and Surgical Hospitals
Assisted Living Services
Home Health Services
Ambulatory Centers
Rehabilitation Centers
Nursing Homes
Physician Network Management
Research

BRANDS/DIVISIONS/AFFILIATES:

MedStar Franklin Square Medical Center
MedStar Good Samaritan Hospital
MedStar Harbor Hospital
MedStar Montgomery Medical Center
MedStar Southern Maryland Hospital Center
MedStar National Rehabilitation Hospital
MedStar Physician Partners
MedStar Health Research Institute

CONTACTS: Note: Officers with more than one job title may be intentionally listed here more than once.

Kenneth A. Samet, CEO
Joy Drass, COO
Kenneth A. Samet, Pres.
Michael J. Curran, CFO
Kevin P. Kowalski, Exec. VP-Mktg.
David P. Noe, VP-Human Resources
Stephen R.T. Evans, Chief Medical Officer
Michael J. Curran, Chief Admin. Officer
Oliver M. Johnson, II, General Counsel
Eric R. Wagner, Exec. VP-Diversified Oper. & External Affairs
Christine M. Swearingen, Exec. VP-Planning & Community Rel.
Jean Hitchcock, VP-Public Affairs & Mktg.
Susan K. Nelson, VP-Finance & Acct. Oper.
Carl Schindelar, Exec. VP-Oper., Baltimore Region
Jennie P. McConagha, Chief of Staff
Joel N. Bryan, Treas.
Pegeen Townsend, VP-Gov't Affairs
William R. Roberts, Chmn.

GROWTH PLANS/SPECIAL FEATURES:

MedStar Health is a nonprofit, community-based health care organization primarily composed of several integrated businesses, including 10 major hospitals, with 30,000 associates and 6,000 affiliated physicians. The hospitals are located within proximity of the Baltimore/Washington, D.C area and include the following: MedStar Franklin Square Medical Center, MedStar Good Samaritan Hospital, MedStar Harbor Hospital, MedStar Montgomery Medical Center, MedStar Southern Maryland Hospital Center, MedStar St. Mary's Hospital, MedStar Union Memorial Hospital, MedStar Georgetown University Hospital, MedStar Washington Hospital Center and MedStar National Rehabilitation Hospital. The hospitals' services include primary, urgent and sub-acute care; behavioral health and psychiatric services; medical education; and research. MedStar also provides assisted living, home health, hospice and long-term care and operates nursing homes, senior housing, adult day care, rehabilitation and ambulatory centers. MedStar serves roughly 140,000 inpatients, over 4.3 million outpatients and conducts 266,778 home health visits annually. The organization manages MedStar Physician Partners, a comprehensive physician network serving in the region. Its MedStar Health Research Institute conducts research and clinical trials; and MedStar Health has one of the largest graduate medical education programs in the country, training more than 1,100 medical residents annually, and is the medical education and clinical partner of Georgetown University. In July 2016, the firm opened its newest healthcare facility in Brandywine, Maryland comprising a state-of-the-art, 60,000-square-foot facility which brings medical specialists from MedStar Georgetown University Hospital, MedStar Washington Hospital Center and MedStar National Rehabilitation Network to one location, along with primary care, radiology and laboratory services.

MedStar's employees are offered health, dental and vision insurance; flexible spending accounts; an employee assistance program; paid leave; a tax deferred retirement savings plan; life & disability insurance; and tuition assistance.

FINANCIAL DATA: Note: Data for latest year may not have been available at press time.

In U.S. $	2016	2015	2014	2013	2012	2011
Revenue		5,030,000,000	4,620,000,000	4,200,000,000	4,175,900,000	4,017,200,000
R&D Expense						
Operating Income						
Operating Margin %						
SGA Expense						
Net Income		160,100,000	110,000,000	79,000,000	69,900,000	312,200,000
Operating Cash Flow						
Capital Expenditure						
EBITDA						
Return on Assets %						
Return on Equity %						
Debt to Equity						

CONTACT INFORMATION:

Phone: 410-772-6500   Fax: 410-715-3905
Toll-Free: 877-772-6505
Address: 5565 Sterrett Place, 5th Fl., Columbia, MD 21044 United States

STOCK TICKER/OTHER:

Stock Ticker: Nonprofit   Exchange:
Employees: 31,000   Fiscal Year Ends: 06/30
Parent Company:

SALARIES/BONUSES:

Top Exec. Salary: $ Bonus: $
Second Exec. Salary: $ Bonus: $

OTHER THOUGHTS:

Estimated Female Officers or Directors: 15
Hot Spot for Advancement for Women/Minorities: Y

Medtronic Inc

NAIC Code: 334510

www.medtronic.com

TYPES OF BUSINESS:

Equipment-Defibrillators & Pacing Products
Neurological Devices
Diabetes Management Devices
Ear, Nose & Throat Surgical Equipment
Pain Management Devices
Cardiac Surgery Equipment

BRANDS/DIVISIONS/AFFILIATES:

Aptus Endosystems Inc
Medina Medical
Lazarus Effect
Twelve Inc
Airlift Medical
Advanced Uro-Solutions
Covidien plc

CONTACTS: Note: Officers with more than one job title may be intentionally listed here more than once.

Omar Ishrak, CEO
Karen Parkhill, CFO
Michael Coyle, Executive VP
Hooman Hakami, Executive VP
Robert Hoedt, Executive VP
Bryan Hanson, Executive VP
Bradley Lerman, General Counsel
Carol Surface, Other Executive Officer
Geoffrey Martha, President, Divisional

GROWTH PLANS/SPECIAL FEATURES:

Medtronic, Inc. is a global leader in medical device technology, serving physicians, clinicians and patients in more than 160 countries worldwide. Its operations consist of four primary segments: the cardiac and vascular group, which includes the cardiac rhythm disease management (CRDM), as well as coronary, structural heart and endovascular therapies; the restorative therapies group, which includes the spinal, neuromodulation, diabetes and surgical technologies divisions; the minimally invasive technologies group, which includes surgical and patient monitoring and recovery solutions;and the diabetes group, which includes advanced diabetes management solutions. Products in the CRDM division manage cardiac rhythm disorders and include pacemakers, implantable defibrillators, ablation products and products for the treatment of atrial fibrillation (AF). The coronary, structural heart and endovascular therapies unit makes technology that supports the interventional treatment of coronary artery disease to help improve blood flow, and includes products such as stents, guide wires, and catheters. The spinal division offers medical devices used to treat spinal and cranial conditions. The neuromodulation division develops devices for the treatment of neurological, urological and gastroenterological disorders. The surgical technologies division develops and manufactures minimally invasive products to treat ear, nose and throat (ENT) and neurological diseases. The patient monitoring and recovery develops and markets sensors, monitors and temperature management products, as well as products and therapies for complication-free recovery. The diabetes unit develops integrated diabetes management systems, insulin pump therapies, continuous glucose monitoring systems and therapy management software. In 2015, the firm acquired Aptus Endosystems, Inc.; Covidien plc; Advanced Uro-Solutions; Medina Medical; Lazarus Effect; Twelve, Inc.; and Airlift Medical. That same year Medtronic agreed to acquire FR Surgical Systems, Inc.

The firm offers employees health care and disability, adoption and elder care assistance, retirement plans and stock options.

FINANCIAL DATA: Note: Data for latest year may not have been available at press time.

In U.S. $	2016	2015	2014	2013	2012	2011
Revenue	28,833,000,000	20,261,000,000	17,005,000,000	16,590,000,000	16,184,000,000	15,933,000,000
R&D Expense	2,224,000,000	1,640,000,000	1,477,000,000	1,557,000,000	1,490,000,000	1,508,000,000
Operating Income	5,291,000,000	3,766,000,000	3,813,000,000	4,251,000,000	4,658,000,000	3,723,000,000
Operating Margin %	18.35%	18.58%	22.42%	25.62%	28.78%	23.36%
SGA Expense	9,469,000,000	6,904,000,000	5,847,000,000	5,698,000,000	5,623,000,000	5,533,000,000
Net Income	3,538,000,000	2,675,000,000	3,065,000,000	3,467,000,000	3,617,000,000	3,096,000,000
Operating Cash Flow	5,218,000,000	4,902,000,000	4,959,000,000	4,883,000,000	4,470,000,000	3,741,000,000
Capital Expenditure	1,046,000,000	571,000,000	396,000,000	457,000,000	499,000,000	548,000,000
EBITDA	8,542,000,000	5,458,000,000	4,934,000,000	5,221,000,000	5,327,000,000	4,977,000,000
Return on Assets %	3.42%	3.69%	8.42%	10.20%	11.39%	10.58%
Return on Equity %	6.72%	7.36%	16.08%	19.37%	21.86%	20.23%
Debt to Equity	0.58	0.63	0.53	0.52	0.43	0.50

CONTACT INFORMATION:

Phone: 763 514-4000   Fax: 763 514-4000
Toll-Free: 800-633-8766
Address: 710 Medtronic Pkwy., Minneapolis, MN 55432 United States

STOCK TICKER/OTHER:

Stock Ticker: MDT
Employees: 92,000
Parent Company:

Exchange: NYS
Fiscal Year Ends: 04/30

SALARIES/BONUSES:

Top Exec. Salary:
$1,548,216
Second Exec. Salary:
$749,039

Bonus: $

Bonus: $250,000

OTHER THOUGHTS:

Estimated Female Officers or Directors: 5

Hot Spot for Advancement for Women/Minorities: Y

Sales, profits and employees may be estimates. Financial information, benefits and other data can change quickly and may vary from those stated here.

Menard Inc

NAIC Code: 444110

TYPES OF BUSINESS:

Home Improvement Stores
Lumber
Housing Materials
Building Materials Manufacturing
Prefabricated Houses

BRANDS/DIVISIONS/AFFILIATES:

Menards
Midwest Manufacturing
MasterForce
MasterCraft
Dakota
Grip Fast
Tuscany
Tool Shop

CONTACTS: Note: Officers with more than one job title may be intentionally listed here more than once.

John R. Menard, Jr., Pres.
Charlie Menard, General Manager

GROWTH PLANS/SPECIAL FEATURES:

Menard, Inc. is a family-owned company that began in 1960 headquartered in Eau Claire, Wisconsin and has 280 home improvement stores. The company's Menards-branded stores are located throughout the Midwest in a 14-state region: Illinois, Indiana, Iowa, Kansas, Kentucky, Michigan, Minnesota, Missouri, Nebraska, North Dakota, Ohio, South Dakota, Wisconsin and Wyoming. The firm's departments include appliances; bath; building materials; doors, windows and millwork; electrical; flooring and rugs; grocery and pet; heating and cooling; home and dÃ©cor; kitchen; lighting and ceiling fans; maintenance, repair and operations; outdoors; paint; plumbing; home and patio; storage and organization; and tools and hardware. Menards provides a number of quality brands such as Midwest Manufacturing, Masterforce, Dakota, Mastercraft, Grip Fast, Tuscany, Tool Shop and Enchanted Garden/Enchanted Forest. The company's subsidiary, Midwest Manufacturing, operates a number of manufacturing facilities in Wisconsin, Illinois, Ohio, Nebraska, Iowa and Minnesota. Menard has four distribution centers in Plato, Illinois; Shelby, Iowa; Holiday City, Ohio; and Eau Claire, Wisconsin.

The company offers employees medical, dental and disability insurance; a profit sharing program; advancement opportunities; 401(k); store discounts; and bonuses.

FINANCIAL DATA: Note: Data for latest year may not have been available at press time.

In U.S. $	2016	2015	2014	2013	2012	2011
Revenue		8,970,000,000	8,710,000,000	7,775,000,000	7,600,000,000	7,475,000,000
R&D Expense						
Operating Income						
Operating Margin %						
SGA Expense						
Net Income						
Operating Cash Flow						
Capital Expenditure						
EBITDA						
Return on Assets %						
Return on Equity %						
Debt to Equity						

CONTACT INFORMATION:

Phone: 715-876-5911   Fax: 715-876-2868
Toll-Free:
Address: 5101 Menard Drive, Eau Claire, WI 54703 United States

STOCK TICKER/OTHER:

Stock Ticker: Private   Exchange:
Employees: 46,500   Fiscal Year Ends: 01/31
Parent Company:

SALARIES/BONUSES:

Top Exec. Salary: $ Bonus: $
Second Exec. Salary: $ Bonus: $

OTHER THOUGHTS:

Estimated Female Officers or Directors:
Hot Spot for Advancement for Women/Minorities:

Mentor Graphics Corp

www.mentor.com

NAIC Code: 0

TYPES OF BUSINESS:

Software-Component Design, Simulation & Testing
Electronic Design Automation Tools
Consulting Services

BRANDS/DIVISIONS/AFFILIATES:

Veloce
Calibre
Questa
Olympus-SoC
Xpedition Series (The)
Flexras Technologies
Tanner EDA
Calypto Design Systems Inc

CONTACTS: Note: Officers with more than one job title may be intentionally listed here more than once.

Walden Rhines, CEO
Gregory Hinckley, CFO
Richard Trebing, Chief Accounting Officer
Michael Ellow, Senior VP, Divisional
Brian Derrick, Vice President, Divisional
Dean Freed, Vice President

GROWTH PLANS/SPECIAL FEATURES:

Mentor Graphics Corp. is a supplier of electronic design automation (EDA) systems, advanced computer software and emulation hardware products used to automate the design, analysis and testing of electronic hardware and embedded systems and components. These products are primarily marketed to large companies in the military, aerospace, communications, computer, consumer electronics, semiconductor, networking, multimedia and transportation industries. The company's offerings include Scalable Verification products, integrated circuit (IC) design and integrated system design. Scalable Verification products help engineers verify that their IC designs function as needed. Products in this category include Questa, a scalable verification platform that includes support, simulation and verification technologies for extended verification of systems and ICs, and hardware emulation systems, such as the Veloce product family. IC design products consist of the Calibre and Olympus-SoC (system-on-chip) product lines. Calibre tools are designed to aid customers in the design process of ICs at the nanometer (nm) level. Olympus-SoC products are designed for creating ICs with geometries of 65 nm and below. Integrated system design products support the printed circuit board (PCB) and field-programmable gate array (FPGA) design process with products such as The Xpedition Series, PADS, I/O Designer, XtremePCB and XtremeAR. Mentor sells and licenses its products through a direct sales force as well as distributors and sales representatives. In 2015, the firm acquired Flexras Technologies, Tanner EDA and Calypto Design Systems, Inc.

Employees of Mentor receive a 401(k); adoption assistance; a discount stock purchase plan; medical, dental, vision and prescription drug coverage; life and AD&D insurance; and tuition reimbursement.

FINANCIAL DATA: Note: Data for latest year may not have been available at press time.

In U.S. $	2016	2015	2014	2013	2012	2011
Revenue	1,180,988,000	1,244,133,000	1,156,373,000	1,088,727,000	1,014,638,000	914,753,000
R&D Expense	381,440,000	381,125,000	348,817,000	313,962,000	310,758,000	284,851,000
Operating Income	136,745,000	187,811,000	183,040,000	161,633,000	112,192,000	52,539,000
Operating Margin %	11.57%	15.09%	15.82%	14.84%	11.05%	5.74%
SGA Expense	425,197,000	444,881,000	418,342,000	412,977,000	401,419,000	421,205,000
Net Income	96,277,000	147,139,000	155,258,000	138,736,000	83,872,000	28,584,000
Operating Cash Flow	228,596,000	138,208,000	149,703,000	139,287,000	103,938,000	82,208,000
Capital Expenditure	43,336,000	48,366,000	30,761,000	45,130,000	41,555,000	47,175,000
EBITDA	199,779,000	245,080,000	234,974,000	213,752,000	167,955,000	107,366,000
Return on Assets %	4.68%	7.44%	8.50%	8.41%	5.63%	2.15%
Return on Equity %	7.42%	11.97%	13.99%	14.60%	10.21%	4.03%
Debt to Equity	0.18	0.18	0.18	0.21	0.24	0.26

CONTACT INFORMATION:

Phone: 503 685-7000   Fax: 503 685-1202
Toll-Free: 800-592-2210
Address: 8005 SW Boeckman Rd., Wilsonville, OR 97070 United States

STOCK TICKER/OTHER:

Stock Ticker: MENT   Exchange: NAS
Employees: 5,558   Fiscal Year Ends: 01/31
Parent Company:

SALARIES/BONUSES:

Top Exec. Salary: $761,000   Bonus: $
Second Exec. Salary: $619,000 Bonus: $

OTHER THOUGHTS:

Estimated Female Officers or Directors:
Hot Spot for Advancement for Women/Minorities:

Mercedes-Benz USA LLC

NAIC Code: 336111

www.mbusa.com

TYPES OF BUSINESS:

Automobile Manufacturing
Marketing & Sales Services
Dealership

BRANDS/DIVISIONS/AFFILIATES:

Daimler AG
Mercedex-Benz U.S. International Inc
AMG Driving Academy

CONTACTS: Note: Officers with more than one job title may be intentionally listed here more than once.

Dietmar Exler, CEO
Harald Henn, CFO
Ola Kallenius, VP-Mktg. & Sales
Norbert H. Litzkow, Chief Technology Officer
Matthew E. Roy, VP-Admin.
Michelle D. Spreitzer, General Counsel
Donna Boland, Mgr.-Corp. Comm.

GROWTH PLANS/SPECIAL FEATURES:

Mercedes-Benz USA LLC (MBUSA), a wholly-owne subsidiary of Daimler AG, sells, services, distributes an markets Mercedes-Benz cars and light trucks and Maybac super-luxury sedans throughout the U.S. MBUSA's vehicle include the C-, E- and S-Class and Maybach sedans; C-, E and S-Class, CLA, CLS and AMG GT S coupes; G- and E Class, GLA, GLC, GLE, GLE Coupe and GLS sport utilit vehicles (SUVs) and wagons; SLC- and SL-Class roadsters the E- and S-Class Cabriolet convertibles; and the B-Class, C Class, S-Class and GLE hybrid and electric sedans and SUVs The firm sells these vehicles through a network of more tha 300 independently owned dealerships in the U.S. MBUSA als provides sales, marketing and other services to Mercedes Benz dealerships. Company certified collision centers are located in Alabama, Alaska, Arizona, California, Colorad Connecticut, Delaware, District of Columbia, Florida, Georgia Hawaii and Idaho. Mercedes-Benz U.S. International, Inc (MBUSI), a division of Mercedes-Benz and a subsidiary o Daimler AG, operates a Mercedes-Benz automobil manufacturing plant near Vance, Alabama, which i approximately 3.2 million square feet in size and sits on a 966 acre plot. In addition, the company operates the AMG Drivin Academy, a teen driving school in Los Angeles; and a 71,000 square-foot research and development facility in Sunnyvale California. In 2015, the firm moved its headquarters from New Jersey to Atlanta, Georgia.

Employee benefits include medical, dental, vision, short- an long-term disability, life, AD&D, automobile, home and pe insurance; domestic partner benefits; flexible spending accounts; paid holidays; and a 401(k). The firm has been liste in Fortune magazine's 100 Best Companies to Work For, an noted by the Great Place to Work Institute.

FINANCIAL DATA: Note: Data for latest year may not have been available at press time.

In U.S. $	2016	2015	2014	2013	2012	2011
Revenue		43,260,000,000	41,197,513,000	38,394,700,000	33,556,967,000	
R&D Expense						
Operating Income						
Operating Margin %						
SGA Expense						
Net Income		152,378,099	219,621,273	94,128,328	409,015,739	
Operating Cash Flow						
Capital Expenditure						
EBITDA						
Return on Assets %						
Return on Equity %						
Debt to Equity						

CONTACT INFORMATION:

Phone: 201-573-0600   Fax: 201-573-0117
Toll-Free: 800-367-6372
Address: 303 Perimeter Ctr. N., Atlanta, GA 30346 United States

STOCK TICKER/OTHER:

Stock Ticker: Subsidiary
Employees: 22,833
Parent Company: Daimler AG

Exchange:
Fiscal Year Ends: 12/31

SALARIES/BONUSES:

Top Exec. Salary: $ Bonus: $
Second Exec. Salary: $ Bonus: $

OTHER THOUGHTS:

Estimated Female Officers or Directors: 2
Hot Spot for Advancement for Women/Minorities:

Sales, profits and employees may be estimates. Financial information, benefits and other data can change quickly and may vary from those stated here.

Mercer LLC

www.mercer.com

NAIC Code: 541612

TYPES OF BUSINESS:

Consulting-Human Resources
Investment/Financial Consulting
Health and Benefits Management
Human Capital Consulting
Outsourced Human Resources Services (BPO)
Investment Management
Retirement Plan Administration
Merger/Acquisition Consulting

BRANDS/DIVISIONS/AFFILIATES:

Marsh & McLennan Companies Inc

CONTACTS: *Note: Officers with more than one job title may be intentionally listed here more than once.*

Julio A. Portalatin, CEO
Ken Haderer, COO
Julio A. Portalatin, Pres.
Helen Shan, CFO
Rian Miller, General Counsel
David Rahill, Pres., Health & Benefits
Phil de Cristo, Pres., Investments
Patricia Milligan, Pres., North America
Orlando Ashford, Pres., Talent
Simon O'Regan, Pres., EuroPac

GROWTH PLANS/SPECIAL FEATURES:

Mercer LLC, a subsidiary of Marsh & McLennan Companies, Inc., offers a broad range of human resource advice and solutions in 42 countries. The firm divides its services into four categories: health & benefits, wealth & investments, workforce & careers and mergers & acquisitions. Health & benefits include private health exchange, employee benefits, global benefits, health benefits administration and affinity benefits. Wealth & investments include retirement plan administration, defined benefit pension plans, pension risk management, defined contribution plans, employee financial wellness, alternative investments, endowments & foundations and financial intermediary partnerships. Workforce & careers include talent strategy, executive compensation, workforce rewards, talent mobility, human resource transformation and employee communication. Mergers & acquisitions (MA) include M&A due diligence, M&A project management office, post-merger integration and private equity advisory. Mercer provides its solutions and services for those in business roles such as CEOs, boards, CFOs, talent leaders, benefits managers, financial advisors, trustees & fiduciaries and employees; for organizations such as corporations, multinational corporations, endowments & foundations, affinity, public sector, wealth management and private equity; and for industries such as energy, insurance, health care, financial services, higher education and retail. Based in New York, USA, the firm has offices throughout the world, including North America, Latin America, Europe, the Middle East, Africa, Asia-Pacific, Australia and New Zealand.

Employees of the firm receive benefits including medical, dental, life, disability and vision coverage; health club discounts; legal assistance; eldercare; continuing education programs; an employee stock purchase plan; paid vacations; tuition reimbursement; and family resource programs.

FINANCIAL DATA: *Note: Data for latest year may not have been available at press time.*

In U.S. $	2016	2015	2014	2013	2012	2011
Revenue		4,313,000,000	4,350,000,000	4,241,000,000	4,147,000,000	3,782,000,000
R&D Expense						
Operating Income						
Operating Margin %						
SGA Expense						
Net Income						
Operating Cash Flow						
Capital Expenditure						
EBITDA						
Return on Assets %						
Return on Equity %						
Debt to Equity						

CONTACT INFORMATION:

Phone: 212-345-7000   Fax: 212-345-7414
Toll-Free:
Address: 1166 Ave. of the Americas, New York, NY 10036 United States

STOCK TICKER/OTHER:

Stock Ticker: Subsidiary   Exchange:
Employees: 21,000   Fiscal Year Ends: 12/31
Parent Company: Marsh & McLennan Companies Inc

SALARIES/BONUSES:

Top Exec. Salary: $ Bonus: $
Second Exec. Salary: $ Bonus: $

OTHER THOUGHTS:

Estimated Female Officers or Directors: 2
Hot Spot for Advancement for Women/Minorities: Y

Mercy

NAIC Code: 622110

TYPES OF BUSINESS:

General Medical and Surgical Hospitals
Outpatient Care
Health Classes
Long-Term Care
Community Service & Outreach

BRANDS/DIVISIONS/AFFILIATES:

Mississippi Health Advocacy
Mercy Ministries of Laredo
Mercy Family Center of New Orleans
Roi

CONTACTS: *Note: Officers with more than one job title may be intentionally listed here more than once.*

Lynn Britton, Pres.
Michael McCurry, COO
Shannon Sock, CFO
Donn Sorensen, Regional Pres., East Communities
Diana Smalley, Regional Pres., West Communities
Shannon Sock, Exec. VP-Organizational Effectiveness
Kim Day, Regional Pres., Central Communities

GROWTH PLANS/SPECIAL FEATURES:

Mercy, established in 1986, is one of the largest Catholic health care systems in the U.S. It is sponsored by the St. Louis Regional Community of the Sisters of Mercy religious order. It operates outpatient clinics, physician practices, hospitals, managed health plans and community outreach programs in seven states: Arkansas, Kansas, Mississippi, Missouri, Texas, Louisiana and Oklahoma. The organization's members include 11 specialty hospitals, including heart, children's, rehab and orthopedic; more than 700 clinic and outpatient care facilities; 46 acute care hospitals; and more than 2,000 Mercy clinic physicians. The group also operates the Mississippi Health Advocacy program, an active advocacy program for issues of social justice, especially in the field of health care, providing participants with updates on issues of concern and the means of contacting elected officials. Mercy offers a variety of free or inexpensive classes at its hospitals, including a healing-through-the-arts program, babysitter skills training, massage classes, infant care and CPR/first aid classes as well as substance abuse and terminal illness support groups. With outreach programs in Louisiana and Mississippi, Mercy allocates money for subsidized care, community outreach ministries and charity care. It also operates Mercy Ministries of Laredo, an outpatient program that provides services primarily for women, children and the poor; and Mercy Family Center of New Orleans, an outpatient behavioral health clinic for treatment of childhood disorders. ROi, the firm's supply chain operating division, provides purchasing, product and pharmaceutical distribution services and custom procedure tray manufacturing services.

The company offers employees medical, dental, vision, life and long-term disability coverage; a pension and 401(k) plan; tuition reimbursement; and a co-worker assistance plan for employees and their immediate family members.

FINANCIAL DATA: *Note: Data for latest year may not have been available at press time.*

In U.S. $	2016	2015	2014	2013	2012	2011
Revenue		5,000,000,000	4,510,184,000	4,380,885,000	4,200,000,000	4,300,000,000
R&D Expense						
Operating Income						
Operating Margin %						
SGA Expense						
Net Income						
Operating Cash Flow						
Capital Expenditure						
EBITDA						
Return on Assets %						
Return on Equity %						
Debt to Equity						

CONTACT INFORMATION:

Phone: 956-718-6810   Fax:
Toll-Free:
Address: 2500 Zacatecas Street, Laredo, TX 78046 United States

STOCK TICKER/OTHER:

Stock Ticker: Nonprofit   Exchange:
Employees: 40,000   Fiscal Year Ends: 06/30
Parent Company:

SALARIES/BONUSES:

Top Exec. Salary: $ Bonus: $
Second Exec. Salary: $ Bonus: $

OTHER THOUGHTS:

Estimated Female Officers or Directors: 10
Hot Spot for Advancement for Women/Minorities: Y

Merrill Lynch & Co Inc

www.ml.com

NAIC Code: 523110

TYPES OF BUSINESS:

Stock Brokerage & Investment Banking
Research Services
Financial Planning Services

BRANDS/DIVISIONS/AFFILIATES:

Bank of America Corp
Merill Edge

CONTACTS: Note: Officers with more than one job title may be intentionally listed here more than once.

John Thiel, Head-Merrill Lynch Wealth Management
John Hogarty, COO-GWIM
Alexandre Bettamio, CEO-Brazilian Oper.
Manuel Ebner, CEO-Merrill Lynch Capital Markets AG
Brian T. Moynihan, Chmn.

GROWTH PLANS/SPECIAL FEATURES:

Merrill Lynch & Co., Inc., a wholly owned subsidiary of Bank of America Corp., is a wealth management, capital markets and advisory firm. The firm is one of the largest brokerages in the world, managing over $2.2 trillion in client assets. The company provides banking, investing, asset management and other financial and risk management products and services to its clients. The company's services include corporate and investment banking services, such as commercial lending, high-yield debt, equity and mergers and acquisitions review; personal wealth management; private banking; and retail brokerage. Merrill Lynch operates in three segments: global wealth and investment management (GWIM), global research and global banking and markets. GWIM primarily provides wealth management services to high-net-worth individuals and institutions, with a focus on retirement plans, philanthropic planning and asset management. This division utilizes Merrill Edge, a self-directing electronic platform that provides clients with access to Merrill Lynch investing and Bank of America banking. GWIM also offers an online Special Needs Calculator to help caregivers of individuals with special needs ensure a lifetime of financial security. The global research segment informs and supports customer decisions by analyzing prospective companies, hedge funds, mutual funds, pension funds, wealth management funds and other investment targets. The global banking and markets segment services corporations, institutions and government entities with debt underwriting, financing and other banking services.

FINANCIAL DATA: Note: Data for latest year may not have been available at press time.

In U.S. $	2016	2015	2014	2013	2012	2011
Revenue		14,898,000,000	15,256,000,000	14,771,000,000	13,800,000,000	13,500,000,000
R&D Expense						
Operating Income						
Operating Margin %						
SGA Expense						
Net Income			2,465,000,000	2,469,000,000	1,876,000,000	1,270,000,000
Operating Cash Flow						
Capital Expenditure						
EBITDA						
Return on Assets %						
Return on Equity %						
Debt to Equity						

CONTACT INFORMATION:

Phone: 212-449-1000   Fax: 212-449-9418
Toll-Free: 800-637-7455
Address: 250 Vesey St., 4 World Financial Center, New York, NY 10080
United States

STOCK TICKER/OTHER:

Stock Ticker: Subsidiary   Exchange:
Employees: 52,000   Fiscal Year Ends: 12/31
Parent Company: BANK OF AMERICA CORP

SALARIES/BONUSES:

Top Exec. Salary: $ Bonus: $
Second Exec. Salary: $ Bonus: $

OTHER THOUGHTS:

Estimated Female Officers or Directors: 2
Hot Spot for Advancement for Women/Minorities:

MetLife Inc
NAIC Code: 524113

www.metlife.com

TYPES OF BUSINESS:
Insurance
Banking
Investment Products
Mutual Funds
Life Insurance
Property & Casualty Insurance
Auto Insurance

BRANDS/DIVISIONS/AFFILIATES:
Administradora de Fondos de Pensiones Provida SA
Brighthouse Financial

CONTACTS: Note: Officers with more than one job title may be intentionally listed here more than once.
Steven Kandarian, CEO
John Hele, CFO
Peter Carlson, Chief Accounting Officer
Ricardo Anzaldua, Executive VP
Frans Hijkoop, Executive VP
Martin Lippert, Executive VP
Maria Morris, Executive VP
Esther Lee, Executive VP
Steven Goulart, Executive VP
Michel Khalaf, President, Geographical
Christopher Townsend, President, Geographical
Timothy Ring, Secretary

GROWTH PLANS/SPECIAL FEATURES:
MetLife, Inc. is a provider of insurance and other financial services with operations throughout the world. Through its domestic and international subsidiaries and affiliates, the company provides insurance, annuities and employee benefit programs. The firm is organized into six segments, reflecting three broad geographic regions: retail; group, voluntary & worksite benefits; corporate benefit funding; Latin America (Americas); Asia; and Europe, the Middle East and Africa (EMEA). The retail segment is organized into two businesses: life & other and annuities. Retail's major products within life & other are: variable life, universal life, term life, whole life, disability and property & casualty insurance. Products within annuities are variable and fixed. The group, voluntary and worksite benefits segment offers life, dental, disability, long-term care and property and casualty. The corporate benefit funding segment provides funding and financing solutions that help institutional customers mitigate and manage liabilities associated with their qualified, nonqualified and welfare employee benefit programs. Products offered in this segment are stable value products, pension closeouts, torts and settlement and capital market investment products. The Americas segment includes operations in seven countries: Argentina, Brazil, Chile, Colombia, Ecuador, Mexico, and Uruguay. It offers accident & health insurance; and private pension funds in Chile through Administradora de Fondos de Pensiones Provida SA. In Asia, the firm provides life, accident & health and credit insurance; and retirement and savings products in 10 countries. The EMEA segment includes 29 countries with business engagements in retirement and savings products; and life, accident & health and credit insurance. In July 2016, the firm announced plans to spin-off its U.S. retail division into a separate company called Brighthouse Financial.

The company offers employees medical, prescription and dental insurance; disability & life insurance; flexible spending accounts; and pension & 401(k) plans.

FINANCIAL DATA: Note: Data for latest year may not have been available at press time.

In U.S. $	2016	2015	2014	2013	2012	2011
Revenue		69,951,000,000	73,316,000,000	68,199,000,000	68,150,000,000	70,262,000,000
R&D Expense						
Operating Income		7,470,000,000	8,804,000,000	4,052,000,000	1,442,000,000	10,026,000,000
Operating Margin %		10.67%	12.00%	5.94%	2.11%	14.26%
SGA Expense		12,460,000,000	12,338,000,000	13,512,000,000	14,662,000,000	14,151,000,000
Net Income		5,310,000,000	6,309,000,000	3,368,000,000	1,324,000,000	6,981,000,000
Operating Cash Flow		14,129,000,000	16,376,000,000	16,131,000,000	17,160,000,000	10,290,000,000
Capital Expenditure						
EBITDA						
Return on Assets %		.57%	.69%	.37%	.14%	.87%
Return on Equity %		7.35%	9.26%	5.15%	1.93%	12.38%
Debt to Equity		0.31	0.27	0.35	0.34	0.44

CONTACT INFORMATION:
Phone: 212 578-2211   Fax: 212 578-3320
Toll-Free: 800-638-5433
Address: 200 Park Ave., New York, NY 10166 United States

STOCK TICKER/OTHER:
Stock Ticker: MET   Exchange: NYS
Employees: 68,000   Fiscal Year Ends: 12/31
Parent Company:

SALARIES/BONUSES:
Top Exec. Salary: Bonus: $
$1,425,000
Second Exec. Salary: Bonus: $199,659
$587,236

OTHER THOUGHTS:
Estimated Female Officers or Directors: 5

Hot Spot for Advancement for Women/Minorities: Y

Microsoft Corp

www.microsoft.com

NAIC Code: 0

TYPES OF BUSINESS:

Computer Software, Operating Systems, Languages & Development Tools
Enterprise Software
Game Consoles
Operating Systems
Software as a Service (SAAS)
Search Engine and Advertising
E-Mail Services
Instant Messaging

BRANDS/DIVISIONS/AFFILIATES:

Xbox LIVE
Microsoft Windows
Microsoft Office
Office 365 Consumer
Xbox
Skype
Microsoft Dynamics

CONTACTS: Note: Officers with more than one job title may be intentionally listed here more than once.

Satya Nadella, CEO
Amy Hood, CFO
John Thompson, Chairman of the Board
Frank Brod, Chief Accounting Officer
William Gates, Co-Founder
Margaret Johnson, Executive VP, Divisional
Kathleen Hogan, Executive VP, Divisional
Christopher Capossela, Executive VP
Jean-Philippe Courtois, Executive VP
Bradford Smith, Other Executive Officer

GROWTH PLANS/SPECIAL FEATURES:

Microsoft Corp. develops and markets software, services and hardware devices. The company operates in two divisions: devices & consumer (D&C) and commercial. The D&C segment develops, manufactures, market and supports products and services designed to increase productivity, simplify tasks, entertain and connect people and help advertisers connect with audiences. The D&C segment is made up of D&C licensing; computing & gaming hardware, phone hardware and D&C other. The principal products of the D&C Licensing unit are: Windows, including original equipment manufacturer licensing and other non-volume licensing and academic volume licensing of the Windows operating system and related software; non-volume licensing of Microsoft Office for consumers; Windows Phone operating system, including related patent licensing; and certain other patent licensing revenue. The principal products of the computing & gaming hardware unit are: Xbox gaming and entertainment consoles and accessories, video game royalties and Xbox Live subscriptions; surface devices and accessories; and Microsoft PC accessories. The principal products of the D&C other unit are: resale, including the Windows Store, Xbox Live transactions and the Windows Phone Store; search advertising; display advertising; Office 365 Consumer; studios; and Microsoft retail stores. The commercial division develops, markets and supports software and services designed to increase productivity and efficiency, and to simplify everyday tasks through seamless operations across hardware and software. This division consists of the commercial licensing and commercial other segments. Products provided by the commercial segments include: server products; Windows Embedded; volume licensing of the Windows operating system, excluding academic; Microsoft Office for business; Skype; and Microsoft Dynamics business solutions.

Microsoft offers its employees health, dental and vision coverage; onsite health screenings; adoption assistance; childcare service discounts; a 401(k) plan; an employee stock purchase plan; and tuition assistance.

FINANCIAL DATA: Note: Data for latest year may not have been available at press time.

In U.S. $	2016	2015	2014	2013	2012	2011
Revenue	85,320,000,000	93,580,000,000	86,833,000,000	77,849,000,000	73,723,000,000	69,943,000,000
R&D Expense	11,988,000,000	12,046,000,000	11,381,000,000	10,411,000,000	9,811,000,000	9,043,000,000
Operating Income	20,182,000,000	18,161,000,000	27,759,000,000	26,764,000,000	21,763,000,000	27,161,000,000
Operating Margin %	23.65%	19.40%	31.96%	34.37%	29.51%	38.83%
SGA Expense	19,260,000,000	20,324,000,000	20,632,000,000	20,425,000,000	18,426,000,000	18,162,000,000
Net Income	16,798,000,000	12,193,000,000	22,074,000,000	21,863,000,000	16,978,000,000	23,150,000,000
Operating Cash Flow	33,325,000,000	29,080,000,000	32,231,000,000	28,833,000,000	31,626,000,000	26,994,000,000
Capital Expenditure	8,343,000,000	5,944,000,000	5,485,000,000	4,257,000,000	2,305,000,000	2,355,000,000
EBITDA	27,616,000,000	25,245,000,000	33,629,000,000	31,236,000,000	25,614,000,000	31,132,000,000
Return on Assets %	9.08%	6.99%	14.02%	16.58%	14.76%	23.76%
Return on Equity %	22.09%	14.35%	26.16%	30.09%	27.50%	44.83%
Debt to Equity	0.56	0.34	0.22	0.15	0.16	0.20

CONTACT INFORMATION:

Phone: 425 882-8080   Fax: 425 936-7329
Toll-Free: 800-642-7676
Address: 1 Microsoft Way, Redmond, WA 98052 United States

STOCK TICKER/OTHER:

Stock Ticker: MSFT
Employees: 118,000
Parent Company:

Exchange: NAS
Fiscal Year Ends: 06/30

SALARIES/BONUSES:

Top Exec. Salary:
$1,200,000
Second Exec. Salary:
$539,204

Bonus: $4,320,000

Bonus: $3,795,000

OTHER THOUGHTS:

Estimated Female Officers or Directors: 4

Hot Spot for Advancement for Women/Minorities: Y

Sales, profits and employees may be estimates. Financial information, benefits and other data can change quickly and may vary from those stated here.

Middleby Corporation (The)

NAIC Code: 333318

www.middleby.com

TYPES OF BUSINESS:

Commercial Kitchen Equipment

BRANDS/DIVISIONS/AFFILIATES:

Blodgett
Bloomfield
CTX
Carter-Hoffman
frifri
Toastmaster
Alkar
Rapidpak

CONTACTS: Note: Officers with more than one job title may be intentionally listed here more than once.

Martin Lindsay, Assistant Secretary
Selim Bassoul, CEO
Timothy Fitzgerald, CFO
David Brewer, COO, Divisional

GROWTH PLANS/SPECIAL FEATURES:

The Middleby Corporation is engaged in the design manufacture, marketing, distribution and service of a line of cooking and warming equipment. The company conducts its business through three main business segments: commercial foodservice equipment (CFE), food processing equipment (FPE) and residential kitchen equipment (RKE). CFE has a broad portfolio of brands and cooking and warming equipment which enable it to serve virtually any cooking or warming application within a commercial restaurant or institutional kitchen. This equipment is used across all types of foodservice operations, including quick-service restaurants, full-service restaurants, convenience stores, retail outlets, hotels and other institutions. Brands include Blodgett, Bloomfield, CTX, Carter-Hoffmann, frifri, Lang, MagiKitch'n, Middleby Marshall Southbend, Star, Toastmaster and Wells. FPE provides an array of products designed for the food processing industry. Products include cooking equipment, including batch ovens belt ovens and convey cooking systems marketed under the Alkar brand; food preparation equipment, such as breading, battering, mixing, forming and slicing machines, marketed under the MP Equipment brand; and packaging and food safety equipment marketed under the Rapidpak brand. RKE manufactures, sells and distributes kitchen equipment for the residential market. Its products include ranges, ovens, refrigerators, dishwashers, microwaves, cooktops and outdoor equipment sold under the Brigade, Jade, TurboChef, U-Line and Viking brands. During 2015, the firm acquired Marsal & Sons Inc.; Induc Commercial Electronics Co. Ltd.; AGA Rangemaster Group plc; Lynx Grills, Inc; and the assets and manufacturing facility of Marel's high speed slicing business unit. In May 2016, it acquired Follett Corporation.

FINANCIAL DATA: Note: Data for latest year may not have been available at press time.

In U.S. $	2016	2015	2014	2013	2012	2011
Revenue		1,826,598,000	1,636,538,000	1,428,685,000	1,038,174,000	855,907,000
R&D Expense						
Operating Income		302,603,000	300,432,000	244,462,000	188,084,000	148,710,000
Operating Margin %		16.56%	18.35%	17.11%	18.11%	17.37%
SGA Expense		375,148,000	346,672,000	305,549,000	214,905,000	195,427,000
Net Income		191,610,000	193,312,000	153,928,000	120,697,000	95,473,000
Operating Cash Flow		249,592,000	233,882,000	146,158,000	128,346,000	130,393,000
Capital Expenditure		22,362,000	13,143,000	19,640,000	7,652,000	7,840,000
EBITDA		352,208,000	337,634,000	284,846,000	210,581,000	168,659,000
Return on Assets %		7.93%	9.95%	10.04%	10.09%	9.45%
Return on Equity %		17.63%	20.95%	20.68%	20.79%	20.40%
Debt to Equity		0.62	0.58	0.68	0.39	

CONTACT INFORMATION:

Phone: 847 741-3300   Fax:
Toll-Free:
Address: 1400 Toastmaster Dr., Elgin, IL United States

STOCK TICKER/OTHER:

Stock Ticker: MIDD
Employees: 4,860
Parent Company:

Exchange: NAS
Fiscal Year Ends: 12/31

SALARIES/BONUSES:

Top Exec. Salary:
$1,000,000
Second Exec. Salary:
$575,000

Bonus: $

Bonus: $

OTHER THOUGHTS:

Estimated Female Officers or Directors:

Hot Spot for Advancement for Women/Minorities:

Modine Manufacturing Company

www.modine.com

NAIC Code: 336300

TYPES OF BUSINESS:
Automobile Parts Manufacturer
Heat Exchangers & Systems
Oil Cores
Electronics Cooling
Heating & Air Conditioning Products
Radiator Cores
Fuel Cells

BRANDS/DIVISIONS/AFFILIATES:

CONTACTS: *Note: Officers with more than one job title may be intentionally listed here more than once.*
Thomas Burke, CEO
Michael Lucareli, CFO
Thomas Marry, COO
Margaret Kelsey, General Counsel
Scott Bowser, Vice President, Divisional
Matthew McBurney, Vice President, Divisional
Holger Schwab, Vice President, Geographical
Scott Wollenberg, Vice President, Geographical

GROWTH PLANS/SPECIAL FEATURES:

Modine Manufacturing Company is a worldwide leader in thermal management technology. The firm serves the vehicular; industrial; commercial; fuel cell; and building heating, ventilating, air conditioning and refrigeration (HVAC&R) markets. Modine develops, produces and markets thermal management products, components and systems such as radiators, charge air coolers, exhaust gas recirculation (EGR) coolers and oil coolers. Its primary customers are original equipment manufacturers (OEMs) in various industries, including the commercial truck, bus and specialty vehicle markets; the firm also caters to construction contractors and wholesalers of plumbing and heating equipment. Modine is organized into four segments: Americas (North and South), Asia, Europe and building HVAC. The three geographic units represent the company's original equipment segments and serve the commercial vehicle, off-highway and automotive markets. These divisions sell radiators, charge-air-coolers, EGR coolers, fan shrouds, engine oil coolers, fuel coolers, intake air coolers and HVAC system modules such as condensers, evaporators and heater cores. The firm's building HVAC segment includes unit heaters such as gas-fired, hydronic, electric and oil-fired; duct furnaces, both indoor and outdoor; infrared units, both high- and low-intensity; hydronic products, including commercial fin-tube radiation, cabinet unit heaters and convectors; roof-mounted direct- and indirect-fired makeup air units; commercial packaged rooftop ventilation units; unit ventilators; single packaged vertical units; geothermal and water-source heat pumps; precision air conditioning units for data center applications; air-handling units; chillers; ceiling cassettes; and condensing units. In 2016, the firm acquired a controlling stake in a Chinese joint venture with Jiangsu Puxin Heat Exchange System Co. Ltd., which produces stainless steel heat exchangers for the China light-, medium- and heavy-duty commercial vehicle markets. Modine already produces these products in other regions.

Modine offers employees medical benefits, educational assistance, retirement plans, life insurance and flexible spending accounts.

FINANCIAL DATA: *Note: Data for latest year may not have been available at press time.*

In U.S. $	2016	2015	2014	2013	2012	2011
Revenue	1,352,500,000	1,496,400,000	1,477,600,000	1,376,000,000	1,577,152,000	1,448,235,000
R&D Expense						
Operating Income	-7,500,000	52,700,000	37,200,000	-600,000	67,524,000	42,794,000
Operating Margin %	-.55%	3.52%	2.51%	-.04%	4.28%	2.95%
SGA Expense	204,500,000	184,500,000	181,700,000	166,300,000	189,046,000	185,300,000
Net Income	-1,600,000	21,800,000	130,400,000	-24,200,000	38,461,000	6,180,000
Operating Cash Flow	72,400,000	63,500,000	104,500,000	48,800,000	45,758,000	20,812,000
Capital Expenditure	62,800,000	58,300,000	53,100,000	49,800,000	64,352,000	55,061,000
EBITDA	51,400,000	104,500,000	94,500,000	55,400,000	118,084,000	102,910,000
Return on Assets %	-.17%	2.22%	14.08%	-2.82%	4.24%	.70%
Return on Equity %	-.43%	5.58%	37.76%	-8.19%	11.18%	1.79%
Debt to Equity	0.33	0.36	0.30	0.49	0.43	0.38

CONTACT INFORMATION:
Phone: 262 636-1200   Fax: 262 636-1424
Toll-Free:
Address: 1500 DeKoven Ave., Racine, WI 53403 United States

STOCK TICKER/OTHER:
Stock Ticker: MOD   Exchange: NYS
Employees: 6,900   Fiscal Year Ends: 02/28
Parent Company:

SALARIES/BONUSES:
Top Exec. Salary: $856,692   Bonus: $
Second Exec. Salary: Bonus: $
$493,077

OTHER THOUGHTS:
Estimated Female Officers or Directors: 4
Hot Spot for Advancement for Women/Minorities: Y

Mohawk Industries Inc

NAIC Code: 314110

www.mohawkind.com

TYPES OF BUSINESS:

Floor Covering Stores
Tile & Stone Products
Extrusion
Laminate Flooring Technology
Roofing Systems

BRANDS/DIVISIONS/AFFILIATES:

Mohawk Carpet Distribution Inc
Dal-Tile Corporation
Unilin BVBA
American Olean
Aladdin
Pergo
Marazzi
Quick-Step

CONTACTS: *Note: Officers with more than one job title may be intentionally listed here more than once.*

Jeffrey Lorberbaum, CEO
Frank Boykin, CFO
James Brunk, Chief Accounting Officer
W. Wellborn, COO
Rodney Patton, General Counsel
Brian Carson, President, Divisional
John Turner, President, Divisional
Bernard Thiers, President, Subsidiary

GROWTH PLANS/SPECIAL FEATURES:

Mohawk Industries, Inc. is a leading producer of floor-covering products for residential and commercial applications in the U.S and residential applications in Europe. Its primary subsidiaries are Mohawk Carpet Distribution, Inc.; Dal-Tile Corporation; and Unilin BVBA. Mohawk's operating segments include carpet, ceramic and laminate & wood. The carpet segment designs, manufactures, sources, distributes and markets its carpet and rug product line in a broad range of colors, textures and patterns. It also markets and distributes ceramic tile, laminate, hardwood, resilient floor covering, carpet pad and flooring accessories. Its brands include Aladdin, Bigelow, Durkan, Horizon, Karastan, Lees, Mohawk, Mohawk ColorCenters, Mohawk Floorscapes, Mohawk Home, Portico and SmartStrand. It sells through independent floor covering retailers, home centers, mass merchandisers, department stores, shop at home, buying groups, commercial dealers and commercial end users. The ceramic segment designs, manufactures, sources, distributes and markets a broad line of ceramic tile, porcelain tile and natural stone products. Its brands include American Olean, Daltile, Marazzi and Mohawk Tile. The laminate & wood segment designs, manufactures, sources, licenses, distributes and markets laminate and hardwood flooring. This segment also licenses certain patents related to laminate flooring installation. Its brands include Columbia Laminate, Mohawk Laminate, Pergo and Quick-Step. In Europe, the laminate & wood segment also produces roofing elements, insulation boards, medium-density fiberboard, chipboards and other wood products. Subsidiary Pergo is a manufacturer of laminate flooring in the U.S. and Europe. In January 2015, subsidiary Unilin BVBA agreed to acquire International Flooring Systems SA (IVC), a global manufacturer, distributor and marketer of vinyl flooring products.

FINANCIAL DATA: *Note: Data for latest year may not have been available at press time.*

In U.S. $	2016	2015	2014	2013	2012	2011
Revenue		8,071,563,000	7,803,446,000	7,348,754,000	5,787,980,000	5,642,258,000
R&D Expense						
Operating Income		837,566,000	772,796,000	546,931,000	379,508,000	315,542,000
Operating Margin %		10.37%	9.90%	7.44%	6.55%	5.59%
SGA Expense		1,573,120,000	1,381,396,000	1,373,878,000	1,110,550,000	1,101,337,000
Net Income		615,302,000	531,965,000	348,786,000	250,258,000	173,922,000
Operating Cash Flow		911,873,000	662,188,000	525,163,000	587,590,000	300,993,000
Capital Expenditure		503,657,000	561,804,000	366,550,000	208,294,000	275,573,000
EBITDA		1,182,594,000	1,107,668,000	846,688,000	659,498,000	599,225,000
Return on Assets %		6.75%	6.34%	4.71%	4.00%	2.82%
Return on Equity %		13.27%	11.98%	8.52%	7.01%	5.20%
Debt to Equity		0.24	0.31	0.47	0.35	0.35

CONTACT INFORMATION:

Phone: 706 629-7721   Fax: 706 625-3851
Toll-Free: 800-241-4494
Address: 160 S. Industrial Blvd., Calhoun, GA 30701 United States

STOCK TICKER/OTHER:

Stock Ticker: MHK
Employees: 32,300
Parent Company:

Exchange: NYS
Fiscal Year Ends: 12/31

SALARIES/BONUSES:

Top Exec. Salary:
$1,109,197
Second Exec. Salary:
$958,433

Bonus: $

Bonus: $

OTHER THOUGHTS:

Estimated Female Officers or Directors: 1

Hot Spot for Advancement for Women/Minorities:

Molex Inc

NAIC Code: 334417

www.molex.com

TYPES OF BUSINESS:

Electronic Connector Manufacturing
Transportation Products
Commercial Products
Micro Products
Automation & Electrical Products
Integrated Products
Global Sales & Marketing Organization

BRANDS/DIVISIONS/AFFILIATES:

Woodhead
Koch Industries Inc
Soligie Inc

CONTACTS: Note: Officers with more than one job title may be intentionally listed here more than once.

Martin P. Slark, CEO
Liam McCarthy, COO
Liam McCarthy, Pres.
David D. Johnson, CFO
Graham C. Brock, Pres., Global Sales & Mktg.
Ana G. Rodriguez, Sr. VP-Global Human Resources
Gary J. Matula, CIO
Robert J. Zeitler, General Counsel
Tim Ruff, Sr. VP-Bus. Dev. & Corp. Strategy
David D. Johnson, Treas.
John H. Krehbiel, Jr., Co-Chmn.
Junichi Kaji, Pres., Global Mirco Prod. Div.
J. Michael Nauman, Pres., Global Integrated Prod. Div.
Joseph Nelligan, Pres., Commercial Prod. Division

GROWTH PLANS/SPECIAL FEATURES:

Molex, Inc., a subsidiary of Koch Industries, Inc., is a manufacturer of electronic components. It designs, manufactures and sells more than 100,000 products, including terminals, connectors, planar cables, cable assemblies, interconnection systems, backplanes, integrated products and mechanical and electronic switches. The company also provides manufacturing services to integrate specific components into a customer's product. The firm's products are sold primarily within seven markets: IT, telecommunications, consumer, industrial, automotive, mobile devices and other. In the IT market, Molex develops signal, power and optical connectors and cables for usage in desktop computers, personal computers, mobile devices and peripheral equipment. The telecommunications division produces products such as backplane connector systems, optical signal products and transmission equipment. The consumer segment specializes in micro-miniature connector engineering, high wattage products and cable and wire application equipment. This unit manufactures the world's smallest connectors for audio players, DVD players and video cameras as well as products for large computer game facilities and machines. The firm's industrial products include network interface cards, cord sets and software for industrial networks. The Woodhead electrical solutions product line is designed to increase worker safety. Automotive products are designed for use in all automobile systems, including infotainment and navigation, powertrain and safety. The mobile devices division produces connectors for mobile phones, tablets and notebook computers. Other offerings include products such as connectors and integrated systems for the military and medical industries. This includes the Solid State Lighting market, which focuses on developing products for general illumination purposes. The firm operates 45 manufacturing facilities in 17 countries throughout the Americas, Asia Pacific and Europe. In 2015, the firm acquired certain assets of Soligie, Inc. a firm specializing in printed and flexible electronic solutions.

FINANCIAL DATA: Note: Data for latest year may not have been available at press time.

In U.S. $	2016	2015	2014	2013	2012	2011
Revenue		3,900,000,000	3,862,540,000	3,620,446,976	3,489,189,120	3,587,333,888
R&D Expense						
Operating Income						
Operating Margin %						
SGA Expense						
Net Income			260,189,372	243,623,008	281,376,992	298,808,000
Operating Cash Flow						
Capital Expenditure						
EBITDA						
Return on Assets %						
Return on Equity %						
Debt to Equity						

CONTACT INFORMATION:

Phone: 630 969-4550   Fax: 630 969-1352
Toll-Free: 800-786-6539
Address: 2222 Wellington Ct., Lisle, IL 60532-1682 United States

STOCK TICKER/OTHER:

Stock Ticker: Subsidiary
Employees: 35,983
Parent Company: Koch Industries, Inc.

Exchange:
Fiscal Year Ends: 06/30

SALARIES/BONUSES:

Top Exec. Salary: $ Bonus: $
Second Exec. Salary: $ Bonus: $

OTHER THOUGHTS:

Estimated Female Officers or Directors: 2
Hot Spot for Advancement for Women/Minorities:

Monro Muffler Brake Inc

NAIC Code: 811100

www.monro.com

TYPES OF BUSINESS:

Automotive Repair & Maintenance
Under-Car Repair Services
Inspection Services
Tires

BRANDS/DIVISIONS/AFFILIATES:

Monro Muffler Brake & Service
Monro Service Corporation
Tread Quarters Discount Tire
Autotire Car Care Center
Tire Warehouse
Mr. Tire
Tire Barn Warehouse
Car-X

CONTACTS: *Note: Officers with more than one job title may be intentionally listed here more than once.*

John Van Heel, CEO
Catherine DAmico, CFO
Robert Gross, Chairman of the Board
Brian DAmbrosia, Chief Accounting Officer
Joseph Tomarchio, Executive VP
Christopher Hoornbeck, President, Subsidiary
Maureen Mulholland, Secretary
Craig Hoyle, Senior VP, Divisional
Raymond Pickens, Vice President, Divisional
John Lamb, Vice President, Divisional

GROWTH PLANS/SPECIAL FEATURES:

Monro Muffler Brake, Inc. operates through a chain of 1,025 company-operated stores, one franchised location and 14 dealer-operated stores, providing automotive under-car repair and tire services in the U.S. These stores are typically located in high-visibility locations in suburban and small towns in Connecticut, Delaware, Florida, Georgia, Illinois, Indiana, Kentucky, Maine, Maryland, Massachusetts, Michigan, Missouri, New Hampshire, New Jersey, New York, North Carolina, Ohio, Pennsylvania, Rhode Island, South Carolina, Tennessee, Vermont, Virginia, West Virginia and Wisconsin. The stores operate under the names Monro Muffler Brake & Service, Tread Quarters Discount Tire, Mr. Tire, Autotire Car Care Center, Tire Warehouse, Tire Barn Warehouse, Ken Towery's Tire & Auto Care and The Tire Choice. The firm's stores service approximately 5.5 million vehicles annually. Monro provides a range of services on passenger cars, light trucks and vans for brakes; mufflers and exhaust systems; and steering, drive train, suspension and wheel alignment. Other products and services offered by the company include tires and routine maintenance services, such as state inspections. The company specializes in the repair and replacement of parts that must be periodically replaced due to normal wear and tear. Typically, the firm does not perform under-the-hood repair, except for oil change services, heating and cooling system flush and fill services and some minor tune-ups. Monro operates one subsidiary, Monro Service Corporation, which provides purchasing, distribution, merchandising, advertising, accounting and other store support functions. In 2015, the firm acquired the Car-X trade name and franchise rights to 146 locations, and will operate as the franchisor.

Monro offers its employees Automotive Service Excellence (ASE) certification reimbursement; recreational discounts; an employee assistance program; tool insurance; and medical, dental, life and disability insurance.

FINANCIAL DATA: *Note: Data for latest year may not have been available at press time.*

In U.S. $	2016	2015	2014	2013	2012	2011
Revenue	943,651,000	894,492,000	831,432,000	731,997,000	686,552,000	636,678,000
R&D Expense						
Operating Income	120,589,000	109,789,000	95,347,000	73,705,000	91,416,000	78,385,000
Operating Margin %	12.77%	12.27%	11.46%	10.06%	13.31%	12.31%
SGA Expense	265,114,000	243,561,000	224,627,000	204,442,000	184,981,000	176,969,000
Net Income	66,805,000	61,799,000	54,459,000	42,567,000	54,612,000	45,841,000
Operating Cash Flow	126,504,000	126,349,000	93,943,000	84,436,000	82,626,000	61,721,000
Capital Expenditure	36,834,000	34,750,000	32,150,000	34,185,000	28,556,000	17,507,000
EBITDA	160,358,000	145,510,000	127,035,000	101,205,000	115,497,000	101,874,000
Return on Assets %	6.95%	7.41%	7.40%	6.96%	11.35%	10.23%
Return on Equity %	13.14%	13.89%	13.94%	12.29%	17.97%	17.87%
Debt to Equity	0.50	0.53	0.44	0.51	0.15	0.16

CONTACT INFORMATION:

Phone: 585-647-6400   Fax: 585-647-0945
Toll-Free:
Address: 200 Holleder Pkwy., Rochester, NY 14615 United States

STOCK TICKER/OTHER:

Stock Ticker: MNRO   Exchange: NAS
Employees: 6,725   Fiscal Year Ends: 03/31
Parent Company:

SALARIES/BONUSES:

Top Exec. Salary: $550,000   Bonus: $
Second Exec. Salary: Bonus: $150,000
$270,000

OTHER THOUGHTS:

Estimated Female Officers or Directors: 1
Hot Spot for Advancement for Women/Minorities:

Moody's Corporation

www.moodys.com

NAIC Code: 561450

TYPES OF BUSINESS:

Credit Bureau
Credit Risk Assessment Products & Services
Credit Processing Software
Credit Training Services

BRANDS/DIVISIONS/AFFILIATES:

Equilibrium

CONTACTS: Note: Officers with more than one job title may be intentionally listed here more than once.

Raymond Mcdaniel, CEO
Michael Crimmins, Chief Accounting Officer
Richard Cantor, Chief Risk Officer
Henry McKinnell, Director
Linda Huber, Executive VP
John Goggins, Executive VP
Robert Fauber, President, Divisional
Mark Almeida, President, Subsidiary
Jane Clark, Secretary
Blair Worrall, Senior VP, Divisional
Lisa Westlake, Senior VP

GROWTH PLANS/SPECIAL FEATURES:

Moody's Corporation is a provider of credit ratings; credit and economic related research, data and analytical tools; risk management software; quantitative credit risk measures, credit portfolio management solutions, training and financial credentialing and certification services; and outsourced research and analytical services to institutional customers. The company maintains offices worldwide. Moody's operates in two segments: Moody's investors service (MIS) and Moody's analytics (MA). MIS publishes rating opinions on a broad range of credit obligors and credit obligations issued in domestic and international markets, including various corporate and governmental obligations, structured finance securities and commercial paper programs. Ratings are distributed via press releases through a variety of print and electronic media, including the Internet and other real-time information systems used by securities traders and investors. MIS has ratings relationships with approximately 11,000 corporate issuers and approximately 20,000 public finance issuers. Additionally, the company has rated and currently monitors ratings on approximately 68,000 structured finance obligations. MA offers a range of products that support the risk management activities of institutional participants in global financial markets. These products and services include in-depth research on major debt issuers, industry studies and commentary on topical credit related events as well as economic research, credit data and analytical tools such as quantitative credit risk scores. MA's customers represent more than 4,700 institutions worldwide operating in approximately 130 countries. During 2015, Moody's research web site was accessed by over 259,000 individuals, including 34,000 client users. In 2015, the firm acquired Equilibrium, a provider of credit rating and research services in Peru and other Latin American countries; and acquired the residential mortgage backed securities data and analytics assets of BlackBox Logic.

FINANCIAL DATA: Note: Data for latest year may not have been available at press time.

In U.S. $	2016	2015	2014	2013	2012	2011
Revenue		3,484,500,000	3,334,300,000	2,972,500,000	2,730,300,000	2,280,700,000
R&D Expense						
Operating Income		1,473,400,000	1,439,100,000	1,234,600,000	1,077,400,000	888,400,000
Operating Margin %		42.28%	43.16%	41.53%	39.46%	38.95%
SGA Expense		921,300,000	869,300,000	822,100,000	752,200,000	629,600,000
Net Income		941,300,000	988,700,000	804,500,000	690,000,000	571,400,000
Operating Cash Flow		1,153,600,000	1,018,600,000	926,800,000	823,100,000	803,300,000
Capital Expenditure		89,000,000	74,600,000	42,300,000	45,000,000	67,700,000
EBITDA		1,618,600,000	1,680,800,000	1,360,000,000	1,191,300,000	986,400,000
Return on Assets %		19.22%	21.81%	19.25%	20.18%	21.09%
Return on Equity %			1325.33%	222.79%	638.29%	
Debt to Equity				6.23	4.17	

CONTACT INFORMATION:

Phone: 212 553-0300   Fax: 212 553-4820
Toll-Free:
Address: 250 Greenwich St., 7 World Trade Center, New York, NY 10007
United States

STOCK TICKER/OTHER:

Stock Ticker: MCO
Employees: 9,900
Parent Company:

Exchange: NYS
Fiscal Year Ends: 12/31

SALARIES/BONUSES:

Top Exec. Salary: Bonus: $
$1,000,000
Second Exec. Salary: Bonus: $
$609,000

OTHER THOUGHTS:

Estimated Female Officers or Directors: 2

Hot Spot for Advancement for Women/Minorities: Y

Morgan Stanley

NAIC Code: 523110

TYPES OF BUSINESS:

Stock Brokerage/Investment Banking
Institutional Securities
Wealth Management
Asset Management
Bank Holding Company

BRANDS/DIVISIONS/AFFILIATES:

CONTACTS: Note: Officers with more than one job title may be intentionally listed here more than once.

James Gorman, CEO
Jonathan Pruzan, CFO
Paul Wirth, Chief Accounting Officer
Keishi Hotsuki, Chief Risk Officer
James Rosenthal, COO
Eric Grossman, Executive VP
Jeffrey Brodsky, Executive VP
Thomas Kelleher, President
Martin Cohen, Secretary

GROWTH PLANS/SPECIAL FEATURES:

Morgan Stanley is a global financial services firm wit
approximately $1.4 billion in assets under management c
supervision and over 1,300 offices in 42 countries. Morga
Stanley provides a wide variety of products and services to
large and diversified group of clients, including corporation:
governments, financial institutions and individuals. The fir
operates in three business segments: institutional securitie:
investment management and wealth management. Th
institutional securities division incorporates activities such a
capital raising; financial advisory services, including advice o
mergers and acquisitions, restructurings, real estate an
project finance; corporate lending; sales, trading, financing an
market-making activities in equity and fixed income securitie:
risk management analytics; research; and investmer
activities. The investment management division provide
global asset management products and services in fixe
income; alternative investments, including hedge funds an
funds of funds; equity; and merchant banking, which include
real estate, private equity and infrastructure, to institutiona
clients through proprietary and third-party distributio
channels. The wealth management division provide
comprehensive financial services to clients through a networ
of 16,000 global representatives in 622 locations. This segmer
serves individual investors and small-to-medium size
businesses and institutions with an emphasis on ultra-high ne
worth, high net worth and affluent investors. Its advisor
services cover equities, options, futures, foreign currencie:
precious metals, fixed income securities, mutual fund:
structured products, alternative investments, unit investmer
trusts, managed futures and mutual fund asset allocatio
programs. Wealth management also engages in fixed incom
principal trading.

FINANCIAL DATA: Note: Data for latest year may not have been available at press time.

In U.S. $	2016	2015	2014	2013	2012	2011
Revenue		35,155,000,000	34,275,000,000	32,417,000,000	26,112,000,000	32,403,000,000
R&D Expense						
Operating Income		8,495,000,000	3,591,000,000	4,482,000,000	515,000,000	6,114,000,000
Operating Margin %		24.16%	10.47%	13.82%	1.97%	18.86%
SGA Expense		18,464,000,000	20,117,000,000	18,683,000,000	18,137,000,000	18,820,000,000
Net Income		6,127,000,000	3,467,000,000	2,932,000,000	68,000,000	4,110,000,000
Operating Cash Flow		3,674,000,000	1,131,000,000	35,553,000,000	24,548,000,000	6,684,000,000
Capital Expenditure		1,373,000,000	992,000,000	1,316,000,000	1,312,000,000	1,304,000,000
EBITDA						
Return on Assets %		.71%	.38%	.32%		.26%
Return on Equity %		8.55%	4.94%	4.30%	-.04%	3.82%
Debt to Equity		2.41	2.54	2.67	3.05	3.38

CONTACT INFORMATION:

Phone: 212 761-4000   Fax: 212 761-0086
Toll-Free:
Address: 1585 Broadway, New York, NY 10036 United States

STOCK TICKER/OTHER:

Stock Ticker: MS
Employees: 55,802
Parent Company:

Exchange: NYS
Fiscal Year Ends: 12/31

SALARIES/BONUSES:

Top Exec. Salary:
$1,500,000
Bonus: $9,023,750

Second Exec. Salary:
$1,000,000
Bonus: $8,798,750

OTHER THOUGHTS:

Estimated Female Officers or Directors: 3

Hot Spot for Advancement for Women/Minorities: Y

Mutual of Omaha Companies (The)

www.mutualofomaha.com

NAIC Code: 524113

TYPES OF BUSINESS:

Life Insurance
Asset Management
Annuities
Medical & Dental Insurance
Supplemental Health Insurance
IT Services & Consulting

BRANDS/DIVISIONS/AFFILIATES:

Companion Life Insurance Company
United of Omaha Life Insurance Company
United World Life Insurance Company
Mutual of Omaha Investor Services Inc
Omaha Financial Holdings Inc
East Campus Realty LLC
Omaha Insurance Company

CONTACTS:
Note: Officers with more than one job title may be intentionally listed here more than once.

James T. Blackledge, CEO
Stacy A. Scholtz, Exec.VP-Oper.
David A. Diamond, CFO
Richard Hrabchak, Exec. VP-CIO
Richard C. Anderl, General Counsel
Stacy A. Scholtz, Exec. VP-Corp. Oper.
David A. Diamond, Treas.
Daniel P. Martin, Exec. VP-Group Benefit Svcs.
Michael C. Weekly, Exec. VP-Individual Financial Svcs.
Richard A. Witt, Chief Investment Officer
Kenneth R. Cook, Pres., East Campus Realty
Daniel P. Neary, Chmn.

GROWTH PLANS/SPECIAL FEATURES:

The Mutual of Omaha Companies provide insurance, annuities and asset management products through several affiliated companies. These firms include Companion Life Insurance Company; Mutual of Omaha Investor Services, Inc.; United of Omaha Life Insurance Company; Omaha Insurance Company; United World Life Insurance Company; Omaha Financial Holdings, Inc.; and East Campus Realty, LLC. Companion Life Insurance Company provides insurance, annuities and investment services to New York residents. Mutual of Omaha Investor Services, Inc. is a registered broker dealer that offers mutual funds and asset management to affiliate companies and directly to consumers. United of Omaha Life Insurance Company provides life insurance, annuities and financial services through the Mutual of Omaha network of sales representatives. Omaha Insurance Company sells accident and health insurance. United World Life Insurance Company offers specialty life plans, as well as health and accident coverage, through independent agents. Omaha Financial Holdings, Inc. is a holding company that handles Mutual of Omaha's banking operation. East Campus Realty, LLC is in the process of developing Midtown Crossing at Turner Park, a mixed-use development offering condominiums, apartments, services, dining and entertainment adjacent to Mutual of Omaha's headquarters.

The firm offers employees benefits including medical, dental, vision, life and disability insurance; flexible spending accounts; and a 401(k).

FINANCIAL DATA:
Note: Data for latest year may not have been available at press time.

In U.S. $	2016	2015	2014	2013	2012	2011
Revenue		7,200,000,000	6,878,021,000	6,600,000,000	6,436,988,000	5,974,057,000
R&D Expense						
Operating Income						
Operating Margin %						
SGA Expense						
Net Income		330,000,000	291,701,000	359,200,000	283,797,000	130,050,000
Operating Cash Flow						
Capital Expenditure						
EBITDA						
Return on Assets %						
Return on Equity %						
Debt to Equity						

CONTACT INFORMATION:

Phone: 402-342-7600   Fax: 402-351-2775
Toll-Free: 800-775-6000
Address: Mutual of Omaha Plz., Omaha, NE 68175 United States

STOCK TICKER/OTHER:

Stock Ticker: Mutual Company
Employees: 5,100
Parent Company:

Exchange:
Fiscal Year Ends: 12/31

SALARIES/BONUSES:

Top Exec. Salary: $ Bonus: $
Second Exec. Salary: $ Bonus: $

OTHER THOUGHTS:

Estimated Female Officers or Directors: 3
Hot Spot for Advancement for Women/Minorities: Y

Sales, profits and employees may be estimates. Financial information, benefits and other data can change quickly and may vary from those stated here.

National Instruments Corp

www.ni.com

NAIC Code: 0

TYPES OF BUSINESS:

Software-Instrumentation
Virtual Instrumentation
Signal Conditioning Hardware
Test & Measurement Software
Motion Control Products
Analysis & Visualization Software
Automation Software
Image Acquisition Products

BRANDS/DIVISIONS/AFFILIATES:

LabVIEW
LabWindows
Measurement Studio
NI TestStand
NI VeriStand
NI DIAdem
NI InsightCM Enterprise
LabVIEW for LEGO MINDSTORMS

CONTACTS: Note: Officers with more than one job title may be intentionally listed here more than once.

Alexander Davern, CFO
James Truchard, Co-Founder
Jeffrey Kodosky, Co-Founder
Eric Starkloff, Executive VP, Divisional
David Hugley, General Counsel
Scott Rust, Senior VP, Divisional

GROWTH PLANS/SPECIAL FEATURES:

National Instruments Corp. (NI) supplies test, measurement and automation products used by engineers and scientists from numerous industries. Its key markets range from the automotive, aerospace, electronics, semiconductors and defense sectors, to the education, government, medical research and telecommunications industries, among others. Products and services include system design software; programming tools; application software; hardware products and related driver software; the Ni education platform, including software and hardware products for teaching; NI services, including hardware services and maintenance; software maintenance services; and training and certification. The company's flagship product is LabVIEW, a system design software for measurement and control. With LabVIEW, users program graphically and can design custom virtual instruments by connecting icons with software wires to create block diagrams, which are natural design notations for scientists and engineers. Users can customize front panels with knobs, buttons, dials and graphs to emulate control panels of instruments or add custom graphics to visually represent the control and operation of processes. In addition to LabVIEW, NI offers LabWindows/CVI and Measurement Studio as alternative programming environments. NI offers a suite of software products, including NI TestStand, NI VeriStand, NI DIAdem, NI InsightCM Enterprise and NI Multisim, which are complimentary to LabVIEW. The NI education platform combines software, hardware and courseware designed to create engaging, authentic learning experiences that prepare students for the next generation of innovation. Teaching software includes LabVIEW for LEGO MINDSTORMS, used in the development of robotics projects in secondary school.

The firm offers its employees a 401(k) plan; stock purchase and profit sharing plans; health, dental and vision coverage; life and disability insurance; tuition assistance; and an onsite fitness center.

FINANCIAL DATA: Note: Data for latest year may not have been available at press time.

In U.S. $	2016	2015	2014	2013	2012	2011
Revenue		1,225,456,000	1,243,862,000	1,172,558,000	1,143,692,000	1,024,173,000
R&D Expense		225,131,000	227,433,000	234,796,000	222,994,000	199,071,000
Operating Income		137,172,000	145,187,000	98,617,000	116,934,000	112,712,000
Operating Margin %		11.19%	11.67%	8.41%	10.22%	11.00%
SGA Expense		546,197,000	553,110,000	535,218,000	523,490,000	471,426,000
Net Income		95,262,000	126,333,000	80,513,000	90,137,000	94,072,000
Operating Cash Flow		162,637,000	195,110,000	169,479,000	132,516,000	169,899,000
Capital Expenditure		68,154,000	73,559,000	67,861,000	102,684,000	71,930,000
EBITDA		210,501,000	215,393,000	166,591,000	175,620,000	162,609,000
Return on Assets %		6.54%	9.02%	6.12%	7.39%	8.90%
Return on Equity %		8.66%	11.80%	8.20%	10.06%	11.78%
Debt to Equity		0.03				

CONTACT INFORMATION:

Phone: 512 338-9119   Fax: 512 683-9300
Toll-Free: 800-433-3488
Address: 11500 N. Mopac Expy., Austin, TX 78759-3504 United States

SALARIES/BONUSES:

Top Exec. Salary: $550,000   Bonus: $
Second Exec. Salary: $331,250   Bonus: $

STOCK TICKER/OTHER:

Stock Ticker: NATI   Exchange: NAS
Employees: 7,441   Fiscal Year Ends: 12/31
Parent Company:

OTHER THOUGHTS:

Estimated Female Officers or Directors: 1
Hot Spot for Advancement for Women/Minorities:

NBCUniversal LLC

NAIC Code: 515120

www.nbcuni.com

TYPES OF BUSINESS:
Television Broadcasting
Online News & Information
TV & Movie Production
Radio Broadcasting
Interactive Online Content
Cable Television Programming
Theme Parks
Film, TV & Home Video Distribution

BRANDS/DIVISIONS/AFFILIATES:
Universal Studios Japan
Comcast Corp
Hulu LLC
Universal Pictures
Universal Orlando Resort
NBC Sports Network
CNBC International
Bravo Media

CONTACTS: *Note: Officers with more than one job title may be intentionally listed here more than once.*
Stephen B. Burke, CEO
Anand Kini, CFO
Linda Yaccarino, Chairman- Advertising, Sales & Client Partnerships
Craig Robinson, Chief Diversity Officer
Jeff Shell, Chmn.-Universal Filmed Entertainment
Kimberley D. Harris, General Counsel
Maggie McLean Suniewick, Sr. VP-Strategic Integration
Cameron Blanchard, Exec. VP-Comm.
Patricia Fili-Krushel, Chmn.-NBCUniversal News Group
Robert Greenblatt, Chmn., NBC Entertainment
Bonnie Hammer, Chmn., NBCUniversal Cable Entertainment Group
Ted Harbert, Chmn., NBC Broadcasting
Kevin MacLellan, Chmn., NBCUniversal Int'l
Matt Bond, Exec. VP-Content Dist.

GROWTH PLANS/SPECIAL FEATURES:
NBCUniversal LLC is one of the world's largest entertainment and media companies in the development, production and marketing of news, entertainment and information to a global audience. The company is a product of a 2004 merger of Vivendi Universal Entertainment and NBC (National Broadcasting Company). The firm is a wholly owned subsidiary of Comcast Corp. The firm operates in eight divisions: cable, broadcast, digital, film, parks, local media, TV studios production and international. The cable division includes Bravo Media, Golf Channel, NBC Sports Network, Sprout, Universal HD, Chiller, E!, MSNBC, NBCUniversal International Television, SYFY, USA Network, CLOO, Esquire Network, CNBC, The Weather Channel Company and Oxygen Media. The broadcast division includes NBC Entertainment, NBC News, NBC Sports, Telemundo, NBC Entertainment and NBC Olympics. The digital division consists of Fandango, GolfNow, Hulu LLC and Seeso. The film division includes Focus Features, Universal Pictures, Universal Pictures International and Universal Pictures Home Entertainment. The parks division includes Universal Orlando Resort, Universal Studios Japan, Universal Studios Singapore and Universal Studios Hollywood. The local media division consists of Cozi TV, NBC Sports Regional Networks, TeleXitos and NBCUniversal owned television stations. The international division includes CNBC International, NBCUniversal International Television. The TV studios production division consists of Universal Cable Productions, Telemundo Studios and Universal Television.

NBC Universal offers its employees medical, dental, vision and prescription drug coverage; a 401(k) plan; health club discounts; same-sex domestic partner benefits; life insurance; and flexible spending accounts.

FINANCIAL DATA: *Note: Data for latest year may not have been available at press time.*

In U.S. $	2016	2015	2014	2013	2012	2011
Revenue		26,000,000,000	25,400,000,000	23,740,000,000	22,349,100,000	21,124,000,000
R&D Expense						
Operating Income						
Operating Margin %						
SGA Expense						
Net Income		5,591,000,000	5,588,000,000	4,732,000,000	3,989,076,000	3,769,000,000
Operating Cash Flow						
Capital Expenditure						
EBITDA						
Return on Assets %						
Return on Equity %						
Debt to Equity						

CONTACT INFORMATION:
Phone: 212-664-4444   Fax: 212-664-4085
Toll-Free:
Address: 30 Rockefeller Plz., New York, NY 10112 United States

STOCK TICKER/OTHER:
Stock Ticker: Subsidiary   Exchange:
Employees: 40,000   Fiscal Year Ends: 12/31
Parent Company: Comcast Corp

SALARIES/BONUSES:
Top Exec. Salary: $ Bonus: $
Second Exec. Salary: $ Bonus: $

OTHER THOUGHTS:
Estimated Female Officers or Directors: 12
Hot Spot for Advancement for Women/Minorities: Y

NCR Corporation

NAIC Code: 334118

TYPES OF BUSINESS:

Computer Manufacturing
Barcode Scanning Equipment
Automatic Teller Machines (ATMs)
Transaction Processing Equipment
Point-of-Sale & Store Automation
Data Warehousing
Printer Consumables

BRANDS/DIVISIONS/AFFILIATES:

Blackstone Group LP (The)

CONTACTS: Note: Officers with more than one job title may be intentionally listed here more than once.

William Nuti, CEO
Robert Fishman, CFO
Frederick Marquardt, Executive VP, Divisional
Edward Gallagher, General Counsel
Andrea Ledford, Other Executive Officer
Andrew Heyman, President, Divisional
Michael Bayer, President, Divisional

GROWTH PLANS/SPECIAL FEATURES:

NCR Corporation provides information technology and related services to various industries, enabling client companies to interact more efficiently with customers. The company offers financial institutions, retailers and other organizations financially oriented self-service technologies, such as ATMs, cash dispensers, self-checkout kiosks and software solutions. Its operations are divided into four segments: financial services, retail solutions, hospitality and emerging industries. Financial services solutions include ATM and payment processing hardware and software designed to quickly and reliably process consumer transactions and incorporate advanced features such as automated check cashing/deposit, automated cash deposit, web-enablement, bill payment and the dispensing of non-cash items. NCR's retail solutions include automated point-of-sale (POS) systems such as POS terminals and bar-code scanners as well as self-checkout kiosks. Through the hospitality segment, the company offers technology solutions to customers in the hospitality, convenience and specialty retail industries, serving businesses that range from a single store or restaurant to global chains and the world's largest sports stadiums. The emerging industries segment provides maintenance and managed and professional services for third-party computer hardware provided to select manufacturers, primarily in the telecommunications industry. The firm also provides maintenance and support services for its products, including complete systems management and site assessment and preparation, staging, installation and implementation. Additionally, NCR develops, produces and markets printer consumables for various print technologies. In December 2015, The Blackstone Group LP acquired a minority stake in NCR for $820 million. In January 2016, NCR agreed to sell its interactive printer solutions division to Atlas Holdings LLC.

FINANCIAL DATA: Note: Data for latest year may not have been available at press time.

In U.S. $	2016	2015	2014	2013	2012	2011
Revenue		6,373,000,000	6,591,000,000	6,123,000,000	5,730,000,000	5,443,000,000
R&D Expense		230,000,000	263,000,000	203,000,000	219,000,000	177,000,000
Operating Income		135,000,000	353,000,000	666,000,000	232,000,000	65,000,000
Operating Margin %		2.11%	5.35%	10.87%	4.04%	1.19%
SGA Expense		1,042,000,000	1,012,000,000	871,000,000	894,000,000	805,000,000
Net Income		-178,000,000	191,000,000	443,000,000	146,000,000	53,000,000
Operating Cash Flow		681,000,000	524,000,000	281,000,000	-294,000,000	351,000,000
Capital Expenditure		229,000,000	258,000,000	226,000,000	160,000,000	163,000,000
EBITDA		386,000,000	602,000,000	865,000,000	390,000,000	230,000,000
Return on Assets %		-2.24%	2.28%	6.11%	2.44%	1.06%
Return on Equity %		-20.30%	10.49%	29.37%	14.27%	6.30%
Debt to Equity			1.85	1.87	1.51	1.06

CONTACT INFORMATION:

Phone: 937 445-5000   Fax: 937 445-5541
Toll-Free: 800-225-5627
Address: 3097 Satellite Blvd, Duluth, GA 30096 United States

STOCK TICKER/OTHER:

Stock Ticker: NCR   Exchange: NYS
Employees: 30,200   Fiscal Year Ends: 12/31
Parent Company:

SALARIES/BONUSES:

Top Exec. Salary: Bonus: $
$1,000,000
Second Exec. Salary: Bonus: $136,500
$575,000

OTHER THOUGHTS:

Estimated Female Officers or Directors: 3

Hot Spot for Advancement for Women/Minorities: Y

NeoPhotonics Corp

NAIC Code: 334210

www.neophotonics.com

TYPES OF BUSINESS:
Optical Integrated Circuits

BRANDS/DIVISIONS/AFFILIATES:
EigenLight Corporation
Advanced Hybrid Photonic Integration

CONTACTS: *Note: Officers with more than one job title may be intentionally listed here more than once.*
Timothy Jenks, CEO
Clyde Wallin, CFO
Chi Yue Cheung, COO
Benjamin Sitler, Senior VP, Divisional
Wupen Yuen, Senior VP

GROWTH PLANS/SPECIAL FEATURES:
NeoPhotonics Corp. develops, manufactures and sells optoelectronic products that transmit, receive and switch high speed digital optical signals for communications networks. The company focuses on growth in its 100 gigabytes per second (Gbps) and beyond products. High speed products include products designed for 100G and beyond; network products comprise all products designed for applications below 100 Gbps, and includes 40 Gbps products. NeoPhotonics' Advanced Hybrid Photonic Integration technology progressively increases performance, reduces costs and reduces product size. This technology is an enabler to the development and manufacturing of products for 100G and beyond applications. The company produces photonic integrated circuits (PICs) that comprise both arrayed and individual photonic functional elements using optimized materials systems and processes from in-house silicon, indium phosphide and gallium arsenide wafer fabrication. NeoPhotonics sells its products to the world's leading network equipment manufacturers, including Alcatel-Lucent SA, Ciena Corporation, Cisco Systems Inc. and Huawei Technologies Co. Ltd., which are among the firm's largest customers, accounting for approximately 79% of 2015 revenue. In 2015, the firm acquired the tunable laser product lines of EMCORE Corporation; and acquired the assets of EigenLight Corporation, along with their precision optical power monitoring technology and product lines.

FINANCIAL DATA: *Note: Data for latest year may not have been available at press time.*

In U.S. $	2016	2015	2014	2013	2012	2011
Revenue		339,439,000	306,177,000	282,242,000	245,423,000	201,029,000
R&D Expense		44,533,000	45,959,000	45,853,000	38,288,000	30,855,000
Operating Income		3,953,000	-19,132,000	-33,673,000	-16,907,000	-28,466,000
Operating Margin %		1.16%	-6.24%	-11.93%	-6.88%	-14.16%
SGA Expense		47,458,000	45,295,000	44,254,000	39,049,000	33,586,000
Net Income		3,668,000	-19,719,000	-34,339,000	-17,530,000	-14,754,000
Operating Cash Flow		26,138,000	-451,000	4,511,000	-8,790,000	-12,510,000
Capital Expenditure		16,837,000	11,027,000	19,566,000	12,738,000	11,677,000
EBITDA		30,890,000	7,472,000	-11,758,000	2,976,000	-882,000
Return on Assets %		1.16%	-6.70%	-11.48%	-6.12%	-14.15%
Return on Equity %		1.97%	-11.72%	-18.33%	-9.43%	-99.38%
Debt to Equity		0.05	0.13	0.13	0.08	0.12

CONTACT INFORMATION:
Phone: 408 232-9200   Fax: 408 456-2971
Toll-Free:
Address: 2911 Zanker Rd., San Jose, CA 95134 United States

SALARIES/BONUSES:
Top Exec. Salary: $435,481   Bonus: $
Second Exec. Salary: $325,948   Bonus: $

STOCK TICKER/OTHER:
Stock Ticker: NPTN
Employees: 2,541
Parent Company:

Exchange: NYS
Fiscal Year Ends: 12/31

OTHER THOUGHTS:
Estimated Female Officers or Directors:
Hot Spot for Advancement for Women/Minorities:

New York Life Insurance Co

www.newyorklife.com

NAIC Code: 524113

TYPES OF BUSINESS:

Life Insurance
Annuities
Mutual Funds
Asset Management
Life Insurance
Real Estate

BRANDS/DIVISIONS/AFFILIATES:

NYLIFE Securities LLC
NYLIFE Distributors LLC
MainStay Investments
IndexIQ

CONTACTS: Note: Officers with more than one job title may be intentionally listed here more than once.

Theodore A. Mathas, CEO
John T. Fleurant, CFO
Katherine R. O'Brien, Sr. VP-Human Resources
John Y. Kim, Chief Investment Officer
John Y. Kim, Pres.
Frank M. Boccio, Chief Admin. Officer
Sheila K. Davidson, General Counsel
Barry Schub, Sr. VP-Strategy & Communications
George Nichols, III, Sr. VP-Office of Gov't Affairs
Christopher O. Blunt, Exec. VP
Mark W. Pfaff, Exec. VP
Susan A. Thrope, Deputy General Counsel
Theodore A. Mathas, Chmn.

GROWTH PLANS/SPECIAL FEATURES:

New York Life Insurance Co. provides life insurance policies, annuities, mutual funds and third-party asset management services. The company has approximately $550 billion assets under management. New York Life operates through two segments: insurance products and investment products. Insurance products include life insurance and long-term care insurance. Types of life insurance includes term life, whole life, universal life, variable universal life, corporate sponsored plans and group membership associations. Subsidiaries within this unit include NYLIFE Securities LLC and NYLIFE Distributors LLC. Long-term insurance helps provide for the cost of long-term care generally not covered by health insurance, Medicare or Medicaid. Investment products include retirement income, investment annuities and mutual funds. Retirement income offers several guaranteed income annuity products such as lifetime income annuities, future income annuities, lifetime mutual income annuities and future mutual income annuities. Investment annuities are types of savings plans that help prepare individuals for retirement, and come in the form of variable annuities and fixed deferred annuities. Mutual funds are provided through New York Life's MainStay Investments subsidiary, which offers a broad selection of mutual funds across multiple asset classes and investment styles. These investments include U.S./international/global stock funds; investment grade, high yield and municipal bond funds; and asset allocation funds that invest in a mix of asset classes and investment styles. In 2015, the firm acquired IndexIQ, a liquid alternative exchange-traded fund provider; and acquired, through reinsurance, 60%, or approximately 1.3 million policies, of John Hancock Financial's closed block portfolio, comprised primarily of participating whole life insurance.

FINANCIAL DATA: Note: Data for latest year may not have been available at press time.

In U.S. $	2016	2015	2014	2013	2012	2011
Revenue		26,127,000,000	27,451,000,000	24,781,000,000	24,709,000,000	23,653,000,000
R&D Expense						
Operating Income						
Operating Margin %						
SGA Expense						
Net Income		1,785,000,000	2,455,000,000	2,045,000,000	2,090,000,000	1,171,000,000
Operating Cash Flow						
Capital Expenditure						
EBITDA						
Return on Assets %						
Return on Equity %						
Debt to Equity						

CONTACT INFORMATION:

Phone: 212-576-7000   Fax: 212-576-8145
Toll-Free: 800-692-3086
Address: 51 Madison Ave., New York, NY 10010 United States

STOCK TICKER/OTHER:

Stock Ticker: Mutual Company   Exchange:
Employees: 12,000   Fiscal Year Ends: 12/31
Parent Company:

SALARIES/BONUSES:

Top Exec. Salary: $ Bonus: $
Second Exec. Salary: $ Bonus: $

OTHER THOUGHTS:

Estimated Female Officers or Directors: 4
Hot Spot for Advancement for Women/Minorities: Y

Nielsen Holdings PLC

www.nielsen.com

NAIC Code: 541910

TYPES OF BUSINESS:

Market Research
Magazine Publishing
Media/Entertainment Audience Research
Trade Publications
Directories
Business Consulting
Internet Audience Research

BRANDS/DIVISIONS/AFFILIATES:

eXelate

CONTACTS: Note: Officers with more than one job title may be intentionally listed here more than once.

Dwight Barns, CEO
Jamere Jackson, CFO
Jeffrey Charlton, Chief Accounting Officer
James Powell, Chief Technology Officer
Stephen Hasker, COO
James Attwood, Director
Eric Dale, Other Executive Officer
Mary Finn, Other Executive Officer
Giovanni Tavolieri, President, Divisional
Arvin Kash, Vice Chairman

GROWTH PLANS/SPECIAL FEATURES:

Nielsen Holdings PLC is a leading global provider of marketing information, audience measurement and business media products and services with operations in over 100 countries and data measurements of 10 million consumers worldwide. The firm has two major segments: what consumers watch (watch) and what consumers buy (buy). Accounting for 44% the company's 2014 revenues, the watch segment provides viewership data and analytics primarily to the media industry, and advertising across three primary platforms that include mobile screens, online and television. Clients of this segment use Nielsen's data to plan and optimize their advertising spending and to better ensure that their advertisements reach the intended audience. The buy segment (responsible for 56% of 2014 revenue) provides consumer behavior information and analytics primarily to businesses in the consumer packaged goods industry. Clients use the data to manage their brands, find new sources of demand, launch and grow new products, improve their marketing mix and establish more effective consumer relationships. In 2015, the firm acquired eXelate, a leading provider of data and technology to facilitate the buying and selling of advertising across programmatic platforms.

FINANCIAL DATA: Note: Data for latest year may not have been available at press time.

In U.S. $	2016	2015	2014	2013	2012	2011
Revenue		6,172,000,000	6,288,000,000	5,703,000,000	5,612,000,000	5,532,000,000
R&D Expense						
Operating Income		1,093,000,000	1,089,000,000	861,000,000	952,000,000	794,000,000
Operating Margin %		17.70%	17.31%	15.09%	16.96%	14.35%
SGA Expense		1,915,000,000	1,917,000,000	1,815,000,000	1,778,000,000	1,888,000,000
Net Income		570,000,000	384,000,000	740,000,000	273,000,000	84,000,000
Operating Cash Flow		1,179,000,000	1,093,000,000	901,000,000	784,000,000	641,000,000
Capital Expenditure		408,000,000	412,000,000	374,000,000	358,000,000	367,000,000
EBITDA		1,846,000,000	1,494,000,000	1,350,000,000	1,341,000,000	1,110,000,000
Return on Assets %		3.71%	2.48%	4.91%	1.87%	.58%
Return on Equity %		12.01%	7.12%	13.88%	5.70%	2.23%
Debt to Equity		1.58	1.27	1.13	1.26	1.42

CONTACT INFORMATION:

Phone: 646 654-5000   Fax:
Toll-Free: 800-864-1224
Address: 85 Broad Street, New York, NY 10004 United States

STOCK TICKER/OTHER:

Stock Ticker: NLSN   Exchange: NYS
Employees: 43,000   Fiscal Year Ends: 12/31
Parent Company:

SALARIES/BONUSES:

Top Exec. Salary: $700,000   Bonus: $325,000
Second Exec. Salary: Bonus: $
$1,000,000

OTHER THOUGHTS:

Estimated Female Officers or Directors: 4
Hot Spot for Advancement for Women/Minorities: Y

Nike Inc
NAIC Code: 424340

TYPES OF BUSINESS:
Footwear Distribution
Athletic Equipment
Sports Accessories
Retail Stores
Sports Apparel
Plastic Products
Hockey Products
Swimwear

BRANDS/DIVISIONS/AFFILIATES:
All Star
Chuck Taylor
Converse Inc
Hurley International LLC
One Star
Jordan
NIKE IHM Inc
Jack Purcell

CONTACTS: Note: Officers with more than one job title may be intentionally listed here more than once.
Mark Parker, CEO
Philip Knight, Chairman Emeritus
Chris Abston, Chief Accounting Officer
Hilary Krane, Chief Administrative Officer
Eric Sprunk, COO
John Slusher, Executive VP, Divisional
David Ayre, Executive VP, Divisional
Andrew Campion, Executive VP
Michael Spillane, President, Divisional
Trevor Edwards, President, Divisional
John Coburn, Vice President

GROWTH PLANS/SPECIAL FEATURES:
Nike, Inc. designs, develops and markets footwear, apparel equipment and accessories. It is one of the largest sellers of athletic footwear and athletic apparel in the world. The company's athletic footwear products are designed primarily for specific athletic use, although a large percentage of its products are worn for casual or leisure purposes. Running, training, basketball and soccer sport-inspired urban shoes and children's shoes are the firm's top-selling product categories. Nike also markets shoes designed for tennis, golf, baseball, football, lacrosse, walking, outdoor activities, skateboarding, bicycling, volleyball, wrestling, cheerleading, aquatic activities and other athletic and recreational uses. The firm maintains several wholly-owned subsidiaries: Converse, Inc., which distributes and licenses footwear, apparel and accessories through brand names Converse, All Star, One Star, Chuck Taylor, Star Chevron and Jack Purcell; Hurley International LLC, which is headquartered in the U.K. and designs/distributes a collection of action sports apparel sold under the Hurley brand; and Jordan, which sells a line of basketball shoes, clothing and gear for men. Another subsidiary, NIKE IHM, Inc. sells small amounts of various plastic products to other manufacturers. Nike sells its products to retail accounts, through Nike-owned retail stores and through a mix of independent distributors and licensees worldwide. Within the U.S. the firm operates 339 Nike Brand and subsidiary retail stores: 218 Nike locations, 92 Converse stores including factory outlets and 29 Hurley locations. In the international market, which includes countries within Europe, Asia, South America and Africa, the firm maintains 592 retail stores (585 Nike and seven Converse). In March 2015, the sportswear giant announced it will launch partnerships with Garmin, TomTom, Wahoo Fitness and Netpulse in an effort to broaden its Nike+ running community.

FINANCIAL DATA: Note: Data for latest year may not have been available at press time.

In U.S. $	2016	2015	2014	2013	2012	2011
Revenue	32,376,000,000	30,601,000,000	27,799,000,000	25,313,000,000	24,128,000,000	20,862,000,000
R&D Expense						
Operating Income	4,502,000,000	4,175,000,000	3,680,000,000	3,254,000,000	3,040,000,000	2,815,000,000
Operating Margin %	13.90%	13.64%	13.23%	12.85%	12.59%	13.49%
SGA Expense	10,469,000,000	9,892,000,000	8,766,000,000	7,780,000,000	7,431,000,000	6,693,000,000
Net Income	3,760,000,000	3,273,000,000	2,693,000,000	2,485,000,000	2,223,000,000	2,133,000,000
Operating Cash Flow	3,096,000,000	4,680,000,000	3,003,000,000	3,027,000,000	1,899,000,000	1,812,000,000
Capital Expenditure	1,143,000,000	963,000,000	880,000,000	636,000,000	597,000,000	432,000,000
EBITDA	5,164,000,000	4,824,000,000	4,312,000,000	3,767,000,000	3,445,000,000	3,206,000,000
Return on Assets %	17.48%	16.28%	14.88%	15.03%	14.59%	14.50%
Return on Equity %	30.12%	27.81%	24.50%	23.07%	21.98%	21.76%
Debt to Equity	0.16	0.08	0.11	0.10	0.02	0.02

CONTACT INFORMATION:
Phone: 503 671-6453   Fax: 503 671-6300
Toll-Free: 800-344-6453
Address: 1 Bowerman Dr., Beaverton, OR 97005 United States

STOCK TICKER/OTHER:
Stock Ticker: NKE   Exchange: NYS
Employees: 62,600   Fiscal Year Ends: 05/31
Parent Company:

SALARIES/BONUSES:
Top Exec. Salary: Bonus: $
$1,550,000
Second Exec. Salary: Bonus: $
$990,000

OTHER THOUGHTS:
Estimated Female Officers or Directors: 2

Hot Spot for Advancement for Women/Minorities: Y

NN Inc

NAIC Code: 332991

www.nninc.com/

TYPES OF BUSINESS:
Ball and Roller Bearing Manufacturing

BRANDS/DIVISIONS/AFFILIATES:
Caprock Manufacturing Inc
Caprock Enclosures LLC
Precision Engineered Products Holdings Inc

CONTACTS: Note: Officers with more than one job title may be intentionally listed here more than once.
Richard Holder, CEO
G. Morris, Chairman of the Board
Thomas Burwell, Chief Accounting Officer
Matthew Heiter, General Counsel
John Manzi, General Manager, Divisional
Warren Veltman, General Manager, Divisional
Jeff Manzagol, General Manager, Divisional
James Widders, Senior VP, Divisional

GROWTH PLANS/SPECIAL FEATURES:
NN, Inc. is a global manufacturer of high precision bearing components, industrial plastic products and precision metal components to a wide array of markets. The company has 42 manufacturing plants in North America, Western & Eastern Europe, South America and China. NN operates through three segments: precision bearing components, precision engineered products and autocam precision components. The precision bearing components segment derives 39% of annual net sales, and manufactures and supplies high precision bearing components, consisting of balls, cylindrical rollers, tapered rollers, spherical rollers and metal retainers for leading bearing and CV-joint (constant velocity) manufacturers on a global basis. The precision engineered products segment (12%) manufactures highly-engineered, difficult-to-manufacture precision metal components and subassemblies for the automotive, HVAC, fluid power and diesel engine end markets. Products within this division include surgical knives, bioresorbable implants, surgical staples, orthopedic system tools, laparoscopic devices, drug delivery devices, catheter components, electrical connectors, precision stampings, optical grade plastics, thermally-conductive plastics, as well as titanium, Iconel, magnesium and gold electroplating. The autocam precision components segment (49%) sells a wide range of highly-engineered, extremely close tolerance, precision-machined metal components and subassemblies primarily to the consumer transportation, industrial technology, HVAC, fluid power and diesel engine end markets. This division has developed an expertise in manufacturing highly-complex, system critical components for fuel systems, engines, transmissions, power steering systems and electromechanical motors. In 2015, the firm acquired Caprock Manufacturing, Inc., Caprock Enclosures LLC; and Precision Engineered Products Holdings, Inc. That same year, it sold Delta Rubber Company.

FINANCIAL DATA: Note: Data for latest year may not have been available at press time.

In U.S. $	2016	2015	2014	2013	2012	2011
Revenue		667,280,000	488,601,000	373,206,000	370,084,000	424,691,000
R&D Expense						
Operating Income		26,797,000	27,687,000	27,827,000	25,071,000	29,432,000
Operating Margin %		4.01%	5.66%	7.45%	6.77%	6.93%
SGA Expense		51,745,000	43,756,000	33,281,000	31,561,000	30,657,000
Net Income		-7,431,000	8,217,000	17,178,000	24,268,000	20,937,000
Operating Cash Flow		33,310,000	30,708,000	31,751,000	37,358,000	14,955,000
Capital Expenditure		38,553,000	27,602,000	15,250,000	17,089,000	20,329,000
EBITDA		51,431,000	48,442,000	44,509,000	41,862,000	48,645,000
Return on Assets %		- .70%	1.68%	6.50%	9.24%	8.24%
Return on Equity %		-3.04%	5.03%	12.21%	21.26%	23.55%
Debt to Equity		2.60	1.97	0.19	0.52	0.75

CONTACT INFORMATION:
Phone: 423 743-9151   Fax: 423 743-2670
Toll-Free:
Address: 207 Mockingbird Lane, Johnson City, TN 37604 United States

STOCK TICKER/OTHER:
Stock Ticker: NNBR
Employees: 3,775
Parent Company:

Exchange: NAS
Fiscal Year Ends: 12/31

SALARIES/BONUSES:
Top Exec. Salary: $596,154   Bonus: $
Second Exec. Salary: $356,625   Bonus: $

OTHER THOUGHTS:
Estimated Female Officers or Directors:
Hot Spot for Advancement for Women/Minorities:

Sales, profits and employees may be estimates. Financial information, benefits and other data can change quickly and may vary from those stated here.

Nordstrom Inc
NAIC Code: 452111

TYPES OF BUSINESS:
Department Stores
Outlet Stores
Online Retailing
Catalog Sales
Financial Services
Federal Savings Bank

BRANDS/DIVISIONS/AFFILIATES:
Nordstrom.com
HauteLook
TrunkClub.com
Nordstrom Rack
Jeffrey
Last Chance
Nordstrom fsb
Nordstrom

CONTACTS: Note: Officers with more than one job title may be intentionally listed here more than once.
Michael Koppel, CFO
Enrique Hernandez, Chairman of the Board
James Howell, Chief Accounting Officer
Daniel Little, Chief Information Officer
Peter Nordstrom, Director
Blake Nordstrom, Director
Erik Nordstrom, Director
Ken Worzel, Executive VP, Divisional
Christine Deputy Ott, Executive VP, Divisional
Brian Dennehy, Executive VP
Robert Sari, Executive VP
Geevy Thomas, Executive VP
James Nordstrom, Executive VP

GROWTH PLANS/SPECIAL FEATURES:

Nordstrom, Inc., founded in 1901, is an upscale fashion apparel and shoe retailer. Nordstrom operates a total of 323 stores in 39 U.S. states, as well as an e-commerce business through Nordstrom.com, HauteLook and TrunkClub.com. The retailer also operates three Nordstrom full-line stores in Canada. The company sells a wide selection of apparel, shoes and accessories for women, men and children. The west and east coasts of the U.S. are the areas where the company has its largest presence. Nordstrom operates through two segments: retail and credit. The retail segment includes 118 Nordstrom branded full-line stores, 197 off-price Nordstrom Rack stores, three Canadian full-line stores, as well as other retail channels Trunk Club showrooms, Jeffrey boutiques and a clearance store that operates under the Last Chance name. The credit segment includes Nordstrom's wholly-owned federal savings bank, Nordstrom fsb, through which it offers a private label credit card, two Nordstrom VISA credit cards and a debit card. It generates income through finance charges and fees on these cards and saves on interchange fees that the retail segment would incur when its customers use third-party cards. In May 2016, the firm announced that it would hire 1,600 local employees (800 each) for its new CF Toronto Eaton Centre and Yorkdale Shopping Centre stores, located in Canada, in the Fall of the same year. The Toronto stores mark the retailer's fourth and fifth Canadian locations. The first Nordstrom Rack is scheduled to open in Toronto in 2018.

Nordstrom offers employees benefits including medical, dental, vision, AD&D, life and short- and long-term disability insurance; wellness programs; 401(k) plan & profit sharing; employee stock purchase plan; access to the company bank and credit union; employee assistance programs; adoption financial assistance; and merchandise discounts.

FINANCIAL DATA: Note: Data for latest year may not have been available at press time.

In U.S. $	2016	2015	2014	2013	2012	2011
Revenue	14,437,000,000	13,506,000,000	12,540,000,000	12,148,000,000	10,877,000,000	9,700,000,000
R&D Expense						
Operating Income	1,101,000,000	1,323,000,000	1,350,000,000	1,345,000,000	1,249,000,000	1,118,000,000
Operating Margin %	7.62%	9.79%	10.76%	11.07%	11.48%	11.52%
SGA Expense	4,168,000,000	3,777,000,000	3,453,000,000	3,371,000,000	3,036,000,000	2,685,000,000
Net Income	600,000,000	720,000,000	734,000,000	735,000,000	683,000,000	613,000,000
Operating Cash Flow	2,451,000,000	1,220,000,000	1,320,000,000	1,110,000,000	1,177,000,000	1,177,000,000
Capital Expenditure	1,082,000,000	861,000,000	803,000,000	513,000,000	511,000,000	399,000,000
EBITDA	1,677,000,000	1,832,000,000	1,805,000,000	1,713,000,000	1,576,000,000	1,451,000,000
Return on Assets %	7.08%	8.08%	8.80%	8.86%	8.56%	8.73%
Return on Equity %	36.24%	31.85%	36.76%	37.99%	34.34%	34.12%
Debt to Equity	3.20	1.27	1.49	1.63	1.60	1.37

CONTACT INFORMATION:
Phone: 206 628-2111   Fax: 206 628-1795
Toll-Free: 888-282-6060
Address: 1617 Sixth Avenue, Seattle, WA 98101 United States

STOCK TICKER/OTHER:
Stock Ticker: JWN   Exchange: NYS
Employees: 67,000   Fiscal Year Ends: 01/31
Parent Company:

SALARIES/BONUSES:
Top Exec. Salary: $764,328   Bonus: $
Second Exec. Salary: Bonus: $
$735,445

OTHER THOUGHTS:
Estimated Female Officers or Directors: 8
Hot Spot for Advancement for Women/Minorities: Y

Nortek Holdings Inc

www.nortek-inc.com

NAIC Code: 333415

TYPES OF BUSINESS:

Warm Air Heating and Air-Conditioning Equipment Manufacturing

BRANDS/DIVISIONS/AFFILIATES:

Broan
Zephyr
Linear
Mighty Mule
OmniMount
Governair
Anthro Corporation
Nuiku

CONTACTS: Note: Officers with more than one job title may be intentionally listed here more than once.

Michael Clarke, CEO
J. Smith, Chairman of the Board
Kevin Donnelly, General Counsel
David LaGrand, President, Divisional
Peter Segar, President, Divisional
Mark DeVincent, President, Divisional
Jeffrey Mueller, President, Divisional
Timothy Burling, Senior VP, Divisional
Donald Reilly, Vice President

GROWTH PLANS/SPECIAL FEATURES:

Nortek, Inc. and its wholly-owned subsidiaries are diversified manufacturers of innovative, branded residential and commercial building products. The company operates within five reporting segments: air quality & home solutions (AQH), security & control solutions (SCS), ergonomic & productivity solutions (ERG), residential & commercial HVAC (RCH) and custom & commercial air solutions (CAS). Through these segments Nortek manufactures and sells a variety of products principally for the remodeling and replacement markets, the residential and commercial new construction markets and the personal and enterprise computer markets. The company primarily manufactures and sells its products in the U.S., Canada and Europe, with additional manufacturing in China and Mexico. AQH products include range hoods, exhaust fans, indoor air quality products and central vacuum systems under brands such as Broan, NuTone, Venmar, Best and Zephyr. SCS products include security, automation and access control equipment and systems under the Linear, 2GIG, Numera, Mighty Mule and GTO/PRO brands. ERG products include wall and desk mounts, carts, arms, workstations, stands and related accessories under the Ergotron, OmniMount and Anthro brands. RCH products include split-system & packaged air conditioners and heat pumps, air handlers, furnaces and heaters under brands such as Frigidaire and Gibson. CAS products include HVAC products under brands such as Mammoth and Governair. In 2015, Nortek acquired Anthro Corporation, as well as the health & wellness technology business from Numera, Inc. In 2016, it acquired Nuiku, a next-generation natural language processing platform that facilitates voice control across home automation and other applications; and agreed to acquire a minority stake (25%) in MiOS Limited. In July of the same year, Nortek agreed to be acquired by U.K.-based Melrose Industries PLC for approximately $2.8 billion.

FINANCIAL DATA: Note: Data for latest year may not have been available at press time.

In U.S. $	2016	2015	2014	2013	2012	2011
Revenue		2,526,099,968	2,546,099,968	2,287,899,904	2,201,299,968	2,140,499,968
R&D Expense						
Operating Income						
Operating Margin %						
SGA Expense						
Net Income		-26,700,000	-45,600,000	-8,300,000	9,500,000	-55,900,000
Operating Cash Flow						
Capital Expenditure						
EBITDA						
Return on Assets %						
Return on Equity %						
Debt to Equity						

CONTACT INFORMATION:

Phone: 401 751-1600   Fax:
Toll-Free:
Address: 500 Exchange Street, Providence, RI 02903 United States

STOCK TICKER/OTHER:

Stock Ticker: NTK   Exchange: NAS
Employees: 11,200   Fiscal Year Ends: 12/31
Parent Company:

SALARIES/BONUSES:

Top Exec. Salary: $ Bonus: $
Second Exec. Salary: $ Bonus: $

OTHER THOUGHTS:

Estimated Female Officers or Directors:
Hot Spot for Advancement for Women/Minorities:

Sales, profits and employees may be estimates. Financial information, benefits and other data can change quickly and may vary from those stated here.

Northwestern Mutual Life Insurance Co

www.northwesternmutual.com
NAIC Code: 524113

TYPES OF BUSINESS:

Life Insurance
Disability Insurance
Employee Benefit Plans
Long-Term Care Insurance
Investment Products & Services
Financial Planning Services

BRANDS/DIVISIONS/AFFILIATES:

Northwestern Long Term Care Insurance Company
Northwestern Mutual Investment Services LLC
Northwestern Mutual Financial Network
Northwestern Mutual Trust Company
Strategic Employee Benefit Services
Network Planning Advisors
Estate Strategies Group

CONTACTS: Note: Officers with more than one job title may be intentionally listed here more than once.

John E. Schlifske, CEO
Gregory C. Oberland, Pres.
Michael G. Carter, CFO
Ronald Paul Joelson, CIO
Jean M. Maier, Exec. VP-Tech.
Raymond J. Manista, General Counsel
Jean M. Maier, Exec. VP-Enterprise Oper.
Ronald P. Joelson, Exec. VP
Todd M. Schoon, Exec. VP-Agencies
John E. Schlifske, Chmn.

GROWTH PLANS/SPECIAL FEATURES:

Northwestern Mutual Life Insurance Co. (NMLIC) is a financial network company. It offers network services, insurance products, investment products and advisory services to 4.3 million policy owners, and has $238.5 billion in assets, $279 billion in revenues and more than $1.6 trillion worth of life insurance protection in force. NMLIC's network services include asset and income protection, personal needs analysis investment services, education funding and retirement products. The firm also offers permanent, term and combination life insurance plans, providing individual and group disability plans to approximately 450,000 policy holders. Long-term care insurance is offered to more than 150,000 policy holders through NMLIC's Northwestern Long Term Care Insurance Company subsidiary, while investment services are provided by Northwestern Mutual Investment Services, LLC. Under its marketing name, Northwestern Mutual Financial Network, NMLIC offers a wide range of products and services through 350 offices across the U.S. Network affiliates include Strategic Employee Benefit Services, which provides custom-designed employee benefit programs; Network Planning Advisors, which offers financial planning services; Estate Strategies Group, an investment advising group specializing in estate and business succession planning; and Northwestern Mutual Trust Company, which offers a full range of investment and trust services.

NMLIC offers its employees flexible spending accounts, training programs, flexible work schedules, adoption assistance, an onsite fitness center, credit union membership, educational assistance and a business casual work environment.

FINANCIAL DATA: Note: Data for latest year may not have been available at press time.

In U.S. $	2016	2015	2014	2013	2012	2011
Revenue		27,880,000,000	26,707,000,000	25,909,000,000	24,621,000,000	23,595,000,000
R&D Expense						
Operating Income						
Operating Margin %						
SGA Expense						
Net Income			679,000,000	802,000,000	783,000,000	645,000,000
Operating Cash Flow						
Capital Expenditure						
EBITDA						
Return on Assets %						
Return on Equity %						
Debt to Equity						

CONTACT INFORMATION:

Phone: 414-271-1444   Fax: 414-299-7022
Toll-Free:
Address: 720 E. Wisconsin Ave., Milwaukee, WI 53202 United States

STOCK TICKER/OTHER:

Stock Ticker: Mutual Company   Exchange:
Employees: 5,000   Fiscal Year Ends: 12/31
Parent Company:

SALARIES/BONUSES:

Top Exec. Salary: $ Bonus: $
Second Exec. Salary: $ Bonus: $

OTHER THOUGHTS:

Estimated Female Officers or Directors: 5
Hot Spot for Advancement for Women/Minorities: Y

Norwegian Cruise Line Holdings Ltd (NCL)

www.ncl.com

NAIC Code: 483112

TYPES OF BUSINESS:
Cruise Line
Luxury Cruise Lines

BRANDS/DIVISIONS/AFFILIATES:
Regent Seven Seas
Oceania Cruises
Prestige Cruises International

CONTACTS: Note: Officers with more than one job title may be intentionally listed here more than once.
Daniel Farkas, Assistant Secretary
Frank Del Rio, CEO
Wendy Beck, CFO
Faye Ashby, Chief Accounting Officer
Jason Montague, COO, Divisional
Walter Revell, Director
Harry Sommer, Executive VP, Divisional
T. Lindsay, Executive VP, Divisional
Andrew Stuart, President, Divisional
Robert Binder, Vice Chairman, Divisional

GROWTH PLANS/SPECIAL FEATURES:
Norwegian Cruise Line Holdings Ltd. (NCLH) is one of the largest cruise line operators in the world. It offers a wide variety of cruises ranging in length from one day to three weeks and itineraries originating from 19 ports (of which 13 are in North America). In addition to the traditional cruise markets in the Caribbean and Mexico, Norwegian sails to destinations in Europe, including the Mediterranean and the Baltic, Bermuda, Alaska and Hawaii. The firm owns Prestige Cruises International, which in turn owns Oceania Cruises and Regent Seven Seas Cruises. These two brands operate a total of eight ships with over 6,400 berths. Oceania operates a fleet of five mid-size ships, providing customers with an upscale and sophisticated experience including personalized service and elegant accommodations. Oceania offers destination-oriented cruises to approximately 330 ports around the globe. Regent offers a luxury all-inclusive cruise vacation experience, including free air transportation, a pre-cruise hotel night stay, premium wines and top shelf liquors, gratuities and unlimited shore excursions. The brand operates three all-suite ships, with itineraries to approximately 300 ports worldwide. Overall, the company has a combined fleet of 22 ships, which offer itineraries to more than 520 destinations worldwide. By 2019, the firm's fleet of major ships will total 27. In January 2015, NCLH expanded its sales presence in Sao Paulo, Brazil, with the establishment of a sales, marketing and reservations center. In October of same year, NCLH announced that it will introduce its first purpose-built ship customized for the China market by 2017.

FINANCIAL DATA: Note: Data for latest year may not have been available at press time.

In U.S. $	2016	2015	2014	2013	2012	2011
Revenue		4,345,048,000	3,125,881,000	2,570,294,000	2,276,246,000	2,219,324,000
R&D Expense						
Operating Income		702,486,000	502,941,000	395,887,000	357,093,000	316,112,000
Operating Margin %		16.16%	16.08%	15.40%	15.68%	14.24%
SGA Expense		554,999,000	403,169,000	301,155,000	251,183,000	251,351,000
Net Income		427,137,000	338,352,000	101,714,000	168,556,000	126,859,000
Operating Cash Flow		1,041,178,000	635,601,000	475,281,000	398,594,000	356,990,000
Capital Expenditure		1,122,734,000	1,051,974,000	894,851,000	303,840,000	184,797,000
EBITDA		1,152,821,000	807,818,000	640,998,000	574,623,000	527,161,000
Return on Assets %		3.58%	3.71%	1.61%	2.93%	2.28%
Return on Equity %		11.70%	11.04%	4.39%	8.72%	7.09%
Debt to Equity		1.52	1.59	1.08	1.36	1.53

CONTACT INFORMATION:
Phone: 305-436-4000   Fax: 305-436-4140
Toll-Free:
Address: 7665 Corporate Center Dr., Miami, FL 33126 United States

STOCK TICKER/OTHER:
Stock Ticker: NCLH   Exchange: NAS
Employees: 2,700   Fiscal Year Ends: 12/31
Parent Company:

SALARIES/BONUSES:
Top Exec. Salary: Bonus: $
$1,837,500
Second Exec. Salary: Bonus: $757,500
$891,027

OTHER THOUGHTS:
Estimated Female Officers or Directors: 4

Hot Spot for Advancement for Women/Minorities: Y

NVIDIA Corp

NAIC Code: 334413

www.nvidia.com

TYPES OF BUSINESS:

Printed Circuit Assembly (Electronic Assembly) Manufacturing
Graphics Processors
Graphics Software

BRANDS/DIVISIONS/AFFILIATES:

GeForce
Quadro
Tesla
GRID
Tegra
DRIVE
SHIELD

CONTACTS: Note: Officers with more than one job title may be intentionally listed here more than once.

David Shannon, Chief Administrative Officer

GROWTH PLANS/SPECIAL FEATURES:

NVIDIA Corp. designs, develops and markets a family of 3D graphics processors, graphics processing units (GPUs) and related software. The company serves virtually all markets that rely on high-quality visuals in PC applications, including manufacturing, science, e-business, entertainment and education. It has two product groups: the GPU and Tegra processors. GPUs, each with billions of transistors, are the engine of visual computing and among the world's most complex processors. Products include GeForce, Quadro, Tesla and GRID. GeForce processors enhance the gaming experience on PCs by improving the visual quality of graphics. Quadro is for professional workstations. Tesla is a GPU-accelerated computing processor used to accelerate scientific, analytics, engineering, consumer and enterprise applications. GRID uses GPUs to deliver graphics performance remotely, from the cloud. GRID's uses include gaming, professional applications provided as a service and improving Citrix and VMware installations. Tegra processors are architected to deliver a superior visual and multimedia experience on tablets, smartphones and gaming devices while consuming minimal power. Tegra is also sold to original equipment manufacturers for devices where graphics and overall performance are of great importance. The processors are primarily designed to enable the firm's branded DRIVE and SHIELD platforms. DRIVE automotive computers provide supercomputing capabilities to make driving safer and more enjoyable. SHIELD is a family of devices designed to harness the power of mobile-cloud in order to revolutionize gaming. NVIDIA's research and development in visual computing has yielded approximately 7,000 patent assets, including inventions essential to modern computing.

Employees of NVIDIA receive medical, dental and vision coverage; a 529 college savings plan; a 401(K) plan; an employee assistance program; flex spending accounts; and discounts with Apple, Microsoft and AT&T.

FINANCIAL DATA: Note: Data for latest year may not have been available at press time.

In U.S. $	2016	2015	2014	2013	2012	2011
Revenue	5,010,000,000	4,681,507,000	4,130,162,000	4,280,159,000	3,997,930,000	3,543,309,000
R&D Expense	1,331,000,000	1,359,725,000	1,335,834,000	1,147,282,000	1,002,605,000	848,830,000
Operating Income	747,000,000	758,989,000	496,227,000	648,239,000	648,299,000	255,747,000
Operating Margin %	14.91%	16.21%	12.01%	15.14%	16.21%	7.21%
SGA Expense	602,000,000	480,763,000	435,702,000	430,822,000	405,613,000	418,513,000
Net Income	614,000,000	630,587,000	439,990,000	562,536,000	581,090,000	253,146,000
Operating Cash Flow	1,175,000,000	905,656,000	835,146,000	824,172,000	909,156,000	675,797,000
Capital Expenditure	86,000,000	122,381,000	255,186,000	183,309,000	138,735,000	97,890,000
EBITDA	987,000,000	1,021,094,000	759,845,000	891,568,000	870,690,000	461,285,000
Return on Assets %	8.42%	8.72%	6.44%	9.40%	11.56%	6.26%
Return on Equity %	13.81%	14.21%	9.47%	12.53%	15.86%	8.65%
Debt to Equity		0.31	0.30			

CONTACT INFORMATION:

Phone: 408 486-2000   Fax: 408 486-2200
Toll-Free:
Address: 2701 San Tomas Expressway, Santa Clara, CA 95050 United States

STOCK TICKER/OTHER:

Stock Ticker: NVDA   Exchange: NAS
Employees: 9,227   Fiscal Year Ends: 01/31
Parent Company:

SALARIES/BONUSES:

Top Exec. Salary: $789,680   Bonus: $1,000,000
Second Exec. Salary: $1,018,941   Bonus: $

OTHER THOUGHTS:

Estimated Female Officers or Directors: 3
Hot Spot for Advancement for Women/Minorities: Y

NVR Inc

NAIC Code: 236117

www.nvrinc.com/

TYPES OF BUSINESS:

Construction, Home Building and Residential
Mortgages
Townhouse Construction
Condominium Construction

BRANDS/DIVISIONS/AFFILIATES:

Ryan Homes
NVHomes
Fox Ridge Homes
NVR Mortgage Finance Inc
VR Mortgage Finance Inc

CONTACTS: *Note: Officers with more than one job title may be intentionally listed here more than once.*

Daniel Malzahn, CFO

GROWTH PLANS/SPECIAL FEATURES:

NVR, Inc. is primarily engaged in the construction and sale of single-family detached homes, townhomes and condominium buildings. Additionally, NVR offers mortgage banking services through its subsidiary NVR Mortgage Finance, Inc. (NVRM). NVRM originates mortgage loans for NVR's homebuilding customers and sells all mortgage loans it closes to investors in the secondary markets on a servicing released basis. The company operates in 14 states, with concentration in the Washington, D.C. and Baltimore, Maryland metropolitan areas, which accounted for 31% and 13% of its 2015 homebuilding revenues. NVR's homebuilding operations include the sale and construction of single-family detached homes, townhomes and condominium buildings under four brand names: Ryan Homes, Fox Ridge Homes, NVHomes and Heartland Homes. The Ryan Homes and Fox Ridge products are moderately priced and marketed primarily to first-time homeowners and first-time move-up buyers. Ryan Homes are currently sold in 28 metropolitan areas located primarily in the eastern U.S. Fox Ridge Homes are sold solely in the Nashville, Tennessee metropolitan area. NVHomes are marketed primarily to move-up and upscale buyers and are sold in Delaware, Washington, D.C., Baltimore and Philadelphia metropolitan areas. Heartland Homes are sold in Pittsburgh. The firm's houses range from approximately 1,000 to 7,000 square feet, typically including two to four bedrooms, and are priced between $136,000 and $1.9 million. NVR also provides mortgage-related services through its mortgage banking operations, which include subsidiaries that broker title insurance and perform title searches.

FINANCIAL DATA: *Note: Data for latest year may not have been available at press time.*

In U.S. $	2016	2015	2014	2013	2012	2011
Revenue		5,169,562,000	4,449,508,000	4,220,908,000	3,193,204,000	2,663,906,000
R&D Expense						
Operating Income		626,771,000	473,055,000	441,081,000	282,606,000	185,605,000
Operating Margin %		12.12%	10.63%	10.44%	8.85%	6.96%
SGA Expense		424,009,000	407,867,000	355,623,000	334,959,000	294,515,000
Net Income		382,927,000	281,630,000	266,477,000	180,588,000	129,420,000
Operating Cash Flow		203,391,000	184,549,000	270,222,000	264,384,000	1,463,000
Capital Expenditure		18,277,000	31,672,000	19,016,000	12,365,000	11,444,000
EBITDA		648,305,000	494,300,000	454,472,000	290,706,000	216,140,000
Return on Assets %		15.73%	11.64%	10.46%	8.23%	6.40%
Return on Equity %		32.40%	23.61%	19.43%	12.64%	8.30%
Debt to Equity		0.48	0.53	0.47	0.40	

CONTACT INFORMATION:

Phone: 703 956-4000   Fax: 703 956-4750
Toll-Free:
Address: 11700 Plz. America Dr., Ste. 500, Reston, VA 20190 United States

STOCK TICKER/OTHER:

Stock Ticker: NVR
Employees: 3,942
Parent Company:

Exchange: NYS
Fiscal Year Ends: 12/31

SALARIES/BONUSES:

Top Exec. Salary: Bonus: $
$1,528,125
Second Exec. Salary: Bonus: $
$462,500

OTHER THOUGHTS:

Estimated Female Officers or Directors:

Hot Spot for Advancement for Women/Minorities:

Old Dominion Freight Line Inc

www.odfl.com

NAIC Code: 484122

TYPES OF BUSINESS:

Trucking
LTL Trucking
Freight Logistics

BRANDS/DIVISIONS/AFFILIATES:

OD-Domestic
OD-Expedited
OD-Global
OD-Technology
OD-Household Services

CONTACTS: Note: Officers with more than one job title may be intentionally listed here more than once.

Adam Satterfield, Assistant Secretary
John Congdon, CEO, Subsidiary
Earl Congdon, Chairman of the Board
Greg Gantt, COO
David Congdon, Director
Ross Parr, General Counsel
Cecil Overbey, Senior VP, Divisional
Kevin Freeman, Senior VP, Divisional
David Bates, Senior VP, Divisional
John Booker, Vice President

GROWTH PLANS/SPECIAL FEATURES:

Old Dominion Freight Line, Inc. is a less-than-truckload (LTL)
multi-regional motor carrier. The firm provides one- to five-day
service among six regions in the U.S. and next-day and
second-day service within these regions. LTL carriers pick up
multiple shipments from multiple customers on a single truck
and then route the goods through service centers where freight
may be transferred to other trucks for delivery. Old Dominion
offers its services through five branded product groups: OD-
Domestic, OD-Household Services, OD-Expedited, OD-Global
and OD-Technology. Through marketing and carrier
relationships, the firm also provides service to and from all of
North America, Central America, South America and the Far
East. Old Dominion conducts operations through
approximately 222 U.S. service center locations. The company
operates major break-bulk facilities in Atlanta, Georgia; Rialto,
California; Indianapolis, Indiana; Greensboro, North Carolina;
Harrisburg, Pennsylvania; Memphis and Morristown,
Tennessee; and Dallas, Texas. Additionally, the company uses
smaller service centers for limited break-bulk activity in order to
serve next-day markets. The service centers are strategically
located in five regions of the country to help minimize freight
handling costs. The firm uses roughly 27,259 trailers (most of
which are 28 feet in length) in its line haul operations, often
combined into tractor-trailer-trailer combinations, allowing
goods to be shipped with minimal unloading and reloading. Old
Dominion operates approximately 6,907 tractors. Tractors are
generally used in long-distance operations for roughly three to
five years and are then transferred to less demanding pickup
and delivery operations.

FINANCIAL DATA: Note: Data for latest year may not have been available at press time.

In U.S. $	2016	2015	2014	2013	2012	2011
Revenue		2,972,442,000	2,787,897,000	2,337,648,000	2,110,483,000	1,882,541,000
R&D Expense						
Operating Income		498,240,000	441,307,000	338,438,000	285,254,000	234,072,000
Operating Margin %		16.76%	15.82%	14.47%	13.51%	12.43%
SGA Expense		1,695,632,000	1,518,575,000	1,306,510,000	1,188,634,000	1,065,465,000
Net Income		304,690,000	267,514,000	206,113,000	169,452,000	139,470,000
Operating Cash Flow		553,880,000	391,674,000	350,666,000	328,056,000	277,380,000
Capital Expenditure		462,059,000	367,680,000	295,606,000	373,193,000	250,214,000
EBITDA		660,570,000	585,590,000	465,378,000	395,382,000	324,971,000
Return on Assets %		12.95%	12.83%	11.31%	10.50%	10.13%
Return on Equity %		19.17%	19.62%	18.25%	18.00%	18.28%
Debt to Equity		0.06	0.08	0.12	0.19	0.26

CONTACT INFORMATION:

Phone: 336 889-5000   Fax: 336 822-5239
Toll-Free: 800-432-6335
Address: 500 Old Dominion Way, Thomasville, NC 27360 United States

STOCK TICKER/OTHER:

Stock Ticker: ODFL   Exchange: NAS
Employees: 16,443   Fiscal Year Ends: 12/31
Parent Company:

SALARIES/BONUSES:

Top Exec. Salary: $575,328   Bonus: $
Second Exec. Salary: Bonus: $
$575,328

OTHER THOUGHTS:

Estimated Female Officers or Directors:
Hot Spot for Advancement for Women/Minorities:

Oliver Wyman Group

www.oliverwymangroup.com

NAIC Code: 541610

TYPES OF BUSINESS:

Management Consulting
Business Strategy Consulting
Financial Services Consulting
Risk Management & Insurance Consulting

BRANDS/DIVISIONS/AFFILIATES:

Oliver Wyman
Lippincott
NERA Economic Consulting
Oliver Wyman Institute
Marsh & McLennan Companies
Mercer LLC
Guy Carpenter
Marsh

CONTACTS: Note: Officers with more than one job title may be intentionally listed here more than once.

Scott McDonald, CEO
Scott McDonald, Pres.
Matthew Cunningham, CFO
Nicky Dingemans, Chief Human Capital Officer
Paula McGlarry, General Counsel
Simon Harris, Chief Strategy & Corp. Dev. Officer
David Fishbaum, Actuarial
Rachel Kirsh, Chief Risk Officer

GROWTH PLANS/SPECIAL FEATURES:

Oliver Wyman Group (OWG), a subsidiary of Marsh & McLennan Companies, is a global consulting group with offices in over 50 cities in 25 countries. The company operates in three units. The largest part of the group is its Oliver Wyman unit, a management consulting firm offering general business consulting with specialized expertise in strategy, operations, risk management, organizational transformation and leadership development. The second unit is Lippincott, a firm offering services related to corporate brand strategy and design consultancy. The group's third unit, NERA Economic Consulting, provides economic analysis and advice related to complex business and legal issues arising from regulation, public policy, litigation, strategy and competition. In addition, as part of the Marsh & McLennan group, OWG works in partnership with sister companies such as Mercer LLC, a human capital consulting firm; Guy Carpenter, a provider of reinsurance advisory services; and Marsh, a risk consulting company. OWG's clients are primarily the CEOs and top management of Fortune 1000 firms across a number of key industries, including automotive, aviation and aerospace, defense, energy, communications and media, financial services, retail and consumer products, health care, life sciences, technology and transportation. Special projects of the firm include the Oliver Wyman Institute, a collaborative group that conducts market research, and the Delta Organization & Leadership Executive Learning Center, which implements custom leadership development and education programs.

FINANCIAL DATA: Note: Data for latest year may not have been available at press time.

In U.S. $	2016	2015	2014	2013	2012	2011
Revenue		1,751,000,000	1,710,000,000	1,483,000,000	1,466,000,000	1,483,000,000
R&D Expense						
Operating Income						
Operating Margin %						
SGA Expense						
Net Income						
Operating Cash Flow						
Capital Expenditure						
EBITDA						
Return on Assets %						
Return on Equity %						
Debt to Equity						

CONTACT INFORMATION:

Phone: 212-345-8000   Fax: 212-345-8075
Toll-Free:
Address: 1166 Ave. of the Americas, New York, NY 10036 United States

STOCK TICKER/OTHER:

Stock Ticker: Subsidiary   Exchange:
Employees: 4,000   Fiscal Year Ends: 12/31
Parent Company: Marsh & McLennan Companies Inc

SALARIES/BONUSES:

Top Exec. Salary: $ Bonus: $
Second Exec. Salary: $ Bonus: $

OTHER THOUGHTS:

Estimated Female Officers or Directors: 3
Hot Spot for Advancement for Women/Minorities: Y

Omnicom Group Inc

www.omnicomgroup.com

NAIC Code: 541810

TYPES OF BUSINESS:

Advertising Services
Public Relations
Market Research
Marketing & Brand Consulting
Interactive & Search Engine Marketing
Media Planning & Buying
Health Care Communications

BRANDS/DIVISIONS/AFFILIATES:

Diversified Agency Services
DDB Worldwide Communications Group Inc
DDB Worldwide Inc
TBWA Worldwide Inc
OMD Worldwide
Omincom Media Group
Wednesday Agency Group
Ketchum Inc

CONTACTS: Note: Officers with more than one job title may be intentionally listed here more than once.

Jonathan Nelson, CEO, Divisional
John Wren, CEO
Bruce Crawford, Chairman of the Board
Peter Swiecicki, Controller
Philip Angelastro, Executive VP
Michael OBrien, General Counsel
Andrew Castellaneta, Senior VP
Dennis Hewitt, Treasurer

GROWTH PLANS/SPECIAL FEATURES:

Omnicom Group, Inc. is a holding company that, through its subsidiaries, is one of the largest advertising, marketing and corporate communications companies in the world. The firm owns subsidiary agencies that operate in over 100 countries, serving over 5,000 clients. Its agencies provide an extensive range of services, mainly focusing on four fundamental disciplines: advertising, customer relationship management, public relations and specialty communications. The company's holdings are managed by the Diversified Agency Services group of companies; this sector includes over 200 public relations, marketing, consulting and special communications firms, such as Ketchum, Inc. and Porter Novelli. Omnicom's advertising is based in three areas: global advertising brands, national advertising agencies and media services. Global advertising brands include BBDO Worldwide Communications Group, Inc., DDB Worldwide, Inc. and TBWA Worldwide, Inc. National advertising agencies include Arnell Group, Goodby Silverstein & Partners, GSD&M, Martin/Williams, Merkley and Partners and Zimmerman Partners. Media services operate as the Omnicom Media Group, which include two full service media companies, OMD Worldwide and PHD Network, and several media specialist companies. Other group activities of note include experiential marketing, mobile marketing, package design, custom printing, reputation consulting and search engine marketing. Omnicom digital oversees the company's digital operations. In 2015, the firm acquired a majority stake in Wednesday Agency Group via BBDO.

FINANCIAL DATA: Note: Data for latest year may not have been available at press time.

In U.S. $	2016	2015	2014	2013	2012	2011
Revenue		15,134,400,000	15,317,800,000	14,584,500,000	14,219,400,000	13,872,500,000
R&D Expense						
Operating Income		1,920,100,000	1,944,100,000	1,825,300,000	1,804,200,000	1,671,100,000
Operating Margin %		12.68%	12.69%	12.51%	12.68%	12.04%
SGA Expense		1,852,400,000	2,023,700,000	1,993,400,000	2,034,500,000	1,950,800,000
Net Income		1,093,900,000	1,104,000,000	991,100,000	998,300,000	952,600,000
Operating Cash Flow		2,172,300,000	1,476,500,000	1,809,000,000	1,451,300,000	1,315,300,000
Capital Expenditure		202,700,000	213,000,000	212,000,000	226,300,000	185,500,000
EBITDA		2,250,800,000	2,281,600,000	2,142,900,000	2,122,000,000	1,980,800,000
Return on Assets %		4.95%	4.96%	4.47%	4.68%	4.75%
Return on Equity %		40.79%	33.69%	28.14%	28.66%	26.89%
Debt to Equity		1.45	1.60	1.12	1.28	0.90

CONTACT INFORMATION:

Phone: 212 415-3600   Fax: 212 415-3393
Toll-Free:
Address: 437 Madison Ave., New York, NY 10022 United States

STOCK TICKER/OTHER:

Stock Ticker: OMC
Employees: 74,900
Parent Company:

Exchange: NYS
Fiscal Year Ends: 12/31

SALARIES/BONUSES:

Top Exec. Salary:
$1,000,000
Second Exec. Salary:
$850,000

Bonus: $

Bonus: $

OTHER THOUGHTS:

Estimated Female Officers or Directors: 6

Hot Spot for Advancement for Women/Minorities: Y

Oracle Corp

www.oracle.com

NAIC Code: 0

TYPES OF BUSINESS:

Computer Software, Data Base & File Management
e-Business Applications Software
Internet-Based Software
Consulting Services
Human Resources Management Software
CRM Software
Middleware

BRANDS/DIVISIONS/AFFILIATES:

Oracle Saas
Oracle Applications
Oracle PaaS
Oracle Database
Java
Oracle Fusion Middleware
Datalogix Holdings Inc
Maxymiser

CONTACTS: Note: Officers with more than one job title may be intentionally listed here more than once.

Brian Higgins, Assistant Secretary
Safra Catz, CFO
Lawrence Ellison, Chairman of the Board
William West, Chief Accounting Officer
Mark Hurd, Co-CEO
Jeffrey Henley, Director
John Fowler, Executive VP, Divisional
Dorian Daley, General Counsel
Thomas Kurian, President, Divisional

GROWTH PLANS/SPECIAL FEATURES:

Oracle Corp. is a leading enterprise software company, providing hardware products and services to over 400,000 customers throughout the world. The firm markets its integrated hardware and software systems directly to corporations. Oracle's products can be categorized into three broad areas: software & cloud, hardware systems and services. The software & cloud division is further divided into new software licenses & cloud software subscriptions, which includes Oracle's Software-as-a-Service (SaaS) and Platform-as-a-Service (PaaS) offerings; cloud infrastructure as a service; and software license updates & product support. This division represents 77% of total revenues. Hardware systems is comprised of hardware systems products and hardware systems support services, representing 14% of total revenues. Services (9% or revenues) offers consulting services, enhanced support services and education services. Applications and technologies of the firm include Oracle SaaS, providing software applications delivered via a cloud-based IT environment that the company hosts, manages and supports; Oracle Applications software are licensed for use in on-premise, data center and related IT environments to manage and automate core business functions across the enterprise; Oracle PaaS is designed to deliver Oracle Database, Java and other platform services in the cloud to enable developers to extend applications; Oracle Database software is licensed to customers and designed to enable reliable & secure storage, retrieval and manipulation of all forms of data; Oracle Fusion Middleware is a broad family of integrated application infrastructure software products; and Java is a software development language platform. In 2014, the firm acquired MICROS Systems, BlueKai, LiveLOOK and TOA Technologies and Datalogix Holdings Inc. In 2015, it acquired cloud-based software provider, Maxymiser. In July 2016, Oracle agreed to acquire NeetSuite Inc. for $9.3 billion.

Oracle offers employees a cafeteria-style benefits plan with a 401(k) plan, an employee assistance plan, an employee stock purchase plan and a Live and Work Well program.

FINANCIAL DATA: Note: Data for latest year may not have been available at press time.

In U.S. $	2016	2015	2014	2013	2012	2011
Revenue	37,047,000,000	38,226,000,000	38,275,000,000	37,180,000,000	37,121,000,000	35,622,000,000
R&D Expense	5,787,000,000	5,524,000,000	5,151,000,000	4,850,000,000	4,523,000,000	4,519,000,000
Operating Income	12,604,000,000	13,871,000,000	14,759,000,000	14,684,000,000	13,706,000,000	12,033,000,000
Operating Margin %	34.02%	36.28%	38.56%	39.49%	36.92%	33.77%
SGA Expense	9,039,000,000	8,732,000,000	8,605,000,000	8,400,000,000	8,253,000,000	7,549,000,000
Net Income	8,901,000,000	9,938,000,000	10,955,000,000	10,925,000,000	9,981,000,000	8,547,000,000
Operating Cash Flow	13,561,000,000	14,336,000,000	14,921,000,000	14,224,000,000	13,743,000,000	11,214,000,000
Capital Expenditure	1,189,000,000	1,391,000,000	580,000,000	650,000,000	648,000,000	450,000,000
EBITDA	15,418,000,000	16,838,000,000	17,526,000,000	17,626,000,000	16,644,000,000	15,015,000,000
Return on Assets %	7.98%	9.87%	12.72%	13.64%	13.14%	12.65%
Return on Equity %	18.55%	20.80%	23.93%	24.73%	23.91%	24.22%
Debt to Equity	0.84	0.82	0.48	0.41	0.30	0.37

CONTACT INFORMATION:

Phone: 650 506-7000   Fax: 650 506-7200
Toll-Free: 800-392-2999
Address: 500 Oracle Pkwy., Redwood City, CA 94065 United States

STOCK TICKER/OTHER:

Stock Ticker: ORCL
Employees: 132,000
Parent Company:

Exchange: NYS
Fiscal Year Ends: 05/31

SALARIES/BONUSES:

Top Exec. Salary: $950,000   Bonus: $
Second Exec. Salary: $950,000   Bonus: $

OTHER THOUGHTS:

Estimated Female Officers or Directors: 6
Hot Spot for Advancement for Women/Minorities: Y

O'Reilly Automotive Inc

www.oreillyauto.com

NAIC Code: 441310

TYPES OF BUSINESS:

Auto Parts, Retail
Tools
Auto Accessories

BRANDS/DIVISIONS/AFFILIATES:

O'Reilly Auto Parts
Power Torque
BrakeBest
Prestone
Master Pro
Omnispark
Super Start
Ultima

CONTACTS: *Note: Officers with more than one job title may be intentionally listed here more than once.*

Gregory Henslee, CEO
Thomas McFall, CFO
David OReilly, Chairman of the Board
Jeff Shaw, Executive VP, Divisional
Gregory Johnson, Executive VP, Divisional
Tricia Headley, Secretary
Brad Beckham, Senior VP, Divisional
Byron Childers, Senior VP, Divisional
Larry Ellis, Senior VP, Divisional
Mike Swearengin, Senior VP, Divisional
Randy Johnson, Senior VP, Divisional
Tony Bartholomew, Senior VP, Divisional
Jeffrey Lauro, Senior VP, Divisional
Scott Kraus, Senior VP, Divisional
Jeffrey Groves, Senior VP, Divisional
Charles OReilly, Vice Chairman of the Board
Lawrence OReilly, Vice Chairman of the Board

GROWTH PLANS/SPECIAL FEATURES:

O'Reilly Automotive, Inc. is one of the largest specialty retailers of automotive aftermarket parts, tools, supplies, equipment and accessories in the U.S., selling products to both do-it-yourself (DIY) customers and professional installers. The company operates 4,571 stores under the O'Reilly Auto Parts name in 44 states across the U.S. Stores carry an average of 44,000 stock keeping units (SKUs) with an extensive product line consisting of new and remanufactured automotive hard parts such as alternators, starters, brake system components, batteries, chassis parts and engine parts; maintenance items such as oil, antifreeze, fluids, wiper blades, lighting, engine additives and appearance products; accessories, such as floor mats, truck accessories and seat covers; and a complete line of auto body paint and related materials, automotive tools and professional service equipment. Store merchandise generally consists of nationally recognized, well-advertised, name-brand products such as AC Delco, Armor All, Bosch, BWD, Cardone, Castrol, Gates Rubber, Monroe, Moog, Pennzoil, Prestone, Quaker State, STP, Turtle Wax, Valvoline, Wagner and Wix. In addition to name-brand products, stores carry a wide variety of high-quality private-label products under the BestTest, BrakeBest, Import Direct, Master Pro, Micro-Gard, Murray, Omnispark, Precision, Power Torque, Super Start and Ultima brands. O'Reilly operates 26 distribution centers and 297 hub stores, each equipped with highly automated material handling equipment that expedites the movement of products to loading areas for shipment to individual stores on a nightly basis. O'Reilly Automotive opened 205 new stores in 2015, with plans to open another 200-plus stores in 2016, in an effort to penetrate existing markets and expand into new, contiguous ones.

O'Reilly offers its employees medical, dental, vision, pharmacy and life insurance; a credit union membership; a 401(k) plan with company match; a profit sharing plan; paid time off; a discount stock purchase plan; and an employee assistance program.

FINANCIAL DATA: *Note: Data for latest year may not have been available at press time.*

In U.S. $	2016	2015	2014	2013	2012	2011
Revenue		7,966,674,000	7,216,081,000	6,649,237,000	6,182,184,000	5,788,816,000
R&D Expense						
Operating Income		1,514,021,000	1,270,374,000	1,103,485,000	977,393,000	866,766,000
Operating Margin %		19.00%	17.60%	16.59%	15.80%	14.97%
SGA Expense		2,648,622,000	2,438,527,000	2,265,516,000	2,120,025,000	1,973,381,000
Net Income		931,216,000	778,182,000	670,292,000	585,746,000	507,673,000
Operating Cash Flow		1,281,476,000	1,190,430,000	908,026,000	1,251,555,000	1,118,991,000
Capital Expenditure		414,020,000	429,987,000	395,881,000	300,719,000	328,319,000
EBITDA		1,727,751,000	1,469,677,000	1,291,196,000	1,158,827,000	1,009,818,000
Return on Assets %		14.09%	12.34%	11.34%	10.41%	9.62%
Return on Equity %		46.79%	39.05%	32.90%	23.65%	16.76%
Debt to Equity		0.70	0.69	0.71	0.51	0.28

CONTACT INFORMATION:

Phone: 417 862-6708   Fax: 417 863-2242
Toll-Free: 800-755-6759
Address: 233 S. Patterson Ave., Springfield, MO 65802 United States

STOCK TICKER/OTHER:

Stock Ticker: ORLY   Exchange: NAS
Employees: 71,621   Fiscal Year Ends: 12/31
Parent Company:

SALARIES/BONUSES:

Top Exec. Salary: Bonus: $
$1,205,769
Second Exec. Salary: Bonus: $
$698,462

OTHER THOUGHTS:

Estimated Female Officers or Directors: 1

Hot Spot for Advancement for Women/Minorities: Y

Oshkosh Corporation

www.oshkoshcorporation.com

NAIC Code: 336120

TYPES OF BUSINESS:

Fire & Emergency Vehicles
Military Trucks
Truck Bodies
Specialty Trucks
Cement Mixers
Refuse Trucks

BRANDS/DIVISIONS/AFFILIATES:

JerrDan
JLG Industries Inc
Pierce
Oshkosh Defense

CONTACTS: Note: Officers with more than one job title may be intentionally listed here more than once.

William Jones, CEO
Marek May, Senior VP, Divisional
Richard Donnelly, Chairman of the Board
Thomas Polnaszek, Chief Accounting Officer
Gary Schmiedel, Executive VP, Divisional
Joseph Kimmitt, Executive VP, Divisional
David Sagehorn, Executive VP
Gregory Fredericksen, Executive VP
Janet Hogan, Executive VP
James Johnson, Executive VP
Frank Nerenhausen, Executive VP
Ignacio Cortina, General Counsel
Bradley Nelson, President, Divisional
Robert Messina, Senior VP, Divisional
Mark Radue, Senior VP, Divisional
Colleen Moynihan, Senior VP, Divisional

GROWTH PLANS/SPECIAL FEATURES:

Oshkosh Corporation is a leading designer, manufacturer and marketer of specialty vehicles and vehicle bodies. The company operates in four segments: defense, access equipment, fire and emergency and commercial. The defense segment, accounting for roughly 15% of the company's sales, supplies severe-duty, heavy-payload tactical trucks to the U.S. Department of Defense (DoD). The access equipment segment (56%), through subsidiary JLG Industries, Inc., manufactures aerial work platforms, telehandlers, scissor lifts and vertical masts used in construction, agricultural, industrial, institutional and general maintenance applications. The fire and emergency segment (13%), through subsidiary Pierce, is a leading domestic manufacturer of fire apparatus assembled on custom chassis. It also manufactures fire apparatus assembled on commercially-available chassis, snow removal vehicles and emergency vehicles, including pumpers; aerial and ladder trucks; tankers; light-, medium- and heavy-duty rescue vehicles; rough terrain response vehicles; mobile command and control centers; bomb squad vehicles; and hazardous materials control vehicles. The segment sells aircraft rescue and fire fighting (ARFF) vehicles to domestic and international airports. Through its Jerr-Dan subsidiary, the segment also manufactures towing and recovery equipment in the U.S. The commercial segment (16%), manufactures rear- and front-discharge concrete mixers, refuse collection vehicles, mobile and stationary compactors and waste transfer units, portable and stationary concrete batch plants and vehicle components. JLG markets its products in over 3,500 locations worldwide. In April 2015, the Oshkosh Defense unit won a contract to build new Joint Light Tactical Vehicles for the U.S. military. The contract could eventually be worth as much as $30 billion and could run until 2040.

The firm offers employees medical, prescription, dental, vision, AD&D, disability and life insurance; a flexible spending account; a 401(k); tuition reimbursement; an employee stock purchase program; and a pension plan.

FINANCIAL DATA: Note: Data for latest year may not have been available at press time.

In U.S. $	2016	2015	2014	2013	2012	2011
Revenue		6,098,100,000	6,808,200,000	7,665,100,000	8,180,900,000	7,584,700,000
R&D Expense						
Operating Income		398,600,000	503,300,000	505,700,000	366,000,000	500,900,000
Operating Margin %		6.53%	7.39%	6.59%	4.47%	6.60%
SGA Expense		587,400,000	624,100,000	620,500,000	567,300,000	513,200,000
Net Income		229,500,000	309,300,000	318,000,000	230,800,000	273,400,000
Operating Cash Flow		82,500,000	170,400,000	438,000,000	268,300,000	387,700,000
Capital Expenditure		158,000,000	124,900,000	59,900,000	64,300,000	86,200,000
EBITDA		520,700,000	630,100,000	637,800,000	493,600,000	651,600,000
Return on Assets %		4.97%	6.58%	6.54%	4.72%	5.73%
Return on Equity %		11.75%	15.05%	16.05%	13.37%	18.70%
Debt to Equity		0.44	0.44	0.42	0.51	0.63

CONTACT INFORMATION:

Phone: 920 235-9151   Fax:
Toll-Free:
Address: 2307 Oregon St., Oshkosh, WI 54902 United States

STOCK TICKER/OTHER:

Stock Ticker: OSK   Exchange: NYS
Employees: 13,300   Fiscal Year Ends: 09/30
Parent Company:

SALARIES/BONUSES:

Top Exec. Salary: Bonus: $
$1,105,578
Second Exec. Salary: Bonus: $
$654,033

OTHER THOUGHTS:

Estimated Female Officers or Directors: 5

Hot Spot for Advancement for Women/Minorities: Y

Owens & Minor Inc

www.owens-minor.com

NAIC Code: 423450

TYPES OF BUSINESS:

Distribution-Medical & Surgical Equipment
Supply Chain Management

BRANDS/DIVISIONS/AFFILIATES:

Movianto
ArcRoyal

CONTACTS: Note: Officers with more than one job title may be intentionally listed here more than once.

P. Phipps, CEO
Nicholas Pace, Senior VP
Richard Meier, CFO
Craig Smith, Chairman of the Board
Richard Mears, Chief Information Officer
Michael Lowry, Controller
Rony Kordahi, Executive VP, Divisional
W. Simpson, Executive VP
Truitt Allcott, Other Corporate Officer
Chuck Graves, Other Corporate Officer
Erika Davis, Other Executive Officer
Charles Colpo, Senior VP, Divisional
M. Romans, Senior VP, Divisional
Geoffrey Marlatt, Senior VP, Divisional
Daniel Healy, Senior VP, Divisional

GROWTH PLANS/SPECIAL FEATURES:

Owens & Minor, Inc., founded in 1882, is a leading health care logistics company that connects the world of medical products to the point of care. The company provides vital supply chain assistance to the providers of health care services and the manufacturers of health care products, supplies and devices in the U.S. and Europe. Owens & Minor's service portfolio covers procurement, inventory management, delivery and sourcing for the health care market. It serves customers ranging from hospitals, integrated health care systems, group purchasing organizations and the U.S. federal government to manufacturers of life-science & medical devices and supplies, including pharmaceuticals in Europe. The firm's operations are divided into two segments: domestic and international. The domestic segment includes all functions in the U.S. relating to the role as a health care services company, providing distribution and logistics services to health care providers and manufacturers. The international segment consists of Movianto, a European contract logistics service provider to the pharmaceutical, biotechnology and health care industry, offering a broad range of supply chain logistics services to manufacturers; and ArcRoyal, a producer of surgical kits and procedure trays for the health care market. This segment has a network of 22 logistics centers and one packaging facility in 11 European countries. The company offers a comprehensive portfolio of products, including branded products purchased in large volume from manufacturers and its own proprietary private-label products. The company also offers additional services to health care providers including supplier management, analytics, inventory management, outsourced resource management, clinical supply management and business process consulting.

OMI offers its employees educational assistance; incentive pay; flexible benefit plans; and medical, dental, vision, life and disability insurance.

FINANCIAL DATA: Note: Data for latest year may not have been available at press time.

In U.S. $	2016	2015	2014	2013	2012	2011
Revenue		9,772,946,000	9,440,182,000	9,071,532,000	8,908,145,000	8,627,912,000
R&D Expense						
Operating Income		200,359,000	159,536,000	198,083,000	196,753,000	203,515,000
Operating Margin %		2.05%	1.68%	2.18%	2.20%	2.35%
SGA Expense		933,596,000	926,977,000	863,656,000	682,595,000	610,657,000
Net Income		103,409,000	66,503,000	110,882,000	109,003,000	115,198,000
Operating Cash Flow		269,597,000	-3,761,000	140,554,000	218,506,000	68,141,000
Capital Expenditure		36,616,000	70,808,000	60,129,000	38,963,000	36,315,000
EBITDA		266,341,000	222,943,000	248,669,000	236,357,000	237,650,000
Return on Assets %		3.71%	2.60%	4.89%	5.24%	6.11%
Return on Equity %		10.33%	6.54%	11.10%	11.53%	12.97%
Debt to Equity		0.57	0.61	0.20	0.22	0.23

CONTACT INFORMATION:

Phone: 804 723-7000　　Fax: 804 270-7281
Toll-Free:
Address: 9120 Lockwood Blvd., Mechanicsville, VA 23116 United States

STOCK TICKER/OTHER:

Stock Ticker: OMI　　　　　　　　　Exchange: NYS
Employees: 8,100　　　　　　　　　Fiscal Year Ends: 12/31
Parent Company:

SALARIES/BONUSES:

Top Exec. Salary: $443,117　　Bonus: $1,125,000
Second Exec. Salary: $863,157　　Bonus: $

OTHER THOUGHTS:

Estimated Female Officers or Directors: 4
Hot Spot for Advancement for Women/Minorities: Y

PACCAR Inc

www.paccar.com

NAIC Code: 336120

TYPES OF BUSINESS:

Truck Manufacturing
Premium Truck Manufacturer
Parts Distribution
Finance, Lease and Insurance Services

BRANDS/DIVISIONS/AFFILIATES:

PACCAR International
DAF Trucks
Peterbilt Motors
Kenworth Truck Company
PACCAR Leasing
PACCAR Financial Services
Braden
Gearmatic

CONTACTS: *Note: Officers with more than one job title may be intentionally listed here more than once.*

Ronald Armstrong, CEO
Robert Christensen, CFO
Mark Pigott, Chairman of the Board
Michael Barkley, Chief Accounting Officer
Gary Moore, Executive VP
David Anderson, General Counsel
Preston Feight, General Manager, Subsidiary
Darrin Siver, General Manager, Subsidiary
Harrie Schippers, President, Subsidiary
M. Walton, Secretary
T. Quinn, Senior VP
Robert Bengston, Senior VP, Divisional
Marco Davila, Vice President
Jack LeVier, Vice President, Divisional

GROWTH PLANS/SPECIAL FEATURES:

PACCAR, Inc. is a leading manufacturer of premium light-, medium- and heavy-duty trucks. The firm operates in three major divisions: trucks, parts and financial services. Truck division subsidiaries include Kenworth Truck Company, Peterbilt Motors and DAF Trucks. The vehicles are used worldwide for over-the-road and off-highway hauling of freight, petroleum, wood products, construction and other materials. The Kenworth and Peterbilt nameplates are manufactured and distributed by separate divisions in the U.S. and foreign plants in Canada, Mexico and Australia. Headquartered in the Netherlands, DAF Trucks comprises the European component of PACCAR, with distribution throughout Europe, Asia and Africa. Products and services are available worldwide, with customer call centers operating continuously. Substantially all trucks and related parts are sold to independent dealers, and this division accounts for 77% of net sales. The parts division includes the distribution of aftermarket parts for trucks and related commercial vehicles in the U.S., Canada, Europe, Australia, Mexico and South America. Aftermarket truck parts are sold and delivered to the company's independent dealers through the firm's 17 strategically-located distribution centers. The parts segment accounts for 16% of net sales. The company's financial services segment (6% of net sales), which operates through wholly-owned subsidiaries PACCAR Financial Services and PACCAR Leasing, maintains a presence in over 22 countries and owns a fleet of over 150,000 vehicles. This division provides financing and leasing arrangements, mainly for its manufactured trucks. The company's share of the U.S. and Canadian Class 8 truck market is roughly 28%. In addition, other businesses (1% of net sales) consists of a manufacturing division, which makes industrial winches in two U.S. plants and markets them under the Braden, Carco and Gearmatic nameplates.

FINANCIAL DATA: *Note: Data for latest year may not have been available at press time.*

In U.S. $	2016	2015	2014	2013	2012	2011
Revenue		19,115,100,000	18,997,000,000	17,123,800,000	17,050,500,000	16,355,200,000
R&D Expense		239,800,000	215,600,000	251,400,000	279,300,000	288,200,000
Operating Income		2,445,600,000	2,134,500,000	1,827,600,000	1,753,900,000	1,660,700,000
Operating Margin %		12.79%	11.23%	10.67%	10.28%	10.15%
SGA Expense		541,500,000	561,400,000	559,500,000	571,600,000	546,900,000
Net Income		1,604,000,000	1,358,800,000	1,171,300,000	1,111,600,000	1,042,300,000
Operating Cash Flow		2,556,000,000	2,123,600,000	2,375,700,000	1,519,000,000	1,592,600,000
Capital Expenditure		1,725,200,000	1,537,300,000	1,872,800,000	1,803,400,000	1,647,300,000
EBITDA		3,374,500,000	3,074,500,000	2,661,600,000	2,488,200,000	2,362,000,000
Return on Assets %		7.68%	6.57%	5.95%	6.21%	6.63%
Return on Equity %		23.42%	20.29%	18.76%	19.83%	19.44%
Debt to Equity		0.83	0.82	0.90	0.77	0.55

CONTACT INFORMATION:

Phone: 425 468-7400   Fax: 425 468-8216
Toll-Free:
Address: 777 106th Ave. NE, Bellevue, WA 98004 United States

SALARIES/BONUSES:

Top Exec. Salary: Bonus: $
$1,186,730
Second Exec. Salary: Bonus: $
$774,769

STOCK TICKER/OTHER:

Stock Ticker: PCAR   Exchange: NAS
Employees: 23,300   Fiscal Year Ends: 12/31
Parent Company:

OTHER THOUGHTS:

Estimated Female Officers or Directors:

Hot Spot for Advancement for Women/Minorities:

PAREXEL International Corp

www.parexel.com

NAIC Code: 541711

TYPES OF BUSINESS:

Clinical Trial & Data Management
Biostatistical Analysis & Reporting
Medical Communications Services
Clinical Pharmacology Services
Consulting Services

BRANDS/DIVISIONS/AFFILIATES:

PAREXEL Consulting Services
PAREXEL Informatics
ClinPhone RTSM
Quantum Solutions India

CONTACTS: Note: Officers with more than one job title may be intentionally listed here more than once.

Emma Reeve, CFO
Ulf Schneider, Chief Administrative Officer
Mark Goldberg, COO
Josef Von Rickenbach, Founder
Xavier Flinois, President, Divisional
Gadi Saarony, Senior VP, Divisional
Thomas Senderovitz, Senior VP, Divisional
Roland Andersson, Senior VP, Divisional
Douglas Batt, Senior VP

GROWTH PLANS/SPECIAL FEATURES:

PAREXEL International Corp. is a leading biopharmaceutical outsourcing services company, providing a broad range of expertise in clinical research, clinical logistics, medical communications, consulting, commercialization and advanced technology products and services to the worldwide pharmaceutical, biotechnology and medical device industries. Operating in approximately 80 locations throughout 51 countries, PAREXEL has three business segments: clinical research services (CRS), PAREXEL Consulting Services (PC) and PAREXEL Informatics (PI). CRS, accounting for 75% of revenue, includes all phases of clinical research from first-in man trials through post-marketing studies. CRS service offerings include clinical trials management, observational studies, patient/disease registries and post-marketing surveillance, data management and biostatistics, epidemiology and health economics/outcomes research, clinical logistics, pharmacovigilance and clinical pharmacology as well as related medical affairs, patient recruitment and investigator site services. PC provides technical expertise and advice in such areas as drug development, regulatory affairs and good manufacturing practice compliance consulting. In addition, it provides market development, product development, commercialization and targeted communications services in support of product launch. PC consultants also identify alternatives and propose solutions to address clients' product development, registration and commercialization issues. The segment provides information technology solutions designed to improve product development processes. Products and services include ClinPhone RTSM, medical imaging services, ePRO, CTMS, EDC, web-based portals, systems integration and patient diary applications. In 2015, the firm acquired Quantum Solutions India, a provider of specialized pharmacovigilance services. In January 2016, it agreed to acquire Health Advances LLC, a life sciences strategy consulting firm.

FINANCIAL DATA: Note: Data for latest year may not have been available at press time.

In U.S. $	2016	2015	2014	2013	2012	2011
Revenue	2,426,300,000	2,330,274,000	2,266,342,000	1,995,966,000	1,618,234,000	1,422,425,000
R&D Expense						
Operating Income	224,000,000	199,852,000	199,498,000	136,123,000	88,802,000	81,630,000
Operating Margin %	9.23%	8.57%	8.80%	6.81%	5.48%	5.73%
SGA Expense	385,300,000	367,192,000	379,800,000	318,806,000	263,462,000	271,049,000
Net Income	154,900,000	147,821,000	129,094,000	95,972,000	63,158,000	48,786,000
Operating Cash Flow	261,300,000	157,843,000	287,201,000	183,815,000	234,457,000	-1,455,000
Capital Expenditure	95,500,000	80,167,000	72,585,000	81,089,000	74,403,000	60,153,000
EBITDA	320,900,000	284,791,000	280,826,000	217,403,000	158,262,000	141,124,000
Return on Assets %	7.94%	7.99%	7.14%	5.79%	4.26%	3.68%
Return on Equity %	23.85%	23.78%	23.12%	16.71%	10.74%	9.70%
Debt to Equity	0.76	0.51	0.57	0.78	0.35	0.42

CONTACT INFORMATION:

Phone: 781 487-9900   Fax: 781 487-0525
Toll-Free:
Address: 195 West St., Waltham, MA 02451 United States

STOCK TICKER/OTHER:

Stock Ticker: PRXL   Exchange: NAS
Employees: 18,660   Fiscal Year Ends: 06/30
Parent Company:

SALARIES/BONUSES:

Top Exec. Salary: $933,600   Bonus: $400,435
Second Exec. Salary: Bonus: $151,417
$597,400

OTHER THOUGHTS:

Estimated Female Officers or Directors: 1
Hot Spot for Advancement for Women/Minorities: Y

Park-Ohio Holdings Corp

www.pkoh.com

NAIC Code: 488510

TYPES OF BUSINESS:

Logistics & Supply Chain Services
Automobile Parts Manufacturing
Aluminum Components
Industrial Equipment Manufacturing

BRANDS/DIVISIONS/AFFILIATES:

Park-Ohio Industries Inc

CONTACTS: Note: Officers with more than one job title may be intentionally listed here more than once.

Edward Crawford, CEO
Patrick Fogarty, CFO
Robert Vilsack, Other Executive Officer
Matthew Crawford, President

GROWTH PLANS/SPECIAL FEATURES:

Park-Ohio Holdings Corp., through its subsidiary Park-Ohio Industries, Inc., is an industrial supply chain logistics and diversified manufacturing business. The company operates through three segments: supply technologies, engineered products and assembly components. The supply technologies segment, which accounted for 40% of the firm's 2015 sales, provides integrated supply chain and logistics services for various high-volume, specialty production components. Supply technologies provides value-added services, such as engineering and design, part usage, cost analysis, supplier selection, quality assurance, bar coding, product packaging and tracking, electronic billing services and ongoing technical support through 54 international logistics centers. The segment's primary customers are in the heavy-duty truck; automotive and vehicle parts; electrical distribution and controls; power sports/fitness equipment; heating, ventilation and air conditioning (HVAC); aerospace and defense; electrical components; appliance; and semiconductor industries. The engineered products segment (21%), with 24 domestic and international manufacturing facilities, operates a diverse group of niche manufacturing businesses that design and manufacture a broad range of high quality products engineered for specific customer applications. The principal customers of engineered products are original equipment manufacturers (OEMs) and end users in the steel, coatings, forging, heavy-duty truck, construction equipment, automotive, oil and gas, rail and locomotive manufacturing and aerospace and defense industries. The assembly components segment (39%), with 25 domestic and international manufacturing facilities, manufactures cast aluminum components, automotive and industrial rubber and thermoplastic products, fuel filler and hydraulic assemblies for automotive, agricultural equipment, construction equipment, heavy-duty truck and marine equipment industries. It also provides value-added services such as design and engineering, machining and assembly.

FINANCIAL DATA: Note: Data for latest year may not have been available at press time.

In U.S. $	2016	2015	2014	2013	2012	2011
Revenue		1,463,800,000	1,378,700,000	1,203,200,000	1,134,042,000	966,573,000
R&D Expense						
Operating Income		97,900,000	97,900,000	86,500,000	76,807,000	56,384,000
Operating Margin %		6.68%	7.10%	7.18%	6.77%	5.83%
SGA Expense		135,100,000	136,600,000	119,300,000	117,209,000	105,582,000
Net Income		48,100,000	45,600,000	43,400,000	31,786,000	29,435,000
Operating Cash Flow		44,700,000	53,600,000	60,300,000	55,881,000	35,861,000
Capital Expenditure		36,500,000	25,800,000	30,100,000	29,625,000	12,673,000
EBITDA		126,600,000	121,100,000	106,300,000	94,798,000	72,561,000
Return on Assets %		5.00%	5.08%	5.61%	4.74%	5.04%
Return on Equity %		24.60%	26.46%	33.28%	38.02%	52.64%
Debt to Equity		2.19	2.34	2.38	3.67	5.28

CONTACT INFORMATION:

Phone: 440 947-2000   Fax: 440 947-2099
Toll-Free:
Address: 6065 Parkland Blvd., Cleveland, OH 44124 United States

STOCK TICKER/OTHER:

Stock Ticker: PKOH   Exchange: NAS
Employees: 5,000   Fiscal Year Ends: 12/31
Parent Company:

SALARIES/BONUSES:

Top Exec. Salary: $550,000   Bonus: $600,000
Second Exec. Salary: Bonus: $
$750,000

OTHER THOUGHTS:

Estimated Female Officers or Directors: 1
Hot Spot for Advancement for Women/Minorities:

Sales, profits and employees may be estimates. Financial information, benefits and other data can change quickly and may vary from those stated here.

Patrick Industries Inc

www.patrickind.com

NAIC Code: 321219

TYPES OF BUSINESS:

Reconstituted Wood Product Manufacturing

BRANDS/DIVISIONS/AFFILIATES:

Parkland Plastics Inc
Progressive Group (The)
Cana Holdings Inc
Mishawaka Sheet Metal LLC
BH Electronics Inc

CONTACTS: Note: Officers with more than one job title may be intentionally listed here more than once.

Joshua Boone, CFO
Jeff Rodino, COO
Todd Cleveland, Director
Paul Hassler, Director
Andy Nemeth, President
Courtney Blosser, Vice President, Divisional

GROWTH PLANS/SPECIAL FEATURES:

Patrick Industries, Inc. is a manufacturer and supplier of building products and materials to the manufactured housing and recreational vehicle industries. Additionally, it is a supplier to certain other industrial markets such as furniture manufacturing, marine, architectural and the automotive aftermarket. Through the firm's manufacturing divisions, it manufactures and fabricates a variety of products such as decorative vinyl & paper laminated panels, wrapped vinyl, paper & hardwood profile mouldings, stiles & battens, hardwood, foil & membrane pressed cabinet doors, solid surface, granite and quartz countertops & sinks, drawer sides & bottoms, hardwood furniture, fiberglass bath & shower surrounds and fixtures, slide-out trim & fascia, interior passage doors, exterior graphics and slotwall panels & components. In conjunction with its manufacturing capabilities, Patrick Industries also provide value added processes, including custom fabrication, edge-banding, drilling, boring and cut-to-size capabilities. The company also distributes pre-finished wall & ceiling panels, drywall & drywall finishing products, electronics, wiring, electrical & plumbing products, cement siding, interior passage doors, roofing products, laminate & ceramic flooring, shower doors, furniture, fireplaces & surrounds, interior & exterior lighting products and other miscellaneous products. More than 80% of consolidated net sales in 2015, were derived from decorative interior products and components, consisting primarily of manufactured panels, mouldings, trim, hardwood, pressed doors, furniture, countertops and fiberglass products. Patrick Industries maintains 42 manufacturing plants and 16 warehouse and distribution facilities in 11 states. In 2016, the firm acquired Parkland Plastics, Inc., The Progressive Group, Cana Holdings, Inc., Mishawaka Sheet Metal LLC and BH Electronics, Inc.

FINANCIAL DATA: Note: Data for latest year may not have been available at press time.

In U.S. $	2016	2015	2014	2013	2012	2011
Revenue		920,333,000	735,717,000	594,931,000	437,367,000	307,822,000
R&D Expense						
Operating Income		69,918,000	51,471,000	40,945,000	27,040,000	13,475,000
Operating Margin %		7.59%	6.99%	6.88%	6.18%	4.37%
SGA Expense		73,523,000	62,525,000	48,137,000	37,419,000	30,248,000
Net Income		42,219,000	30,674,000	24,040,000	28,095,000	8,470,000
Operating Cash Flow		65,630,000	45,741,000	22,431,000	20,997,000	11,815,000
Capital Expenditure		7,958,000	6,542,000	8,669,000	7,895,000	2,436,000
EBITDA		86,693,000	61,904,000	48,242,000	30,895,000	17,692,000
Return on Assets %		13.16%	14.27%	15.13%	24.51%	10.54%
Return on Equity %		36.49%	33.14%	33.45%	62.26%	36.05%
Debt to Equity		1.50	0.98	0.66	0.80	1.10

CONTACT INFORMATION:

Phone: 574 294-7511   Fax: 574 522-5213
Toll-Free:
Address: 107 West Franklin Street, Elkhart, IN 46515 United States

STOCK TICKER/OTHER:

Stock Ticker: PATK   Exchange: NAS
Employees: 2,799   Fiscal Year Ends: 12/31
Parent Company:

SALARIES/BONUSES:

Top Exec. Salary: $539,424   Bonus: $
Second Exec. Salary: $265,000 Bonus: $70,029

OTHER THOUGHTS:

Estimated Female Officers or Directors:
Hot Spot for Advancement for Women/Minorities:

Patterson Companies Inc

www.pattersoncompanies.com

NAIC Code: 423450

TYPES OF BUSINESS:

Dental Products & Related Services
Veterinary Products
Non-Wheelchair Assistive Products

BRANDS/DIVISIONS/AFFILIATES:

Patterson Dental Supply Inc
Patterson Veterinary Supply Inc
Patterson Dental Holdings Inc
Dolphin Imaging Systems LLC
Animal Health International Inc

CONTACTS: *Note: Officers with more than one job title may be intentionally listed here more than once.*

John Adent, CEO, Divisional
Paul Guggenheim, CEO, Subsidiary
Scott Anderson, CEO
Ann Gugino, CFO
Kelly Baker, Other Executive Officer
Les Korsh, Vice President

GROWTH PLANS/SPECIAL FEATURES:

Patterson Companies, Inc. is a firm engaged in the distribution of products to the dental, veterinary and medical industries. The company operates in two segments: dental supply and veterinary supply. The dental supply segment, Patterson Dental Supply Inc., is one of the largest distributors of dental products in North America. The division provides consumable products, including X-ray film, restorative materials, hand instruments and sterilization products; basic and advanced technology dental equipment; practice management and clinical software; patient education systems; and office forms and stationery. Patterson Dental also offers related services including dental equipment installation, maintenance and repair, dental office design and equipment financing. The veterinary supply segment, Patterson Veterinary Supply Inc., provides products for the diagnosis, treatment and/or prevention of diseases in companion pets and equine animals. This segment offers over 56,000 products that are sold by field sales representatives. The segment also has an agency commission business with several pharmaceutical manufacturers. Patterson Companies' other subsidiaries include Patterson Dental Holdings Inc. and Dolphin Imaging Systems LLC. In 2015, the firm acquired Animal Health International Inc.; and sold its medical business, Patterson Medical Supply Inc., to Madison Dearborn Partners for $715 million.

Employee benefits include medical, dental and vision coverage; flexible spending accounts; short- and long-term disability; life and accident insurance; a 401(k); employee stock purchase and ownership plans; education and employee assistance; and employee discounts.

FINANCIAL DATA: *Note: Data for latest year may not have been available at press time.*

In U.S. $	2016	2015	2014	2013	2012	2011
Revenue	5,386,703,000	4,375,020,000	4,063,715,000	3,637,212,000	3,535,661,000	3,415,670,000
R&D Expense						
Operating Income	347,713,000	373,427,000	345,756,000	354,455,000	358,009,000	376,008,000
Operating Margin %	6.45%	8.53%	8.50%	9.74%	10.12%	11.00%
SGA Expense	975,035,000		852,522,000			768,217,000
Net Income	187,184,000	223,261,000	200,612,000	210,272,000	212,815,000	225,385,000
Operating Cash Flow	156,329,000	262,691,000	195,836,000	299,195,000	321,158,000	262,612,000
Capital Expenditure	79,354,000	62,945,000	40,387,000	21,983,000	29,650,000	36,822,000
EBITDA	434,141,000	427,694,000	398,611,000	403,516,000	402,364,000	423,066,000
Return on Assets %	5.78%	7.68%	7.23%	7.75%	8.02%	9.03%
Return on Equity %	12.66%	14.95%	13.99%	15.18%	14.49%	15.01%
Debt to Equity	0.70	0.47	0.49	0.51	0.52	0.33

CONTACT INFORMATION:

Phone: 651 686-1600   Fax: 651 686-9331
Toll-Free: 800-328-5536
Address: 1031 Mendota Heights Rd., St. Paul, MN 55120 United States

STOCK TICKER/OTHER:

Stock Ticker: PDCO   Exchange: NAS
Employees: 7,000   Fiscal Year Ends: 04/30
Parent Company:

SALARIES/BONUSES:

Top Exec. Salary: $770,477   Bonus: $
Second Exec. Salary: $399,167   Bonus: $

OTHER THOUGHTS:

Estimated Female Officers or Directors: 4
Hot Spot for Advancement for Women/Minorities: Y

Sales, profits and employees may be estimates. Financial information, benefits and other data can change quickly and may vary from those stated here.

Penske Automotive Group Inc

www.penskeautomotive.com

NAIC Code: 441110

TYPES OF BUSINESS:

Auto Dealers, Retail
Automotive Leasing
Parts & Service

BRANDS/DIVISIONS/AFFILIATES:

Western Star Trucks Australia
Penske Truck Leasing Co LP
Nicole Group
Harper Truck Centres

CONTACTS: Note: Officers with more than one job title may be intentionally listed here more than once.

Gregory Penske, CEO, Subsidiary
Roger Penske, CEO
J. Carlson, Chief Accounting Officer
Shelley Hulgrave, Controller
Robert Kurnick, Director
Bud Denker, Executive VP, Divisional
Shane Spradlin, Executive VP

GROWTH PLANS/SPECIAL FEATURES:

Penske Automotive Group, Inc. (PAG) is an international transportation services company operating automotive dealerships and commercial vehicle distribution principally in the U.S., Western Europe, Australia and New Zealand. It operates 355 automotive retail franchises, of which 181 are located in the U.S. and 174 outside of the U.S. The franchises outside the U.S. are located primarily in the U.K. In 2015, the company retailed and wholesaled more than 523,000 vehicles. The commercial vehicle segment includes the operations of subsidiary Western Star Trucks Australia, the exclusive importer and distributor of Western Star heavy duty trucks (a Daimler brand), MAN heavy and medium duty trucks and buses (a VW Group brand), and Dennis Eagle refuse collection vehicles, together with associated parts across Australia, New Zealand and portions of Southeast Asia. The company also holds a 9% interest in Penske Truck Leasing Co., L.P. (PTL), a leading provider of transportation services and supply chain management. PTL operates and maintains approximately 220,000 vehicles and serves customers in North America, South America, Europe, Australia and Asia, and is one of the largest purchasers of commercial trucks in North America. In 2016, the firm acquired a 49% stake in the Nicole Group, a luxury dealership with operations in Kanagawa and Tokyo, Japan; and Harper Truck Centres, a commercial truck dealership group based in Ontario, Canada.

Employee benefits include medical, dental, prescription, vision and life insurance; a 401(k) with company match; flexible spending accounts; an employee assistance program; and paid time off.

FINANCIAL DATA: Note: Data for latest year may not have been available at press time.

In U.S. $	2016	2015	2014	2013	2012	2011
Revenue		19,284,900,000	17,177,200,000	14,705,400,000	13,163,520,000	11,556,230,000
R&D Expense						
Operating Income		566,500,000	504,100,000	436,200,000	364,858,000	298,190,000
Operating Margin %		2.93%	2.93%	2.96%	2.77%	2.58%
SGA Expense		2,223,000,000	1,999,600,000	1,761,900,000	1,594,095,000	1,478,297,000
Net Income		326,100,000	286,700,000	244,200,000	185,540,000	176,881,000
Operating Cash Flow		391,500,000	366,600,000	314,800,000	323,400,000	63,475,000
Capital Expenditure		199,500,000	174,800,000	256,300,000	161,286,000	133,115,000
EBITDA		683,800,000	630,900,000	528,600,000	428,672,000	370,826,000
Return on Assets %		4.27%	4.20%	4.14%	3.75%	4.12%
Return on Equity %		18.94%	18.16%	17.38%	15.20%	16.24%
Debt to Equity		0.70	0.79	0.68	0.70	0.74

CONTACT INFORMATION:

Phone: 248 648-2500   Fax: 248 648-2525
Toll-Free:
Address: 2555 Telegraph Rd., Bloomfield Hills, MI 48302 United States

STOCK TICKER/OTHER:

Stock Ticker: PAG
Employees: 22,100
Parent Company:

Exchange: NYS
Fiscal Year Ends: 12/31

SALARIES/BONUSES:

Top Exec. Salary:
$1,200,000
Second Exec. Salary:
$479,327

Bonus: $

Bonus: $250,000

OTHER THOUGHTS:

Estimated Female Officers or Directors: 2

Hot Spot for Advancement for Women/Minorities:

Penske Corporation

www.penske.com

NAIC Code: 532120

TYPES OF BUSINESS:

Truck Rental
Auto Racing
Auto Sales & Service
Supply Chain Solutions
Auto Accessories Manufacturing & Retail
Fuel Management Systems
Fleet Management Services
Vehicle Components & Systems

BRANDS/DIVISIONS/AFFILIATES:

Penske Automotive Group
Penske Motor Group
Penske Truck Rental
Penske Logistics
Truck-Lite Global
Penske Racing
Truck-Lite Co LLC
Davco Technology LLC

CONTACTS: Note: Officers with more than one job title may be intentionally listed here more than once.

Roger S. Penske, CEO
Robert H. Kurnick Jr., Pres.
Gregory J. Houfley, VP-Finance
Robert H. Kurnick, Jr., Pres., Penske Automotive Group
Calvin C. Sharp, Exec. VP-Human Resources, Penske Automotive Group
David K. Jones, CFO
Shane M. Spradlin, General Counsel
Roger S. Penske, Chmn.
Marc Althen, Pres., Penske Logistics

GROWTH PLANS/SPECIAL FEATURES:

Penske Corporation is a diversified transportation company that participates in a variety of automotive markets through its network of subsidiaries. Its markets include auto sales and service, truck rental, supply chain solutions, vehicle headlight design and development, vehicle lighting and harness safety systems, fluid management and automobile racing. Penske Automotive Group (PAG) is an international transportation services company that operates retail automotive dealerships, Hertz car rental franchises and commercial vehicle distribution. It operates primarily in the U.S., Western Europe, Australia and New Zealand. Penske Motor Group owns and operates automobile dealerships in California. Penske Truck Leasing is a partnership between the firm and General Electricals. It operates over 200,000 vehicles and consists of Penske Truck Rental, which offers fleet management services including service leasing, truck rentals, logistics, used trucks for sale and felt services for utility and transit companies with municipalities at almost 1,000 Penske facilities nationwide. Penske Logistics focuses on supply chain solutions, providing services designed to cut costs, reduce cycle time, improve service and integrate technology into the operations of its customers. Penkse Logistics operates 300 locations, 15 million square feet of warehousing space and a 3,000 vehicle fleet. Truck-Lite Global is responsible for creating vehicle lighting and harness safety systems for fleet vehicles through its affiliated subsidiaries: Truck-Lite Co., LLC and Truck-Lite Europe Limited. Davco Technology, LLC provides diesel fuel management with its line of filters, fuel/water separators and fuel warmers. Davco products include the Sea Pro for marine applications, Diesel Pro for medium trucks and the REN line of industrial automatic oil replenishment systems. Penske Racing's operations include teams competing in NASCAR Sprint Cup Series, IndyCar Series, NASCAR Nationwide Series and American Le Mans Series.

FINANCIAL DATA: Note: Data for latest year may not have been available at press time.

In U.S. $	2016	2015	2014	2013	2012	2011
Revenue		23,000,000,000	20,500,000,000	20,000,000,000	19,000,000,000	17,000,000,000
R&D Expense						
Operating Income						
Operating Margin %						
SGA Expense						
Net Income						
Operating Cash Flow						
Capital Expenditure						
EBITDA						
Return on Assets %						
Return on Equity %						
Debt to Equity						

CONTACT INFORMATION:

Phone: 248-648-2000   Fax: 248-648-2525
Toll-Free:
Address: 2555 Telegraph Rd., Bloomfield Hills, MI 48302 United States

STOCK TICKER/OTHER:

Stock Ticker: Private   Exchange:
Employees: 50,000   Fiscal Year Ends: 12/31
Parent Company:

SALARIES/BONUSES:

Top Exec. Salary: $ Bonus: $
Second Exec. Salary: $ Bonus: $

OTHER THOUGHTS:

Estimated Female Officers or Directors:
Hot Spot for Advancement for Women/Minorities:

Sales, profits and employees may be estimates. Financial information, benefits and other data can change quickly and may vary from those stated here.

PepsiCo Inc

NAIC Code: 312111

www.pepsico.com

TYPES OF BUSINESS:

Soft Drink Manufacturing
Snack Food Manufacturing
Juice & Sports Drink Manufacturing
Cereal Manufacturing
Rice & Pasta Product Manufacturing
Oatmeal Product Manufacturing
Bottled Water Production
Cereal Bar Manufacturing

BRANDS/DIVISIONS/AFFILIATES:

Frito-Lay North America Inc
Wimm-Bill-Dann Foods OJSC
Lay's
Quaker Foods North America
Tropicana Products Inc
Ruffles
Cheetos
Doritos

CONTACTS: *Note: Officers with more than one job title may be intentionally listed here more than once.*

Albert Carey, CEO, Geographical
Cynthia Trudell, Executive VP, Divisional
Sanjeev Chadha, CEO, Geographical
Laxman Narasimhan, CEO, Geographical
Ramon Laguarta, CEO, Geographical
Indra Nooyi, CEO
Hugh Johnston, CFO
Marie Gallagher, Chief Accounting Officer
Mehmood Khan, Chief Scientific Officer
Tony West, Executive VP, Divisional
Cynthia Nastanski, Other Corporate Officer
Jamie Caulfield, Senior VP, Divisional

GROWTH PLANS/SPECIAL FEATURES:

PepsiCo, Inc. is a leading global food, snack and beverage company operating in six business units: Frito-Lay North America (FLNA); Quaker Foods North America (QFNA); North America Beverages (NAB); Latin America; Europe Sub-Saharan Africa (ESSA); and Asia, Middle East & North Africa (AMENA). FLNA manufactures markets, sells and distributes branded snacks including Lay's potato chips, Doritos, Cheetos, Fritos, Ruffles, Tostitos and SunChips. QFNA makes Aunt Jemima mixes and syrups, Quaker grits, Life cereal, and Rice-a-Roni and Near East side dishes. NAB makes, markets, distributes and sells beverage concentrates, fountain syrups and finished goods under various beverage brands including Pepsi, Gatorade, Mountain Dew, Diet Pepsi, Aquafina, Diet Mountain Dew, Tropicana Pure Premium, Sierra Mist and Mug. Latin America offers a number of snack foods including Gamesa, Doritos, Cheetos, Ruffles, Lay's and Sabritas as well as Quaker brand cereals and snacks in Latin America. ESSA makes, markets, distributes and sells a number of leading snack food brands including Lay's, Walkers, Doritos, Cheetos and Ruffles, as well as many Quaker-branded cereals and snacks, through consolidated businesses as well as through noncontrolled affiliates. AMENA makes, markets, distributes and sells a number of leading snack food brands including Lay's, Kurkure, Chipsy, Doritos, Cheetos and Crunchy through consolidated businesses, as well as through noncontrolled affiliates.

PepsiCo offers employees medical, dental, vision, life, auto, home and disability insurance; flexible spending accounts; wellness programs; a 401(k); retirement benefits; employee assistance; adoption assistance; family leave; tuition reimbursement; child and elder care support; and employee discounts on cell phones, electronics and entertainment.

FINANCIAL DATA: *Note: Data for latest year may not have been available at press time.*

In U.S. $	2016	2015	2014	2013	2012	2011
Revenue		63,056,000,000	66,683,000,000	66,415,000,000	65,492,000,000	66,504,000,000
R&D Expense						
Operating Income		8,353,000,000	9,581,000,000	9,705,000,000	9,112,001,000	9,633,000,000
Operating Margin %		13.24%	14.36%	14.61%	13.91%	14.48%
SGA Expense		24,885,000,000	26,126,000,000	25,357,000,000	24,970,000,000	25,145,000,000
Net Income		5,452,000,000	6,513,000,000	6,740,000,000	6,178,000,000	6,443,000,000
Operating Cash Flow		10,580,000,000	10,506,000,000	9,688,001,000	8,479,000,000	8,944,000,000
Capital Expenditure		2,758,000,000	2,859,000,000	2,795,000,000	2,714,000,000	3,339,000,000
EBITDA		10,828,000,000	12,291,000,000	12,465,000,000	11,892,000,000	12,427,000,000
Return on Assets %		7.77%	8.78%	8.85%	8.36%	9.12%
Return on Equity %		37.24%	31.23%	28.96%	28.83%	30.89%
Debt to Equity		2.45	1.36	1.00	1.05	1.00

CONTACT INFORMATION:

Phone: 914 253-2000   Fax:
Toll-Free:
Address: 700 Anderson Hill Rd., Purchase, NY 10577 United States

STOCK TICKER/OTHER:

Stock Ticker: PEP   Exchange: NYS
Employees: 263,000   Fiscal Year Ends: 12/31
Parent Company:

SALARIES/BONUSES:

Top Exec. Salary: Bonus: $
$1,642,308
Second Exec. Salary: Bonus: $
$900,000

OTHER THOUGHTS:

Estimated Female Officers or Directors: 10

Hot Spot for Advancement for Women/Minorities: Y

PerkinElmer Inc

www.perkinelmer.com

NAIC Code: 325413

TYPES OF BUSINESS:

Diagnostic Systems
Mechanical Components
Optoelectronics
Pharmaceutical Manufacturing
Life Science Systems
Environmental Safety Equipment

BRANDS/DIVISIONS/AFFILIATES:

DELFIA Xpress
NeoGram
ViaCord
Clarus
Altus UPLC/HPLC
NexION
PerkinElmber-GIS Centre for Precision Oncology
Vanadis Diagnostics AB

CONTACTS: *Note: Officers with more than one job title may be intentionally listed here more than once.*

Robert F. Friel, CEO
Robert F. Friel, Pres.
Frank Wilson, CFO
Deborah Butters, Chief Human Resources Officer
Robert F. Friel, Chmn.

GROWTH PLANS/SPECIAL FEATURES:

PerkinElmer, Inc. provides technology, services and solutions to the diagnostics, research, environmental, safety and security, industrial and laboratory services markets. The firm designs, manufactures, markets and services products and systems throughout 150 countries. The company operates in two business units: human health and environmental health. The human health segment develops diagnostics, tools and applications with the goal of detecting disease earlier and more accurately and accelerating the discovery and development of critical new therapies. Products in this segment include DELFIA Xpress, a prenatal screening solution; NeoGram, an in vitro diagnostic kit; GSP Neonatal nTSH kits for screening congenital neonatal conditions from a drop of blood; and ViaCord umbilical cord blood banking services for the banking of stem cells harvested from umbilical cord blood. The environmental health segment provides products, services and solutions to facilitate a cleaner and safer environment, including the creation of secure food and consumer products. This division serves the environmental, industrial and laboratory services market. Its Clarus product offers a series of gas chromatographs used to identify and quantify compounds in the environmental, forensics, food & beverage, hydrocarbon processing/biofuels, materials testing, pharmaceutical and semiconductor industries. Other products from this segment include the Altus UPLC/HPLC advanced liquid chromatography systems; the NexION family of mass spectrometers; and the LAMBDA UV/Vis series of spectrophotometers. In 2016, the firm, along with Genome Institute of Singapore, opened PerkinElmer-GIS Centre for Precision Oncology. The R&D laboratory supports real-time biomarker development for predicting therapeutic response that may pave the way for delivery of precision medicine for cancer. That same year, PerkinElmer acquired Vanadis Diagnostics AB, which is developing a novel solution for non-invasive prenatal testing based on digital analysis of cell-free DNA; and sold its U.S. prenatal screening laboratory services business, PerkinElmer Labs/NTD, to Eurofins Scientific.

FINANCIAL DATA: *Note: Data for latest year may not have been available at press time.*

In U.S. $	2016	2015	2014	2013	2012	2011
Revenue		2,262,359,000	2,237,219,000	2,166,232,000	2,115,205,000	1,921,287,000
R&D Expense		125,928,000	121,141,000	133,023,000	132,639,000	115,821,000
Operating Income		286,134,000	210,742,000	217,442,000	98,543,000	91,128,000
Operating Margin %		12.64%	9.41%	10.03%	4.65%	4.74%
SGA Expense		598,848,000	659,335,000	585,850,000	632,734,000	627,172,000
Net Income		212,425,000	157,778,000	167,212,000	69,940,000	7,655,000
Operating Cash Flow		287,098,000	281,597,000	158,591,000	152,170,000	224,874,000
Capital Expenditure		29,632,000	29,072,000	38,991,000	42,408,000	30,592,000
EBITDA		395,515,000	322,609,000	331,727,000	223,239,000	200,058,000
Return on Assets %		5.11%	3.90%	4.26%	1.80%	.21%
Return on Equity %		10.23%	7.81%	8.50%	3.69%	.40%
Debt to Equity		0.47	0.51	0.46	0.48	0.51

CONTACT INFORMATION:

Phone: 781 663-6900   Fax:
Toll-Free: 800-762-4000
Address: 940 Winter St., Waltham, MA 02451 United States

STOCK TICKER/OTHER:

Stock Ticker: PKI   Exchange: NYS
Employees: 7,700   Fiscal Year Ends: 01/31
Parent Company:

SALARIES/BONUSES:

Top Exec. Salary: Bonus: $
$1,029,054
Second Exec. Salary: Bonus: $
$510,385

OTHER THOUGHTS:

Estimated Female Officers or Directors: 1

Hot Spot for Advancement for Women/Minorities: Y

Petco Animal Supplies Inc

NAIC Code: 453910

TYPES OF BUSINESS:

Pets & Pet Supplies, Retail
Online Sales
Pet Grooming
Veterinary Services
Obedience Training
Pet Photography

BRANDS/DIVISIONS/AFFILIATES:

CVC Capital Partners
Canada Pension Plan Investment Board
Think Adoption First
P.A.L.S.
Petco Foundation (The)

CONTACTS: Note: Officers with more than one job title may be intentionally listed here more than once.

Jim Myers, CEO
Brad Weston, Pres.
Michael Nuzzo, CFO
Michael Zuna, Exec. VP-Mktg.
Charlie Piscitello, Exec. VP-Human Resources
Brad Williams, Dir.-IT
Thomas A. Farello, Sr. VP-Oper.
Lisa Epstein, Sr. Comm. Specialist
Jim Myers, Chmn.

GROWTH PLANS/SPECIAL FEATURES:

Petco Animal Supplies, Inc. is a leading specialty retailer of premium pet food, supplies and services. The company currently operates over 1,450 stores and more than 115 Unleashed by Petco neighborhood shops. Petco's superstores carry more than 10,000 products including premium pet food and treats; small animals such as fish, birds and reptiles as well as related supplies; collars and leashes; grooming products; toys; pet carriers; cat furniture; dog houses and beds; vitamins and veterinary supplies. Most stores also provide a variety of pet services, including professional grooming, veterinary clinics, vaccinations, obedience training and pet photography. Several services are performed in glass-walled stations in order to increase customer awareness and confidence in the services. In light of overpopulation problems, Petco chooses not to sell dogs and cats, though it does support adoption programs such as Petfinder.com through in-store Think Adoption First kiosks in many stores. The firm also operates the P.A.L.S. (Petco animal lovers save) customer loyalty program. Members receive special benefits and savings through the use of the P.A.L.S. card, which allows Petco to target customers and track shopping habits. In addition to its retail stores, the company operates an e-commerce site, which offers Petco merchandise, pet tips, a community forum, online specials and information about The Petco Foundation, an animal welfare and rights group. In February 2016, Petco was acquired by CVC Capital Partners and Canada Pension Plan Investment Board for $4.6 billion.

Petco offers its employees medical, dental, disability, vision, life and AD&D insurance plans; discounted pet insurance; a 401(k); flexible spending accounts; an employee assistance program; fitness discounts; paid time off; and merchandise discounts.

FINANCIAL DATA: Note: Data for latest year may not have been available at press time.

In U.S. $	2016	2015	2014	2013	2012	2011
Revenue		4,000,000,000	3,925,000,000	3,550,000,000	3,200,000,000	2,855,000,000
R&D Expense						
Operating Income						
Operating Margin %						
SGA Expense						
Net Income			75,000,000			
Operating Cash Flow						
Capital Expenditure						
EBITDA						
Return on Assets %						
Return on Equity %						
Debt to Equity						

CONTACT INFORMATION:

Phone: 858-453-7845   Fax:
Toll-Free:
Address: 9125 Rehco Rd., San Diego, CA 92121 United States

STOCK TICKER/OTHER:

Stock Ticker: Private   Exchange:
Employees: 25,500   Fiscal Year Ends: 01/31
Parent Company:

SALARIES/BONUSES:

Top Exec. Salary: $ Bonus: $
Second Exec. Salary: $ Bonus: $

OTHER THOUGHTS:

Estimated Female Officers or Directors: 2
Hot Spot for Advancement for Women/Minorities:

PetSmart Inc

NAIC Code: 453910

www.petsmart.com

TYPES OF BUSINESS:

Pets & Pet Supplies, Retail
Online & Catalog Sales
Pet Training
In-Store Adoption Centers
Veterinary Services
Pet Boarding
Pet Grooming

BRANDS/DIVISIONS/AFFILIATES:

Argos Holdings Inc
PetSmart.com
PetPerks
Medical Management International Inc
Banfield, The Pet Hospital
PetSmart PetHotels

CONTACTS: Note: Officers with more than one job title may be intentionally listed here more than once.

Michael J. Massey, CEO
Gregg Scanlon, Sr. VP-Operations
David Lenhardt, CEO
Robin S. Anderson, CFO
Erick Goldberg, Sr. VP-Human Resources
Donald Beaver, Chief Information Officer
Michael Goodwin, Sr. VP-CIO
Paulette Dodson, General Counsel
Erick Goldberg, Senior VP, Divisional
Bruce Thorn, Senior VP, Divisional
Jaye Perricone, Senior VP, Divisional
Matthew McAdam, Senior VP, Divisional
Melvin Tucker, Senior VP, Divisional
Gene Burt, Senior VP, Divisional

GROWTH PLANS/SPECIAL FEATURES:

PetSmart, Inc. is a leading operator of superstores specializing in pet food, supplies and services. The company operates over 1,466 stores in the U.S., Puerto Rico and Canada, which offer an assortment of pet services and products. Its stores range in size from 12,000 to 27,500 square feet and carry roughly 11,000 distinct items in store and 9,000 additional items online through PetSmart.com. These items include nationally recognized brand names and a selection of proprietary or private label brands. PetSmart stores sell supplies for dogs, cats, fresh-water tropical fish, reptiles, birds and other small pets. The firm offers a PetPerks loyalty program to its customers. PetSmart stores also offer value-added pet services including grooming, training, boarding and day camp; and it operates full-service veterinary hospitals in many of its stores. Medical Management International, Inc., an operator of veterinary hospitals, operates more than 800 of PetSmart's hospitals under the name Banfield, The Pet Hospital. The remaining seven hospitals are located in Canada and operated by other third parties. PetSmart offers pet boarding in more than 200 stores through its PetSmart PetsHotels. PetsHotels provide boarding for dogs and cats, which includes 24-hour supervision by caregivers who are PetSmart-trained to provide personalized pet care, temperature controlled rooms and suites and play time as well as day camp for dogs. The company also actively supports pet adoption through its in-store adoption centers. In 2015, PetSmart was acquired by Argos Holdings, Inc., operating as its wholly-owned subsidiary.

PetSmart offers its employees medical, dental and vision insurance; life and AD&D insurance; short- and long-term disability; a 401(k) plan; an employee stock purchase plan; adoption assistance; associate discount; tuition assistance; flexible spending accounts; and a work/life balance program.

FINANCIAL DATA: Note: Data for latest year may not have been available at press time.

In U.S. $	2016	2015	2014	2013	2012	2011
Revenue		7,110,000,000	6,916,626,944	6,758,237,184	6,113,304,064	5,693,796,864
R&D Expense						
Operating Income						
Operating Margin %						
SGA Expense						
Net Income			419,520,000	389,528,992	290,243,008	239,867,008
Operating Cash Flow						
Capital Expenditure						
EBITDA						
Return on Assets %						
Return on Equity %						
Debt to Equity						

CONTACT INFORMATION:

Phone: 623 580-6100   Fax:
Toll-Free: 800-738-1385
Address: 19601 N. 27th Ave., Phoenix, AZ 85027 United States

SALARIES/BONUSES:

Top Exec. Salary: $ Bonus: $
Second Exec. Salary: $ Bonus: $

STOCK TICKER/OTHER:

Stock Ticker: Subsidiary   Exchange:
Employees: 53,000   Fiscal Year Ends: 01/31
Parent Company: Argos Holdings Inc

OTHER THOUGHTS:

Estimated Female Officers or Directors: 3
Hot Spot for Advancement for Women/Minorities: Y

Sales, profits and employees may be estimates. Financial information, benefits and other data can change quickly and may vary from those stated here.

Pfizer Inc

NAIC Code: 325412

www.pfizer.com

TYPES OF BUSINESS:

Pharmaceuticals
Infusion Technologies

BRANDS/DIVISIONS/AFFILIATES:

Xeljanc
Eliquis
Lyrica
Hospira Inc

CONTACTS: Note: Officers with more than one job title may be intentionally listed here more than once.

Ian Read, CEO
John Young, President, Divisional
Frank DAmelio, CFO
Loretta Cangialosi, Chief Accounting Officer
Freda Lewis-Hall, Chief Medical Officer
Rady Johnson, Chief Risk Officer
Sally Susman, Executive VP, Divisional
Laurie Olson, Executive VP, Divisional
Charles Hill, Executive VP, Divisional
Douglas Lankler, Executive VP
Anthony Maddaluna, Executive VP
Margaret Madden, Other Executive Officer
William Meury, President, Divisional
Albert Bourla, President, Divisional
Mikael Dolsten, President, Divisional
Brenton Saunders, President

GROWTH PLANS/SPECIAL FEATURES:

Pfizer, Inc. is a research-based, global pharmaceutical company. It discovers, develops, manufactures and markets health care products. The company operates in two segments. innovative products and established products. Innovative products is composed of two divisions: global innovative pharmaceuticals (GIP) and global vaccines/oncology/consumer healthcare (VOC). GIP is focused on developing, registering and commercializing novel value-creating medicines that significantly improve patients lives. These therapeutic areas include inflammation, cardiovascular metabolic, neuroscience, pain, rare diseases and women's/men's health under brands such as Xeljanc, Eliquis and Lyrica. VOC focuses on the development and commercialization of vaccines and products for oncology and consumer health care. Each of the three businesses in VOC operate as a separate, global business. The established products segment consists of the global established pharmaceutical (GEP) division, and includes the brands that have lost market exclusivity and, generally, the mature, patent-protected products that are expected to lose exclusivity through the coming year in most major markets. Additionally, GEP includes Pfizer's sterile injectable products and biosimilar development portfolio. In 2015, the firm acquired Hospira, Inc. for $16 billion. Hospira is a leader in injectable drugs and infusion technologies. In August 2016, Pfizer agreed to acquire Medivation, Inc. for $14 billion.

FINANCIAL DATA: Note: Data for latest year may not have been available at press time.

In U.S. $	2016	2015	2014	2013	2012	2011
Revenue		48,851,000,000	49,605,000,000	51,584,000,000	58,986,000,000	67,425,000,000
R&D Expense		7,690,000,000	8,393,000,000	6,678,000,000	7,870,000,000	9,112,001,000
Operating Income		11,824,000,000	13,249,000,000	16,727,000,000	13,221,000,000	15,241,000,000
Operating Margin %		24.20%	26.70%	32.42%	22.41%	22.60%
SGA Expense		14,809,000,000	14,097,000,000	14,355,000,000	16,616,000,000	19,468,000,000
Net Income		6,960,000,000	9,135,000,000	22,003,000,000	14,570,000,000	10,009,000,000
Operating Cash Flow		14,512,000,000	16,883,000,000	17,765,000,000	17,054,000,000	20,240,000,000
Capital Expenditure		1,496,000,000	1,583,000,000	1,465,000,000	1,327,000,000	1,660,000,000
EBITDA		15,321,000,000	19,137,000,000	23,540,000,000	21,215,000,000	23,469,000,000
Return on Assets %		4.13%	5.35%	12.29%	7.79%	5.22%
Return on Equity %		10.23%	12.38%	27.94%	17.83%	11.78%
Debt to Equity		0.44	0.44	0.39	0.38	0.42

CONTACT INFORMATION:

Phone: 212 733-2323   Fax: 212 573-7851
Toll-Free:
Address: 235 E. 42nd St., New York, NY 10017 United States

STOCK TICKER/OTHER:

Stock Ticker: PFE   Exchange: NYS
Employees: 78,300   Fiscal Year Ends: 12/31
Parent Company:

SALARIES/BONUSES:

Top Exec. Salary: Bonus: $
$1,858,750
Second Exec. Salary: Bonus: $
$1,293,750

OTHER THOUGHTS:

Estimated Female Officers or Directors: 7

Hot Spot for Advancement for Women/Minorities: Y

Sales, profits and employees may be estimates. Financial information, benefits and other data can change quickly and may vary from those stated here.

PG&E Corporation

www.pgecorp.com

NAIC Code: 221111

TYPES OF BUSINESS:

Hydroelectric Power Generation
Electric and Gas Utility
Electricity Generation
Pipelines
Nuclear Generation
Natural Gas

BRANDS/DIVISIONS/AFFILIATES:

Pacific Gas and Electric Co

CONTACTS: *Note: Officers with more than one job title may be intentionally listed here more than once.*

Anthony Earley, CEO
Linda Cheng, Secretary
Dinyar Mistry, CFO, Subsidiary
David Thomason, CFO, Subsidiary
Jason Wells, CFO
Barry Williams, Chairman of the Board, Subsidiary
John Simon, Executive VP, Divisional
Hyun Park, General Counsel
Julie Kane, Other Executive Officer
Edward Halpin, Other Executive Officer
Loraine Giammona, Other Executive Officer
Karen Austin, Other Executive Officer
Nickolas Stavropoulos, President, Subsidiary
Geisha Williams, President, Subsidiary
Kent Harvey, Senior VP, Divisional
Desmond Bell, Senior VP, Subsidiary
Fong Wan, Senior VP, Subsidiary

GROWTH PLANS/SPECIAL FEATURES:

PG&E Corporation is a holding company that markets energy services and products in northern and central California through subsidiary Pacific Gas and Electric Co. The subsidiary is one of the largest electric and natural gas utilities in the U.S., serving roughly 16 million customers. With approximately 142,000 circuit miles of distribution lines, the company's electricity distribution network extends through most of northern and central California. Pacific owns and operates power plants producing nearly half of the power it sells including 104 hydroelectric, one nuclear (with two units), 13 photovoltaic and 12 fossil fuel facilities. The company's hydroelectric generation system covers 16 counties in northern and central California. This system consists of approximately 6,400 miles of backbone and local transmission pipelines, 42,800 miles of distribution pipelines and eight natural gas compressor and storage facilities. Through interconnections with various interstate pipelines, the company can receive gas from every major natural gas basin in western North America, including basins in Canada, the southwestern U.S. and the Rocky Mountains.

The company offers employees supplemental life, disability, medical, dental and vision insurance; flexible spending accounts for health care and dependent care; paid time off; paid sick leave; a wellness program; GlobalFit program; a 401(k); retiree medical and life insurance; post-retirement life insurance; an employee assistance program; adoption reimbursement; and tuition reimbursement opportunities. Other benefits include a company-matching program for educational or environmental charitable contributions, employee organized activities and employee discounts and volunteer opportunities.

FINANCIAL DATA: *Note: Data for latest year may not have been available at press time.*

In U.S. $	2016	2015	2014	2013	2012	2011
Revenue		16,833,000,000	17,090,000,000	15,598,000,000	15,040,000,000	14,956,000,000
R&D Expense						
Operating Income		1,508,000,000	2,450,000,000	1,762,000,000	1,693,000,000	1,942,000,000
Operating Margin %		8.95%	14.33%	11.29%	11.25%	12.98%
SGA Expense						
Net Income		888,000,000	1,450,000,000	828,000,000	830,000,000	858,000,000
Operating Cash Flow		3,753,000,000	3,677,000,000	3,427,000,000	4,882,000,000	3,739,000,000
Capital Expenditure		5,173,000,000	4,833,000,000	5,207,000,000	4,624,000,000	4,038,000,000
EBITDA		4,246,000,000	4,962,000,000	3,888,000,000	4,042,000,000	4,213,000,000
Return on Assets %		1.41%	2.48%	1.50%	1.59%	1.76%
Return on Equity %		5.40%	9.54%	5.93%	6.48%	7.21%
Debt to Equity		0.96	0.95	0.88	0.95	0.97

CONTACT INFORMATION:

Phone: 415 973-8200   Fax: 415 973-8719
Toll-Free: 800-719-9056
Address: 77 Beale Street, 24/F, San Francisco, CA 94177 United States

STOCK TICKER/OTHER:

Stock Ticker: PCG   Exchange: NYS
Employees: 22,581   Fiscal Year Ends: 12/31
Parent Company:

SALARIES/BONUSES:

Top Exec. Salary: Bonus: $
$1,281,250
Second Exec. Salary: Bonus: $
$795,967

OTHER THOUGHTS:

Estimated Female Officers or Directors: 15

Hot Spot for Advancement for Women/Minorities: Y

Pharmaceutical Product Development Inc

www.ppdi.com

NAIC Code: 541711

TYPES OF BUSINESS:

Contract Research
Drug Discovery & Development Services
Clinical Data Consulting Services
Medical Marketing & Information Support Services
Drug Discovery Services
Medical Device Development

BRANDS/DIVISIONS/AFFILIATES:

Carlyle Group (The)
Hellman & Friedman

CONTACTS: Note: Officers with more than one job title may be intentionally listed here more than once.

David Simmons, CEO
Christine A. Dingivan, Chief Medical Officer
B. Judd Hartman, General Counsel
William W. Richardson, Sr. VP-Global Bus. Dev.
Randy Buckwalter, Head-Media
Luke Heagle, Head-Investor Rel.
Lee E. Babiss, Chief Science Officer
David Johnston, Exec. VP-Global Lab Svcs.
David Simmons, Chmn.
Paul Colvin, Exec. VP-Global Clinical Dev.

GROWTH PLANS/SPECIAL FEATURES:

Pharmaceutical Product Development, Inc. (PPD), jointly owned by The Carlyle Group and Hellman & Friedman provides drug discovery and development services to pharmaceutical, biotechnology, medical device, academic and government organizations. PPD's services are divided into six segments: early development, which offers a range of early development services, phase 1 clinical trial services and non-clinical consulting; clinical development, which helps advance drug research and development for products; PPD Laboratories, which provides comprehensive lab services; post-approval, which provides post-approval studies and late stage clinical trials management; PPD Consulting, which acts as a consulting partner that assists companies with their biopharmaceutical product's success from pre-clinical through post-approval; and technology/innovation/performance, which helps companies deliver life-changing medicines, cutting-edge technologies, real-time analytics and customized training. Therapeutic areas of studies include cardiovascular, critical care, dermatology, dental pain research, endocrine & metabolics, gastroenterology, hemotology & oncology, immunology, infectious diseases, neuroscience, ophthalmology, respiratory and urology. In 2015, the firm opened a central laboratory in Shanghai, China, to deliver global scientific and technical laboratory expertise.

FINANCIAL DATA: Note: Data for latest year may not have been available at press time.

In U.S. $	2016	2015	2014	2013	2012	2011
Revenue		1,200,000,000	1,222,000,000	1,023,100,000	749,100,032	700,000,000
R&D Expense						
Operating Income						
Operating Margin %						
SGA Expense						
Net Income						
Operating Cash Flow						
Capital Expenditure						
EBITDA						
Return on Assets %						
Return on Equity %						
Debt to Equity						

CONTACT INFORMATION:

Phone: 910-251-0081   Fax: 910-762-5820
Toll-Free:
Address: 929 N. Front St., Wilmington, NC 28401-3331 United States

STOCK TICKER/OTHER:

Stock Ticker: Private   Exchange:
Employees: 16,000   Fiscal Year Ends: 12/31
Parent Company: The Carlyle Group

SALARIES/BONUSES:

Top Exec. Salary: $ Bonus: $
Second Exec. Salary: $ Bonus: $

OTHER THOUGHTS:

Estimated Female Officers or Directors: 2
Hot Spot for Advancement for Women/Minorities:

Phillips 66

NAIC Code: 324110

www.phillips66.com

TYPES OF BUSINESS:

Petroleum Refineries
Natural Gas Gathering
Gasoline Marketing
Chemicals Interests

BRANDS/DIVISIONS/AFFILIATES:

DCP Midstream LLC
Phillips 66 Partners LP
Chevron Phillips Chemical Company LLC

CONTACTS: Note: Officers with more than one job title may be intentionally listed here more than once.

Greg Garland, CEO
Kevin Mitchell, CFO
Lawrence Ziemba, Executive VP, Divisional
Robert Herman, Executive VP, Divisional
Paula Johnson, Executive VP, Divisional
Timothy Taylor, President
Chukwuemeka Oyolu, Vice President

GROWTH PLANS/SPECIAL FEATURES:

Phillips 66 is a downstream energy company engaged in refining, marketing and distributing petroleum products as well as power generation. Previously a unit of ConocoPhillips, Phillips 66 is organized into four operating segments: refining, marketing & specialties (M&S), midstream and chemicals. The company's refining operations include 14 refineries with a net crude oil capacity of 4.7 million barrels per day (bpd), 2.4 million barrels of refined product storage capacity, and 2 mill barrels of incremental crude storage capacity under construction (expected to be completed by late-2016). This segment buys, sells and refines crude oil and other feedstocks into petroleum products such as gasolines, distillates and aviation fuels. The M&S segment purchases refined petroleum products such as gasolines, distillates and aviation fuels for resale and markets, mainly in the U.S. and Europe. This segment includes the manufacturing and marketing of specialty products as well as power generation operations. The midstream segment comprises three business lines: transportation, which transports crude oil and other feedstocks to refineries and other locations, delivers refined and specialty products to market and provides storage services for crude oil and petroleum products; DCP Midstream LLC, which gathers, processes, transports and markets natural gas and transports, fractionates and markets natural gas liquids (NGL); and NGL, which transports, fractionates and markets NGL. The midstream segment also includes subsidiary Phillips 66 Partners LP, which owns, operates, develops and acquires fee-based crude oil, refined petroleum product and NGL pipelines and terminals as well as other transportation and midstream assets. The chemicals segment manufactures and markets petrochemicals and plastics on a worldwide basis. This segments includes its 50% interest in Chevron Phillips Chemical Company LLC, one of the world's top producers of olefins and polyolefins.

FINANCIAL DATA: Note: Data for latest year may not have been available at press time.

In U.S. $	2016	2015	2014	2013	2012	2011
Revenue		100,949,000,000	164,093,000,000	174,809,000,000	182,922,000,000	200,614,000,000
R&D Expense						
Operating Income		6,410,000,000	6,188,000,000	5,761,000,000	8,006,000,000	7,079,000,000
Operating Margin %		6.34%	3.77%	3.29%	4.37%	3.52%
SGA Expense		1,670,000,000	1,663,000,000	1,478,000,000	1,722,000,000	1,409,000,000
Net Income		4,227,000,000	4,762,000,000	3,726,000,000	4,124,000,000	4,775,000,000
Operating Cash Flow		5,713,000,000	3,529,000,000	6,027,000,000	4,296,000,000	5,006,000,000
Capital Expenditure		5,764,000,000	3,773,000,000	1,779,000,000	1,721,000,000	1,022,000,000
EBITDA		7,405,000,000	7,007,000,000	6,748,000,000	7,790,000,000	7,549,000,000
Return on Assets %		8.68%	9.66%	7.60%	9.03%	10.83%
Return on Equity %		18.91%	21.87%	17.41%	18.71%	19.38%
Debt to Equity		0.38	0.36	0.27	0.33	0.01

CONTACT INFORMATION:

Phone: 281-293-6600   Fax:
Toll-Free:
Address: 3010 Briarpark Dr., Houston, TX 77042 United States

STOCK TICKER/OTHER:

Stock Ticker: PSX   Exchange: NYS
Employees: 13,500   Fiscal Year Ends: 12/31
Parent Company:

SALARIES/BONUSES:

Top Exec. Salary: Bonus: $
$1,549,164
Second Exec. Salary: Bonus: $
$1,004,712

OTHER THOUGHTS:

Estimated Female Officers or Directors: 4

Hot Spot for Advancement for Women/Minorities: Y

Sales, profits and employees may be estimates. Financial information, benefits and other data can change quickly and may vary from those stated here.

Pinnacle Entertainment Inc

www.pnkinc.com

NAIC Code: 721120

TYPES OF BUSINESS:

Casinos
Hospitality & Entertainment Facilities
Racetrack Facilities

BRANDS/DIVISIONS/AFFILIATES:

Gaming and Leisure Properties Inc
L'Auberge Casino Resort
L'Auberge Baton Rouge
River City Casino & Hotel
Belterra Casino Resort
Boomtown Casino Hotel
Cactus Petes and The Horseshu Jackpot
Heartland Poker Tour

CONTACTS: *Note: Officers with more than one job title may be intentionally listed here more than once.*

Anthony Sanfilippo, CEO
Carlos Ruisanchez, CFO
James Martineau, Chairman of the Board
Virginia Shanks, Chief Administrative Officer
Neil Walkoff, Executive VP, Divisional
Troy Stremming, Executive VP, Divisional
John Godfrey, Executive VP

GROWTH PLANS/SPECIAL FEATURES:

Pinnacle Entertainment, Inc. is a developer, owner and operator of casinos and other hospitality facilities. The company owns and operates 15 gaming entertainment properties, located in Colorado, Indiana, Iowa, Louisiana, Mississippi, Missouri, Nevada and Texas. The company's largest casino resort, L'Auberge Casino Resort located in Lake Charles, Louisiana, offers 995 guestrooms, suites and villas, as well as 1,616 slot machines, 75 table games, a golf course and a full-service spa. L'Auberge Casino Hotel in Baton Rouge, Louisiana, features 1,480 slot machines, 56 table games, a hotel with 205 guestrooms and a rooftop pool, three dining outlets, an amphitheater style event lawn feature and a multi-purpose event center. The River City Casino & Hotel in St Louis, Missouri includes 200 hotel rooms, 2,018 slot machines and 62 table games. Other properties include Belterra Casino Resort located near Vevay, Indiana; six Ameristar Casino Hotels in Iowa, Indiana, Missouri, Mississippi and Colorado; two Boomtown Casino Hotels featuring dockside riverboat casinos in New Orleans and Bossier City, Louisiana; and Cactus Petes and The Horseshu Jackpot, featuring a hotel, gaming, dining, golf course and showroom entertainment. The company also owns the Heartland Poker Tour, a live and televised poker tournament series; and owns a majority interest in Retama Park Racetrack outside of San Antonio, Texas. In April 2016, the firm was acquired by Gaming and Leisure Properties, Inc. in an all-stock transaction, operating as GLP's wholly-owned subsidiary. Prior to the acquisition, Pinnacle spun off Belterra Park Gaming & Entertainment, located in Cincinnati, Ohio, into a stand-alone publicly-traded company.

FINANCIAL DATA: *Note: Data for latest year may not have been available at press time.*

In U.S. $	2016	2015	2014	2013	2012	2011
Revenue		2,291,848,000	2,210,543,000	1,487,836,000	1,002,836,000	
R&D Expense		14,247,000	12,962,000	89,009,000	21,508,000	
Operating Income		301,166,000	310,473,000	104,387,000	136,695,000	
Operating Margin %		13.14%	14.04%	7.01%	13.63%	
SGA Expense		426,064,000	421,399,000	287,381,000	181,175,000	
Net Income		48,887,000	43,843,000	-255,870,000	-31,805,000	
Operating Cash Flow		408,226,000	328,486,000	161,067,000	186,906,000	
Capital Expenditure		109,032,000	255,815,000	292,623,000	300,521,000	
EBITDA		543,933,000	543,536,000	142,773,000	201,831,000	
Return on Assets %		-1.74%	.87%	-4.95%		
Return on Equity %		-33.65%	17.83%	-119.73%		
Debt to Equity		4.78	14.30	20.42		

CONTACT INFORMATION:

Phone: 702 541-7777   Fax:
Toll-Free:
Address: 3980 Howard Hughes Pkwy, Las Vegas, NV 89169 United States

STOCK TICKER/OTHER:

Stock Ticker: PNK   Exchange: NAS
Employees: 14,738   Fiscal Year Ends: 12/31
Parent Company: Gaming and Leisure Properties Inc

SALARIES/BONUSES:

Top Exec. Salary: Bonus: $
$1,200,000
Second Exec. Salary: Bonus: $
$800,000

OTHER THOUGHTS:

Estimated Female Officers or Directors: 3

Hot Spot for Advancement for Women/Minorities: Y

PPG Industries Inc

www.ppg.com

NAIC Code: 325510

TYPES OF BUSINESS:

Automotive Paints
Coatings
Glass
Chemicals
Fiberglass
Industrial Products

BRANDS/DIVISIONS/AFFILIATES:

PPG
Glidden
Comex
Olympic
Dulux
Homax
REVOCOAT
Chemfil Canada Limited

CONTACTS: *Note: Officers with more than one job title may be intentionally listed here more than once.*

Anne Foulkes, Assistant General Counsel
Michael McGarry, CEO
Frank Sklarsky, CFO
Charles Bunch, Chairman of the Board
Viktoras Sekmakas, Executive VP
Glenn Bost, General Counsel
Cynthia Niekamp, Senior VP, Divisional

GROWTH PLANS/SPECIAL FEATURES:

PPG Industries, Inc. is a global manufacturer of decorative and protective coatings that operates in three business segments: performance coatings, industrial coatings and glass. Performance coatings is comprised of the refinish, aerospace, protective, marine and architectural coatings businesses. Refinish coatings supplies coatings products for automotive and commercial transport, fleet repair and refurbishing, industrial coatings purposes and for signs. Aerospace coatings supplies sealants, coatings, maintenance cleaners and transparencies for commercial, military, regional jet and general aviation aircraft and transparent armor for specialty applications and also provides chemical management services for the aerospace industry. Protective and marine coatings supplies coatings and finishes for the protection of metals and structures to metal fabricators, heavy duty maintenance contractors and manufacturers of ships, bridges and rail cars. Architectural coatings produces coatings used by painting and maintenance contractors and by consumers for decoration and maintenance of residential and commercial building structures. These coatings are sold under the PPG, Glidden, Comex, Olympic, Dulux, Sikkens, Mulco, Flood, Liquid Nails, Sico, CIL, Renner, Taubman's, White Knight, Bristol and Homax brands. Architectural coatings offers its products in the Americas, Asia Pacific and EMEA (Europe, Middle East and Africa). The glass business consists of flat glass and fiber glass, supplying its products to commercial and residential construction companies, as well as the wind energy, energy infrastructure, transportation and electronics industries. Most glass products are sold directly to manufacturing companies. In 2015, PPG acquired REVOCOAT, a supplier of sealants, adhesives and damper products; and the remaining interest in Chemfil Canada Limited, becoming the firm's wholly-owned subsidiary. In April 2016, PPG sold its minority stake (40%) in Pittsburgh Glass Works.

Employees receive medical, dental and vision coverage; life insurance; and dependent care benefit accounts.

FINANCIAL DATA: *Note: Data for latest year may not have been available at press time.*

In U.S. $	2016	2015	2014	2013	2012	2011
Revenue		15,330,000,000	15,360,000,000	15,108,000,000	15,200,000,000	14,885,000,000
R&D Expense		486,000,000	492,000,000	488,000,000	455,000,000	430,000,000
Operating Income		2,079,000,000	1,843,000,000	1,701,000,000	1,573,000,000	1,673,000,000
Operating Margin %		13.56%	11.99%	11.25%	10.34%	11.23%
SGA Expense		3,679,000,000	3,758,000,000	3,699,000,000	3,335,000,000	3,234,000,000
Net Income		1,406,000,000	2,102,000,000	3,231,000,000	941,000,000	1,095,000,000
Operating Cash Flow		1,837,000,000	1,528,000,000	1,791,000,000	1,787,000,000	1,436,000,000
Capital Expenditure		476,000,000	587,000,000	515,000,000	411,000,000	390,000,000
EBITDA		2,503,000,000	2,079,000,000	2,160,000,000	2,077,000,000	2,274,000,000
Return on Assets %		8.11%	12.56%	20.35%	6.21%	7.45%
Return on Equity %		27.66%	41.57%	71.83%	25.73%	31.79%
Debt to Equity		0.81	0.68	0.68	0.82	1.10

CONTACT INFORMATION:

Phone: 412 434-3131   Fax: 412 434-2571
Toll-Free:
Address: 1 PPG Pl., Pittsburgh, PA 15272 United States

STOCK TICKER/OTHER:

Stock Ticker: PPG
Employees: 44,400
Parent Company:

Exchange: NYS
Fiscal Year Ends: 12/31

SALARIES/BONUSES:

Top Exec. Salary:
$1,441,667
Second Exec. Salary:
$845,833

Bonus: $

Bonus: $

OTHER THOUGHTS:

Estimated Female Officers or Directors: 6

Hot Spot for Advancement for Women/Minorities: Y

Precision Castparts Corp

NAIC Code: 331529

www.precast.com

TYPES OF BUSINESS:

Cast Metal Products
Machine Parts Manufacturing

BRANDS/DIVISIONS/AFFILIATES:

Berkshire Hathaway Inc
AEREX
INCOLOY
MULTIPHASE
NIMONIC
Yangzhou Chengde Steel Tube Co., Ltd.
MONEL

CONTACTS: Note: Officers with more than one job title may be intentionally listed here more than once.

Mark Donegan, CEO
Shawn Hagel, CFO
Steven Hackett, Executive VP
Andrew Masterman, Executive VP
Ruth Beyer, General Counsel
James Pieron, Senior VP
Alan Power, Senior VP
Kirk Pulley, Vice President, Divisional

GROWTH PLANS/SPECIAL FEATURES:

Precision Castparts Corp. is a worldwide manufacturer of complex metal components and products. Precision Castparts operates in three principal business segments: Investment Cast Products, Forged Products and Airframe Products. The Investment Cast Products segment manufactures investment castings for aircraft engines, IGT engines, airframes, medical implants, armament, unmanned aerial vehicles and other industrial applications. The Forged Products segment is a leading manufacturer of forged components for the aerospace and power generation markets. Forged components manufactured from titanium and nickel-based alloys for commercial and military aircraft engines and IGT power plants including fan discs, compressor discs, turbine discs, seals, spacers, shafts, hubs and cases. The Airframe Products segment is a leading developer and manufacturer of highly engineered fasteners, fastener systems, aerostructures and precision components, primarily for critical aerospace applications. General Electric, the company's biggest client, accounts for roughly 15% of its sales. Precision Castparts' alloy brands include INCONEL, INCOLOY, MONEL, NIMONIC, UDIMET, BRIGHTRAY and NILO, and its fastener and components brands include AEREX, MULTIPHASE, MP35N and MP159. In January 2016, the firm was acquired by Berkshire Hathaway, Inc.

Precision Castparts offers its employees health and life insurance, flexible spending accounts, short- and long-term disability, employee assistant programs, 401(k) with company match plan, a health and fitness club reimbursement program and tuition assistance.

FINANCIAL DATA: Note: Data for latest year may not have been available at press time.

In U.S. $	2016	2015	2014	2013	2012	2011
Revenue		10,005,000,192	9,616,000,000	8,377,800,192	7,214,600,192	6,220,100,096
R&D Expense						
Operating Income						
Operating Margin %						
SGA Expense						
Net Income		1,530,000,000	1,776,999,936	1,426,599,936	1,224,099,968	1,013,500,032
Operating Cash Flow						
Capital Expenditure						
EBITDA						
Return on Assets %						
Return on Equity %						
Debt to Equity						

CONTACT INFORMATION:

Phone: 503 946-4800   Fax: 503 417-4817
Toll-Free:
Address: 4650 S.W. Macadam Ave., Ste. 440, Portland, OR 97239-4262
United States

STOCK TICKER/OTHER:

Stock Ticker: Subsidiary   Exchange:
Employees: 30,100   Fiscal Year Ends: 03/31
Parent Company: Berkshire Hathaway Inc

SALARIES/BONUSES:

Top Exec. Salary: $ Bonus: $
Second Exec. Salary: $ Bonus: $

OTHER THOUGHTS:

Estimated Female Officers or Directors: 1
Hot Spot for Advancement for Women/Minorities:

Sales, profits and employees may be estimates. Financial information, benefits and other data can change quickly and may vary from those stated here.

Priceline Group Inc (The)

www.priceline.com

NAIC Code: 519130

TYPES OF BUSINESS:

Online Retail-Travel Services
Auction-Based Travel Sales
Online Financial Services

BRANDS/DIVISIONS/AFFILIATES:

Name Your Own Price
Booking.com
Agoda.com
RentalCars.com
Priceline.com
Kayak Software Corporation
OpenTable Inc
PriceMatch

CONTACTS: Note: Officers with more than one job title may be intentionally listed here more than once.

Gillian Tans, CEO, Subsidiary
Jeffery Boyd, CEO
Daniel Finnegan, CFO
Maelle Gavet, Executive VP, Divisional
Glenn Fogel, Executive VP, Divisional
Peter Millones, Executive VP

GROWTH PLANS/SPECIAL FEATURES:

The Priceline Group, Inc. is a leading online travel company that offers its customers a broad range of travel services, including airline tickets, hotel rooms, car rentals, vacation packages, cruises and destination services primarily through its proprietary Priceline.com website. Within the U.S., the firm offers customers the ability to purchase travel services in a traditional, price-disclosed manner or the opportunity to use the Name Your Own Price service, which allows customers to make offers on travel goods and services at discounted prices. To make an offer, a customer specifies the origin and destination of the trip, the dates on which the customer wishes to depart and return, the price the customer is willing to pay and the customer's valid credit card to guarantee the offer. In total, Priceline is affiliated with eight domestic airlines and 13 international airlines. The company enables customers to make hotel reservations on a worldwide basis, primarily under the Booking.com and Agoda.com brands internationally, and primarily under the Priceline.com brand in the U.S. Through these operations, Priceline works with more than 600,000 chain-owned and independently owned hotels, offering hotel reservations on various web sites and in 42 different languages. Through subsidiary RentalCars.com, the company offers retail price-disclosed rental car reservations through over 28,000 locations. The firm's international business represents approximately 87% of the company's gross bookings and contributes more than 94% of Priceline's consolidated operating income. Subsidiary KAYAK Software Corporation provides a price comparison service allowing consumers to search and compare prices for travel services. In 2014, Priceline acquired OpenTable, Inc., a restaurant booking service. In May 2015, the firm acquired PriceMatch, a cloud-based data and analytics solution for hotels.

Employee benefits include annual bonuses; medical, life, AD&D, disability and dental coverage; a 401(k) savings and investment plan with company match; tuition reimbursement; an employee assistance plan; flexible spending accounts; and travel agent discount benefits.

FINANCIAL DATA: Note: Data for latest year may not have been available at press time.

In U.S. $	2016	2015	2014	2013	2012	2011
Revenue		9,223,987,000	8,441,971,000	6,793,306,000	5,260,956,000	4,355,610,000
R&D Expense		113,617,000	97,498,000	71,890,000	43,685,000	33,813,000
Operating Income		3,258,907,000	3,073,312,000	2,412,414,000	1,829,793,000	1,398,922,000
Operating Margin %		35.33%	36.40%	35.51%	34.78%	32.11%
SGA Expense		4,946,789,000	4,205,500,000	3,113,607,000	2,145,062,000	1,593,321,000
Net Income		2,551,360,000	2,421,753,000	1,892,663,000	1,419,566,000	1,056,371,000
Operating Cash Flow		3,102,231,000	2,914,397,000	2,301,436,000	1,785,750,000	1,341,812,000
Capital Expenditure		173,915,000	131,504,000	84,445,000	55,158,000	46,833,000
EBITDA		3,561,043,000	3,285,621,000	2,497,801,000	1,889,074,000	1,453,339,000
Return on Assets %		15.76%	19.08%	22.24%	26.93%	30.72%
Return on Equity %		29.38%	31.29%	35.02%	43.87%	48.15%
Debt to Equity		0.70	0.44	0.25	0.22	0.03

CONTACT INFORMATION:

Phone: 203-2998000   Fax:
Toll-Free:
Address: 800 Connecticut Ave., Norwalk, CT 06854 United States

STOCK TICKER/OTHER:

Stock Ticker: PCLN   Exchange: NAS
Employees: 12,700   Fiscal Year Ends:
Parent Company:

SALARIES/BONUSES:

Top Exec. Salary: $865,000   Bonus: $
Second Exec. Salary: Bonus: $
$360,335

OTHER THOUGHTS:

Estimated Female Officers or Directors: 1
Hot Spot for Advancement for Women/Minorities: Y

PriceSmart Inc

NAIC Code: 452910

TYPES OF BUSINESS:

Warehouse Clubs, Retail
Merchandise
Warehouse Club Membership

BRANDS/DIVISIONS/AFFILIATES:

CONTACTS: *Note: Officers with more than one job title may be intentionally listed here more than once.*

Jose Laparte, CEO
John Heffner, CFO
Robert Price, Chairman of the Board
William Naylon, COO
Jesus Von Chong, Executive VP, Divisional
Rodrigo Calvo, Executive VP, Divisional
Brud Drachman, Executive VP, Divisional
John Hildebrandt, Executive VP, Divisional
Robert Gans, Executive VP
Thomas Martin, Executive VP

GROWTH PLANS/SPECIAL FEATURES:

PriceSmart, Inc. is one of the largest operators of warehouse membership clubs in Central America, the Caribbean and South America. The company serves over 2.9 million cardholders at 37 owned and operated warehouse clubs in Central America, South America and the Caribbean. PriceSmart's membership club model is similar to U.S. clubs like Costco and Sam's, with some differences: smaller store size, lower membership fees (average $30), and merchandise is tailored to local preferences as well as for retail and wholesale customers. PriceSmart warehouse clubs can be found in Colombia, 6; Costa Rica, 6; Panama, 5; Trinidad and Tobago, 4; Guatemala, 3; Dominican Republic, 3; Honduras, 3; El Salvador, 2; Nicaragua, 2; and one each in Aruba, Barbados, Jamaica and the U.S. Virgin Islands. Online shopping is available to its members in all countries. Merchandise departments include electronics, computers, baby, automotive, restaurant/institutional, sporting goods, outdoor, hardware, toys and games, appliances, housewares, bed and bath, luggage, health care, furniture, office and fashion accessories. In 2016, the firm expected to open its seventh warehouse club in Colombia, by year's end.

FINANCIAL DATA: *Note: Data for latest year may not have been available at press time.*

In U.S. $	2016	2015	2014	2013	2012	2011
Revenue		2,802,603,000	2,517,567,000	2,299,812,000	2,050,745,000	1,714,247,000
R&D Expense						
Operating Income		146,366,000	136,707,000	127,935,000	107,926,000	90,880,000
Operating Margin %		5.22%	5.43%	5.56%	5.26%	5.30%
SGA Expense		301,393,000	265,751,000	242,449,000	224,039,000	192,663,000
Net Income		89,124,000	92,886,000	84,265,000	67,621,000	61,750,000
Operating Cash Flow		110,503,000	137,275,000	130,633,000	89,889,000	75,599,000
Capital Expenditure		89,185,000	118,101,000	69,927,000	52,705,000	47,033,000
EBITDA		177,481,000	167,019,000	151,871,000	132,644,000	114,426,000
Return on Assets %		9.10%	10.51%	10.79%	9.65%	9.98%
Return on Equity %		15.78%	18.04%	18.72%	17.01%	17.34%
Debt to Equity		0.12	0.14	0.12	0.17	0.16

CONTACT INFORMATION:

Phone: 858 404-8800   Fax: 858 404-8848
Toll-Free:
Address: 9740 Scranton Rd., San Diego, CA 92121 United States

STOCK TICKER/OTHER:

Stock Ticker: PSMT   Exchange: NAS
Employees: 7,592   Fiscal Year Ends: 08/31
Parent Company:

SALARIES/BONUSES:

Top Exec. Salary: $596,310   Bonus: $12,100
Second Exec. Salary: Bonus: $7,073
$425,177

OTHER THOUGHTS:

Estimated Female Officers or Directors: 4
Hot Spot for Advancement for Women/Minorities: Y

PricewaterhouseCoopers (PWC)

www.pwc.com

NAIC Code: 541211

TYPES OF BUSINESS:

Accounting Services
Business Advisory
Corporate Finance Services
Employee Benefits Services
Tax Services
Business Publications
Management Consulting

BRANDS/DIVISIONS/AFFILIATES:

CONTACTS: *Note: Officers with more than one job title may be intentionally listed here more than once.*

Carol Sawdye, CFO
Rob Gittings, Mktg. & Sales
Gary Price, Chief Admin. Officer
Diana Weiss, General Counsel
Robert E. Moritz, Chmn.
Mitch Cohen, Vice Chmn.
Terri McClements, Head-U.S. Human Capital & Public Policy
Laura Cox Kaplan, Head-Regulation Affairs & Public Policy
Bob Moritz, Chmn.

GROWTH PLANS/SPECIAL FEATURES:

PricewaterhouseCoopers (PwC) is a global accounting firm with over 200,000 employees across 150+ countries. PwC provides accounting and advisory services to a large number of mid-sized and small companies. The firm provides industry-focused services for public and private clients primarily in eight areas: audit and assurance, consulting, deals, human resources, risk assurance, forensic services, IFRS (International Financial Reporting Standards) reporting and tax. Audit and assurance provides financial statement audits, regulatory and Sarbanes-Oxley compliance and financial accounting, while a crisis management division offers business recovery services with dispute analysis and investigations. The consulting sector offers services in technology, operations, sustainability, investigations and finance. The deals sector specializes in mergers and acquisitions, strategic and valuation advice and growth and divestments. The human resources services segment helps clients with international assignments; HR management; and employee growth, benefits and rewards. Risk assurance services include internal auditing; third party assurance; process assurance; IT and project assurance; and governance, risk and compliance. Forensic sciences services includes fraud protection, cybercrime and data breach response and intellectual property protection. IFRS reporting helps businesses navigate the financial and industry standards of IFRS. Lastly, the tax sector helps businesses reduce tax risks, improve operating efficiency and manage total tax contributions to governments. PwC also produces a number of publications that provide authoritative information on better business practices and emerging issues facing management and breaking trends in the business world.

The company offers employees a formal work-life balance program; substantial sick leave and family care leave; flexible work arrangements that may include job-sharing, flex time, sabbaticals and a compressed work week; and access to training at the PwC Open University.

FINANCIAL DATA: *Note: Data for latest year may not have been available at press time.*

In U.S. $	2016	2015	2014	2013	2012	2011
Revenue		35,400,000,000	34,000,000,000	32,100,000,000	31,500,000,000	29,200,000,000
R&D Expense						
Operating Income						
Operating Margin %						
SGA Expense						
Net Income						
Operating Cash Flow						
Capital Expenditure						
EBITDA						
Return on Assets %						
Return on Equity %						
Debt to Equity						

CONTACT INFORMATION:

Phone: 646-471-4000   Fax: 813-286-6000
Toll-Free:
Address: 300 Madison Ave., 24th Fl., New York, NY 10017 United States

STOCK TICKER/OTHER:

Stock Ticker: Private   Exchange:
Employees: 208,109   Fiscal Year Ends: 06/30
Parent Company:

SALARIES/BONUSES:

Top Exec. Salary: $ Bonus: $
Second Exec. Salary: $ Bonus: $

OTHER THOUGHTS:

Estimated Female Officers or Directors: 5
Hot Spot for Advancement for Women/Minorities: Y

Principal Financial Group (The)

NAIC Code: 524113

www.principal.com

TYPES OF BUSINESS:

Asset Management
Life Insurance
Health Insurance
Annuities
Disability Insurance
Investment Services
Specialty Benefits Insurance

BRANDS/DIVISIONS/AFFILIATES:

CONTACTS: Note: Officers with more than one job title may be intentionally listed here more than once.

Terrance Lillis, CFO
Nick Cecere, Senior VP, Divisional
Gary Scholten, Chief Information Officer
Gregory Elming, Chief Risk Officer
Renee Schaaf, COO, Divisional
Timothy Dunbar, Executive VP
Luis Valdes, Other Corporate Officer
Leanne Valentine, Other Corporate Officer
Mark Lagomarcino, Other Corporate Officer
Nora Everett, President, Divisional
Deanna Strable-Soethout, President, Divisional
James Mccaughan, President, Divisional
Daniel Houston, President
Karen Shaff, Secretary

GROWTH PLANS/SPECIAL FEATURES:

The Principal Financial Group is a leading provider of retirement savings, investment and insurance products and services. It holds a total of $527.4 billion in assets and serves 19.1 million customers globally, with a focus on small and medium sized businesses (companies with less than 1,000 employees). The company is organized into four segments: retirement & income solutions, principal global investors, principal international and U.S. insurance solutions. The retirement & income solutions segment offers products and services for retirement savings and retirement income: to small- and medium-sized businesses, including 401k and 403b plans, benefit pension plans, non-qualified executive benefit plants, employee stock ownership plans, as well as SIMPLE individual retirement accounts (IRA) and payroll deduction plans; to large institutional clients, offering investment-only products such as guaranteed investment contracts; and employees of businesses and other individuals, offering accumulate savings for retirement plans, as well as mutual funds, individual annuities and bank products. The principal global investors segment manages assets for sophisticated investors worldwide, including equity, fixed income, real estate and other alternative investments. This division maintains offices in Australia, Beijing, Brazil, Dubai, Germany, Hong Kong, Japan, the Netherlands, Singapore, the U.K. and the U.S. The principal international segment focuses on countries and territories with growing middle classes, favorable demographics and increasing long-term savings. This division has operations in Brazil, Chile, China, Hong Kong Special Administrative Region, India, Mexico and Southeast Asia. The U.S. insurance solutions segment offers group and individual insurance solutions, providing comprehensive insurance solutions for small- and medium-sized businesses and their owners and executives. These solutions include both group and individual dental, vision, life and disability insurance; and both group and individual life insurance options.

Employee benefits include medical, dental and vision coverage; retirement plans and 401(k); employee stock purchase plan; financial services; and health and wellness programs.

FINANCIAL DATA: Note: Data for latest year may not have been available at press time.

In U.S. $	2016	2015	2014	2013	2012	2011
Revenue		11,964,400,000	10,477,600,000	9,289,500,000	9,215,100,000	8,709,600,000
R&D Expense						
Operating Income		1,430,800,000	1,494,900,000	1,124,000,000	959,400,000	987,600,000
Operating Margin %		11.95%	14.26%	12.09%	10.41%	11.33%
SGA Expense		3,672,400,000	3,574,300,000			3,057,700,000
Net Income		1,234,000,000	1,144,100,000	912,700,000	805,900,000	715,000,000
Operating Cash Flow		4,377,100,000	3,102,900,000	2,221,200,000	3,080,900,000	2,713,300,000
Capital Expenditure		136,400,000	136,000,000	59,400,000	38,900,000	56,900,000
EBITDA						
Return on Assets %		.55%	.52%	.47%	.49%	.46%
Return on Equity %		12.40%	11.18%	9.05%	7.97%	7.04%
Debt to Equity		0.35	0.24	0.26	0.27	0.16

CONTACT INFORMATION:

Phone: 515 247-5111　　Fax:
Toll-Free: 800-986-3343
Address: 711 High St., Des Moines, IA 50392 United States

STOCK TICKER/OTHER:

Stock Ticker: PFG
Employees: 14,895
Parent Company:

Exchange: NYS
Fiscal Year Ends: 12/31

SALARIES/BONUSES:

Top Exec. Salary:
$1,038,462
Second Exec. Salary:
$735,577

Bonus: $

Bonus: $

OTHER THOUGHTS:

Estimated Female Officers or Directors: 10

Hot Spot for Advancement for Women/Minorities: Y

Progressive Corporation (The)

www.progressive.com

NAIC Code: 524126

TYPES OF BUSINESS:

Insurance, Direct Property & Casualty
Automobile Insurance

BRANDS/DIVISIONS/AFFILIATES:

American Strategic Insurance Corp
Progressive Home Advantage
Progressive Commercial Advantage
ARX Holding Corp
ASI

CONTACTS: Note: Officers with more than one job title may be intentionally listed here more than once.

John Auer, CEO, Subsidiary
John Sauerland, CFO
Glenn Renwick, Chairman of the Board
Jeffrey Basch, Chief Accounting Officer
Steven Broz, Chief Information Officer
Jeffrey Charney, Chief Marketing Officer
William Cody, Other Executive Officer
Valerie Krasowski, Other Executive Officer
Charles Jarrett, Other Executive Officer
John Barbagallo, President, Divisional
Michael Sieger, President, Divisional
Patrick Callahan, President, Divisional
John Murphy, President, Divisional
Susan Griffith, President
Thomas King, Treasurer

GROWTH PLANS/SPECIAL FEATURES:

The Progressive Corporation, together with its subsidiaries and affiliates, is one of the largest auto insurers in the U.S. Progressive is divided into six business segments. The personal lines segment writes insurance for personal autos and recreational and other vehicles in all 50 states and the District of Columbia. This division also writes personal auto insurance in Australia. The commercial lines segment primarily writes liability, physical damage and other auto-related insurance for automobiles and trucks owned and/or operated predominantly by small businesses as a part of the commercial auto market. This division offers its products in 49 states. The property segment, through American Strategic Insurance Corp. (ASI), is one of the 20 largest homeowners carriers in the U.S. ASI specializes in personal and commercial property insurance, personal umbrella insurance and primary and excess flood insurance. The other indemnity segment consists of managing The Progressive Corporation's run-off businesses, including the run-off of its professional liability business, with five professional liability policies currently in force. The service businesses segment includes the servicing of the company's commercial auto insurance procedures and plans, as well as the company's two commission-based service businesses: Progressive Home Advantage and Progressive Commercial Advantage. Progressive Home Advantage offers home, condominium and renter's insurance; and Progressive Commercial Advantage offers customers the ability to package their auto coverage with other commercial coverages that are written by unaffiliated insurance companies or placed with additional companies through unaffiliated insurance agencies. Last, the claims segment manages the vehicle claims handling on a company-wide basis through approximately 215 stand-alone claims offices throughout the U.S. In 2015, the firm acquired ARX Holding Corp., the parent company of ASI.

Progressive offers its employees health, dental and vision insurance; fitness centers & wellness programs; maternity services; 401(k); and other assistive benefits.

FINANCIAL DATA: Note: Data for latest year may not have been available at press time.

In U.S. $	2016	2015	2014	2013	2012	2011
Revenue		20,853,800,000	19,391,400,000	18,170,900,000	17,083,900,000	15,508,100,000
R&D Expense						
Operating Income		1,911,600,000	1,907,400,000	1,720,000,000	1,317,700,000	1,487,000,000
Operating Margin %		9.16%	9.83%	9.46%	7.71%	9.58%
SGA Expense		77,500,000	69,800,000	38,800,000	36,100,000	19,400,000
Net Income		1,267,600,000	1,281,000,000	1,165,400,000	902,300,000	1,015,500,000
Operating Cash Flow		2,292,900,000	1,725,600,000	1,899,900,000	1,691,400,000	1,497,900,000
Capital Expenditure		130,700,000	108,100,000	140,400,000	127,700,000	78,900,000
EBITDA						
Return on Assets %		4.55%	5.10%	4.94%	4.05%	4.72%
Return on Equity %		17.83%	19.53%	19.11%	15.27%	17.13%
Debt to Equity		0.37	0.31	0.30	0.34	0.42

CONTACT INFORMATION:

Phone: 440 461-5000   Fax:
Toll-Free: 800-776-4737
Address: 6300 Wilson Mills Rd., Mayfield Village, OH 44143 United States

STOCK TICKER/OTHER:

Stock Ticker: PGR   Exchange: NYS
Employees: 28,580   Fiscal Year Ends: 12/31
Parent Company:

SALARIES/BONUSES:

Top Exec. Salary: $318,750   Bonus: $2,800,000
Second Exec. Salary: $750,000   Bonus: $

OTHER THOUGHTS:

Estimated Female Officers or Directors: 2
Hot Spot for Advancement for Women/Minorities: Y

Providence St. Joseph Health

www.psjhealth.org

NAIC Code: 622110

TYPES OF BUSINESS:

General Medical and Surgical Hospitals
Assisted Living Facilities
Low Income Living Facilities
Counseling

BRANDS/DIVISIONS/AFFILIATES:

Providence Health & Services
St. Joseph Health
Covenant Health
Facey Medical Foundation
Hoag Memorial Presbyterian
Kadlec
Pacific Medical Centers
Institute for Mental Health and Wellness

CONTACTS: Note: Officers with more than one job title may be intentionally listed here more than once.

Rodney F. Hochman, CEO
Myron Berdischewsky, Chief Medical & Quality Officer
Cindy Strauss, Sr. VP
Mike Butler, Pres., Oper. & Svcs.
David Brown, VP-Strategy & Bus. Dev.
Deborah Burton, VP
Jack Friedman, Sr. VP-Accountable Care & Payor Relations
Joel Gilbertson, VP-Gov't. & Public Affairs
John O. Mudd, Sr. VP-Mission leadership
Dave Hunter, VP-Supply Chain Mgmt.

GROWTH PLANS/SPECIAL FEATURES:

Providence St. Joseph Health, formed by the 2016 merger of Providence Health & Services and St. Joseph Health, comprises 50 hospitals, 829 clinics, 23,000 physicians, 14 supportive housing facilities and 106,000 caregivers with the goal of improving the health of the communities it serves especially the poor and the vulnerable. The firm provides a comprehensive range of services across Alaska, California, Montana, New Mexico, Oregon, Texas and Washington. The Providence St. Joseph Health family includes: Providence Health & Services (Alaska, Washington, Montana, Oregon and California), St. Joseph Health (California, New Mexico and Texas), Covenant Health (Texas), Facey Medical Foundation (California), Hoag Memorial Presbyterian (California), Kadlec (Washington), Pacific Medical Centers (Washington), as well as Swedish Health Services (Washington). The company established the Institute for Mental Health and Wellness in order to provide effective mental health services for those who struggle with mental health stigmatization, diagnosis and treatment. The Foundation for Mental Health and Wellness will oversee this work, and the funds derived by the foundation will support research and startup operations for mental health awareness, diagnosis and treatment.

FINANCIAL DATA: Note: Data for latest year may not have been available at press time.

In U.S. $	2016	2015	2014	2013	2012	2011
Revenue		14,434,000,000	12,261,825,000	11,099,009,000	10,608,249,000	8,420,847,000
R&D Expense						
Operating Income						
Operating Margin %						
SGA Expense						
Net Income		77,000,000	771,422,000	253,270,000	1,216,516,000	361,727,000
Operating Cash Flow						
Capital Expenditure						
EBITDA						
Return on Assets %						
Return on Equity %						
Debt to Equity						

CONTACT INFORMATION:

Phone: 425-525-3355   Fax:
Toll-Free:
Address: 1801 Lind Avenue SW, Renton, WA 98057 United States

STOCK TICKER/OTHER:

Stock Ticker: Nonprofit   Exchange:
Employees: 100,000   Fiscal Year Ends: 12/31
Parent Company:

SALARIES/BONUSES:

Top Exec. Salary: $ Bonus: $
Second Exec. Salary: $ Bonus: $

OTHER THOUGHTS:

Estimated Female Officers or Directors: 5
Hot Spot for Advancement for Women/Minorities: Y

Prudential Financial Inc

www.prudential.com

NAIC Code: 524113

TYPES OF BUSINESS:

Insurance-Life
Property & Casualty Insurance
Asset Management
Life Insurance

BRANDS/DIVISIONS/AFFILIATES:

Administradora de Fondos de Pensiones Habitat SA

CONTACTS: Note: Officers with more than one job title may be intentionally listed here more than once.

Andrew Hughes, Assistant Secretary
Richard Lambert, Other Executive Officer
John Strangfeld, CEO
Robert Falzon, CFO
Robert Axel, Chief Accounting Officer
Barbara Koster, Chief Information Officer
Nicholas Silitch, Chief Risk Officer
Charles Lowrey, COO, Divisional
Stephen Pelletier, COO, Geographical
Mark Grier, Director
Timothy Harris, Executive VP
Susan Blount, Executive VP
Margaret Foran, Other Executive Officer
Scott Sleyster, Other Executive Officer
Sharon Taylor, Senior VP, Divisional
Scott Sleyster, Other Executive Officer

GROWTH PLANS/SPECIAL FEATURES:

Prudential Financial, Inc. provides financial products and services, including life insurance, annuities, retirement-related services, mutual funds and investment management. Prudential is a financial leader with approximately $1.184 trillion of assets under management, and has operations in the U.S., Asia, Europe and Latin America. The company's products and services are offered to individual and institutional customers through proprietary and third party distribution networks. The businesses of Prudential are divided into the financial services businesses and the closed block businesses. The financial business consists of four operating divisions, which together has seven segments, as well as corporate and other operations. The U.S. retirement solutions and investment management division, contains the individual annuities, retirement and asset management segments. The U.S. individual life and group insurance division consists of its individual life and group insurance segments. The international insurance division contains the international insurance segment. The closed block division is designed to provide for the reasonable expectations for future policy dividends after demutualization of holders of participating individual life insurance policies and annuities by allocating assets that will be used exclusively for payment of benefits, including policy-holder dividends, expenses and taxes with respect to these products. The corporate and other operations include items and initiatives that are not allocated to business segments, as well as businesses that have been or will be divested. In 2016, the firm acquired Administradora de Fondos de Pensiones Habitat SA, in Chile.

Employee benefits include medical, dental, disability, life and accident insurance; a 401(k); fitness and wellness centers; and employee discounts.

FINANCIAL DATA: Note: Data for latest year may not have been available at press time.

In U.S. $	2016	2015	2014	2013	2012	2011
Revenue		57,119,000,000	54,105,000,000	41,461,000,000	84,815,000,000	49,045,000,000
R&D Expense						
Operating Income		7,769,000,000	1,759,000,000	-1,684,000,000	676,000,000	5,117,000,000
Operating Margin %		13.60%	3.25%	-4.06%	.79%	10.43%
SGA Expense		10,912,000,000	11,807,000,000	11,011,000,000	11,094,000,000	9,815,000,000
Net Income		5,642,000,000	1,381,000,000	-667,000,000	469,000,000	3,666,000,000
Operating Cash Flow		13,895,000,000	19,396,000,000	8,445,000,000	20,909,000,000	12,377,000,000
Capital Expenditure						
EBITDA						
Return on Assets %		.74%	.19%	-.09%	.07%	.62%
Return on Equity %		13.48%	3.84%	-1.80%	1.23%	10.52%
Debt to Equity		0.67	0.47	0.76	0.68	0.66

CONTACT INFORMATION:

Phone: 973 802-6000   Fax: 973 367-6476
Toll-Free: 877-998-7625
Address: 751 Broad Street, Newark, NJ 07102 United States

STOCK TICKER/OTHER:

Stock Ticker: PRU   Exchange: NYS
Employees: 49,384   Fiscal Year Ends: 12/31
Parent Company:

SALARIES/BONUSES:

Top Exec. Salary: Bonus: $
$1,190,000
Second Exec. Salary: Bonus: $
$770,000

OTHER THOUGHTS:

Estimated Female Officers or Directors: 6

Hot Spot for Advancement for Women/Minorities: Y

Publix Super Markets Inc

NAIC Code: 445110

www.publix.com

TYPES OF BUSINESS:

Grocery Stores
Dairy, Deli & Bakery Products
Convenience Stores
Liquor Stores
Restaurants

BRANDS/DIVISIONS/AFFILIATES:

Publix

CONTACTS: *Note: Officers with more than one job title may be intentionally listed here more than once.*

Sharon Miller, Assistant Secretary
David Bornmann, Vice President
William Crenshaw, CEO
David Phillips, CFO
Laurie Zeitlin, Chief Information Officer
Charles Jenkins, Director
Hoyt Barnett, Director
Randall Jones, President
John Hrabusa, Senior VP
John Attaway, Senior VP
Linda Hall, Vice President
Dale Myers, Vice President
David Duncan, Vice President
David Bridges, Vice President
Michael Smith, Vice President
Thomas Mclaughlin, Vice President
William Fauerbach, Vice President
Alfred Ottolino, Vice President
Mark Irby, Vice President
John Frazier, Vice President
Marc Salm, Vice President

GROWTH PLANS/SPECIAL FEATURES:

Publix Super Markets, Inc. is a leading operator c supermarkets, with 1,114 locations in Alabama, Florida Georgia, South Carolina, North Carolina and Tennessee. The firm's supermarkets sell groceries, dairy products, produce, de foods, bakery items, meat, seafood, housewares and healt and beauty merchandise. Many stores also feature pharmacies, floral departments, photo labs, liquor stores and in-store banking areas. It also owns several pharmacy and convenience store locations under various names. Publix's lines of merchandise include a variety of nationally advertise and private label brands as well as some unbranded merchandise, such as produce, meat and seafood. In addition to its retail operations, Publix manufactures dairy, bakery and deli products through manufacturing facilities located in Lakeland, Miami, Jacksonville, Sarasota, Orlando, Deerfield Beach and Boynton Beach, Florida and Lawrenceville Georgia. The firm is one of the largest employee-owned grocery stores in the U.S. In July 2016, the firm agreed to acquire 10 Virginia stores from Ahold USA, Inc.'s affiliate GIANT/MARTIN'S, dependent upon FTC approval and clearance of the merger between Ahold and Delhaize Group.

Publix offers its employees health, dental and vision coverage quarterly retail bonuses; an employee stock ownership plan holiday bonuses; free hot lunches; prescription discounts; a 401(k) plan; a profit sharing plan; access to a credit union tuition reimbursement; and an employee assistance plan.

FINANCIAL DATA: *Note: Data for latest year may not have been available at press time.*

In U.S. $	2016	2015	2014	2013	2012	2011
Revenue		32,618,760,000	30,802,470,000	29,147,520,000	27,706,770,000	27,178,760,000
R&D Expense						
Operating Income		2,678,241,000	2,400,861,000	2,319,738,000	2,165,251,000	2,134,925,000
Operating Margin %		8.21%	7.79%	7.95%	7.81%	7.85%
SGA Expense		6,480,908,000	6,168,955,000	5,890,461,000	5,630,537,000	5,523,469,000
Net Income		1,965,048,000	1,735,308,000	1,653,954,000	1,552,255,000	1,491,966,000
Operating Cash Flow		2,941,365,000	2,777,232,000	2,567,303,000	2,604,207,000	2,341,187,000
Capital Expenditure		1,235,648,000	1,374,124,000	668,485,000	697,112,000	602,952,000
EBITDA		3,260,133,000	2,914,254,000	2,821,427,000	2,795,833,000	2,627,564,000
Return on Assets %		12.49%	12.12%	12.80%	13.18%	13.92%
Return on Equity %		16.58%	16.12%	17.13%	20.36%	22.23%
Debt to Equity		0.01	0.01	0.01	0.01	0.01

CONTACT INFORMATION:

Phone: 863 688-1188   Fax: 863 688-5532
Toll-Free: 800-242-1227
Address: 3300 Publix Corporate Pkwy., Lakeland, FL 33811 United States

STOCK TICKER/OTHER:

Stock Ticker: PUSH   Exchange: GREY
Employees: 180,000   Fiscal Year Ends: 12/31
Parent Company:

SALARIES/BONUSES:

Top Exec. Salary: $777,400   Bonus: $
Second Exec. Salary: $622,193   Bonus: $

OTHER THOUGHTS:

Estimated Female Officers or Directors: 5
Hot Spot for Advancement for Women/Minorities: Y

PulteGroup Inc

NAIC Code: 236117

pultegroupinc.com

TYPES OF BUSINESS:

Construction, Home Building and Residential
Financial Services
Mortgages
Land Development

BRANDS/DIVISIONS/AFFILIATES:

Pulte Home Corp
Del Webb Corp
Centex Corp
Pulte Mortgage LLC

CONTACTS: Note: *Officers with more than one job title may be intentionally listed here more than once.*

Robert OShaughnessy, CFO
James Ossowski, Chief Accounting Officer
Richard Dugas, Director
James Ellinghausen, Executive VP, Divisional
Harmon Smith, Executive VP
Steven Cook, Executive VP
Ryan Marshall, President

GROWTH PLANS/SPECIAL FEATURES:

PulteGroup, Inc. is a holding company with subsidiaries in the homebuilding and financial services industries. These subsidiaries include Del Webb Corp.; Pulte Home Corp.; Centex Corp.; and Pulte Mortgage LLC. PulteGroup's core homebuilding business is engaged in the acquisition and development of land, primarily for residential purposes within the U.S. The firm builds a wide variety of homes targeted for first-time, first and second move-up and active adult home buyers, including detached units, townhouses, condominium apartments and duplexes, with varying prices, models, options and lot sizes. Its homebuilding business operates in 50 markets spanning 26 states and offers homes in about 620 communities. During 2015, the firm closed 17,127 homes, with the average unit selling price of $338,000. Sales prices range from less than $100,000 to more than $1,500,000, 85% of which fall between $150,000 and $500,000. PulteGroup's homebuilding operations consist of six geographic segments: Northeast (including Connecticut, Maryland, Massachusetts, New Jersey, New York, Pennsylvania, Rhode Island and Virginia), Florida, Texas, Midwest (including Illinois, Indiana, Kentucky, Michigan, Minnesota, Missouri and Ohio), Southeast (consisting of Georgia, North Carolina, South Carolina and Tennessee) and West (including Arizona, California, Nevada, New Mexico and Washington). The firm's strategy is based on extensive market research that reveals well-defined buying profiles, job demographics and lifestyle choices. PulteGroup's financial services segment consists principally of mortgage operations conducted through Pulte Mortgage LLC and its subsidiaries. In 2015, the firm acquired 507 acres in North Naples, Florida that includes an existing 18-hole golf course and 548 new single family home sites; and agreed to acquire assets of John Wieland Homes & Neighborhood that December.

The company offers employees medical, dental and vision insurance; a 401(k); life and AD&D insurance; business travel accident insurance; short- and long-term disability; tuition reimbursement; an employee assistance program; and time off for volunteering.

FINANCIAL DATA: Note: *Data for latest year may not have been available at press time.*

In U.S. $	2016	2015	2014	2013	2012	2011
Revenue		5,981,964,000	5,822,363,000	5,679,595,000	4,819,998,000	4,136,690,000
R&D Expense						
Operating Income		820,486,000	703,279,000	587,540,000	241,699,000	-24,236,000
Operating Margin %		13.71%	12.07%	10.34%	5.01%	-.58%
SGA Expense		589,780,000	667,815,000	568,500,000	514,457,000	519,583,000
Net Income		494,090,000	474,338,000	2,620,116,000	206,145,000	-210,388,000
Operating Cash Flow		-348,129,000	309,249,000	881,136,000	760,140,000	17,222,000
Capital Expenditure		45,440,000	48,790,000	28,899,000	13,942,000	21,238,000
EBITDA		863,033,000	730,471,000	560,121,000	214,400,000	-276,889,000
Return on Assets %		5.59%	5.44%	33.87%	3.02%	-2.88%
Return on Equity %		10.26%	9.96%	76.62%	9.98%	-10.32%
Debt to Equity		0.49	0.40	0.46	1.14	1.59

CONTACT INFORMATION:

Phone: 404-978-6400   Fax:
Toll-Free: 866-785-8325
Address: 3350 Peachtree Road NE, Ste 150, Atlanta, GA 30326 United States

STOCK TICKER/OTHER:

Stock Ticker: PHM
Employees: 4,542
Parent Company:

Exchange: NYS
Fiscal Year Ends: 12/31

SALARIES/BONUSES:

Top Exec. Salary:
$1,200,000
Second Exec. Salary:
$700,000

Bonus: $

Bonus: $

OTHER THOUGHTS:

Estimated Female Officers or Directors: 4

Hot Spot for Advancement for Women/Minorities: Y

Sales, profits and employees may be estimates. Financial information, benefits and other data can change quickly and may vary from those stated here.

Qualcomm Inc

www.qualcomm.com

NAIC Code: 334413

TYPES OF BUSINESS:

Telecommunications Equipment
Digital Wireless Communications Products
Integrated Circuits
Mobile Communications Systems
Wireless Software & Services
E-Mail Software
Code Division Multiple Access

BRANDS/DIVISIONS/AFFILIATES:

Guizhou Huaxintong Semi-Conductor Technology Co
RF360 Holdings Singapore Pte Ltd

CONTACTS: Note: Officers with more than one job title may be intentionally listed here more than once.

Steven Mollenkopf, CEO
George Davis, CFO
Paul Jacobs, Chairman of the Board
John Murphy, Chief Accounting Officer
Matthew Grob, Chief Technology Officer
Michelle Sterling, Executive VP, Divisional
Brian Modoff, Executive VP, Divisional
James Thompson, Executive VP, Subsidiary
Cristiano Amon, Executive VP, Subsidiary
Donald Rosenberg, Executive VP
Derek Aberle, President

GROWTH PLANS/SPECIAL FEATURES:

Qualcomm, Inc. provides digital wireless communications products, technologies and services. Its operations are divided into three segments: Qualcomm CDMA Technologies (QCT), Qualcomm Technology Licensing (QTL) and Qualcomm Strategic Initiatives (QSI). QCT designs application-specific integrated circuits based on Code Division Multiple Access (CDMA), Orthogonal Frequency-Division Multiple Access (OFDMA) and other technologies for use in voice and data communications, networking, application processing multimedia functions and GPS products. QTL grants licenses and provides rights to use portions of Qualcomm's intellectual property portfolio to third-party manufacturers of wireless products and networking equipment. QSI makes strategic investments in various companies and technologies that Qualcomm believes will open new opportunities for its technologies. In January 2016, the firm partnered with Guizhou Province in order to form joint venture Guizhou Huaxintong Semi-Conductor Technology Co. Ltd., which will design and sell world-class server chipset technology in China; and partnered with TDK Corporation to form joint venture RF360 Holdings Singapore Pte. Ltd., which will deliver RF front-end modules and RF filters into fully integrated systems for mobile devices and fast-growing business segments such as the Internet of Things, drones, robotics, automotive applications and more.

U.S. employees of the company receive medical, dental and vision insurance; dependent/health care reimbursement accounts; tuition reimbursement; a 401(k); and an employee stock purchase plan.

FINANCIAL DATA: Note: Data for latest year may not have been available at press time.

In U.S. $	2016	2015	2014	2013	2012	2011
Revenue		25,281,000,000	26,487,000,000	24,866,000,000	19,121,000,000	14,957,000,000
R&D Expense		5,490,000,000	5,477,000,000	4,967,000,000	3,915,000,000	2,995,000,000
Operating Income		5,776,000,000	7,550,000,000	7,230,000,000	5,682,000,000	5,026,000,000
Operating Margin %		22.84%	28.50%	29.07%	29.71%	33.60%
SGA Expense		2,344,000,000	2,290,000,000	2,518,000,000	2,324,000,000	1,945,000,000
Net Income		5,271,000,000	7,967,000,000	6,853,000,000	6,109,000,000	4,260,000,000
Operating Cash Flow		5,506,000,000	8,887,000,000	8,778,000,000	5,998,000,000	4,900,000,000
Capital Expenditure		994,000,000	1,185,000,000	1,048,000,000	1,284,000,000	593,000,000
EBITDA		7,805,000,000	8,700,000,000	9,234,000,000	7,549,000,000	6,862,000,000
Return on Assets %		10.60%	16.93%	15.48%	15.38%	12.71%
Return on Equity %		14.93%	21.17%	19.68%	20.20%	17.82%
Debt to Equity		0.31				

CONTACT INFORMATION:

Phone: 858 587-1121   Fax: 858 658-2100
Toll-Free:
Address: 5775 Morehouse Dr., San Diego, CA 92121 United States

STOCK TICKER/OTHER:

Stock Ticker: QCOM   Exchange: NAS
Employees: 33,000   Fiscal Year Ends: 09/30
Parent Company:

SALARIES/BONUSES:

Top Exec. Salary: Bonus: $
$1,141,886
Second Exec. Salary: Bonus: $
$805,394

OTHER THOUGHTS:

Estimated Female Officers or Directors: 2

Hot Spot for Advancement for Women/Minorities: Y

Sales, profits and employees may be estimates. Financial information, benefits and other data can change quickly and may vary from those stated here.

Quality Systems Inc

NAIC Code: 0

TYPES OF BUSINESS:

Computer Software, Healthcare & Biotechnology

BRANDS/DIVISIONS/AFFILIATES:

ViaTrack Systems LLC
Clinical Product Suite
Opus Healthcare Solutions LLC
NextGen Healthcare Information Systems LLC
Mirth Corporation
Quality Systems India Healthcare Private Limited
HealthFusion Holdings Inc
Gennius Inc

CONTACTS: *Note: Officers with more than one job title may be intentionally listed here more than once.*

John Frantz, CEO
Sheldon Razin, Chairman Emeritus
John Stumpf, Chief Accounting Officer
David Metcalfe, Chief Technology Officer
Daniel Morefield, COO
Jeffrey Margolis, Director
Craig Barbarosh, Director
Mark Davis, Executive VP, Divisional
James Arnold, Executive VP
Jocelyn Leavitt, Executive VP

GROWTH PLANS/SPECIAL FEATURES:

Quality Systems, Inc. develops and provides computer-based practice management, medical records and e-business applications. The firm operates through four divisions: QSI dental, hospital solutions, NextGen and RCM services. All four develop and market products that streamline patient records and administrative functions such as billing and scheduling at health care facilities. The QSI dental division, which includes ViaTrack Systems LLC, focuses on developing, marketing and supporting software suites for dental and niche medical practices. Its Clinical Product Suite is a UNIX-based medical practice management software suite that incorporates clinical tools including periodontal charting and digital imaging of x-ray and inter-oral camera images. The hospital solutions division, which includes Opus Healthcare Solutions LLC, develops and markets practice management software products for rural and community hospitals, which perform administrative functions required for operating a small hospital as well as physician documentation and computerized physician order entry (CPOE) charting. The NextGen division, operated by both NextGen Healthcare Information Systems LLC and Mirth Corporation, develops and sells proprietary electronic medical records software and practice management systems. Its primary product categories include the NextGen ambulatory product suite, which streamlines patient care through the use of standardized, real-time clinical and administrative workflows within a physician's practice. NextGen's products also includes tools for measuring and evaluating patient outcomes. The firm's RCM services segment primarily provides revenue cycle management (RCM) services for medical practices through a combination of web-based software as a service (SaaS) and the NextGen software platform. Quality Systems India Healthcare Private Limited, the firm's India-based subsidiary, was established to offshore technology application development and business processing services. In 2015, the firm acquired HealthFusion Holdings, Inc., a developer of web-based, cloud computing software for physicians, hospitals and medical billing services; and Gennius, Inc. a provider of health care data analytics.

FINANCIAL DATA: *Note: Data for latest year may not have been available at press time.*

In U.S. $	2016	2015	2014	2013	2012	2011
Revenue	492,477,000	490,225,000	444,667,000	460,229,000	429,835,000	353,363,000
R&D Expense	65,661,000	69,240,000	41,524,000	30,865,000	31,369,000	21,797,000
Operating Income	7,362,000	35,956,000	23,088,000	69,100,000	116,199,000	94,092,000
Operating Margin %	1.49%	7.33%	5.19%	15.01%	27.03%	26.62%
SGA Expense	156,234,000	158,172,000	149,214,000	148,353,000	128,846,000	108,310,000
Net Income	5,657,000	27,332,000	15,680,000	42,724,000	75,657,000	61,606,000
Operating Cash Flow	40,796,000	82,758,000	104,140,000	68,041,000	76,786,000	70,064,000
Capital Expenditure	28,688,000	21,132,000	28,718,000	39,424,000	10,323,000	24,303,000
EBITDA	37,363,000	65,223,000	51,825,000	93,255,000	134,149,000	108,742,000
Return on Assets %	1.14%	6.03%	3.53%	9.67%	18.47%	17.88%
Return on Equity %	2.04%	9.44%	5.20%	14.18%	29.10%	29.83%
Debt to Equity	0.38					

CONTACT INFORMATION:

Phone: 949 255-2600   Fax:
Toll-Free: 800-888-7955
Address: 18111 Von Karman, Ste. 700, Irvine, CA 92612 United States

STOCK TICKER/OTHER:

Stock Ticker: QSII   Exchange: NAS
Employees: 2,939   Fiscal Year Ends: 02/28
Parent Company:

SALARIES/BONUSES:

Top Exec. Salary: $460,682   Bonus: $
Second Exec. Salary: Bonus: $
$450,006

OTHER THOUGHTS:

Estimated Female Officers or Directors:
Hot Spot for Advancement for Women/Minorities:

Quanta Services Inc

NAIC Code: 237130

www.quantaservices.com

TYPES OF BUSINESS:

Construction, Power & Communication Lines
Network Installation & Support Services
Network Design Services
Electric Power Transmission Systems
Gas Pipeline Systems

BRANDS/DIVISIONS/AFFILIATES:

CONTACTS: *Note: Officers with more than one job title may be intentionally listed here more than once.*

Earl Austin, CEO
Derrick Jensen, CFO
Bruce Ranck, Director
Randall Wisenbaker, Executive VP, Divisional
Jesse Morris, Executive VP, Divisional
Dale Querrey, President, Divisional
Carolyn Campbell, Secretary
Nicholas Grindstaff, Treasurer
Dorothy Upperman, Vice President, Divisional

GROWTH PLANS/SPECIAL FEATURES:

Quanta Services, Inc. is a specialty contract provider c
infrastructure services. The company designs, installs an
maintains networks for the electric power, natural gas and o
pipeline industries. Quanta Services operates in two segments
electric power infrastructure services (EPIS) and oil & ga
infrastructure services (OGIS). EPIS derives the majority of th
firm's annual revenue and provides comprehensive networl
solutions to customers in the electric power industry. Service:
performed by this segment include the design, installation
upgrade, repair and maintenance of electric powe
transmissions and distribution infrastructure and substatio
facilities along with other engineering and technical services. I
also provides emergency restoration services, including the
repair of infrastructure damaged by inclement weather, the
energized installation, maintenance and upgrade of electri
power infrastructure utilizing unique bare hand and hot stick
methods and Quanta's proprietary robotic arm technologies, a:
well as the installation of smart grid technologies on electri
power networks. OGIS provides infrastructure solutions tc
customers involved in the development and transportation o
natural gas, oil and other pipeline products. Services performec
by this segment include the design, installation, repair anc
maintenance of pipeline transmission and distribution systems
gathering systems, production systems and compressor anc
pump stations, as well as related trenching, directional borinç
and automatic welding services. This division also provide:
pipeline protection, integrity testing, rehabilitation anc
replacement and fabrication of pipeline support systems anc
related structures and facilities. During 2015, the firm sold it:
fiber optic licensing operations to Crown Castle fo
approximately $1 billion; and acquired 11 companies which
were merged into the EPIS segment.

FINANCIAL DATA: *Note: Data for latest year may not have been available at press time.*

In U.S. $	2016	2015	2014	2013	2012	2011
Revenue		7,572,436,000	7,851,250,000	6,522,842,000	5,920,269,000	4,623,829,000
R&D Expense						
Operating Income		237,503,000	475,575,000	526,928,000	465,122,000	217,683,000
Operating Margin %		3.13%	6.05%	8.07%	7.85%	4.70%
SGA Expense		592,863,000	722,038,000	501,010,000	434,894,000	372,963,000
Net Income		310,907,000	296,714,000	401,921,000	306,629,000	132,515,000
Operating Cash Flow		618,183,000	310,824,000	446,592,000	106,217,000	218,030,000
Capital Expenditure		210,179,000	301,728,000	263,558,000	210,986,000	172,005,000
EBITDA		434,392,000	671,899,000	803,542,000	626,320,000	364,212,000
Return on Assets %		5.39%	4.90%	7.35%	6.23%	2.93%
Return on Equity %		8.18%	6.78%	10.04%	8.57%	3.92%
Debt to Equity		0.15	0.01			

CONTACT INFORMATION:

Phone: 713 629-7600   Fax: 713 629-7676
Toll-Free:
Address: 2800 Post Oak Blvd, Ste 2600, Houston, TX 77056 United
States

STOCK TICKER/OTHER:

Stock Ticker: PWR   Exchange: NYS
Employees: 24,600   Fiscal Year Ends: 12/31
Parent Company:

SALARIES/BONUSES:

Top Exec. Salary: Bonus: $
$1,075,000
Second Exec. Salary: Bonus: $
$875,000

OTHER THOUGHTS:

Estimated Female Officers or Directors:

Hot Spot for Advancement for Women/Minorities:

Quest Diagnostics Inc

www.questdiagnostics.com

NAIC Code: 621511

TYPES OF BUSINESS:

Services-Testing & Diagnostics
Clinical Laboratory Testing
Clinical Trials Testing
Esoteric Testing Laboratories

BRANDS/DIVISIONS/AFFILIATES:

Nichols Institute
Athena Diagnostics
Superior Mobile Medics

CONTACTS: Note: Officers with more than one job title may be intentionally listed here more than once.

Stephen Rusckowski, CEO
Mark Guinan, CFO
Daniel Stanzione, Chairman of the Board
Michael Prevoznik, General Counsel
Jon Cohen, Other Corporate Officer
Catherine Doherty, Other Corporate Officer
James Davis, Other Corporate Officer
William OShaughnessy, Secretary
Everett Cunningham, Senior VP, Divisional
Robert Klug, Vice President

GROWTH PLANS/SPECIAL FEATURES:

Quest Diagnostics, Inc. is a U.S. clinical laboratory testing company, offering diagnostic testing and related services to the health care industry. The firm's operations consist of routine, esoteric and clinical trials testing. Quest operates through its national network of over 2,300 patient service centers, principal laboratories in several major metropolitan areas, rapid-response laboratories, outpatient anatomic pathology centers, hospital-based laboratories and esoteric testing laboratories on both coasts. Routine tests measure various important bodily health parameters. Tests in this category include blood cholesterol level tests, complete blood cell counts, urinalyses, pregnancy and prenatal tests, substance-abuse tests and allergy tests such. The company also provides cancer diagnostics, including anatomic pathology services in the U.S. Gene-based and other esoteric tests require more sophisticated technology and highly skilled personnel. Quest's two esoteric testing laboratories, comprising the Nichols Institute and Athena Diagnostics, are among the leading esoteric clinical testing laboratories in the world. Esoteric tests involve endocrinology, genetics, immunology, microbiology, oncology, serology, endocrinology, hematology and toxicology. Clinical trial testing primarily involves assessing the safety and efficacy of new drugs to meet FDA requirements. The company has clinical trials testing centers in the U.S. and the U.K., and also provides clinical trials testing in Argentina, Brazil, China and Singapore through affiliated laboratories. Additionally, Quest provides risk management services to the life insurance industry in the U.S. and Canada as well as many other countries. In 2015, the firm acquired MemorialCare Heath System's laboratory outreach service business; and Superior Mobile Medics, a national provider of paramedical & health data collection services. In 2016, Quest Diagnositcs acquired Clinical Laboratory Partners' outreach laboratory testing business; and sold Focus Diagnostics' molecular and immunoassay product business to DiaSorin SpA.

The firm offers employees medical, dental and life insurance; employee assistance program; and flexible spending accounts.

FINANCIAL DATA: Note: Data for latest year may not have been available at press time.

In U.S. $	2016	2015	2014	2013	2012	2011
Revenue		7,493,000,000	7,435,000,000	7,146,000,000	7,382,562,000	7,510,490,000
R&D Expense						
Operating Income		1,399,000,000	983,000,000	1,475,000,000	1,200,797,000	995,048,000
Operating Margin %		18.67%	13.22%	20.64%	16.26%	13.24%
SGA Expense		1,679,000,000	1,728,000,000	1,704,000,000	1,745,200,000	1,814,315,000
Net Income		709,000,000	556,000,000	849,000,000	555,721,000	470,567,000
Operating Cash Flow		810,000,000	938,000,000	652,000,000	1,187,168,000	895,474,000
Capital Expenditure		263,000,000	308,000,000	231,000,000	182,234,000	161,556,000
EBITDA		1,561,000,000	1,330,000,000	1,793,000,000	1,522,679,000	1,310,683,000
Return on Assets %		7.14%	5.90%	9.31%	5.97%	5.27%
Return on Equity %		15.78%	13.48%	20.93%	14.14%	12.18%
Debt to Equity		0.74	0.75	0.79	0.80	0.91

CONTACT INFORMATION:

Phone: 973 520-2700   Fax:
Toll-Free: 800-222-0446
Address: 3 Giralda Farms, Madison, NJ 07940 United States

STOCK TICKER/OTHER:

Stock Ticker: DGX   Exchange: NYS
Employees: 45,000   Fiscal Year Ends: 12/31
Parent Company:

SALARIES/BONUSES:

Top Exec. Salary: Bonus: $
$1,128,846
Second Exec. Salary: Bonus: $
$596,819

OTHER THOUGHTS:

Estimated Female Officers or Directors: 3

Hot Spot for Advancement for Women/Minorities: Y

QuikTrip Corporation

www.quiktrip.com

NAIC Code: 447110

TYPES OF BUSINESS:

Convenience Stores
Gas Stations
Truck Stops

BRANDS/DIVISIONS/AFFILIATES:

QT Distribution
IQ
QuikTrip
Hotzi
QT Kitchens
Wally
QT Twister
Quikshakes

CONTACTS: *Note: Officers with more than one job title may be intentionally listed here more than once.*

Chester Cadieux, III, CEO
Chester Cadieux, III, Pres.
Stuart Sullivan, CFO
Gina Hitz, CIO
Mike Thornbrugh, Mgr.-Public & Gov't Affairs
Troy DeVos, Dir.-Real Estate
Chester Cadieux, III, Chmn.

GROWTH PLANS/SPECIAL FEATURES:

QuikTrip Corporation (QT), a privately-held company headquartered in Tulsa, Oklahoma, is a convenience and gasoline retailer. QuikTrip has more than 700 stores in 11 states. The company maintains high detergent levels in its gasoline and offers unique brands of food and beverage products. Because of its IQ detergent additive, QuikTrip gasoline has been named a TOP TIER Detergent Gasoline by a group of major automobile manufacturers. The additive removes engine deposits, thereby increasing efficiency and reducing pollutants. The firm's wholly-owned subsidiary, QT Distribution, is the exclusive distribution center and manufacturing facility for QuikTrip. More than 70% of products sold in QuikTrip stores are shipped via the QT warehouse system. QT Distribution operates warehouses located in or nearby Kansas City, Atlanta, Dallas and Phoenix. The company's convenience stores feature various food and beverage products including, but not limited to, Hotzi breakfast and QuikTrip sandwiches, QT Kitchens prepared meals, taquitos, egg rolls, hot dogs, Wally drinks, QT Twister frozen treats, Quikshakes and Freezoni frozen drinks, coffee and energy drinks. In addition, QuikTrip sells surplus real estate in Arizona, Georgia, Kansas, Missouri, North Carolina, Oklahoma, South Carolina and Texas.

QuikTrip offers its employees medical, dental and vision coverage; life insurance; a 401(k) plan; a profit sharing program; a stock option plan; vacation benefits that increase with the number of years of service; a credit union; a seniority awards program; tuition reimbursement; an employee assistance program; free employee uniform shirts; disability; medical and child care reimbursement accounts; and a scholarship program. Part-time workers receive a more limited benefits package. QuikTrip believes in promotion-from-within, with nearly all executives and managers having risen from the bottom.

FINANCIAL DATA: *Note: Data for latest year may not have been available at press time.*

In U.S. $	2016	2015	2014	2013	2012	2011
Revenue		10,960,000,000	11,450,000,000	11,210,000,000	10,770,000,000	8,770,000,000
R&D Expense						
Operating Income						
Operating Margin %						
SGA Expense						
Net Income						
Operating Cash Flow						
Capital Expenditure						
EBITDA						
Return on Assets %						
Return on Equity %						
Debt to Equity						

CONTACT INFORMATION:

Phone: 918-615-7700   Fax: 918-615-7377
Toll-Free: 800-848-1966
Address: 4705 S. 129th East Ave., Tulsa, OK 74134 United States

STOCK TICKER/OTHER:

Stock Ticker: Private   Exchange:
Employees: 17,000   Fiscal Year Ends: 04/30
Parent Company:

SALARIES/BONUSES:

Top Exec. Salary: $ Bonus: $
Second Exec. Salary: $ Bonus: $

OTHER THOUGHTS:

Estimated Female Officers or Directors:
Hot Spot for Advancement for Women/Minorities:

Quintiles Transnational Holdings Inc

www.quintiles.com

NAIC Code: 541711

TYPES OF BUSINESS:

Contract Research
Pharmaceutical, Biotech & Medical Device Research
Consulting & Training Services
Sales & Marketing Services

BRANDS/DIVISIONS/AFFILIATES:

IMS Health Holdings Inc
Quintiles IMS Holdings

CONTACTS: *Note: Officers with more than one job title may be intentionally listed here more than once.*

Thomas Pike, CEO
Michael Mcdonnell, CFO
Charles Williams, Chief Accounting Officer
Kevin Gordon, COO
Jack Greenberg, Director
James Erlinger, Executive VP
Trudy Stein, Executive VP
Jon Resnick, President, Divisional
Scott Evangelista, President, Divisional
Kevin Knightly, President, Divisional
Jose Fernandez, President, Divisional

GROWTH PLANS/SPECIAL FEATURES:

Quintiles Transnational Holdings, Inc. provides full-service contract research, sales and marketing services to the global pharmaceutical, biotechnology and medical device industries. The company is one of the world's top contract research organizations, offering a broad range of contract services to speed the process from development to peak sales of a new drug or medical device. Quintiles, conducting business in approximately 100 countries, is organized in two primary business segments: product development and integrated health care services. The product development group provides a full range of drug development services, from strategic planning and preclinical services to regulatory submission and approval. Integrated health care services provides the health care industry with both broad geographic presence and commercial capabilities. Commercialization services are designed to accelerate the commercial success of biopharmaceutical and other health-related products by promoting, delivering and proving value. Commercial services include contract sales, market entry/market exit, integrated multichannel management, patient engagement services and market access and commercialization consulting. The company also provides a consulting service that focus on product commercialization, market intelligence, market access, regulatory and quality consulting. In May 2016, Quintiles agreed to merge with IMS Health Holdings, Inc. in an all-stock deal worth about $8.75 billion. The new company will be called Quintiles IMS Holdings.

FINANCIAL DATA: *Note: Data for latest year may not have been available at press time.*

In U.S. $	2016	2015	2014	2013	2012	2011
Revenue		5,737,619,000	5,459,998,000	5,099,545,000	4,865,513,000	4,327,748,000
R&D Expense				604,663,000		548,784,000
Operating Income		646,612,000	590,390,000	462,333,000	396,435,000	345,251,000
Operating Margin %		11.26%	10.81%	9.06%	8.14%	7.97%
SGA Expense		920,985,000	882,338,000	255,847,000	817,755,000	213,515,000
Net Income		387,205,000	356,383,000	226,591,000	177,546,000	241,772,000
Operating Cash Flow		475,691,000	431,754,000	397,370,000	335,701,000	160,953,000
Capital Expenditure		78,391,000	82,650,000	92,346,000	71,336,000	75,679,000
EBITDA		768,529,000	723,791,000	554,128,000	500,087,000	385,744,000
Return on Assets %		10.70%	11.18%	8.14%	7.36%	10.40%
Return on Equity %						
Debt to Equity						

CONTACT INFORMATION:

Phone: 919-998-2000   Fax:
Toll-Free: 866-267-4479
Address: 4820 Emperor Blvd., Durham, NC 27703 United States

STOCK TICKER/OTHER:

Stock Ticker: Q
Employees: 36,100
Parent Company:

Exchange: NYS
Fiscal Year Ends: 12/31

SALARIES/BONUSES:

Top Exec. Salary: $1,040,000   Bonus: $
Second Exec. Salary: $800,000   Bonus: $

OTHER THOUGHTS:

Estimated Female Officers or Directors: 3

Hot Spot for Advancement for Women/Minorities: Y

Rackspace Hosting Inc

www.rackspace.com

NAIC Code: 517110

TYPES OF BUSINESS:

Web Hosting Services
Data Centers
Cloud Computing Services
Server Farms

BRANDS/DIVISIONS/AFFILIATES:

OpenStack
OnMetal Cloud Servers
RackConnect

CONTACTS: *Note: Officers with more than one job title may be intentionally listed here more than once.*

William Rhodes, CEO
Karl Pichler, CFO
Graham Weston, Chairman of the Board
Joseph Saporito, Chief Accounting Officer
Alex Pinchev, Executive VP
Eugene DeFelice, General Counsel
Mark Roenigk, General Manager
William Alberts, Secretary
Scott Crenshaw, Senior VP, Divisional

GROWTH PLANS/SPECIAL FEATURES:

Rackspace Hosting, Inc. provides hosting services fo businesses, specializing in web sites, web-based informatio technology (IT) systems and computing-as-a-service. I actively offers four service categories: dedicated cloud, publi cloud, private cloud and hybrid cloud. Dedicated cloud is know as managed hosting, referring to IT services provided on server or servers reserved for specific customers. subscription-based business, this service provides management portal and tools. Public cloud services delive pooled computing resources on-demand over the Internet. Thi division offers cloud servers for computing; cloud sites fo website hosting; cloud block storage and cloud files for storage cloud databases for hosting MySQL instances; cloud loa balances for traffic management; cloud backup for fil protection; cloud monitoring for infrastructure control; clou Domain Name System (DNS) for domain management; an cloud applications, which includes email, collaboration and fil back-ups. Private cloud, used widely by large corporat customers, refers to a pool of computing resources that i virtualized for greater efficiency and nimbleness, but that i dedicated to one particular customer rather than being used b multiple customers. The hardware can be located in dat centers or in the customer's facilities. Hybrid cloud allow customers to seamlessly utilize the benefits of both dedicate and public cloud through its RackConnect service. Through th hybrid cloud, the technologies can be combined to addres each customer's changing needs. Rackspace serves mor than 300,000 customers in over 120 countries. Additionally, th firm is the co-founder, with NASA, of OpenStack, the world' fastest-growing open cloud platform and developer community In August 2016, Rackspace agreed to be acquired by th private equity firm Apollo Global Management LLC for $4. billion.

The firm offers employees medical, dental and visio insurance; a 401(k) plan; profit sharing; employee training; an an onsite fitness facility.

FINANCIAL DATA: *Note: Data for latest year may not have been available at press time.*

In U.S. $	2016	2015	2014	2013	2012	2011
Revenue		2,001,300,000	1,794,357,000	1,534,786,000	1,309,239,000	1,025,064,000
R&D Expense		124,900,000	117,006,000	90,213,000		
Operating Income		206,100,000	163,529,000	133,136,000	172,741,000	123,471,000
Operating Margin %		10.29%	9.11%	8.67%	13.19%	12.04%
SGA Expense		594,900,000	559,604,000	505,937,000	519,174,000	397,086,000
Net Income		126,200,000	110,553,000	86,737,000	105,418,000	76,411,000
Operating Cash Flow		583,600,000	542,510,000	444,060,000	399,499,000	342,985,000
Capital Expenditure		474,900,000	430,335,000	452,596,000	270,374,000	269,804,000
EBITDA		604,800,000	535,413,000	446,884,000	422,601,000	317,689,000
Return on Assets %		6.93%	7.09%	6.22%	9.07%	8.54%
Return on Equity %		12.31%	10.38%	9.13%	14.61%	14.71%
Debt to Equity		0.67	0.11	0.02	0.07	0.12

CONTACT INFORMATION:

Phone: 210 312-4000　　　　Fax: 210 312-4300
Toll-Free: 800-961-2888
Address: 5000 Walzem Rd., San Antonio, TX 78218 United States

STOCK TICKER/OTHER:

Stock Ticker: RAX　　　　　　　　　Exchange: NYS
Employees: 6,189　　　　　　　　　Fiscal Year Ends: 12/31
Parent Company:

SALARIES/BONUSES:

Top Exec. Salary: $298,883　　Bonus: $500,000
Second Exec. Salary:　　　　　Bonus: $
$702,606

OTHER THOUGHTS:

Estimated Female Officers or Directors: 1
Hot Spot for Advancement for Women/Minorities:

Sales, profits and employees may be estimates. Financial information, benefits and other data can change quickly and may vary from those stated here.

Ralph Lauren Corporation

www.polo.com

NAIC Code: 424300

TYPES OF BUSINESS:

Apparel and Clothing Brands, Designers, Importers and Distributors
Apparel Design & Marketing
Accessories
Fragrances
Home Furnishings
Cosmetics
Retail Stores

BRANDS/DIVISIONS/AFFILIATES:

Polo
Ralph by Ralph Lauren
Romance
Purple Label
Ralph Lauren Blue
RLX Golf
Big Pony
Club Monaco

CONTACTS: Note: Officers with more than one job title may be intentionally listed here more than once.

Robert Madore, CFO
Ralph Lauren, Chairman of the Board
Stefan Larsson, Director
David Lauren, Director
Valerie Hermann, President, Divisional
Jeffrey Kuster, President, Geographical

GROWTH PLANS/SPECIAL FEATURES:

Ralph Lauren Corporation (Polo) designs, markets and distributes premium lifestyle products. Polo licenses the manufacturing of its products to companies worldwide. Capitalizing on the creative force of its founder, Ralph Lauren, the firm's various brand names have become recognizable cultural symbols across the globe. The firm offers four categories of lifestyle products: apparel products (including extensive collections of men's, women's and children's clothing), home products (including bedding and bath products, furniture, fabric, wallpaper, paints, tabletop and giftware), accessories (including footwear, eyewear, jewelry, leather goods, handbags and luggage) and fragrance products (consisting of fragrances and skin care products). The company markets its products through department, specialty, golf and Ralph Lauren stores as well as via the Internet and mail order catalogs. Polo also offers wholesale products to upscale (and certain mid-tier) department stores, specialty stores and golf/pro shops worldwide. Its brands include Ralph by Ralph Lauren, Romance, Polo, Purple Label, Ralph Lauren Blue, Polo Black, RRL, RLX Golf, Denim & Supply Ralph Lauren, Big Pony, Pink Pony, Chaps and Club Monaco. Ralph Lauren Corporation sells its merchandise through its wholesale distribution channels at approximately 13,000 different retail locations worldwide. It also sells directly to customers through its 493 retail stores, its 583 concession-based shop-within-shops and its various eCommerce sites. Additionally, its international licensing partners operate 93 Ralph Lauren stores, 133 Club Monaco stores and 42 Ralph Lauren concession shops.

FINANCIAL DATA: Note: Data for latest year may not have been available at press time.

In U.S. $	2016	2015	2014	2013	2012	2011
Revenue	7,405,000,000	7,620,000,000	7,450,000,000	6,944,800,000	6,859,500,000	5,660,300,000
R&D Expense						
Operating Income	582,000,000	1,035,000,000	1,130,000,000	1,126,700,000	1,039,400,000	845,100,000
Operating Margin %	7.85%	13.58%	15.16%	16.22%	15.15%	14.93%
SGA Expense	3,389,000,000	3,301,000,000	3,142,000,000	2,971,600,000	2,915,200,000	2,442,700,000
Net Income	396,000,000	702,000,000	776,000,000	750,000,000	681,000,000	567,600,000
Operating Cash Flow	1,007,000,000	894,000,000	907,000,000	1,018,900,000	885,300,000	688,700,000
Capital Expenditure	418,000,000	391,000,000	390,000,000	276,500,000	272,200,000	255,000,000
EBITDA	883,000,000	1,298,000,000	1,374,000,000	1,343,700,000	1,264,800,000	1,037,800,000
Return on Assets %	6.42%	11.51%	13.48%	13.84%	13.09%	11.78%
Return on Equity %	10.37%	17.71%	19.85%	20.16%	19.57%	17.67%
Debt to Equity	0.23	0.13	0.13		0.07	0.10

CONTACT INFORMATION:

Phone: 212 318-7000   Fax:
Toll-Free: 800-377-7656
Address: 650 Madison Ave., New York, NY 10022 United States

STOCK TICKER/OTHER:

Stock Ticker: RL   Exchange: NYS
Employees: 25,000   Fiscal Year Ends: 03/31
Parent Company:

SALARIES/BONUSES:

Top Exec. Salary: $528,846   Bonus: $2,750,000
Second Exec. Salary: $1,783,654   Bonus: $

OTHER THOUGHTS:

Estimated Female Officers or Directors: 2
Hot Spot for Advancement for Women/Minorities: Y

Sales, profits and employees may be estimates. Financial information, benefits and other data can change quickly and may vary from those stated here.

Raymond James Financial Inc

www.raymondjames.com

NAIC Code: 523110

TYPES OF BUSINESS:

Stock Brokerage/Investment Banking
Trust Services
Asset Management
Banking

BRANDS/DIVISIONS/AFFILIATES:

Raymond James & Associates Inc
Raymond James Financial Services Inc
Raymond James Financial Services Advisors Inc
Raymond James Bank NA
Raymond James Ltd
Eagle Asset Management Inc
Raymond James Investment Services Limited
Raymond James Financial International Ltd

CONTACTS: *Note: Officers with more than one job title may be intentionally listed here more than once.*

Paul Allison, CEO, Subsidiary
John Carson, President
Dennis Zank, CEO, Subsidiary
Steven Raney, CEO, Subsidiary
Paul Reilly, CEO
Jeffrey Julien, CFO
Thomas James, Chairman of the Board
Jennifer Ackart, Chief Accounting Officer
George Catanese, Chief Risk Officer
Francis Godbold, Director
Jeffrey Dowdle, Executive VP, Divisional
Bella Allaire, Executive VP, Subsidiary
Paul Matecki, General Counsel
Scott Curtis, President, Subsidiary
Tashtego Elwyn, President, Subsidiary
Jeffrey Trocin, President, Subsidiary

GROWTH PLANS/SPECIAL FEATURES:

Raymond James Financial, Inc. (RJF) is a diversified financial services holding company with subsidiaries engaged in investment and financial planning primarily in the U.S. and Canada. Services include securities, brokerage, investment banking, asset management, banking and cash management and trust products. The firm's principal subsidiaries are Raymond James & Associates, Inc. (RJ&A); Raymond James Financial Services, Inc. (RJFS); Raymond James Financial Services Advisors, Inc. (RJFSA); Raymond James, Ltd. (RJ Ltd); Eagle Asset Management, Inc. (Eagle); and Raymond James Bank, NA (RJ Bank). RJF operates through five segments: private client group, capital markets, asset management, RJ Bank and other. The private client group provides securities transaction and financial planning services to roughly 2.7 million client accounts through the branch office systems of RJ&A, RJFS, RJFSA, RJ ltd. and in the U.K through Raymond James Investment Services Limited (RJIS) The capital markets segment's activities consist primarily of equity and fixed income products and services in which institutional clients are serviced through the RJ&A fixed income department and its European offices; Raymond James Financial International, Ltd. (headquartered in London); and James European Securities, Inc. The asset management segment includes proprietary asset management operations, internally sponsored mutual funds, non-affiliated private account portfolio management alternatives, a national bank and other fee based programs. The segment includes Eagle, the Eagle Family of Funds, the asset management operations of RJ&A, Raymond James Trust, National Association (RJT) and other fee-based programs. RJ Bank is a federally-chartered bank that provides residential, consumer and commercial loans, as well as deposit accounts, to clients of the company's broker-dealer subsidiaries and to the general public. The other segment includes principal capital and private equity activities as well as various corporate overhead costs of RJF. In August 2015, the firm acquired Producers Choice, LLC, a private insurance and annuity marketing organization.

FINANCIAL DATA: *Note: Data for latest year may not have been available at press time.*

In U.S. $	2016	2015	2014	2013	2012	2011
Revenue		5,200,210,000	4,861,369,000	4,485,427,000	3,806,531,000	3,334,056,000
R&D Expense			139,672,000			
Operating Income		776,712,000	715,948,000	593,910,000	467,921,000	450,745,000
Operating Margin %		14.93%	14.72%	13.24%	12.29%	13.51%
SGA Expense		3,851,343,000	3,617,741,000	3,472,892,000	2,845,163,000	2,438,440,000
Net Income		502,140,000	480,248,000	367,154,000	295,869,000	278,353,000
Operating Cash Flow		899,177,000	507,587,000	659,805,000	391,289,000	1,558,441,000
Capital Expenditure		74,111,000	60,149,000	72,879,000	77,515,000	37,200,000
EBITDA						
Return on Assets %		2.00%	2.06%	1.65%	1.51%	1.55%
Return on Equity %		11.55%	12.30%	10.59%	10.10%	11.38%
Debt to Equity		0.41	0.45	0.36	0.43	0.27

CONTACT INFORMATION:

Phone: 727 567-1000   Fax:
Toll-Free: 800-248-8863
Address: 880 Carillon Pkwy., St. Petersburg, FL 33716 United States

STOCK TICKER/OTHER:

Stock Ticker: RJF   Exchange: NYS
Employees: 6,700   Fiscal Year Ends: 09/30
Parent Company:

SALARIES/BONUSES:

Top Exec. Salary: $445,000   Bonus: $4,325,030
Second Exec. Salary: Bonus: $2,337,506
$305,000

OTHER THOUGHTS:

Estimated Female Officers or Directors: 1
Hot Spot for Advancement for Women/Minorities: Y

Recreational Equipment Inc (REI)

www.rei.com

NAIC Code: 451110

TYPES OF BUSINESS:

Outdoor Gear & Clothing, Retail
Sporting Equipment Retail & Rental
Adventure Travel Services
Catalog & Online Sales

BRANDS/DIVISIONS/AFFILIATES:

REI
REI Adventures
REI Gear and Apparel
Novara

CONTACTS: Note: Officers with more than one job title may be intentionally listed here more than once.

Jerry Stritzke, CEO
Eric Artz, Interim-COO
Jerry Stritzke, Pres.
Catherine Walker, CFO
Michelle Clements, Sr. VP-Human Resources
Susan Viscon, VP-Merch.
Catherine Walker, General Counsel
Brad Brown, Sr. VP-e-Commerce & Direct Sales
Michael Collins, VP-Public Affairs
Sue Sallee, VP-Finance & Acct.
Tim Spangler, Sr. VP-Retail
Kathleen Peterson, VP-REI Private Brands
John Hamlin, Chmn.
Rick Bingle, VP-Supply Chain

GROWTH PLANS/SPECIAL FEATURES:

Recreational Equipment, Inc. (REI) is one of the largest consumer cooperatives in the U.S. The firm offers quality outdoor gear, clothing and footwear selected for performance and durability in outdoor recreation, including hiking, climbing, camping, bicycling, paddling and winter sports. Today, REI has more than 5.5 million active members served by approximately 143 retail stores in 35 states. Stores include a variety of facilities for testing equipment, including bike test trails, climbing pinnacles and camp stove demonstration tables. While anyone may shop at the stores, customers who pay a small fee to become members receive special discounts and a share in the company's profits through an annual patronage refund based on their purchases. REI's e-commerce site is one of the largest outdoor online stores, offering a comprehensive library of product information, expert gear advice and outdoor recreation information. In addition to nationally recognized brands, the company sells private label apparel and accessories under the REI Gear and Apparel brand. It also offers mountain, road and touring bikes under the private Novara name. Through REI Adventures, the company has been operating small group tours throughout the world for more than 20 years, avoiding standard tourist routes and emphasizing outdoor activities. Each year, REI Adventures plans domestic and international bicycling, trekking, kayaking, hiking, camping and mountaineering adventures. The firm invests millions of dollars on an annual basis to build trails, clean up the environment and teach children outdoor ethics. In February 2016, the firm announced plans to deepen its roots in New York and Florida with new stores at CityGate in Rochester, NY in fall 2016 and Winter Park Village in Winter Park, FL in spring 2017.

The firm offers employees health, life and disability plans; tuition reimbursement; adoption and relocation assistance; an employee discount program; and a public transit subsidy.

FINANCIAL DATA: Note: Data for latest year may not have been available at press time.

In U.S. $	2016	2015	2014	2013	2012	2011
Revenue		2,423,221,000	2,217,130,000	2,017,476,000	1,930,635,000	1,798,009,000
R&D Expense						
Operating Income						
Operating Margin %						
SGA Expense						
Net Income		35,372,000	44,183,000	19,031,000	29,005,000	30,168,000
Operating Cash Flow						
Capital Expenditure						
EBITDA						
Return on Assets %						
Return on Equity %						
Debt to Equity						

CONTACT INFORMATION:

Phone: 253-891-2500   Fax: 253-891-2523
Toll-Free: 800-426-4840
Address: 6750 S. 228th St., Kent, WA 98032 United States

STOCK TICKER/OTHER:

Stock Ticker: Private   Exchange:
Employees: 12,000   Fiscal Year Ends: 12/31
Parent Company:

SALARIES/BONUSES:

Top Exec. Salary: $ Bonus: $
Second Exec. Salary: $ Bonus: $

OTHER THOUGHTS:

Estimated Female Officers or Directors: 7
Hot Spot for Advancement for Women/Minorities: Y

Red Hat Inc

NAIC Code: 0

www.redhat.com

TYPES OF BUSINESS:

Computer Software-Linux Operating Systems
Open-Source Software

GROWTH PLANS/SPECIAL FEATURES:

Red Hat, Inc. is a provider of open-source software solutions
The firm's solutions include its core enterprise operating
system platform Red Hat Enterprise Linux, the enterprise
middleware platform Red Hat JBoss Middleware Suite, virtual
solutions, cloud storage and other Red Hat enterprise
technologies. The company offers a choice of operating system
platforms for servers, work stations and desktops that support
multiple application areas, including the data center, edge-of-
the-network applications, IT infrastructure, corporate desktop
and technical/developer workstation. Red Hat JBoss
Middleware delivers a suite of middleware products for service
oriented architectures, permitting web-enabled applications to
run on open source and other platforms. The software provides
an application infrastructure for building and deploying
distributed applications that are accessible via the Internet
corporate intranets, extranets and virtual private networks
Applications deployed on JBoss include online e-business
hotel and airline reservations, online banking, credit card
processing, securities trading, health care systems, customer
and partner portals, retail and point of sale systems (POS)
telecommunications network infrastructure and grid-based
systems. The integrated management services, Red Hat
Satellite and Red Hat JBoss Operations Network, permit Red
Hat enterprise technologies to be updated and configured as
well as the performance of these and other technologies to be
monitored and managed in an automated fashion. Red Hat
Virtualization allows a single system to run more than one
operating systems by abstracting the operating systems and
application software from the underlying hardware
infrastructure. The firm's suite of training and other professional
service offerings enable enterprise customers to adapt Red
Hat's technologies to their needs. In 2014, the firm announced
that it would be shifting its focus from client-server to cloud
mobile architectures. In 2015, Red Hat agreed to acquire
Ansible, Inc., a provider of powerful IT automation solutions.

BRANDS/DIVISIONS/AFFILIATES:

Red Hat JBoss Middleware Suite
Red Hat Satellite
Red Hat JBoss Operations Network
Red Hat Enterprise Linux
Red Hat Virtualization

CONTACTS: Note: Officers with more than one job title may be intentionally listed here more than once.

James Whitehurst, CEO
Henry Shelton, Chairman of the Board
Eric Shander, Chief Accounting Officer
Arun Oberoi, Executive VP, Divisional
Frank Calderoni, Executive VP, Divisional
Michael Cunningham, Executive VP
DeLisa Alexander, Executive VP
Paul Cormier, President, Divisional

FINANCIAL DATA: Note: Data for latest year may not have been available at press time.

In U.S. $	2016	2015	2014	2013	2012	2011
Revenue	2,052,230,000	1,789,489,000	1,534,615,000	1,328,817,000	1,133,103,000	909,277,000
R&D Expense	413,322,000	367,856,000	317,263,000	263,150,000	208,662,000	171,253,000
Operating Income	288,048,000	249,994,000	232,289,000	201,038,000	199,913,000	145,676,000
Operating Margin %	14.03%	13.97%	15.13%	15.12%	17.64%	16.02%
SGA Expense	1,041,231,000	898,440,000	752,463,000	664,029,000	545,980,000	442,061,000
Net Income	199,365,000	180,201,000	178,292,000	150,204,000	146,626,000	107,278,000
Operating Cash Flow	716,092,000	622,795,000	540,580,000	465,297,000	391,883,000	290,748,000
Capital Expenditure	55,517,000	51,771,000	97,559,000	120,038,000	51,618,000	46,852,000
EBITDA	374,074,000	341,155,000	306,694,000	263,379,000	251,285,000	193,673,000
Return on Assets %	5.01%	5.21%	6.02%	5.66%	6.25%	5.27%
Return on Equity %	15.20%	12.69%	11.61%	10.29%	10.90%	8.93%
Debt to Equity	0.54	0.55		0.03		

CONTACT INFORMATION:

Phone: 919 754-3700   Fax: 919 754-3701
Toll-Free: 888-733-4281
Address: 1801 Varsity Dr., Raleigh, NC 27606 United States

STOCK TICKER/OTHER:

Stock Ticker: RHT   Exchange: NYS
Employees: 7,300   Fiscal Year Ends: 02/28
Parent Company:

SALARIES/BONUSES:

Top Exec. Salary: $474,830   Bonus: $4,000,000
Second Exec. Salary: Bonus: $
$975,000

OTHER THOUGHTS:

Estimated Female Officers or Directors: 3
Hot Spot for Advancement for Women/Minorities: Y

Regal-Beloit Corporation

www.regal-beloit.com

NAIC Code: 335312

TYPES OF BUSINESS:

Mechanical Products Manufacturing
HVAC Components

BRANDS/DIVISIONS/AFFILIATES:

Power Transmission Solutions

CONTACTS: Note: Officers with more than one job title may be intentionally listed here more than once.

Mark Gliebe, CEO
Charles Hinrichs, CFO
Jonathan Schlemmer, COO
Terry Colvin, Vice President, Divisional
John Avampato, Vice President
Robert Rehard, Vice President

GROWTH PLANS/SPECIAL FEATURES:

Regal-Beloit Corporation is a U.S.-based multinational corporation that manufactures electric motors and controls, electric generators and power transmission products. The company operates through three segments: commercial & industrial systems (CIS), climate solutions & power transmission solutions (CPTS). CIS designs, manufactures and sells fractional, integral and large horsepower AC and DC motors and controls for commercial and industrial applications. These motors are sold directly to original equipment manufacturer (OEM) and end-user customers through direct and independent sales representatives, as well as through regional and national distributors. CPTS designs, manufactures and sells fractional motors, electronic variable speed controls and blowers used in a variety of residential and light commercial air moving applications including HVAC systems and commercial refrigeration. Power transmission solutions designs, manufactures and markets standard, modified and highly engineered enclosed gear drives, gearmotors, transmissions and custom open gearing used for motion control within complex equipment systems. This gearing reduces the speed and increases the torque from an electric motor or other prime mover to meet the requirements of equipment such as a conveyor drive. Regal manufactures the majority of the products that it sells at its facilities located in the U.S., Canada, Mexico, India, China, Thailand and Europe. In 2015, the firm acquired Power Transmission Solutions from Emerson Electric Co. for $1.4 billion, which designs, manufactures and sells services belt & chain drives, helical & worm gearing, mounted & unmounted bearings, high-performance couplings, belts & conveying chains and components.

FINANCIAL DATA: Note: Data for latest year may not have been available at press time.

In U.S. $	2016	2015	2014	2013	2012	2011
Revenue		3,509,700,000	3,257,100,000	3,095,700,000	3,166,900,000	2,808,332,000
R&D Expense						
Operating Income		252,800,000	121,500,000	208,000,000	312,800,000	255,713,000
Operating Margin %		7.20%	3.73%	6.71%	9.87%	9.10%
SGA Expense				494,200,000		
Net Income		143,300,000	31,000,000	120,000,000	195,600,000	152,290,000
Operating Cash Flow		381,100,000	298,200,000	305,000,000	351,700,000	265,296,000
Capital Expenditure		92,200,000	88,200,000	91,000,000	82,300,000	57,621,000
EBITDA		416,500,000	268,100,000	341,400,000	440,400,000	355,691,000
Return on Assets %		3.58%	.87%	3.32%	5.72%	5.32%
Return on Equity %		7.40%	1.55%	5.98%	11.21%	10.51%
Debt to Equity		0.88	0.32	0.29	0.38	0.59

CONTACT INFORMATION:

Phone: 608 364-8800   Fax: 608 364-8818
Toll-Free:
Address: 200 State Street, Beloit, WI 53511 United States

STOCK TICKER/OTHER:

Stock Ticker: RBC   Exchange: NYS
Employees: 24,100   Fiscal Year Ends: 12/31
Parent Company:

SALARIES/BONUSES:

Top Exec. Salary: $947,500   Bonus: $
Second Exec. Salary: $586,250   Bonus: $

OTHER THOUGHTS:

Estimated Female Officers or Directors:
Hot Spot for Advancement for Women/Minorities:

Sales, profits and employees may be estimates. Financial information, benefits and other data can change quickly and may vary from those stated here.

ResMed Inc
NAIC Code: 339100

www.resmed.com

TYPES OF BUSINESS:
Sleep Disordered Breathing Medical Equipment
Diagnosis & Treatment Products

BRANDS/DIVISIONS/AFFILIATES:
S9
AirSense 10
AirCurve 10
Curative Medical

CONTACTS: *Note: Officers with more than one job title may be intentionally listed here more than once.*
Michael Farrell, CEO
Brett Sandercock, CFO
Peter Farrell, Chairman of the Board

GROWTH PLANS/SPECIAL FEATURES:
ResMed, Inc. is an Australian-founded company that develops manufactures and distributes medical equipment for treating diagnosing and managing sleep disordered breathing (SDB) and other respiratory disorders. SDB includes obstructive sleep apnea (OSA) and other related respiratory disorders that occur during sleep. The company was originally founded to commercialize a continuous positive airway pressure (CPAP) treatment for OSA, which delivers pressurized air, typically through a nasal mask, to prevent collapse of the upper airway during sleep. Since the introduction of nasal CPAP, the firm has developed a number of innovative products for SDB, including mask systems, headgear, airflow generators, diagnostic products and other accessories. The firm's CPAP products include the S9, AirSense 10 Elite and AirSense 10 CPAP. Its variable positive airway pressure (VPAP) products include the S9 family: VPAP ST-A and COPD (chronic obstructive pulmonary disease; and the AirCurve 10 family: S, V Auto, ST, ASV and CS. Other product categories include automatic positive airway pressure (APAP) products, diagnostic products and data/patient management products. The company's business strategy includes expanding into new clinical applications by seeking to identify new uses for its technologies, as well as increasing consumer awareness of the little-known condition, which may afflict up to 20% of Americans. The firm sells products in over 100 countries through wholly-owned subsidiaries and independent distributors. ResMed's market is divided into three regions, North & Latin America, Europe and Asia Pacific. Through various subsidiaries, the company owns approximately 1,043 issued U.S. patents (including approximately 413 design patents) and approximately 2,020 issued foreign patents. In October 2015, the firm acquired Curative Medical, a provider of non-invasive ventilation and sleep-disordered breathing medical devices and accessories. This acquisition allowed ResMed to invest in the China market and expand its growth potential in SDB, COPD and respiratory care in China.

FINANCIAL DATA: *Note: Data for latest year may not have been available at press time.*

In U.S. $	2016	2015	2014	2013	2012	2011
Revenue	1,838,713,000	1,678,912,000	1,554,973,000	1,514,457,000	1,368,515,000	1,243,148,000
R&D Expense	118,651,000	114,865,000	118,226,000	144,889,000	109,733,000	92,007,000
Operating Income	428,952,000	409,236,000	405,087,000	354,824,000	294,407,000	266,924,000
Operating Margin %	23.32%	24.37%	26.05%	23.42%	21.51%	21.47%
SGA Expense	488,057,000	478,627,000	450,414,000	430,802,000	401,621,000	372,249,000
Net Income	352,409,000	352,886,000	345,273,000	307,133,000	254,850,000	226,986,000
Operating Cash Flow	547,933,000	383,180,000	391,268,000	402,823,000	383,159,000	283,190,000
Capital Expenditure	67,829,000	71,944,000	81,156,000	71,782,000	61,107,000	74,996,000
EBITDA	537,621,000	514,750,000	510,661,000	469,786,000	422,587,000	337,540,000
Return on Assets %	12.94%	15.52%	15.10%	14.12%	12.11%	12.28%
Return on Equity %	21.47%	21.09%	20.49%	19.08%	15.26%	15.04%
Debt to Equity	0.51	0.18	0.17		0.15	0.05

CONTACT INFORMATION:
Phone: 858 836-5000   Fax: 858 746-2900
Toll-Free: 800-424-0737
Address: 9001 Spectrum Ctr. Blvd., San Diego, CA 92123 United States

STOCK TICKER/OTHER:
Stock Ticker: RMD   Exchange: NYS
Employees: 4,340   Fiscal Year Ends: 06/30
Parent Company:

SALARIES/BONUSES:
Top Exec. Salary: $800,000   Bonus: $
Second Exec. Salary: $669,500   Bonus: $

OTHER THOUGHTS:
Estimated Female Officers or Directors: 2
Hot Spot for Advancement for Women/Minorities:

Resources Connection Inc

www.resourcesglobal.com

NAIC Code: 541612

TYPES OF BUSINESS:

Business Process Outsourcing
Accounting
Human Resources Outsourcing
IT Outsourcing
Supply Chain Management
Legal Services
Risk Management & Internal Audit Services
Corporate Advisory

BRANDS/DIVISIONS/AFFILIATES:

Resources Global Professionals
Sitrick Brincko Group
policyIQ

CONTACTS: *Note: Officers with more than one job title may be intentionally listed here more than once.*

Anthony Cherbak, CEO
Nathan Franke, CFO
Donald Murray, Chairman of the Board
John Bower, Chief Accounting Officer
Tracy Stephens, COO
Kate Duchene, Executive VP, Divisional

GROWTH PLANS/SPECIAL FEATURES:

Resources Connection, Inc., operating primarily as Resource Global Professionals (RGP), is an international professional services firm that assists its clients with projects requiring specialized expertise in a number of fields. Resources Connection maintains 45 offices in the U.S. and 23 abroad. The firm's service offerings include finance & accounting services; information management; governance, risk & compliance; corporate advisory and restructuring; supply chain management; human capital; and legal & regulatory services. In the finance & accounting segment, the company provides assistance for corporate reorganizations; financial analyses, such as product cost and margin analyses; budgeting and forecasting; public-entity reporting; and audit preparation. The information management services segment offers financial system/enterprise resource planning implementation and post-implementation optimization. The governance, risk & compliance segment provides compliance reviews, assistance services and internal audit co-sourcing. Through the Sitrick Brincko Group, the company offers a combination of strategic counsel, execution and organizational and logistical support critical to companies undergoing restructuring and change. The firm's supply chain management services include leading strategic sourcing efforts, negotiating contracts and purchasing strategies. The human capital segment includes change management, organization development & effectiveness, as well as optimization of human resources technology and operations. The firm offers legal services by providing attorneys, paralegals and contract managers to assist clients, including law firms, with project-based or peak period needs. In addition, the company offers policyIQ, an online content management system to help companies create and manage business information.

The company offers employees continuing education & training, certification programs, comprehensive benefits & bonus programs and participation in the employee stock purchase plan.

FINANCIAL DATA: *Note: Data for latest year may not have been available at press time.*

In U.S. $	2016	2015	2014	2013	2012	2011
Revenue	598,521,000	590,589,000	567,181,000	556,334,000	571,763,000	545,546,000
R&D Expense						
Operating Income	53,803,000	50,258,000	37,975,000	39,702,000	73,092,000	51,452,000
Operating Margin %	8.98%	8.50%	6.69%	7.13%	12.78%	9.43%
SGA Expense	174,806,000	173,797,000	172,531,000	168,318,000	170,992,000	172,622,000
Net Income	30,443,000	27,508,000	19,886,000	20,504,000	41,142,000	24,855,000
Operating Cash Flow	38,262,000	31,751,000	32,018,000	34,959,000	36,370,000	26,064,000
Capital Expenditure	2,381,000	2,364,000	3,725,000	3,147,000	2,786,000	3,852,000
EBITDA	57,360,000	54,565,000	43,291,000	45,976,000	82,187,000	63,705,000
Return on Assets %	7.25%	6.57%	4.74%	4.83%	9.07%	5.23%
Return on Equity %	8.91%	8.01%	5.69%	5.70%	11.14%	6.84%
Debt to Equity						

CONTACT INFORMATION:

Phone: 714 430-6400   Fax: 714 433-6100
Toll-Free: 800-900-1131
Address: 17101 Armstrong Ave., Irvine, CA 92614 United States

STOCK TICKER/OTHER:

Stock Ticker: RECN
Employees: 3,258
Parent Company:

Exchange: NAS
Fiscal Year Ends: 05/31

SALARIES/BONUSES:

Top Exec. Salary: $583,000   Bonus: $190,000
Second Exec. Salary: $583,000   Bonus: $190,000

OTHER THOUGHTS:

Estimated Female Officers or Directors: 6
Hot Spot for Advancement for Women/Minorities: Y

Sales, profits and employees may be estimates. Financial information, benefits and other data can change quickly and may vary from those stated here.

Rite Aid Corporation

www.riteaid.com

NAIC Code: 446110

TYPES OF BUSINESS:

Drug Stores

BRANDS/DIVISIONS/AFFILIATES:

GNC
Riteaid.com

CONTACTS: Note: Officers with more than one job title may be intentionally listed here more than once.

Kenneth Martindale, CEO, Divisional
John Standley, CEO
Darren Karst, CFO
Anthony Montini, Executive VP, Divisional
David Abelman, Executive VP, Divisional
Bryan Everett, Executive VP, Divisional
Jocelyn Konrad, Executive VP, Divisional
Dedra Castle, Executive VP
James Comitale, Secretary
Douglas Donley, Senior VP

GROWTH PLANS/SPECIAL FEATURES:

Rite Aid Corporation is a U.S.-based retail drugstore company which operates over 4,561 drug stores in 31 states and Washington, D.C. Rite Aid stores primarily markets prescription drugs, which account for approximately 69.1% of its revenues. Other marketed merchandise, which accounts for the remaining 30.9% of revenues, includes non-prescription medications, health and beauty aids, personal care items, cosmetics, household items, beverages, convenience foods, greeting cards and seasonal merchandise. In addition to its marketed products, the firm offers an automated refill option for customers with ongoing prescriptions; and it also makes prescription refill reminder phone calls. Customers can order prescription refills through the company's e-commerce site Riteaid.com. The firm's average store size is approximately 12,600 square feet. Its larger stores are located in the western U.S. Rite Aid offers approximately 3,000 products under the Rite Aid private brand. The company maintains a strategic alliance with GNC, which enables Rite Aid to sell GNC branded and co-branded products. Rite Aid operates more than 2,300 GNC store-within-Rite Aid-stores. Approximately 62% of Rite Aid's stores are freestanding, 54% include a drive-through pharmacy, and 51% include a GNC store-within-Rite Aid-store. A majority of stores also include one-hour photo shops. In October 2015, the firm announced it would be acquired by Walgreens Boot Alliance, Inc. Stockholders voted to approve the Walgreens acquisition/merger in February 2016, and the transaction was expected to close by the end of 2016.

The company offers its employees health, dental, vision and prescription plans; vision discount plan; basic and supplemental life and AD&D insurances; flexible spending accounts; bereavement leave; employee assistance; 401(k); stock purchase plan; and more.

FINANCIAL DATA: Note: Data for latest year may not have been available at press time.

In U.S. $	2016	2015	2014	2013	2012	2011
Revenue	30,736,660,000	26,528,380,000	25,526,410,000	25,392,260,000	26,121,220,000	25,214,910,000
R&D Expense						
Operating Income	764,486,000	839,145,000	721,268,000	646,652,000	161,871,000	23,778,000
Operating Margin %	2.48%	3.16%	2.82%	2.54%	.61%	.09%
SGA Expense	7,013,346,000	6,695,642,000	6,561,162,000	6,600,765,000	6,531,411,000	6,457,833,000
Net Income	165,465,000	2,109,173,000	249,414,000	118,105,000	-368,571,000	-555,424,000
Operating Cash Flow	997,402,000	648,959,000	702,046,000	819,588,000	266,537,000	395,849,000
Capital Expenditure	669,995,000	539,386,000	421,223,000	382,980,000	250,137,000	186,520,000
EBITDA	1,237,190,000	1,241,060,000	1,078,550,000	937,037,000	577,580,000	507,545,000
Return on Assets %	1.64%	26.68%	3.07%	1.48%	-5.07%	-7.23%
Return on Equity %	51.83%					
Debt to Equity	11.98	97.17				

CONTACT INFORMATION:

Phone: 717 761-2633   Fax: 717 975-5905
Toll-Free: 800-748-3243
Address: 30 Hunter Lane, Camp Hill, PA 17011 United States

STOCK TICKER/OTHER:

Stock Ticker: RAD   Exchange: NYS
Employees: 90,000   Fiscal Year Ends: 02/28
Parent Company:

SALARIES/BONUSES:

Top Exec. Salary: Bonus: $
$1,150,000
Second Exec. Salary: Bonus: $
$900,000

OTHER THOUGHTS:

Estimated Female Officers or Directors: 3

Hot Spot for Advancement for Women/Minorities: Y

Ritz-Carlton Hotel Company LLC (The)

www.ritzcarlton.com

NAIC Code: 721110

TYPES OF BUSINESS:

Hotels, Luxury
Condominiums
Golf Courses
Spas
Time Share Units

BRANDS/DIVISIONS/AFFILIATES:

Marriott International Inc
Six Senses
La Prairie
ESPA
Ritz-Carlton Destination Club (The)
Residencies at the Ritz-Carlton (The)
Ritz-Carlton Koh Samui
Ritz-Carlton Reserve

CONTACTS: Note: Officers with more than one job title may be intentionally listed here more than once.

Herve Humler, COO
Herve Humler, Pres.

GROWTH PLANS/SPECIAL FEATURES:

The Ritz-Carlton Hotel Company, LLC, a subsidiary of Marriott International, Inc., is one of the world's best-known luxury hotel chains, operating 91 hotels in 30 countries and territories. The firm maintains international sales offices in locations such as Chicago, New York, Los Angeles, Dubai, Shanghai, Tokyo and London. In an attempt to cater to an upscale client base, full-service luxury spas are offered at most of the company's resorts. Some spas at Ritz-Carlton hotels operate under the brand names Six Senses, La Prairie and ESPA. Besides its hotels, the firm provides vacation properties and residential suites under The Ritz-Carlton Destination Club and The Residencies at the Ritz-Carlton. The Ritz-Carlton Destination Club is the firm's time-share ownership unit, offering a flexible alternative to a second home. Membership is currently available in locations such as Aspen Highlands, Bachelor Gulch and Vail, Colorado; St. Thomas, U.S. Virgin Islands; San Francisco and North Lake Tahoe, California; Jupiter, Florida; Abaco, Bahamas; and Kauai Lagoons and Maui, Hawaii. The Residencies at the Ritz-Carlton offer luxury condominiums and estate homes throughout the U.S. and in Canada, Thailand, Israel, the Bahamas and Malaysia. Ritz-Carlton also markets its 12 luxury golf courses (many designed by leading names in the golf world such as Greg Norman and Jack Nicklaus) and fitness facilities to both local residents and visitors and hosts many PGA and Senior PGA tournaments. In November 2015, the firm signed with YTL Hotels for the development of two new hotels in Asia Pacific, the Ritz-Carlton, Koh Samui, in Thailand, and Ritz-Carlton Reserve in Niseko Village, Japan.

The firm offers employees health care & dependent care spending accounts; tuition reimbursement; dental & vision insurance; short- and long-term disability coverage; credit union membership; and employee assistance programs.

FINANCIAL DATA: Note: Data for latest year may not have been available at press time.

In U.S. $	2016	2015	2014	2013	2012	2011
Revenue		2,400,000,000	2,355,320,000	2,222,213,400	2,126,520,000	2,217,060,000
R&D Expense						
Operating Income						
Operating Margin %						
SGA Expense						
Net Income						
Operating Cash Flow						
Capital Expenditure						
EBITDA						
Return on Assets %						
Return on Equity %						
Debt to Equity						

CONTACT INFORMATION:

Phone: 301-547-4700   Fax:
Toll-Free: 888-241-3333
Address: 4445 Willard Ave., Ste. 800, Chevy Chase, MD 20815 United States

STOCK TICKER/OTHER:

Stock Ticker: Subsidiary   Exchange:
Employees: 40,000   Fiscal Year Ends: 12/31
Parent Company: Marriott International Inc

SALARIES/BONUSES:

Top Exec. Salary: $ Bonus: $
Second Exec. Salary: $ Bonus: $

OTHER THOUGHTS:

Estimated Female Officers or Directors: 1
Hot Spot for Advancement for Women/Minorities:

Robert Half International Inc

www.rhi.com

NAIC Code: 561320

TYPES OF BUSINESS:

Staffing
Risk Consulting
Internal Audit Services
Litigation Consulting & Forensic Accounting

BRANDS/DIVISIONS/AFFILIATES:

Accountemps
Robert Half Finance & Accounting
Robert Half Management Resources
Robert Half Technology
OfficeTeam
Robert Half Legal
Creative Group (The)
Protiviti Inc

CONTACTS: Note: Officers with more than one job title may be intentionally listed here more than once.

Harold Messmer, CEO
M. Waddell, CFO
Michael Buckley, Chief Accounting Officer
Paul Gentzkow, COO, Divisional
Robert Glass, Executive VP, Divisional
Evelyn Crane-Oliver, Secretary

GROWTH PLANS/SPECIAL FEATURES:

Robert Half International, Inc. (RHI) is a staffing firm that provides professional staffing and risk consulting services. RHI operates through more than 400 company-operated or -owned locations around the world. It provides temporary, project and full-time workers to firms in areas such as accounting, finance, administrative and legal support, IT, advertising and marketing. RHI consists of seven staffing divisions: Accountemps, for the staffing of accounting, tax and finance professionals; Robert Half Finance & Accounting and Robert Half Management Resources, for senior-level accounting and finance professionals; OfficeTeam, a division for highly skilled temporary administrative support staff; Robert Half Technology, for IT professionals; Robert Half Legal, which provides attorneys, paralegals and legal support personnel; and The Creative Group, for advertising, marketing and web design professionals. RHI has increased its focus on providing workers for small to mid-size businesses, and it has a growing number of highly-experienced, older workers on its list. Protiviti Inc., the company's wholly-owned subsidiary, provides internal audit and risk consulting services by aiding clients in identifying, measuring and managing operational and technology-related risks in areas such as the media, hospitality, communications, energy, financial services, real estate, health care, government, education, non-profit, manufacturing, distribution and technology. Business risk consultations involve areas such as anti-money laundering, capital projects and construction, energy commodity risks, fraud investigation and forensic accounting. Technology risk consultations provide solutions for security and privacy, continuity, change management, IT assets and application effectiveness.

The firm offers employees medical, dental, vision and life insurance; a savings plan; short- and long-term disability coverage; an employee assistance program; and travel accident insurance.

FINANCIAL DATA: Note: Data for latest year may not have been available at press time.

In U.S. $	2016	2015	2014	2013	2012	2011
Revenue		5,094,933,000	4,695,014,000	4,245,895,000	4,111,213,000	3,776,976,000
R&D Expense						
Operating Income		580,480,000	496,625,000	396,577,000	343,048,000	250,216,000
Operating Margin %		11.39%	10.57%	9.34%	8.34%	6.62%
SGA Expense		1,533,799,000	1,425,734,000	1,324,815,000	1,305,614,000	1,240,184,000
Net Income		357,796,000	305,928,000	252,195,000	209,942,000	149,922,000
Operating Cash Flow		438,236,000	340,698,000	309,217,000	289,177,000	256,316,000
Capital Expenditure		75,057,000	62,830,000	53,725,000	64,449,000	56,535,000
EBITDA		633,945,000	546,306,000	445,349,000	394,166,000	301,631,000
Return on Assets %		21.35%	19.50%	17.56%	15.59%	11.42%
Return on Equity %		36.07%	32.21%	28.63%	25.56%	18.07%
Debt to Equity						

CONTACT INFORMATION:

Phone: 650 234-6000 Fax:
Toll-Free:
Address: 2884 Sand Hill Rd., Menlo Park, CA 94025 United States

STOCK TICKER/OTHER:

Stock Ticker: RHI			Exchange: NYS
Employees: 16,100			Fiscal Year Ends: 12/31
Parent Company:

SALARIES/BONUSES:

Top Exec. Salary: $525,000	Bonus: $
Second Exec. Salary:	Bonus: $
$265,000

OTHER THOUGHTS:

Estimated Female Officers or Directors: 1
Hot Spot for Advancement for Women/Minorities:

Rockwell Automation Inc

www.rockwellautomation.com

NAIC Code: 334513

TYPES OF BUSINESS:

Architecture & Software Products
Control Products & Services

BRANDS/DIVISIONS/AFFILIATES:

Allen-Bradley
Rockwell Software
A-B
ICS Triplex
FactoryTalk
MagneMotion

CONTACTS: *Note: Officers with more than one job title may be intentionally listed here more than once.*

Keith Nosbusch, Chairman of the Board
David Dorgan, Chief Accounting Officer
Sujeet Chand, Chief Technology Officer
Blake Moret, President
Frank Kulaszewicz, Senior VP
John Mcdermott, Senior VP
Martin Thomas, Senior VP, Divisional
Susan Schmitt, Senior VP, Divisional
Theodore Crandall, Senior VP
Douglas Hagerman, Senior VP
Rondi Rohr-Dralle, Vice President, Divisional
John Miller, Vice President
Steven Etzel, Vice President

GROWTH PLANS/SPECIAL FEATURES:

Rockwell Automation, Inc. is a global provider of industrial automation power, control and information products and services. It operates in two segments: architecture & software (A&S); and control products & solutions (CP&S). The A&S operating segment contains all elements of the company's integrated control and information architecture capable of connecting the customer's entire manufacturing enterprise. The division's integrated architecture and Logix controllers perform multiple types of control and monitoring applications, including discrete, batch, continuous process, drive system, motion and machine safety across various industrial machinery, plants and processes; and supply real time information to supervisory software and plant-wide information systems. Products include control platforms, software, I/O devices, communication networks, high performance rotary and linear motion control systems, electronic operator interface devices, condition based monitoring systems, sensors, industrial computers and machine safety components. These products are marketed primarily under the FactoryTalk, A-B, Allen-Bradley and Rockwell Software brand names. The CP&S segment's portfolio includes low voltage and medium voltage electro-mechanical and electronic motor starters, motor and circuit protection devices, AC/DC variable frequency drives, contractors, push buttons, signaling devices, termination and protection devices, relays and timers and condition sensors. The segment also offers value-added packaged solutions that range from configured drives and motor control centers to automation and information solutions where Rockwell provides design, integration and start-up services for custom-engineered hardware and software systems. Additionally, the CP&S segment provides life-cycle support services designed to help maximize a customer's automation investment, including multi-vendor customer technical support and repair, asset management, training and maintenance. Rockwell's control products are marketed through the Allen-Bradley, A-B and ICS Triplex brands. In February 2016, the firm agreed to acquire MagneMotion, a leading manufacturer of intelligent conveying systems.

FINANCIAL DATA: *Note: Data for latest year may not have been available at press time.*

In U.S. $	2016	2015	2014	2013	2012	2011
Revenue		6,307,900,000	6,623,500,000	6,351,900,000	6,259,400,000	6,000,400,000
R&D Expense						
Operating Income		1,196,700,000	1,183,800,000	1,036,100,000	1,031,000,000	867,600,000
Operating Margin %		18.97%	17.87%	16.31%	16.47%	14.45%
SGA Expense		1,506,400,000	1,570,100,000	1,537,700,000	1,491,700,000	1,461,200,000
Net Income		827,600,000	826,800,000	756,300,000	737,000,000	697,800,000
Operating Cash Flow		1,187,700,000	1,033,300,000	1,014,800,000	718,700,000	643,700,000
Capital Expenditure		122,900,000	141,000,000	146,200,000	139,600,000	120,100,000
EBITDA		1,353,700,000	1,346,000,000	1,187,000,000	1,164,600,000	1,058,400,000
Return on Assets %		13.08%	13.69%	13.17%	13.49%	13.90%
Return on Equity %		33.64%	31.53%	34.08%	40.94%	43.49%
Debt to Equity		0.66	0.34	0.35	0.48	0.51

CONTACT INFORMATION:

Phone: 414 382-2000   Fax: 414 382-8520
Toll-Free:
Address: 1201 S. 2nd St., Milwaukee, WI 53204 United States

STOCK TICKER/OTHER:

Stock Ticker: ROK   Exchange: NYS
Employees: 22,500   Fiscal Year Ends: 09/30
Parent Company:

SALARIES/BONUSES:

Top Exec. Salary: Bonus: $
$1,216,115
Second Exec. Salary: Bonus: $
$635,431

OTHER THOUGHTS:

Estimated Female Officers or Directors: 1

Hot Spot for Advancement for Women/Minorities:

Sales, profits and employees may be estimates. Financial information, benefits and other data can change quickly and may vary from those stated here.

Roper Technologies Inc

www.ropertech.com

NAIC Code: 334513

TYPES OF BUSINESS:

Controls Manufacturing
Energy Controls
Medical Systems
Flow Controls

BRANDS/DIVISIONS/AFFILIATES:

Roper Industries Inc

CONTACTS: Note: Officers with more than one job title may be intentionally listed here more than once.

Brian Jellison, CEO
John Humphrey, CFO
Paul Soni, Chief Accounting Officer
John Stipancich, General Counsel

GROWTH PLANS/SPECIAL FEATURES:

Roper Technologies, Inc., formerly known as Roper Industries, Inc., designs, manufactures and distributes energy systems and controls, scientific and industrial imaging products and software, industrial technology products and radio frequency (RF) products and services. The company's operations are reported in four segments: Medical & Scientific Imaging, Energy Systems & Controls, Industrial Technology and RF Technology. The company's Medical & Scientific Imaging segment principally offers products and software in medical applications and high performance digital imaging products. These products and solutions are provided through 1 reporting units. The firm's Energy Systems & Controls segment mainly produces control systems, fluid properties testing equipment, industrial valves and controls, vibration sensors and other non-destructive inspection and measurement products and solutions, which are provided through six reporting units. The firm's Industrial Technology segment produces industrial pumps, equipment and consumables for materials analysis, industrial leak testing equipment, flow measurement and metering equipment and water meter and automatic meter reading (AMR) products and systems. These products and solutions are provided through six reporting units. The company's RF Technology segment provides radio frequency identification (RFID) and other communication related technology and software solutions that are used mainly in comprehensive toll and traffic systems and processing, security and access control, campus card systems, freight matching, food industries, metering and remote monitoring applications. These products and solutions are provided through nine reporting units. The firm markets its products and services to selected segments of a range of industries including healthcare, transportation, food, water, RF applications, energy, research and medical, education, security and other niche markets.

FINANCIAL DATA: Note: Data for latest year may not have been available at press time.

In U.S. $	2016	2015	2014	2013	2012	2011
Revenue		3,582,395,000	3,549,494,000	3,238,128,000	2,993,489,000	2,797,089,000
R&D Expense						
Operating Income		1,027,918,000	999,473,000	842,361,000	757,587,000	660,539,000
Operating Margin %		28.69%	28.15%	26.01%	25.30%	23.61%
SGA Expense		1,136,728,000	1,102,426,000	1,040,567,000	914,130,000	855,025,000
Net Income		696,067,000	646,033,000	538,293,000	483,360,000	427,247,000
Operating Cash Flow		928,825,000	840,441,000	802,553,000	677,852,000	601,618,000
Capital Expenditure		36,260,000	37,644,000	42,528,000	38,405,000	40,702,000
EBITDA		1,232,179,000	1,196,757,000	1,031,359,000	908,954,000	800,682,000
Return on Assets %		7.49%	7.78%	7.05%	7.80%	8.22%
Return on Equity %		13.84%	14.40%	13.62%	14.04%	14.37%
Debt to Equity		0.61	0.46	0.58	0.40	0.31

CONTACT INFORMATION:

Phone: 941 556-2601   Fax: 941 556-2670
Toll-Free:
Address: 6901 Professional Parkway East, Sarasota, FL 34240 United States

STOCK TICKER/OTHER:

Stock Ticker: ROP
Employees: 10,806
Parent Company:

Exchange: NYS
Fiscal Year Ends: 12/31

SALARIES/BONUSES:

Top Exec. Salary:
$1,225,000
Second Exec. Salary:
$767,000

Bonus: $

Bonus: $

OTHER THOUGHTS:

Estimated Female Officers or Directors:

Hot Spot for Advancement for Women/Minorities:

Rosendin Electric

www.rosendin.com

NAIC Code: 238210

TYPES OF BUSINESS:

Electrical Contractor

BRANDS/DIVISIONS/AFFILIATES:

KST Electric

GROWTH PLANS/SPECIAL FEATURES:

Rosendin Electric is a San Jose, California-based electrical contractor that has been operating since the early 1900s. The services provided by the firm include preconstruction services that assist general contractors and owners during the development phase of a project. Other services include engineering, prefabrication, 24-hour/seven-days-a-week service response, network services, electric utility work along highways and the construction of solar & wind farms. Its project portfolio includes services for the following industries: biotechnology, pharmaceuticals, data centers, education, health care, high tech, institutions, multi-family residences, solar power, transportation, commercial, design-build, entertainment, heavy industrial, hotels, power, telecom and wind energy. Rosendin is also experienced in meeting LEED regulations. Subsidiary KST Electric is a Texas-based electrical, data and communication contracting company.

Rosendin is an employee-owned firm.

CONTACTS: Note: Officers with more than one job title may be intentionally listed here more than once.

Tom Sorley, CEO
Larry Beltramo, Pres.
Sam Lamonica, CIO

FINANCIAL DATA: Note: Data for latest year may not have been available at press time.

In U.S. $	2016	2015	2014	2013	2012	2011
Revenue		1,300,000,000	1,100,000,000	935,000,000	887,000,000	820,000,000
R&D Expense						
Operating Income						
Operating Margin %						
SGA Expense						
Net Income						
Operating Cash Flow						
Capital Expenditure						
EBITDA						
Return on Assets %						
Return on Equity %						
Debt to Equity						

CONTACT INFORMATION:

Phone: 480-286-2800   Fax:
Toll-Free:
Address: 880 Mabury Rd., San Jose, CA 95133 United States

STOCK TICKER/OTHER:

Stock Ticker: Private   Exchange:
Employees: 5,300   Fiscal Year Ends:
Parent Company:

SALARIES/BONUSES:

Top Exec. Salary: $ Bonus: $
Second Exec. Salary: $ Bonus: $

OTHER THOUGHTS:

Estimated Female Officers or Directors:
Hot Spot for Advancement for Women/Minorities:

Sales, profits and employees may be estimates. Financial information, benefits and other data can change quickly and may vary from those stated here.

Ross Stores Inc

NAIC Code: 448140

www.rossstores.com

TYPES OF BUSINESS:

Discount Apparel Stores
Home Furnishings

BRANDS/DIVISIONS/AFFILIATES:

Ross Dress for Less
dd's DISCOUNTS

CONTACTS: Note: Officers with more than one job title may be intentionally listed here more than once.

Ken Jew, Assistant Secretary
Barbara Rentler, CEO
Michael Hartshorn, CFO
Norman Ferber, Chairman Emeritus
Michael OSullivan, Co- President
James Fassio, Co- President
Michael Balmuth, Director
John Call, Executive VP, Divisional
Brian Morrow, Other Executive Officer
Bernard Brautigan, President, Divisional

GROWTH PLANS/SPECIAL FEATURES:

Ross Stores, Inc. operates 1,274 off-price retail apparel and home accessories stores in 34 states, Washington, D.C. and Guam, most of which operate under the Ross Dress for Less brand. The company also operates 172 dd's DISCOUNTS locations in 15 states. Most of the stores are located in community and neighborhood strip shopping centers in heavily populated urban and suburban areas. The company's chains target value-conscious women and men ages 18-54. Ross offers new, in-season, name-brand and designer apparel accessories, footwear and home merchandise at savings of 20%-60% off department and specialty store regular prices while dd's DISCOUNTS, targeting lower-income customers, offers similar merchandise, but at savings of up to 70% off department and specialty store prices. The company's stores are supplied by four distribution processing facilities. Ross has combined a network of approximately 8,300 vendors and manufacturers, purchasing the vast majority of its merchandise directly from the manufacturer. By purchasing later in the merchandise buying cycle than department and specialty stores, Ross takes advantage of imbalances between retailers demand for products and manufacturers' supply of those products. In addition, the company typically does not require that manufacturers provide promotional and markdown allowances, return privileges, split shipments, drop shipments to stores or delayed deliveries of merchandise, further enabling Ross to provide significant discounts on in-season merchandise. Sales of lady's products account for approximately 29% of the firm's revenues; home accents/bed and bath, 25%; men's products, 13%; accessories, lingerie, jewelry and fragrances, 13%; shoes, 12%; and children's products, 8%. In fiscal 2015, Ross Stores opened a total of 70 Ross Dress for Less and 20 dd's DISCOUNTS stores.

Ross offers its employees medical, dental, vision and life insurance; sick pay; health care spending accounts; holiday and personal days; a commuter reimbursement account; a 401(k) plan; and an employee stock purchasing plan.

FINANCIAL DATA: Note: Data for latest year may not have been available at press time.

In U.S. $	2016	2015	2014	2013	2012	2011
Revenue	11,940,000,000	11,041,680,000	10,230,350,000	9,721,065,000	8,608,291,000	7,866,100,000
R&D Expense						
Operating Income	1,624,371,000	1,488,350,000	1,343,063,000	1,271,751,000	1,053,144,000	906,590,000
Operating Margin %	13.60%	13.47%	13.12%	13.08%	12.23%	11.52%
SGA Expense	1,738,755,000	1,615,371,000	1,526,366,000	1,437,886,000	1,304,065,000	1,229,775,000
Net Income	1,020,661,000	924,724,000	837,304,000	786,763,000	657,170,000	554,797,000
Operating Cash Flow	1,326,252,000	1,372,865,000	1,022,003,000	979,644,000	820,105,000	673,066,000
Capital Expenditure	366,960,000	646,691,000	550,515,000	424,434,000	416,271,000	198,651,000
EBITDA	1,899,877,000	1,721,720,000	1,549,674,000	1,457,842,000	1,224,036,000	1,068,414,000
Return on Assets %	21.32%	21.50%	22.12%	22.57%	20.48%	18.85%
Return on Equity %	42.96%	43.14%	44.37%	48.26%	46.51%	44.56%
Debt to Equity	0.16	0.17	0.07	0.08	0.10	0.11

CONTACT INFORMATION:

Phone: 925 965-4400   Fax:
Toll-Free:
Address: 5130 Hacienda Drive, Dublin, CA 94568-7579 United States

STOCK TICKER/OTHER:

Stock Ticker: ROST   Exchange: NAS
Employees: 77,800   Fiscal Year Ends: 01/31
Parent Company:

SALARIES/BONUSES:

Top Exec. Salary: $140,152   Bonus: $2,000,000
Second Exec. Salary: Bonus: $
$1,276,250

OTHER THOUGHTS:

Estimated Female Officers or Directors: 4
Hot Spot for Advancement for Women/Minorities: Y

Royal Caribbean Cruises Ltd

www.royalcaribbean.com

NAIC Code: 483112

TYPES OF BUSINESS:
Cruise Line
Rail Tours
Online Travel Services
Academic Tours

BRANDS/DIVISIONS/AFFILIATES:
Royal Caribbean International
Celebrity Cruises
Azamara Club Cruises
Pullmantur
CDF Croisieres de France
TUI Cruises
Celebrity Xpedition
SkySea Cruises

CONTACTS: *Note: Officers with more than one job title may be intentionally listed here more than once.*
Lawrence Pimentel, CEO, Subsidiary
Michael Bayley, CEO, Subsidiary
Lisa Lutoff-Perlo, CEO, Subsidiary
Jorge Vilches, CEO, Subsidiary
Richard Fain, CEO
Jason Liberty, CFO
Henry Pujol, Chief Accounting Officer
Adam Goldstein, COO
Harri Kulovaara, Executive VP, Divisional
Bradley Stein, General Counsel

GROWTH PLANS/SPECIAL FEATURES:
Royal Caribbean Cruises, Ltd. is a global cruise vacation firm, serving the contemporary, premium and deluxe cruise markets, including the budget and luxury segments. With 44 ships offering 110,900 berths, the firm operates five brand names: Royal Caribbean International, Celebrity Cruises, Azamara Club Cruises, Pullmantur and CDF Croisieres de France. It also has a 50% joint venture investment in TUI Cruises with TUI AG. Royal Caribbean's ships have itineraries that call on approximately 490 destinations worldwide. Royal Caribbean International operates 23 ships with 68,600 berths, offering cruise itineraries that range from 2-24 nights. Its destinations include Alaska, Asia, Australia, Bahamas, Bermuda, Canada, the Caribbean, Europe, the Panama Canal, South America and New Zealand. The Celebrity Cruises brand operates 10 ships with 23,100 berths targeted toward higher-end clientele. It also operates Celebrity Xpedition, a ship that travels to the Galapagos Islands and offers pre-cruise tours of Ecuador. Azamara Club Cruises consists of two smaller ships, of about 1,400 passengers each, that focus on cruises to unique destinations, with an emphasis on on-board lectures and fine dining. Its ships sail in Asia, the Mediterranean, South America and less traveled Caribbean Islands. Pullmantur serves the Spanish, Portuguese and Latin American cruise markets, and it operates three ships with 6,200 berths. CDF Croisieres de France serves the French market and operates two ships with an aggregate capacity of 2,800 births. TUI Cruises operates four ships, Mein Schiff 1, 2, 3 and 4, with a capacity of 8,800 berths. Mein Schiff 5 and 6 are on order for a late-2016/mid-2017 delivery, and will bring aggregate capacity to 5,000 berths. Moreover, 35%-owned SkySea Cruises, which offers a custom-tailored product for Chinese cruise guests. In June 2016, the firm signed an agreement with Miami-Dade Country to build and operate a new cruise terminal at PortMiami.

FINANCIAL DATA: *Note: Data for latest year may not have been available at press time.*

In U.S. $	2016	2015	2014	2013	2012	2011
Revenue		8,299,074,000	8,073,855,000	7,959,894,000	7,688,024,000	7,537,263,000
R&D Expense						
Operating Income		874,902,000	941,859,000	798,148,000	403,110,000	931,628,000
Operating Margin %		10.54%	11.66%	10.02%	5.24%	12.36%
SGA Expense		1,086,504,000	1,048,952,000	1,044,819,000	1,011,543,000	960,602,000
Net Income		665,783,000	764,146,000	473,692,000	18,287,000	607,421,000
Operating Cash Flow		1,946,366,000	1,743,759,000	1,412,068,000	1,381,734,000	1,455,739,000
Capital Expenditure		1,613,340,000	1,811,398,000	763,777,000	1,291,499,000	1,173,626,000
EBITDA		1,770,516,000	1,794,890,000	1,560,825,000	1,104,565,000	1,634,054,000
Return on Assets %		3.19%	3.74%	2.37%	.09%	3.07%
Return on Equity %		8.14%	8.94%	5.53%	.21%	7.43%
Debt to Equity		0.96	0.92	0.73	0.83	0.93

CONTACT INFORMATION:
Phone: 305 539-6000   Fax: 305 539-0562
Toll-Free:
Address: 1050 Caribbean Way, Miami, FL 33132 United States

STOCK TICKER/OTHER:
Stock Ticker: RCL   Exchange: NYS
Employees: 66,000   Fiscal Year Ends: 12/31
Parent Company:

SALARIES/BONUSES:
Top Exec. Salary: Bonus: $
$1,038,462
Second Exec. Salary: Bonus: $300,000
$568,939

OTHER THOUGHTS:
Estimated Female Officers or Directors: 3

Hot Spot for Advancement for Women/Minorities: Y

Sales, profits and employees may be estimates. Financial information, benefits and other data can change quickly and may vary from those stated here.

RR Donnelley & Sons Co

NAIC Code: 323111

www.rrdonnelley.com

TYPES OF BUSINESS:

Commercial Printing
Distributors-Books, Magazines, Catalogs & Direct Mail
Digital Content Management
Creative Services
Logistics Services

BRANDS/DIVISIONS/AFFILIATES:

Courier Corporation

CONTACTS: Note: Officers with more than one job title may be intentionally listed here more than once.

Thomas Quinlan, CEO
John Pope, Chairman of the Board
Andrew Coxhead, Chief Accounting Officer
Daniel Knotts, COO
Daniel Leib, Executive VP
Suzanne Bettman, Executive VP

GROWTH PLANS/SPECIAL FEATURES:

R.R. Donnelley & Sons Co. is a provider of print and related services. The firm markets its services, including business process outsourcing (BPO), to customers in the advertising, publishing, health care, retail, technology and financial services industries. R.R. Donnelley operates through five segments: publishing and retail services, accounting for 22.7% of net sales, which offers magazines, catalogs, retail inserts, books, directories and packaging products; variable print, 32.5%, which includes commercial and digital print, direct mail, office products, labels, statement printing, forms and packaging; strategic services, 22.5%, which includes the company's logistics services, financial print products, print management offerings and digital and creative solutions; international, 22.3%, its non-U.S. printing operations in Asia, Europe, Latin America and Canada, with primary offerings consisting of magazines, catalogs, retail inserts, books, directories, direct mail, packaging, forms, labels, manuals, statement printing, commercial and digital print, logistics services and digital and creative solutions; and corporate, 22.5%, which consists of unallocated selling, general and administrative activities and associated expenses including executive, legal, finance, communications, facility costs and inventory provisions. In 2015, the firm acquired Courier Corporation, a digital printing, publishing and content management company. That same year, it announced plans to split into three independent public companies: a financial communications services company, a publishing & retail-centric print services company and a multi-channel communications management company. The split transactions are expected to close before the end of 2016.

FINANCIAL DATA: Note: Data for latest year may not have been available at press time.

In U.S. $	2016	2015	2014	2013	2012	2011
Revenue		11,256,800,000	11,603,400,000	10,480,300,000	10,221,900,000	10,611,000,000
R&D Expense						
Operating Income		587,400,000	515,900,000	579,700,000	-369,800,000	65,200,000
Operating Margin %		5.21%	4.44%	5.53%	-3.61%	.61%
SGA Expense		1,300,000,000	1,427,000,000	1,181,500,000	1,102,600,000	1,236,300,000
Net Income		151,100,000	117,400,000	211,200,000	-651,400,000	-122,600,000
Operating Cash Flow		652,000,000	722,700,000	694,800,000	691,900,000	946,300,000
Capital Expenditure		207,600,000	223,600,000	216,600,000	205,900,000	250,900,000
EBITDA		1,003,100,000	912,100,000	917,700,000	108,600,000	572,300,000
Return on Assets %		2.02%	1.57%	2.91%	-8.38%	-1.41%
Return on Equity %		23.67%	19.15%	61.70%	-118.92%	-7.50%
Debt to Equity		4.67	5.77	5.67	64.77	3.27

CONTACT INFORMATION:

Phone: 312 326-8000   Fax: 312 326-8001
Toll-Free:
Address: 111 S. Wacker Dr., Chicago, IL 60606 United States

SALARIES/BONUSES:

Top Exec. Salary: $725,000   Bonus: $700,000
Second Exec. Salary: Bonus: $
$1,183,333

STOCK TICKER/OTHER:

Stock Ticker: RRD   Exchange: NYS
Employees: 68,000   Fiscal Year Ends: 12/31
Parent Company:

OTHER THOUGHTS:

Estimated Female Officers or Directors: 1
Hot Spot for Advancement for Women/Minorities: Y

Ryder System Inc

www.ryder.com

NAIC Code: 532120

TYPES OF BUSINESS:

Truck Rental & Leasing
Trucking
Logistics & Consulting Services
Supply Chain Management
Dedicated Fleet Services
Fleet Management Services

BRANDS/DIVISIONS/AFFILIATES:

CONTACTS: Note: Officers with more than one job title may be intentionally listed here more than once.

Art Garcia, CFO
Scott Allen, Chief Accounting Officer

GROWTH PLANS/SPECIAL FEATURES:

Ryder System, Inc. is a global provider of transportation and supply chain management solutions. It operates in two segments: fleet management solutions and supply chain solutions. The fleet management solutions segment, which accounts for approximately 63% of Ryder's revenues, provides full service leasing, contract maintenance, contract-related maintenance and commercial rental of trucks, tractors and trailers to customers principally in the U.S., Canada and the U.K. The division also offers transaction fleet solutions, including commercial truck rental; maintenance services; and value-added fleet support services, such as insurance, vehicle administration and fuel services. In addition, it provides customers with access to a large selection of used trucks, tractors and trailers through its used vehicle sales program. The supply chain solutions segment, from which Ryder derives roughly 37% of its revenues, provides supply chain solutions such as distribution and transportation services throughout North America and Asia. The division's products are organized into four primary categories: dedicated services, distribution management, transportation management and professional services. Dedicated services combines the equipment, maintenance & administrative services of a full-service lease with drivers and additional services; its services are offered on a stand-alone basis or as part of an integrated supply chain solution. Distribution management offers services relating to a customer's distribution operations, such as its distribution network or managing its distribution facilities. Transportation management relates to all aspects of a customer's transportation network, such as shipment planning & execution, through a series of technological and web-based solutions. Professional services provides solutions and support related to a customer's supply chain. In 2015, the firm opened a new truck maintenance & rental facility in Santa Fe Springs, California.

FINANCIAL DATA: Note: Data for latest year may not have been available at press time.

In U.S. $	2016	2015	2014	2013	2012	2011
Revenue		6,571,893,000	6,638,774,000	6,419,285,000	6,256,967,000	6,050,534,000
R&D Expense						
Operating Income		505,909,000	451,031,000	490,249,000	350,909,000	344,234,000
Operating Margin %		7.69%	6.79%	7.63%	5.60%	5.68%
SGA Expense		844,497,000	816,975,000	790,681,000	766,704,000	771,244,000
Net Income		304,768,000	218,575,000	237,792,000	209,979,000	169,777,000
Operating Cash Flow		1,441,788,000	1,369,991,000	1,223,082,000	1,130,905,000	1,041,456,000
Capital Expenditure		2,667,978,000	2,259,164,000	2,140,464,000	2,133,235,000	1,698,589,000
EBITDA		1,830,333,000	1,568,146,000	1,519,621,000	1,432,560,000	1,324,741,000
Return on Assets %		2.95%	2.32%	2.72%	2.63%	2.37%
Return on Equity %		16.03%	11.76%	14.13%	15.07%	12.47%
Debt to Equity		2.45	2.47	2.07	2.35	2.35

CONTACT INFORMATION:

Phone: 305 500-3726   Fax: 305 500-4129
Toll-Free:
Address: 11690 NW 105th St., Miami, FL 33178 United States

STOCK TICKER/OTHER:

Stock Ticker: R   Exchange: NYS
Employees: 30,600   Fiscal Year Ends: 12/31
Parent Company:

SALARIES/BONUSES:

Top Exec. Salary: $768,825   Bonus: $
Second Exec. Salary: Bonus: $
$533,050

OTHER THOUGHTS:

Estimated Female Officers or Directors: 4
Hot Spot for Advancement for Women/Minorities: Y

Sales, profits and employees may be estimates. Financial information, benefits and other data can change quickly and may vary from those stated here.

Safeco Insurance Company of America

www.safeco.com

NAIC Code: 524126

TYPES OF BUSINESS:

Direct Property & Casualty Insurance
Personal Insurance

BRANDS/DIVISIONS/AFFILIATES:

Liberty Mutual Group Inc
Safeco Package
Liberty Northwest
Colorado Casualty Insurance
America First Insurance
Golden Eagle Insurance
Ohio Casualty Montgomery Insurance
Safeco Insurance Fund

CONTACTS: Note: Officers with more than one job title may be intentionally listed here more than once.

Gary R. Gregg, CEO
Michael Joseph Fallon, CFO
Donald J. DeShaw, General Counsel

GROWTH PLANS/SPECIAL FEATURES:

Safeco Insurance Company of America (Safeco) is a property and casualty insurance provider for homeowners and drivers. The company is a subsidiary of life, auto and home insurance provider Liberty Mutual Group, Inc. Safeco's personal insurance services include auto, homeowners, condo, rental and specialty insurance products for individuals. Specialty insurance products include umbrella, classic car, motorcycle, recreational vehicle and boat/watercraft owners' insurance coverage for individuals. The company also offers The Safeco Package, a combined auto and home property insurance product. Safeco maintains regional offices in California, Texas, Indiana, Ohio, Colorado, Washington, New Hampshire and Georgia. It also has service offices in Missouri, Oregon, Illinois and Connecticut; and customer care centers in Indiana, Washington and Colorado. The firm's business insurance activities are operated by Safeco's sister companies, such as Liberty Northwest, Colorado Casualty Insurance, America First Insurance, Golden Eagle Insurance, Ohio Casualty Montgomery Insurance and Peerless Insurance. These companies provide business-owner policies, surety bonds, commercial auto, commercial multi-peril, workers compensation, commercial property and general liability policies for small- and mid-sized businesses. The company holds naming rights to the Seattle Mariners' baseball stadium, Safeco Field. In addition, the Safeco Insurance Fund, a fund within the Liberty Mutual Foundation, supports nonprofit organizations within the state of Washington. The fund's grands program focuses on educational opportunities of underprivileged youth, ensuring security through life-saving basic services to homeless persons and promoting accessibility for individuals of all abilities.

Through Liberty Mutual Group, Safeco offers its employees benefits including a 401(k) plan; flexible spending accounts; medical, vision, disability, life, AD&D, dependent life and long-term care insurance; paid time off; and tuition reimbursement.

FINANCIAL DATA: Note: Data for latest year may not have been available at press time.

In U.S. $	2016	2015	2014	2013	2012	2011
Revenue		1,650,000,000	1,595,200,000	1,461,447,245	1,631,937,130	1,709,915,290
R&D Expense						
Operating Income						
Operating Margin %						
SGA Expense						
Net Income						
Operating Cash Flow						
Capital Expenditure						
EBITDA						
Return on Assets %						
Return on Equity %						
Debt to Equity						

CONTACT INFORMATION:

Phone: 206-545-5000   Fax:
Toll-Free:
Address: 1001 Fourth Ave., Safeco Plz., Seattle, WA 98154 United States

STOCK TICKER/OTHER:

Stock Ticker: Subsidiary   Exchange:
Employees: 3,000   Fiscal Year Ends: 12/31
Parent Company: Liberty Mutual Group Inc

SALARIES/BONUSES:

Top Exec. Salary: $ Bonus: $
Second Exec. Salary: $ Bonus: $

OTHER THOUGHTS:

Estimated Female Officers or Directors:
Hot Spot for Advancement for Women/Minorities: Y

Safeway Inc

www.safeway.com

NAIC Code: 445110

TYPES OF BUSINESS:

Grocery Stores
Food Processing & Packaging
Online Grocery Sales & Home Delivery
Pharmacies
Gift Cards & Payment Processing Technology

BRANDS/DIVISIONS/AFFILIATES:

AB Acquisition LLC
Safeway
Carrs
Genuardi's
Pavilions
Tom Thumb
Dominick's
Randall's

CONTACTS: *Note: Officers with more than one job title may be intentionally listed here more than once.*

Robert G. Miller, CEO
Peter J. Bocian, CFO
Larree Renda, Executive VP
Kelly Griffith, Executive VP, Divisional
Diane Dietz, Executive VP
Melissa Plaisance, Senior VP, Divisional
David Stern, Senior VP, Divisional
Donald Wright, Senior VP, Divisional
Jerry Tidwell, Senior VP, Divisional
Russell Jackson, Senior VP, Divisional
Robert Gordon, Senior VP
Robert G. Miller, Chmn.

GROWTH PLANS/SPECIAL FEATURES:

Safeway, Inc. is one of the largest food retailers in the U.S., operating stores in 33 states and the District of Columbia. These stores operate regionally under the names Safeway, Carrs, Genuardi's, Pavilions, Tom Thumb, Dominick's, Randall's and Vons, each of which offer a wide selection of both food and general merchandise and feature a variety of special departments such as bakery, delicatessen, pharmacy and floral departments. In addition, the company offers online grocery shopping and home delivery through its wholly-owned subsidiary GroceryWorks. Safeway has developed a line of Safeway SELECT brand products, ranging from packaged foods to laundry detergent, and offers corporate-branded products under the Safeway labels: O Organics, Eating Right, Bright Green and Open Nature. Beyond these operations, Safeway manages its Blackhawk Network subsidiary, which is one of the largest providers of third-party prepaid gift cards in the country. In December 2014, Safeway sold its real estate subsidiary, Property Development Centers LLC, as well as its 49% stake in Mexico-based food retailer Casa Ley, SA de CV. In June 2015, AB Acquisition LLC (Albertson's) completed a merger with Safeway. The combined companies have a total of 2,230 stores, 27 distribution centers and 19 manufacturing plants, with 250,000 employees nationwide.

Safeway offers its employees medical, prescription drug, vision and dental coverage; an employee assistance plan; flexible spending accounts; life insurance; short- and long-term disability; paid time off; a stock purchase plan; a retirement plan; and a 401(k) plan.

FINANCIAL DATA: *Note: Data for latest year may not have been available at press time.*

In U.S. $	2016	2015	2014	2013	2012	2011
Revenue		36,980,000,000	36,330,000,000	36,139,098,112	44,206,501,888	43,630,198,784
R&D Expense						
Operating Income						
Operating Margin %						
SGA Expense						
Net Income			111,600,000	3,507,500,032	596,499,968	516,700,000
Operating Cash Flow						
Capital Expenditure						
EBITDA						
Return on Assets %						
Return on Equity %						
Debt to Equity						

CONTACT INFORMATION:

Phone: 925 467-3000   Fax: 925 467-3323
Toll-Free: 877-723-3929
Address: 5918 Stoneridge Mall Rd., Pleasanton, CA 94588-3229 United States

STOCK TICKER/OTHER:

Stock Ticker: Private   Exchange:
Employees: 138,000   Fiscal Year Ends: 12/31
Parent Company: AB Acquisition LLC

SALARIES/BONUSES:

Top Exec. Salary: $ Bonus: $
Second Exec. Salary: $ Bonus: $

OTHER THOUGHTS:

Estimated Female Officers or Directors: 4
Hot Spot for Advancement for Women/Minorities: Y

SalesForce.com Inc

www.salesforce.com

NAIC Code: 0

TYPES OF BUSINESS:

Software-Sales & Marketing Automation
Customer Relationship Management Software
Software Subscription Services

GROWTH PLANS/SPECIAL FEATURES:

SalesForce.com, Inc. builds and delivers customer relationship management (CRM) applications through an on-demand web services platform. The firm's web-based services enable clients to track sales and marketing by delivering enterprise software as an online service, making software purchases similar to paying for a utility as opposed to a packaged product. The firm offers core cloud based services such as sales force automation, customer service & support, marketing automation, community management, analytics, as well as a platform for building custom application. Products include Sales Cloud, Service Cloud, Marketing Cloud, Community Cloud, Analytics Cloud, IoT (Internet of Things) Cloud and App Cloud. Sales Cloud is a platform for sales force automation and solutions for partner relationship management; Service Cloud addresses customer service and support needs; Marketing Cloud is a digital marketing platform that manages customer interactions across email, mobile, social, web and connected products; Community Cloud creates trusted, branded destinations for customers, partners and employees to collaborate; Analytics Cloud is an app and platform for business intelligence; IoT Cloud connects billions of events from devices, sensors, apps and more from the IoT to SalesForce, enabling companies to take action with the connected world; and App Cloud, an app development platform that includes Force, Heroku, Enterprise and Lightning, to share identity, data and network services. In July 2016, the firm aquired Demandware, Inc. for $2.8 billion, becoming the firm's new commerce cloud platform.

SalesForce.com offers its employees paid time off, parental/family care, employee stock purchase plans, educational reimbursement, wellness allowances, volunteer time off and a 401(k) plan.

BRANDS/DIVISIONS/AFFILIATES:

Sales Cloud
Service Cloud
Marketing Cloud
Community Cloud
Analytics Cloud
IoT Cloud
App Cloud
Demandware Inc

CONTACTS:

Note: Officers with more than one job title may be intentionally listed here more than once.

Marc Benioff, CEO
Mark Hawkins, CFO
Joe Allanson, Chief Accounting Officer
Parker Harris, Co-Founder
George Hu, COO
Keith Block, Director
Cynthia Robbins, Executive VP, Divisional
Amy Weaver, Executive VP
Burke Norton, Executive VP
Alexandre Dayon, Other Executive Officer
Maria Martinez, President, Divisional

FINANCIAL DATA:

Note: Data for latest year may not have been available at press time.

In U.S. $	2016	2015	2014	2013	2012	2011
Revenue	6,667,216,000	5,373,586,000	4,071,003,000	3,050,195,000	2,266,539,000	1,657,139,000
R&D Expense	946,300,000	792,917,000	623,798,000	429,479,000	295,347,000	187,887,000
Operating Income	114,923,000	-145,633,000	-286,074,000	-110,710,000	-35,085,000	97,497,000
Operating Margin %	1.72%	-2.71%	-7.02%	-3.62%	-1.54%	5.88%
SGA Expense	3,988,062,000	3,437,032,000	2,764,851,000	2,047,847,000	1,517,391,000	1,047,942,000
Net Income	-47,426,000	-262,688,000	-232,175,000	-270,445,000	-11,572,000	64,474,000
Operating Cash Flow	1,612,585,000	1,173,714,000	875,469,000	736,897,000	591,507,000	459,081,000
Capital Expenditure	709,852,000	416,889,000	299,110,000	179,707,000	171,300,000	368,831,000
EBITDA	662,514,000	308,448,000	88,699,000	119,949,000	141,014,000	204,953,000
Return on Assets %	-.40%	-2.64%	-3.16%	-5.58%	-.31%	2.32%
Return on Equity %	-1.05%	-7.49%	-8.66%	-13.85%	-.80%	5.55%
Debt to Equity	0.29	0.37	0.44			0.39

CONTACT INFORMATION:

Phone: 415 901-7000   Fax: 415 901-7040
Toll-Free:
Address: 1 Market St., Ste. 300, The Landmark, San Francisco, CA 94105 United States

STOCK TICKER/OTHER:

Stock Ticker: CRM   Exchange: NYS
Employees: 16,000   Fiscal Year Ends: 01/31
Parent Company:

SALARIES/BONUSES:

Top Exec. Salary: $1,550,000   Bonus: $
Second Exec. Salary: $1,077,000   Bonus: $40,564

OTHER THOUGHTS:

Estimated Female Officers or Directors: 4

Hot Spot for Advancement for Women/Minorities: Y

Sam's Club

www.samsclub.com

NAIC Code: 452910

TYPES OF BUSINESS:

Warehouse Clubs, Retail

BRANDS/DIVISIONS/AFFILIATES:

Wal-Mart Stores Inc
Member's Mark
Bakers & Chefs
Sam's Club
Sam's CafÃ©
Sam's Savings
Sam's Business
Sam's Plus

CONTACTS: *Note: Officers with more than one job title may be intentionally listed here more than once.*

Rosalind G. Brewer, CEO
Don Frieson, Exec.VP-Operations
Rosalind G. Brewer, Pres.
Charles Redfield, Exec. VP-Merch.
Whitney Head, General Counsel
P. Todd Harbaugh, Exec. VP-Oper.
Don Frieson, Sr. VP-Planning & Replenishment
John Boswell, Sr. VP-e-Commerce
Bill Durling, Sr. Dir.-Corp. Comm.
Mike Turner, Sr. VP-Sam's Club Membership
Whitney Head, Sr. VP- Asset Protection & Compliance

GROWTH PLANS/SPECIAL FEATURES:

Sam's Club, a subsidiary of Wal-Mart Stores, Inc., is an American chain of membership-only retail warehouse clubs. There are more than 650 clubs across the U.S. and Puerto Rico, with in-club benefits including pharmacy, fuel stations, optical centers, hearing aid centers, photo centers, tire & battery centers, daily Tastes & Tips sampling demonstrations and free monthly health screenings. Sam's Club offers discounted prices on items, including appliances & electronics, office supplies, food, clothing, optical & pharmacy services, home furnishings, books and auto supplies. It also sells selected private-label items under the Member's Mark, Bakers & Chefs and Sam's Club brands. Most locations also offer fresh departments such as bakery, meat, produce, floral and Sam's Cafe. Sam's Club requires a customer to become a member, providing three options for an annual fee: Sam's Savings ($45 annual fee), Sam's Business ($45 annual fee) and Sam's Plus ($100 annual fee). In addition to merchandise discounts, the firm offers its members discounted services that include various types of insurance, a travel club, an auto purchase program, discount credit card processing, mail-order pharmacy services, Internet access and long-distance services. Sam's Club 5-3-1 MasterCard option is a credit card cash back program issued by Synchrony Financial. Sam's Club stores, averaging 70,000-190,000 square feet, are designed to resemble a warehouse, with merchandise displayed on shipping pallets or in large freezer/cooler units. The company's merchandise consists of five categories: grocery & consumables; fuel & other categories; technology, office and entertainment; home & apparel; and health & wellness. In February 2016, the firm began accepting Visa credit cards at most of its stores.

Parent company Wal Mart offers employees health reimbursement accounts, health savings accounts, HMO plans, life insurance, AD&D insurance, short- and long-term disability and a 401(k) with company match.

FINANCIAL DATA: *Note: Data for latest year may not have been available at press time.*

In U.S. $	2016	2015	2014	2013	2012	2011
Revenue		57,000,000,000	57,157,000,000	56,423,000,000	53,795,000,000	49,459,000,000
R&D Expense						
Operating Income						
Operating Margin %						
SGA Expense						
Net Income			1,975,000,000	1,960,000,000	1,865,000,000	1,711,000,000
Operating Cash Flow						
Capital Expenditure						
EBITDA						
Return on Assets %						
Return on Equity %						
Debt to Equity						

CONTACT INFORMATION:

Phone: 479-277-7000   Fax:
Toll-Free: 888-746-7726
Address: 2101 S. E. Simple Savings Drive, Bentonville, AR 72716 United States

STOCK TICKER/OTHER:

Stock Ticker: Subsidiary   Exchange:
Employees: 110,000   Fiscal Year Ends: 01/31
Parent Company: Wal-Mart Stores Inc

SALARIES/BONUSES:

Top Exec. Salary: $ Bonus: $
Second Exec. Salary: $ Bonus: $

OTHER THOUGHTS:

Estimated Female Officers or Directors: 3
Hot Spot for Advancement for Women/Minorities: Y

Sanmina Corp

NAIC Code: 334418

TYPES OF BUSINESS:

Printed Circuit Assembly (Electronic Assembly) Manufacturing
Assembly & Testing
Logistics Services
Support Services
Product Design & Engineering
Repair & Maintenance Services

BRANDS/DIVISIONS/AFFILIATES:

Viking Technology
SCI Technology Inc

CONTACTS: Note: Officers with more than one job title may be intentionally listed here more than once.

Jure Sola, CEO
Bob Eulau, CFO
Alan Reid, Exec. VP-Global Human Resources
Jure Sola, Chmn.

GROWTH PLANS/SPECIAL FEATURES:

Sanmina Corp. is a global provider of customized, integrated electronics manufacturing services (EMS). With production facilities in 25 countries, the firm is one of the largest global EMS providers. The firm has two business segments: integrated manufacturing solutions (IMS) and components, products and services (CPS). The IMS includes printed circuit board assembly and test, which involves attaching electronic components such as integrated circuits, capacitors, microprocessors to printed circuit boards; final system assembly and test, which consists of combining assemblies and modules to form finished products; and direct-order fulfillment, which involves receiving customer orders, configuring products and delivering the products either to the OEM, a distribution channel. The CPS segment includes interconnect systems (printed circuit board fabrication, backplane and cable assemblies) and mechanical systems (enclosures, precision machining and plastic injection molding). This segment also includes the operations of Viking Technology, a manufacturer of flash memory and related storage products and SCI Technology, Inc.'s defense and aerospace products, as well as logistics and repair services. The company caters to defense and aerospace, computing and storage, automotive, multi-media, clean technology, medical systems and communications network industries.

Employee benefits include a 401(k); tuition reimbursement; credit union membership; an employee assistance program; flexible spending accounts; and medical, prescription, dental, vision, life and AD&D insurance.

FINANCIAL DATA: Note: Data for latest year may not have been available at press time.

In U.S. $	2016	2015	2014	2013	2012	2011
Revenue		6,374,541,000	6,215,106,000	5,917,124,000	6,093,334,000	6,602,411,000
R&D Expense		33,083,000	32,495,000	25,571,000	21,899,000	20,802,000
Operating Income		203,101,000	199,682,000	157,629,000	137,490,000	211,997,000
Operating Margin %		3.18%	3.21%	2.66%	2.25%	3.21%
SGA Expense		239,288,000	242,288,000	238,072,000	240,863,000	247,127,000
Net Income		377,261,000	197,165,000	79,351,000	180,234,000	68,917,000
Operating Cash Flow		174,896,000	307,382,000	317,889,000	215,413,000	234,908,000
Capital Expenditure		119,097,000	69,507,000	75,950,000	78,631,000	107,574,000
EBITDA		301,771,000	290,220,000	240,431,000	221,164,000	303,223,000
Return on Assets %		11.08%	6.25%	2.57%	5.52%	2.07%
Return on Equity %		27.26%	16.86%	7.72%	20.78%	9.62%
Debt to Equity		0.27	0.31	0.51	0.86	1.53

CONTACT INFORMATION:

Phone: 408-964-3500   Fax: 408-964-3636
Toll-Free:
Address: 2700 N. First St., San Jose, CA 95134 United States

STOCK TICKER/OTHER:

Stock Ticker: SANM   Exchange: NAS
Employees: 43,854   Fiscal Year Ends: 09/30
Parent Company:

SALARIES/BONUSES:

Top Exec. Salary: $900,000   Bonus: $
Second Exec. Salary: Bonus: $
$510,000

OTHER THOUGHTS:

Estimated Female Officers or Directors:
Hot Spot for Advancement for Women/Minorities:

Sapient Corporation

www.sapient.com

NAIC Code: 541512

TYPES OF BUSINESS:
IT Consulting
Internet Strategy Consulting
Interactive Marketing Software

BRANDS/DIVISIONS/AFFILIATES:
Sapient Government Services
Sapient Global Markets
SapientNitro
Campfire
Publicis Groupe

CONTACTS: *Note: Officers with more than one job title may be intentionally listed here more than once.*
Alan Herrick, CEO
Joseph Tibbetts, CFO
William Kanarick, CMO
Alan Wexler, Executive VP
J. Moore, Founder
Joseph LaSala, General Counsel
Harry Register, Managing Director, Divisional
Christian Oversohl, Managing Director, Geographical
Laurie MacLaren, Senior VP, Divisional

GROWTH PLANS/SPECIAL FEATURES:
Sapient Corporation is a business consulting and technology services firm that designs and manages information technology to improve business performance for clients in the U.S. and abroad. Sapient has offices in the U.S., Europe, Asia, Australia and South America. The firm operates through three primary business units: SapientNitro, Sapient Global Markets and Sapient Government Services. SapientNitro, a leading global interactive marketing agency, provides interactive marketing and creative services, web site and interactive development, media planning and buying, strategic planning and market analytics and marketing technologies. Sapient Global Markets offers financial and commodity market customer advisory services, analytics, technology and business process solutions. Sapient Government Services provides consulting, technology and marketing services to several agencies of the U.S. government, including the Library of Congress, Federal Bureau of Investigation, National Institutes of Health and U.S. Department of Homeland Security. The group also serves provincial and other governmental entities in Canada and Europe. Sapient works on both long- and short-term consulting projects. Sapient operates through a proprietary Global Distributed Delivery (GDD) model, which allows associates in widely disparate locations to work together efficiently. The firm's clients consist of companies within the following industries: financial services, technology, communications, consumer, automotive, energy services, government, health and education. In 2014, Sapient acquired marketing agency, Campfire. In February 2015, the firm was acquired by Publicis Groupe.

FINANCIAL DATA: *Note: Data for latest year may not have been available at press time.*

In U.S. $	2016	2015	2014	2013	2012	2011
Revenue		1,562,781,000	1,451,000,000	1,305,232,000	1,161,548,032	1,062,204,032
R&D Expense						
Operating Income						
Operating Margin %						
SGA Expense						
Net Income						
Operating Cash Flow						
Capital Expenditure						
EBITDA						
Return on Assets %						
Return on Equity %						
Debt to Equity						

CONTACT INFORMATION:
Phone: 617 621-0200   Fax: 617 621-1300
Toll-Free:
Address: 131 Dartmouth St., Boston, MA 02116 United States

STOCK TICKER/OTHER:
Stock Ticker: Subsidiary
Employees: 11,900
Parent Company: PUBLICIS GROUPE
Exchange:
Fiscal Year Ends: 12/31

SALARIES/BONUSES:
Top Exec. Salary: $ Bonus: $
Second Exec. Salary: $ Bonus: $

OTHER THOUGHTS:
Estimated Female Officers or Directors: 2
Hot Spot for Advancement for Women/Minorities:

Sales, profits and employees may be estimates. Financial information, benefits and other data can change quickly and may vary from those stated here.

SAS Institute Inc

www.sas.com

NAIC Code: 0

TYPES OF BUSINESS:

Software-Statistical Analysis
Business Intelligence Software
Data Warehousing
Online Bookstore
Consulting

BRANDS/DIVISIONS/AFFILIATES:

SAS 9.4
SAS Visual Analytics
Decisions & Systems Inc
IDeaS Revenue Optimization
JMP Software
SAS Curriculum Pathways
RiskAdvisory
SAS Cloud

CONTACTS: *Note: Officers with more than one job title may be intentionally listed here more than once.*

James Goodnight, CEO
Don Parker, CFO
Jim Davis, Chief Mktg. Officer
Jennifer Mann, VP-Human Resources
Keith Collins, Sr. VP
John Boswell, Chief Legal Officer
Carl Farrell, Exec. VP-SAS Americas
John Sall, Exec. VP
Mikael Hagstrom, Exec. VP-EMEA & Asia Pacific

GROWTH PLANS/SPECIAL FEATURES:

SAS Institute, Inc. provides statistical analysis software. The company's products are designed to extract, manage an analyze large volumes of data, often assisting in financia reporting and credit analysis. Individual contracts can b tailored to specific global and local industries, such as banking manufacturing and government. The firm's popular SAS Visua Analytics software product is a single application for E (business intelligence), data exploration and analytics, allowin users to design and distribute BI reports and dashboards an explore data through interactive data visualization. SAS 9. provides high-performance analytics, with the ability to deplo in cloud environments. SAS Cloud helps companies transitio from a traditional IT structure to cloud-based applications providing options for clients such as whether they will stor information in a public cloud or private cloud. In addition, th firm operates an online bookstore offering a library of SAS produced books, documentation and training materials. SAS serves more than 75,000 business, government and universit sites in over 138 different countries, including 93 of the top 10 companies on the Fortune Global 500 list. The firm's softwar is used in a number of industries, including aerospace defense, banking, government, financial services, insurance manufacturing and retail. SAS extends focused solutions int targeted markets to further support analytically drive customers through its wholly-owned subsidiary Decisions Systems, Inc. Other subsidiaries and divisions include IDeaS Revenue Optimization, JMP Software, RiskAdvisory and SAS Curriculum Pathways.

SAS offers its employees life, disability, medical, dental, auto home and vision insurance; flexible spending accounts; onsite health care and fitness centers; an employee assistance program; adoption assistance; scholarship programs; a 401(k) and a profit sharing plan.

FINANCIAL DATA: *Note: Data for latest year may not have been available at press time.*

In U.S. $	2016	2015	2014	2013	2012	2011
Revenue		3,160,000,000	3,090,000,000	3,020,000,000	2,870,000,000	2,725,000,000
R&D Expense						
Operating Income						
Operating Margin %						
SGA Expense						
Net Income						
Operating Cash Flow						
Capital Expenditure						
EBITDA						
Return on Assets %						
Return on Equity %						
Debt to Equity						

CONTACT INFORMATION:

Phone: 919-677-8000　　　Fax: 919-677-4444
Toll-Free: 800-727-0025
Address: 100 SAS Campus Dr., Cary, NC 27513 United States

STOCK TICKER/OTHER:

Stock Ticker: Private　　　　　　　　Exchange:
Employees: 13,814　　　　　　　　　Fiscal Year Ends: 12/31
Parent Company:

SALARIES/BONUSES:

Top Exec. Salary: $　　　Bonus: $
Second Exec. Salary: $　　　Bonus: $

OTHER THOUGHTS:

Estimated Female Officers or Directors: 1
Hot Spot for Advancement for Women/Minorities: Y

SC Johnson & Son Inc

www.scjohnson.com

NAIC Code: 325600

TYPES OF BUSINESS:

Household Products Manufacturing
Household Products
Cleaning Products
Auto Care Products
Insect Repellents

BRANDS/DIVISIONS/AFFILIATES:

Drano
Pledge
Shout
Windex
Off!
Raid
ALLOUT
Glade

CONTACTS: *Note: Officers with more than one job title may be intentionally listed here more than once.*

Fisk Johnson, CEO
Salman Amin, COO
Mark H. Eckhardt, Exec. VP
Fisk Johnson, Chmn.

GROWTH PLANS/SPECIAL FEATURES:

S.C. Johnson & Son, Inc. is one of the world's largest manufacturers of household chemical products, with many proprietary brand names. The firm was established in 1886 as a flooring company and has since been managed by the Johnson family for over five generations. The company produces home cleaning, home storage, insect control, auto care and air care products. Its home cleaning products include the Drano home drain cleaner, Pledge dust and pet hair cleaner, Shout stain remover for clothes and fabrics, Fantastik surface cleaner, Scrubbing Bubbles bathroom cleaner, Windex glass and window cleaner and Duck bathroom cleaner. Other products include Saran plastic wrap and Ziploc plastic bags for home storage; Off!, Raid, Baygon, Autan and ALLOUT insect repellent; Grand Prix waxes, protectants and cleaners for auto care; and Oust air fresheners and Glade candles and home fragrances for the air care market. The company's patented Greenlist process allows scientific and environmental organizations to review and rate ingredients for use in the firm's products. This system allows the company to improve and update its products by health and environmental standards. The firm has operations in more than 70 countries worldwide. S.C. Johnson & Son also operates an online mail order service, which allows customers to order a select number of company products, available for shipping anywhere in the USA. In November 2015, the firm announced plans to invest between $50 to $80 million to upgrade its corporate office in Racine, Wisconsin, but also is moving about 175 sales & marketing jobs out of state from Racine to Chicago.

FINANCIAL DATA: *Note: Data for latest year may not have been available at press time.*

In U.S. $	2016	2015	2014	2013	2012	2011
Revenue		9,600,000,000	9,600,000,000	9,600,000,000	9,400,000,000	9,100,000,000
R&D Expense						
Operating Income						
Operating Margin %						
SGA Expense						
Net Income						
Operating Cash Flow						
Capital Expenditure						
EBITDA						
Return on Assets %						
Return on Equity %						
Debt to Equity						

CONTACT INFORMATION:

Phone: 262-260-2000   Fax: 262-260-6004
Toll-Free: 800-494-4855
Address: 1525 Howe St., Racine, WI 53403 United States

SALARIES/BONUSES:

Top Exec. Salary: $ Bonus: $
Second Exec. Salary: $ Bonus: $

STOCK TICKER/OTHER:

Stock Ticker: Private   Exchange:
Employees: 13,000   Fiscal Year Ends: 06/30
Parent Company:

OTHER THOUGHTS:

Estimated Female Officers or Directors:
Hot Spot for Advancement for Women/Minorities: Y

Sales, profits and employees may be estimates. Financial information, benefits and other data can change quickly and may vary from those stated here.

SCANA Corporation

NAIC Code: 221112

TYPES OF BUSINESS:

Electricity & Natural Gas
Telecommunications Services
Ethernet Services & Data Center Facilities
Communications Towers Management
Management & Maintenance Services
Service Contracts
Risk Management Services

BRANDS/DIVISIONS/AFFILIATES:

South Carolina Electric and Gas Company
PSNC Energy
SCANA Energy
SCANA Energy Marketing Inc
SCANA Services Inc
South Carolina Generating Company Inc
South Carolina Fuel Company Inc

CONTACTS: Note: Officers with more than one job title may be intentionally listed here more than once.

Ronald Lindsay, Assistant Secretary
Kevin Marsh, CEO
Jimmy Addison, CFO
J. Swan, Controller
Stephen Byrne, COO, Subsidiary
Don Harris, COO, Subsidiary
Gina Champion, Other Corporate Officer
Jeffrey Archie, Other Executive Officer
William Kissam, President, Subsidiary
Martin Phalen, Senior VP, Divisional
Sarena Burch, Senior VP, Subsidiary
Kenneth Jackson, Senior VP

GROWTH PLANS/SPECIAL FEATURES:

SCANA Corporation is an energy-based holding company that has brought power and fuel to homes in the Carolinas and Georgia for over 160 years. Through its subsidiaries, SCANA is engaged in regulated electric and natural gas utility operations and other non-regulated energy-related businesses. South Carolina Electric and Gas Company (SCE&G) is a regulated utility that generates, transmits, distributes and sells electricity to over 698,000 customers in 24 counties, and provides natural gas to approximately 347,000 customers. PSNC Energy is a regulated public utility that purchases, sells and transports natural gas to more than 534,000 residential, commercial and industrial customers. SCANA Energy is a natural gas marketer that serves approximately 450,000 residential, commercial and industrial customers throughout Georgia. Other subsidiaries include SCANA Energy Marketing, Inc., which provides natural gas and energy services; SCANA Services, Inc., which provides administration, management and other services to SCANA subsidiaries; South Carolina Generating Company, Inc., which supplies electricity for SCE&G; and South Carolina Fuel Company, Inc., a fuel supplier for SCE&G. In 2015, the firm sold Carolina Gas Transmission Corporation to Dominion Resources, Inc., and sold SCANA Communications, Inc. to Spirit Communications.

The company offers its employees medical, dental and vision insurance; a retirement plan; and a 401(k) plan.

FINANCIAL DATA: Note: Data for latest year may not have been available at press time.

In U.S. $	2016	2015	2014	2013	2012	2011
Revenue		4,380,000,000	4,951,000,000	4,495,000,000	4,176,000,000	4,409,000,000
R&D Expense						
Operating Income		1,308,000,000	1,007,000,000	910,000,000	859,000,000	813,000,000
Operating Margin %		29.86%	20.33%	20.24%	20.56%	18.43%
SGA Expense						
Net Income		746,000,000	538,000,000	471,000,000	420,000,000	387,000,000
Operating Cash Flow		1,059,000,000	730,000,000	1,050,000,000	839,000,000	811,000,000
Capital Expenditure		1,153,000,000	1,092,000,000	1,106,000,000	1,077,000,000	884,000,000
EBITDA		1,871,000,000	1,546,000,000	1,441,000,000	1,309,000,000	1,233,000,000
Return on Assets %		4.38%	3.36%	3.16%	2.98%	2.92%
Return on Equity %		14.30%	11.14%	10.68%	10.44%	10.19%
Debt to Equity		1.08	1.10	1.15	1.19	1.18

CONTACT INFORMATION:

Phone: 803 217-9000   Fax: 803 343-2389
Toll-Free: 800-251-7234
Address: 100 SCANA Pkwy., Cayce, SC 29033 United States

SALARIES/BONUSES:

Top Exec. Salary: $1,202,590   Bonus: $
Second Exec. Salary: $138,462   Bonus: $500,000

STOCK TICKER/OTHER:

Stock Ticker: SCG   Exchange: NYS
Employees: 5,829   Fiscal Year Ends: 12/31
Parent Company:

OTHER THOUGHTS:

Estimated Female Officers or Directors: 4

Hot Spot for Advancement for Women/Minorities: Y

Science Applications International Corp (SAIC)   www.saic.com

NAIC Code: 541512

TYPES OF BUSINESS:
IT Consulting
IT Infrastructure Management
Research & Development
Software Development
Engineering

BRANDS/DIVISIONS/AFFILIATES:
Scitor Holdings Inc

CONTACTS: *Note: Officers with more than one job title may be intentionally listed here more than once.*
Anthony Moraco, CEO
John Hartley, CFO
Edward Sanderson, Chairman of the Board
Maria Bishop, Controller
Steven Mahon, Executive VP
Paul Greiner, Other Corporate Officer
Kimberly Admire, Other Executive Officer
Nazzic Keene, President, Divisional
Douglas Wagoner, President, Divisional

GROWTH PLANS/SPECIAL FEATURES:
Science Applications International Corporation (SAIC) provides technical, engineering and enterprise IT services to commercial operations and government agencies. The company's clients include all four branches of the U.S. military (Army, Air Force, Navy and Marines), the U.S. Defense Logistics Agency, the National Aeronautics and Space Administration, the U.S. Department of State and the U.S. Department of Homeland Security. In 2015, 90% of total revenues were derived from contracts with the U.S. government or from subcontracts with other contractors engaged in work for the U.S. government, all of which were entities located in the U.S. The firm offers services in five areas: technology solutions, which include big data and analytics, cybersecurity, IT managed services, cloud, software and mobility services and network & communications; mission, SETA & program support, which consists of systems engineering, advisory and business transformation services; simulation and training; logistics & supply chain, which includes wholesale and retail distribution, aftermarkets parts distribution, product support & sustainment and proprietary software; and crisis management and security, which consists of critical infrastructure, force protection, public safety communications and security & surveillance. In 2015, the firm acquired Scitor Holdings, Inc.

FINANCIAL DATA: *Note: Data for latest year may not have been available at press time.*

In U.S. $	2016	2015	2014	2013	2012	2011
Revenue	4,315,000,000	3,885,000,000	4,121,000,000	11,173,000,000	10,587,000,000	10,798,000,000
R&D Expense						
Operating Income	227,000,000	240,000,000	183,000,000	734,000,000	311,000,000	929,000,000
Operating Margin %	5.26%	6.17%	4.44%	6.56%	2.93%	8.60%
SGA Expense	158,000,000	95,000,000	92,000,000	592,000,000	670,000,000	495,000,000
Net Income	117,000,000	141,000,000	113,000,000	526,000,000	56,000,000	611,000,000
Operating Cash Flow	226,000,000	277,000,000	183,000,000	343,000,000	769,000,000	717,000,000
Capital Expenditure	20,000,000	22,000,000	16,000,000	48,000,000	65,000,000	73,000,000
EBITDA	289,000,000	261,000,000	196,000,000	865,000,000	435,000,000	1,043,000,000
Return on Assets %	6.64%	9.91%	3.08%	8.38%	.83%	
Return on Equity %	32.27%	39.05%	7.60%	22.58%	2.71%	
Debt to Equity	2.66	1.32	1.29	0.49	0.63	

CONTACT INFORMATION:
Phone: 703 676-4300   Fax:
Toll-Free:
Address: 1710 SAIC Dr., McLean, VA 22102 United States

STOCK TICKER/OTHER:
Stock Ticker: SAIC
Employees: 13,000
Parent Company:
Exchange: NYS
Fiscal Year Ends: 01/31

SALARIES/BONUSES:
Top Exec. Salary: $985,577   Bonus: $
Second Exec. Salary: $570,192   Bonus: $

OTHER THOUGHTS:
Estimated Female Officers or Directors: 5
Hot Spot for Advancement for Women/Minorities: Y

Scotts Miracle-Gro Co (The)

NAIC Code: 325320

www.scottsmiraclegro.com/

TYPES OF BUSINESS:

Horticulture & Turf Products Manufacturer
Fertilizers
Herbicides
Plant Foods
Lawn Services
Outdoor & Garden Products
Plants & Seeds
Mowers & Tractors

BRANDS/DIVISIONS/AFFILIATES:

EverGreen
Fertiligene
Miracle-Gro Patch Magic
Scotts
Turf Builder EdgeGuard
Scotts OxiClean
General Hydroponics Inc
Bio-Organic Solutions Inc

CONTACTS: Note: Officers with more than one job title may be intentionally listed here more than once.

James Hagedorn, CEO
Thomas Coleman, CFO
Jim Gimeson, COO, Divisional
Michael Lukemire, COO
Denise Stump, Executive VP, Divisional
Ivan Smith, Executive VP

GROWTH PLANS/SPECIAL FEATURES:

The Scotts Miracle-Gro Co. (SMG) is a marketer of do-it
yourself (DIY) lawn, garden and home protection products t
consumers globally. Its products are divided into three
categories: lawn care, gardening & landscaping and controls
The lawn care division is designed to help consumers obtai
and enjoy the lawn they want. Internationally, products withi
this category include brands such as EverGreen, Fertiligene
Substral, Miracle-Gro Patch Magic, Weedol, Pathclear, KB an
Celaflor. This division also includes spreaders and othe
durables under the Scotts brand name, including Turf Builde
EdgeGuard spreaders, Snap spreaders and Handy Green
handheld spreaders. The firm also markets outdoor cleaner
under the Scotts OxiClean brand name. The gardening &
landscape division is designed to help consumers grow & enjo
flower and vegetable gardens, as well as beautiful landscape
areas. This category also includes the company's hydroponi
gardening. The controls division is designed to help consumer
protect their homes from pests and maintain external hom
areas. In 2015, the firm acquired General Hydroponics, Inc., a
manufacturer of hydroponic nutrients and systems; and Bio
Organic Solutions, Inc., a manufacturer of potting soil, so
amendments, soilless mediums, dry fertilizers and compost fo
outdoor gardening and indoor hydroponics. In April 2016, the
company sold subsidiary Scotts LawnService to TruGreer
which provided residential & commercial lawn care, tree &
shrub care and pest control services in the U.S.

Employees receive medical, dental, vision and prescription
drug coverage; fitness club reimbursement; flexible spending
accounts; life insurance; an employee assistance plan; an
adoption assistance.

FINANCIAL DATA: Note: Data for latest year may not have been available at press time.

In U.S. $	2016	2015	2014	2013	2012	2011
Revenue		3,016,500,000	2,841,300,000	2,816,500,000	2,826,100,000	2,835,700,000
R&D Expense						
Operating Income		294,600,000	314,600,000	313,200,000	243,600,000	247,000,000
Operating Margin %		9.76%	11.07%	11.12%	8.61%	8.71%
SGA Expense		698,400,000	680,500,000	661,100,000	713,500,000	699,900,000
Net Income		159,800,000	166,500,000	161,100,000	106,500,000	167,900,000
Operating Cash Flow		246,900,000	240,900,000	342,000,000	153,400,000	122,100,000
Capital Expenditure		361,700,000	87,600,000	60,100,000	69,400,000	72,700,000
EBITDA		363,600,000	368,300,000	379,300,000	306,000,000	307,500,000
Return on Assets %		6.96%	8.33%	8.03%	5.16%	7.96%
Return on Equity %		27.21%	26.34%	24.55%	18.33%	25.35%
Debt to Equity		1.65	1.25	0.67	1.29	1.41

CONTACT INFORMATION:

Phone: 937 644-0011   Fax: 937 644-7614
Toll-Free:
Address: 14111 Scottslawn Rd., Marysville, OH 43041 United States

STOCK TICKER/OTHER:

Stock Ticker: SMG
Employees: 7,900
Parent Company:

Exchange: NYS
Fiscal Year Ends: 09/30

SALARIES/BONUSES:

Top Exec. Salary:
$1,100,000
Second Exec. Salary:
$616,250

Bonus: $

Bonus: $

OTHER THOUGHTS:

Estimated Female Officers or Directors: 3

Hot Spot for Advancement for Women/Minorities: Y

Select Comfort Corporation

www.selectcomfort.com

NAIC Code: 337910

TYPES OF BUSINESS:

Mattress Manufacturing

BRANDS/DIVISIONS/AFFILIATES:

DualAir
Sleep Number
Classic Series
Performance Series
Innovation Series
Memory Foam Series
x12 Series
Select Comfort

CONTACTS:
Note: Officers with more than one job title may be intentionally listed here more than once.

Shelly Ibach, CEO
Jean-Michel Valette, Chairman of the Board
Robert Poirier, Chief Accounting Officer
Joseph Saklad, Chief Information Officer
Kevin Brown, Chief Marketing Officer
Mark Kimball, Chief Risk Officer
Suresh Krishna, COO, Divisional
Andrew Carlin, Executive VP
Melissa Barra, Other Executive Officer
Patricia Dirks, Other Executive Officer
Andrea Bloomquist, Other Executive Officer
David Callen, Senior VP

GROWTH PLANS/SPECIAL FEATURES:

Select Comfort Corporation was founded as a Minnesota-based corporation in 1987, and its business is to develop, manufacture, market and distribute adjustable-firmness beds and other sleep-related accessory products. The DualAir technology of its proprietary Sleep Number bed allows adjustable firmness on each side of the mattress and provides a sleep surface. In addition, the company markets and sells accessories and other sleep related products which focus on providing personalized comfort to complement the Sleep Number bed. The company offers Sleep Number beds in five series to help consumers choose the bed that is best for them- The Sleep Number bed Classic Series is the classic design with personal adjustability, and includes Sleep Number c2 and c4 models. The Sleep Number bed Performance Series features comfort and value, and includes the Sleep Number p5 and p6 models. The Sleep Number bed Innovation Series offers personalized comfort combined with leading innovations in sleep technology, and includes the Sleep Number i8 and i10 models. The Memory Foam Series is breathable and contouring, and includes the Sleep Number m6 and m7 models. The Sleep Number x12 Series bed features the integration of multiple technology options, including Select's FlexFit 3 adjustable base and its SleepIQ technology, which monitor each individual's sleep patterns. The company uses information technology systems to operate, analyze and manage its business, to reduce operating costs and to enhance its customers' experience. Sleep Number beds are only sold at Sleep Number stores. Select Comfort has a number of other registered trademarks, including Double Arrow logo, Select Comfort, Know Better Sleep, ComfortFit, CoolFit LuxFit and PillowFit. In June 2016, Select Comfort opened its first store in Alaska, and its first outside the lower 48 U.S. states, in the city of Anchorage.

FINANCIAL DATA:
Note: Data for latest year may not have been available at press time.

In U.S. $	2016	2015	2014	2013	2012	2011
Revenue		1,213,699,000	1,156,757,000	960,171,000	934,978,000	743,203,000
R&D Expense		15,971,000	8,233,000	9,478,000	6,194,000	4,175,000
Operating Income		75,096,000	101,746,000	90,688,000	119,787,000	90,453,000
Operating Margin %		6.18%	8.79%	9.44%	12.81%	12.17%
SGA Expense		649,684,000	596,871,000	501,996,000	470,417,000	375,608,000
Net Income		50,519,000	67,974,000	60,081,000	78,094,000	60,478,000
Operating Cash Flow		107,942,000	144,468,000	88,105,000	100,626,000	91,046,000
Capital Expenditure		85,586,000	76,594,000	76,811,000	51,593,000	23,527,000
EBITDA		122,726,000	141,555,000	121,874,000	140,498,000	104,151,000
Return on Assets %		10.23%	15.88%	16.60%	25.82%	27.95%
Return on Equity %		21.08%	28.19%	28.68%	48.34%	64.55%
Debt to Equity						

CONTACT INFORMATION:

Phone: 763 551-7000   Fax: 763 694-3300
Toll-Free:
Address: 9800 59th Avenue North, Minneapolis, MN 55442 United States

STOCK TICKER/OTHER:

Stock Ticker: SCSS
Employees: 3,484
Parent Company:

Exchange: NAS
Fiscal Year Ends: 12/31

SALARIES/BONUSES:

Top Exec. Salary: $779,231   Bonus: $
Second Exec. Salary: $396,835   Bonus: $

OTHER THOUGHTS:

Estimated Female Officers or Directors:
Hot Spot for Advancement for Women/Minorities:

Select Medical Holdings Corporation

www.selectmedicalcorp.com

NAIC Code: 622310

TYPES OF BUSINESS:

Extended Care Hospitals
Long-Term Acute Care
Outpatient Rehabilitation Clinics
Contract Therapy Services
Medical Equipment Distribution
Billing Services
Recruiting

BRANDS/DIVISIONS/AFFILIATES:

Select Medical Corporation
SSM WorkHealth
Physiotherapy Associates Holdings Inc

CONTACTS: Note: Officers with more than one job title may be intentionally listed here more than once.

David Chernow, CEO
Martin Jackson, CFO
Robert Ortenzio, Chairman of the Board
Scott Romberger, Chief Accounting Officer
Rocco Ortenzio, Co-Founder
Michael Tarvin, Executive VP
John Saich, Executive VP
Robert Breighner, Other Corporate Officer

GROWTH PLANS/SPECIAL FEATURES:

Select Medical Holdings Corporation, through its subsidiary Select Medical Corporation, operates specialty acute care hospitals for long-term stay patients in the U.S. The firm operates 127 specialty hospitals in 27 states, and 1,038 outpatient rehabilitation clinics in 31 states and the District of Columbia. Select Medical's business is divided between specialty hospitals and outpatient rehabilitation. The company's hospitals treat patients with complex medical conditions, such as respiratory failure, neuromuscular disorders, cardiac disorders, renal disorders and cancer. The majority of Select Medical's specialty hospitals are located in leased space within a host general hospital. The firm's outpatient rehabilitation segment is designed to help patients minimize physical and cognitive impairments and maximize functional ability. Services at its clinics include physical, occupational and speech rehabilitation programs, work injury prevention and management, sports performance and athletic training services. In addition, the company provides clinical program development, billing support, staff retention strategies, training and assistance with equipment. In 2016, the firm sold its contract therapy business to an affiliate of Encore Rehabilitation Services LLC for $65 million; acquired SSM WorkHealth based in St. Louis, Missouri; and acquired Physiotherapy Associates Holdings, Inc. That same year, Select transferred a hospital in Atlanta, Georgia to Kindred Healthcare, Inc.; and Kindred transferred a hospital in San Antonio, Texas to Select.

Employee benefits include health, dental, vision and prescription coverage; life insurance; short- and long-term disability; tuition reimbursement; and a 401(k).

FINANCIAL DATA: Note: Data for latest year may not have been available at press time.

In U.S. $	2016	2015	2014	2013	2012	2011
Revenue		3,742,736,000	3,065,017,000	2,975,648,000	2,948,969,000	2,804,507,000
R&D Expense						
Operating Income		274,790,000	284,476,000	301,436,000	336,859,000	310,719,000
Operating Margin %		7.34%	9.28%	10.13%	11.42%	11.07%
SGA Expense		92,052,000	85,247,000	76,921,000	66,194,000	62,354,000
Net Income		130,736,000	120,627,000	114,390,000	148,230,000	107,846,000
Operating Cash Flow		208,415,000	170,642,000	192,523,000	298,682,000	217,128,000
Capital Expenditure		182,642,000	95,246,000	73,660,000	68,185,000	46,016,000
EBITDA		426,229,000	357,597,000	349,557,000	401,811,000	354,463,000
Return on Assets %		3.45%	4.08%	4.10%	5.35%	3.92%
Return on Equity %		15.87%	15.37%	15.21%	19.25%	13.42%
Debt to Equity		2.54	2.08	1.81	2.03	1.68

CONTACT INFORMATION:

Phone: 717 972-1100   Fax:
Toll-Free: 888-735-6332
Address: 4714 Old Gettysburg Rd., Mechanicsburg, PA 17055 United States

STOCK TICKER/OTHER:

Stock Ticker: SEM
Employees: 31,200
Parent Company:

Exchange: NYS
Fiscal Year Ends: 12/31

SALARIES/BONUSES:

Top Exec. Salary: $995,000   Bonus: $
Second Exec. Salary: $950,000   Bonus: $

OTHER THOUGHTS:

Estimated Female Officers or Directors: 1
Hot Spot for Advancement for Women/Minorities:

Service Corporation International Inc   www.sci-corp.com

NAIC Code: 812210

TYPES OF BUSINESS:
Funeral Homes and Funeral Services

BRANDS/DIVISIONS/AFFILIATES:
Dignity Memorial
Dignity Planning
National Cremation Society
Advantage Funderal Cremation Services
Funeraria del Angel
Making Everlasting Memories
Neptune Society
Trident Society

CONTACTS: *Note: Officers with more than one job title may be intentionally listed here more than once.*
Thomas Ryan, CEO
Tammy Moore, Chief Accounting Officer
Michael Webb, COO
Robert Waltrip, Founder
Gregory Sangalis, General Counsel
Sumner Waring, Senior VP, Divisional
Steven Tidwell, Senior VP, Divisional
Eric Tanzberger, Senior VP

GROWTH PLANS/SPECIAL FEATURES:
Service Corporation International, Inc. is a provider of deathcare products and services in North America. The company's funeral service and cemetery operations consist of funeral service locations, cemeteries, funeral service/cemetery combination locations, crematoria and related businesses. The firm provides all professional services relating to funerals and cremations, including the use of funeral facilities and motor vehicles and preparation and embalming services. Funeral related merchandise, including caskets, burial vaults, cremation receptacles, flowers and other ancillary products and services are sold at funeral service locations. Service Corporation's cemeteries provide cemetery property interment rights, including mausoleum spaces, lots and lawn crypts, and sell cemetery related merchandise and services, including stone and bronze memorials, burial vaults, casket and cremation memorialization products, merchandise installations and burial openings and closings. The firm's funeral segment also includes the operation of twelve funeral homes in Germany that it intends to exit when economic values and conditions are conducive to a sale. Service Corporation has branded the company's funeral operations in North America under the name Dignity Memorial. Other brands include Dignity Planning, National Cremation Society, Advantage Funeral and Cremation Services, Funeraria del Angel, Making Everlasting Memories, Neptune Society and Trident Society.

FINANCIAL DATA: *Note: Data for latest year may not have been available at press time.*

In U.S. $	2016	2015	2014	2013	2012	2011
Revenue		2,986,380,000	2,994,012,000	2,556,382,000	2,410,481,000	2,316,040,000
R&D Expense						
Operating Income		550,279,000	607,549,000	388,170,000	399,789,000	363,699,000
Operating Margin %		18.42%	20.29%	15.18%	16.58%	15.70%
SGA Expense		128,188,000	184,877,000	155,136,000	123,905,000	103,860,000
Net Income		233,772,000	172,469,000	143,848,000	152,546,000	144,903,000
Operating Cash Flow		472,186,000	317,355,000	384,709,000	369,246,000	388,112,000
Capital Expenditure		150,986,000	144,499,000	113,084,000	115,628,000	118,375,000
EBITDA		778,570,000	817,252,000	580,884,000	569,807,000	543,102,000
Return on Assets %		1.97%	1.38%	1.27%	1.60%	1.56%
Return on Equity %		18.31%	12.39%	10.43%	11.15%	10.09%
Debt to Equity		2.59	2.16	2.23	1.42	1.33

CONTACT INFORMATION:
Phone: 713 522-5141   Fax: 713 525-5586
Toll-Free:
Address: 1929 Allen Parkway, Houston, TX 77019 United States

STOCK TICKER/OTHER:
Stock Ticker: SCI   Exchange: NYS
Employees: 23,785   Fiscal Year Ends: 12/31
Parent Company:

SALARIES/BONUSES:
Top Exec. Salary: $1,241,154   Bonus: $
Second Exec. Salary: $988,616   Bonus: $

OTHER THOUGHTS:
Estimated Female Officers or Directors:

Hot Spot for Advancement for Women/Minorities:

ServiceNow Inc

www.service-now.com

NAIC Code: 0

TYPES OF BUSINESS:

Cloud-Based Workflow Software

BRANDS/DIVISIONS/AFFILIATES:

Itapp

CONTACTS: *Note: Officers with more than one job title may be intentionally listed here more than once.*

Frank Slootman, CEO
Michael Scarpelli, CFO
Paul Barber, Chairman of the Board
Daniel McGee, COO
Frederic Luddy, Director
David Schneider, Other Executive Officer

GROWTH PLANS/SPECIAL FEATURES:

ServiceNow, Inc. is a provider of cloud-based services tha automate enterprise IT operations. The company's servic includes a suite of applications built on its proprietary platforr that automates workflow and provides integration betwee related business processes. The firm focuses on transformin enterprise IT by automating and standardizing busines processes and consolidating IT across the global enterprise Organizations deploy its service to create a single system c record for enterprise IT, lower operational costs and enhanc efficiency. Additionally, customers use its extensible platforr to build custom applications for automating activities unique t their business requirements. ServiceNow helps transform l organizations from reactive, manual and task-oriented, to prc active, automated and service-oriented organizations. Th company's on-demand service enables organizations to defin their IT strategy, design the systems and infrastructure that wi support that strategy, and implement, manage and automat that infrastructure throughout its lifecycle while leveraging it self-service capability. The firm provides a broad set c integrated functionality that is highly configurable an extensible and can be efficiently implemented and upgradec Its multi-instance architecture has proven scalability for globa enterprises as well as having advantages in security, reliabilit and deployment location. The company offers its service unde a Software-as-a-Service (SaaS) business model. Customer can rapidly deploy its service in a modular fashion, allowin them to solve immediate business needs and access, configur and build new applications as their requirements evolve. Th firm's service, which is accessed through an intuitive web based interface, can be easily configured to adapt to custome workflow and processes. In April 2016, the firm agreed t acquire ITApp, a cloud management software developer.

FINANCIAL DATA: *Note: Data for latest year may not have been available at press time.*

In U.S. $	2016	2015	2014	2013	2012	2011
Revenue		1,005,480,000	682,563,000	424,650,000	243,712,000	92,641,000
R&D Expense		217,389,000	148,258,000	78,678,000	39,333,000	7,004,000
Operating Income		-166,365,000	-151,835,000	-66,267,000	-37,584,000	10,560,000
Operating Margin %		-16.54%	-22.24%	-15.60%	-15.42%	11.39%
SGA Expense		625,043,000	437,364,000	256,980,000	137,954,000	43,502,000
Net Income		-198,426,000	-179,387,000	-73,708,000	-37,348,000	9,830,000
Operating Cash Flow		315,091,000	138,900,000	81,746,000	48,766,000	37,468,000
Capital Expenditure		89,231,000	54,379,000	55,321,000	42,066,000	8,733,000
EBITDA		-101,559,000	-109,776,000	-42,115,000	-24,078,000	12,032,000
Return on Assets %		-12.27%	-13.83%	-8.95%	-7.81%	12.27%
Return on Equity %		-39.86%	-43.59%	-23.11%	-15.34%	
Debt to Equity						

CONTACT INFORMATION:

Phone: 408-501-8550   Fax:
Toll-Free:
Address: 2225 Lawson Lane, Santa Clara, CA 95054 United States

STOCK TICKER/OTHER:

Stock Ticker: NOW   Exchange: NYS
Employees: 3,686   Fiscal Year Ends: 12/31
Parent Company:

SALARIES/BONUSES:

Top Exec. Salary: $450,000   Bonus: $
Second Exec. Salary: Bonus: $
$350,000

OTHER THOUGHTS:

Estimated Female Officers or Directors:
Hot Spot for Advancement for Women/Minorities:

Sherwin-Williams Company (The)

www.sherwin-williams.com

NAIC Code: 325510

TYPES OF BUSINESS:

Paints & Coatings Manufacturing
Retail Paint Stores
Wall Coverings
Automotive Finishing Products
Design Consulting

BRANDS/DIVISIONS/AFFILIATES:

Sherwin-Williams
Sayerlack
Pratt & Lambert
Martin Senour
Dutch Boy
Thompson's
Minwax
Krylon

CONTACTS: *Note: Officers with more than one job title may be intentionally listed here more than once.*

John Morikis, CEO
Sean Hennessy, CFO
Christopher Connor, Chairman of the Board
Allen Mistysyn, Chief Accounting Officer
Catherine Kilbane, General Counsel
Joel Baxter, General Manager, Divisional
Mike Conway, Other Corporate Officer
David Sewell, President, Divisional
Robert Davisson, President, Divisional
Robert Wells, Senior VP, Divisional
Thomas Gilligan, Senior VP, Divisional
Timothy Knight, Senior VP, Divisional

GROWTH PLANS/SPECIAL FEATURES:

The Sherwin-Williams Company is one of the largest international manufacturers, distributors and retailers of paint and related products to professional, industrial, commercial and retail customers. The company operates in four segments: paint stores group, consumer group, global finishes group and Latin America coatings group. The paint stores group consists of 4,086 company-operated stores, which sell Sherwin-Williams brand architectural paint, coatings and other associated products and brands. Several subsidiaries operate under this division, including Duron, Inc., a Maryland paint producer. It has operations in the U.S., Canada, Puerto Rico, Jamaica, St. Maarten, Curacao, Trinidad and Tobago and the Virgin Islands. This division also sells industrial products, marine products and finishes for original equipment manufacturers (OEM). The consumer group produces and distributes paint, coatings and related products to third-party customers and to the paint stores group (which represented 63% of the consumer group's sales in 2015). The global finishes group, through 296 branches, manufactures, licenses, distributes and sells paints and coatings, industrial and marine products, automotive finishes, refinish products and OEM coatings throughout Europe, North and South American and Asia. The Latin America coatings group develops, licenses, manufactures and sells architectural paint and coatings, OEM product finishes and protective and marine products in North and South America. The segment maintains 291 company-operated stores. In all segments, the company's varnish, applicators, paint, finishes and coatings are marketed under various name brands, including several private labels such as Sherwin-Williams, Sayerlack, Pratt & Lambert, Martin Senour, Dutch Boy, Thompson's, Minwax and Krylon. In March 2016, Sherwin-Williams agreed to acquire rival Valspar Corp. for approximately $9 billion.

FINANCIAL DATA: *Note: Data for latest year may not have been available at press time.*

In U.S. $	2016	2015	2014	2013	2012	2011
Revenue		11,339,300,000	11,129,530,000	10,185,530,000	9,534,462,000	8,765,699,000
R&D Expense						
Operating Income		1,645,708,000	1,304,036,000	1,146,366,000	946,578,000	775,525,000
Operating Margin %		14.51%	11.71%	11.25%	9.92%	8.84%
SGA Expense		3,913,518,000	3,822,966,000	3,467,681,000	3,259,648,000	2,963,545,000
Net Income		1,053,849,000	865,887,000	752,561,000	631,034,000	441,860,000
Operating Cash Flow		1,447,463,000	1,081,528,000	1,083,766,000	887,886,000	735,812,000
Capital Expenditure		234,340,000	200,545,000	166,680,000	157,112,000	153,801,000
EBITDA		1,809,319,000	1,521,376,000	1,336,466,000	1,129,299,000	964,949,000
Return on Assets %		18.25%	14.32%	11.92%	11.00%	8.49%
Return on Equity %		112.57%	63.42%	43.94%	41.41%	32.14%
Debt to Equity		2.21	1.12	0.64	0.96	0.47

CONTACT INFORMATION:

Phone: 216 566-2000   Fax:
Toll-Free: 800-474-3794
Address: 101 W. Prospect Ave., Cleveland, OH 44115 United States

STOCK TICKER/OTHER:

Stock Ticker: SHW   Exchange: NYS
Employees: 40,706   Fiscal Year Ends: 12/31
Parent Company:

SALARIES/BONUSES:

Top Exec. Salary: Bonus: $
$1,221,987
Second Exec. Salary: Bonus: $
$877,054

OTHER THOUGHTS:

Estimated Female Officers or Directors: 2

Hot Spot for Advancement for Women/Minorities: Y

Smithfield Foods Inc

www.smithfieldfoods.com

NAIC Code: 311612

TYPES OF BUSINESS:

Meat Processing, Pork
Hog Production

BRANDS/DIVISIONS/AFFILIATES:

Smithfield Packing Company Inc (The)
John Morrell Food Group
Farmland Foods Inc
Murphy-Brown LLC
Campofrio Food Group SA
WH Group Limited

CONTACTS: *Note: Officers with more than one job title may be intentionally listed here more than once.*

C. Larry Pope, CEO
Kenneth M. Sullivan, COO
Glenn T. Nunziata, CFO
William B. Brunt, Sr. VP-Mktg.
Mark Garrett, Chief People Officer
Julia Anderson, CIO
Henry L. Morris, Sr. Corp. VP-Eng.
Michael H. Cole, Chief Legal Officer
Henry L. Morris, Sr. Corp. VP-Oper.
Keira L. Lombardo, VP-Corp. Comm.
Keira L. Lombardo, VP-Investor Rel.
Jeffrey A. Deel, Corp. Controller
George H. Richter, Pres.
Parul Stevens, VP-Risk Mgmt.
Timothy Dykstra, Treas.
Dennis H. Treacy, Chief Sustainability Officer
Dariusz Nowakowski, Pres., Smithfield Europe

GROWTH PLANS/SPECIAL FEATURES:

Smithfield Foods, Inc. is a leading hog producer and one of the largest processors and suppliers of fresh pork and processed meat products in the U.S. and internationally. The firm conducts its operations via four segments: pork, hog production, international and corporate. The pork segment operates through three primary subsidiaries: The Smithfield Packing Company, Inc.; John Morrell Food Group; and Farmland Foods, Inc. Together, these companies produce a range of fresh pork and packaged meats products in the U.S. and markets them nationwide and to numerous foreign markets, including China, Japan, Mexico, Russia and Canada. The segment operates approximately 40 processing plants. The hog production segment, which operates through Murphy-Brown LLC, is comprised of the company's hog production facilities in the U.S. It operates numerous hog production facilities, with approximately 894,000 sows producing about 16.2 million market hogs annually. The international segment includes the company's meat processing and distribution facilities in Poland, Romania and the U.K.; interests in meat processing operations in Western Europe and Mexico, including a 37% interest in Campofrio Food Group SA; hog production operations in Poland and Romania; and interests in hog production operations in Mexico. The corporate segment provides management and administrative support to the other segments. The firm is a subsidiary of WH Group Limited.

FINANCIAL DATA: *Note: Data for latest year may not have been available at press time.*

In U.S. $	2016	2015	2014	2013	2012	2011
Revenue		14,438,400,000	15,031,300,000	13,221,100,000	13,094,299,648	12,202,699,776
R&D Expense						
Operating Income						
Operating Margin %						
SGA Expense						
Net Income		556,100,000		183,800,000	361,300,000	521,000,000
Operating Cash Flow						
Capital Expenditure						
EBITDA						
Return on Assets %						
Return on Equity %						
Debt to Equity						

CONTACT INFORMATION:

Phone: 757 365-3000   Fax: 757 365-3017
Toll-Free: 888-366-6767
Address: 200 Commerce St., Smithfield, VA 23430 United States

STOCK TICKER/OTHER:

Stock Ticker: Subsidiary   Exchange:
Employees: 48,000   Fiscal Year Ends: 04/30
Parent Company: WH Group Lmited

SALARIES/BONUSES:

Top Exec. Salary: $ Bonus: $
Second Exec. Salary: $ Bonus: $

OTHER THOUGHTS:

Estimated Female Officers or Directors: 1
Hot Spot for Advancement for Women/Minorities: Y

Sodexo Inc

www.sodexousa.com

NAIC Code: 722310

TYPES OF BUSINESS:

Food Service Outsourcing
Facilities Management
Laundry Services
Sports Arena Management
Plant Management
Grounds Keeping
Asset Management
Outsourced Procurement Services

BRANDS/DIVISIONS/AFFILIATES:

Sodexho Group
Sodexo Foundation
Entegra Procurement Services

CONTACTS: Note: Officers with more than one job title may be intentionally listed here more than once.

Michel Landel, CEO
Sian Herbert-Jones, CFO
Elisabeth Carpentier, Group Chief Human Resources Officer
Michel Landel, Pres.
Debbie White, CEO-Sodexo U.K. & Ireland
Pierre Bellon, Chmn.

GROWTH PLANS/SPECIAL FEATURES:

Sodexo, Inc. is the North American subsidiary of French firm Sodexo Group, a global contract foodservice supplier. The company is one of the largest providers of contract food and facilities management services in the U.S., Mexico and Canada, with more than 32,000 sites. In total, it serves 75 million consumers each day. Sodexo offers a wide variety of outsourcing solutions in food service, facilities management, business strategy, wellness, motivation solutions and corporate citizenship. The company provides these services to corporations; health care, long-term care and retirement centers; conference centers; schools; college campuses; military bases; and government and remote sites. Services to college stadiums and arenas involve concession stands, catering, physical plant management and sports field management. The firm also has a contract to manage the food operations for the U.S. Marine Corps, which includes meal preparation, operation of clean dining facilities and bringing national brands to Navy bases, Army bases and international locations. In addition, the company sponsors the Sodexo Foundation, an independent charitable organization that supports initiatives addressing the problems of hunger in children and families. The Entegra Procurement Services unit provides food and supplies purchasing management for 10,000 clients in hospitality and other industries.

The firm offers employees a pension plan; a 401(k) savings plan; health and family care spending accounts; employee assistance plans; tuition reimbursement; and medical, life, disability, dental and vision insurance.

FINANCIAL DATA: Note: Data for latest year may not have been available at press time.

In U.S. $	2016	2015	2014	2013	2012	2011
Revenue		9,200,000,000	8,800,000,000	9,350,000,000	9,200,000,000	9,000,000,000
R&D Expense						
Operating Income						
Operating Margin %						
SGA Expense						
Net Income						
Operating Cash Flow						
Capital Expenditure						
EBITDA						
Return on Assets %						
Return on Equity %						
Debt to Equity						

CONTACT INFORMATION:

Phone: 301-987-4000   Fax: 301-987-4438
Toll-Free: 800-763-3946
Address: 9801 Washingtonian Blvd., Gaithersburg, MD 20878 United States

STOCK TICKER/OTHER:

Stock Ticker: Subsidiary   Exchange:
Employees: 132,600   Fiscal Year Ends: 08/31
Parent Company: Sodexo Group

SALARIES/BONUSES:

Top Exec. Salary: $ Bonus: $
Second Exec. Salary: $ Bonus: $

OTHER THOUGHTS:

Estimated Female Officers or Directors: 2
Hot Spot for Advancement for Women/Minorities: Y

Sales, profits and employees may be estimates. Financial information, benefits and other data can change quickly and may vary from those stated here.

Sonoco Products Company

www.sonoco.com

NAIC Code: 322220

TYPES OF BUSINESS:

Coated and Laminated Packaging Paper Manufacturing

BRANDS/DIVISIONS/AFFILIATES:

Graffo Paranaense de Embalagens SA
iPS Studio

CONTACTS: Note: Officers with more than one job title may be intentionally listed here more than once.

M. Sanders, CEO
Allan McLeland, Vice President, Divisional
Barry Saunders, CFO
Harris Deloach, Chairman of the Board
Bond Ritchie, Secretary
Robert Tiede, Senior VP, Divisional
Kevin Mahoney, Senior VP, Divisional
R. Coker, Vice President, Divisional
Rodger Fuller, Vice President, Divisional
Roger Schrum, Vice President, Divisional
Arthur Vicki, Vice President, Divisional
Robert Puechl, Vice President, Divisional
Marty Pignone, Vice President, Divisional
Marcy Thompson, Vice President, Divisional
Adam Wood, Vice President, Geographical
James Harrell, Vice President, Geographical

GROWTH PLANS/SPECIAL FEATURES:

Sonoco Products Company manufactures industrial an consumer packaging products and provides various packagin services, with 330 locations in 34 countries. Its operations ar divided into four segments: consumer packaging, paper industrial converted products (PICP), display & packaging an protective solutions. Consumer packaging, which accounts fo 43% of sales revenue, consists of 86 plants located worldwid which produces packaging solutions such as round composit cans, shaped rigid paperboard containers, fiber caulk/adhesiv tubes, as well as aluminum, steel & peelable membrane easy open closures for composite and metal cans; plastic bottles jars, jugs, cups and trays; and printed flexible packaging an rotogravure cylinder engraving. PICP accounts for 35% c sales revenue and consists of 182 plants which provides th primary raw material for the company's fiber-based packaging Sonoco uses approximately 56% of the paper this divisio manufactures and the remainder is sold to third parties. Thi vertical integration is supported by 20 paper mills with 30 pape machines and 23 recycling facilities throughout the world Display & packaging accounts for 12% of sales revenue an consists of 26 plants which produce point-of-purchas displays, custom packaging, retail packaging and printe backer cards. This division also provides thermoformed blister and heat sealing equipment, as well as supply chai management and paperboard specialties. Protective solution derives 10% of sales revenue and produces custom engineered, paperboard-based and expanded foam protectiv packaging. This division also produces temperature-assure packaging for pharmaceutical and food products. In 2015, th firm acquired a majority stake (67%) in Graffo Paranaense d Embalagens SA, a Brazilian flexible packaging business. I early 2016, it opened state-of-the-art iPS Studio, a leadin edge research, development and innovation center tha connects consumer and market insights to the invention of ne packaging solutions, all under one roof. iPS stands fo innovative packaging solutions, and is based in Hartsville South Carolina.

FINANCIAL DATA: Note: Data for latest year may not have been available at press time.

In U.S. $	2016	2015	2014	2013	2012	2011
Revenue		4,964,369,000	5,014,534,000	4,848,092,000	4,786,129,000	4,498,932,000
R&D Expense						
Operating Income		382,544,000	391,511,000	361,295,000	347,059,000	322,480,000
Operating Margin %		7.70%	7.80%	7.45%	7.25%	7.16%
SGA Expense		496,241,000	506,996,000	487,171,000	463,715,000	397,477,000
Net Income		250,136,000	239,165,000	219,113,000	196,010,000	217,517,000
Operating Cash Flow		452,930,000	417,915,000	538,027,000	403,915,000	245,275,000
Capital Expenditure		192,295,000	177,076,000	172,442,000	214,862,000	173,372,000
EBITDA		598,080,000	592,978,000	562,153,000	551,591,000	506,109,000
Return on Assets %		6.07%	5.84%	5.37%	4.80%	5.98%
Return on Equity %		16.56%	14.86%	13.69%	13.51%	14.98%
Debt to Equity		0.67	0.79	0.55	0.73	0.87

CONTACT INFORMATION:

Phone: 843 383-7000   Fax: 843 383-7008
Toll-Free:
Address: 1 N. 2nd St., Hartsville, SC 29550 United States

STOCK TICKER/OTHER:

Stock Ticker: SON   Exchange: NYS
Employees: 20,800   Fiscal Year Ends: 12/31
Parent Company:

SALARIES/BONUSES:

Top Exec. Salary: $993,632   Bonus: $
Second Exec. Salary: Bonus: $
$551,928

OTHER THOUGHTS:

Estimated Female Officers or Directors:
Hot Spot for Advancement for Women/Minorities:

Southwest Airlines Co

www.southwest.com

NAIC Code: 481111

TYPES OF BUSINESS:

Airline
Air Freight

BRANDS/DIVISIONS/AFFILIATES:

EarlyBird Check-in

CONTACTS: Note: Officers with more than one job title may be intentionally listed here more than once.

Gary Kelly, CEO
Tammy Romo, CFO
Michael Van De Ven, COO
Thomas Nealon, Executive VP, Divisional
Jeff Lamb, Executive VP, Divisional
Robert Jordan, Executive VP
Mark Shaw, Secretary
Ron Ricks, Vice Chairman of the Board

GROWTH PLANS/SPECIAL FEATURES:

Southwest Airlines Co. is one of the largest U.S. domestic air travel providers, primarily engaged in short haul, high-frequency airline services. The firm operates an all-Boeing 737 fleet, 692 total, serving 97 cities in 40 states throughout the U.S., Washington, D.C., Puerto Rico, Mexico, Jamaica, the Bahamas, Aurba and the Dominican Republic. In 2014, 73% of the company's customers flew nonstop, with an average aircraft trip being 721 miles, with an average duration of approximately two hours. Southwest served 581 nonstop city pairs. The busiest routes include those to Chicago, Las Vegas, Phoenix, Baltimore, Denver, Houston, Dallas, Los Angeles, Oakland and St. Louis. Southwest primarily flies to conveniently located, secondary or downtown airports such as Houston-Hobby, Dallas-Love Field and Chicago-Midway, which are typically less congested than other airlines' hub airports. Southwest employs a point-to-point route system, which allows for more direct nonstop routing, thereby minimizing connections, delays and total trip time. It also offers the EarlyBird Check-in service, which allows customers to reserve a boarding position prior to general check-in for a fee. In December 2014, the firm integrated its wholly-owned subsidiary AirTran Airways into Southwest. In January 2015, the firm announced that it will offer daily nonstop flights to nine cities from Dallas, including Memphis, Milwaukee, and Seattle, and will increase the number of nonstop flights to recently introduced destinations added after the October 2014 expiration of the Wright Amendment restrictions on long-haul flying at the Love Field.

Southwest Airlines' employee benefits include free, discounted and guest passes on Southwest Airlines flights; medical, vision, dental, life and long-term disability insurance; an employee assistance program; 401(K) plan; a profit-sharing plan; and an employee stock purchase plan.

FINANCIAL DATA: Note: Data for latest year may not have been available at press time.

In U.S. $	2016	2015	2014	2013	2012	2011
Revenue		19,820,000,000	18,605,000,000	17,699,000,000	17,088,000,000	15,658,000,000
R&D Expense						
Operating Income		4,116,000,000	2,225,000,000	1,278,000,000	623,000,000	693,000,000
Operating Margin %		20.76%	11.95%	7.22%	3.64%	4.42%
SGA Expense		6,383,000,000	5,434,000,000	5,035,000,000	4,749,000,000	4,371,000,000
Net Income		2,181,000,000	1,136,000,000	754,000,000	421,000,000	178,000,000
Operating Cash Flow		3,238,000,000	2,902,000,000	2,477,000,000	2,064,000,000	1,385,000,000
Capital Expenditure		2,143,000,000	1,828,000,000	1,447,000,000	1,348,000,000	968,000,000
EBITDA		4,584,000,000	2,861,000,000	2,183,000,000	1,655,000,000	1,220,000,000
Return on Assets %		10.50%	5.74%	3.97%	2.29%	1.06%
Return on Equity %		30.86%	16.10%	10.52%	6.07%	2.71%
Debt to Equity		0.36	0.35	0.33	0.46	0.45

CONTACT INFORMATION:

Phone: 214 792-4000   Fax: 214 792-5015
Toll-Free:
Address: 2702 Love Field Dr., Dallas, TX 75235 United States

STOCK TICKER/OTHER:

Stock Ticker: LUV   Exchange: NYS
Employees: 49,583   Fiscal Year Ends: 12/31
Parent Company:

SALARIES/BONUSES:

Top Exec. Salary: $675,000   Bonus: $232,875
Second Exec. Salary: Bonus: $129,720
$468,750

OTHER THOUGHTS:

Estimated Female Officers or Directors: 14
Hot Spot for Advancement for Women/Minorities: Y

Sales, profits and employees may be estimates. Financial information, benefits and other data can change quickly and may vary from those stated here.

Spectrum Health
NAIC Code: 622110

www.spectrumhealth.org

TYPES OF BUSINESS:
General Medical and Surgical Hospitals
Trauma Center
Neonatal Center
Burn Center
Poison Center
HMO
Long-Term Care
Children's Hospital

BRANDS/DIVISIONS/AFFILIATES:
Priority Health

CONTACTS: *Note: Officers with more than one job title may be intentionally listed here more than once.*
Richard C. Breon, CEO
Richard C. Breon, Pres.
Michael P. Freed, CFO
Carrie Manders, Dir.-Public Relations
Patrick O'Hare, CIO
Thomas Malvitz, Chmn.

GROWTH PLANS/SPECIAL FEATURES:
Spectrum Health is one of the largest health systems in western Michigan. The firm's not-for-profit system of care is dedicated to improving the health of families and individuals. Spectrum's organization includes 12 hospitals, 180 ambulatory & service sites, more than 3,400 affiliated physicians and its nationally-recognized health plan, Priority Health. Priority Health has 738,500 members. Spectrum Health provides inpatient and outpatient services throughout Michigan and facilities are located in in cities such as Grand Rapids, Holland, Zeeland, Belding, Reed City, Fremont, Kentwood, Rockford, Cutlerville, Greenville, Wyoming, Big Rapids, Canadian Lakes, East Grand Rapids, Allendale, Hastings, Lake Odessa, Grand Blanc, Grand Haven, Coopersville, Stanwood, Evart and many more. The organization is also West Michigan's largest provider of post-acute care including skilled nursing, long-term acute, home and residential care. Spectrum Health's services include insurance, wellness products, state-of-the-art technology and medical treatments. Major services offered by the firm include cancer, continuing care, diabetes, endocrinology, digestive disease, heart & vascular, neurosciences, orthopaedics, pediatrics, rehabilitation, transplant and women's health.

Employees of the company receive benefits including medical, dental, vision, life, disability and AD&D coverage; flexible spending accounts; retirement plans; employee assistance services; tuition assistance; and paid time off.

FINANCIAL DATA: *Note: Data for latest year may not have been available at press time.*

In U.S. $	2016	2015	2014	2013	2012	2011
Revenue	5,220,515,000	4,625,176,000	4,107,828,000	3,937,360,000	3,849,984,000	3,667,801,000
R&D Expense						
Operating Income						
Operating Margin %						
SGA Expense						
Net Income	212,044,000	367,311,000	147,747,000	212,257,000	144,114,000	73,816,000
Operating Cash Flow						
Capital Expenditure						
EBITDA						
Return on Assets %						
Return on Equity %						
Debt to Equity						

CONTACT INFORMATION:
Phone: 616-391-1774   Fax: 616-391-2780
Toll-Free: 866-989-7999
Address: 100 Michigan St. NE, Grand Rapids, MI 49503 United States

STOCK TICKER/OTHER:
Stock Ticker: Nonprofit
Employees: 23,000
Parent Company:

Exchange:
Fiscal Year Ends: 06/30

SALARIES/BONUSES:
Top Exec. Salary: $ Bonus: $
Second Exec. Salary: $ Bonus: $

OTHER THOUGHTS:
Estimated Female Officers or Directors:
Hot Spot for Advancement for Women/Minorities:

Spirit Aerosystems Holdings Inc

www.spiritaero.com

NAIC Code: 336413

TYPES OF BUSINESS:

Aircraft Fuselage Wing Tail and Similar Assemblies Manufacturing
Aerostructures
Fuselages
Wings & Flight Control Components
Engineering, Design & Materials Testing
Custom Tool Fabrication
Spare Parts & Maintenance Services
Supply Chain Management

BRANDS/DIVISIONS/AFFILIATES:

Onex Corp

CONTACTS: *Note: Officers with more than one job title may be intentionally listed here more than once.*

Sanjay Kapoor, CFO
Robert Johnson, Chairman of the Board
Mark Suchinski, Chief Accounting Officer
Samantha Marnick, Chief Administrative Officer
John Pilla, Chief Technology Officer
Thomas Gentile, Director
Michelle Lohmeier, General Manager, Divisional
Michelle Lohmeie, General Manager, Divisional
Stacy Cozad, Secretary
Heidi Wood, Senior VP, Divisional
Krisstie Kondrotis, Senior VP, Divisional
Duane Hawkins, Senior VP, Divisional
Philip Anderson, Senior VP, Divisional
Ronald Rabe, Senior VP, Divisional
James Sharp, Vice President, Subsidiary

GROWTH PLANS/SPECIAL FEATURES:

Spirit Aerosystems Holdings, Inc. is an independent designer and manufacturer of aircraft parts and aerostructures for commercial and military aircraft. The firm operates through three principal segments: fuselages, propulsion systems and wing systems. The fuselages segment produces forward, mid and rear fuselage sections and offers services that include numerical control programming, materials testing, onsite planning and global supply chain management. The propulsion systems segment primarily produces nacelles (aerodynamic engine enclosures that enhance propulsion installation efficiency, dampen engine noise and provide thrust reversing capabilities), struts/pylons (structures that attach engines to airplane wings) and engine structural components. The wing systems segment produces wings, wing components and flight control surfaces. Spirit Aerosystems is also engaged in tooling, the fabrication of custom tools and the manufacturing of structural components for military aircraft. The firm's tooling capabilities include tool design, computer numerical control (CNC) programming, machining, composite, aluminum and invar tooling. The company offers spare parts and components for all items of which it is the original production supplier and provides maintenance, repair and overhaul work for nacelles, fuselage doors, structural components and modification kits. Spirit Aerosystems is the largest independent supplier of aerostructures to Boeing and one of the largest to Airbus. The company is majority-controlled by Onex Corp. With its headquarters in Wichita, Kansas, the firm operates throughout the U.S., Europe and Asia.

Employee benefits include a company profit sharing bonus; 401(k); relocation benefits; medical, vision and life insurance; health care spending accounts; disability coverage; and tuition assistance.

FINANCIAL DATA: *Note: Data for latest year may not have been available at press time.*

In U.S. $	2016	2015	2014	2013	2012	2011
Revenue		6,643,900,000	6,799,200,000	5,961,000,000	5,397,700,000	4,863,800,000
R&D Expense		27,800,000	29,300,000	34,700,000	34,100,000	35,700,000
Operating Income		863,000,000	354,000,000	-364,300,000	92,300,000	356,100,000
Operating Margin %		12.98%	5.20%	-6.11%	1.71%	7.32%
SGA Expense		220,800,000	233,800,000	200,800,000	172,200,000	159,900,000
Net Income		788,700,000	358,800,000	-621,400,000	34,800,000	192,400,000
Operating Cash Flow		1,289,700,000	361,600,000	260,600,000	544,400,000	-47,300,000
Capital Expenditure		360,100,000	220,200,000	272,600,000	249,000,000	249,700,000
EBITDA		1,041,900,000	526,500,000	-199,400,000	250,500,000	491,900,000
Return on Assets %		14.41%	6.98%	-11.81%	.66%	3.79%
Return on Equity %		42.16%	23.13%	-35.74%	1.75%	10.19%
Debt to Equity		0.51	0.70	0.77	0.58	0.58

CONTACT INFORMATION:

Phone: 316 526-9000   Fax:
Toll-Free: 800-501-7597
Address: 3801 S. Oliver St., Wichita, KS 67210 United States

STOCK TICKER/OTHER:

Stock Ticker: SPR
Employees: 13,496
Parent Company: Onex Corp

Exchange: NYS
Fiscal Year Ends: 12/31

SALARIES/BONUSES:

Top Exec. Salary: Bonus: $
$1,255,284
Second Exec. Salary: Bonus: $250,000
$424,840

OTHER THOUGHTS:

Estimated Female Officers or Directors: 2

Hot Spot for Advancement for Women/Minorities: Y

Spirit Airlines Inc

NAIC Code: 481111

www.spiritair.com

TYPES OF BUSINESS:

Airline
Low-Fare Carrier

BRANDS/DIVISIONS/AFFILIATES:

Free Spirit
Big Front Seat
$9 Fare Club

CONTACTS: Note: Officers with more than one job title may be intentionally listed here more than once.

Edward Christie, CFO
H. Gardner, Chairman of the Board
Edmundo Miranda, Chief Accounting Officer
Robert Fornaro, Director
Thomas Canfield, General Counsel
Martha Villa, Other Executive Officer
John Bendoraitis, Senior VP

GROWTH PLANS/SPECIAL FEATURES:

Spirit Airlines, Inc. is a leading private low-fare airline in the U.S. The company flies to 56 destinations including the U.S, Mexico, the Caribbean, the Bahamas and Central and Latin America and offers over 400 daily flight departures. Its all Airbus fleet currently consists of A321s, A320s and A319s, with an average age of 5.1 years. Approximately 45 A320neo and 10 A321neo aircraft are on order, along with 19 A320s and 1 A321s (which are scheduled for delivery through 2018). The firm also offers personalized packages through both scheduled and charter flights to its destinations. Spirit Airlines reduces it costs by offering typically standard services, such as checked baggage, on an optional, pay-for-service basis. The airline operates a fully integrated Spanish-language customer service plan that includes a web site and dedicated reservation line. Some of the other benefits the company offers its customers include the Big Front Seat seating option, with more leg room and side room than the standard six inches, more side room than the standard and fewer adjacent seats. The company's frequent flyer program is called Free Spirit. In addition, the firm offers a $9 Fare Club program if customers pay a membership fee of $59.95 for the first year, and $69.95 per year afterward without written cancellation. Members receive offers on exclusive deals on flights before promotions are offered to the public, and have access to reduced bag fee options. In 2015 the firm launched its first international flight departing from Houston's George Bush Intercontinental Airport to Cancun Mexico, the first of seven international flights the carrier added that month.

FINANCIAL DATA: Note: Data for latest year may not have been available at press time.

In U.S. $	2016	2015	2014	2013	2012	2011
Revenue		2,141,463,000	1,931,580,000	1,654,385,000	1,318,388,000	1,071,186,000
R&D Expense						
Operating Income		509,122,000	355,263,000	282,292,000	173,990,000	144,382,000
Operating Margin %		23.77%	18.39%	17.06%	13.19%	13.47%
SGA Expense		464,786,000	388,811,000	329,631,000	275,587,000	233,091,000
Net Income		317,220,000	225,464,000	176,918,000	108,460,000	76,448,000
Operating Cash Flow		472,985,000	260,512,000	195,376,000	113,631,000	171,198,000
Capital Expenditure		558,959,000	186,569,000	19,812,000	23,771,000	14,093,000
EBITDA		585,140,000	399,965,000	314,357,000	189,840,000	152,482,000
Return on Assets %		15.34%	16.19%	16.84%	13.02%	12.51%
Return on Equity %		28.47%	25.44%	26.17%	20.67%	42.27%
Debt to Equity		0.48	0.13			

CONTACT INFORMATION:

Phone: 954 447-7920   Fax: 248-727-2688
Toll-Free: 800-772-7117
Address: 2800 Executive Way, Miramar, FL 33025 United States

STOCK TICKER/OTHER:

Stock Ticker: SAVE   Exchange: NAS
Employees: 4,326   Fiscal Year Ends: 12/31
Parent Company:

SALARIES/BONUSES:

Top Exec. Salary: $496,025   Bonus: $
Second Exec. Salary: Bonus: $
$336,900

OTHER THOUGHTS:

Estimated Female Officers or Directors: 1
Hot Spot for Advancement for Women/Minorities:

St Jude Medical Inc

www.sjm.com

NAIC Code: 339100

TYPES OF BUSINESS:

Cardiovascular Medical Devices
Cardiac Rhythm Management Devices
Cardiac Surgery Devices
Cardiology Devices
Atrial Fibrillation Devices

BRANDS/DIVISIONS/AFFILIATES:

Thoratec
Thoratec Corporation

CONTACTS: Note: Officers with more than one job title may be intentionally listed here more than once.

Michael Rousseau, CEO
Jeff Fecho, Vice President, Divisional
Donald Zurbay, CFO
Daniel Starks, Chairman of the Board
Mark Murphy, Chief Information Officer
Lisa Andrade, Chief Marketing Officer
Mark Carlson, Chief Medical Officer
Philip Ebeling, Chief Technology Officer
Jeffrey Dallager, Controller
John Heinmiller, Executive VP
Jason Zellers, General Counsel
I. Bae, Other Executive Officer
Joel Becker, President, Divisional
Denis Gestin, President, Divisional
Eric Fain, President, Divisional
Scott Thome, Vice President, Divisional
Rachel Ellingson, Vice President, Divisional

GROWTH PLANS/SPECIAL FEATURES:

St. Jude Medical, Inc. is a developer, manufacturer and distributor of cardiovascular medical devices and neurostimulation medical devices. Its cardiovascular medical devices are produced for the global cardiac rhythm management, cardiovascular and atrial fibrillation therapy areas; and its interventional pain therapy & neurostimulation devices are produces for the management of chronic pain and movement disorders. The company derives its revenues from seven principal product categories: tachycardia implantable cardio defibrillator (ICD) systems; bradycardia pacemaker systems; atrial fibrillation products such as electrophysiology introducers & catheters, advanced cardiac mapping, navigation & recording systems and ablation systems; vascular products such as vascular closure products, pressure measurement guidewires, optical coherence tomography imaging products, vascular plugs and heart failure monitoring devices; structural heart products such as heart valve replacement and repair products and structural heart defect devices; neuromodulation products such as spinal cord stimulation and radiofrequency ablation to treat chronic pain & deep brain stimulation, as well as to treat movement disorders; and Thoratec products such as ventricular assist devices and percutaneous heart pumps, both of which facilitate blood flow from the chambers of the heart throughout the entire body. In October 2015, the firm acquired Thoratec Corporation for $3.3 billion. In April 2016, St. Jude agreed to be acquired by Abbott Laboratories for $25 billion, with the transaction expected to close by year's end.

The company offers its employees benefits including medical, dental and vision coverage; flexible spending accounts; an employee assistance program; access to a credit union; life and disability insurance; a physical fitness program; a LiveWell program; a matching gift program; a scholarship program; paid time off; an employee stock purchase plan; referral bonuses; a 401(k); and tuition reimbursement.

FINANCIAL DATA: Note: Data for latest year may not have been available at press time.

In U.S. $	2016	2015	2014	2013	2012	2011
Revenue		5,541,000,000	5,622,000,000	5,501,000,000	5,503,000,000	5,611,696,000
R&D Expense		676,000,000	692,000,000	691,000,000	676,000,000	709,464,000
Operating Income		1,030,000,000	1,151,000,000	1,051,000,000	1,100,000,000	1,114,244,000
Operating Margin %		18.58%	20.47%	19.10%	19.98%	19.85%
SGA Expense		1,878,000,000	1,856,000,000	1,884,000,000	1,891,000,000	2,084,538,000
Net Income		880,000,000	1,002,000,000	723,000,000	752,000,000	825,793,000
Operating Cash Flow		1,039,000,000	1,304,000,000	961,000,000	1,335,000,000	1,286,843,000
Capital Expenditure		186,000,000	190,000,000	222,000,000	280,000,000	306,494,000
EBITDA		1,365,000,000	1,463,000,000	1,162,000,000	1,362,000,000	1,384,789,000
Return on Assets %		7.56%	9.79%	7.40%	8.22%	9.39%
Return on Equity %		21.35%	23.77%	17.36%	17.55%	18.66%
Debt to Equity		1.29	0.54	0.83	0.62	0.60

CONTACT INFORMATION:

Phone: 651 756-2000   Fax: 651 766-3045
Toll-Free: 800-328-9634
Address: 1 St. Jude Medical Dr., St. Paul, MN 55117 United States

STOCK TICKER/OTHER:

Stock Ticker: STJ
Employees: 16,000
Parent Company:

Exchange: NYS
Fiscal Year Ends: 12/31

SALARIES/BONUSES:

Top Exec. Salary:
$1,110,000
Second Exec. Salary:
$800,000

Bonus: $

Bonus: $

OTHER THOUGHTS:

Estimated Female Officers or Directors: 4

Hot Spot for Advancement for Women/Minorities: Y

Sales, profits and employees may be estimates. Financial information, benefits and other data can change quickly and may vary from those stated here.

Stanley Black & Decker Inc

www.stanleyblackanddecker.com

NAIC Code: 333991

TYPES OF BUSINESS:

Power Tools & Accessories Manufacturer
Security Solutions
Household Appliances
Home Improvement Products
Fastening & Assembly Systems
Plumbing Products
Automotive Machinery

BRANDS/DIVISIONS/AFFILIATES:

Bostitch
Black & Decker
Stanley
FatMax
Porter-Cable
DeWALT
GripCo
Sargent & Greenleaf

CONTACTS: *Note: Officers with more than one job title may be intentionally listed here more than once.*

Kathryn Sherer, Assistant General Counsel
James Loree, President
John Lundgren, CEO
Lee McChesney, CFO, Divisional
Donald Allan, CFO
Jocelyn Belisle, Chief Accounting Officer
Rhonda Gass, Chief Information Officer
Bruce Beatt, General Counsel
Jeffery Ansell, Other Corporate Officer
James Cannon, Other Corporate Officer
John Wyatt, President, Divisional
Ben Sihota, President, Divisional
William Taylor, President, Divisional
Jaime Ramirez, President, Divisional
Joseph Voelker, Senior VP, Divisional
Craig Douglas, Treasurer
Michael Bartone, Vice President, Divisional

GROWTH PLANS/SPECIAL FEATURES:

Stanley Black & Decker, Inc. is a global manufacturer an marketer of power tools and accessories, hardware and home improvement products, security solutions and technology based fastening systems. The firm is also a worldwide supplie of engineered fastening and assembly systems. Stanley Black & Decker products and services are marketed in hardware and home improvement stores around the globe. The firm operate in three business tools & storage, security and industrial. Th tools & storage segment includes professional and consume power tools and accessories, lawn and garden tools, consume mechanics tools, storage systems and pneumatic tools an fasteners. The security segment provides both mechanical an electric access and security systems primarily for retailers educational, financial and health care institutions; an commercial, government and industrial customers. Th industrial segment manufactures and markets professiona industrial and automotive mechanics tools and storag systems; metal and plastic fasteners and engineered fastening systems; hydraulic tools and accessories; plumbing, heating and air conditioning tools; assembly tools and systems; an specialty tools. The company sells these products to industria clients in the automotive, transportation, aerospace electronics and machine tool industries primarily through third party distributors. Brand names include DeWALT, Porter Cable, Bostitch, FatMax, Powers, Oldham, Guaranteed Tough and Black & Decker as well as Mac Tools, GripCo, CRC LaBounty, Dubuis and Sargent & Greenleaf.

Employee benefits include medical, dental, life and disability insurance; and a 401(k).

FINANCIAL DATA: *Note: Data for latest year may not have been available at press time.*

In U.S. $	2016	2015	2014	2013	2012	2011
Revenue		11,171,800,000	11,338,600,000	11,001,200,000	10,190,500,000	10,376,400,000
R&D Expense						
Operating Income		1,585,600,000	1,506,800,000	734,200,000	707,200,000	920,100,000
Operating Margin %		14.19%	13.28%	6.67%	6.93%	8.86%
SGA Expense		2,459,100,000	2,575,000,000	2,700,900,000	2,509,100,000	2,536,000,000
Net Income		883,700,000	760,900,000	490,300,000	883,800,000	674,600,000
Operating Cash Flow		1,182,300,000	1,295,900,000	868,000,000	966,200,000	998,900,000
Capital Expenditure		311,400,000	291,000,000	365,600,000	386,000,000	302,100,000
EBITDA		1,745,200,000	1,711,800,000	1,188,300,000	1,117,100,000	1,330,200,000
Return on Assets %		5.69%	4.69%	3.02%	5.55%	4.33%
Return on Equity %		14.43%	11.50%	7.28%	12.92%	9.62%
Debt to Equity		0.66	0.59	0.55	0.52	0.41

CONTACT INFORMATION:

Phone: 860 225-5111   Fax: 860 827-3895
Toll-Free:
Address: 1000 Stanley Dr., New Britain, CT 06053 United States

SALARIES/BONUSES:

Top Exec. Salary:
$1,350,000

Bonus: $

Second Exec. Salary:
$835,000

Bonus: $

STOCK TICKER/OTHER:

Stock Ticker: SWK
Employees: 51,815
Parent Company:

Exchange: NYS
Fiscal Year Ends: 12/31

OTHER THOUGHTS:

Estimated Female Officers or Directors: 5

Hot Spot for Advancement for Women/Minorities: Y

Starbucks Corporation

www.starbucks.com

NAIC Code: 722515

TYPES OF BUSINESS:

Coffee Houses & Coffee Stores
Coffee-Related Accessories & Equipment
Wholesale Coffee Distribution
Tea and Accessories

BRANDS/DIVISIONS/AFFILIATES:

Starbucks
Starbucks Coffee Korea Co Ltd
President Starbucks Coffee Corporation
President Starbucks Coffee Co Ltd
Tata Starbucks Limited (India)
Teavana
La Boulange
Ethos

CONTACTS: *Note: Officers with more than one job title may be intentionally listed here more than once.*

Sophie Hume, Assistant General Counsel
Howard Schultz, CEO
Scott Maw, CFO
Kevin Johnson, Director
Lucy Helm, Executive VP
Michael Conway, President, Divisional
John Culver, President, Divisional
Clifford Burrows, President, Divisional

GROWTH PLANS/SPECIAL FEATURES:

Starbucks Corporation is a roaster, marketer and retailer of specialty coffee, operating in 73 countries, with more than 24.305 retail stores. The firm purchases and roasts high-quality coffees that it sells, along with handcrafted coffee, tea and other beverages and a variety of fresh food items, through company-operated stores. Starbucks also licenses its trademarks through other channels such as grocery stores and national foodservice accounts. In addition to its flagship Starbucks brand, the company's portfolio includes goods and services offered under the following brands: Teavana, Tazo, Seattle's Best Coffee, Starbucks VIA, Starbucks Refreshers, Evolution Fresh, La Boulange and Ethos. The firm has four operating segments: Americas (the U.S., Canada and Latin America), accounting for 69% of total 2015 net revenues; Europe, Middle East and Africa (EMEA), 6%; China/Asia Pacific (CAP), 13%; and channel development, 9%; with all other segments, 3%. The Americas, EMEA and CAP segments include both company-operated and licensed stores. The Americas and EMEA segments include certain food service accounts, primarily in Canada and the UK. Additionally, the Americas includes the company's La Boulange retail stores. Seattle's Best Coffee is reported in a minor other segment, with less than 1% of total net revenues. The company owns a 50% interest in each of the following companies: Starbucks Coffee Korea Co. Ltd., President Starbucks Coffee Corporation (Taiwan), President Starbucks Coffee (Shanghai) Company Limited and Tata Starbucks Limited (India). It also licenses the rights to produce and distribute Starbucks-branded products to its 50% joint venture with Pepsi-Cola Company, The North American Coffee Partnership, which develops and distributes bottled Starbucks beverages. The company's updated mobile app labelled Order and Pay App, allows customers to place, pay and pick up orders.

Starbucks offers employee benefits including 401(k), adoption assistance, health coverage, employee discounts, education assistance, time off and discount stock purchase plans.

FINANCIAL DATA: *Note: Data for latest year may not have been available at press time.*

In U.S. $	2016	2015	2014	2013	2012	2011
Revenue		19,162,700,000	16,447,800,000	14,892,200,000	13,299,500,000	11,700,400,000
R&D Expense						
Operating Income		3,601,000,000	3,081,100,000	-325,400,000	1,997,400,000	1,728,500,000
Operating Margin %		18.79%	18.73%	-2.18%	15.01%	14.77%
SGA Expense		6,607,800,000	5,629,500,000	5,224,000,000	4,719,300,000	4,301,200,000
Net Income		2,757,400,000	2,068,100,000	8,300,000	1,383,800,000	1,245,700,000
Operating Cash Flow		3,749,100,000	607,800,000	2,908,300,000	1,750,300,000	1,612,400,000
Capital Expenditure		1,303,700,000	1,160,900,000	1,151,200,000	856,200,000	531,900,000
EBITDA		4,907,300,000	3,972,200,000	453,800,000	2,672,400,000	2,394,400,000
Return on Assets %		23.77%	18.57%	.08%	17.76%	18.12%
Return on Equity %		49.72%	42.41%	.17%	29.15%	30.91%
Debt to Equity		0.40	0.38	0.29	0.10	0.12

CONTACT INFORMATION:

Phone: 206 447-1575   Fax: 206 447-0828
Toll-Free: 800-782-7282
Address: 2401 Utah Ave. S., Seattle, WA 98134 United States

STOCK TICKER/OTHER:

Stock Ticker: SBUX   Exchange: NAS
Employees: 238,000   Fiscal Year Ends: 09/30
Parent Company:

SALARIES/BONUSES:

Top Exec. Salary: Bonus: $
$1,500,000
Second Exec. Salary: Bonus: $500,000
$576,923

OTHER THOUGHTS:

Estimated Female Officers or Directors: 5

Hot Spot for Advancement for Women/Minorities: Y

Sales, profits and employees may be estimates. Financial information, benefits and other data can change quickly and may vary from those stated here.

Starwood Hotels & Resorts Worldwide Inc www.starwoodhotels.com

NAIC Code: 721110

TYPES OF BUSINESS:

Hotels & Resorts
Financial Services
Hotel Management & Franchising
Spa Services

BRANDS/DIVISIONS/AFFILIATES:

Sheraton
W
Four Points
Westin
Le Meridien
St. Regis
Marriott International Inc
Aloft

CONTACTS: Note: Officers with more than one job title may be intentionally listed here more than once.

Thomas Mangas, CEO
Bruce Duncan, Chairman of the Board
Alan Schnaid, Chief Accounting Officer
Kenneth Siegel, Chief Administrative Officer
Martha Poulter, Chief Information Officer
Robyn Arnell, Controller
Jeffrey Cava, Executive VP
Kristen Prohl, Other Executive Officer
Simon Turner, President, Divisional
Sergio Rivera, President, Geographical

GROWTH PLANS/SPECIAL FEATURES:

Starwood Hotels & Resorts Worldwide, Inc. is involved in the global operation of hotels and resorts, primarily in the luxury and upscale segments of the industry. It owns, leases, manages or franchises approximately 1,222 properties with approximately 354,200 rooms in nearly 100 countries. The company's hotel brand names include St. Regis, The Luxury Collection, Phoenician, Tremont, Hotel Alfonso, Hotel Imperial, Hotel Maria Cristina, The Gritti Palace, Hotel Goldener Hirsch, W, Westin, Sheraton, Four Points, Le Meridien, Aloft and Element. The firm's earnings are derived mainly from its hotel and leisure operations; the receipt of franchise fees; and the development, ownership and operation of vacation ownership resorts. Additionally, Starwood provides financing to customers who purchase interests in resorts. The firm's frequent guest loyalty program, Starwood Preferred Guest, is unique in the hotel industry for its lack of capacity controls and blackout dates. In September 2016, Marriott International, Inc. completed an acquisition of Starwood.

The firm offers employees dental, vision and health insurance; life insurance; wellness programs; dependent care flexible spending accounts; an employee assistance program; and adoption assistance.

FINANCIAL DATA: Note: Data for latest year may not have been available at press time.

In U.S. $	2016	2015	2014	2013	2012	2011
Revenue		5,762,999,808	5,983,000,064	6,114,999,808	6,320,999,936	5,624,000,000
R&D Expense						
Operating Income						
Operating Margin %						
SGA Expense						
Net Income		489,000,000	633,000,000	635,000,000	562,000,000	489,000,000
Operating Cash Flow						
Capital Expenditure						
EBITDA						
Return on Assets %						
Return on Equity %						
Debt to Equity						

CONTACT INFORMATION:

Phone: 914 640-8100   Fax: 914 640-8310
Toll-Free:
Address: 1 StarPoint, White Plains, NY 06902 United States

STOCK TICKER/OTHER:

Stock Ticker: Subsidiary   Exchange:
Employees: 180,400   Fiscal Year Ends: 12/31
Parent Company: Marriott International Inc

SALARIES/BONUSES:

Top Exec. Salary: $ Bonus: $
Second Exec. Salary: $ Bonus: $

OTHER THOUGHTS:

Estimated Female Officers or Directors: 4
Hot Spot for Advancement for Women/Minorities: Y

State Farm Insurance Companies   www.statefarm.com

NAIC Code: 524126

TYPES OF BUSINESS:

Insurance, Direct Property & Casualty
Accident Insurance
Health Insurance
Life Insurance
Annuities
Automobile Insurance
Banking/Savings Association
Mutual Funds

BRANDS/DIVISIONS/AFFILIATES:

State Farm Mutual Automobile Insurance Co
State Farm Life & Accident Assurance Company
State Farm Fire & Casualty Company
State Farm General Insurance Company
State Farm Lloyds
State Farm Guaranty Insurance Company
State Farm Bank FSB
State Farm Associate & Retail Mutual Funds

CONTACTS: *Note: Officers with more than one job title may be intentionally listed here more than once.*

Michael L. Tipsord, CEO
Michael L. Tipsord, Pres.
Edward B. Rust, Jr., Chmn.

GROWTH PLANS/SPECIAL FEATURES:

State Farm Insurance Companies is a mutual company providing personal property and casualty insurance through over 18,000 agent offices, 55 operation centers and more than 300 claim offices across the U.S. and Canada. The company provides auto, homeowners, renters, life and annuities, health, disability, long-term care, business, boat, farm and ranch, flood, motorcycle, personal and volcano damage insurance. Over half of its 82 million policies are auto policies. The group's major insurance companies include State Farm Mutual Automobile Insurance Company, State Farm Life & Accident Assurance Company, State Farm Fire & Casualty Company, State Farm General Insurance Company, State Farm Lloyds and State Farm Guaranty Insurance Company. Through State Farm Bank, F.S.B., the company provides bank account, credit card and loan services including individual retirement accounts (IRA), money market, checking, savings and health savings accounts; and home mortgage and home equity, vehicle and business loans. The firm also manages mutual fund accounts through State Farm Associate & Retail Mutual Funds and State Farm Investment Management Corp. In addition, State Farm is a leading insurer in Canada, serving households in Alberta, New Brunswick and Ontario. In 2015, the firm received FAA approval to test unmanned aircraft systems for commercial use, enabling the insurer to research this new technology and potentially deploy it in ways that could benefit customers. Its plans are to explore the use of drones to assess potential roof damage during the claims process and respond to natural disasters.

Employee benefits include medical, dental and life coverage; a 401(k); a company retirement plan; and a wellness program.

FINANCIAL DATA: *Note: Data for latest year may not have been available at press time.*

In U.S. $	2016	2015	2014	2013	2012	2011
Revenue		75,700,000,000	71,200,000,000	68,291,000,000	65,285,700,000	64,305,100,000
R&D Expense						
Operating Income						
Operating Margin %						
SGA Expense						
Net Income		6,200,000,000	4,200,000,000	5,189,000,000	3,159,200,000	845,000,000
Operating Cash Flow						
Capital Expenditure						
EBITDA						
Return on Assets %						
Return on Equity %						
Debt to Equity						

CONTACT INFORMATION:

Phone: 309-766-2311   Fax: 309-766-3621
Toll-Free: 877-734-2265
Address: 1 State Farm Plaza, Bloomington, IL 61710 United States

STOCK TICKER/OTHER:

Stock Ticker: Mutual Company   Exchange:
Employees: 70,000   Fiscal Year Ends: 12/31
Parent Company:

SALARIES/BONUSES:

Top Exec. Salary: $ Bonus: $
Second Exec. Salary: $ Bonus: $

OTHER THOUGHTS:

Estimated Female Officers or Directors: 3
Hot Spot for Advancement for Women/Minorities: Y

Sales, profits and employees may be estimates. Financial information, benefits and other data can change quickly and may vary from those stated here.

Stericycle Inc

NAIC Code: 562112

TYPES OF BUSINESS:

Medical Waste Treatment

BRANDS/DIVISIONS/AFFILIATES:

Bio-Systems
Ster-Safe
Shred-It International ULC

CONTACTS: *Note: Officers with more than one job title may be intentionally listed here more than once.*

Charles Alutto, CEO
Dan Ginnetti, CFO
Mark Miller, Director
Brent Arnold, Executive VP
John Schetz, Executive VP
Brenda Frank, Executive VP
Michael Collins, Executive VP

GROWTH PLANS/SPECIAL FEATURES:

Stericycle, Inc. is engaged in the business of medical waste disposal. Through its national networks of 253 processing facilities, 358 transfer sites and 137 other service facilities, the firm is able to serve the U.S. and 21 other countries, including Argentina, Brazil, Canada, Chile, Ireland, Japan, Mexico, Portugal, Romania, Korea, Spain, and the U.K. In order to dispose of medical waste, Stericycle utilizes various technologies, including autoclaving, an electro-thermal deactivation system (ETD), chemical treatment and incineration. While Stericycle's customers are mainly hospitals, clinics, acute care facilities and dental offices, it also handles disposal of expired or surplus products from pharmacies and pharmaceutical manufacturers. The company generally provides its customers with its own waste containers, such as the plastic Bio Systems containers, to avoid needle sticks and leakages. After treatment, the residual ash is passed on to a third-party landfill and the containers are returned to customers. Stericycle utilizes its own branded methodologies, which include Steri-Safe, a compliance program designed to familiarize clients with regulatory policies, mail-back programs, product recalls, returns and onsite waste disposal services. The company serves more than 1 million customers worldwide, including large-quantity generators such as hospitals, blood banks and pharmaceutical manufacturers; and small-quantity generators such as outpatient clinics, medical and dental offices, long-term and sub-acute care facilities and retail pharmacies. In October 2015, the firm acquired document destruction company Shred-it International ULC, for about $2.3 billion, increasing its international footprint via 19 U.S. and 24 international businesses, as well as 2,400 trucks and 5,400 team members.

The company offers its employees medical, dental, vision, life, AD&D, long-term care, auto and home insurance; flexible spending accounts; an employee assistance program; tuition reimbursement; short- and long-term disability; a prepaid legal program; a 401(k) plan; an employee stock purchase plan; and paid vacation, holidays and funeral leave.

FINANCIAL DATA: *Note: Data for latest year may not have been available at press time.*

In U.S. $	2016	2015	2014	2013	2012	2011
Revenue		2,985,908,000	2,555,601,000	2,142,807,000	1,913,149,000	1,676,048,000
R&D Expense						
Operating Income		487,612,000	556,336,000	535,619,000	468,836,000	424,311,000
Operating Margin %		16.33%	21.76%	24.99%	24.50%	25.31%
SGA Expense		712,803,000	489,937,000	390,610,000	356,817,000	311,522,000
Net Income		267,046,000	326,456,000	311,372,000	267,996,000	234,751,000
Operating Cash Flow		390,328,000	448,500,000	403,467,000	387,448,000	306,104,000
Capital Expenditure		114,761,000	86,496,000	73,109,000	65,236,000	53,301,000
EBITDA		615,817,000	658,326,000	621,397,000	545,154,000	487,801,000
Return on Assets %		4.47%	7.88%	8.38%	7.97%	8.07%
Return on Equity %		11.11%	17.91%	18.91%	19.56%	20.89%
Debt to Equity		1.11	0.80	0.73	0.82	1.07

CONTACT INFORMATION:

Phone: 847 367-5910   Fax: 847 367-9493
Toll-Free: 800-643-0240
Address: 28161 N. Keith Dr., Lake Forest, IL 60045 United States

STOCK TICKER/OTHER:

Stock Ticker: SRCL   Exchange: NAS
Employees: 14,170   Fiscal Year Ends: 12/31
Parent Company:

SALARIES/BONUSES:

Top Exec. Salary: $488,269   Bonus: $
Second Exec. Salary: Bonus: $
$346,923

OTHER THOUGHTS:

Estimated Female Officers or Directors:
Hot Spot for Advancement for Women/Minorities:

Stifel Financial Corp

NAIC Code: 523110

TYPES OF BUSINESS:
Stock Brokerage/Investment Banking
Underwriting
Broker-Dealer
Investment Advisory Services
Research
Insurance
Annuities

BRANDS/DIVISIONS/AFFILIATES:
Stifel Nicolaus & Company Inc
Century Securities Associates Inc
Stifel Nicolaus Europe Limited
Stifel Bank & Trust
Sterne Agee Group Inc
Stifel Trust Company NA
Bruyette & Woods Inc
De La Rosa & Co

CONTACTS: Note: Officers with more than one job title may be intentionally listed here more than once.
Ronald Kruszewski, CEO
James Zemlyak, CFO
James Marischen, Chief Accounting Officer
Thomas Weisel, Co-Chairman
Richard Himelfarb, Director
Ben Plotkin, Director
Thomas Mulroy, Director
Victor Nesi, Director
Thomas Michaud, Director
David Minnick, General Counsel
Mark Fisher, General Counsel
David Sliney, Senior VP

GROWTH PLANS/SPECIAL FEATURES:
Stifel Financial Corp. is a financial services holding company that provides, through its subsidiaries, retail brokerage, securities trading, investment banking, investment advisory, retail, consumer and commercial banking and related financial services. Its principal subsidiary is Stifel, Nicolaus & Company, Inc., a full service retail/institutional brokerage and investment banking firm. Other subsidiaries include Century Securities Associates, Inc.; Keefe, Bruyette & Woods, Inc.; De La Rosa & Co.; Stifel Nicolaus Europe Limited; Stifel Bank & Trust; and Stifel Trust Company NA. The firm operates in three business segments: global wealth management, institutional group and other. The global wealth management segment includes two businesses: the private client group, which provides brokerage services through 329 branch offices and independent contractor offices in 45 states and Washington, D.C.; and Stifel Bank, which provides residential, consumer and commercial lending. The institutional group segment offers institutional sales and trading services, investment research and corporate and public finance underwriting. The other segment includes revenues and expenses associated with certain corporate activities. Internationally, Stifel Financial operates in the U.K. and Europe. In 2015, the firm acquired Sterne Agee Group, Inc.

The company offers its employees medical, dental, vision and prescription drug coverage; health care, dependent care and commuter flexible spending accounts; life insurance; short- and long-term disability; tuition assistance; business travel accident insurance; an employee assistance program; a 401(k) plan; and an employee stock ownership plan (ESOP).

FINANCIAL DATA: Note: Data for latest year may not have been available at press time.

In U.S. $	2016	2015	2014	2013	2012	2011
Revenue		2,331,594,000	2,208,424,000	1,973,446,000	1,612,650,000	1,396,831,000
R&D Expense						
Operating Income		141,567,000	290,794,000	185,229,000	225,872,000	118,877,000
Operating Margin %		6.07%	13.16%	9.38%	14.00%	8.51%
SGA Expense		1,742,058,000	1,547,413,000	1,448,337,000	1,135,754,000	1,003,050,000
Net Income		92,336,000	176,067,000	162,013,000	138,573,000	84,134,000
Operating Cash Flow		-379,509,000	250,269,000	702,219,000	-264,267,000	45,888,000
Capital Expenditure		69,822,000	26,632,000	32,278,000	18,837,000	59,730,000
EBITDA						
Return on Assets %		.80%	1.90%	2.02%	2.32%	1.83%
Return on Equity %		3.83%	8.03%	9.11%	9.90%	6.58%
Debt to Equity		0.33	0.30	0.19	0.31	0.06

CONTACT INFORMATION:
Phone: 314 342-2000   Fax: 314 342-1159
Toll-Free: 800-679-5446
Address: 501 N. Broadway, St. Louis, MO 63102 United States

STOCK TICKER/OTHER:
Stock Ticker: SF
Employees: 5,862
Parent Company:

Exchange: NYS
Fiscal Year Ends: 12/31

SALARIES/BONUSES:
Top Exec. Salary: $250,000   Bonus: $350,000
Second Exec. Salary: Bonus: $350,000
$250,000

OTHER THOUGHTS:
Estimated Female Officers or Directors:
Hot Spot for Advancement for Women/Minorities:

Strategy&

NAIC Code: 541610

TYPES OF BUSINESS:

Management Consulting

BRANDS/DIVISIONS/AFFILIATES:

PricewaterhouseCoopers (PWC)
Katzenbach Center
Capabilities-Driven Strategy

CONTACTS: *Note: Officers with more than one job title may be intentionally listed here more than once.*

Leslie Moeller, Global Managing Director
Mark Berlind, General Counsel
Jochim Rotering, Sr. Partner-Oper.
Peter B. Mensing, Managing Dir.-Europe
Mike Connolly, Sr. Partner-Health Svcs.
Leslie Moeller, Sr. Partner
Jay Davis, Global Dir.-Oper.
Ivan de Souza, Managing Dir.-Global Markets

GROWTH PLANS/SPECIAL FEATURES:

Strategy& is a management consulting firm which provide
services to businesses and government institutions worldwide
Strategy& serves industries as diverse as aerospace and
defense, automotive, chemicals, consumer products, energ
and utilities, financial services, health, industrials, media an
entertainment, oil and gas, private equity, public sector, retai
technology, telecommunications and transportation. The firr
offers consulting services in the fields of corporate finance
deals, digital business and technology, enterprise strategy
marketing and sales, operations
organization/change/leadership, as well as product and servic
innovation. Strategy&'s Capabilities-Driven Strategy focuse
on evaluating pragmatic choices before implementin
strategies in order to achieve the highest level of coherence
competitive sustainability outpace and reliability. The
Katzenbach Center at Strategy& develops client-centere
organizational models, applications and innovations focuse
on producing new thinking and higher performance throug
cultural change. The company has offices around the world
including Africa, Asia-Pacific, Europe, the Middle East, Nort
America and South America. The firm's clients have include
Deutsche Post World Net, Mediaset, Quest Diagnostics an
Wolters Kluwer. Strategy& is owned b
PricewaterhouseCoopers.

The firm offers employees a formal work-life balance program
substantial sick leave and family care leave; flexible wor
arrangements that may include job-sharing, flex time
sabbaticals and a compressed work week; and access t
training at the PwC Open University.

FINANCIAL DATA: *Note: Data for latest year may not have been available at press time.*

In U.S. $	2016	2015	2014	2013	2012	2011
Revenue		1,147,000,000	1,300,000,000	1,050,000,000	1,000,000,000	
R&D Expense						
Operating Income						
Operating Margin %						
SGA Expense						
Net Income						
Operating Cash Flow						
Capital Expenditure						
EBITDA						
Return on Assets %						
Return on Equity %						
Debt to Equity						

CONTACT INFORMATION:

Phone: 212-697-1900   Fax: 212-551-6732
Toll-Free:
Address: 101 Park Ave., 18th Fl., New York, NY 10178 United States

SALARIES/BONUSES:

Top Exec. Salary: $ Bonus: $
Second Exec. Salary: $ Bonus: $

STOCK TICKER/OTHER:

Stock Ticker: Subsidiary   Exchange:
Employees: 3,000   Fiscal Year Ends:
Parent Company: PricewaterhouseCoopers (PWC)

OTHER THOUGHTS:

Estimated Female Officers or Directors: 1
Hot Spot for Advancement for Women/Minorities:

Stryker Corp

NAIC Code: 339100

www.stryker.com

TYPES OF BUSINESS:

Equipment-Orthopedic Implants
Powered Surgical Instruments
Endoscopic Systems
Patient Care & Handling Equipment
Imaging Software
Small Bone Innovations

BRANDS/DIVISIONS/AFFILIATES:

CHG Hospital Beds Inc
Muka Metal AS

CONTACTS: Note: Officers with more than one job title may be intentionally listed here more than once.

Kevin Lobo, CEO
Glenn Boehnlein, CFO
William Berry, Chief Accounting Officer
Bijoy Sagar, Chief Information Officer
Michael Hutchinson, General Counsel
David Floyd, President, Divisional
Timothy Scannell, President, Divisional
Lonny Carpenter, President, Divisional
Dean Bergy, Secretary
Yin Becker, Vice President, Divisional
M. Fink, Vice President, Divisional
Katherine Owen, Vice President, Divisional

GROWTH PLANS/SPECIAL FEATURES:

Stryker Corp. develops, manufactures and markets specialty surgical and medical products for the global market. Products include orthopedic implants, patient care and handling equipment, powered surgical instruments and endoscopic systems. The firm's products are produced by three segments: orthopaedics; MedSurg; and neurotechnology and spine. The orthopaedics segment's products consist primarily of implants for knee and hip joint replacements and trauma surgeries as well as products designed for upper and lower extremity small bone indications, with a focus on small joint replacement. The MedSurg segment includes surgical instruments and surgical navigation systems; endoscopic and communications systems; patient handling and emergency medical equipment; and reprocessed and remanufactured medical devices. The neurotechnology and spine segment's products primarily include neurosurgical and neurovascular devices, including products for traditional brain and open skull base procedures. This segment's offerings also include products used for minimally invasive endovascular techniques; orthobiologic and biosurgery products, including synthetic bone grafts and vertebral augmentation products; minimally invasive products for the treatment of acute ischemic and hemorrhagic stroke; and spinal implant products such as cervical, thoracolumbar and interbody systems. The company's products are sold in over 100 countries worldwide. In 2015, it acquired CHG Hospital Beds, Inc.; received FDA clearance for its Mako total knee application; and acquired Muka Metal AS.

Stryker offers its employees medical, vision, prescription, dental, long- and short-term disability and life insurance; an employee stock purchase plan; a 401(k); flexible spending; an employee assistance program; onsite fitness centers and cafeteria; wellness programs; maternity leave; adoption assistance; and tuition reimbursement.

FINANCIAL DATA: Note: Data for latest year may not have been available at press time.

In U.S. $	2016	2015	2014	2013	2012	2011
Revenue		9,946,000,000	9,675,000,000	9,021,000,000	8,657,000,000	8,307,000,000
R&D Expense		625,000,000	614,000,000	536,000,000	471,000,000	462,000,000
Operating Income		1,861,000,000	1,246,000,000	1,256,000,000	1,741,000,000	1,686,000,000
Operating Margin %		18.71%	12.87%	13.92%	20.11%	20.29%
SGA Expense		3,610,000,000	4,336,000,000	4,066,000,000	3,466,000,000	3,150,000,000
Net Income		1,439,000,000	515,000,000	1,006,000,000	1,298,000,000	1,345,000,000
Operating Cash Flow		899,000,000	1,782,000,000	1,886,000,000	1,657,000,000	1,434,000,000
Capital Expenditure		270,000,000	233,000,000	195,000,000	210,000,000	226,000,000
EBITDA		2,258,000,000	1,624,000,000	1,563,000,000	2,018,000,000	2,201,000,000
Return on Assets %		8.47%	3.07%	6.95%	10.13%	11.54%
Return on Equity %		16.82%	5.83%	11.40%	15.94%	18.10%
Debt to Equity		0.38	0.37	0.30	0.20	0.22

CONTACT INFORMATION:

Phone: 269 385-2600   Fax: 269 385-1062
Toll-Free:
Address: 2825 Airview Blvd., Kalamazoo, MI 49002 United States

STOCK TICKER/OTHER:

Stock Ticker: SYK
Employees: 27,000
Parent Company:

Exchange: NYS
Fiscal Year Ends: 12/31

SALARIES/BONUSES:

Top Exec. Salary:
$1,093,333
Second Exec. Salary:
$584,333

Bonus: $

Bonus: $

OTHER THOUGHTS:

Estimated Female Officers or Directors: 7

Hot Spot for Advancement for Women/Minorities: Y

SunGard Data Systems Inc

www.sungard.com

NAIC Code: 0

TYPES OF BUSINESS:

Computer Software, Security & Anti-Virus
Software for Schools
Consulting
Software for Investment Firms

BRANDS/DIVISIONS/AFFILIATES:

SunGard Financial Systems
SunGard Public Sector

CONTACTS: Note: Officers with more than one job title may be intentionally listed here more than once.

Russ Fradin, CEO
Mairanne Brown, COO-Financial Systems
Russ Fradin, Pres.
Charles Neral, CFO
Patti Cassidy, Chief Human Resources Officer
Steven Silberstein, Chief Technology Officer
Steven Silberstein, CTO
Victoria Silbey, General Counsel
Anthony Calenda, Sr. VP-Corp. Dev. & Strategy
Karen Mullane, Controller
Harold Finders, CEO-Financial Systems
Andrew Stern, CEO-Availability Svcs.
Mike Borman, CEO-Public Sector
George Pepper, Pres., K-12 Education
Vince Coppola, Sr. VP-Global Bus. Svcs. & Tech.

GROWTH PLANS/SPECIAL FEATURES:

SunGard Data Systems, Inc. is a leading global provider of integrated software and information technology services for financial services companies, higher education and the public sector. The firm serves more than 16,000 clients in over 100 countries. SunGard is organized into three business segments: financial systems, K-12 education and public sector. SunGard Financial Systems serves financial services companies specializing in alternative investments, banking, benefit administration, brokerage and clearance, capital markets and investment banking, energy trading and risk management, institutional asset management, insurance, trading, treasury management and wealth management. The K-12 education segment provides specialized enterprise resource planning and administrative software to support over eight million students in the U.S. SunGard Public Sector serves school districts; nonprofit organizations; and local, state and federal government agencies with solutions for accounting, human resources, payroll; utility billing, land management, public safety and criminal justice and grant and project management. In 2014, the company split off its Sungard Availability Services business into an independent company. In 2015, the firm agreed to be acquired by Fidelity National Information Services, Inc. for $9.1 billion.

SunGard offers its employees medical, dental and vision insurance; an employee assistance program; a flexible compensation plan; short- and long-term disability; life and AD&D insurance; a retirement savings plan; a college tuition savings plan; tuition reimbursement; and adoption assistance

FINANCIAL DATA: Note: Data for latest year may not have been available at press time.

In U.S. $	2016	2015	2014	2013	2012	2011
Revenue		2,950,000,000	2,800,000,000	4,134,000,000	4,213,000,000	4,381,000,000
R&D Expense						
Operating Income						
Operating Margin %						
SGA Expense						
Net Income			87,000,000	-107,000,000	-317,000,000	-376,000,000
Operating Cash Flow						
Capital Expenditure						
EBITDA						
Return on Assets %						
Return on Equity %						
Debt to Equity						

CONTACT INFORMATION:

Phone: 484-582-2000 Fax:
Toll-Free: 800-825-2518
Address: 680 E. Swedesford Rd., Wayne, PA 19087 United States

STOCK TICKER/OTHER:

Stock Ticker: Private
Employees: 13,000
Parent Company:

Exchange:
Fiscal Year Ends: 12/31

SALARIES/BONUSES:

Top Exec. Salary: $ Bonus: $
Second Exec. Salary: $ Bonus: $

OTHER THOUGHTS:

Estimated Female Officers or Directors: 3
Hot Spot for Advancement for Women/Minorities: Y

Supervalu Inc

www.supervalu.com

NAIC Code: 445110

TYPES OF BUSINESS:

Grocery Stores
Food Distribution & Logistics

BRANDS/DIVISIONS/AFFILIATES:

Retail Food
Save-A-Lot
Shopper's Value
Culinary Circle
Java Delight
Stockman & Dakota
Wild Harvest
Essential Everyday

CONTACTS: *Note: Officers with more than one job title may be intentionally listed here more than once.*

Eric Claus, CEO, Subsidiary
Gerald Storch, Chairman of the Board
Susan Grafton, Chief Accounting Officer
Randy Burdick, Chief Information Officer
Bruce Besanko, COO
Michele Murphy, Executive VP, Divisional
Michael Stigers, Executive VP, Divisional
Mark Van Buskirk, Executive VP, Divisional
James Weidenheimer, Executive VP, Divisional
Karla Robertson, Executive VP
Robert Woseth, Executive VP
Mark Gross, President

GROWTH PLANS/SPECIAL FEATURES:

Supervalu, Inc. is a supermarket retailer and food distributor. Supervalu conducts its operations through three business segments: independent business, Save-A-Lot and retail food. The independent business segment provides wholesale distribution of products to independent retailers and is the largest public company food wholesaler in the nation. This segment's network spans 41 states and serves as primary grocery supplier to approximately 1,825 stores, in addition to its own stores, as well as serving as a secondary grocery supplier to approximately 208 stores of independent retail customers. The Save-A-Lot segment consists of 1,334 stores, including 903 licensed Save-A-Lot stores, located throughout the U.S. This segment's operations are supplied by 17 distribution centers providing wholesale distribution to the company's own stores and to licensed stores. Supervalu owns 431 Save-A-Lot stores. The retail food segment operates its business through 194 company-owned retail food stores throughout the U.S. under five regionally-based retail banners of Cub Foods, Shoppers Food & Pharmacy, Shop 'n Save, Farm Fresh and Hornbacher's and two Rainbow stores. Products include a wide variety of nationally-advertised brand name and private-label products, primarily grocery (both perishable and non-perishable); general merchandise; home, health and beauty care; and pharmacy. Supervalu's private label products include: Culinary Circle, Java Delight, Stockman & Dakota, Wild Harvest, Essential Everyday, equaline, Artic Shores Seafood Company, Baby Basics, Carlita, Farm Stand, Stone Ridge Creamery and SuperChill. The firm's value brand is Shopper's Value. In July 2015, the firm announced that it has begun preparations to allow for a possible spin-off of Save-A-Lot into a stand-alone, publicly traded company.

Supervalu offers its employees medical, dental and life insurance; short- and long-term disability coverage; a 401(k) plan; profit sharing; tuition reimbursement; flexible spending accounts; and an employee assistance program.

FINANCIAL DATA: *Note: Data for latest year may not have been available at press time.*

In U.S. $	2016	2015	2014	2013	2012	2011
Revenue	17,529,000,000	17,820,000,000	17,155,000,000	17,097,000,000	36,100,000,000	37,534,000,000
R&D Expense						
Operating Income	454,000,000	424,000,000	418,000,000	-157,000,000	-519,000,000	-976,000,000
Operating Margin %	2.59%	2.37%	2.43%	-.91%	-1.43%	-2.60%
SGA Expense	2,124,000,000	2,154,000,000	2,114,000,000	2,445,000,000	7,106,000,000	7,516,000,000
Net Income	178,000,000	192,000,000	182,000,000	-1,466,000,000	-1,040,000,000	-1,510,000,000
Operating Cash Flow	424,000,000	408,000,000	19,000,000	898,000,000	1,056,000,000	1,163,000,000
Capital Expenditure	261,000,000	239,000,000	111,000,000	228,000,000	661,000,000	597,000,000
EBITDA	730,000,000	714,000,000	720,000,000	211,000,000	370,000,000	-44,000,000
Return on Assets %	4.02%	4.33%	2.36%	-12.69%	-8.05%	-10.00%
Return on Equity %					-152.82%	-71.44%
Debt to Equity					279.42	4.73

CONTACT INFORMATION:

Phone: 952 828-4000   Fax: 952 828-8998
Toll-Free:
Address: 7075 Flying Cloud Dr., Eden Prairie, MN 55344 United States

STOCK TICKER/OTHER:

Stock Ticker: SVU
Employees: 38,500
Parent Company:

Exchange: NYS
Fiscal Year Ends: 02/28

SALARIES/BONUSES:

Top Exec. Salary: Bonus: $
$1,500,000
Second Exec. Salary: Bonus: $
$705,289

OTHER THOUGHTS:

Estimated Female Officers or Directors: 3

Hot Spot for Advancement for Women/Minorities: Y

Sutter Health Inc
NAIC Code: 622110

TYPES OF BUSINESS:
General Medical and Surgical Hospitals
Neonatal Care
Pregnancy & Birth
Training Programs
Medical Research Facilities
Home Health Services
Hospice Networks
Long-Term Care

BRANDS/DIVISIONS/AFFILIATES:
Memorial
Sutter
Kahi Mohala
Alta Bates
Eden
Menlo Park Surgical
California Pacific
Sutter Health Plus

CONTACTS: Note: Officers with more than one job title may be intentionally listed here more than once.
Sarah Krevans, CEO
Sarah Krevans, Pres.

GROWTH PLANS/SPECIAL FEATURES:
Sutter Health, Inc. is one of the nation's largest nonprofit healt
care systems. Through its affiliates, the firm serves 10
Northern California communities via 5,000 physicians, whic
are members of the Sutter medical network. Sutter Healt
operates approximately 27 hospitals, nine medical foundatio
groups, 12 cancer centers, 23 emergency room locations, fiv
education and training centers, 10 home health and hospic
services companies, four imaging laboratories, as well a
surgery centers, research institutes, urgent cares, walk-i
clinics and long-term care centers. The company's hospital
are branded under the Memorial, Sutter, Kahi Mohala, Alt
Bates, Eden, Menlo Park Surgical, California Pacific an
Novato Community names. Many of the hospitals operat
charitable foundations. Sutter Health is a regional leader i
labor and delivery, neonatology and pediatrics services, as we
as orthopedics, bariatric, cosmetic, diabetes, heart an
vascular, mental health, sleep disorders, transplant service
and cancer care services. The company was one of the firs
health networks in its area to implement two eICU (electroni
ICU) centers, which allow more comprehensive and consisten
monitoring of ICU patients by feeding monitoring data to
central location. Sutter Health Plus is an HMO that offer
affordably-priced health plans to individuals and employe
groups.

FINANCIAL DATA: Note: Data for latest year may not have been available at press time.

In U.S. $	2016	2015	2014	2013	2012	2011
Revenue		10,998,000,000	10,161,000,000	9,600,000,000	9,560,000,000	9,079,000,000
R&D Expense						
Operating Income						
Operating Margin %						
SGA Expense						
Net Income		81,000,000	402,000,000	300,000,000	549,000,000	697,000,000
Operating Cash Flow						
Capital Expenditure						
EBITDA						
Return on Assets %						
Return on Equity %						
Debt to Equity						

CONTACT INFORMATION:
Phone: 916-733-8800   Fax:
Toll-Free:
Address: 2200 River Plaza Dr., Sacramento, CA 95833 United States

STOCK TICKER/OTHER:
Stock Ticker: Nonprofit
Employees: 55,000
Parent Company:

Exchange:
Fiscal Year Ends: 12/31

SALARIES/BONUSES:
Top Exec. Salary: $ Bonus: $
Second Exec. Salary: $ Bonus: $

OTHER THOUGHTS:
Estimated Female Officers or Directors: 3
Hot Spot for Advancement for Women/Minorities: Y

Symantec Corp

NAIC Code: 0

www.symantec.com

TYPES OF BUSINESS:

Computer Software, Security & Anti-Virus
Remote Management Products
Consulting-Cyber Security
Information Protection Products

BRANDS/DIVISIONS/AFFILIATES:

Norton

CONTACTS: *Note: Officers with more than one job title may be intentionally listed here more than once.*

Thomas Seifert, CFO
Daniel Schulman, Chairman of the Board
Mark Garfield, Chief Accounting Officer
Gregory Clark, Director
Francis Rosch, Executive VP, Divisional
Scott Taylor, Executive VP
Nicholas Noviello, Executive VP
Michael Fey, President
Amy Cappellanti-Wolf, Senior VP

GROWTH PLANS/SPECIAL FEATURES:

Symantec Corp. provides a range of software, appliances and services designed to secure and manage information technology (IT) infrastructure. The company provides customers worldwide with software and services that protect, manage and control information risks related to security, data protection, storage, compliance and systems management. Symantec conducts business in three geographical regions: the Americas, Asia and the Middle East and Africa. The firm has three operating segments: enterprise security, consumer security and information management. The enterprise security segment offers products to secure confidential information such as Secure Socket Layer Certificates, authentication, mail and web security, data center security, data loss prevention, information security services, endpoint security and management, encryption, and mobile security solutions. The consumer security segment provides multi-layer security and identity protection on major desktop and mobile operating systems through Norton products. The information management segment focuses on backup and recovery, archiving and eDiscovery, storage and high availability solutions, helping to ensure that customers' IT infrastructure and mission-critical applications are protected, managed and available. Symantec operates in over 50 countries. In August 2015, it agreed to sell Veritas to an investor group led by The Carlyle Group together with GIC, Singapore's sovereign wealth fund, and other expected co-investors for $8 billion in cash.

Symantec offers employees a 401(k) with company match, tuition reimbursement and adoption assistance.

FINANCIAL DATA: *Note: Data for latest year may not have been available at press time.*

In U.S. $	2016	2015	2014	2013	2012	2011
Revenue	3,600,000,000	6,508,000,000	6,676,000,000	6,906,000,000	6,730,000,000	6,190,000,000
R&D Expense	748,000,000	1,144,000,000	1,038,000,000	1,012,000,000	969,000,000	862,000,000
Operating Income	457,000,000	1,149,000,000	1,183,000,000	1,123,000,000	1,079,000,000	880,000,000
Operating Margin %	12.69%	17.65%	17.72%	16.26%	16.03%	14.21%
SGA Expense	1,587,000,000	2,702,000,000	2,880,000,000	3,185,000,000	3,251,000,000	3,012,000,000
Net Income	2,488,000,000	878,000,000	898,000,000	765,000,000	1,172,000,000	597,000,000
Operating Cash Flow	796,000,000	1,312,000,000	1,281,000,000	1,593,000,000	1,901,000,000	1,794,000,000
Capital Expenditure	272,000,000	381,000,000	260,000,000	336,000,000	286,000,000	268,000,000
EBITDA	766,000,000	1,611,000,000	1,731,000,000	1,800,000,000	2,241,000,000	1,519,000,000
Return on Assets %	19.90%	6.55%	6.43%	5.58%	9.10%	4.98%
Return on Equity %	51.77%	14.96%	16.00%	14.55%	24.36%	13.15%
Debt to Equity	0.60	0.29	0.36	0.38	0.40	0.43

CONTACT INFORMATION:

Phone: 650 527-8000   Fax:
Toll-Free:
Address: 350 Ellis St., Mountain View, CA 94043 United States

STOCK TICKER/OTHER:

Stock Ticker: SYMC
Employees: 19,000
Parent Company:

Exchange: NAS
Fiscal Year Ends: 03/31

SALARIES/BONUSES:

Top Exec. Salary: $536,750   Bonus: $500,000
Second Exec. Salary: Bonus: $
$1,000,000

OTHER THOUGHTS:

Estimated Female Officers or Directors: 3
Hot Spot for Advancement for Women/Minorities: Y

SYNNEX Corp
NAIC Code: 423430

TYPES OF BUSINESS:
IT Supply Chain Services
Distribution Services
Contract Assembly Services
Outsourcing Services

BRANDS/DIVISIONS/AFFILIATES:
SYNNEX Canada Ltd
SYNNEX de Mexico SA de CV
SYNNEX Infotec Corporation
Concentrix

CONTACTS: Note: Officers with more than one job title may be intentionally listed here more than once.
Kevin Murai, CEO
Marshall Witt, CFO
Matthew Miau, Chairman Emeritus
Dwight Steffensen, Chairman of the Board
Dennis Polk, COO
Christopher Caldwell, Executive VP
Simon Leung, General Counsel
Peter Larocque, President, Divisional

GROWTH PLANS/SPECIAL FEATURES:
SYNNEX Corp. is a leading business process services company, serving resellers, retailers and original equipment manufacturers (OEMs) around the world. The firm operates in two segments: technology solutions and Concentrix. The technology solutions segment distributes computer systems and complimentary products to a variety of customers including value-added resellers, system integrators and retailers. This segment also provides assembly services to OEMs, including integrated supply chain management; build-to-order and configure-to-order system configurations; materials; and management and logistics. Subsidiary SYNNEX Infotec Corporation distributes IT equipment, electronic components and software in Japan. The Concentrix segment offers a range of services, including customer management software development, web hosting, hosted software, domain name registration and back office processing. SYNNEX delivers these services through various methods, including voice, chat, web, e-mail and digital print. The company purchases IT systems from OEM suppliers, such as Acer, Hewlett-Packard Co., Panasonic, Lenovo and Seagate and sells them to its reseller and retail customers. It currently distributes over 30,000 technology products from over 300 OEM suppliers to more than 20,000 resellers. The firm operates approximately 40 distribution facilities in the U.S., Canada, Japan and Mexico. Foreign subsidiaries include SYNNEX Canada Ltd. and SYNNEX de Mexico, SA de CV. In late 2013, the firm acquired IBM's customer care outsourcing business and combined it with Concentrix, a wholly owned subsidiary of SYNNEX, to become one of the world's foremost customer engagement outsourcing company in the $55 billion+ CRM BPO market.

SYNNEX employees receive medical, dental and vision insurance; flexible spending accounts; a 401(k); life and AD&D insurance; short- and long-term disability insurance; a discount stock purchase plan; an employee assistance program; a product purchase plan; pet insurance; and tuition reimbursement.

FINANCIAL DATA: Note: Data for latest year may not have been available at press time.

In U.S. $	2016	2015	2014	2013	2012	2011
Revenue		13,338,400,000	13,839,590,000	10,845,160,000	10,285,510,000	10,409,840,000
R&D Expense						
Operating Income		354,552,000	308,507,000	240,828,000	255,012,000	256,228,000
Operating Margin %		2.65%	2.22%	2.22%	2.47%	2.46%
SGA Expense		837,239,000	790,497,000	414,142,000	401,725,000	374,270,000
Net Income		208,525,000	180,034,000	152,237,000	151,376,000	150,331,000
Operating Cash Flow		643,609,000	-234,772,000	35,707,000	242,793,000	219,153,000
Capital Expenditure		100,106,000	57,377,000	28,965,000	14,481,000	40,153,000
EBITDA		458,062,000	400,206,000	265,290,000	279,642,000	280,901,000
Return on Assets %		4.50%	4.47%	4.84%	5.22%	5.63%
Return on Equity %		11.93%	11.74%	11.15%	12.22%	13.97%
Debt to Equity		0.35	0.15	0.04	0.06	0.19

CONTACT INFORMATION:
Phone: 510 656-3333   Fax: 510 668-3777
Toll-Free: 800-756-9888
Address: 44201 Nobel Dr., Fremont, CA 94538 United States

STOCK TICKER/OTHER:
Stock Ticker: SNX   Exchange: NYS
Employees: 72,500   Fiscal Year Ends: 11/30
Parent Company:

SALARIES/BONUSES:
Top Exec. Salary: $624,582   Bonus: $
Second Exec. Salary: Bonus: $
$452,820

OTHER THOUGHTS:
Estimated Female Officers or Directors: 2
Hot Spot for Advancement for Women/Minorities:

Synopsys Inc

www.synopsys.com

NAIC Code: 0

TYPES OF BUSINESS:

Computer Software-Electronic Design Automation
Consulting & Support Services

BRANDS/DIVISIONS/AFFILIATES:

Galaxy Design Platform
Verification Continuum Platform
DesignWare
Yield Explorer
Odyssey Yield Management
Codenomicon
Atrenta
Elliptic Technologies

CONTACTS: Note: Officers with more than one job title may be intentionally listed here more than once.

Aart de Geus, Co-CEO
Chi-Foon Chan, Pres.
Aart de Geus, Chmn.

GROWTH PLANS/SPECIAL FEATURES:

Synopsys, Inc. is a supplier of electronic design automation (EDA) software and related services for the design, creation and testing of integrated circuits (IC). The firm also offers pre-designed circuits used as components in larger chip designs as well as technical and support services. Synopsys' products and services are divided into four groups: Core EDA, intellectual property (IP) and software solutions, manufacturing solutions and professional services. The company's Core EDA products, which include the Galaxy Design Platform (GDP), the Verification Continuum Platform and the FPGA (Field Programmable Gate Array) design products, are used by semiconductor manufacturers to automate the integrated circuit design process and reduce errors. GDP provides a single, integrated IC design, while the Verification Continuum provides virtual prototyping, static and formal verification, simulation, emulation, FPGA-based prototyping, and debug in a unified environment. FPGA design products are complex chips that can be programmed to perform a specific function. The IP and software solutions group includes IP products and components, providing high-quality, silicon-proven IP solutions for systems on a chip (Socs), marketed under the DesignWare brand. Manufacturing solutions enable semiconductor manufacturers to more quickly develop new fabrication processes. Solutions include Technology-CAD (TCAD) device and process simulation products, Proteus optical proximity correction (OPC) products, CATS mask data preparation product and Yield Explorer and Odyssey Yield Management solutions. The professional services group provides consulting and design services which address all phases of the SoC development process. In 2015, the firm acquired Codenomicon, a Finland-based software security company; Elliptic Technologies; the Bluetooth Smart IP from Silicon Vision; certain assets of Quotium, including the Seeker product and R&D team; and Atrenta, a provider of SoC realization solutions.

Employee benefits include medical, dental and vision coverage; life, AD&D and disability insurance; an employee assistance program; educational assistance; adoption benefits; and a wellness program.

FINANCIAL DATA: Note: Data for latest year may not have been available at press time.

In U.S. $	2016	2015	2014	2013	2012	2011
Revenue		2,242,211,000	2,057,472,000	1,962,214,000	1,756,017,000	1,535,643,000
R&D Expense		776,229,000	718,768,000	669,197,000	581,628,000	491,871,000
Operating Income		266,466,000	248,717,000	246,493,000	190,024,000	212,843,000
Operating Margin %		11.88%	12.08%	12.56%	10.82%	13.86%
SGA Expense		639,504,000	608,294,000	569,773,000	573,088,000	475,878,000
Net Income		225,934,000	259,124,000	247,800,000	182,402,000	221,364,000
Operating Cash Flow		495,160,000	550,953,000	496,705,000	486,068,000	440,316,000
Capital Expenditure		90,647,000	106,913,000	69,068,000	57,493,000	60,230,000
EBITDA		496,245,000	466,863,000	464,766,000	359,966,000	341,393,000
Return on Assets %		4.60%	5.67%	5.82%	4.85%	6.65%
Return on Equity %		7.29%	8.86%	9.36%	7.92%	10.53%
Debt to Equity			0.01	0.02	0.04	

CONTACT INFORMATION:

Phone: 650 584-5000   Fax: 650 965-8637
Toll-Free: 800-541-7737
Address: 700 E. Middlefield Rd., Mountain View, CA 94043 United States

STOCK TICKER/OTHER:

Stock Ticker: SNPS
Employees: 10,284
Parent Company:

Exchange: NAS
Fiscal Year Ends: 10/31

SALARIES/BONUSES:

Top Exec. Salary: $500,000   Bonus: $
Second Exec. Salary: Bonus: $
$500,000

OTHER THOUGHTS:

Estimated Female Officers or Directors: 3
Hot Spot for Advancement for Women/Minorities: Y

Syntel Inc

NAIC Code: 518210

www.syntelinc.com

TYPES OF BUSINESS:

Business Process Outsourcing
Outsourcing Services
e-Business Solutions
Application Development & Management

BRANDS/DIVISIONS/AFFILIATES:

CONTACTS: *Note: Officers with more than one job title may be intentionally listed here more than once.*

Sanjay Garg, CEO, Subsidiary
Anil Agrawal, CFO
Bharat Desai, Chairman of the Board
Daniel Moore, Chief Administrative Officer
Rakesh Khanna, COO
Prashant Ranade, Director
Neerja Sethi, Director
Anil Jain, Other Corporate Officer
Srinath Mallya, Other Corporate Officer
Murlidhar Reddy, Other Corporate Officer
Raja Ray, Other Corporate Officer
Nitin Rakesh, President
Rajiv Tandon, Senior VP, Divisional
Srikanth Karra, Senior VP, Divisional
Rajesh Save, Senior VP, Divisional
V. S. Raj, Senior VP, Divisional
Christopher Mason, Senior VP, Divisional
Avinash Salelkar, Vice President, Divisional

GROWTH PLANS/SPECIAL FEATURES:

Syntel, Inc. is a global provider of digital transformation
information technology (IT) and knowledge proces
outsourcing services to Global 2000 companies. The fir
operates through five business segments which each he
Syntel customers adapt to market change by providing an arra
of technology-based, industry-specific solutions. Thes
segments include banking & financial services, healthcare
life sciences, insurance, manufacturing and retail, logistics
telecom (RLT). Banking & financial services include
companies that provide banking, capital markets, cards
payments, investments and transaction processing services
third parties. The healthcare & life sciences segment include
healthcare payers & providers, as well as pharmaceutical
medical device providers, among others. This division focuse
on addressing regulatory requirements and emerging industr
trends such as integrated care, wider use of electronic heal
records and the increasing prevalence of healthcare banking
The insurance segment serves the needs of global property
casualty insurers, insurance brokers, as well as persona
commercial, life and retirement insurance service providers
The manufacturing segment provides technology services an
business consulting in a range of sub-sectors, includin
industrial products, aerospace & automotive manufacturing, a
well as to processors of raw materials, natural resources an
chemicals. The RLT segment serves retailers & distributors
including supermarkets, specialty premium retailers
department stores and large mass-merchandise discounter
who seek Syntel's assistance in becoming more efficient an
cost-effective, as well as in helping to drive busines
transformation. This division also serves the entire travel
hospitality industry, including airlines, hotels & restaurants, a
well as online & retail travel, global distribution systems
intermediaries and real estate companies.

FINANCIAL DATA: *Note: Data for latest year may not have been available at press time.*

In U.S. $	2016	2015	2014	2013	2012	2011
Revenue		968,612,000	911,429,000	824,765,000	723,903,000	642,404,000
R&D Expense						
Operating Income		283,745,000	268,350,000	267,602,000	211,940,000	138,228,000
Operating Margin %		29.29%	29.44%	32.44%	29.27%	21.51%
SGA Expense		100,256,000	109,217,000	96,587,000	103,044,000	108,721,000
Net Income		252,526,000	249,740,000	219,658,000	185,543,000	122,856,000
Operating Cash Flow		223,521,000	233,400,000	199,966,000	188,688,000	109,052,000
Capital Expenditure		17,013,000	19,218,000	20,495,000	32,255,000	38,232,000
EBITDA		299,312,000	284,492,000	282,076,000	226,385,000	155,108,000
Return on Assets %		19.07%	22.48%	25.49%	28.04%	21.49%
Return on Equity %		23.97%	29.90%	34.10%	35.04%	26.01%
Debt to Equity			0.13	0.19		

CONTACT INFORMATION:

Phone: 248 619-2800   Fax: 248 619-2888
Toll-Free:
Address: 525 E. Big Beaver Rd., Ste. 300, Troy, MI 48083 United States

STOCK TICKER/OTHER:

Stock Ticker: SYNT   Exchange: NAS
Employees: 24,537   Fiscal Year Ends: 12/31
Parent Company:

SALARIES/BONUSES:

Top Exec. Salary: $399,066   Bonus: $31,562
Second Exec. Salary: Bonus: $26,495
$311,488

OTHER THOUGHTS:

Estimated Female Officers or Directors:
Hot Spot for Advancement for Women/Minorities:

SYSCO Corporation

www.sysco.com

NAIC Code: 424410

TYPES OF BUSINESS:
Food-Wholesale Distribution
Restaurant Supplies Distribution
Medical & Surgical Supplies Distribution
Cleaning Supplies Distribution

BRANDS/DIVISIONS/AFFILIATES:
SYGMA
Tannis Trading Inc
Brakes Group
North Star Seafood
Supplies on the Fly

CONTACTS: *Note: Officers with more than one job title may be intentionally listed here more than once.*
William Delaney, CEO
Joel Grade, CFO
Jackie Ward, Chairman of the Board
Wayne Shurts, Chief Technology Officer
Paul Moskowitz, Executive VP, Divisional
R. Charlton, Executive VP, Divisional
William Day, Executive VP, Divisional
Russell Libby, Executive VP, Divisional
Thomas Bene, President
Shannon Mutschler, Vice President, Divisional

GROWTH PLANS/SPECIAL FEATURES:
SYSCO Corporation, through its subsidiaries, is one of the largest distributors of food and food-related products to the foodservice industry in North America. The firm provides products and services to more than 425,000 customers, including restaurants, health care companies, educational facilities and lodging establishments. Restaurants account for approximately 64% of the company's sales; health care, 9%; education and government, 8%; travel, leisure and retail, 8%; and other sources, 11%. SYSCO distributes a wide variety of frozen and imported foods; fresh meats and seafood; dairy items; fresh produce; and nonfood items, including tableware, restaurant/kitchen equipment, medical/surgical supplies and cleaning supplies. Subsidiary SYGMA distributes a full line of food products, non-food products and customer-specific proprietary products to certain chain restaurant customer locations. The company operates 197 distribution facilities throughout the U.S., Bahamas, Canada and Ireland, with a fleet of approximately 9,600 delivery vehicles (consisting of tractor and trailer combinations, vans and panel trucks). In June 2015, the firm terminated its merger agreement with US Foods after a U.S. Federal judge ruled that Sysco-US Foods would control 75% of the U.S. foodservice industry and stifle competition. That same year, SYSCO acquired Tannis Trading, Inc., a broadline foodservice distributor in Ontario, Canada. In 2016, it acquired Brakes Group, a foodservice distributor in the U.K., France and Sweden, for $3.1 billion; North Star Seafood, a distributor of high-quality fresh and frozen seafood; and Supplies on the Fly, an eCommerce platform that provides restaurant supplies.

The firm offers employees life, disability, medical, dental and vision insurance; annual performance incentives; an assistance program; tuition assistance; a stock purchase plan; matching charity gifts; a 401(k); direct deposit; and product discounts.

FINANCIAL DATA: *Note: Data for latest year may not have been available at press time.*

In U.S. $	2016	2015	2014	2013	2012	2011
Revenue	50,366,920,000	48,680,750,000	46,516,710,000	44,411,230,000	42,380,940,000	39,323,490,000
R&D Expense						
Operating Income	1,850,500,000	1,229,362,000	1,587,122,000	1,658,478,000	1,890,632,000	1,931,502,000
Operating Margin %	3.67%	2.52%	3.41%	3.73%	4.46%	4.91%
SGA Expense	7,189,972,000	7,322,154,000	6,593,913,000	6,209,113,000	5,785,945,000	5,389,646,000
Net Income	949,622,000	686,773,000	931,533,000	992,427,000	1,121,585,000	1,152,030,000
Operating Cash Flow	1,933,142,000	1,555,484,000	1,492,815,000	1,511,594,000	1,404,180,000	1,091,518,000
Capital Expenditure	527,346,000	542,830,000	523,206,000	511,862,000	784,501,000	636,442,000
EBITDA	2,401,863,000	1,815,975,000	2,155,427,000	2,188,498,000	2,314,341,000	2,348,309,000
Return on Assets %	5.47%	4.40%	7.21%	8.01%	9.55%	10.61%
Return on Equity %	21.73%	13.04%	17.81%	20.09%	23.88%	27.00%
Debt to Equity	2.10	0.43	0.45	0.50	0.58	0.48

CONTACT INFORMATION:
Phone: 281 584-1390   Fax: 281 584-2880
Toll-Free:
Address: 1390 Enclave Pkwy., Houston, TX 77077 United States

STOCK TICKER/OTHER:
Stock Ticker: SYY   Exchange: NYS
Employees: 51,700   Fiscal Year Ends: 06/30
Parent Company:

SALARIES/BONUSES:
Top Exec. Salary: Bonus: $
$1,220,583
Second Exec. Salary: Bonus: $
$732,875

OTHER THOUGHTS:
Estimated Female Officers or Directors: 8

Hot Spot for Advancement for Women/Minorities: Y

Sales, profits and employees may be estimates. Financial information, benefits and other data can change quickly and may vary from those stated here.

T Rowe Price Group Inc

NAIC Code: 523920

TYPES OF BUSINESS:

Investment Management & Mutual Funds
Retirement Accounts
Advisory Services

BRANDS/DIVISIONS/AFFILIATES:

T Rowe Price Associates Inc
T Rowe Price International Ltd
T Rowe Price Singapore Private Ltd
T Rowe Price Hong Kong Limited
Emerging Markets Value Stock Fund

CONTACTS: Note: Officers with more than one job title may be intentionally listed here more than once.

Kenneth Moreland, CFO
Brian Rogers, Chairman of the Board
Jessica Hiebler, Chief Accounting Officer
William Stromberg, Director
Edward Bernard, Director
Christopher Alderson, Other Corporate Officer
Eric Veiel, Other Corporate Officer
David Oestreicher, Other Executive Officer
Edward Wiese, Vice President

GROWTH PLANS/SPECIAL FEATURES:

T. Rowe Price Group, Inc. is a financial services holding company. The firm derives revenue primarily from investment advisory services that it provides to individual and institutional investors. The firm manages approximately $772.7 billion in assets. T. Rowe Price operates its investment advisory business through subsidiaries T. Rowe Price Associates, Inc. and T. Rowe Price International, Ltd. In Hong Kong and Singapore, T. Rowe Price operates through T. Rowe Price Hong Kong Limited and T. Rowe Price Singapore Private Ltd. respectively. Products and services for the individual investor include mutual funds, retirement accounts, rollover IRAs, college savings plans, private asset management, high-net-worth services, banking services and advisory services. In addition to investment services, T. Rowe Price offers institutional clients retirement plan services, including small business and corporate retirement plans as well as public sector plans for religious institutions, schools and hospitals. The company introduces new mutual funds and other investment portfolios in an attempt to complement and expand its investment offerings and respond to competitive developments in the marketplace. The firm manages a broad range of domestic and international stock, bonds and mutual funds and other investment portfolios. T. Rowe Price also offers administrative services to its clients, including mutual fund transferring, accounting and shareholder services, record keeping and transfer agent services for defined contribution retirement plans, discount brokerages and trust services. In 2015, the firm launched the Emerging Markets Value Stock Fund, which invests in emerging markets companies that are out of favor and undervalued but possess identified catalysts that could drive their stock prices higher.

The firm offers its employees medical, dental, prescription, vision, retiree, travel, life, AD&D, short- and long-term disability insurance; a nurse hotline; Lasik vision discount; fitness club reimbursement; a 401(k); flexible spending accounts; adoption assistance; tuition reimbursement; and community support programs.

FINANCIAL DATA: Note: Data for latest year may not have been available at press time.

In U.S. $	2016	2015	2014	2013	2012	2011
Revenue		4,200,600,000	3,982,100,000	3,484,200,000	3,022,500,000	2,747,100,000
R&D Expense						
Operating Income		1,898,900,000	1,890,900,000	1,637,400,000	1,364,300,000	1,226,900,000
Operating Margin %		45.20%	47.48%	46.99%	45.13%	44.66%
SGA Expense		1,523,300,000	1,405,600,000	1,498,600,000	1,137,400,000	1,060,600,000
Net Income		1,223,000,000	1,229,600,000	1,047,700,000	883,600,000	773,200,000
Operating Cash Flow		1,506,400,000	1,291,300,000	1,233,200,000	902,800,000	948,400,000
Capital Expenditure		151,300,000	126,200,000	105,800,000	76,900,000	82,300,000
EBITDA		2,025,200,000	2,002,600,000	1,728,400,000	1,445,600,000	1,299,300,000
Return on Assets %		22.45%	22.76%	22.48%	22.16%	20.76%
Return on Equity %		23.76%	23.80%	23.96%	24.31%	22.91%
Debt to Equity						

CONTACT INFORMATION:

Phone: 410 345-2000   Fax: 410 345-2394
Toll-Free: 800-638-7890
Address: 100 E. Pratt St., Baltimore, MD 21202 United States

STOCK TICKER/OTHER:

Stock Ticker: TROW   Exchange: NAS
Employees: 5,999   Fiscal Year Ends: 12/31
Parent Company:

SALARIES/BONUSES:

Top Exec. Salary: $350,000   Bonus: $
Second Exec. Salary: Bonus: $
$350,000

OTHER THOUGHTS:

Estimated Female Officers or Directors:
Hot Spot for Advancement for Women/Minorities:

Team Health Holdings Inc

www.teamhealth.com

NAIC Code: 621111

TYPES OF BUSINESS:

Physicians and Hospital Staff Services
Hospital Administrative Services
Pediatrics
Radiology & Teleradiology Services
Urgent Care

BRANDS/DIVISIONS/AFFILIATES:

TeamHealth Medical Call Center
Children's Emergency Services
Tri-City Emergency Medical Group
Lake County Anesthesia Associates
Signature Healthcare Solutions

CONTACTS: Note: Officers with more than one job title may be intentionally listed here more than once.

David Jones, CFO
H. Massingale, Chairman of the Board
Miles Snowden, Chief Medical Officer
Oliver Rogers, Executive VP
Steven Clifton, Executive VP

GROWTH PLANS/SPECIAL FEATURES:

Team Health Holdings, Inc. is a provider of clinical outsourcing services such as emergency department administration and staffing. The company serves approximately 990 civilian and military hospitals, clinics and physician groups in 47 states with a team of approximately 13,000 affiliated health care professionals including physicians, physician assistants, nurse practitioners, and nurses. Team Health also manages recruiting, hiring, payroll, billing, collection and benefits functions. The company provides both permanent and temporary assistance to its clients. It also provides a full range of outsourced physician staffing and administrative services in emergency medicine, inpatient services (hospitalists comprising the specialties of internal medicine, orthopedic surgery, general surgery, and OB/GYN), anesthesiology, urgent care, pediatrics and other hospital-based functions. Additionally, it provides a full range of health care management services to military treatment and government facilities. Moreover, the company provides non-physician staffing services, including such services as para-professional providers, nursing, specialty technicians and administrative staffing to military and government facilities. The TeamHealth Medical Call Center provides services to hospitals, physician groups and managed care organizations, and are designed to be the one source for expertise in both clinical and non-clinical inbound and outbound call models. The call center is available 24 hours a day, every day. In 2015, the firm acquired Ruby Crest Emergency Medicine, Professional Anesthesia Service, Inc., Princeton Emergency Physicians, as well as Brookhaven Anesthesia Associates. It also agreed to acquire IPC Healthcare for $1.6 billion.

The company offers employees health, dental and vision insurance; life insurance; a 401(k); flexible spending accounts; disability coverage; and supplementary retirement plans.

FINANCIAL DATA: Note: Data for latest year may not have been available at press time.

In U.S. $	2016	2015	2014	2013	2012	2011
Revenue		3,597,247,000	2,819,643,000	2,383,595,000	2,069,023,000	1,745,328,000
R&D Expense						
Operating Income		236,913,000	184,610,000	162,598,000	125,281,000	131,738,000
Operating Margin %		6.58%	6.54%	6.82%	6.05%	7.54%
SGA Expense		308,193,000	281,054,000	228,911,000	220,799,000	169,147,000
Net Income		82,711,000	97,738,000	87,409,000	63,772,000	65,521,000
Operating Cash Flow		145,824,000	198,663,000	154,409,000	78,171,000	98,799,000
Capital Expenditure		40,690,000	24,576,000	21,378,000	22,005,000	11,977,000
EBITDA		345,075,000	261,143,000	217,218,000	164,979,000	161,702,000
Return on Assets %		2.74%	5.85%	6.82%	5.99%	7.54%
Return on Equity %		15.56%	28.42%	45.51%	94.94%	
Debt to Equity		3.63	1.37	1.80	4.28	22.12

CONTACT INFORMATION:

Phone: 865 693-1000   Fax:
Toll-Free: 800-818-1498
Address: 265 Brookview Ctr. Way, Ste. 400, Knoxville, TN 37919 United States

STOCK TICKER/OTHER:

Stock Ticker: TMH   Exchange: NYS
Employees: 13,200   Fiscal Year Ends: 12/31
Parent Company:

SALARIES/BONUSES:

Top Exec. Salary: $972,115   Bonus: $
Second Exec. Salary: $682,770   Bonus: $

OTHER THOUGHTS:

Estimated Female Officers or Directors: 3
Hot Spot for Advancement for Women/Minorities: Y

Sales, profits and employees may be estimates. Financial information, benefits and other data can change quickly and may vary from those stated here.

Team Inc

NAIC Code: 237120

www.teamindustrialservices.com

TYPES OF BUSINESS:

Piping System Maintenance & Construction Services

BRANDS/DIVISIONS/AFFILIATES:

Quest Integrity Group
Qualspec Group
Furmanite Corporation

CONTACTS: Note: Officers with more than one job title may be intentionally listed here more than once.

Greg Boane, CFO
Philip Hawk, Chairman of the Board
Andre Bouchard, Executive VP
Arthur Victorson, President, Divisional
Jeffrey Ott, President, Divisional
Declan Rushe, President, Divisional
Peter Wallace, President, Divisional
Ted Owen, President

GROWTH PLANS/SPECIAL FEATURES:

Team, Inc. is an industrial services provider. These service
include the inspection & assessment required in maintainin
high temperature and high pressure piping systems an
vessels utilized in the refining, petrochemical, power, pipelin
and other heavy industries. Team operates through thre
segments: inspection & heat treating services (IHT
mechanical services and Quest Integrity Group. IHT provide
both inspection services and heat treating services generall
associated with turnaround or project activities. These activitie
include non-destructive evaluation & testing services
radiographic testing, ultrasonic testing, magnetic particl
inspection, liquid penetrant inspection, positive materia
identification, electromagnetic testing, eddy current testing
long-range guided ultrasonics, phased array ultrasonic testing
tank inspection & management, rope access, mechanica
services and field heat treating services. The mechanica
services segment offers both on-stream services an
turnaround/project related services such as leak repair, fugitiv
emissions control, hot tapping, field machining, technica
bolting, valve repair, heat exchanger & maintenance, isolatio
& test plug solutions and valve insertion. Quest Integrit
provides integrity management solutions to the energy industr
in the form of advanced quantitative inspection and engineerin
assessment services and projects. Its advanced quantitativ
inspection services utilize proprietary non-destructive testing
examination instrumentation to provide technology-enable
inspections of fired heaters, piping systems and stear
reformers, primarily to the process, pipeline and powe
industries. Quest Integrity also offers engineering assessmer
services by Team's proprietary software and analytic models
The company maintains over 150 locations throughout th
world. During 2015, the firm acquired Qualspec Group,
provider of non-destructive testing services in the U.S. In Marc
2016, it acquired Furmanite Corporation, a provider of on-sit
industrial plant turnaround maintenance and on-line contractc
engineered services.

FINANCIAL DATA: Note: Data for latest year may not have been available at press time.

In U.S. $	2016	2015	2014	2013	2012	2011
Revenue		842,047,000	749,527,000	714,311,000	623,740,000	508,020,000
R&D Expense						
Operating Income		68,465,000	53,421,000	55,602,000	56,497,000	42,475,000
Operating Margin %		8.13%	7.12%	7.78%	9.05%	8.36%
SGA Expense		189,528,000	171,455,000	158,355,000	139,737,000	115,698,000
Net Income		40,070,000	29,855,000	32,436,000	32,911,000	26,585,000
Operating Cash Flow		43,471,000	52,861,000	58,643,000	36,652,000	28,480,000
Capital Expenditure		28,769,000	33,016,000	26,068,000	23,933,000	13,158,000
EBITDA		91,252,000	74,889,000	74,323,000	73,966,000	57,059,000
Return on Assets %		7.94%	6.31%	7.50%	8.66%	8.56%
Return on Equity %		12.50%	9.98%	12.31%	14.81%	14.38%
Debt to Equity		0.23	0.23	0.25	0.35	0.37

CONTACT INFORMATION:

Phone: 281-331-6154　　　Fax:
Toll-Free: 800-662-8326
Address: 13131 Dairy Ashford Rd., Sugar Land, TX 77478 United States

STOCK TICKER/OTHER:

Stock Ticker: TISI　　　　　　　　Exchange: NYS
Employees: 4,800　　　　　　　　Fiscal Year Ends: 05/31
Parent Company:

SALARIES/BONUSES:

Top Exec. Salary: $788,040　　Bonus: $
Second Exec. Salary:　　　　　Bonus: $225,000
$493,378

OTHER THOUGHTS:

Estimated Female Officers or Directors:
Hot Spot for Advancement for Women/Minorities:

Sales, profits and employees may be estimates. Financial information, benefits and other data can change quickly and may vary from those stated here.

Tech Data Corp

www.techdata.com

NAIC Code: 423430

TYPES OF BUSINESS:
Computer & Software Products, Distribution
Training
Assembly Services

BRANDS/DIVISIONS/AFFILIATES:

CONTACTS: *Note: Officers with more than one job title may be intentionally listed here more than once.*
Robert Dutkowsky, CEO
Alain Amsellem, CFO, Geographical
Joseph Trepani, CFO, Geographical
Charles Dannewitz, CFO
Steven Raymund, Chairman of the Board
John Tonnison, Chief Information Officer
Richard Hume, COO
David Vetter, General Counsel
Beth Simonetti, Other Corporate Officer
Joseph Quaglia, President, Geographical
Nestor Cano, President, Geographical
Jeffrey Taylor, Senior VP

GROWTH PLANS/SPECIAL FEATURES:
Tech Data Corp. is a worldwide distributor of information technology (IT) products, logistics management and other value-added services. The company serves more than 115,000 value-added resellers (VARs), direct marketers, retailers and corporate resellers in over 100 countries throughout Europe, Latin America and North America. It offers a variety of products from manufacturers and publishers, including Lenovo, Apple Computer, Autodesk, Toshiba, Xerox, Kodak and Panasonic. Products are typically purchased directly from manufacturers or software publishers on a non-exclusive basis and then shipped to customers from one of Tech Data's 32 regionally located logistics centers. The company's vendor agreements do not restrict it from selling similar products manufactured by competitors. The firm also provides resellers with extensive pre- and post-sale training, service and support as well as configuration and assembly services and e-commerce tools. Tech Data provides products and services to the online reseller channel and does business with thousands of resellers through its web site. The firm's entire electronic catalog is available online, and its electronic software distribution initiative allows resellers and vendors to easily access software titles directly from a secure location on the web site. In May 2015, the firm agreed to acquire certain assets of Signature Technology Group, Inc., a leading provider of data center and professional services. In Spetember 2016, the firm agreed to purchase Avnet Inc.'s technology solutions unit for approximately $2.6 billion.

FINANCIAL DATA: *Note: Data for latest year may not have been available at press time.*

In U.S. $	2016	2015	2014	2013	2012	2011
Revenue	26,379,780,000	27,670,630,000	26,821,900,000	25,358,330,000	26,488,120,000	24,375,970,000
R&D Expense						
Operating Income	401,428,000	267,635,000	227,513,000	263,720,000	327,858,000	333,985,000
Operating Margin %	1.52%	.96%	.84%	1.04%	1.23%	1.37%
SGA Expense	990,934,000	1,114,234,000	1,116,553,000	1,009,872,000	1,037,839,000	949,303,000
Net Income	265,736,000	175,172,000	179,932,000	176,255,000	206,396,000	214,243,000
Operating Cash Flow	188,993,000	119,381,000	379,148,000	120,753,000	503,412,000	103,843,000
Capital Expenditure	33,972,000	28,175,000	30,388,000	38,365,000	44,370,000	31,902,000
EBITDA	454,159,000	334,478,000	303,894,000	317,945,000	383,997,000	380,826,000
Return on Assets %	4.25%	2.63%	2.57%	2.79%	3.36%	3.45%
Return on Equity %	13.40%	8.63%	8.95%	9.05%	10.09%	10.19%
Debt to Equity	0.17	0.18	0.16	0.18	0.02	0.02

CONTACT INFORMATION:
Phone: 727 539-7429   Fax: 727 538-7808
Toll-Free: 800-237-8931
Address: 5350 Tech Data Dr., Clearwater, FL 33760 United States

STOCK TICKER/OTHER:
Stock Ticker: TECD
Employees: 9,000
Parent Company:

Exchange: NAS
Fiscal Year Ends: 01/31

SALARIES/BONUSES:
Top Exec. Salary: $1,089,421
Bonus: $
Second Exec. Salary: $790,726
Bonus: $

OTHER THOUGHTS:
Estimated Female Officers or Directors: 1

Hot Spot for Advancement for Women/Minorities:

Sales, profits and employees may be estimates. Financial information, benefits and other data can change quickly and may vary from those stated here.

Tenet Healthcare Corporation

www.tenethealth.com

NAIC Code: 622110

TYPES OF BUSINESS:

General Medical and Surgical Hospitals
Specialty Care Facilities
Outpatient Centers
Diagnostic Imaging Centers
Rural Health Care Clinics
HMOs

BRANDS/DIVISIONS/AFFILIATES:

Conifer Holdings Inc
Centennial Medical Center
Doctors Hospital
Lake Pointe Medical Center
Regional Medical Center
Baylor Scott & White Medical Center

CONTACTS: *Note: Officers with more than one job title may be intentionally listed here more than once.*

Trevor Fetter, CEO
Daniel Cancelmi, CFO
R. Ramsey, Chief Accounting Officer
Audrey Andrews, General Counsel
Paul Castanon, Other Corporate Officer
J. Evans, President, Divisional
Keith Pitts, Vice Chairman

GROWTH PLANS/SPECIAL FEATURES:

Tenet Healthcare Corporation specializes in the provision c
health care services, primarily through the operation of genera
hospitals. The company operates 86 hospitals, 20 short-sta
surgical hospitals, over 475 outpatient centers, nine facilities i
the U.K. and six health plans via subsidiaries, partnerships an
joint ventures. Subsidiary Conifer Holdings, Inc. provide
healthcare business process services in the areas of revenu
cycle management, technology-enabled performance an
health management to health systems, individual hospitals
physician practices, self-insured organizations and healt
plans. Each of the company's general hospitals offers acut
care services, operating and recovery rooms, radiolog
services, respiratory therapy services, clinical laboratories an
pharmacies. In addition, most offer intensive care, critical car
or coronary care units, physical therapy, as well as orthopedic
oncology and outpatient services. Some of the hospitals als
offer tertiary care services such as open-heart surgery
neonatal intensive care and neuroscience. Along wit
hospitals, Tenet's subsidiaries operate three academic medica
centers, two children's hospitals, two specialty hospitals an
two critical access hospitals, with a total of 22,525 license
beds, serving primarily urban and suburban communities in 1
states. In 2016, the firm sold two North Carolina and fiv
Atlanta-area hospitals and related operations; and formed
joint venture with Baylor Scott & White Health to own fiv
hospitals in North Texas, including Centennial Medical Cente
Doctors Hospital, Lake Pointe Medical Center, Regiona
Medical Center and Baylor Scott & White Medical Center.

The company offers its employees medical, dental and visio
insurance; life and AD&D insurance; a 401(k) plan; a
employee stock purchase plan; and credit union membership

FINANCIAL DATA: *Note: Data for latest year may not have been available at press time.*

In U.S. $	2016	2015	2014	2013	2012	2011
Revenue		18,634,000,000	16,615,000,000	11,102,000,000	9,119,000,000	8,854,000,000
R&D Expense						
Operating Income		1,056,000,000	925,000,000	663,000,000	749,000,000	650,000,000
Operating Margin %		5.66%	5.56%	5.97%	8.21%	7.34%
SGA Expense						
Net Income		-140,000,000	12,000,000	-134,000,000	152,000,000	82,000,000
Operating Cash Flow		1,026,000,000	687,000,000	589,000,000	593,000,000	497,000,000
Capital Expenditure		293,000,000	933,000,000	683,000,000	508,000,000	475,000,000
EBITDA		1,853,000,000	1,750,000,000	861,000,000	1,176,000,000	949,000,000
Return on Assets %		-.66%	.06%	-1.06%	1.61%	.68%
Return on Equity %		-20.86%	1.70%	-14.12%	12.63%	4.60%
Debt to Equity		20.81	17.96	14.15	4.51	3.94

CONTACT INFORMATION:

Phone: 469-893-2200   Fax:
Toll-Free:
Address: 1445 Ross Ave., Ste. 1400, Dallas, TX 75202 United States

STOCK TICKER/OTHER:

Stock Ticker: THC   Exchange: NYS
Employees: 130,000   Fiscal Year Ends: 12/31
Parent Company:

SALARIES/BONUSES:

Top Exec. Salary: Bonus: $
$1,316,346
Second Exec. Salary: Bonus: $
$828,577

OTHER THOUGHTS:

Estimated Female Officers or Directors: 5

Hot Spot for Advancement for Women/Minorities: Y

Sales, profits and employees may be estimates. Financial information, benefits and other data can change quickly and may vary from those stated here.

Tenneco Inc

NAIC Code: 336300

TYPES OF BUSINESS:

Automotive Parts Manufacturer
Advanced Suspension Technologies
Ride Control Products
Emissions Systems
Performance Mufflers
Noise Control Systems

BRANDS/DIVISIONS/AFFILIATES:

Clevite
Marzocchi
Elastomers
Monroe
Walker
DynoMax
Rancho
Axios

CONTACTS: *Note: Officers with more than one job title may be intentionally listed here more than once.*

Gregg Sherrill, CEO
Brian Kesseler, COO
Timothy Jackson, Executive VP, Divisional
Josep Fornos, Executive VP, Divisional
Kenneth Trammell, Executive VP
James Harrington, General Counsel
Joseph Pomaranski, General Manager, Divisional
Peng Guo, General Manager, Geographical
Gregg Bolt, Senior VP, Divisional
Michael Charlton, Senior VP, Divisional
Henry Hummel, Senior VP
Paul Novas, Vice President, Divisional
John Kunz, Vice President

GROWTH PLANS/SPECIAL FEATURES:

Tenneco, Inc. is a leading manufacturer of automotive emission control and ride control products and systems for both original equipment manufacturers (OEMs) and aftermarket retailers. The firm designs, manufactures and sells individual components for vehicles as well as groups of components that are combined as modules or systems within vehicles. The firm maintains 90 emission control manufacturing facilities and 15 engineering centers across six continents. Tenneco's primary brands are Monroe ride control products and Walker, Fonos and Dynomax emission control products. Other brands include Rancho, Clevite, Elastomers, Marzocchi, Axios, Kinetic and Fric-Rot ride control products and Thrush emission control products. Tenneco sells to more than 70 OEMs worldwide. Its leading customers are General Motors, which accounts for 15% of net sales, and Ford, 13%. In the aftermarket sector, Tenneco's customers serves more than 500 full-line and specialty warehouse distributors, retailers, jobbers, installer chains and car dealers such as National Auto Parts Association (NAPA), Advance Auto Parts, Uni-Select and O'Reilly Automotive in North America; Temot Autoteile GmbH, Autodistribution International, Group Auto Union, Auto Teile Ring and AP United in Europe; and Rede Presidente in South America. The firm's products are sold primarily in North America (48% of sales) and Europe, South America, Asia and India (52%).

FINANCIAL DATA: *Note: Data for latest year may not have been available at press time.*

In U.S. $	2016	2015	2014	2013	2012	2011
Revenue		8,209,000,000	8,420,000,000	7,964,000,000	7,363,000,000	7,205,000,000
R&D Expense		146,000,000	169,000,000	144,000,000	126,000,000	133,000,000
Operating Income		524,000,000	499,000,000	428,000,000	435,000,000	389,000,000
Operating Margin %		6.38%	5.92%	5.37%	5.90%	5.39%
SGA Expense		491,000,000	519,000,000	453,000,000	427,000,000	428,000,000
Net Income		247,000,000	226,000,000	183,000,000	275,000,000	157,000,000
Operating Cash Flow		517,000,000	341,000,000	503,000,000	365,000,000	245,000,000
Capital Expenditure		309,000,000	341,000,000	269,000,000	269,000,000	228,000,000
EBITDA		722,000,000	700,000,000	629,000,000	633,000,000	586,000,000
Return on Assets %		6.19%	5.76%	4.92%	7.91%	4.82%
Return on Equity %		53.11%	48.60%	53.90%	223.57%	
Debt to Equity		2.59	2.15	2.35	4.33	

CONTACT INFORMATION:

Phone: 847 482-5000   Fax: 847 482-5940
Toll-Free:
Address: 500 N. Field Dr., Lake Forest, IL 60045 United States

STOCK TICKER/OTHER:

Stock Ticker: TEN   Exchange: NYS
Employees: 29,000   Fiscal Year Ends: 12/31
Parent Company:

SALARIES/BONUSES:

Top Exec. Salary: $850,000   Bonus: $1,207,188
Second Exec. Salary: Bonus: $341,402
$1,120,500

OTHER THOUGHTS:

Estimated Female Officers or Directors: 4
Hot Spot for Advancement for Women/Minorities: Y

Tesla Motors Inc

www.teslamotors.com

NAIC Code: 336111

TYPES OF BUSINESS:

Automobile Manufacturing, All-Electric
Battery Manufacturing
Lithium Ion Battery Storage Technologies
Energy Storage Systems

BRANDS/DIVISIONS/AFFILIATES:

Model S
70D
Model X
Model 3
Tesla Powerwall
Gigafactory

CONTACTS: *Note: Officers with more than one job title may be intentionally listed here more than once.*

Elon Musk, CEO
Jason Wheeler, CFO
Jeffrey Straubel, Chief Technology Officer
Jon McNeill, President, Divisional
Gregory Reichow, Vice Chairman, Divisional
Douglas Field, Vice President, Divisional

GROWTH PLANS/SPECIAL FEATURES:

Tesla Motors, Inc. manufactures high-performance all-electri automobiles and energy storage products. Its sales have bee impressive, despite the relatively high price of its initial models and the company is widely admired for its innovation, design engineering and marketing. Tesla's Model S family sedan saw its first deliveries in June 2012. The Model S features lightweight aluminum body. The car can be ordered with either of two battery packs. The 70kWh battery version, called th 70D, offers all-wheel drive at a price of about $75,000. The 8 kWh model features 265-mile range and 0-60 acceleration c 5.4 seconds in the standard edition or 4.2 seconds in th performance model. Batteries come with an 8-year, 125,00C mile warranty. The company began deliveries of its Model crossover featuring gullwing doors in October 2015, which ca cost more than $130,000 when fully equipped. Tesla also plan to launch a Model 3 sedan in 2017 with a base price of abou $35,000, capable of traveling about 200 miles per charge Battery-wise, each Tesla car has thousands of small, lithium ion batteries linked together, similar to the batteries found i consumer electronics. The firm's system of convenient ca charger stations in high traffic urban areas, called Tesl Superchargers, are located in North America, Europe and Asia The Tesla Powerwall is an easy-to-install home-sized energ storage system intended to store local, solar-generated powe for later use. The company's Gigafactory near Reno, Nevada manufactures battery packs for the company's energy storag products, and plans to do the same for its vehicles. The factor is expected to have an annual capacity equal to 35 gigawat hours' worth of batteries (the equivalent of generating on billion watts for a single hour). Full capacity is expected to b reached by 2020. In 2016, the firm agreed to a $2.6 billion stoc merger with SolarCity Corp.

FINANCIAL DATA: *Note: Data for latest year may not have been available at press time.*

In U.S. $	2016	2015	2014	2013	2012	2011
Revenue		4,046,025,000	3,198,356,000	2,013,496,000	413,256,000	204,242,000
R&D Expense		717,900,000	464,700,000	231,976,000	273,978,000	208,981,000
Operating Income		-716,629,000	-186,689,000	-61,283,000	-394,283,000	-251,488,000
Operating Margin %		-17.71%	-5.83%	-3.04%	-95.40%	-123.13%
SGA Expense		922,232,000	603,660,000	285,569,000	150,372,000	104,102,000
Net Income		-888,663,000	-294,040,000	-74,014,000	-396,213,000	-254,411,000
Operating Cash Flow		-524,499,000	-57,337,000	257,994,000	-266,081,000	-114,364,000
Capital Expenditure		1,634,850,000	969,885,000	264,224,000	239,228,000	197,896,000
EBITDA		-334,183,000	48,181,000	67,591,000	-366,998,000	-236,960,000
Return on Assets %		-12.74%	-7.11%	-4.19%	-43.35%	-46.27%
Return on Equity %		-88.83%	-37.24%	-18.69%	-227.22%	-118.03%
Debt to Equity		1.87	2.05	0.89	3.29	1.21

CONTACT INFORMATION:

Phone: 650 681-5000   Fax:
Toll-Free:
Address: 3500 Deer Creek, Palo Alto, CA 94304 United States

STOCK TICKER/OTHER:

Stock Ticker: TSLA   Exchange: NAS
Employees: 10,161   Fiscal Year Ends: 12/31
Parent Company:

SALARIES/BONUSES:

Top Exec. Salary: $339,300   Bonus: $
Second Exec. Salary: Bonus: $
$306,923

OTHER THOUGHTS:

Estimated Female Officers or Directors: 1
Hot Spot for Advancement for Women/Minorities:

Sales, profits and employees may be estimates. Financial information, benefits and other data can change quickly and may vary from those stated here.

Textron Inc

NAIC Code: 336411

www.textron.com

TYPES OF BUSINESS:

Helicopters & General Aviation Aircraft Manufacturing
Aerospace
Electrical Test & Measurement Equipment
Fiber Optic Equipment
Off-Road Vehicles
Financing

BRANDS/DIVISIONS/AFFILIATES:

Bell Helicopter
Greenlee
Textron Aviation
Textron Financial Corporation
Jacobsen
Kautex
E-Z-GO
Textron Systems

CONTACTS: *Note: Officers with more than one job title may be intentionally listed here more than once.*

Scott Donnelly, CEO
Frank Connor, CFO
Mark Bamford, Chief Accounting Officer
Cheryl Johnson, Executive VP, Divisional
Robert Lupone, Executive VP

GROWTH PLANS/SPECIAL FEATURES:

Textron, Inc. is a global multi-industry company active in the aircraft, defense, industrial and finance industries. The company divides its operations into five segments: Bell Helicopter, Textron Systems, Textron Aviation, industrial and finance. Bell Helicopter supplies helicopters, tilt rotor aircraft and helicopter-related spare parts and services for military and commercial applications. It also offers commercially-certified helicopters to corporate; offshore petroleum exploration; utility; charter; and police, fire, rescue and emergency medical helicopter operators. Textron Systems manufactures weapons systems and surveillance and intelligence products for the defense, aerospace, homeland security and general aviation markets. It sells most of its products to U.S. government customers, but also to customers outside the U.S. through foreign military sales sponsored by the U.S. government and directly through commercial sales channels. Textron Aviation is home to the Beechcraft, Cessna and Hawker brands, which account for more than half of all general aviation aircraft flying. Its product portfolio includes five business lines: business jets, general aviation and special mission turboprop aircraft, high performance piston aircraft, military trainer and defense aircraft and a customer service organization. The industrial segment includes the business of E-Z-GO, Jacobsen, Kautex and Greenlee. These companies design, manufacture and sell diverse products such as golf carts, off-road utility vehicles, turf maintenance equipment, blow-molded fuel systems, electrical test and measurement instruments and fiber optic connectors. The finance segment consists of Textron Financial Corporation and its subsidiaries, which mostly support the company's other segments. In 2014, the firm acquired Beech Holdings LLC, and merged it with its Cessna business to form business segment, Textron Aviation.

Textron offers its employees medical, prescription, dental and vision coverage; flexible spending accounts; life, AD&D, business travel and disability insurance; adoption assistance; discounts on products and auto and home insurance; and educational assistance.

FINANCIAL DATA: *Note: Data for latest year may not have been available at press time.*

In U.S. $	2016	2015	2014	2013	2012	2011
Revenue		13,423,000,000	13,878,000,000	12,104,000,000	12,237,000,000	11,275,000,000
R&D Expense						
Operating Income		1,140,000,000	1,096,000,000	847,000,000	1,053,000,000	337,000,000
Operating Margin %		8.49%	7.89%	6.99%	8.60%	2.98%
SGA Expense		1,304,000,000	1,361,000,000	1,126,000,000	1,168,000,000	1,183,000,000
Net Income		697,000,000	600,000,000	498,000,000	589,000,000	242,000,000
Operating Cash Flow		1,090,000,000	1,208,000,000	810,000,000	927,000,000	1,063,000,000
Capital Expenditure		420,000,000	429,000,000	444,000,000	480,000,000	423,000,000
EBITDA		1,601,000,000	1,503,000,000	1,236,000,000	1,436,000,000	986,000,000
Return on Assets %		4.75%	4.35%	3.83%	4.42%	1.67%
Return on Equity %		15.09%	13.86%	13.50%	20.53%	8.46%
Debt to Equity		0.67	0.90	0.72	1.15	1.56

CONTACT INFORMATION:

Phone: 401 421-2800   Fax: 401 421-2878
Toll-Free:
Address: 40 Westminster St., Providence, RI 02903 United States

STOCK TICKER/OTHER:

Stock Ticker: TXT
Employees: 34,000
Parent Company:

Exchange: NYS
Fiscal Year Ends: 12/31

SALARIES/BONUSES:

Top Exec. Salary: Bonus: $
$1,151,154
Second Exec. Salary: Bonus: $
$925,000

OTHER THOUGHTS:

Estimated Female Officers or Directors: 10

Hot Spot for Advancement for Women/Minorities: Y

Thermo Fisher Scientific Inc

www.thermofisher.com

NAIC Code: 423450

TYPES OF BUSINESS:

Laboratory Equipment & Supplies Distribution
Contract Manufacturing
Equipment Calibration & Repair
Clinical Trial Services
Laboratory Workstations
Clinical Consumables
Diagnostic Reagents
Custom Chemical Synthesis

BRANDS/DIVISIONS/AFFILIATES:

Thermo Scientific
Applied Biosystems
Invitrogen
Fisher Scientific
Unity Lab Services
Alchematrix
Ecochem
Affymetrix Inc

CONTACTS: Note: Officers with more than one job title may be intentionally listed here more than once.

Marc Casper, CEO
Jim Manzi, Chairman of the Board
Peter Wilver, Executive VP
Mark Stevenson, Executive VP
Thomas Loewald, Other Executive Officer
Patrick Durbin, President, Divisional
Stephen Williamson, Senior VP
Daniel Shine, Senior VP
Seth Hoogasian, Senior VP
Peter Hornstra, Vice President

GROWTH PLANS/SPECIAL FEATURES:

Thermo Fisher Scientific, Inc. is a distributor of products an
services principally to the scientific-research and clinica
laboratory markets. The firm serves over 400,000 customer
including biotechnology and pharmaceutical companies
colleges and universities; medical-research institutions
hospitals; reference, quality control, process-control an
research and development labs in various industries; an
government agencies. It operates in four segments: lif
sciences solutions, analytical instruments, specialty
diagnostics and laboratory products & services. Life science
solutions provides a portfolio of reagents, instruments an
consumables used in biological and medical research, discove
and production of new drugs and vaccines. This division als
provides diagnosis of disease. Analytical instruments provide
a broad offering of instruments, consumables, software an
services used for a range of applications in the laboratory, o
the production line and in the field. These products are used b
customers in pharmaceutical, biotechnology, academic
government, environmental, research, industrial markets, a
well as clinical laboratories. Specialty diagnostics offers
range of diagnostic test kits, reagents, culture media
instruments and associated products in order to serv
customers in health care, clinical, pharmaceutical, industria
and food safety laboratories. Laboratory products & service
offers everything needed for the laboratory to enabl
customers to focus on core activities and become mor
efficient, productive and cost-effective. This segment'
products are used primarily for drug discovery & developmen
as well as for life science research in order to advance th
prevention and cure of diseases and enhance quality of life
The company's five primary brands include Thermo Scientific
Applied Biosystems, Invitrogen, Fisher Scientific and Unity La
Services. The firm has over 600 subsidiaries, includin
Alchematrix; Ecochem; Flux Instruments; LambTrack Ltd.; an
Fermentas International, Inc. In 2016, the firm acquire
Affymetrix, Inc.; and agreed to acquire FEI Company.

Employee benefits include tuition reimbursement, retiremen
plans and training & development opportunities. Benefits var
by country.

FINANCIAL DATA: Note: Data for latest year may not have been available at press time.

In U.S. $	2016	2015	2014	2013	2012	2011
Revenue		16,965,400,000	16,889,600,000	13,090,300,000	12,509,900,000	11,725,900,000
R&D Expense		692,300,000	691,100,000	395,500,000	376,400,000	340,600,000
Operating Income		2,336,200,000	2,503,000,000	1,609,600,000	1,482,100,000	1,245,200,000
Operating Margin %		13.77%	14.81%	12.29%	11.84%	10.61%
SGA Expense		4,612,100,000	4,896,100,000	3,446,300,000	3,354,900,000	3,126,500,000
Net Income		1,975,400,000	1,894,400,000	1,273,300,000	1,177,900,000	1,329,900,000
Operating Cash Flow		2,816,900,000	2,619,600,000	2,010,700,000	2,039,500,000	1,691,000,000
Capital Expenditure		422,900,000	427,600,000	282,400,000	315,100,000	266,500,000
EBITDA		4,039,500,000	4,251,900,000	2,581,500,000	2,494,700,000	2,165,400,000
Return on Assets %		4.71%	5.07%	4.29%	4.34%	5.52%
Return on Equity %		9.42%	10.12%	7.87%	7.72%	8.74%
Debt to Equity		0.53	0.60	0.56	0.45	0.38

CONTACT INFORMATION:

Phone: 781 622-1000   Fax: 781 933-4476
Toll-Free: 800-678-5599
Address: 81 Wyman St., Waltham, MA 02454 United States

STOCK TICKER/OTHER:

Stock Ticker: TMO
Employees: 52,000
Parent Company:

Exchange: NYS
Fiscal Year Ends: 12/31

SALARIES/BONUSES:

Top Exec. Salary:
$1,339,692
Second Exec. Salary:
$817,237

Bonus: $

Bonus: $

OTHER THOUGHTS:

Estimated Female Officers or Directors: 1

Hot Spot for Advancement for Women/Minorities: Y

Thomson Reuters Corp

www.thomsonreuters.com

NAIC Code: 0

TYPES OF BUSINESS:

Information Services & Software
Legal & Regulatory Information Services
Financial Information & Technology
Health Care Information Tools
Scientific Data Tools

BRANDS/DIVISIONS/AFFILIATES:

WestlawNext
Thomson IP Manager
Pangea3
Thomson Reuters Eikon
Dominio Sistemas
UBS Convertible Indices
K'Origin

CONTACTS: *Note: Officers with more than one job title may be intentionally listed here more than once.*

James Smith, CEO
David Craig, President, Divisional
Stephane Bello, CFO
David Thomson, Chairman of the Board
Rick King, Chief Information Officer
David Binet, Deputy Chairman
Neil Masterson, Executive VP
Brian Scanlon, Executive VP
Peter Warwick, Executive VP
Gustav Carlson, Executive VP
Deirdre Stanley, General Counsel
Mark Schlageter, Other Executive Officer
Vin Caraher, President, Divisional
Gonzalo Lissarrague, President, Divisional
Susan Martin, President, Divisional
Brian Peccarelli, President, Divisional
David Craig, President, Divisional

GROWTH PLANS/SPECIAL FEATURES:

Thomson Reuters provides specialized information in digital and print formats, with operations in 100 countries. The company is organized in two divisions: markets, which consists of the firm's financial and media businesses; and professional, which consists of the legal, tax and accounting, health care and science business segments. The markets division includes four units: sales & trading, which provides information, trading and post-trade connectivity requirements for the trading floor activities of clients; investment & advisory, which provides information to aid in investment management, wealth management and investment banking; enterprise, a technology and real and non-real time content provider for financial clients; and media, a journalist supported division providing news and information for the media and business industries. The professional division includes three units: legal, tax & accounting and intellectual property & science. The legal segment provides information, decision support tools and research services to legal professionals worldwide, primarily through the firm's WestlawNext online platform, which is offered through country-specific versions. The tax & accounting segment provides technology solutions, tax compliance and accounting software through two businesses: workflow & service solutions and business compliance & knowledge solutions. The intellectual property & science segment provides decision support solutions to assist professionals in the science and biopharmaceutical industry in managing expenditures and legal work. Major brands of the firm include Thomson IP Manager, an asset management solution for patents, trademarks, licensing agreements and more; Pangea3, which provides legal process outsourcing services; and Thomson Reuters Eikon, the company's flagship desktop product that provides pre-trade decision-making tools, news, pricing and charting. In 2014, the firm acquired Dominio Sistemas, as well as UBS Convertible Indices. In 2015, it acquired K'Origin, a content solution software that allows customers to take full advantage of the FTA and manage global operations more efficiently.

FINANCIAL DATA: *Note: Data for latest year may not have been available at press time.*

In U.S. $	2016	2015	2014	2013	2012	2011
Revenue		12,209,000,000	12,607,000,000	12,702,000,000	13,278,000,000	13,807,000,000
R&D Expense						
Operating Income		1,734,000,000	2,545,000,000	1,516,000,000	2,651,000,000	-705,000,000
Operating Margin %		14.20%	20.18%	11.93%	19.96%	-5.10%
SGA Expense						
Net Income		1,255,000,000	1,909,000,000	137,000,000	2,070,000,000	-1,390,000,000
Operating Cash Flow		2,838,000,000	2,366,000,000	2,103,000,000	2,704,000,000	2,597,000,000
Capital Expenditure		1,003,000,000	968,000,000	1,004,000,000	977,000,000	1,041,000,000
EBITDA		3,455,000,000	4,285,000,000	3,255,000,000	4,447,000,000	1,008,000,000
Return on Assets %		4.19%	6.05%	.42%	6.36%	-4.08%
Return on Equity %		9.35%	12.68%	.82%	12.33%	-7.78%
Debt to Equity		0.54	0.53	0.46	0.36	0.43

CONTACT INFORMATION:

Phone: 646 223-4000   Fax:
Toll-Free:
Address: 3 Times Square, New York, NY 10036 United States

STOCK TICKER/OTHER:

Stock Ticker: TRI
Employees: 52,000
Parent Company:

Exchange: NYS
Fiscal Year Ends: 12/31

SALARIES/BONUSES:

Top Exec. Salary:
$1,550,000
Second Exec. Salary:
$939,315

Bonus: $

Bonus: $

OTHER THOUGHTS:

Estimated Female Officers or Directors: 2

Hot Spot for Advancement for Women/Minorities: Y

Sales, profits and employees may be estimates. Financial information, benefits and other data can change quickly and may vary from those stated here.

Thor Industries Inc

www.thorindustries.com

NAIC Code: 336214

TYPES OF BUSINESS:

Recreational Vehicle Manufacturing
Motor Homes
Automotive Parts & Accessories
Buses

BRANDS/DIVISIONS/AFFILIATES:

Airstream Inc
CrossRoads RV
Thor Motor Coach Inc
Keystone RV Company
Postle Operating LLC
Cruiser RV
DRV Luxury Suites
Jayco Inc

CONTACTS: *Note: Officers with more than one job title may be intentionally listed here more than once.*

Robert Martin, CEO
Colleen Zuhl, CFO
Peter Orthwein, Chairman of the Board
W. Woelfer, General Counsel
Kenneth Julian, Vice President, Divisional

GROWTH PLANS/SPECIAL FEATURES:

Thor Industries, Inc. is a leading manufacturer of a wide range of recreational vehicles (RVs). The company's primary RV subsidiaries are Airstream, Inc., CrossRoads RV, Thor Motor Coach, Inc., Keystone RV Company, Heartland Recreational Vehicles LLC, Livin' Lite RV, Inc., Bison Coach, K.Z., Inc. and Postle Operating LLC. Together they produce towable RVs which account forf 77% of annual net sales, as well as motorized RVs, which account for 22% of net sales (1% goes toward other/related sales). Towable RVs include conventional travel trailers, fifth wheels and park models; truck and folding campers; and equestrian and other specialty towable vehicles. Park models are recreational dwellings towed to a permanent site such as a lake, woods or park, with the maximum size of park models in the U.S. being 400 square feet. Motorized RVs include Class A, B and C motorhomes, which are self-powered vehicles built on a chassis and self-contained with their own lighting, heating, cooking, refrigeration, sewage holding and water storage facilities. Thor also manufactures and sells related parts and accessories. In 2015, Thor acquired towable RV maker Cruiser RV and luxury fifth wheel maker DRV Luxury Suites, both based in Howe, Indiana; and Postle Aluminum Co., a producer of extruded aluminum and specialized components for the RV and other industries. In July 2016, it acquired Jayco Inc. for $576 million, a manufacturer of recreation vehicles such as camping, travel and fifth-wheel trailers, as well as motorhomes.

FINANCIAL DATA: *Note: Data for latest year may not have been available at press time.*

In U.S. $	2016	2015	2014	2013	2012	2011
Revenue		4,006,819,000	3,525,456,000	3,241,795,000	3,084,660,000	2,755,508,000
R&D Expense						
Operating Income		290,639,000	248,764,000	217,429,000	176,487,000	138,549,000
Operating Margin %		7.25%	7.05%	6.70%	5.72%	5.02%
SGA Expense		250,891,000	208,712,000	194,650,000	169,154,000	180,858,000
Net Income		199,385,000	179,002,000	152,862,000	121,739,000	106,273,000
Operating Cash Flow		247,860,000	149,261,000	145,066,000	118,841,000	114,802,000
Capital Expenditure		42,283,000	30,406,000	24,305,000	10,063,000	33,749,000
EBITDA		324,456,000	278,663,000	246,965,000	206,229,000	176,848,000
Return on Assets %		13.69%	13.08%	11.88%	9.97%	9.83%
Return on Equity %		19.51%	19.14%	17.53%	14.43%	14.23%
Debt to Equity						

CONTACT INFORMATION:

Phone: 574-970-7460   Fax:
Toll-Free:
Address: 601 E. Beardsley Ave., Elkhart, IN 46514-3305 United States

STOCK TICKER/OTHER:

Stock Ticker: THO   Exchange: NYS
Employees: 10,450   Fiscal Year Ends: 07/31
Parent Company:

SALARIES/BONUSES:

Top Exec. Salary: $750,000   Bonus: $
Second Exec. Salary: Bonus: $
$750,000

OTHER THOUGHTS:

Estimated Female Officers or Directors:
Hot Spot for Advancement for Women/Minorities:

TIBCO Software Inc

www.tibco.com

NAIC Code: 0

TYPES OF BUSINESS:

Software-Business Process
Data Management Software
Consulting & Support Services

BRANDS/DIVISIONS/AFFILIATES:

Jaspersoft
Spotfire
TIBCO Clarity
TIBCO Live Datamart
TIBCO Business Events
TIBCO Cloud Bus
TIBCO Foresight
TIBCO Cloud MDM

CONTACTS: Note: Officers with more than one job title may be intentionally listed here more than once.

Murray Rode, CEO
Tom Berquit, CFO
Thomas Been, CMO
Michele Haddad, Sr. VP-Global Human Resources
Matt Quinn, Chief Technology Officer
Thomas Laffey, Executive VP, Divisional
Ram Menon, Executive VP
William Hughes, Executive VP
R. Bradley, President
John Ederer, Vice President, Divisional

GROWTH PLANS/SPECIAL FEATURES:

TIBCO Software, Inc. is a provider of middleware and infrastructure software, focused on creating and marketing software for use in the integration of business information, processes and applications. The company offers a range of standards-based infrastructure software products that help customers streamline business process management by offering real-time access to information. TIBCO's software products are capable of instantly correlating information about an organization's operations and performance with information about expected behavior and business rules, allowing customers to anticipate and respond to business developments. TIBCO offers products in five main categories: analytics, cloud, customer loyalty, Integration and event processing. The analytics products such as Jaspersoft and Spotfire offer analytics, visualization, reporting and business intelligence. Some of the clouds products are TIBCO Cloud Bus, TIBCO Clarity, TIBCO Formvine and TIBCO Cloud MDM. TIBCO Reward is the firm's customer loyalty product and some of the Integration products include TIBCO Connectors, TIBCO API Exchange and TIBCO Foresight. Event processing products are TIBCO Live Datamart and TIBCO Business Events among others. TIBCO's products are designed to address three primary areas of operational efficiency: service oriented architecture (SOA), process automation and collaboration (PAC) and business optimization. The company additionally offers professional services, including consulting, planning, maintenance and support of information systems. In 2015, the firm agreed to acquire Mashery, an industry leader in Application Programming Interface (API) management.

TIBCO offers its employees medical, dental, vision, disability, life and AD&D insurance; a 401(k) program; credit union membership; an employee assistance program; a discount stock purchase plan; and tuition reimbursement.

FINANCIAL DATA: Note: Data for latest year may not have been available at press time.

In U.S. $	2016	2015	2014	2013	2012	2011
Revenue		1,000,000,000	1,022,400,000	1,069,950,016	1,024,612,992	920,246,016
R&D Expense						
Operating Income						
Operating Margin %						
SGA Expense						
Net Income						
Operating Cash Flow						
Capital Expenditure						
EBITDA						
Return on Assets %						
Return on Equity %						
Debt to Equity						

CONTACT INFORMATION:

Phone: 650 846-1000   Fax: 650 846-1218
Toll-Free: 800-420-8450
Address: 3307 Hillview Ave., Palo Alto, CA 94304 United States

SALARIES/BONUSES:

Top Exec. Salary: $ Bonus: $
Second Exec. Salary: $ Bonus: $

STOCK TICKER/OTHER:

Stock Ticker: Private   Exchange:
Employees: 2,965   Fiscal Year Ends: 11/30
Parent Company: Vista Equity Partners

OTHER THOUGHTS:

Estimated Female Officers or Directors: 2
Hot Spot for Advancement for Women/Minorities:

Time Warner Inc

NAIC Code: 515210

TYPES OF BUSINESS:

Cable TV Networks
Digital Entertainment
Film Production
Video Game Publishing
Entertainment Investments
Digital Media Production

BRANDS/DIVISIONS/AFFILIATES:

Turner
Home Box Office
Warner Bros
HBO Go
MAX Go
HBO Nordic
HBO Asia
iStreamPlanet Co LLC

CONTACTS: Note: Officers with more than one job title may be intentionally listed here more than once.

Howard Averill, CFO
Jeffrey Bewkes, Chairman of the Board
Douglas Horne, Chief Accounting Officer
Olaf Olafsson, Executive VP, Divisional
Gary Ginsberg, Executive VP, Divisional
Carol Melton, Executive VP, Divisional
Paul Cappuccio, Executive VP
Karen Magee, Executive VP
Paul Washington, Secretary

GROWTH PLANS/SPECIAL FEATURES:

Time Warner, Inc. is a global media and entertainmer
conglomerate. The firm operates in three segments: Turner
consisting of cable networks and digital media; Home Bo
Office, a basic tier service internationally and a premium pa
service internationally and domestically; and Warner Bros
made up of feature film, television, home video and videogam
production and distributions. The Turner segment consist
principally of domestic and international networks; digital medi
properties, which primarily include brand-aligned web sites
and basic tier and premium pay television programming. Thi
division includes domestic and international cable network
such as TBS, TNT and CNN. Additionally, in Latin America
Turner brands include Space, Infinito and I-Sat. Home Bo
Office consists of premium pay services such as HBO an
Cinemax. In 2015, this segment had approximately 82 millio
worldwide subscribers. This segment also produces origina
programing via DVDs, Blu-ray and electronic sell-through
Revenue is also generated through content licensing
Internationally, HBO distributes HBO Go and MAX G
streaming services, basic tier and premium pay televisio
services. HBO wholly-owns both HBO Nordic and HBO Asia
The Warner Bros. segment generates revenues throug
production and distribution of feature films, televisio
programming and video games. Warner Bros. produce even
films such as Batman, The Hangover and Harry Potter; along
with minor original films. This segment is also responsible fo
production of television shows both domestically an
internationally. Additionally, interactive entertainment fo
consoles, PC/Mac and handheld platforms are created an
distributed through Warner Bros. 2015, it acquired a majorit
interest in iStreamPlanet Co., LLC, a provider of streaming an
cloud-based video and technology services.

Time Warner offers employees health and wellness programs
flexible work arrangements, dependent care and child car
options.

FINANCIAL DATA: Note: Data for latest year may not have been available at press time.

In U.S. $	2016	2015	2014	2013	2012	2011
Revenue		28,118,000,000	27,359,000,000	29,795,000,000	28,729,000,000	28,974,000,000
R&D Expense						
Operating Income		6,865,000,000	5,975,000,000	6,605,000,000	5,918,000,000	5,805,000,000
Operating Margin %		24.41%	21.83%	22.16%	20.59%	20.03%
SGA Expense		4,824,000,000	5,190,000,000	6,465,000,000	6,333,000,000	6,439,000,000
Net Income		3,833,000,000	3,827,000,000	3,691,000,000	3,019,000,000	2,886,000,000
Operating Cash Flow		3,851,000,000	3,681,000,000	3,714,000,000	3,442,000,000	3,432,000,000
Capital Expenditure		423,000,000	474,000,000	602,000,000	643,000,000	772,000,000
EBITDA		7,509,000,000	6,765,000,000	14,734,000,000	6,687,000,000	6,609,000,000
Return on Assets %		6.03%	5.83%	5.41%	4.43%	4.29%
Return on Equity %		15.93%	14.07%	12.34%	10.09%	9.17%
Debt to Equity		0.99	0.87	0.67	0.64	0.65

CONTACT INFORMATION:

Phone: 212 484-8000   Fax: 703 265-1000
Toll-Free:
Address: 1 Time Warner Ctr., New York, NY 10019 United States

STOCK TICKER/OTHER:

Stock Ticker: TWX   Exchange: NYS
Employees: 25,600   Fiscal Year Ends: 12/31
Parent Company:

SALARIES/BONUSES:

Top Exec. Salary: Bonus: $
$2,000,000
Second Exec. Salary: Bonus: $
$1,400,000

OTHER THOUGHTS:

Estimated Female Officers or Directors: 3

Hot Spot for Advancement for Women/Minorities: Y

TJX Companies Inc (The)

NAIC Code: 448140

TYPES OF BUSINESS:

Discount Apparel Stores
Domestics
Footwear
Jewelry
Home Furnishings
Accessories

BRANDS/DIVISIONS/AFFILIATES:

Marmaxx
HomeGoods
TJX Canada
T J Maxx
Marshalls
Winners
HomeSense
Trade Secret

CONTACTS: *Note: Officers with more than one job title may be intentionally listed here more than once.*

Scott Goldenberg, CFO
Carol Meyrowitz, Chairman of the Board
Richard Sherr, President, Divisional
Kenneth Canestrari, President, Geographical
Michael MacMillan, President, Geographical
Ernie Herrman, President
Ann McCauley, Secretary

GROWTH PLANS/SPECIAL FEATURES:

The TJX Companies, Inc. is a low-price apparel and home fashion retailer, operating over 3,600 stores in the U.S. and worldwide. TJX's stores offer merchandise sold at 20% to 60% below department and specialty store regular prices. The firm operates through four major divisions: Marmaxx, made up of T.J. Maxx and Marshalls; HomeGoods, made up of the HomeGoods retail chain; TJX Canada, comprised of Winners, HomeSense and Marshalls; and TJX international, operating T.K. Maxx, HomeSense and Trade Secret. The Marmaxx group is the largest off-price retailer in the U.S., with 2,163 stores. T.J. Maxx and Marshalls stores offer brand-name family apparel, including footwear and accessories, and home fashions, including home basics, accent furniture and giftware. The chains are similar, although Marshalls features a full-line shoe department and larger men's and juniors' departments, while T.J. Maxx carries an extended line of jewelry and accessories. The HomeGoods segment offers discounted home fashions in 526 stores throughout the U.S. TJX Canada operates a total of 245 Winners, 101 HomeSense and 41 Marshalls locations throughout Canada. The TJX international segment operates 456 T.K. Maxx stores in the U.K., Ireland, Poland, Austria, the Netherlands and Germany; 39 HomeSense locations in the U.K.; and 35 Trade Secret stores in Australia. In addition, this segment operates Sierra Trading Post, an off-price Internet retailer (sierratradingpost.com) of brand name and quality outdoor gear, family apparel and footwear, sporting goods and home fashions. Sierra Trading Post also operates eight retail stores in the U.S. The company purchases its inventory from over 17,000 vendors worldwide. In 2015, the firm acquired the Trade Secret off-price retail businesses in Australia, from Gazal Corporation Limited.

TJX offers its employees medical, dental, vision, disability and life insurance; 401(k) & profit sharing plans; auto/home insurance; savings & discount programs; paid vacation; and adoption assistance.

FINANCIAL DATA: *Note: Data for latest year may not have been available at press time.*

In U.S. $	2016	2015	2014	2013	2012	2011
Revenue	30,944,940,000	29,078,410,000	27,422,700,000	25,878,370,000	23,191,460,000	21,942,190,000
R&D Expense						
Operating Income	3,704,700,000	3,606,501,000	3,350,570,000	3,106,526,000	2,411,414,000	2,203,229,000
Operating Margin %	11.97%	12.40%	12.21%	12.00%	10.39%	10.04%
SGA Expense	5,205,715,000	4,695,384,000	4,467,089,000	4,250,446,000	3,890,144,000	3,710,053,000
Net Income	2,277,658,000	2,215,128,000	2,137,396,000	1,906,687,000	1,496,090,000	1,343,141,000
Operating Cash Flow	2,937,343,000	3,008,369,000	2,590,329,000	3,045,614,000	1,916,034,000	1,976,481,000
Capital Expenditure	889,380,000	911,522,000	946,678,000	978,228,000	803,330,000	707,134,000
EBITDA	4,335,265,000	4,194,239,000	3,914,403,000	3,627,112,000	2,943,798,000	2,671,158,000
Return on Assets %	20.13%	20.77%	21.68%	21.43%	18.40%	17.40%
Return on Equity %	53.14%	52.15%	54.13%	55.46%	47.42%	44.85%
Debt to Equity	0.39	0.39	0.30	0.21	0.24	0.25

CONTACT INFORMATION:

Phone: 508 390-1000   Fax: 508 390-2091
Toll-Free:
Address: 770 Cochituate Rd., Framingham, MA 01701 United States

STOCK TICKER/OTHER:

Stock Ticker: TJX   Exchange: NYS
Employees: 198,000   Fiscal Year Ends: 01/31
Parent Company:

SALARIES/BONUSES:

Top Exec. Salary: Bonus: $
$1,575,002
Second Exec. Salary: Bonus: $
$1,382,309

OTHER THOUGHTS:

Estimated Female Officers or Directors: 4

Hot Spot for Advancement for Women/Minorities: Y

T-Mobile US Inc

www.t-mobile.com

NAIC Code: 517210

TYPES OF BUSINESS:

Cellular Telephone Service
Wireless Internet Services

BRANDS/DIVISIONS/AFFILIATES:

Deutsche Telekom AG
T-Mobile International AG
T-Mobile USA
MetroPCS Communications Inc

CONTACTS: Note: Officers with more than one job title may be intentionally listed here more than once.

J. Carter, CFO
Timotheus Hottges, Chairman of the Board
Neville Ray, Chief Technology Officer
G. Sievert, COO
John Legere, Director
Peter Ewens, Executive VP, Divisional
Larry Myers, Executive VP, Divisional
David Carey, Executive VP, Divisional
David Miller, Executive VP
Thomas Keys, President, Divisional
Michael Morgan, Senior VP, Divisional
Peter Osvaldik, Senior VP, Divisional

GROWTH PLANS/SPECIAL FEATURES:

T-Mobile US, Inc. (T-Mobile) is a national provider of wireless voice, messaging and data services, and is one of the larges cellular companies in America. The company represents th combined operations of T-Mobile USA and MetroPC Communications, Inc. The firm offers wireless service unde both the T-Mobile and MetroPCS brands. T-Mobile uses GSM (global system for mobile communications) technology and i a member of the North American GSM Alliance, a group of U.S and Canadian digital wireless carriers that provide seamles GSM wireless communications for its members in Nor America and internationally. Along with GSM, the firm use technology platforms based on HSPA+ (high speed packe access plus), CDMA (code division multiple access) and LT (long-term evolution) to service over 63 million customers in th postpaid, prepaid and wholesale markets. The company products include Internet and e-mail; games and application for mobile devices; messaging; voicemail; mobile devic wallpapers; music and sounds; and handset protectio services in case of loss, theft, malfunction or accidenta damage to the product. T-Mobile US operates as a subsidiar of T-Mobile International AG, which itself is the mobil communications subsidiary of Deutsche Telekom AG. In 201! T-Mobile completed transactions for the 700 MHz A-Block advanced wireless service (AWS) and person communications service (PCS) spectrum licenses from Verizo Communications, Inc., covering approximately 97 millic people. Spectrum licenses grant permission to use a portion the radio frequency spectrum in a given geographical area fo broadcasting purposes.

FINANCIAL DATA: Note: Data for latest year may not have been available at press time.

In U.S. $	2016	2015	2014	2013	2012	2011
Revenue		32,053,000,000	29,564,000,000	24,420,000,000	5,101,278,000	4,847,382,000
R&D Expense						
Operating Income		2,065,000,000	1,416,000,000	996,000,000	823,969,000	747,538,000
Operating Margin %		6.44%	4.78%	4.07%	16.15%	15.42%
SGA Expense		10,189,000,000	8,863,000,000	7,382,000,000	696,789,000	643,959,000
Net Income		733,000,000	247,000,000	35,000,000	394,172,000	301,310,000
Operating Cash Flow		5,414,000,000	4,146,000,000	3,545,000,000	1,181,451,000	1,061,808,000
Capital Expenditure		6,659,000,000	7,217,000,000	4,406,000,000	840,323,000	956,029,000
EBITDA		7,162,000,000	6,176,000,000	4,901,000,000	1,524,377,000	1,279,564,000
Return on Assets %		1.13%	.46%	.11%	4.00%	3.46%
Return on Equity %		4.20%	1.65%	.39%	12.54%	11.01%
Debt to Equity		1.57	1.55	1.18	1.40	1.60

CONTACT INFORMATION:

Phone: 425-378-4000   Fax: 425-378-4040
Toll-Free: 800-318-9270
Address: 12920 SE 38th St., Bellevue, WA 98006-1350 United States

STOCK TICKER/OTHER:

Stock Ticker: TMUS   Exchange: NAS
Employees: 45,000   Fiscal Year Ends: 12/31
Parent Company: Deutsche Telekom AG

SALARIES/BONUSES:

Top Exec. Salary: Bonus: $
$1,492,358
Second Exec. Salary: Bonus: $
$792,308

OTHER THOUGHTS:

Estimated Female Officers or Directors:

Hot Spot for Advancement for Women/Minorities:

Toll Brothers Inc

www.tollbrothers.com

NAIC Code: 236117

TYPES OF BUSINESS:

Construction, Home Building and Residential
Mortgages & Insurance
Property Management
Landscaping
Country Club Communities
Golf Courses
Security Monitoring
Lumber Distribution

BRANDS/DIVISIONS/AFFILIATES:

Gramercy Park

CONTACTS: *Note: Officers with more than one job title may be intentionally listed here more than once.*

Douglas Yearley, CEO
Martin Connor, CFO
Robert Toll, Chairman of the Board
Richard Hartman, COO
Michael Snyder, Secretary
Joseph Sicree, Senior VP

GROWTH PLANS/SPECIAL FEATURES:

Toll Brothers, Inc. designs, builds, markets and arranges financing for single-family detached and attached homes in luxury residential communities. The firm is also involved, both directly and through joint ventures, in building or converting existing rental apartment buildings into high-, mid- and low-rise luxury homes. Toll Brothers markets its services to move-up, empty-nester, active-adult, age-qualified and second-home buyers through its operations in 19 U.S. states. The company is present in major suburban and urban residential areas including the Philadelphia, Pennsylvania metropolitan area; Virginia and Maryland suburbs of Washington, D.C.; central and northern New Jersey; Boston, Massachusetts; Westchester, Dutchess and Ulster Counties, New York; San Diego and Palm Springs, California; the San Francisco Bay area; Phoenix, Arizona; Las Vegas and Reno, Nevada; and Chicago, Illinois. The average base sales price of the company's homes is roughly $646,000. Toll Brothers operates its own land development, architectural, engineering, mortgage, title, landscaping, lumber distribution, house component assembly and manufacturing operations. In addition, the company owns and operates golf courses in conjunction with several of its master planned communities. The company operates a portfolio of 539 communities with 44,253 homes sites. In 2015, the firm acquired Gramercy Park in order to expand its presence in New York City.

The firm offers employees discounts on homes, mortgages, titles, home appliances and kitchen cabinets; life, medical and dental insurance; long- and short-term disability coverage; a 401(k); and educational reimbursement. After two years of service, employees are able to use the company's furnished resort luxury guesthouses for their personal vacations.

FINANCIAL DATA: *Note: Data for latest year may not have been available at press time.*

In U.S. $	2016	2015	2014	2013	2012	2011
Revenue		4,171,248,000	3,911,602,000	2,674,299,000	1,882,781,000	1,475,881,000
R&D Expense						
Operating Income		446,870,000	397,249,000	201,067,000	63,429,000	-47,748,000
Operating Margin %		10.71%	10.15%	7.51%	3.36%	-3.23%
SGA Expense		455,108,000	432,516,000	339,932,000	287,257,000	261,355,000
Net Income		363,167,000	340,032,000	170,606,000	487,146,000	39,795,000
Operating Cash Flow		60,182,000	313,200,000	-568,963,000	-168,962,000	52,850,000
Capital Expenditure		9,447,000	15,074,000	26,567,000	14,495,000	9,553,000
EBITDA		559,119,000	528,237,000	292,907,000	135,528,000	-4,720,000
Return on Assets %		4.12%	4.46%	2.62%	8.67%	.77%
Return on Equity %		8.99%	9.46%	5.28%	17.06%	1.54%
Debt to Equity		0.89	0.88	0.75	0.72	0.63

CONTACT INFORMATION:

Phone: 215 938-8000   Fax: 215 938-8023
Toll-Free:
Address: 250 Gibraltar Rd., Horsham, PA 19044 United States

STOCK TICKER/OTHER:

Stock Ticker: TOL
Employees: 3,500
Parent Company:

Exchange: NYS
Fiscal Year Ends: 10/31

SALARIES/BONUSES:

Top Exec. Salary:
$1,000,000

Bonus: $

Second Exec. Salary:
$1,000,000

Bonus: $

OTHER THOUGHTS:

Estimated Female Officers or Directors:

Hot Spot for Advancement for Women/Minorities:

Sales, profits and employees may be estimates. Financial information, benefits and other data can change quickly and may vary from those stated here.

Total System Services Inc (TSYS)

NAIC Code: 522320

TYPES OF BUSINESS:

Credit Card Processing
Risk Management Tools
Fraud Detection
Debt Collection Services
Printing Services
Customer Relationship Management
Business Process Management

BRANDS/DIVISIONS/AFFILIATES:

China Unionpay Data Services Co Ltd
Columbus Productions Inc
Total System Services de Mexico
TSYS Acquiring Solutions LLC

CONTACTS: Note: Officers with more than one job title may be intentionally listed here more than once.

M. Woods, CEO
Paul Todd, CFO
Dorenda Weaver, Chief Accounting Officer
Patricia Watson, Chief Information Officer
Pamela Joseph, Director
William Pruett, Other Executive Officer
G. Griffith, Secretary

GROWTH PLANS/SPECIAL FEATURES:

Total System Services, Inc. (TSYS) is one of the world's larges
electronic payment processors of consumer credit, retail, debi
stored value, government services and commercial car
accounts for financial and non-financial institutions. TSYS
serves clients throughout the Americas, Africa, Europe, th
Middle East and the Asia Pacific region. The company als
offers value-added products and services, including ris
management tools and techniques like fraud detection an
prevention and behavior analysis tools as well as revenu
enhancement tools, such as customer relationshi
management (CRM) and client advising. TSYS's operation
are divided into four segments: North America services
accounting for approximately 45% of revenues; merchar
services, accounting for 21%; international services
accounting for 15%; and NetSpend, accounting for 19%
Merchant services include processing services, acquirin
applications, related systems and integrated support services
NetSpend provides general purpose reloadable prepaid deb
and payroll cards to underbanked and other consumers in th
U.S. The company also offers additional services, such a
business process management, mail and correspondenc
processing, teleservicing, data documentation, offset printing
collections and account solicitation and client services. Th
firm's subsidiaries include Columbus Productions, Inc., whic
provides commercial printing and finishing solutions; and TSYS
Acquiring Solutions LLC, a supplier of transaction processing
related systems and integrated support services. The compan
also owns a 49% equity interest in a joint venture compan
called Total System Services de Mexico as well as a 44.5%
interest in China Unionpay Data Services Co., Ltd.

The company offers U.S. employees life, AD&D, disability
medical, dental and vision insurance; flexible spendin
accounts; and adoption assistance.

FINANCIAL DATA: Note: Data for latest year may not have been available at press time.

In U.S. $	2016	2015	2014	2013	2012	2011
Revenue		2,779,541,000	2,446,877,000	2,132,353,000	1,870,972,000	1,808,966,000
R&D Expense						
Operating Income		534,107,000	431,640,000	386,247,000	357,652,000	322,456,000
Operating Margin %		19.21%	17.64%	18.11%	19.11%	17.82%
SGA Expense		390,253,000	343,128,000	295,555,000	251,010,000	228,540,000
Net Income		364,044,000	322,872,000	244,750,000	244,280,000	220,559,000
Operating Cash Flow		600,194,000	560,201,000	452,398,000	455,753,000	436,319,000
Capital Expenditure		203,316,000	235,923,000	137,833,000	118,065,000	95,945,000
EBITDA		795,853,000	679,658,000	591,598,000	525,464,000	488,916,000
Return on Assets %		9.44%	8.61%	8.57%	12.58%	11.57%
Return on Equity %		20.41%	19.52%	16.28%	17.91%	17.35%
Debt to Equity		0.75	0.83	0.90	0.13	0.04

CONTACT INFORMATION:

Phone: 706 649-2310   Fax: 706 649-2456
Toll-Free:
Address: One TSYS Way, Columbus, GA 31901 United States

STOCK TICKER/OTHER:

Stock Ticker: TSS   Exchange: NYS
Employees: 9,900   Fiscal Year Ends: 12/31
Parent Company:

SALARIES/BONUSES:

Top Exec. Salary: $843,000   Bonus: $
Second Exec. Salary: Bonus: $550,000
$142,195

OTHER THOUGHTS:

Estimated Female Officers or Directors: 3
Hot Spot for Advancement for Women/Minorities: Y

Toyota Motor Sales USA Inc (TMS)   www.toyota.com/usa/operations

NAIC Code: 336111

TYPES OF BUSINESS:

Automobile Manufacturing

BRANDS/DIVISIONS/AFFILIATES:

Toyota Motor Corporation
Toyota Motor Manufacturing Alabama Inc
Toyota Motor Manufacturing Indiana Inc
Toyota Motor Manufacturing Kentucky Inc
Toyota Motor Manufacturing Mississippi Inc
Toyota Motor Manufacturing Texas Inc
Toyota Motor Manufacturing West Virginia Inc
Toyota Auto Body California Inc

CONTACTS: *Note: Officers with more than one job title may be intentionally listed here more than once.*

Jim Lentz, CEO

GROWTH PLANS/SPECIAL FEATURES:

Toyota Motor Sales, USA, Inc.'s operations include Toyota Motor Engineering & Manufacturing North America, Inc. (TEMA), which is responsible for the engineering design and development, R&D and manufacturing activities in the U.S., Mexico and Canada for Toyota. The firm operates through various subsidiaries that together operate 10 factories/plants in the U.S. and manufactures 13 different models. Toyota Motor Manufacturing, Alabama, Inc. is an engine plant that produces engines for the Tacoma, Tundra, Sequoia, Camry, RAV4, Venza and Highlander. Toyota Motor Manufacturing, Indiana, Inc. manufactures approximately 350,000 of the Sequoia, Highlander, Highlander Hybrid and Sienna each year. Toyota Motor Manufacturing, Kentucky, Inc. is the largest North American manufacturing facility and produces over 500,000 vehicles each year, including the Avalon, Avalon Hybrid, Camry, Camry Hybrid, Venza and Lexus ES. Toyota Motor Manufacturing, Mississippi, Inc. is TEMA's newest plant and produces approximately 170,000 Corolla each year. Toyota Motor Manufacturing, Texas, Inc. manufactures the Tundra and Tacoma Pickups and is the first plant to integrate production facilities for many of its suppliers on the same grounds. Toyota Motor Manufacturing, West Virginia, Inc. produces engines and transmissions for vehicles such as the Camry, Lexus RX350, Matrix, Corolla and Highlander. Toyota Auto Body California, Inc., acting primarily as a supplier of parts for Tacoma trucks, was TEMA's first manufacturing facility in the U.S. Bodine Aluminum, Inc., with plants in St. Louis and Troy, Missouri and Jackson, Tennessee, produces engine and transmission components for use in all U.S. manufacturing facilities. Finally, in collaboration with Subaru's parent company, Fuji Heavy Industries, Ltd., Subaru of Indiana Automotive, Inc. assembles approximately 100,000 of the Camry each year. In total, Toyota produced about 1.337 million vehicles in the U.S. in 2015.

FINANCIAL DATA: *Note: Data for latest year may not have been available at press time.*

In U.S. $	2016	2015	2014	2013	2012	2011
Revenue		93,053,000,000	78,110,000,000	61,283,000,000	46,338,000,000	52,941,000,000
R&D Expense						
Operating Income						
Operating Margin %						
SGA Expense						
Net Income						
Operating Cash Flow						
Capital Expenditure						
EBITDA						
Return on Assets %						
Return on Equity %						
Debt to Equity						

CONTACT INFORMATION:

Phone: Fax: 310-468-7814
Toll-Free: 800-331-4331
Address: 19001 South Western Ave., Dept. WC11, Torrance, CA 90501
United States

STOCK TICKER/OTHER:

Stock Ticker: Subsidiary   Exchange:
Employees: 43,809   Fiscal Year Ends: 03/31
Parent Company: Toyota Motor Corporation

SALARIES/BONUSES:

Top Exec. Salary: $ Bonus: $
Second Exec. Salary: $ Bonus: $

OTHER THOUGHTS:

Estimated Female Officers or Directors:
Hot Spot for Advancement for Women/Minorities:

Trader Joe's Company Inc

NAIC Code: 445110

TYPES OF BUSINESS:

Grocery Stores
Specialty Groceries
Vitamins & Dietary Supplements
Organic Foods

BRANDS/DIVISIONS/AFFILIATES:

ALDI Group

CONTACTS: Note: Officers with more than one job title may be intentionally listed here more than once.

Dan Bane, CEO
Tara Miller, Dir.-Mktg.
Laurie Mead, VP-Human Resources
Charles Pillitier, Sr. VP-Oper.
Brandt Sharrock, VP-Real Estate
Dan Bane, Chmn.

GROWTH PLANS/SPECIAL FEATURES:

Trader Joe's Company, Inc. operates a chain of approximate 457 company-owned and -operated specialty grocery stores i over 38 states and Washington, D.C., with about half of it stores located in California, where the company was founde Although the stores sell some brand-name products, the va majority of the selection comprises more than 3,000 Trade Joe's private-label products, including specialty vegetarian kosher, organic food and vitamin supplement products as we as regional fare, such as Thai and Mexican foods. Prices ten to be comparable to or lower than traditional groceries, as result of Trader Joe's efforts to buy many items and ingredient directly from suppliers and the chain's focus on its private lab lines. The company also keeps costs down by eliminatin service departments and using spaces of 15,000 square fe or less for its stores. Selections and inventory tend to vary fro state to state and store to store because of the company commitment to experimentation, regional and season products and bringing variety to its customers. The firm owned by a trust created by Theo Albrecht, co-founder German supermarket chain ALDI.

Trader Joe's offers employees medical, dental and visio insurance; a company-paid retirement plan; a 10% employe discount; and paid time off. Medical, dental and vision coverag is available to both full and part-time employees of the firm.

FINANCIAL DATA: Note: Data for latest year may not have been available at press time.

In U.S. $	2016	2015	2014	2013	2012	2011
Revenue		13,000,000,000	12,000,000,000	9,725,000,000	9,500,000,000	9,000,000,000
R&D Expense						
Operating Income						
Operating Margin %						
SGA Expense						
Net Income						
Operating Cash Flow						
Capital Expenditure						
EBITDA						
Return on Assets %						
Return on Equity %						
Debt to Equity						

CONTACT INFORMATION:

Phone: 626-599-3700   Fax: 626-301-4431
Toll-Free:
Address: 800 S. Shamrock Ave., Monrovia, CA 91016 United States

STOCK TICKER/OTHER:

Stock Ticker: Subsidiary   Exchange:
Employees: 12,500   Fiscal Year Ends: 06/30
Parent Company: ALDI GROUP

SALARIES/BONUSES:

Top Exec. Salary: $ Bonus: $
Second Exec. Salary: $ Bonus: $

OTHER THOUGHTS:

Estimated Female Officers or Directors: 2
Hot Spot for Advancement for Women/Minorities:

Travelers Companies Inc (The)

www.travelers.com

NAIC Code: 524126

TYPES OF BUSINESS:

Direct Property & Casualty Insurance
Reinsurance
Automobile & Homeowners' Insurance
General Liability & Commercial Multi-Peril Insurance
Marine Insurance
Risk Management Services

BRANDS/DIVISIONS/AFFILIATES:

National Property
Inland Marine
Ocean Marine
Boiler & Machinery

CONTACTS: Note: Officers with more than one job title may be intentionally listed here more than once.

Doreen Spadorcia, CEO, Divisional
Wendy Skjerven, Secretary
Alan Schnitzer, CEO
Jay Benet, CFO
Jay Fishman, Chairman of the Board
Douglas Russell, Chief Accounting Officer
Andy Bessette, Chief Administrative Officer
Brian MacLean, COO
John Clifford, Executive VP, Divisional
Maria Olivo, Executive VP, Divisional
Kenneth Spence, Executive VP
William Heyman, Other Executive Officer

GROWTH PLANS/SPECIAL FEATURES:

The Travelers Companies, Inc. is a holding company principally engaged in providing commercial and personal property and casualty (P&C) insurance products and services to businesses, government units, associations and individuals. The company operates in three segments: business & international insurance (BII), bond & specialty insurance (BSI) and personal insurance. BII offers an array of P&C insurance and insurance related services to its clients, primarily in the U.S., as well as in Canada, the U.K., Ireland and other select parts of the world. Domestically, this segment provides small-, mid- and large-sized businesses with P&C products, including multi-peril, commercial property, general liability, commercial auto and workers' compensation insurance. It provides traditional and customized property insurance programs to large- and mid-sized customers through National Property; builders' risk insurance through Inland Marine; international trade services through Ocean Marine; and comprehensive breakdown coverages for equipment through Boiler & Machinery. Internationally, the BII segment offers P&C insurance and risk management services to customers in the technology, public services, financial and professional services sectors. BSI provides surety, crime, management and professional liability coverages and risk management services to primarily domestic customers, utilizing various degrees of financially-based underwriting approaches. The personal insurance segment writes a broad range of P&C insurance covering individual's personal risks. The primary products within this segment include automobile and homeowner's insurance.

FINANCIAL DATA: Note: Data for latest year may not have been available at press time.

In U.S. $	2016	2015	2014	2013	2012	2011
Revenue		26,800,000,000	27,162,000,000	26,191,000,000	25,740,000,000	25,446,000,000
R&D Expense						
Operating Income		4,740,000,000	5,089,000,000	4,945,000,000	3,166,000,000	1,352,000,000
Operating Margin %		17.68%	18.73%	18.88%	12.29%	5.31%
SGA Expense		4,079,000,000	3,952,000,000	3,757,000,000	3,610,000,000	3,556,000,000
Net Income		3,439,000,000	3,692,000,000	3,673,000,000	2,473,000,000	1,426,000,000
Operating Cash Flow		3,434,000,000	3,693,000,000	3,816,000,000	3,230,000,000	2,169,000,000
Capital Expenditure						
EBITDA						
Return on Assets %		3.35%	3.54%	3.49%	2.34%	1.34%
Return on Equity %		14.09%	14.76%	14.52%	9.83%	5.66%
Debt to Equity		0.26	0.25	0.25	0.22	0.25

CONTACT INFORMATION:

Phone: 917 778-6000   Fax:
Toll-Free: 800-328-2189
Address: 485 Lexington Ave., New York, NY 10017 United States

STOCK TICKER/OTHER:

Stock Ticker: TRV   Exchange: NYS
Employees: 30,200   Fiscal Year Ends: 12/31
Parent Company:

SALARIES/BONUSES:

Top Exec. Salary: Bonus: $
$1,000,000
Second Exec. Salary: Bonus: $
$925,000

OTHER THOUGHTS:

Estimated Female Officers or Directors: 7

Hot Spot for Advancement for Women/Minorities: Y

TreeHouse Foods Inc

www.treehousefoods.com

NAIC Code: 311421

TYPES OF BUSINESS:

Food Manufacturing & Distribution

BRANDS/DIVISIONS/AFFILIATES:

Bay Valley Foods LLC
Sturm Foods
S T Foods
Cains
Associated Brands Inc
Protenergy Natural Foods Inc
Flagstone foods
TreeHouse Private Brands

CONTACTS: *Note: Officers with more than one job title may be intentionally listed here more than once.*

Sam Reed, CEO
Thomas ONeill, Chief Administrative Officer
Christopher Sliva, COO
David Vermylen, Director
Rachel Bishop, Other Executive Officer
Lori Roberts, Senior VP, Divisional
Erik Kahler, Senior VP, Divisional

GROWTH PLANS/SPECIAL FEATURES:

TreeHouse Foods, Inc. is a food manufacturer servicing primarily the retail grocery and foodservice distribution industry. The firm operates through its wholly-owned U.S subsidiaries Bay Valley Foods LLC, Sturm Foods, S.T. Foods, Cains, Associated Brands Inc. (ABI), Protenergy Natural Foods Inc. (Protenergy) and Flagstone Foods. Its wholly-owned Canadian subsidiaries include E.D. Smith, ABI Canada and Protenergy Canada. The company's products include salad dressings and sauces, non-dairy powdered and liquid coffee creamer, Mexican sauces, pickles, private label soups and jams and pie fillings. The firm manufactures these products under private labels for retailers such as mass merchandisers and supermarkets. TreeHouse Foods also markets its products to the foodservice industry, industrial customers who use the firm's products as ingredients in other products or repackage them in portion control packages and sells items under its own brands, primarily on a regional basis to retail customers. The company operates in three segments: North American retail grocery, food away from home and industrial & export. The North American retail grocery division sells branded and private label products to customers within the U.S. and Canada under brand names such as Bennett's, Hoffman House, Farman's, Peter Piper and Grove Square. The food away from home segment sells products such as pickles, salsas, non-dairy powdered creamers and aseptic and refrigerated products to the U.S. and Canadian food service industries under the label Schwartz and Saucemaker. TreeHouse Foods' industrial & export group offers co-pack business and non-dairy powdered creamers for use in industrial applications. In February 2016, the firm acquired ConAgra Foods' private brands operations for $2.7 billion, expanding its presence in private label dry and refrigerated grocery. This operation is now called TreeHouse Private Brands.

FINANCIAL DATA: *Note: Data for latest year may not have been available at press time.*

In U.S. $	2016	2015	2014	2013	2012	2011
Revenue		3,206,405,000	2,946,102,000	2,293,927,000	2,182,125,000	2,049,985,000
R&D Expense						
Operating Income		239,736,000	218,154,000	178,164,000	176,827,000	188,275,000
Operating Margin %		7.47%	7.40%	7.76%	8.10%	9.18%
SGA Expense		342,152,000	333,395,000	256,063,000	239,752,000	244,158,000
Net Income		114,910,000	89,880,000	86,988,000	88,363,000	94,407,000
Operating Cash Flow		285,318,000	211,957,000	216,690,000	204,559,000	156,071,000
Capital Expenditure		86,096,000	99,218,000	81,183,000	79,520,000	77,796,000
EBITDA		338,805,000	294,521,000	282,856,000	274,033,000	275,839,000
Return on Assets %		3.02%	2.71%	3.31%	3.58%	3.93%
Return on Equity %		6.35%	5.92%	7.09%	7.84%	9.20%
Debt to Equity		0.65	0.82	0.73	0.76	0.84

CONTACT INFORMATION:

Phone: 708 483-1300   Fax:
Toll-Free:
Address: 2021 Spring Rd., Ste. 600, Oakbrook, IL 60523 United States

STOCK TICKER/OTHER:

Stock Ticker: THS   Exchange: NYS
Employees: 6,181   Fiscal Year Ends: 12/31
Parent Company:

SALARIES/BONUSES:

Top Exec. Salary: Bonus: $
$1,009,500
Second Exec. Salary: Bonus: $
$539,667

OTHER THOUGHTS:

Estimated Female Officers or Directors: 3

Hot Spot for Advancement for Women/Minorities: Y

Sales, profits and employees may be estimates. Financial information, benefits and other data can change quickly and may vary from those stated here.

Trimble Navigation Ltd

www.trimble.com

NAIC Code: 334511

TYPES OF BUSINESS:

GPS Technologies
Surveying & Mapping Equipment
Navigation Tools
Autopilot Systems
Data Collection Products
Fleet Management Systems
Outdoor Recreation Information Service
Telecommunications & Automotive Components

BRANDS/DIVISIONS/AFFILIATES:

Embedded Technologies
Applanix
Trimble Outdoors
ThingMagic
Linear Project GmbH
Fifth Element
HarvestMark
AGRI-TREND

CONTACTS: *Note: Officers with more than one job title may be intentionally listed here more than once.*

Steven Berglund, CEO
Robert Painter, CFO
Julie Shepard, Chief Accounting Officer
Ulf Johansson, Director
Nickolas Vande Steeg, Director
James Kirkland, General Counsel
Sachin Sankpal, Other Corporate Officer
Darryl Matthews, Senior VP, Divisional
Mark Harrington, Vice President, Divisional
Christopher Gibson, Vice President, Divisional
James Veneziano, Vice President, Divisional
Jurgen Kliem, Vice President, Divisional
Bryn Fosburgh, Vice President, Divisional

GROWTH PLANS/SPECIAL FEATURES:

Trimble Navigation, Ltd. provides global positioning products to industrial, commercial, governmental and agricultural customers. With offices in 43 countries, the firm operates in four segments: engineering/construction, field solutions, mobile solutions and advanced devices. Engineering and construction products incorporate global positioning systems (GPS); optical, global navigation satellite systems (GNSS); and radio, laser and cellular technologies to facilitate precise surveying, site preparation and interior measurement by small crews. The field solutions segment offers handheld geographic information system (GIS) data collectors for fieldwork and manual and automated navigation systems for tractors and other agricultural equipment. The mobile solutions segment offers a fleet management tool for large enterprise clients, consisting of vehicle-mounted hardware together with a web-based subscription service. The combined businesses within the advanced devices segment are hardware centric, generally rely on original equipment manufacturer (OEM) distribution and have products that can be utilized in a number of different end-user markets. Products sold by this segment include the product lines from the company's Embedded Technologies, Timing, Applanix, Trimble Outdoors, Military and Advanced Systems (MAS) and ThingMagic businesses. Trimble holds roughly 1,100 unique issued and enforceable patents, the majority of which cover GNSS technology and other applications such as optical and laser technology. In 2015, the firm acquired Linear Project GmbH, a provider of scheduling software for linear infrastructure projects; Fifth Element, a forestry enterprise and mobile software solutions for logistics and harvest operations; HarvestMark, a provider of food traceability and quality inspection solutions; and AGRI-TREND, a North American agricultural consultancy.

Employee benefits include medical, dental and vision coverage; life and AD&D insurance; 401(k); an employee stock purchase plan; profit sharing; health care and dependent care flexible spending accounts; short- and long-term disability; business travel accident insurance; and an employee assistance program.

FINANCIAL DATA: *Note: Data for latest year may not have been available at press time.*

In U.S. $	2016	2015	2014	2013	2012	2011
Revenue		2,290,400,000	2,395,546,000	2,288,124,000	2,040,113,000	1,644,065,000
R&D Expense		336,700,000	317,992,000	299,421,000	256,458,000	197,007,000
Operating Income		154,400,000	260,823,000	251,737,000	212,568,000	156,402,000
Operating Margin %		6.74%	10.88%	11.00%	10.41%	9.51%
SGA Expense		629,900,000	634,689,000	564,982,000	509,494,000	425,179,000
Net Income		121,100,000	214,118,000	218,855,000	191,060,000	150,755,000
Operating Cash Flow		354,900,000	407,083,000	414,635,000	340,700,000	241,629,000
Capital Expenditure		44,000,000	54,945,000	70,877,000	55,241,000	24,944,000
EBITDA		376,500,000	452,464,000	441,314,000	395,179,000	281,764,000
Return on Assets %		3.20%	5.65%	6.10%	6.24%	6.67%
Return on Equity %		5.29%	9.35%	10.62%	11.02%	10.27%
Debt to Equity		0.27	0.28	0.29	0.46	0.31

CONTACT INFORMATION:

Phone: 408 481-8000   Fax: 408 481-2218
Toll-Free: 800-874-6253
Address: 935 Stewart Dr., Sunnyvale, CA 94085 United States

STOCK TICKER/OTHER:

Stock Ticker: TRMB   Exchange: NAS
Employees: 8,451   Fiscal Year Ends: 12/31
Parent Company:

SALARIES/BONUSES:

Top Exec. Salary: $860,000   Bonus: $
Second Exec. Salary: $425,000   Bonus: $

OTHER THOUGHTS:

Estimated Female Officers or Directors: 5
Hot Spot for Advancement for Women/Minorities: Y

Trinity Health

NAIC Code: 622110

www.trinity-health.org

TYPES OF BUSINESS:

General Medical and Surgical Hospitals
Assisted Living Facilities
Hospice Programs
Senior Housing Communities
Management & Consulting Services

BRANDS/DIVISIONS/AFFILIATES:

Senior Emergency Departments

CONTACTS: *Note: Officers with more than one job title may be intentionally listed here more than once.*

Richard J. Gilfillan, CEO
Judith M. Persichilli, Interim Pres.
Benjamin R. Carter, CFO
Clayton Fitzhugh, Chief Human Resource Officer
P. Terrence O'Rourke, Exec. VP-Clinical Transformation
Benjamin R. Carter, Exec. VP-Finance
James Bosscher, Chief Investment Officer
Paul Conlon, Sr. VP-Clinical Quality & Patient Safety
Rebecca Havlisch, Chief Nursing Officer
Louis Fierens, Sr. VP-Supply Chain & Capital Projects Mgmt.

GROWTH PLANS/SPECIAL FEATURES:

Trinity Health is one of the nation's largest multi-institutiona Catholic health care delivery systems, serving patients an communities in 22 states. Trinity Health operates 93 hospitals 120 continuing care facilities, which include home care hospice, PACE and senior living facilities that provide nearl 2.5 million visits annually. The organization return approximately $1 billion to its communities annually in the form of charity care and other community benefits programs. Trinit Health is known for its focus on the country's aging population and is the innovator of Senior Emergency Departments, th largest non-profit provider of home health care services in th nation. Trinity Health is also the nation's leading provider c PACE (Program of All Inclusive Care for the Elderly) based o the number of available programs. In August 2016, Waterbury Connecticut-based Saint Mary's Health System joined Trinit Health, becoming the fifth hospital to affiliate with the regiona health ministry of New England.

The firm offers employees health and dental coverage, shor and long-term disability, paid time-off, life insurance, flexibl spending accounts, 403(b) and 401(k) plans, tuitio reimbursement and professional education as well as adoptio assistance.

FINANCIAL DATA: *Note: Data for latest year may not have been available at press time.*

In U.S. $	2016	2015	2014	2013	2012	2011
Revenue		14,388,150,000	13,600,000,000	8,978,385,000	8,469,453,000	
R&D Expense						
Operating Income						
Operating Margin %						
SGA Expense						
Net Income		671,630,000	951,405,000	666,439,000	367,053,000	
Operating Cash Flow						
Capital Expenditure						
EBITDA						
Return on Assets %						
Return on Equity %						
Debt to Equity						

CONTACT INFORMATION:

Phone: 734-343-1000   Fax:
Toll-Free:
Address: 20555 Victor Parkway, Livonia, MI 48152-7018 United States

STOCK TICKER/OTHER:

Stock Ticker: Nonprofit   Exchange:
Employees: 97,000   Fiscal Year Ends: 06/30
Parent Company:

SALARIES/BONUSES:

Top Exec. Salary: $ Bonus: $
Second Exec. Salary: $ Bonus: $

OTHER THOUGHTS:

Estimated Female Officers or Directors: 4
Hot Spot for Advancement for Women/Minorities: Y

Trinity Industries Inc

www.trin.net

NAIC Code: 336510

TYPES OF BUSINESS:

Railroad Car Manufacturing
Railroad Car Leasing & Management
Inland Barge Manufacturing & Services
Construction Materials Manufacturing
Highway Guardrails
Metal Containers
Steel Beams & Girders
Ready-Mix Concrete

BRANDS/DIVISIONS/AFFILIATES:

Trinity Rail Group LLC
Trinity Industries Leasing Company
TRIP Rail Holdings LLC
RIV 2013 Rail Holdings LLC
Trinity Marine Products Inc
Trinity Highway Products LLC
Trinity Structural Towers Inc
Platinum Energy Services Corporation

CONTACTS:
Note: Officers with more than one job title may be intentionally listed here more than once.

Bryan Stevenson, Assistant General Counsel
Jack Todd, Vice President, Divisional
Timothy Wallace, CEO
James Perry, CFO
Mary Henderson, Chief Accounting Officer
Stephen Smith, Chief Technology Officer
S. Rice, Other Executive Officer
Steven McDowell, Other Executive Officer
William Mcwhirter, President, Divisional
D. Menzies, President, Divisional
Melendy Lovett, Senior VP
Gail Peck, Treasurer
Heather Randall, Vice President, Divisional
Virginia Gray, Vice President, Divisional
W. Howard, Vice President, Divisional
Kathryn Collins, Vice President, Divisional
John Lee, Vice President, Divisional

GROWTH PLANS/SPECIAL FEATURES:

Trinity Industries, Inc. is a holding company overseeing diversified leading industrial companies that manufacture various transportation, construction and industrial products. The company operates through five principal segments. Trinity Rail Group, LLC, one of the largest producers of freight and tank railcars in North America, manufactures railroad freight cars, principally pressure and non-pressure tank cars, hoppers and gondola cars used for transporting liquids, gases and dry cargo. Trinity's railcar leasing and management services group, which operates primarily through subsidiary Trinity Industries Leasing Company, TRIP Rail Holdings LLC and RIV 2013 Rail Holdings LLC, provides comprehensive railcar fleet management services such as leasing and financing options; administration; regulatory compliance and tax preparation; and maintenance. The inland barge group, through subsidiary Trinity Marine Products, Inc., is a top manufacturer of flat-deck, tank and hopper barges used to transport cargo on U.S. inland waterways. The construction products group includes Trinity Highway Products, LLC, a full-line manufacturer of highway guardrail and crash cushions. Trinity's energy segment includes subsidiaries Trinity Structural Towers, Inc., a leading manufacturer of structural wind towers; and Platinum Energy Services Corporation, which manufactures and sells oil and gas process and storage equipment, including various types of containers, separator and treaters used at the well-site and in midstream locations. In 2014, the firm acquired WesMor Cyrogenic Companies; Alloy Custom Products, Inc.; Platinum Energy Services Corporation; and assets of Meyer Steel Structures, the utility steel structures division of Thomas & Betts Corporation.

FINANCIAL DATA:
Note: Data for latest year may not have been available at press time.

In U.S. $	2016	2015	2014	2013	2012	2011
Revenue		6,392,700,000	6,170,000,000	4,365,300,000	3,811,900,000	3,075,100,000
R&D Expense						
Operating Income		1,438,900,000	1,251,000,000	772,900,000	574,800,000	425,300,000
Operating Margin %		22.50%	20.27%	17.70%	15.07%	13.83%
SGA Expense		476,400,000	403,600,000	291,300,000	224,100,000	209,100,000
Net Income		796,500,000	678,200,000	375,500,000	255,200,000	142,200,000
Operating Cash Flow		939,700,000	819,200,000	662,200,000	527,400,000	104,300,000
Capital Expenditure		1,029,800,000	464,600,000	731,000,000	469,200,000	340,000,000
EBITDA		1,713,100,000	1,502,100,000	989,300,000	774,300,000	615,700,000
Return on Assets %		9.04%	8.45%	5.37%	3.99%	2.39%
Return on Equity %		23.95%	25.12%	16.85%	13.03%	7.83%
Debt to Equity		0.87	1.18	1.24	1.48	1.59

CONTACT INFORMATION:

Phone: 214 631-4420   Fax: 214 589-8501
Toll-Free:
Address: 2525 Stemmons Fwy., Dallas, TX 75207-2401 United States

STOCK TICKER/OTHER:

Stock Ticker: TRN
Employees: 22,070
Parent Company:

Exchange: NYS
Fiscal Year Ends: 12/31

SALARIES/BONUSES:

Top Exec. Salary:
$1,050,000
Second Exec. Salary:
$650,000

Bonus: $

Bonus: $

OTHER THOUGHTS:

Estimated Female Officers or Directors: 2

Hot Spot for Advancement for Women/Minorities: Y

Sales, profits and employees may be estimates. Financial information, benefits and other data can change quickly and may vary from those stated here.

TripAdvisor Inc

NAIC Code: 519130

www.tripadvisor.com

TYPES OF BUSINESS:

Online Travel Information

BRANDS/DIVISIONS/AFFILIATES:

tripadvisor.com
airfarewatchdog.com
bookingbuddy.com
cruisecritic.com
everytrail.com
familyvacationcritic.com
independenttraveler.com
jetsetter.com

CONTACTS: Note: Officers with more than one job title may be intentionally listed here more than once.

Barrie Seidenberg, CEO, Divisional
Stephen Kaufer, CEO
Gregory Maffei, Chairman of the Board
Noel Watson, Chief Accounting Officer
Seth Kalvert, General Counsel
Dermot Halpin, President, Divisional
Ernst Teunisssen, Senior VP

GROWTH PLANS/SPECIAL FEATURES:

TripAdvisor, Inc. operates a major web-based travel network through its primary web site, tripadvisor.com, offering traveling advice, reviews, flight searches and planning services such as TripAdvisor mobile. TripAdvisor's sites offer over 320 million reviews/opinions and receive more than 350 million unique monthly visitors. It features information about over 6.2 million accommodations, restaurants and attractions. The sites operate in 46 countries worldwide. In addition, it features over 625,000 traveler attraction photos and videos. The company also operates 23 sites that are available in several countries and languages, such as airfarewatchdog.com, bookingbuddy.com, cruisecritic.com, everytrail.com, familyvacationcritic.com, flipkey.com, gateguru.com, holidaylettings.co.uk, holidaywatchdog.com, independenttraveler.com, jetsetter.com, thefork.com, niumba.com and onetime.com. The company's TripAdvisor for Business division offers access to TripAdvisor's monthly visitors to the tourism industry. TripAdvisor for Business provides services such as vacation rental listings, helping property managers and individual home owners list their properties and showcase hotel alternatives; and business listings, allowing hoteliers to connect directly to millions of researching travelers.

The firm offers employees benefits including medical, dental, discounted vision, life and disability insurance; flexible spending accounts; paid vacation; tuition assistance; fitness subsidies; sick and parental leave; adoption assistance; product discounts; free lunches, snacks and beverages; a 401(k); and a matching charitable gift program.

FINANCIAL DATA: Note: Data for latest year may not have been available at press time.

In U.S. $	2016	2015	2014	2013	2012	2011
Revenue		1,492,000,000	1,246,000,000	944,661,000	762,966,000	637,063,000
R&D Expense		207,000,000	171,000,000	130,673,000	86,640,000	57,448,000
Operating Income		232,000,000	340,000,000	294,574,000	296,296,000	272,757,000
Operating Margin %		15.54%	27.28%	31.18%	38.83%	42.81%
SGA Expense		902,000,000	630,000,000	466,474,000	341,880,000	253,946,000
Net Income		198,000,000	226,000,000	205,443,000	194,069,000	177,677,000
Operating Cash Flow		382,000,000	387,000,000	349,523,000	239,066,000	217,882,000
Capital Expenditure		109,000,000	81,000,000	55,455,000	29,282,000	21,323,000
EBITDA		342,000,000	396,000,000	330,002,000	318,922,000	297,932,000
Return on Assets %		9.68%	13.17%	14.82%	18.17%	22.79%
Return on Equity %		15.60%	22.71%	25.81%	38.03%	42.65%
Debt to Equity		0.20	0.23	0.34	0.46	1.29

CONTACT INFORMATION:

Phone: 781-800-5000   Fax:
Toll-Free:
Address: 400 1st Ave., Needham, MA 02494 United States

STOCK TICKER/OTHER:

Stock Ticker: TRIP   Exchange: NAS
Employees: 3,008   Fiscal Year Ends: 12/31
Parent Company:

SALARIES/BONUSES:

Top Exec. Salary: $700,000   Bonus: $630,000
Second Exec. Salary: Bonus: $211,336
$433,177

OTHER THOUGHTS:

Estimated Female Officers or Directors: 4
Hot Spot for Advancement for Women/Minorities: Y

Trustmark Companies

www.trustmarkins.com

NAIC Code: 524113

TYPES OF BUSINESS:
Life Insurance
Health Insurance
Employee Benefits Management

BRANDS/DIVISIONS/AFFILIATES:
CoreSource
Starmark
Trustmark Voluntary Benefit Solutions
HealthFitness Corporation
Trustmark Critical LifeEvents

CONTACTS: *Note: Officers with more than one job title may be intentionally listed here more than once.*
Joseph L. Pray, CEO
Joseph L. Pray, Pres.
Phil Goss, CFO
Krsitin Zelkowitz, Chief Human Resources Officer
Dan Simpson, CIO
J. Grover Thomas, Jr., Chmn.

GROWTH PLANS/SPECIAL FEATURES:
Trustmark Companies offer health and life insurance and benefits administration services to employer groups through four major operating subsidiaries. These subsidiaries include CoreSource, Starmark, Trustmark Voluntary Benefit Solutions and HealthFitness Corporation, CoreSource is one of the nation's largest employee benefit administrators, managing health care for over 1.4 million people across the U.S. It serves self-insured employers with claims administration, case management, provider network development, information management, fraud detection, COBRA administration and prescription-drug benefit administration. Starmark serves the health and life insurance needs of employers for businesses with 2 to 99 employees. Trustmark Voluntary Benefit Solutions offers voluntary dental, universal life, disability and critical illness plans through businesses and credit unions. HealthFitness offers onsite and web-based workplace programs that help improve employee health and fitness. HealthFitness programs include medical screenings, risk assessment, fitness management and coaching. Trustmark Disability Advisors specializes in disability claims, providing service in negotiated settlements when and if appropriate, adjudication and appeals and financial consulting. In March 2015, the firm launched a new, patent-pending critical illness insurance product, Trustmark Critical LifeEvents, which will allow more benefits for early identification and early stage diagnosis, pay multiple benefits as a disease progresses and help eliminate consumer confusion over what triggers a benefit and how they are paid.

FINANCIAL DATA: *Note: Data for latest year may not have been available at press time.*

In U.S. $	2016	2015	2014	2013	2012	2011
Revenue		882,683,041	917,505,556	947,327,068	932,700,000	963,300,000
R&D Expense						
Operating Income						
Operating Margin %						
SGA Expense						
Net Income		8,645,781	11,716,081	29,017,258		
Operating Cash Flow						
Capital Expenditure						
EBITDA						
Return on Assets %						
Return on Equity %						
Debt to Equity						

CONTACT INFORMATION:
Phone: 847-615-1500 Fax: 847-615-3910
Toll-Free:
Address: 400 Field Dr., Lake Forest, IL 60045 United States

STOCK TICKER/OTHER:
Stock Ticker: Mutual Company Exchange:
Employees: 4,150 Fiscal Year Ends: 12/31
Parent Company:

SALARIES/BONUSES:
Top Exec. Salary: $ Bonus: $
Second Exec. Salary: $ Bonus: $

OTHER THOUGHTS:
Estimated Female Officers or Directors:
Hot Spot for Advancement for Women/Minorities: Y

Sales, profits and employees may be estimates. Financial information, benefits and other data can change quickly and may vary from those stated here.

TRW Automotive Holdings Corp

NAIC Code: 336300

TYPES OF BUSINESS:

Automotive Systems & Components
Safety Systems

BRANDS/DIVISIONS/AFFILIATES:

ZF Friedrichshafen AG

CONTACTS: Note: Officers with more than one job title may be intentionally listed here more than once.

Franz Kleiner, CEO
Tammy Mitchell, Controller
Christophe Marnat, CFO
John Harju, Exec. VP-Human Resources
Neil Marchuk, Executive VP, Divisional
Peter Lake, Executive VP, Divisional
Joseph Cantie, Executive VP
Robin Walker-Lee, Executive VP

GROWTH PLANS/SPECIAL FEATURES:

TRW Automotive Holdings Corp. is one of the world's larges
suppliers of automotive systems, modules and components t
global automotive original equipment manufacturers (OEMs
and related aftermarkets. Through an extensive network c
subsidiaries, TRW supplies products and services to over 4
major vehicle manufacturers and 250 nameplates. Th
company supplies products in three principal categorie:
chassis systems, occupant safety systems and electronic:
The firm's chassis systems segment focuses on the desigr
manufacture and sale of products and systems relating t
modules, steering, braking and linkage, actuation an
suspension. The occupant safety systems segment design
products and systems relating to airbags, seat belts an
steering wheels, including airbag sensors, active seat be
pretensioning and retractor systems and a full range of steerin
wheels. The electronics segment designs and manufacture
electronics components and systems in the areas of safet
chassis, Radio Frequency (RF), powertrain and camera an
radar-based driver assistance. Its products in this categor
consist of active safety electronics such as crash sensors an
vehicle rollover sensors; RF electronics, which include keyles
entry systems and direct tire pressure monitoring systems; an
driver assist systems such as active cruise control and lan
keeping/lane departure warning systems. The compan
maintains over 22 technical centers and 13 test tracks facilitie
in 20 countries. Some of TRW's largest customers ar
Volkswagen, Ford, Chrysler and General Motors. In May 201!
the firm was acquired by ZF Friedrichshafen AG.

FINANCIAL DATA: Note: Data for latest year may not have been available at press time.

In U.S. $	2016	2015	2014	2013	2012	2011
Revenue		16,400,000,000	17,539,000,320	17,435,000,832	16,444,000,256	16,243,999,744
R&D Expense						
Operating Income						
Operating Margin %						
SGA Expense						
Net Income		319,574,976	293,000,000	970,000,000	1,008,000,000	1,156,999,936
Operating Cash Flow						
Capital Expenditure						
EBITDA						
Return on Assets %						
Return on Equity %						
Debt to Equity						

CONTACT INFORMATION:

Phone: 734 855-2600   Fax: 734 266-2696
Toll-Free:
Address: 12001 Tech Center Dr., Livonia, MI 48150 United States

STOCK TICKER/OTHER:

Stock Ticker: Subsidiary   Exchange:
Employees: 66,900   Fiscal Year Ends: 12/31
Parent Company: ZF Friedrichshafen AG (ZF)

SALARIES/BONUSES:

Top Exec. Salary: $ Bonus: $
Second Exec. Salary: $ Bonus: $

OTHER THOUGHTS:

Estimated Female Officers or Directors: 2
Hot Spot for Advancement for Women/Minorities: Y

Tutor Perini Corporation

www.tutorperini.com

NAIC Code: 237310

TYPES OF BUSINESS:

Construction Services
Hospitality & Casino Construction
Construction Management Services
Civic & Infrastructure Construction
Design Services

BRANDS/DIVISIONS/AFFILIATES:

CONTACTS: *Note: Officers with more than one job title may be intentionally listed here more than once.*

Craig Shaw, CEO, Divisional
Ronald Tutor, CEO
Gary Smalley, CFO
Ronald Marano, Chief Accounting Officer
James Frost, COO
Michael Klein, Director
Robert Band, Executive VP, Subsidiary
John Barrett, Secretary
Jorge Casado, Vice President, Divisional

GROWTH PLANS/SPECIAL FEATURES:

Tutor Perini Corporation and its subsidiaries provide general contracting, construction management and design-build services worldwide. It operates in three segments: building, civil and specialty contractors. The building segment focuses on large, complex projects in the hospitality and gaming, transportation, health care, municipal offices, sports and entertainment, education, correctional facilities, biotech, pharmaceutical, industrial and high-tech markets. The civil segment focuses on public works construction, including the new construction, repair, replacement and reconstruction of public infrastructure such as highways, bridges, mass transit systems and wastewater treatment facilities. The company's customers primarily award contracts through the public competitive bid, in which price is the major determining factor; or through a request for proposals, where contracts are awarded based on a combination of technical capability and price. The specialty contractors segment engages in electrical, mechanical, HVAC (heating, ventilation and air conditioning), plumbing and pneumatically paced concrete for construction projects in the commercial, industrial, hospitality, transportation and gaming markets.

The firm offers employees medical, dental, vision and life insurance; a flexible spending account; an employee assistance program; educational assistance; and reimbursement on health club memberships.

FINANCIAL DATA: *Note: Data for latest year may not have been available at press time.*

In U.S. $	2016	2015	2014	2013	2012	2011
Revenue		4,920,472,000	4,492,309,000	4,175,672,000	4,111,471,000	3,716,317,000
R&D Expense						
Operating Income		105,413,000	241,690,000	203,822,000	-221,811,000	168,376,000
Operating Margin %		2.14%	5.38%	4.88%	-5.39%	4.53%
SGA Expense		250,840,000	263,752,000	263,082,000	260,369,000	226,965,000
Net Income		45,292,000	107,936,000	87,296,000	-265,400,000	86,148,000
Operating Cash Flow		14,072,000	-56,678,000	50,728,000	-67,863,000	-30,524,000
Capital Expenditure		35,912,000	75,013,000	42,360,000	41,352,000	66,747,000
EBITDA		161,595,000	288,126,000	244,657,000	-162,211,000	220,428,000
Return on Assets %		1.15%	3.01%	2.60%	-7.68%	2.69%
Return on Equity %		3.25%	8.26%	7.30%	-20.86%	6.35%
Debt to Equity		0.51	0.57	0.49	0.58	0.43

CONTACT INFORMATION:

Phone: 818 362-8391   Fax:
Toll-Free:
Address: 15901 Olden St., Sylmar, CA 91342 United States

STOCK TICKER/OTHER:

Stock Ticker: TPC   Exchange: NYS
Employees: 10,939   Fiscal Year Ends: 12/31
Parent Company:

SALARIES/BONUSES:

Top Exec. Salary: Bonus: $3,750,000
$1,750,000
Second Exec. Salary: Bonus: $950,000
$233,333

OTHER THOUGHTS:

Estimated Female Officers or Directors:

Hot Spot for Advancement for Women/Minorities:

Twitter Inc

NAIC Code: 519130

TYPES OF BUSINESS:

Real-Time Short Messaging
Advertising Services

BRANDS/DIVISIONS/AFFILIATES:

Tweet
Twitterers
Twitter.com
Twitter International Company
Periscope

CONTACTS: Note: Officers with more than one job title may be intentionally listed here more than once.

Anthony Noto, CFO
Omid Kordestani, Chairman of the Board
Robert Kaiden, Chief Accounting Officer
Adam Messinger, Chief Technology Officer
Adam Bain, COO
Jack Dorsey, Director
Vijaya Gadde, General Counsel

GROWTH PLANS/SPECIAL FEATURES:

Twitter, Inc. operates a social networking web site, Twitter.com
which encourages users to post a constant stream of updates
or Tweets, to their profile page answering the question, What
are you doing? Each message is limited to 140 characters, the
size of one short message service (SMS) text message. The
website has over 302 million active users and generates over
500 million Tweets per day. Users can send and receive
Tweets via the Twitter web site, text messages or external
applications. Users of Twitter, known as Twitterers, can make
their profile page public or private and can include hash tags
around certain words to make their public posts searchable.
They can reTweet others' Tweets and post the Tweet on their
profile and send direct messages to other Twitterers. In
addition, users can attach poll questions to tweets, with polls
being open for 24 hours and voters are not identifiable.
Twitterers can elect to follow the Tweets of family, friends, co-
workers, celebrities, news organizations and many others via
Twitter's messaging service. Twitter makes the Twitter API
(application programming interface) publicly available on its
web site, providing developers with all the tools necessary to
create new Twittering applications for a variety of operating
systems and platforms, including Windows, Mac OSX, Google
Desktop, Android OS, iPhone and iPod Touch. Twitter and its
products and services are available in multiple languages. In
2015, the firm acquired Periscope. Effective May 2015, users
outside of the U.S. are legally served by the Ireland-based
Twitter International Company instead of Twitter, Inc.; these
users are now subject to Irish and European data protection
lawns.

Twitter employees receive benefits including paid parental
leave, medical and dental coverage, wireless discounts,
catered breakfast and lunch, a 401(k), Zipcar discounts, gym
membership reimbursement and a commuter program.

FINANCIAL DATA: Note: Data for latest year may not have been available at press time.

In U.S. $	2016	2015	2014	2013	2012	2011
Revenue		2,218,032,000	1,403,002,000	664,890,000	316,933,000	106,313,000
R&D Expense		806,648,000	691,543,000	593,992,000	119,004,000	80,176,000
Operating Income		-450,036,000	-538,866,000	-635,831,000	-77,083,000	-127,411,000
Operating Margin %		-20.28%	-38.40%	-95.62%	-24.32%	-119.84%
SGA Expense		1,132,164,000	804,016,000	440,011,000	146,244,000	91,745,000
Net Income		-521,031,000	-577,820,000	-645,323,000	-79,399,000	-128,302,000
Operating Cash Flow		383,066,000	81,796,000	1,398,000	-27,935,000	-70,597,000
Capital Expenditure		347,280,000	201,630,000	75,744,000	50,599,000	11,546,000
EBITDA		-122,304,000	-330,701,000	-524,937,000	-4,577,000	-103,219,000
Return on Assets %		-8.66%	-12.91%	-30.74%	-10.23%	-22.77%
Return on Equity %		-13.03%	-17.57%	-47.76%		
Debt to Equity		0.34	0.41	0.03		

CONTACT INFORMATION:

Phone: 415-222-9670   Fax: 415-222-0922
Toll-Free:
Address: 1355 Market Street, Ste 900, San Francisco, CA 94103 United States

STOCK TICKER/OTHER:

Stock Ticker: TWTR
Employees: 3,898
Parent Company:

Exchange: NYS
Fiscal Year Ends: 12/31

SALARIES/BONUSES:

Top Exec. Salary: $375,000   Bonus: $
Second Exec. Salary: Bonus: $
$375,000

OTHER THOUGHTS:

Estimated Female Officers or Directors: 2
Hot Spot for Advancement for Women/Minorities: Y

Tyson Foods Inc

www.tyson.com

NAIC Code: 311615

TYPES OF BUSINESS:

Poultry Processing
Beef & Pork Products
Ethnic Foods
Soups & Sauces
Frozen & Refrigerated Food

BRANDS/DIVISIONS/AFFILIATES:

Cobb-Vantress Inc
Tyson Rizhao
Tyson Dalong
Tyson Nantong
Godrej Tyson Foods
Tyson Mexico Trading Company
Hillshire Brands Company

CONTACTS: *Note: Officers with more than one job title may be intentionally listed here more than once.*

R. Hudson, Assistant General Counsel
Jon Kathol, Vice President, Divisional
Donald Smith, CEO
Dennis Leatherby, CFO
John Tyson, Chairman of the Board
Mike Roetzel, Executive VP, Divisional
Howell Carper, Executive VP, Divisional
David Van Bebber, Executive VP
Mary Oleksiuk, Executive VP
Sally Grimes, Other Executive Officer
Thomas Hayes, President
Andrew Callahan, President, Divisional
Donnie King, President, Divisional
Noel White, President, Divisional
Stephen Stouffer, President, Divisional
Wes Morris, President, Divisional
Curt Calaway, Senior VP

GROWTH PLANS/SPECIAL FEATURES:

Tyson Foods, Inc. is a producer, distributor and marketer of chicken, beef, pork, prepared foods and related products. The company operates in five segments: chicken, beef, pork, prepared foods and international. The chicken operations include breeding and raising chickens as well as processing live chickens into fresh, frozen and value-added chicken products. Through subsidiary Cobb-Vantress, Inc., Tyson is one of the world's top poultry breed stock suppliers. The beef operations include processing live cattle and fabricating dressed beef carcasses into primal and sub-primal meat cuts and case-ready products. This segment also includes sales from allied products, such as hides and variety meats. The pork operations include processing live market hogs and fabricating pork carcasses into primal and sub-primal cuts and case-ready products. This segment also includes the live swine group and related allied product processing activities. Prepared food operations include the manufacture and marketing of frozen and refrigerated food products. Products include pepperoni, bacon, beef and pork pizza toppings, pizza crusts, flour and corn tortilla products, appetizers, prepared meals, ethnic foods, soups, sauces, side dishes, meat dishes and processed meats. Products are marketed domestically to food retailers, foodservice distributors, restaurant operators and noncommercial foodservice establishments such as schools, hotel chains, health care facilities, the military and other food processors as well as to international markets. The company's international operations include Cobb-Vantress, Tyson Rizhao, Tyson Dalong, Tyson Nantong, Godrej Tyson Foods and Tyson Mexico Trading Company. In 2014, the firm acquired Hillshire Brands Company; and acquired the assets of Bosco's Pizza Co. During 2015, it sold Tyson de Mexico. The company also announced plans to eliminate human antibiotics from broiler chicken flocks by 2017; aspires to be the global innovative leader of selling branded protein-centric food; and plans to discontinue operations at its Jefferson, Wisconsin and Chicago, Illinois plants by mid-2016.

FINANCIAL DATA: *Note: Data for latest year may not have been available at press time.*

In U.S. $	2016	2015	2014	2013	2012	2011
Revenue		41,373,000,000	37,580,000,000	34,374,000,000	33,278,000,000	32,266,000,000
R&D Expense						
Operating Income		2,169,000,000	1,430,000,000	1,375,000,000	1,248,000,000	1,285,000,000
Operating Margin %		5.24%	3.80%	4.00%	3.75%	3.98%
SGA Expense		1,748,000,000	1,255,000,000	983,000,000	912,000,000	914,000,000
Net Income		1,220,000,000	864,000,000	778,000,000	583,000,000	750,000,000
Operating Cash Flow		2,570,000,000	1,178,000,000	1,314,000,000	1,187,000,000	1,046,000,000
Capital Expenditure		854,000,000	632,000,000	558,000,000	690,000,000	643,000,000
EBITDA		2,925,000,000	1,914,000,000	1,921,000,000	1,782,000,000	1,822,000,000
Return on Assets %		5.19%	4.78%	6.46%	5.07%	6.87%
Return on Equity %		13.13%	11.45%	12.74%	9.99%	13.85%
Debt to Equity		0.62	0.84	0.30	0.31	0.37

CONTACT INFORMATION:

Phone: 479 290-4000   Fax: 479 290-7984
Toll-Free: 800-643-3410
Address: 2200 Don Tyson Pkwy., Springdale, AR 72762 United States

STOCK TICKER/OTHER:

Stock Ticker: TSN
Employees: 113,000
Parent Company:

Exchange: NYS
Fiscal Year Ends: 09/30

SALARIES/BONUSES:

Top Exec. Salary:
$1,124,228
Second Exec. Salary:
$910,089

Bonus: $

Bonus: $

OTHER THOUGHTS:

Estimated Female Officers or Directors: 4

Hot Spot for Advancement for Women/Minorities: Y

Sales, profits and employees may be estimates. Financial information, benefits and other data can change quickly and may vary from those stated here.

Uber Inc

NAIC Code: 561599

uber.com

TYPES OF BUSINESS:

Car Rental Referral Service
Computer Software, Telecom, Communications & VOIP

BRANDS/DIVISIONS/AFFILIATES:

UberX
Uber

CONTACTS: *Note: Officers with more than one job title may be intentionally listed here more than once.*

Travis Kalanick, CEO
Ryan Graves, Head-Global Oper.
Thuan Pham, CTO
Salle Yoo, General Counsel
Ryan Graves, Head-Global Oper.
Salle Yoo, General Counsel

GROWTH PLANS/SPECIAL FEATURES:

Uber, Inc. is a California-based creator of the Uber mobile app which connects drivers and ridesharing services with passengers. The application serves over 200 cities in the U.S plus cities in about 68 countries throughout the Americas Europe, the Middle East, Africa and Asia Pacific. Drivers fc Uber, called UberX drivers, must be over 23 years old with the driver's license and their own vehicle which passes a inspections and background check, and must pay a fee eac time a trip is set up through the app. Drivers receive an iPhon upon approval in order to receive ride requests and are paid vi a weekly direct deposit. Upon receiving a ride request, Ube sends the closest driver to fulfill it. Riders can rate the experiences with drivers for other riders to view. The compan retains a 20% fee from each ride that it books and then passe the balance of the fare to the drivers. Gross fares are estimate to run as high as $3 billion in 2014 and could hit $10 billion i 2015 as the company continues its rapid expansion. Growt rates are estimated at about 300% for each of 2014 and 2015

FINANCIAL DATA: *Note: Data for latest year may not have been available at press time.*

In U.S. $	2016	2015	2014	2013	2012	2011
Revenue		2,000,000,000	1,000,000,000	104,000,000	85,000,000	30,000,000
R&D Expense						
Operating Income						
Operating Margin %						
SGA Expense						
Net Income						
Operating Cash Flow						
Capital Expenditure						
EBITDA						
Return on Assets %						
Return on Equity %						
Debt to Equity						

CONTACT INFORMATION:

Phone: 866-576-1039   Fax:
Toll-Free:
Address: 182 Howard St #8, San Francisco, CA 94105 United States

SALARIES/BONUSES:

Top Exec. Salary: $ Bonus: $
Second Exec. Salary: $ Bonus: $

STOCK TICKER/OTHER:

Stock Ticker: Private   Exchange:
Employees: 20,313   Fiscal Year Ends:
Parent Company:

OTHER THOUGHTS:

Estimated Female Officers or Directors: 1
Hot Spot for Advancement for Women/Minorities:

Under Armour Inc

www.underarmour.com

NAIC Code: 424300

TYPES OF BUSINESS:

Apparel and Clothing Brands, Designers, Importers and Distributors
Outdoor and Sports Apparel
Shirts
Footwear
Gloves

BRANDS/DIVISIONS/AFFILIATES:

HEATGEAR
COLDGEAR
ALLSEASONGEAR
Endomondo
MyFitnessPal
UA Record
UA HealthBox
UA SpeedForm

CONTACTS: Note: Officers with more than one job title may be intentionally listed here more than once.

Kevin Plank, CEO
Lawrence Molloy, CFO
Paul Fipps, Chief Information Officer
Kip Fulks, Chief Marketing Officer
James Hardy, Executive VP, Divisional
John Stanton, General Counsel
Karl-Heinz Maurath, Other Executive Officer
Kerry Chandler, Other Executive Officer
Henry Stafford, Other Executive Officer
Matthew Mirchin, President, Geographical

GROWTH PLANS/SPECIAL FEATURES:

Under Armour, Inc. (UA) develops, markets and distributes branded performance apparel, footwear and accessories for men, women and youth. It offers several lines of apparel and accessories that utilize a variety of synthetic microfiber fabrications engineered to replace traditional cotton products in the world of athletics and fitness. UA's active wear and sports apparel accessories are designed to wick perspiration away from the skin, help regulate body temperature, enhance comfort and mobility and improve performance regardless of weather conditions. Its products are designed and merchandised along three gear lines: HEATGEAR, for hot weather; COLDGEAR, for cold weather; and ALLSEASONGEAR, for weather between the extremes. Within each product line, UA's garments come in three fit types: compression (tight fitting), fitted (athletic cut) and loose (relaxed). Annually, apparel accounts for 74% of the firm's revenues, while footwear and accessories (such as gloves for baseball batting, football, golf and running) account for 14% and 9% respectively. Licensing arrangements for the sale of UA products represent the remaining 3% of revenue. UA's larger customer, Dick's Sporting Goods, accounted for 14.4% of annual revenue, with no other customer accounting for more than 10% of net revenue. Unaffiliated manufacturers operating in 14 countries manufacture virtually all of the company's products. International professional football, baseball, basketball, hockey, rugby and soccer players as well as athletes in major collegiate sports and junior athletes of all levels use the firm's products. The company is the official supplier of footwear to the NFL (National Football League). In February 2015, the firm acquired Endomondo and MyFitnessPal. In Jan 2016, the company launched a new suite of connected fitness products including UA Record app, UA HealthBox, UA SpeedForm and UA Heart Rate. The company is keen on maintaining a strong line of athleisure apparel, and it has made major investments in fitness apps and apparel technologies that track physical activities.

Employees are referred to as Teammates; approximately 70% of them played high school sports. The headquarters includes a giant gym and basketball court.

FINANCIAL DATA: Note: Data for latest year may not have been available at press time.

In U.S. $	2016	2015	2014	2013	2012	2011
Revenue		3,963,313,000	3,084,370,000	2,332,051,000	1,834,921,000	1,472,684,000
R&D Expense						
Operating Income		408,547,000	353,955,000	265,098,000	208,695,000	162,767,000
Operating Margin %		10.30%	11.47%	11.36%	11.37%	11.05%
SGA Expense		1,497,000,000	1,158,251,000	871,572,000	670,602,000	550,069,000
Net Income		232,573,000	208,042,000	162,330,000	128,778,000	96,919,000
Operating Cash Flow		-44,104,000	219,033,000	120,070,000	199,761,000	15,218,000
Capital Expenditure		298,928,000	140,528,000	87,830,000	50,650,000	79,392,000
EBITDA		502,253,000	426,048,000	315,647,000	251,777,000	197,004,000
Return on Assets %		9.37%	11.32%	11.87%	12.40%	12.15%
Return on Equity %		15.40%	17.31%	17.35%	17.72%	17.10%
Debt to Equity		0.37	0.18	0.04	0.06	0.11

CONTACT INFORMATION:

Phone: 410 454-6428   Fax: 410 367-2400
Toll-Free: 888-727-6687
Address: 1020 Hull St., Fl. 3, Baltimore, MD 21230 United States

STOCK TICKER/OTHER:

Stock Ticker: UA   Exchange: NYS
Employees: 7,800   Fiscal Year Ends: 12/31
Parent Company:

SALARIES/BONUSES:

Top Exec. Salary: $552,884   Bonus: $250,000
Second Exec. Salary: $675,000   Bonus: $

OTHER THOUGHTS:

Estimated Female Officers or Directors:
Hot Spot for Advancement for Women/Minorities:

United Continental Holdings Inc   newsroom.united.com/corporate-fact-sheet

NAIC Code: 481111

TYPES OF BUSINESS:

Airline
Air Freight
Regional Airlines

BRANDS/DIVISIONS/AFFILIATES:

United Airlines Inc

CONTACTS: *Note: Officers with more than one job title may be intentionally listed here more than once.*

Oscar Munoz, CEO
Jennifer Kraft, Other Corporate Officer
Gerald Laderman, CFO
Chris Kenny, Chief Accounting Officer
Linda Jojo, Chief Information Officer
Gregory Hart, COO
Robert Milton, Director
Michael Bonds, Executive VP, Divisional
Brett Hart, Executive VP
Julia Haywood, Executive VP
James Compton, Other Executive Officer
J. Kirby, President

GROWTH PLANS/SPECIAL FEATURES:

United Continental Holdings, Inc. is the holding company fo
United Airlines, Inc. The airline operates approximately 5,05
flights per day to 373 airports across six continents, serving 23
domestic destinations and 140 international destinations. Hub
are located in major cities around the world, including Chicago
Cleveland, Denver, Houston, Los Angeles, Newark, Sa
Francisco, Washington D.C., Guam and Tokyo. Unite
provided transportation to 138 million passengers in 2014. Th
company is a member of the Star Alliance, which has 18,50(
daily flights to 1,300 airports in 190 countries through it
member airlines. The firm's fleet includes 1,257 internationa
aircraft, regional jets and turbo props, consisting of Airbus
Boeing, Bombardier, Embraer and Canadair aviation bran(
lines.

United offers its employees travel passes; medical, denta
vision, life, personal and business accident insurance; flexibl(
spending accounts; a 401(k) plan and profit sharing plans;
perfect attendance program; and on-time bonuses.

FINANCIAL DATA: *Note: Data for latest year may not have been available at press time.*

In U.S. $	2016	2015	2014	2013	2012	2011
Revenue		37,864,000,000	38,901,000,000	38,279,000,000	37,152,000,000	37,110,000,000
R&D Expense						
Operating Income		5,166,000,000	2,373,000,000	1,249,000,000	39,000,000	1,822,000,000
Operating Margin %		13.64%	6.10%	3.26%	.10%	4.90%
SGA Expense		11,809,000,000	11,191,000,000	10,951,000,000	9,297,000,000	9,087,000,000
Net Income		7,340,000,000	1,132,000,000	571,000,000	-723,000,000	840,000,000
Operating Cash Flow		5,992,000,000	2,634,000,000	1,444,000,000	935,000,000	2,408,000,000
Capital Expenditure		2,747,000,000	2,005,000,000	2,164,000,000	2,016,000,000	700,000,000
EBITDA		6,658,000,000	3,490,000,000	2,962,000,000	1,596,000,000	3,309,000,000
Return on Assets %		18.76%	3.05%	1.53%	-1.91%	2.16%
Return on Equity %		129.20%	42.08%	32.95%	-63.22%	47.55%
Debt to Equity		1.15	4.46	3.66	23.35	6.32

CONTACT INFORMATION:

Phone: 872-825-4000　　　Fax: 847 700-2214
Toll-Free:
Address: 233 South Wacker Drive, Chicago, IL 60606 United States

STOCK TICKER/OTHER:

Stock Ticker: UAL　　　　　　　　　Exchange: NYS
Employees: 87,000　　　　　　　　　Fiscal Year Ends: 12/31
Parent Company:

SALARIES/BONUSES:

Top Exec. Salary: $261,218　　　Bonus: $5,200,000
Second Exec. Salary:　　　　　　Bonus: $246,154
$715,000

OTHER THOUGHTS:

Estimated Female Officers or Directors: 2
Hot Spot for Advancement for Women/Minorities: Y

United Natural Foods Inc

NAIC Code: 424410

TYPES OF BUSINESS:

Food Distribution
Natural & Organic Foods Distribution
Nutritional Supplements Distribution
Personal Care Products Distribution
Retail Stores

BRANDS/DIVISIONS/AFFILIATES:

United Natural Trading Co
Woodstock Farms Manufacturing
UNFI Canada Inc
Earth Origins
Drive Organics
Nor-Cal Produce Inc
Haddon House Food Products Inc
Gourmet Guru Inc

CONTACTS: *Note: Officers with more than one job title may be intentionally listed here more than once.*

Steven Spinner, CEO
Eric Dorne, Chief Information Officer
Sean Griffin, COO
Michael Funk, Director
Thomas Dziki, Other Executive Officer
Chirstopher Testa, President, Divisional
Craig Smith, President, Divisional
Michael Zechmeister, Senior VP
Joseph Traficanti, Senior VP

GROWTH PLANS/SPECIAL FEATURES:

United Natural Foods, Inc. (UNFI) is a national distributor of natural and organic foods and related products. The company, which is a Certified Organic Distributor, carries more than 85,000 natural and organic products. These are sold under regional brand, national brand, private and master distribution labels. The firm offers six types of products: grocery and general merchandise; personal care items; produce; nutritional supplements; sports nutrition perishables; and frozen foods and bulk and food service products. UNFI serves over 40,000 customers, including supernatural chains (large chains of natural foods supermarkets), independently owned natural products retailers and conventional supermarkets located across the U.S. The company also distributes through the food service, international and buying club channels. The company has been the primary distributor to one of the largest natural food chains in the U.S., Whole Foods Market, Inc. for more than 17 years, with its agreement to expire in 2020. The firm's operations consist of three principal divisions: wholesale, which includes the operations of its 31 distribution centers; retail, which consists of UNFI's 13 owned and managed retail store through its subsidiary which does business as Earth Origins Market, and one natural products retail store in British Columbia which does business as Drive Organics; and manufacturing, which is comprised of its subsidiaries United Natural Trading Co. (which does business as Woodstock Farms Manufacturing) and UNFI Canada Inc. Woodstock Farms is an importer, processor, packager and wholesale distributor of natural and organic products, trail mixes, nuts, seeds, dried fruit and confections. Distribution members of UNFI include Albert's Organics and Select Nutrition. During 2016, the firm acquired Nor-Cal Produce, Inc.; Haddon House Food Products, Inc.; and Gourmet Guru, Inc.

UNFI offers employees medical, dental, life and disability insurance; an assistance program; and educational assistance.

FINANCIAL DATA: *Note: Data for latest year may not have been available at press time.*

In U.S. $	2016	2015	2014	2013	2012	2011
Revenue		8,184,978,000	6,794,447,000	6,064,355,000	5,236,021,000	4,530,015,000
R&D Expense						
Operating Income		241,957,000	210,788,000	185,494,000	155,158,000	129,681,000
Operating Margin %		2.95%	3.10%	3.05%	2.96%	2.86%
SGA Expense		1,017,755,000	916,857,000	837,953,000	755,744,000	688,859,000
Net Income		138,734,000	125,482,000	107,854,000	91,342,000	76,673,000
Operating Cash Flow		48,864,000	62,419,000	44,331,000	66,244,000	49,844,000
Capital Expenditure		129,134,000	147,303,000	66,554,000	31,492,000	40,778,000
EBITDA		308,067,000	263,919,000	222,411,000	195,077,000	166,731,000
Return on Assets %		5.72%	6.23%	6.69%	6.31%	5.78%
Return on Equity %		10.55%	10.71%	10.38%	9.88%	10.22%
Debt to Equity		0.38	0.36	0.14	0.11	

CONTACT INFORMATION:

Phone: 401 528-8634   Fax:
Toll-Free:
Address: 313 Iron Horse Way, Providence, RI 02908 United States

STOCK TICKER/OTHER:

Stock Ticker: UNFI   Exchange: NAS
Employees: 8,700   Fiscal Year Ends: 07/31
Parent Company:

SALARIES/BONUSES:

Top Exec. Salary: $872,300   Bonus: $
Second Exec. Salary: Bonus: $
$440,300

OTHER THOUGHTS:

Estimated Female Officers or Directors: 3
Hot Spot for Advancement for Women/Minorities: Y

Sales, profits and employees may be estimates. Financial information, benefits and other data can change quickly and may vary from those stated here.

United Parcel Service Inc (UPS)

www.ups.com

NAIC Code: 492110

TYPES OF BUSINESS:

Couriers and Express Delivery Services
Logistics Services
Supply Chain Services
International Products & Services
Ground & Air Delivery Services
Visibility & Technology Services

BRANDS/DIVISIONS/AFFILIATES:

UPS Hundredweight Services
UPS Next Day Air
Mail Boxes Etc
UPS Supply Chain Solutions
UPS Capital
Poltraf Sp zoo
Coyote Logistics Midco Inc
Parcel Pro Inc

CONTACTS: Note: Officers with more than one job title may be intentionally listed here more than once.

David Abney, CEO
Richard Peretz, CFO
David Barnes, Chief Information Officer
Alan Gershenhorn, Other Executive Officer
Teri Mcclure, Other Executive Officer
James Barber, President, Divisional
Myron Gray, President, Divisional
Teresa Finley, Senior VP, Divisional
Kate Gutmann, Senior VP, Divisional
Mark Wallace, Senior VP, Divisional
Norman Brothers, Senior VP

GROWTH PLANS/SPECIAL FEATURES:

United Parcel Service, Inc. (UPS) is one of the world's larges package delivery companies and a global provider of suppl chain management. It delivers packages each business day 8.2 million receivers in over 220 countries. The firm delivers a average of 18 million pieces per day worldwide. It is also major provider of LTL transportation services. Offerings includ domestic and international package products and services an supply chain and freight services. The U.S. domestic packag products and services business delivers packages traveling b ground or air transportation. In addition to the standard groun delivery products, UPS Hundredweight Services offer guaranteed, time-definite service to customers sendin multiple package shipments. UPS Next Day Air offers severa service options guaranteeing next business day delivery b 8:00AM, 10:30AM, noon, 3-4:30PM or by the end of the day the 48 contiguous U.S. states and limited areas of Alaska International services include guaranteed early morning morning and noon delivery to major cities around the world a well as scheduled day-definite air and ground services. Th supply chain and freight segment consists of its forwarding an logistics operations, UPS Freight and other related businesse The division provides services in more than 195 countries an territories and includes supply chain design and managemen freight distribution, customs brokerage, mail and consultin services. UPS Freight offers a variety of LTL/truckload service to customers in North America. Other business units within th segment include Mail Boxes, Etc.; UPS Supply Chai Solutions; and UPS Capital. In 2015, the firm acquired Polanc based pharmaceutical logistics company, Poltraf Sp. z.o.o Coyote Logistics Midco, Inc.; Parcel Pro, Inc.; and the insure parcel services division of G4S International Logistics.

U.S. employees at UPS receive benefits including tuitio assistance; medical, prescription, dental, life and visio coverage; and health care spending accounts.

FINANCIAL DATA: Note: Data for latest year may not have been available at press time.

In U.S. $	2016	2015	2014	2013	2012	2011
Revenue		58,363,000,000	58,232,000,000	55,438,000,000	54,127,000,000	53,105,000,000
R&D Expense						
Operating Income		7,668,000,000	4,968,000,000	7,034,000,000	1,343,000,000	6,080,000,000
Operating Margin %		13.13%	8.53%	12.68%	2.48%	11.44%
SGA Expense		31,028,000,000	32,045,000,000	28,557,000,000	33,102,000,000	27,575,000,000
Net Income		4,844,000,000	3,032,000,000	4,372,000,000	807,000,000	3,804,000,000
Operating Cash Flow		7,430,000,000	5,726,000,000	7,304,000,000	7,216,000,000	7,073,000,000
Capital Expenditure		2,379,000,000	2,328,000,000	2,065,000,000	2,153,000,000	2,005,000,000
EBITDA		9,767,000,000	6,913,000,000	8,921,000,000	3,225,000,000	7,906,000,000
Return on Assets %		13.13%	8.45%	11.64%	2.19%	11.13%
Return on Equity %		210.10%	70.38%	78.58%	13.80%	50.67%
Debt to Equity		4.58	4.60	1.67	2.38	1.57

CONTACT INFORMATION:

Phone: 404 828-6000   Fax: 404 828-6562
Toll-Free: 800-874-5877
Address: 55 Glenlake Pkwy. NE, Atlanta, GA 30328 United States

STOCK TICKER/OTHER:

Stock Ticker: UPS
Employees: 435,000
Parent Company:

Exchange: NYS
Fiscal Year Ends: 12/31

SALARIES/BONUSES:

Top Exec. Salary: $381,327   Bonus: $1,000,000
Second Exec. Salary: $1,018,764   Bonus: $

OTHER THOUGHTS:

Estimated Female Officers or Directors: 4
Hot Spot for Advancement for Women/Minorities: Y

Sales, profits and employees may be estimates. Financial information, benefits and other data can change quickly and may vary from those stated here.

United States Cellular Corp

www.uscellular.com

NAIC Code: 517210

TYPES OF BUSINESS:

Cell Phone Service

BRANDS/DIVISIONS/AFFILIATES:

Telephone and Data Systems Inc

CONTACTS: *Note: Officers with more than one job title may be intentionally listed here more than once.*

Leroy Carlson, CEO, Subsidiary
Kenneth Meyers, CEO
Steven Campbell, CFO
Douglas Shuma, Chief Accounting Officer
Michael Irizarry, Chief Technology Officer
Kristin MacCarthy, Controller
Leroy Carlson, Director Emeritus
Jay Ellison, Executive VP, Divisional
Deirdre Drake, Other Executive Officer
Edward Perez, Senior VP, Divisional
Jane McCahon, Vice President, Divisional

GROWTH PLANS/SPECIAL FEATURES:

United States Cellular Corp. (U.S. Cellular) is a leading U.S. wireless telecommunications firm, providing wireless voice and data services to 4.9 million customers across 23 states. The company maintains interests in consolidated and investment wireless licenses that cover portions of 23 states and a total population of 32 million people. U.S. Cellular offers a range of wireless devices such as handsets, modems, mobile hotspots, home phone and tablets for use by its customers. The firm has also installed service repair programs at certain facilities, which assist customers with over-the-counter exchanges, Smartphone advance exchanges, loaner phones, device recycling and device returns. U.S. Cellular sells wireless devices to agents and other third-party distributors for resale. The wireless services segment provides a variety of packaged voice and data pricing plans. The company offers post-pay plans and prepaid plans. Moreover, U.S. Cellular services include connected home, a self-installed home security and automation system for home monitoring purposes. The company also offers data-services and app-like experiences to non-smartphone devices via a technology known as binary runtime environment for wireless (BREW). These enhanced data services include downloading news, weather, sports information, games, ring tones and other services. Telephone and Data Systems, Inc. owns approximately 84% of the company.

Employee benefits include medical, dental and vision coverage; life insurance and AD&D; short- and long-term disability; a 401(k) and Roth IRA; a pension plan; and tuition reimbursement.

FINANCIAL DATA: *Note: Data for latest year may not have been available at press time.*

In U.S. $	2016	2015	2014	2013	2012	2011
Revenue		3,996,853,000	3,892,747,000	3,918,836,000	4,452,084,000	4,343,346,000
R&D Expense						
Operating Income		312,942,000	-143,390,000	146,865,000	156,656,000	280,780,000
Operating Margin %		7.82%	-3.68%	3.74%	3.51%	6.46%
SGA Expense		1,493,730,000	1,591,914,000	1,677,395,000	1,764,933,000	1,779,203,000
Net Income		241,347,000	-42,812,000	140,038,000	111,006,000	175,041,000
Operating Cash Flow		555,114,000	172,342,000	290,897,000	899,291,000	987,862,000
Capital Expenditure		580,593,000	605,083,000	734,402,000	949,090,000	771,798,000
EBITDA		1,096,278,000	604,679,000	1,105,400,000	856,079,000	951,993,000
Return on Assets %		3.56%	-.66%	2.14%	1.71%	2.85%
Return on Equity %		7.03%	-1.27%	3.93%	3.01%	4.93%
Debt to Equity		0.45	0.34	0.25	0.23	0.24

CONTACT INFORMATION:

Phone: 773 399-8900   Fax: 773 399-8936
Toll-Free: 888-944-9400
Address: 8410 W. Bryn Mawr Ave., Ste. 700, Chicago, IL 60631 United States

STOCK TICKER/OTHER:

Stock Ticker: USM   Exchange: NYS
Employees: 6,600   Fiscal Year Ends: 12/31
Parent Company: Telephone and Data Systems Inc

SALARIES/BONUSES:

Top Exec. Salary: $905,300   Bonus: $964,000
Second Exec. Salary: $605,750   Bonus: $181,362

OTHER THOUGHTS:

Estimated Female Officers or Directors: 6
Hot Spot for Advancement for Women/Minorities: Y

United Technologies Corporation

www.utc.com

NAIC Code: 336412

TYPES OF BUSINESS:

Aircraft Engine and Engine Parts Manufacturing
Elevator & Escalator Systems
HVAC Systems
Aircraft Parts & Maintenance

BRANDS/DIVISIONS/AFFILIATES:

Otis
UTC Climate, Controls & Security
UTC Aerospace Systems
Pratt & Whitney

CONTACTS: Note: Officers with more than one job title may be intentionally listed here more than once.

Gregory Hayes, CEO

GROWTH PLANS/SPECIAL FEATURES:

United Technologies Corporation (UTC) provides high technology products and services to the building systems and aerospace industries worldwide. The company operate through four principle segments: Otis; UTC climate, controls & security; Pratt & Whitney; and UTC aerospace systems. Otis manufactures, sells, installs and services a wide range of passenger and freight elevators for low-, medium-, and high speed applications, as well as a broad line of escalators and moving walkways. UTC climate, controls & security is the leading provider of HVAC (heating, ventilation and air conditioning) and refrigeration systems, including controls for residential, commercial, industrial and transportation applications. This segment is also a global provider of security and fire safety products and services such as alarms, access control systems and video surveillance systems. Pratt & Whitney supplies aircraft engines and maintenance services for the commercial, military, business jet and general aviation markets. Pratt & Whitney Canada (P&WC) is a world leader in the production of engines powering general and business aviation, as well as regional airline, utility and military airplane and helicopters, and provides maintenance, repair and overhaul services, including the sale of spare parts. UTC Aerospace Systems supplies technologically advanced aerospace products and aftermarket solutions for aircraft manufacturers, airlines, regional, business and general aviation markets, military, space and undersea operations.

UTC offers employees benefits including medical and dental insurance, health care reimbursement accounts, long-term disability coverage, an Employee Scholar Program that features paid time off for academic pursuits as well as academic expense reimbursement, employee assistance programs, a retirement plan and select benefits for part time employees.

FINANCIAL DATA: Note: Data for latest year may not have been available at press time.

In U.S. $	2016	2015	2014	2013	2012	2011
Revenue		56,098,000,000	65,100,000,000	62,626,000,000	57,708,000,000	58,190,000,000
R&D Expense		2,279,000,000	2,635,000,000	2,529,000,000	2,371,000,000	2,058,000,000
Operating Income		7,291,000,000	9,769,000,000	9,209,000,000	7,684,000,000	8,099,000,000
Operating Margin %		12.99%	15.00%	14.70%	13.31%	13.91%
SGA Expense		5,886,000,000	6,500,000,000	6,718,000,000	6,452,000,000	6,464,000,000
Net Income		7,608,000,000	6,220,000,000	5,721,000,000	5,130,000,000	4,979,000,000
Operating Cash Flow		6,326,000,000	7,336,000,000	7,505,000,000	6,646,000,000	6,590,000,000
Capital Expenditure		2,089,000,000	2,304,000,000	2,410,000,000	2,932,000,000	983,000,000
EBITDA		9,275,000,000	11,894,000,000	11,167,000,000	9,328,000,000	9,625,000,000
Return on Assets %		8.51%	6.83%	6.35%	6.80%	8.30%
Return on Equity %		25.97%	19.72%	19.80%	21.46%	23.01%
Debt to Equity		0.70	0.57	0.61	0.83	0.43

CONTACT INFORMATION:

Phone: 860 728-7000   Fax: 860 728-7028
Toll-Free:
Address: 1 Financial Plz., Hartford, CT 06103 United States

STOCK TICKER/OTHER:

Stock Ticker: UTX   Exchange: NYS
Employees: 211,000   Fiscal Year Ends: 12/31
Parent Company:

SALARIES/BONUSES:

Top Exec. Salary: Bonus: $850,000
$1,300,000
Second Exec. Salary: Bonus: $710,000
$1,087,500

OTHER THOUGHTS:

Estimated Female Officers or Directors: 2

Hot Spot for Advancement for Women/Minorities: Y

UnitedHealth Group Inc

www.unitedhealthgroup.com

NAIC Code: 524114

TYPES OF BUSINESS:

Medical Insurance
Wellness Plans
Dental & Vision Insurance
Health Information Technology

BRANDS/DIVISIONS/AFFILIATES:

United Healthcare
OptumHealth
OptumInsight
OptumRX
United Healthcare Employer & Individual
UnitedHealthcare Medicare & Retirement
UnitedHealthcare Community & State
Catamaran Corporation

CONTACTS: *Note: Officers with more than one job title may be intentionally listed here more than once.*

Larry Renfro, CEO, Subsidiary
Stephen Hemsley, CEO
John Rex, CFO
Richard Burke, Chairman of the Board
Tom Roos, Chief Accounting Officer
Dirk McMahon, Executive VP, Divisional
D. Wilson, Executive VP, Divisional
Marianne Short, Executive VP
David Wichmann, President
Dannette Smith, Secretary

GROWTH PLANS/SPECIAL FEATURES:

UnitedHealth Group, Inc. is a diversified health and insurance firm that serves over 75 million people worldwide. The company provides individuals with access to health care services and resources through approximately 1 million physicians and other care providers and 6,000 hospitals across the U.S. The company has four operating segments: UnitedHealthcare (which includes United Healthcare Employer & Individual, UnitedHealthcare Medicare & Retirement and UnitedHealthcare Community & State), OptumHealth, OptumInsight and OptumRX. The United Healthcare segment provides consumer-oriented health benefit plans and services for large national employers, public sector employers, mid-sized employers, small businesses and individuals nationwide; health and well-being services for individuals age 50 and older; and network-based health services for beneficiaries of government-sponsored health care programs. The OptumHealth segment is engaged in care services, behavioral solutions, specialty benefits and financial services in fields such as dental, vision, disability, therapy and stop-loss coverage. The OptumInsight segment provides technology, operational and consulting services to participants in the health care industry. The OptumRX segment offers a comprehensive suite of integrated pharmacy benefit management (PBM) services to more than 66 million people through over 67,000 retail network pharmacies as well as mail order service facilities. In 2015, the firm acquired pharmacy-benefit manager Catamaran Corporation for $12.8 billion.

The company offers its employees medical, vision, dental, life and disability insurance; flexible spending accounts; an employee assistance program; a 401(k); adoption assistance; and tuition reimbursement.

FINANCIAL DATA: *Note: Data for latest year may not have been available at press time.*

In U.S. $	2016	2015	2014	2013	2012	2011
Revenue		157,107,000,000	130,474,000,000	122,489,000,000	110,618,000,000	101,862,000,000
R&D Expense						
Operating Income		11,021,000,000	10,274,000,000	9,623,000,000	9,254,000,000	8,464,000,000
Operating Margin %		7.01%	7.87%	7.85%	8.36%	8.30%
SGA Expense		24,312,000,000	21,681,000,000	19,362,000,000	17,306,000,000	15,557,000,000
Net Income		5,813,000,000	5,619,000,000	5,625,000,000	5,526,000,000	5,142,000,000
Operating Cash Flow		9,740,000,000	8,051,000,000	6,991,000,000	7,155,000,000	6,968,000,000
Capital Expenditure		1,556,000,000	1,525,000,000	1,307,000,000	1,070,000,000	1,067,000,000
EBITDA		12,714,000,000	11,752,000,000	10,998,000,000	10,563,000,000	9,588,000,000
Return on Assets %		5.87%	6.67%	6.91%	7.42%	7.85%
Return on Equity %		17.53%	17.39%	17.76%	18.58%	19.00%
Debt to Equity		0.75	0.49	0.46	0.45	0.46

CONTACT INFORMATION:

Phone: 952 936-1300   Fax: 952 936-0044
Toll-Free: 800-328-5979
Address: 9900 Bren Rd. E., Minnetonka, MN 55343 United States

STOCK TICKER/OTHER:

Stock Ticker: UNH
Employees: 200,000
Parent Company:

Exchange: NYS
Fiscal Year Ends: 12/31

SALARIES/BONUSES:

Top Exec. Salary:
$1,350,000
Second Exec. Salary:
$1,150,000

Bonus: $

Bonus: $

OTHER THOUGHTS:

Estimated Female Officers or Directors: 4

Hot Spot for Advancement for Women/Minorities: Y

Universal Health Services Inc

www.uhsinc.com

NAIC Code: 622110

TYPES OF BUSINESS:

General Medical and Surgical Hospitals
Radiation Oncology Centers
Behavioral Health Hospitals
Surgical Hospitals
Administrative Services
Physician Recruitment
Facilities Planning

BRANDS/DIVISIONS/AFFILIATES:

Cygnet Hospital-Taunton
Orchard Portman House Hospital
Alpha Hospitals Holdings Limited
Desert View Regional Medical Center

CONTACTS: Note: Officers with more than one job title may be intentionally listed here more than once.

Alan Miller, CEO
Steve Filton, CFO
Marc Miller, Director
Debra Osteen, President, Divisional
Marvin Pember, Senior VP

GROWTH PLANS/SPECIAL FEATURES:

Universal Health Services, Inc. (UHS) owns and operate through its subsidiaries acute care hospitals, behavioral healt centers, surgical hospitals, ambulatory surgery centers an radiation oncology centers. UHS has 24 acute care hospital and 229 behavioral health care facilities located in 37 state Washington, D.C., the U.S. Virgin Islands, the U.K. and Puert Rico. As part of its ambulatory treatment centers division, th firm manages or partially/wholly owns five surgical hospital and surgery and radiation oncology centers located in fou states. UHS hospitals provide general surgery, pharmaceutic services, internal medicine, pediatric services, obstetric emergency room care, radiology, oncology, diagnostic car coronary care and behavioral health services. The compan also provides non-medical services to its facilities, including variety of management services such as central purchasing facilities planning, administrative personnel managemen finance and control systems, information services, physicia recruitment services, marketing and public relations. In 201 acute care hospitals, surgery centers, surgical hospitals an radiation oncology centers made up approximately 51% of th firm's revenue, with behavioral health care facilities accountin for the remaining 49%. In 2015, the firm acquired Orchar Portman House Hospital (now called Cygnet Hospital-Taunton in the U.K.; and Alpha Hospitals Holdings Limited, also base in the U.K. In 2016, it acquired Desert View Regional Medic Center in Nevada, U.S.

The company offers its employees medical, dental, vision, lif AD&D and disability insurance; coverage availability fc blended families; family and caregiving support; wellnes support; a savings plan; an employee stock purchase plan; an flexible spending accounts.

FINANCIAL DATA: Note: Data for latest year may not have been available at press time.

In U.S. $	2016	2015	2014	2013	2012	2011
Revenue		9,043,451,000	8,065,326,000	7,283,822,000	6,961,400,000	7,500,198,000
R&D Expense						
Operating Income		1,259,395,000	1,063,305,000	1,015,463,000	942,581,000	897,128,000
Operating Margin %		13.92%	13.18%	13.94%	13.54%	11.96%
SGA Expense		4,307,360,000	3,975,625,000	97,758,000	129,771,000	91,765,000
Net Income		680,528,000	545,343,000	510,733,000	443,446,000	398,167,000
Operating Cash Flow		1,020,898,000	1,035,876,000	884,241,000	815,271,000	718,251,000
Capital Expenditure			404,638,000	408,304,000	417,554,000	323,931,000
EBITDA		1,560,558,000	1,438,929,000	1,358,573,000	1,251,271,000	1,192,989,000
Return on Assets %		7.31%	6.30%	6.18%	5.58%	5.24%
Return on Equity %		17.03%	15.61%	17.12%	17.70%	18.62%
Debt to Equity		0.79	0.85	0.98	1.37	1.59

CONTACT INFORMATION:

Phone: 610 768-3300   Fax: 610 768-3336
Toll-Free:
Address: 367 S. Gulph Rd., King Of Prussia, PA 19406 United States

STOCK TICKER/OTHER:

Stock Ticker: UHS   Exchange: NYS
Employees: 68,700   Fiscal Year Ends: 12/31
Parent Company:

SALARIES/BONUSES:

Top Exec. Salary: Bonus: $
$1,568,310
Second Exec. Salary: Bonus: $
$695,027

OTHER THOUGHTS:

Estimated Female Officers or Directors: 2

Hot Spot for Advancement for Women/Minorities: Y

US Bancorp
NAIC Code: 522110

www.usbank.com/en/AboutHome.cfm

TYPES OF BUSINESS:
Banking
Lease Financing
Consumer Finance
Credit Cards
Discount Brokerage
Investment Advisory Services
Trust Services
Insurance

BRANDS/DIVISIONS/AFFILIATES:
US Bank

CONTACTS: *Note: Officers with more than one job title may be intentionally listed here more than once.*
Richard Davis, CEO
Kent Stone, Vice Chairman, Divisional
Craig Gifford, Chief Accounting Officer
Mark Runkel, Chief Credit Officer
P. Parker, Chief Risk Officer
Andrew Cecere, COO
Jennie Carlson, Executive VP, Divisional
James Chosy, Executive VP
Katherine Quinn, Executive VP
Jeffry von Gillern, Vice Chairman, Divisional
John Elmore, Vice Chairman, Divisional
James Kelligrew, Vice Chairman, Divisional
Leslie Godridge, Vice Chairman, Divisional
Terrance Dolan, Vice Chairman, Divisional

GROWTH PLANS/SPECIAL FEATURES:
U.S. Bancorp (USB) is a financial services holding company, with $429 billion in assets. USB operates 3,133 banking offices and 4,936 ATMs in the Midwest and Western regions of the U.S. Through U.S. Bank and other subsidiaries, the company is engaged in general banking, primarily in domestic markets, and serves individuals, businesses, institutional organizations, financial institutions and government entities. Lending services include traditional credit products, credit card services, financing, leasing, asset-backed lending and agricultural finance. Depository services include checking and savings accounts and time certificate contracts. Ancillary services include foreign exchange, treasury management and lock-box collection for corporate customers. A full range of asset management and fiduciary services are available for individuals, estates, business corporations, foundations and charitable organizations. USB's non-banking subsidiaries provide investment and insurance products as well as mutual fund processing services to a range of mutual funds. Mortgage services are available through the bank's offices, while consumer lending products are originated through banking offices, indirect correspondents and brokers. In April 2016, the firm sold its 50.1% majority stake in Sao Paulo-based Elavon do Brasil to Stone Pagamentos SA.

The company offers employees benefits including medical, dental and vision insurance; flexible spending accounts; disability and life insurance; 401(k) and pension plans; an employee assistance plan; adoption benefits; and tuition reimbursement.

FINANCIAL DATA: *Note: Data for latest year may not have been available at press time.*

In U.S. $	2016	2015	2014	2013	2012	2011
Revenue		20,093,000,000	19,939,000,000	19,378,000,000	20,064,000,000	18,883,000,000
R&D Expense		887,000,000	863,000,000	848,000,000	821,000,000	758,000,000
Operating Income		8,030,000,000	7,995,000,000	7,764,000,000	7,726,000,000	6,629,000,000
Operating Margin %		39.96%	40.09%	40.06%	38.50%	35.10%
SGA Expense		6,637,000,000	6,274,000,000	6,178,000,000	5,957,000,000	5,558,000,000
Net Income		5,879,000,000	5,851,000,000	5,836,000,000	5,647,000,000	4,872,000,000
Operating Cash Flow		8,782,000,000	5,332,000,000	11,446,000,000	7,958,000,000	9,820,000,000
Capital Expenditure						
EBITDA						
Return on Assets %		1.36%	1.45%	1.54%	1.55%	1.45%
Return on Equity %		14.13%	14.87%	15.73%	16.41%	16.01%
Debt to Equity		0.78	0.83	0.55	0.74	1.01

CONTACT INFORMATION:
Phone: 651 466-3000 Fax:
Toll-Free:
Address: 800 Nicollet Mall, Minneapolis, MN 55402 United States

STOCK TICKER/OTHER:
Stock Ticker: USB Exchange: NYS
Employees: 65,433 Fiscal Year Ends: 12/31
Parent Company:

SALARIES/BONUSES:
Top Exec. Salary: $1,300,000 Bonus: $
Second Exec. Salary: $750,000 Bonus: $

OTHER THOUGHTS:
Estimated Female Officers or Directors: 5

Hot Spot for Advancement for Women/Minorities: Y

Sales, profits and employees may be estimates. Financial information, benefits and other data can change quickly and may vary from those stated here.

USAA
NAIC Code: 524126

TYPES OF BUSINESS:
Insurance, Direct Property & Casualty
Banking
Life Insurance
Real Estate Development
Discount Brokerage
Investment Management
Mutual Funds

BRANDS/DIVISIONS/AFFILIATES:
United Services Automobile Association
USAA Investment Management Company
USAA Alliance Services LLC
USAA Educational Foundation
USAA Casualty Insurance Company
USAA General Indemnity Company
USAA County Mutual Insurance Company
USAA Life Insurance Company

CONTACTS:
Note: Officers with more than one job title may be intentionally listed here more than once.

Stuart Parker, CEO
Stuart Parker, Pres.
Shon Manasco, Chief Admin. Officer
Steven A. Bennett, General Counsel
Wendi E. Strong, Exec. VP-Enterprise Affairs
F. David Bohne, Pres., USAA Federal Savings Bank
Kevin J. Bergner, Pres., USAA Property & Casualty Insurance Group
Christopher W. Claus, Exec. VP-Enterprise Advice Group
Wayne Peacock, Pres., USAA Capital Corporation
Lester L. Lyles, Chmn.

GROWTH PLANS/SPECIAL FEATURES:
USAA (United Services Automobile Association) is a mutual insurance company that serves over 11 million members comprised exclusively of U.S. military personnel and their families. It owns and manages over $137 billion in assets from offices in Texas, Colorado, Arizona, Virginia and Florida; and international offices in London and Frankfurt. USAA offers more than 150 financial services and products, primarily automobile, property and life insurance as well as automobile, mortgage and home equity loans. The company also manages checking accounts, savings accounts, credit cards and personal loans for its military customers. In addition, customers have access to mutual funds and brokerage services through USAA Investment Management Company. Members can access their accounts and conduct investing, banking and insurance business online. Additionally, subsidiary USAA Alliance Services, LLC has formed a series of partnerships to provide members with discounts on home security, travel services and insurance, floral services, car rentals and diamond and fine jewelry. The firm's USAA Educational Foundation division, a nonprofit entity, provides consumer education to the general public on topics including personal finance, safety and quality of life. Other subsidiaries include USAA Casualty Insurance Company, USAA General Indemnity Company, USAA County Mutual Insurance Company, USAA Life Insurance Company, USAA Financial Advisors, Inc. and USAA Federal Savings Bank.

Employee benefits include medical and dental coverage, 401(k), military leave, an employee assistance program, educational assistance and adoption assistance.

FINANCIAL DATA:
Note: Data for latest year may not have been available at press time.

In U.S. $	2016	2015	2014	2013	2012	2011
Revenue		20,971,000,000	24,033,000,000	20,971,000,000	20,729,000,000	19,036,000,000
R&D Expense						
Operating Income						
Operating Margin %						
SGA Expense						
Net Income		2,726,000,000	3,410,000,000	2,726,000,000	2,832,000,000	2,128,000,000
Operating Cash Flow						
Capital Expenditure						
EBITDA						
Return on Assets %						
Return on Equity %						
Debt to Equity						

CONTACT INFORMATION:
Phone: 210-498-2211   Fax: 210-498-9940
Toll-Free: 800-531-8722
Address: 9800 Fredericksburg Rd., San Antonio, TX 78288 United States

STOCK TICKER/OTHER:
Stock Ticker: Mutual Company   Exchange:
Employees: 26,000   Fiscal Year Ends: 12/31
Parent Company:

SALARIES/BONUSES:
Top Exec. Salary: $ Bonus: $
Second Exec. Salary: $ Bonus: $

OTHER THOUGHTS:
Estimated Female Officers or Directors: 4
Hot Spot for Advancement for Women/Minorities: Y

UST Global Inc

www.ust-global.com

NAIC Code: 541512

TYPES OF BUSINESS:

IT Services & BPO
IT Services
Business Process Outsourcing (BPO)
Mortgage BPO
Consulting
Data Management
Enterprise Resource Planning
Business Intelligence

BRANDS/DIVISIONS/AFFILIATES:

Comcraft Group
Kanchi Technologies

CONTACTS: *Note: Officers with more than one job title may be intentionally listed here more than once.*

Sajan Pillai, CEO
Saurabh Ranjan, COO
Joe Nalkara, Pres.
Krishna Sudheendra, CFO
Nikki Arora, Corp. Mktg. Officer
Manu Gopinath, Global Head-Human Resources
David Whitehouse, Chief Medical Officer
Jaya Kumar, CIO
Alexander Varghese, Chief Admin. Officer
Catherine Gardner, Global Head-Legal, Risk & Compliance
Saurabh Ranjan, Managing Dir.-Global Oper.
Shaun Mitra, Chief Bus. Officer
Adam Krajchir, Chief Customer Officer
Gaurav Agarwal, VP
BG Moore, Chief of Staff
Krishna Prasad, Chief Solutions Officer
Bipin Thomas, Pres., Health Group
John Gustafson, Pres., Diversified Bus.
Dan Gupta, Chmn.
Michael E. Hopewell, Managing Dir.-Europe

GROWTH PLANS/SPECIAL FEATURES:

UST Global, Inc., a division of Comcraft Group, provides information technology (IT) services and business process outsourcing (BPO) through its international facilities. The firm divides its services into ten divisions. Consulting services encompasses the firm's IT strategy, architecture, process management and change management service offerings. Technology build services builds custom applications or entire systems for clients. Application managed services provides end-to-end management for applications, helping clients to reduce total cost of ownership, improve service quality and enable business growth. Infrastructure managed services provides management for IT infrastructures. QA and testing services develop and execute quality assurance and testing strategies for optimal performance and results. Business process outsourcing (BPO) helps reduce costs while simultaneously driving innovation and delivering value to meet and exceed customer expectations and satisfaction. S+CC services (Smart plus connected communities) features energy management, asset management, enhanced safety/security, connected health care, connected transportation, connected sports, connected entertainment, connected education and connected maintenance. Mobility services help enterprises realize their mobile initiatives by performing assessments, building roadmaps, identifying and designing applications, and then testing, deploying and managing the apps. Smarter cities services builds cities with tools to coordinate and analyze data for better decisions, anticipate problems and coordinate resources in order to operate efficiently. Engineering services is operated through Kanchi Technologies, and offers consultancy services, project management, business process improvement, integration of business technology, execution of global delivery strategies as well as auditing services.

FINANCIAL DATA: *Note: Data for latest year may not have been available at press time.*

In U.S. $	2016	2015	2014	2013	2012	2011
Revenue		455,000,000	450,000,000	435,000,000	420,000,000	
R&D Expense						
Operating Income						
Operating Margin %						
SGA Expense						
Net Income						
Operating Cash Flow						
Capital Expenditure						
EBITDA						
Return on Assets %						
Return on Equity %						
Debt to Equity						

CONTACT INFORMATION:

Phone: 949-716-8757   Fax: 949-716-8396
Toll-Free:
Address: 20 Enterprise, 4th Fl., Aliso Viejo, CA 92656 United States

STOCK TICKER/OTHER:

Stock Ticker: Private   Exchange:
Employees: 14,000   Fiscal Year Ends:
Parent Company: Comcraft Group

SALARIES/BONUSES:

Top Exec. Salary: $ Bonus: $
Second Exec. Salary: $ Bonus: $

OTHER THOUGHTS:

Estimated Female Officers or Directors: 2
Hot Spot for Advancement for Women/Minorities:

Valassis Communications Inc (RedPlum)   www.valassis.com
NAIC Code: 541800

TYPES OF BUSINESS:
Coupon Marketing Products & Services
Direct Mail
Newspaper Advertising
Sampling
Software

BRANDS/DIVISIONS/AFFILIATES:
MacAndrews & Forbes Inc
Harland Clarke Holdings Corp
RedPlum
Intelligent Media Delivery
Clipper Magazine
Printed Deals

CONTACTS: Note: Officers with more than one job title may be intentionally listed here more than once.
Robert A. Mason, CEO
Ron Goolsby, COO
Robert L. Recchia, CFO
Suzie Brown, Exec. VP-Sales & Mktg.
Jim Parkinson`, Chief Digital & Tech. Officer
Todd L. Wiseley, Exec. VP-Admin.
Todd L. Wiseley, General Counsel
Brian J. Husselbee, Pres.

GROWTH PLANS/SPECIAL FEATURES:

Valassis Communications, Inc. operates under the bran
RedPlum, and is a provider of media and marketing service:
The company provides its services to more than 15,00
consumer packaged goods, financial, food service, genera
marketing, grocery & drug, specialty retail an
telecommunications sectors. Its offerings are divided into fiv
segments: direct mail, in-store advertising, newspape
advertising, digital advertising and marketing analysis. Dire
mail distributes advertisements mid-week in order to engag
consumers as they are planning weekend shopping trip:
Direct mail ads include inserts, wraps and postcards; and thi
division also provides mailing lists and design templates. Ir
store advertising provides innovative, at-shelf solutions tha
garner attention, engage customers and drive action. In-stor
ads include coupon dispensers, floor graphics, shelf talker
and more. Newspaper advertising provides ads withi
newspapers such as coupons and product/bran
advertisement. This division also provides coupon books, a
well as newspaper inserts. Digital advertising includes displa
advertisements on computer and mobile screens, ema
marketing and digital couponing. Marketing analysis comprise
Valassis' Intelligent Media Delivery platform in order fc
companies to engage and activate consumers wherever the
plan, shop, share and/or buy. The data-driven intelliger
solution targets responses, stimulates activity and predict
performance. Valassis is a wholly-owned subsidiary of Harlan
Clarke Holdings Corp., which itself is a subsidiary c
MacAndrews & Forbes, Inc. In 2015, the firm acquired Clippe
Magazine; and Printed Deals.

Valassis Communications offers its employees medical, denta
life, vision and AD&D insurance; an employee assistance plar
a retirement plan and 401(k); adoption assistance; and shor
and long-term disability.

FINANCIAL DATA: Note: Data for latest year may not have been available at press time.

In U.S. $	2016	2015	2014	2013	2012	2011
Revenue		2,285,000,000	2,225,000,000	2,200,000,000	2,162,084,096	2,235,959,040
R&D Expense						
Operating Income						
Operating Margin %						
SGA Expense						
Net Income						
Operating Cash Flow						
Capital Expenditure						
EBITDA						
Return on Assets %						
Return on Equity %						
Debt to Equity						

CONTACT INFORMATION:
Phone: 734 591-3000   Fax:
Toll-Free: 800-437-0479
Address: 19975 Victor Pkwy., Livonia, MI 48152 United States

STOCK TICKER/OTHER:
Stock Ticker: Subsidiary   Exchange:
Employees: 7,000   Fiscal Year Ends: 12/31
Parent Company: Harland Clarke Holdings Corp

SALARIES/BONUSES:
Top Exec. Salary: $ Bonus: $
Second Exec. Salary: $ Bonus: $

OTHER THOUGHTS:
Estimated Female Officers or Directors: 4
Hot Spot for Advancement for Women/Minorities: Y

Varian Medical Systems Inc

www.varian.com

NAIC Code: 334510

TYPES OF BUSINESS:

Radiation Oncology Systems
X-Ray Equipment
Software Systems
Security & Inspection Products

BRANDS/DIVISIONS/AFFILIATES:

Linatron
Ginzton Technology Center
Varian Particle Therapy

CONTACTS: Note: Officers with more than one job title may be intentionally listed here more than once.

Dow R. Wilson, CEO
Elisha W. Finney, CFO
Wendy Scott, Chief Human Resources Officer
Jessica Denecour, CIO

GROWTH PLANS/SPECIAL FEATURES:

Varian Medical Systems, Inc. designs, manufactures, sells and services equipment and software products for treating cancer with radiotherapy, stereotactic radiosurgery and brachytherapy. The firm operates in two segments: oncology systems and imaging components. The oncology systems segment designs, manufactures, sells and services hardware and software products for treating cancer with radiotherapy, stereotactic radiotherapy, stereotactic body radiotherapy (SBRT), stereotactic radiosurgery (SRS) and brachytherapy. Products include linear accelerators, brachytherapy afterloaders, treatment simulation and verification equipment and accessories as well as information management, treatment planning and image processing software. The imaging components segment designs, manufactures, sells and services medical imaging components for use in a range of applications, including radiographic or fluoroscopic imaging, mammography and computed tomography. It also designs, manufactures, sells and services security inspection products, which include Linatron x-ray accelerators, imaging processing software and image detection products for cargo screening at ports and borders and for non-destructive examination and testing in a variety of industrial applications. Varian's other businesses include Ginzton Technology Center, a research facility that develops technologies that enhance the firm's current businesses; and Varian Particle Therapy, which develops, manufactures and sells products and systems for delivering proton therapy, another form of external beam radiotherapy using proton beams. In 2016, the firm announced plans to spin off its imaging components business into a stand-alone public company to be named Varex Imaging Corporation. The transaction was expected to close by year's end.

Varian offers employees medical, life, AD&D, disability, dental and vision plans; a 401(k); educational reimbursement; an employee assistance program; and a stock purchase plan.

FINANCIAL DATA: Note: Data for latest year may not have been available at press time.

In U.S. $	2016	2015	2014	2013	2012	2011
Revenue		3,099,111,000	3,049,800,000	2,942,897,000	2,807,015,000	2,596,666,000
R&D Expense		245,211,000	234,840,000	208,208,000	185,742,000	170,725,000
Operating Income		548,967,000	571,155,000	608,890,000	594,074,000	588,451,000
Operating Margin %		17.71%	18.72%	20.69%	21.16%	22.66%
SGA Expense		488,514,000	495,680,000	432,589,000	416,520,000	376,713,000
Net Income		411,485,000	403,703,000	438,248,000	427,049,000	398,933,000
Operating Cash Flow		469,556,000	448,986,000	455,185,000	492,775,000	472,779,000
Capital Expenditure		91,384,000	89,649,000	76,277,000	61,103,000	70,928,000
EBITDA		631,117,000	644,126,000	679,071,000	660,325,000	643,900,000
Return on Assets %		11.82%	11.82%	13.80%	15.88%	16.54%
Return on Equity %		24.72%	24.24%	27.18%	31.01%	31.67%
Debt to Equity		0.19	0.23	0.26		

CONTACT INFORMATION:

Phone: 650 493-4000   Fax:
Toll-Free: 800-544-4636
Address: 3100 Hansen Way, Palo Alto, CA 94304 United States

SALARIES/BONUSES:

Top Exec. Salary: Bonus: $
$1,062,823
Second Exec. Salary: Bonus: $
$658,154

STOCK TICKER/OTHER:

Stock Ticker: VAR   Exchange: NYS
Employees: 7,300   Fiscal Year Ends: 09/30
Parent Company:

OTHER THOUGHTS:

Estimated Female Officers or Directors: 6

Hot Spot for Advancement for Women/Minorities: Y

VCA Antech Inc

www.vcaantech.com

NAIC Code: 541940

TYPES OF BUSINESS:

Animal Health Care Services
Veterinary Diagnostic Laboratories
Full-Service Animal Hospitals
Veterinary Equipment
Ultrasound Imaging

BRANDS/DIVISIONS/AFFILIATES:

Abaxis Veterinary Reference Laboratory
Companion Animal Practices

CONTACTS: Note: Officers with more than one job title may be intentionally listed here more than once.

Robert Antin, CEO
Tomas Fuller, CFO
Arthur Antin, Co-Founder
Neil Tauber, Co-Founder
Josh Drake, President, Subsidiary

GROWTH PLANS/SPECIAL FEATURES:

VCA Antech, Inc. is a leading animal healthcare company operating in the U.S. and Canada. The firm provides services and diagnostic testing to support veterinary care, and sells diagnostic equipment and other medical technology products to the veterinary market. VCA's hospitals offer a full range of general medical and surgical services for companion animals as well as specialized treatments, including advanced diagnostic services, internal medicine, oncology, ophthalmology, dermatology and cardiology. In addition, the company provides pharmaceutical products and performs a variety of pet wellness programs such as health examinations, diagnostic testing, routine vaccinations, spaying, neutering and dental care. VCA's network of animal hospitals is supported by nearly 3,000 veterinarians and sees more than 9 million patient visits annually. In 2015, the firm acquired Abaxis Veterinary Reference Laboratory from Abaxis; and sold nearly all of the assets of subsidiary Vetstreet, Inc. to Henry Schein, Inc (retaining a 19.9% interest). In 2016, it acquired a majority interest (80%) in Companion Animal Practices, North America based in Las Vegas, Nevada. Companion operates a network of 56 free-standing animal hospitals.

VCA offers its employees health, life, dental and vision insurance; tuition reimbursement; disability coverage; and veterinary care discounts.

FINANCIAL DATA: Note: Data for latest year may not have been available at press time.

In U.S. $	2016	2015	2014	2013	2012	2011
Revenue		2,133,675,000	1,918,483,000	1,803,369,000	1,699,642,000	1,485,361,000
R&D Expense						
Operating Income		329,770,000	247,268,000	249,014,000	92,936,000	195,653,000
Operating Margin %		15.45%	12.88%	13.80%	5.46%	13.17%
SGA Expense		183,995,000	171,506,000	157,911,000	157,155,000	121,112,000
Net Income		211,049,000	135,438,000	137,511,000	45,551,000	95,405,000
Operating Cash Flow		317,545,000	270,210,000	256,372,000	237,253,000	191,051,000
Capital Expenditure		95,234,000	72,948,000	73,270,000	76,807,000	63,485,000
EBITDA		454,537,000	324,939,000	326,712,000	175,838,000	250,360,000
Return on Assets %		8.72%	5.92%	6.35%	2.22%	5.07%
Return on Equity %		17.25%	10.80%	11.04%	3.97%	9.05%
Debt to Equity		0.67	0.64	0.43	0.49	0.52

CONTACT INFORMATION:

Phone: 310 571-6500   Fax: 310 571-6700
Toll-Free: 800-966-1822
Address: 12401 W. Olympic Blvd., Los Angeles, CA 90064 United States

STOCK TICKER/OTHER:

Stock Ticker: WOOF   Exchange: NAS
Employees: 11,500   Fiscal Year Ends: 12/31
Parent Company:

SALARIES/BONUSES:

Top Exec. Salary: Bonus: $
$1,031,391
Second Exec. Salary: Bonus: $
$653,645

OTHER THOUGHTS:

Estimated Female Officers or Directors:

Hot Spot for Advancement for Women/Minorities:

Verisk Analytics Inc

www.verisk.com

NAIC Code: 541612

TYPES OF BUSINESS:

Actuarial & Insurance Underwriting Consulting
Risk Assessment
Loss Prediction & Quantification
Fraud Identification & Detection

BRANDS/DIVISIONS/AFFILIATES:

Insurance Services Office Inc
Inovatus LLC
Aspect Loss Prevention LLC
Risk Intelligence Ireland

CONTACTS: *Note: Officers with more than one job title may be intentionally listed here more than once.*

Scott Stephenson, CEO
Mark Anquillare, COO
Kenneth Thompson, Executive VP
Steven Halliday, Group President
Nana Banerjee, Other Corporate Officer
Vincent McCarthy, Senior VP, Divisional
Eva Huston, Senior VP, Divisional

GROWTH PLANS/SPECIAL FEATURES:

Verisk Analytics, Inc. is a leading provider of information about risk to professionals in insurance, financial services, government, supply chain and risk management. Verisk provides solutions in fraud prevention, actuarial science, insurance coverages, fire protection, catastrophe and weather risk and data management. The firm's activities are grouped into two primary business segments: risk assessment and decision analytics. The risk assessment segment serves property and casualty (P&C) insurance customers and focuses on the first two decision making processes in the company's risk analysis framework: prediction of loss and selection and pricing of risk. This segment also provides solutions to help its insurance customers comply with reporting requirements in each U.S. state in which they operate. This segment operates in part through Verisk's largest subsidiary, Insurance Services Office, Inc. (ISO), which provides services for the property/casualty insurance industry as well as through other business units, such as Inovatus LLC, which operates in the auto insurance field, and Aspect Loss Prevention LLC, which offers loss prevention software and analytic services to a variety of industries. The company's decision analytics segment develops predictive models to forecast scenarios and produces both standard and customized analytics that help customers better predict loss, select and price risk; detect fraud before and after a loss event and qualify losses. In 2016, the firm acquired Risk Intelligence Ireland; sold its health care services business to Veritas Capital for $820 million; and agreed to acquire Greentech Media, Inc.

FINANCIAL DATA: *Note: Data for latest year may not have been available at press time.*

In U.S. $	2016	2015	2014	2013	2012	2011
Revenue		2,068,010,000	1,746,726,000	1,595,703,000	1,534,320,000	1,331,840,000
R&D Expense						
Operating Income		736,562,000	660,446,000	614,267,000	591,588,000	513,381,000
Operating Margin %		35.61%	37.81%	38.49%	38.55%	38.54%
SGA Expense		312,690,000	227,306,000	228,982,000	231,359,000	209,469,000
Net Income		507,577,000	400,042,000	348,380,000	329,142,000	282,758,000
Operating Cash Flow		623,687,000	489,452,000	506,920,000	468,229,000	375,721,000
Capital Expenditure		166,138,000	146,818,000	145,976,000	74,373,000	59,829,000
EBITDA		1,054,236,000	804,087,000	749,454,000	695,915,000	592,887,000
Return on Assets %		12.75%	16.49%	14.32%	16.87%	20.50%
Return on Equity %		64.12%	105.46%	86.75%	419.01%	
Debt to Equity		1.67	5.21	2.32	4.95	

CONTACT INFORMATION:

Phone: 201 469-2000   Fax:
Toll-Free: 800-888-4476
Address: 545 Washington Blvd., Jersey City, NJ 07310 United States

STOCK TICKER/OTHER:

Stock Ticker: VRSK   Exchange: NAS
Employees: 7,918   Fiscal Year Ends: 12/31
Parent Company:

SALARIES/BONUSES:

Top Exec. Salary: $860,000   Bonus: $
Second Exec. Salary: Bonus: $
$525,200

OTHER THOUGHTS:

Estimated Female Officers or Directors: 1
Hot Spot for Advancement for Women/Minorities: Y

Sales, profits and employees may be estimates. Financial information, benefits and other data can change quickly and may vary from those stated here.

Verizon Communications Inc

www.verizon.com

NAIC Code: 517110

TYPES OF BUSINESS:

Telephone Service
Telecommunications Services
Wireless Services
Long-Distance Services
High-Speed Internet Access
Video-on-Demand Services
e-Commerce & Online Services

BRANDS/DIVISIONS/AFFILIATES:

AOL Inc

CONTACTS: *Note: Officers with more than one job title may be intentionally listed here more than once.*

Matthew Ellis, CFO, Divisional
Francis Shammo, CFO
Lowell McAdam, Chairman of the Board
Anthony Skiadas, Chief Accounting Officer
Marc Reed, Chief Administrative Officer
Roger Gurnani, Chief Information Officer
Diego Scotti, Chief Marketing Officer
Craig Silliman, Executive VP, Divisional
John Stratton, Executive VP
Marni Walden, Executive VP
William Horton, Other Corporate Officer

GROWTH PLANS/SPECIAL FEATURES:

Verizon Communications, Inc. is one of the world's larges
providers of communications services. Its primary networ
technology platforms are 3G CDMA, based on spread
spectrum digital radio technology, and 4G LTE, which provide
higher throughput performance and more improved efficiencie
than 3G. It operates in two segments: wireless and wirelin
The wireless segment's products and services include wireles
voice, data products and other value added services an
equipment sales across the U.S. The segment's networ
provides services to a customer base of nearly 108.2 millior
Wireless' 4G LTE network is deployed in more than 50
markets, covering more than 309 million people. The wirelin
segment comprises four units: mass markets, globa
enterprise, global wholesale and other. The mass markets un
provides local exchange, long distance, broadband service
and FiOS bundled services to residential and small busines
subscribers. Global enterprise offers voice, data and Interne
communications services to medium and large busines
customers, multi-national corporations and state and federa
government customers. Global wholesale provides switche
access and special access services to long distance and othe
carriers. The other division provides local exchange and lon
distance services from former MCI mass market customer
operator services, pay phone, card services and supply sale
Wireless contributes approximately 70% of Verizon's tota
revenues. The company invested about $23 billion in upgrade
to FiOS systems in recent years. In 2015, the firm acquire
AOL, Inc. In March 2016, Verizon and Hearst agreed to jointl
acquire Complex in a 50/50 ownership structure. Tha
February, Verizon sold its exchange business and relate
landline activities in California, Florida and Texas, to Frontie
Communications Corporation. In July 2016, the firm acquire
the core internet operations and land holdings of Yahoo Inc. fo
$4.8 billion.

Employee benefits include 401(k); corporate discounts; healt
and dependent care spending accounts; life and AD&
insurance; commuter spending accounts; medical, dental an
vision coverage; disability; adoption reimbursement; and tuitio
assistance.

FINANCIAL DATA: *Note: Data for latest year may not have been available at press time.*

In U.S. $	2016	2015	2014	2013	2012	2011
Revenue		131,620,000,000	127,079,000,000	120,550,000,000	115,846,000,000	110,875,000,000
R&D Expense						
Operating Income		33,060,000,000	19,599,000,000	31,968,000,000	13,160,000,000	12,880,000,000
Operating Margin %		25.11%	15.42%	26.51%	11.35%	11.61%
SGA Expense		29,986,000,000	41,016,000,000	27,089,000,000	39,951,000,000	35,624,000,000
Net Income		17,879,000,000	9,625,000,000	11,497,000,000	875,000,000	2,404,000,000
Operating Cash Flow		38,930,000,000	30,631,000,000	38,818,000,000	31,486,000,000	29,780,000,000
Capital Expenditure		27,717,000,000	17,545,000,000	17,184,000,000	20,110,000,000	16,244,000,000
EBITDA		49,177,000,000	36,718,000,000	48,550,000,000	28,928,000,000	29,806,000,000
Return on Assets %		7.49%	3.79%	4.60%	.38%	1.06%
Return on Equity %		124.47%	37.64%	31.93%	2.53%	6.45%
Debt to Equity		6.31	8.98	2.30	1.43	1.39

CONTACT INFORMATION:

Phone: 212 395-1000   Fax:
Toll-Free: 800-837-4966
Address: 1095 Avenue of the Americas, New York, NY 10036 United States

STOCK TICKER/OTHER:

Stock Ticker: VZ
Employees: 177,300
Parent Company:

Exchange: NYS
Fiscal Year Ends: 12/31

SALARIES/BONUSES:

Top Exec. Salary: $1,661,538   Bonus: $

Second Exec. Salary: $1,028,846   Bonus: $

OTHER THOUGHTS:

Estimated Female Officers or Directors: 5

Hot Spot for Advancement for Women/Minorities: Y

Sales, profits and employees may be estimates. Financial information, benefits and other data can change quickly and may vary from those stated here.

VF Corp

NAIC Code: 424300

TYPES OF BUSINESS:

Apparel and Clothing Brands, Designers, Importers and Distributors
Swimsuits
Outdoor Gear & Apparel
Image Wear
Outlet Stores
Footwear

BRANDS/DIVISIONS/AFFILIATES:

Vans Inc
lucy
SmartWool
Wrangler
Timberland
North Face (The)
Nautica
Majestic

CONTACTS: *Note: Officers with more than one job title may be intentionally listed here more than once.*

Bryan McNeill, Chief Accounting Officer
Eric Wiseman, Director
Steven Rendle, Director
Laura Meagher, General Counsel
Craig Hodges, Other Corporate Officer
Karl Salzburger, President, Divisional
Scott Baxter, President, Divisional
Scott Roe, Vice President

GROWTH PLANS/SPECIAL FEATURES:

VF Corp., organized in 1899, is one of the world's largest brand-name apparel manufacturers and a leading producer of jeanswear, outerwear, footwear, sportswear and occupational apparel. VF products are sold globally throughout the U.S., Canada, Europe, Asia and Latin America. The company divides its brands into five business groups, called coalitions: outdoor & action sports, which includes outerwear, sportswear, footwear, equipment, backpacks, daypacks, luggage and accessories; jeanswear, which consists of jeans as well as shorts, casual pants, knit and woven tops and outerwear; imagewear, which includes occupational apparel, uniforms and owned and licensed sports and lifestyle apparel; sportswear, which includes outerwear, underwear, swimwear, sleepwear, luggage and accessories; and contemporary brands, which focuses on lifestyle brands. The outdoor & action sports coalition includes the firm's largest brand, The North Face, as well as Timberland, SmartWool, Vans, JanSport, Eastpak, Kipling, Napapijri, Reef and lucy. In jeanswear, Lee and Wrangler are its largest brand names. The image business includes the firm's uniforms and career occupational clothing. These brands include Red Kap work clothes; Bulwark flame resistant and protective clothing; and Horace Small apparel for law enforcement and public safety officials. The licensed business consists of VF's owned and licensed high profile apparel, marketed under the Majestic and Harley-Davidson brand names. Sportswear brands include Nautica and Kipling. The company's contemporary brands coalition includes its premium upscale lifestyle brands such as Splendid, Ella Moss and 7 For All Mankind.

FINANCIAL DATA: *Note: Data for latest year may not have been available at press time.*

In U.S. $	2016	2015	2014	2013	2012	2011
Revenue		12,376,740,000	12,282,160,000	11,419,650,000	10,879,850,000	9,459,232,000
R&D Expense						
Operating Income		1,660,996,000	1,437,724,000	1,647,147,000	1,465,267,000	1,244,791,000
Operating Margin %		13.42%	11.70%	14.42%	13.46%	13.15%
SGA Expense		4,178,386,000	4,159,885,000	3,841,032,000	3,596,708,000	3,085,839,000
Net Income		1,231,593,000	1,047,505,000	1,210,119,000	1,085,999,000	888,089,000
Operating Cash Flow		1,146,510,000	1,697,629,000	1,506,041,000	1,275,000,000	1,081,371,000
Capital Expenditure		317,784,000	302,020,000	325,142,000	282,830,000	249,128,000
EBITDA		1,941,878,000	1,713,974,000	1,900,536,000	1,753,436,000	1,441,056,000
Return on Assets %		12.55%	10.32%	12.13%	11.46%	11.26%
Return on Equity %		22.36%	17.89%	21.60%	22.50%	21.17%
Debt to Equity		0.26	0.25	0.23	0.27	0.40

CONTACT INFORMATION:

Phone: 336 424-6000   Fax:
Toll-Free:
Address: 105 Corporate Ctr. Blvd., Greensboro, NC 27408 United States

STOCK TICKER/OTHER:

Stock Ticker: VFC   Exchange: NYS
Employees: 59,000   Fiscal Year Ends: 12/31
Parent Company:

SALARIES/BONUSES:

Top Exec. Salary: Bonus: $
$1,350,001
Second Exec. Salary: Bonus: $
$832,308

OTHER THOUGHTS:

Estimated Female Officers or Directors: 5

Hot Spot for Advancement for Women/Minorities: Y

Victoria's Secret

www.victoriassecret.com

NAIC Code: 448120

TYPES OF BUSINESS:

Intimate Apparel-Women's, Retail
Cosmetics
Fragrances
Personal Care Products
Online Sales
Catalogs
Women's Shoes
General Women's Apparel

BRANDS/DIVISIONS/AFFILIATES:

PINK
Victoria's Secret Direct
Victoria's Secret Beauty
Angels
IPEX
Body by Victoria
La Senza
Limited Brands Inc

CONTACTS: *Note: Officers with more than one job title may be intentionally listed here more than once.*

Sharen Jester Turney, CEO
Brian VanOoyen, VP-Merch. Planning
Bridget Ryan-Berman, CEO-Victoria's Secret Direct
Sharen Jester Turney, CEO

GROWTH PLANS/SPECIAL FEATURES:

Victoria's Secret, a wholly-owned subsidiary of Limited Brands Inc., purchases, distributes and sells lingerie, personal car products and women's apparel through over 1,139 retail stores the Internet and direct mail channels. The stores offer brande merchandise such as IPEX, PINK, Very Sexy, Body by Victoria VS Cotton, Dream Angels, Beauty Rush and Angels. The firr also owns several standalone PINK stores in the U.S. an Canada, which sell intimate apparel, denim, casual apparel an body products targeted to young women ages 13-25, an standalone Victoria's Secret Beauty and Accessories Stores Victoria's Secret Beauty offers a complete line of fragrance cosmetics and body products for skin and hair. In addition to it retail stores, the company operates Victoria's Secret Direc which consists of the famous Victoria's Secret Catalog and a e-commerce site, VictoriasSecret.com. Street apparel such a dresses, pants, skirts, shorts, tops and shoes are available from the catalog and online, but not in stores. Once each yea Victoria's Secret conducts a televised fashion show featurin some of the world's top models and performances b acclaimed musicians such as Maroon 5 or Kanye West. Th Victoria's Secret group also includes the operations of La Senza, a Canadian lingerie store chain owned by Limite Brands. Approximately 25% of the firm's sales are made via th catalogs and online.

The company offers employees medical, dental, vision an prescription drug coverage; a 401(k) plan; a discount stoc purchase plan; life insurance; discounts on products; tuitio reimbursement; a commuter discount program; and a employee assistance program.

FINANCIAL DATA: *Note: Data for latest year may not have been available at press time.*

In U.S. $	2016	2015	2014	2013	2012	2011
Revenue		7,672,000,000	7,207,600,000	6,884,200,000	6,574,000,000	6,121,000,000
R&D Expense						
Operating Income						
Operating Margin %						
SGA Expense						
Net Income			1,042,000,000	903,000,000		
Operating Cash Flow						
Capital Expenditure						
EBITDA						
Return on Assets %						
Return on Equity %						
Debt to Equity						

CONTACT INFORMATION:

Phone: 614-577-7111   Fax:
Toll-Free: 800-411-5116
Address: 4 Limited Pkwy. E, Reynoldsburg, OH 43068 United States

STOCK TICKER/OTHER:

Stock Ticker: Subsidiary   Exchange:
Employees: 65,000   Fiscal Year Ends: 01/31
Parent Company: L Brands Inc

SALARIES/BONUSES:

Top Exec. Salary: $ Bonus: $
Second Exec. Salary: $ Bonus: $

OTHER THOUGHTS:

Estimated Female Officers or Directors: 3
Hot Spot for Advancement for Women/Minorities: Y

Visa Inc

www.visa.com

NAIC Code: 522320

TYPES OF BUSINESS:
Credit Cards
Debit Cards
Prepaid Cards

BRANDS/DIVISIONS/AFFILIATES:
VisaNet
Tokenization
Visa Checkout
payWave
Visa Canada Corporaiton
CyberSource Corporation
Inovant LLC
Visa Europe Limited

CONTACTS: *Note: Officers with more than one job title may be intentionally listed here more than once.*
Charles Scharf, CEO
Vasant Prabhu, CFO
Robert Matschullat, Chairman of the Board
James Hoffmeister, Chief Accounting Officer
Rajat Taneja, Executive VP, Divisional
William Sheedy, Executive VP, Divisional
Kelly Tullier, Executive VP
Ryan McInerney, President
Mary Richey, Vice Chairman, Divisional

GROWTH PLANS/SPECIAL FEATURES:
Visa, Inc. is a global payments technology company that connects consumers, businesses, financial institutions and governments in over 200 countries. The company's processing network, VisaNet, facilitates authorization, clearing and settlement of payment transactions worldwide. It also offers fraud protection for account holders and rapid payment for merchants. Visa is not a bank and does not issue cards, extend credit or set rates and fees for account holders in Visa-branded cards and payment products. In most cases, account holder and merchant relationships belong to, and are managed by, Visa's financial institution clients. Visa's Tokenization replaces account numbers with digital tokens for online and mobile payments, benefiting merchants and issuers by removing sensitive account information and reducing fraud risk. Visa's EMV chip payment technology addresses fraud at the physical point-of-sale by working with merchants and Visa financial institution clients in the U.S. Visa Checkout is a fast, simple and intuitive payment experience that allows consumers to pay for goods online, on any device, in just a few clicks. Visa payWave technology allows consumers to pay for products and services via smart phone and by using contactless cards at physical retailers. The company's core products and services can be condensed into three divisions: debit, providing debit solutions that support issuers' payment products that draw on demand deposit accounts; prepaid, providing prepaid payment solutions that support issuer's products that access a pre-funded amount; and credit, providing credit payment solutions that support issuers' deferred payment and customized financing products. Subsidiaries of the company include Visa Canada Corporation; CyberSource Corporation; Visa U.S.A., Inc.; Visa International Service Association; PlaySpan, Inc. and Inovant LLC. In June 2016, the firm bought its European counterpart, Visa Europe Limited, for $23.4 billion, a deal consolidating the payment network's global operations.

FINANCIAL DATA: *Note: Data for latest year may not have been available at press time.*

In U.S. $	2016	2015	2014	2013	2012	2011
Revenue		13,880,000,000	12,702,000,000	11,778,000,000	10,421,000,000	9,188,000,000
R&D Expense						
Operating Income		9,063,999,000	7,697,000,000	7,239,000,000	2,139,000,000	5,456,000,000
Operating Margin %		65.30%	60.59%	61.46%	20.52%	59.38%
SGA Expense		1,755,000,000	1,735,000,000	1,739,000,000	1,709,000,000	1,621,000,000
Net Income		6,328,000,000	5,438,000,000	4,980,000,000	2,144,000,000	3,650,000,000
Operating Cash Flow		6,584,000,000	7,205,000,000	3,022,000,000	5,009,000,000	3,872,000,000
Capital Expenditure		414,000,000	553,000,000	471,000,000	376,000,000	353,000,000
EBITDA		9,558,000,000	8,132,000,000	7,636,000,000	2,472,000,000	5,976,000,000
Return on Assets %		16.05%	14.59%	13.11%	5.73%	10.70%
Return on Equity %		22.10%	20.03%	18.27%	7.93%	14.18%
Debt to Equity						

CONTACT INFORMATION:
Phone: 650-432-3200   Fax:
Toll-Free: 800-847-2911
Address: P.O. Box 8999, San Francisco, CA 94128 United States

STOCK TICKER/OTHER:
Stock Ticker: V
Employees: 11,300
Parent Company:

Exchange: NYS
Fiscal Year Ends: 09/30

SALARIES/BONUSES:
Top Exec. Salary: $547,616   Bonus: $6,875,000
Second Exec. Salary: $1,000,038   Bonus: $

OTHER THOUGHTS:
Estimated Female Officers or Directors: 6
Hot Spot for Advancement for Women/Minorities: Y

VMware Inc

www.vmware.com

NAIC Code: 0

TYPES OF BUSINESS:

Computer Software, Network Management, System Testing & Storage
Virtual Infrastructure Automation
Virtual Infrastructure Management

BRANDS/DIVISIONS/AFFILIATES:

vSphere
Horizon
Fusion
Workstation
AirWatch
vCloud Hybrid Service
VMware vCloud Service Provider Program
vCHS Business Ventures

CONTACTS: *Note: Officers with more than one job title may be intentionally listed here more than once.*

Patrick Gelsinger, CEO
Zane Rowe, CFO
Michael Dell, Chairman of the Board
Ray O'Farrell, Executive VP
Rangarajan Raghuram, Executive VP, Divisional
Maurizio Carli, Executive VP, Geographical
Sanjay Poonen, Executive VP
William Fathers, Executive VP
Dawn Smith, Other Executive Officer

GROWTH PLANS/SPECIAL FEATURES:

VMware, Inc. is a leader in virtualization infrastructure software
It develops and markets its products through three area:
software-defined data center (SDDC), end-user computing an
hybrid cloud computing. SDDC consists of four main produ
categories: compute, providing a hypervisor layer of softwar
that enables compute virtualization through its flagshi
vSphere; storage and availability, offering cost-effective holist
data storage and protection options to all applications runnir
on vSphere; network and security, which abstracts physic
networks and simplifies the provisioning and consumption
networking resources; and management and automatior
which automates overarching IT processes involved
provisioning IT services and resources to users from initi
deployment to retirement. The firm's end-user computin
products enable IT organizations to deliver secure access
data, applications and devices to end-users. This segment'
solutions include desktop applications through its Horizor
Fusion and Workstation brands, which control and deliver dat
store images, provide cloud delivery and virtualization solution
for Macintosh and Windows; mobile solutions throug
AirWatch, which offer enterprise mobile management an
security solutions; and social computing and other workspac
services through Socialcast, an enterprise social platform, a
well as through App Manager, a single sign-on identity servic
that delivers applications, desktops and data in a single port
of entry, called Workspace. VMware's hybrid cloud computin
product enables customers to utilize off-premises vSpher
based hybrid cloud computing capacity through thre
programs: vCloud Hybrid Service, a service cloud that allow
seamless extension from the customer's data center to th
cloud; VMware vCloud Service Provider Program, a hostin
and cloud computing vendor; and vCHS Business Venture
which co-invests with large in-country telecommunication
providers to enable user experience with the firm's vClou
Hybrid Service.

FINANCIAL DATA: *Note: Data for latest year may not have been available at press time.*

In U.S. $	2016	2015	2014	2013	2012	2011
Revenue		6,571,000,000	6,035,000,000	5,207,000,000	4,605,047,000	3,767,096,000
R&D Expense		1,300,000,000	1,239,000,000	1,082,000,000	999,214,000	775,051,000
Operating Income		1,197,000,000	1,027,000,000	1,093,000,000	871,943,000	735,171,000
Operating Margin %		18.21%	17.01%	20.99%	18.93%	19.51%
SGA Expense		3,033,000,000	2,836,000,000	2,234,000,000	2,012,567,000	1,634,887,000
Net Income		997,000,000	886,000,000	1,014,000,000	745,702,000	723,936,000
Operating Cash Flow		1,899,000,000	2,180,000,000	2,535,000,000	1,897,524,000	2,025,633,000
Capital Expenditure		333,000,000	352,000,000	345,000,000	234,458,000	455,172,000
EBITDA		1,574,000,000	1,417,000,000	1,488,000,000	1,252,636,000	1,114,190,000
Return on Assets %		6.44%	6.43%	8.84%	7.73%	9.35%
Return on Equity %		12.86%	12.30%	16.15%	14.19%	16.87%
Debt to Equity		0.18	0.19	0.06	0.07	0.09

CONTACT INFORMATION:

Phone: 650 427-5000   Fax: 650 475-5005
Toll-Free: 877-486-9273
Address: 3401 Hillview Ave., Palo Alto, CA 94304 United States

STOCK TICKER/OTHER:

Stock Ticker: VMW
Employees: 18,000
Parent Company:

Exchange: NYS
Fiscal Year Ends: 12/31

SALARIES/BONUSES:

Top Exec. Salary: $1,000,000   Bonus: $ 650

Second Exec. Salary: $730,000   Bonus: $ 650

OTHER THOUGHTS:

Estimated Female Officers or Directors: 3

Hot Spot for Advancement for Women/Minorities: Y

W R Berkley Corporation

www.wrberkley.com

NAIC Code: 524126

TYPES OF BUSINESS:

Insurance, Direct Property & Casualty
Reinsurance
Regional Insurance
Specialty Insurance
Risk Management
Liability Insurance

BRANDS/DIVISIONS/AFFILIATES:

Berkley International Seguros Colombia SA
Berkley Global Product Recall Management

CONTACTS: *Note: Officers with more than one job title may be intentionally listed here more than once.*

William Berkley, CEO
Richard Baio, CFO
William Berkley, Chairman of the Board
Eugene Ballard, Executive VP, Divisional
James Shiel, Executive VP, Divisional
Ira Lederman, Executive VP
Matthew Ricciardim, General Counsel

GROWTH PLANS/SPECIAL FEATURES:

W.R. Berkley Corporation is one of the largest insurance holding companies in the U.S. The firm operates in three segments of the property & casualty insurance business: insurance-domestic, insurance-international and reinsurance-global. The insurance-domestic segment underwrites risks associated with specialty lines of business including premises operations, commercial automobile, property, products liability, and professional liability lines. It also provides insurance products and services to small-to-mid-sized businesses and state and local governmental entities primarily in 45 states and Washington, D.C.; insurance products, analytical tools and risk management services such as loss control and claims management that enable clients to select their risk tolerance and manage it appropriately; and services comprising claims, administrative and consulting services. This segment specializes in insuring, reinsuring and administering self-insurance programs and other alternative risk transfer mechanisms for clients, such as commercial and governmental entity employers, employer groups, insurers and other groups or entities seeking ways to manage their exposure to risks. The insurance-international segment underwrites specialty, casualty, property, automobile, group life and health and workers' compensation, professional indemnity, directors' and officers' liability, medical malpractice, general liability, personal accident and travel, engineering and construction and surety lines of business in almost 60 countries worldwide, with branches or offices in 19 locations outside the U.S. The reinsurance-global segment offers other insurance companies and self-insureds with assistance in managing their net risk through reinsurance on either a portfolio basis, through treaty reinsurance, or on an individual basis, through facultative reinsurance. In 2015, the firm established Berkley International Seguros Colombia SA, entering the Colombian reinsurance market; and established Berkley Global Product Recall Management to aid worldwide businesses in the prevention and management of product recall incidences. In August 2016, it sold wholly-owned subsidiary, Aero Precision Industries, for $130 million.

FINANCIAL DATA: *Note: Data for latest year may not have been available at press time.*

In U.S. $	2016	2015	2014	2013	2012	2011
Revenue		7,206,457,000	7,128,928,000	6,408,534,000	5,823,554,000	5,155,984,000
R&D Expense						
Operating Income		732,030,000	952,196,000	698,888,000	701,928,000	518,283,000
Operating Margin %		10.15%	13.35%	10.90%	12.05%	10.05%
SGA Expense		127,365,000	2,157,456,000	2,000,684,000	1,799,623,000	1,621,329,000
Net Income		503,694,000	648,884,000	499,925,000	510,592,000	394,803,000
Operating Cash Flow		881,304,000	734,847,000	819,798,000	675,458,000	670,279,000
Capital Expenditure		63,562,000	41,958,000	63,150,000	40,556,000	45,320,000
EBITDA						
Return on Assets %		2.31%	3.07%	2.45%	2.64%	2.19%
Return on Equity %		10.96%	14.53%	11.56%	12.28%	10.23%
Debt to Equity		0.47	0.53	0.46	0.49	0.43

CONTACT INFORMATION:

Phone: 203 629-3000   Fax:
Toll-Free:
Address: 475 Steamboat Rd., Greenwich, CT 06830 United States

STOCK TICKER/OTHER:

Stock Ticker: WRB   Exchange: NYS
Employees: 7,621   Fiscal Year Ends: 12/31
Parent Company:

SALARIES/BONUSES:

Top Exec. Salary: $645,833   Bonus: $415,000
Second Exec. Salary: Bonus: $725,000
$332,692

OTHER THOUGHTS:

Estimated Female Officers or Directors: 16
Hot Spot for Advancement for Women/Minorities: Y

Walgreens Boots Alliance Inc   www.walgreens.com

NAIC Code: 446110

TYPES OF BUSINESS:

Drug Stores
Mail-Order Pharmacy Services
Pharmacy Benefit Management
Health Care Center Management
Online Pharmacy Services
Photo Printing Services
Specialty Pharmacy Services
Home Infusion Services

BRANDS/DIVISIONS/AFFILIATES:

boots.com
BootsWebMD.com
Walgreens
Duane Reade
Boots and Alliance Healthcare
No7
Botanics
Liz Earl

CONTACTS: Note: *Officers with more than one job title may be intentionally listed here more than once.*

Stefano Pessina, CEO
George Fairweather, CFO
James Skinner, Chairman of the Board
Kimberly Scardino, Chief Accounting Officer
Marco Pagni, Chief Administrative Officer
Alexander Gourlay, Co-COO
Ornella Barra, Co-COO
Theodore Heidloff, Controller
Kathleen Wilson-Thompson, Executive VP
Ken Murphy, Executive VP
Simon Roberts, Executive VP
Jan Reed, General Counsel

GROWTH PLANS/SPECIAL FEATURES:

Walgreens Boots Alliance, Inc. is a global pharmacy-led health and wellbeing enterprise, with more than 13,100 stores worldwide. The company's global pharmaceutical wholesale and distribution network comprises more than 350 distribution centers delivering to over 200,000 pharmacies, doctors, health centers and hospitals on an annual basis. The firm operates through three business segments: retail pharmacy USA, retail pharmacy international and pharmaceutical wholesale. Retail pharmacy USA oversees pharmacy-led health and beauty retail businesses in 50 states, the District of Columbia, Puerto Rico and the U.S. Virgin Islands. It operates more than 8,100 retail stores, and fill approximately 723 million prescriptions (including immunizations) annually. The retail pharmacy international segment oversees pharmacy-led health & beauty retail businesses in eight countries. It operates more than 4,500 retail stores located in the U.K., Thailand, Norway, Ireland, The Netherlands, Mexico and Chile. Websites boots.com and BootsWebMD.com continue to be two of the most visited health websites, averaging 19 million and 11 million visits monthly. The pharmaceutical wholesale segment operates primarily under the Alliance Healthcare brand, and supplies medicines and other health care products to more than 140,000 pharmacies, doctors, health centers and hospitals from 302 distribution centers, mainly located in Europe. Walgreens' portfolio of retail and business global brands include Walgreens, Duane Reade, Boots and Alliance Healthcare, as well as global health & beauty product brands such as No7, Botanics, Liz Earl and Soap & Glory. In October 2015, Walgreens agreed to acquire Rite Aid Corporation. The purchase would give the firm an additional 4,600 stores in 31 states. The acquisition is still awaiting regulatory approval, and was expected to close by the end or 2016.

The company offers employees medical, prescription and dental coverage; life and accident insurance; profit sharing and stock purchase plans; employee discounts; and a flexible spending account.

FINANCIAL DATA: Note: *Data for latest year may not have been available at press time.*

In U.S. $	2016	2015	2014	2013	2012	2011
Revenue		103,444,000,000	76,392,000,000	72,217,000,000	71,633,000,000	72,184,000,000
R&D Expense						
Operating Income		4,668,000,000	4,194,000,000	3,940,000,000	3,464,000,000	4,365,000,000
Operating Margin %		4.51%	5.49%	5.45%	4.83%	6.04%
SGA Expense		22,571,000,000	17,992,000,000	17,543,000,000	16,878,000,000	16,561,000,000
Net Income		4,220,000,000	1,932,000,000	2,450,000,000	2,127,000,000	2,714,000,000
Operating Cash Flow		5,664,000,000	3,893,000,000	4,301,000,000	4,431,000,000	3,643,000,000
Capital Expenditure		1,251,000,000	1,106,000,000	1,212,000,000	1,550,000,000	1,213,000,000
EBITDA		6,410,000,000	5,029,000,000	5,223,000,000	4,630,000,000	5,451,000,000
Return on Assets %		7.96%	5.31%	7.10%	6.98%	10.10%
Return on Equity %		16.44%	9.68%	13.00%	12.85%	18.55%
Debt to Equity		0.43	0.18	0.23	0.22	0.16

CONTACT INFORMATION:

Phone: 847 315-2500   Fax: 847 914-2804
Toll-Free: 800-925-4733
Address: 108 Wilmot Rd., Deerfield, IL 60015 United States

STOCK TICKER/OTHER:

Stock Ticker: WBA   Exchange: NAS
Employees: 251,000   Fiscal Year Ends: 08/31
Parent Company:

SALARIES/BONUSES:

Top Exec. Salary: Bonus: $
$1,381,667
Second Exec. Salary: Bonus: $
$932,465

OTHER THOUGHTS:

Estimated Female Officers or Directors: 7

Hot Spot for Advancement for Women/Minorities: Y

Wal-Mart Stores Inc (Walmart)

www.walmartstores.com

NAIC Code: 452910

TYPES OF BUSINESS:

Supercenters
Supermarkets
Warehouse Membership Clubs
Online Sales
Pharmacies
Vision Centers
Auto Repair Centers

BRANDS/DIVISIONS/AFFILIATES:

Wal-Mart
Wal-Mart Supercenter
Sam's Club
Neighborhood Market
walmart.com
Marketside

CONTACTS: *Note: Officers with more than one job title may be intentionally listed here more than once.*

Neil Ashe, CEO, Divisional
Rosalind Brewer, CEO, Divisional
David Cheesewright, CEO, Divisional
Gregory Foran, CEO, Divisional
C. McMillon, CEO
Brett Biggs, CFO
Steven Whaley, Chief Accounting Officer
Rollin Ford, Chief Administrative Officer
Gregory Penner, Director
Jacqueline Canney, Executive VP, Divisional
Daniel Bartlett, Executive VP, Divisional
Jeffrey Gearhart, Executive VP, Divisional
Gordon Allison, General Counsel

GROWTH PLANS/SPECIAL FEATURES:

Wal-Mart Stores, Inc., one of the world's largest retailers, operates through a massive base of Wal-Mart stores, Supercenters, Sam's Clubs, Marketside, Neighborhood Markets and walmart.com. The company operates in three business segments: Wal-Mart U.S., Wal-Mart international and Sam's Club. Wal-Mart U.S. is a mass merchandiser of consumer products, groceries and drugs, operating under the Wal-Mart brand, as well as walmart.com. This segment operates retail stores in the USA, including all 50 states, Washington D.C. and Puerto Rico, with Supercenters in 49 states, Washington D.C. and Puerto Rico and Wal-Mart discount stores in 41 states and Puerto Rico. Wal-Mart U.S. also operates a relatively small number Neighborhood Markets, which are about 40,000 square feet each. Its main line of business, the Wal-Mart Supercenters, average 178,000 square feet each. Wal-Mart International consists of operations in 26 countries outside the USA, and includes numerous formats divided into three major categories: retail, wholesale and other. These categories consist of formats such as Supercenters, supermarkets, hypermarkets, warehouse clubs (including Sam's Clubs), cash & carry, home improvement, specialty electronics, restaurants, apparel stores, drug stores and convenience stores. Sam's Club operates membership-only warehouse clubs, as well as samsclub.com in the U.S. All memberships include a spouse/household card at no additional cost and Plus Members are eligible for cash rewards which provides $10 for every $500 in qualifying Sam's Club purchases up to a $500 cash reward annually. In early 2016, Wal-Mart announced it would end its experiment with small format Wal-Mart Express stores. That September, it acquired eCommerce website, Jet.com, for approximately $3 billion.

FINANCIAL DATA: *Note: Data for latest year may not have been available at press time.*

In U.S. $	2016	2015	2014	2013	2012	2011
Revenue	482,130,000,000	485,651,000,000	476,294,000,000	469,162,000,000	446,950,000,000	421,849,000,000
R&D Expense						
Operating Income	24,105,000,000	27,147,000,000	26,872,000,000	27,801,000,000	26,558,000,000	25,542,000,000
Operating Margin %	4.99%	5.58%	5.64%	5.92%	5.94%	6.05%
SGA Expense	97,041,000,000	93,418,000,000	91,353,000,000	88,873,000,000	85,265,000,000	81,020,000,000
Net Income	14,694,000,000	16,363,000,000	16,022,000,000	16,999,000,000	15,699,000,000	16,389,000,000
Operating Cash Flow	27,389,000,000	28,564,000,000	23,257,000,000	25,591,000,000	24,255,000,000	23,643,000,000
Capital Expenditure	11,477,000,000	12,174,000,000	13,115,000,000	12,898,000,000	13,510,000,000	12,699,000,000
EBITDA	33,640,000,000	36,433,000,000	35,861,000,000	36,489,000,000	34,850,000,000	33,384,000,000
Return on Assets %	7.28%	8.01%	7.85%	8.57%	8.39%	9.32%
Return on Equity %	18.14%	20.75%	20.99%	23.02%	22.45%	23.53%
Debt to Equity	0.54	0.53	0.58	0.54	0.66	0.63

CONTACT INFORMATION:

Phone: 479 273-4000   Fax: 479 273-1986
Toll-Free: 800-925-6278
Address: 702 SW 8th St., Bentonville, AR 72716 United States

STOCK TICKER/OTHER:

Stock Ticker: WMT   Exchange: NYS
Employees: 2,200,000   Fiscal Year Ends: 01/31
Parent Company:

SALARIES/BONUSES:

Top Exec. Salary: Bonus: $500,939
$1,033,037
Second Exec. Salary: Bonus: $
$1,263,231

OTHER THOUGHTS:

Estimated Female Officers or Directors: 13

Hot Spot for Advancement for Women/Minorities: Y

Walt Disney Company (The)
NAIC Code: 515210

corporate.disney.go.com

TYPES OF BUSINESS:
Cable TV Networks, Broadcasting & Entertainment
Filmed Entertainment
Merchandising
Television Networks
Music & Book Publishing
Online Entertainment Programs
Theme Parks, Resorts & Cruise Lines
Comic Book Publishing

BRANDS/DIVISIONS/AFFILIATES:
ABC Television Network
Hulu
ESPN Inc
Fusion
A&E
Walt Disney Pictures
Touchstone Pictures
Pixar Animation Studios

CONTACTS: *Note: Officers with more than one job title may be intentionally listed here more than once.*
Robert Iger, CEO
Christine Mccarthy, CFO
Brent Woodford, Executive VP, Divisional
Mary Parker, Executive VP
Kevin Mayer, Other Executive Officer
Alan Braverman, Senior Executive VP

GROWTH PLANS/SPECIAL FEATURES:
The Walt Disney Company is an international entertainme
company operating in five primary business segments: med
networks, studio entertainment, Disney consumer product
parks and resorts and Disney interactive. The media network
segment, which operates ABC Television Network, is involve
in domestic broadcast television, cable/satellite network
international broadcast operations, television production an
distribution, domestic broadcast radio and Internet operation
The company also owns interest in and/or operates numerou
cable networks, including ESPN Inc., ABC Family, Hulu, Fusio
and A&E. The studio entertainment segment produces an
acquires feature films, direct-to-video programming, music
recordings and live stage plays. Its motion picture subsidiarie
include Walt Disney Pictures, Touchstone Pictures, Pix
Animation Studios and Marvel. The Disney consumer product
segment designs, promotes and sells merchandise based o
the firm's intellectual property. The parks and resorts segmer
owns and operates Florida's Walt Disney World Resort, Disne
Cruise Line, the Disneyland resort in California, Adventures b
Disney and the Disney Vacation Club. It also holds interest i
the Disneyland Paris and Hong Kong Disneyland resorts an
licenses the Tokyo Disney Resort in Japan. The Disne
interactive segment creates and delivers company-brande
entertainment and lifestyle content across interactive med
platforms. The segment's primary operating businesses ar
Disney Interactive Studios, which produces video games; an
Disney Online, which produces web sites and online virtu
worlds. Additionally, the segment maintains the firm's Japar
based Disney-branded mobile phone business. The company'
Shanghai Disney Resort is set to open in 2016. In 2014, Disne
acquired Maker Studios, a leading network of online vide
content on YouTube.

FINANCIAL DATA: *Note: Data for latest year may not have been available at press time.*

In U.S. $	2016	2015	2014	2013	2012	2011
Revenue		52,465,000,000	48,813,000,000	45,041,000,000	42,278,000,000	40,893,000,000
R&D Expense						
Operating Income		13,224,000,000	11,540,000,000			
Operating Margin %		25.20%	23.64%			
SGA Expense		8,523,000,000	8,565,000,000			
Net Income		8,382,000,000	7,501,000,000	6,136,000,000	5,682,000,000	4,807,000,000
Operating Cash Flow		10,909,000,000	9,780,000,000	9,452,000,000	7,966,000,000	6,994,000,000
Capital Expenditure		4,265,000,000	3,311,000,000	2,796,000,000	3,784,000,000	3,559,000,000
EBITDA		16,487,000,000	14,828,000,000	12,161,000,000	11,719,000,000	10,319,000,000
Return on Assets %		9.72%	9.06%	7.85%	7.72%	6.80%
Return on Equity %		18.73%	16.59%	14.40%	14.73%	12.83%
Debt to Equity		0.28	0.28	0.28	0.27	0.29

CONTACT INFORMATION:
Phone: 818 5601000   Fax:
Toll-Free:
Address: 500 S. Buena Vista St., Burbank, CA 91521 United States

STOCK TICKER/OTHER:
Stock Ticker: DIS   Exchange: NYS
Employees: 185,000   Fiscal Year Ends: 09/30
Parent Company:

SALARIES/BONUSES:
Top Exec. Salary: Bonus: $
$2,548,077
Second Exec. Salary: Bonus: $
$1,963,541

OTHER THOUGHTS:
Estimated Female Officers or Directors: 7

Hot Spot for Advancement for Women/Minorities: Y

Waste Management Inc

www.wm.com

NAIC Code: 562000

TYPES OF BUSINESS:

Waste Disposal
Recycling Services
Landfill Operation
Hazardous Waste Management
Transfer Stations
Recycled Commodity Trading
Waste Methane Generation

BRANDS/DIVISIONS/AFFILIATES:

Deffenbaugh Disposal Inc
Think Green

CONTACTS: Note: Officers with more than one job title may be intentionally listed here more than once.

David Steiner, CEO
James Fish, CFO
W. Reum, Chairman of the Board
James Trevathan, COO
Barry Caldwell, Other Executive Officer
Courtney Tippy, Secretary
John Morris, Senior VP, Divisional
Mark Schwartz, Senior VP, Divisional
Jeff Harris, Senior VP, Divisional
Puneet Bhasin, Senior VP, Divisional
Devina Rankin, Treasurer

GROWTH PLANS/SPECIAL FEATURES:

Waste Management, Inc. provides comprehensive waste management services to municipal, commercial, industrial and residential customers throughout North America. Waste Management is the nation's largest collector of recyclables from businesses and households, collecting recyclable materials and depositing them at about a hundred local materials recovery facilities. The firm recycles several different materials including plastics, rubber, electronics and commodities. The company also has a pulp and paper trading group that reduces paper's overall long-term commodity price exposure. Waste Management owns or operates 249 landfill sites, as well as 297 transfer stations that consolidate, compact and transport waste. Its hazardous waste management services include geosynthetic manufacturing, radioactive waste services and landfill liner installation. Additionally, Waste Management promotes environmental initiatives such as Keep America Beautiful and Wildlife Habitat Council as well as its own Think Green. In 2015, the firm acquired Deffenbaugh Disposal, Inc., a collection and disposal firm with assets including five collection operations, seven transfer stations, two recycling facilities, one subtitle-D landfill and one construction/demolition landfill.

Waste Management offers its employees life, AD&D, medical, dental and vision insurance; prescription drug coverage; family assistance programs; flexible spending accounts; adoption assistance; education savings accounts; an employee stock purchase plan; and tuition reimbursement.

FINANCIAL DATA: Note: Data for latest year may not have been available at press time.

In U.S. $	2016	2015	2014	2013	2012	2011
Revenue		12,961,000,000	13,996,000,000	13,983,000,000	13,649,000,000	13,378,000,000
R&D Expense						
Operating Income		2,045,000,000	2,299,000,000	1,079,000,000	1,851,000,000	2,028,000,000
Operating Margin %		15.77%	16.42%	7.71%	13.56%	15.15%
SGA Expense		1,343,000,000	1,481,000,000	1,468,000,000	1,472,000,000	1,551,000,000
Net Income		753,000,000	1,298,000,000	98,000,000	817,000,000	961,000,000
Operating Cash Flow		2,498,000,000	2,331,000,000	2,455,000,000	2,295,000,000	2,469,000,000
Capital Expenditure		1,233,000,000	1,151,000,000	1,271,000,000	1,510,000,000	1,324,000,000
EBITDA		3,290,000,000	3,591,000,000	2,308,000,000	3,088,000,000	3,230,000,000
Return on Assets %		3.60%	5.89%	.42%	3.57%	4.36%
Return on Equity %		13.43%	22.43%	1.62%	13.15%	15.58%
Debt to Equity		1.63	1.42	1.66	1.44	1.50

CONTACT INFORMATION:

Phone: 713 512-6200   Fax:
Toll-Free:
Address: 1001 Fannin St., Ste. 4000, Houston, TX 77002 United States

STOCK TICKER/OTHER:

Stock Ticker: WM   Exchange: NYS
Employees: 39,800   Fiscal Year Ends: 12/31
Parent Company:

SALARIES/BONUSES:

Top Exec. Salary: Bonus: $
$1,275,891
Second Exec. Salary: Bonus: $
$678,462

OTHER THOUGHTS:

Estimated Female Officers or Directors: 1

Hot Spot for Advancement for Women/Minorities: Y

Sales, profits and employees may be estimates. Financial information, benefits and other data can change quickly and may vary from those stated here.

Waters Corporation

www.waters.com

NAIC Code: 334516

TYPES OF BUSINESS:

Equipment-Liquid Chromatography Instruments
Mass Spectrometry Systems
Thermal Analyzers
Rheometry Equipment
Software Development
Food Safety Technology

BRANDS/DIVISIONS/AFFILIATES:

ACQUITY UPLC
ACQUITY Arc System
Mpe Orbur Group Ltd
Midland Precision Equipment Company Ltd

CONTACTS: *Note: Officers with more than one job title may be intentionally listed here more than once.*

Christopher OConnell, CEO
Eugene Cassis, CFO
Douglas Berthiaume, Chairman of the Board
Terrance Kelly, President, Divisional
Rohit Khanna, Senior VP, Divisional
Ian King, Senior VP, Divisional
Michael Harrington, Senior VP, Divisional
David Terricciano, Senior VP, Divisional
Elizabeth Rae, Senior VP, Divisional
Mark Beaudouin, Senior VP

GROWTH PLANS/SPECIAL FEATURES:

Waters Corporation is an analytical instrument manufacturer. The firm operates in two segments: waters division and TA division. The waters division offers high-performance liqui chromatography (HPLC) and ultra-performance LC (UPLC). HPLC is a standard technique used to identify and analyze th constituent components of a variety of chemicals and othe materials and has the capabilities to separate and identif approximately 80% of all known chemicals and materials. HPLC is also used in a variety of other applications such a analyses of foods and beverages for nutritional labeling an compliance with safety regulations, the testing of water and a purity within the environmental testing industry as well a applications in other industries, such as chemical an consumer products. ACQUITY UPLC is a proprietar technology that utilizes a packing material with small, uniform diameter particles to accommodate the increased pressure an narrow chromatographic bands that are generated by these small particles. By using ACQUITY UPLC, researchers an analysts achieve chemical separations and faster analysi times in comparison with many analyses performed by HPLC. The TA division, which stands for thermal analysis, measure the physical characteristics of materials as a function c temperature. TA techniques are widely used in th development, production and characterization of materials i various industries such as plastics, chemicals, automobiles pharmaceuticals and electronics. This division also include rheometry instruments, which characterize the flow propertie of materials and measures their viscosity, elasticity an deformation. Its ACQUITY Arc System is a quaternary liqui chromatograph (LC) that gives analytical laboratories runnin established LC methods a choice for replicating or improvin their separations performance. In November 2015, the firr acquired Mpe Orbur Group Ltd., along with its sole subsidiary Midland Precision Equipment Company Ltd.

Waters offers employees medical insurance, retiremer planning programs, sickness/disability programs, life insuranc and an employee assistance program.

FINANCIAL DATA: *Note: Data for latest year may not have been available at press time.*

In U.S. $	2016	2015	2014	2013	2012	2011
Revenue		2,042,332,000	1,989,344,000	1,904,218,000	1,843,641,000	1,851,184,000
R&D Expense		118,545,000	107,726,000	100,536,000	96,004,000	92,347,000
Operating Income		567,451,000	517,908,000	517,343,000	511,490,000	528,600,000
Operating Margin %		27.78%	26.03%	27.16%	27.74%	28.55%
SGA Expense		495,747,000	512,707,000	492,965,000	477,270,000	490,011,000
Net Income		469,053,000	431,620,000	450,003,000	461,443,000	432,968,000
Operating Cash Flow		560,293,000	511,648,000	484,876,000	449,280,000	497,374,000
Capital Expenditure		103,012,000	106,248,000	118,450,000	104,749,000	85,436,000
EBITDA		668,149,000	619,162,000	599,850,000	584,529,000	597,610,000
Return on Assets %		11.51%	11.57%	13.33%	15.66%	17.14%
Return on Equity %		23.72%	23.59%	27.85%	34.25%	37.72%
Debt to Equity		0.72	0.65	0.67	0.71	0.57

CONTACT INFORMATION:

Phone: 508 478-2000   Fax: 508 872-1990
Toll-Free: 800-252-4752
Address: 34 Maple St., Milford, MA 01757 United States

STOCK TICKER/OTHER:

Stock Ticker: WAT   Exchange: NYS
Employees: 6,594   Fiscal Year Ends: 12/31
Parent Company:

SALARIES/BONUSES:

Top Exec. Salary: $234,808   Bonus: $1,700,000
Second Exec. Salary: Bonus: $
$743,982

OTHER THOUGHTS:

Estimated Female Officers or Directors: 3
Hot Spot for Advancement for Women/Minorities: Y

Wells Fargo & Co

www.wellsfargo.com

NAIC Code: 522110

TYPES OF BUSINESS:

Banking
Credit & Debit Cards
Personal Trust Accounts Management
Mutual Fund Administration
Mortgages
Insurance Services
Investment Banking
Asset Management

BRANDS/DIVISIONS/AFFILIATES:

CONTACTS: *Note: Officers with more than one job title may be intentionally listed here more than once.*

John Stumpf, CEO
Anthony Augliera, Secretary
John Shrewsberry, CFO
Richard Levy, Chief Accounting Officer
Kevin Rhein, Chief Information Officer
Michael Loughlin, Chief Risk Officer
Hope Hardison, Executive VP, Divisional
James Strother, General Counsel
Mary Mack, President, Subsidiary
Timothy Sloan, President
Carrie Tolstedt, Senior Executive VP, Divisional
Avid Modjtabai, Senior Executive VP, Divisional
David Carroll, Senior Executive VP, Divisional

GROWTH PLANS/SPECIAL FEATURES:

Wells Fargo & Co. (WFC) is a financial services holding company that provides banking, insurance, investments, mortgage and consumer and commercial finance. Headquartered in San Francisco, the company operates in all 50 U.S. states; Washington, D.C.; and 36 countries, including those in Europe, Africa, Central America and the Asia Pacific region. The firm operates primarily through Wells Fargo Bank, NA, with assets of $1.9 trillion. WFC operates in three business segments: personal, small business and commercial. The personal segment includes banking, loans and credit, insurance, investing and retirement and wealth management. Banking involves checking and savings accounts, CDs, debit and prepaid cards, credit cards, foreign exchange, global remittance services, online banking, online bill pay, transfers, online statements, mobile banking and ATM services. The small business segment includes banking, loans and credit, merchant services, insurance and payroll and other. Loans and credit involves business lines of credit, credit cards, business loans, real estate financing, equipment or vehicle loans and financing for health care practice. The commercial segment includes products and services, industry expertise and insights. Industry expertise involves auto dealerships, beverage companies, education, energy, environment and waste, financial institutions, food and agribusiness, gaming, government, health care, media communications, restaurants, retail and technology banking. In August 2016, the firm acquired the Australian and New Zealand segments of GE Capital's commercial distribution finance business.

Wells Fargo offers its employees a 401(k) plan, tuition reimbursement, adoption assistance, discounted checking and savings accounts and scholarships for dependent children.

FINANCIAL DATA: *Note: Data for latest year may not have been available at press time.*

In U.S. $	2016	2015	2014	2013	2012	2011
Revenue		86,057,000,000	84,347,000,000	83,780,000,000	86,086,000,000	80,948,000,000
R&D Expense						
Operating Income		33,641,000,000	33,915,000,000	32,629,000,000	28,471,000,000	23,656,000,000
Operating Margin %		39.09%	40.20%	38.94%	33.07%	29.22%
SGA Expense		31,654,000,000	30,870,000,000	31,097,000,000	30,160,000,000	28,933,000,000
Net Income		22,894,000,000	23,057,000,000	21,878,000,000	18,897,000,000	15,869,000,000
Operating Cash Flow		14,772,000,000	17,529,000,000	57,641,000,000	58,540,000,000	13,665,000,000
Capital Expenditure		135,000,000	150,000,000			
EBITDA						
Return on Assets %		1.23%	1.35%	1.41%	1.31%	1.16%
Return on Equity %		12.78%	13.67%	13.99%	13.16%	12.18%
Debt to Equity		1.16	1.11	0.99	0.88	0.97

CONTACT INFORMATION:

Phone: 866 249-3302   Fax:
Toll-Free: 800-869-3557
Address: 420 Montgomery St., San Francisco, CA 94163 United States

STOCK TICKER/OTHER:

Stock Ticker: WFC
Employees: 264,900
Parent Company:

Exchange: NYS
Fiscal Year Ends: 12/31

SALARIES/BONUSES:

Top Exec. Salary:
$2,800,000
Second Exec. Salary:
$2,000,000

Bonus: $

Bonus: $

OTHER THOUGHTS:

Estimated Female Officers or Directors: 8

Hot Spot for Advancement for Women/Minorities: Y

Whirlpool Corp

www.whirlpoolcorp.com

NAIC Code: 335224

TYPES OF BUSINESS:

Home Appliance Manufacturer
Laundry Appliances
Refrigerators & Freezers
Air Conditioning Equipment
Kitchen Appliances

BRANDS/DIVISIONS/AFFILIATES:

Whirlpool
KitchenAid
Maytag
Brastemp
Bauknecht
Amana
American Dryer Corporation
Consul

CONTACTS: Note: Officers with more than one job title may be intentionally listed here more than once.

Jeff Fettig, CEO
Christopher Kuehn, CFO, Divisional
Joseph Lovechio, CFO
James Peters, Chief Accounting Officer
David Szczupak, Executive VP, Divisional
Esther Berrozpe-Galindo, Executive VP
Joseph Liotine, Executive VP
Joao Brega, Executive VP
Bridget Quinn, General Counsel
Marc Bitzer, President
Kirsten Hewitt, Senior VP, Divisional

GROWTH PLANS/SPECIAL FEATURES:

Whirlpool Corp. is a worldwide manufacturer and marketer major home appliances. It manufactures products in countries under nine principal brand names, includin Whirlpool, Maytag, KitchenAid, Consul, Brastemp, Aman Bauknecht, Jenn-Air and Indesit. The firm operates manufacturing and technology research centers internationa and markets products in nearly every country around the worl The company's principal products are laundry appliance refrigerators and freezers, cooking appliances, dishwashe and mixers and other small household appliances. Additionall the company aims to produce Energy Star grade appliance with increased overall efficiency than normal grade appliance In North America, Whirlpool markets and distributes maj home appliances and portable appliances. In addition to i extensive operations in Western and Eastern Europ Whirlpool has sales subsidiaries in Russia, Dubai, Turkey an Morocco. In Latin America, the company manages applianc sales and distribution in Brazil, Argentina, Chile, Ecuado Colombia, Guatemala and Peru through its Brazilia subsidiary, and in Bolivia, Paraguay, Venezuela, th Caribbean, Uruguay and Central American countries throug its distributors. In Asia, the firm markets and distributes i major home appliances in China, Hong Kong, Taiwan, Indi Nepal, Pakistan, Australia, New Zealand, the Pacific Island and Southeast Asia. Whirlpool sells its products to dealer distributors, retailers and builders. Major customers includ Lowe's, Sears, Home Depot, Best Buy, hhgregg, Grupo Pa De Acuacar, Suning, IKEA and Alno. In 2015, the firm acquire American Dryer Corporation (ADC), a private manufacturer coin-operated, on premise, industrial and specialty laundr equipment.

Whirlpool offers its employees health, dental and visio coverage; educational leave; flexible spending account scholarship programs for employees' dependents; and fitnes and weight loss rebates.

FINANCIAL DATA: Note: Data for latest year may not have been available at press time.

In U.S. $	2016	2015	2014	2013	2012	2011
Revenue		20,891,000,000	19,872,000,000	18,769,000,000	18,143,000,000	18,666,000,000
R&D Expense						
Operating Income		1,285,000,000	1,188,000,000	1,249,000,000	869,000,000	792,000,000
Operating Margin %		6.15%	5.97%	6.65%	4.78%	4.24%
SGA Expense		2,130,000,000	2,038,000,000	1,828,000,000	1,757,000,000	1,621,000,000
Net Income		783,000,000	650,000,000	827,000,000	401,000,000	390,000,000
Operating Cash Flow		1,225,000,000	1,479,000,000	1,262,000,000	696,000,000	530,000,000
Capital Expenditure		689,000,000	720,000,000	578,000,000	476,000,000	608,000,000
EBITDA		1,953,000,000	1,748,000,000	1,634,000,000	1,420,000,000	743,000,000
Return on Assets %		4.01%	3.65%	5.34%	2.62%	2.53%
Return on Equity %		16.26%	13.25%	18.00%	9.50%	9.27%
Debt to Equity		0.73	0.72	0.37	0.45	0.50

CONTACT INFORMATION:

Phone: 269 923-5000   Fax: 269 923-3978
Toll-Free:
Address: 2000 N. M-63, Benton Harbor, MI 49022-2692 United States

STOCK TICKER/OTHER:

Stock Ticker: WHR   Exchange: NYS
Employees: 100,000   Fiscal Year Ends: 12/31
Parent Company:

SALARIES/BONUSES:

Top Exec. Salary: $1,475,000   Bonus: $

Second Exec. Salary: $949,167   Bonus: $

OTHER THOUGHTS:

Estimated Female Officers or Directors: 4

Hot Spot for Advancement for Women/Minorities: Y

William Morris Endeavor Entertainment LLC (WME-IMG)
www.wma.com
NAIC Code: 711410

TYPES OF BUSINESS:

Talent Agency
Literary Agency
Sports Marketing & Agents
Media Consulting
Book Publishing

BRANDS/DIVISIONS/AFFILIATES:

William Morris Agency Inc
Endeavor Agency (The)
Silver Lake Partners

CONTACTS: *Note: Officers with more than one job title may be intentionally listed here more than once.*

Ari Emanuel, Co-CEO
Patrick Whitesell, Co-CEO
David Wirtschafter, Pres.
David Wirtschafter, Co-CEO

GROWTH PLANS/SPECIAL FEATURES:

William Morris Endeavor Entertainment LLC, formed by the merger of the former William Morris Agency and the Endeavor Agency, is one of the largest talent and literary agencies in the world. The firm operates in departments including books, commercials, lectures, motion pictures, music, athletics, television, voice-overs and theater. The books department represents a multitude of fiction and non-fiction authors. The department works closely with the motion picture and television departments to bring books to both large and small screens. The commercials department creates special interest home videos, infomercials, home shopping and industrial programming as well as overseeing sponsorships and promotional events. The lectures division represents a roster of speakers across a broad spectrum of issues and topics. The motion pictures department represents both established and up-and-coming directors and actors. The music group represents clients across a range of musical genres. The athletics department represents athletes and sports properties and seeks to secure endorsements, sponsorships and other opportunities on behalf of its clients. The television group represents television programming and creative talent. The voice-over division represents a range of voice-over talent including Spanish language voice-over actors. The company also represents Broadway and theatrical tours; books agency clients into fairs and special events; and coordinates public, corporate and private speaking engagements. The firm's consulting segment offers entertainment marketing strategies to customers such as General Motors, Hasbro, Starbucks, Swarovski and Bluefly.com. The firm represents celebrities such as television personalities, Whoopi Goldberg, Ryan Seacrest and Emeril Legasse; actors such as Adam Sandler, Clint Eastwood, Denzel Washington, Russell Crowe, Robert de Niro and Matt Damon; and directors such as Martin Scorsese and Danny Boyle. William Morris is partly owned by private equity firm Silver Lake Partners.

FINANCIAL DATA: *Note: Data for latest year may not have been available at press time.*

In U.S. $	2016	2015	2014	2013	2012	2011
Revenue		2,200,000,000	2,100,000,000	365,000,000	450,000,000	400,000,000
R&D Expense						
Operating Income						
Operating Margin %						
SGA Expense						
Net Income						
Operating Cash Flow						
Capital Expenditure						
EBITDA						
Return on Assets %						
Return on Equity %						
Debt to Equity						

CONTACT INFORMATION:

Phone: 310-285-9000   Fax: 310-285-9010
Toll-Free:
Address: 1 William Morris Pl., Beverly Hills, CA 90212 United States

STOCK TICKER/OTHER:

Stock Ticker: Private
Employees: 4,500
Parent Company: Silver Lake Partners

Exchange:
Fiscal Year Ends: 12/31

SALARIES/BONUSES:

Top Exec. Salary: $ Bonus: $
Second Exec. Salary: $ Bonus: $

OTHER THOUGHTS:

Estimated Female Officers or Directors:
Hot Spot for Advancement for Women/Minorities:

WW Grainger Inc

NAIC Code: 423830

www.grainger.com

TYPES OF BUSINESS:

Industrial Equipment & Products-Wholesale
Maintenance & Repair Products
Online Sales
Safety Products
Logistics Services

BRANDS/DIVISIONS/AFFILIATES:

Grainger.com
Acklands-Grainger
Zoro
Zoro.com
Fabory Group (The)
MonotaRO
Grainger Mexico
Cromwell Group Limited

CONTACTS: *Note: Officers with more than one job title may be intentionally listed here more than once.*

James Ryan, CEO
Ronald Jadin, CFO
William Lomax, Chief Accounting Officer
Michael Ali, Chief Information Officer
Donald Macpherson, COO
John Howard, General Counsel
D. L. Rawlinson, Other Corporate Officer
Joseph High, Other Executive Officer
Laura Brown, Senior VP, Divisional

GROWTH PLANS/SPECIAL FEATURES:

W. W. Grainger, Inc. (Grainger) offers facilities maintenanc products and related services and information solutions t approximately 3 million businesses and institutions. Th company is divided into two segments: U.S. and Canada. Th U.S. segment markets over 1 million products, includin material handling equipment, safety and security supplies lighting and electrical products, power and hand tools, pump and plumbing supplies, cleaning and maintenance supplies forestry and agriculture equipment, building and hom inspection supplies and vehicle and fleet components. Th U.S. business operates through its website, Grainger.com, an in over 330 branches and 41 regional contact centers in all 5 states as well as through a network of 19 distribution centers The Canada segment, operating as Acklands-Grainger, is leading broad-line distributor of industrial and safety supplies including tools, fasteners, instruments and welding and sho equipment. This business operates through 165 branches an five distribution centers across Canada. Grainger has a singl channel online business called Zoro, which operates in th U.S., Europe, Asia and Latin America. Zoro is an onlin distributor of MRO (maintenance, repair and operating products serving U.S. businesses and consumers through it Zoro.com website. Other businesses, include The Fabor Group, a European distributor of fasteners, tools and industri supplies; 51%-owned MonotaRO, a provider of small- and mic sized Japanese businesses with products that help ther operate and maintain their facilities; and Grainger Mexicc which provides local businesses with MRO supplies and othe related products primarily from Mexico and the U.S. Durin 2015, Grainger closed its business operations in Brazil; an acquired Cromwell Group Limited, a broad line distributor c MRO supplies in the U.K.

Employee benefits include health, dental and prescriptio coverage; a profit sharing plan; an employee assistanc program; adoption benefits; dependant care assistance; critica illness insurance; and a group legal plan.

FINANCIAL DATA: *Note: Data for latest year may not have been available at press time.*

In U.S. $	2016	2015	2014	2013	2012	2011
Revenue		9,973,384,000	9,964,953,000	9,437,758,000	8,950,045,000	8,078,185,000
R&D Expense						
Operating Income		1,300,320,000	1,347,117,000	1,296,854,000	1,131,125,000	1,052,429,000
Operating Margin %		13.03%	13.51%	13.74%	12.63%	13.02%
SGA Expense		2,931,108,000	2,967,125,000	2,839,629,000	2,785,035,000	2,458,363,000
Net Income		768,996,000	801,729,000	797,036,000	689,881,000	658,423,000
Operating Cash Flow		989,904,000	959,814,000	986,498,000	816,195,000	746,108,000
Capital Expenditure		373,868,000	387,390,000	272,145,000	249,860,000	196,942,000
EBITDA		1,512,243,000	1,552,805,000	1,481,437,000	1,292,916,000	1,209,818,000
Return on Assets %		13.66%	15.19%	15.50%	14.17%	15.27%
Return on Equity %		27.80%	24.82%	25.40%	24.40%	27.24%
Debt to Equity		0.61	0.12	0.13	0.15	0.06

CONTACT INFORMATION:

Phone: 847 535-1000   Fax:
Toll-Free: 800-323-0620
Address: 100 Grainger Pkwy., Lake Forest, IL 60045 United States

STOCK TICKER/OTHER:

Stock Ticker: GWW
Employees: 23,600
Parent Company:

Exchange: NYS
Fiscal Year Ends: 12/31

SALARIES/BONUSES:

Top Exec. Salary: $1,150,169   Bonus: $

Second Exec. Salary: $725,750   Bonus: $

OTHER THOUGHTS:

Estimated Female Officers or Directors:

Hot Spot for Advancement for Women/Minorities: Y

Wyndham Worldwide Corporation   www.wyndhamworldwide.com

NAIC Code: 721110

TYPES OF BUSINESS:

Hotels, Motels & Resorts
Property Management
Hotel Development
Vacation Property Exchange and Rental
Timeshare Resorts
Franchising
Vacation Ownership

BRANDS/DIVISIONS/AFFILIATES:

Wyndham Hotel Group
Wyndham Destination Network
Wyndham Vacation Ownership
Margaritaville Vacation Club
Baymont Inn & Suites
Wyndham Vacation Rentals
Club Wyndham
WorldMark

CONTACTS: *Note: Officers with more than one job title may be intentionally listed here more than once.*

Franz Hanning, CEO, Divisional
Geoffrey Ballotti, CEO, Divisional
Gail Mandel, CEO, Divisional
Stephen Holmes, CEO
Thomas Conforti, CFO
Scott McLester, Executive VP
Mary Falvey, Executive VP
Thomas Anderson, Executive VP
Nicola Rossi, Senior VP

GROWTH PLANS/SPECIAL FEATURES:

Wyndham Worldwide Corporation (WW) is a hospitality company offering individual consumers and business customers an array of hospitality products and services as well as various accommodation alternatives and price ranges through its portfolio of world-renowned brands. WW's Wyndham Hotel Group is a world renowned hotel company with 7,812 hotels and more than 678,000 hotel rooms. The group franchises in the upscale, upper midscale, midscale, economy and extended stay segments with a concentration on economy brands. It also provides property management services for full-service and select limited-service hotels, which is predominantly a fee-for-service business. Group brands include Dolce Hotels & Resorts, Wyndham Grand Hotels & Resorts, Wyndham Hotels & Resorts, Wyndham Garden Hotels, TRYP, Wingate, Hawthorn, Microtel, Ramada Worldwide, Baymont Inn & Suites, DaysInn, Super 8, Howard Johnson, Travelodge and Knights Inn. Wyndham Destination Network (formerly Wyndham Exchange & Rentals) operates more than 110,000 vacation properties worldwide under the following brands: cottages4you, Hoseasons, James Villa Hollidays, Landal GreenParks, Novasol, RCI, The Registry Collection and Wyndham Vacation Rentals. Wyndham Vacation Ownership (WVO) is a timeshare/vacation ownership business with 213 resorts and approximately 897,000 owners. WVO develops and markets vacation ownership interests (VOI) to individual consumers, provides consumer financing, as well as property management services at the resorts. WVO brands include Club Wyndham, WorldMark, Shell Vacations Club, Margaritaville Vacation Club, Club Wyndham Asia, WorldMark South Pacific Club and Wyndham Club Brasil. In January 2016, Wyndham Exchange & Rentals changed its name to Wyndham Destination Network.

The firm offers employees medical, dental, vision and life insurance; domestic partner benefits; flexible spending accounts; an educational assistance program; an employee assistance program; adoption reimbursement; and travel discounts on Wyndham properties and the firm's affiliated car rental partners.

FINANCIAL DATA: *Note: Data for latest year may not have been available at press time.*

In U.S. $	2016	2015	2014	2013	2012	2011
Revenue		5,536,000,000	5,281,000,000	5,009,000,000	4,534,000,000	4,254,000,000
R&D Expense						
Operating Income		1,015,000,000	941,000,000	910,000,000	852,000,000	767,000,000
Operating Margin %		18.33%	17.81%	18.16%	18.79%	18.03%
SGA Expense		1,574,000,000	1,557,000,000	1,471,000,000	1,389,000,000	1,221,000,000
Net Income		612,000,000	529,000,000	432,000,000	400,000,000	417,000,000
Operating Cash Flow		991,000,000	984,000,000	1,008,000,000	1,004,000,000	1,003,000,000
Capital Expenditure		222,000,000	235,000,000	238,000,000	208,000,000	239,000,000
EBITDA		1,275,000,000	1,191,000,000	1,030,000,000	945,000,000	980,000,000
Return on Assets %		6.31%	5.44%	4.49%	4.32%	4.52%
Return on Equity %		55.51%	36.76%	24.31%	19.22%	16.19%
Debt to Equity		5.21	3.81	2.83	2.08	1.69

CONTACT INFORMATION:

Phone: 973 753-6000   Fax: 973 496-7658
Toll-Free:
Address: 22 Sylvan Way, Parsippany, NJ 07054 United States

SALARIES/BONUSES:

Top Exec. Salary: Bonus: $
$1,595,784
Second Exec. Salary: Bonus: $
$794,824

STOCK TICKER/OTHER:

Stock Ticker: WYN   Exchange: NYS
Employees: 37,700   Fiscal Year Ends: 12/31
Parent Company:

OTHER THOUGHTS:

Estimated Female Officers or Directors: 2

Hot Spot for Advancement for Women/Minorities: Y

Wynn Resorts Limited

www.wynnresorts.com

NAIC Code: 721120

TYPES OF BUSINESS:

Hotel Casinos
Online Poker

BRANDS/DIVISIONS/AFFILIATES:

Wynn Las Vegas
Encore at Wynn Macau
Wynn Macau
Encore Theater
Palo Real Estate Company Limited
Wynn Resorts
Wynn Palace

CONTACTS: Note: Officers with more than one job title may be intentionally listed here more than once.

Stephen A. Wynn, CEO
Matt Maddox, Pres.
Stephen Cootey, CFO
Stephen A. Wynn, Chmn.

GROWTH PLANS/SPECIAL FEATURES:

Wynn Resorts Limited is a developer, owner and operator destination casino resorts. It owns and operates tw destination casino resorts: The Wynn Las Vegas on the Stri in Las Vegas, Nevada, which includes Encore at Wynn La Vegas; and the Wynn Macau in the Macau Speci Administrative Region of China. The firm's Las Vega operations offer 4,748 rooms and suites. The 186,000 squar foot casino features 232 table games, a poker room, 1,849 sl machines and a race and sports book. The resort also feature 34 food and beverage outlets; three nightclubs; two spas an salons; a Ferrari and Maserati automobile dealership; weddin chapels; an 18-hole golf course; 290,000 square feet meeting space; and a 99,000 square foot retail promenad featuring boutiques from Alexander McQueen, Cartier, Chan and Louis Vuitton. At the Encore Theater, the company offe headlining entertainment acts from personalities such a Beyonce. The company's Wynn Macau resort operation including Encore at Wynn Macau, features 1,008 rooms an suites, approximately 284,000 square feet of casino gamin space with 625 slot machines and 498 table games, eigl restaurants, two luxury spas and 57,000 square feet of reta space. Wynn Palace is a resort development scheduled open by mid-2016, featuring 1,700 rooms and suites, an 8-acr performance lake, air-conditioned SkyCabs, floral sculpture gaming space, meeting facilities, spa, salon, retail spaces an fine dining.

FINANCIAL DATA: Note: Data for latest year may not have been available at press time.

In U.S. $	2016	2015	2014	2013	2012	2011
Revenue		4,075,883,000	5,433,661,000	5,620,936,000	5,154,284,000	5,269,792,000
R&D Expense						
Operating Income		658,814,000	1,266,278,000	1,290,091,000	1,029,276,000	1,008,240,000
Operating Margin %		16.16%	23.30%	22.95%	19.96%	19.13%
SGA Expense		552,951,000	533,047,000	469,095,000	482,143,000	519,702,000
Net Income		195,290,000	731,554,000	728,652,000	502,036,000	613,371,000
Operating Cash Flow		572,813,000	1,098,317,000	1,676,642,000	1,185,718,000	1,515,835,000
Capital Expenditure		1,925,152,000	1,345,940,000	506,786,000	240,985,000	184,146,000
EBITDA		912,782,000	1,588,043,000	1,656,596,000	1,394,956,000	1,433,524,000
Return on Assets %		1.99%	8.38%	9.30%	7.08%	9.03%
Return on Equity %					54.86%	28.35%
Debt to Equity						1.34

CONTACT INFORMATION:

Phone: 702 770-7555   Fax: 702 733-4681
Toll-Free:
Address: 3131 Las Vegas Blvd. S., Las Vegas, NV 89109 United States

STOCK TICKER/OTHER:

Stock Ticker: WYNN   Exchange: NAS
Employees: 16,800   Fiscal Year Ends: 12/31
Parent Company:

SALARIES/BONUSES:

Top Exec. Salary: Bonus: $
$2,500,000
Second Exec. Salary: Bonus: $
$1,500,000

OTHER THOUGHTS:

Estimated Female Officers or Directors: 3

Hot Spot for Advancement for Women/Minorities: Y

Xerox Corporation

www.xerox.com

NAIC Code: 561110

TYPES OF BUSINESS:

Business Process Outsourcing
Managed Print Services Outsourcing
Software
Multipurpose Office Machines
Consulting Services
Desktop Printers
Computer Facilities Management Services
Equipment Financing

BRANDS/DIVISIONS/AFFILIATES:

Phaser
Xerox ConnectKey
WorkCentre 3215
Xerox WorkCentre 7970
WorkCentre 5945
DocuTech
Xerox Nuvera
Xerox iGen

CONTACTS: *Note: Officers with more than one job title may be intentionally listed here more than once.*

J Peffer, Assistant General Counsel
Ursula Burns, CEO
Joseph Mancini, Chief Accounting Officer
Don Liu, Executive VP
James Firestone, Executive VP
Darrell Ford, Other Executive Officer
Thomas Maddison, Other Executive Officer
Robert Zapfel, President, Divisional
Jeffrey Jacobson, President, Divisional
Herve Tessler, President, Divisional
Leslie Varon, Vice President

GROWTH PLANS/SPECIAL FEATURES:

Xerox Corporation is a document systems and services company operating in the global document market. It operates in three segments: document technology, services and other. The document technology segment includes the production and supply of document technology and related services and equipment financing. Products in this category are subcategorized as entry, mid-range and high-end. Entry products are sold to small- and mid-sized businesses and include desktop color and monochrome printers with Xerox ConnectKey technology, such as WorkCenter 3215 and Phaser series. Mid-range products are sold to enterprises of varying sizes through Xerox-branded partners and include multifunction printers, copiers, digital printing presses and light production products. The firm's mid-range product line includes multifunction printers, such as Xerox WorkCentre 7970 and WorkCentre 5945. Xerox produces high-end digital monochrome and color systems for larger companies and those in the graphics industry. These products allow for on-demand printing, digital full-color printing and enterprise printing and include DocuTech, Xerox Nuvera and Xerox iGen. The services segment includes the firm's business process outsourcing and documenting outsourcing services. Business process outsourcing ranges from government health care solutions to human resources services to customer care to transportation solutions. Document outsourcing helps companies to optimize their printing infrastructure by means of managed print services, as well as communication and marketing services. The other segment includes paper sales in developing market countries, wide-format systems, licensing revenue, Global Imaging Systems network integration solutions and non-allocated corporate items. During 2015, the company acquired California-based, Healthy Communities Institute and sold its information technology outsourcing business to Atos. In January 2016, the firm announced plans to separate into two independent companies: a document technology company, Xerox Corporation; and a business process outsourcing company, Conduent, Inc.

Xerox employees receive health care, life insurance, employee assistance programs, retirement plans and child care/elder care resources.

FINANCIAL DATA: *Note: Data for latest year may not have been available at press time.*

In U.S. $	2016	2015	2014	2013	2012	2011
Revenue		18,045,000,000	19,540,000,000	21,435,000,000	22,390,000,000	22,626,000,000
R&D Expense		563,000,000	577,000,000	601,000,000	655,000,000	721,000,000
Operating Income		831,000,000	1,566,000,000	1,462,000,000	1,802,000,000	2,044,000,000
Operating Margin %		4.60%	8.01%	6.82%	8.04%	9.03%
SGA Expense		3,559,000,000	3,788,000,000	4,137,000,000	4,288,000,000	4,497,000,000
Net Income		474,000,000	969,000,000	1,159,000,000	1,195,000,000	1,295,000,000
Operating Cash Flow		1,611,000,000	2,063,000,000	2,375,000,000	2,580,000,000	1,961,000,000
Capital Expenditure		342,000,000	452,000,000	427,000,000	513,000,000	501,000,000
EBITDA		1,825,000,000	2,869,000,000	2,913,000,000	2,847,000,000	3,047,000,000
Return on Assets %		1.71%	3.33%	3.84%	3.89%	4.18%
Return on Equity %		4.64%	8.36%	9.81%	10.16%	10.64%
Debt to Equity		0.73	0.59	0.57	0.66	0.59

CONTACT INFORMATION:

Phone: 203 968-3000   Fax:
Toll-Free: 800-275-9376
Address: 45 Glober Ave., Norwalk, CT 06856 United States

STOCK TICKER/OTHER:

Stock Ticker: XRX   Exchange: NYS
Employees: 147,500   Fiscal Year Ends: 12/31
Parent Company:

SALARIES/BONUSES:

Top Exec. Salary: $1,100,000   Bonus: $374,453
Second Exec. Salary: $603,750   Bonus: $600,000

OTHER THOUGHTS:

Estimated Female Officers or Directors: 11

Hot Spot for Advancement for Women/Minorities: Y

Sales, profits and employees may be estimates. Financial information, benefits and other data can change quickly and may vary from those stated here.

Yum! Brands Inc

NAIC Code: 722513

TYPES OF BUSINESS:

Fast Food Restaurants

BRANDS/DIVISIONS/AFFILIATES:

KFC
Pizza Hut
Taco Bell
Little Sheep
Third Point Management

CONTACTS: *Note: Officers with more than one job title may be intentionally listed here more than once.*

John Daley, Assistant General Counsel
Tracy Skeans, Other Executive Officer
Roger Eaton, CEO, Divisional
Joey Wat, CEO, Divisional
Peter Kao, CEO, Divisional
Brian Niccol, CEO, Divisional
Muktesh Pant, CEO, Subsidiary
Greg Creed, CEO
David Russell, Chief Accounting Officer
Marc Kesselman, General Counsel
Elizabeth Grenfell, Other Corporate Officer
Virginia Ferguson, Other Corporate Officer
Jonathan Blum, Other Corporate Officer
Christian Campbell, Other Executive Officer
David Gibbs, President
Steve Schmitt, Vice President, Divisional

GROWTH PLANS/SPECIAL FEATURES:

Yum! Brands, Inc. is a fast-food restaurant company with ove 42,000 restaurants in more than 130 countries and territories The firm's brands include KFC, Pizza Hut and Taco Bell. Th company operates in four segments: YUM China, KFC, Pizz Hut and Taco Bell. YUM China includes all operations i mainland China. The KFC and Pizza Hut segments includes a operations of the KFC concept outside China. The Taco Be segment includes all operations of the Taco Bell concep outside of India. KFC operates in 125 countries and territorie with 5,003 units in China, 372 units in India and 14,577 unit within the KFC division. Pizza Hut operates in 95 countries an territories with 1,903 units in China, 432 units in India an 13,728 units within the Pizza Hut division. Taco Bell operate in 21 countries and territories with 6,400 Taco Bell units withi the Taco Bell division, primarily located in the USA and 7 unit in India. The firm also owns a controlling interest in Little Sheep, a chain of restaurants in the Inner Mongolia region o China. In 2015, Third Point Management acquired a unspecified stake in the company. That October, the compan announced plans to spin off its YUM China business separating into two independent, publicly-traded companies.

The firm offers employees benefits including life, acciden disability, medical, dental, vision and hearing insurance; healt and fitness programs; a 401(k); paid time off; child care; flexibl spending accounts; an employee assistance program adoption assistance; discount programs; and tuitio reimbursement.

FINANCIAL DATA: *Note: Data for latest year may not have been available at press time.*

In U.S. $	2016	2015	2014	2013	2012	2011
Revenue		13,105,000,000	13,279,000,000	13,084,000,000	13,633,000,000	12,626,000,000
R&D Expense						
Operating Income		1,921,000,000	1,557,000,000	1,798,000,000	2,294,000,000	1,815,000,000
Operating Margin %		14.65%	11.72%	13.74%	16.82%	14.37%
SGA Expense		1,504,000,000	1,419,000,000	1,412,000,000	1,510,000,000	1,372,000,000
Net Income		1,293,000,000	1,051,000,000	1,091,000,000	1,597,000,000	1,319,000,000
Operating Cash Flow		2,139,000,000	2,049,000,000	2,139,000,000	2,294,000,000	2,170,000,000
Capital Expenditure		973,000,000	1,033,000,000	1,049,000,000	1,099,000,000	940,000,000
EBITDA		2,668,000,000	2,296,000,000	2,542,000,000	2,939,000,000	2,471,000,000
Return on Assets %		15.74%	12.33%	12.32%	17.89%	15.38%
Return on Equity %		105.20%	56.61%	50.50%	80.31%	77.61%
Debt to Equity		3.35	1.98	1.34	1.36	1.64

CONTACT INFORMATION:

Phone: 502 874-8300   Fax:
Toll-Free:
Address: 1441 Gardiner Ln., Louisville, KY 40213 United States

STOCK TICKER/OTHER:

Stock Ticker: YUM
Employees: 537,000
Parent Company:

Exchange: NYS
Fiscal Year Ends: 12/31

SALARIES/BONUSES:

Top Exec. Salary: Bonus: $
$1,104,615
Second Exec. Salary: Bonus: $
$1,100,000

OTHER THOUGHTS:

Estimated Female Officers or Directors: 3

Hot Spot for Advancement for Women/Minorities: Y

Zimmer Biomet Holdings Inc

www.zimmerbiomet.com/

NAIC Code: 339100

TYPES OF BUSINESS:

Orthopedic Supplies
Human Bone Joint Replacement Systems
Orthopedic Support Devices
Operating Room Supplies
Powered Surgical Instruments
Dental Implants

BRANDS/DIVISIONS/AFFILIATES:

Persona
Zimmer
Transposal
JuggerKnot
3i T3
Timerline
TraumaOne
Cayenne Medical Inc

CONTACTS: Note: Officers with more than one job title may be intentionally listed here more than once.

David Dvorak, CEO
Larry Glasscock, Director
Daniel Williamson, President, Divisional
Adam Johnson, President, Divisional
David Nolan, President, Divisional
Stuart Kleopfer, President, Geographical
Katarzyna Mazur-Hofsaess, President, Geographical
Sang Yi, President, Geographical
Daniel Florin, Senior VP
Chad Phipps, Senior VP
Derek Davis, Vice President, Divisional
Tony Collins, Vice President

GROWTH PLANS/SPECIAL FEATURES:

Zimmer Biomet Holdings, Inc. designs, manufactures and markets musculoskeletal products for the health care industry. These include orthopedic reconstructive products; sports medicine, biologics, extremities and trauma products; spine, bone healing, craniomaxillofacial and thoracic products; dental implants; and related surgical products. Zimmer Biomet collaborates with health care professionals worldwide to advance the pace of innovation. The company's products and solutions help treat patients suffering from disorders of, or injuries to, bones, joints or supporting soft tissues. Knee products include the Persona, NexGen, Vanguard and Oxford branded systems. Hip products include the Zimmer, Taperloc, Arcos, Continuum and G7 branded systems. Surgical, sports medicine, biologics, foot & ankle, extremities and trauma products include the Transposal & Transposal Ultra fluid waste management systems, automatic tourniquet systems, JuggerKnot soft anchor system, Gel-One cross-linked hyaluronate, Travecular Metal reverse shoulder system, Comprehensive shoulder system, Zimmer Natural Nail system and DVR plating system. Dental products include the Tapered Screw-Vent implant system, 3i T3 implant system and Puros allograft products. Spine and craniomaxillofacial and thoracic products include the Polaris spinal system, Timberline lateral fusion system, PathFinder NXT pedicle screw system and TraumaOne plating system brand lines. Other products include PALACOS bone cement and SinalPak fusion stimulator. In 2016, Zimmer Biomet acquired Cayenne Medical, Inc., which designs, develops and markets technically-advanced soft tissue repair and reconstruction solutions of the knee, shoulder and extremeties. That June, it agreed to acquire LDR Holding Corporation, a global medical device company that designs and commercializes novel and proprietary surgical technologies for the treatment of patients suffering from spine disorders.

FINANCIAL DATA: Note: Data for latest year may not have been available at press time.

In U.S. $	2016	2015	2014	2013	2012	2011
Revenue		5,997,800,000	4,673,300,000	4,623,400,000	4,471,700,000	4,451,800,000
R&D Expense		268,800,000	188,300,000	204,200,000	225,600,000	238,600,000
Operating Income		467,300,000	1,034,700,000	1,035,600,000	1,047,400,000	1,024,100,000
Operating Margin %		7.79%	22.14%	22.39%	23.42%	23.00%
SGA Expense		2,291,900,000	1,844,000,000	1,880,800,000	1,822,100,000	1,991,900,000
Net Income		147,000,000	720,100,000	761,000,000	755,000,000	760,800,000
Operating Cash Flow		816,700,000	1,052,800,000	963,100,000	1,151,900,000	1,176,900,000
Capital Expenditure		434,100,000	342,300,000	292,900,000	264,500,000	288,100,000
EBITDA		1,152,200,000	1,382,800,000	1,409,700,000	1,426,100,000	1,394,100,000
Return on Assets %		.79%	7.49%	8.18%	8.61%	9.21%
Return on Equity %		1.79%	11.23%	12.51%	13.28%	13.49%
Debt to Equity		1.16	0.21	0.26	0.29	0.28

CONTACT INFORMATION:

Phone: 574-267-6639   Fax: 574-267-8137
Toll-Free: 800-613-6131
Address: 1800 W. Center St., Warsaw, IN 46580 United States

SALARIES/BONUSES:

Top Exec. Salary: $334,646   Bonus: $750,000
Second Exec. Salary: Bonus: $
$1,056,258

STOCK TICKER/OTHER:

Stock Ticker: ZBH   Exchange: NYS
Employees: 10,000   Fiscal Year Ends: 05/31
Parent Company:

OTHER THOUGHTS:

Estimated Female Officers or Directors: 3
Hot Spot for Advancement for Women/Minorities: Y

Sales, profits and employees may be estimates. Financial information, benefits and other data can change quickly and may vary from those stated here.

Zumiez Inc

NAIC Code: 448140

www.zumiez.com

TYPES OF BUSINESS:

Action Sports Apparel
Action Sports Footwear, Equipment & Accessories

BRANDS/DIVISIONS/AFFILIATES:

Zumiez
Blue Tomato

CONTACTS: Note: Officers with more than one job title may be intentionally listed here more than once.

Richard Brooks, CEO
Christopher Work, CFO
Troy Brown, Executive VP, Divisional
Chris Visser, Executive VP
Thomas Campion, Founder

GROWTH PLANS/SPECIAL FEATURES:

Zumiez, Inc. is a mall-based specialty retailer of action sports related apparel, footwear, equipment and accessorie operating under the Zumiez brand name. The compan operates more than 603 stores (550 in the U.S., 35 in Canad and 18 in Europe) which cater to young men and wome between the ages of 12 and 24 who seek popular brand representing a lifestyle centered on action sports such a skateboarding, surfing, snowboarding, BMX (bicycl motocross) and motocross. In addition to apparel and footwea the stores offer sports equipment, including skateboard snowboards, boots and bindings; and accessories, includin wallets, jewelry and other miscellaneous novelties and DVD Zumiez promotes its brand through a multi-faceted marketin approach featuring extensive grassroots marketing events a well as through a differentiated merchandising strategy, stor design and comprehensive training programs aimed a providing an experience for its customers that it believes consistent with their attitudes, fashion tastes and identities. Th company's stores, which average 3,000 square feet, featur couches and action sports oriented video game stations tha are intended to encourage customers to stay in the store longe and to interact with each other and store associates. T increase customer traffic, Zumiez generally locates its store near busy areas of the mall such as food courts, movi theaters, music or game stores and other popular tee retailers. Besides store operations, Zumiez manages an e commerce site that provides current information regardin upcoming events and promotions, store locations an merchandise selection. In Europe, the company additional operates under the brand name Blue Tomato, a leading mult channel retailer for board sports and related apparel an footwear.

The firm's employees receive a 401(k) retirement plan and a employee stock purchase plan, among other benefits.

FINANCIAL DATA: Note: Data for latest year may not have been available at press time.

In U.S. $	2016	2015	2014	2013	2012	2011
Revenue	804,183,000	811,551,000	724,337,000	669,393,000	555,874,000	478,849,000
R&D Expense						
Operating Income	46,165,000	71,571,000	72,842,000	68,542,000	60,232,000	37,367,000
Operating Margin %	5.74%	8.81%	10.05%	10.23%	10.83%	7.80%
SGA Expense	222,459,000	215,512,000	188,918,000	172,742,000	141,444,000	133,030,000
Net Income	28,785,000	43,192,000	45,948,000	42,164,000	37,351,000	24,203,000
Operating Cash Flow	48,607,000	89,937,000	66,894,000	66,225,000	68,065,000	48,692,000
Capital Expenditure	34,834,000	35,758,000	35,969,000	41,070,000	25,508,000	29,361,000
EBITDA	76,575,000	100,738,000	99,438,000	91,499,000	79,976,000	55,290,000
Return on Assets %	6.33%	9.21%	10.77%	10.93%	11.25%	8.61%
Return on Equity %	8.76%	12.42%	14.37%	14.64%	14.97%	11.54%
Debt to Equity		0.01	0.01	0.01		

CONTACT INFORMATION:

Phone: 425 551-1500   Fax: 425 551-1555
Toll-Free: 877-828-6929
Address: 4001 204th St. SW, Lynnwood, WA 98036 United States

STOCK TICKER/OTHER:

Stock Ticker: ZUMZ
Employees: 6,500
Parent Company:

Exchange: NAS
Fiscal Year Ends: 01/31

SALARIES/BONUSES:

Top Exec. Salary: $689,327   Bonus: $
Second Exec. Salary: $398,597   Bonus: $

OTHER THOUGHTS:

Estimated Female Officers or Directors: 1
Hot Spot for Advancement for Women/Minorities:

ADDITIONAL INDEXES

CONTENTS:

INDEX OF FIRMS NOTED AS HOT SPOTS FOR ADVANCEMENT FOR WOMEN & MINORITIES

3M Company
Abbott Laboratories
ABM Industries Inc
Accenture LLP
Acosta Inc
Adobe Systems Inc
Advance Auto Parts Inc
Adventist Health System
Advocate Health Care
Aegion Corporation
Aetna Inc
AFLAC Inc
Agero Inc
Alaska Air Group Inc
Alliance Data Systems Corporation
Allscripts Healthcare Solutions Inc
Amazon.com Inc
American Airlines Group Inc
American Express Co
American Financial Group Inc
American International Group Inc (AIG)
Amerigroup Corporation
AmerisourceBergen Corp
Amgen Inc
AMSURG Corporation
Anthem Inc
Applied Materials Inc
Arrow Electronics Inc
Arthur J Gallagher & Co
Ascena Retail Group Inc
Ascension Health
AT&T Inc
Automatic Data Processing Inc (ADP)
Avnet Inc
Bank of America Corp
Bank of New York Mellon Corp
BB&T Corporation
Becton Dickinson & Co
Belden Inc
Best Buy Co Inc
Bio Rad Laboratories Inc
Biogen Inc
Black & Veatch Holding Company
BlackRock Inc
BMC Software Inc
Boeing Company (The)
Booz Allen Hamilton Holding Corp
BorgWarner Inc
Boston Consulting Group Inc (The, BCG)
Boston Scientific Corp
Brinker International Inc
Brown & Brown Inc
Buffalo Wild Wings Inc
CACI International Inc
Capital One Financial Corp
Cardinal Health Inc
CarMax Inc
Carnival Corporation

Casey's General Stores Inc
Caterpillar Inc
Catholic Health Initiatives
CBS Corporation
CDW Corporation
Celanese Corporation
Celgene Corporation
CenturyLink Inc
Cerner Corporation
CH Robinson Worldwide Inc
Charles Schwab Corp (The)
Chemed Corporation
Chevron Phillips Chemical Company LLC
Chico's FAS Inc
Cigna Corporation
Cisco Systems Inc
Citigroup Inc
Cleveland Clinic Foundation (The)
Clorox Company (The)
Coca-Cola Bottling Co Consolidated
Coca-Cola Company (The)
Colgate Palmolive Co
Comcast Corp
Community Health Systems Inc
Container Store (The)
Convergys Corporation
Cooper Companies Inc
Corning Inc
Costco Wholesale Corp
Cox Enterprises Inc
CR Bard Inc
Crown Holdings Inc
Cullen-Frost Bankers Inc
CVS Health Corporation
Dana Holding Corporation
Danaher Corporation
Darden Restaurants Inc
DaVita Healthcare Partners Inc
Dell-EMC
Deloitte Consulting LLP
Deloitte LLP
Delta Air Lines Inc
DENTSPLY International Inc
Dick's Sporting Goods Inc
DIRECTV
Discovery Communications Inc
DTE Energy Company
Duke Energy Corporation
Eastman Chemical Company
Edward D Jones & Co LP
Edwards Lifesciences Corporation
EMCOR Group Inc
Enterprise Holdings Inc
Equity Lifestyle Properties Inc
Estee Lauder Companies Inc (The)
Exelon Corporation
Express Scripts Holding Co
EY LLP
F5 Networks Inc
Facebook Inc
FactSet Research Systems Inc
Fairview Health Services
FCA US LLC
FedEx Corporation
Fidelity National Information Services Inc

FirstEnergy Corporation
FirstMerit Corporation
Fluor Corp
Foot Locker Inc
Ford Motor Co
Fossil Group Inc
Frito-Lay North America Inc
FTI Consulting Inc
Gartner Inc
General Dynamics Corp
General Electric Co (GE)
General Motors Company (GM)
Gilead Sciences Inc
Goldman Sachs Group Inc
Google (Alphabet Inc)
Greenbrier Companies Inc (The)
Group 1 Automotive Inc
Hanesbrands Inc
Hartford Financial Services Group Inc (The)
Health Care Service Corporation (HCSC)
HealthSouth Corporation
HEB Grocery Company LP
Henry Schein Inc
Hershey Co
Hertz Global Holdings Inc
Hibbett Sports Inc
Hillenbrand Inc
Hillshire Brands Company
Home Depot Inc
Houston Methodist
Hub International Limited
Humana Inc
Hyatt Hotels Corporation
IAC/InterActiveCorp
IDEXX Laboratories Inc
Illinois Tool Works Inc
IMS Health Holdings Inc
Ingram Micro Inc
Ingredion Inc
Intel Corp
Interpublic Group of Companies Inc
Intuit Inc
inVentiv Health Inc
Jabil Circuit Inc
Jack Henry & Associates Inc
Jackson National Life Insurance Company
Jacobs Engineering Group Inc
JB Hunt Transport Services Inc
JetBlue Airways Corporation
Johnson & Johnson
Johnson Controls Inc
Jones Lang LaSalle Inc
JP Morgan Chase & Co Inc
Kaiser Permanente
Kate Spade & Company Inc
Kelly Services Inc
Kimpton Hotel & Restaurant Group LLC
Kindred Healthcare Inc
Kohl's Corporation
Kroger Co (The)
L Brands Inc
Laboratory Corp of America Holdings
Lam Research Corp
Land O'Lakes Inc

Lennar Corporation
Level 3 Communications Inc
Liberty Global Inc
Liberty Mutual Group Inc
LifePoint Health Inc
Lilly (ELI) & Company
Lincoln National Corporation
LinkedIn Corp
Lockheed Martin Corp
Loews Hotels Holding Corporation
Lowe's Companies Inc
Marriott International Inc
Marsh & Mclennan Companies Inc
Mary Kay Inc
MassMutual Financial Group
MasterCard Inc
MAXIMUS Inc
Mayo Foundation for Medical Education
and Research
McAfee Inc
McCormick & Company Inc
McDonald's Corp
McKesson Corporation
McKinsey & Company Inc
Medical Information Technology Inc
(MEDITECH)
MedStar Health
Medtronic Inc
Mercer LLC
Mercy
MetLife Inc
Microsoft Corp
Modine Manufacturing Company
Moody's Corporation
Morgan Stanley
Mutual of Omaha Companies (The)
NBCUniversal LLC
NCR Corporation
New York Life Insurance Co
Nielsen Holdings PLC
Nike Inc
Nordstrom Inc
Northwestern Mutual Life Insurance Co
Norwegian Cruise Line Holdings Ltd
(NCL)
NVIDIA Corp
Oliver Wyman Group
Omnicom Group Inc
Oracle Corp
O'Reilly Automotive Inc
Oshkosh Corporation
Owens & Minor Inc
PAREXEL International Corp
Patterson Companies Inc
PepsiCo Inc
PerkinElmer Inc
PetSmart Inc
Pfizer Inc
PG&E Corporation
Phillips 66
Pinnacle Entertainment Inc
PPG Industries Inc
Priceline Group Inc (The)
PriceSmart Inc
PricewaterhouseCoopers (PWC)

Principal Financial Group (The)
Progressive Corporation (The)
Providence St. Joseph Health
Prudential Financial Inc
Publix Super Markets Inc
PulteGroup Inc
Qualcomm Inc
Quest Diagnostics Inc
Quintiles Transnational Holdings Inc
Ralph Lauren Corporation
Raymond James Financial Inc
Recreational Equipment Inc (REI)
Red Hat Inc
Resources Connection Inc
Rite Aid Corporation
Ross Stores Inc
Royal Caribbean Cruises Ltd
RR Donnelley & Sons Co
Ryder System Inc
Safeco Insurance Company of America
Safeway Inc
SalesForce.com Inc
Sam's Club
SAS Institute Inc
SC Johnson & Son Inc
SCANA Corporation
Science Applications International Corp
(SAIC)
Scotts Miracle-Gro Co (The)
Sherwin-Williams Company (The)
Smithfield Foods Inc
Sodexo Inc
Southwest Airlines Co
Spirit Aerosystems Holdings Inc
St Jude Medical Inc
Stanley Black & Decker Inc
Starbucks Corporation
Starwood Hotels & Resorts Worldwide Inc
State Farm Insurance Companies
Stryker Corp
SunGard Data Systems Inc
Supervalu Inc
Sutter Health Inc
Symantec Corp
Synopsys Inc
SYSCO Corporation
Team Health Holdings Inc
Tenet Healthcare Corporation
Tenneco Inc
Textron Inc
Thermo Fisher Scientific Inc
Thomson Reuters Corp
Time Warner Inc
TJX Companies Inc (The)
Total System Services Inc (TSYS)
Travelers Companies Inc (The)
TreeHouse Foods Inc
Trimble Navigation Ltd
Trinity Health
Trinity Industries Inc
TripAdvisor Inc
Trustmark Companies
TRW Automotive Holdings Corp
Twitter Inc
Tyson Foods Inc

United Continental Holdings Inc
United Natural Foods Inc
United Parcel Service Inc (UPS)
United States Cellular Corp
United Technologies Corporation
UnitedHealth Group Inc
Universal Health Services Inc
US Bancorp
USAA
Valassis Communications Inc (RedPlum)
Varian Medical Systems Inc
Verisk Analytics Inc
Verizon Communications Inc
VF Corp
Victoria's Secret
Visa Inc
VMware Inc
W R Berkley Corporation
Walgreens Boots Alliance Inc
Wal-Mart Stores Inc (Walmart)
Walt Disney Company (The)
Waste Management Inc
Waters Corporation
Wells Fargo & Co
Whirlpool Corp
WW Grainger Inc
Wyndham Worldwide Corporation
Wynn Resorts Limited
Xerox Corporation
Yum! Brands Inc
Zimmer Biomet Holdings Inc

INDEX OF SUBSIDIARIES, BRAND NAMES AND AFFILIATIONS

INDEX OF SUBSIDIARIES, BRAND NAMES AND AFFILIATIONS, CONT.

Andaz; **Hyatt Hotels Corporation**
Android Auto; **FCA US LLC**
Angels; **Victoria's Secret**
Animal Health International Inc; **Patterson Companies Inc**
Ankylos; **DENTSPLY International Inc**
Ann Inc; **Ascena Retail Group Inc**
Ann Sacks; **Kohler Company**
Ann Taylor; **Ascena Retail Group Inc**
Annuity Investors Life Insurance Company; **American Financial Group Inc**
ANOVO; **Ingram Micro Inc**
Anthem Blue Cross Blue Shield; **Anthem Inc**
Anthem Inc; **Amerigroup Corporation**
Anthro Corporation; **Nortek Holdings Inc**
AO Smith; **A.O. Smith Corporation**
AOL Inc; **Verizon Communications Inc**
Apex; **Avis Budget Group Inc**
App Cloud; **SalesForce.com Inc**
Applanix; **Trimble Navigation Ltd**
Apple TV; **Apple Inc**
Apple Watch; **Apple Inc**
AppleCarPlay; **FCA US LLC**
Application Security Manager; **F5 Networks Inc**
Applied Biosystems; **Thermo Fisher Scientific Inc**
Aptus Endosystems Inc; **Medtronic Inc**
Aquasource; **Lowe's Companies Inc**
Aramis; **Estee Lauder Companies Inc (The)**
Aranesp; **Amgen Inc**
ARCHITECT; **Abbott Laboratories**
ArcRoyal; **Owens & Minor Inc**
Area 31; **Kimpton Hotel & Restaurant Group LLC**
Argos Holdings Inc; **PetSmart Inc**
Aromax; **Chevron Phillips Chemical Company LLC**
Artisan Confections Company; **Hershey Co**
ARX; **F5 Networks Inc**
ARX Holding Corp; **Progressive Corporation (The)**
Ascend; **MAXIMUS Inc**
Ascension; **Ascension Health**
ASI; **Progressive Corporation (The)**
Aspect; **Fastenal Co**
Aspect Loss Prevention LLC; **Verisk Analytics Inc**
Associated Brands Inc; **TreeHouse Foods Inc**
AT Kearney Procurement & Analytic Solutions; **AT Kearney Inc**
AT&T Inc; **DIRECTV**
AT&T Mobility LLC; **AT&T Inc**
ATDOnline; **American Tire Distributors**
Athena Diagnostics; **Quest Diagnostics Inc**
athenaClinicals; **Athenahealth Inc**

athenaCollector; **Athenahealth Inc**
athenaCommunicator; **Athenahealth Inc**
athenaCoordinator; **Athenahealth Inc**
athenaNet; **Athenahealth Inc**
Atlantic City Electric; **Exelon Corporation**
Atlantic Credit & Finance Inc; **Encore Capital Group Inc**
Atrenta; **Synopsys Inc**
Atripla; **Gilead Sciences Inc**
ATX Group; **Agero Inc**
Audit Committee Institute; **KPMG LLP**
Aurora Products Group LLC; **Matthews International Corporation**
Autogrill SpA; **HMSHost Corporation**
Autopart International; **Advance Auto Parts Inc**
Autostack Company LLC; **Greenbrier Companies Inc (The)**
Autotire Car Care Center; **Monro Muffler Brake Inc**
Aveda; **Estee Lauder Companies Inc (The)**
Avis; **Avis Budget Group Inc**
AVONEX; **Biogen Inc**
Axios; **Tenneco Inc**
Axium Pharmacy Holdings Inc; **Kroger Co (The)**
Ayudin; **Clorox Company (The)**
Azamara Club Cruises; **Royal Caribbean Cruises Ltd**
Babson Capital Management LLC; **MassMutual Financial Group**
Backcountry.com Inc; **Liberty Interactive Corp**
Badger Licensing LLC; **ExxonMobil Chemical**
Bahama Breeze; **Darden Restaurants Inc**
Bakers & Chefs; **Sam's Club**
Baldwin & Mattson Inc; **Acosta Inc**
Baltimore Gas and Electric Company; **Exelon Corporation**
Banamex; **Citigroup Inc**
Band-Aid; **Johnson & Johnson**
Banfield, The Pet Hospital; **PetSmart Inc**
Bank of America Corp; **Merrill Lynch & Co Inc**
Bank of New York Mellon (The); **Bank of New York Mellon Corp**
Bank of New York Mellon Trust Company; **Bank of New York Mellon Corp**
Banno; **Jack Henry & Associates Inc**
Baring Asset Management Limited; **MassMutual Financial Group**
Bass Pro Shop; **Bass Pro Shops Inc**
Batesville Casket Company; **Hillenbrand Inc**
Bath & Body Works; **L Brands Inc**
Battle.net; **Activision Blizzard Inc**
Bauknecht; **Whirlpool Corp**
Bay Valley Foods LLC; **TreeHouse Foods Inc**

Baycorp Holdings Pty Ltd; **Encore Capital Group Inc**
Baylor Scott & White Medical Center; **Tenet Healthcare Corporation**
Baymont Inn & Suites; **Wyndham Worldwide Corporation**
Bayside Business Solutions; **Jack Henry & Associates Inc**
BB&T Equipment Finance Corporation; **BB&T Corporation**
BB&T Insurance Services Inc; **BB&T Corporation**
BB&T Investment Services Inc; **BB&T Corporation**
BB&T Securities; **BB&T Corporation**
BD Hypak; **Becton Dickinson & Co**
BD Life Sciences; **Becton Dickinson & Co**
BD Medical; **Becton Dickinson & Co**
BD Vacutainer; **Becton Dickinson & Co**
B-Dubs; **Buffalo Wild Wings Inc**
B-Dubs Radio; **Buffalo Wild Wings Inc**
Bean and Body; **Coca-Cola Bottling Co Consolidated**
Beanstalk Data; **Heartland Payment Systems Inc**
Beaudevin; **HMSHost Corporation**
Beckman Coulter; **Danaher Corporation**
Bed Bath & Beyond; **Bed Bath & Beyond Inc**
Behr Premium Plus; **Home Depot Inc**
Belara; **Mary Kay Inc**
Bell Helicopter; **Textron Inc**
Belterra Casino Resort; **Pinnacle Entertainment Inc**
Berkley Global Product Recall Management; **W R Berkley Corporation**
Berkley International Seguros Colombia SA; **W R Berkley Corporation**
Berkshire Hathaway Inc; **Precision Castparts Corp**
Berkshire Hathaway Primary Group; **Berkshire Hathaway Inc**
Berkshire Hathaway Reinsurance Group; **Berkshire Hathaway Inc**
Best Buy; **Best Buy Co Inc**
Best Buy Canada; **Best Buy Co Inc**
Best Buy Direct; **Best Buy Co Inc**
Best Buy Express; **Best Buy Co Inc**
Best Buy Mobile; **Best Buy Co Inc**
Beverage Partners Worldwide; **Coca-Cola Company (The)**
BH Electronics Inc; **Patrick Industries Inc**
BHE U.S. Transmission; **Berkshire Hathaway Energy Company**
Big Cedar Lodge; **Bass Pro Shops Inc**
Big Front Seat; **Spirit Airlines Inc**
Big Mac; **McDonald's Corp**
Big Pony; **Ralph Lauren Corporation**
Big Ten Network; **Fox Entertainment Group Inc**
BIG-IP; **F5 Networks Inc**

INDEX OF SUBSIDIARIES, BRAND NAMES AND AFFILIATIONS, CONT.

INDEX OF SUBSIDIARIES, BRAND NAMES AND AFFILIATIONS, CONT.

INDEX OF SUBSIDIARIES, BRAND NAMES AND AFFILIATIONS, CONT.

INDEX OF SUBSIDIARIES, BRAND NAMES AND AFFILIATIONS, CONT.

INDEX OF SUBSIDIARIES, BRAND NAMES AND AFFILIATIONS, CONT.

Epocrates; **Athenahealth Inc**
EPOGEN; **Amgen Inc**
Epsilon; **Alliance Data Systems Corporation**
Equilibrium; **Moody's Corporation**
eSecuritel; **Brightstar Corporation**
ESP/SurgeX; **Ametek Inc**
ESPA; **Ritz-Carlton Hotel Company LLC (The)**
ESPN Inc; **Walt Disney Company (The)**
Essential Everyday; **Supervalu Inc**
Estane; **Lubrizol Corporation (The)**
Estate Strategies Group; **Northwestern Mutual Life Insurance Co**
Estee Lauder; **Estee Lauder Companies Inc (The)**
Esthet.X; **DENTSPLY International Inc**
Estrobond; **Eastman Chemical Company**
Estron; **Eastman Chemical Company**
Ethos; **Starbucks Corporation**
etrinity NV; **Computer Task Group Inc**
EV1000; **Edwards Lifesciences Corporation**
EVER; **AFLAC Inc**
EverGreen; **Scotts Miracle-Gro Co (The)**
everytrail.com; **TripAdvisor Inc**
Evite Inc; **Liberty Interactive Corp**
EXACT; **Henry Schein Inc**
Executive Agenda; **AT Kearney Inc**
eXelate; **Nielsen Holdings PLC**
Exelon Generation Company LLC; **Exelon Corporation**
exp.o; **Expeditors International of Washington Inc**
exp.o Booking; **Expeditors International of Washington Inc**
exp.o ISF; **Expeditors International of Washington Inc**
Expedia CruiseShipCenters; **Expedia Inc**
Expedia.com; **Expedia Inc**
Expeditors Tradewin LLC; **Expeditors International of Washington Inc**
Experian plc; **Experian North America**
Experian.com; **Experian North America**
Exxon Mobil Corporation (ExxonMobil); **ExxonMobil Chemical**
EY; **EY LLP**
E-Z-GO; **Textron Inc**
Fabory Group (The); **WW Grainger Inc**
Facebook Platform; **Facebook Inc**
Facey Medical Foundation; **Providence St. Joseph Health**
FactoryTalk; **Rockwell Automation Inc**
Fairfield Inn & Suites by Marriott; **Marriott International Inc**
Fairview Foundation (The); **Fairview Health Services**
Fairview Lakes Medical Center; **Fairview Health Services**
Fairview Northland Medical Center; **Fairview Health Services**

Fairview Ridges Hospital; **Fairview Health Services**
Fairview Southdale Hospital; **Fairview Health Services**
familyvacationcritic.com; **TripAdvisor Inc**
FAMPYRA; **Biogen Inc**
Farmland Foods Inc; **Smithfield Foods Inc**
FatMax; **Stanley Black & Decker Inc**
FCI Asia Pte Ltd; **Amphenol Corporation**
Federal Express Corp; **FedEx Corporation**
FedEx Custom Critical Inc; **FedEx Corporation**
FedEx Freight Inc; **FedEx Corporation**
FedEx Ground Package System Inc; **FedEx Corporation**
FedEx SmartPost Inc; **FedEx Corporation**
FedEx SupplyChain System; **FedEx Corporation**
FedEx Trade Networks Inc; **FedEx Corporation**
Fertiligene; **Scotts Miracle-Gro Co (The)**
Fiat Chrysler Automobiles NV; **FCA US LLC**
Fidelity Advisor; **Fidelity Investments Financial Services**
Fidelity Brokerage Services; **Fidelity Investments Financial Services**
Fidelity Management & Research Company; **Fidelity Investments Financial Services**
Fidelity National Title Insurance Company; **Fidelity National Financial Inc**
Field & Stream; **Dick's Sporting Goods Inc**
Fifth & Pacific Companies Inc; **Kate Spade & Company Inc**
Fifth Element; **Trimble Navigation Ltd**
Filet O'Fish; **McDonald's Corp**
Filtrete; **3M Company**
final-score.com; **Foot Locker Inc**
Firefly; **Hertz Global Holdings Inc**
FirePass; **F5 Networks Inc**
FirstEnergy Transmission LLC; **FirstEnergy Corporation**
FirstMerit Bank NA; **FirstMerit Corporation**
FirstMerit Equipment Finance Company Inc; **FirstMerit Corporation**
FirstMerit Insurance Agency Inc; **FirstMerit Corporation**
FirstMerit Insurance Group Inc; **FirstMerit Corporation**
FirstMerit Mortgage Corporation; **FirstMerit Corporation**
FirstMerit Title Agency Ltd; **FirstMerit Corporation**
Fisher Scientific; **Thermo Fisher Scientific Inc**
Flagstone foods; **TreeHouse Foods Inc**
Flex; **Lam Research Corp**

Flexras Technologies; **Mentor Graphics Corp**
FlightSafety International Inc; **Berkshire Hathaway Inc**
Flint Hills Resources; **Koch Industries Inc**
Florida Hospital; **Adventist Health System**
FloTrac; **Edwards Lifesciences Corporation**
Fluor Constructors International Inc; **Fluor Corp**
FMT; **Fastenal Co**
FNL; **Fastenal Co**
FNL G9; **Fastenal Co**
Food 4 Less; **Kroger Co (The)**
Foot Locker; **Foot Locker Inc**
Footaction; **Foot Locker Inc**
Foote, Cone & Belding; **Interpublic Group of Companies Inc**
Ford; **Ford Motor Co**
Ford Escape Hybrid SUV; **Ford Motor Co**
Ford F150; **Ford Motor Co**
Ford Focus; **Ford Motor Co**
Ford Motor Credit Co; **Ford Motor Co**
Ford Mustang; **Ford Motor Co**
Formula 409; **Clorox Company (The)**
Forte Design Systems; **Cadence Design Systems Inc**
Fortive Corporation; **Danaher Corporation**
Forum Analytics LLC; **CBRE Group Inc**
Fossil; **Fossil Group Inc**
Fotolia; **Adobe Systems Inc**
Four Points; **Starwood Hotels & Resorts Worldwide Inc**
Fox College Sports; **Fox Entertainment Group Inc**
Fox Ridge Homes; **NVR Inc**
Fox Sports Enterprises; **Fox Entertainment Group Inc**
Fred Meyer; **Kroger Co (The)**
Free Spirit; **Spirit Airlines Inc**
freecreditscore.com; **Experian North America**
Freedom Fertility; **Express Scripts Holding Co**
Freightquote.com; **CH Robinson Worldwide Inc**
FreshKO Produce Services Inc; **C&S Wholesale Grocers Inc**
frifri; **Middleby Corporation (The)**
Frito-Lay North America Inc; **PepsiCo Inc**
Frost Bank; **Cullen-Frost Bankers Inc**
Frost Brokerage Services Inc; **Cullen-Frost Bankers Inc**
Frost Insurance Agency Inc; **Cullen-Frost Bankers Inc**
Frost Investment Advisors LLC; **Cullen-Frost Bankers Inc**
Frye Regional Medical Center; **LifePoint Health Inc**

INDEX OF SUBSIDIARIES, BRAND NAMES AND AFFILIATIONS, CONT.

INDEX OF SUBSIDIARIES, BRAND NAMES AND AFFILIATIONS, CONT.

INDEX OF SUBSIDIARIES, BRAND NAMES AND AFFILIATIONS, CONT.

INDEX OF SUBSIDIARIES, BRAND NAMES AND AFFILIATIONS, CONT.

INDEX OF SUBSIDIARIES, BRAND NAMES AND AFFILIATIONS, CONT.

INDEX OF SUBSIDIARIES, BRAND NAMES AND AFFILIATIONS, CONT.

INDEX OF SUBSIDIARIES, BRAND NAMES AND AFFILIATIONS, CONT.

INDEX OF SUBSIDIARIES, BRAND NAMES AND AFFILIATIONS, CONT.

INDEX OF SUBSIDIARIES, BRAND NAMES AND AFFILIATIONS, CONT.

Robert Half Technology; **Robert Half International Inc**
Robinson Fresh; **CH Robinson Worldwide Inc**
Rock River; **Fastenal Co**
Rockwell Software; **Rockwell Automation Inc**
Rocky Mountain Power; **Berkshire Hathaway Energy Company**
Roi; **Mercy**
Rold Gold; **Frito-Lay North America Inc**
Romance; **Ralph Lauren Corporation**
Rona Inc; **Lowe's Companies Inc**
Roper Industries Inc; **Roper Technologies Inc**
Ross Dress for Less; **Ross Stores Inc**
Rotex Global LLC; **Hillenbrand Inc**
Roto-Rooter Corporation; **Chemed Corporation**
Royal Caribbean International; **Royal Caribbean Cruises Ltd**
Royce Funds (The); **Legg Mason Inc**
RPM Data Solutions LLC; **ExlService Holdings Inc**
RPM Direct LLC; **ExlService Holdings Inc**
Ruffles; **PepsiCo Inc**
Ruffles; **Frito-Lay North America Inc**
Rusty Taco Inc; **Buffalo Wild Wings Inc**
RxWorks Inc; **Henry Schein Inc**
Ryan Homes; **NVR Inc**
Ryobi; **Home Depot Inc**
S T Foods; **TreeHouse Foods Inc**
S9; **ResMed Inc**
SaaS Email Security; **McAfee Inc**
Sacred Heart's Health System; **Ascension Health**
Safeco Insurance Fund; **Safeco Insurance Company of America**
Safeco Package; **Safeco Insurance Company of America**
Safeway; **Safeway Inc**
SAIC-GMAC Automotive Finance Co Ltd; **General Motors Company (GM)**
Sales Cloud; **SalesForce.com Inc**
Sam's Business; **Sam's Club**
Sam's Café; **Sam's Club**
Sam's Club; **Wal-Mart Stores Inc (Walmart)**
Sam's Club; **Sam's Club**
Sam's Plus; **Sam's Club**
Sam's Savings; **Sam's Club**
Samsung Corning Precision Materials Co Ltd; **Corning Inc**
Sands China Ltd; **Las Vegas Sands Corp (The Venetian)**
Sands Expo and Convention Center (The); **Las Vegas Sands Corp (The Venetian)**
Sands Macao Casino (The); **Las Vegas Sands Corp (The Venetian)**
Sani-Tip; **DENTSPLY International Inc**

SAP SE; **Concur Technologies Inc**
Sapient Global Markets; **Sapient Corporation**
Sapient Government Services; **Sapient Corporation**
SapientNitro; **Sapient Corporation**
Sargent & Greenleaf; **Stanley Black & Decker Inc**
SAS 9.4; **SAS Institute Inc**
SAS Cloud; **SAS Institute Inc**
SAS Curriculum Pathways; **SAS Institute Inc**
SAS Visual Analytics; **SAS Institute Inc**
Save-A-Lot; **Supervalu Inc**
Sayerlack; **Sherwin-Williams Company (The)**
Sazerac; **Kimpton Hotel & Restaurant Group LLC**
Scala's Bistro; **Kimpton Hotel & Restaurant Group LLC**
SCANA Energy; **SCANA Corporation**
SCANA Energy Marketing Inc; **SCANA Corporation**
SCANA Services Inc; **SCANA Corporation**
Scharffen Berger; **Hershey Co**
Schawk Inc; **Matthews International Corporation**
Schneider Electric SA; **APC by Schneider Electric**
Schuh; **Genesco Inc**
SCI Technology Inc; **Sanmina Corp**
Sciex; **Danaher Corporation**
Scitor Holdings Inc; **Science Applications International Corp (SAIC)**
Scotch; **3M Company**
Scotts; **Scotts Miracle-Gro Co (The)**
Scotts OxiClean; **Scotts Miracle-Gro Co (The)**
Seabourn Cruise Line; **Carnival Corporation**
Seamless Technologies Inc; **Avnet Inc**
Seasons 52; **Darden Restaurants Inc**
Security for Business; **McAfee Inc**
Seeds of Change; **Mars Inc**
Select Comfort; **Select Comfort Corporation**
Select Medical Corporation; **Select Medical Holdings Corporation**
Senior Emergency Departments; **Trinity Health**
Sensipar; **Amgen Inc**
Service Cloud; **SalesForce.com Inc**
ServiceLink Holdings LLC; **Fidelity National Financial Inc**
Servicos e Tecnologia de Pagamentos SA; **Fleetcor Technologies Inc**
ServiTrade; **Fluor Corp**
Seventh-day Adventist Church; **Adventist Health System**

SGK Brand Solutions; **Matthews International Corporation**
Sheraton; **Starwood Hotels & Resorts Worldwide Inc**
Sherwin-Williams; **Sherwin-Williams Company (The)**
SHIELD; **NVIDIA Corp**
ShoeBuy; **IAC/InterActiveCorp**
Shopper's Value; **Supervalu Inc**
Shout; **SC Johnson & Son Inc**
Shred-It International ULC; **Stericycle Inc**
Signature Healthcare Solutions; **Team Health Holdings Inc**
SII Investments Inc; **Jackson National Life Insurance Company**
Sikorsky Aircraft; **Lockheed Martin Corp**
Silfex Inc; **Lam Research Corp**
Silver Lake Partners; **William Morris Endeavor Entertainment LLC (WME-IMG)**
Silverlake; **Jack Henry & Associates Inc**
Silverleaf Tavern; **Kimpton Hotel & Restaurant Group LLC**
Similac; **Abbott Laboratories**
Simon & Schuster; **CBS Corporation**
Simply Asia; **McCormick & Company Inc**
SircleIT Inc; **Gartner Inc**
Sitehawk Retail Real Estate; **CBRE Group Inc**
Sitrick Brincko Group; **Resources Connection Inc**
Six Senses; **Ritz-Carlton Hotel Company LLC (The)**
SIX; 02; **Foot Locker Inc**
Skagen; **Fossil Group Inc**
Sky Brasil Servicos Ltda; **DIRECTV**
Sky Mexico; **DIRECTV**
Skype; **Microsoft Corp**
SkySea Cruises; **Royal Caribbean Cruises Ltd**
Sleep Number; **Select Comfort Corporation**
SmartBeam; **Gentex Corporation**
SmartWool; **VF Corp**
SMF-28e; **Corning Inc**
Smithfield Packing Company Inc (The); **Smithfield Foods Inc**
Smith's; **Kroger Co (The)**
Smithsonian Institution; **CBS Corporation**
SNAPshot DX; **IDEXX Laboratories Inc**
Sodexho Group; **Sodexo Inc**
Sodexo Foundation; **Sodexo Inc**
Sofitel; **Accor North America**
SoftBank Group Corp; **Brightstar Corporation**
Softsoap; **Colgate Palmolive Co**
Softswitch; **Level 3 Communications Inc**
Software Advice Inc; **Gartner Inc**
Solar Turbines; **Caterpillar Inc**
Solaris Mobile; **EchoStar Corp**

INDEX OF SUBSIDIARIES, BRAND NAMES AND AFFILIATIONS, CONT.

INDEX OF SUBSIDIARIES, BRAND NAMES AND AFFILIATIONS, CONT.

INDEX OF SUBSIDIARIES, BRAND NAMES AND AFFILIATIONS, CONT.

INDEX OF SUBSIDIARIES, BRAND NAMES AND AFFILIATIONS, CONT.

CPSIA information can be obtained
at www.ICGtesting.com
Printed in the USA
LVOW02s2156071016

507914LV00003B/5/P

9 781628 314199